JANE'S FIGHTING AIRCRAFT
OF WORLD WAR II

JANE'S FIGHTING AIRCRAFT
OF WORLD WAR II

FOREWORD BY BILL GUNSTON

CRESCENT BOOKS
NEW YORK • AVENEL, NEW JERSEY

Jane's Fighting Aircraft of WW II
Originally published by Jane's Publishing Company
1946/7

This 1994 edition published by Crescent Books,
distributed by Outlet Book Company, Inc., a Random House
Company,
40 Engelhard Avenue, Avenel, New Jersey 07001.

Reprinted 1989, 1992, 1994

By arrangement with the proprietor

Copyright © for this edition 1989 Studio Editions Ltd.

Printed in Singapore

ISBN 0 517 67964 7

8 7 6 5 4 3

PUBLISHER'S NOTE

This volume is reproduced from the 1945/6 edition of
Jane's All The World's Aircraft, which was the first wholly
uncensored issue of the famous book to appear following
the opening of hostilities in 1939. The publication of this
original volume was delayed following the emergence of
numerous, until then, confidential reports from the Allied
nations and indeed from Germany and Japan. Much of
this newly released information was incorporated by the
original editor. This volume has been specifically reformatted
and the amendments and additions to the original edition
have been incorporated into the text at the appropriate
place. It should be remembered that this volume represents
what was known at the time, and therefore follows the
contemporary official reports, although new facts about
the Second World War have inevitably since emerged.
This edition does nevertheless represent the best com-
pendium of information on the airforces of the world at
the time of first publication.

RANDOM HOUSE

New York ● Toronto ● London ● Sydney ● Auckland

CONTENTS

FOREWORD

In February 1946, as an RAF Cadet Pilot at the University of Durham, I somehow managed to scrape together three guineas (£3.15) and bought the newly published 1945/46 Edition of *Jane's All The World's Aircraft*. I have not over-dramatized the task of finding the money. The average wage for someone in full employment was somewhere around £1 per week. My friends knew I was the proverbial 'nut-case' where aircraft were concerned, but such extravagance was thought rather idiotic. One pointed out that three guineas would have kept me in beer and chips (Durham is pretty far north) for a full year.

Today that copy of the most famous *Jane's* of all is showing the effect of well over 40 years of intensive use. Not to put too fine a point on it, it is tatty, though no pages are actually missing. Yet today, over the secondhand bookshop counter, it would still fetch much more than ten times what I gave for it.

It is only natural that 1945/46 should be rather special. Like the corresponding edition at the end of World War I, it collected together everything then known about the aircraft that were important at the close of mankind's greatest ever conflict. But this bald statement needs a lot of qualification, and this will make this Foreword much longer.

The Editor at the time was Leonard Bridgman. A most courteous and kindly man, he compiled each edition almost single-handed. He told me that until the 1945/46 edition there had been no problem. Not a lot had changed between one year and the next. Suddenly, as the 1945/46 volume was going to press, an avalanche of information descended on him. An enormous amount comprised details of new British and American aircraft, suddenly released for publication as the new types poured from literally hundreds of mighty factories. A little of it lifted a corner of the curtain of secrecy – or, rather, simply poor communications – that had previously almost hidden from view the aircraft of the Soviet Union, the West's mighty ally that had done more than any other nation to defeat Nazi Germany. The name of that country appeared as 'Russia', though that is in fact just one of the fifteen republics of the USSR. And the famous Central Aerodynamics and Hydro-dynamics Institute was abbreviated to ZAGI, and the corresponding engine laboratory to ZIAM, simply because that is the abbreviation in German! Today, for no good reason, we still abbreviate 'Central' as 'Ts'. But at least the 1945/46 edition got rid of the spate of Western aircraft wrongly thought to be mass-produced in the Soviet Union.

What really knocked Bridgman for six was the information that arrived by the truck-load on new aircraft from Germany and Japan. Wisely, publication was postponed in order to get in as much of the new material as possible. The late appearance of the volume resulted in its title, for the first time, combining two years (I have tried, unsuccessfully, to get this practice discontinued!). Even so, such was the torrent of new information that, again for the first time, Bridgman was forced to insert a 24-page Addenda. Of these, three were devoted to new German photographs and details, and 21 to new aircraft suddenly released for publication in what was then very rightly called Great Britain.

Just for the record, the 1945/46 volume added these 21 pages of last-minute British news to a British section of 75 tightly packed pages. Today the British section, in a vastly expanded *Jane's*, amounts to just 45 pages, many of which are devoted to light-plane projects, prototypes and one-offs. But such comparisons prove little.

Thumbing through those well-used pages one is struck by the wording used to describe such situations as the enforced takeover by the State of Frank Whittle's company Power Jets – special emphasis is laid on the fact that the shares were 'voluntarily sold', which perhaps eased someone's conscience. One sympathizes with whoever had the job of reporting on Brewster's contribution to the war effort; and the next entry, Budd, is just another of many programmes which began with high hopes and massive orders and ended with a zero. As for that other Zero, the Japanese navy fighter, this entry at least began to describe the major versions, but still listed only one of the six types of gun armament and one of the five possible loads of bombs or rockets. Frankly, the links between the people reading the captured books and studying the once-enemy hardware, and open publications, even of the stature of *Jane's*, were extremely poor. We can be thankful for the many later researchers – in the case of Japanese aircraft most notably Rene J. Francillon – who followed trails that were cold and yet left for posterity thousands of facts that never reached the pages of this great volume.

Even in the case of Germany, another of the later researchers, Bill Green, had to dig and delve laboriously for twenty years to compile an epic volume that – by starting from scratch, and certainly not merely believing everything in this volume of *Jane's* – has likewise put the aircraft of Hitler's *Luftwaffe* on permanent and accurate record. This is not to suggest that overworked Bridgman did a

shoddy job, but he started with too many precon-ceived notions. One was that 'With the reconstruc-tion of the company as Messerschmitt A.G. the designation of the 109 was changed to Me 109, the first production version to carry this designation being the Me 109E . . .' The mind boggles at the tenacity with which this belief was adhered to. We were ankle-deep in shot-down Bf 109 nameplates!

One even finds odd 'non-facts' in the Great Britain section, where there is less justification for error. The Hawker Siddeley firms seem to have had a penchant for exaggeration, claiming that 'well over 15,000 Hurricanes were built', and that 'Avro war production included 7,500 Lancasters' (their true figure was, I believe, 3,670). In addition, consider-ing the pressure under which the Editor worked, a reasonable number of typographical errors were sprinkled through the book. At the time I jotted down a few, on a sheet of design-office memo paper rescued from the shattered Focke-Wulf plant at Bremen (along with various other things which I still use).

There is one final point, and it is important. To some degree the title of this re-formatted reprint is misleading. A nitpicker might agree the title JANE'S FIGHTING AIRCRAFT AT THE END OF WORLD WAR TWO. The *Jane's* annuals have, as one might expect, concentrated on what was important at the time of publication. This volume ignored the air-craft of France, Poland Czechoslovakia, Denmark, Finland, the Netherlands, Belgium, Yugoslavia and many other countries, all of which had participated in the war. It also ignored such types as the Battle (except for mention of a testbed), Lysander, Hampden, Albacore, Blenheim and many other once-famous aircraft which by the end of the war were no longer in production.

There are also plenty of anomalies. For example, while the Curtiss XP-42 is included, despite the fact that this pre-war prototype (incorrectly said to have 'first flown on May 31, 1941') was used early in the war only for research, the same maker's O-52 Owl AT-9 Jeep are missing, even though they served in numbers. And, of course, Pan Am never used the 'DC-7 Globemaster', which instead became the USAF C-74, biggest vehicle on the Berlin Airlift. One could go on, but we must be a little humble. We have the enormous benefit of hindsight, and almost complete knowledge of what actually happened. Bridgman didn't.

Bill Gunston

PREFACE

THIS volume of *"All the World's Aircraft"* appears a little later than usual but the delay has made it possible to include therein a very extensive documentation of the aircraft and aero-engines used by the combatant air forces right up to the end of the war. It has, in fact been the most difficult to of all the war editions to compile and produce. Although the war in Europe came to an end in May, 1945, and the surrender of the last enemy took place in the following August, this edition is still essentially a war edition.

Actually the major part of the revision had been completed when the cease fire sounded in Europe. This event, however, threatened to make available for publication a vast amount of material concerning German aircraft and equipment and a decision had to be made whether to proceed to press with what was then know to be out-of-date wartime information or to postpone publication in order to include the latest authoritative material which the Air Ministry very readily promised to make available as soon as it could be prepared.

To have accepted the first alternative would have resulted in earlier publication of this volume but it would also have necessitated holding over all subsequently released information on enemy aircraft for publication in the next volume where it would not only be out of place but also by that time sadly out of date. It was therefore decided to await the impending release of new material. By the time this had been received and incorporated in the completely revised German sections, Japan had surrendered.

With this event the need for stringent security regulations no longer existed, but official recognition of the fact that the war was over took some time to make itself felt. Here again it was necessary to decide whether to pass information already in print which, written under the influence of the dead hand of official wartime control, was utterly inadequate and frequently wrong, or to endeavour to make use of as much as possible of the information that was then becoming available without involving too much disturbance of standing matter. Production of the book at this stage was too advanced to incorporate all new material in its rightful place and consequently for the first time *"All the World's Aircraft"* carries a number of Addenda pages ahead of the Aeroplane Section, wherein are included details of all new British aircraft released for publication up to the beginning of 1946, together with a number of photographs of German aircraft which were acquired too late to be included in the German pages.

THE AEROPLANE AND ENGINE SECTIONS

From what has already been said it will be obvious that this edition contains a greater amount of information on aircraft and aero-engines than any other wartime edition. Including the Addenda pages, there are 339 pages in the Aeroplane Section, 101 more than last year. This is the first time that this section has exceeded 300 pages since 1938. The Aero-Engine Section contains 94 pages, 26 more than last year.

A very considerable amount of new information relating to the development of all the important British and American combat aircraft has been worked into the pages and this, taken into conjunction with the extensive information now presented in detail concerning German and Japanese aircraft and aero-engines, makes this particular issue of *"All the World's Aircraft"* of more than usual interest and historical value. Well over 700 illustrations, of which 550 are new, are used and the three-view silhouettes have been almost completely revised and renewed.

After this issue the blacked-in silhouette type of three-view drawing will disappear from these pages. The silhouette served its purpose during the war in recognition training, and the silhouettes used in *"All the World's Aircraft"* were standard with those used by both the British and American training organizations, but it is felt that the three-view line drawing is more satisfactory for the purpose for which drawings are used in *"All the World's Aircraft"* and in future all drawings published will be of the open line type.

The Aero-engine Section contains much that is new, including completely revised German section. It also contains for the first time two sections, one British and one German, devoted to gas turbines. Unfortunately, nothing was available concerning American development in this field before closing for press.

THE HISTORICAL SECTIONS

The two historical sections—covering Service and Civil Aviation throughout the World—are more truly historical this year than normally. The information concerning the Air Forces of all nations relates in most cases to conditions existing during the last year of the war, the review of the operations of the British and Dominion Air Forces up to the end of the war; the outline of the organization of the Air Forces of the United States in 1945; and the final summing up of events leading to the complete eclipse of the Luftwaffe, all taking their places in the history of Air Power. The Allied air structure which worked as an integrated whole with such devastating effect during the latter stages of the war is now in process of drastic demobilisation and it will be for future issues of the Annual to record the ultimate establishment of the World's Air Forces which, whether under national or international control, will be responsible for maintaining World peace.

The Civil Aviation Section likewise serves as a historical record of what organizations existed throughout the World in the last year of the war. During the war purely civil aviation suffered in varying degrees from the usual civilian handicaps while air transport under Allied military control grew to full stature as an essential branch of the armed forces.

The transitional period from war to peace at the stage at which it is at the time writing does not permit of coherent recording, for what is written one day is out of date the next. International negotiation and agreement, the rehabilitation of war-torn nations, shortages of aircraft and equipment and the lack of ground organization, lingering military control, etc., are all matters which await solution before post-war civil aviation assumes some semblence of orderliness.

The International Civil Aviation Conference held at Chicago in the Winter of 1944 and attended by the representatives of 52 nations, was the first attempt to establish an International starting point for post-war civil aviation. A summary of the agreements reached at Chicago, together with an outline of the organization of the Provisional International Civil Aviation Organization (P.I.C.A.O.) set up under one of the agreements, is published in the Civil Aviation Section. Summaries are also included covering organization of the Commonwealth Air Transport Council, the Southern African Air Transport Conference and the new International Air Traffic Association.

ACKNOWLEDGEMENTS

My thanks are again due to Mrs. Joan Bradbrooke for her assistance in preparing the review of the operations of the Royal Air Force and the Air Forces of the Dominians in the Service Section. I also acknowledge the help I have received from many different sources, both at home and abroad, In particular I am grateful to the Public Relations Officers of the Air Ministry and the Ministry of Aircraft Production for their courtesy and co-operation. Thanks are also due to the representatives of foreign governments and the technical and publicity officials of the British and foreign aircraft industries.

For those who are interested in the more intimate side of this publication, it is now permissible to say that the premises, warehouse, stock and files of the publishers, Sampson Low, Marston & Co. Ltd., were entirely destroyed in the great fire raid on the city of London in December, 1941. They were driven from temporary offices on two further occasions (in 1942 and 1944) by the effects of enemy action and suffered many other wartime inconveniences.

The printer's problems, apart from a near miss or two, were mainly concerned with extreme shortage of labour and materials and to those few loyal patient and long-suffering men and women who over the past four years have submitted without complaint to my whims and coped with the truly comprehensive task of producing this volume which, I feel has fulfilled a definite need during the past war years, I offer my most grateful thanks.

This and the last three volumes I have produced single-handed without office or personal staff of any kind in spare time left over from full-time employment elsewhere. I have now been given the services of an editorial assistant, Mr. H. J. Cooper, who brings both experience and enthusiasm to his new task. With his help I look forward to the production of the next edition, the first for six years which will be free from all hindrances, frustrations, disappointments and, one may even be tempted to hope, the shortages of wartime publication.

L.B.

VICTORY

BY

J. M. SPAIGHT, C.B., C.B.E.

IN the tremendous events of the months of May and August, 1945, all those who have steadfastly believed in the power of the air can find justification of the faith that was in them. It was in the Far East that the triumph of air power was most glittering and unmistakeable. There, effect followed hotfoot upon cause. In the west the results were produced more slowly, but the part which the air arms of the Allies played in the great drama of the liberation of Europe was manifest to all who had eyes to see.

The victory in Europe was one to which all arms of war contributed. The 2coup-de-grace was given to Nazidom, as all informed opinion held that it would have to be given, by the Allies' armies. Those armies owed their triumph in no small degree to the support afforded to them by the air arms. How unfailing and valuable the support was has been freely acknowledged by the army commanders. Still more striking as evidence of the effect of the strategic air offensive are the words of two enemy commanders.

A few days after Field Marshal Von Rundstedt was captured on May 1, 1945, he gave an interview to a number of war correspondents and told them some illuminating things.2 Inter alia,2 he said that air power was the first decisive factor in Germany's defeat; lack of petrol and oil was the second; and the destruction of the railways was the third. Field Marshal Kesselring was captured a few days later, on May 9, and he, too, bore testimony to the effect of the Allies' air power. He told war correspondents that there were three reasons for Germany's defeat: Allied strategic bombing behind the lines; attacks by low flying fighter aircraft; and terror raids against the civilian population.

Discounting the last propogandist allegation, one can agree whole-heartedly with what the two Field Marshals said. Germany was beaten not by air power alone but by a combination of air, land and sea power of which the first was assuredly not the weakest partner in the team. Had it been absent we might have witnessed in 1935-45 in the West a repetition on a more terrible scale of the mass-slaughter of 1914-18. It is no exaggeration to say that there are probably alive today a million or more young men of British and American stock who, but for air power, would be dead.

The period from January, 1944 to May, 1945, saw in Europe a march of events without parallel. When it began the Battle of Berlin was still in progress. It had begun on November 18, 1943, and in the course of it a number of very damaging attacks had been made on the German capital, the most destructive being that of the night of November 22. The new year brought little respite to the Berliners. On the night of February 15, 1944, their city received a greater weight of bombs than had ever been dropped on any objective in air warfare - 2,500 tons of high explosives and incendiaries. (Greater loads still were to be deposited on other targets in the months that followed). Between November 18 and February 15, 326 war factories in Berlin were destroyed or damaged, it was officially announced in March. That the city was grievously devestated there was ample evidence even then, much of it from witnesses who would be unlikely to exaggerate for this purpose, at any rate. M. Philippe Henriot the Vichy Minister of Propaganda, stated on June 7 after a visit: "Berlin is a sight which grips one with fear. The destruction is terrible. The sight of empty spaces covering entire areas is symptomatic and frightening". Perhaps the savage murder of 50 flying officers at Stalag Luft III in March was the Gestapo's characteristic reaction to the wrecking of the city.

The Anglo-American air offensive left Berlin a broken shell of a city. No capital has ever suffered as it did, at any rate since the dark ages. "Berlin is dead" said a correspondent who was there on May 10, 1945. "It has been wiped off the map. As a city Berlin no longer exists. I used

to work in Berlin, at an office in Unter den Linden. Today I had the utmost difficulty in identifying the site where that office used to stand. The extent of the catastrophe that has overtaken Berlin is difficult for the mind to grasp. It is not merely a street here and there, or even a whole block of buildings wiped out. The whole city has been practically obliterated. From the fashionable Kurfuerstendamm in the west to the Alexanderplatz and the Frankfurter Allee — a distance of about 4½ miles — and the same distance north to south, the city is an eerie echoing waste of ruins and bomb craters, with the bombed-out skeletons of tall buildings".

The devastation of Berlin was paralleled through the length and breadth of the Ruhr; and all the time the British and American air forces were conducting three great campaigns-against Germany's aircraft production, against her oil, and against her railway network.

The main object of the American air offensive in the Spring of 1944 was the immobilising of the fighter branch of the German air force. An intensive campaign for this purpose was started on February 20 and in the week that followed the 8th Air Force, from Great Britain, and the 15th Air Force, from Italy, attacked a great number of fighter aircraft factories throughout Germany and Austria, as well as many aerodromes. As a result of these and subsequent attacks a plan which the Germans had adopted in 1942 for the doubling of their fighter strength by April, was completely upset. It had been well on the way to achievement at the beginning of 1944, but actually the fighter establishment of the Luftwaffe was no greater by the summer of that year than it had been in 1942, notwithstanding the efforts made to expand it. It was quite inadequate in consequence to meet the demands made upon it by the war of encirclement to which Germany was now being subjected. Its culminating disasters came in April, 1945. On April 10, a huge flotilla of 1,300 Fortresses and Liberators, escorted by 850 fighters, attacked airfields and other targets in the Berlin area; 284 enemy aircraft were destroyed on the ground by the fighters, and 55 more were destroyed elsewhere on the ground, while 57 were shot down in addition. This destruction of some 396 aircraft in one day stood as the record for less than a week. On April 16, at least 827 enemy aircraft were destroyed, it was stated in the S.H.A.E.F. *communique* of April 17. It was for all practical purposes the end of the *Luftwaffe*.

The enormous advantage possessed by the belligerent who has superiority in the air was made speedily apparent when the Anglo-American invasion of the continent began on June 6. For over two months before that date the British and American airmen had been "softening" the invasion coast. On D-Day Allied aircraft flew the all-time record of 13,000 sorties, between dawn on June 6 and dawn on June 7. They maintained a giant umbrella of 600 miles square from Le Have to Cherbourg, with at least 200 machines always in the air over this area. The subsequent operations in France, the Low Countries and Germany afforded the British and American air forces countless opportunities for assisting their comrades on the ground. The close support given by the heavy bombers, notably in the tremendous attacks near Caen on July 7 and 18 and August 8, were a new and unparalleled example of co-operation between the air and the ground. Not less remarkable was the help which the fighters-bombers and the rocket-firing fighters gave. On one day alone (August 7), the rocket-firing Typhoons put 135 tanks out of action. That was but one example of the air arm's contribution to the great victory in France. Another—out of many—was the softening of the defences of Calais with such good effect that the garrison of 11,000 Germans was captured on October 1 at the extraordinarily low cost to the Canadian army of 300 casualties. It was the weather alone

which prevented the Allies from exploiting to the full their mastery of the air. The *Luftwaffe* seldom intervened.

The demarcation between strategical and tactical bombing tends to become blurred when the belligerent whose air operations are in question stands at his enemy's gates. It would be difficult to assign confidently to either category many of the raids carried out by the Allies in the autumn of 1944. In regard to some of them, however, no doubt can arise. The connection between the land battle and the recurring air attacks on the enemy's communications, his railway lines and junctions, marshalling yards, roads, bridges and barges, was too evident to be misunderstood.

The Allies, said an Air Ministry Bulletin of December 4, 1944, had their "railway plan for Germany". Its object was to cut off the western front from the enemy's main industrial centres, and it was a continuation of a programme which had already been completed successfully in France. "The railway plan which blocked the movement of German reserves and supplies to Normandy", said the Bulletin, "made possible the great victory there; a similar plan will do much to weaken the defence of Germany". In France the object in view was achieved by the smashing of the bridges over the Seine and the Loire and the devastation of the railway junctions or yards of Trappe, La Chapelle, Juvisy, Vaires, Villeneuve-St. Georges, etc. By D-Day 50 of the 82 important railway centres between the Vosges and the Belgian frontier had been completely destroyed, 8 had been mainly destroyed and 17 had been severely damaged.

The task in Germany was more formidable, for there the railway network was a more elaborate one. It was a network planned for war and admirably constructed for that purpose. But it was planned and constructed with insufficient regard to one important consideration. "The railways of Germany," said the Bulletin already quoted, "are built for all forms of war but bombing." It was a fatal oversight.

During November and December Bomber Command of the Royal Air Force set itself to wreck the railway centres which served Germany's western front. Essen, with its 22 railway yards, in the heart of the Ruhr; Dortmund, the eastern entrance; Duisburg, the western exit; Hamm, the greatest marshalling yard in Germany; Soest, hardly less important than Hamm; Hagen, an alternative route to the line *via* Dortmund; Oberhausen, towards the west of the Ruhr; Witten, the junction of two routes by-passing the devastated areas of the Ruhr; were all heavily attacked. So were the neighbouring railway centres of Osnabruck and Giessen, and those of Karlsruhe and Heilbronn in the Rhineland, while Freiburg-im-Breisgau in the Black Forest and Ulm away on the Danube were also attacked. The yards at Frankfurt, Giessen and Hanau were raided on December 11 by the largest force ever sent out by the U.S. 8th Air Force—1,600 Fortresses and Liberators, escorted by more than 800 Thunderbolts and Mustangs. The campaign against the railways went on until the end of the year. It was necessarily a lengthy campaign; its purpose was to immobilise a system of communications which the Germans had been building up since the days of Bismarck and Von Moltke.

A second major air campaign was being conducted at the same time. It was aimed at Germany's liquid fuel production. With the capture of the Ploesti oilfields by the Russians the synthetic oil plants in Germany, Austria and Czecholslovakia assumed an enhanced importance. The Bomber Commands of the Royal Air Force, the U.S. 8th Air Force in Great Britain, and the U.S. 15th Air Force in Italy took due cognizance of that fact. They had begun to attack the oil plants even before the Rumanian supplies were cut off. By the middle of the year Germany's oil production had been cut to 30 per cent of its former volume accord-

VICTORY

ing to a statement made by General H. H. Arnold at Washington on July 3, 1944 by September, all the ten plants in the Ruhr had been temporarily put out of action and production throughout Greater Germany had dropped to 310 thousand metric tons a month this was only 23 per cent of the potential output at the beginning of 1944 which had been (including the Ploesti supplies) one and one third million metric tons. The Germans made frantic efforts to repair the damaged plants. The greatest single source of supply was the Leuna plant at Merseburg near Leipzig. Here 600,000 tons a year were produced and 50,000 workers were employed. It was attacked on many occasions by the Allies' heavy bombers. So serious had the position become," said an Air Ministry Bulletin of December 7, that the Germans decided to give the plants first priority both in defence and in repairs Guns were even take away from the industrial cities and rushed to Leuna, and it has been calculated that the plant has now about 400 heavy guns defending it as many as there used to be defending Berlin." By mid November the output at Leuna had been halved it was still producing more oil than any of the ten Rhur plants except Nordstern and Scholven. It was attacked repeatedly by the 8th Air Force as well as by the Royal Air Force the effect became apparent in 1945; lack of oil was undoubtedly one of the chief reasons for Germany's defeat. There was already evidence before the close of 1944 of a definite stringency in the position of the petrol supply for the *Luftwaffe*. How short was the supply of petrol is evident from the efforts which the enemy made to maintain the production of benzol. Benzol is a by-product of coke ovens and tar distillation plants, coke being the main product. Though the demand for coke had decreased and it had in fact become a drug in the market as a result of the destruction of many steel plants and the shortage of tungsten, chrome and other metals, the Germans still kept their plants which produced it in operation. There can have been only one reason for their doing so, namely, the need for benzol, small as the output of this was; the largest coke oven produces only 2,000 tons of benzol a month, as compared with 33,000 tons of petrol from the largest synthetic oil plant. The benzol plants in the Ruhr were repeatedly attacked by Bomber Command.

The shortage of fuel was one of the reasons why the *Luftwaffe* was unable to mount a counter offensive against Britain or even to give the German armies the close support which they needed. Another effect was the curtailment of training of pilots and aircrews. The mighty air arm which had been in the forefront of the *Blitzkrieg* in the early stages of the war had fallen on evil days. The glory had departed. Its bankruptcy was manifest when it was driven to entrust the task of raiding Britain to the nasty mechanical contrivance known officially as the flying-bomb and unofficially as the doodlebug."

The bombardment of London with this weapon —V.1. *Vergeltungswaffe Eins* began in mid-June. It would have begun at an earlier date and would have been a far more formidable onslaught but for the sustained offensive conducted by Bomber Command against the launching sites on the Channel coast during the winter of 1943-44. Even before that time the Command had gone far to spike the guns of this new *eratz* artillery. On the night of August 17, 1943, a force of Lancasters, Halifaxes and Stirlings raided the experimental station at Peenemunde near the Baltic. The official *communique* stated that the attack was highly success ful": how successful, we did not learn until later, It wiped out the brain-centre of the secret weapon organization. The head scientist and a large number of the staff at Peenemunde were killed in the raid, and the preparations for the Vweapon campaign were set back by many months. A further precious respite was won for us by the airmen when they smashed the first series of about 100 launching sites between Le Havre and Calais. The permanent platforms there were replaced by prefabricated and more mobile ramps Which were well camouflaged and more difficult to destroy. Nevertheless, a high proportion of them were wrecked, and so was a large structure at Watten,

in the Pas de Calais, which appeared to be intended for use with the longrange rocket.

In September, V.2, *Vergeltungswaffe Zwie,* was brought into use. Defence against it was more difficult. The flying-bomb had been defeated by a combination of fighter aircraft (the most successful being the new Hawker Tempest and the still newer jet-propelled Gloster Meteor). and anti-aircraft guns and barrage balloons. The menace was reduced to small dimensions when the Allied armies swept into Belgium at the beginning of September. After that time the V.1. was launched from the air. It was carried by a Heinkel He 111, and both the carrier and the missile were a mark for our interceptors. Thus launched, the bomb was more erratic than ever. The rocket bomb was still more haphazard. It was launched from sites near The Hague and to the north of it, and with the advance of the Allied armies towards this part of Holland, the V.2 menace was brought to an end.

Both the V.1 and the V.2 were militarily futile weapons, with no influence whatever upon the course of the war. Apart from their inaccuracy, they were not even very efficient as infernal machines. The bomb-load was not impressive. The warhead of each was about one ton in weight, that is, less than onefifth of the weight of the earthquake" bomb carried by our Lancasters; and the range was trivial in comparison with that of the latter. The chief value of the weapons was, in fact, the psychological effect within the Reich. The German newspapers of June 19, pictured London as a city on fire, with all roads leading out of it choked with refugees, most of them carrying pots and pans on hand-drawn carts and other improvised vehicles. Those of us who were travelling to and from London daily by train and bus at that time without noticing any great change from normal conditions were highly edified by such fairy tails, but no doubt they were eagerly swallowed in Germany.

Undoubtedly the flying-bombs and rockets were unpleasant things, and they did cause substantial damage and very regrettable casualties. The effect, however, was merely to harden the British people's will to win. We whose houses suffered knew, too, that this was the price which we had to pay for our own tremendous air onslaught on Germany and that, so regarded, it was a small price. When a question was asked in the House of Commons on December 12 about retaliation upon German cities Mr. Eden replied that there was really no comparison between what the Germans were able to do to us and what we were able to do to them. Of that, indeed, there could be no doubt whatever. They were scourging us with whips but we were scourging them with scorpions. Our own bombing offensive became more and more devastating as the war progressed. Our bombs became bigger and bigger. The 12,000lb. bomb was first used against the Gnome-Rhone woks at Limoges in the Spring of 1944. A year later the 22,000lb. bomb came into use; it was first dropped on March 14, 1945, by Lancasters on a railway viaduct at Bielefeld in Germany. Others were dropped next day on a viaduct at Arnsburg. Europe was spared the atomic bomb. The effectiveness of our offensive was due in part to the adoption of new technique in air raids by night and in part to the fact that we were at last in a position to attack also by day. Bomber Command had sent its heavies into the Reich by day on a few special occasions before 1944. Its offensive was, however, essentially a nightly one. It ceased to have that almost exclusive character in 1944. On August 27 our bombers penetrated the Rhur in daylight for the first time; a force of Lancasters and Halifaxes, escorted by fighters, attacked the Homberg-Meerbeck synthetic oil plant on that day. A number of other daylight raids followed in the Autumn and Winter. The fact that the bombers could now be escorted by fighters, usually Spitfires and Mustangs, ensured a rate of loss that was extraordinarily low for day light raids.

The rate was low, too, in later raids by night in 1944 (and 1945). It had been high in the earlier raids of the year; in the raid on Nuremburg on the night of March 30, 1944, 94 aircraft were missing. The losses in the following Autumn and Winter

were in comparison, extraordinarily light. The improvement was due to a number of causes. The most important of these was the adoption of what amounted to a system of fighter escort by nighta system which had at one time been considered to be impracticable. Bomber Command developed its own organization of night fighters and intruders, using Mosquitos for the purpose and sending them to keep away the German night fighters from the bombers and to attack the air fields from which the German interceptors took off. The system was very successful and large numbers of German night-fighters were destroyed, while our own bombers were free to carry out their attacks with much less interference than before. The loss by the enemy of the forward observation posts and radar stations which he had been using on the Channel coast was a further handicap for his defence system. The technique of diversionary raids and feints was also considerably elaborated on our side.

The accuracy of our bombing improved at the same time. In August,1942, the Pathfinder Force had been formed. That Force produced in time a number of very highly skilled experts who became known as master bombers." These were the pathfinders *d'elite*. Their task was to shepherd the bombers to the target area, to direct the ground marking of it, or, if the clouds were too thick, the sky-marking, and to see that the markers were maintained and the bombing concentrated on them. The work of the master bombers and · the Pathfinder Force as a whole was facilitated by the use of an ingenious instrument some particulars of which were disclosed in November, 1944.

This was the British-developed gen box" or black box"the mickey" of the American airmen—containing a small radio transmitter which, fitted in the fuselage of the aircraft, sends out a succession of electrical impulses which bounce back from the ground on impact and, on their rebound, are caught and reproduced electronically (through a cathode-ray tube) on a glass screen set before the bomb-aimer. The outline of the target can thus be discerned even through tentenths cloud. The system is a development of radiolocation, in which we succeeded in keeping a lead over the Germans.

We were not quite so far ahead in another technical advance that was disclosed during the year, jet-propulsion. The Whittle engine was being developed, it appears, in good time, but the Germans undoubtedly had aircraft propelled in a somewhat similar way in action at an earlier date than we. Their Me 262's were not available in substantial numbers, however, and their rocket-propelled Me 163's were also comparatively few. When the *Luftwaffe* tried to stage a come-back" in support of the German counter-offensive which began on the morning of December 16 against the American First Army, the Me 109's and Fw 190's still constituted the great bulk of the fighters. They were up in large numbers but were unable seriously to disturb the Allies' virtual mastery of the air. At sea the most spectacular event in the West of the air warfare of 1944-45 was the sinking of the battleship *Tirpitz*. She was caught in Tromso Fjord on November 12 by a force of 29 Lancasters, which made a round flight of more than 12 hours' duration to attack her with 12,000lb. bombs, causing her to capsize and settle on the bottom with her keel out of the water. The Lancasters' success was contributed to indirectly by an earlier achievemant for which the credit goes to the Fleet Air Arm. In May, a force of naval Barracudas, escorted by Hellcats and Wildcats, made a daring attack on the *Tirpitz* and obtained a number of direct hits. She was so damaged that she was unable to leave her anchorage in northern Norway, where she was still six months later when Bomber Command returned to the hunt. That Command in actually sinking her, stole the limelight from both the Royal Navy and Coastal Command. It was to them, however, that it fell to play again the chief part in the grim drama of the war at sea; and, again, they played it well to the very end. They continued to harry unceasingly the enemy's surface and underwater craft, his E and R and U-boats. In the east the war in the air was predominantly waged by the American Army and Naval Air Forces.

The carrier-borne aircraft of the United States fleets won a number of resounding successes in October and December, 1944, and April, 1945. The first was in the region of Formosa, where in a two-days' action the naval airmen sank or damaged 63 ships and 35 small craft and destroyed 398 aircraft, for the loss of 45 American aircraft. The Japanese made the usual fantastic claims to a great victory in this encounter—and, apparently, were misled by their own propaganda. They sent another naval force to mop up the "survivors" and the American Third Fleet met it in the Philippines and dealt with it faithfully. 58 Japanese ships were sunk or damaged in this second encounter of October and 171 aircraft were destroyed. Admiral Halsey's fleet lost 3 light cruisers and 3 destroyers. Another disaster for the Japanese in the Philippines followed on December 13-15, when 94 of their vessels and 269 of their aircraft were destroyed. On April 7, 1945, carrier-borne aircraft of the 3rd American Fleet sand the 45,000-ton battleship2 Yamato and five other Japanese warships off Okinawa, destroying in addition nearly 600 aircraft. To these losses at sea the Japanese had to record another debit addition in the account of relative air power in the east. It represented the opening of the offensive by the Superfortresses (B-29's) against the Japanese homeland. That was an event of ominous implications.

How ominous it was became apparent when on August 6, 1945, a Superfortress launched against the city of Hiroshima a projectile which surpassed in destructive force anything yet contrived by man. The effect of the atomic bomb, developed by British and American scientists and manufactured in the United States, was comparable to that of a major earthquake such as Tokyo itself had experienced in 1923. Three days later Nagasaki suffered no less terribly. In the early hours of the same day (August 9) Russian forces crossed the Manchurian borders. Two days later (August 11) Japan made known her readiness to surrender. Statements made by her rulers and the inherent evidence of the events themselves justify the conclusion that her sudden collapse was due to the bombing of the two cities. That was what smashed her will to war.

That final triumph should not blind one to the truth that well before August 6 the combination of Allied air, sea and land power had made Japan's position hopeless. Her doom was already sealed by the early Summer of 1945. Her power of resistance had been worn down in the operations conducted in the Pacific by Admiral Nimitz and General MacArthur, and in Burma by those under Admiral Mountbatten. The latter forces' share in the final victory should never be forgotten.

In Burma the Royal and Indian Air Forces asserted their ascendancy over the Japanese, and —an even more formidable antagonist—the weather. It was because of their superiority in the air that they, with their American comrades, were able in March to ensure the success of the most remarkable operation by air-borne forces ever attempted up to that time. An Army was leap-frogged over the enemy's head and deposited behind him and then kept supplied with everything it needed— men, munitions, rations, supplies of all kinds, all by air and without the help of any communications on the ground. Nor was that the end of the story. In the 18 months that ended at the beginning of May, 1945, R.A.F. aircraft dropped half a million tons of supplies to the troops in Burma. The Combat Cargo Task Force of Eastern Air Command made the capture of Rangoon on May 3 possible. On every day of the two months preceding the taking of the city 2,000 tons or more of supplies and munitions were brought up by air for the 14th Army. It was a landmark in logistics.

PART A

A
REVIEW OF THE WORLD'S
AIR POWER
DURING THE YEARS 1944-45

(Corrected to August 31st, 1945)

ARRANGED IN

ALPHABETICAL ORDER OF NATIONS

A RECORD OF THE ARMY AND NAVY AIR SERVICES AND OF THE INDEPENDENT AIR FORCES OF ALL NATIONS DURING 1944-1945, TOGETHER WITH AN ACCOUNT OF THEIR ORGANIZATION AND THE ADDRESSES OF THEIR VARIOUS DEPARTMENTS AND COMMANDS.

HISTORICAL (SERVICE AVIATION)

AFGHANISTAN

(The Kingdom of Afghanistan)

NATIONAL MARKINGS

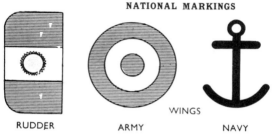

BLACK

RED

GREEN

RUDDER   WINGS ONLY

The Afghan Air Force is an integral part of the Army under the administration of the Ministry of War. The Commandant of the Air Force, Firqa Mishar (Major-General) Muhammad Ihsan Khan, is responsible to the Minister of War through the Chief of the General Staff of the Ministry of War.

ORGANIZATION

The aircraft of the Afghan Air Force are organized into three squadrons. All squadrons, which come directly under the disciplinary control of the Commandant of the Air Force, are normally concentrated at the Kabul (Sherpur) Aerodrome, the Headquarters of the Air Force.

ADMINISTRATION

Headquarters, Afghan Air Force, Kabul (Sherpur).

The Headquarters of the Air Force is organized as follows :—

Organization Branch

Responsible for operations, equipment and supply.

Control Branch

Responsible for finance, personnel and pay.

Engineering Branch

Responsible for aircraft and material.

Aerodrome Guard

An Army Detachment detailed for guard duties. It is also responsible for ordinary soldiers recruited as aircraft hands.

TRAINING

There is a small Flying Training School and an Engineering School at Kabul, with capacities for nine student pilots and nine mechanics respectively. A Royal Air Force officer is attached to the Afghan Air Force for general instruction and performs the duties of pilot instructor for the Flying Training School.

EQUIPMENT

The Afghan Air Force is equipped with Hawker Hind and Meridionali RO.37 aircraft. Although several Breda 25's and one Stearman biplane are available for training, the Hawker Hinds only are used for this purpose.

ARGENTINA

(The Argentine Republic—Republica Argentina)

NATIONAL MARKINGS

AZURE

YELLOW

BLACK

RUDDER   ARMY   WINGS   NAVY

On January 4, 1945, a Ministry of Aeronautics was established in Argentina to co-ordinate and administer all matters concerning Military and Civil Aviation, with the exception of the Naval Air Service, which continues under control of the Ministry of Marine. The responsible Minister is Brigadier Bartolome de la Colina.

ORGANIZATION

Secretaría de Aeronáutica (Secretariat of Aeronautics), Juncal 1116, Buenos Aires.

The organization of the Secretariat (Ministry of Aeronautics) includes :—

(1) Comando de las Fuerzas Aéreas Argentinas (Command of the Argentine Air Forces).

(2) Dirección General de Aeronáutica Civil (General Directorate of Civil Aeronautics).

(3) Dirección de Institutos Aeronáuticos (Directorate of Air Training).

(4) Cuartelmaestre General de Aeronáutica (Department of Material, Works and Buildings).

(5) Instituto Aerotecnico (Technical Research and Development Institute).

(6) Comando de la Defensa Antiaérea (Command of Anti-aircraft Defense).

THE ARGENTINE AIR FORCES

Subordinate to the Comando de las Feurzas Aéreas Argentinas are :—four Military Air Bases, three Air Regiments, one Observation unit, one Transport Group and one Training Group.

The units of the Argentine Air Forces (Fuerzas Aéreas Argentinas are :—

Air Regiment No. 1. Military Air Base "El Palomar," Province of Buenos Aires.

Air Regiment No. 2. Military Air Base "El Palomar," Province of Buenos Aires.

Air Regiment No. 3. Military Air Base "El Plumerillo," Mendoza, Province of Mendoza.

Reconnaissance Group No. 1. Military Air Base "General Urquiza," Paraná, Province of Entre Ríos.

Subordinate to the Direccion de Institutos Aeronauticos are :—

Escuela de Aviación Militar (School of Military Aviation), Córdoba, Province of Córdoba.

Escuela de Especialidades (School of Specialists for non-commissioned officers), Córdoba, Province of Córdoba.

Escuala de Paracaidistas (Paratroop School), Córdoba, Province of Córdoba.

EQUIPMENT

Fighting :—Curtiss Hawk III, Curtiss Hawk 75 (Argentine-built).

Attack :—Northrop 8-A2.

Bombing :—Glenn Martin 139, Ae. M.B.2 (Argentine-built).

Reconnaissance :—Junkers K.43, Fairchild 82 (photography).

Training :—Focke-Wulf Fw 44 and Fw 58, (Argentine-built) North American NA-16, Fairchild M-62, DL-22 (Argentine-built).

Transport :—Junkers Ju 52, Lockheed 10E and 12B.

THE NAVAL AIR SERVICE

Naval Aviation is administered by a Director-General of Naval Aviation, who is directly responsible to the Minister of Marine.

ORGANIZATION

Dirección-General de Aviación Naval, Ministerio de Marine, Moreno 1921, Buenos Aires. Director-General : Rear-Admiral Horacio Smith.

Under the technical control of the Director-General and the operational control of the Commander-in-Chief of the Fleet are :—

The Puerto Belgrano Naval Air Base (land and sea).

The Punta Indio Naval Air Base (land and sea).

The Naval Air Detachment at Fuerte Barragan.

The Naval Air Detachment at Mar del Plata.

Naval Air Detachment at Madryn.

The School of Naval Aviation at Puerto Belgrano.,

Three Air Squadrons.

The School of Aviation mentioned above gives instruction to naval air pilots, engineers and mechanics.

There are also naval airfields at Puerto Belgrano, Martin Garcia and Ushuaia.

The following air units are also included in the Naval Air Service : The Puerto Belgrano Air Defence Force, the Rio de la Plata Air Defence Force and the Naval Air Squadron.

EQUIPMENT.

Training :—Curtiss-Wright 16E, Stearman 76D1, Vought Corsair O2U-1, Junkers W34, Stinson Reliant.

Reconnaissance :—Vought Corsair V-142 and V-65F, Grumman G-15 and G-21, Supermarine Walrus.

Bombing :—Glenn Martin 139W.

Patrol :—Consolidated P2Y-3.

Transport :—Fokker, Douglas Dolphin, Consolidated Fleetster, Curtiss-Wright Condor.

General Purposes :—Fairchild 82, Fairchild 45, Lockheed Electra 10E.

The cruiser *La Argentina*, built by Vickers-Armstrongs Ltd. at Barrow and delivered in January, 1939, is equipped with one catapult amidships and has accommodation for two Supermarine Walrus reconnaissance amphibians. The Cruisers *Almirante Brown* and *Veinticinco de Mayo* are equipped with catapults and Grumman reconnaissance amphibians.

BELGIUM

(The Kingdom of Belgium—Royaume de Belgique)

When Belgium was invaded and the armed forces were finally forced to lay down their arms on May 28, 1940, a small proportion of the personnel of the Belgian Military Air Arm which survived the heavy fighting over its own soil managed to escape to France where efforts were made to re-form and re-equip a small Air Force to continue the fight under its own accredited Government alongside the Allies. The collapse of France six weeks later, however, caught the Belgian forces completely unprepared, but a certain number of officer and non-commissioned pilots managed to escape by various means to Great Britain.

Arrangements were thereupon made with the British Air Ministry for the experienced Belgian pilots to join the Royal Air Force Volunteer Reserve and these pilots were posted to several squadrons in the Fighter and Coastal Commands. So it was that about thirty Belgian pilots took part in the operations over England and the English Channel during the Battle of Britain in August-October, 1940. The number of victories achieved by Belgian pilots during the Battle of Britain amounted to twenty-seven for a cost of five airmen killed in action.

In October, 1940, by the escape from France of the most representative of the Belgian Ministers, the legal Belgian Government was re-constituted in London and the Belgian armed forces were re-formed in the United Kingdom.

Belgian Military Aviation has been maintained in the form of a Belgian Section of the Royal Air Force Volunteer Reserve, the members of which are employed according to their usefulness in units of the R.A.F.

During the past four years Belgian airmen, soldiers and young civilians managed to find their way out of enemy-occupied territories and most of them on arriving in England volunteered for the Air Force. After undergoing training at R.A.F. stations in England and Canada nearly seven hundred had been posted to operational units up to the end of 1944. Belgian airmen have served in India, the Middle East, Crete, Malta, Sicily, the Azores, Iceland, as well as in Great Britain.

Now that Belgium is liberated it has become possible to recruit all ground personnel required and a specific Belgian training centre under Belgian supervision has been established in England within the organization of Technical Training Command, R.A.F.

In November, 1941, the first Belgian squadron, equipped with Supermarine Spitfire single-seat fighters, took up its duties as an operational unit in R.A.F. Fighter Command. The occasion was marked by the presentation of the flag of a pre-war Belgian air regiment to the squadron by M. Camille Gutt, the Belgian Minister of National Defence. This flag, which had been hidden in occupied Belgium since May, 1940, had been brought to England just prior to the presentation by two Belgian officers who had been entrusted with the perilous mission of fetching it from their native land.

This squadron has had considerable operational experience since its formation. On August 19, 1942, in the course of four sorties during the Dieppe operations the squadron destroyed seven and damaged twelve enemy aircraft for the loss of one pilot missing.

At the beginning of 1943 a second Belgian fighter squadron was formed in West Africa. This unit was later transferred to England and served in the R.A.F. 2nd Tactical Air Force.

Several Belgian officers were appointed to command British squadrons. The first Allied officer to command a British squadron was a Belgian.

At the time of writing thirty Belgian officers who have served in the Belgian Section of the R.A.F. had been awarded the Distinguished Flying Cross, three of whom hold a bar to this distinction. Two Belgian squadron leaders have received the D.S.O. for their work in Bomber and Coastal Command respectively. The devotion to duty of Belgian airmen has also been recognised by the award of three French Croix de Guerre and more than 160 Belgian Croix de Guerre.

In addition to the several hundred airmen serving as ground personnel, there were also 165 Belgian girls serving in the W.A.A.F.

All costs incurred by the Air Ministry for pay, allowances, lodging, instruction, materiel, etc., in connection with Belgian Military Aviation have been borne entirely by the Belgian Government.

On the cessation of hostilities in Europe the Air Council sent the following message to Air Commodore L. F. E. Wouters, C.B.E., M.C., Inspector-General of the Belgian Air Force :—

The long awaited defeat of our common enemy has at last been achieved and after more than five years the shadow of tyranny is lifted from Europe.

In this hour of victory the Air Council wish to express their admiration for the courage and endurance of your airmen who, separated from their country, have won great glory among the forces of freedom. The spirit which led your countrymen to fight their way to these Islands to take up arms again and showed itself in the exploits of your squadrons in the air is the spirit by which her

friends have ever known Belgium—undaunted against odds and unconquerable.

The Air Council look on it as a source of honour that the Belgian Air Force decided to associate itself so closely with the Royal Air Force and they hope that this close and trusted association may continue far into the years of peace.

Plans for the establishment of a permanent Belgian Air Force visualise the formation of four Fighter Wings, one Night Fighter Wing, one Transport Wing and one Liaison Wing.

BOLIVIA

(The Bolivian Republic—República de Bolivia)

NATIONAL MARKINGS

RED

GREEN

YELLOW

RUDDER   FUSELAGE & WINGS

The Bolivian Air Force, which used to be part of the Army, was organized as a separate service at the end of 1944. It is controlled by the Minister of Defence, through a Chief of Staff who is an Air Force officer of Colonel's rank.

The Bolivian Air Force is divided among four Regiones Aereas with headquarters at La Paz, Santa Cruz, Sucre and Tarija. There are four aviation groups, one to each area, and each comprising one or two squadrons (escuadrillas) of seven aircraft each.

ORGANIZATION

Ministerio de Defensa Nacional, La Paz.
Minister of National Defence : Colonel Jorge Jordan.
Direccion de Aviacion, La Paz.
Director of Military Aviation : Lieut.-Col. Jose C. Pindo.
Región Aérea No. 1, "El Alto," La Paz.
Región Aérea No. 2, "El Trompillo," Santa Cruz.
Región Aérea No. 3, "La Florida," Sucre.
Región Aérea No. 4, "El Tejar," Tarija.
Escuela de Pilotaje (Flying Training School), "Colcapirua," Cochabamba.
Escuela de Application (Operational Training Unit), "El Alto, La Paz.

The aerodrome of "El Alto" at La Paz is on a plateau 4,100 m. (13,500 ft.) above sea level and is 500 m. (1,640 ft.) above the city of La Paz, the capital. The aerodrome of "El Trompillo," Santa Cruz is 600 m. (1,970 ft.) above sea level ; "La Florida," Sucre, 2,460 m. (8,070 ft.) above sea level ; "El Tejar," Tarija, 2,100 m. (6,900 ft.) above sea level ; and "Colcapirua," Cochabamba, 2,500 m. (8,200 ft.) above sea level.

EQUIPMENT

Fighting :—Curtiss Hawk, Curtiss CW-22.
Training :—Curtiss R-19, North American AT-6A, Beechcraft AT-17 and AT-11, Vultee BT-13 Valiant, Ryan PT-16, Boeing PT-17, Stinson Voyager, Interstate L-8.
Transport :—Douglas C-47 Dakota, Junkers Ju 86.
Miscellaneous :—Grumman OA-9, Curtiss Osprey, Focke Wulf.

BRAZIL

(The United States of Brazil—Estados Unidos do Brasil)

NATIONAL MARKINGS

GREEN

BLUE

YELLOW

RUDDER   WINGS ONLY

By Presidential Decree dated January 20, 1940, an Air Ministry was created to co-ordinate all branches of aeronautics within the Republic. The administration and units of the former Army and Naval Air Services have been transferred from the Ministries of War and Marine to the new Ministry and the new independent Air Force has been given the name Forças Aereas Brasileiras (F.A.B.).

ORGANIZATION

The Air Ministry (Ministeria do Ar), Rio de Janeiro.
Air Minister : Major-General Armando Trompowski.
The organization of the Air Ministry includes :—

The Air Staff (Estado Major da Aeronautica)
Responsible for training, war plans and tactical use of the Air Force and the anti-aircraft defences, either independently or in collaboration with the General Staffs of the Army, the Navy or the Civil Defence authorities.
There are also Departments responsible for **Personnel, Training, Research and Technical Development, Material, Works and Buildings, Anti-Aircraft Defence, Commercial Air Services** and **Civil Flying.**

AIR ZONE COMMANDS.

By a Decree Law dated October 25, 1941, the territory of Brazil was divided into five Air Zones. A further Decree Law dated March 5, 1942, modified the Air Zones created by the earlier Decree Law. Decree Law dated July 14, 1942, foreshadowed the possibility of existing Zones being sub-divided and at the same time mentioned the formation of Air Base Groups to include all personnel, fixed installations and equipment at Air Bases. The Air Regiments, however, remain and are to

be divided into Groups (Squadrons) of one type of aircraft. The Zones, with the Air Bases and Establishments they administer, are as follow :—

No. 1 Air Zone. Headquarters : Belém.
Officer Commanding : Tte-Coronel E. Ferrara da Silva.
Covers the States of Amazones, Pará, Maranhão, and Acre Territory.

No. 2 Air Zone. Headquarters : Recife.
Officer Commanding : Brigadier A. Vieira Macarenhas.
Covers the States of Piauí, Ceará, Rio Grande de Norte, Paraíba, Pernambuco, Alagõas, Sergipe, and Bahia.

No. 3 Air Zone. Headquarters : Rio de Janeiro.
Officer Commanding : Brigadier Ivo Borges.
Covers the States of Espirito Santo, Rio de Janeiro, Minas Geraes, Goiás and the Federal District.
Under this command are the Central Air Park, the Air Technical Services, the Central Aeronautical Stores and the Air Medical Centre, all based at the Campo dos Alfonsos Air Base, Rio de Janeiro ; and the Aircraft Factory, Central Aeronautical Stores, Air Medical Centre and Flying Training Unit attached to the School of Technical Training at the Ponto do Galeão Marine Air Base, on the Ilha do Governador, Buenos Aires.

No. 4 Air Zone. Headquarters : São Paulo.
Officer Commanding : Brigadier Antonio Appel Neto.
Covers the States of São Paulo and Matto Grosso.

No. 5 Air Zone. Headquarters : Porto Alegre.
Officer Commanding : Brigadier G. D. de Lima Rodriquez.
Covers the States of Paraná, Santa Catarina and Rio Grande do Sul.

TRAINING ESTABLISHMENTS

Escola de Aeronautica (Air Force College), Campo dos Alfonsos, Rio de Janeiro.
Established in 1941 in the buildings formerly occupied by the Escola de Aviação Militar at the Campo dos Alfonsos, Rio de Janeiro. This establishment trains officers for both the Military and Naval wings. The training course lasts three years. The first course began on April 1, 1941.
Escola de Especialistas de Aeronautica (School of Technical Training), Ponto do Galeão.
This establishment has taken over the former separate training schools of the Army and Naval Air Services. It trains all engineer officers and mechanics.
Escola Tecnica de Aviação (Technical School of Aviation), São Paulo.
Established in 1943 for the training of technicians and specialists for the Air Force and airlines. Operated by the

Embry-Riddle School of Aviation and is staffed by American instructors.

THE MILITARY MAIL SERVICE

The Air Force operates air mail services, under the name Correio Aerea Brasileira, to places in the hinterland, the traffic to which would be too small to be handled profitably by commercial companies. It also provides useful training for service pilots. All mail is carried at normal postage rates.

EQUIPMENT

Fighting :—Boeing P-12E, Vought V-65 and V-66, Curtiss P-36 and P-40, Republic P-47.
Bombing :—Vultee V-11GB, North American NA-44, Douglas B-18, North American Mitchell, Consolidated Catalina, Lockheed Hudson.
Training :—Avro 626, Muniz M-9, Focke-Wulf Fw 44J and Fw 58B, Stearman 75L3 and 76 C3, Waco F-5, D.H. Moth, Vultee 54 Valiant, Fairchild M-62.
Transport and Miscellaneous :—Douglas Dakota, Bellanca Pacemaker, Lockheed 12 and 14, Beechcraft D-17A and Waco C-8.

Brazil declared War on Germany and Italy on August 22, 1942, following the sinking of several Brazilian ships by U-boats. Prior to this Brazil had instituted a system of anti-submarine patrols along its long coastline and had attacked and sunk several submarines.

In January, 1944, a group of fighter pilots and ground personnel all volunteers from the Brazilian Air Force, left Rio de Janeiro for the United States to undergo advanced and operational training before proceeding overseas as the First Brazilian Fighter Squadron to serve with the U.S. Army Air Forces. Under the command of Lieut.-Col. Nero Moura, the squadron arrived in Italy on October 6, 1944, and was attached to the 12th Air Force. It went on its first mission on November 11, equipped with Republic P-47 Thunderbolts.

Between October 31, 1944 and January 22, 1945, the squadron flew 897 sorties, dropped 339 bombs and destroyed 159 enemy road vehicles, one locomotive, 33 railway vehicles, 6 bridges, 3 fuel dumps, 2 ammunition dumps, one supply dump and one aircraft. In addition, the squadron scored 94 cuts on vital railways, exploded or left burning 9 enemy-occupied buildings, damaged 105 enemy vehicles, 36 locomotives, 306 railway vehicles, 7 bridges, 5 ships and small boats and one aircraft. Five P-47's were lost from A-A fire.

THE BRITISH COMMONWEALTH OF NATIONS
1—THE BRITISH EMPIRE

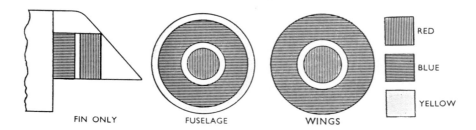

FIN ONLY   FUSELAGE   WINGS   RED   BLUE   YELLOW

GREAT BRITAIN AND NORTHERN IRELAND

THE ROYAL AIR FORCE
The Royal Air Force was formed on April 1, 1918, by the amalgamation of the Royal Flying Corps and the Royal Naval Air Service. The basic organization of the Royal Air Force begins at the Air Ministry. The controlling authority of the Air Ministry is the Air Council, which is charged by Parliament with the administration of matters relating to the Air Force and the defence of the Realm by air. The President of the Air Council is the Secretary of State for Air and the four Air Members of the Council and the Permanent Under Secretary of State are constituted as the five departmental heads among whom the main duties of the Air Ministry are divided.

Marshal of the Royal Air Force : H.M. King George VI.

THE AIR COUNCIL
The Rt. Hon. Viscount Stansgate, D.S.O., D.F.C., Secretary of State for Air (President).

Mr. E. J. St. L. Strachey, M.P., Parliamentary Under-Secretary of State for Air (Vice-President).

Air Chief Marshal Lord Portal of Hungerford, G.C.B., D.S.O., M.C., Chief of the Air Staff (to be succeeded on January 1, 1946, by Air Chief Marshal Sir Arthur Tedder, G.C.B.).

Air Marshal Sir Douglas C. S. Evill, K.C.B., D.S.O., A.F.C., Vice-Chief of the Air Staff.

Air Marshal Sir John Slessor, K.C.B., D.S.O., M.C., Air Member for Personnel.

Air Marshal Sir Leslie N. Hollinghurst, K.B.E., C.B., D.F.C., Air Member for Supply and Organization.

Air Marshal Sir Roderick M. Hill, K.C.B., M.C., A.F.C., Air Member for Training.

Sir William Brown, K.C.B., K.C.M.G., C.B.E., Permanent Under-Secretary of State.

Sir Harold Howitt, D.S.O., M.C., F.C.A., who gives advice and assistance on financial policy.

Air Vice-Marshal Sir Alec Coryton, K.B.E., C.B., M.V.O., D.F.C., Controller of Research and Development, Ministry of Aircraft Production.

Lord Henderson, Additional Member.

HOME COMMANDS
British Air Forces of Occupation (Germany).
Air Chief Marshal Sir Sholto Douglas, K.C.B., M.C., D.F.C.

Bomber Command
Air Marshal Sir Norman Bottomley, K.C.B., C.I.E., D.S.O., A.F.C.

Fighter Command
Air Marshal Sir James Robb, K.B.E., C.B., D.S.O., D.F.C., A.F.C.

Coastal Command
Air Marshal Sir Leonard Slatter, K.B.E., C.B., D.S.C., D.F.C.

Flying Training Command
Air Marshal Sir Arthur Coningham, K.C.B., D.S.O., M.C., D.F.C., A.F.C.

Technical Training Command
Air Marshal Sir Ralph Sorley, K.C.B., O.B.E., D.S.C., D.F.C.

Maintenance Command
Air Marshal Sir Graham Donald, K.C.B., D.F.C., A.F.C.

Air Transport Command
Air Marshal The Hon. Sir Ralph Cochrane, K.B.E., C.B., A.F.C.

OVERSEAS COMMANDS
Royal Air Force, Mediterranean/Middle East
Air Commander-in-Chief : Air Marshal Sir Charles E. H. Medhurst, K.C.B., O.B.E., C.B.E.

This Command represents the merging of the former Mediterranean and Middle East Command (formerly located at Naples) and H.Q.R.A.F. Middle East. It covers air activities in the Central Mediterranean, North Africa, the Middle East Area, including the Levant, Iraq and Sudan, Aden and East Africa. Air Headquarters, Italy, under the same Command, supervises R.A.F. units remaining in Italy and Austria.

Air Headquarters, Malta
Air Officer Commanding : Air Vice-Marshal K. B. Lloyd, C.B.E., A.F.C.

Air Headquarters, Egypt
Air Officer Commanding : Air Cdre. S. O. Bufton, C.B., D.F.C.

Air Headquarters, Iraq
Air Officer Commanding : Air Vice-Marshal S. C. Strafford, C.B., C.B.E., D.F.C.

H.Q. British Forces, Aden
Air Officer Commanding : Air Vice-Marshal H. T. Lydford, C.B.E., A.F.C.

Air Headquarters, East Africa
Officer Commanding : Brigadier H. G. Willmott, C.B.E., S.A.A.F.

Air Headquarters, Eastern Mediterranean
Air Officer Commanding : Air Vice-Marshal S. E. Toomer, C.B.E., D.F.C.

Royal Air Force, Gibraltar
Air Officer Commanding : Air Cdre. A. D. Rogers, C.B.E., A.F.C.

Royal Air Force, West Africa
Air Officer Commanding : Air Vice-Marshal Sir Ranald M. Reid, K.C.B., D.S.O., M.C.

Royal Air Force, India
Air Officer Commanding : Air Vice-Marshal M. Thomas, C.B.E., D.F.C., A.F.C.

South-East Asia Command
Air Commander-in-Chief : Air Chief Marshal Sir Keith Park, K.C.B., K.B.E., M.C., D.F.C.

This Command includes the following :—

Base Air Forces, South-East Asia
Air Officer Commanding : Air Marshal Sir Roderick Carr, K.B.E., C.B., D.F.C., A.F.C.

Air Headquarters, Burma
Air Officer Commanding : Air Marshal Sir Hugh W. L. Saunders, K.B.E., C.B., M.C., D.F.C., M.M.

Air Headquarters, Malaya
Air Officer Commanding : Air Vice-Marshal J. D. Breakey, C.B., D.F.C.

THE FIFTH AND SIXTH YEAR OF THE WAR

During the fifth and sixth years of the War Allied Air Power was deployed at its full might and in all theatres of operations the Anglo-American forces worked more closely together than ever. The three main centres of operations for the Royal Air Force were the European, the Mediterranean and the Far Eastern theatres.

The most spectacular of these was the European theatre, where operations during the first half of 1944 were devoted to preparations for the Allied invasion of Europe. The tremendous air forces of the Allies, based in Great Britain, kept up a 24-hour attack, each component force having its particular job. The concerted Allied programme was designed to ensure that when the land assault began the enemy's air opposition would be reduced to a minimum. Attacks against the enemy's defensive air power and against his wide-spread communications system were carried on side by side by Bomber Command of the Royal Air Force, the U.S. Eighth Air Force and the Allied Expeditionary Air Force of the R.A.F. and units of Fighter Command, together with the U.S. Ninth Air Force.

Aircraft factories, war industries, airfields, railways, roads, bridges, canals and radiolocation centres were strewn with wreckage. And while these attacks were being made from bases in Great Britain blows were being struck with increasing effect on the Balkans and Southern Europe by Allied aircraft based in Italy. Also, when the attacks on communications were stepped up they were co-ordinated with similar attacks from Italy.

By D-Day—June 6, 1944—when the Allied landings were made in Normandy, of 80 major railway centres between the Vosges and the Belgian frontier 51 had been completely destroyed and 25 severely damaged. To accomplish this some 22,000 sorties were flown and some 66,000 tons of bombs were dropped by R.A.F. Bomber Command, the U.S. Eighth Air Force and the Allied Expeditionary Air Force. In addition, of the 10 railway and 14 road bridges across the Seine, only one of each was usable. Thus, with the destruction also of the enemy's radiolocation centres, the Allied Air Forces enabled the landings to achieve tactical surprise.

Meanwhile preparations for co-operation between the Air Forces and the Armies in land attacks were being worked out, not only to provide a comprehensive air umbrella to cover the troops, but a striking force to be employed far behind the enemy lines. Plans were made for 90 per cent. of this advanced air striking force to carry bombs when the time came.

Throughout the land battles in Europe, leading to the unconditional surrender of Germany on May 4, 1945, co-operation between the land forces and the Air Forces was on an unparalleled scale. During the rapid advance through North-Eastern France and Belgium into Holland new methods of giving close support to the Armies were introduced and heavy bombers were used tactically on a large scale for the first time, while the role played by the fighter-bombers was of vital importance.

Simultaneously with the preparations for the invasion, the Allied Air Forces kept up incessant attacks against the enemy's threatened use of flying bombs and rockets. Counter-measures against these attacks, planned to divert the impact of the Allied Air Forces on Germany, were first taken in August, 1943, when Bomber Command made a heavy attack on the German experimental station at Peenemunde. Heavy assaults were then made on the enemy's production centres where various weapons and component parts were being built and in December, 1943, attacks were begun on the launching installations discovered by constant photographic reconnaissance of Northern France. As a result of this persistent offensive Germany's attacks with pilotless aircraft were delayed for six months and when launched, shortly after D-Day, the attacks were on less than a quarter the scale originally planned.

Towards the end of the flying-bomb attacks the enemy introduced long-range rockets. The task of interrupting supplies of these weapons and bombing their launching sites and storage depots devolved on Spitfire fighter-bombers which kept up a constant assault until the enemy capitulated.

All home commands of the R.A.F. shared in the European operations, Coastal Command keeping ceaseless watch on and making continuous attacks on enemy shipping, while operations of Transport Command of the R.A.F. expanded tremendously and the Airborne Forces were used on a greater scale than ever before.

Although less spectacular than those in Europe, operations of the Mediterranean Allied Air Forces continued on a large scale. In addition to co-ordinated attacks in connection with the European invasion, full strategic and tactical support was given to the Eighth and Fifth Armies in their advance up the Italian peninsula, culminating in the surrender of all German forces in Italy on May 3, 1945.

In the Far East, in spite of the fact that the prosecution of the War against Japan in this theatre was, by agreement between the Allies, relegated to second place in strategy and equipment until the defeat of Germany, the threat to India was removed and by the end of 1944 the Japanese had been swept out of the length of Burma.

In the Pacific American forces, island-hopping by way of Guam, the Marianas, the Philippines, Iwojima and Okinawa, and the Allied fleets navigating Japanese home waters and bombarding the mainland without opposition, were closing in for the final kill, while the British in Burma and the Australian forces in New Guinea and the Indies were slowly cancelling out Japanese conquests in the South. The gigantic air campaign waged on the Japanese mainland from the Marianas, Guam and Iwojima had by mid-1945 so reduced Japan's capacity for war that the dramatic events of August merely precipitated the inevitable.

On August 6, the first atomic bomb was dropped on Hiroshima, on August 8 Russia declared war on Japan and began the invasion of Manchuria and Karafuto, and on August 9, the second atom bomb was dropped on Nagasaki. On August 10, Japan signified its readiness to discuss surrender and, on August 15, accepted the Potsdam terms of unconditional surrender. The actual surrender document was signed by the Allied chiefs and the Japanese envoys in the U.S.S. *Missouri* in Sagami Bay, Tokyo, on September 2, 1945.

General Aircraft Hamilcar tank-carrying gliders with their Halifax tugs lined-up in readiness for the invasion of Europe.

BOMBER COMMAND

During 1944 Bomber Command dropped more than 525,000 tons of bombs, or more than twice the weight dropped in the first four and a quarter years of the War, and despatched seven per cent. more aircraft on operational flights than in all the previous years of the War put together. In spite of this, the casualty rate was well under half that of 1943. The greatest weight of bombs dropped in any one night of the year was just under 5,500 tons and the greatest weight dropped in 24 hours was 10,300 tons.

Of the total of 525,000 tons, 35 per cent. was dropped on industrial towns in Germany, 18 per cent. on enemy transport, 16 per cent. in direct support of the Allied Armies, 11 per cent. on V-weapon sites and supply depôts, 7 per cent. on the German oil industry, three per cent. on oil storage depots, four per cent. on the German aircraft industry, three per cent. on ports and shipping and three per cent. on miscellaneous industrial targets. By the end of the year the total area which had been devastated in German industrial towns was at least 36,000 acres and the number of German towns which had received 10,000 tons (the majority had received considerably more) was 13. They were Berlin, Essen, Cologne, Dusseldorf, Stuttgart, Duisburg, Kiel, Hamburg, Frankfurt, Gelsenkirchen, Dortmund, Mannheim, and Hanover. Duisburg, in fact, received 10,000 tons of bombs, including 500,000 incendiaries, in the middle of October in one period of 18 hours, during which it was attacked twice by a total of some 2,000 aircraft.

During 1944 200 bombers caused as much destruction as 1,000 in 1942. The first time that Bomber Command sent out 1,000 heavy bombers, as compared with the "1,000 bomber" raids of 1942, (which were composed mainly of twin-engined aircraft) was on the night of March 16, 1944, when some 1,200 heavy bombers dropped 3,000 tons of bombs on Stuttgart. Throughout the rest of the year attacks by 1,000 and up to 1,400 heavy bombers at night were commonplace and before the end of the year 1,000 bomber raids by daylight were no unusual occurrence.

New devices, equipment and tactics all added to the effectiveness of Bomber Command. These included Radar; the Mark XIV bomb sight (used by the U.S.A.A.F. as the T.1); saturation bombing, by which vast loads were dropped simultaneously to swamp the defences and disorganize counter-measures; precision bombing by day and by night by means of the "Pathfinder" technique and the "Master" Bomber; new incendiary bombs and 12,000-lb. and 22,000-lb. bombs. The 12,000-lb. "blast" bomb was used first on the night of February 8 and the newer streamlined 12,000-lb. "earthquake"—or penetration—bomb later in the year. The 22,000-lb. "volcano" bomb was first used on March 14, 1945, on the Bielefeld Viaduct which carried a double-track railway from the Ruhr to Central Germany. Only the Avro Lancaster could carry these two "outsize" bombs.

The "Master" Bomber, first tried out in the raid on the Möhne and Eder dams in 1943 and again for a special raid on Peenemünde on August 18, 1943, controls and directs the main force, guiding them, checking the position of the target indicators, and in area bombing, ensuring the even distribution of attack over the whole area. These tactics were first used regularly in March, 1944, for attacks on individual French factories working for the Germans. They later became a regular feature of many of Bomber Command's attacks and but for them, the tactical bombing which prepared the way for the invasion might have been a much longer and more uncertain business.

Another innovation introduced during 1944 was the formation of "Bomber Support" Squadrons, composed of Mosquito night fighters which accompanied the bombers on their night operations, greatly reducing the casualty rate in spite of the fact that enemy night fighters were more numerous and active than ever before. Bomber Command's greatest loss during the year was on the night of March 31, during a raid on Nuremburg when 94 out of a force of between 900 and 1,000 bombers were lost. Exceptionally heavy concentrations of night fighters and moonlight were mainly responsible.

One of the outstanding features of operations during the year was the amount of daylight raiding done by Bomber Command. The first daylight high-level attack since 1942 was made on June 14 when two forces of Lancasters, escorted by Spitfire fighters bombed the E-boat pens at Le Havre. From then on daylight operations became almost as frequent as those at night and, in fact, during the months of August and September the total daylight sorties exceeded night sorties. On August 27 a strong force of Halifax bombers was over Germany in daylight for the first time with fighter protection—afforded by Spitfires—all the way to the target in the Ruhr.

At the beginning of 1944 Bomber Command was still maintaining the Battle of Berlin, which had begun in November, 1943, and which continued until the end of March, the heaviest raid being in February, when 2,500 tons of bombs were dropped. In February a number of attacks were interlocked with operations of the U.S.A.A.F., the same targets being raided by day and by night. At the same time Bomber Command was beginning to develop the double raid in one night. By the end of the year as many as six targets in one night were receiving concentrated attacks.

In March, Bomber Command began attacking targets in occupied territory. These called for precision attacks and were usually made during the moonlight periods, raids on Germany being concentrated in the darker periods.

There followed for the next two months a sustained assault on various targets in the occupied countries, particularly on railways, ammunition dumps, airfield buildings, factories and military objects generally, as the prelude to the invasion. By May 9 the Allied Air Forces had attacked 51 separate railway targets in France and Belgium in the course of some 140 operations and of the 34,000 tons of bombs dropped, Bomber Command dropped 26,000. Of 80 important railway centres in France, Belgium and Western Germany scheduled for bombing before the invasion about 40 were assigned to Bomber Command and 37 of them had been gravely damaged by D-Day.

Another of Bomber Command's special invasion tasks was the assault upon enemy coastal batteries, which began on May 7. By June 5, 40 attacks had been made on 24 sites. The heaviest attack was made a few hours before the invasion when 5,000 tons of bombs were dropped on the 10 coastal batteries defending the beaches where the landings were to be made.

For the next few months after D-Day Bomber Command concentrated mainly on military targets in the field and close support to the Armies. Among the outstanding examples of tactical support given by the Command were the bombing at Caen and Falaise, and the bombing of the Channel ports. Both day and night low-level precision attacks were made on enemy concentrations of armour and strong points, frequently only some 2,000 yards ahead of the Allied Armies. The most concentrated attack of all was made early on the morning of July 18 when more than 2,200 Allied bombers dropped over 7,000 tons of bombs in an area of some 70 square miles in just over three hours to prepare the way for the Allied break-through in Normandy. Bomber Command's share in this operation was 5,000 tons dropped by 1,000 bombers.

The German-held ports of Brest, Boulogne, Le Havre and Calais received some 26,000 tons of bombs before the capture of Calais on September 30.

The liberation by September of the greater part of France and Belgium relieved the Command of one of its greatest tasks

The result of the R.A.F. attack on the night of February 21-22, 1945, on the Mitelland Canal, near Gravenhorst.

A Halifax over the inferno created by a daylight attack on troop and tank concentrations near Caen on July 7, 1944.

The 22,000-lb. "volcano" bomb, the first of which was dropped by the R.A.F. on March 14, 1945. Of the streamlined deep-penetration type, the bomb is 35 ft. 5 in. long, 3 ft. 10 in. diameter, and has a tail unit 13 ft. 6 in. long with aerodynamic fins which cause it to spin when falling.

since the beginning of the year—the persistent bombing of V-weapon sites and storage depots in Northern France. One hundred launching sites prepared for the flying bombs—mostly in the Pas de Calais—were destroyed and although new sites were built, the attacks by flying bombs were delayed until June.

German synthetic oil plants were also priority targets for the Command. The assault began in June and by September the 10 plants in the Ruhr were all temporarily out of action. The attack was sustained and although the enemy's production showed a slight increase in November, the plants were out of action again by December. Meanwhile the offensive against the Reich continued and in October the second battle of the Ruhr was opened. The battle front was then only 40 miles away and the main targets were factories, road, rail and water communications. The Dortmund-Ems and Mitteland canals were kept effectively blocked by air attacks. By the end of the year the Dortmund-Ems canal had been drained for the fourth time and the Mitteland canal three times.

Parallel with the bombing of tactical and strategical targets behind the enemy lines, Bomber Command continued its close support to the Armies whenever necessary. The heaviest attack of all was made on November 16 when more than 1,150 heavy bombers gave direct support to the American Army for the first time by dropping 5,600 tons of bombs on three towns North-East of Aachen before the Americans attacked.

One of the most dramatic achievements of the year was the sinking of the battleship "*Tirpitz*" in Tromsoe Fjord in daylight on November 12. The attack was made by 29 Lancaster bombers carrying 12,000-lb. bombs. This was the third attack to be made with 12,000-lb. bombs and although the "*Tirpitz*" had previously been damaged, it had remained a potential threat. The first attack, on September 15, was launched from a Russian base near Archangel, to which Lancasters each carrying a 12,000 lb. bomb and more than 2,000 gals. of petrol, had flown on September 11. The flight to Russia, of 1,750 miles, was made in 11 hours and was the longest flight ever made by any aircraft carrying such a bomb load.

Mosquito aircraft continued to make an important contribution to Bomber Command's offensive throughout 1944. With a bomb load increased to 4,000 lb. and with new Mosquito XVI equipped with a pressure cabin, both high and low level attacks were maintained throughout the year on Berlin and other industrial and railway centres. Formed into the Light Night Striking Force, as part of the Pathfinder Force, these attacks were frequently made by more than 50 Mosquitos at a time. By the end of the year over 12,000 tons of bombs had been dropped on the Reich by Mosquitos, of which Berlin had received more than 2,200 tons in 67 attacks.

Among the other activities of Bomber Command during the year was the dropping of arms and supplies to the Maquis who

The Mosquito B. Mk. XVI high-speed unarmed bomber. Each carrying one 4,000-lb. bomb, Mosquitos of the Light Night Striking Force played an important part in Bomber Command's massive offensive. Over 7,000 tons were dropped by Mosquitos on Berlin alone.

liberated Paris and to the underground forces of Occupied Europe, minelaying and leaflet dropping. On an average, more than 10 per cent. of the Command's effort is engaged on mine-laying and during the first four years of operations—up to the Spring of 1944—more than 13,000 sorties had been flown and over 500 ships sunk or damaged. In three months between May and August, 1944, aircraft of Bomber Command flew nearly 2,000,000 miles on mine-laying and dropped more mines than in any other quarter since the war began. Mosquito bombers made their first mine-laying attack, on the Keil Canal, on May 12.

In the first four and a half years of the War the R.A.F. dropped 1,264,456,656 leaflets, newspapers and magazines over enemy and enemy-occupied territory.

In the opening months of 1945 practically the whole weight of the bomber offensive was directed against Germany proper, and as the new Western Front offensive developed the strategic and tactical aspects of bombing were even more closely intermingled than ever before. The industrial output of towns close to the front became more vulnerable as the land forces approached but at the same time the towns became of even greater importance to the enemy because of their value as communications and supply centres. They were, therefore, destroyed.

In February, of the total of 45,750 tons of bombs dropped 45,200 fell on targets in Germany. Industrial targets, railways, waterways, etc., received over 27,000 tons and oil targets 14,000 tons. In March the entire tonnage dropped, some 67,500, fell on Germany, 39,000 by night and 27,600 by day. Seventeen towns received some 28,000 tons, 8,500 tons were dropped in tactical bombing of enemy troops, vehicles, supplies, defended positions and communications, more than 5,000 tons were dropped in daylight on specific rail targets, and 19,000 tons on oil targets. During the daylight attacks the first 22,000-lb. bombs were used for attacks on viaducts and bridges, and later on U-boat shelters.

With Bomber Command's score approaching the million-ton mark, its strategic mission in Europe was drawing to a close. In April the tonnage dropped amounted to 34,850, the weightiest effort, with some 14,000 tons, being directed against ports, naval installations and shipping, and included in the results were the sinking of Germany's last two pocket battleships,—the *Admiral Scheer* at Kiel on April 9 and the *Lutzow* at Swinemünde on April 19. 6,000 tons were dropped on tactical targets, including 1,200 tons on Hitler's chalet and eyrie at Berchtesgaden, and over 5,400 tons on oil targets. In April Mosquitos completed their 170th raid and dropped their 7,000th ton of bombs on Berlin.

In the last weeks of the war aircraft of Bomber Command were employed on dropping medical supplies on prisoner-of-war camps and, as the camps were overrun, evacuating prisoners -of-war to Great Britain. Food and supplies were also flown to Holland and dropped from the bomb-bays of Lancasters on flare-marked areas in The Hague, Leyden and Rotterdam before the enemy forces had capitulated.

Some Figures.

During the war in Europe Bomber Command flew a total of 391,137 sorties, during which 955,040 tons (1,069,645 U.S. short tons) of bombs were dropped, 657,674 tons on Germany. The total load was made up of 758,685 tons of high explosive and 196,355 tons of incendiary bombs. In addition, 47,250 mines were laid, which sank more than 1,000 ships. Further more detailed figures will be found in statistical form on later pages.

THE ALLIED EXPEDITIONARY AIR FORCE

The Allied Expeditionary Air Force, the greatest single air component ever created, was formed towards the end of 1943 as the main Tactical Air Force for the Allied invasion of Europe. It consisted of three separate and distinct forces equipped with fighter, fighter-bomber and medium bomber aircraft—the 2nd Tactical Air Force of the Royal Air Force, the United States Ninth Air Force, and Fighter Command (formerly Air Defence of Great Britain), R.A.F. The first two were essentially offensive forces, the latter primarily a defensive force. Although each was complete in itself these forces operated in unison and with complete unity of strategy and purpose under the supreme command of the Air Commander, Allied Expeditionary Air Force, Air Chief Marshal Sir Trafford Leigh-Mallory, until his appointment towards the end of 1944 to the South-East Asia Command. He was, unfortunately posted missing, believed killed, during his flight to the Far East to take up his new command.

During the first few months of 1944 the A.E.A.F. maintained almost "round-the-clock" bombing of the occupied countries, attacking targets of every kind. But when the real "softening

Airspeed Horsa troop-carrying gliders lined up on June 6, 1944, in readiness for the invasion of Normandy.

Handley Page Halifaxes on the Gardarmoen airfield near Oslo. These aircraft landed thousands of tons of supplies in the early stages of the R.A.F.'s bloodless invasion to liberate Norway.

up" process began, in April, attacks were concentrated on the enemy's communications system, mainly important road and rail bridges, notably across the Seine. Targets were pounded over a wide area so that the enemy should have no hint as to where the landings were to be made and, in fact, more bombs were dropped outside the invasion area than inside.

By D-Day, June 6, the A.E.A.F. had made 80,000 sorties against and had dropped 5,600 tons of bombs on railway centres in France while 5,209 sorties had been made and 5,370 tons of bombs had been dropped in attacks against road and rail bridges.

Plans had been made before the invasion, to ensure adequate support for the Armies, the American Air Forces attaching squadrons to each American Army group whereas the R.A.F. 2nd Tactical Air Force maintained a system of visual control posts, equipped with wireless and near the battle area, so that air support could be called up at any point when needed. Wherever necessary the component parts of the A.E.A.F. worked together in direct support of the Armies and behind them, ready to be summoned at need, were the R.A.F. and U.S. Eighth Air Force Bomber Commands.

In May a total of 65,000 sorties was flown by the A.E.A.F. and from D-Day to the end of August light and medium bombers flew 268,054 sorties and dropped 103,000 tons of bombs, mainly on bridges, airfields, ammunition dumps and other pin-point targets. The highest number of sorties in one month—in June —was 99,980. During the first month of operations in Normandy from June 6 to July 6, the Allied Air Forces as a whole flew approximately 158,500 sorties and losses were under one per cent. During the first 70 days of the invasion, 2,990 enemy aircraft were destroyed in combat and 651 on the ground, making a total of 3,641. During the same period Allied losses totalled 2,959 aircraft.

In addition to the "softening up" process and, after the invasion, their direct support to the Armies, the Allied Expeditionary Air Forces dropped more than 19,000 tons of bombs during the five months to the middle of June, 1944, on launching sites for the Flying Bombs. More than 23,500 sorties were flown in this connection and between April and May 420 carefully planned attacks were completed by aircraft of the A.E.A.F.,

Mitchell medium bombers of the Second Tactical Air Force. The aircraft in the foreground belong to a Dutch Naval squadron which had served with the R.A.F. since 1940.

mostly by Mosquito, Marauder, Mitchell, Boston and R.P. Typhoon aircraft.

Some account of the activities of the two Royal Air Force component forces of the Allied Expeditionary Air Force follows.

FIGHTER COMMAND

Although the official announcement was not made until Feb. 29, 1944, Fighter Command was reorganized in November, 1943, as the Air Defence of Great Britain, a component of the A.E.A.F. Its functions were : to give air defence to the base from which the Allied invasion was to be launched and to shipping in the nearer waters ; to assist the invasion forces with air cover before air bases could be established firmly on the Continent ; and in general to back up the 2nd Tactical Air Force.

R.A.F. Airfield Construction units building an airfield in Normandy. From the first clearing of the site to the landing of the first aircraft took about a week.

Bombing-up a Supermarine Spitfire F.IX.E fighter-bomber with one 500-lb. and two 250-lb. bombs. The "E" armament consists of two 20 m/m. cannon and two .50-in. machine-guns.

The title A.D.G.B. was retained until October, 1944, when the rebirth of Fighter Command was announced, with the same functions as before.

The year 1944 was the most varied of Fighter Command's existence. During the first half of the year and whenever the moon was down the enemy renewed his night attacks against London and Southern England—the heaviest night attacks launched by the Luftwaffe since 1940-1941—and these were continued, on a receding scale during April and May, until the Allied landings in June. These attacks cost the Luftwaffe some 250 aircraft shot down by night fighters and the A.A.—a higher percentage than had ever been obtained before. In addition, in the six weeks before D-Day the enemy attempted 129 reconnaissance flights over Great Britain but only on 11 occasions were German aircraft able to penetrate the defensive fighter screen.

On June 13 Germany opened the threatened attack against London and South-Eastern England with Flying Bombs. The attack began in earnest on June 15 and continued, almost nonstop, until the end of August. Throughout this period Fighter Command (A.D.G.B.) maintained continuous day and night patrols between the areas over which the bombs were known to travel.

Between June 13 and August 24 about 7,250 Flying Bombs were launched against Great Britain and of these nearly 2,000 were destroyed by Fighter Command. Three squadrons of one Tempest Wing accounted for over 600. The top-scoring pilot had a total of 60 shot down.

In the initial stages the fighters encountered some difficulty in tackling the Flying Bombs, but after a few days were destroying about 50 per cent. of those intercepted and after the first few weeks so improved their tactics that they were shooting down about 80 per cent. The attacks had been expected and defensive plans involving A.D.G.B., the A.A. Command, R.A.F. Balloon Command and the Royal Observer Corps, were ready. The parts played by the Balloon Barrage and the R.O.C. during these attacks are given under their respective headings and fuller details of the campaign are given under the account of Enemy Action during the year.

When the greater part of France had been liberated by the end of August and the Flying Bombs could no longer be launched from the ground the enemy used obsolescent Heinkel He 111 bombers from which to launch the Flying Bombs over the North Sea. A number of these "carrier" aircraft were shot down before these attacks—usually at night and on a much smaller scale—also waned.

Meanwhile throughout the earlier part of the year Fighter Command maintained offensive operations across the Channel escorting bombers of the 2nd T.A.F. on daylight raids and, after D-Day, heavy bombers of Bomber Command. One of the specialist arms of Fighter Command, Mosquito "Intruder" squadrons maintained their patrols over enemy airfields at night and the biggest force of "intruders" ever sent out was despatched a few hours before the Allied landings in Normandy to bomb airfields, gun positions, bridges, searchlights, trains and railway installations. Typhoons of the Command also had a share in the destruction of the enemy's coastal radio network before D-Day.

Fighters of the Command provided protection for the shipping taking part in the landings and maintained continuous day and night patrols over the beachheads. Operating in direct support of the Allied land, sea and air forces engaged in the invasions, pilots of the Command destroyed 149 enemy aircraft between June 6 and July 21. Mosquito fighter-bombers made skip-bombing attacks against special targets in the battle areas and thousands of sorties were flown by the Command in support of the ground forces. During the first month of the invasion aircraft of Fighter Command flew 21,000 sorties over Normandy.

By September well over three-quarters of the sorties flown were offensive and during the first two weeks of this month 3,000 sorties were flown over the Continent by one Group alone. Fighter Command provided much of the cover for the Airborne Landings at Arnhem at this time and also assisted in the Air/Sea Rescue work in this connection, spotting ditched gliders and transport aircraft for Air/Sea Rescue launches. Long-range Spitfire, Mustang and Tempest fighters supported the Arnhem operations by providing cover over the battlefields and for each new landing, as well as blasting enemy strong points.

One of the biggest fighter forces despatched by Fighter Command during the latter half of the year was on October 6 when more than 300 Spitfire and Mustang fighters escorted Lancaster and Halifax bombers attacking Emmerich and Kleve. A special squadron of Spitfires also accompanied the Mosquito Pathfinder force which went ahead to mark the target area. On October 7 two Mosquito fighters made one of the longest flights ever made by home-based fighters when they attacked airfields on the outskirts of Vienna—a trip of 1,700 miles there and back. A landing for re-fuelling was made in France.

Spitfire fighters of the Command acted as spotters for the naval bombardment of German gun positions on Walcheren Island during the Commando landings there in October. Flying in pairs—one Spitfire as watch-dog in case of interference by German fighters—they directed the naval gunners by radio.

In October when the Germans launched their long-range rockets against the South of England Spitfire fighter-bombers of the Command with specially trained pilots began pin-point attacks upon the launching and storage sites for the V-2 weapons in Holland and cannon-strafing attacks were made against enemy transport serving the sites with supplies. Many of the launching sites were located amidst populated districts in Holland and were strongly defended by German A.A. guns. But the Spitfires pressed home their attacks successfully with remarkably little destruction to the surrounding Dutch property. Although these attacks on the sites and on all railways and roads feeding the sites kept the menace within limits, the V-2 rocket was not defeated until Holland was overrun.

In 1944 aircraft of Fighter Command destroyed more than 700 enemy aircraft, over 500 by night.

In 1945 aircraft of the Command had to fly deep into Germany to win their victories over the reluctant Luftwaffe. In February they flew more than 3,000 sorties over enemy-held Holland and Germany, mainly as escort to aircraft of Bomber Command. In the following month nearly 3,000 sorties were flown in attacks on rocket sites in Holland and nearly 4,000 on bomber escort duties. In rail and road cuts to impede enemy transport one squadron alone flew over 1,000 operational hours during March, a record for this kind of work. Long-range Mustangs escorted many shipping strikes to the coast of Norway, flying for five or six hours over the sea out of sight of land. Altogether 27 enemy aircraft were destroyed in March as compared with 17 in the previous month. In April some 4,000 sorties were made and 23 enemy aircraft destroyed.

By the middle of April Fighter Command aircraft based in the British Isles were shooting down enemy aircraft over Berlin a fitting victory gesture by the Command which, to quote Mr. Winston Churchill, "broke the teeth of the German Air Fleet at odds of seven and eight to one" over London and the towns and fields of Southern England in 1940.

No. 11 Group, Fighter Command, which bore the brunt of the Battle of Britain, destroyed a total of 5,524 enemy aircraft during the war; 402 during the Battle of France including Dunkirk, 2,033 during the Battle of Britain, and 3,089 between January, 1941, and the cease fire in Europe. Further details of Fighter Command operations will be found in the statistical information published on later pages.

SECOND TACTICAL AIR FORCE.

Formed late in 1943, the Second Tactical Air Force of the R.A.F. had the advantage of being able to benefit from the experience of its Commander—Air Marshal Sir Arthur Coningham who controlled the First Tactical Air Force in Tunisia, Sicily and Italy. Two months before D-Day he was joined by Air Vice-Marshal Harry Broadhurst, D.S.O., D.F.C., A.F.C., who had succeeded him in Italy and was then appointed to command No. 84 (Fighter) Group, which was the spear-head of the Second Tactical Air Force during the invasion operations.

The functions of the Tactical Air Force were extremely diverse and mobile and included many activities besides complete integrity with the Army Command. The squadrons comprised Royal Air Force, Dominion and Allied Units (French, Dutch, Belgian and Polish) equipped with North American Mitchell, Douglas Boston and de Havilland Mosquito medium bombers, Supermarine Spitfire, Hawker Typhoon, Mosquito (and, in the first few months, Hawker Hurricane) fighter-bombers and R P. Typhoon, Tempest, Spitfire and Mustang fighters.

Besides the new Tempest, the Typhoon with its bomb load of 2,000 lb. and its devastating effect as an anti-tank weapon when armed with eight rocket projectiles, new Marks of Spitfire fighters for low and high level operations, and the long-range Mustang added greatly to the strength of the Command. Spitfire fighter-bombers were officially mentioned in an offensive sweep over France for the first time on April 8 and long-range Mustangs of the Command on the 20th of that month.

During the first part of the year the medium bomber operations were concentrated mainly against the V-weapon sites and installations in the Pas de Calais area, which became almost a day-by-day routine. Thousands of sorties were flown by one Mitchell wing alone in this campaign. Meanwhile the fighters and fighter-bombers were extensively engaged in escorting the medium bombers of the T.A.F. and of the U.S. Eighth and Ninth Air Forces on daylight raids against V-sites, airfields and other military objectives, and attacking enemy ground defences, communications and factories deep inside France, Holland and Belgium. One fighter group flew 7,000 such sorties between February and March. Mosquitos and Typhoons frequently operated as "free-booters," ranging over Northern and Central France in search of enemy aircraft which, with enemy communications, were given priority over other targets during the early months of the year.

From April on, activities were greatly increased to prepare the way for the land forces, the targets including bridges, railway centres, fuel dumps and wireless installations. With Fighter Command, one of T.A.F.'s most important pre-invasion tasks was to eliminate the German radio-location stations in Northern France. Operations were almost continuous throughout the days and nights, the medium bombers and "intruder" aircraft operating by night as well as by day.

Once the Allied landings had begun the Second T.A.F. maintained continuous day and night cover over the beachheads, at the same time keeping up ceaseless attacks on enemy targets of all kinds and disrupting large enemy forces which were massing for counter-attacks. Working intimately with Army ground schemes, T.A.F. fighters developed their close-support tactics, destroyed gun positions, strong-points and observation points within sight of the Allied troops. Use of what became known as the "cab rank" system of control brought Army-Air co-operation to perfection. Squadrons of Typhoon and other fighters circled over the forward troops and could be directed instantaneously by radio to any target the Army Commander wished removed.

Supermarine Spitfires of a Royal Canadian Air Force Squadron serving with the Second Tactical Air Force in Holland.

A Hawker Typhoon fighter-bomber of the Second Tactical Air Force taxying on a waterlogged airfield in Holland.

With the first tide on D-Day the first R.A.F. Beach Squadron consisting of highly-trained specialist officers and men whose task it was to pave the way for the steady flow of R.A.F. ground personnel, petrol, supplies and equipment, landed in Normandy. As soon as the landings had made sufficient progress the airfield construction units and Servicing Commandos were put ashore. Equipped with bulldozers, levellers and graders they moved to inland sites which had been selected previously from photographs and in a very short time the ground had been prepared, the portable runways laid down and the Servicing Commandos were ready to refuel and rearm the fighters.

Four days after D-Day, on June 10, the first Spitfire fighters were operating from forward landing strips in Normandy. Three days later there were five such landing grounds in Normandy and three months later the Tactical Air Force was operating from France, Belgium and Holland. Throughout the rest of the year as the fighting progressed on the Western front the landing grounds were moved farther forward with every advance made by the Armies.

As a result of the Allied wearing down and destruction of the Luftwaffe in the months before D-Day Allied superiority over the battle-fronts was at no time seriously challenged, although towards the end of the year German fighters took a more active part in the land fighting than at any time, while more of the jet-propelled Me 262 and Ar 234 fighter-bombers came into service.

At each stage of the battles for the liberation of France and Belgium the air operations had a decisive effect on the land situation. Because of the frequent bad weather the fighters and fighter-bombers bore the brunt of most situations. During July the Tactical Air Force flew almost 27,000 sorties, mainly in direct support of the British-Canadian Second Army while August was the greatest month and the most disastrous for the German Army. During that month Typhoons and Spitfires in road-strafing operations claimed some 3,000 vehicles knocked out when the enemy was trying to escape from the trap at Falaise and in the subsequent land operations, when the enemy's convoy discipline was lost, the T.A.F. took toll of approximately 1,000 vehicles a day. Altogether that month the T.A.F. claimed

Mitchell medium bombers of the Second Tactical Air Force taxying out for an attack on a bridge at Venlo in Holland.

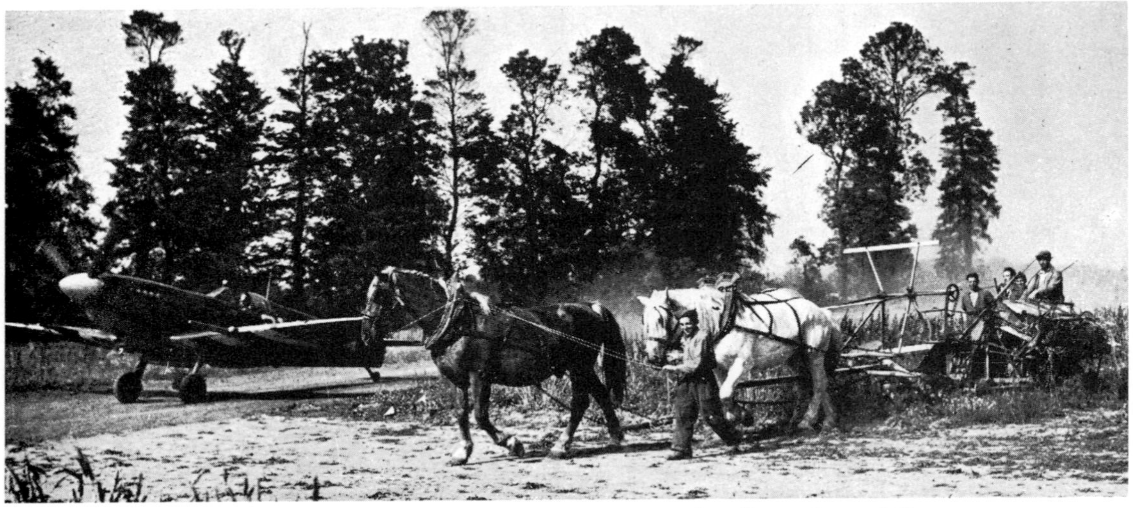

A Supermarine Spitfire on an airstrip running through a Normandy cornfield.

10,500 German transport vehicles and 850 tanks. More than 33,000 sorties were flown. The Rocket Typhoon proved the ideal anti-tank weapon, while the Spitfire dominated the attacks against "soft-skinned" vehicles. At Mortain, the Falaise Gap and the Seine crossings, during the advances to Eindhoven and at Walcheren, T.A.F. played a vital part in the operations.

Towards the end of the year T.A.F. took its share in the dislocation of the railway system in Western Germany and against railway lines in Central Holland which became priority targets. Weather during October was almost continuously adverse while in November there were six days on which no flying was possible.

In December, when Runstedt began his counter-offensive, T.A.F. shot down 100 enemy aircraft and during several critical days of the attack flew in conditions which in other circumstances would have kept them grounded. During the first six days of the offensive the weather was so bad that on three days flying was impossible. Despite these handicaps some 15,000 sorties were flown, one-third of them on armed reconnaissance and army support, during which much German armour was crippled.

During the whole of 1944 the 2nd Tactical Air Force flew more than 1,024,000 sorties on nearly 20,000 operations and the bomb tonnage for the year exceeded 38,000 tons, while about 130,000 rockets were fired. One Typhoon Wing fired more than one million rounds of cannon shells and 40,000 rockets between D-Day and the end of the year.

One Group of T.A.F., known as Base Defence Group, was formed to provide air defence for the base headquarters of operational Groups in the Continent with units based from North-east France, across Belgium and deep into Holland. A miniature air force on its own, it comprised night fighter Mosquitos, Air-Sea Rescue aircraft, a communications squadron, mobile balloon squadrons, contingents of the R.A.F. Regiment and Technical, Maintenance and Constructing units. The Airfield Construction Wing of this Group was responsible for building many of the forward landing grounds in Normandy, Belgium and Holland. Between D-Day and the end of 1944 night fighters of this Group destroyed more than 200 enemy aircraft.

On July 15, 1945 the 2nd T.A.F. ceased to exist, its place being taken in Europe by British Air Forces of Occupation (Germany) under the Command of Air Chief Marshal Sir W. Sholto Douglas.

With the passing of the 2nd T.A.F. one of the greatest fighting units of the British armed forces passed into history. Formed out of experience against the Afrika Korps in the desert, 2nd T.A.F. grew in the hands of Air Marshal Sir Arthur Coningham from a desert compromise into a first-class striking force. Its fighters, fighter-bombers and medium bombers covered the landings in Normany, crippled the enemy thrust to the sea at Avranches, plugged the Falaise Gap with blasted transport, tanks and men, and assisted in the Walcheren landing operation. They helped to stop the Rundstedt drive in the Ardennes, supported the Allied forces all the way to the Rhine, covered the Rhine crossing and, finally, in an all-out five-day assault destroyed some 4,500 road transports, put out of action 150 ships including many U-boats, shot down 116 enemy aircraft and put out of action 100 on the ground, as its contribution to the final capitulation. In the eleven months from D-Day to the end of the war in Europe 2nd T.A.F. formations destroyed more than 13,000 vehicles, including tanks.

ENEMY ACTION AGAINST GREAT BRITAIN

Enemy activity over Great Britain during 1944 was divided into two phases—the first half of the year when orthodox air raids were made and the second half which was entirely given over to "pilotless," or "V" weapons—flying bombs and long-range rockets.

At the beginning of the year the Luftwaffe maintained spasmodic bombing raids, mainly against London and South-East England. These attacks were increased considerably during February and March, reaching the heaviest scale since 1940-41.

Many incendiaries as well as H.E.s were dropped and the enemy obviously copied tactics and devices used by the Royal Air Force over Germany, including the Pathfinder technique, and the dropping of strips of metalised paper designed to interfere with the radiolocation system. Frequently the enemy crossed the coast some way to the North and attacked London and South-East England by round-about routes, flying in close formation and thus achieving a greater concentration. But the attacks were devoid of any plan and the bombing was scattered and indiscriminate.

The usual method was for the bombers to fly in across the coast at a great height and to take advantage of this height on their way out by diving steeply and crossing the coast again at 2,000 ft. or less. The types of aircraft used for these attacks included the Messerschmitt Me 210 and 410, Junkers Ju 88 and Ju 188, Dornier Do 217 and a few Heinkel He 177 heavy bombers.

The greatest number to cross the coast on any night during this period was some 175 aircraft and the general rate of casualties inflicted throughout the raids was on a higher scale than that suffered by R.A.F. bombers over Germany. About 54 enemy aircraft were destroyed over Great Britain in February, and 58 in March. During April and May the raids continued but on a smaller scale and less frequently. Then there was a lull until the opening of the second phase—the so-called V weapons.

The first flying bombs, known officially in Germany as the FZG-76 but popularly called V.1, were launched against Great Britain on the night of June 13. The attack began in earnest on June 15. For the next 80 days it was kept up almost continuously, mainly against the London area and Southern England.

The existence of the flying bomb had been known and counter-measures had been taken to meet the attack. In February, 1944, the Prime Minister warned the country that the Germans were preparing on the French coast new means of attack on Great Britain.

As a result of searching investigations by agents and reconnaissance, the main experimental stations for both the flying bomb and the long-range rocket had been located at Peenemünde, on the Baltic. The heavy attack by Bomber Command on Peenemünde on August 17-18, 1943, and the serious damage and many casualties inflicted, caused a severe set-back to the enemy's plans. Factories and plants manufacturing special weapons and production plants building weapons and component parts, as well as storage depots, were heavily attacked by the British and American Air Forces.

Reconnaissance photographs of Northern France, covering many hundreds of square miles, showed the construction of launching points for the flying bombs, including launching ramps and scattered small buildings, usually well hidden and camouflaged in thick woods. Heavy bombing attacks on these installations were begun in December, 1943, by R.A.F., United States, Dominion and Allied Air Forces whenever the weather and operational requirements permitted. Large structures which appeared to be connected with the firing of the long-range rocket were also located in the Pas de Calais area and heavily and continuously attacked, as well as many other structures along the French coast between Le Havre and Calais.

All the 100 firing sites which had been discovered and bombed were destroyed. As they were repaired, so they were bombed again. Under the pressure of these counter-measures the enemy developed a new series of pre-fabricated structures which could be assembled rapidly and well camouflaged. From these the attack was finally launched.

But the attack, planned to bolster up German morale and to divert the impact of the Allied Air Forces on German industries and communications, was delayed for six months at least, and when it was eventually launched was on less than a quarter the scale originally planned.

Altogether, before and during the attacks, more than 100,000 tons of bombs were dropped on the flying bomb targets, involving a loss of 450 British and American aircraft and approximately 2,900 pilots and members of air crews.

Detailed arrangements for the defence of London were made, providing for three defence belts; a balloon barrage just outside London, a gun belt beyond, and beyond that a fighter zone.

During the pre-invasion period the majority of the A.A. guns and balloons were concentrated round the British ports of departure. When the flying bomb attack was launched the guns and balloons were moved immediately to prepared sites to the South East of London, the guns along the Southern edge of the Balloon Barrage, stretching roughly from Maidstone to East Grinstead. About the middle of July the entire gun belt was moved down to the South Coast so that the guns could have an uninterrupted field. Fighters then had an area between the coast and the balloons, and over the channel. After this deployment the guns shot down 17 per cent. of the bombs and in the last week of the attack, 74 per cent.

Altogether, 800 heavy and nearly 2,000 light guns were in action, of which American batteries provided about one-eighth of the total number of heavy guns.

The Balloon Barrage consisted at first of some 500 balloons, but these were increased to nearly 2,000.

When the first flying bomb crossed the coast on June 13 Fighter Command's (A.D.G.B. as it was at that time) plan for the defences went into action together with the Royal Observer Corps, the A.A. Defences and the Balloon Barrage. Constant standing patrols were maintained by Fighter Command day and night throughout the 24 hours, over land and sea. Many bombs were intercepted and destroyed over the Channel and along the coast of France. Others were shot down over the open country before they could reach the built-up areas farther inland.

The fighters had to contend with many difficulties and entirely new tactics had to be worked out to intercept the flying bombs. Only the fastest fighters could overtake the bomb in level flight as it flew between 350 and 400 m.p.h. and at a height of a few thousand feet only. Also, the bombs were launched in salvos. During daylight the fighters had difficulty in seeing the small, fast moving object, although over land a running commentary was kept up by radio to tell the pilots where the bombs were in relation to local landmarks.

At night the problem was easier because the flaming tail of the bomb could be seen many miles away. Another difficulty was that to bring the bombs down the pilots had to fire at a range of about 300 yards. After much experiment a simple and ingenious range-finder was produced and this problem was solved.

Aircraft used against the flying bomb included the Mosquito, Spitfire, Typhoon, the Tempest—which first went into action against the flying bomb—and the Gloster Meteor jet-propelled aircraft, which also first went into action at this time.

Beginning on June 15, the flying bomb attack lasted for 80 days almost non-stop. During this time the enemy launched more than 8,000 bombs, of which some 2,300 got through to the London area. About 25 per cent. of the bombs which were launched were inaccurate and erratic; many dived into the sea of their own accord; others strayed as far North as Norfolk and Northampton; and the remainder were brought down.

In the first week of the attack about 33 per cent. of the bombs were destroyed by the defences. By the end of the attack some 70 per cent. of those launched were brought down and only about nine per cent. were reaching London. The record was on August 28 when of the total of 101 bombs which approached the coast, 97 were destroyed before they reached London.

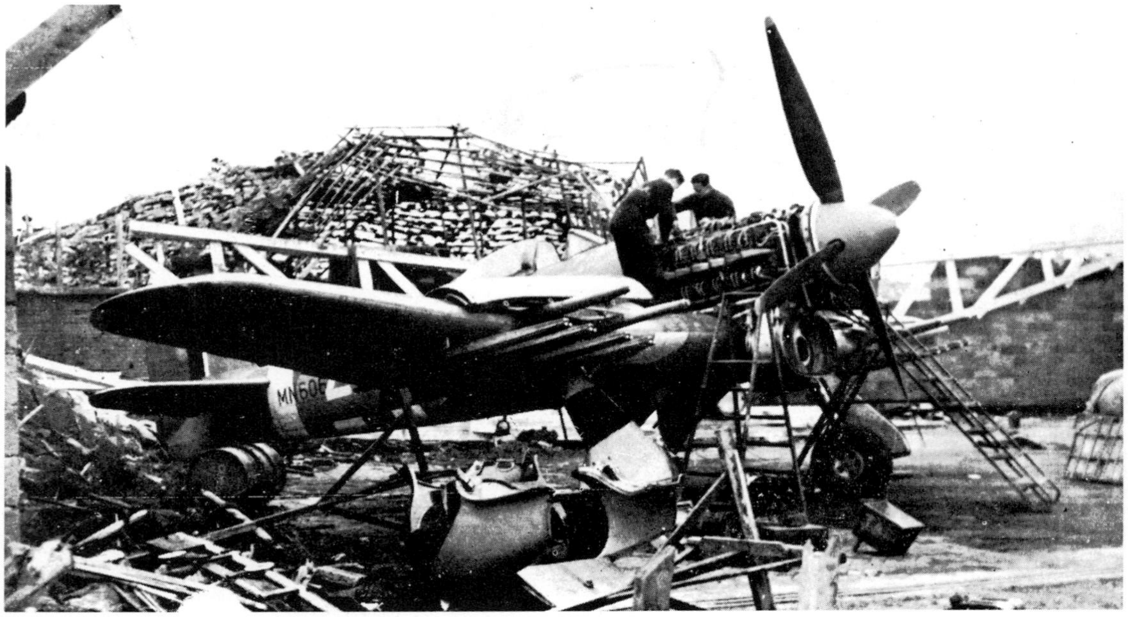

A Repair and Salvage unit of the Second Tactical Air Force servicing a Rocket-firing Typhoon on a German airfield in N.W. Europe.

On certain dull and cloudy days as many as 200 flying bombs were launched within 24 hours. In one 24-hour period London had 15 alerts and on two occasions, 11 alerts in 24 hours. The longest alert was three minutes less than 12 hours and the longest lull was towards the end of August when the attacks had tended to become spasmodic and there were several lulls, including one period of 30 hours.

A light-scale attack was made on Portsmouth and Southampton during five days in July but during the whole of the rest of the period the attack was aimed at London. About 92 per cent. of all fatal casualties occurred in the London region.

At the beginning there was an average of one death for every bomb launched ; at the end, three bombs were launched for every one person killed.

Of the total number shot down, the various defences accounted for the following :—Fighter Command, more than 1,900 ; A.A. guns, 1,560 ; and Balloon Barrage, 279 ; making a total of more than 3,739.

The main bombardment with flying bombs, or V.1s, ended at the beginning of September when the flying bomb sites were over-run and captured by the Allied forces in France. But during the month intermittent attacks were made, mainly at night, by flying bombs launched from specially-adapted Heinkel He 111s. During the earlier months a small proportion of the bombs had come in from the East. These had also been launched from He 111 aircraft which flew out over the North Sea to launch their bombs. A number of these carriers were shot down.

The first long-range rockets, or V.2s, were launched about the third week in September. The rockets, launched mainly from Holland, arrived unheralded, travelling at a speed of some 3,000 m.p.h. With a range of about 200 miles the total time of flight from launching to impact with the ground was about five minutes. Because the speed of the V.2 was greater than that of sound the noise of the passage of the V.2 was not heard until after it had exploded. The weight of the explosive carried was about the same as in the flying bomb—about one ton—and the damage caused was generally about the same.

The task of countering the rocket attacks devolved almost entirely on fighter bombers of Fighter Command and the Second Tactical Air Force. Pin-point attacks on V.2 storage and launching sites, well hidden in woods and populated districts, were continuously made by Spitfire fighter-bombers of Fighter Command. In addition, Spitfires, Tempests, Typhoons and Mosquitos of the Second Tactical Air Force incessantly attacked depots, railways and the communications systems used between the Rhine and Meuse Fronts to bring up the rockets to their sites. Unlike the flying bombs the rockets were launched from small areas and needed little special equipment. Constant harrying of the rail systems and depots was one of the few means of curtailing the supply.

Again the attacks were against Southern England, including the London area, but because of security restrictions to avoid giving the enemy any information and assistance, no details of the V.2 attacks had been permitted up to the end of March, 1945.

From October to the end of 1944 enemy action was mainly confined to the long-range rocket attacks, with a few flying bomb raids, including one against the North of England on December 24. Throughout December there were only three 24-hour periods when there was no enemy action over Great Britain.

The V.2 attacks continued in 1945 on a varying scale and early in March the Luftwaffe made its first appearance over Great Britain for almost a year by making one or two sharp attacks against the North of England. Also there was a renewal of intermittent flying bomb attacks launched from aircraft over the North Sea.

CIVILIAN AIR RAID CASUALTIES.

	Killed	Seriously Injured
January	107	270
February	961	1,712
March	279	633
April	146	226
May	68	75
June	1,935	5,906
July	2,441	7,107
August	1,103	2,921
September	170	360
October	172	416
November	716	1,511
December	367	847
Totals	8,465	21,984
Totals since September, 1940	55,280	92,611
Grand total, killed and seriously injured, Sept., 1940 to Dec., 1944		147,891

COASTAL COMMAND

Working from bases in the United Kingdom and Northern Ireland, Iceland, Gibraltar and the Mediterranean, the Azores, Ceylon and West Africa, Coastal Command maintained continuous operations throughout the year from the Arctic to the Equator, from Norway to mid-Atlantic, over the South Atlantic and in the Far East and always in close co-operation with the Royal Navy. Escorting and protecting convoys, maintaining constant anti-submarine patrols and attacking enemy shipping of all kinds continued to be the chief functions of the Command, together with Photographic and Meteorological Reconnaissance and Air/Sea Rescue Duties. One Meteorological Flight equipped with Hudson aircraft made two 500-mile flights Westward over the Atlantic from Reykjavik, Iceland, every 24 hours. The Photographic Reconnaissance Group contributed greatly to the battle against the flying bomb by locating many launching sites.

The types in service continued to include the Short Sunderland and Consolidated Catalina flying-boats, Handley Page Halifax bombers for anti-submarine and shipping patrols, the Vickers-Armstrongs Wellington and Consolidated Liberator equipped with Leigh Lights, the Vickers-Armstrongs Warwick for G.R. and Air/Sea Rescue duties and the de Havilland Mosquito and

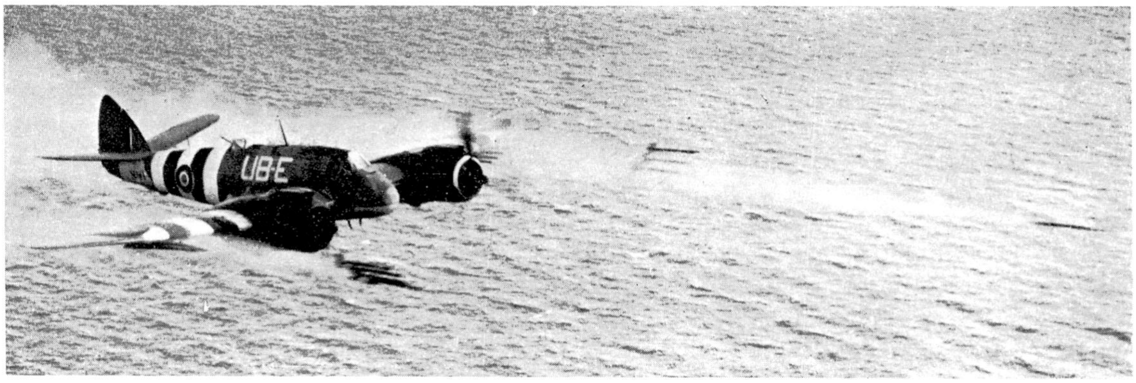

A Rocket-firing Bristol Beaufighter of a squadron of the Royal Australian Air Force which served in the British Isles with R.A.F. Coastal Command.

Bristol Beaufighter. The outstanding additions to Coastal Command during the year were the Beaufighter and Mosquito equipped with rocket projectiles and the Mosquito XVIII armed with the six-pounder (57 m/m.) cannon.

Throughout the year aircraft of the Royal Navy, including Fairey Albacore and Swordfish and Grumman Avenger units operated under Coastal Command and participated in attacks against enemy "E" and "R" boats with torpedoes and mines.

Without at any time coming much into the limelight Coastal Command's greatest and most important achievements during the year were in the European theatre, where D-Day marked for the Command the culmination of many months' preparation and a triumph over enemy submarines. According to the Secretary of State for Air, Sir Archibald Sinclair, had the German submarines been sinking even a fraction of the number of Allied ships which they were sinking in every month of 1943, the weight of the Allied invasion of Europe on June 6, 1944, would have been greatly reduced. But Coastal Command and the Royal Navy had obtained an increasing mastery of the submarines and the seas and the Channel were kept open.

In the three weeks before D-Day the Germans endeavoured to move up reserves of submarines from bases in Norway but their every move was anticipated. In the continuous daylight of the Northern Summer the battle was fought off the coasts of Norway, the Shetlands, the Faröe Islands and in the Arctic. Many submarines were sunk and damaged.

The main campaign was fought in the English Channel and its Western approaches. This campaign began on D-Day when the German Biscay submarine fleet made its way to the Western approaches of the Channel on the surface. This fleet was constantly engaged by Coastal Command which, during the first four critical days from D-Day, made 38 sightings that resulted in many successful attacks, the U-boats fighting back.

These successes were decisive, as were the incessant attacks on enemy motor gun-boats and motor torpedo-boats on which the Germans had also relied to interfere with the invasion fleet.

In addition to continuous anti-submarine patrols, which frequently involved 30,000 flying hours a month, Coastal Command maintained throughout the year persistent and mounting attacks —or "strikes"—against enemy shipping of all kinds round the coasts of Europe.

The tremendous effect of the R.P. Mosquito and Beaufighter aircraft, together with the Mosquito XVIII, all of which went into service late in 1943 but were not announced officially until early in 1944, made the anti-shipping "strikes" even more devastating.

The first attack against an enemy submarine by a Mosquito XVIII was made early in November, 1943, against a surfaced submarine returning to Brest from a patrol. From then on even the waters close to the French coast were no longer safe for unescorted surfaced submarines and shortly after the first attack the Germans were forced to provide escorts for surface ships and fighter aircraft to protect submarines entering or leaving harbour.

During the twelve months to March 31, 1944, Coastal Command made 4,500 sorties on anti-shipping operations and from April onward these attacks increased. The effect of the attacks by Bomber Command and the Second Tactical Air Force on enemy communications forced the enemy to an increasing use of his coastal shipping resources, thus providing Coastal Command with more numerous targets. These targets were attacked with torpedoes, bombs, rocket projectiles and cannon so effectively that the enemy was forced to supply his convoys with protection and it was estimated that some 40 per cent. of the German naval strength was deployed on escorting inshore shipping. As many as 20 escorts were provided for one merchant ship. The Norwegian coast was a specially good hunting ground but enemy shipping along the coasts of Denmark, Holland, Belgium and France was attacked day and night.

Strike wings of torpedo or R.P. Beaufighters and R.P. Mosquitos were usually accompanied by a large escort either of cannon-firing Mosquitos or by aircraft of Fighter Command.

Frequently the torpedo-carrying Beaufighter "Strike Wings" would be escorted by R.P. Beaufighters. The escorting aircraft went in first to shoot up the enemy escort and "flak" ships with cannon and rocket projectiles, thus reducing the opposition and enabling more accurate attacks to be made by the Strike Wings.

During June a total of 8,000 sorties was flown by Coastal Command, more than 3,000 on P.R. and anti-shipping sorties during which some 600 vessels were attacked. The following month 2,000 sorties were flown against shipping and 550 individual attacks were made against approximately 225 vessels.

An important part in the battle for the French ports, especially the U-boat bases in the Brest Peninsula, was played by the Command. Immediately the fall of the ports appeared imminent Coastal Command aircraft and surface vessels of the Royal Navy threw a ring around them, thus preventing the beleaguered garrisons from obtaining reinforcements. In addition, by destroying a large proportion of the enemy's minesweeper fleet operating in the Bay of Biscay, air and surface craft prevented the movement of U-boats and enemy shipping. In three weeks, Mosquito, Beaufighter and Halifax aircraft made nearly 300 attacks on nearly 150 separate targets from Ostend to Bordeaux, during which more than 30 enemy vessels were sunk, damaged or set on fire.

The biggest force of Beaufighters ever engaged on a shipping strike attacked on Sept. 25 a concentration of some twenty enemy vessels in the heavily defended anchorage of Den Helder, the most likely "escape port" for German forces trapped in Holland by the British Second Army. More than 70 Beaufighters, escorted by Mustang and Tempest fighters of Fighter Command, made sea-level attacks on the ships and on shore batteries and radio installations with cannon, rockets and torpedoes.

The liberation of Belgium provided a new base for Coastal Command aircraft, including Swordfish of the Navy operating with the Command, and towards the end of the year the main battle area was concentrated round the Dutch and Norwegian coasts.

Darkness brought the enemy no relief, strike aircraft co-operating with flame-dropping aircraft continuing the attacks at night while small ships were persistently sought in a campaign of individual night attacks. A new technique was adopted for these night attacks known as the "Drem" system. This consisted of a striking force of Beaufighter aircraft armed with torpedoes or rockets and Halifax and Wellington flare-dropping aircraft which went out singly under cover of darkness to patrol areas round the Norwegian coast. When targets were located powerful flares were dropped by the Halifax and Wellington bombers to indicate the position of the enemy ships and guided by these lights, the striking force of Beaufighters formed up for the attack.

Anti-shipping activities were continued into 1945 when Coastal Command introduced a new phase. On February 4, 1945, Leigh Light Liberators attacked enemy submarines and destroyers in the Baltic port of Danzig. This attack, the first of its kind to be made by the Command, involved a flight of more than 1,600 miles.

Anti U-boat patrols steadily increased as the enemy made his last despairing effort to interfere with the operations in Northern Europe. In February sorties from home bases involved over 16,500 hours, and in March the total increased to 28,000 flying hours, but dropped to 27,000 hours in April.

Shipping strikes in the waters between Scandinavia and Germany were a conspicuous feature in April. More than 1,650 anti-shipping sorties were flown and 234 targets were attacked. The grand finale of shipping destruction took place on May 3 and 4 when the enemy was attempting a frantic evacuation from his remaining Baltic ports to Denmark. Every type of vessel from 10,000-ton liners to E-boats was involved and Coastal Command joined in the general massacre.

Coastal Command's war activities came to an end on June 4, when the 2,853rd and last convoy protection patrol was completed.

SOUTH-EAST ASIA COMMAND

Throughout 1944 air power was the deciding factor in every major campaign fought in the South-East Asia Command. The most effective collaboration between the air and ground forces of any theatre of War was claimed for the Burma front and R.A.F. Advisers were attached to Army Brigades for all matters connected with air support. One of the outstanding features of this theatre in 1944 was the transport and supplying by air of the ground forces, which became a model for all other fronts.

In 1944 enemy-held territory in the South-East Asia Command extended some 2,500 miles southwards from the North of Burma. The front in Burma covered some 700 miles over the wildest and most impenetrable jungle and mountainous country in the World, and was second in length only to the Russian front.

On its formation in 1943 the South-East Asia Command was intended to become an increasingly offensive theatre, but shortly afterwards the Allies decided to concentrate in the European theatre and equipment intended for Burma was transferred. In fact all the landing ships allotted to S.E.A.C. were withdrawn and were used during the landings at Anzio in the Mediterranean and later in the invasion of Normandy. S.E.A.C. was instructed to carry on as best it could with what was left. Throughout 1944 it had the lowest priority of any of the commands in the East and West.

In spite of this handicap the British 14th Army and American and Chinese forces, together with the Anglo-American air forces drove the Japanese out of India, inflicting the greatest defeat of the War so far on the Japanese Imperial armies. By the end of the year a large part of Northern Burma had been re-captured and in the first four months of 1945 the Burma and Ledo roads had been re-opened and Meiktila and Mandalay had been captured. On May 3, British forces entered Rangoon.

The Anglo-American Air Forces in this theatre were probably more closely integrated than in any other theatre. Eastern Air Command, under the command of Major-General George E. Stratemayer, who was also Deputy Air Commander S.E.A.C., comprised a Strategical Air Force, under the Command of Major-Gen. Howard C. Davidson, consisting of the U.S. 10th Air Force and units of the R.A.F., mainly Liberator and Wellington bombers; The Third Tactical Air Force, under the operational control of Air Marshal Sir John Baldwin, also A.O.C., R.A.F. Bengal-Burma, who was succeeded towards the end of the year by Air Marshal W. A. Coryton, C.B., M.V.O., D.F.C., Troop Carrier Command, under the operational control of Brig.-Gen. William D. Old, U.S. Army, which consisted of units of R.A.F. Transport Command and the U.S. Air Transport Command. R.A.F. squadrons based in Southern India, Ceylon, East Africa and Arabia all operated with Eastern Air Command.

Types of aircraft used in this theatre included:—Spitfire fighters and fighter-bombers, Mosquito VI fighters and fighter-bombers and P.R. Mosquitos, Mustang fighters and fighter-bombers, Thunderbolt fighters, Hawker Hurricane fighter-bombers, rocket-projectile Hurricanes and Beaufighters, Vengeance dive-bombers and Auster light aeroplanes.

Throughout the year the Allied Air Forces operated in continuous support of the Armies. Japanese road, rail and river communications over the whole of Burma were kept crippled in round-the-clock attacks and constant attacks by the Strategic Air Force reduced the use by Japan of the main Burma ports. But the most spectacular operations of the year were those of the transport units which kept all ground troops in forward areas supplied by air and flew out the wounded from forward bases.

Supply dropping was developed to a fine art in the Burma theatre. Supplies dropped by the R.A.F. in containers both with and without parachutes included fresh eggs, blood plasma, live poultry, clothing, ammunition, weapons, petrol (dropped in 55 gallon drums roped to three parachutes) and 75 m/m. pack howitzers, the parts for which were dropped in special containers. C-47 Dakotas and C-46 Commandos were the main types of transport used by the Allies for supply dropping. A division fighting and marching light in the hills was estimated to require 100 tons of supplies a day. A division as fighting in Central Burma towards the end of 1944 was estimated to require 130 tons daily. Dakotas circled forward areas two and three times a day to drop supplies by parachute. In some areas, and circumstances, landing strips were prepared and the transports landed, sometimes with gliders. R.A.F. transports dropped between 1,300 and 3,000 tons a month.

Between May and October, inclusive, transport aeroplanes of the Combat Cargo Task Force flew 25,049 sorties and delivered 76,169 tons of supplies. Even the Monsoon did not stop the transports, the longest single period during which the dropping of supplies was impossible because of the weather being five days.

Another great service was performed by small liaison aircraft including L-4, L-5, and D.H. Tiger Moths and Fox Moths. These small aeroplanes flew in liaison officers and reinforcements and evacuated wounded from landing strips only some 100 yards long in the heart of the jungle. Many of the landing strips were only a few hundred yards from enemy positions and were frequently under fire. R.A.F. Tiger Moths and Fox Moths, modified to take stretcher cases, operated in the remote reaches of the River Kaladan, in Arakan, saving many lives. Pilots flew an average of 10 hours a day to evacuate wounded and between February 16, and May 8, 1944, these light aeroplanes brought out to forward bases more than 2,000 casualties. Frequently Hurricane or Spitfire fighters strafed Japanese positions close to the landing strips to silence enemy opposition so that the light aeroplanes could land and take on their loads.

A special R.A.F. organization known as Forward Airfields Maintenance Organization was developed to overcome the supply problems. It was developed from the First Wingate Chindit expedition of 1943. By means of F.A.M.O., main bases kept pace with the Army advances through the jungle. Sites were chosen during reconnaissance flights and within two to three days strips of some 70 yards long would be ready for light aeroplanes to land. Within a week of the first operation Dakotas would be landing on strips 1,000 yards long, and medical supplies and equipment of all kinds, troops and petrol would have been flown in.

Operations in Burma during 1944 were divided into three major sectors—Arakan, or the Southern Front; Imphal or the Central Front; and Myitkyina, or the Northern Front. The main object of the campaigns was to drive the Japanese out of the North-East corner of Burma so as to improve communications with China. In April, headquarters of S.E.A.C. were moved from Delhi to Kandy, Ceylon.

The first victory was in the Arakan sector where the Japanese attempted to invade India from the south in February. At first they had some success, driving a wedge between two divisions and encircling some 8,000 British troops in what became known as the "Admin. Box." At the beginning of this Japanese thrust Japanese Zeke fighters appeared over the Battle area but were met by Spitfires of the Third Tactical Air Force. Ten days later the challenge was broken off by the Japanese after Spitfires had destroyed and damaged 65 Japanese fighters for a loss of three Spitfires. Meanwhile, transport aircraft flew by day and night to drop supplies to the besieged "boxes," 500 sorties delivering 1,500 tons of supplies with the loss of only one transport. After 17 days' siege and battle the encircled troops, together with reinforcements which had been brought up, inflicted the first severe defeat on the Japanese in Burma. This Arakan battle was important also because it was the first vindication of the land-air technique of combat and supply. The British advance on this front then continued until the Monsoon broke in June, by which time the fortress of Razabil and the commanding heights of Buthidaung had been taken. Meanwhile, throughout the Monsoon the R.A.F., operating from all-weather landing strips, continued to harry the Japanese.

The second Japanese attempt to invade India was launched on March 17 across the Chindwin towards the Imphal Plain, while aircraft of the Tactical Air Force struck hard at their bases along the Chindwin. But the Japanese advanced across the Kohima-Imphal road, reached within striking distance of Imphal and all but took Kohima. About the middle of May British forces attacked from both Kohima and Imphal, had cleared the road by June 22 and by August 25 the last Japanese had been driven from India with the British still in pursuit down the Tiddim road.

The battles of Imphal and Kohima were two of the outstanding achievements of the year. Completely cut off from India by the surrounding Japanese, except by air, the Imphal Valley was completely enclosed by hills rising to a height at some points of 7,000 ft. The main airstrip in the valley was about 4,000 yards long. Regular transport services were organized, Dakotas and Mitchells flying in every day from bases in India some 200 miles away, bringing food, petrol, ammunition, ordnance stores, medical supplies, men and water, and evacuating casualties. Wellington bombers alone ferried in a million pounds of bombs for the fighter-bombers. Throughout the siege about 300 transport aircraft arrived and left each day. Two fully-equipped divisions were flown up from Arakan.

Meanwhile R.A.F. squadrons operating from the Imphal "Box" included two squadrons of Spitfire fighters and four squadrons of Hurricane fighter-bombers. Besides giving close support to the ground forces and protecting them from the Japanese fighter-bombers, these squadrons had to protect the constant stream of transports. Another Spitfire squadron not based in the Valley, flew in each morning from outside and flew home again at night. So effectively did the fighters protect the transports that out of the thousands which flew in and out, only 20 were lost by enemy action. Meanwhile the Japanese positions were constantly attacked from Imphal. One Hurricane Group dropped over 2½ million pounds of bombs in April. Flying was continued throughout the Monsoon and in the first four months fighters and medium bombers of the Tactical Air Force flew 24,000 sorties.

Simultaneously the Strategical Air Force was bombing enemy-held Burma and penetrating as far as Bangkok. The Irrawaddy and Chindwin rivers were swept for river traffic and Japanese communications of every kind were systematically pounded.

Kohima, also besieged, was in a worse position than Imphal because it had no air strip. Instead, supplies were dropped from the air and the siege was held until supplies had been built up inside both Kohima and Imphal and reinforcements had fought their way up and the break-out was made. During these two great battles a total of 30,000 non-combatant troops were flown out of Imphal and 30,000 casualties were evacuated. Two and a half divisions and all their equipment, almost as many replacements and 50,000 tons of supplies were flown in.

In preparation for the break-out Hurricane fighter-bombers and Vengeance dive-bombers bombed and machine-gunned the Japanese positions. Once the siege of Kohima and Imphal was lifted the enemy was pursued down the Tiddim road, the 14th Army and the Air Forces passing completely to the offensive and working in the closest co-operation. In fact, the Hurricane and Vengeance bombers were credited with virtually liquidating some Japanese positions without infantry assistance.

Following this break-out the Japanese were pushed out of India, the Chin Hills were re-captured and the Chindwin crossed on a wide front in November—many of the troops crossing on rafts dropped from the air. On December 2, Kalewa, known as the "gateway to Burma," was captured and by April, 1945 the Battle of Arakan, after two and a half years, was won.

On May 3 Rangoon was captured. The entry into Rangoon was the story of victory through air power, a story which began over a year previously at Imphal, when an encircled British army, its land communications cut on every side, was fully supplied and reinforced by air until it was ready to break the siege. In the weary months that followed that army had battled south to Rangoon through the most arduous fighting country in the world, with the Allied Air Forces as its constant provider and shield and battering ram.

With the 14th Army almost at the gates of Rangoon, a new threat to the city developed from the south. On May 2, troops came ashore from landing craft to link up with paratroops who had dropped near the Rangoon River the day previously, but for days before that, Eastern Air Command had been paving the way for final, pulverising assault.

On May 2 R.A.F. supply-dropping aircraft of Eastern Air Command's Combat Cargo Task Force flew 850 miles to Rangoon and back through pre-monsoon storms to parachute supplies of water and ammunition to paratroops on the banks of the Rangoon River. This was the longest operation ever undertaken by R.A.F. transports in this theatre and lasted seven hours. It came as the climax to eighteen months of effort during which transport crews flew thousands of hours to drop more than half a million tons of essential war supplies to the 14th Army. Rangoon set the seal to the finest sustained operation in air transport history.

One of the greatest exploits in Burma during 1944 was the Second Wingate "Chindit" expedition on the Northern Front. In February an American-Chinese force operating under General Stillwell invaded Northern Burma from Assam in order to sieze air fields giving better communications with China and to re-open the Burma Road. British and Imperial airborne forces—Chindits—were landed in advance of the Chinese forces and thus enabled General Stillwell to clear the Kukwang Valley.

This first airborne invasion of Burma has been called the test, and then the model, for the airborne invasion of Normandy. An Anglo-American operation, it was planned by Lord Louis Mountbatten, C.-in-C., S.E.A.C. and General Wingate, and details were worked out at the Quebec Conference in 1943. An Air Commando Force was organized by Col. P. G. Cockran, U.S.A.A.F., to transport, supply and evacuate the Wingate forces. In addition, the Air Commando added an Air Striking Force to the organization for close support work with the Wingate columns. This force comprised P-51 Mustang fighter-bombers, a squadron of B-25 Mitchell bombers, C-47 Dakota transports, UC-61 Fairchild transports, L-1 and L-5 Grasshopper liaison aircraft and CG-4A gliders.

Besides the Air Commando Force, which was under the operational control of Air Marshal Sir John Baldwin, A.O.C.-in-C., the Tactical Air Force, the Tactical Air Force and Troop Carrier Command were involved.

Two sites were selected as landing grounds 150 miles inside Burma and more than 100 miles behind the Japanese lines, but 15 minutes before the departure of the first transports and gliders, one site had to be abandoned because a reconnaissance photograph showed that the Japanese had hopelessly obstructed the ground. All transports were directed to the other site.

The invasion was launched on the night of March 5, gliders and their Dakota tugs taking off from the base in India at 5-10 minute intervals. Of the 54 gliders despatched 37 arrived, eight landed west of the Chindwin in friendly territory and nine landed in enemy territory. Almost all the gliders were damaged or destroyed in the landing but more than 500 men were brought in that first night, including many engineers, and work was started on clearing the field. Thirteen hours later, on the night of March 6, 62 Dakota sorties were flown to the field, which had been named "Broadway," and all casualties had been evacuated.

In seven days 12,000 men, 500,000 lbs. of stores, 1,183 mules and 175 ponies were flown in at a cost of 121 men. Transports landed and took-off at the rate of one every three minutes. Four days after the first landing the troops had marched into the jungle to start work on the Japanese communications. Unfortunately, General Wingate was killed on the night of March 24, when, after touring the forward positions, the aeroplane in which he was flying was lost in a storm and crashed on a mountain-side.

Three days after the first landing a second site was chosen to relieve the congestion and not until the eighth day did the Japanese discover the landing strips and send in their fighters, which were beaten off.

The full story of the Long-Range Penetration Forces, as they were officially called, has yet to be told, but this expedition helped the advance of General Stillwell's forces, which captured the aerodrome at Myitkyina after a hard fight on May 17,although not until August was the town captured.

With the occupation of Rangoon the reconquest of Burma was virtually complete, the principal task of the air forces thereafter being to harass the enemy and block his ways of escape eastward into Siam.

On June 1, 1945, Eastern Air Command was disbanded, the U.S. forces serving therein being withdrawn for service elsewhere. General Stratemayer handed over his command to Air Vice-Marshal W. A. Coryton, his former assistant.

For eighteen months Eastern Air Command had put an inpenetrable air umbrella over the men who swept the enemy out of Burma. It cleared the skies of Japanese aircraft, bombed the enemy's supply bases, ports and communications and,its greatest achievement, kept the ground forces supplied with all its requirements along the 1,200 miles from Kohima to Rangoon. From January, 1944, to April, 1945, transport aircraft of Eastern Air Command carried supplies, ammunition and reinforcements totalling 504,165 tons and 315,120 men.

The appointment of Air Chief Marshal Sir Trafford Leigh-Mallory, C.-in-C. Allied Expeditionary Air Force for the invasion of Europe, as Allied Air C.-in-C., South East Asia Command in October, 1944, and Lt.-Gen. F. A. M. Browning, Deputy Commander, Allied First Airborne Army, as Chief of Staff to

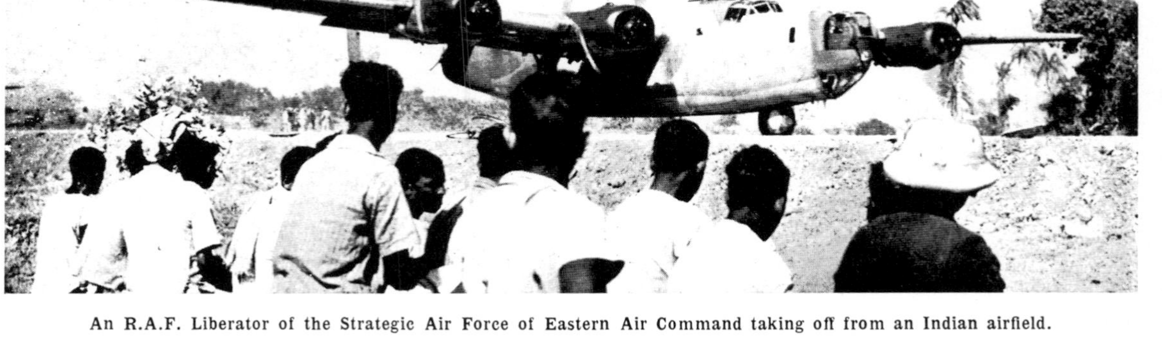

An R.A.F. Liberator of the Strategic Air Force of Eastern Air Command taking off from an Indian airfield.

Admiral Lord Louis Mountbatten in November, foreshadowed the growing importance of the S.E.A.C. theatre.

Air Chief Marshal Leigh-Mallory lost his life while flying out to the Far East to take up his new appointment in December, and early in 1945 Air Marshal Sir Keith R. Park, K.B.E., C.B., M.C., D.F.C., formerly A.O.C.-in-C., Middle East Command, was appointed to take his place as Allied Air C.-in-C., S.E.A.C. Preparations were also being made for the transfer of R.A.F. squadrons and supporting units to the Far East when the European War was over.

THE MEDITERRANEAN AIR COMMAND

Progress in Italy and the Mediterranean theatre during 1944 was slow but steady against a stubbornly retreating enemy. Operations were frequently hampered by unusually wet and stormy weather and, towards the middle of the year, by the withdrawal of large numbers of troops for the invasion of Southern France. Activities of the Mediterranean Allied Air Forces were extended during the year to Austria, France, Greece and the whole of the Balkans, in addition to Italy.

In 1944 the Mediterranean Allied Air Forces, under the command of General Ira C. Eaker, U.S.A.A.F., comprised the following :—

Strategic Air Forces. This Command included the 15th U.S. Army Air Force and No. 205 Group, the only R.A.F. heavy and medium bomber group in the Mediterranean.

Tactical Air Forces. This included the 12th U.S. Army Air Force, the R.A.F. Desert Air Force, squadrons of the Dominions Air Forces and units of the French and Brazilian Air Forces.

Coastal Air Force. This included R.A.F., Dominions, American and French units.

Balkan Air Force. This was a new R.A.F. Command formed in June for operations in the Balkans and in the Adriatic and to support the partisan forces, especially in Yugoslavia.

Although the Allied offensive in Italy was slowed it tied down some 23-27 German divisions which the enemy would have found useful for the East and West European fronts. Allied air activities throughout the year were concentrated mainly on supporting the land forces in Italy, and the strategic bombing of North Italy, France, Austria and the Balkans. Although comparatively little was heard of its activities, R.A.F. Middle East Command played an active part, with the M.A.A.F., in the ceaseless campaign against German lines of communication —mainly shipping—which radiated from Greece down the Aegean and Ionian seas. Aircraft from bases all over the Middle East Command, including Liberators, Halifaxes, Mitchells, Marauders, Wellingtons and Beaufighters took part in these activities.

Allied air attacks against industrial targets in Northern Italy and Austria and oil targets at such places as Leghorn, Fiume, Trieste, and Ploesti, were fitted into the strategic bombardment of Germany itself, while the continuous assault on the enemy's land and sea transport systems created tremendous confusion. An important contribution to the offensive against Germany's lines of Communication was made by R.A.F. Wellington and Liberator bombers which mined the Danube for hundreds of miles in Bulgaria, Rumania and Hungary. The heavy bomber strategic attacks by daylight were made by Fortress and Liberator bombers of the 15th Air Force while R.A.F. Wellingtons Halifaxes and Liberators maintained the attacks at night.

The Mediterranean Allied Tactical Air Force, or M.A.T.A.F. as it was called, was mainly employed in support of the ground forces and in disrupting enemy communications of all kinds. Aircraft of the R.A.F. Desert Air Force included Spitfire fighters and fighter-bombers, Mustang fighters and fighters-bombers, Kittyhawk fighter-bombers, Mitchell and Marauder medium bombers and a wing of Boston bombers for special night work.

Coastal Air Force, comprising squadrons of rocket-projectile Beaufighters, Hurricane and Mosquitos, Spitfire and Airacobra fighters and Wellington, Baltimore and Marauder bombers, maintained a ceaseless war on enemy shipping and submarines in the Adriatic and in the Gulf of Genoa, made reconnaissance flights over the seas and gave fighter protection to Allied convoys, bases and lines of communication both by day and night. During the first part of the year especially, fighters of this Command kept up raids against German sea, rail and road transport in Yugoslavia, Albania and Greece in support of the Russian and partisan operations in the Balkans. In one week these sweeps on the Dalmatian coast destroyed or damaged 150 German vehicles and up to the beginning of May nearly 1,000 casualties had been inflicted on German coastal transport of all kinds. One Group of fighters alone in May destroyed 23 enemy aircraft, about 100 goods waggons and a number of enemy ships in these operations.

One outstanding exploit of R.P. Beaufighters of Coastal Air Force was the sinking of the 51,000 ton Italian liner *Rex* on September 8, south of Trieste. Escorted by Mustangs the Beaufighters attacked by daylight without loss and of 64 rockets, 55 ripped the *Rex* below the waterline and four above it, while 3,000 cannon shells were pumped into the hull.

At the beginning of the year the 5th and 8th Armies in Italy were tied down by strong enemy forces, difficult terrain and bad weather, the 8th on the Adriatic side and the 5th in front of the strongly-defended Cassino Abbey. In an attempt to relieve this position a surprise landing by units of the 5th Army was made on January 22 at Anzio, some 30 miles down the coast from Rome.

An offensive by the Air Force during the last few weeks of 1943 and the first weeks of 1944 prepared the way for the landings by intensive attacks directed first against the ring of aerodromes round Rome, then by day and night attacks against communications which sealed off, temporarily, the North of Italy from the South. The night attacks were made by R.A.F. Wellington bombers and by Mosquito bombers of Middle East Command which had the special task of crippling road communications at night.

In December, 1943, the M.A.A.F. sent out an average of 1,000 aircraft of all types each day and by January this had increased to an average of 1,200. Between January 1 and January 26, 1944, some 29,000 sorties were flown by the M.A.A.F. and 11,000 tons of bombs dropped.

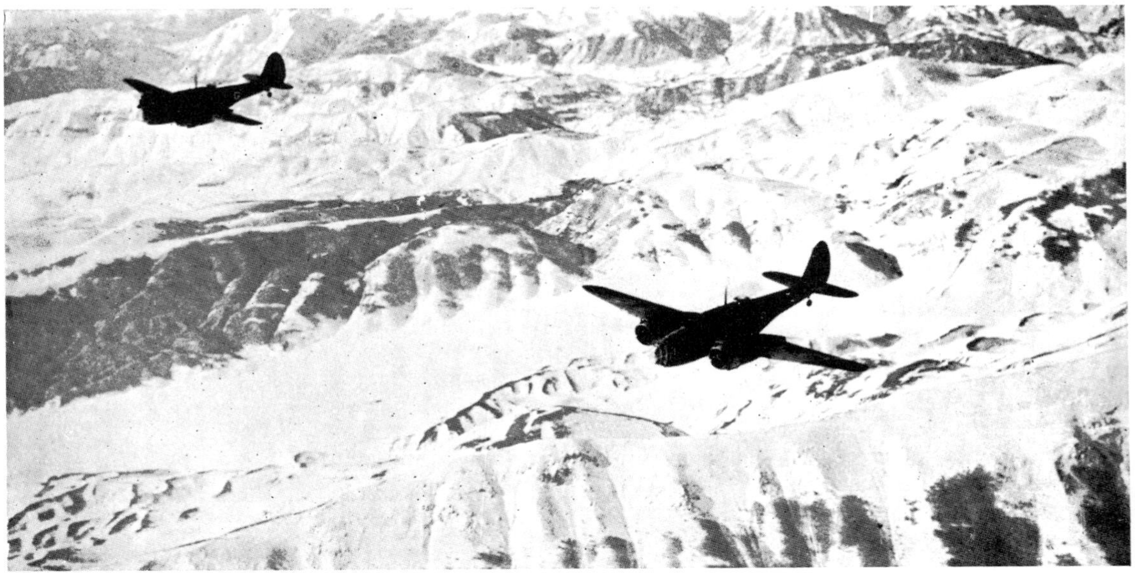

R.A.F. Baltimores of the Mediterranean Air Command over the snow-covered mountains of Central Italy.

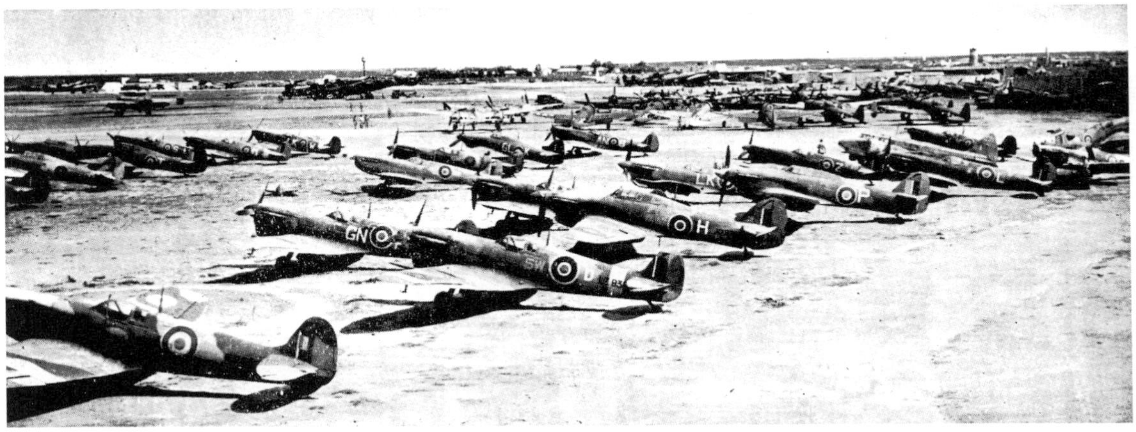

An R.A.F. maintenance base in Southern Italy. Aircraft wearing the colours of the R.A.F., U.S.A.A.F. and the co-belligerent Italian Air Force are seen in the picture.

Air cover during the initial stages of the Anzio landings was provided from aircraft-carriers and then by R.A.F. Spitfire fighters operating from Sicily. In two days alone, some 900 aircraft protected the beach-head. In spite of the intensive flying of all commands during this time losses were less than one per cent.

Although the landings went well the position was not exploited and at the beginning of February the Germans launched strong counter-attacks and managed to prevent the Allied forces from breaking out of the narrow foothold—of some three or four miles only—which had been secured. Hemmed in and subjected to constant attacks, the Anzio beach-head held, but again the land fighting was checked.

Meanwhile Cassino Abbey was subjected to the heaviest air attack ever made by the M.A.A.F. up to that time, in an effort to put the stronghold out of action. Bombers of all types took part but although the Abbey was reduced to rubble the Germans managed to retain their positions. Cassino was finally captured by ground forces on May 18. Cassino was regarded as proof that neither bombing from the air nor artillery bombardment could wholly exterminate a dug-in enemy—a lesson that was profited from in the Normandy landings.

The next big-scale offensive was launched against the Gustav line on May 11. In preparation for this attack the 5th and 8th Armies had been re-grouped, an undertaking which involved bringing up divisions from the Adriatic coast and the Apennines across Italy. These operations were completed without enemy interference, mainly because of the M.A.A.F. In addition to maintaining standing patrols of fighters to prevent the enemy noting troop movements, bombers of all types concentrated on isolating the enemy's forward positions by cutting the German supply lines.

The railway network linking Rome with Florence, bridges, road junctions and a number of small ports which the enemy had been using as unloading bases, were subjected to continuous attack. By May 3 the railways had been cut in 83 places between Rome and Florence. This damage caused supplies to pile up in Florence and other places farther North, and they in turn were bombed by heavy bombers by day and night. Meanwhile the enemy was forced to send supplies by road and the road convoys were kept under continuous attack by fighter-bombers of the Tactical Air Force by day and by special R.A.F. Boston units at night. In preparation for the major offensive British aircraft alone made more than 10,000 sorties against enemy shipping and port facilities on the Italian and Dalmatian coasts during April.

Launched on May 11 the battle continued for three weeks practically without interruption, but after about a fortnight the Germans began a rapid retreat. In support of the Armies at this time the R.A.F. made an average of some 2,000 sorties a day and, on three occasions, more than 3,000.

Rome was captured on June 4 and the pursuit of the enemy continued, fighters, fighter-bombers and medium bombers of the Tactical Air Force maintaining continuous attacks against the retreating Germans so that the roads as far as 80 miles North of Rome were littered with wrecked vehicles. In less than one month some 10,000 motor transport vehicles were wrecked. In one day Mustang and Kittyhawk fighter-bombers of the Desert Air Force destroyed a complete convoy of more than 200 vehicles.

Thereafter followed a long arduous pursuit up through Italy of the enemy, who was retiring with skill and in good order, in spite of intensive operations by the Air Forces. One R.A.F. fighter-bomber wing operating in close support of the Armies in June flew one million miles and dropped more than 7,000 tons of bombs on enemy motor transports, gun positions, bridges, rail targets, ammunition and petrol dumps and road junctions.

Florence was captured on August 4 and this phase of the Italian campaign ended when the Germans took up defensive positions along the line of the Apennines.

August marked the beginning of more extended operations by the Mediterranean Allied Air Forces than ever before, in France, Poland and the Balkans. This month marked the culmination of the air preparations for the landings in Southern France on August 15. The softening-up process had started as far back as the end of April when aircraft from the Mediterranean Command began attacks on harbours, rail yards, bridges, viaducts and airfields. By August 15 all the rail bridges except one, across the Rhône between Lyons and the sea had been cut by Allied bombers. Between April 29 and the beginning of August 6,000 sorties were flown by M.A.A.F. against targets in Southern France and in the six days to August 15 more than 4,000 sorties.

The landings in Southern France were made by American and French troops of the 7th U.S. Army between Toulon and Cannes. The thoroughness of the preparations were seen when glider-borne forces landed in daylight with no air and little ground opposition. The entire strategic bomber force from the Mediterranean was thrown into the tactical attack while hundreds of fighters protected the landings and naval forces. R.A.F. and U.S.A.A.F. Beaufighters escorted the convoys during the night as they approached the coast. At dawn R.A.F. Spitfires and aircraft of the French Air Force took over the fighter cover while fighters, fighter-bombers, light and medium bombers of the M.A.T.A.F. joined in offensive support of the ground forces. Before the invasion Coastal Air Force had largely prevented enemy reconnaissance of the ports in Italy, Corsica, Sardinia, Sicily and North Africa where the invasion craft had assembled and enemy opposition to the landings was almost non-existent until the end of the first day.

By August 21 R.A.F. Spitfire fighters were operating from landing strips on the beach-head. During August R.A.F. bombers from the Mediterranean operating in this theatre made nearly 7,000 sorties by day and 2,000 by night, dropping a total of 7,500 tons of bombs. R.A.F. fighter sorties in the same month exceeded 10,000.

Operations in these landings proceeded rapidly and with magnificent support from the M.A.A.F. the Germans had been pursued north to the Vosges within a few weeks. A model of air co-operation in this campaign was the miracle of supply, which was exclusively by the Air Force, that kept rations, gasoline, bombs and ammunition always available to the front-line fighter-bombers in one of the fastest moving campaigns of the War.

August was remarkable also for one of the outstanding operations of the R.A.F. in the Mediterranean Command. Halifax and Liberator bombers flown by R.A.F., S.A.A.F. and Polish crews dropped weapons and supplies to the Polish patriots who had risen in Warsaw on August 1. These operations were continued for many weeks, more than 100 tons of weapons being delivered by parachute up to early in September. The supplies included ammunition, various types of guns and special material suitable for close street fighting.

These flights involved round trips of 1,750 miles across strong German fighter belts and over Warsaw the Halifax and Liberator aircraft had to come in at very low heights and fly at slow speeds in order to drop their containers accurately in the city in face of intense enemy ground fire. Up to the middle of September some 250 Allied airmen had been lost in the attempt to give help to the Polish patriots.

Meanwhile on August 26 the Allied forces in Italy began a methodical assault against the Apennine line, the main weight of the attack being on the Adriatic side. Fighting in difficult mountain country and handicapped by unusually wet and stormy weather but strongly supported by the Tactical Air Force whenever weather permitted, the enemy was gradually driven back to prepared positions and Rimini was captured on September 21. During the battle for Rimini Spitfires of the Desert Air Force had probably the most sustained period of concerted attacks against enemy targets—pilots flying at least three sorties a day, sometimes five, for three weeks.

Almost simultaneously with the intensified Italian operations the Russians launched an offensive against Rumania and during the next few months made progress in Rumania, Bulgaria, Hungary and Yugoslavia. Early in September the German withdrawal from Greece began, this action and their subsequent flight through the Balkans being largely caused by the support given to the Armies by R.A.F. Spitfire fighter-bombers.

Operations of the M.A.A.F. during the next few months were intensified in the Balkans to help the Russian campaigns and almost every type of aeroplane shared in bombing and strafing targets, especially in Albania and Yugoslavia. One of the features of activities in November was the increasing use in daylight of R.A.F. Wellington, Halifax and Liberator bombers which had previously operated mainly by night. These daylight operations included the bombing of German communications in North Italy and Yugoslavia and the dropping of supplies to Marshal Tito's forces in Yugoslavia.

The Balkan operations continued throughout the remainder of the year and into 1945, while at the same time constant support was given the armies in Italy which continued to advance slowly. Forli was captured on November 9, Ravenna on December 5 and Faenza on December 17, in spite of almost impossible weather during nearly the whole of December. After the fall of Ravenna the Desert Air Force acted as the spearhead of the advance, bombing and strafing only 300 yards ahead of the troops.

At the beginning of 1945 operations in the Mediterranean continued to be divided between Italy and the Balkans, much of the bombing, both by day and by night, being concentrated against German supply routes from the North of Italy deep into Southern Germany and Austria. In March the activities of the Desert Air Force extended over thousands of square miles from the 8th Army front to Austria and Yugoslavia. By the beginning of April the R.A.F. had established a base in Crete and was carrying supplies to partisans there and evacuating thousands of British troops left behind after the evacuation of Crete in 1941 who had been operating with the partisans. R.A.F. Wellington bombers were withdrawn from the Strategic Air Force at this time and were replaced by R.A.F. Liberators.

What turned out to be the final and decisive battle for the liberation of Italy was launched on April 10, 1945, the 8th Army advancing up the Po valley and the 5th Army towards Spezia. The Allied Air Forces provided 24-hour non-stop support. Spitfires, Kittyhawks, Mustangs, Marauders, American-piloted Thunderbolts and night-flying Bostons and Baltimores made an all-out effort. As the enemy reeled under the land and air blows, the Desert Air Force, which had provided air support for the 8th Army from Alamein to the Alps and had been in at the death of the enemy in Africa and Sicily, smashed strong-points and transport throughout the Po valley. Its aircraft flew 21,000 sorties in April and put out of action nearly 5,000 vehicles of all kinds. Thousands of close-support sorties were flown for the 8th Army, smashing about half of the enemy tank force and destroying nearly 2,000 enemy-occupied buildings.

On May 2, the German Armies in Italy surrendered unconditionally to Field Marshal Sir Harold Alexander, Allied Supreme Commander, Mediterranean. On that day Sir Guy Garrod, Commander-in-Chief of the R.A.F. in the Mediterranean and Middle East, sent the following signal to all air officers under his command : "On this great day I wish to offer you all and those under your command my heartfelt congratulations and appreciation of the fine work you have done to bring this victory about."

On July 31, 1945, the Mediterranean Allied Air Force was disbanded and thereafter the R.A.F. and U.S. Air Forces reverted to independent commands. More than a quarter of a million officers and men wearing the uniforms of several nations and flying thirty different types of aircraft made up the M.A.A.F. The Force was at its peak strength in August-September, 1944, when there were 68,896 R.A.F. and 173,845 U.S.A.A.F. personnel serving under its command.

Aircraft of the M.A.A.F. dropped over 650,000 tons of bombs on enemy objectives and more than 8,700 enemy aircraft were destroyed in the air and on the ground. More than 9,000 Allied aircraft were lost and about 40,000 airmen were killed, wounded, prisoners-of-war or missing.

THE BALKAN AIR FORCE

The Balkan Air Force, a Royal Air Force component of the Mediterranean Allied Air Force, was formed in June, 1944, to operate in direct support of, and with, the partisan forces in the Balkans, especially those of Marshal Tito in Yugoslavia. From early in 1942 British Liberators and Halifax bombers had been flying from the Suez Canal zone to drop parachutists to make contact with the resistance movements in Greece, Albania and Yugoslavia. Throughout 1944 air support was given by the M.A.A.F. but the formation of the Balkan Air Force for this special task was announced in August, 1944.

From its headquarters on the Italian mainland the Balkan Air Force operated in two main spheres :—direct support to Marshal Tito's forces, and supplying the Yugoslav partisans and bringing out wounded. As well as working in close conjunction with the partisans the fighters, fighter-bombers and bombers were also closely co-ordinated with Land Forces Adriatic and ships of the British and American Navies. Land Forces Adriatic, formed during the first half of 1944, operated on a wide front in the Adriatic country, including the islands off Yugoslavia and Albania, and the Dalmation coast generally, harassing German troops occupying this territory. Somewhat resembling a special Commando force, its tactical air support was supplied in all its operations by the Balkan Air Force.

Aircraft of the Balkan Air Force included Spitfire, Mustang and Mosquito fighters and fighter-bombers, rocket-firing Beaufighter and Hurricane aircraft, Marauder and Baltimore bombers and Dakota transports. Italian pilots flying Spitfire, Macchi and Airacobra fighters also operated with the Command and by September a number of Yugoslav pilots, trained by the R.A.F. and flying Spitfires and Baltimores were also serving with the Balkan Air Force.

In its offensive rôle in support of the Partisans, the Balkan Air Force was mainly employed on bombing and strafing German communications of all kinds, ammunition dumps and targets of every description—many at the request of Marshal Tito's headquarters—in the Balkans and along the Dalmation coast. During the first four months of its existence 114 enemy ships, 211 locomotives, 643 motor vehicles, and 63 enemy aircraft were destroyed behind a 700 mile coastline of the Balkans held by the Germans.

The Allied landings in Southern Greece in October were covered by the Command, Spitfire fighter-bombers landing on the Greek mainland (on landing fields specially prepared by R.A.F. ground crews flown in by Transport Command) before the troops were ashore. The Balkan Air Force supported the subsequent operations in Greece, including the fighting between E.L.A.S. and British troops which broke out on December 5 and continued until early in 1945. During this time bombers of the Command operated from the Greek mainland and the people of Greece were kept informed of events by means of leaflets and specially prepared newspapers dropped by the bombers. The transport section of the Balkan Air Force also kept the R.A.F. units in Greece supplied.

Supply missions flown by the Balkan Air Force to Yugoslavia, Czechoslavokia, Poland, Austria, Northern Italy, Bulgaria and Greece were as important as the offensive missions, or even more, though little has been revealed about them through security considerations.

By air 22,299 gross tons of arms and ammunition, food, clothing and medical supplies were taken to the Partisan forces mainly in Yugoslavia, being dropped by parachute or landed on secret airfields behind the enemy lines. Empty transports carried out loads of wounded who would otherwise have died and who in any case encumbered the Partisan forces. In all, the Balkan Air Force aircraft rescued almost 20,000 men, women and children and brought them safely to Italy.

The Balkan Air Force was disbanded on July 11, 1945.

TRANSPORT COMMAND.

The work of R.A.F. Transport Command in 1944 may be divided into four sections : the operation of regular military services carrying military passengers, mails and freight over some 100,000 miles of scheduled air routes that include the United Kingdom, North America, part of South America, North and West Africa, Egypt, the Persian Gulf, India and the Antipodes ; the ferrying of reinforcements and new aircraft across the Atlantic to the United Kingdom and North Africa, and from the United Kingdom to the Middle and Far East ; close support operations in connection with airborne invasions on all fronts ; and the supplying of forward ground forces, and the evacuation of wounded.

In preparation for the invasion of Normandy a special Close Support Unit—No. 46 Group—was formed and squadrons were given special training for operational duties in carrying airborne and parachute troops, towing gliders, and the evacuation of wounded. Equipped mainly with Dakota aircraft, the Group first dropped leaflets in the landing area, and then a few hours before the first seaborne landings in Normandy on June 6, towed in Horsa and Hadrian gliders filled with airborne troops. No. 38 Group, equipped with Halifax and Stirling glider-tugs towing the bigger Hamilcar gliders.

For the Normandy invasion No. 46 Group carried 2,300 parachute troops, 1,000 glider-borne troops, 200 vehicles, and much equipment was dropped in containers. A few days after the invasion several R.A.F. Wings, comprising some 2,000 men and many tons of supplies including 500-lb. bombs, drop-tanks, wireless and spare parts were flown to the Continent.

Once landing strips were available the Dakotas landed with supplies and the evacuation of wounded by air began on June 12. By the end of 1944 more than 50,000 casualties had been evacuated, over three-quarters of them stretcher cases. Although more than 4,000 sorties representing some 1,500,000 miles of flying were involved in the evacuation of these 50,000 casualties not a single Transport Command aircraft met with any mishap when carrying wounded.

In addition, between D-Day and the end of 1944 approximately 15,000 tons of war freight, mails and passengers had been flown to the Continent.

During the rapid advance across Northern France and into Belgium both the Armies and the Air Forces outstripped their supplies and the continued advance was only possible because of the work of Transport Command and the United States Troop Carrier Command. Non-stop shuttle services from England to France and Belgium were operated, the transports carrying petrol, ammunition of all kinds, food, equipment, maps and mails. One airfield handled about 1,000 tons of supplies in one

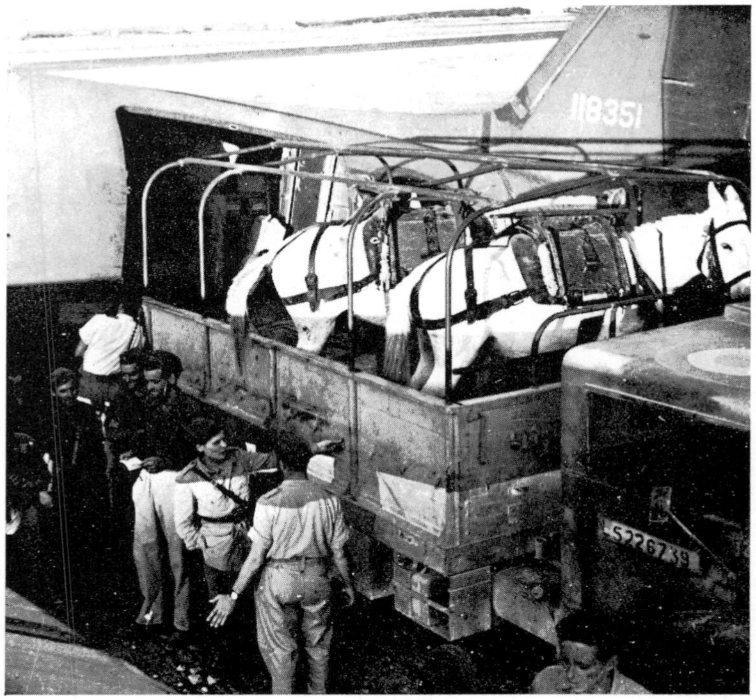

Mules being loaded into a Dakota of the Balkan Air Force for transport to Yugoslavia for the use of the Partisans in mountain warfare.

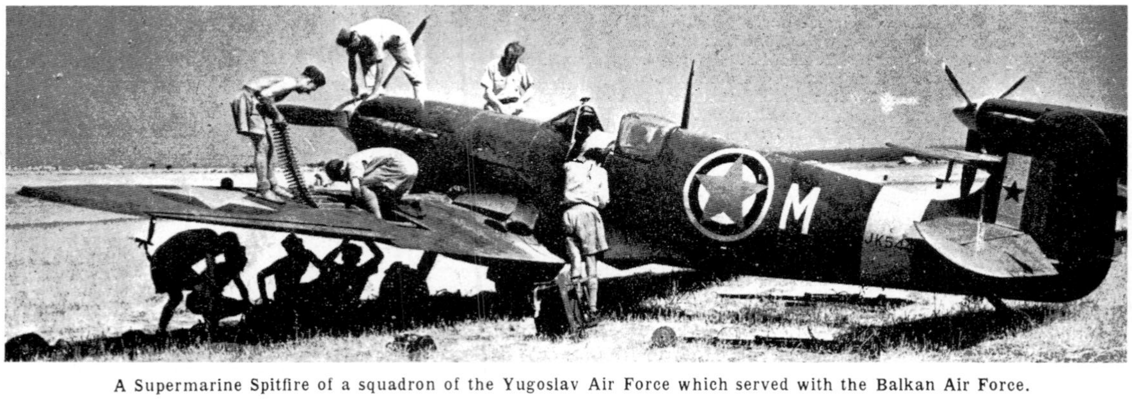

A Supermarine Spitfire of a squadron of the Yugoslav Air Force which served with the Balkan Air Force.

day, aircraft landing at two-and-a-half minute intervals from dusk to dawn.

One aerodrome in Belgium was taken over by a Wing of Transport Command two days after its capture and the following day was in full operation. In one month 3,438 aircraft were received from the United Kingdom, more than 7,000 tons of freight were handled, 4,280 passengers were received and despatched and 7,200 casualties were evacuated to England, many of them brought to the aerodrome by air from front-line landing strips.

In addition to supplying the Armies and Air Forces, Transport Command also carried medical supplies, food, clothing and Red Cross supplies of all kinds to liberated Paris, Holland and Belgium. In one day one Group conveyed 167 tons of food to Paris.

Aircraft of Transport Command were also in the spearhead of the airborne landings at Arnhem. No. 46 Group played an outstanding part in these operations. Troops of the First Airborne Division as well as jeeps, guns and other equipment were taken over in gliders on September 17 and 18 and for a week afterwards Dakotas of the Group dropped vital war supplies, food and medical supplies to the isolated Arnhem bridgehead in spite of intense enemy opposition and bad weather, until the troops were withdrawn. In the glider operations the speeds of the unarmed Dakotas were slowed down to little more than 100 m.p.h. by the gliders and evasive action was not possible. Losses on the subsequent supply-dropping operations were inevitably heavy because the enemy was able to concentrate his anti-aircraft defences and fighter formations. But the vast majority of supplies were dropped and in little more than a week No. 46 Group made more than 500 sorties.

During 1944 more than 5,000 parachute troops were dropped behind the enemy lines and about 14,000 soldiers and airmen were landed on forward airfields on the Western Front by Transport Command.

The Command also took part in all important campaigns on the other fronts. A vital share was taken by transport aircraft in both the opening and final phases of the liberation of Greece. The first operations were in the Peloponnese in late September, when Dakotas flew in parachute troops to prepare a landing strip for Spitfire fighters. The following day, when the landing strip was still unfinished, Dakotas landed—some on roads nearby—with picks and shovels, arms, ammunition, jeeps and transport. Later a re-arming and refuelling party was flown in. On October 19 a flight of Dakotas dropped parachute troops 12 miles West of Athens and once the city was liberated Transport squadrons from Italy and Africa moved fighter squadrons to the aerodromes round Athens and brought in petrol and ammunition, meteorological units, flying control units, jeeps and equipment of all kinds.

Dakotas of the Mediterranean Group also played a vital rôle in operations in the Balkans. More than 2,000,000 lbs. of supplies were dropped or landed for Marshal Tito's forces in Yugoslavia and more than 6,000 wounded men and women and sick children were evacuated. These operations required flying skill of the highest order as many of the landing grounds were only roughly prepared strips in the mountains and only a few miles from the Germans.

Dakotas of No. 216 Group in the Mediterranean took part in the landings in Southern France. Fighter squadrons and their equipment were flown from Corsica for the landings in Southern France and airborne forces were also landed.

Altogether, from its formation in September, 1942 until the end of the war in Europe, No. 216 Group carried 26,800 tons of war material, 400,000 passengers and over 8,000 tons of mail. In addition, ferry pilots of the group flew thousands of replacement aircraft to all fronts in and beyond the Mediterranean theatre.

Something of the work of Transport Command squadrons on the Burma front has already been described in the South-East Asia Command Section. In Burma air transport was the joint responsibility of both British and American forces serving in Eastern Air Command. In the twelve months ending March 31, 1945, R.A.F. and U.S.A.A.F. transport aircraft flew into Burma more than 550,000 tons, a deadweight equal to the cargo of 55 Liberty ships. This huge tonnage was flown over high mountains and through some of the worst weather in the World in unarmed and generally unescorted transports.

With the opening of a regular military service across the Pacific to Australia, Transport Command's routes formed a World system. Main routes crossed the North and South Atlantic and operated from the United Kingdom to Africa, the Mediterranean, Egypt and the Middle East, India and Ceylon. From Montreal the Australian route crosses North America to San Francisco, thence by way of Honolulu, Canton, Fiji and Auckland, New Zealand, to Sydney—a total of 11,520 miles. The Pacific route was inaugurated in November, 1944, the actual flying time for the initial flight being 50 hours. The service, which carries military passengers, freight and mails is operated twice weekly in each direction by the R.A.F. Transport Command formation in Canada. Connections are made with services already operated by the Command to the United Kingdom, Near East, West Africa and South America.

As an indication of the scope of the Command, in December alone 47,000 passengers, more than 781 tons of mail and 5,134 tons of freight were carried on regular and special flights operated over the military routes. Some 5,850,000 track miles were flown on those services, including reinforcement flights of the Group based in Canada but excluding other ferry and reinforcement flights.

Aircraft controlled by Transport Command on the North Atlantic service, including those operated by Trans-Canada Airlines and the Return Ferry Service of B.O.A.C., delivered 3,183,160 lb. of mail and freight, in addition to passengers, from the United States and Canada to one British terminal in 1944. Nearly 3,000 aircraft were involved. From Great Britain to North America more than 500,000 lb. of mail and freight were carried.

In May, 1944, the 15,000th Trans-Atlantic air crossing since the War began was completed. R.A.F. Transport Command alone was flying more than one million miles a month over the North and South Atlantic routes at that time. By the beginning of 1945 well over 37,000 trans-Atlantic flights had been made.

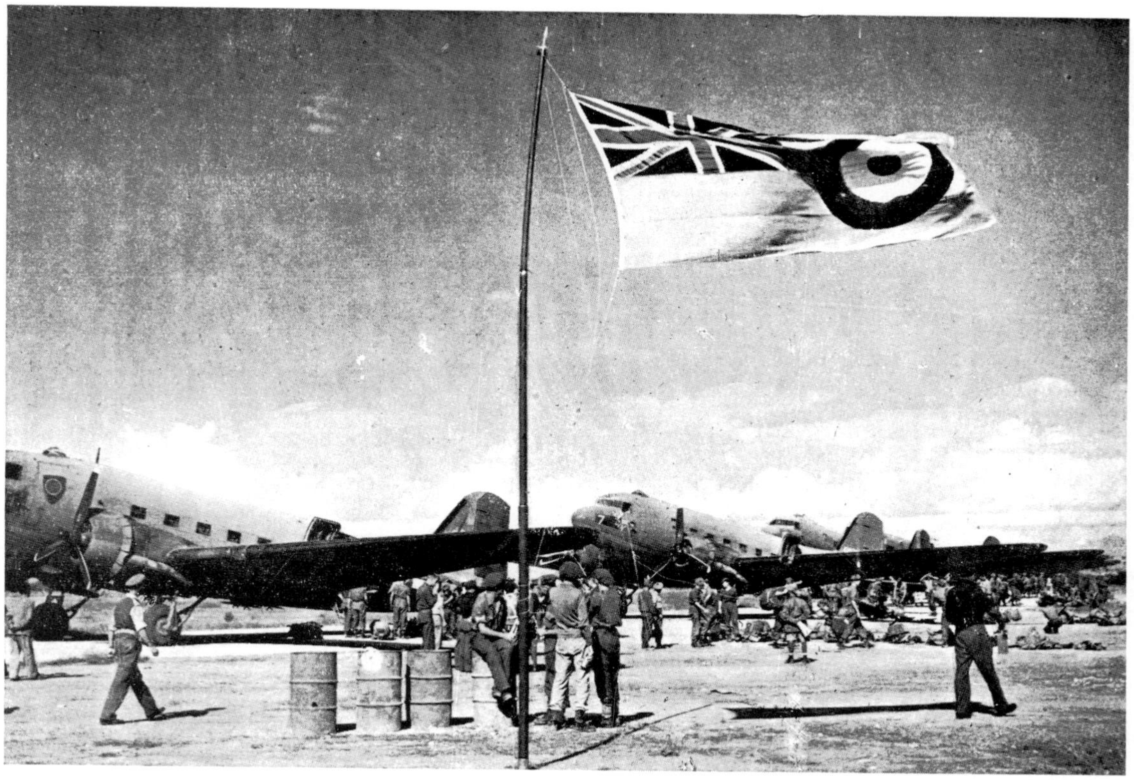

R.A.F. and U.S.A.A.F. Dakota transports on an airfield in Southern Greece after bringing in men and supplies for the liberation of the Country.

During 1944 the Command opened its own school of Air Transport to instruct new officers in the technique of transport operations, with particular attention being paid to the movement of troops and equipment, the towing of gliders and airborne operations. Plans were already advanced by the end of the year for the development of airport and staging post facilities for the increase of traffic on routes to South East Asia Command and for the intensification of the War in the Pacific. By February, 1945, training was being undertaken by the Command in some 25 special units located in the United Kingdom, Canada, the Middle East and India.

In 1944 special flights were made by aircraft of the Command which involved hazardous landings in France before the invasion and in Poland to rescue patriots.

At the beginning of 1945 Air Chief Marshal Sir Frederick Bowhill was succeeded as A.O.C.-in-C., Transport Command, by Air Vice-Marshal the Hon. Sir Ralph Cochrane.

In March, 1945, the Command took part in the greatest airborne operation of the War when on the 24th of the month 120 gliders were towed to the East of the Rhine to set in motion the crossings by the British and Canadian Armies which resulted in the ultimate unconditional surrender of all German forces in North-West Germany, Holland and Denmark.

Despite heavy anti-aircraft fire all the gliders were cast off over the dropping zone and only one of the Dakota tugs was lost.

As the Allied advanced armoured columns swept on into Germany transport aircraft were used on a bigger scale than ever to keep the armoured columns on the move. Supplies of all kinds were flown to advanced strips but the most traffic was in petrol and oil. The biggest quantity supplied in a single day was flown in on April 4 when 669,465 gallons of petrol were delivered to advanced bases in Germany by nearly 2,000 aircraft. An average of some 500,000 gallons a day were flown in during one week. On their return journeys the transports brought home liberated prisoners of war. During April and May No. 46 Group lifted some 80,000 Allied repatriates from Continental airfields and flew them to England. Dakotas, Halifaxes and Stirlings were used for this dual task.

TRAINING COMMANDS.

At the outbreak of the War one Training Command of the Royal Air Force dealt with all training, both ground trades and flying personnel, but on May 28, 1940, two commands were formed—Flying Training Command and Technical Training Command.

Flying Training Command is responsible for all flying training done in Great Britain from the time the air crew cadet goes to a reception centre until he leaves the advanced unit for the operational training unit. In addition, the Empire Central Flying School, which was formed in 1943 to succeed the Central Flying School, comes under Flying Training Command. The Empire Central Flying School is attended by pilots and instructors of the R.A.F., the Dominions Air Forces, the United States, and other members of the United Nations.

Special flights made during 1944 by the Empire Navigation School included a flight of four Wellington bombers to India, and a Stirling to Canada to make a navigational demonstration tour to the Canadian Navigation schools. In October, 1944, the first round-the-World flight by the R.A.F. was made by an Avro Lancaster I to study navigation and demonstrate the latest equipment likely to be of use in the Pacific area.

In May, 1945, a Lancaster of the School studying navigation and testing special equipment under Polar conditions, flew over the North Pole from Iceland and over the Magnetic Pole from Goose Bay. In ten days the Lancaster flew 17,720 miles and completed its tests by flying non-stop from Whitehorse, Yukon, back to the school at Shawbury in 18 hrs. 26 min.

In 1944 the Central Navigation and Air Armament Schools of the Royal Air Force were organised on similar lines to form the Empire Navigation School and the Empire Air Armament School.

Technical Training Command includes schools for every ground trade in the Royal Air Force and also administers the aircraft apprentices schools at Halton and Cranwell. The R.A.F. College, Cranwell, celebrated its jubilee on February 5, 1945.

The Commonwealth Air Training Plan. The British Commonwealth Joint Air Training Plan in Canada was discontinued on March 31, 1945, although skeleton training staffs and aerodromes were retained. The original agreement provided for joint training in Canada from December 17, 1939 to March 31, 1943, but by a further agreement in March, 1942, the scale of training was increased and the plan extended to March 31, 1945. The discontinuation of the plan was possible because of the favourable war situation towards the end of 1944, when the decision was made, and because the casualty rate among pilots had been lower than expected and a surplus of air-crews had been built up.

The slowing down of training in Canada began in February, 1944, and some 4,200 Canadians waiting for training were released to the Army and recruiting for the Air Forces was discontinued from June until October. As from June, there was a progressive closing of a number of training units and schools, the first to shut being R.A.F. schools transferred to Canada earlier in the War. The last R.A.F. school in Canada closed on February 2, 1945.

The cumulative total of trainees from all sources entered for training under the plan in Canada, from its inception to August 25, 1944 was 152,925, excluding 5,296 R.A.F. and Fleet Air Arm personnel which graduated from R.A.F. Schools in Canada. Of the 152,925, a total of 108,957 had been graduated by August 25, 1944, and 20,109 were unsuccessful in completeng their courses. Of the total pupils trained in Canada 60,603 were R.C.A.F. personnel, 34,361 R.A.F. (including the 5,296 trained at R.A.F. schools), 8,067 were R.A.A.F., and 6,026 R.N.Z.A.F. personnel.

The original agreement called for a peak air-crew production at the rate of 20,864 a year but with the expanded programme a peak of 52,503 was planned for June, 1944. That figure was reached in February, 1944, when 3,854 air crews were graduated in the month. In that month the eventual objective was lowered to a rate of 20,965 a year, which was to be reached in the Spring of 1945. By October there were more than 15,000 air-crews in training, of whom more than 8,000 were R.C.A.F.

At the peak of the Commonwealth Plan there were 154 flying schools in operation in Canada. Between December 15, 1944, and January 1, 1945, 28 schools were closed and some 56 remained open. At its height, the Plan was operated by a staff of 101,418 of which 69,753 were Canadians and 31,665 were from Great Britain and other Empire countries. By the end of August, 1944, more than 12,000 training aircraft were operating in Canada and training aircraft under the Training Plan had flown 1,750,000,000 miles.

By the end of 1944 the air-crews trained consisted of (approximate figures):—42,500 Pilots, 37,500 Navigators, 15,000 Wireless Operators/Air Gunners, 12,500 Air Gunners and some

900 Flight Engineers and other specialist categories. In addition more than 114,000 ground crews had been trained in 50 different trades.

Simultaneously with the Plan for closing down the British Commonwealth Air Training Plan, announced on November 17, 1944, training was also considerably reduced in South Africa and Southern Rhodesia. Both Australia and New Zealand stopped sending air crews to Canada for training in the middle of the year.

Altogether the cost of the Plan amounted to $2,192,000,000. Of this total Canada expected to pay $1,324,000,000; the United Kingdom $862,000,000; Australia $96,000,000; and New Zealand $46,000,000.

THE BALLOON COMMAND.

In 1944 Balloon Command took part in the Allied invasion of Normandy and in the defence against the flying-bombs. Throughout the preparations for the Allied landings balloons guarded the dispatching ports and when the invasion began balloons flew above the invasion craft and ships during the crossing and off the French coast during the landings. Specially-picked two-men crews with a smaller type of balloon were used to protect the ships on the crossing. Units of the Balloon Barrage were among the first R.A.F. troops to land in Normandy, where balloons flying from the beaches protected the unloading of the ships and the landing of the troops.

The greatest balloon barrage in the history of the R.A.F. was massed to support the defences against the flying-bombs. Arrangements were first planned in December, 1943, when Balloon Command received instructions that a barrage of 500 balloons would be required by Air Defence of Great Britain as a line of defence in front of London. The planning for the arrangements was personally supervised by Air Vice-Marshal W. C. C. Gell, C.B., D.S.O., M.C., Air Officer Commanding, Balloon Command.

This first curtain of balloons was to be in an area outside the normal London balloon barrage where there were no facilities in existence for this type of defence. Within eight days of receiving initial instructions, a reconnaissance party of eight officers and a corporal had selected the sites needed. Most of the sites were in remote places only accessible by footpaths or across fields. But where no roads existed they were built with the help of the R.A.F. Airfield Construction Unit, an anchorage was laid on each site and hutted camps were set up to house the headquarters staff and officers of each squadron. Work on the 500 sites was completed in 10 days.

On June 16 Balloon Command Headquarters received a signal ordering the deployment of the barrage and although 18 days had been calculated as the time required, all 500 balloons were in position and flying in five days. On June 21 another 500 balloons were ordered; more sites were chosen and within two days the second 500 had been brought from all parts of the country to the South of England. Some came from Scapa Flow and were rushed by sea to the London docks. Before they were in position the strength of the barrage had been ordered to be increased to 1,750. The total barrage occupied a space 31 miles long and 11 miles deep.

The first flying-bomb to be brought down by the barrage was reported two days after its deployment. Altogether, the balloons destroyed 279 flying-bombs out of those which escaped the outer defence rings of anti-aircraft guns and fighters and headed towards London.

On February 5, 1945, the closing down of Balloon Command was announced because of the reduced need of British cities, towns and industrial buildings for defence against air attack. Balloons were no defence against rockets.

The London Balloon Barrage came into existence on March 17, 1937, when No. 30 (Balloon Barrage) Group was formed within R.A.F. Fighter Command. The barrage was flown for the first time over London during the Munich crisis week of 1938 and on November 1 that year Balloon Command was formed. In September, 1939, some 600 balloons were flying; by the end of the blitz some 2,400, although the expansion of the barrage was difficult because factories making the equipment were damaged by air attack and a large number of the balloons were shot down by the enemy. In 1943 more than 1,000 balloon sites were staffed by members of the W.A.A.F. which enabled many balloon squadrons to be released for overseas service.

Besides the Home Command and the invasion of Normandy, squadrons of the Balloon Barrage during the five years of the Command flew in defence of the Suez Canal, the Persian Gulf and Ceylon; over the beaches of Sicily and Italy; and in co-operation with the Royal Navy helped to guard conveys and naval establishments. A number was also sent to the United States in 1942.

THE AIR/SEA RESCUE SERVICE

The Air/Sea Rescue Service was inaugurated in May, 1941, and is controlled by the Directorate of Aircraft Safety in the Air Ministry, although it is organized jointly by the Admiralty and the Air Ministry. The organization works in conjunction with the Royal National Lifeboat Institution, the Coastguards, U.S. Air Forces and others and is mainly intended to pick up aircrews forced down at sea and crews of ships which have been sunk by the enemy. Both surface craft, including fast specially-armed high-speed launches, and aeroplanes are used by the Service. The air search is conducted by Fighter Command aeroplanes if the lost crews are near the coasts of England or by Coastal Command if the airmen are down farther out to sea.

In 1944 the Vickers-Armstrongs Warwick, equipped with the Mk. IA airborne lifeboat, was added to the types of aeroplane serving with the Command. One of the biggest operations during the year was during the airborne invasion of Holland in September, 1944. When the invasion armada set out it found a chain of rescue launches stretching right across the North Sea from the East coast of Great Britain to within a few miles of the enemy shore, with rescue aircraft of Fighter Command patrolling overhead. More than 100 lives were saved by the Service during the first day—September 17, when gliders ran into trouble and were forced to "ditch." These rescue operations were on the largest scale ever known since the formation of the Service.

Air/Sea Rescue services were also established at Malta, in the Middle East, in Italy and in India. In the Mediterranean area the R.A.F. and the Emergency Rescue Squadrons of the United States Army Air Forces co-operated on Air/Sea Rescue work. They operated under the control of the Mediterranean Coastal Air Force and the aircraft used included R.A.F. Walruses, American Catalinas and Italian Cants.

During the war the Air/Sea Rescue Service saved the lives of 5,721 British and American airmen from the waters around Great Britain and of 4,665 soldiers, sailors and civilians in areas other than around Britain. Well over 3,000 lives were saved in overseas theatres of war.

THE R.A.F. REGIMENT

Commandant: Major-General C. F. Liardet, C.B., D.S.O., T.D.

Assistant Commandant: Air Commodore A. P. M. Saunders, R.A.F.

The Royal Air Force Regiment, which was formed in January, 1942, is responsible for the defence of aerodromes and is fully trained in all combatant duties.

Units of the R.A.F. Regiment served on all fronts throughout the war. In the United Kingdom gunners of the R.A.F. Regiment joined in the battle against the flying-bomb, operating from airfields in the South.

On the Western Front, units of the Regiment were stationed at one of the first airfields established on liberated soil. Part of their duties was to inspect and make safe for the advancing ground forces buildings and roads in which the enemy had laid booby traps. Several times units of the Regiment engaged enemy forces during the advance across Europe and towards the end of 1944 troops of the Regiment were in the line in Holland as a fighting force for the first time.

THE WOMEN'S AUXILIARY AIR FORCE

Director: Air Commandant Lady Welsh.

The Women's Auxiliary Air Force was formed in June, 1939, on lines similar to those of the Women's Royal Air Force which was formed in the last war but was disbanded in 1919.

When formed there were only five different trades open to recruitment for women but so successfully have they undertaken other work which releases men for more active duty that there are now more than 70 trades.

The practice of substituting members of the W.A.A.F. for R.A.F. personnel increased during 1944, particularly in the maintenancing and servicing of aircraft and in photographic work. By the end of 1944 more than 90 per cent of R.A.F. Home Communications were operated by the W.A.A.F. and 75 per cent. of the messes and cookhouses in Fighter Command were manned by W.A.A.F. Over 800 members served with the Balloon Barrage sites during the flying-bomb campaign. One of the new duties introduced for the W.A.A.F. during the year was that of Nursing Orderly to accompany all seriously wounded men evacuated from the Western Front by air. By the end of the year most of the W.A.A.F. Nursing Orderlies had made 40 operational flights each, involving some 200 flying hours.

The W.A.A.F. is serving in every R.A.F. Command at home and by the end of the war was also working in France, Belgium, Gibralter, Malta, Italy, North Africa, the Middle East, India, Ceylon, Canada, the U.S.A., the West Indies and Bermuda. The first 500 members, serving in 12 trades, to be posted to the South-East Asia Command arrived in Ceylon in November, 1944.

THE AIR TRAINING CORPS

Air Commodore-in-Chief: H.M. the King.

Chief Commandant and Director-General: Air Marshal Sir Leslie Gossage, K.C.B., C.V.O., D.S.O., M.C.

With the approval of H.M. the King, the Air Training Corps came into being on February 1, 1941. Its formation was in reality achieved by the Air Ministry taking over the Air Defence Cadet Corps which had been formed in 1938 by the Air League of the British Empire. The 200 or so squadrons of the former Air Defence Cadet Corps formed the basis of the new corps and hundreds of new units, including University Air Squadrons and air sections of school Officer's Training Corps, have since been formed.

The Air Training Corps exists primarily to give boys who wish to join the Royal Air Force or the Fleet Air Arm such training as will fit them for aircrew duties or for certain duties on the ground, although it is not guaranteed that they will be drafted to the air services on being called up.

Enrolment is open to boys of 15 to 18 years of age who are physically fit. Training is similar to that given at Initial Training Wings in the R.A.F. but young men who wish to serve as pilots or observers in the R.A.F. and are likely to be suitable for commissioned rank are given a special six months' course at a University Air Squadron. Those taking this course become full members of the university and the cost of training and board and lodging is borne by the Air Ministry.

In addition to training boys of 15 to 18 years of age, the Corps also undertook during 1943 the training of young men who had been accepted for aircrew service with the Royal Air Force but who were waiting their turn to be called up for duty.

Up to the end of the war more than 150,000 trained cadets had joined the fighting services and Mercantile Marine. Of this number over 100,000 cadets were drafted into the R.A.F. and 10,000 into the Fleet Air Arm. About 63,000 of the 100,000 R.A.F. entries became air crew members.

The strength of the Corps at the end of the war totalled about 95,000 cadets in about 1,500 squadrons.

THE ROYAL OBSERVER CORPS

Commandant: Air Cdre. Lord Bandon, C.B., D.S.O., R.A.F.

The Royal Observer Corps, which received permission from His Majesty the King to assume its "Royal" title in April, 1941, is a civil volunteer force which is administered by the Air Ministry and is controlled operationally by Fighter Command. Its function is to detect and keep continuous track of every hostile aircraft flying over the British Isles by day or by night.

Enemy aircraft crossing the sea were detected by Radar but near the coast they came under observation by the R.O.C. who identified them. As the aircraft passed over the countryside their movements were reported by successive R.O.C. posts and the continuous "track" thus obtained was one of the factors of Fighter Command's success.

All aircraft, both friendly and hostile were tracked by the Corps and in conjunction with other means it was responsible for guiding the home-based bomber returning from raids and reporting friendly aircraft in difficulties. The Corps helped to save the lives of many Allied airmen.

During the Allied invasion of Normandy in 1944 members of the Corps were carried on board merchant ships to act as aircraft recognition officers and to advise the anti-aircraft defences on the identity of aircraft, both friendly and hostile. More than 1,500 observers of all ages between 18 and 72 volunteered for this task. They were given an intensive course before being posted to merchant ships and wore a "Seaborne" shoulder flash.

The Corps also played an important part in the defence against the flying-bombs, the tracks obtained by the Corps being one of the factors in the defeat of the attacks. A member of the Corps was the first person to sight and report the first flying-bomb.

By the end of 1944 the Corps consisted of 32,000 members, of whom 23,000 were spare-time watchers, and more than 1,000 R.O.C. posts were scattered throughout the country, often in remote and isolated places, so that the entire sky over Great Britain was under observation 24 hours of every day, as it had been since the moment the War began.

On May 1, 1945, the stand-down of the Corps was announced but the Corps is to be maintained on a voluntary spare-time basis, its duties co-ordinated to whatever peacetime structure is evolved for the air defence of Great Britain.

THE ARMY AIR CORPS

The Army Air Corps was officially constituted on February 27, 1942. It consists of The Glider Pilot Regiment, The Airborne Infantry Units and The Parachute Regiment, all of which work closely with the Royal Air Force, especially for training purposes. Personnel in all three sections are recruited from the Army and are nearly all volunteers.

At the end of 1944 newly-formed Glider squadrons were manned by R.A.F. pilots who had been trained under the Commonwealth Air Training Plan and who were not needed for other commands because air casualties over Europe during the year had been fewer than had been expected.

All units of the Army Air Corps took part in the Allied in-

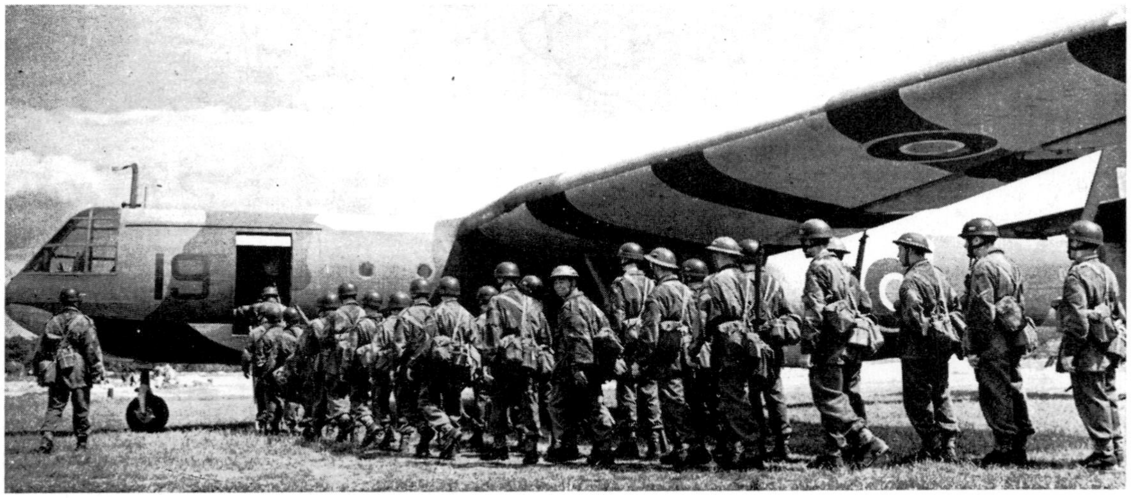

Airborne Infantry emplaning in an Airspeed Horsa I glider of the type which was used in the airborne invasions of Sicily, Southern France and Normandy.

vasion of Normandy. With United States airborne units they formed the spearhead of the invasion and were dropped behind the enemy lines at each end of the wide coastal sector on which the sea landings were made. British forces were dropped at points a little to the North-east of Caen. Parachute troops landed in the dark ahead of the glider-borne forces to clear the area chosen for the glider-landings, which reconnaissance had shown to have been obstructed by the enemy. The main objectives in this area were two bridges over which the enemy might attempt to bring reinforcements. The airborne landings were so successful that the bridges were captured intact within a few hours.

Gliders brought in troops and equipment, including light tanks and anti-tank guns. One of the elements of surprise in the airborne landings was the General Aircraft Hamilcar glider which had been specially designed to carry a light tank and other heavy equipment. By the time the Germans had counter-attacked in the British airborne landing area reinforcements had been flown in, and more landings were made on succeeding nights. Although the airborne forces, in this instance the British Sixth Airborne Division, had a hard fight it accomplished all the special tasks which had been allotted it and fought in Normandy for several months.

THE FIRST ALLIED AIRBORNE ARMY

On August 10, 1944, the formation of a new command was announced to consolidate the airborne troops of the Allied Expeditionary Force as the First Allied Airborne Army under the command of Lieut.-Gen. Lewis H. Brereton, U.S.A.A.F. Lieut.-Gen. F. A. M. Browning, formerly Commanding the British Airborne Forces, was the original Deputy Commander but in November, 1944, he was appointed Chief of Staff to Admiral Lord Louis Mountbatten, South-East Asia Command. On Jan. 19, 1945, Maj.-Gen. R. N. Gale, British Army, was appointed Deputy Commander of the Airborne Army.

The First Allied Airborne Army included British, American and Polish troops and combined both the combat troops and the aircraft and gliders which transported them. In size it approximated an Army. The gliders used were :—the American Waco CG-4A (Hadrian) and the British Airspeed Horsa (also used by the Americans under reverse Lend/Lease) and the General Aircraft Hamilcar. Aircraft tugs included the Douglas C-47 Dakota, Armstrong Whitworth Albemarle, Handley Page Halifax and Short Stirling.

The first operation of the First Allied Airborne Army was made on September 17, when strong forces were landed in Holland in daylight. More than 1,000 aircraft took part in the landings and the whole of the Allied Air Forces co-operated. The purpose of the landings was to enable the Allied Armies in Belgium and Holland to "jump" the Siegfried Line and cross the Lower Rhine. The task of the Airborne forces was to save the bridges over the Rhine at Arnhem and Nijmegen and to prevent the enemy from destroying them or using them.

One part of the task was accomplished—at Nijmegen, where

Short Stirling IV parachute troop carriers lined up in readiness for D-Day on June 6, 1944.

American airborne troops captured the bridge and linked up with the armoured forces.

At Arnhem the British First Airborne Division held out for nine days and although the bridge was reached and held for a time, enemy opposition in the area was stronger than had been supposed and the armoured columns were unable to relieve the Airborne Division. In addition, bad weather helped to tip the scales against the venture and prevented the dropping of adequate supplies and reinforcements. It also hindered support from the Tactical Air Forces while it helped the German counter-attacks.

Valiant attempts were made by transport aircraft to drop supplies in face of the constant enemy fire from the Germans surrounding the area. During the first four days more than 4,000 aircraft and 2,800 glider sorties were flown, but at the end of nine days the British First Airborne Division was withdrawn and brought back over the Lower Rhine. Of some 6,500 troops which had been dropped at Arnhem, about 2,000 returned unwounded.

The Arnhem operation was a gamble which, had it succeeded, would probably have shortened the War by some months. It did not succeed but was not a complete failure. The stand at Arnhem contributed greatly to the success of operations as a whole in that corridor and made a powerful contribution to the success at the Nijmegen bridge. The heroic nine days at Arnhem and the attempts of the Air Force to assist them was one of the great stories of the War.

The greatest airborne operation of the War was made on March 24, 1945, when two divisions, the British Sixth and the United States 17th, were dropped across the Rhine in front of the British Second Army. On this occasion the Ground forces began their crossing of the Rhine at night and the Airborne Divisions—preceded by parachute troops—were dropped the following morning. The Force included 1,300 gliders and 200 paratroop-carrying aircraft. The total weight lifted from Great Britain, including tanks, weapons, transport and supplies, amounted to more than 1,500 tons. On this occasion each tug towed two gliders.

The landings were completely successful and the British Sixth Airborne Division was one of the spearheads of the Second Army's advance through North-West Germany.

The last airborne operation in the Western Front was the dropping of parachute troops in Northern Holland on April 7, 1945.

R.A.F. STATISTICS ON CEASE FIRE IN EUROPE

Operational Sorties—Bomb Tonnage and aircraft losses for European and Mediterranean War Theatres, 1939-45.

Losses

Security considerations precluded the announcement of certain operational losses of Royal Air Force Commands during the course of hostilities. With certain exceptions it was permissible to publish only those aircraft losses of which the enemy could be presumed to be aware—i.e. aircraft lost over enemy or enemy-occupied territory or in sight of enemy vessels. Losses of aircraft given in the tables below include not only those not previously announced for the above reasons but the additional losses of aircraft so badly damaged in combat that upon landing at their base or in Allied territory they were unfit for further service.

BOMBER COMMAND

	Sorties	Tonnage	Aircraft Lost
1939	591	31	40
1940	22,473	13,033 (510)	509
1941	32,012	31,704 (707)	985
1942	35,338 (1,088)	45,561 (6,367)	1,517 (26)
1943	65,068 (1,240)	157,457 (9,136)	2,457 (17)
1944	166,844	525,518 (13,170)	2,904
1945	67,483	181,740 (3,373)	708
	389,809 (2,328)	955,044 (33,263)	9,120 (43)
	392,137	988,307	9,163

Figures in brackets under sorties show additional aircraft of Bomber Command operating under Coastal Command and the losses in those operations are correspondingly marked. Under "tonnage" the figures in brackets are the tonnages of mines laid.

ARMY CO-OPERATION COMMAND

Sorties	Tonnage	Aircraft Lost
4,474	63	70

FIGHTER COMMAND
(including Air Defence of Great Britain)

	Sorties	Tonnage	Aircraft Lost
1939	3,217	—	3
1940	121,079	1	1,186
1941	150,828	129	651
1942	147,087	207	688
1943	136,167	986	569
1944	122,136	1,232	397
1945	19,712	926	64
	700,226	3,481	3,558

2nd TACTICAL AIR FORCE

	Sorties	Tonnage	Aircraft Lost
1943	23,695	3,627	177
1944	214,592	38,729	1,305
1945	89,426	19,482	633
	327,713	61,838	2,115

COASTAL COMMAND (All Bases)

	*Sorties	Tonnage	Aircraft Lost
1939 and 1940	41,001	917 (241)	288
1941	30,544	766 (240)	233
1942	31,676	529 (100)	302
1943	43,231	494 (21)	279
1944	66,362	1,411	305
1945	22,935	661	132
	235,749	4,778 (602)	1,579
		5,380	

*Does not include sorties by Bomber Command aircraft which are shown under Bomber Command.

Figures in brackets under tonnage show weight of mines laid.

MEDITERRANEAN AND MIDDLE EAST
Including Dominion and Allied Squadrons Serving with the R.A.F., June, 1940—May, 1945.

	Sorties		Tonnage		Aircraft Lost
1940	Bomber	5,158	Germany (including Austria, Czechoslovakia and Poland)	—	133
	Fighter	9,168			
	Coastal	1,304			
	Tactical, Reconnaissance and Army Co-operation	2,032	Other Occupied Countries	2,503	
	Miscellaneous	49	Targets at Sea	22	
1941	Bomber	14,850	Germany (as above)	—	671
	Fighter	33,211			
	Coastal	4,845	Other Occupied Countries	12,562	
	Tactical, Reconnaissance and Army Co-operation	3,554	Targets at Sea	220	
	Miscellaneous	568			
1942	Bomber	19,896	Germany (as above)	—	1,189
	Fighter	79,478			
	Coastal	11,116	Other Occupied Countries	22,153	
	Tactical, Reconnaissance and Army Co-operation	2,603	Targets at Sea	398	
	Miscellaneous	1,642			
1943	Bomber	18,968	Germany (as above)	—	1,349
	Fighter	107,671			
	Coastal	21,644	Other Occupied Countries	32,148	
	Tactical, Reconnaissance and Army Co-operation	2,681	Targets at Sea	587	
	Miscellaneous	13,631			
1944	Bomber	33,621	Germany (as above)	636	1,853
	Fighter	167,008			
	Coastal	7,608	Other Occupied Countries	58,673	
	Tactical, Reconnaissance and Army Co-operation	16,597	Targets at Sea	1,133	
	Miscellaneous	18,852			
1945	Bomber	15,959	Germany (as above)	1,715	540
	Fighter	57,245			
	Coastal	59	Other Occupied Countries	27,932	
	Tactical, Reconnaissance and Army Co-operation	(a)	Targets at Sea	158	
	Miscellaneous	4,986			
Totals 1940 to 1945	Bomber	108,452	Germany (as above)	2,351	5,735
	Fighter	453,781			
	Coastal	46,576	Other Occupied Countries	155,971	
	Tactical, Reconnaissance and Army Co-operation	27,467	Targets at Sea	2,518	
	Miscellaneous	39,728			

(a) Included with fighter.

Miscellaneous Sorties include :— Special Duties, General Reconnaissance, Photo-Reconnaissance, Air/Sea Rescue, etc.

R.A.F. BOMBER COMMAND
Tonnage of Bombs dropped and number of Sea-Mines laid
By Category of Target, monthly from September, 1939 to May, 1945
British Tons (2,240 lbs.).

1939	Industrial Towns	Troops & Defences	Transportation	Naval Targets	Oil Targets	Airfields and Aircraft Factories	Specific Industries	Military Installations	Misc. Targets	Total Tons	No. of Mines Laid
September	—	—	—	6	—	—	—	—	—	6	—
October	—	—	—	—	—	—	—	—	—	—	—
November	—	—	—	—	—	—	—	—	—	—	—
December	—	—	—	25	—	—	—	—	—	25	—
Total 1939	—	—	—	31	—	—	—	—	—	31	—
1940											
January	—	—	—	—	—	1	—	—	—	1	—
February	—	—	—	1	—	—	—	—	—	1	—
March	—	—	—	11	—	20	—	—	—	31	—
April	—	—	—	18	—	76	—	—	18	112	118
May	—	1,245	249	—	117	50	7	—	—	1,668	70
June	—	621	616	22	375	274	192	—	200	2,300	97
July	—	—	225	176	219	488	39	—	110	1,257	156
August	—	—	147	97	297	445	201	—	178	1,365	138
September	—	—	241	1,399	120	184	172	—	223	2,339	49
October	—	—	167	623	299	275	187	—	100	1,651	56
November	—	—	338	264	204	231	183	—	96	1,316	31
December	137	—	165	281	88	105	104	—	112	992	47
Total 1940	137	1,866	2,148	2,892	1,719	2,149	1,085	—	1,037	13,033	762 = 510 tons
1941											
January	97	—	107	372	112	25	45	—	19	777	45
February	513	—	80	491	140	96	45	—	66	1,431	66
March	716	—	18	687	153	101	3	—	66	1,744	70
April	972	—	21	1,035	79	108	32	—	149	2,396	129
May	1,513	—	32	941	34	59	152	—	115	2,846	121
June	2,138	—	768	865	4	103	115	—	317	4,310	76
July	1,348	—	1,532	901	48	122	424	—	9	4,384	133
August	1,411	—	1,874	546	6	144	103	—	158	4,242	81
September	962	—	708	901	—	80	204	—	34	2,889	101
October	910	—	1,029	686	—	164	144	—	51	2,984	75
November	1,062	—	—	482	—	38	8	—	317	1,907	111
December	697	—	—	940	—	8	58	—	91	1,794	47
Total 1941	12,339	—	6,169	8,847	576	1,048	1,333	—	1,392	31,704	1,055 = 707 tons

R.A.F. BOMBER COMMAND—*continued*
Tonnage of Bombs dropped and number of Sea-Mines laid
By Category of Target, monthly from September, 1939 to May, 1945
British Tons (2,240 lbs.).

	Industrial Towns	Troops & Defences	Transportation	Naval Targets	Oil Targets	Airfields & Aircraft Factories	Specific Industries	Military Installations	Misc. Targets	Total Tons	No. of Mines Laid
1942											
January	853	—	—	1,219	—	82	—	—	138	2,292	62
February	285	—	—	376	—	36	—	—	314	1,011	306
March	1,711	—	—	298	—	32	510	—	124	2,675	356
April	2,667	—	70	847	—	243	397	—	209	4,433	569
May	2,383	—	11	231	—	304	211	—	94	3,234	1,023
June	6,087	—	—	223	11	390	36	—	98	6,845	1,167
July	5,246	—	11	896	—	99	22	—	94	6,368	897
August	3,828	61	—	110	—	34	15	—	114	4,162	968
September	5,256	—	—	103	—	125	16	—	95	5,595	1,101
October	3,124	—	—	394	1	183	37	—	70	3,809	982
November	1,700	—	9	662	—	8	9	—	35	2,423	1,156
December	2,497	—	34	24	—	7	88	—	64	2,714	987
Total 1942	35,637	61	135	5,383	12	1,543	1,341	—	1,449	45,561	9,574= 6,367 tons
1943											
January	2,925	—	30	1,212	—	66	49	—	63	4,345	1,285
February	6,329	—	6	4,403	—	16	127	—	78	10,959	1,129
March	6,606	—	73	1,668	24	15	2,072	—	133	10,591	1,159
April	9,097	—	108	1,335	—	750	41	—	136	11,467	1,869
May	11,904	—	113	32	21	600	79	—	171	12,920	1,148
June	13,948	—	106	124	—	189	751	—	153	15,271	1,174
July	16,099	—	206	6	3	4	391	—	121	16,830	927
August	15,674	—	5	—	—	2	1,830	2,072	566	20,149	1,103
September	12,066	670	775	—	—	18	1,026	153	147	14,855	1,188
October	13,101	—	—	5	6	17	337	—	307	13,773	1,076
November	12,537	—	1,456	2	—	7	219	—	274	14,495	976
December	11,178	—	—	—	—	7	97	346	174	11,802	800
Total 1943	131,464	670	2,878	8,787	54	1,691	7,019	2,571	2,323	157,457	13,834= 9,136 tons
1944											
January	16,566	—	7	78	—	20	63	1,482	212	18,428	1,101
February	11,592	—	145	12	—	139	46	9	111	12,054	1,661
March	19,456	—	6,243	—	—	1,380	339	14	266	27,698	1,472
April	11,997	633	19,230	6	—	1,175	380	7	68	33,496	2,643
May	5,296	12,634	15,013	15	—	2,648	1,488	5	53	37,252	2,760
June	710	13,729	17,433	3,133	4,496	1,346	50	15,907	463	57,267	1,778
July	9,594	8,847	9,475	298	4,407	514	19	24,292	169	57,615	708
August	10,181	9,915	4,300	2,988	11,129	5,316	2,543	19,376	107	65,855	1,586
September	12,527	26,364	2,633	458	4,835	4,447	3	859	461	52,587	748
October	42,246	12,366	536	972	3,682	47	1,082	—	273	61,204	1,133
November	27,696	5,689	4,892	159	14,385	19	63	—	119	53,022	750
December	16,727	3,677	18,454	1,529	5,109	1,858	1,604	—	82	49,040	1,160
Total 1944	184,688	93,854	98,361	9,648	48,043	18,909	7,680	61,951	2,384	525,518	17,500= 13,170 tns.
1945											
January	11,931	2,072	8,459	129	9,028	—	1,221	—	83	32,923	668
February	21,888	3,756	5,505	561	14,109	—	—	—	70	45,889	1,354
March	30,278	8,042	6,229	3,924	18,936	5	11	—	212	67,637	1,198
April	2,322	12,056	7,909	6,526	5,437	596	4	—	104	34,954	1,362
May	63	155	—	—	—	36	—	—	83	337	—
Total 1945	66,482	26,081	28,102	11,140	47,510	637	1,236	—	552	181,740	4,582= 3,373 tns.
Grand Total	~430,747	122,532	137,793	46,728	97,914	25,977	19,694	64,522	9,137	955,044	47,307= 33,263 tns.

MEDITERRANEAN THEATRE OF OPERATIONS
Tonnage distribution by Type of Target
Heavy Bombers and Wellingtons only
British Tons (2,240 lbs.)

	Oil Plants, Storage Etc.	Aircraft Factories	Other Industries	Airfields	Communications	Harbours	Military Targets/ Army Support	Targets at sea	Miscellaneous	Total Tons	Tonnage of Mines Laid
1940	14.3	—	1.2	193.0	20.4	146.6	53.6	—	26.3	455.4	—
1941	36.3	41.1	37.3	3,368.3	205.0	3,352.2	852.0	54.2	51.9	7,998.3	43.5
1942	—	—	—	2,601.0	14.5	8,524.4	4,983.7	204.0	9.5	16,337.1	383.0
1943	40.3	123.5	65.0	5,832.0	6,780.7	4,400.3	3,943.5	34.4	82.2	21,301.9	160.7
1944	2,496.1	287.7	419.3	1,449.8	10,564.7	2,280.1	3,311.7	49.0	476.8	21,335.2	1,147.1
1945	244.2	—	—	—	6,643.4	1,232.2	938.1	—	—	9,057.9	—
Totals	2,831.2	452.3	522.8	13,444.1	24,228.7	19,935.8	14,082.6	341.6	646.7	76,485.8	1,734.3

TONNAGE OF BOMBS DROPPED BY BOMBER COMMAND BY CITIES

Target	Tons (of 2,240 lbs.)	Dates of First and Last Attacks	
Berlin	45,517	25/26th August, 1940	— 20/21st April, 1945.
Essen	36,420	24/25th May, 1940	— 11th March, 1945.
Cologne	34,711	15th May, 1940	— 2nd March, 1945.
Duisburg	30,025	16/17th May, 1940	— 21/22nd February, 1945.
Hamburg	22,580	17/18th May, 1940	— 17/18th April, 1945
Dortmund	22,242	24/25th June, 1940	— 29th March. 1945
Stuttgart	21,016	24/25th August, 1940	— 17/18th March, 1945.
Gelsenkirchen	19,606	14/15th May, 1940	— 24th March, 1945.
Mannheim/Ludwigshaven	18,114	4/5th June, 1940	— 17/18th March, 1945.
Dusseldorf	17,769	15/16th May, 1940	— 23rd February, 1945.
Kiel	16,712	1/2nd July, 1940	— 2/3rd May, 1945.
Frankfurt	15,696	2/3rd June, 1940	— 13/14th March, 1945.
Hanover	14,776	18/19th May, 1940	— 29/30th March, 1945.
Le Havre	13,449	18/19th September, 1940	— 11th September, 1944.
Nuremberg	13,021	8/9th November, 1940	— 11th April, 1945.
Bremen	12,831	17/18th May, 1940	— 22/23rd April, 1945.
Bochum	10,784	21/22nd June, 1940	— 22/23rd March, 1945.
Calais	9,736	3/4th September, 1940	— 27th September, 1944.
Brest	8,428	28/29th July, 1940	— 5th September, 1944.
Boulogne	7,827	11th July, 1940	— 17th September, 1944.

THE NAVAL AIR ARM, 1944-45

One of the most important years in the history of British naval aviation came to its end with an announcement of great significance. This was the brief statement that Rear Admiral T. H. Troubridge, D.S.O., R.N., had been appointed Fifth Sea Lord in succession to Vice-Admiral D. W. Boyd, C.B., C.B.E., D.S.C., R.N.

In quick succession came news of other appointments, and honours. Commodore M. S. Slattery, R.N., who had for long served as Chief Naval Representative in the Ministry of Aircraft Production was promoted Rear Admiral and given an appointment in the Admiralty as Vice-Controller (Air), which he holds in parallel with the position of C.N.R. in M.A.P.

Rear-Admiral L. D. Mackintosh, who had recently served as Captain of the *Implacable* from which he became Assistant Chief of Naval Staff (Air), was appointed Flag Officer, Carrier Training and Administration, being succeeded as A.C.N.S. (Air) by Rear-Admiral Charles Lambe, lately Captain of the *Illustrious* in the British Pacific Fleet.

These appointments carried with them numerous other changes in lower ranks, and it is interesting to note that among these was the promotion of E. W. Anstice to the rank of Commodore, R.N., he having been one of the original naval pilots of the 1924 course at Netheravon, and in this war commanding officer of the Escort-Carrier *Fencer*.

Vice-Admiral Boyd received the honour of the K.C.B. at an Investiture held by The King in July, and took up the appointment of Admiral (Air)—the first of its kind—with headquarters at Lee-on-Solent after handing over the office of Fifth Sea Lord to Rear Admiral Troubridge.

As Admiral (Air), Sir Denis Boyd takes over and further extends work which had been done by the Rear-Admiral, Naval Air Stations.

This change at the top of the naval air arm was the first indication outwardly of an inner revolution of basic ideas in the Navy. The new ideas concern weapons, aircraft, ships and above all personnel.

Chief impetus to the advance of the Navy's air arm has sprung from the dynamic influence of Vice-Admiral Boyd who took up the dual appointment of Fifth Sea Lord and Chief of Naval Air Equipment on January 14, 1943.

This appointment, as Fifth Sea Lord, had an almost immediate effect on every branch of naval aviation, and it was badly needed for especially on the aircraft side the Navy was in the doldrums. The Fairey Barracuda torpedo-bomber, designed for 1940, had been held back in priority by a Cabinet decision to concentrate production on certain specified types of fighters and bombers for the R.A.F. so that the main striking force of the naval air arm was chiefly the Fairey Swordfish augmented by a few squadrons of Fairey Albacore torpedo-bombers (the Albacore having gone out of production to give way for a scheduled appearance of the Barracuda in 1940). Indeed, one of the most stirring production stories of the war concerns the efforts of Blackburn Aircraft, Ltd., in building Fairey Swordfish at a new factory specially laid down in 1940 as an emergency measure to continue the flow of at least some aircraft to the Navy. In these dark years of development the Fairey Aviation Co. Ltd. continued development progress of the Barracuda and the new Firefly two-seat reconnaissance fighter.

Admiral Boyd advanced the case for re-instating the Barracuda and Firefly on high priority for production, and both were so restored by mid-summer 1943. The original trickle of aircraft, inseparable from production of a new type, soon swelled to a strong running river, the Firefly especially proving an outstanding success. Both these types were officially "released" from a thick mist of secrecy in 1944.

Coupled with the soaring rate of recruitment and aircraft production, the ship problem was solved in a typically British compromise manner. At the outbreak of war there was with the Fleet only one modern aircraft-carrier, but the Naval Estimates had covered the building of six successors,—*Illustrious, Indomitable, Formidable, Victorious, Implacable* and *Indefatigable*—rated as "Fleet-type carriers." However, the construction and equipment to modern standards—especially as regards radio—of a Fleet carrier takes a long time. The deteriorating position, particularly in the Atlantic, in the anti-U-boat war had become most serious; so serious indeed that the War Cabinet constituted a special U-boat Warfare Committee with, significantly, the Minister of Aircraft Production as its head.

One of the many measures accepted and advanced by this committee, and fostered on all sides, was the development of the Escort Carrier, in which a merchant ship hull was to be internally adapted with hangar accommodation and aircraft facilities and a "roof" put on the hull for use as a flying deck. These makeshift carriers, ugly ducklings of the Fleets, turned out to be operational swans. More than 40 of these ships, together capable of carrying more than 1,000 operational aircraft, have already been cited as being with the British Fleet. Their successes are World-wide and their influence on the war almost inestimable.

In addition, and as an indication of the desperate demands for air cover against submarines, what were termed Macships (merchant aircraft carrier ships) were introduced; these being an even more simplified version of the already utility-only Escort classes.

Although the escort carriers have faced every hazard from the North Cape to the Far East their losses have been infinitesimal though several have been damaged by air and U-boat attacks. They have proved a stop-gap of great worth, though there are grave limitations to their operational value with a Fleet.

The net result of these developments was that the Navy, despite the loss of the *Courageous, Glorious, Hermes, Eagle* and *Ark Royal*, had by 1945 augmented its sea-going air fleets to the extent of at least 1,500 aircraft—and probably many more. In June, 1945 *Furious* was officially announced as released from operational duty.

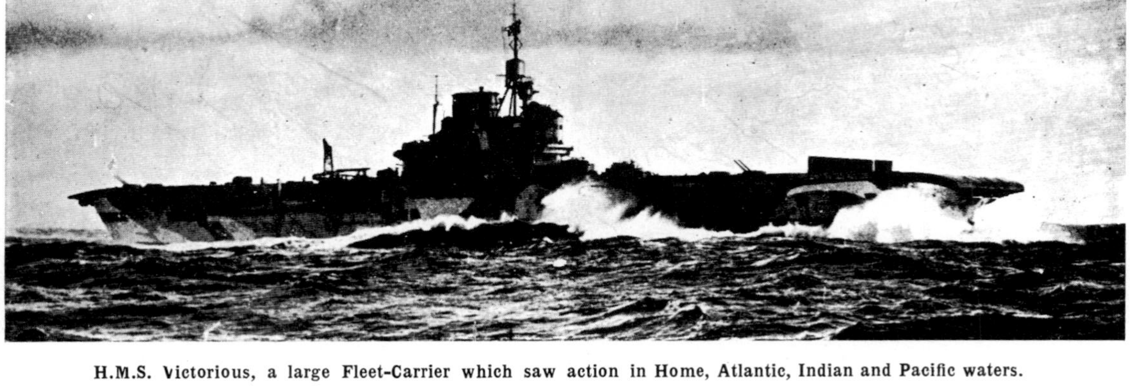

H.M.S. Victorious, a large Fleet-Carrier which saw action in Home, Atlantic, Indian and Pacific waters.

On the aircraft side, the technical advance has likewise been marked. From decks where once no more than a slow biplane could be contemplated, fast fighters (Seafire, Hellcat, Wildcat, Corsair), the two-seat Firefly (successor to the Fulmar) and heavy torpedo-bombers (Barracuda and Avenger) are now operated. Though obsolete in design before 1939, in the sixth year of war the Swordfish continues on operational duty.

Yet another change concerns the introduction of rockets. These have been adapted for accelerating take-off from the deck of a carrier and as the motive force in rocket projectiles. The Firefly, Barracuda and Swordfish have all been officially cited during the past year as being armed with rockets, though attacks of this kind were used by the naval air arm in the Atlantic as long ago as early 1943. Moreover, the fighters such as the Seafire have been nominated as able to carry heavy bombs, thus following the R.A.F. practice of making a good aeroplane into a better by increasing its flexibility of employment in war.

By January, 1943, the first Barracudas were embarked in *Illustrious* which was then planned for action in the Mediterranean. By late Summer several Barracuda squadrons had been embarked in ships off Malta and were waiting for the signal to attack the Italian Fleet. The enemy, however, pusillanimously capitulated and the glorious opportunity for a Barracuda debut in force and reminiscent of the attack at Taranto vanished. Thus deprived of its targets, the Barracuda still remained on the secret list.

In fact the Barracuda had what might be termed a double-debut. On April 3, 1944, the 45,000-ton German battleship *Tirpitz* was the target for a surprise attack by squadrons of Barracudas which, with fighter escort, made dive-bomb attacks and secured numerous hits. Though much damage was done superficially, the *Tirpitz* was not sunk. Its second appearance in the headlines came shortly after, on April 19, when a Barracuda force attacked Sabang in Northern Sumatra, without loss.

These initial successes were followed up closely. Barracuda squadrons, with fighter protection, struck at two enemy convoys off Kristiansund (Norway) on May 6, 1944, with full success. Two weeks later, naval Hellcat squadrons armed with bombs and escorted by purely fighter Wildcats and Hellcats, struck at numerous shore installations on the Norwegian coast and hit ships, oil tanks and the fish oil factory at Statlandet. This was done despite enemy interception and without damage to our warships.

Without mentioning exact dates, on May 19 the Admiralty gave details of a successful convoy to Russia in which aircraft from the escort-carrier *Chaser* played an important part, its Wildcat fighters shooting down enemy reconnaissance aircraft. Close-range attacks on U-boats were successfully made by Swordfish. Two U-boats were sunk and more damaged severely.

The assault on enemy ships and installations by British carrier aircraft continued, the sixth in the series in northern waters being mounted on June 1. Three supply ships were hit with bombs and four escort vessels raked with gun and cannon fire. The attacks were widespread and were made with aircraft from the carriers *Victorious, Furious, Searcher, Emperor, Pursuer, Fencer*, and *Striker*—an indication of the gathering forces at sea.

Meanwhile, Sea Hurricanes operating from the *Nairana* were intercepting and shooting down long-range reconnaissance aircraft far out in the Atlantic, their protection to the convoys being inestimable.

The naval air arm also took part in the D-Day landings in Normandy (June 6, 1944). One naval wing flew 430 sorties on D-Day alone, and 8 days later had completed 1,248 hours flying. Outside the mouth of the English Channel aircraft-carriers were diligently on patrol watching for possible U-boats.

Public interest in the progress of the Normandy landings obscured the fact of another successful Russian convoy, of which details were given on June 24. British naval aircraft from the carriers *Tracker* and *Activity* not only sank U-boats but fought off attacking aircraft, these successes going to Swordfish, Avenger and Wildcat aircraft.

Meanwhile the pace in Far East attacks was quickening. In the first week of July, 1944, the Eastern Fleet raided Sourabaya, Corsairs delivering a hit-and-run attack on Jap protective airfields, leaving aircraft blazing on all sides and sinking a small transport ship. This was followed by a parallel raid on the Jap-

anese-held base at Port Blair in the Andaman Islands, ground installations and transport of all categories being shot up. On July 25 a full-scale attack by battleships, cruisers and destroyers was made, supported by British carrier aircraft. Port Blair was badly battered, and a formation of enemy attack aircraft was shot out of the sky by defending fighters before it could close the Fleet.

On the other side of the World naval aircraft attacked ground installations at Alesund and Kristiansund on August 12, 1944, in particular destroying Me 110 fighters on the ground at Gossen, radio-location stations at Lepsoy and sinking two of three armed vessels in the same area.

Early in September the Admiralty saw fit to release first information on the Seafire III (the folding-wing naval version of the Spitfire). The engineering feat of "cutting" the canti-lever wing of a Spitfire to permit folding must stand as a triumph for the Supermarine designers. Though in service in large numbers long before, the Seafire III made its operational debut on D-Day, operating from land bases. Shortly afterwards Seafire III's were prime operators from escort-carriers in the landings in the South of France.

A series of strikes which was to culminate in the sinking of the *Tirpitz* by R.A.F. Lancasters was then staged. In each of these enemy ships were sunk and, in particular, radar ground stations used to warn the enemy of approaching aircraft were wrecked. These attacks also got the enemy "jumpy" and caused the *Tirpitz* to be moved nearer to German bases—and nearer for the attacking Lancasters on November 12, 1944. On Sept-ember 5, it was announced that over a period of days several strikes had been made against the *Tirpitz* at Alten Fjord and in the Hammerfest area, the attacks being made by Barracudas, Hellcats, Seafires and Corsairs, and on September 12 aircraft from the *Furious* and *Trumpeter* carried on the good work off Stat-landet.

On September 15, R.A.F. Lancasters attacked the *Tirpitz* with 12,000-lb. bombs, and one direct hit was claimed. At least, the damage caused the ship to be moved and another 12,000-lb. Lancaster attack was made on September 29—again with a claim of one direct hit. The *Tirpitz* was now at Tromsœ and, in part as a diversionary raid and in part to continue ground devastation, British carrier aircraft made attacks at Bodœ, sinking six ships and causing a U-boat to run ashore. In a follow-up raid they sank 19 ships by cannon fire and bombs, as well as wrecking radar and other installations and laying mines by night. Thus cornered the *Tirpitz* waited her inevitable fate, and on November 12, 1944 the R.A.F. completed the job which had begun in March, 1942, when a flight of 12 Albacores had attacked with small bombs without visible damage to the enemy.

This major sea defeat by air forces did not result in a relax-ation of the stranglehold placed on Norwegian sea movements by the aircraft-carriers. On November 15, Wildcats from the *Pursuer* successfully bombed shore installations.

By now first details of the Fairey Firefly two-seat reconn-aissance fighter had been made known, though this aircraft had already figured conspicuously in many attacks on ground install-ations along the Norwegian littoral. Details were announced on December 1, 1944, of a series of attacks in which, flying through snowstorms and in atrocious Arctic weather, Barracuda Firefly and Seafire aircraft with the Home Fleet made attacks on convoys off Mosjoen and Rorvik, Central Norway. Another series of attacks made with Firefly and Wildcat fighters on supply convoys near Haugesund was successfully completed in appalling weather without loss of more than one aircraft. To round off the year concerning Norway, bombs, rockets and cannon fire were used to deal with two convoys off Statlandet by aircraft from the small carriers *Nairana* and *Campania*.

Most of the Russian convoy actions off Norway were running actions covering several consecutive days. Thus, operating daringly close inshore on January 12, near Egersund Harbour a cruiser force with the escort carriers *Premier* and *Trumpeter* made night aircraft and gunnery attacks on a defended convoy. A month later aircraft from *Campania* and *Nairana* fought a seven-day battle in blinding snowstorms and blizzards of gale force and with visibility down to 1,000 yards. U-boats and enemy aircraft made repeated attempts to attack, but achieved only near misses for the loss of two U-boats and several aircraft.

Yet another important convoy was fought through at the end of March, 1945. Torpedo-bombers and U-boats attacked in strength, but more than 94% of the convoy got through the 2,000 mile journey safely, escorted by aircraft from the *Campania*. Almost immediately afterwards (on April 1, 1945) naval aircraft form the *Searcher*, *Queen*, *Nairana* and *Puncher* made a series of raids to cover the leads in Trondheim and Aalesund areas, three intercepting Me 109's being destroyed by Wildcat fighters. And so the grim story went fearlessly on, with the balance of success heavily in favour of the carrier aircraft.

To switch to warmer climes, important naval air actions were taking place in the Mediterranean. Here the escort-carriers had not acquired a good reputation, for at the Salerno landings in windless conditions of flat calm they had not sufficient speed to make deck flying as straightforward as it can be and had, at full speed for long periods, rapidly exhausted their oil fuel. There had been many crashed aircraft in these conditions and though the task of Salerno had been successfully completed the percenta e loss in naval aircraft had been high.

It was again the Mediterranean Summer when, following successes in Normandy, landings in the South of France were scheduled. For these a force of some 300 warships had been mustered, ranging from the battleship *Ramillies* to gunboats, from corvettes to minesweepers, and including seven British carriers under the command of Rear-Admiral Troubridge.

In view of the Salerno naval aircraft story it may be well to state the facts of the successful landings in the South of France. The carriers operating were the *Emperor*, *Khedive*, *Searcher*, *Pursuer*, *Attacker*, *Hunter* and *Stalker*. The aircraft undertook full-scale air co-operation and attack support. On an average, during the period August 15 to 23, one aircraft took off every six minutes between dawn and dusk. Each pilot flew an average of 2,300 miles and the total distance flown was 275,605 miles. The landings were an unqualified success and the naval air action

H.M.S. Indefatigable passing through the Suez Canal on passage to the Far Eastern Theatre of Operations.

The Escort Carrier Atheling of the "Ruler" Class of fourteen ships built in the United States for the Royal Navy.

was described by the American General present as "a model of perfection."

As it has long been a theory that naval aircraft must be "inferior" to land-based, and as these attacks were made well within the range of German and Italian air squadrons, the results claimed are not without interest. Officially nominated as being "conservative," the results are given as :—Motor Transport 160 destroyed, 190 damaged ; Rail trucks 64 destroyed, 83 damaged ; Armoured vehicles 4 destroyed, 18 damaged ; Bridges 4 destroyed, 5 damaged ; Roads cut 18 ; Railways cut 14 ; Military installations 53 direct hits ; Ships sunk 7. These results, quite apart from reconnaissance sorties of the utmost value, were obtained by Seafire, Hellcat and Wildcat fighters.

In the Far East, since April, 1944, almost regular monthly attacks have been made against Japanese-held bases, as well as constant patrols against submarines and enemy shipping. Attacks included Sabang (2), Sourabaya, Andaman Islands, Indiaroeng, Emmahaven, Sigli, Nicobar Islands, and the sinking of six ships in Nancouvry Island. Many of these actions were not disclosed in detail by the Admiralty or even mentioned at all at the time, since security declined to satisfy Japanese broad-casts which sought information.

However, on February 5, 1945, details were released of a series of important attacks on Japanese oil refineries in Sumatra, extending from 20 December, 1944, onwards. The attacks aimed to knock-out the oil plants at Pangkalan-Brandan where 75% of all aviation fuel used by the Japanese was produced. Bombs and rockets were used with outstanding success. The attacks were mounted from the Fleet carriers *Illustrious*, *Victor-ious*, *Indomitable* and *Indefatigable*. The first three of these are of the order of 23,000 tons, but the *Indefatigable* (with her sister-ship the *Implacable*) is officially listed as "in the neighbour-hood of 30,000 tons" and with a speed of "considerably more than 30 knots." The *Indefatigable* is the first four-screw aircraft-carrier in the Royal Navy and (perhaps of more interest to aviators) she incorporates many advanced ideas internally, particularly for maintenance of aircraft and crew comfort.

The Sumatra attacks were followed up by two days of heavy British air attacks on the Sakishima islands of Miyako and Ishigaki, from which interference might have been made to the U.S. landings on Okinawa. Seafires, Hellcats, Corsairs and Avengers ran a shuttle service to attack Japanese ground install-ations and airfields and also kept a standing patrol over the British warships of the Pacific Fleet.

Two days before, in the Indian Ocean some 11 days of hard flying by the naval air arm had wound up the assault on the Arakan Islands, which included the occupation of Ramree and Cheduba islands—the latter being a 100% naval party.

Over a two month's combat period off the Sakishima Islands, 170 miles South of Okinawa, seven ships of the British Pacific

Fleet, including the aircraft-carriers *Indefatigable* and *Victorious*, were hit by Japanese "suicide" aircraft, but no ship was put out of action and all continued normally within two hours of the attacks.

In the heavy attacks on the Japanese mainland by the U.S. Third Fleet and ships of the British Pacific Fleet serving under the unified command of Admiral Nimitz, U.S.N., the British Carrier Force commanded by Vice-Admiral Phillip Vian con-tributed its quota of aircraft to the air forces engaged. During the week ending July 21, 1945, British and U.S. naval aircraft

The Escort Carrier Chaser seen from an aircraft which has just taken off.

attacking targets on the Japanese east coast destroyed or damaged 128 ships and 92 aircraft. In 22 days at least 1,230 ships and 1,257 aircraft were put out of action by the U.S. Third Fleet and units of the British Pacific Fleet.

In an attack on the Tokyo area on July 30, British naval aircraft sank a destroyer and three other ships, while 33 ships were hit, some being heavily damaged. In the combined British and U.S. assault 89 Japanese vessels were destroyed or damaged and 178 aircraft were shot down.

In the last 42 days of the war in the Pacific the British Aircraft-Carrier Force was responsible for the destruction of 148 enemy aircraft, with a further 199 damaged. It sank 9 combatant and 99 non-combatant ships and damaged 21 combatant and 18 non-combatant vessels.

When the "cease fire" in the Pacific was sounded on August 14, the British and U.S. Fleets were cruising 100 miles off the Japanese coast and carrier aircraft were on their way to Tokyo. The aircraft, after dropping their bombs in the sea, returned to their carriers.

Details of a new class of Light Fleet Carrier were announced on September 1. This type of carrier is virtually a scaled-down version of the larger Fleet Carrier with a displacement of 14,000 tons, a designed speed of 25 knots and accommodation for 33 aircraft. Four units of this class,—*Colossus, Glory, Venerable* and *Vengeance*—served with the British Pacific Fleet. It was on the deck of the *Glory*, lying off Rabaul, New Britain, that the surrender of the Japanese forces in the South-West Pacific was signed on September 6, 1945. The "*Colossus*" Class has been followed by "*Majestic*" Class of similar characteristics but embodying various improvements. In addition to the *Majestic* the following ships in this Class have been launched :— *Hercules, Leviathan* and *Powerful*.

These operations in the Far East stress the point of spares and maintenance far from home supply sources. The corrosion problem was particularly acute in Ceylon where the sea breezes carried acids of such virility that in a few hours they would corode the finest steel and rendered useless valuable aircraft unless they had been carefully tended and greased in advance. Since Ceylon, the base of the East Indies Fleet, and Sydney, the base of the British Pacific Fleet, were many hundred of miles from the scenes of many actions, a new class of ship—Fleet Train—was introduced to cope with running repairs. This type of ship is virtually an aeronautical floating workshop and has proved of immense value as a "camp follower" to the aircraft-carrier fleets.

These actions and the review of the development of the naval air arm indicate the powerful influence the aircraft-carrier is likely to exert on all future naval action.

This article may well conclude with the significant words spoken by Vice-Admiral Sir Denis Boyd in an address to naval air apprentices :—"The main striking power of the Navy is its aircraft. The whole future of the Navy lies in its correct assimilation of the lessons of war. Our aircraft will in future be comparable to anything of their size that flies. The air is the background to your lives."

These words, coming from the man who was Fifth Sea Lord during the Years of Endurance, must be regarded as a signpost to an ascendant future and imply a new determination in the highest quarters to master the hazards of the air, as for so many centuries have the perils of the sea been faced and overcome.

B.J.H.

The Escort Carrier Searcher, one of many which played a vitally important part in the protection of Russian and trans-Atlantic convoys.

During the most critical period of the Battle of the Atlantic a number of British merchant ships were provided with flying decks to provide air cover to the convoys in which they sailed. These ships, known as Merchant Aircraft-carriers or Macships, combined the functions of laden merchantmen and aircraft-carriers. The illustration above shows the Macship Empire McColl.

SOUTHERN RHODESIA

In 1936 the Government of Southern Rhodesia formed the nucleus of an Air Section of the Permanent Staff Corps and six recruits were sent to Great Britain for a course of technical training with the Royal Air Force. In the following year two R.A.F. officers were seconded for duty with the Air Section. On the outbreak of War in September, 1939, the Government offered to bring the air unit up to the strength of a full squadron, to man two more squadrons and maintain them in the field with the R.A.F. on any front. This offer was accepted by the British Government and the first Rhodesian Squadron was despatched to serve with the R.A.F., Middle East Command.

Meanwhile Southern Rhodesia became a partner in the British Empire Air Training Scheme and formed the Rhodesian Air Training Group to train personnel exclusively for the R.A.F.

The Air Officer Commanding, Southern Rhodesian Air Training Group, is Air Vice-Marshal C. W. Meredith, C.B.E., A.F.C.

The Minister for Air is Colonel Sir E. Guest.

For the year 1944-45 Southern Rhodesia had an estimated expenditure of £3,410,232 for military, air and police services.

OPERATIONS

By April, 1944, out of a total white population of 70,000, there were 8,514 Southern Rhodesians serving with the Army and the Royal Air Force. Of this number, some 2,000 were with the R.A.F. serving in three Southern Rhodesian squadrons and in all Commands of the R.A.F.

Rhodesia had two squadrons operating on the Western Front. No. 44 Squadron—which was the first squadron in the R.A.F. to be equipped with Lancaster bombers—and No. 266 Squadron equipped with Typhoons. Both squadrons played a full part in all R.A.F. operations preceding and during the liberation of Europe.

In the Middle East a third Rhodesian squadron, No. 237, equipped with Spitfires, served with the First Tactical Air Force throughout the Italian campaign and covered the Allied landings in Southern France in August, 1944. This squadron, formerly No. 1 (Rhodesia) Squadron, was the first Dominion squadron in the field when the War broke out. It was at its station at Nairobi two days before the outbreak of the War on Sept. 3, 1939.

In September, 1944, a gold cup bearing the inscription "To the Southern Rhodesian Air Force from the Royal Air Force as a token of comradeship and esteem" was flown from Great Britain to Southern Rhodesia.

TRAINING

Southern Rhodesia's greatest contribution to the War was its training organization. The Southern Rhodesian Air Training Group was the first to open an Elementary Flying Training School under the British Commonwealth Air Training Plan—in May, 1940. The Group was also the first to turn out trained pilots and the first to complete its scheme.

The original scheme was greatly expanded and men from the United Kingdom, African Colonies and Territories, the Belgian Congo, Australia, and from the Middle East and Allied Nations were trained in Rhodesia.

Towards the end of 1944 a number of the training stations were closed down when the need for air crew members was reduced.

The Colony contributed £800,000 a year to the general cost of the Air Training Group and also bore the cost of the Headquarters staff, maintenance, camps and aerodromes.

THE RHODESIAN AIR ASKARI CORPS

The Rhodesian Air Askari Corps consists almost entirely of native personnel and has two branches; a labour division which is responsible for all labour duties required on Air Force stations in the Colony; and Askaris, who are armed and carry out guard and defence duties at all aerodromes and Air Force Stations.

AIR TRAINING CORPS

An Air Training Corps on the lines of the British organization was formed in 1941 under the supervision of Wing Commander Lord Douglas Hamilton, of the Rhodesian Air Training Group.

SOUTHERN RHODESIAN WOMEN'S AUXILIARY AIR SERVICES

The Southern Rhodesia Women's Auxiliary Air Services was formed on June 1, 1941, as an independent organization administered on a full-time basis by the Departments of Air. The S.R.W.A.A.S. is employed only in the Colony, has 19 trades and some 500 members.

INDIA

THE ROYAL INDIAN AIR FORCE

The Indian Air Force was constituted with effect from October 8, 1932, by the Governor-General in Council in pursuance of the Indian Air Force Act, 1932. The first flight of No. 1 Squadron of the Indian Air Force was formed on April 1, 1933. In March 1945, His Majesty the King approved the designation "Royal Indian Air Force."

By the middle of 1944 the strength of the Indian Air Force had grown to about 30,000 compared with 200 in 1939. By the end of 1944 there were 10 squadrons and in addition a number of Indian Air Force ground and flying crews were serving with the Royal Air Force in the Eastern Air Command to gain experience.

During 1944 a number of Indian pilots served with R.A.F. Fighter Command in operations over Europe and at least one

pilot served with the Pathfinder Force of Bomber Command. In addition, several Armament officers of the Indian Air Force completed courses in Great Britain before becoming instructors with the Indian Air Force.

The first Distinguished Service Order to be awarded an officer of the Indian Air Force was won in March, 1944 by Squadron Leader Mehar Singh who commanded an Indian Air Force

Hurricane squadron on the Arakan front. The first Indian Air Force officer to command an operational station was Wing Commander S. Mukerjee, who was appointed to command a station at Kohat during 1944.

In 1944 the Indian Air Force had more squadrons serving on operations than ever before. The first squadron went into action on the Burma front in November, 1943, and was followed at regular intervals by other squadrons. Throughout the whole of the Army operations on the Arakan front Hurricane and Vengeance squadrons of the I.A.F. served with the Third Tactical Air Force and supported the 14th Army by dive bombing and strafing enemy troops, communications, supplies and dumps. In addition a Hurricane squadron on this front operated on tactical and photographic reconnaissance duties, strafing, and numerous secret operational missions which ranged from dropping medical supplies to delivering official instructions to army units surrounded by the enemy.

One Indian squadron, on its second tour of operations in the Burma theatre, flew 3,360 sorties and a total of 4,000 operational hours between February and December, 1944. Another squadron operating from a forward position on the Assam front had a record of 98.5 serviceability for the month of July, 1944, the highest in the Third Tactical Air Force. Hurricane squadrons of the I.A.F. flew on both day and night duties.

Towards the end of 1944 the first Spitfire squadron of the Indian Air Force went into action on the Arakan front.

Indian Air Force squadrons in the Burma theatre were congratulated on several occasions by the Army for their close support work and by the Third Tactical Air Force.

In addition to the Burma theatre, squadrons of the I.A.F. continued to serve throughout the war on the North-West Frontier and to patrol the Indian coasts.

Early in 1945 His Majesty The King approved the formation of an Indian Parachute Regiment. Training of the nucleus of the Regiment had begun in 1942 with the R.A.F.

The Indian Government has announced that it is their intention to maintain the R.I.A.F. at an initial peacetime strength of ten squadrons, plus the necessary training and other ancilliary units required to provide a fully balanced force. It is emphasised that this in only an initial minimum strength which will be expanded as rapidly as conditions permit and as personnel becomes available.

As a first step towards meeting anticipated requirements of regular officers for the R.I.A.F., the Government of India decided, before the war with Japan was over, to grant a number of Government commissions to Indian officers serving in the Air Force. At the time this decision was made the number of such commissions to be granted was determined at ninety.

TRAINING

During 1944-45 there was a total of some 104 Indian Air Force establishments in India. Flying training continued on an increased scale, the Fairchild Cornell trainer being added to the D.H. Moth and North American Harvard types already in service.

During the 12 months to July, 1944 the technical side of the Air Force expanded some 600 per cent. and in order to bring the technical and non-combatant sections up to strength a number of men training for the Army was diverted to the Indian Air Force. Altogether there were 17 technical and non-technical training schools for trades in the Indian Air Force at which more than 50 per cent. of the instructors were Indian.

In January, 1945, a display flight of the Indian Air Force was formed to stimulate public interest in the Air Force and to assist recruiting. The flight, equipped with Cornell and Hurricane aircraft made a tour of Northern India.

Combined training centres for the Indian Air Force, Army and Navy were set up during 1944 on the coasts of India for special training in amphibious warfare.

By the beginning of 1945 the scheme covered all the 19 Indian universities, including three universities in Indian States. In addition to receiving instruction in ground subjects students were also given at least three hours flying experience during their course.

In 1944 a scheme for giving pre-entry training facilities was introduced at certain public and secondary schools by the formation of special "air classes" to encourage air-mindedness. The first part of the scheme was to be limited to a small number of schools in the provincial capitals and Indian States, but if successful the scheme was to be extended to one school in each of the principal cities in India.

AIR TRAINING CORPS

An Air Training Corps Scheme was approved for the Universities of India and inaugurated in January, 1943, at Aligarh University. The scheme is designed to assist young students who may consider entering the technical or clerical trade groups of the Indian Air Force by giving them a course of preliminary training in subjects they would be required to learn on joining the Service.

The course consists of three months' training on technical and non-technical Air Force subjects and is an optional subject added to the normal university curriculum. The syllabus includes an initial course to give preliminary instruction in service organization and other general matters, followed by an elementary course divided into technical and non-technical subjects according to the branch of the service the student intends to enter. Trainees who complete the course successfully are awarded a diploma similar to the British Air Training Corps certificate.

Uniforms and distinctive badges are provided for students taking the course and during training they are paid Rs20 a month.

THE WOMEN'S AUXILIARY CORPS (India)

The Women's Auxiliary Corps (India) was formed in 1943 and consists of Army, Navy and Air Force Wings comprised of women of Indian and various nationalities. In 1944 the Air Force Wing of the W.A.C. (I) was employed with the Royal Air Force on plotting and photographic duties, among others. Early in 1945 the first course for advanced training for the W.A.C. (I) was opened at the Staff College, Quetta, and permission was given for the members of the W.A.C. (I) to serve outside India.

2—THE SELF-GOVERNING DOMINIONS

THE DOMINION OF CANADA

THE ROYAL CANADIAN AIR FORCE.

The Royal Canadian Air Force is administered by the Department of National Defence, Canada, through the Minister of National Defence for Air, who is advised by an Air Council consisting of the following members :—

THE CANADIAN AIR COUNCIL

The Minister for Air, Hon. Colin Gibson, M.C., K.C., V.D., M.P.

The Deputy Air Minister, Mr. H. F. Gordon.

Chief of the Air Staff, Air Marshal R. Leckie, C.B., D.S.O., D.S.C., D.F.C.

Air Member for Personnel, Air Commodore H. L. Campbell, C.B.E. (effective 15th April, 1945).

Air Member for Training, Air Vice-Marshal J. L. E. A. de Niverville, C.B.

Air Member for Air Staff, Air Vice-Marshal W. A. Curtis, C.B.E., D.S.C.

Air Member for Supply and Organization, Air Vice-Marshal F. S. McGill.

Administration of the Force is exercised by R.C.A.F. Headquarters, Ottawa, through five Commands—three operational and two Air Commands, as follow :—

OPERATIONAL COMMANDS

Eastern Air Command, Halifax, Nova Scotia.

Air Officer Commanding-in-Chief : Air Vice-Marshal A. L. Morfee, C.B.E.

Western Air Command, Victoria, British Columbia.

Air Officer Commanding : Air Vice-Marshal F. V. Heakes, C.B.

North Western Air Command, Edmonton, Alberta.

Air Officer Commanding : Air Vice-Marshal T. A. Lawrence.

AIR COMMANDS

No. 1 Air Command, Trenton, Ontario.

Air Officer Commanding : Air Vice-Marshal A. Raymond, C.B.E.

No. 2 Air Command, Winnipeg, Manitoba.

Air Officer Commanding : Air Vice-Marshal K. M. Guthrie, C.B.E.

The Air Officer Commanding-in-Chief, R.C.A.F. Overseas (with headquarters in the United Kingdom) is Air Marshal G. O. Johnson, C.B., M.C., and the Deputy A.O.C.-in-C. is Air Commodore C. R. Slemon, C.B.E.

The Canadian Air Attaché in Washington is Group Captain F. H. Smith, O.B.E. Air Vice-Marshal V. G. Walsh, C.B.E., is R.C.A.F. member of the Permanent Joint Defence Board in Washington.

The strength of the Royal Canadian Air Force in 1944 numbered 202,000 compared with 4,000 before the War. The total strength overseas amounted to some 100,000 and the greater proportion of Canadian air-crews overseas was lent to the Royal Air Force as there were not enough Royal Canadian Air Force squadrons to absorb them all. More than one-fifth of the air-crews of the Royal Air Force were Canadian and some 45 per cent. of the strength of Royal Air Force radio mechanics were Canadian. The Canadian Government bears the entire cost of pay, allowances, maintenance and equipment of all Royal Canadian Air Force squadrons operating overseas and the pay, allowances and maintenance of all R.C.A.F. personnel in the Royal Air Force.

The Canadian Air Estimates for 1944-1945 provided for nearly $1,400,000,000 of which about $48,000,000 was recoverable from Great Britain, Australia and New Zealand in respect of pay for Royal Air Force personnel and for the training of Commonwealth air crews in Canada. The maintenance of Canadian squadrons overseas was estimated as $345,000,000, some $13,000,000 more than for 1934-1944.

Total estimated expenditure from September, 1939 to March 31, 1945 was :—

R.C.A.F. overseas operations	$910,819,643
Western Hemisphere operations	$963,053,377
B.C.A.T.P.	$1,635,408,265
Total ..	$3,509,281,285

In 1944 the Royal Canadian Navy took over two aircraft-carriers from the Royal Navy. Flying personnel on these carriers were British but in September, 1944, the first four Canadian naval officers to take air training for eventual service with Canadian aircraft-carriers, graduated from a Service Flying Training School in Canada. After further advanced training in the United Kingdom these officers were to serve with the Royal Navy, subject to recall by the Royal Canadian Navy. At that time there was a total of 31 such officers undergoing training in Canada for aircraft-carrier duties.

R.C.A.F. ACTIVITIES AT HOME

The functions of the operational commands in Canada are the air defence of Canada and co-operation with Great Britain in convoy protection. Throughout the year R.C.A.F. Liberator squadrons and squadrons of Canso flying-boats (Canadian-built Catalina flying boats) of Eastern Air Command patrolled the Atlantic and operated between Canada and Iceland, while Western Air Command patrolled and kept watch on the Pacific coast.

On June 1, 1944, a new Canadian Home Command was established, the North-West Air Command, with headquarters at Edmonton. Its principal responsibility is the control and operation of the North-West Staging Route, the chain of aerodromes and intermediate airfields stretching from Edmonton to the Yukon and Alaska. The geographical boundaries of this new Command stretch from Edmonton to the Arctic Ocean, thence along the seaboard to the international boundary with Alaska and British Columbia and southwards along the British Columbia-Alberta highway.

The North-West Staging Route had previously been controlled by No. 2 Wing of the Western Air Command but the development of the route, with its strategic and international implications arising from its extensive use by the United States and Russia, made necessary the establishment of a new command.

On August 1, 1944, the Canadian Government announced that arrangements had been made for the reimbursment of the United States for all expenditure on air bases made by that country in Canada during the War which were of permanent value. This consisted mainly of airfields which had been constructed by both Canadian and United States funds across Canada in connection with the ferry routes to Europe and Russia.

The North-East Staging Route, which was revealed for the first time when the new arrangement was announced, was established to relieve the pressure on the ferry route from Gander. Goose Bay, to which Canada was given a 99 year lease by Newfoundland, became the second great base for the ferrying of aircraft and was used by the R.C.A.F., R.A.F. and United States forces.

After the entry of the United States into the War on December 7, 1941, another route was built with shorter stages. This stretched from The Pas and Churchill, Manitoba, to Southampton Island, N.W. Territories, Frobisher Bay, Baffin Island, Greenland and Iceland, with another route from the United States by way of Ontario and Quebec to Frobisher. The Hudson's Bay leg (via Churchill) of the North-East route was not used to the extent anticipated but construction of these bases completed an interlocking network of more than 300 airfields across Canada.

Under the arrangement of 1944, Canada will own all these bases and will pay the following amounts for construction in Canada by the United States :—

	U.S. Dollars.
North-West Staging Route (including contracts not completed)	31,311,196
Flight Strips along the Alaska Highway	3,262,687
Flight Strips along the Mackenzie River	1,264,150
Hudson's Bay Route	27,460,330
Airfield at Mingan, Quebec	3,627,980
Airfield at Goose Bay, Labrador ..	543,000
Telephone—telegraph—teletype line from Edmonton to Alsaka boundary ..	9,342,208
Total ..	$76,811,551

Costs incurred by Canada on United States' account which Canada will assume are :—

	Canadian Dollars
North-West Staging Route	$18,359,953
Hudson's Bay Route	1,290,010
Airfield at Goose Bay, Labrador ..	9,950,680
Total ..	$29,600,643

In addition Canada will pay $5,151,000 for a projected improvement on the North-West Staging Route. Canada's total expenditures on war-time developments in the North-East and North-West alone amount to about $120,000,000.

The Directorate of Air Transport Command

Officer Commanding : Group Captain L. Leigh, O.B.E.

At the end of 1943 transport activities of the R.C.A.F. in Canada and overseas had expanded to such an extent that a Directorate of Air Transport Command was formed under which all R.C.A.F. air service activities have been centralised.

The first heavy transport squadron of the R.C.A.F. was formed in January, 1943, to fly supplies from Moncton, N.B. to Goose Bay, Labrador. In January and February, 1944, this squadron was carrying more than a million pounds of freight a month in a fleet of Dakota and Lodestar transports. Other squadrons operate over the North-West Staging Route. A Communications Wing operated special services between squadrons and undertakes any special flights necessary in Canada. Other activities of the Command are the ferrying of aircraft in Canada, and flying aircraft in connection with the training in Canada of parachute troops.

In addition, the Command operates services across the Altantic carrying mail for the Canadian forces overseas. During 1944

Canadian-built Avro Lancaster X bombers of the R.C.A.F. "Moose" Squadron which served with No. 6 (R.C.A.F.) Group, R.A.F. Bomber Command.

Loading 500-lb. bombs into a Handley Page Halifax of the R.C.A.F. French-Canadian "Allonette" Squadron which served with No 6. (R.C.A.F.) Group, R.A.F. Bomber Command.

two R.C.A.F. squadrons were formed for transport work in Western Europe and Burma.

THE R.C.A.F. OVERSEAS

During 1944 more than 100,000 R.C.A.F. men and women served overseas and the number of Canadian squadrons increased to more than 40. These included fighter, fighter-bomber, night-fighter and "Intruder" squadrons, the Canadian Bomber Group, a Pathfinder squadron, R.C.A.F. squadrons serving with Coastal Command of the Royal Air Force both at home and in Ceylon, and two R.C.A.F. Transport squadrons.

No. 6 (R.C.A.F.) Bomber Group, based in Yorkshire had a full complement of squadrons in 1944 completely equipped with Handley Page Halifax and Avro Lancaster bombers, an increasing proportion of the latter being Canadian-built Mark X's. In 1944 the Bomber Group flew 25,353 operational sorties and dropped 86,503 tons of bombs with the lowest loss percentage of four-engined aircraft in the whole of Bomber Command.

Between dusk of June 5 and dawn of June 7, 1944, the Group flew 478 sorties for the loss of one bomber and attacked five targets. Between dusk and dawn on D-Day, the R.C.A.F. dropped 1,000 tons of bombs but the heaviest tonnage was recorded after D-Day. A new record was established in August when 3,700 sorties were flown and 13,000 tons of bombs were dropped. On many occasions the Group operated alone. A record for the number of Canadian bombers despatched against a single target was made in the Duisburg raids on October 14 and 15 when more than 500 R.C.A.F. bombers took part, the first time that more than 500 sorties had been flown by Canadian bombers during 24 hours. In the first 10 months of 1944 the Canadian bomber Group received 1,242 awards for gallantry, seven for chivalry and 318 mentions in despatches. The heaviest loss recorded by the Command was on July 28 when 23 aircraft failed to return.

In addition to the Canadian Bomber Group, thousands of R.C.A.F. personnel served with Bomber Command of the R.A.F. and 19 Canadians flew in the 29 Lancasters which sank the *Tirpitz*. On August 11, 1944, H.M. The King, accompanied by the Queen and Princess Elizabeth spent a day with the R.C.A.F. Bomber Group.

Four R.C.A.F. wings equipped with Spitfire, Typhoon, Mustang and Mosquito aircraft served with the R.A.F. Second Tactical Air Force during the year. Twelve R.C.A.F. fighter squadrons formed part of the air protection for the Allied landings in Normandy and a Canadian Spitfire squadron was among the first to operate from a base in France—four days after D-Day.

Of the 170 enemy aircraft destroyed by fighters of the Second T.A.F. based in France in the first month of its operations, 135 were destroyed by fighters of an R.C.A.F. sector. Between D-Day and the middle of August, of 356 enemy aircraft destroyed by one fighter-bomber group commanded by Air Vice-Marshal Broadhurst, 249 were destroyed by R.C.A.F. pilots.

R.C.A.F. squadrons equipped with Leigh-Light Wellington, Albacore, Sunderland and R.P. Beaufighter aircraft operated with Coastal Command of the R.A.F. throughout the year and Canadian air-crews formed part of Coastal Command's Meteorological Flight stationed at Reykjavik, Iceland.

The first all-Canadian Transport squadron in the European theatre was formed in September, 1944. Known as the "Husky" squadron and equipped with Dakota aircraft, it took part in the Arnhem operations, ferried supplies to the Western Front and evacuated wounded and maintained a daily service to the continent.

In the Mediterranean theatre the Canadian "City of Windsor" squadron, equipped with Spitfire VIII fighter-bombers continued to serve throughout the year with the First R.A.F. Tactical Air Force. R.C.A.F. air crews were members of the R.A.F. Halifax squadrons operating with the Balkan Air Force

which supported Marshal Tito's Partisan forces in Yugoslavia and some Canadians flew with a South African bomber squadron. Canadian ground crews were attached to airfields in Italy.

In the Far East the Canadian Catalina squadron based on Ceylon continued to operate over the Indian Ocean and Bay of Bengal. During the Summer of 1944 Canadian ground crews of R.C.A.F. Transport squadrons were flown from the United Kingdom to a base in North-West India in four days. They were the first squadron ground crews to be flown to India.

A Dakota squadron manned by R.C.A.F. crews operated with the R.A.F. in Burma and in January, 1945, a second R.C.A.F. Dakota squadron began operations in this theatre. Canadian strength in R.A.F. Dakota squadrons in the Burma theatre was estimated at 25 per cent. In addition many Canadians flew with the Third Tactical Air Force throughout the year and more than 50 Canadians flew with an R.A.F. Liberator squadron based in India which was commanded by a Canadian.

Besides the R.C.A.F. squadrons operating in Europe, the Mediterranean and Burma, R.C.A.F. personnel served with every Royal Air Force Command at home and overseas. R.C.A.F. casualties from the beginning of the War to September 30, 1944, amounted to 16,985, of which 10,658 were killed or presumed killed.

A Catalina flying-boat of the R.C.A.F. "Tusker" Squadron in Ceylon.

The first Victoria Cross won by the R.C.A.F. in this War was awarded to Flight-Lieut. D. E. Hornell, R.C.A.F. for pressing home a skilful and successful attack against an enemy submarine in the Atlantic, although his aeroplane, a Catalina, was on fire and was shot down. The all-Canadian crew of the Catalina, which was operating with R.A.F. Coastal Command, spent 21 hours in icy water before being picked up but Flight-Lieut. Hornell died from exposure shortly after being rescued.

Plans for the participation of the R.C.A.F. in the War against Japan were made during the Summer of 1944 when a number of R.C.A.F. officers under Air Vice-Marshal L. F. Stevenson were attached to R.A.F. Headquarters, South East Asia Command, to make a survey of tropical conditions under which air forces operate in that theatre and to acquire the information needed for the establishment of Canadian squadrons in the Pacific zone.

In April, 1945, Canada announced that Canadian squadrons would be represented in any Air Police Force which might be established in Europe after the defeat of Germany.

TRAINING

Training in Canada under the British Commonwealth Air Training Plan was gradually reduced after February, 1944, because of the changing War situation, the success of the Allied air effort and because casualties had been lower than had been expected, particularly among fighter pilots. Because of this a substantial reserve of pilots and air-crews had been built up. Both Australia and New Zealand stopped sending men for training.

The peak effort under the Training Plan was achieved in February when 3,854 air crews graduated. Recruiting for the R.C.A.F. in Canada was stopped between June and October and a number of prospective air-crews were released to the Army. In addition, the length of the pilot training course was extended by eight weeks.

Before the end of 1944 the four Training Commands in Canada were reduced to two, Nos. 1 and 3 being amalgamated to form a new No. 1 Command and Nos. 2 and 4 to form a new No. 2 Command.

Altogether more than 131,000 trained air-crews graduated from the British Commonwealth Air Training Plan, of which 55 per cent. were members of the R.C.A.F. Although the Commonwealth Training Plan was considered to have fulfilled its purpose (to plan and provide not only for immediate needs but for operational requirements from 18 months to two years ahead) and was closed down on March 31, 1945, arrangements were made to continue training R.A.F. men at 11 schools of different kinds. In addition, six Operational Training Units were to be maintained for the R.A.F. and R.C.A.F. in Canada as well as seven schools for refresher and specialised courses. The number of persons on the training and administrative staffs of the Training Commands in Canada, which was 64,300 in December, 1943, was to be reduced by at least one half by March, 1945.

THE AIR CADET LEAGUE OF CANADA

The Air Cadet League of Canada was formed in June, 1941, to organize Air Cadet units throughout the Dominion on lines similar to those of the Air Training Corps of Great Britain. Under an Order in Council in May, 1943, the League was incorporated as part of the R.C.A.F.

Only boys of 15 to 18 years of age who can pass examinations similar to those for aircrew duties in the R.C.A.F. are enrolled. Those who complete 50 per cent. of the cadet training syllabus may enlist in the R.C.A.F. without being obliged to spend the usual six months on ground duties. The equipment of the Corps is provided by the R.C.A.F. and during the Summer the cadets spend 10 days in camp at R.C.A.F. stations. The strength of the League is some 20,000 cadets with 230 squadrons.

Spitfires of the R.C.A.F. "City of Windsor" Squadron in Italy. This squadron was the only all-Canadian air unit to have served overseas from 1940 to the final victory in Europe.

THE ROYAL CANADIAN AIR FORCE (WOMEN'S DIVISION)

Founded in July, 1941, the Royal Canadian Air Force (Women's Division) was the first Canadian women's service organized in this War to release men for more active duties and the first service to send a contingent overseas. The first Canadian contingent of the Women's Division arrived in Great Britain on August 31, 1942, and the second in March, 1943.

By November, 1944, the strength of the Women's Division was more than 16,800 of which over 1,300 were on active service overseas. There were over 40 trades.

THE COMMONWEALTH OF AUSTRALIA

THE ROYAL AUSTRALIAN AIR FORCE

The Australian Air Force was formed by Proclamation on March 31, 1921, pending the passage of the Air Defence Act. On August 13, 1921, it became the Royal Australian Air Force. The Air Defence Act received Royal Assent on September 1, 1923, under which the Royal Australian Air Force became a separate service of the defence forces of the Commonwealth, with equal status to the Royal Australian Navy and the Commonwealth Military Forces.

ORGANIZATION

In March, 1942, headquarters of the Allied South-West Pacific Command, with General Douglas MacArthur as Supreme Commander-in-Chief, were established in Australia. Lieut.-General George H. Brett, of the U.S. Army Air Forces was appointed Deputy Commander-in-Chief of the Allied Forces and Officer Commanding the Air Forces in the South-West Pacific. Air Vice-Marshal W. D. Bostock, R.A.A.F., was appointed second in command to Lieut.-General Brett, who was later succeeded by Major General G. C. Kenney. This arrangement was changed later in the year when Air Vice-Marshal W. D. Bostock became Air Officer Commanding R.A.A.F. Command, Allied Air Forces.

ALLIED AIR FORCES, SOUTH-WEST PACIFIC

General Officer Commanding: Lieut.-General George C. Kenney, U.S. Army Air Forces.

Air Officer Commanding R.A.A.F. Command: Air Vice-Marshal W. D. Bostock, C.B., O.B.E.

All operational units of the Royal Australian Air Force are now under the command of the General Officer Commanding. Allied Air Forces.

THE AIR BOARD

The Air Board is responsible for the administration, training, equipment and maintenance of the R.A.A.F., as well as for works and buildings. Maintenance of personnel and equipment in connection with actual war operations is also a function of the Board, which in close collaboration with the American command, co-ordinates the supply and works services for the combined Air Forces.

The constitution of the Air Board is as follows:—

The Hon. A. S. Drakeford, M.P., Minister of State for Air.

Air Vice-Marshal G. Jones, C.B., C.B.E., D.F.C., Chief of the Air Staff.

Air Commodore F. R. Scherger, D.S.O., A.F.C., Acting Air Member for Personnel.

Air Commodore E.C. Wackett, O.B.E., Air Member for Engineering and Maintenance.

Air Commodore G. J. W. Mackinolty, O.B.E., Air Member for Supply and Equipment.

H. C. Elvons, Esq., Finance Member.

R. H. Nesbitt, Esq., Business Member.

F. J. Mulrooney, Esq., Secretary.

M. C. Langslow, Esq., M.B.E. The Secretary, Department of Air, is an ex-officio member of the Board, as is P. E. Coleman. Esq., O.B.E., The Assistant Secretary, Department of Air.

R.A.A.F. OVERSEAS

Overseas Headquarters, Royal Australian Air Force: Kodak House, Kingsway, London, W.C.2.

Air Officer Commanding: Air Vice-Marshal H. N. Wrigley, C.B.E., D.F.C., A.F.C.

Overseas Headquarters, R.A.A.F., has taken over the duties formerly undertaken by the Air Liaison Office, London, which ceased to function on November 30, 1941.

The High Commissioner remains the representative of the Commonwealth Government in the United Kingdom and deals with all matters of Government policy. Otherwise Overseas Headquarters is the channel of communication between the Department of Air, Melbourne, and the Air Ministry, London.

Personnel of the R.A.A.F. serving in Mediterranean Allied Air Forces and Air Command South East Asia come within the sphere of administrative control of Overseas Headquarters to the same extent as personnel serving in the United Kingdom and on the Continent.

R.A.A.F. Air Member, Australian Joint Staff Mission, U.S.A.:—Air Marshal R. Williams, C.B., C.B.E., D.S.O.

R.A.A.F. Liaison Officer, Canada:—Air Vice-Marshal S. J. Goble, C.B.E., D.S.O., D.S.C.

R.A.A.F. Liaison Officer, Middle East:—Group Capt. J. E. Graham.

R.A.A.F. Liaison Officer, India:—Wing Cdr. G. Pape.

TRAINING

Director of Training: Air Commodore F. N. Wright, O.B.E., M.V.O.

There are two training groups as shown hereunder:—

H.Q. No. 1 Training Group, Melbourne, Victoria.

H.Q. No. 2 Training Group, Wagga Wagga, N.S.W.

By the end of 1944 the strength of the Royal Australian Air Force was more than 40 times greater than in 1939. Total expenditure on the R.A.A.F. from the beginning of the War to December 31, 1944, was £386,618,000—excluding expenditure on behalf of United States forces in Australia and joint Australia-America projects.

Casualties in the R.A.A.F. up to December 31, 1944, totalled 13,109. Of these 8,264 were in Europe, the Middle East and Canada (including 4,525 killed) and 4,845 in the South-West Pacific Area, Far East and the India-Burma theatre (including 2,352 killed).

By the end of 1944 Australian airmen had won 3,136 awards for gallantry, including 649 in the South-West Pacific Area. The total awards included three Victoria Crosses, 23 United States awards and nine foreign decorations.

At the beginning of 1945 the announcement was made that the R.A.A.F. would spend some £4,000,000 on aerodromes and buildings for the shore-based requirements of the Fleet Air Arm of the Royal Navy's Pacific fleet.

TRAINING

During the Summer of 1944 far-reaching changes in air-crew training were announced in Australia, following the unexpectedly light casualty rate in the European theatre of the War and the success of Australia in meeting to the full its commitments of trained crews under the British Commonwealth Air Training Plan. In August, 1944, Australia decided to send no more fully-trained pilots to Great Britain, the Middle East and India, but small drafts of trained navigators, wireless operators and air gunners were sent until the end of the year. The last draft of R.A.A.F. men to complete their training in Canada under the British Commonwealth Plan left Australia in August.

The Pacific requirements of the R.A.A.F. were taking about three-fifths of the normal output of trained men in 1944 and, with an expanding effort in that area, new R.A.A.F. squadrons were being formed. But with the surplus of air-crews which had been built up a reduction in the number of volunteers for the R.A.A.F. in Australia was possible and several thousand were released to the Army. In addition, the opportunity of remustering as ground crew was given a number of men to meet the requirements of the new units and the increasing number of forward bases of the R.A.A.F.

Australian air-crews trained under the British Commonwealth Air Training Plan were estimated to comprise nine per cent. of the R.A.F. bomber air crews engaged in the offensive against Germany. Up to the end of September, 1944, more than 25,000 had been fully trained in Australia under the Commonwealth Plan and another 600 in Rhodesia. Altogether, Australia provided 35,000 fully-trained pilots, navigators, wireless operators and air-gunners under the British Commonwealth Air Training Plan from its inception to its close in March, 1945. Australia's cash contribution to the Plan amounted to some £145,000,000.

THE R.A.A.F. AT HOME

The strength of the R.A.A.F. squadrons serving in the South-West Pacific Area in 1944 increased by 15 per cent. and by the beginning of 1945 the R.A.A.F. was operating on almost the entire Eastern flank of the Pacific from the Solomon Islands in the South to Mindoro in the North.

Throughout 1944 R.A.A.F. squadrons operated from 20 bases in the Pacific islands, flew 45,000 sorties and dropped 9,000 tons of bombs. From the beginning of the Japanese War to the end of 1944 they had flown more than 415,000 operational hours on 85,000 sorties, an aggregate of approximately 66,000,000 miles. R.A.A.F. aircraft sank a total of 57 Japanese ships, two submarines and 437 barges in 1944 and probably sank an additional 125 ships, 11 submarines and 569 barges.

Transport squadrons of the R.A.A.F. in this theatre flew 16,000,000 miles and carried 63,000 short tons of war freight in 1944.

From the beginning of the Japanese War to the end of 1944 R.A.A.F. and United States aircraft in this theatre destroyed 10,342 Japanese aeroplanes, probably destroyed 1,742 and damaged 1,946.

Throughout 1944 the campaigns in the South-West Pacific area were designed to reach the Philippines by the quickest possible route and in the shortest possible time, by a series of leap-frog moves to new bases and by-passing Japanese strongholds. From the invasion of the Admiralty Islands in March, 1944, the R.A.A.F. shared in every landing that carried General MacArthur's forces to—and through—the Philippine Islands.

In January, 1944, a new operational group of the R.A.A.F., later named the First Tactical Air Force, was established at Nadzab, some 20 miles up the Markham Valley from Lae. The runways and dispersal bays at this base were built in the record time of 27 days by the R.A.A.F. Airfield Construction squadrons.

This new Group was established under the command of Air Commodore F. R. W. Scherger, D.S.O., R.A.A.F., who was succeeded in July, 1944 by Air Commodore A. H. Cobby, C.B.E., D.S.O., D.F.C. and two Bars, G.M. The First Tactical Air Force, designed as a mobile force, operated as an integral part of the U.S. 5th Air Force and was equipped with Vengeance dive-bombers, which were later replaced, Kittyhawk fighter-bombers, Beauforts, Bostons, Beaufighters, and towards the end of the year, Spitfires.

During the first three months of the year the Vengeance dive-bombers and Kittyhawk fighter-bombers gave constant support to the Australian and American ground forces in New Guinea while squadrons of Beaufighters and Kittyhawks maintained constant attacks on Japanese shipping plying along the shores of New Britain and New Guinea from Rabaul.

In March Allied forces began landings at three points in North East New Guinea at Aitape, Hollandia and Tanahmera Bay by-passing the main Japanese bases at Madang, Hansa Bay and Wewak. They then seized Wakde Island, Biak Island, Noemfoor Island and Sansapor, on the extreme West of Dutch New Guinea, before moving out of New Guinea to Morotai, in the Halmaheras, in September, 1944, and so to the Philippines.

R.A.A.F. Mobile Works Units accompanied U.S. troops landing at Aitape and within 42 hours had an air strip ready for use at Tadji, 24 hours ahead of schedule. The strip was occupied by R.A.A.F. Kittyhawks which were the spearhead of the R.A.A.F., provided top cover over Hollandia and later gave close support to troops landing at Wakde and Biak islands. During the hard fighting on Biak the Kittyhawks helped to frustrate the Japanese counter-attacks, on one occasion shooting down 10 out of 12 attacking Japanese aircraft for the loss of one Kittyhawk. Later, joined by R.A.A.F. Beaufighters and Bostons, the Kittyhawks maintained shipping sweeps and offensive reconnaissances along the jungle and river escape routes of the Japanese.

Meanwhile Australian ground forces, assisted by the R.A.A.F. were at work clearing the back-areas of by-passed Japanese in New Guinea, New Britain and the Northern Solomon Islands. Beaufighter aircraft, although maintaining their offensive shipping duties, also operated against ground targets and in June made almost daily attacks against encircled Japanese troops at Wewak, and Japanese villages and targets in other districts, assisted by Beauforts and Bostons.

Australian Boomerang and Wirraway aircraft had special tasks throughout the year with the Australian Army. Operating under the direct control of the Army, the Boomerangs were used mainly for tactical spotting duties and to lead bomber formations to specific pin-pointed targets. In mountainous and difficult country the Boomerang aircraft indicated the targets to fighter-bombers and medium bombers by strafing the targets with tracer bullets or dropping smoke bombs and then, some-

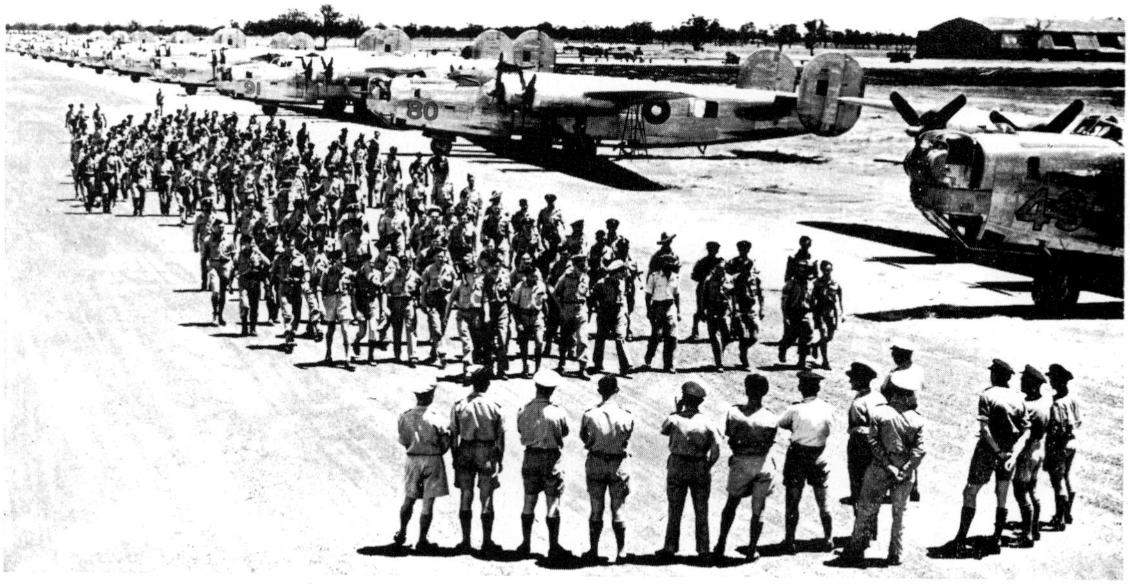

Instructional staff and aircrews under training at an R.A.A.F. Liberator Operational Training Unit.

Aircrews of an Australian Beaufort squadron in the Wewak area in New Guinea.

Australian Kittyhawk fighters being serviced in the Hollandia area in New Guinea after the return from a mission over Biak.

Pilots and Kittyhawk aircraft of an R.A.A.F. fighter squadron serving in the Pacific theatre.

what like the R.A.F. pathfinder tactics and "master-bombers" kept watch and corrected the bombing by radio. In the Solomon Islands the Wirraways and Boomerangs acted in close co-operation with Corsair fighter-bombers of the R.N.Z.A.F. serving as Pathfinders for them. They were also used to drop "comforts" to the troops.

During the Allied landings at Sansapor on August 1, 1944, R.A.A.F. Kittyhawks provided air cover in greater strength than ever before. Later in the year R.A.A.F. Kittyhawks and Beaufighters were based on Morotai, in the Halmaheras, to eliminate Japanese resistance in those islands and begin attacks in the Celebes. At the end of December, 1944, they were joined by R.A.A.F. Spitfire VIII's which had hitherto been based at Darwin. From Morotai, the R.A.A.F. maintained constant attacks on Japanese aerodromes and targets in Dutch territory, with little opposition from Japanese aircraft.

Some of the most spectacular work during the last quarter of 1944 was undertaken by Catalina flying-boats of the R.A.A.F. which did extensive mine-laying in Japanese ports, especially in the Netherlands East Indies. They also assisted in the U.S. landings in the Philippine Islands, mining selected ports, and early in 1945 moved to a base at Leyte. These crews were the first R.A.A.F. men to operate from the Philippines.

During 1944 Liberator bombers of the R.A.A.F. went into service and before the end of the year were making increasingly longer bombing attacks on Japanese-held targets. In addition, the first Australian-built Beaufighters went into service in the middle of 1944 and the first deliveries of Australian-built Mosquito fighter-bombers were made to the R.A.A.F. in July, 1944. Other types serving with the R.A.A.F. in the South-West Pacific Area during the year were :—Sunderland flying-boats, a number of which were flown out from England ; Ventura patrol-bombers ; Mitchell bombers, Kingfisher and Walrus sea-going aircraft, and Dakota transports.

Early in 1945 a surprise mine-laying raid at night in the South-West Pacific by Catalina flying-boats of the R.A.A.F. completely bottled up a Japanese battle fleet which included four battleships, an aircraft carrier, six cruisers and many destroyers. Mine-laying operations of the Catalinas closed, at least temporarily, every important harbour in the Dutch East Indies during the last months of 1944 and early 1945 and took an increasing toll of Japanese shipping.

The Australian Catalina squadrons were at that time the only heavy aircraft employed on mine-laying in the South-West Pacific and were employed on mining in the Philippines at the special request of the United States fleet.

On May 2, 1945, Australian forces undertook their biggest operations so far in the Pacific when they landed on Tarakan Island, off the North-East coast of Borneo. Aircraft of the R.A.A.F. played a vital part in the landings by blasting all airfields within range of the invasion convoy and by smashing the beachhead and garrison defences. This softening-up process was mainly accomplished by R.A.A.F. Liberator bombers.

In preparation for the landings a large number of Liberators were diverted from a base in North-West Australia to Morotai. As the convoy neared Tarakan, R.A.A.F. Liberators went out in force to neutralise airfields to the North and to guard the other flanks. The airfields in the Southern Celebes, Java and Borneo were particularly heavily bombed and the attacks were carefully orientated so as to confuse the Japanese.

R.A.A.F. Beaufighters escorted Mitchell bombers to Tarakan and adjoining targets. The Beaufighters were making their longest mission and drew the fire of the ground defences while the Mitchells, equipped with special photographic equipment, secured vital photographs of such of the enemy dispositions and beach defences which had escaped the bombing.

The R.A.A.F. squadrons operating from Morotai accomplished their pre-invasion rôle without loss, the Liberators flying deep into enemy territory by daylight without fighter cover.

Two R.A.A.F. Airfield Construction Squadrons also took part in the Tarakan landings. They were part of the Mobile Works Wing which had operated with American forces in the landings along the North New Guinea coast, in the Halmaheras and in the Philippines.

This first All-Australian landing in the South-West Pacific presaged the beginning of an even bigger Commonwealth share in the Pacific following the end of the European war and the release of men and aircraft for the Pacific.

THE R.A.A.F. OVERSEAS

At the end of the war in Europe, there were 13,000 R.A.A.F. air-crews serving in the European theatre. Of this total 2,000 were in R.A.A.F. squadrons, 4,000 in R.A.F. squadrons, 2,500 in non-operational R.A.F. units and nearly 5,000 were still under training. Altogether at this time, including the Mediterranean and India-Burma theatres, more than 19,000 R.A.A.F. airmen were serving overseas, although a number of air-crews returned to Australia in September, 1944.

Sixteen R.A.A.F. squadrons, formed under the British Commonwealth Air Training Plan, were serving overseas during 1944-45—twelve in Great Britain and France and the rest in the Middle East. Those in the European theatre included three Lancaster and one Halifax squadrons, a squadron of Mosquito night fighters, a squadron of Mosquitos operating with the Second Tactical Air Force, three squadrons of Spitfires with the Tactical Air Force and Nos. 10 and 461 Sunderland squadrons and No. 455 Beaufighter squadron with Coastal Command. R.A.A.F. Squadrons in the Middle-East included two equipped with Kittyhawk fighter-bombers, a squadron of Baltimore medium bombers and a Wellington squadron.

The first R.A.A.F. Fighter Wing in the European theatre was equipped with Spitfires, and based in the United Kingdom. It was devoted almost entirely to counter-measures against the V-2 rocket. Operating from bases in Great Britain, and then on the Continent, two R.A.A.F. Squadrons made 1,328 sorties over Holland and dropped 2,309 bombs on V-2 objectives.

One of the squadrons made the first direct assault against a V-2 launching site in the Hague. Later it was employed on shooting up German transport in Holland.

In 1944 more than 37,000 tons of bombs were dropped by the R.A.A.F. Lancaster and Halifax squadrons based in Great Britain in operations involving a total mileage of approximately 8,296,000. Of this total tonnage more than 27,000 tons were dropped between D-Day and the end of the year. During 1944 these squadrons attacked 160 targets a total of 289 times, including 26 attacks on Berlin. One new Lancaster squadron and one new Halifax squadron were formed during 1944. The senior R.A.A.F. Lancaster squadron, No. 460, which converted to Lancaster bombers in 1942, made its 5,000th sortie at the beginning of 1945.

Up to VE-Day this squadron alone had dropped nearly 25,000 tons of bombs and made 6,264 sorties during its service in Europe.

R.A.A.F. squadrons operated with Coastal Command throughout the year and in June, 1944, No. 10 Sunderland squadron broke all records by flying a total of more than 1,100 hours. Nos. 10 and 461 squadrons each flew more than a million miles in 1944 and at the end of the year had flown a total of 4,287,000 and 2,000,000 miles respectively since they began operations. No. 10 Squadron recorded the greatest war mileage of all Australian squadrons operating in Europe—4,000,000 in 33,700 flying hours.

R.A.A.F. Mosquito squadrons claimed 24½ flying bombs destroyed and 27 trains and three power stations damaged besides many armoured vehicles, tanks and enemy transports. One Mosquito squadron took part in the raid on the Amiens prison, winning the toss for the second squadron to go in to the attack.

A squadron of Spitfire bombers began operations from France a few days after D-Day, returning to Great Britain in October.

Five R.A.A.F. squadrons operated in the Mediterranean and Balkans areas during 1944 and in the quarter ended January 31, 1945, flew 4,000 hours on 1,700 sorties. No. 3 (R.A.A.F.) Squadron equipped with Kittyhawk fighter-bombers, which served continuously in this theatre from the early days of the Western Desert fighting, flew 837 hours on 400 sorties. One

R.A.A.F. squadron of Spitfires, operating from Corsica, after service in Egypt, Western Desert, Palestine, Syria and Cyprus, provided air cover for some of the convoys which landed the Allied forces in the invasion of Southern France, and later patrolled the beaches. Later it formed part of the R.A.A.F. Wing in Great Britain. The R.A.A.F. Baltimore squadron shared in the liberation of Greece.

During 1944, the first R.A.A.F. Air Ambulance Unit which was equipped with D.H. 86 aircraft, returned to Australia after serving for three years in the Middle East, taking up supplies to troops in the forward areas and evacuating more than 8,250 casualties with a loss of only one D.H. 86.

R.A.A.F. squadrons based in Great Britain and Europe since they began operations in 1940 and up to VE-Day, had flown 195,200 operational hours on 44,000 sorties, and had dropped nearly 60,000 tons of high explosive bombs and 9,000 tons of incendiaries. The R.A.A.F. in Great Britain and Europe had destroyed 103 enemy aircraft probably destroyed 53 and damaged 163. At least 34 enemy ships had been destroyed (including submarines) and 186 damaged. Total mileage covered by all British-based Australian squadrons from 1940 to the end of the war was:—Bomber Command Units, 12,615,000 ; Coastal Command units, 7,933,000 ; and Fighter Command and T.A.F. Units, 4,662,000.

In addition to the work of the R.A.A.F. squadrons many hundreds of Australian airmen served throughout the War in the Royal Air Force, and other Dominion squadrons in all Commands in Great Britain, the Mediterranean and South-East Asia. In the India-Burma Theatre R.A.A.F. air crews served with Liberator, Thunderbolt, Mosquito, Spitfire, Beaufighter, Dakota and Catalina squadrons.

WOMEN'S AUSTRALIAN AUXILIARY AIR FORCE

Director : Group Officer Clare G. Stevenson.

The Women's Australian Auxiliary Air Force was established in March, 1941, and organized on similar lines to the British W.A.A.F. At the beginning the intention was to recruit some 300 members, whose tasks were to be limited to three trades. By the end of 1944 the strength of the W.A.A.A.F. was 18,280 and there were some 60 trades. Of the total W.A.A.A.F. some 4,000 served on signals and communications duties, 3,000 as

cooks and stewardesses, 3,000 on clerical duties, 2,000 on equipment and stores, 1,500 on aircraft duties and 1,000 in the medical and dental branches.

THE AIR TRAINING CORPS

The Australian Air Training Corps was formed in July, 1941, and is administered as an integral part of the R.A.A.F. The object of the Corps is to provide training and educational courses for boys between the ages of 16 and 18 who wish eventually to join the R.A.A.F. Service is on a voluntary part-time basis but the boys are required to give an honourable undertaking that they will join the Air Force when eligible to do so, if their services are required.

The A.A.T.C. will be continued in peacetime but the extent and composition of the Corps will depend on decisions regarding the ultimate strength of the R.A.A.F.

More than 12,000 A.A.T.C. cadets passed into the R.A.A.F. and had operational experience overseas.

AIR OBSERVER CORPS

Since the start of the War in the Pacific a Volunteer Air Observer Corps has been established in Australia with a network of posts throughout the country.

Both men and women are members and take their turns of duty. Like the Royal Observer Corps in Great Britain, the Australian V.A.O.C. keeps track of all aircraft and has been the means of aiding many R.A.A.F., United States and transport aircraft. Many of the posts co-operate with the Meterological services by providing accurate weather reports. By the end of 1944 the strength of the V.A.O.C. was 18,510.

VOLUNTARY EMERGENCY NATIONAL TRAINING SCHOOLS

In 1940 a system of Voluntary Emergency National Training Schools was founded in Sydney to give free training to the aircrew reservists of the Royal Australian Air Force and members of the W.A.A.F. in morse code, signalling and in radio and electrical theory. The Schools are officially recognised by the Royal Australian Air Force and there are plans to increase the instruction given at the schools. Between September, 1940, and August, 1942, a total of 3,050 reservists were trained of which 2,750 are now serving with the R.A.A.F. Approximately 1,000 girls joined the educational schools, of whom some 500 have been enrolled in the W.A.A.A.F.

THE DOMINION OF NEW ZEALAND

THE ROYAL NEW ZEALAND AIR FORCE

The Royal New Zealand Air Force was constituted a separate branch of the Defence Forces of the Dominion by the Air Force Act of 1937. Its control is vested in an Air Board, with the Minister of Defence, who is also in charge of the Air Department, as its President.

ORGANIZATION

The Air Department, Bunny Street, Wellington, C.1.
Minister in Charge of Aviation : The Hon. F. Jones, Minister of Defence.

Air Secretary : Mr. T. A. Barrow.

The Air Board

The Hon. F. Jones, M.P., Minister of Defence (President).

Air Vice-Marshal L. M. Isitt, C.B.E., R.N.Z.A.F., Chief of the Air Staff and Air Officer Commanding the Royal New Zealand Air Force.

Air Cdre. G. T. Jarman, D.S.O., D.F.C., R.A.F., Deputy Chief of the Air Staff.

Air Cdre. R. B. Bannerman, D.F.C., R.N.Z.A.F., Air Member for Personnel.

Air Cdre. F. E. T. Hewlett, D.S.O., O.B.E., R.N.Z.A.F., Air Member for Supply.

Mr. T. A. Barrow, Air Secretary.

The increasingly important part played by the Royal New Zealand Air Force in the Pacific theatre of the War led to the appointment of a senior officer of that force as head of the New Zealand Joint Staff Mission in Washington. Air Cdre. J. C. Findlay was the head of the Mission and is also the R.N.Z.A.F. representative with the Combined Chiefs of Staff Committee in Washington.

The strength of the Royal New Zealand Air Force continued to expand and by the end of 1944 was well over 45,000. The estimated cost of the R.N.Z.A.F. for the year 1944-1945 was £35,500,000.

By June, 1945, 1,345 honours and awards had been won by members of the R.N.Z.A.F.

TRAINING

As with the other Dominions, an adjustment in the training plans for the R.N.Z.A.F. was announced in the middle of 1944 whereby no more members of the R.N.Z.A.F. were to be sent to Canada for training under the B.C.A.T.P.

A Lockheed Hudson of the Royal New Zealand Air Force on patrol off Guadalcanal.

Throughout 1944 the responsibilities of the R.N.Z.A.F. in the South-West Pacific area increased gradually and as a result some 1,200 new air-crew members were estimated to be needed each year. They were to be fully-trained in New Zealand, but because men were no longer expected to be needed overseas in such large numbers a progressive reduction in the Home training establishments was expected and some 2,000 men were released by the end of 1944. Up to Aug. 25, 1944, a total of 6,026 members of the R.N.Z.A.F. had graduated for air training schools in Canada under the British Commonwealth Air Training Plan and New Zealand's contribution to the Plan was estimated at some $46,000,000.

THE R.N.Z.A.F. IN THE PACIFIC

By the end of 1944 more than 80 per cent. of the bomber and fighter-bomber squadrons of the R.N.Z.A.F. had been transferred from defensive duties in the South Pacific to offensive duties in the South-West Pacific theatre. A New Zealand Air Task Force, with a high degree of mobility, was based on Bougainville and other islands to the North under the operational command of Group Capt. G. N. Roberts. One of the duties performed by units of the Air Task Force during the year was the ferrying of a number of Corsair fighter-bombers to Leyte for the U.S. Marine Corps.

Throughout 1944 New Zealand squadrons took a greater share in operations in the Pacific and there was an increasing measure of collaboration with units of the R.A.A.F., especially in the Solomons area. Three R.N.Z.A.F. squadrons equipped with Corsair fighter-bombers and, operating in conjunction with R.A.A.F. Wirraway and Boomerang aircraft, played a large part in the softening-up process before the Australian advance in Bougainville.

During the eight months to November, 1944, R.N.Z.A.F. fighter-bombers based on Bougainville made 15,356 sorties involving 32,000 flying hours. During December, 1944, R.N.Z.A.F squadrons and U.S. Marine Corps squadrons flew a total of 2,929 sorties and dropped 1,404 tons of bombs. Of that total, 619 tons were dropped on New Britain, 224 tons on Bougainville and 539 tons on New Ireland.

A New Zealand squadron of Catalina flying-boats was also based in the Solomon Islands and maintained constant anti-shipping and submarine patrols as well as operating on Air/Sea Rescue duties. Other New Zealand squadrons were equipped with Ventura aircraft.

During 1944 the R.N.Z.A.F. operated its own transport and ferry services within New Zealand, and between New Zealand and R.N.Z.A.F. units based in the forward areas in the Pacific.

A detached flight from Nos. 40 and 41 Transport Squadrons, based on Guadalcanal and equipped with Dakotas, was responsible for the R.N.Z.A.F. Pacific transport service. With seven Dakotas it was transporting an average of 415,000 lb. of freight, mail and personnel per month. A New Zealand flight crew also operated with the R.A.F. Transport Command trans-Pacific service from San Diego, Cal. to New Zealand.

New Zealand airmen in the Pacific won 75 awards, including 19 U.S. decorations and 81 were mentioned in despatches.

THE R.N.Z.A.F. OVERSEAS

By the end of the war in Europe New Zealand had sent over 25,000 men overseas. In addition to seven R.N.Z.A.F. squadrons overseas, New Zealanders were serving with all Commands of the Royal Air Force in all theatres of the War. The seven New Zealand squadrons comprised No. 490 Squadron equipped with Sunderland flying-boats stationed in West Africa and six operating in the European theatre. These six squadrons consisted of No. 75 (N.Z.) Squadron equipped with Lancaster bombers; No. 485 Squadron equipped with Spitfires; No. 486 Squadron equipped successively with Hurricanes, Typhoons and Tempests; No. 487 Squadron equipped with Venturas and, later, Mosquitos; No. 488 Squadron which first operated with Beaufighters and was later re-equipped with Mosquitos; and No. 489 Squadron which first flew Hampdens and was later re-equipped with Beaufighter X torpedo-fighters.

No. 75 Squadron took part in all Bomber Command's major day and night operations throughout the year and established an outstanding operational record with its group. In March, 1945 the squadron set up a new record by operating on 19 days and three nights, dropping a tonnage of bombs three and a half times greater than that dropped in the corresponding month in 1944. During the preliminary operations at Wesel before the crossing of the Rhine, the squadron gave spectacular close-support to the Armies, bombing targets within 2,000 yards of the advanced troops. Every bomb fell in the target area with such accuracy that special messages of congratulation were received from Field Marshal Montgomery, General Dempsey and the Commando Force. From May, 1940, to December, 1944, No. 75 Squadron flew 34,500 hours on 6,923 sorties, dropped 18,076 tons of bombs and fired 652,578 rounds of ammunition.

The New Zealand Spitfire Squadron (485) serving with the Second T.A.F. did not lose a single aeroplane to the enemy during 1944. During the early part of the year it took part in cross-Channel sweeps and escorted bombers, then shared in the D-Day operations and gave close-support to the Army, bombing and strafing. It was one of the first squadrons to patrol over the invasion fleet. Between April, 1941, and December, 1944, the squadron flew 13,811 hours on 10,195 sorties, fired 235,000 rounds of ammunition, destroyed 63, probably destroyed 25 and damaged 32 enemy aircraft, and dropped 147 tons of bombs.

No. 486 Squadron, which was formed in 1942 and first operated as a night fighter squadron with Hurricanes and was later equipped with Typhoons and Tempests, took part in the Allied invasion of Normandy, patrolling the beach-heads until the flying bomb attack began, when it was recalled to the defence of Great Britain. Up to December, 1944, it had flown 11,010 hours on 9,851 sorties, fired 194,895 rounds of ammunition, destroyed 17, probably destroyed 7 and damaged 18 enemy aircraft, shot down 231 flying-bombs and destroyed several E-boats and R-boats in the Channel.

No. 487 Squadron was formed in August, 1942, and first operated with Venturas. Re-equipped with Mosquitos, it took part in many special operations, including the attack on Amiens prison and on the Gestapo headquarters at Atthus and Copenhagen. It also operated as a night intruder unit. From December, 1942, to December, 1944, the squadron flew 558 hours in 2,337 sorties and dropped 1,249 tons of bombs.

No 488 Squadron reformed in Britain in June, 1942, after Singapore. Equipped with Beaufighters it operated as a night fighter unit. Early in 1944 it was re-equipped with Mosquitos and by June of that year it had destroyed 20 enemy aircraft. During the Battle of Normandy it destroyed 27 more. By the time it was disbanded its score had risen to 67, with 4 probably destroyed and 10 damaged. To December, 1944, the hours flown on 2,261 sorties totalled 5,345.

No. 489 Squadron was a torpedo-bomber squadron. Formed early in 1941 it first flew Hampdens and later was re-equipped with Beaufighters. Its score was 19 motor vessels totalling 73,000 tons destroyed and 15 motor vessels totalling 36,000 tons seriously damaged. Up to December, 1944, it flew 8,285 hours on 2,040 sorties, fired 86,431 rounds of ammunition and 185 torpedoes and dropped 54 tons of bombs.

Of the 10,363 members of the R.N.Z.A.F. who operated in the European theatre, 919 were killed, 77 were missing believed killed, 385 missing, 1,504 presumed dead, 89 injured and 427 taken prisoner. The honours won were: orders, 42; decorations 643; medals, 178; foreign and Allied awards, 9; mentioned in despatches, 164. 1,385 men were awarded the 1939-43 Star and 197 the Africa Star.

A Typhoon Wing of the R.A.F. commanded by a New Zealander pioneered the use of R.P. Typhoons.

The R.N.Z.A.F. squadrons and New Zealanders serving with R.A.F. squadrons took a full share in the liberation of Europe.

THE AIR TRAINING CORPS

A Cadet Corps similar in constitution and aims to the British Air Training Corps was formed in New Zealand in 1941 to give preliminary training to boys from 16 to 18 years of age to prepare them for entry into the R.N.Z.A.F. There were more than 50 "town" squadrons and 60 school units.

WOMEN'S AUXILIARY AIR FORCE.

A Women's Auxiliary Air Force was formed in New Zealand in March, 1941, and by June, 1943, some 3,500 women were serving with the R.N.Z.A.F. in New Zealand.

UNION OF SOUTH AFRICA

(Unie van Suid Afrika)

The South African Air Force is a branch of the South African Permanent Force and is administered by the Minister of Defence.

At the beginning of the War the Force consisted of one squadron and a total of 1,500 men. On its 21st birthday, on August 20, 1941, its strength had grown to more than 2,000 officers and 25,000 men. It is expected that the total figure will eventually reach 50,000.

ORGANIZATION

Chief of the Union Defence Forces Staff: Lieut.-General Sir Pierre van Ryneveld, K.C.B., D.S.O., M.C.

Air Force Headquarters: Roberts Heights, Pretoria.

Director-General of the S.A.A.F.: Major-General C. J. Venter, D.F.C., S.A.A.F.

Training Headquarters: Kimberley.

Director of Air Training: Air Vice-Marshal M. B. Frew, D.S.O., M.C., A.F.C., R.A.F.

Commander, Coastal Air Defences, Air Commodore F. R. Drew.

By the end of 1944 the South African Air Force had a total of 34 active squadrons including heavy, medium and fighter-bombers, fighters and photographic reconnaissance units. At the end of the European War some 12 squadrons and some 40 engineer, signal, transport, workshop and security units were expected to be retained in the North so as to help maintain lines of communication through to the Far East and help with other garrison forces. In addition some squadrons were expected to share in the war in the Far East.

TRAINING

By February, 1944, a total of about 16,000 air crews including 5,000 pilots, a similar number of observers, 2,000 navigators, 2,000 bomb aimers and 2,000 air gunners had been trained in the Union. By March, 1944 there were 33 schools operating in the Union involving some 30,000 airmen. The majority of the air crews received their Operational Training at schools in the Middle East. In addition, a large number of ground crews were trained in the Union.

Towards the end of 1944 the training scheme was operating on a reduced scale and 18 schools were expected to close down by the middle of 1945.

OPERATIONS IN 1944

Squadrons of the South African Air Force continued to operate throughout 1944 with the Royal Air Force in the Middle East, Mediterranean, in Italy and in the Balkans. The strength of the S.A.A.F. in this theatre was estimated as being then equivalent to a division of troops. Many of the squadrons served with the First Tactical Air Force of the R.A.F. and in addition South African squadrons shared in the defence and patrolling of the Mediterranean from Alexandria to Algiers, of the seas from West Africa to Cape Town, and the Indian coast from Cape Point to the Red Sea. A number of these squadrons on Coastal patrol duties were part of the Coastal Air Defence Arm stationed in the Union and equipped with Ventura aircraft. They worked with R.A.F. Catalina squadrons.

South African squadrons shared in all the operations in the Italian theatre until the successful conclusion of that campaign in May, 1945. They were equipped with Liberator heavy bombers, Marauder and Baltimore medium bombers, R.P. Beaufighters, Kittyhawk and Spitfire fighters and Mustang fighter-bombers. The senior Marauder Wing of the S.A.A.F. had flown more than 21,000 operational sorties against the enemy up to the end of 1944. A number of S.A.A.F. airmen were seconded to the R.A.F. to fly Liberator and Wellington bombers.

One Spitfire squadron completed its 2,000th operation, which also included its 7,224th sortie, early in 1945. Spitfires of another S.A.A.F. squadron were responsible for photographing the Germans' defence system in the Central Sector of the Hitler Line in Italy before the start of the Allied offensive in May, 1944.

During May, 1944, Spitfire fighter-bombers in Italy flew a record number of sorties, cutting railway lines 129 times and dropping more than 400 tons of bombs on communication centres. On three occasions special messages of congratulation from the Army were received by the S.A.A.F. In addition, medium bombers and R.P. Beaufighters of the S.A.A.F. achieved many successes against enemy shipping in the Aegean sea.

In addition to operations in direct support of the Armies in Italy throughout the year, squadrons of the S.A.A.F. served with the R.A.F. Balkan Air Force in support of Marshal Tito's forces in Yugoslavia. South Africans flying Liberators shared in the carrying of supplies to Warsaw during the Patriot rising in the Summer of 1944.

A South African transport squadron equipped with Dakotas and operating with a Mediterranean Group of R.A.F. Transport Command completed more than one million miles flying during 1944 and had carried five million lb. war freight and mail, including 13,000 passengers.

A Shuttle Service was operated during 1944 by S.A.A.F. transport aircraft between Pretoria and Rome. The service was flown in six days. By the end of 1944 about 40,000 passengers, 779,000 lb. mail, 1,734,000 lb. of freight had been carried and a mileage of more than 9½ million had been established.

In August 1944 troop carriers flown by the S.A.A.F. shared in the movement of new recruits for the South African 6th Division from Pretoria to a base in the Middle East where they were to complete their training. The flight involved some 4,000 miles.

In addition to the squadrons of the S.A.A.F. in the Mediterranean theatre a number of South African airmen served throughout the year with the Royal Air Force in all commands and in all theatres. The only South African to be seconded to the Pathfinder Force of Bomber Command, Captain Edwin Swales, was awarded the Victoria Cross early in 1945.

At the beginning of 1945 a small number of air crews of the S.A.A.F. had started training to fly Sunderland flying-boats at a base in Scotland.

South African casualties in all forces from the beginning of the War to Nov. 30, 1944 totalled 28,943.

THE S.A.A.F. REGIMENT

Officer Commanding: Major Craig Anderson.

The S.A.A.F. Regiment was in process of formation towards the end of 1943. This new branch of the Air Force is modelled on the British R.A.F. Regiment, its principal functions being the capturing, protecting and servicing of aerodromes. All personnel are trained in Commando tactics at the Battle School, Premier Mine, selected candidates later taking a parachute-jumping course before joining the Parachute Section of the Regiment.

THE SOUTH AFRICAN WOMEN'S AUXILIARY AIR FORCE

The South African Women's Auxiliary Air Force was formed for service with the South African Air Force in November, 1939.

The South African W.A.A.F. was founded on the Civil Air Guard and South African Women's Aviation Association which had been formed in 1938. In February, 1941 the Women's Volunteer Air Service was formed as a separate unit but it includes all part-time workers training for the W.A.A.F.

The South African W.A.A.F. provides auxiliary military services throughout the Union. Members have also served in Kenya and East Africa and there is a contingent in the Middle East.

THE AIR SECTION OF THE YOUTH TRAINING BRIGADE

South Africa has no separate Air Training Corps. Its counterpart is the Air Section of the Youth Training Brigade which is controlled by the Army and gives full-time training for the services to boys over 16 years of age. The Air Section is organized on the same general lines as the Air Training Corps and a high proportion of the boys join the South African Air Force.

In addition, a number of University Air Squadrons have been formed at Universities in the Union.

EIRE

Military Aviation, organized in the Irish Air Corps, is a component of the Defence Forces and is controlled by the Department of Defence (Roinn Cosanta), Parkgate, Dublin. The Officer Commanding the Air Corps (Aer Chor) is Major W. P. Delamere.

ORGANIZATION

The Irish Air Corps comprises a Headquarters, a Depôt, a maintenance unit, a Flying Training School and Service Units.

The Headquarters, Depôt, Maintenance Unit and Flying Training School are situated at Baldonnel Aerodrome, Dublin.

PERSONNEL

A Short Service Commission Scheme together with direct recruiting for new pilots provides the necessary flying personnel. Technical and other ranks are obtained through the medium of a Boy Apprentice Scheme.

EQUIPMENT

Training:—Miles Magister, Miles Master II and Avro Anson.
Fighting:—Hawker Hurricane.
Army Co-operation:—Westland Lysander.

CHILE

(The Chilean Republic—República de Chile)

NATIONAL MARKINGS

RED

BLUE

RUDDER   WINGS ONLY

The Chilean Air Force, or Fuerza Aerea de Chile, was formed as an autonomous fighting service, including Army and Naval Aviation, under the Ministry of National Defence in 1930. To facilitate relations between the Air Force and the Ministry of National Defence, there exists an Under-Secretariat of Aviation, which likewise functions under the Ministry.

ORGANIZATION

Subsecretaria de Aviacion, Ministerio de Defensa, El Bosque.
Commander-in-Chief of the Fuerza Aerea de Chile : Air-General Manuel Tovarias Arroyo.
Chief of the General Staff : Brig.-General Oscar Herreros Walker.
Directly under the control of the Commander-in-Chief are :—
(1) General Headquarters.
(2) The Air Council.
(3) The General Administration.

The Maintenance Directorate is responsible for the supply, distribution and maintenance of material for the Fuerza Aerea de Chile, and includes the Air Arsenals and Repair Shops.

MILITARY AERODROMES.

"Los Condores," Iquique.
    Headquarters of Aviation Group No. 1.
"Quintero," Valparaiso.
    Headquarters of Naval Aviation Group No. 2.
    Air Gunnery and Bombing School.
"El Bosque," Santiago.
    Headquarters of Aviation Group No. 4.
    Headquarters of the Anti-Aircraft Defence Group.
    The Aviation School.
    Mechanics Training School.
    Central Repair Shops.
    Aviation Arsenals.
Control is further sub-divided under the following directorates or commands :—
(a) Headquarters Staff. Chief : Group Cdr. David Yuseff Urrea.
(b) Directorate of Personnel.
(c) Aeronautical Directorate.
(d) Directorate of Maintenance.
(e) Accountancy Directorate.
(f) Training Directorate.
(g) Air Brigade Commands.
The Training Directorate includes :—
(1) The Air Academy.
(2) The Aviation School.
(3) The Specialists' Training School.
(4) Mechanics' Training School.
(5) Air Gunnery and Bombing School.

"Maquehua," Temuco.
    Headquarters of Aviation Group No. 3.
"Chamiza," Puerto Montt.
    Headquarters of Aviation Group No. 5.
"Punta Arenas," Magallanes.
    Headquarters of Aviation Group No. 6.
There are also numerous intermediary aerodromes and emergency landing grounds throughout the 2,800 miles of territory. Many of the emergency aerodromes which are maintained by the civil air lines are under the control of the military authorities.

EQUIPMENT
Primary Training :— Focke-Wulf Fw 44, Avro 626, Fairchild PT-19.
Advanced Training :—North American AT-6, Vultee BT-13.
Fighting :—Curtiss P-40.
Bombing :—Junkers Ju 86, Douglas A-24.
General Purpose :—Arado Ar 95.
Naval Reconnaissance :—Chance-Vought OS2U-3.
Naval Patrol :—Consolidated Catalina.
Amphibian :—Sikorsky S-43.

TRAINING
Since 1941, Chile has had her own Air Cadet Schools open to all Chilean nationals who have passed their MatriculationExamination and who are not less than 23 years old. The Cadet Course lasts three years.
An American Air Mission has taken over the training of the Chilean Air Force and is reorganizing the old system on similar lines to those of the U.S. Army Air Forces. A number of Chilean pilots are also training in the United States.

CHINA

(The Great Chinese Republic—Chang-Hua Min-Kuo)

NATIONAL MARKINGS

BLUE

RUDDER   WINGS ONLY

Control of the Armed Forces in China is vested in the National Military Council, of which General Chiang Kai-Shek is the head.

The Chinese Air Force is controlled by a Commission of Aeronautical Affairs, with headquarters at Chungking.
The Chinese Air Force, never very large, suffered heavily at the hands of the Japanese. Organization, according to Western standards, is poor but efforts have been made to re-organize and re-equip the Air Force with Allied assistance.
American air assistance for China originated with the American Volunteer Group. This Group, which was independent of the Chinese Air Force, was recruited in the United States by Colonel Chennault, who commanded it. It was originally under contract to the Chinese Government to protect the Burma Road and the assembly plants on the Burmese border.
Until July 4, 1942, when the A.V.G. was disbanded and absorbed into the U.S. Army Air Forces as the 23rd Pursuit Group of the Air Task Force operating in China, the Group had been completely self-contained and was equipped with Curtiss P-40 single-seat fighters. When the Japanese invaded Burma the Group took an active part in assisting British units in the

delaying action, conducting operations into Indo-China, Siam and occupied China. Up to the time of disbandment the A.V.G. had destroyed 284 Japanese aircraft and probably damaged as many more. The personnel of the Group never numbered more than 250. Ten pilots were killed in action, four were presumably killed in action and nine were accidentally killed.
The American Army Air Forces in China were steadily built up, and in March, 1943, the Air Task Force, already referred to, was constituted as the 14th Air Force under the command of Brigadier-General Chennault. This Air Force, under the administrative control of the Commanding General, India, Burma and China, comprised a well-balanced force of Fighter, Bomber, Attack and Transport units with ancilliary services.
The American authorities have also giving assistance to the Chinese Air Force. Large numbers of Chinese pupils have received instruction in Army Air Force schools in the United States and assistance was also given by American personnel in China in operational training repair, and maintenance.

COLOMBIA

(The Republic of Colombia—República de Columbia).

NATIONAL MARKINGS

RED

BLUE

YELLOW

RUDDER   WINGS ONLY

As an outcome of re-organization in 1943, the Columbian Air Force (Fuerza Aérea Colombiana) is now a separate air arm under the control of the Ministry of War.

EQUIPMENT
Fighting :—Curtiss Hawk.
Reconnaissance :—Curtiss Falcon.
Bombing :—Bellanca Twin-engined Bomber.
Training :—Fairchild, North American AT-6.
Miscellaneous and Transport:—Sikorsky amphibian, Curtiss Condor, Junkers W 33, W 34, K43 and Ju 52, Ford Trimotor and Consolidated P2Y.

ORGANIZATION
Ministerio de Guerra, Direccion-General de Aviacion, Bogota.
Director-General of Aviation : Lieut.-Col. Lema Posada.
The Colombian Air Force consists of fighting, reconnaissance and training units, details of which are not available.
The Military Aviation School is situated at Cali.

CUBA

(The Republic of Cuba—Republica de Cuba)

NATIONAL MARKINGS

RED

BLUE

RUDDER   WINGS ONLY

The Cuban Aviation Corps, or Cuerpo de Aviacion, is administered by an aviation section of the Secretariat of National Defence. It is a small service using modern aircraft of American origin. It has naval and military branches.

ORGANIZATION
Secretaria de Defensa Nacional, Departamento de Direccion, Seccion de Aviacion, Havana.
Aviacion de Ejercito (Military Aviation) : H.Q. Campo de Columbia, Havana.
    Officer Commanding : Colonel Otalio Soca de Llanez.
Aviacion Naval (Naval Aviation) : H.Q. Rancho Boyeros near Havana.
    Officer Commanding : Comandante Ernesto Usatorres.

TRAINING
Escuela del Cuerpo de Aviacion, Campo de Columbia, Havana.
This establishment has a capacity for 75 cadets. It is

provided with laboratories, workshops, radio and meteorological office.
To provide a reserve of pilots for the Aviation Corps the Academia Nacional de Aviacion Cubana Reserva Aerea was formed in 1941. This organization will eventually acquire its own aircraft but for the present it uses obsolete types owned by the Cuban Aviation Corps and operates at the Campo Teniente Brihuegas Army Airport. It is expected that it will eventually be taken over by the Aviation Corps.

EQUIPMENT
Training :—Stearman A73-B1, Aeronca.
Advanced Training :—Waco, Curtiss-Wright 19-R, North American AT-6.
Transport :—Bellanca, Howard DGA-15.
Amphibian :—Grumman G-21.

CZECHOSLOVAKIA

(The Czechoslovak Republic—Ceskoslovenska Republika)

The year 1938, in which Czechoslovakia was, as a result of the Munich Agreement, deprived of its historic mountainous frontiers, fortifications and almost one third of its territory, will always remain one of the most fateful in the history of the Czechoslovak Air Force.

March 15, 1939, the day on which the German forces invaded Czechoslovakia, was to have been the last day in the life of its Air Force. The result of twenty years of pioneer and research work, both in military and civil aviation, should according to Nazi plans, have been blotted out of history.

The German Army did succeed in destroying practically everything connected with the Czechoslovak Air Force, but it could not destroy the determination of Czechoslovak airmen to fight on. Large numbers of both flying and ground personnel escaped from the country in order to join the Air Force of any nation which was prepared to fight and check the progress of the avalanche of German aggression which had already engulfed their country.

As early as the Summer of 1939, the first group of these men enlisted in the Polish Air Force. In later days, it was one of these pilots, Sergeant Josef Frantisek, who, fighting with the Polish Air Force in the Battle of Britain, won the distinction of being among the first Allied pilots to be awarded the Distinguished Flying Medal (and a Bar only a week later).

At the same time other groups were forming and assembling on French territory.

They were given short instruction and refresher courses and soon were being posted to various Fighter and Bomber units of the French Air Force for operational duties. Thus, in the Spring of 1940, there were more than one hundred Czechoslovak Fighter pilots operating over the Western Front where, despite the overwhelming superiority possessed by the Germans both in numbers and material, they achieved many victories. Two of them were ranked among the top-scoring French Fighter pilots, having destroyed fifteen and thirteen enemy aircraft respectively.

Apart from the total of 138 German aircraft shot down, Czechoslovak airmen took part in the air operations against the Nazi motorised columns which had broken into France, destroying a number of tanks and armoured vehicles.

Six Czechoslovak fighter pilots were posted for operational duty with a French Squadron in Syria and, after the fall of France, succeeded in making an adventurous escape into Palestine. Upon reaching the Syrian border, they were in danger of being captured and only the intervention of an armed British patrol helped them to safety and thus, eventually, to rejoin their comrades of the Czechoslovak Air Force, by that time reorganized in Great Britain.

When France collapsed in June, 1940, the majority of the Czechoslovak airman managed to reach England. Some of them flew their aircraft over but by far the greatest number were saved from capture by the gallantry of the British, Polish and Dutch seamen. On their arrival in Great Britain, these men were immediately organized into a fighting force. The Czechoslovak Air Force was then re-grouped within the framework of the Royal Air Force. Its own Inspectorate was established at the Air Ministry to be responsible for the administration of all Czechoslovak Air Force Units in the United Kingdom.

Within a fortnight the first Czechoslovak Fighter Squadron had been formed to operate from Great Britain. This Squadron became operational on August 26, 1940, only six weeks after its formation. On that day, they had their first success in battle, destroying four enemy aircraft (two bombers and two fighters). At first the Squadron was equipped with the Hawker Hurricane; later, however, it was re-armed with the Supermarine Spitfire. It played a prominent part in the Battle of Britain and by the end of October, 1940, its members had 42 enemy aircraft destroyed to their credit.

Subsequently, two further Czechoslovak Fighter Squadrons were formed and went into action in October, 1940, and June, 1941, respectively.

After June, 1942, these Fighter Squadrons operated as an independent Czechoslovak Fighter Wing, taking part in many offensive sweeps over enemy occupied territory. Their other activities included escorting bombers, attacking ground targets and enemy shipping, dive-bombing the German anti-invasion defences, and reconnaissance and defensive patrols.

After the formation of the 2nd Tactical Air Force in the Autumn of 1943, this Czechoslovak Wing operated as one of its units and thus took part in the air operations preceding the invasion of Europe. It was also privileged to be one of the Air Force units operating on D-Day.

From July, 1944, the Czechoslovak Fighter Squadrons operated with Fighter Command, escorting bombers during their attacks on important military objectives behind the enemy lines and in the Rhineland. They also carried out a number of offensive operations against enemy defences and communications. One of their tasks was to provide air cover for the Allied airborne troops at Arnhem and to attack gun-emplacements in that area.

Czechoslovak fighter pilots also served with various British units, including day and night fighter Squadrons. As far back as the Summer of 1942, one of these Czechoslovak pilots gained the distinction of becoming the first Czechoslovak Commander of a British Fighter Squadron; since then several others achieved the same honour.

The first Czechoslovak Bomber Squadron was formed on August 4, 1940, and equipped with twin-engined Vickers Wellingtons. The difficulties of language and lack of experience of these aircraft were among the main problems which had to be overcome before it could become operational. This was done, however, in record time and in September, 1940, the Squadron took off on its first operational mission. From that time up to April 1942, it operated in Bomber Command, attacking 70 different targets in Germany, Italy, and German-occupied Europe. During these sorties more than 1,300 tons of bombs were dropped. In April, 1942, the Squadron was transferred to Coastal Command and in its first year of service with that Command completed several hundred sorties, covering a distance equal to thirty-six times round the World. In addition to destroying or damaging several U-boats, the squadron shot down three enemy fighters and damaged seven others in the course of its anti-submarine patrols and sweeps. Later it was re-equipped with four-engined long-range Liberator bombers.

Up to 31 October, 1944, the Czechoslovak Coastal Command crews had attacked twenty-six U-boats and achieved victories in twenty-nine encounters with enemy fighters. One of their most outstanding successes was the sinking of an enemy blockade-runner carrying valuable cargo in the Bay of Biscay on December 27, 1943.

After completing their operational tours Czechoslovak airmen were employed as Instructors at various Schools, as pilots in Maintenance Units or Delivery Flights or were posted for duty with Transport Command. In April, 1942, the first Czechoslovak pilot to be employed on Trans-Atlantic ferrying crossed the Atlantic from the U.S.A.

In June, 1944, a Czechoslovak Air Regiment was formed on territory of the U.S.S.R. and this unit played an important part in the fighting in eastern Czechoslovakia operating from aerodromes in Czechoslovak territory. Its flying personnel consisted partly of airmen who had fought both in France and in Great Britain, and partly of those pilots who had succeeded in escaping from Czechoslovakia and made their way into the U.S.S.R.

The following decorations have been awarded to Czechoslovak airmen in recognition of their distinguished service within the Polish Air Force, the French Air Force, and the R.A.F.:—Czechoslovak Military Cross 565 awards (with 388 bars), Czechoslovak Gallantry Medal 477 awards (with 209 bars), Distinguished Service Order 2 awards, Distinguished Flying Cross 30 awards (1 bar), Distinguished Flying Medal 17 awards, Air Force Cross 3 awards, Air Force Medal 2 awards, Légion d' Honneur 7 awards, Croix de Guerre 81 awards, and Polish Military Cross 60 awards.

On the cessation of hostilities in Europe the Air Council sent the following message to Air Vice-Marshal K. Janousek, K.C.B., Inspector-General of the Czechoslovak Air Force:—

Now that the infamous Third Reich is at last destroyed, the Air Council send to you and all the officers and other ranks of the Czechoslovak Air Force their deepest thanks for your unswerving help throughout the long and arduous struggle against the common enemy.

The Royal Air Force will long remember how your countrymen, by devious ways, came to these Islands with the single thought of continuing the struggle for the freedom of Europe and how when the enemy's forces were thrown against us your pilots fought with ours in the immortal Battle of Britain. In this hour your comrades in the Royal Air Force will feel no greater cause for rejoicing than that the usurper of your country has been finally overthrown. May this brotherhood in arms continue as a lasting friendship in the days of peace.

On August 16, 1945, an official reception was held on the Prague airfield at Ruzin to celebrate the return, after six years of war, of the three Czechoslovak fighter squadrons (Nos. 310, 312 and 313) equipped with Spitfires, and the long-range bomber-reconnaissance squadron (No. 311) equipped with Liberators, which had served with the R.A.F. for five years.

DENMARK

(The Kingdom of Denmark—Kongeriget Danmark)

Denmark was invaded without warning by Germany on April 9, 1940, and the country was occupied with little opposition. At the time of the invasion Danish Military and Naval Aviation was under the control of the Minister of Defence.

The Army Air Force (Haerens Flyvertropper) consisted of two fighter squadrons and three reconnaissance and army co-operation squadrons. The Naval Air Service (Marinens Flyvevœsenet) consisted of one squadron of reconnaissance seaplanes, one squadron of single-seat fighters and two Hawker Dantorp torpedo-bomber seaplanes. Both services had their own training organizations and aircraft factories.

After the occupation the Army and Naval Air Services were disarmed. All permanent personnel were transferred to their former regiments or units and all reserve personnel were demobilised.

All Danish military and civil aerodromes were taken over by the German Luftwaffe as bases for the campaign against Norway and several were bombed by the Royal Air Force.

The situation on May 5, 1945, when the German forces in Denmark capitulated, was that cadres of the Army and Navy Air Forces existed but all training had ceased. The Army and Navy Aircraft Factories, both of which were fully equipped to build complete airframes were inactive.

In the Summer of 1945 the Danish Minister of Defence charged Wing-Cdr. Berksted, who had served in the Royal Air Force during the war, with the task of reconstructing the Danish Air Force.

DOMINICAN REPUBLIC

(Santo Domingo—Republica Dominicana)

An Aviation Company forms part of the National Army. This Company, commanded by Captain Mario Lovaton, is under the direction and supervision of the Secretary for War and Marine, who is also Commander-in-Chief of the National Army, and is based at the General Andrews Airport, Ciudad Trujillo. There the Company has established schools for the training of both pilots and technicians.

The equipment of the company consists of the following types of aircraft:—

Primary Training:—Boeing PT-17.

Intermediate Training:—Consolidated-Vultee BT-13.

Advanced Training:—North American AT-6A, Curtiss R-19.

Artillery Liaison:—Aeronca L-3.

In addition, there are a few miscellaneous types, one of which is a Piper AE-1 light ambulance.

ECUADOR

(The Republic of El Ecuador—República del Ecuador)

NATIONAL MARKINGS

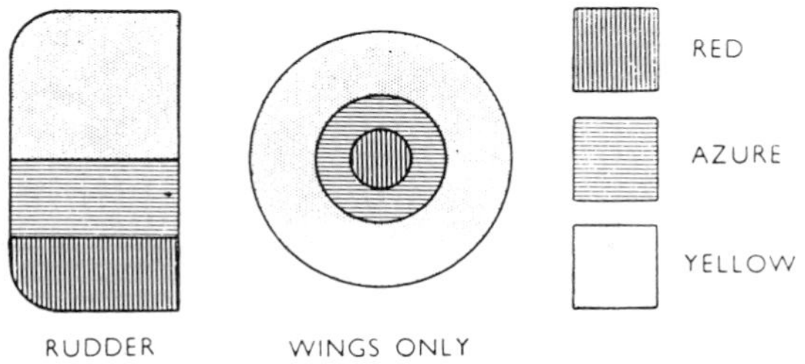
RED
AZURE
YELLOW
RUDDER
WINGS ONLY

The Air Force of Ecuador is part of the Army and is administered by a Commandant of Military Aviation who is responsible through the Superior Army Command to the Minister of Defence, General Alberto C. Romero.

An Italian Air Mission was originally assisting the Ecuadorean authorities but this has been replaced by an American Air Mission which arrived in Ecuador early in 1941. This Mission is now co-operating with the Air Force in the development of its training scheme.

By an agreement between the Ecuadorian and American Governments facilities have been placed at the disposal of the latter for the establishment of an air base at Punta Salinas for the defence of the Canal Zone. The School of Aviation has been transferred from Quito to Punta Salinas, where the U.S. Air mission is based.

ORGANIZATION

The organization of the Ecuadorean Air Force, or Fuerza Aerea Ecuatoriana, is composed of the following:—

- **Comandancia de Aeronautica,** Quito.
  - Commandant of the Air Force: Major Bayordo Tobar.
- **Air Base Commands.**
- **Group Commands.**
- **School of Aviation,** Guayaquil (Primary) and Punta Salinas (Advanced).
- **Aerial Bases and smaller airports.**

TRAINING

Commissioned flying personnel is recruited from different branches of the Army, from the Military Cadet College, from non-commissioned personnel (with a degree) or university students and from students of secondary schools.

Students before entering the Aviation School receive preliminary training on the Link Trainer. Those from the civil schools are graded as Cadets on entry.

Specialist personnel complete their training with special courses after joining their units.

EQUIPMENT

Fighting:—Republic P-35.
Transport:—Junkers Ju 52, Bellanca.
Training:—North American NA-16, Curtiss-Wright R-19, Curtiss-Wright 16E, Fairchild M-62, Ryan PT-20.

MILITARY AERODROMES

Military Aerodromes are situated at PUNTA SALINAS, QUITO, GUAYAQUIL, LATACUNGA, CUENCA, LOJA, SALINAS, MANTA and RIOBAMBA.

EGYPT

(The Kingdom of Egypt—Misr)

NATIONAL MARKINGS

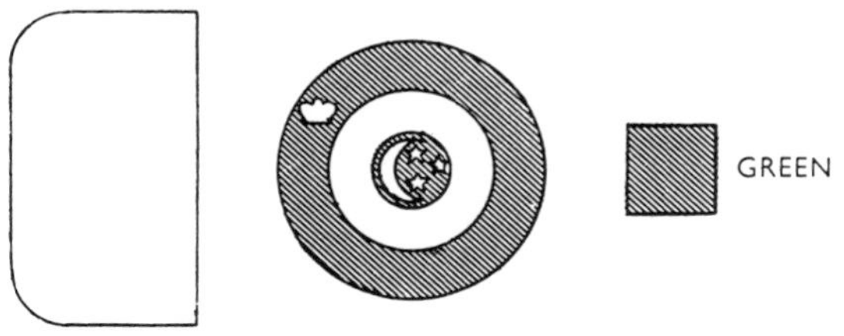

RUDDER FUSELAGE & WINGS

The Royal Egyptian Air Force was formed in 1932 under the command of a British Royal Air Force officer. The second-in-command was also an R.A.F. officer and there were six Egyptian officers, six British N.C.O's. and forty Egyptian military and civilian mechanics. The aircraft consisted of five D.H. Moths.

In April, 1937, in accordance with the Anglo-Egyptian Treaty signed in 1936, the command of the Air Force was taken over by an Egyptian officer and the British officer previously in command was appointed Air Adviser to both the Egyptian Ministry of War and the British Military Mission. At the same time the British officers commanding squadrons handed over their commands to Egyptian officers and assumed duties with these units as advisers and instructors.

ADMINISTRATION

The Command and administration of the Air Force is under the Air Officer Commanding, Royal Egyptian Air Force, Lewa (Major-General) Husni Taher Pasha, who is directly responsible to the Minister of Defence. Although the Air Force is an independent unit it is dependent on the Army for certain ancillary services and, to some extent, operational control is exercised by the Chief of the Army Staff. The Air Force is advised by the R.A.F. officers of the Air Wing of a British Military Mission.

ORGANIZATION

The Air Force is organized in six squadrons, of which five are operational and one a communications unit.

All squadrons are located at Almaza with the exception of No. 2, which in stationed at Edku.

Air Headquarters, Almaza.

Air Officer Commanding: Lewa (Major-General) Husni Taher Pasha.

Station Headquarters, Almaza.
No. 1 (Fighter-Reconnaissance) Squadron (Hurricane I).
No. 2 (Fighter) Squadron .. (Hurricane IIC).
No. 3 (Communications) Squadron .. (Anson).
No. 4 (Bomber) Squadron .. .. (Anson).
No. 5 (Fighter) Squadron .. (Gladiator).
No. 6 (Fighter) Squadron .. (Tomahawk).

TRAINING

Between 1932 and 1937 pupil-pilots selected from the Army and the Military School were trained by the Royal Air Force at No. 4 Flying Training School at Abu Sueir. In 1938 a Flying Training School was formed at Almaza with both British and Egyptian instructors.

Training in the Royal Egyptian Air Force has always been either wholly or partly undertaken by British Officers and N.C.O's. and all *ab initio*, intermediate and advanced training is based on R.A.F. methods.

The following are the principal training establishments :—

Flying Training School.

This consists of an Elementary, an Intermediate and an advanced Flying Training Squadron. Elementary training is carried out at Khanka and the Intermediate and advanced Training at Almaza.

Technical Training Schools.

These consist of a Technical Training School, a Signals and Electrical School and an Air Armament School, all located at Almaza.

All mechanic and specialist recruits are taken from trade and technical schools.

FINLAND

(The Finnish Republic—Suomen Tasavalta)

The Finnish Air Force, or Ilmavoimat, was administered by the Ministry of Defence and was controlled by the Chief of the Air Force, who was under the direct operational command of the Commander-in-Chief of the Finnish Military Forces.

Before the first Russo-Finnish War (30/11/39–30/3/40) the Finnish Air Force consisted of an Air Staff, three Air Regiments, one Naval Co-operation Squadron, a Central Flying School, a Mechanics' School, an Aircraft Depôt and two Anti-Aircraft Artillery Regiments.

This small force, equipped with Fokker D.21, Bristol Bulldog and Gloster Gamecock single-seat fighters and Bristol Blenheim, Fokker C.V-E and C.X multi-seat aircraft, put up a valiant fight in the face of overwhelming numbers of Russian aircraft. It received some reinforcements of new aircraft, notably further Fokker D.21 and some Brewster Buffalo and Fiat C.R.42 fighters, but being virtually cut off from the outside world Finland was forced to accept the Russian terms of surrender, which included a rearrangement of the frontier and the surrender of naval and air bases.

Finland, as an ally of Germany, again took up arms against Russia on June 22, 1941, but was compelled to accept peace terms on September 4, 1944.

FRANCE

(The French Republic—République Française)

THE ARMÉE DE L'AIR.

The Allied landings in North Africa in November, 1942, were the first to liberate French soil, for Algeria is governed as part of Metropolitan France. With French soil thus free again the Comité Français de Liberation Nationale was formed to replace the Free French movement established on British soil in June, 1940, by General de Gaulle, and the seat of Government was transferred from London to Algiers.

The Free French Air Force which since the dark days of 1940 had kept alive the honour and traditions of the Armée de l'Air under the proud emblem of the Cross of Lorraine, formed the corner stone on which a new Armée de l'Air was reborn. Air Headquarters were transferred to Algiers, leaving behind a subsidiary command responsible for the units of the Air Force operating within the framework of the Royal Air Force in the United Kingdom.

Headquarters in North Africa established two objectives—to continue to take part in operations in Tunisia, and later in Italy ; and, with the co-operation and assistance of the British and American authorities, to form new units for service on all fronts. As fast as Anglo-American equipment and fresh personnel trained in North African schools, in the United States and in Great Britian could be made available new formations were established.

Fighter Groups II 7 "Nice," I 3 "Corse," III 6 "Rousaillon," I 4 "Navarre," I 5 "Champagne" and II 3 "Dauphiné" were formed and went into action during 1943. They took part in the Corsican and Italian campaigns and protected Allied convoys in the Mediterranean. Group II/33, equipped with P.R. Lightnings, undertook long-range reconnaissance over occupied territory, particularly on the Italian front. In March, 1944 the Medium Bomber Group "Maroc," equipped with Marauders, went into service in Italy.

In Great Britain, alongside the "Lorraine," "Ile de France" and "Alsace" Groups, Fighter Groups I/2 "Cigogne" and II/2 "Berry," transferred from North Africa, went into action in March and April, 1944, after re-equipment with Spitfires.

Towards the end of 1943 the Royal Air Force undertook the responsibility of training personnel sent from North Africa to Great Britain to form air-crews and ground staff for future heavy bomber groups, as well as to provide reinforcements for formations which had already been in service since the beginning of hostilities within the framework of the R.A.F. Flying Training Command provided the instruction, which followed the standard British air-crew training programme, but a French commandant and French administrative officers were responsible for the enlistment and discipline of their formations.

Thus, at the beginning of 1944, after eight or ten months preparation, virtually the entire resources of French aviation were once again ready to participate in the struggle for the liberation of France and, ultimately, the defeat of Germany.

To the four Fighter Groups and the "Lorraine" Medium Bomber Group operating from the British Isles in preparation for the invasion of the continent, were added two Heavy Bomber Groups, II/23 "Guyanne" and I/25 "Tunisie," which, after passing through all stages of training with the R.A.F., were equipped with four-engined Halifaxes and posted to No. 4 Group, R.A.F. Bomber Command.

ORGANISATION IN 1944

After arduous training, the 2ème Regiment de Chasseurs Parachutistes, forming part of the Special Air Services Brigade, was dropped into Britanny where it took part in many operations in liaison with the Forces Françaises de l'Interieur (F.F.I.).

From Italy, Corsica and North Africa, six Fighter Groups, six Medium Bomber Groups and one Reconnaissance Group prepared the way for and supported the invasion of the South of France on August 15, 1944.

The strategic situation evolved rapidly. With the heart of France liberated French units, operating within the framework of Allied command, attacked the enemy in Holland, the Ardennes, the Vosges and Alsace, while the heavy bomber units, always penetrating deeper into enemy territory, took part in Bomber Commands' massive raids on Magdeburg, Leipzig, Chemnitz and other centres.

Meanwhile, on the periphery of the "Fortress Europe" the enemy clung to the Atlantic ports. Already in January, 1944, the need had been foreseen for a special air group to assist the F.F.I. as soon as the hour of rising struck. Using old aircraft of the 1939-40 campaign and employed in the meantime in the North African schools, the Group "Patrie" was formed and later equipped with Douglas A-24 Dauntless dive-bombers this group landed on Toulouse aerodrome, only just liberated, on August 29. After taking part in numerous low attack missions on German columns in retreat the Group, reinforced with personnel recruited locally and using aircraft abandoned by the enemy, became the Forces Aériennes de l'Atlantique which, with the Fighter Groups, two Medium Bomber Groups and one Reconnaissance Group, played a vital part in the reduction of the German Atlantic pockets.

With the liberation of Paris and the installation in the capital of the Headquarters of the Forces Aériennes Francaises, a new organization was created. A General Staff of the Air exercised command over all the forces of the Armée de l'Air, which operated within the general tactical framework of the Allied Command. The distribution of the French air forces operating under Allied tactical control was as follows :—

Bomber Command, R.A.F.

Groupement de Bombardement Lourd No. 1 (Groupes II/23 and I/25).

2nd Tactical Air Force, R.A.F.

Groupes de Chasse I/2, II/2, III/2 and IV/2, forming No. 145 Fighter Wing, R.A.F.

Mediterranean Allied Tactical Air Force.

31ème Escadre de Bombardement Moyen (Groupes I/22, II/22 and I/19).

34ème Escadre de Bombardement Moyen (Groupes II/63, II/52 and I/32).

Mediterranean Allied Photo Reconnaissance Wing.

1ère Escadrille de G.R. II/33.

Mediterranean Allied Coastal Air Force.

1ère Escadre de Chasse (Groupes I/3, I/7 and II/7).
3ème Escadre de Chasse (Groupes I/5, III/6 and I/4).
4ème Escadre de Chasse (Groupes II/5, II/3 and III/3).

In addition, Groupe II/6 of the Section d'Aviation Cotière, dependent from a section of the French Staff, operated within the framework of the M.A.C.A.F.

In Russia, under Russian tactical control.

Régiment de Chasse III/5.

In addition, the Forces Aeriennes Françaises included the following :—

3 Regiments of Parachutists, of which one served under the tactical control of the French Army and the others in the cadre of the S.A.S. Brigade.

1 Brigade of Anti-aircraft Artillery.

1 Battalion of Engineers.

1 French Servicing Section, forming part of the Allied Air Forces Service Command.

An Air Staff responsible for all French air units stationed in the British Isles constituted a subsidiary command known as the Forces Aériennes Françaises de Grande-Bretagne.

The territorial commands in Algeria, Tunisia, Morocco, Corsica, A.O.F., A.E.F., Levant and Somalia exercised responsibility for their respective non-combatant personnel serving with the air forces in the European theatre.

ORGANIZATION IN 1945

With the complete liberation of France and the new phase of the war which began with the invasion of Germany, further re-organization was called for, and from the beginning of 1945 the Forces Aériennes Françaises conformed to the following organization :—

1er Corps Aerien Francais (forming part of the 1st Tactical Air Force).
1ère Escadre de Chasse (Groupes I/3, I/7 and II/7).
3ème Escadre de Chasse (Groupes I/4, I/5 and III/6).
4ème Escadre de Chasse (Groupes II/3, II/5 and III/3).
33ème Escadre de Reconnaissance (Groupes I/33 and II/33).
Groupe de Reconnaissance I/35.
Groupe de Transport I/15.
1er Régiment d'Artillerie de l'Air.
One Battalion and two Air Support Companies of the Groupement de Détection Electro-Magnétique (Air Defence Wing No. 550).

IIeme Brigade de Bombardement Moyen (part of the 1st Tactical Air Force but under the direct orders of the 42ème Wing de Bombardement Moyen).
31ème Escadre de Bombardement Moyen (Groupes I/19, II/20 and I/22).
34ème Escadre de Bombardement Moyen (Groupes I/32, II/52 and II/63).

Forces Aeriennes de L'Atlantique.
Groupes de Chasse I/18 and II/18.
Groupes de Bombardement I/31 and I/34.
Groupes de Reconnaissance III/33.
Two Flotillas of Naval Dive-bombers.
1 Régiment d'Information de l'Air.

Forces Aeriennes Françaises de Grande-Bretagne (operating under British tactical command).
2ème Escadre de Chasse (Groupes I/2, II/2, III/2 and IV/2).
Groupe de Bombardement Moyen I/20.
Groupement de Bombardement Lourd No. 1 (Groupes I/23 and II/25).
Two Parachute Regiments included in the S.A.S. Brigade.

Division operating under Russian tactical command.
Régiment de Chasse III/5.

Formations with the Allied Service Command and under directive of the 1st Tactical Air Force.
One Parc de Depôt of the 61st A.D.G.
Three Secteurs de l'Air.
Ambulance Chirurgicale No. 401.
Fifty Servicing Companies.

Home Defence Organization.
5ème Escadre de Chasse (Groups I/9, II/9 and II/6).
Three Naval flotillas 2S., 4S., 8E.
Two Groupements de Détection Electro-Magnétique (502 and 505).
One Battalion of Engineers.
One Parachute Regiment.

The re-organization of French territory into Aerial Regions and sub-divisions has been revived, while in overseas territories the local commands, corresponding to territorial divisions, are being maintained or have been re-created. These commands, in addition to being responsible for the recruitment, maintenance and equipment of local forces, are also responsible for the administration of Police and Security units and border patrol squadrons.

EQUIPMENT

On the cessation of hostilities in Europe the operational units of the Armée de l'Air were equipped with the following types of aircraft :—

Fighting : Supermarine Spitfire (8 groups), Republic Thunderbolt (6 groups), Bell Airacobra (2 groups), Yak-3 (1 group), Dewoitine D.520 (1 group).
Medium Bombing : Martin Marauder (8 groups), North American Mitchell (1 group).
Heavy Bombing : Handley Page Halifax (2 groups).
Reconnaissance : Lockheed Lightning (1 group), Northrop Black Widow (1 group), M.500 (Fieseler Storch) (2 groups).
Transport : Douglas Dakota (2 groups), Beechcraft Expeditor (1 group), Junkers Ju 52 (1 group).

Border patrol, police and security units were equipped with Bristol Blenheim, Avro Anson, Martin Baltimore and various French types.

GERMANY

(The German Empire—Deutsches Reich)

NATIONAL MARKINGS

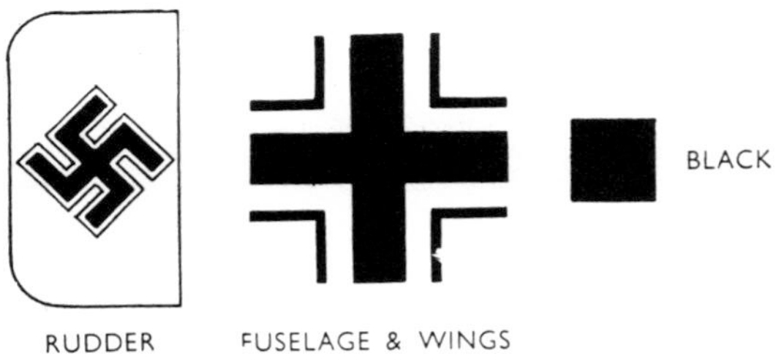
BLACK
RUDDER
FUSELAGE & WINGS

During the last year of the war, the organization of the German Air Force underwent considerable changes. These were the result of the Allies closing the ring in the West, South and East around the "European Fortress" and compressing the operational area of the Luftwaffe. Previously, the German Air Force was organized on a territorial basis. Each of the six Luftflotten (Air Fleets) was allotted an area in which it exercised administrative and operational authority. When the Luftwaffe squadrons began to operate from German soil, with the exception of those in Norway, the Balkans and in Courland, all units came under the command of the Oberbefehlhaber Luftflotte Reich (Commander-in-Chief Air Fleet Reich) Generaloberst Anas Stumpff who was previously in command of Luftflotte 5 in Norway. The Air Officers Commanding Luftflotte 3 and Italy, Generalfeldmarschall Hugo Sperrle and Baron von Richthofen respectively, retired.

Generaloberst Stumpff created a number of operational commands (for fighters, night fighters, bombers, reconnaissance aeroplanes, dive-bombers, ground-attack aircraft, seaplanes, etc.) which were mainly headed by officers who had distinguished themselves in the field. Stumpff's main task was the defence of the Reich, but on his initiative offensive operations, such as the abortive fighter-bomber sweep on January 1, 1945, against allied airfields in Belgium were sometimes made, their execution being entrusted to the Kommandierender General der Jäger or Jagdbomber (A.O.C. Fighters or Fighter-Bombers.)

The difficulties of the numerically inferior Luftwaffe to stem the onslaught of the Allied Air Forces were aggravated not only by shortages of practically all raw materials (in particular of petrol) and spare parts, but also by the transport chaos, a result of the Allied bombing offensive. These shortages forced the Luftwaffe Command to curtail training which, in the second half of 1944, came practically to a standstill, with the exception of conversion training for reaction-propelled types. During the last six months of hostilities, a sharp decline of the moral of German airmen, in particular of fighter pilots, became noticeable. These and many other causes speeded up the downfall of the Luftwaffe which, after the Allies had crossed the Rhine, was no longer able to put up resistance.

There were also some changes among the heads of departments of the German Air Ministry. On the occasion of the attempt on Hitler's life on July 20, 1944, the Chief of the Air Staff General der Flieger Günther Korten was mortallly wounded and had to be replaced by the former Chief of Staff of Luftflotte 3 General der Flieger Koller. The Chief of the Ministerial Office Generaloberst Karl Bodenschatz was also injured and did not appear to have recovered before the unconditional surrender of the Wehrmacht. Towards the end of April, 1945, Reich Marshal Hermann Göring, the Commander-in-Chief, resigned for "health reasons" and was replaced by General-oberst Robert Ritter von Greim, the Commander-in-Chief of the Luftflotte 6 (Central Sector of the Eastern Front) who by taking over the new post became the 23rd Field Marshal of the Wehrmacht and the 5th of the Luftwaffe.

The re-organization of the Luftwaffe resulted in the apparent abolition of practically all the mobile and operational commands, the Fliegerkorps and Fliegerdivisionen (Air Corps and Air Divisions), the only exception being the Fallschirmjäger-divisionen (Parachute Divisions), which were greatly increased by personnel from flying units, signal formations, and other detachments. There was even a Fallschirmjäger Armee, commanded by the Inspector of Parachutists Generaloberst Kurt Student, which tried unsuccessfully to defend North-Western Europe and, towards the end, North-Western Germany. At least one Fallschirmjäger Division operated in Italy while elements of others were distributed among the units on the Eastern Front or formed the nucleus of the Luftwaffe Field Divisions, of which some twenty seem to have been in existence in the beginning of 1945.

With one exception, Fallschirmjäger fought as infantry; the exception being the operation "Greif" when, during the first two days of Runstedt's push in the Ardennes in December, 1944, some 1,500 parachutists divided into so-called battle groups were dropped in front of the Panzers for sabotage purposes. Yet, the men lacked the skill and experience of the Fallschirmjäger who captured the Waalhaven-Rotterdam aerodrome in 1940 and overcame the dogged British resistance on Crete in May/June, 1941.

Lack of transport aircraft seems also to have hampered the full employment of the German parachutists in the Ardennes offensive. Because Ju 52/3m's had been lost in great numbers in North Africa, Russia, and Western Europe, and losses could no longer be replaced from production because of the great destruction in the factories, operational types were used, as for instance, for the supply of the beseiged Channel strongholds and those along the Atlantic Coast. Losses of men and material among the already decimated Transportgeschwader (Air Transport Groups) were, however, so great that regular supply flights could not be maintained. Lack of transport aircraft also sealed the fate of the German garrisons in Greece and on the Aegean islands, which were unable to evacuate their strongholds in time.

FORMATIONS AND FLYING UNITS

While, theoretically, the strength of the Staffel, Gruppe, and Geschwader (Squadron, Wing, and Group) remained the same during the whole war (see previous issues) serviceability in the operational units steadily decreased because it became impossible to keep pace with the rate of destruction. Perhaps the only exception were the units equipped with reaction-propelled types—the rocket-propelled Me 163 and the jet-propelled Me 262 and Ar 234.

ARMY CO-OPERATION

Because of lack of fuel, Tactical reconnaissance flights had to be restricted severely as far back as the middle of 1944. Most Army Co-operation units were equipped with obsolete types (mainly Hs 126, but also Fw 189) which even under a strong "fighter umbrella" had little chance of carrying out the orders given to them. Tactical reconnaissance was, therefore, entrusted to single-seat fighter squadrons, equipped with the Me 109 or Fw 190, which made these missions between two Combat sorties. The former close co-operation between Panzer and Stuka—at least one Gruppe of Ju 87 Stukas was attached to each Panzer Division in 1942—could also no longer be maintained as the production of the Ju 87 was practically abandoned towards the end of 1944 after most of the factories building this type were either destroyed by bombs or re-tooled for the manufacture of fighters. Furthermore, most of the operational Ju 87's were converted for ground-attack work. Shortly before D-Day, Ju 87 ground attack squadrons began to operate only by night in order to avoid heavy loses.

NAVAL CO-OPERATION

With the exception of a few attempts by German torpedo-aircraft and submarines to intercept Allied convoys sailing to Murmansk and reconnaissance and weather flights, mainly undertaken by Bv 138 flying-boats, from Northern Norway, the German Air Force had hardly any opportunity of co-operating with the German Navy. This was another result of the shortage of aircraft which, as in the case of the Luftflotte 5 in Norway, was so great that not even a complete single-seat fighter squadron was available to protect the *Tirpitz* at her moorings in the Alten Fjord when it was attacked by the Royal Air Force. No change in the equipment of naval co-operation squadrons was observed during the past year. The only new type which was put into service was a "rotor-kite" which was used by U-boats for reconnaissance purposes.

ADMINISTRATION AND SUPPLY

When Generaloberst Stumpff became practically the Commander-in-Chief of all the operational Luftwaffe units, he also took over the air defence organization which had been previously entrusted to the Luftgaue (Air Districts). From then onwards, their tasks were purely administrative, as the supply organisation appeared to have been re-organized by concentrating it under the control of a General of Supply.

TRAINING

Although the Directorate of Education and Training was still in existence shortly before the cessation of hostilities, it had hardly anything to do since training came to a standstill. Its educational functions had been taken over by the so-called Educational Officers who were, in fact, representatives of the Nazi Party and/or the Gestapo.

The training of flying personnel, which was thorough in pre-war days and up to the Autumn of 1941, had to be gradually curtailed. The first to suffer were the bomber crew pupils; their operational training aircraft and instructors were transferred at first temporarily then permanently, to the air transport units which were engaged in flying supplies, firstly to the armies advancing through Russia and latterly to the besieged garrisons on the Eastern Front. Then, unless these transferees showed extraordinary abilities, they were transferred to the Luftwaffe Field Divisions.

In the meantime, the Western Allies had so increased the weight of their bombing offensive against the German Air Force and its production plants that the German High Command was compelled to concentrate practically all productive capacities on the manufacture of fighters aircraft. Training was concentrated on the instruction of fighter pilots and on conversion training of bomber pilots. This training was mainly done in the East and South-East—in Poland, Eastern Germany and Hungary. Schools in the West could not maintain their programmes because of the continuous interruptions by Allied raiders. When the Russians overran the great training installations in the East, it was the beginning of the end. The few remaining schools did not have the capacity to instruct the number of pupils necessary to replace the steadily-mounting losses, and the supply difficulties and the incessant fighter sweeps over Reich territory did the rest.

As to the training itself, the following comparison may give an indication of how it deteriorated during the past year. While before the War, a fighter pupil flew almost a dozen different training and operational types, before he joined a fighting unit, by the beginning of 1944 he was flying only four : the Bü 131 Jungmann elementary trainer, the Ar 96 advanced trainer, the Me 108, and the operational Me 109 single-seat fighter. The number of flying hours amounted to hardly more than 25 per cent. of those flown in pre-war days, when the German Air Force claimed that its pupils had to fly roughly 200 hours before being sent to an operational unit.

AIRBORNE FORCES

Since the capture of Crete air-borne forces played no decisive part in German operations. As far as could be ascertained, such units were employed only twice. One occasion was during Rundstedt's "Christmas offensive" in 1944, the other, the "liberation" of Mussolini. The latter is interesting because the parachutists which were used were not Luftwaffe Fallschirmjäger but members of the S.S. Security Service. Although German propaganda claimed that the training of parachutists was continued right into 1945, the operation "Greif" disproved such claims, as many men employed in it had had only theoretical instruction, while some had never previously been inside an aeroplane.

The production of gliders, which at one time had been given priority over some operational types, was abandoned completely to free productive capacity for fighters or V-weapon manufacture. The production of air transport types was, before D-Day, practically restricted to two factories—the Junkers-owned Villacoublay plant near Paris and the A.T.G. aircraft factory in Leipzig-Mockau, also part of the Junkers-Argus combine. Towards the end of 1944, the equipment of the existing air transport units was very mixed, including even such obsolete types as the Junkers W 33 and 34 of 1928 vintage.

AIR SIGNAL UNITS

One of the most important tasks of these units before the invasion of the Continent was the manning of the Fernortungs-geräte (the radiolocation installations), which were mainly set up in the occupied Western territories, and also the devices for the direction of the night fighters. When the Allies overran France. Belgium, and part of Holland, these installations had to be abandoned and the personnel was sent to infantry units.

THE HERMANN GÖRING PANZER CORPS

This unit, the development of which was described in previous editions, was ultimately increased to the strength of an Army Corps. Parts of it fought in Italy and on the East Prussian Front where they suffered severe losses, in particular the Panzer Grenadier Regiments.

GREECE
(The Kingdom of Greece—Hellas)

At the outbreak of the Greco-Italian War in November, 1940, the Royal Hellenic Air Force was suffering some initial disadvantage from its size and from the lack of an individual tradition. The fact that its senior officers were recruited from the Army and the Navy, although advantageous to co-operation, did not assist the formation of this tradition. Shortage of material, due to the lack of a domestic aircraft industry, and financial restrictions hampered, until quite recently, the development of effective striking forces in peace and increased difficulties of maintenance and replacement during war.

The flying equipment in use in October, 1940, was made up as follows :—

(1) **Two Fighter Squadrons** equipped with Polish PZL single-seat monoplanes. These aircraft are obsolete, they were slow and their radio equipment was unsatisfactory.

(2) **Three Light Bomber Squadrons** equipped with Bristol Blenheim, Potez 63 and Fairy Battle monoplanes respectively. These units were not complete in establishment nor were the individual aircraft fully equipped.

(3) **Two Army Co-operation Squadrons** equipped with Henschel Hs 126 monoplanes and Breguet XIX biplanes respectively. The former is a standard type in the German Luftwaffe but the Breguet XIX, bought some 15 years before, was obsolete, slow and ill-equipped.

(4) **Three Naval Co-operation Squadrons** incompletely equipped with Avro Anson, Fairey IIIF and Dornier aircraft respectively. These forces were augmented after the outbreak of the Greco-Italian War by certain aircraft made available by the Royal Air Force, but the extent of this reinforcement was limited by the strategical situation at the time. The personnel of the Royal Hellenic Air Force was insufficient to provide an adequate trained reserve and was naturally deficient in training under war conditions.

These special conditions and, in particular, the shortage of equipment placed certain marked limitations upon the tactical employment of the Royal Hellenic Air Force. For example, the bomber squadrons, owing to lack of bomb-sights, could only be used for dive-bombing. Similarly, lack of communications, equipment, fuel and oil, repair facilities and, above all, of highly-trained personnel, placed the Air Force under a great disadvantage in comparison with the enemy. Finally, the absence of sufficient permanent operational aerodromes and shortage of staff put a severe strain on both officers and men.

In practice, however, the adaptability and high moral of the Air Force overcame some of these difficulties and many operations were successfully undertaken. Fighter protection was given to ports and aerodromes and successful bomber sorties were repeatedly made over the enemy's rear positions in Albania, on aerodromes at Corytsa and Agyrocastro, ammunition stores at Premeti and elsewhere and on many other strategic objectives. In addition, the Army Co-operation squadrons, in spite of their great inferiority, successfully fulfilled their roles in reconnaissances and other tactical operations over land and sea. Numerous Italian aircraft were destroyed both in the air and on the ground, and at no time could Italy be said to have secured general (as opposed to local) air superiority over Greece.

In the course of these successes, however, losses of trained pilots and material were incurred faster than they could be replaced. A strategical reinforcement of fighter squadrons of the Royal Air Force was provided with most satisfactory results and the combined force remained in action until the Allied withdrawal from Greece on April 23, 1941.

After that date considerable numbers of Royal Hellenic Air Force personnel and some aircraft succeeded in reaching Egypt and from these, implemented from other sources, the nucleus of a Royal Hellenic Air Force came into being.

It was organized along the lines of the Royal Air Force, which gave every assistance and established a liaison organization through which the Greeks could become familiar not only with the administration and operation of the R.A.F. but with the best means and methods whereby their own problems could be solved and progress facilitated.

The first operational unit of the Royal Hellenic Air Force went into service early in 1942 equipped with Hawker Hurricane single-seat fighters. All pilots, both officers and N.C.O.s, had previously been engaged on flying duties either on the Albanian front against the Italians or during the German invasion which followed. This squadron was initially engaged in shipping protection, both by day and by night, in the Mediterranean, and it later took part in the Italian campaign. It was later equipped with the Supermarine Spitfire.

Bomber pilots of the Royal Hellenic Air Force had, since 1942, undertaken anti-submarine patrols and long range reconnaissance patrols over the Mediterranean and took part in operations in Italy and Yugoslavia. The Hellenic bomber squadron served as a mixed unit as, although all pilots and navigators were Greek. insufficient trained personnel made it necessary for R.A.F. air-gunners and some ground staff to be employed. In 1944 the squadron joined the R.A.F. Balkan Air Force on its formation. It took part in the disruption of enemy communications in Yugoslavia in support of the Partisans' ground operations and made many successful bombing missions by daylight on enemy strongpoints, power installations, stores and ammunition dumps, shipping and docks. Originally equipped with the Bristol Blenheim, it was later armed with the Martin Baltimore.

On the conclusion of hostilities in Europe the Air Council sent the following message to Air Vice-Marshal J. Cassimatis, commanding the Royal Hellenic Air Force :—

On this memorable Day of Victory over Germany the Air Council send greetings and congratulations to you and to all officers and other ranks of the Royal Hellenic Air Force.

They warmly appreciate the comradeship in arms and association with the Royal Air Force which have grown up and which they hope will continue.

They will never forget the courage and skill of your Countrymen in their gallant resistance to the treacherous Fascist onslaught, and their superb endurance in the face of the Germans.

The Council are deeply mindful of the sufferings which Greece has so heroically borne and earnestly hope that the future will bring to your Country a lasting peace and happiness.

GUATEMALA
(The Republic of Guatemala—República del Guatemala)

NATIONAL MARKINGS

RUDDER   WINGS ONLY   AZURE

The Air Force of Guatemala, or Cuerpo de Aeronautica Militar, is under the administration of the Army Command. It has recently been modernised, the system of training has been brought up-to-date and a number of Ryan and Waco trainers have been acquired.

In return for facilities to build defence bases the United States has granted cash credits to Guatemala under the Lease-Lend Act for the purchase of defence materials, including aircraft and equipment.

ORGANIZATION

Aeronautica Militar, Secretaria de Guerra, Guatemala City.

Chief of Military Aviation and Director-General of Civil Aviation : General Jose Ovidio Sierra.

Technical Inspector of Military Aviation : Coronel Henri Massot.

Escuela de Aeronautica Militar, "La Aurora" Airport, Guatemala City.

The Military Aviation School is equipped with Ryan ST training monoplanes and operates on the "La Aurora" Airport at Guatemala City. Pilots of the Military Aviation School have made many formation flights to the capitals of neighbouring republics.

HONDURAS
(Republic of Honduras—República de Honduras)

NATIONAL MARKINGS

RUDDER   WINGS ONLY   BLUE

Military Aviation in Honduras is administered by the Department of War, Marine and Aviation.

ORGANIZATION

Departamento de Guerra, Marina y Aviacion, Tegucigalpa.
Director of Military Aviation : Lieut.-Col. H. A. White.
Assistant-Director : Capt. L. A. Fiallos.
The Director of Military Aviation also controls all Civil Aviation in the Republic. The Directorate comprises the following departments :—
Estado Mayor e Inspeccion (Headquarters and Inspection).
Intendencia y Administration (Finance and Administration).
Justicia Militar (Military Justice).
The Honduras Military Air Arm is a small force equipped with modern American aircraft. The Military Aviation School is situated at Tegucigalpa, the capital. North American NA-16, Waco and Ryan ST trainers are used.

The Honduras Government is planning a programme of expansion whereby enlisted men will join the Military Aviation School for a period of two years, during which they will be taught mechanics, carpentry and other trades connected with aviation. Those who qualify to a certain standard of competence at the conclusion of their training will be promoted to the rank of cadet and trained as pilots.

HUNGARY
(The Kingdom of Hungary—Magyarorszag)

The Hungarian Air Force was founded in 1936, when a small military air arm was formed under the sponsorship of the Directorate of Civil Aviation. At the end of 1938 a new organization known as the Air Force Command came into being. This Command was directly subordinate to the Ministry of National Defence, as was the Anti-Aircraft Defence Command.

At the time Germany undertook the organization and instruction of the Hungarian Air Force. Subsequent control of Hungarian air routes took place as and when required for the conduct of operations. Units engaged in the defence of Hungarian targets were probably more independent of Luftwaffe control than units which operated on the Russian front.

The Air Force originally consisted of five Air Regiments comprising bomber, fighter and tactical units equipped with German and Italian types of aircraft. After 1941 new units were formed which were equipped with more modern German aircraft types for service on the Russian Front.

The Commander-in-Chief of the Hungarian Air Force in 1944-45 was Air Commodore V. S. Banfalvy.

IRAN (PERSIA)
(The Kingdom of Iran—Mamalik-i-mahrousseh-i-iran)

NATIONAL MARKINGS

RED

GREEN

RUDDER   WINGS ONLY

The Air Force of Iran, which was created in 1924, is an integral part of the Army. It is administered by the Aviation Department of the Ministry of War and is subordinated to the General Staff of the Army. The Commander of the Air Force and Head of the Aviation Department is Brigadier General Ahmed Khsorovani. The headquarters of the Air Force is at Teheran.

British and Russian forces entered Teheran on August 25th, 1941, following the Iranian Government's failure to give a satisfactory reply to joint overtures made by Russia and Britain concerning the presence and activities of German "tourists" in the country. The British Forces, which made their entries from the South and the West, were under the direction of General Sir Archibald Wavell, Commander-in-Chief, India, but the air contingents were supplied by the Royal Air Force, Middle East Command. These included fighters for the support of air-borne troops and for offensive action against the Iranian Air Force.

At the end of four days all resistance ceased by agreement and terms were drawn up for the occupation by the British and Russians.

On September 9th, 1943, Iran declared war on Germany. After the Teheran Conference, which was held between November 28 and December 1, Great Britain, Russia and the United States issued a joint declaration wherein their Governments recognised Iranian assistance, undertook to give Iran economic aid wherever possible and expressed their desire for the maintenance of Iranian independence, sovereignty and territorial integrity.

From 1942 and until the Mediterrean was re-opened to traffic, Iran served as one of the principal channels of supply for Russia and large numbers of British and American aircraft were delivered to bases in Iran, erected and handed over to Russian pilots for final delivery to the Soviet Union.

ORGANIZATION

The Air Force is made up of two Regiments, one Bomber and one Reconnaissance. Both the Regiments are stationed at Teheran (Doshan Teppeh). The Reconnaissance Regiment has three detachments disposed at Ahwaz, Kermanshah and Isfahan.

TRAINING

Up to 1932 all pilots for the Iranian Air Force were trained abroad, either in France or Soviet Russia. In 1932 a Flying Training School was established at Mehrabad and, with the exception of twelve officers who were sent to Great Britain in 1935, all pilots have since been trained in Iran.

The Flying Training School at Doshan Teppeh, consists of three Groups, Elementary, Service and Advanced. There is also one Ground Training Group. The majority of the F.T.S. pupils are officers, but N.C.O.'s are also trained.

MAINTENANCE AND REPAIR

There is a Maintenance and Repair Unit located at Teheran (Doshan Teppeh) where major repairs and overhauls are undertaken and where assistance is rendered by a small Advisory Staff of R.A.F. personnel.

EQUIPMENT

The Iranian Air Force is equipped as follows :—
No. 1 Bomber Regiment : Avro Anson and D.H. Tiger Moths.
No. 2 Reconnaissance Regiment : Hawker Hind, Audax and Fury, D.H. Tiger Moth.

'IRAQ
(The Kingdom of 'Iraq—Mesopotamia)

NATIONAL MARKINGS

RED

GREEN

BLACK

FIN ONLY   FUSELAGE & WINGS

The Royal 'Iraqi Air Force was formed in 1931. The first few officer pilots were trained in England at the R.A.F. College at Cranwell, but a Training School of the R.I.A.F. was opened in Baghdad in June, 1933. The instructors were Royal Air Force and 'Iraqi officers who had passed through the R.A.F. Central Flying School. Originally the mechanics of the R.I.A.F. were trained at the R.A.F. Depôt at Hinaidi but later an Apprentices' Training School, modelled on R.A.F. lines and employing R.A.F. instructors, was instituted within the R.I.A.F.

ADMINISTRATION

The Royal 'Iraqi Air Force is a part of the Army and comes under the direction of the Ministry of Defence. The command and administration of the Air Force is under an officer known as the Officer Commanding, Royal 'Iraqi Air Force, who is directly responsible to the Chief of the General Staff. The system of internal administration and command is similar to corresponding formations in the British Royal Air Force.

ORGANIZATION

The Royal 'Iraqi Air Force consists of the following units :—
No. 1 (Army Co-operation) Squadron, Mosul.
No. 4 (Fighter) Squadron, Kirkuk.
No. 5 (Fighter) Squadron, Al Rashid, Baghdad.
No. 7 (Fighter-Bomber) Squadron, Al Rashid, Baghdad.
Communications Flight, Al Rashid, Baghdad.
Flying Training School, Al Rashid, Baghdad.

The Commanding Officer, 'Aqid (Colonel) Semi Fattah, who was trained at Sandhurst and at various R.A.F. schools, is reorganizing the Air Force with the co-operation of R.A.F. officers and N.C.O's, who are now employed in the Royal 'Iraqi Air Force and form part of the British Military Mission to the 'Iraqi Army.

The R.A.F. in the Middle East has offered a number of aircraft to the R.I.A.F. and further aircraft will be purchased from R.A.F. sources.

In October, 1943, cadets were sent to England for training, and a number of 'Iraqi pilots have been sent to R.A.F. Middle East establishments for advanced flying training.

THE NATIONAL MARKING

The triangular marking worn on fuselage and wings of all 'Iraqi military aircraft incorporates a formalised representation of the initial letter of the word Jaish, the Arabic word for Army. The four colour bands of the fin marking are the colours of the 'Iraqi flag and represent the four dynasties of 'Iraqi history.

ITALY
(The Kingdom of Italy—Regno d'Italia)

On September 8, 1943, the Italian Government under the leadership of General Badoglio surrendered unconditionally to the Allies and on October 13 this Government, whose sphere of influence was limited to the territory captured by the Allies, declared war on Germany. On the following day Italy was accepted by the Allies as a co-belligerent. The remainder of the country came under the complete domination of Germany.

THE ITALIAN CO-BELLIGERENT AIR FORCE

From the Italian airmen who, after the fall of the Fascist Government in July, 1943, joined the Allied air forces in the Mediterranean, three Wings were formed, a Fighter Wing with headquarters at Lecce ; a Seaplane Wing with headquarters at Taranto (under the operational control of No. 323 Wing, Mediterranean Coastal Air Forces) ; and a Bomber and Transport Wing with headquarters at Lecce.

These wings, although under Italian command, were directed and controlled by an air sub-commission of the Allied Control Commission, and were, by agreement between the Allied Command and the Italian authorities, based on the eastern coast of Italy.

The Fighter Wing consisted of five squadrons, Squadrons 10 and 12 (Airacobra) stationed at Canne ; Squadron 20 (Spitfire VB) stationed at Canne ; Squadron 102 (Macchi 202) and Squadron 155 (Macchi 205) both stationed at Lecce.

The Seaplane Wing was made up of four squadrons, Squadron 82 (Cant Z.506B) stationed at Taranto ; Squadron 83 (Cant Z.501, Z.506B and Z.506S) stationed at Brindisi ; Squadron 84 (Cant Z.506B, 506C and 506S) stationed at Taranto and Elmas ; and Squadron 85 (Cant Z.501, Z.506B, Z.506S and Fiat R.S.14).

The Bomber and Transport Wing consisted of five squadrons, Squadron 1 (S.M.82) stationed at Lecce ; Squadron 2 (S.M. 73, 75, 79, 82 and Fiat G.12) stationed at Rome ; Squadrons 28 and 132 (Baltimore IV and V) stationed at Littorio ; and Squadron 88 (Cant Z.1007) at Lecce.

Between October, 1943, and May 8, 1945, aircraft of the Co-Belligerent Air Force flew 8,542 sorties, during which 4 enemy aircraft were destroyed and 41 Italian aircraft were lost. During the same period 1,188 tons of bombs were dropped. The main activity of the co-belligerent units was in co-operating with the Balkan Air Force, chiefly over Yugoslavia.

At the end of hostilities in the Mediterranean the Co-Belligerent Air Force consisted of 512 aircraft, of which 433 were operational types. Serviceability was about 46 per cent.

THE FASCIST REPUBLICAN AIR FORCE

This force was formed after the Armistice with Italy, with General Tessari as Under-Secretary of State for Air. It consisted of a number of fighter squadrons, together with a torpedo-bomber unit and a squadron of reconnaissance seaplanes, all equipped with Italian aircraft. This force, which became operational in March, 1944, was virtually under the control of the Luftwaffe. Actual strength was probably never higher than 150 serviceable aircraft, of which 100-120 were fighters.

During the Summer of 1944 one Fighter Gruppo was re-equipped with the Me 109 and early in 1945 a second Gruppo was similarly re-equipped. Upon his retirement General Tessari was succeeded by Dr. Molfese who, after a short period as Under-Secretary of State for Air, was ultimately replaced by General R. Bonomi.

The Republican Air Force carried out routine fighter patrols and provided air defence on a small scale after the withdrawal of the Luftwaffe fighters from Northern Italy. The fact that these units were active, although their fighting value was not of a high order, was probably worth a good deal from the propaganda point of view. They also helped to relieve the Luftwaffe in the defence of Northern Italy at a time when Germany was hard-pressed on all sides.

JAPAN
(The Japanese Empire—Nippon)

NATIONAL MARKINGS

RED

RUDDER   FUSELAGE & WINGS

Japan surrendered to the Allies on August 14, 1945, the surrender terms including the disbandment of the Air Forces, the prohibition of all flying within Japan and the destruction of all aircraft manufacturing plants. The following gives a brief outline of the organization of the Army and Navy Air Forces as they existed before the capitulation.

Service Aviation in Japan was subordinated to the Army and the Navy, Army Aviation under the jurisdiction of the Ministry of War and the Naval Air Service under the control of the Admiralty. H.I.M. The Emperor Hirohito was the supreme commander of the fighting forces.

MILITARY AVIATION

Re-organization of the Japanese High Command in the Autumn of 1941 resulted in the creation of a National Defence Headquarters, which was charged with the defence of the Japanese islands, Korea, Formosa and Karafuto (Sakhalin) and controlled the field and air forces in those areas.

Within the organization of the Minister of War the Army Air Service was directed by a Chief of Military Aviation who was directly responsible to the Emperor for all specialized air operations.

The Army Air Force was organized into Air Armies, Flying Divisions, Flying Brigades and Flying Regiments. Early in 1945 the greatest concentration of strength was in Japan and its southern approaches ; but there was also one Air Army in Manchuria, another in China and another in the S.W. area.

These Air Armies were subordinated, generally speaking, to Area (ground) Armies. All Army Air Forces in the territories occupied by Japan after its entry into the war were included in the Southern Army.

The basic unit of the Army Air Force was the Flying Regiment. The number of aircraft in a Flying Regiment varied according to the type of aircraft of which it was composed; there were some 48 aircraft in a Regiment composed of Fighters, 36 in a Bomber Regiment, and 27 in a Reconnaissance Regiment. The Regiments subdivided into 3 Squadrons apiece for tactical purposes, and the Squadrons into smaller tactical units.

Two to five Flying Regiments usually formed a Flying Brigade, which was generally a mixed formation including Regiments of more than one type of aircraft. Brigades were organized into Divisions, and again Divisions into Armies, the number of Brigades in a Division and of Divisions in an Army depending on operational requirements.

NAVAL AVIATION

Naval Aviation was administered by a Directorate of Naval Aviation under a Vice-Admiral, who was directly responsible to the Minister of Marine.

Shore based naval air forces were grouped into a number of Base Air Forces for operational purposes. These corresponded to a number of Air Fleets on the administrative side. In addition naval commands at home and overseas controlled aircraft for patrol and defensive purposes.

The basic naval air unit was the Air Group, which was subdivided into Flying Units and Base Unit—the latter comprising administrative, maintenance and other services. The Flying Units were each equipped with one type of aircraft. Standard establishments for Fighter and Bomber Units were 36 with 12 in immediate reserve, for Night Fighters and Reconnaissance Units 18 with 6 in immediate reserve, and for Flying-Boat units 12 with 4 in immediate reserve.

An Air Group could contain one to four Flying Units but the usual number was two.

TRAINING

All training establishments came under the jurisdiction of the Bureau of Training at Naval Air Headquarters. A single Combined Air Training Command based at Gifu was responsible for carrying out the policy thus laid down. Apart from a few training establishments in Formosa, the greater part of naval air training was carried out in Japan, unlike the Army Air Force, many of whose training units were located overseas.

Units embarked in aircraft-carriers, seaplane-tenders and other ships were under the control of the Commander-in-Chief of the Naval station or the Admiral commanding the Fleet to which they were assigned.

Apart from units embarked in aircraft-carriers and seaplane-tenders, aircraft were carried in battleships and cruisers and in certain other classes of surface vessels.

MEXICO

(The United States of Mexico—Estados Unidos Mexicanos)

NATIONAL MARKINGS

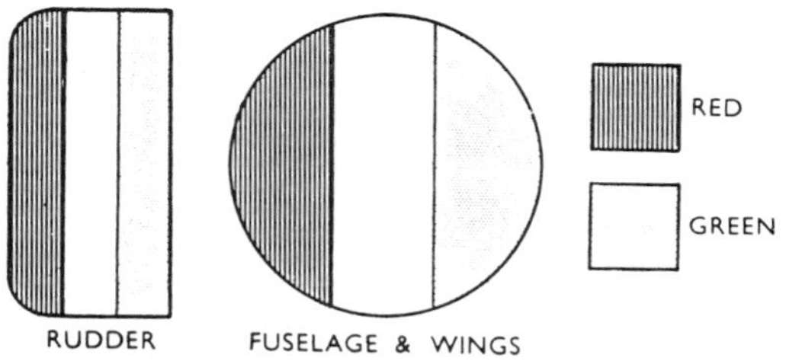
RED
GREEN
RUDDER
FUSELAGE & WINGS

Military Aviation in Mexico is administered by the Direccion de Aeronautica, a branch of the Ministry of National Defence. A naval air service is in course of being built up.

ORGANIZATION

Ministerio de Guerra y Marina, Mexico City.

President of the Republic and Minister for National Defence :—General Manuel Avila Camacho.

Direccion de Aeronautica, Campo de Aviacion Militar.

Officer Commanding Military Aviation :—General Gustavo Salinas Camina.

The Mexican Air Force, or Fuerza Aerea Mexicana, has its headquarters at the Valbuena Air Base, Mexico City.

The Military Flying School is situated at Guadalajara and is under the direction of the Direccion-General de Educacion Militar but the directors and staff are supplied by the Air Force. Cadet pilots receive their primary training at Guadalajara and after completion of both primary and basic training in Mexico proceed to U.S. Army flying schools for advanced training.

The ground staff forms the Corps of Aeronautical Mechanics, the technical personnel of which are trained at Valbuena.

The Direccion de Aeronautica is responsible for the administration of the Talleres Nacionales de Construcciones Aeronauticas, or National Aircraft Factory, Valbuena, which is equipped to build complete aircraft. It also undertakes all overhaul and repair of military aircraft.

On April 1, 1941, the Mexican and United States Governments signed an agreement which provided for practically unlimited reciprocal use of the ground organizations of the two countries.

Mexico declared war on the Axis on May 29, 1942. In the following month the Commander-in-Chief of the Mexican Air Force placed a number of training sites at the disposal of the U.S. Army Air Forces for the instruction of several thousand flying cadets.

For pilot training Mexico has adopted the American WTS system and two flying training schools have been established with the co-operation of the American authorities and, at the request of Mexico, American supervisors. Instructors were detailed by the Civil Aeronautics Authority to instruct Mexicans in U.S. training methods.

Early in 1945 No. 201 Fighter Squadron of the Mexican Air Force was due to leave Mexico to proceed to the South West Pacific theatre of war to serve with the American Army Air Forces. This squadron received operational training in the United States and was equipped with aircraft supplied by the United States Government.

TYPES OF AIRCRAFT USED

Training :—Ryan ST, North American AT-6, Vultee BT-13 and BT-15, Fairchild PT-19, Fleet Finch (Canadian-built), Tezuitlan (Mexican-built).
Reconnaissance :—Vought O2U-1 Corsair, Vought-Sikorsky OS2U-1 Kingfisher, North American AT-6 (with armament).
Light Bomber :—Douglas A-24 Dauntless.
Transport :—Lockheed Lodestar, Beechcraft C-45.

An expansion programme provides for the acquisition of further aircraft from the United States. It has been reported that these will include the North American B-25 Mitchell and the Chance Vought F4U Corsair.

THE NETHERLANDS

(The Kingdom of the Netherlands—Nederland)

THE ROYAL NETHERLANDS NAVAL AIR SERVICE

On May 15, 1940, the Commander-in-Chief of the Royal Netherlands Navy, Vice-Admiral J. Th. Furstner, gave orders to captains of all ships and aircraft to proceed to France or England so that they could continue to fight against the aggressor.

Early in the morning of May 15 all available naval air service personnel flew from various points in the Netherlands to a number of seaplane bases in France. Their aircraft consisted of Fokker T.VIIIW torpedo-bomber seaplanes, Fokker C.XIVW reconnaissance seaplanes and Fokker C.XIIIW training seaplanes. On arrival in France the bomb-racks on the T.VIIIW seaplanes were changed to accommodate French anti-submarine bombs and for several days these aircraft, manned by their own personnel, patrolled the French coast. They were then ordered to proceed to England.

On arrival in England the T.VIIIW seaplanes were sent to an R.A.F. operational seaplane base and once again their bomb-racks were changed to accommodate British types of anti-submarine bombs. The training aircraft were sent to the Netherlands East Indies.

All Dutch naval aviation personnel were attached to the R.A.F. Coastal Command and two squadrons were formed to co-operate with the Royal Air Force. One squadron, equipped with Fokker T.VIIIW seaplanes, started operational work immediately, protecting convoys and making anti-submarine, and rescue patrols over the Irish Sea. The other squadron after training on Anson aircraft, became an operational unit soon after. Both squadrons had several engagements with enemy aircraft over the Irish Sea but none of the convoys under their care ever suffered any losses. On several occasions they were responsible for the rescue of stranded flying crews and shipwrecked personnel.

By the end of 1940 the two squadrons had been combined into one and their Fokkers and Ansons were gradually replaced by Lockheed Hudsons. After several months' patrolling the Irish Sea the squadron was transferred to a North-Eastern aerodrome to operate over the North Sea. At the outset the fully-trained crews continued anti-submarine patrols and convoy duties over the North Sea and as trained crews increased the squadron gradually increased its duties to include offensive patrols, scouting and bombing along the Norwegian coast and the attack of enemy shipping. Early in 1942 the squadron was again transferred, this time to a South-Eastern aerodrome from which it operated against enemy shipping along the Dutch coast.

Early in 1943 the squadron was re-equipped with the North American Mitchell and transferred to the 2nd Tactical Air Force. It became operational with its new equipment in July, 1943.

The operational record of this squadron up to September, 1944, can be summarised as follows :—

The Fokker T-VIIIW floatplanes flew 135 sorties on convoy protection and U-boat search over the Irish Sea.

The Avro Anson landplanes flew 371 sorties and Hudsons added a further 39 over the North Sea.

The combined squadron after transference to the North-east coast flew 418 sorties along the Norwegian coast, in addition to which 50 strikes were made on enemy shipping.

After transference to a South-eastern aerodrome 116 air/sea rescue sorties were flown over the North Sea, after which followed a period during which 337 sorties were flown against enemy shipping along the Dutch coast. The result was 36 enemy merchant ships sunk or damaged, representing a total of 112,000 tons. The squadron also took part in a 1,000 bomber raid on Bremen.

After re-equipment with Mitchell medium bombers and from July, 1943, to September, 1944, the squadron flew 1,800 sorties, during which 3,600 tons of bombs were dropped.

In 1943 a start was made with the forming of a fighter squadron and a torpedo-bomber-reconnaissance squadron. The latter squadron is now serving afloat in a British aircraft-carrier.

Squadrons of the Royal Netherlands Naval Air Service operating in Great Britain served under their own commanding officers and all personnel wore the Netherlands Naval uniform. The Netherlands Government was responsible for the payment of all personnel, the upkeep of aircraft and the supply of fuel, bombs, ammunition, etc.

THE ROYAL NETHERLANDS ARMY AIR CORPS.

When Germany invaded the Netherlands the Army Air Corps, against everwhelming odds, fought to the limit of their resources and by the time the Army had surrendered, the fighting units had lost all their aircraft. Only a few aircrews were able to escape from the Fortress Holland (*i.e.* territory enclosed by artificial inundations). They were ordered to proceed to England or France in order to continue the fight against the aggressor on free soil. Two Flying Training Schools, namely the Primary and the Advanced Flying Schools, succeeded, as nearly complete units, in making their way via Belgium and France to England. Training aircraft (Fokker S-4 and S-9) which were not too badly damaged by the attacks of the Luftwaffe were flown to France by the pupil-pilots, but an arrival on a French airfield they were dismantled and prepared for transportation.

After the necessary re-grouping in September, 1940, all personnel was attached to the Royal Netherlands Naval Air Service; the qualified pilots were immediately given operational duties while the pupils were sent to the Netherlands East Indies to complete their training.

The latter returned to England in 1941 for operational flying. By that time many young Dutchmen who had escaped since the occupation of the mother country by the Germans had started their flying training in Canada and were incorporated into the Royal Air Force. Their number was augmented by pilots of the Army Air Corps, who had also made their way to England. Numerous Dutch pilots later served in various R.A.F. Squadrons.

On June 12, 1943, a Fighter Squadron was formed, equipped with the Supermarine Spitfire, complete with Dutch ground personnel, of which the greater part had been trained in England. From January 4, 1944, the Squadron was engaged on escort duties, defensive patrols, the interception of flying bombs—of which they shot down a considerable number (110)—long-range escorts over Germany, offensive patrols—such as the shooting-up of enemy rail and road transport, enemy troop concentrations, bridges, etc. The latter operational sorties were flown under the auspices of the 2nd Tactical Air Force, R.A.F.

During the first operational period the Squadron was equipped with Supermarine Spitfire Mk. V and Mk. XIV; afterwards it was re-equipped with Supermarine Spitfire Mk. IX.

The Army Air Corps, although it formed part of the Royal Air Force, had their own commanding officers and all personnel wore R.A.F. uniform with the flash "Netherlands."

On the conclusion of hostilities in Europe the Air Council sent the following message to Vice-Admiral J. W. Termijtelen, Director of Netherlands Air Forces :—

Now that victory in Europe has finally rewarded our long struggle, the Air Council hasten to send their greetings and congratulations to you and to the Dutch officers and airmen who have fought so gallantly with the Royal Air Force against our common enemy. Together we have battled throughout the years since your Air Forces valiantly joined us in the Battle of the Atlantic and the Western approaches in the summer of 1940 when your Country had tragically fallen into the hands of a treacherous and bloodthirsty invader. Together we will go forward to sweep our Japanese enemy from the territories which he has usurped.

The Council are deeply mindful of the trials which your Country has so bravely borne through the years of occupation and of the havoc wrought by the aggressor. Their heartfelt sympathy goes out to all your countrymen and with it the resolve that the comradeship of war shall develop into a guarantee of lasting peace.

THE NETHERLANDS EAST INDIES

When the Japanese launched their attack against the Netherlands East Indies, both the Army Air Corps and the Naval Air Service, details of the organization of which were published in previous editions of this Annual, were in process of expansion. Although the decision for a considerable expansion had been decided upon some time previously, the outbreak of War in Europe had interfered with the realization of these plans. Both forces were therefore modest in size.

Before actual hostilities against the Netherlands East Indies began the Army Air Corps and the Naval Air Service had for some time been in action assisting their British and American Allies to the best of their abilities. This, however, had still further depleted their strength. In spite of this, the Dutch airmen fought most gallantly with hardly a moment of rest, destroying many aircraft, sinking many ships and opposing the invader with all possible means. Their heroism won for both the Army Air Corps and the Naval Air Service the "Militaire Willemsorde," the highest honour of the Dutch armed forces.

When their bases became untenable, the remnants of both forces proceeded to Australia and Ceylon to continue the fight from there. One week after their arrival in Ceylon in March, 1942, a flying-boat squadron of the Naval Air Service equipped with Consolidated Catalinas was again fully operational. Other Naval Catalinas made a record non-stop flight from Australia to Ceylon, a distance of about 2,800 miles, to join those already there. Since then the Naval Air Service in Ceylon was considerably increased. Like its counterpart in the United Kingdom it was under the operational control of the Royal Air Force. All flying and ground personnel were Dutch.

The Army Air Corps on arrival in Australia immediately started to reorganize. A medium bomber squadron was soon formed and was placed under the operational control of the Allied Air Force Command in Australia. By the middle of 1943 it had made a great many highly successful attacks on enemy bases and shipping.

Apart from the fully-trained and operational personnel of the two services which managed to get away from the Indies as mentioned above, a total of about 500 air trainees were evacuated to Australia, together with their instructors and training aircraft.

The Australian Government placed the facilities of a Flying Training School at the disposal of the Dutch authorities, but it was later deemed advisable and more practical to move the training establishment to the United States where the American authorities made the Army Air Base at Jackson, Miss., available for its use.

Here the Royal Netherlands Military Flying School was established under the command of Major-General L. H. Van Oyen, Chief of the Netherlands East Indies Army Air Corps. By the end of 1943 the school had trained sufficient aircrews to permit the formation of a second medium bomber squadron and a fighter squadron for service in Australia. Dutch ground personnel was not available but Australian ground crews were loaned by the R.A.A.F.

NICARAGUA

(The Republic of Nicaragua—República de Nicaragua)

NATIONAL MARKINGS

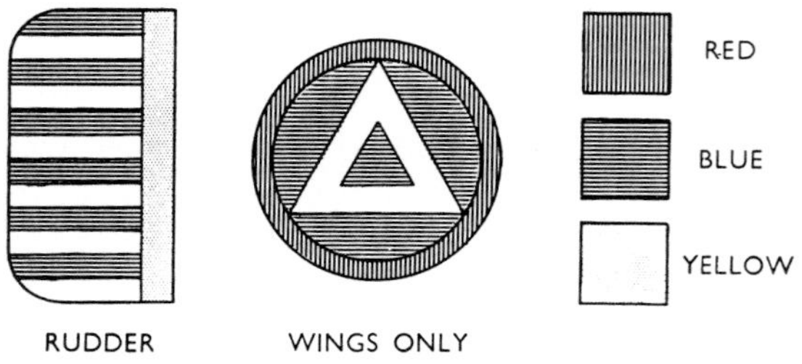

The Army Air Force, or Fuerza Aerea de la Guardia Nacional, was formed on June 9, 1938. Its function is to police the Republic, keep order, render assistance in an emergency and to protect the country against enemy invasion. It is administered by the Ministerio de Guerra, Marina y Aviacion.

Ministerio de Guerra, Marina y Aviacion, Managua.

The Minister of War, Marine and Aviation: Capt. Benjamin Argüello.

The Officer Commanding the Fuerza Aerea de la Guardia Nacional: Colonel Guillermo Rivas Cuadra, G.N.

The Fuerza Aerea de la Guardia Aviacion is equipped with modern aircraft of American design and of American and Canadian manufacture, including Waco D light fighters and Grumman G-23 two-seat biplanes, the latter built by the Canadian Car & Foundry Co., Ltd.

A meteorological station was established at Archibald Field, the U.S. Marine Corps base at Managua City, in 1929 and this station is now operated by Pan-American Airways. Weather reports are transmitted daily from all Nicaraguan aerodromes to Managua by the Guardia Nacional radio system.

The only purchaser of aircraft and aeronautical supplies in Nicaragua is the Ministry of War and the only flying school in operation is the Aviation School of the Guardia Nacional.

NORWAY

(The Kingdom of Norway—Norge)

NATIONAL MARKINGS

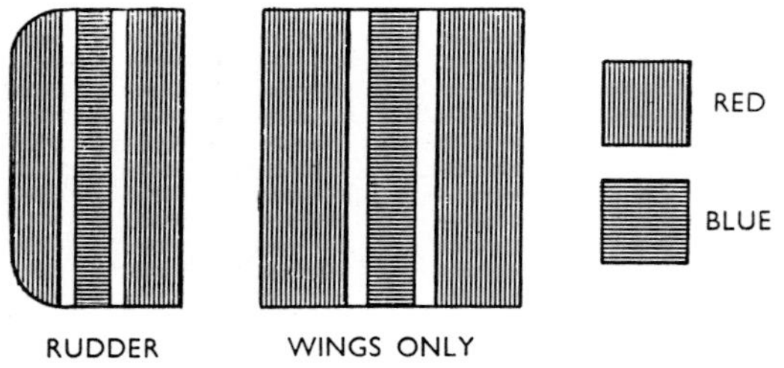

When the Germans launched their attack on Norway on April 9, 1940, the Norwegian air forces consisted of two separate units—the Royal Norwegian Army Air Force and the Royal Norwegian Naval Air Service. Each was respectively an integral part of the Army and the Navy, and under their direct control.

Both forces were modest in size. Their aeroplanes were mainly obsolete types, built in the years 1925 to 1930. Existing aerodromes were comparatively few and mainly situated in coastal areas.

During the Summer and Autumn of 1939 and the Spring of 1940, it was decided to expand both forces and equip them with more up-to-date types of aircraft; American Curtiss Hawk 75A Fighters and Douglas 8-A5 Attack Bombers for the Army Air Force; American Northrop N-3PB Patrol-Bomber and German Heinkel He 115 Reconnaissance Seaplanes for the Naval Air Service. In addition, funds were provided for the construction of air bases further inland. The Germans, however, attacked before the major part of this new programme could materialise.

In spite of this, and the fact that the invader had already succeeded by noon of April 9 in occupying all the existing aerodromes and seaplane bases south of Narvik, and that the German Luftwaffe during the first weeks after the invasion had recklessly thrown in a force of from 1,500 to 2,000 aircraft, the small Norwegian air forces managed to retain their ability to operate right up to the moment when the last Allied forces had to abandon the North of Norway, two months after the attack had started.

The outnumbered Norwegian Gloster Gladiators, all of which were disposed for the air defence of Oslo, put up a gallant fight on the morning of April 9 against the endless waves of German bombers, fighters and troop transports, but the fight was short mainly owing to lack of suitable landing fields within range. The Gladiators which were not shot down were, after having exhausted the stocks of petrol and ammunition, more or less damaged during forced landings on snow-covered fields and lakes.

The Naval Heinkel He 115 and M.F. 11 seaplanes rendered valuable service during the whole campaign in Southern Norway. Night and day, operating from the fjords and from frozen lakes, they bombed and harassed German transports and positions on the West Coast. Together with the Army Fokker C-V's and Tiger Moths, they carried out communication flights, serving as links between the isolated groups of the fighting forces in various fjords and valleys.

At the conclusion of the fighting in Southern Norway, Army staff officers were flown to the North of Norway in the Naval aircraft which were still able to make the long flight. Naval seaplanes too damaged to do this flight flew over to Scotland. Some of these latter aircraft, which were repaired with British assistance, were again flown across to Northern Norway and continued the struggle there.

In Northern Norway the Naval Heinkel He 115 and M.F. 11 seaplanes, and the Army Fokkers and Tiger Moths put up an almost continuous service for reconnaissance and communication purposes. The three first-mentioned types also rendered remarkably good service by bombing and machine-gunning German military objectives—transports, troop concentrations, airfields, machine-gun and artillery positions, etc.

After the withdrawal of the Allied forces, some of the seaplanes were flown to the Shetlands.

When the struggle in Southern Norway had to be given up at the beginning of May, some senior air officers were ordered to proceed to England. Together with the air personnel from that part of the country which could be provided with shipping accommodation to England, they were to organize fighter squadrons with British equipment (preferably Hurricanes) for transfer to the North of Norway later on. But the campaign in Northern Norway was relinquished before this plan could be put into action.

The Norwegian Air Command in London then took up the work of establishing their air crews on the Western Front in France. Here the French Armée de l'Air was operating with the same type of fighter aircraft as ordered by the Norwegian Army Air Force in the U.S.A. (Curtiss Hawk 75A). Again plans and preparations were frustrated. France collapsed on June 17, 1940.

Preliminary investigations had already been initiated by the Norwegian authorities with a view to establish training facilities in Canada. In conference with the Air Ministry and representatives of the Canadian Government, a new future was once more visualised for the remnants of the shattered Norwegian air forces. During June and July, 1940, it was decided to establish a Norwegian Air Training Camp in Canada to train pilots to fight in Europe with the R.A.F. and to provide a reserve to satisfy future demands.

Preceded by a small advance-party, the first contingent of air and ground personnel arrived in Canada at the beginning of August, 1940. These men—some 120 in number—immediately proceeded with the task of rebuilding a modern Norwegian Air Force. In less than six weeks the training of pilots was begun with Norwegian aircraft purchased in the United States.

THE ROYAL NORWEGIAN AIR FORCE

A Norwegian Order in Council dated November 10, 1944, united the former separate Army and Naval air services into the Royal Norwegian Air Force. The Commander-in-Chief is Major-General Hjalmar Riiser-Larsen, K.C.B. The former joint command continues to operate the new organization.

The Norwegian squadrons on active service with the R.A.F. in Europe included several squadrons in Fighter and Coastal Commands. A Norwegian Fighter Wing of two Spitfire Squadrons took part in many operations during 1942. Many of its victories were won in the Dieppe operations, when the Wing shot down 11 enemy aircraft and severely damaged many others.

During the Spring of 1943 the Norwegian Wing became the top-scoring wing of Fighter Command and at the end of the year one of the two squadrons was heading the scoring list of fighter squadrons in the British Isles.

After the invasion of Western Europe the Wing was used extensively in close support of the ground forces. This change of rôle, as well as the weak opposition put up by the enemy resulted in a decrease in the number of enemy aircraft destroyed. On the other hand, the appreciation from the Armies of the work carried out by the Wing showed a good balance.

The squadrons in Coastal Command were equipped with Sunderlands, Catalinas and Mosquitos. These squadrons were engaged in convoy escort, shipping reconnaissance and anti-U-boat warfare in the North Atlantic and achieved an excellent record on these operations.

In addition, a considerable number of Norwegian air and ground personnel served at various R.A.F. stations in the United Kingdom, some with the Operational Training Units and at Schools of Technical Training, and some with Operational Squadrons of both the Fighter and Coastal Commands.

The entire cost of the Royal Norwegian Air Forces serving in the United Kingdom, as with all other Norwegian expenditure, was borne by the Norwegian Government in Great Britain, mainly from the income derived from the operations of the maritime fleet.

On the cessation of hostilities in Europe the Air Council sent the following message to Major-General H. Riiser-Larsen, K.C.B., Commander-in-Chief, Royal Norwegian Air Force:—

The bitter struggle against the common foe is at an end and at this memorable time the Air Council send you a message of congratulation and fellowship from your comrades in the Royal Air Force.

The Council well remember how your Air Force challenged, with devoted courage, the overwhelming might of the Luftwaffe in the Spring of 1940 and how since that time it vigilantly defended the shores of Britain, this citadel of freedom, and staunchly engaged the enemy in the skies of Europe.

When your airmen return to their own land they will carry with them the good wishes and warm friendship of the Royal Air Force, who earnestly hope that the links which have bound our two air forces in adversity and war will be maintained and developed in peace.

In reply, Major-General Riiser-Larsen sent the following message to the Air Council:—

Please accept my very best thanks for your kind telegram on the cessation of hostilities.

On behalf of all the personnel in the Royal Norwegian Air Force, I beg to express sincere thanks for the great friendship shown to every one of us by our comrades-in-arms of the Royal Air Force.

These five years will certainly be the most memorable years in the history of Norway, who will not forget to render honour to the Royal Air Force especially for the Battle of Britain. If that had not been victorious there would not have been a free Norway again. In commemoration of this, and as a remembrance of the personnel of the Royal Norwegian Air Force and the people of Norway, I am grateful for your permission for the Royal Norwegian Air Force to wear "Air Force Blue" uniform.

Whenever called upon, be certain that the Royal Norwegian Air Force will be at the side of the Royal Air Force.

On May 22, the two Norwegian squadrons of R.A.F. Fighter Command landed at the Gardarmoen airfield near Oslo, the first Allied fighters to land in Norway after the liberation. They were welcomed on their home soil by H.R.H. the Crown Prince Olaf and met by their Norwegian ground crews who had arrived by sea and by transport aircraft previously.

PANAMA
(The Republic of Panama—República de Panama)

Early in 1933 the Republic of Panama decided to replace its marine protective service with a small Air Corps for general police and patrol work. The initial equipment consisted of one Keystone "Commuter" biplane (300 h.p. Wright "Whirlwind" engine) and two Travel Air "Speedwing" biplanes (240 h.p. Wright "Whirlwind" engines). The latter were equipped with

In September, 1941, the Air Corps took delivery of a Luscombe "Silvaire" two-seat cabin monoplane which will be used for the flight training of Panama police and Government officials.

In 1941 the Republic of Panama granted rights to the United light armament. The Officer Commanding the Panama Air Corps is Capt. Marcos A. Gelabert.

States Government for the establishment of air bases and defence stations in Panamanian territory to strengthen the Panama Canal defences. These bases and stations come under the jurisdiction of the 6th Air Force of the U.S. Army Air Forces (which see).

PARAGUAY
(Republic of Paraguay—República del Paraguay)

NATIONAL MARKINGS

BLUE

RED

YELLOW

WINGS   FUSELAGE

Military Aviation in Paraguay is organized as part of the Army under the Ministry of War and Marine, General de Brigada Don Vincente Manchuca, and includes some naval aircraft and personnel. The Officer Commanding, who may be either a naval or military officer, is responsible to the Minister of War and Marine and also controls Civil Aviation.

The headquarters of the Fuerzas Aereas Nacionales are at the Campo Grande Airport, near Asuncion, which is also the principal Customs Aerodrome in the Republic. There are both landplane and seaplane schools.

The officer Commanding is Major Pablo Stagni.

EQUIPMENT
Fighting :—Fiat CR.32, Bergamaschi A.P.1.
Training :—Breda 25, Savoia-Marchetti flying-boat, Fairchild M-62, Vultee 54, North American NA-16; Muniz M-9 (Brazilian).
Transport :—Breda 44.
Bombing :—Caproni.

PERU
(The Republic of Peru—República del Perú)

NATIONAL MARKINGS

RED

RUDDER   WINGS ONLY

The Air Arm of Peru, uniting under one command both Naval and Military Aviation, was instituted by a Supreme Decree dated May 20, 1929.

A Decree signed by President Manuel Prado on November 1, 1941, created an independent Ministry of Aeronautics to control all Military and Civil Aviation in Peru. The new Ministry began to function on January 1, 1942.

ORGANIZATION
Ministerio de Aeronautica, Miraflores, Lima.
Minister of Aeronautics : General de Aeronautica Don Fernando Melgar.
The Air Officer Commanding the Air Arm controls all the air

services in the country, Civil as well as Military. The administration of aviation is sub-divided among the following Departments or Directorates :—
Estado-Mayor General de Aeronautica.
Direccion-General des los Servicios Technicos.
Direccion de Abastecimientos y Contabilidad de Aeronautica.
Direccion del Personal de Aeronautica.
Direccion de Aviacion Comercial y Civil.
Direccion de Construcciones Civiles.
Direccion de Sanidad de Aeronautica.
Operational Units
Escuadron de Aviacion No. 1, Chiclayo.
Escuadron de Aviacion No. 4, Ancon.
Escuadron de Aviacion No. 5, Iquitos-Montana.
Escuadrilla No. 6 de Transportes, San Ramon-Montana.
Parque Central de Aeronautica, Callao.
Flying Schools
Escuela Central de Aeronautica "George Chavez," Las Palmas.
Escuela de Hydroaviacion, Ancon.

The Liga Nacional de Aviacion, a Government-sponsored organization, has formulated a plan to build up a reserve of 1,200 pilots and mechanics for the Peruvian Air Force. Ten Taylor-craft light training monoplanes have been acquired by the Liga Nacional de Aviacion and instruction will be centred at the Limatambo Airport, Lima.

Some years ago the Peruvian Government invited an Italian Air Mission to undertake the reorganization and modernization

of the Air Arm. At the same time an agreement was signed with the Caproni Company for the establishment of an aircraft factory for the construction and repair of military aircraft. On the advice of the Mission a number of Italian military aircraft of various types were bought for the Air Arm but these gave endless trouble and were the cause of many fatalities. The aircraft factory was similarly unsuccessful and failed to produce the stipulated number of training aircraft in its first two years' operations.

Soon after the outbreak of the European War the Italian Mission was withdrawn. In June, 1941, the Peruvian Government purchased the Aircraft Factory with the intention of operating it as a Government Air Arsenal.

In 1941 Colonel James T. Moore, U.S. Marine Corps, was appointed Inspector-General of Aviation to advise on air force matters. A number of Peruvian flying officers have been assigned to receive training in the United States and the Canal Zone.

EQUIPMENT
Training :—Stearman, Vultee 54.
Reconnaissance :—Douglas O-17, Fairey Fox.
Bombing :—Fairey Gordon, Douglas 8A-3P.
Fighting :—Curtiss Falcon, Curtiss Hawk, Vought Corsair, North American NA-50.
Transport and Miscellaneous :—Barkley-Grow 8TP, Grumman G-21A, Stinson, Junkers Ju 52, Faucett F.19 seaplane.

POLAND
(The Polish Republic—Rzeczpospolita Polska)

Poland was ruthlessly attacked by Germany on September 1, 1939, and although the Polish Air Force was quickly over-whelmed by the vastly superior size of the Luftwaffe it put up a gallant fight in the face of tremendous odds. When Poland was eventually defeated a large number of Polish pilots and airmen succeeded in escaping from their country and by various means reached France, where preparations were made for Polish units to be formed to continue the fight against the aggressor.

With the collapse of France all Polish Air Force personnel crossed to England where, for the third time in one year, the Air Force went into action against the Luftwaffe.

In accordance with the Anglo-Polish Agreement, signed on behalf of the Polish Government by General Sikorski, units of the Polish Air Force were reorganized within the framework of the Royal Air Force.

The Polish Air Force was the largest of the Allied Air Forces which had been reformed in the British Isles since the outbreak of War and from the point of view of numbers took fourth place (after Great Britain and Russia) among the Allied Air Forces. On the cessation of hostilities in Europe it consisted of fourteen squadrons and the total personnel amounted to 13,000.

Its traditions are those of the pre-War Air Force of Poland, every squadron formed on British soil, having associations with the former Air Regiments of Poland. The Polish Air Force in Great Britain is administered by an Inspector General, Air Vice-Marshal M. Izycki.

The first Polish squadrons to be formed in the British Isles were fighter units—Nos. 302 and 303 (Koscuiszko) Squadrons. The latter squadron during its operational training period shot down its first enemy aircraft on August 20, 1940, and again on August 30 during gunnery practice another enemy aircraft was destroyed.

During the first period of the Battle of Britain Polish pilots played their part in R.A.F. units as it was not until the end of September, 1940, that Polish squadrons went into action as autonomous units.

In that famous battle Polish squadrons destroyed a total of

203 enemy aircraft, to which should be added 35 probably destroyed and 36 damaged. During September alone, of the 662 enemy aircraft shot down by the R.A.F. 131 fell to Polish guns. No. 303 Squadron's record for the whole battle, was 125 for certain and 14 probables, a number which was surpassed by only one British squadron.

After September came a period of comparative quiet and the Polish squadrons were withdrawn from operations for re-equipment. Activities were resumed in April, 1941. During the period June 1—August 23, 1941, in offensive operations over France and Belgium out of a total of 601 enemy aircraft destroyed the Poles accounted for 102½, or 12 per cent.

Polish fighter pilots took part in most of the major daylight offensives during the year 1942 and 1943, their greatest triumph being when they emerged top scorers in the Dieppe operations on August 19, 1942, with seventeen bombers and fighters destroyed. The "Kosciuszko" Squadron accounted for nine for the loss of only one pilot. On December 31, 1942, the Polish Air Force celebrated the destruction of its 500th enemy aircraft.

On D-Day the whole of the Polish Air Force was present. In the first four months of the invasion of the continent Polish fighters shot down 80 aircraft for certain, with 6 probably destroyed and 22 damaged. In one air battle fifteen Poles attacked an enemy formation of sixty Fw 190's and destroyed 16 for the loss of one pilot. Not a single German pilot baled out. A Polish Mosquito squadron destroyed the School of Camouflage in Chateau Maulnay and blew up four big petrol dumps containing over 3 million gallons of petrol.

In the battle against the flying-bomb, out of a total of 1,900 shot down 223 were destroyed by Polish fighters. Later Polish squadrons took an active part in operations against V-2 rocket installations and rail communications in Holland.

On September 14, 1940, the first Polish bomber squadron was formed and, equipped with Fairey Battles, the squadron made its first operational sorties over Boulogne. By October of that year the squadron had been equipped with Vickers Wellingtons.

On the night of March 23-24, 1941, Nos. 300 and 301 Squadrons took part in their first raid on Berlin. They also participated in all four 1,000-bomber raids on the Ruhr, Essen, Cologne and Bremen, in the first two with 102 aircraft.

Throughout 1942-43 Polish bomber squadrons took part in the steadily growing bombing offensive against Germany and Occupied Europe. Between August 4 and September 14, 1942, No. 301 Squadron carried food and arms to besieged Warsaw, and in these operations the squadron lost fifteen crews, or 100 per cent. of its cadre. For this work the squadron, at the orders of the Commander-in-Chief of the Polish Air Force, was given the honour of bearing the name "Defenders of Warsaw."

In 1943 a Polish bomber squadron co-operated with Coastal Command in mine-laying, convoy protection and anti-submarine patrols. At least nine U-boats were claimed to have been sunk and four more damaged. They also took part in the attack on the German warships Scharnhorst, Gneisenau and Prinz Eugen during their escape from Brest in January, 1943. During January, 1943, one aircraft of the squadron had a gallant fight with four Ju 88's, beating them off after 58 minutes of hard fighting. This squadron flew a total of 2,497 sorties, and in addition to the U-boats already mentioned, it sunk seven surface vessels and took part in 50 defensive battles against aircraft, in which three were shot down for certain, one probably destroyed and two others damaged.

On November 5, 1943, the 25th Anniversary of the formation of the Polish Air Force, a Polish bomber squadron equipped with the Mitchell medium bomber, made its first day bomber operation over Northern France.

While the bulk of the Polish Air Force operated from bases in Great Britain, some units were in service overseas. In 1942, Polish airmen went into action in the Middle East, a volunteer flight taking part in air operations in the Libyan campaign. During the victorious North African campaign in 1943 a Polish flight attached to a R.A.F. fighter squadron in a period of seven weeks destroyed 25 enemy aircraft for the loss of only one pilot. During those seven weeks the flight made over 400 operational sorties. Flying Spitfire IX fighters these Polish pilots played a prominent part in harassing the enemy's lines of air communication with Tunisia.

Polish pilots, flying with R.A.F. operational squadrons also took part in the defence of Malta, in the Tunisian campaign, as well as in air fighting over Sicily and the Italian mainland.

Apart from operational units, the Polish Air Force operated its own Flying Training Schools and Technical Training School. A large number of Polish Air Force personnel continued its training in various R.A.F. schools and establishments. R.A.F. Technical Training Command was responsible for the training of nearly 4,000 Polish airmen as fitters, flight mechanics, wireless-operator/air-gunners, motor drivers, etc., as well as 600 Polish W.A.A.F. A Polish Air Force Apprentice Squadron was formed in 1943 from Polish youths brought to Great Britain from the Middle East. This Squadron was a part of the R.A.F. Apprentice Wing.

Many Polish pilots of considerable experience were appointed as instructors at various Polish R.A.F. training schools. A large number of Polish officers, qualified aeronautical engineers and some mechanics have been employed in the British Aircraft Industry.

Many Polish pilots, especially those belonging to the older generation, have been engaged in non-operation flying of the greatest importance. Thus a group of about 70 pilots served in Transport Command. About 2,500 aircraft were flown by them from the Gold Coast to the Middle East, as well as to the fronts in Africa and Italy. Another group consisting of 12 Polish pilots transported aircraft from Canada to Great Britain across the Atlantic, making a total of 265 flights, of which 250 were via the North or South Atlantic, and 15 to India. Polish pilots assigned to the British Overseas Airways Corpn. made about 20 flights with passengers and mails. Ten Polish pilots and three Polish women have served with Air Transport Auxiliary ferrying aircraft from factories to R.A.F. stations. Polish transport pilots have an average of 2,800 hours to their credit.

Summarising the achievements of the Polish Air Force up to May 8, 1945—Polish fighters shot down 741¾ enemy aircraft, with 175 probably destroyed and 238 damaged. In addition, hundreds of locomotives, trucks, tanks, ships, vehicles, etc. were destroyed or damaged. During the same period Polish fighters dropped 3,881,000 lbs. of bombs. Polish bomber squadrons serving in Bomber Command, Coastal Command and with the 2nd Tactical Air Force took part in 1,455 raids with 11,600 aircraft, and dropped 32,000,000 lbs. of bombs on enemy targets. Polish losses were heavy exceeding 200 per cent. of their original cadre.

On the conclusion of hostilities in Europe the Air Council sent the following message to Air Vice-Marshal Izycki, Commander-in-chief of the Polish Air Force :—

In this hour of victory over a resolute, vindictive and barbarous enemy the Air Council send their greetings and congratulations to all ranks of the Polish Air Force.

They do not forget that you were the first to resist the aggressor. Neither do they forget that you came, after manifold trials, to our aid, when we most needed your help. Your valiant squadrons, fighting alongside our own, were in the forefront of the Battle of Britain, and so helped to restore the fortunes of the Allies. Throughout the years of struggle, in good times and bad, you have stood by us and shared with the Royal Air Force their losses and their victories.

The Council would ask you to convey to the officers and other ranks of the Polish Air Force their admiration for their indomitable courage in the air and for their industry and skill on the ground. They trust that the comradeship which has grown up between the air forces of Poland and Great Britain will prove a lasting bond, and that their exploits may have laid the foundations of enduring peace.

In recognition of their gallantry many members of the Polish Air Force have been awarded the highest Polish awards for gallantry—the "Virtuti Militari"—and the Polish Cross of Valour—"Krazyz Walecznych." British awards to officers, N.C.Os. and men of the Polish Air Force include : 1 K.C.B., 5 C.B.E., 6 O.B.E., 2 M.B.E., 1 George Medal, 8 D.S.O., 1 D.F.C. with 2 Bars, 4 D.F.C., with 1 Bar, 154 D.F.C., 1 D.F.M. with Bar, 66 D.F.M., 15 A.F.C., 2 M.C., 1 C.G.M., 3 B.E.M., 6 A.F.M., 1 D.C.M. and 1 M.M. Polish airmen have also received the following American awards: 1 Silver Star, 3 Distinguished Flying Cross, 1 Soldier's Medal and 8 Air Medals, some of them with bars.

PORTUGAL

(The Republic of Portugal—República Portuguesa)

NATIONAL MARKINGS

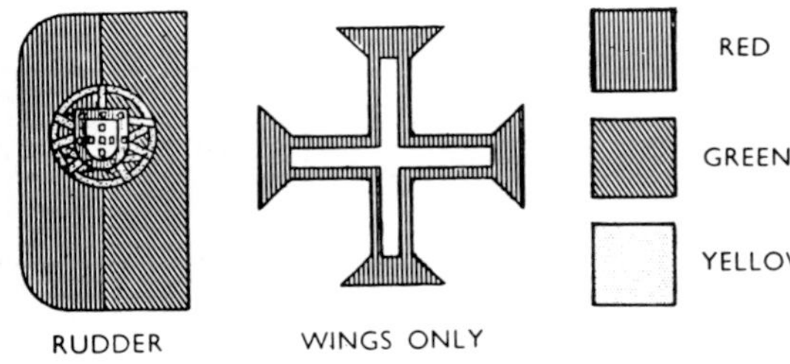
RED
GREEN
YELLOW
RUDDER
WINGS ONLY

Portuguese Service Aviation consists of two branches, the Aeronautica Militar (Army Air Force) and the Aeronautica Naval (Naval Air Service). They belong respectively to and are controlled by the Portuguese Army and Navy.

In 1944, the Aeronautica Militar continued to receive supplies of all kinds from Great Britain. It now consists of several hundred assorted aircraft, including many modern fighters and some modern bombers, both British and American.

MILITARY AVIATION

The Aeronautica Militar forms part of the Army, being classed as the "5a Arma" (Fifth Arm).

The Command Headquarters is situated in Lisbon at No. 7, Avenida Antonio Augusto de Aguiar. The Officer Commanding is Brig-General Alfredo Delesque dos Santos Sintra, who is responsible to, and is under the control of the Minister of War, Lieut. Col. Fernando dos Santos Costa.

ARMY AIR BASES AND ESTABLISHMENTS

The following are the principal Army Air Bases and Establishments :—

Granja do Marquez (Sintra)—Aerial Base No. 1. At this base functions the Army Flying School.

Ota—Aerial Base No. 2. Day and Night Bomber Station.

Tancos—Aerial Base No. 3. Fighter Station.

Portela de Sacavem (Lisbon Airport)—Army Air Force aircraft are much in evidence at this airport, at which a Defence of Lisbon Fighter Squadron is to be established.

Emergency Landing Grounds

Alijó, Amareleja, Alpalhão (Portalegre), Carregado, d'Anciães, Chaves, Colos, Espinho, Faro, Figueira da Foz, Mirandela (Campo Brito Pais), Macedo de Cavaleiros, Ponte de Sôr, Santa Cruz (Torres Vedras), Vila Nova de Milfontes, Vizeu.

Aircraft and personnel are stationed in the Azores but no details are available.

EQUIPMENT

The Aeronautica Militar flies a variety of types of aircraft including :—Supermarine Spitfire (various marks), Hawker Hurricane (at least two marks), Bell Airocobra, Bristol Blenheim IV, Consolidated Vultee Liberator, Junkers Ju 86 and Ju 52, Miles Master and Magister, Airspeed Oxford, Avro 626 and D.H. Tiger Moth.

At Alverca do Ribatejo are the Aeronautical Supply Depôt and the General Aeronautical Material Workshops, at which aircraft are overhauled, repaired or reconstructed.

NAVAL AVIATION

The Aeronautica Naval forms part of the Portuguese Navy. It is under the control of the Minister of Marine who, at the time of writing, was Captain Arnerico Tomaz.

The Director (Commanding Officer) of the Aeronautica Naval is Frigate-Captain Leal da Camara. Command Headquarters are situated in one of the buildings of the old Naval Arsenal in the Rua do Arsenal, Lisbon.

NAVAL AIR ESTABLISHMENTS

The Bom Sucesso Naval Air Base, Lisbon.

The S. Jacinto (Aveiro) Naval Aviation Centre, S. Jacinto Island Aveiro, comprising the Base proper and a Naval Aviation School.

Both the above Bases are fully equipped with buildings and installations.

The Faro Emergency Base, Culatra Island. In the extreme South. An emergency base only, having no hangers or other buildings and installations.

Portela de Sacavem (Lisbon Airport). The Naval Air Service maintains a large number of assorted aircraft, namely landplanes, and some personnel for maintenance, repair, etc., on a site adjacent to the main airport building. This is of a temporary nature and will have to give way to the proposed airport extension work which will shortly be undertaken.

The Montijo Naval Air Base. Although this does not exist as a Base proper, work is well advanced to make it a combined sea and landplane base. When completed it will replace Bom Sucesso, which for years has been marked for extinction. Montijo is on the South bank of the Tagus, near Lisbon. Establishments also exist in the Azores and at Macau (China) but no details are available.

The Aeronautica Naval does not possess the wide diversity of types of aircraft as the Army. Aircraft flown include :—Short Sunderland I, Grumman G-21B and G-44 Widgeon, Bristol Blenheim, Airspeed Oxford, Miles Martinet and Master, Avro 626, Fleet Trainer (with two different engine installations), D.H. Tiger Moth.

RUSSIA

(The Union of Soviet Socialist Republics—Soyuz Sovietskikh Sotsialistficheskikh Respublik)

NATIONAL MARKINGS

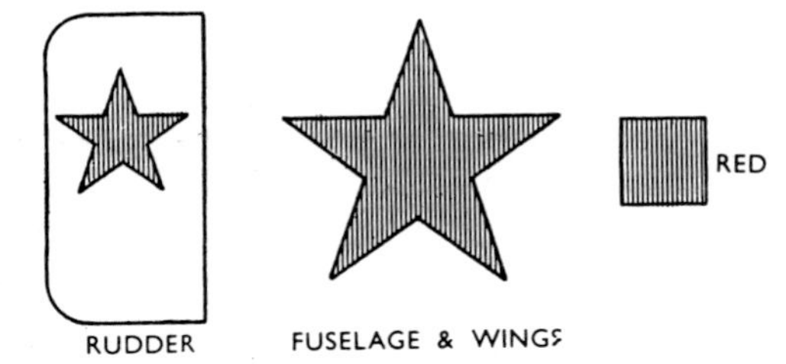
RED
RUDDER
FUSELAGE & WINGS

The Air Forces of the Soviet Union form integral parts of the Army and the Navy, and are divided as follow :—

(1) **Air Forces of the Air Armies**
Commander-in-Chief : Marshal S. H. Khudiakov.

(2) **Fighter Defence Force**

(3) **Long-Range Bomber Force**

Both the above Forces are Commanded by Marshal Novikov.

(4) **Air Forces of the Red Fleets**
Commander-in-Chief : Marshal S. F. Javronkov.

The Soviet Air Forces, like the Army and the Navy, are strategically divided between Far East and West. The forces so divided are designed to be independent, with the aim in view of enabling Russia to fight on two fronts. A considerable degree of independence has, indeed, been achieved, the Air Forces of the Far East even maintaining an independent aircraft industry.

Since the outbreak of war the Air Forces of the West have undergone considerable developments. From a pre-war organization based on territorial conceptions, wherein control was exercised through the Military Districts, the Army Air Force has now become a force organized in some dozen Air Armies, each Air Army covering one of the dozen or so Army Groups deployed against Germany, and subordinate to the Commander-in-Chief of the Army Group.

In addition to the Air Armies there exist, as integral parts of the Red army, a Fighter Defence for the defence of isolated points of importance in the deep rear, and an independent strategic Long-Range Bomber Force, both under the command of Marshal Novikov.

During the four years of war the Red Army Air Force played a part of the utmost importance in the campaigns on the Eastern front, and, from the black days of retreat in 1941, had developed by 1944 to a position of consistent air superiority over its enemy. It ended the war a massive force, with a high standard of efficiency, and unequalled in the field of war experience.

TACTICAL ORGANIZATION

The largest permanent formation of the Air Forces of the Air Armies is the Air Division, which consists of three Air Regiments, each Air Regiment being normally made up of three Squadrons. Guards Air Divisions and Guards Air Regiments exist, these being units which have been specially so designated as a mark of honour for distinguished service in the field.

THE AIR COMPONENTS OF THE RED FLEETS

The Naval Air Components of the Red Fleets are four in number, being those of the Baltic, the Black Sea, the Northern and the Pacific Fleets. They consist of shore-based aircraft, seaplanes and flying-boats. These components are administered by the respective Naval Commands.

The Naval Air Components are organised in Naval Air Divisions and Naval Air Regiments in the same way as the Air Forces of the Red Army. There also exists in these Naval Air Components a considerable number of independent Naval Air Squadrons.

The rôle of the Naval Air Components is predominantly sea reconnaissance, naval escort duties, and anti-shipping operations, but, if occasion demands, they are capable of being, and were frequently used for the support of Army formations in land operations.

ROLE OF THE RED ARMY AIR FORCES

The Air Forces of the Red Army are designed, organized and equipped predominantly for the task of supporting the Red Army, and not in order to undertake an independent strategic task. The emphasis of this aspect of an Air Force in the Russian Military mind has profoundly affected the direction in which the Air Force has been developed. The Long-Range Bomber Force, which hitherto had been regarded as in the nature of an appendage, played an increasing part in operations towards the end of the war in Eastern Europe, yet its activities were seldom divorced from contemporary Army operations.

SALVADOR
(Republic of El Salvador—República de El Salvador)

NATIONAL MARKINGS

RUDDER   WINGS ONLY   BLUE

Military Aviation is administered by a department of the Ministry of National Defence.

ORGANIZATION

Ministerio de Guerra, Marina y Aviacion, Palacio Nacional, San Salvador.

President of the Republic and Minister of National Defence :—General Salvador Castaneda Castro.

Departamento de Aviacion

Director :—Major Herman Barón.

This Department is responsible for the administration of both Military and Civil flying in Salvador.

The Military Air Arm is based at Ilopango, where are situated the Headquarters, the Flying Training School, the Technical Training School and Schools for Specialisation.

The Air Arm consists of one Reconnaissance Flight and one Fighter Flight. Each Flight consists of three aircraft in service with one in reserve, and one mobile unit.

MILITARY AERODROMES

Military aerodromes are established at Ilopango, Principal base (Ilopango, Depto. San Salvador), San Miguel, Depto. de San Miguel, Ahuachapan, Depto. de Ahuachapan, Sonsonate, Depto. de Sonsonate, Zacatecoluca, Depto. de La Paz, San Vicente, Depto. de San Vicente, Chalatenango Depto. de Chalatenango, and Usulutan, Depto. de Usulutan.

SPAIN
(The Spanish State—España)

NATIONAL MARKINGS

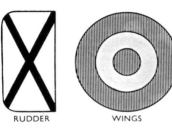

RUDDER   WINGS   FUSELAGE
(Arrows & Yoke—Red on Black)

RED

YELLOW

BLACK

Military Aviation in Spain is organized as an independent Army of the Air under the jurisdiction of the Air Ministry.

ORGANIZATION

The Army of the Air (Ejercito del Aire) was created in October, 1939, as an independent arm on terms of equality with the Army and the Navy. It is administered by the Air Ministry.

On occasions when the Army, Navy and Air Force may be required to co-operate in a particular mission, the joint command may be undertaken by a general officer of any one of the three services. In such a case his staff will consist of officers drawn from the three services. The Minister of State for each one of the services will continue to control administration and organization within his particular mandate.

ADMINISTRATION

The Air Ministry (Ministerio del Aire).

The Air Ministry was created in August, 1939, and now conforms to the following organization :—

(1) **The Air Minister** (Ministro del Aire).

(2) **The Air Staff** (Estado Mayor del Aire), consisting of a Chief of Staff, Assistant Chief of Staff, General Secretariat, five Sections and a Control Service (Intervencion).

The Air Staff deals with the organization, instruction and maintenance of the Air Force in peace, and with its mobilisation and operations in time of war.

(3) **The Under-Secretariat** (Sub-secretaria), which controls the following departments :—

(a) **The General-Directorate of Personnel** (Direccion General de Personal), which deals with all questions of recruitment, promotion, commissioning, etc., of military and civil personnel.

(b) **The General-Directorate of Industry and Material** (Direccion General de Industria y Material) which is responsible for the preparation of programmes and the acquisition of aircraft and equipment in accordance with the requirements of the Higher Command. This Directorate consists of the following sections :—Manufacture, Supplies, and Administration. There is also an Advisory Council on aeronautical matters. Forming part of the Supply Department there is a Council of Aircraft Industry (Jurisdiccion Industrial Aeronautics) to arbitrate with and exercise control over all industries of an aeronautical nature.

(c) **The General-Directorate of Ground Services and Facilities** (Direccion General de Infraestructura), which is responsible for the construction and maintenance of aerodromes, buildings and other ground services.

(d) **The General-Directorate of Air Navigation Aids** (Direccion General de Proteccion de Vuelo), which controls all radio services, the issue of meteorological information, and is responsible for airway lighting, beacons, radio beam and direction finding, etc. The National Meteorological Service forms part of this Directorate.

(e) **The General-Directorate of Ground Defence** (Direccion General de Antiaeronautica), which is responsible for all aspects of anti-aircraft ground defence.

(f) **The General-Directorate of Civil Aviation** (Direccion General de Aviacion Civil), which controls all aspects of civil aviation, including commercial flying, private flying, gliding and soaring, pre-military air instruction etc.

(g) **The General-Directorate of Instruction** (Direccion General de Instruccion) which controls the training of all the personnel of the Air Army.

(h) **The Sections of Supply** (Intendencia), Control (Intervencion), Medical (Sanidad), Pharmacy (Farmacia) and Legal Advice (Asesoria Juridica).

(4) **The National Institute of Aeronautical Science** (Instituto Nacional de Tecnica Aeronautica—I.N.T.A.). Undertakes the study and investigation of all technical problems associated with airframes, aero-engines, propellers, materials, armament, radio, photography, meteorology, etc. This Institute, created in 1942, consists of a Director, Secretary, an Advisory Committee, various sections, experimental workshops and installations, and an aerodrome. It has direct contacts with the Air Minister, the General-Directorate of Industry and Material, the managements of private aeronautical concerns, and similar organizations in the Army and the Navy and the Ministry of National Education.

For the general study of research there is a High Committee (Patronado), which is made up of senior technical and administrative officers of the Air Ministry and other officers and scientists appointed by the War Ministry, the Ministry of Marine, the Academy of Science and other research institutes, and the Aeronautical Industry.

THE ARMY OF THE AIR

The Army of the Air (Ejercito del Aire) consists of a High Command, the formations of flying and ground personnel, anti-aircraft units, airborne troops, transport, technical and communication services, and supply, medical, legal and other units.

Spanish territory is divided into Air Regions in the peninsula and into Air Zones in Africa and the Colonies. Each Region or Zone, which is commanded by a General or Colonel of the Air Force and has its own Regional Air Staff, includes operational and training units and various ancillary services and establishments.

For the administration of Military Justice and the legal control of the personnel of the Air Army and that of the Spanish jurisdictional air space, there is the Aerial Jurisdiction (Jurisdiccion Aérea).

TRAINING

Instruction in the Air Army is co-ordinated and controlled by the General-Directorate of Instruction (Direccion General de Instruccion), under which are the following establishments :—

Academia General del Aire (General Academy of the Air), San Javier. Here all candidates for commissions in all the Air Army Branches and Services must undergo their initial training. Those for the Air Force, Ground Force or Supply, must complete two courses ; those for the Engineering, Medical, Pharmacy, Control and Legal Corps complete half a course. The remainder of the training for all candidates must be completed in the respective specialist academies. This Academy was opened in the Spring of 1945.

Escuela Superior del Aire (Air Staff College).

Academia Especial del Arma de Aviacion (Academy for the Aviation Arm), Alcalá de Henares. Opened in 1944.

Academia Especial del Arma de Tropas de Aviacon (Special Academy for Aviation Troops), Los Alcázares. Opened in 1944.

Academia Militar de Ingenieros Aeronauticos (Military Academy for Aeronautical Engineers).

Escuela Superior Aérontecnica (Higher Aeronautical Technical School).

Institutos de Sanidad Aeronautica (Institute of Aeronautical Medicine).

Academias de Intendencia (Supply), **Intervencion** (Control), **Sanidad** (Medical), **Farmacia** (Pharmacy) and **Juridica** (Legal).

Escuela Inicial Militar Aérea (Military Ab-initio School). For non-commissioned officers (officialidad de complemento) of the Air Force.

Flying personnel receive their instruction in the various elementary and transitional training schools (Escuelas elementales o de transformación) and in the advanced or tactical schools for fighter aircraft, seaplanes, multi-engined aircraft, instrument flying, navigation, etc.

Ground personnel receive their training in the various apprentice schools (Escuelas de Aprendices) attached to the Air Regions. There are specialised schools for engine mechanics, fitters, wireless operators, photographers, armourers, electricians, etc.

Non-flying commissioned personnel in the Control, Supply, Medical and Legal Sections receive their final training in the appropriate military academies or schools of instruction.

Numerous schools under the control of the General-Directorate of Civil Aviation exist for the pre-military training of youth.

EQUIPMENT

The Spanish Aircraft Industry is in an advanced stage of reorganization. The Directorate of Industry and Material is responsible for the purchase and construction of aircraft and equipment and the industry has been given State assistance to enable it to undertake the manufacture on a large scale of bomber and fighter aircraft.

The present equipment of the Spanish Air Force is made up of those types which at the end of the Civil War existed in both zones. These are, however, being steadily replaced by more modern types as the capacity of the national industry increases.

The Spanish Aircraft Industry can be mobilised both in war and peace. There are three groups of concerns ; (a) Aeronautical Military Industries (owned or managed by the Air Ministry), (b) Mobilised Aeronautical Industries (private firms in which the Air Ministry has secured a military control), and (c) Private firms (not yet mobilised).

PROPAGANDA AND PUPLICATIONS

Aeronautical propaganda is in charge of the General Secretary of the Air Ministry. Aeronautical publications are controlled by the 4th Sub-section, 2nd Section of the Air Staff.

The official organ of the Ejercito de Aire is the "Revista de Aeronautica," issued monthly. Postal address : Apartado oficial, Madrid. Offices : Juan de Mena, 8 Madrid. Price : 5.00 ptas. per copy.

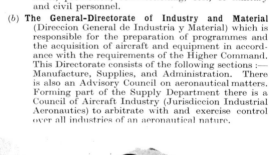

The Prototype Hispano-Suiza H.S.42 Trainer with the 430 h.p. Piaggio engine and fixed landing gear.

SWEDEN
(The Kingdom of Sweden—Sverige)

NATIONAL MARKINGS

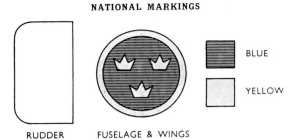

RUDDER   FUSELAGE & WINGS

BLUE

YELLOW

The Swedish Air Force, or Flygvapnet, was organized as an independent force in 1926. Considerable expansion and modernization has been introduced in recent years.

ADMINISTRATION

The Chief of the Air Force (Chefen för Flygvapnet) is in direct subordination to the Commander-in-Chief of the Armed Forces (Överbefälhavaren). In direct subordination to the Chief of the Air Force are the Air Staff (Flygstaben) and the Royal Air Board (Kungl. Flygförvaltnengen), both in Stockholm.

ORGANIZATION

Chief of the Air Force (Chefen för Flygvapnet) : Lieut.-General B. G. Nordenskiöld.
The Air Staff (Flygstaben). Chief : Major-General Axel Ljungdahl. Deputy Chief : Colonel K. J. A. Silfverberg. Responsible for organization, training of personnel and other matters. It comprises the following departments :—
Operations (Operationsavdelningen).
Organization (Organisationsavdelningen).
Training (Utbildningsavdelningen).
Signals (Signalavdelningen).
Flying Safety (Flygsäkerhets-och haveriavdelningen).
Meteorological (Väderleksavdelningen).
Press (Pressektionen).
Staff Headquarters (Expeditionen).
The Royal Air Board (Kungl. Flygförvaltnningen). Chief : The Chief of the Air Force. Deputy Chief : Colonel N. O. F. Söderberg.
Responsible for the supply and maintenance of aircraft, aero-engines, fuel equipment, ordnance and finance, as well as of aerodromes and buildings. It comprises :—
Department of Technical Equipment (Materielavdelningen).
Department of Commissariat (Intendenturavdelningen).
Department of Aerodromes and Buildings (Byggnadsavdelningen).
In addition, there is a **Chief Medical Officer** (Flygöverläkaren). and a **Civil Bureau** (Civilbyran), for matters of pay, law, etc.

OPERATIONAL UNITS

The Chief of the Air Force commands the central administration of the units comprising the Air Force. Under him are four groups (Flydeskadrar), five Air Base Areas and the following wings :—

F 1 Kungl. Vastmanlands Flygflottilj (Heavy Bomber Wing), Västerås.
F 2 Kungl. Roslagens Flygflottilj (Naval Co-operation Wing), Hägernäs.
F 3 Kungl. Ostgöta Flygflottilj (Army Co-operation Wing), Malmslätt.
F 4 Kungl. Jämtlands Flygflottilj (Dive-Bomber Wing, Ostersund.
F 5 Kungl. Krigsflyskolan (Flying Training School). Ljungbyhed.
F 6 Kungl. Västögta Flygflottilj (Dive Bomber-Wing), Karlsborg.
F 7 Kungl. Skaraborgs Flygflottilj (Dive-Bomber Wing, Sätenäs.
F 8 Kungl. Svea Flygflottilj (Fighter Wing), Barkarby.
F 9 Kungl. Göta Flygflottilj (Fighter Wing), Göteborg-Säve.
F10 Kungl. Skånska Flygflottilj (Fighter Wing), Angelholm.
F11 Kungl. Sodermanlands Flygflottilj (Long-range Reconnaissance Wing), Nyköping.
F12 Kungl. Kalmar Flygflottilj (Dive-Bomber Wing), Kalmar.
F13 Kungl. Bråvalla Flygflottilj (Fighter Wing), Norrköping.
F14 Kungl. Hallands Flygflottilj (Heavy Bomber Wing), Halmstad.
F15 Kungl. Hälsinge Flygflottilj (Fighter Wing), Söderhamn.
F16 Kungl. Upplands Flygflottilj (Fighter Wing), Uppsala.
F17 Kungl. Blekinge Flygflottilj (Torpedo-Bomber Wing), Ronneby.
F20 Kungl. Flygkadettskolan (Air Force College), Uppsala.
F21 Kungl. Norrbottens Flygbaskar (Air Training Centre), Luleå.

Each Operational Wing includes a Headquarters Staff, with Meteorological, Photographic, Signals, Ordnance and Material, Commissariat and Medical Sections, four Squadrons (Divisioner). Motor Transport and certain aircraft for transport and liaison. Of the four squadrons in each Wing, two are fully operational, one is devoted to training new personnel and one is reserved for special duties.
The strength of a Squadron is normally made up of three Flights (Grupper), each of three aircraft, plus a reserve Flight.
The sixteen Operational Wings, with the exception of the Army Co-operation Wing (Armespaningsflottilj) assigned to the land forces, are grouped into four Groups. These Groups are constituted as follow :—
1st Air Group (Forsta Flygeskadern). H.Q. : Stockholm. Nos. 1, 4, 12, and 15 Wings.
2nd Air Group (Andra Flygeskadern). H.Q. : Göteborg. Nos. 6, 7, 9 and 14 Wings.
3rd Air Group (Tredje Flygeskadern). H.Q. : Stockholm. Nos. 8, 10, 13 and 16 Wings.
4th Air Group (Fjarde Flygeskadern). H.Q. : Stockholm. Nos. 2, 11 and 17 Wings.
The improvement of ground facilities in Norrland, in the extreme North, has been completed. A main Training Centre (No. 21 Kungl. Norrbottens Flygbaskår) for all branches of the Service has been established at Luleå.
There are two Aircraft Depots (Centrala Flygverkstäder) with repair workshops at Malmslätt and Västeras respectively. A third at Arboga, which will be largely underground, is due for completion in 1945.

The Air Estimates for the fiscal year 1944/45, beginning July 1, 1944, amount to Kr. 235,600,000.

TRAINING

Until 1938 all officers of the Air Force were seconded from the Army or Navy for five years. Since 1938 however the Air Force has recruited its personnel independently.
Officer aspirants are trained at the Aspirant School at Ljungbyhed and the Cadet School at Uppsala. Engineering aspirants also receive training at the Central Aircraft Works or any technical High School in the country.
The training periods are :—
Officer aspirants : about 34 months.
Reserve aspirants : about 21 months.
Engineer aspirants : about 20½ months.
Second year training includes service with an Air Force Wing to give pupils specialized experience in various operational duties.
Observers for service in units for co-operation with the Army and Navy are generally Army or Navy officers who have applied for such training.
The period of enlistment for N.C.O's. and other ranks is from three to four years. Conscripts include those selected for regular service and those in the untrained reserve. Recent legislation has extended the period of training of all Air Force conscripts to 450 days, of which 360 days are served in one sequence. The remaining 90 days are spread over training periods in the second, third and seventh years following the initial period.

DESIGNATION OF MILITARY AIRCRAFT

All Swedish service aircraft are officially indentified by the following class letters :—
B Bombers.
J Fighters.
S Army or Naval Co-operation, Reconnaissance, Observation, etc.
P Experimental.
Tp. Transport or Ambulance.
Sk. Training.
In each class the different types of aircraft are numbered consecutively. A capital letter (A, B, C, etc.) after the type number denotes variations in engines, equipment, etc.

EQUIPMENT

Bombing (B) :— B 17 (SAAB-17), B 18 (SAAB-18).
Fighting (J) :— J 9 (Republic EP-1) J 20 (Reggiane Re. 2000), J 21 (SAAB-21), J 22, J 26 (North American Mustang P-51D).
Army or Naval Co-operation, Reconnaissance, Observation, etc. (S) :— S 2 (Heinkel He 115 seaplane), S 12 (Heinkel He 114 seaplane), S 14 (Fieseler Storch), S 16 (Caproni Ca 313 Reconnaissance), S 17 (SAAB-17).
Transport or Ambulance (Tp) :— Tp 2A (Junkers W.34 ambulance) Tp 3 (Beechcraft 18 S ambulance), Tp 5 (Junkers Ju 52).
Training (Sk) :— Sk 12 (Focke-Wulf Stieglitz), Sk 14 (North American NA-16), Sk 15 (Klemm Kl 25), Sk 25 (Bücker Bestmann).

SWITZERLAND
(The Swiss Federation—Schweizerische Eidgenossenschaft)

NATIONAL MARKINGS

RUDDER   WINGS ONLY   RED

The Swiss Air Force became an independent service by virtue of a Decree dated October 13, 1936. It is administered by a Branch of the Federal Military Department.

ORGANIZATION

Federal Military Department (Eidgenössisches Militärdepartement) Berne.
Air Force and Anti-Aircraft Division (Abteilung fur Flugwesen und Fliegerabwehr)
Officers Commanding : Colonel-Divisionnaire F. Rihner.
This division or branch has sections for Organization ; Personnel and Material ; Technical Services ; Air Defence Warning Service ; Military Aerodromes and Ground Defence.
The Air Force, the headquarters and principal services of which are situated at Dübendorf, near Zürich, is composed of four Regiments, each containing two Groups. A Group is made up of three squadrons and, of the twenty-four squadrons so formed, fifteen are fighter, six are reconnaissance and three are training squadrons (two fighter and one reconnaissance).

Training.

Operational training is carried out in a Training Group which is the nucleus of the regular Air Force and the only tactical training unit. In this Group officers and N.C.O.'s are trained as air-crews. Until 1943 officers only were trained as pilots but since that date specially selected N.C.O.'s have been trained.

TRAINING SCHOOLS

Officers
Officers' School : Dübendorf.
Flying School : Dübendorf.
Mechanics
Radio Operators and Photographers : Dübendorf.
All other Technical Specialists : Payerne.

EQUIPMENT

Reconnaissance :— C.35, C.36 and Potez 63.
Fighting :— Messerschmitt Me 109E, Morane-Saulnier 405, 406.
Training :— Bücker Bü 131 Jungmann, Bü 133 Jungmeister, Messerschmitt Me 108 Taifun.
The only aircraft types in production in Swiss factories are the C.36 and Morane 406.
The chief assembly factories are the branch of the Dornier Werke at Altenrhein, the Federal Aircraft Works at Thun and Emmen and the Pilatus Works at Stan. The last mentioned is occupied mainly with repair work.
Certain spare parts for the Me 109E are made in Switzerland.

TURKEY
(The Turkish Republic—Türkiye)

COMMAND AND ADMINISTRATION

The Turkish Air Force forms an integral part of the Turkish Army. It is controlled politically by the Minister of National Defence and operationally by the Air Bureau of the Turkish General Staff.
Ministry of National Defence, Ankara.
Minister of National Defence : General Ali Riza Artunkal.
Chief of the General Staff : Marshal Kiazim Orbay.
Under Secretary of State for Air : Lieut.-Gen. Yahya Razi Biltan, who is responsible to the Minister of National Defence for administration, personnel, schools and factories, as well as for the purchase of aircraft and supplies.

Chief of the General Staff : Marshal Kiazin Orbay, who is also Director-General of Military Aviation and in supreme command of the Air Force and responsible for operations and training.
The General Staff includes an Air Bureau, under Major-General Zeki Dogan, who is assisted by a number of General Staff officers of both the military and air branches.

ORGANIZATION

The Turkish Air Force is organized in two Air Divisions, the 1st with its Headquarters at Eskishehr, the 2nd with its Headquarters at Gaziemir. The Air Division contains a variable number of Wings, a Wing normally being made up of two

Squadrons. There are altogether approximately fifteen Wings, containing about thirty Squadrons, in the Air Force.
The Squadron is the tactical unit, the first line strength of a Squadron being nine aircraft in the case of Fighter and Army co-operation Squadrons, and six aircraft in the case of Bomber Squadrons.

TRAINING

Prior to 1938 the Turkish Air Force grew chiefly under French tuition, but from that date R.A.F. instructors were brought in and the training system was remodelled on British lines.
Flying training is carried out at Eskishehr where there are the Initial, Elementary, Intermediate and Advanced Training

NATIONAL MARKINGS

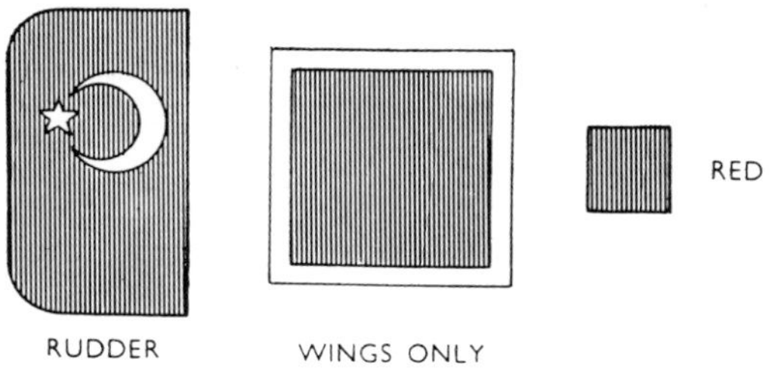
RED
RUDDER
WINGS ONLY

Wings. Operational training for bomber pilots is also undertaken at Eskishehr. Fighter pilots, however, pass straight to their units after completion of their Advanced Training course.

Since 1941, batches of Turkish Air Force officer cadets have been proceeding to Great Britain for training as pilots by the Royal Air Force. Trainees sent to Britain are representative of the normal intake to the Turkish Air Force and are not specially chosen.

Pre-military training is undertaken by the Turkkusu Association, an offshoot of the semi-official Turkish Air League. Branches are established in all the principal towns. Its object is the building up of a reserve of pilots and mechanics for the Air Force. Initial Training is carried out on gliders, and Advanced Training on powered aircraft. Attention is also given to parachute training, and parachute-jumping towers have been installed at several places.

EQUIPMENT

The Turkish Air Force is equipped with the following operational types :—

Heavy Bomber : Consolidated Liberator.
Medium Bomber : Martin 139 and Baltimore.
Light Bomber : Bristol Blenheim.
Fighter : Hawker Hurricane IIB and IIC, Supermarine Spitfire, Focke-Wulf Fw 190.
Army Co-operation : Westland Lysander.
Torpedo Bomber : Bristol Beaufort.
Training :—A wide variety of types is used for training, including the following :—

Miles Magister, Vultee V-11, Curtiss Hawk, Curtiss Falcon, Gotha Go 145, Miles Master, Airspeed Oxford, P.Z.L. 24 and Morane-Saulnier 406.

The Aircraft Factory at Kaiseri builds a number of types under licence. It is the principal repair centre, but another repair depôt exists at Eskishehr.

THE UNITED STATES OF AMERICA

NATIONAL MARKINGS

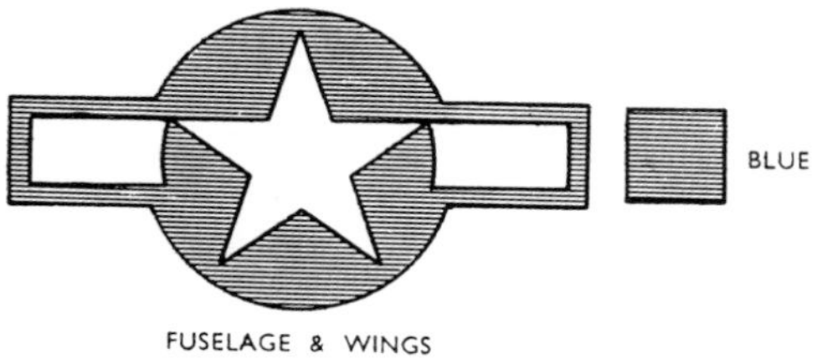
BLUE
FUSELAGE & WINGS

Service Aviation in the United States is organized in two separate arms—the Army Air Forces and the Naval Air Service, the latter including Marine Corps Aviation and, for the duration of the War, the Coast Guard Air Service.

The Commander-in-Chief of the Fighting Forces is the President of the United States.

THE ARMY AIR FORCES

On March 2, 1942, a drastic reorganization was approved whereby all branches of the Army were abolished in favour of three main autonomous commands,—Air Forces, Ground Forces and Service of Supply,—all of which are responsible directly to the General Staff.

The placing of the Air Forces under a single command resulted in the abolition of the Air Corps and Combat Command. General of the Army H. H. Arnold was Commander-in-Chief of the Air Forces from March, 1942, until the victory over Japan. On retirement he will be succeeded by General Carl Spaatz.

Further reorganization, which became effective on March 29, 1943, established six Assistant Chiefs of Staff, to direct and control the activities of the Air Forces. This reorganization results in (*a*) H.Q. Army Air Forces being relieved of details of execution and being left free to determine overall policy ; (*b*) the creation of a more cohesive organization within H.Q. ; and (*c*) the delegation of greater responsibility to field commanders.

In 1944 a Continental Air Forces Headquarters was established at Camp Springs, Va. The new organization is responsible for the air defence of the United States. It takes over the operational functions of the A.A.F. H.Q. in the War Department, the latter continuing to handle high-level policies and planning.

The chart overleaf outlines the train of organization of the Army Air Forces as it was at the closing stages of the war and shows the primary interest, supervision and administrative channels of communication between the Assistant Chiefs of Staff and various Commands and Air Forces.

ORGANIZATION

The War Department, Washington, D.C.
Secretary of War : Robert L. Patterson.
Chief of the General Staff : General of the Army Dwight W. Eisenhower.
Air Forces, Commanding General : General of the Army H. H. Arnold (to be succeeded in 1946 by General Carl Spaatz).

The Commanding General, Army Air Forces, is responsible for the fulfilment of the mission of the Air Forces under policies prescribed by the Chief of the General Staff.

This Mission is set forth by the War Department as follows : "The mission of the Army Air Forces is to procure and maintain equipment peculiar to the Army Air Forces and to provide air force units properly organized, trained and equipped for combat operations."

The Commanding General serves as a member of the Joint U.S. Chiefs of Staff and Combined Chiefs of Staff, is chairman of the Joint Aircraft Committee and participates in formulating and executing policies and plans concerning the strategic conduct of the war, programme of requirements, allocations of munitions resources, and requirements for overseas transportation based on approved strategic policy and priority.

While the overall policies of the Army Air Forces are determined by the Commanding General, the Assistant Chiefs of the Air Staff translate them into needs in terms of men and machines. They direct acquisition of the man power and creation of the machines and allocate them for training and for combat use.

The Assistant Chief of the Air Staff, Personnel, supervises the personnel programme of the Army Air Forces, including procurement, classification and assignment of individuals, both military and civilian.

The Assistant Chief of the Air Staff, Intelligence, is responsible for the collection and dissemination of intelligence information.

The Assistant Chief of the Air Staff, Operations, Commitments and Requirements, determines the tactics and technique of aerial warfare. He determines requirements for trained personnel and for aircraft, equipment and supplies, allocates the finished products of the training and service requirement for operational training as fighting teams, and makes them available to the theatres of operations.

The Assistant Chief of the Air Staff, Material, Maintenance and Distribution, supervises the material procurement and logistical programme of the Air Forces, including research, experimentation, development and procurement of aircraft, equipment and supplies and their maintenance and distribution.

The Assistant Chief of the Air Staff, Plans, represents the Commanding General in the formulation of strategic plans by the staff planning agencies of the United States and its Allies.

The Air Forces outside the continental Circuits of the United States are under the technical supervision of the Commanding General, Army Air Forces, and under the administrative and tactical jurisdiction of the Commander of the theatre or task force to which they are assigned. The four metropolitan Air Forces are now mainly responsible for operational training and are under the direct supervision of the Commanding General, Army Air Forces, through the Assistant Chief of the Air Staff, Training.

THE AIR FORCES

At the end of the war with Japan there were sixteen Air Forces, each theoretically composed of Fighter, Bomber, Air Support and Air Service Commands. The Fighter and Bomber Commands, as their names imply, were made up of fighters and medium and heavy bomber units respectively. The Fighter Commands were responsible for the co-ordination of all types of fighter aircraft, anti-aircraft batteries, balloon-barrages and other air defence elements ranging from searchlights to air-raid warning systems.

The Air Support Commands provided air support for the ground forces of the Army, and operated Fighters, Light and Medium Bombers and Communication aircraft.

Each Air Force had its separate command and staff. The combatant Commands of each Air Force were divided into Divisions, comprising from three to five Wings, the Wing, which generally corresponds to an Army Brigade, being the basic tactical unit. Each Wing was further sub-divided into three Groups, a Group consisting of three to four squadrons of the same category, all based on one airfield. The Group, which generally corresponds to a Regiment, is the basic operational unit. A Squadron may consist of from twelve to twenty-four aircraft according to type. Squadrons are further divided for purposes of flight control into Flights (six aircraft) and Elements (three aircraft).

HOME COMMANDS

There are four Air Forces in the United States. These Air Forces were originally intended for metropolitan defence but after 1942 they became responsible mainly for the operational training of combat groups and units and replacement crews for service in overseas Air Forces.

1st Air Force. H.Q. : Mitchel Field, Long Island, N.Y.
2nd Air Force. H.Q. : Fort George Wright, Spokane, Wash.
3rd Air Force. H.Q. : National Guard Armoury, Tampa, Fla.
4th Air Force. H.Q. : Presidio, San Francisco, Cal.

OVERSEAS COMMANDS

Overseas Air Forces operated in the United Kingdom, Iceland, North and West Africa, Sicily and Italy, the Middle East, India, China, Australia, New Zealand, the Southern Pacific Islands, Hawaii, Alaska, the Caribbean Area, Panama, and at bases outside the Canal Zone and along the Atlantic coast outside the territorial limits of the United States from Newfoundland to the West Indies.

The location of the overseas Air Forces at the end of the war were as follow :—

5th Air Force, Far East Air Force, Okinawa.
First based in Australia. Later incorporated in the U.S. Far East Air Force.

6th Air Force, Caribbean.
Responsible for the defence of the Panama Canal and the Caribbean area.

7th Air Force, Far East Air Force, Okinawa.
Originally based in the Philippines.

8th Air Force, Strategic Air Force, Okinawa.
Originally formed in the British Isles for service in the European

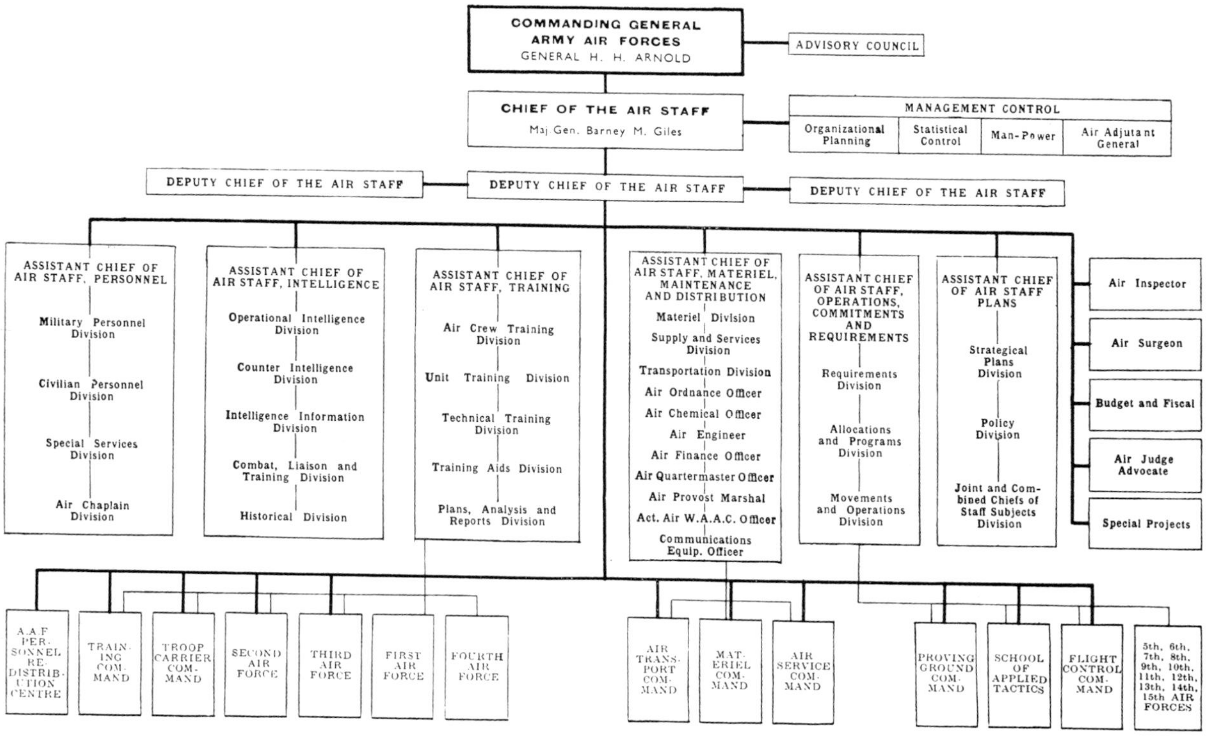
COMMANDING GENERAL
ARMY AIR FORCES
GENERAL H. H. ARNOLD
ADVISORY COUNCIL
CHIEF OF THE AIR STAFF
Maj Gen. Barney M. Giles
MANAGEMENT CONTROL
Organizational Planning
Statistical Control
Man-Power
Air Adjutant General
DEPUTY CHIEF OF THE AIR STAFF
DEPUTY CHIEF OF THE AIR STAFF
DEPUTY CHIEF OF THE AIR STAFF
ASSISTANT CHIEF OF AIR STAFF, PERSONNEL
Military Personnel Division
Civilian Personnel Division
Special Services Division
Air Chaplain Division
ASSISTANT CHIEF OF AIR STAFF, INTELLIGENCE
Operational Intelligence Division
Counter Intelligence Division
Intelligence Information Division
Combat, Liaison and Training Division
Historical Division
ASSISTANT CHIEF OF AIR STAFF, TRAINING
Air Crew Training Division
Unit Training Division
Technical Training Division
Training Aids Division
Plans, Analysis and Reports Division
ASSISTANT CHIEF OF AIR STAFF, MATERIEL, MAINTENANCE AND DISTRIBUTION
Materiel Division
Supply and Services Division
Transportation Division
Air Ordnance Officer
Air Chemical Officer
Air Engineer
Air Finance Officer
Air Quartermaster Officer
Air Provost Marshal
Act. Air W.A.A.C. Officer
Communications Equip. Officer
ASSISTANT CHIEF OF AIR STAFF, OPERATIONS, COMMITMENTS AND REQUIREMENTS
Requirements Division
Allocations and Programs Division
Movements and Operations Division
ASSISTANT CHIEF OF AIR STAFF PLANS
Strategical Plans Division
Policy Division
Joint and Combined Chiefs of Staff Subjects Division
Air Inspector
Air Surgeon
Budget and Fiscal
Air Judge Advocate
Special Projects
A.A.F. PERSONNEL REDISTRIBUTION CENTRE
TRAINING COMMAND
TROOP CARRIER COMMAND
SECOND AIR FORCE
THIRD AIR FORCE
FIRST AIR FORCE
FOURTH AIR FORCE
AIR TRANSPORT COMMAND
MATERIEL COMMAND
AIR SERVICE COMMAND
PROVING GROUND COMMAND
SCHOOL OF APPLIED TACTICS
FLIGHT CONTROL COMMAND
5th, 6th, 7th, 8th, 9th, 10th, 11th, 12th, 13th, 14th, 15th AIR FORCES

The Train of Organization of the U.S. Army Air Forces as it existed in the last year of the war.

Theatre. On the conclusion of the European war, was transferred to the Pacific and re-equipped with B-29 Superfortresses to form part of the Strategic Air Force to bomb Japan.

9th Air Force.
Originally served in the Mediterranean and later in the British Isles and Europe. Was in process of transference to the Pacific on the conclusion of the war. Certain units remained in Germany as part of the forces of occupation.

10th Air Force, China.
Originally formed part of the Allied South-East Asia Command.

11th Air Force, Alaska.
A component of the U.S. Navy North Pacific Command.

12th Air Force.
Formed part of the Mediterranean Allied Air Command in Italy.

13th Air Force, Far East Air Force, Philippines.
Originally served in the Southern Pacific area. Later incorporated in the Far East Air Force.

14th Air Force, China.
Constituted from the former China Air Task Force. Later formed part of the China Theatre Command.

15th Air Force.
Formed in 1943 as part of the U.S. Strategic Bombing Force in Europe to bomb Germany from Italian bases in collaboration with the 8th Air Force (also forming part of the Strategic Bombing Force), which did likewise from British bases.

20th Air Force, Strategic Air Force, Marianas.
Formed to bomb Japan from Indian and, later, Pacific island bases. The first Air Force to be equipped with the B-29 Superfortress.

MATERIEL, MAINTENANCE AND DISTRIBUTION

The Army Air Forces, unlike the Ground Forces, retain their own organizations for supply, maintenance and distribution of equipment. These activities, previously administered by the now-defunct Air Corps, are now divided among the following Commands which report direct to the Commanding General of the Air Forces through the Assistant Chief of Staff, Materiel, Maintenance and Distribution.

Materiel Command. H.Q.: Wright Field, Dayton, Ohio.

Materiel Command is responsible for the conception, experimental development, testing and the ordering, inspection and supervision of production of all aircraft, aero-engines, accessories and equipment used by the Air Forces.

The Command has four separate operating units, Engineering Division, Procurement Division, Production Division and Inspection Division.

The Engineering Division is responsible for research, development and testing of all aeronautical equipment. It develops prototype equipment to the point where it is ready for quantity production. It is composed of the following laboratories and sections :—Aircraft, Power-plant, Equipment, Materials, Propeller, Aero-medical research, Technical Data, Armament, Photography, Aircraft Radio, Engineering Workshops and a Flight Section.

The Procurement Division is responsible for the purchase of all equipment and material supplies for the Air Forces. It includes six Procurement Districts—Eastern, South-eastern, Central, Midcentral, Midwestern and Western, with district headquarters at New York City, N.Y., Atlantic, Ga., Detroit, Mich., Chicago, Ill., Kansas City, Mo., and Los Angeles, Cal., respectively.

The Production Division is responsible for industrial planning and the engineering administration of all contracts for the purchase and manufacture of production aircraft.

Air Service Command. H.Q. Patterson Field, Dayton, Ohio.

The Air Service Command is responsible for furnishing supplies, for all A.A.F. aircraft throughout the World ; for the repair, overhaul and rebuilding of all aircraft at home and overseas ; for the training of personnel for the supply and maintenance branches ; for the preparation for shipment overseas of all American and Lend-Lease aircraft ; and the final inspection of all American aircraft flown overseas. For Lend-Lease aircraft flown to Central and South American countries the Command furnishes supplies, routes and other assistance for the flight from the U.S.A. to destination.

The United States is divided into eleven areas, each designated an area Air Service Command. In each area are located one main depot and a number of sub-depots and specialised depots. A similar organization exists in each overseas theatre of war under the technical control of the Air Service Command. The Command area main depots within the United States are situated at Fairfield, Ohio ; Rome, N.Y. ; Middletown, Pa. ; Mobile, Ala. ; Macon, Ga. ; San Antonio, Tex ; Oklahoma City, Okla. ; Ogden, Utah ; Sacramento, Cal. ; San Bernardino, Cal. ; and Spokane, Wash. The domestic sub-depots and specialised depots total over 300.

The Air Service Command operates the 39th Air Freight Wing, which handles all Command freight, as well as air shipments for all War Department agencies, flown within the United States by Air Transport Command. The 39th Wing has 117 air freight terminals distributed throughout the United States.

Air Transport Command. H.Q.: Gravelly Point, Va.

Air Transport Command was formed on July 1, 1942, to take over duties formerly performed by the Ferrying Command : the Air Division of the Transportation Service, Services of Supply ; and the Cargo Division, Air Service Command. The Command now comprises a domestic Ferrying Division and nine foreign operating Divisions, North Atlantic, Caribbean, South Atlantic, Pacific, North Africa, Central Africa, Alaskan, European and India-China.

Air Transport Command is responsible for the ferrying of all aircraft to destinations throughout the World ; the transport by air of personnel, material and mail for all Army agencies ; and the control, operation and maintenance of establishments and facilities on air routes outside the United States which are or which may be the responsibility of the Commanding General, Army Air Forces.

By the end of 1944 Air Transport Command was flying over 50,000,000 miles a month, most of the mileage being compiled in oversea flights and over foreign lands. Roughly half the flying entailed the ferrying of military aircraft, and half in transport service. The route mileage amounted to approximately 160,000. The strength of the Command was 150,000 officers and men.

OPERATIONS, COMMITMENTS AND REQUIREMENTS

The Assistant Chief of the Air Staff, Operations, Commitments and Requirements, has supervision of the Proving Ground Command, the School of Applied Tactics and Flight Control Command, as well as all the operational Air Forces, except the First and Fourth.

Proving Ground Command. H.Q.: Eglin Field, Fla.

Proving Ground Command is responsible for testing aircraft and equipment under every combat condition to prove their fitness for war. It also furnishes to the Materiel and Air Service Commands any necessary aid, services and facilities to complete engineering and development tests. There are five Proof Sections ; Bombing, Armament, Radio, Tactical and Miscellaneous.

The Bombing Section test bomb-sights, all types of bombs, bomb-fuses, bombing equipment in different types of aircraft, bombing attack techniques, etc.

The Armament Section specialises in tests of machine-guns, cannon, ammunition, gun-sights, gun lubricants, turrets, fire-control systems, gun-firing, bullet-proof fuel tanks, etc.

The Radio Section conducts tests of radio apparatus and accessories, electrically-controlled bombing equipment and turrets, radio-controlled aircraft, etc.

The Tactical Section tests the tactical suitability of specific aircraft types and demonstrates tactical techniques for using characteristics of specific aircraft types with maximum effectiveness.

The Miscellaneous Section covers the testing of all other combat equipment, such as landing-mats, portable runways, life-saving equipment, camouflage, photographic equipment, oxygen suits, fuel and oil containers, etc.

The Command also administers an Arctic, Desert and Tropical Information Centre, which investigates operational problems under the widest climatic conditions.

The Headquarters at Eglin Field has seven satellite fields, and there are Proving Ground Detachments at Aberdeen, Md., Edgewood, Ind., Hope, Ark. and Madison, Ind.

Flight-Control Command.

Flight Control Command was formed in March, 1943, by the merging of the functions of the former Directorate of Air Traffic and Safety, the Army Air Forces Communications Services and the Army Air Forces Weather Services. Its functions are to teach self-preservation under six headings : flight control, weather, communications, air/sea-rescue, flying safety and safety education.

School of Applied Tactics. H.Q.: Orlando, Fla.

The functions of the School of Applied Tactics are to train Air Force cadres, the personnel framework around which all new combat groups are formed ; to test and develop new techniques in fighter, bomber and air support tactics.

The School is virtually a complete Air Force in miniature and its operational area covers an 8,000 square mile "theatre" on the Florida peninsula and over the Gulf of Mexico.

TRAINING

The Assistant Chief of the Air Staff, Training, supervises the Flying Training Command, Troop Carrier Command and the 2nd and 3rd Air Forces. This office also provides technical supervision of the operational training of the 1st and 4th Air Forces.

Training Command. H.Q.: Forth Worth, Texas.

In 1943 the former separate Flying Training and Technical Training Commands were combined to form a unified Training Command, in order to achieve maximum economy of operation, most efficient use of personnel, and maximum co-ordination of training schedules and use of training facilities.

For Flight Training there are three Training Commands, each made up of four Training Wings. Each Wing, commanded by a general officer, administers all Primary, Basic and Advanced Training Schools devoted to the training of pilots, bombardiers, navigators, observers and air-gunners in its area.

Eastern Flying Training Command. H.Q.: Maxwell Field, Ala.

Central Flying Training Command. H.Q.: Randolph Field, Texas.

Western Flying Training Command. H.Q.: Santa Ana, Cal.

The technical training of mechanics and ground personnel is administered through three Technical Training Commands, each of which administers all schools, camps, posts and detachments within its area. Each of the main activities within the Technical Training Commands is commanded by the Brigadier-General. The three Commands are :—

Western Technical Training Command. H.Q.: Denver, Colo.

Central Technical Training Command. H.Q.: St. Louis, Mo.

Eastern Technical Training Command. H.Q.: Greensboro, N.C.

Operational training is undertaken in the four Air Forces based in the United States. The 2nd Air Force trains heavy bombardment units and replacement crews and the 3rd Air Force trains medium, light and dive bombardment units and replacement crews.

Troop-Carrier Command. H.Q.: Stout Field, Indianapolis, Ind.

Officer Commanding : Brig.-General F. S. Borum.

This Command was formed in the Summer of 1942 to be responsible for the training of troop-carrier units which provide for the air movement of air landing troops and equipment, including glider-borne and parachute troops and equipment, and the evacuation by air of sick and wounded personnel.

The Troop-Carrier Command provides aircraft and pilots that carry all airborne troops. It also flies the gliders loaned to the Ground Forces by the Army Air Forces to transport troops.

The training of Army Air Forces officers in glider operations was initiated in June, 1941. Students are trained on light powered aircraft before undergoing glider training.

Pilot Training Centre is at South Plains Army Flying School, Lubbock, Texas. In April, 1943 elementary and basic glider training was temporarily suspended in order to concentrate on operational and combat training.

The Army Ground Forces Airborne Command embraces all parachute and recognized airborne units, and is responsible for the formulation and development of tactical and training doctrine and the development and standardization of material and equipment.

The Ground Forces fly no aircraft of their own except the small liaison types operated by the artillery for spotting or for short-range liaison work. Field Artillery liaison pilot-observers undergo a ten weeks' course at an Air Force Primary training school, followed by five weeks of instruction at the Field Artillery School at Fort Sill, Okla., after which they become liaison pilots.

NAVAL AVIATION

United States Naval Aviation is part of the Naval Organization and is under the direction of the Secretary of the Navy.

ADMINISTRATION

The Navy Department, Washington, D.C.

Secretary of the Navy : James V. Forrestal.

Assistant Secretary of the Navy for Air : Artemus L. Gates.

Chief of Naval Operations : Fleet Admiral Chester W. Nimitz.

Vice-Chief of Naval Operations : Vice-Admiral Dewitt C. Ramsey.

Deputy Chief of Naval Operations for Air : Vice-Admiral Arthur W. Radford.

The function of the office of the Assistant Secretary of the Navy for Air is the supervision of naval aeronautics and the co-ordination of its activities with other Government agencies. It also acts as liaison between the Bureau of Aeronautics and the aircraft manufacturers and handles details of aircraft procurement.

The Deputy Chief of Naval operations for Air correlates and co-ordinates all military aspects of Naval Aviation within the Navy Department.

The Fleet Air Force Commanders assume a certain authority over the aircraft-carrier divisions of the Fleets and serve as principal air advisers to the Commanders-in-Chief.

Bureau of Aeronautics, Washington, D.C.

Chief of the Bureau : Rear Admiral Harold B. Sallada.

The Bureau of Aeronautics is responsible for the design, procurement and upkeep of naval aircraft and aircraft equipment, and the training of naval air personnel.

ORGANIZATION

The Aircraft Squadron is the standard administrative and tactical unit in all naval operations. Carrier-based squadrons comprise eighteen aircraft, sub-divided into two divisions of nine aircraft each. Patrol squadrons comprise six or twelve aircraft but squadrons operating from battleships and cruisers vary in their complement. Three sections of three aircraft form an Observation Squadron attached to each Battleship Division of three ships. Four cruisers usually form a Division and each cruiser carries a section of four aircraft, the four sections forming a Cruiser Scouting Squadron.

NAVAL AIR STATIONS

On the entry of the United States in the War there were thirty-four naval operational, training, overhaul, test and airship bases in commission in continental United States, the West Indies, the Pacific and Alaska. There were also sixteen Naval Reserve Aviation Bases.

During the fiscal year 1942-43 twenty-three new shore establishments were commissioned, twenty-one naval air stations—eighteen for heavier-than-air and three for lighter-than-aircraft—and two Naval Reserve Aviation Bases. There were to be 134 naval air stations in operation in 1945.

The Naval Reserve Aviation Bases are used as centres for elimination training of candidates seeking enrolment as aviation cadets and to give successful candidates the necessary preparatory flight training to qualify them for further instruction at the Naval Air Training Centres at Pensacola, Jacksonville, Miami, and Corpus Christi.

TRAINING

The personnel of U.S. Naval Aviation is composed of (1) regular Naval officers who, on completion of training are designated as Naval Aviators ; (2) enlisted men of the regular Navy who receive designations as Naval Aviation Pilots ; and (3) Naval Aviation Cadets who, upon graduation, are designated as Naval Aviators and receive commissions as Ensigns in the Naval Reserve.

To train pilots under the War programme, the Navy has retained its old training framework, but has expanded it greatly. The facilities of four large universities, one each in the East, the West, the Midwest and the South, have been leased for the duration of the War. At these universities, Naval pilot candidates undergo a rigorous three-months' toughening process covering four phases :—(a) proper physical conditioning ; (b) indoctrination of naval history and customs ; (c) military drill and seamanship ; and (d) training in communications, ordnance and other specialities.

After the preliminary three-months' course candidates proceed to one of the nineteen Naval Reserve elimination centres for a 30-day primary flight training course, after which successful candidates move on to one of the four Naval advanced training bases at Pensacola, Jacksonville, Miami, Fla., and Corpus Christi, Tex., for a six-months' advanced flying training course. During the advanced training Aviation Cadets in addition to becoming pilots receive instruction in engine construction, radio, celestial and dead reckoning navigation, gunnery, warfare tactics and aerodynamics.

On the successful completion of this course the Aviation Cadets are commissioned as Ensigns in the Naval Reserve, and pilots are selected for duty in one of the three specialised branches of naval aviation—patrol-plane (flying-boat), catapult seaplane (operating from cruisers and battleships) and carrier-type landplane—the pilots finally proceeding to one of the twelve operational training bases for tactical experience in the latest type of naval aircraft, prior to posting to active service duties.

NAVAL AIR TRANSPORT

A Naval Air Transport Service was authorised on December 12, 1941, as a section of the Naval Transportation Service, a division of the Office of the Chief of Naval Operations. Early in 1942 it was transferred, together with all other aviation activities, to a newly-formed Aviation Division of the Office of the Chief of Naval Operations.

The Naval Transport Service began operations in February, 1942, and one year after authorisation the Service was operating over 40,000 route-miles to Australia, Alaska, the Aleutians, Newfoundland, Brazil, throughout the Caribbean area and all over continental United States.

The Service operates in three main divisions; Atlantic, West Coast and Pacific.

The Atlantic Command (H.Q.: Patuxent River, Md.) consists of squadrons serving the Atlantic coasts of North, Central and South America, and extending across the Atlantic to Europe and Africa.

The West Coast Command (H.Q.: Alameda, Cal.) operates schedules for the trans-continental service and also serves Western Canada and Alaska.

The Pacific Command (H.Q.: Pearl Harbour, T.H.) operates throughout the Pacific Ocean area.

Pan-American Airways and American Export Airlines supplement the work of the Naval Air Transport Service by operating under contract to the U.S. Navy, air-transport services to naval establishments and fleet units in the War area.

The types of naval transport aircraft used include the Martin PBM-3R Mariner, Consolidated PB2Y-3R Coronado, Douglas R4D and R5D, Lockheed R50, etc.

U.S. MARINE CORPS AVIATION

Headquarters, U.S. Marine Corps, Washington, D.C.

Director of Marine Corps Aviation: Brigadier-General Field Harris.

Marine Corps Aviation is an integral part of Naval Aviation and its mission is to furnish the Air Forces necessary to the Fleet Marine Force, Carrier Operations with the Fleet and for expeditionary duty, marine advanced base operations and the defence of naval bases outside the continental United States which are defended on shore by the Marines. Its officers are either detailed to aviation duty from permanent line officers of the Corps or are recruited as aviation cadets and appointed to the Marine Corps Reserve. Its enlisted men are marines specially trained for aviation duty. A number of enlisted men are selected each year for flight training.

The Marine Corps also includes Parachute battalions and Airborne troops and all parachute training and air training in both powered aircraft and gliders is undertaken by Marine Corps Aviation. All troop-carrying gliders used by the Marines are amphibians, capable of operating either on land or water.

The Marine Corps is also responsible for the organization and training of barrage balloon units for the protection of Navy and Marine shore establishments.

The administration, training and operations of Marine Corps Aviation are directed by the Director of Aviation Headquarters, U.S. Marine Corps, who is also attached to the Bureau of Aeronautics and whose office also constitutes a division of Headquarters, U.S. Marine Corps.

The following are the principal Marine Air Commands:—

1st Marine Aircraft Wing. Philippine Islands.
2nd Marine Aircraft Wing. Central Pacific.
4th Marine Aircraft Wing. Central Pacific.
Marine Fleet Air. West Coast.
9th Marine Aircraft Wing. East Coast.

The air training of Marine Corps aviation personnel has been co-ordinated with Naval air training since July 1, 1941. Qualified personnel recruited by the Marine Corps now pass through the prescribed course for naval aviation cadets at Pensacola and on completion of the course may apply for appointment as Second Lieutenants, U.S. Marine Corps Reserve.

All aviation material used in Marine aviation is procured by the Navy. In general the same types of aircraft are used. Tactical squadrons have a similar organization. Radio, ordnance equipment and motor transport are identical to those of the Navy.

Marine aviation is responsible for the operation, maintenance and overhaul of its aircraft, aero-engines and equipment and there are two large Marine overhaul bases, one on the East coast and one on the West coast.

LIGHTER-THAN-AIR BRANCH

The Airship Branch of the U.S. Navy has shared in the general expansion of Naval Aviation. A widespread network of major and auxiliary bases has been established, including six new major bases for the East Coast and Gulf of Mexico area, three for the Pacific Coast and others for undisclosed points outside the continental limits of the United States. A greatly augmented training programme was initiated at the Lakehurst base and a second school was established at Moffet Field, Sunnyvale, Cal.

Purchase of 48 non-rigid airships was authorised in June, 1940. Following on the successful demonstration of the value of the airship in anti-submarine patrol in areas where there is no likelihood of attack by enemy aircraft, a Bill was passed on June 8, 1942, which authorised the Navy to build or acquire 200 lighter-than-aircraft of the G, K and M non-rigid types for training, patrol and anti-submarine duties.

AIRCRAFT-CARRIERS

The first few months of hostilities revealed the importance of air striking power in naval warfare and the U.S. Navy took immediate steps to augment its aircraft-carrier fleet.

To make up for the deficiency in the number of regular carriers in commission the U.S. Navy had, prior to the entry of the United States into the War, ordered the conversion of an undisclosed number of commercial vessels into Escort Carriers. *Long Island*, the first example of this type of carrier, was commissioned in June, 1941. Since then large numbers of Escort Carriers have been completed, both by conversion and by new construction.

In October, 1943, the Secretary of the Navy announced that three 45,000-ton aircraft-carriers were to be built. Two more

The U.S.S. Lexington, a Fleet Carrier of the "Essex" Class of 27,000 tons displacement and with accommodation for 80 aircraft.

The U.S.S. Cabot, a Light Aircraft Carrier of the "Independence" Class. Ships of this class were originally laid down as 10,000-ton cruisers.

The U.S.S. Ranger, the first American ship to be built from the keel up as an aircraft-carrier. She was commissioned in June, 1934.

The Escort Carrier Charger, a conversion from a merchant hull. Large numbers of this type of ship were built for both the U.S. and British Navies.

have since been authorised. The new vessels will be capable of carrying twin-engined bombers and in armament and armour they will be better protected than any other carriers. Two were laid down in October, 1943, the third early in 1944, and two more in 1945. The first two were launched early in 1945.

A proportion of the 10,000-ton cruisers of the *Cleveland* Class have been completed as aircraft-carriers of the *Independence* class.

AIRCRAFT CARRIERS, LARGE (CVB).

Midway, Franklin D. Roosevelt, and three others.
This new class includes the three 45,000-ton aircraft-carriers authorised in 1943 and laid down in 1943-44, and two additional ships to be laid down in 1945. They will carry more than 80 twin-engined aircraft and will have a complement of 3,000. *Midway* was launched on March 20, 1945.

AIRCRAFT CARRIERS (CV).

Saratoga. Originally laid down as a battle-cruiser in 1921 but under the Washington Treaty re-designed as an aircraft-carrier. Ordered as such on October 30, 1922, launched on April 7, 1925, and first commissioned on November 6, 1927. Sister-ship *Lexington* lost in the Battle of the Coral Sea, May 8, 1942.

Displacement : 33,000 tons. Length overall : 888 ft. Beam : 105.5 ft. Speed : 33.9 knots. Complement : 1,900. Accommodates 83 aircraft.

Ranger. The first ship in the U.S. Navy to be built from the keel up as an aircraft-carrier. Authorised on February 15, 1929, laid down on September 26, 1931, launched on February 25, 1933, and first commissioned on June 4, 1934.

Displacement : 14,500 tons. Length overall : 769 ft. Beam : 80 ft. Speed : 29.5 knots. Complement : 1,800. Accommodates 84 aircraft.

Enterprise. Authorised on June 16, 1933, laid-down on July 16, 1934, launched on October 3, 1936, and first commissioned on May 12, 1938. Sister-ships *Yorktown* lost in Battle of Midway Island, June 7, 1942, and *Hornet* lost in Battle of Santa Cruz Island, October 26, 1942.

Displacement : 19,900 tons. Overall length : 810 ft. Beam 83.25 ft. Speed : 34 knots. Complement : 2,072. Accommodates 81 aircraft.

Essex, Yorktown, Intrepid, Hornet, Franklin, Hancock, Randolph, Lexington, Bunker Hill, Wasp, Ticonderoga, Shangri-La, Bennington, Tarawa, Bonhomme Richard, Kearsage, Oriskany, Boxer, Antietam and others First eleven ordered in 1940, and a further thirteen authorised in 1942. Ten in commission at the end of 1944.

Displacement : 27,000 tons. Overall length : approx. 800 ft. Speed : 30 knots. Accommodates 80 aircraft.

AIRCRAFT CARRIERS, LIGHT (CVL).

Independence, Belleau Wood, Cowpens, Monterey, Cabot, Langley, Bataan, San Jacinto. Originally units of the *Cleveland* 10,000-ton cruiser class but redesigned and renamed. *Princetown* lost in the Battle of the Philippine Sea, October 22-27, 1944.

Displacement : 10,000 tons (as cruiser). Overall length : 600 ft. Beam : 61.5 ft. Complement : 1,500. Accommodates 60 aircraft.

AIRCRAFT CARRIERS, ESCORT (CVE).

Altamaha, Barnes, Bogue, Breton, Card, Charger, Copahee, Core, Croatan, Long Island, Nassau, Prince William and others. These are conversions from C-3 merchant hulls. By mid-1944 fifty-one had been completed, thirty-eight of which were transferred to the Royal Navy. *Block Island* torpedoed in the Atlantic, May, 1944.

Displacement : 14,000 tons. Overall length : 500 ft. Accommodates 20 aircraft.

Chenango, Sangamon, Santee, Suwanee. Converted from *Cimarron* class twin-screw Fleet oilers. Slightly longer and faster than the *Altamaha* class. Greater operating range. Four completed in 1944 and more being built.

Admiralty Islands, Alava Bay, Alazon Bay, Algiers, Attu, Bougainville, Bucareli Bay, Cape Esperence, Cape Gloucester, Casablanca, Anzio, Chapin Bay, Corregidor, Didrickson Bay, Dolomi Bay, Fanshaw Bay, Frosty Bay, Gilbert Islands, Guadalcanal, Hoggatt Bay, Kadashan Bay, Kalinin Bay, Kasaan Bay, Kitkun Bay, Kwajalein, Macassar Strait, Makin Island, Manila Bay, Marcus Island, Matanikou, Mission Bay, Natoma Bay, Nehentor Bay, Ommaney Bay, Oran, Petrof Bay, Rudyerd Bay, St. Andrews Bay, Saginaw Bay, Salamaua, Savo Island, Sergent Island, Shamrock Bay, Shipley Bay, Siboney, Sitkoh Bay, Steamer Bay, Solomons, Takanis Bay, Thetis Bay, Totem Bay, Tripoli, Tulagi, White Plains, Willopa Bay, Windham Bay, Vella Gulf. Built by Henry Kaiser from the keel up as light aircraft-carriers. About the same length as the *Altamaha* class but 1,500 tons lighter, of finer lines and slightly faster. Construction began in May, 1942, and by July, 1944, fifty had been built. *Liscombe Bay* torpedoed off Makin Island, November 24, 1943. *Gambier Bay* and *St. Lo* lost in the Battle of the Philippine Sea, October 22-27, 1944.

SEAPLANE TENDERS, LARGE (AV).

Curtiss, Albemarle, Currituck, Norton Sound, Pine Island, Puget Sound and **Salisbury Sound.** First tenders built as such. Serve as mobile bases for two or more patrol squadrons. All fitted as flagships.

Standard displacement : 8,625 tons. Length : over 500 ft. Armament : 4—5 in. No further details available.

Tangier, Pocomoke, Chandeleur, Cumberland Sound, Hamlin and **St. George.** Former Maritime Commission vessels.

Displacement : 7,500 tons. Length overall : 49 ft. Beam : 69 ft. 6 in. Mean draught : 27 ft. 3 in. Shaft horse power : 8,500. Speed : 16.5 kts.

The Large Seaplane Tender Currituck. This type of vessel serves as a mobile base for one or more flying-boat Squadrons.

The Training Carrier Wolverine, converted from a Great Lakes side-wheel pleasure steamer. She was commissioned in August, 1942.

Wright. Begun as transport and completed as seaplane tender in 1921.

Displacement : 8,675 tons. Length overall : 448 ft. Beam : 58 ft. 3 in. Mean draught : 19 ft. 2 in. Shaft horse-power : 6,000. Speed : 15 kts. Armament : 2—5 in., 2—3 in. A.A. Complement : 300. Fitted as flagship.

SEAPLANE TENDERS, SMALL (AVP).

Barnegat, Biscayne, Casco, Mackinac, Humbolt, Matagorda, Chincoteague, Absecon, Coos Bay, Half Moon, Mobjack, Oyster Bay, Rockaway, San Pablo, Unimak, Yakutat, Behring Strait, Barataria, Onslow, Orcha, Rehoboth, San Carlos, Shelikof, Suisun, Timblier and **Valcour.**

Displacement : 1,695 tons. Armament : 4-5 in., etc. Machinery : Diesel. Speed : 20 knots. No further details.

Childs, Williamson, George E. Badger, Clemson, Goldsborough, Hulbert, William B. Preston, Belknap, Osmond Ingram, Ballard, Thornton, Gillis, Greene and **McFarland.** Former flush-deck destroyers (1919-20) converted into seaplane tenders in 1938-40. Forward boilers and two stacks, two 4 in. guns and all torpedo-tubes removed. A.A. guns and large refuelling tanks installed.

Displacement : 1,190 tons. Length overall : 314 ft. 4 in. Beam : 30 ft. 8 in. Mean draught : 9 ft. 3 in. Complement : 122.

Lapwing, Heron, Thrush, Avocet, Teal, Pelican, Swan, Gannet and **Sandpiper.** Ex-minesweepers, originally commissioned in 1918-19. More recently have been classed as Seaplane Tenders (Small).

Displacement : 840 tons. Length overall : 187 ft. 10 in. Beam : 35 ft. 8 in. Mean draught : 8 ft. 10 in. Shaft horsepower : 1,400. Speed : 14 kts. Complement : 72.

AVIATION REPAIR VESSELS (ARV(A) and ARV(E)).

Designed to service aircraft and aero-engines at sea as part of the Fleet Train. Built on tank landing ship hulls and fitted with all equipment for aircraft and engine repair, including test-stands. Do not accompany carriers, but intended to anchor near air bases or air-strips in forward operational areas.

TRAINING AIRCRAFT CARRIERS.

Wolverine. Formerly the *Seeandbee*, a large passenger ship operating between Cleveland and Buffalo on Lake Erie. Converted into a training carrier with overall flying deck and superstructure on starboard side. Operates on the Great Lakes.

Sable. Formerly the *Greater Buffalo*, a Great Lakes passenger vessel and one of the largest fresh-water vessels in existence. Conversion similar to that of *Wolverine*. Both ships have paddle-wheel propulsion and neither has accommodation for aircraft as all used for training are shore-based.

THE U.S. COAST GUARD

The U.S. Coast Guard constitutes a part of the military forces of the United States, operating under the Treasury in time of peace and the Navy in war. Its principal peacetime duties are the enforcement of maritime and customs laws, operation of aids to navigation, protection of fisheries, iceberg patrol, the saving of life at sea and the rendering of assistance to ships in distress.

The Coast Guard was transferred from the Treasury Department to Naval jurisdiction by Presidential Decree on November 1, 1941.

All Coast Guard Stations and aviation bases are now under the jurisdiction of the U.S. Navy Sea Frontier Command, which embraces the Eastern, Western and Gulf Coasts. Four types of War operations are undertaken : submarine patrol, convoy protection, search and rescue.

Coast Guard pilots receive their training at the Naval Air Station at Pensacola, Fla., after having had at least three years' service at sea as commissioned officers.

Headquarters, U.S. Coast Guard:—Washington, D.C.
Commandant : Rear Admiral R. R. Waesche, U.S.C.G.
Assistant Commandant (Chief Operations Officer) : Rear Admiral L. C. Covell, U.S.C.G.
Chief Aviation Operations Officer : Commander S. C. Linholm, U.S.C.G.

Coast Guard Air Stations
Salem, Mass. (Winter Island). Seaplanes only.
New York, N.Y. (Floyd Bennett Field). Seaplanes and landplanes.
Elizabeth City, N.C. (Davis Bay, Pasquotank River). Seaplanes and landplanes.
Miami, Fla. (Dinner Key). Seaplanes only.
St. Petersburg, Fla. (Albert Whitted Field). Seaplanes and landplanes.
Biloxi, Miss. (Cadet Point). Seaplanes only.
San Diego, Cal. (Lindbergh Field). Seaplanes and landplanes.
San Francisco, Cal. (San Francisco Municipal Field). Seaplanes and landplanes.
Port Angeles, Wash. (Ediz Hook). Seaplanes and landplanes.
There are air patrol detachments at Cape May, N.J., Traverse City, Mich., and El Paso, Texas.

Coast Guard Equipment
Flying-boats :—Hall PH-2, PH-3, Consolidated PBY-5, Martin PBM-3.
Seaplane :—Vought OS2U-3.
Amphibians :—Douglas RD-4, Grumman JF-2, JRF-2, J4F-1.
Landplanes :—Curtiss SOC-4, Lockheed R3O-1, R5O-1, Waco JRW-1, Fairchild JK-1, JK-2.

THE NAMES OF AMERICAN SERVICE AIRCRAFT.

Design Firm	Army Designation	Navy Designation	U.S. Name Army and Navy	British Name
Boeing	B-17	—	Fortress	Fortress
Consolidated Vultee	B-24	PB4Y-1	Liberator	Liberator
Consolidated Vultee	—	PB4Y-2	Privateer	—
North American	B-25	PBJ	Mitchell	Mitchell
Martin	B-26	JM	Marauder	Marauder
Boeing	B-29	—	Superfortress	—
Consolidated Vultee	B-32	—	Dominator	—
Lockheed	B-34 and 37	PV-1	Ventura	Ventura
Lockheed	—	PV-2	Harpoon	—
Douglas	A-20 (P-70)	BD	Havoc	Boston
Douglas	A-24	SBD	Dauntless	—
Curtiss	A-25	SB2C	Helldiver	—
Fairchild (Canada)	—	SBF		
Canadian Car & Foundry	—	SBW		
Douglas	A-26	—	Invader	—
Lockheed	A-28 and 29	PBO	Hudson	Hudson
Vultee	A-31 and 35	—	Vengeance	Vengeance
Grumman	—	TBF	Avenger	Avenger
General Motors (Eastern Divn.)	—	TBM		
Consolidated Vultee	—	TBV	Seawolf	—
Consolidated Vultee	OA-10	PBY	Catalina	Catalina
Naval Aircraft Factory	—	PBN		
Boeing (Canada)	—	PB2B		
Consolidated Vultee	—	PB2Y	Coronado	Coronado
Martin	—	PBM	Mariner	Mariner
Lockheed	P-38	—	Lightning	—
Bell	P-39	—	Airacobra	—
Curtiss	P-40	—	Warhawk	Kittyhawk
Republic	P-47	—	Thunderbolt	Thunderbolt
North American	P-51	—	Mustang	Mustang
Bell	P-59A	—	Airacomet	—
Northrop	P-61	FT	Black Widow	—
Bell	P-63	—	Kingcobra	—
Douglas	P-70 (A-20)	—	Havoc	—
Lockheed	P-80A	—	Shooting Star	—
Grumman	—	F4F	Wildcat	Wildcat
General Motors (Eastern Divn.)	—	FM		
Grumman	—	F6F	Hellcat	Hellcat
Grumman	—	F7F	Tigercat	—
Grumman	—	F8F	Bearcat	—
Vought	—	F4U	Corsair	Corsair
Goodyear	—	FG		
Ryan	—	FR	Fireball	—
Curtiss	—	SC	Seahawk	—
Curtiss	—	SO3C	Seamew	Seamew
Vought	—	OS2U	Kingfisher	Kingfisher
Naval Aircraft Factory	—	OS2N		
Beech	UC-43	GB	Traveller	Traveller
Beech	C-45	JRB	Expeditor	Expeditor
Curtiss	C-46	R5C	Commando	—
Douglas	C-47	R4D	Skytrain	Dakota
Douglas	C-53	R4D	Skytrooper	Dakota
Douglas	C-54	R5D	Skymaster	Skymaster
Lockheed	C-56 and 60	R5O	Lodestar	Lodestar
Fairchild	UC-61	GK	Forwarder	Argus
Noorduyn	C-64	—	Norseman	Norseman (R.C.A.F.)
Cessna	UC-78	JRC	Bobcat	—
Consolidated Vultee	C-87	RY	Liberator	Liberator
Martin	—	JRM	Mars	—
Boeing	PT-13, 17, 18 & 27	N2S	Caydet	—
Fairchild	PT-19, 23 and 26	—	Cornell	Cornell (R.C.A.F.)
Timm	—	N2T	Tutor	—
Ryan	PT-21 and 22	NR	Recruit	—
Fleetwings	BT-12	—	Sophomore	—
Consolidated Vultee	BT-13 and 15	SNV	Valiant	—
North American	AT-6	SNJ	Texan	Harvard
Beech	AT-7	SNB	Navigator	—
Curtiss	—	SNC	Falcon	—
Cessna	AT-8 and 17	—	Bobcat	Crane (R.C.A.F.)
Beech	AT-10	—	Wichita	—
Beech	AT-11	SNB	Kansan	—
Stinson	AT-19	—	Reliant	Reliant
Fairchild	AT-21	—	Gunner	—
Consolidated Vultee	L-1 (O-49)	—	Vigilant	Vigilant
Taylorcraft	L-2 (O-57)	—	Taylorcraft Grasshopper	—
Aeronca	L-3 (O-58)	—	Aeronca Grasshopper	—
Piper	L-4 (O-59)	ME	Piper Grasshopper	—
Stinson	L-5 (O-62)	OY	Sentinel	Sentinel
Waco	CG-4A	LRW	—	Hadrian

URUGUAY
(The Republic of Uruguay—República Oriental del Uruguay)

NATIONAL MARKINGS

RUDDER   WINGS ONLY

RED

BLUE

A Department of Military Aviation and a School of Military Aeronautics was created on November 20, 1916. The first Director was Capt. Don Juan M. Boiso Lanza, after whom the chief military aerodrome is named. He was killed at Pau, France, while on a mission to France.

In 1936 Uruguayan military aviation was reorganized, the newly-created Directorate of Military Aeronautics being placed under the supervision of the Minister of National Defence. The Director, Colonel Don Oscar D. Gestido, is responsible for Military and Civil Aviation to the Minister of Defence through the Inspector-General of the Army.

ORGANIZATION

Ministerio de Defensa Nacional, Calle 25 de Mayo, 279, Montevideo.

Dirección General de la Aeronautica Militar, Avenida Agraciada 3544, Montevidio. Director-General : Colonel Don Oscar D. Gestido. Chief of Staff of Aeronautics : Major Don Tomás R. Mega.

The General-Directorate and Headquarters Staff control the School of Military Aeronautics, two Active Service units and the Air Arsenal. The Headquarters Staff includes the Central Department and the following divisions :—

Central Department. Chief : Capt. Arturo Sasso Alegre.

Division I (Organization). Chief : Capt Saúl C. Baccino.

Division II (Service). Chief : Capt. Adolfo E. Roca.

Division III (Information). Chief : Capt. Héctor R. Caetano.

Division IV (Operations). Chief : Major Juan C. Aragón.

The active service units are :—

Base Aeronáutica No. 1, "Capitan Boiso Lanza" Aerodrome. Camino Pedro de Mendoza No. 5553, Montevideo. Commanding Officer : Lieut.-Col. Don Mariano Rios. Reconnaissance and Attack Squadrons and the Bombing Group. Also Communications Service.

Base Aeronautica No. 2, "Teniente 2 Mario W. Parallada" Aerodrome, Estacion Yi, Dpto. de Durazno. Commanding Officer : Lieut.-Col. Don Oscar M. Sanchez. Reconnaissance and Fighter Squadrons. Also Communications Service.

Escuela Militar de Aeronautica, "General Artigas" Aerodrome, Pando, Dpt. de Canelones. Director of the School of Aeronautics : Lieut.-Col. Don Isaias F. Sanchez. Trains pilots up to qualifying for the rank of First Lieutenant Aviator.

The Air Arsenal, "Capitan Boiso Lanza" Aerodrome, Montevideo. Commanding Officer : Major Don Conrado A. Saez. Includes a Workshop Division, General Stores, Medical Service and Laboratory.

EQUIPMENT

Mainly of American origin. However, British, French and Italian aircraft of pre-war origin are still in service.

NAVAL AIR SERVICE

The **Servicio Aeronautica de la Marina** is under the control of the Inspector-General of the Navy. Its Chief is Capitan de Corbeta Don Horacio del Pilar Bogarin.

The General Command of this Service is on the Isla de la Liberta, where also is the Air Base No. 1. Other Bases are on the Laguna Negra, Laguna del Sauce, in the port of La Paloma and at Punta del Este, all on the River Plate estuary. It is only of late that naval flying has had any significance and the service is still in its infancy. All the material is new—of American production—and ambitious plans are under consideration for the enlargement of its general capacity, equipment and facilities. Many flying officers have proceeded to the United States for advanced instruction.

VENEZUELA
(The Republic of Venezuela—Estados Unidos de Venezuela)

NATIONAL MARKINGS

RUDDER   WINGS ONLY

YELLOW

BLUE

RED

A Venezuelan School of Military Aviation was established under a Presidential Decree dated April 17, 1920. The Military Aviation Regiment was formed in January, 1936.

Military Aviation is directly controlled by the Inspector-General of the Army, under the administration of the Ministry for War and Marine.

ORGANIZATION

Ministerio de Guerra y Marina, Direccion General de Aviacion, Caracas.

Inspector-General of Aviation : Major Jorge Marcano.

Director of Military Aviation : Major Guillermo Pacanins.

Regimiento de Aviacion Militar.

Headquarters : Maracay.

This regiment includes all operational units.

Escuela de Aviacion Militar, Maracay.

This school trains pilots and specialists in rigging, aero-engines, armament, radio, and photography. Both pilotage and technical courses are of one year's duration.

Escuela de Aviacion Civil, Maracay.

This school was formed by Presidential Decree in 1937 and is administered by the Ministry of War and Marine. It is in receipt of a subsidy. Although primarily for civil training it is recognised because of its value in building up a reserve of pilots.

Air Force pilots do tours of duty as First Pilots with the Government-operated Linea Aeropostal Venezolana to give them navigational and cross-country flying experience.

EQUIPMENT

Training :—Waco F-7, Stearman A75L3.

Advanced Training :—North American AT-6A.

Fighting :—Fiat CR.32.

Bombing :—Fiat BR.20.

YUGOSLAVIA
(The Kingdom of Yugoslavia—Kraljevina Jugoslavija)

In April, 1944 an agreement was signed between the British Government and Marshal Tito, commanding the Yugoslav National Army of Liberation, whereby a special Yugoslav air contingent was formed within the framework of the Royal Air Force.

To ensure effective working this agreement provided that the contingent should form part of the R.A.F.V.R. for the duration of the war or for such period as may be subsequently defined by mutual consent.

In the Summer of 1944 a Yugoslav fighter squadron, completely manned by Yugoslav personnel and equipped with Supermarine Spitfires went into action as a unit of the Tactical Wing of the R.A.F. Balkan Air Force in support of Partisan operations. This squadron was trained by the R.A.F. and had developed from a Yugoslav seaplane squadron which was formed in the Middle East in 1942. The numbers of Yugoslav airmen becoming available were such that a second fighter squadron was in training in 1945.

A

REVIEW OF THE WORLD'S
CIVIL AVIATION
1944-45

———

ARRANGED IN

ALPHABETICAL ORDER OF NATIONS

———

A RECORD OF CIVIL AVIATION DURING THE YEARS
1944-45, INCLUDING THE NAMES AND ADDRESSES OF
THE AERONAUTICAL DEPARTMENTS, ASSOCIATIONS,
PUBLICATIONS, TRANSPORT COMPANIES, FLYING
CLUBS AND SCHOOLS OF ALL NATIONS

INTERNATIONAL AIRCRAFT MARKINGS

The nationality and registration marks of civil aircraft of countries which are members of the International Commission for Air Navigation (C.I.N.A.) consist of groups of five letters. The nationality of the aircraft is indicated by the first letter or first two letters of such groups. The letters that follow a hyphen are the registration letters of the aircraft in the country concerned. The following are the identity letters of the various nations, not all of which are, or were, necessarily members of the C.I.N.A. :—

CC-	China.
CF-	Canada.
CL- or **CM-**	Cuba.
CN-	Morocco.
CP-	Bolivia.
CR-	Portuguese Colonies.
CS-	Portugal.
CX-	Uruguay.
D-	Germany.
EC-	Spain.
EI-	Eire.
F-	France, Colonies and Protectorates, less Morocco.
G-	Great Britain.
HA-	Hungary.
HB-	Switzerland.
HC-	Ecuador.
HH-	Haiti.
HI-	Dominican Republic.
HK-	Colombia.
HS-	Siam.
I-	Italy.
J-	Japan.
LB-	Czechoslovakia.
LG-	Guatemala.
LN-	Norway.
LV-	Argentine Republic.
LZ-	Bulgaria.
N	United States of America (*see below*)
OB-	Peru.
OH-	Finland.
OO-	Belgium.
OY-	Denmark.
PH-	Netherlands.
PJ-	Curaçao (Netherlands West Indies).
PK-	Netherlands East Indies
PP-	Brazil.
PZ-	Suriname (Netherlands Guiana).
SE-	Sweden.
SP-	Poland.
SU-	Egypt.
SX-	Greece.
TC-	Turkey.
TF-	Iceland.
TI-	Costa Rica.
URSS	Russia (national letters followed by a number).
VH-	Australia.
VO-	Newfoundland.
VP- **VQ-** **VR-**	British Colonies and Protectorates as below :—

VP-AAA—VP-AZZ	Gold Coast with Ashanti, Northern Territories of Gold Coast in British Togoland.
VP-BAA—VP-BZZ	Bahamas.
VP-CAA—VP-CZZ	Ceylon.
VP-FAA—VP-FZZ	Falkland Islands.

VP-GAA—VP-GZZ	British Guiana.
VP-HAA—VP-HZZ	British Honduras.
VP-JAA—VP-JZZ	Jamaica.
VP-KAA—VP-KZZ	Colonies and the Protectorate of Kenya.
VP-MAA—VP-MZZ	Malta.
VP-NAA—VP-NZZ	Protectorate of Nyasaland.
VP-PAA—VP-PZZ	Islands under the rule of the Western Pacific High Commission.
VP-RAA—VP-RZZ	Northern Rhodesia.
VP-SAA—VP-SZZ	Protectorate of Somaliland.
VP-TAA—VP-TZZ	Trinidad and Tobago.
VP-UAA—VP-UZZ	Protectorate of Uganda.
VP-VAA—VP-VZZ	St. Vincent.
VP-XAA—VP-XZZ	Colonies and Protectorate of Gambia.
VP-YAA—VP-YZZ	Southern Rhodesia.
VP-ZAA—VP-ZZZ	Protectorate of Zanzibar.
VQ-BAA—VQ-BZZ	Barbados.
VQ-CAA—VQ-CZZ	Cyprus.
VQ-FAA—VQ-FZZ	Fiji Islands.
VQ-GAA—VQ-GZZ	Grenada.
VQ-HAA—VQ-HZZ	St. Helena.
VQ-LAA—VQ-LZZ	St. Lucia.
VQ-MAA—VQ-MZZ	Mauritius.
VQ-PAA—VQ-PZZ	Palestine.
VQ-SAA—VQ-SZZ	Seychelle Islands.
VR-BAA—VR-BZZ	Bermuda.
VR-GAA—VR-GZZ	Gibraltar.
VR-HAA—VR-HZZ	Hong Kong.
VR-JAA—VR-JZZ	Johore.
VR-LAA—VR-LZZ	Colonies and Protectorate of Sierra Leone.
VR-NAA—VR-NZZ	Colonies and Protectorate of Nigeria, including British Cameroons.
VR-RAA—VR-RZZ	Federated Malay States.
VR-SAA—VR-SZZ	Straits Settlements.
VR-TAA—VR-TZZ	Tanganyika.
VR-UAA—VR-UZZ	State of Brunei (British North Borneo).
VT-	India.
XA- or **XB-**	Mexico.
XH-	Honduras.
XT-	China.
XY-	Burma.
YA-	Afghanistan.
YI-	'Iraq.
YJ-	New Hebrides Condominium.
YN-	Nicaragua.
YR-	Rumania.
YS-	Salvador.
YU-	Yugoslavia.
YV-	Venezuela.
ZK-	New Zealand.
ZP-	Paraguay.
ZS-	Union of South Africa.

U.S.A.—The letter N is followed either by the letter X for civil aircraft with an experimental licence, the letter C for civil aircraft with an Approved Type Certificate, the letter R for aircraft of restricted use, such as racers, crop-dusters or others with special modifications, or S for State-owned aircraft, such as those belonging to Government or State departments or bureaux. The two letters are followed by a registration number.

HISTORICAL (CIVIL AVIATION 1944-45)

THE INTERNATIONAL PATTERN

In the field of Civil aviation the most important event of 1944 was the Chicago Conference, which was in session throughout November and for the first week in December. It was at once a success and a failure, a success in so far as it achieved the revision and improvement of the International Air Navigation Convention signed at Paris in 1919; a failure in so far as it was unable to settle the two most important questions discussed. These were, first, the question of the freedom, or freedoms, of the air, and, secondly the question of the establishment of an international authority empowered to fix frequencies of air transport services, national quotas, and rates of charges. It was found impossible in either of these matters to reconcile the views of the United States, and, in general, the South American countries, on the one hand, and of the British Commonwealth and a number of other States, on the other. The result was, while a multilateral Convention was agreed (and that is in itself a reason for satisfaction), it does not go as far as some of the States represented at Chicago desired.

It includes two supplementary agreements, either of which the participating countries may elect to sign. In the first of these agreements there is provision for two freedoms of the air only, the right of transit and the right to land for refuelling or servicing but not to pick up or set down traffic. The second agreement provides not only for these two freedoms but for three others as well, namely, the right to land passengers and freight from the (foreign) aircraft's country of origin, the right to embark passengers and freight for that country, and the right to set down or take up intermediate traffic other than internal traffic (to which the rule of cabotage would apply). It was on this last right—the "fifth freedom"—that controversy mainly centred. It was complicated by its connection with another question, that of the escalator clause, which would allow an operator to put extra aircraft into service if he had been carrying 65 per cent. or more of his payload capacity for a year. The question whether the intermediate traffic contemplated in the fifth freedom should count for this purpose was one on which opinions differed. As regards the other main question upon which divergent views were held, while the proposal for an authority with executive powers was not accepted, it was agreed that an Interim Council should be established, to act as an advisory, and, within limits, regulatory, body. This body, known as the Provisional International Civil Aviation Organization (P.I.C.A.O.), was established on June 6, 1945, and the first meeting of the Interim Council, elected at the Chicago Conference, was held in Montreal on August 15, 1945.

Following meetings held between delegates of the British Commonwealth of Nations attending the Chicago Conference, a Commonwealth Air Transport Council was established, the principal function of which will be to plan trunk air routes within the Commonwealth. Complementary to this Commonwealth body is the Southern Africa Air Transport Council which was set up in March, 1945, to promote the progress and development of civil air communications in Southern Africa.

An indirect outcome of Chicago was the establishment of a new International Air Transport Association, representing the air transport operators of all States eligible for membership in the International Civil Aviation Organization.

Because of their international character and their bearing on the future development of civil aviation, summaries of the International Conference at Chicago and the Southern Africa Conference at Cape Town, and details of the composition and functions of the Provisional International Civil Aviation Organization, the Commonwealth Air Transport Council, the Southern Africa Air Transport Council and the International Air Transport Association are given hereafter.

THE INTERNATIONAL CIVIL AVIATION CONFERENCE

The International Civil Aviation Conference was held in Chicago between November 1 and December 7, 1944, and was attended by the representatives of fifty-two nations.

The four principal agreements reached at the conference were: (1) The Interim Agreement on International Civil Aviation (2) The Convention on International Civil Aviation; (3) The International Air Services Transit Agreement; and (4) The International Air Transport Agreement. These are summarised below.

The Interim Agreement on International Civil Aviation

Signed by 34 nations. The signatories were: Afghanistan, Australia, Canada, China, Dominican Republic, Egypt, France, Greece, Haiti, Honduras, Iceland, India, Iraq, Ireland, Lebanon, Mexico, the Netherlands, New Zealand, Nicaragua, Peru, Philippine Commonwealth, Poland, Portugal, Spain, Sweden, Switzerland, Syria, Turkey, United Kingdom, United States, Uruguay, Venezuela, Ministers for Denmark and Thailand.

This agreement sets up a Provisional International Civil Aviation Organization of a technical and advisory nature to last until a permanent organization is created, but not longer than three years. This organization was established on June 6, 1945, with headquarters in Montreal, Canada. Its composition and functions are fully dealt with under a separate heading.

The Convention on International Civil Aviation

Signed by 32 nations. The signatories were: Afghanistan, Australia, Canada, Chile, China, Dominican Rupublic, Ecuador, Egypt, France, Greece, Haiti, Honduras, Iceland, Iraq, Ireland, Lebanon, Mexico, the Netherlands, New Zealand, Nicaragua, Peru, Philippine Commonwealth, Poland, Portugal, Spain, Sweden, Syria, Turkey, United Kingdom, United States, Ministers from Denmark and Thailand. The delegate from Switzerland was not empowered to sign this agreement.

This convention set up a Permanent International Civil Aviation Organization. The pattern of this organization, upon which the interim body is modelled, comprises an Assembly in which all members are equally represented, each having one vote (a majority constituting a quorum), and a Council composed of 21 states elected by the Assembly for three years.

Subject to approval by any general international organization set up by the nations of the World to preserve peace, other States may be admitted to participation in the Convention by means of a four-fifths vote of the Assembly and on such conditions as the Assembly may prescribe; provided that in each case the assent of any State invaded or attacked during the war by the State seeking admission shall be necessary.

The 96 articles of this document establish the privileges and restrictions of all contracting States on a non-discriminating basis; set up codes of operations for aircraft and personnel: provide health and safety rules for aviation; recommend duty, customs and immigration methods and navigation facilities for member States; and arrange for a 12-member Air Navigation Commission of technical experts.

Pursuant to the recognition of the principle that every State has complete and exclusive sovereignty over the air space above its territory (including territorial waters), it is agreed that no scheduled international air service may operate over or into the territory of a contracting State without previous authorisation. The right of cabotage is dependent upon such permission, but each state undertakes not to grant or obtain exclusive cabotage rights.

Each contracting State undertakes to collaborate in securing the highest practicable degree of uniformity in regulations, standards, procedures and organization in relation to aircraft, personnel, airways and auxiliary services in all matters in which such uniformity will facilitate and improve air navigation. To this end the International Civil Aviation Organization will adopt and amend from time to time as may be necessary standards and recommended practices and procedures dealing with: (*a*) Communications systems and air navigation aids, including ground markings; (*b*) characteristics of airports and landing areas; (*c*) rules of the air and air traffic control practices; (*d*) licensing of operating and mechanical personnel; (*e*) airworthiness of aircraft; (*f*) registration and identification of aircraft; (*g*) collection and exchange of meteorological information; (*h*) log books; (*i*) aeronautical maps and charts; (*j*) customs and immigration procedures; and (*k*) investigation of accidents and all matters concerned with the safety, regularity and efficiency of air navigation.

The International Air Services Transit Agreement

Signed by 26 nations. The signatories were: Afghanistan, Ecuador, France, Greece, Haiti, Honduras, India, Iraq, Lebanon, Mexico, the Netherlands, New Zealand, Nicaragua, Peru, Philippine Commonwealth, Poland, Spain, Sweden, Turkey, United Kingdom, United States, Uruguay, Venezuela, Ministers from Denmark and Thailand. The delegate from Switzerland was not empowered to sign this agreement.

This agreement provides for contracting states to grant to other states the following "two freedoms" of the air in respect of scheduled international air services:—

(1) the privilege to fly across its territory without landing;
(2) the privilege to land for non-traffic purposes.

These privileges are granted subject to certain conditions, including the right to designate the route to be followed and the airports to be used for such services; the right to impose reasonable charges for the use of airports and other facilities; and the right of each contracting State to withhold such privileges from any air transport enterprise of which it is not satisfied that substantial ownership and effective control are vested in nationals of a contracting State.

The International Air Transport Agreement

Signed by 16 nations. The signatories were:—Afghanistan, China, Dominican Republic, Ecuador, Haiti, Honduras, Mexico, Nicaragua, Peru, Sweden, Turkey, United States, Uruguay, Venezuela, Ministers from Denmark and Thailand. The delegate from Turkey made a reservation withholding the "fifth freedom of the air." The delegate from the Philippine Commonwealth indicated that the document might be signed later. The delegate from Switzerland was not authorised to sign this document.

This agreement provides for contracting States to grant to other contracting states the following "five freedoms" of the air in respect of scheduled international air services:—

(1) the privilege to fly across its territory without landing:
(2) the privilege to land for non-traffic purposes;
(3) the privilege to put down passengers, mail and cargo taken on in the territory of the State whose nationality the aircraft possesses;
(4) the privilege to take on passengers, mail and cargo destined for the territory of the State whose nationality the aircraft possesses;
(5) the privilege to take on passengers, mail and cargo destined for the territory of any other member State and to put down passengers, mail and cargo coming from any such territory.

Contracting States will have the right to refuse permission to aircraft of other States to take on in its territory passengers mail and cargo destined for another point within its territory. No State shall grant to or obtain from any other State or an airline of any other State any such privilege on an exclusive basis.

Each contracting State undertakes that in the establishment and operation of through services due consideration shall be given to the interests of the other contracting States so as not to interfere unduly with their regional services nor hamper the development of their through services.

Technical Annexes

Various sub-committees on technical standards and procedures, in the limited time available during the Conference, drew up a number of technical annexes containing numerous recommendations which, when studied, revised and agreed upon, will standardise the technical aspects of aviation, such as:—

Airways Systems,
Communications Procedures and Systems,
Rules of the Air,
Air Traffic Control Practices,
Standards governing the Licensing of Operating and Mechanical Personnel,
Log Book requirements,
Airworthiness Requirements for Civil Aircraft engaging in International Air Navigation,
Aircraft Registration and Identification Marks,
Meteorological Protection of International Aeronautics,
Aeronautical Maps and Charts,
Customs Procedures and Manifests,
Search and Rescue, and Investigation of Accidents.

The annexes completely define aviation terms and explain and diagram aircraft construction as affecting safety and load factors. For example, on the subject of land airports the annexes divide into three classifications, for uniformity, the types to be provided, calling them "transoceanic," "transcontinental" and "interstate." The section describes the length of runway required for each type as related to the maximum gross weight of the aircraft landing on the runway.

THE PROVISIONAL INTERNATIONAL CIVIL AVIATION ORGANIZATION (P.I.C.A.O.)

THE INTERIM COUNCIL

President: Dr. Edward P. Warner (U.S.A.).

Vice-Presidents: Dr. F. H. Copes Van Hassault (Netherlands); Mr. Chang Kiangau (China); and Mr. G. E. Saurex (Columbia).

Secretary-General: Dr. Albert Roper (France).

Member States: Australia, Belgium, Brazil, Canada, Chile, China, Columbia, Czechoslovakia, Egypt, El Salvador, France, India, Iraq, Mexico, the Netherlands, Norway, Peru, Turkey, United Kingdom, and United States. A seat on the Council has been reserved for Russia.

Headquarters: Montreal, Canada.

The Provisional International Civil Aviation Organization was established when the Interim Agreement on International Civil Aviation came into force on June 6, 1945, after 30 nations had announced their formal acceptance of the Agreement.

The Organization was established for an interim period to last until a new permanent convention on international civil aviation shall have come into force or another conference on international civil aviation has agreed on other arrangements. The interim period is not to exceed three years.

The Organization consists of an Assembly and a Council.

The Assembly

To meet annually and be convened by the Council. Extraordinary meetings of the Assembly may be held at any time when called by the Council or at the request of any ten member States. All member States have equal right to be represented at the meetings of the Assembly and each member is entitled to one vote. The powers and duties of the Assembly are: (*a*) to elect at each meeting its president and officers; (*b*) to elect the member States to be represented on the Council; (*c*) to examine and take action upon the reports of the Council; (*d*) to determine its own rules of procedure and establish such subsidiary commissions and committees as are needed; approve an annual budget and determine the financial arrangements of the Organization; (*e*) to refer any specific matters to the Council; (*f*) to delegate the necessary powers and authority to the Council which are needed for the duties of the organization; and (*g*) to deal with any matters not specifically assigned to the Council.

The Council

The Council to be composed of not more that 21 member States elected by the Assembly for a period of two years, adequate representation to be given to: (1) those member States of chief importance in air transport; (2) those member States not otherwise included which make the largest contribution to the provision of facilities for international civil air navigation; (3) those member States not otherwise included whose election will ensure that all major geographical areas of the World are represented. No representative of a member State on the Council may be actively associated with or financially interested with the operation of an international air service.

The Council shall elect a President, who will have no vote. One or more vice-presidents to be elected from among the members, who will retain the right to vote when serving as acting president. Decisions of the Council to be deemed valid when approved by a majority of all members. Any member State not a member of the Council may participate in deliberations whenever any decision is to be taken which especially concerns such a member State. But such a State may not vote. In any case in which there is a dispute between one or more member States not members of the Council and one or more member States who are members of the Council, any State within the second category which is party to the dispute shall have no right to vote on that dispute.

The duties and powers of the Council are :—

(1) to discharge the directives of the Assembly.

(2) to determine its own organization of the Assembly.

(3) to determine the method of appointment, emoluments and conditions of service of the employees of the organization.

(4) to appoint a Secretary-General.

(5) to provide for the establishment of any subsidiary working groups which may be considered desirable, including the following interim Committees :—

(*a*) A Committee on Air Transport.
(*b*) A Committee on Air Navigation.
(*c*) A Committee on International Convention on Civil Aviation.

(6) to prepare and submit to the Assembly budget estimates of the Organization and statemounts of accounts of all reports and expenditures.

(7) to enter into agreements with other international bodies when deemed advisable for the maintenance of common service and for common arrangements concerning personnel and, with the approval of the Assembly, enter into such other arrangements as may facilitate the work of the Organization.

In addition, the functions of the Council are to maintain liaison with the member States, calling on them for such data and information as may be required ; receive, register and hold open to inspection by member States, all existing contracts and agreements covering routes, services, landing rights, airport facilities, or other international air matters to which any member State or its airlines is a party ; supervise and co-ordinate the works of the three Committees, consider their reports and transmit the Committee's reports and the findings of the Council to the member States. In addition, the Council is to make recommendations on technical matters to the member States of the Assembly, submit an annual report to the Assembly and, on the direction of the Assembly, convene another conference on international civil aviation or, at such time as the Convention is ratified, convene the first Assembly under the Convention. When requested by all the parties concerned, the Council will act as an arbitral body on any difference arising among member States relating to international civil aviation matters which may be submitted to it.

The expenses of the Provisional Organisation are borne by the member States in proportions to be decided by the Assembly and funds are to be advanced by member States to cover the initial expenses of the Organization. Each member State bears the expenses of its own delegation to the Assembly and those of its delegates on the Council and its representatives on committees or subsidiary groups.

Each contracting State undertakes that its international airlines shall file traffic reports, cost statistics and financial states with the Council. Each contracting State may designate the route to be followed within its territory by any international air service, and the airports which any such service may use. If the Council is of the opinion that the airports or other navigation facilities of a contracting State are not reasonably adequate the Council may consult with the State and others affected, to find means of correcting the position and may make recommendations. If requested by the State, the Council may provide all or a portion of the costs needed for the remedies.

A contracting State may at any time discharge any obligation into which it has entered and take over airports and other facilities which the Council has established in its territory by paying to the Council an amount considered reasonable.

The Council may suggest to contracting States that they form joint organizations to operate air services on any routes or in any regions.

The duties of the Committees established under the Council shall be :—

The Committee on Air Transport : To observe, correlate and continuously report on facts concerning the origin and volume of international air traffic and the relation of such traffic, or the demand for it, to the facilities provided ; collect, analyse and report on subsidies, tariffs and costs of operation ; study matters affecting the organization and operation of international air services, including the international ownership and operation of international trunk lines ; and study and report, with recommendations to the Assembly as soon as practicable on matters on which agreement was not reached at the Chicago International Civil Aviation Conference.

The Committee on Air Navigation : Study and advise on standards and procedures for communications systems and air navigation aids including rules of the air, traffic control practices, licensing of operating and mechanical personnel, airworthiness, registration and identification of aircraft, meteorological protection of international aeronautics, log books, maps and charts, airports, customs, accident investigation and so forth. In addition the Committee will work towards the adoption of minimum requirements and standard procedures for all the above and continue the preparation of technical documents in accordance with the recommendations of the Chicago Conference.

THE COMMONWEALTH AIR TRANSPORT COUNCIL

A Commonwealth Air Transport Council, of a consultative character, was established following meetings between members of the British Commonwealth of Nations before and following the International Civil Aviation Conference at Chicago. The work of the Commonwealth and Empire Conference on Radio for Civil Aviation (C.E.R.C.A.) is under the Council.

A permanent secretariat is attached to the Council and is filled by the Department of Civil Aviation in London, to which are attached liaison officers representing Canada, Australia, New Zealand, South Africa, India, Southern Rhodesia, Newfoundland and the Colonial Empire.

The work of the Council is to plan trunk air routes within the Commonwealth including: United Kingdom to South Africa, by way of Egypt, East Africa and Rhodesia ; United Kingdom to India ; United Kingdom to Australia and New Zealand by way of India ; United Kingdom—Canada, via the Atlantic route ; and the Pacific route from Australia and New Zealand to Canada, by way of Fiji. The Council is not an executive body and its recommendations and conclusions are subject to confirmation by the Commonwealth Governments.

The Council has recommended the setting up of a Council of Co-ordination of Aeronautical Research within the Empire and a Committee for Air Navigation and Ground Organization to deal with the operational planning necessary in the Empire countries.

The first full meeting of the Council was held in London from July 9 to July 14, 1945, to make arrangements for Commonwealth routes.

The principle of parallel partnership which was agreed at the Cape Town Conference between the United Kingdom and the Union of South Africa was taken as the general guide for arrangements for particular routes within the Empire. These arrangements may be summarised as follows :—

In general, the capacity to be operated on a route connecting two Commonwealth countries should be related to the traffic offering on a Third and Fourth Freedom basis between those two countries. The capacity available for Fifth Freedom traffic would accordingly be of a fill-up nature.

Normally, the capacity operated on a route should be divided initially on a 50-50 basis between the two partners, subject to review, at the request of either party, on the basis of traffic embarked and in the light of experience. Mails, freight and passengers to be included for the purpose of settling and dividing capacity.

Where one partner does not wish to take up his own quota of services and invites the other partner to operate the whole or part of his quota for it, the first partner should bear any deficit. If a partner takes up an unwanted quota on his own and with the permission of the other partner, he should bear the deficit. Where one partner, whose share in full or in part is being operated temporarily by the other, wishes to operate on the route, the first partner should transfer the requisite capacity under agreed arrangements which are fair to both.

In general, revenue should be pooled and divided between the two partners in proportion to the frequencies operated, such arrangements to be open to review. The Council consider that in pooling arrangements both operators should use the same aircraft. So long as the Empire Air Mail Scheme remains in operation, the appropriate contributions under that scheme will be included in the pool of revenue.

The arrangement agreed at the Cape Town Conference under which expenditure shall be charged to the operator on whose behalf it is incurred, should be adopted. Where two operators are operating in parallel partnership their joint commercial and technical interests should be the responsibility of one party, or a common agency, in defined zones to be agreed between them.

Aircraft operated by parallel operators, although they will be owned and operated by each, should be regarded, so far as practicable, as a pooled fleet.

The reports and recommendations of the three Committees appointed at the opening of the Conference, were adopted and approved by the Council at its plenary session. The Technical Committee's work covered meteorological, telecommunication and aerodrome facilities required along the routes, existing civil and military facilities, and recommend full co-operation between the civil and Service organizations and system established by Commonwealth countries on these routes.

Pooled services to be operated in parallel between Great Britain and India and between Great Britain and Australia were proposed. The extension of the Australian service to New Zealand is under discussion but New Zealand is not expected to participate directly in the whole service.

A service linking Australia, New Zealand and Canada is proposed by a joint company formed by Great Britain, Australia and New Zealand to operate from the western end of the route across the Pacific. Canada may provide the opposite member to operate a parallel service and may agree to pooling on this service. The principle of parallel partnership is not accepted by Canada for the trans-Atlantic route.

THE SOUTHERN AFRICAN AIR TRANSPORT CONFERENCE

A Southern African Air Transport Conference, attended by delegates representing the United Kingdom, the Union of South Africa, Southern Rhodesia, Northern Rhodesia, Nyasaland, Kenya and the British Protectorates, was held at Cape Town from March 20 to 24, 1945. The objects of the conference were to discuss and formulate action on matters of common interest to the countries concerned in the provision of air services for Southern Africa.

The conference decided to recommend to their governments the establishment of a Southern Africa Air Transport Council, with a permanent secretariat to provide machinery for consultation and to advise the Commonwealth and Empire Governments concerned on all matters connected with the co-ordination of their civil air transport services in Southern Africa.

A number of resolutions were adopted by the Conference dealing with various operational and technical aspects of the development of Commonwealth and Empire air services in Southern Africa.

Arrangements were completed for the early inauguration of main trunk route services between the United Kingdom and South Africa to be operated reciprocally throughout by the British Overseas Airways Corporation and South African Airways, the conference recommending that the initial arrangements for the conveyance of mail on the projected trunk route should be within the general framework of the Empire Air Mail Scheme.

On the subject of regional and local services which it is contemplated will be established within and between the Southern African territories, the Conference recommended that the following principles should apply :—

(*a*) Local services should both serve the requirements for air transport within the territories and afford suitable connections with the main trunk route and with regional routes.

(*b*) The routing of regional services within the territories of Commonwealth and Empire countries in Southern Africa will normally be a matter for discussion by the Southern Africa Air Transport Council, so that the interests of regional and local services may be co-ordinated and protected to their mutual advantage and the convenience of the travelling public. The recommendations of the Council will be submitted to the Governments concerned for approval.

(*c*) It shall be competent for the Southern Africa Air Transport Council to make representations, inter alia, in regard to internal services in Commonwealth and Empire countries in Southern Africa, where these services are not satisfactorily co-ordinated with the trunk and regional services.

The Conference expressed the hope that, in planning and development of regional services in Southern Africa, satisfactory arrangements for co-operation would be made with foreign governments.

It recognises that foreign participation in regional air services is desirable and recommends that the planning of such services should afford scope for co-operation within the orbit of a general operational scheme, or, alternatively, if such general co-operation should not prove feasible, for co-operation on the basis of bilateral agreements confined to particular routes and services.

The Conference formally adopted the following resolutions :—

(1) It is agreed that the resolutions and recommendations of the Conference shall be in harmony with, and subject to, the obligations undertaken by the Commonwealth Governments concerned as a result of the International Civil Aviation Conference at Chicago.

(2) The Conference endorses, so far as it is concerned, the proposal which has already been accepted in principle by Commonwealth countries, that on the technical committees of the Interim Council constituted in accordance with the terms of Article 3 of the Interim Agreement on International Civil Aviation, Commonwealth countries should pool their representation so far as may be practicable and desirable on a mutual basis.

(3) It is agreed that any Southern African organization that may be established by the Conference shall co-operate with the Commonwealth Air Transport Council in formulating proposals, to be submitted in due time by the appropriate authority to the Interim Council, to promote multilateral agreement on air transport questions left undecided by the International Civil Aviation Conference at Chicago.

The United Kingdom—South Africa Trunk Service. At the Conference it was decided that the trunk service between London and Johannesburg would be a parallel one operated jointly by the British Overseas Airways Corpn. and South African Airways, British aircraft flying through to Johannesburg and South African aircraft to London. There would be pooling of revenue and repair and maintenance facilities on the basis that South African Airways would provide the necessary ground personnel and be responsible for operative and administrative functions on the route up to, but excluding, Nairobi, and British Airways would undertake similar responsibility on the remainder of the route.

It was decided to use Avro York four-engined transports, carrying 14 passengers and 3,000 lbs. of freight, at the start of the service, but that ultimately these would be replaced by Avro Tudor aircraft capable of carrying more than double the number of passengers.

Initially, the aerodromes to be used for the trunk service would be at Johannesburg, Kasama (temporary), Nairobi, Khartoum, Cairo, Malta (ultimately Rome) and London.

Representations were to be made to the Southern Rhodesian

Government for the construction of a new airport at Salisbury capable of accommodating the multi-engined aircraft to be used on the trunk service. The proposals have since been approved by the Southern Rhodesian Government. It was not certain whether the use of Kasama as a temporary refuelling point until the proposed Salisbury airport was ready would be approved and it is possible that technical considerations would necessitate the aircraft flying non-stop between Johannesburg and Nairobi in the meantime.

The Johannesburg terminal would be located at Palmietfontein Airport, which was being prepared for the purpose, pending the construction of the Union's permanent international airport at Kempton Park, between Johannesburg and Pretoria.

The Southern African Air Transport Council

The membership of the Southern Africa Air Transport Council includes the United Kingdom, the Union of South Africa, British High Commission Territories, Southern Rhodesia, Northern Rhodesia, Nyasaland, Kenya, Tanganyika, Uganda and Zanzibar.

The functions of the Council will be : (*a*) to keep under review and promote the progress and development of civil air communications in Southern Africa ; (*b*) to serve as a medium for the exchange of views and information between member countries on civil air transport matters ; (*c*) to consider and advise on such civil aviation matters as any member Government may desire to refer to the Council ; (*d*) to furnish a link and to co-operate with the Commonwealth Air Transport Council and to keep the Council fully informed on its deliberations.

The Council, which may appoint technical and other committees, will meet at regular intervals, the meetings to be held in various countries of Southern Africa as may be agreed to be convenient and appropriate on each occasion. The Chairman on each occasion will be designated by the country in which the meeting is held, the Governments concerned deciding on each occasion whether representation shall be on a ministerial or official level. Each country will bear the cost of its own representation on the Council, on the Committees of the Council and on the Secretariat.

Pending the organization of a permanent Secretariate, the Ministry of Transport of the Government of the Union of South Africa provides an interim Secretariat.

THE INTERNATIONAL AIR TRANSPORT ASSOCIATION

A new International Air Transport Association was formally inaugurated on April 19, 1945, at Havana, following a conference of international airline operators. Invitations to the conference and plans for the new organization were drawn up at a conference held in Chicago in December, 1944, on the initiative of the American Air Transport Association and attended by 34 representatives of 21 nations. The new Association succeeds the original International Air Traffic Association founded in 1919.

Headquarters of the new I.A.T.A. are at Montreal, Canada, and the association consists of a General Assembly, comprising 60 air transport companies, and an Executive Committee, in which is vested the management of the association. The post of President is an honarary position.

There are two categories of membership—Active and Associate. Any air transport undertaking is eligible for active membership if it operates a scheduled air service under proper authority for passengers, mail or cargo, between the territories of two or more States, under the flag of a State eligible for membership in the International Civil Aviation Organization.

The original Active Members were :—A.B. Aerotransport (Sweden) ; Aer Lingus Teoranta (Eire) ; American Airlines Inc. ; American Export Airlines Inc. ; Braniff Airways ; British Overseas Airways Corporation ; British West Indian Airways ; Ceskoslovenska Letecka Spolecnost ; Ceskoslovenska Statni Aerolinie ; China National Aviation Corporation ; Cia Mexicana de Aviacion ; Colonial Airlines ; Compania Iberia ; Det Danske Luftfartselskab ; Det Norske Luftfartselskap ; Empresa de Viacaõ Aerea Rio Grandense, Expreso Aereo Inter-Americano ; Indian National Airways ; K.L.M. ; K.N.I.L.M. ; Northeast Airlines ; Northwest Airlines ; Panair do Brasil ; Pan American Airways ; Pan American-Grace Airways ; Polskie Linie Lotnieze Qantas Empire Airways ; Servicios Aereos Cruzeiro do Sul ; Sabena ; Svensk Inter-Kontinental Lufttrafik ; Swissair ; Tasman Empire Airways ; Trans-Canada Air Lines ; Transcontinental and Western Air, Inc. ; Transportes Aereos Centro-Americanos ; United Air Lines ; Western Air Lines ; and Wrightways, Ltd.

Associate membership may be obtained by any air transport concern operating an authorised scheduled air service under the flag of a State eligible for membership in the International Civil Aviation Organization. The original Associate Member companies were :—Aerovias Paraguayas ; All-American Aviation ; Allied Airways (Gander Dower) Ltd. ; Compania Cubana de Aviacion ; T.A.C.A. de Costa Rica ; Compania Nacional Taca de Nicaragua ; Delta Air Lines ; Eastern Airlines ; Empresa de Transportes Aerovias Brasil ; Lineas Aereas Taca de Colombia ; Linea Aerea Taca de Venezuela ; Linea Aeropostal Venezolana ; National Airlines ; Pennsylvania-Central Airlines, Portsmouth Aviation ; Taca Airways ; and Taca de Mexico.

The Executive Committee of I.A.T.A. is to consist of not less than nine or more than 13 members. The first Executive Committee is :—M. René Briand (Air France) ; A. F. T. Cambridge (Indian National Airways, Ltd.) ; John C. Cooper (Pan-American Airways) ; Benito Ribeiro Dantas (Servicios Aereos Cruzeiro do Sul, Ltda.) ; W. Hudson Fysh (Qantas Empire Airways) ; Major J. R. McCrindle (British Overseas Airways) ; Per A. Norlin (Svenska Inter-Kontinental) ; Albert Plesman (K.L.M.) ; and John E. Slater (American Airlines System).

The Committee has recommended that six Regional Offices of the Association should be established at Paris, New York, Rio de Janeiro, Cairo, Johannesburg and Sydney.

ARGENTINA

(The Argentine Republic—República Argentina)

ADMINISTRATION

The controlling authority is the Director-General of Civil Aeronautics (Dirección-General de Aeronáutica Civil), who is directly responsible to the Secretary (Minister) of Aeronautica. Director-General of Civil Aviation : Air Vice-Commodore Francisco José Velez. Offices : Avenida Quintana 591, Buenos Aires.

Subordinate to the Dirección-General de Aeronáutica Civil are :

Dirección de Aeronáutica Comercial, (Directorate of Commercial Flying).

Dirección de Aeronáutica Deportiva, (Directorate of Private Flying).

ASSOCIATIONS

Aero-Club Buenos Aires, Rodriguez Peña 240, Buenos Aires. Affiliated to the *Fédération Aéronautique Internationale* (*F.A.I.*).

PUBLICATIONS

Revista de Informaciones Aeronáuticas, Monthly. Published at Calle Juncal 1116, Buenos Aires. $12.00 Argentine pesos per annum.

Mundo Aeronáutico. Monthly. Published at Calle Rivadavia 945, Buenos Aires. $3.50 Argentine pesos per annum.

Aeronáutica. Monthly. Published at Avenida de Mayo 1370, Buenos Aires. $3.50 Argentine pesos per annum.

Avia. Monthly. Published at Calle Rivadavia 659, Buenos Aires. $6.00 Argentine pesos per annum.

Rutas del Aire. monthly. Published at Dolores 194, Buenos Aires. $3.5 Argentine pesos per annum.

Boletin de Aeronáutica Civil. Published annually at Calle Quintana 591, Buenos Aires.

TRANSPORT COMPANIES

Aeroposta Argentina, S.A. Offices at Avenida de Mayo 560, Buenos Aires.

President : Almirante Ismael Galindez.

This airline started in 1931 under the guidance of the French Aeropostale Company. Later, however, the Syndicato Condor took over the controlling interest. The Company is officially an Argentine concern, and its operations are confined to that country, with headquarters at the "General Pacheco" Airport, Buenos Aires.

Routes :—

Buenos Aires—Bahia Blanca—Carmen Patagones—Trelew—Comodoro Rivadavia—Puerto Deseado—San Julian—Santa Cruz—Rio Gallegos. bi-weekly both ways. Continues on from Rio Gallegos to Rio Grande (Tierra del Fuego). Weekly.

Buenos Aires—Bahía Blanca—Carmen de Patagones—Trelew—Comodoro Rivadavia—Lago Buenos Aires—Cañadón León—Lago Argentino—Rio Gallegos—Rio Grande. Weekly both ways.

Equipment : Four Junkers Ju 52.

Corporacion Sud-Americana de Servicios Aereos. Offices at 25 de Mayo 299, Buenos Aires.

President : Dr. Carlos Rueda.

This airline was started in Argentina early in 1939 with the backing of certain Italian aeronautical interests. It is, however, officially rated as an Argentine Company having local capital, a Government subsidy and Argentine operating personnel.

Routes :—

Buenos Aires—Montevideo, twice daily (except Sundays) both ways.

Buenos Aires—Santa Fé—Barranqueras and Corrientes—Formosa—Asuncion, twice weekly.

Compania Argentina de Aeronavegacion Dodero.

This company has been formed by the Dodero shipping interests to establish air services between Argentina and the neighbouring countries. It has acquired four Short Sunderland flying-boats.

Pan American World Airways. Local representatives are the Compañia de Aviacion Pan Americana S.A., with offices at Avenida Roque Saenz Peña 788, Buenos Aires.

Pan American Airways operates from Buenos Aires to Brazil, both via Montevideo (Uruguay) and Asuncion (Paraguay). Both services continue from Rio de Janeiro up the East coast to Miami (U.S.A.).

Routes :—

Buenos Aires—Montevideo (Uruguay) — Porto Alegre (Brazil), then to Rio de Janeiro and on to Miami, six times weekly.

Buenos Aires—Asuncion (Paraguay)—Iguassú—Curytiba—São Paulo—Rio de Janeiro and the U.S.A., weekly both ways.

Pan American Grace Airways (Panagra). Represented locally by the Compañia de Aviacion Pan Americana S.A., with offices at Avenida Roque Saenz Peña 788, Buenos Aires.

Panagra operate three trans-Andean routes from Argentina through Chile and Bolivia. The Chile service to Santiago crosses the Andes via the Uspallata Pass, in the province of Mendoza, at an altitude of from 11,000 to 14,000 feet. The second Chilean service, opened in September, 1942, crosses the mountains between Salta and Antofagasta. The Bolivian route crosses the border north of Jujuy where the ground level rises sharply to about 13,000 feet to the Bolivian *alte plano* ; this high plateau is flown over for some 500 or 600 miles and the Andes crossing is made west of La Paz at 18,000 to 20,000 feet altitude.

Routes :—

Buenos Aires—Cordoba—Tucuman—Salta — Antofagasta (Chile) and on to Balboa. Thrice weekly.

Buenos Aires — Cordoba — Mendoza — Santiago — Antofagasta (Chile) and on to Balboa. Seven times weekly.

Buenos Aires — Cordoba — Tucuman — Salta — Uyuni (Bolivia) and on to Balboa. Twice weekly.

Sociedade Aerea Cruzeiro Do Sul Limitada. Offices at Calle Corrientes 336, Buenos Aires.

This is the former Brazilian Sindicato Condor Ltd., a German-operated concern which was taken over by the Brazilian Government in 1940. For further information see under "Brazil."

Route :—

Buenos Aires—Porto Allegre—São Paulo—Rio de Janeiro. Three times weekly each way.

Operations in Argentina are centred at the "Presidente Rivadavia" Airport, Buenos Aires.

Aeravias Argentinas S.A. Offices at Calle Corrientes 545, Buenos Aires.

President : Eduardo Bradley.

Originally formed in 1942. In January, 1944, Mr. Lowell Yerex, President of TACA bought the operating rights of the company. Future plans handicapped owing to the difficulties of buying aircraft and equipment.

Línea Aérea Sudoeste (L.A.S.E.).

The Línea Aérea Sudoeste began operations in January, 1940 with a freight-carrying service from Buenos Aires to Esquel. It was developed, and is being operated by the Argentine Air Force, one of the main functions of the service being the training of air force personnel in navigation and long cross-country flights.

Although it is at present a military service, the Air Force may cease operations when an Argentine commercial organization is in a position to operate the routes subject to conditions laid down by the Directorate-General of Civil Aeronautics.

In July, 1940, the service was opened to passengers. The Decree which officially approved this stated that any service operated by the Air Force must function on a non-profit basis. All surplus funds must be applied to improvements to the Ground organization of the routes flown over.

Route :—

Buenos Aires—Santa Rosa—Neuquen—San Carlos de Bariloche—Esquel. Weekly both ways.

Línea Aérea Noreste (L.A.N.E.). Offices at Corrientes 480, Buenos Aires.

This is a military airline similar to the Línea Aérea Sudoeste. It commenced operating from Buenos Aires to the Falls of Iguazu in November, 1943, and in July, 1944, the service was extended to Asunción (Paraguay). The route is now as follows :—

Buenos Aires — Concordia — Monte Caseros — Posadas—Cataratas del Iguazu—Asunción, weekly both ways.

In May, 1945, this airline was authorised to operate a branch service from Posadas to Clorinda, via Resistencia. The service will carry mail only when first inaugurated ; passengers will be carried when the safety conditions meet the requirements demanded by that traffic.

Equipment : Junkers Ju 52.

Servicios Aéreos del Estado.

On May 22, 1945, four Air Mail services organized by the Directorate-General of Civil Aeronautics began to operate along the following routes :—

Service No. 1. Buenos Aires—Gualeguaychú—Concepción del Uruguay—Colonia Yeruá—Villaguay—La Paz—Paraná—Victoria—Buenos Aires, three times weekly.

Service No. 2. Esquina—Feliciano—Colonia Yeruá—Monte Caseros—Feliciano—La Paz—Esquina, three times weekly.

Service No. 3. Corrientes—Bella Vista—Goya—Mercedes—Curuzu Cuatiá—Monte Caseros, three times weekly both ways.

Service No. 4. Posadas—Oberá—San Javier—Apóstales—Santo Tomé—Alvear—Paso de los Libres—Monte Caseros, three times weekly both ways.

STATISTICS

The following summary of operations of national and international airlines during 1944 was issued by the Argentine Aviation Department :—

Distance flown (km.)	3,103,027
Hours flown	13,602
Passengers carried	78,537
Mail carried (kg.)	106,279
Express carried (kg.)	401,001
Freight carried (kg.)	433,384

FLYING SCHOOLS

A National School of Aeronautics gives ground instruction and flying courses, while the Argentine Weather Bureau is organizing a service of upper air weather observations, using military aircraft and pilots.

The Universities of Buenos Aires and Córdoba have added a seat of Aeronautical Engineering to their curricula.

FLYING CLUBS

State aid for flying clubs (financial and material, in the shape of aircraft) is contingent on compliance with strict regulations, the principal of which are the obligation to maintain a school for training pilots, to facilitate the training of as many pilots as possible, to maintain stocks of aircraft fuel and lubricants for machines in transit, and to provide instruction in aeronautics. Aviation material is exempt from customs duty.

The Government sponsors a program to develop private flying. The Government bear the flying costs based on actual hours flown and pays the salaries of instructors. The flying clubs pay for maintenance and repair of the aircraft.

The following is a list of the existing clubs :—

Aero Club Buenos Aires, Rodríguez Pena 240, Buenos Aires. Aerodrome : "Presidente Rivadavia," 6 de Septiembre, Province of Buenos Aires.
Centro Universitario de Aviación, Bmé. Mitre 367, Buenos Aires. Aerodrome : "Presidente Rivadavia," 6 de Septiembre, Province of Buenos Aires.
Asociación Aeronáutica Azul, Uriburu 737, Azul, Province of Buenos Aires.
Aero Club Bahía Blanca, Chiclana 311, Bahía Blanca, Province of Buenos Aires.
Aero Club Bolívar, Bolívar, Province of Buenos Aires.
Aero Club Cañada de Gómez, Ocampo 967, Cañada de Gómez, Province of Santa Fé.
Aero Club Catamarca, Salta 1030, Catamarca, Province of Catamarca.
Aero Club Chaco, Edison 338, Resistencia, Chaco.
Aero Club Ciudad de Paraná, Laprida y Buenos Aires, Paraná, Province of Entre Ríos.
Aero Club Comodoro Rivadavia, Comodoro Rivadavia, Chubut.
Aero Club Concepción del Uruguay, Galarza y Colon, Concepción del Uruguay, Province of Entre Ríos.
Aero Club Coronel Pringles, Coronel Pringles, Province of Buenos Aires.
Aero Club Coronel Suarez, Lavalle 53, Coronel Suarez, Province of Buenos Aires.
Aero Club Córdobo, Aerodrome : "Las Players," Córdobo, Province of Córdobo.
Aero Club Corrientes, Corrientes, Province of Corrientes.
Circulo de Aviación, Rosario. Aerodrome : Paganini, Rosario, Province of Santa Fé.
Centro de Aviación Civil San Juan, Laprida 945, San Juan, Province of San Juan.
Aero Club Dolores, Dolores, Province of Buenos Aires.
Aero Club Esquel, Esquel, Chubut.
Aero Club Esquina, Esquina, Province of Corrientes.
Aero Club Formosa, Saavedra 276, Formosa.
Aero Club General Alvear, Avda. Alvear Este 74, General Alvear, Province of Mendoza.
Aero Club General Acha, General Acha, La Pampa.
Aero Club General Villegas, General Villegas, Province of Buenos Aires.
Aero Club Gualeguaychú, Presidente Wilson 97, Gualeguaychú, Province of Entre Ríos.
Aero Club Huinca Renancó, Huinca Renancó.
Aero Club Junin, Junin, Province of Buenos Aires.
Aero Club Jujuy, Belgrano 817, Jujuy, Province of Jujuy.
Aero Club La Plata, Calle 46 y 126, La Plata, Province of Buenos Aires.
Aero Club Las Flores, Avda. Carmen 612, Las Flores, Province of Buenos Aires.
Aero Club Neuquén, Neuquén.
Aero Club Nueve de Julio, Nueve de Julio, Province of Buenos Aires.
Aero Club Mar del Plata, San Martin 2726, Mar del Plata, Province of Buenos Aires.
Aero Club Mendoza, 9 de Julio 1122, Mendoza, Province of Mendoza.
Aero Club Pampeano, Avellaneda 245, Santa Rosa, La Pampa.
Aero Club Pergamino, 9 de Julio 874, Pergamino, Province of Buenos Aires.
Aero Club Plaza Huincul, Neuquén.
Aero Club Pigüé, Pigüé, Province of Buenos Aires.
Aero Club Posadas, Buenos Aires 320, Posadas, Misiones.
Aero Club Patagones, Patagones. Province of Buenos Aires.
Aero Club Quimillí, Quimillí, Province of Santiago del Estero.
Aero Club Rio Cuarto, Constitución 840, Rio Cuarto, Province of Córdoba.
Aero Club Río Gallegos, Roca 631, Río Gallegos, Santa Cruz.
Aero Club Rosario, Corrientes 321, Rosario, Province of Buenos Aires.
Aero Club Rafaela, Rafaela, Province of Santa Fé.
Aero Club Santa Fé, Suipacha y Rivadavia, Santa Fé, Province of Santa Fé.
Aero Club Saenz Peña, Calle 17-780, Saenz Peña, Chaco.
Aero Club Saladillo, Calle San Martín. Saladillo, Province of Buenos Aires.
Aero Club Salta, España 459, Salta, Province of Salta.
Aero Club San Francisco, San Francisco, Córdoba.
Aero Club San Luís, San Martin 329, San Luís, Province of San Luis.
Aero Club San Rafael, Godoy Cruz 155, San Rafael, Province of Mendoza.
Aero Club Santiago del Estero, 24 de Septiembre 256, Santiago del Estero, Province of Santiago del Estero.
Aero Club Tandil, Tandil, Province of Buenos Aires.
Aero Club Trelew, Trelew, Chubut.
Aero Club Tres Arroyos, Sarmiento 210, Tres Arroyos, Province of Buenos Aires.
Aero Club Tucumân, Avda. B. Teran 5a, Cuadra, Tucumán, Province of Buenos Aires.
Aero Club Veinticinco de Mayo, Calle 11-28-29. Veinticinco de Mayo, Province of Buenos Aires.
Aero Club Villa Maria, San Juan 1233, Villa María, Province of Córdoba.
Aero Club Venado Tuerto, Venado Tuerto, Province of Santa Fé.
Aero Club Villaguay, Balcarce 464, Villaguay, Province of Entre Ríos.
Aero Club Villa Mercedes, Villa Mercedes, Province of San Luis.
Aero Club Aapala, Zapala, Neuquén.

GLIDING CLUBS

Club Argentino de Planeadores "Albatros," Av. de Mayo 1370, Buenos Aires. Aerodrome : Merlo, Province of Buenos Aires.
Club de Planeadores "Otto Ballod," Sarmiento 345, González Chavez, Province of Buenos Aires.
"Condor" Aero Club de Planeadores, Leandro N. Alem 16;, Buenos Aires.
Club de Planeadores "Tandil," Constitución 485, Tandil, Province of Buenos Aires.
Club de Planeadores "Mar del Plata," Santiago del Estero 2376, Mar del Plata, Province of Buenos Aires.
Centro Aeronáutico de la Facultad de Ingeniería de La Plata, Calle 1 esq. 47, La Plata, Province of Buenos Aires.
Club de Planeadores "Paraná," Paraná, Province of Entre Ríos.
Centro de Aviación Popular "Los Tucanes," Ar. Avellaneda 456, Tucumán, Province of Tucumán.
Club Argentino de Planeadores "Las Golondrinas," Rivadavia 771, Punta Alta, Province of Buenos Aires.
Club de Planeadores "Golondrina," Av. Alvear 646, San Cristóbal, Province of Santa Fé.
Club de Planeadores "Urdinarrain," Urdinarrain, Province of Entre Rios.
Club de Planeadores "Nancú," Rivarola 570, Pehuajó, Province of Buenos Aires.
Aero Club Ceres, Ceres, Province of Santa Fé.
Club de Planeadores Esperanza, Esperanza, Province of Santa Fé.
Centro Argentino de Planeadores "Cañuelas," Canuelas, Province of Buenos Aires.
Club de Planeadores "Chajá," General Madariaga, Province of Buenos Aires.
Club de Planeadores San Juan, Laprida 736, San Juan, Province of San Juan.
Club Argentino de Planeadores Rosario, Rioja 2399, Rosario, Province of Santa Fé.
Club de Planeadores Córdoba, Dean Funes 252, Córdoba, Province of Córdoba.
Club de Planeadores Bell-Ville, Córdoba 72, Bell-Ville, Province of Córdoba.
Club de Planeadores Condor, Fuerte General Roca, Rio Negro.
Club Atlético Sarmiento, Villaguay, Province of Entre Rios.
Club de Planeadores Los Halcones, Catamarca, Province of Catamarca.
Club Argentino de Planeadores "Constitución," Villa Constitución, Province of Santa Fé.
Aero Club Bandera, Bandera, Province of Santiago del Estero.
Club de Planeadores Halcones, Tres de Febrero 3639, Santa Fé. Province of Santa Fé.
Aero Club Morteros, Morteros, Province of Córdoba.
Aero Club de Planeadores La Cumbre, La Cumbre, Province of Córdoba.
Centro Deportivo Industrial de Jóvenes "Jorge Newbery," Carhúe, Province of Buenos Aires.
Club de Planeadores Canals, Córdoba 84, Canals, Province of Córdoba.
Club de Planeadores Son Antonio Oeste, San Antonio Oeste, Rio Negro.
Club de Planeadores Tres Arroyos, Saens Peña 433, Tres Arroyos, Province of Buenos Aires.
Club de Planeadores "Chingolo," Perú 155, Santiago del Estero, Province of Santiago del Estero.
Club de Planeadores del Personal del Instituto Aerotécnico, Córdoba, Province of Córdoba.
Club de Planeadores Venado Tuerto, Deptp. General López, Province of Santa Fé.
Club de Planeadores "Tte. Luis Candelaria," Cutral-có, Neuquén.
Club de Planeadores Mendoza, Reg. Aéreo 3, Mendoza, Province of Mendoza.
Club de Planeadores Pilmaiken, Trenque Lauquen, Province of Buenos Aires.
Club Argentino de Planeadores "Nahuel-Pan," Esquel, Chubut.
Aero Club Oran, Coronel Echague 554, Oran, Province of Salta.
Club de Planeadores "Halcon." C. Falcon 3161, Victoria, Province of Buenos Aires.
Club de Planeadores General Pirán, General Pirán, Mar Chiquita, Province of Buenos Aires.
Club de Planeadores y Aeromodelismo "Punta Indio," Verónica, Province of Buenos Aires.
Aero Club General Pico, General Pico, La Pampa.
Club de Planeadores Catriló, Catriló, La Pampa.
Club de Planeadores General Conesa, General Conesa, La Pampa.

AERODROMES

During 1944 the Argentine Government decided to proceed with the construction of a new international airport in the Department of Esteban Echeverria, 40 miles from the City of Buenos Aires. The site covers an area of nearly 15,000 acres and the cost of the airport is estimated to be 30 million pesos.

For complete details regarding existing aerodromes in Argentina, reference should be made to *Guia Aeronautica de Aeropistas*, issued by E. B. Covey, at Avenida Roque Saens Peña 615, Buenos Aires.

BELGIUM

(**Kingdom of the Belgians—Royaume de Belgique**)

Since the liberation of Belgium and the re-establishment of the Government in Brussels the administration of all matters dealing with Civil Aviation has been the responsibility of the Ministère de Communications.

Belgian air transport is in the hands of the Société Anonyme Belge d'Exploitation de la Navigation Aérienne (S.A.B.E.N.A.) which is owned jointly by the Belgian Government, the Congo Colonial Government and the principal Belgian banks. Regular services have been re-established between Brussels and the Belgian Congo, Brussels and Paris and Brussels and London, but details were incomplete at the time of writing.

THE BELGIAN CONGO

ADMINISTRATION

By order of the Governor-General, dated December 27, 1939, an Aeronautical Service was created within the Service of Public Works of the Government to administer all matters concerning aviation in the Colony.

During the war the Belgian Congo in company with its neighbour state French Equatorial Africa, enjoyed a strategic position lying athwart the lines of communication by air between West Africa, the Sudan and South Africa. Several important air routes were operated across the territory and these are enumerated below.

At the end of 1944 a direct mail and passenger service (Lockheed Lodestars) between Leopoldville and Great Britain, by way of Lisbon was started but was discontinued when services were resumed in the Summer of 1945 between Belgium and the Belgian Congo.

TRANSPORT COMPANIES

Société Anonyme Belge D'Exploitation de la Navigation Aérienne (S.A.B.E.N.A.) (Congo).

Routes :—

- Léopoldville—Coquilhatville—Stanleyville. Fortnightly
- Léopoldville—Lulabourg—Elisabethville. Fortnightly.
- Stanleyville — Kindu — Manono—Elisabethville—Ndola—Lusaka — Bulawayo — Johannesburg — Bloemfontein — Cape Town. Fortnightly.
- Luluabourg—Tshikapa—Kikwit—Léopoldville. Weekly.
- Léopoldville — Banningville — Inongo — Coquilhatville — Libenge — Lisala — Bumba — Basoko — Stanleyville. Fortnightly.
- Stanleyville — Irumu — Costermansville — Usumbura — Kindu—Kabalo—Manono—Elisabethville. Fortnightly.

The following freight services were operated under contract to British Airways.

- Léopoldville — Pointe Noire — Libreville — Duala — Lagos. Weekly.
- Takoradi — Lagos — Duala — Libenge — Stanleyville — Entebbe — Juba — Khartoum — Wadi Halfa — Cairo. Twice weekly.

South African Airways

The bi-monthly service inaugurated in March, 1941, from Entebbe (Uganda) to Léopoldville was suspended in July, 1942, and a new weekly service commenced from Johannesburg to Léopoldville with stops in the Belgian Congo at Elisabethville, Irumu, Stanleyville and Coquilhatville.

PRINCIPAL METEOROLOGICAL POSTS

Léopoldville, Coquilhatville, Elisabethville, Costermansville, Stanleyville.

AERODROMES

BANNINGVILLE (Prov. Léopoldville) :—Civil Customs Aerodrome. Wireless, hangar, repairs, petrol, sanitary service.

BOMA (Prov. Léopoldville) :—Civil Customs Aerodrome. Petrol hangar, repairs, sanitary service.

EOLO-BAMBINGA (Prov. Léopoldville) :—Civil Aerodrome. Petrol.

INONGO (Prov. Léopoldville) :—Civil Aerodrome. Wireless, petrol.

KIKWIT (Prov. Léopoldville) :—Civil Aerodrome. Petrol, Meteorological facilities, Radio.

LÉOPOLDVILLE (Prov. Léopoldville) :—Civil Customs Aerodrome. Wireless, hangers, repairs, meteorological station, sanitary service.

MATADI (Prov. Léopoldville) :—Civil Aerodrome.

THYSVILLE (Prov. Léopoldville) :—Civil Aerodrome.

BASANKUSU (Prov. Coquilhatville) :—Civil Aerodrome. Hangar, wireless, repairs, petrol.

BUMBA (Prov. Coquilhatville) :—Civil Aerodrome. Wireless.

COQUILHATVILLE (Prov. Coquilhatville) :—Civil Customs Aerodrome. Hangar, wireless, repairs, petrol, meteorological station, sanitary service.

LIBENGE (Prov. Coquilhatville) :—Civil Customs Aerodrome. Hangar, wireless, petrol, repairs, sanitary service.

LISALA (Prov. Coquilhatville) :—Civil Aerodrome. Wireless, petrol, sanitary service.

BASOKO (Prov. Stanleyville) :—Civil Aerodrome. Wireless, petrol.

LOWA (Prov. Stanleyville) :—Civil Aerodrome.

KASENYI (Prov. Stanleyville) :—Civil Aerodrome. Sanitary service.

STANLEYVILLE (Prov. Stanleyville) :—Civil Customs Aerodrome. Hangar, wireless, repairs, sanitary service.

LUEBO (Prov. Lusambo) :—Civil Aerodrome. Hangars, petrol.

LULUABOURG (Prov. Lusambo) :—Civil Aerodrome. Hangar, petrol, repairs.

LUSAMBO (Prov. Lusambo) :—Civil Aerodrome. Hangar, wireless, petrol, repairs.

LUPUTA (Prov. Lusambo) :—Civil Aerodrome. Petrol.

PORT FRANCQUI (Prov. Lusambo) :—Civil Aerodrome. Hangar, wireless, petrol, repairs.

TSHIKAPA (Prov. Lusambo) :—Civil Aerodrome. Petrol, Meteorological facilities, radio and repairs.

BUKAMA (Prov. Elisabethville) :—Civil Aerodrome. Petrol.

ELISABETHVILLE (Prov. Elisabethville) :—Civil Customs Aerodrome. Hangar, repairs, petrol, meteorological station, sanitary service. Manager : Jose de la Reza.

KAMINA (Prov. Elisabethville) :—Civil Aerodrome.

KONGOLO (Prov. Elisabethville) :—Civil Aerodrome. Wireless.

KABALO (Prov. Elisabethville) :—Civil Aerodrome. Hangar.

MANONO (Prov. Elisabethville) :—Civil Aerodrome.

N'GULE (Prov. Elisabethville) :—Civil Aerodrome. Hangar, repairs, petrol.

KINDU (Prov. Costermansville) :—Civil Aerodrome.

KASONGO (Prov. Costermansville) :—Civil Aerodrome.

USUMBURA (Ruanda-Urundi) :—Civil Aerodrome. Sanitary service.

BOLIVIA

(The Bolivian Republic—República Boliviana)

ADMINISTRATION

Civil Aviation in Bolivia is under the jurisdiction of the Ministry of Defence.

Minister of National Defence : Lieut Col. José Pinto.

Director of Aeronautics : Colonel Alfredo Santalla E.

TRANSPORT COMPANIES

Lloyd Aéreo Boliviano (L.A.B.)

Offices : Nataniel Aguirre 166, Cochabamba.

Commercial Manager : Coronel Meliton Brito.

This airline which began operations in 1926 was largely fostered by German aviation interests, chiefly the Deutsche Lufthansa. On May 14, 1941, the company was expropriated by the Bolivian Government. In order to improve the operations of the company an agreement was concluded on June 9, 1941, between the General Loan Administrator in the U.S.A., the Bolivian Government and L.A.B. whereby Pan American Grace Airways loaned personnel for instruction purposes, etc. The agreement provides that only American nationals shall be employed. The Government continues to subsidize the company by monthly payments of 16,000 Bolivians (13.333 Bol. = £1 at par).

Considerable reorganization has taken place since 1941, including improvements in aerodromes, equipment, meteorological services and schools, and the company may now be considered to be as modern and as well run as any in Latin America. As part of the reorganization, two Lockheed Lodestars were acquired from the U.S.A.

Routes :—

Cobija—Cochabamba. Weekly, via Riberalta.
Cobija—Riberalta. Weekly.
Riberalta—Cochabamba. Weekly, via Guayaramerin, San Joaquin, Magdalena, Trinidad.
Cochabamba—Santa Cruz. Weekly, via Trinidad.
Santa Cruz—Cochabamba. Weekly. via Trinidad, Santa Ana.
Cochabamba—La Paz. Twice weekly, via Oruro.
La Paz—San Borja. Fortnightly.
La Paz—Apolo. Fortnightly.

Aircraft :—Two Lockheed Lodestars, two Junkers Ju 52, three Junkers Ju 86 (two for freight purposes), and one Grumman G-21 amphibian.

Compagnie Aramayo de Mines en Bolivie, Casilla 634, La Paz.

This Company operates a private service from La Paz to Tipuany for gold transportation, using amphibians of American manufacture.

Pan American-Grace Airways Inc. (Panagra).

Headquarters in Bolivia : W. R. Grace & Co., La Paz.

The Company has three routes operating through Bolivia as part of its Balboa—Buenos Aires main services :—

The "La Diagonal" service stops twice weekly at La Paz, Oruro, Uyuni.

The "El Transcontinental" service stops weekly at La Paz, Oruro, Cochabamba, Santa Cruz.

An additional service from Arica (Chile) to Corumba (Brazil) and connecting with Panair do Brasil, stops weekly at La Paz, Oruro, Cochabamba, Santa Cruz, Concepcion, San Ignacio, San José, Robore, Puerto Suarez.

In addition to the above internal routes the company is assisting in the development programme of Lloyd Aéreo Boliviano under the terms of a five-year management contract.

AERODROMES

The principal aerodromes in Bolivia are :—AIQUILE, APOLO, CACHUELA ESPERANZA, CAÑADA LARGA, CHARAGUA, CHORETI, COBIJA, COCHABAMBA, COMARAPA, CONCEPCION, GUAYARAMERIN, IPIAS, JOROCHITO, LAJAS, LA PAZ, MAGDALENA, MIZQUE, MOTACUSITO, ORURO, POZO DEL TIGRE, PULQUINA, PUERTO SUAREZ, RIBERALTA, ROBORÉ, SAN BORJA, SAN IGNACIO, SAN JAVIER, SAN JOSÉ, SAN LORENZO, SANTA ANA, SANTA CRUZ, SUCRE, TARIJA, TODOS SANTOS, TRINIDAD, TRES CRUCES, UYUNI, VALLE ABAJO, VALLE GRANDE, VILLA MONTES, VILLAZON, YACUIBA.

BRAZIL

(The United States of Brazil—Estados Unidos do Brasil)

ADMINISTRATION

On January 20, 1941, by Decree No. 2,961, an Air Ministry was formed to control and co-ordinate all flying activities in Brazil. The Minister for Air is Major-General Armando Trompowski. The Department of Civil Aeronautics, under the Director of Civil Aviation, Dr. Junqueira Ayres, is divided into four branches :—Administration, Traffic, Operations and Meteorology. The address of the Department is :—Departamento de Aeronautica Civil, Aeroporto Santos Dumont, Rio de Janeiro, Brazil.

ASSOCIATIONS

Aero Club do Brasil, Rua Alvaro Alvim No. 31, Rio de Janeiro. Founded : 1911. President : Colonel João Correa Dias Costa. Affiliated with the *Fédération Aéronautique Internationale* (F.A.I.). Controls the activities of all Flying Clubs in Brazil.

PUBLICATIONS

Azas (Wings). Founded in 1922. Published monthly. Official organ of the Aero Club do Brasil. Office : Rua Alvaro Alvim No. 31 and Rua 1° de Março 101, Rio de Janeiro. Director in charge : Cap. Salvador C. de Sá e Benevides. Chief Editor : José Garcia de Souza.

Aviacão. Founded in 1937. Published monthly. Technical Director : L. Nobre de Almeida. Office : Rua Uruguayana No. 104—Sala 407.

Boletim do Ministerio da Aeronautica. Founded in 1941. Official monthly bulletin published by the Ministry of Aeronautics and containing all decrees, laws, dispatches, etc., concerning Brazilian air activities.

Revista Aerea Latina Americana. Published monthly in Spanish by the Aeronautical Digest Publishing Corporation, New York, U.S.A. Representative for South America : José Garcia de Souza. Address : Rua 1° de Marco No. 101, Rio de Janeiro.

TRANSPORT COMPANIES

Pan American World Airways.

Routes :—

The "East Coast Flyer" service stops 3 times weekly in each direction at Belem, Barreiras and Rio de Janeiro. This service also stops four times weekly in each direction at the following towns on the coast route :—

Belem — São Luiz — Fortaleza — Natal — Recife — Maceio—Salvador—Rio de Janeiro. 2,497 miles.

Rio de Janeiro—São Paulo—Curityba—Iguassu Falls—

Asuncion (Paraguay)—Buenos Aires (Argentina). 1,601 miles. Weekly.

Rio de Janeiro- São Paulo Porto Alegre—Montevideo (Uruguay)—Buenos Aires (Argentina). Seven times weekly in each direction.

Belem—Miami (U.S.A.). A weekly cargo service only.

Panair do Brasil, S.A., Avenida Rio Branco 85, Rio de Janeiro. President : Dr. Paulo Sampaio. Manager : Mr. Frank Sampaio.

This Company was started as a Brazilian concern on Sept. 15, 1930, shortly after the general consolidation of Pan American Airways' services in South America. Panair do Brasil is in close contact with the parent company. Its operations headquarters are at the Santos Dumont Airport, Rio de Janeiro, and its flying operations are confined to Brazil, except for the extension to Asuncion.

Early in September, 1943, the Company began flying between Belem, Fortaleza and Rio de Janeiro by night. This is the first illuminated section of any air route in South America.

Routes :—

Rio de Janeiro—Belem, via S. Salvador, Maceio, Recife, Natal, Fortaleza, Parnahyba and Sã Louiz. Four times weekly.

Rio de Janeiro—Recife, via Victoria, Cannavieras, Behia, Aracaju and Maceio. Once weekly.

Rio de Janeiro—Cuyaba, via São Paulo, Bauru, Campo Grande and Corumba. Twice weekly.

Rio de Janeiro—Campo Grande, via São Paulo, Curityba, Iguassu Falls, Asuncion (Paraguay) and Ponta Pora. Once weekly.

Rio de Janeiro—Porto Alegre, via São Paulo (four times weekly), via São Paulo and Florianapolis (once weekly), and via São Paulo and Curitiba (twice weekly).

Rio de Janeiro—Goyania, via Bello Horizonte and Guaratinga. Once weekly.

Rio de Janeiro—Uberaba, via Bello Horizonte and Araxa. Thrice weekly.

Rio de Janerio—Gov. Valladares, via Bello Horizonte. Once weekly.

Rio de Janeiro—Montes Claros, via Bello Horizonte. Once weekly.

Rio de Janeiro—São Paulo, via Bello Horizonte and Pocos de Caldas. Four times weekly.

Rio de Janeiro—Bello Horizonte. Four times weekly.

Belem—Manaõs, via Santarem (once weekly), via Curralinho, Monte Allegre, Santarem and Parintins (once weekly), and via Grupa, Santarem, Obidos and Itacoatiara (once weekly).

Manaõs—Porto Velho, via Borba and Manicore (once weekly), and via Manicore and Humayta (once weekly).

Manaõs—Iquitos (Peru), via Codajaz, Coary, Teffe, Fonte Boa, Sto. Antonio de Ica, S. Paulo de Olivenca, Tabatinga and Benjamin Constant. Once weekly.

Pan American-Grace Airways, Inc. (Panair). Passenger Ticket and Air Express Office : Corumba Airport.

Operates from Corumba to Lima (Peru) via Bolivia. Weekly.

S.A. Empresade Viação Aerea Rio Grandense (Varig) P.O. Box 243, Porto Alegre.

This airline was started in conjunction with the Sindicato Condor in 1927 and took over services in the South of Brazil which for a short time previously had been flown by Condor itself. The Company operates from headquarters at Porto Alegre entirely in the State of Rio Grande do Sul, from which state it has received a subsidy since 1932.

Routes :—

Porto Alegre—Rio Grande. Four times weekly.

Porto Alegre — Estrela — Cruz Alta — Carasinha — Passo Fundo—Estrela—Porto Alegre. Twice weekly.

Porto Alegre — Pacheca — Pelotas — Bagé — Don Pedrito —Livramento—Quarahy—Uruguaiana. Weekly.

Porto Alegre — Pacheco — Pelotas — Bagé — Don Pedrito —Livramento—Alegrete—Urugaiana. Weekly.

Porto Alegre—São Gabriel—Alegrete—Uruguayan. Twice weekly.

Porto Alegre — Pacheca — Pelotas — Jaguarao — Montevideo. Twice weekly.

Porto Alegre—Pelotas. Twice weekly.

Viação Aerea São Paulo, S.A., Rue Libero Badaro No. 92, São

Paulo. President: Napoleao Lorena Marianho. Superintendent: Marcos Melega.

This airline, usually called the "Vasp," was started in 1934 with Brazilian capital, 75% of the shares being controlled by the State and Municipality of São Paulo.

Routes:—

Sao Paulo—Rio de Janeiro. Four round trips daily, two on Sundays.

São Paulo—Ribeirão Preto—Franca—Uberaba—Uberlandia—Araguary—Catalão—Ipamery—Annapolis—Goyania. Weekly.

Sociedade Aerea Cruzeiro do Sul, Limitada, Avenida Rio Branco 128, Rio de Janeiro. President: Dr. Jose Bento Ribeiro Dantas.

This Company, formerly known as Sindicato Condor Limitada, was taken over by the Brazilian Government in 1940 and renamed Serviços Aereos Condor Limitada. The reorganization was completed in November, 1942, when the present name was adopted.

In order to strengthen this airline arrangements were made with the Defense Supplies Corporation (U.S.A.) to obtain aircraft and technical assistance. Four Douglas DC-3 aircraft were delivered in 1943, and these aircraft carried a group of twenty-five American technicians who were in a purely advisory capacity for a period not to exceed eighteen months, in order to train Brazilian personnel in the operation, maintenance and overhaul of American equipment.

German aircraft, taken over at the time of the reorganization, are still being used, including twelve Junkers Ju 52 and two Focke-Wulf Fw 200 Condor airliners.

Routes:—

Rio de Janeiro — Vitoria — Caravelas — Canavieiras — Ilheus — San Salvador — Maceió or Aracajú — Recife — Natal. Twice weekly.

Natal—Fernando de Noronha. Weekly.

Natal — Mossoro — Fortaleza — Acaraú — Sobral — São Benedito — Sta Quitéria — Cratens — Tauá — Saboeiro — C. Sales — Jaicos — Picos — Oeiras — Floriano — Regeneração — San Pedro — Teresina. Weekly

Rio de Janeiro—São Paulo—Porto Alegre—Buenos Aires. Weekly.

Rio de Janeiro—São Paulo—Curitiba—Joinville—Itajai—Florianopolis—Porto Alegre. Weekly.

São Paulo—Curitiba—Porto Alegre. Weekly.

São Paula—Curitiba—Florianopolis. Weekly.

São Paulo—Aracatuba—Tres Lagaos—Campo Grande—Corumba—Cuiaba. Weekly.

Navegação Aerea Brasileira S/A., Avenida Nilo Pechanha 31, Rio de Janeiro. President: Dr. Paulo Rocha Vianna.

Commonly called "NAB," this Company inaugurated its first service on September 9, 1941.

Routes:—

Rio de Janeiro—Bello Horizonte—Lapa—Petrolina—Fortaleza. Twice weekly.

Rio de Janeiro—Bello Horizonte—Lapa—Letrolina—Recife. Weekly.

Rio de Janeiro — Bello Horizonte — Lapa — Teresina. Weekly.

Aerovias do Brasil S.A. Avenida Aparecio Borges 123, Rio de Janeiro.

President: Luiz Felipe de Souza Sampaio.

This Company, a subsidiary of the Taca organization, is operating an unscheduled charter freight service from Rio de Janeiro to Miami about every ten days, using a Lockheed 14.

Viacas Aerea Santos Dumont.

This company, formed in 1944, operates a bi-weekly freight service from Rio de Janeiro to Salvador, Aracaju and Recife. Its fleet consists of three Consolidated Catalina flying-boats and one Budd RB-1 twin-engined freight carrier.

Linha Aerea Transcontinental Brasiliera S.A.

A new company formed in 1944 which plans to establish airlines throughout the interior of Brazil. It has bought six Canadian-built Avro Ansons from the War Assets Corpn. in Canada and these aircraft were ferried by air from Montreal to Rio de Janeiro over the year end.

MILITARY AIR MAIL SERVICE

Correio Aéreo Nacional

The air mail services operated under this title are flown by military aircraft and at the same time are used for the training of pilots of the Forças Aereas Brasileiras (Brazilian Air Force). Waco and Beechcraft single-engined aircraft are used principally, flying about 50,000 kilometres weekly.

FLYING CLUBS

The Directorate of Civil Aviation, through a special Aero Club Department, gives help an encouragement to the Flying Clubs in many ways, one of the most important being the distribution of suitable instructional aircraft. Approximately 350 light aeroplanes of American and national manufacture are now owned by the approved clubs.

AERODROMES

Although the number of aerodromes in 1930 totalled only 31, this number has rapidly increased until at the end of 1941 the number was nearly 600. Reference should be made to the *Guia Aeronautica de Aeropistas*, obtainable through E. B. Covey, Avenida Roque Saenz Peña 615, Buenos Aires.

THE BRITISH COMMONWEALTH OF NATIONS

1—THE BRITISH EMPIRE

GREAT BRITAIN

ADMINISTRATION

The control of Civil Aviation in the United Kingdom is vested in the Minister of Civil Aviation, and orders are issued from time to time under his authority for the safety and benefit of all concerned with Civil flying in the British Isles.

The Ministry of Civil Aviation

Minister of Civil Aviation: Lord Winster.

Parliamentary Secretary to the Ministry of Civil Aviation: Ivor Thomas, M.P.

Permanent Secretary of the Ministry of Civil Aviation: Sir Henry Self, K.C.M.G., K.B.E., C.B., B.A., B.Sc., B.D.

Air Registration Board

Address: Brettenham House, Lancaster Place, Strand, London, W.C.2.

Lord Brabazon of Tara, M.C., P.C. (Chairman), Guy F. Johnson (Hon. Treasurer), Major R. H. Thornton.

Representing Aircraft Operators: F. C. R. Jaques, The Viscount Knollys, Capt. G. P. Olley and Col. R. Preston.

Representing Aircraft Manufacturers: R. H. Dobson, J. D. North, Sir Frederick Handley Page and C. C. Walker.

Representing Aircraft Insurers: Capt. A. G. Lamplugh, L. Murray Stewart, A. B. Stewart and A. J. Whittall.

Members Appointed by the Minister of Civil Aviation: Wing-Cdr. R. H. Stocken.

Secretary: T. R. Thomas, B.Sc.

The Air Registration Board, set up in February, 1937, undertakes such functions in connection with design, construction and maintenance of civil aircraft as may be delegated to it by the Minister of Civil Aviation. It is responsible for the issue of Certificates of Airworthiness to all British civil aircraft.

The Board was incorporated as a company trading not for profit, limited by guarantee and without share capital. Before the War it received a measure of assistance from Air Votes to enable it to perform the functions delegated to it. Those functions continued during the War on a reduced scale and the assistance from public funds was reduced accordingly, but, owing to the development of present and post-war civil aviation, the Board's activities are now expanding.

ASSOCIATIONS

The Royal Aeronautical Society (with which is incorporated the Institution of Aeronautical Engineers). Founded: 1866. Offices: 4, Hamilton Place, W.1.

President: Sir Frederick Handley Page, C.B.E., F.R.Ae.S. Vice-Presidents: Dr. H. Roxbee Cox, Ph.D., D.I.C., B.Sc., F.R.Ae.S., and Sir Oliver Simmonds, M.A., F.R.Ae.S., M.P. Librarian: Mr. J. E. Hodgson, Hon. F.R.Ae.S. Secretary: Captain J. Laurence Pritchard, Hon. F.R.Ae.S.

The Royal Aeronautical Society, founded in 1866, is the oldest institution in the World devoted to flying. It exists for the furtherance of the Science of Aeronautics, and its activities fall under the following headings:—

(1) Protecting the interests of the aeronautical profession by conferring a technical status on those qualified for such distinction. It acts as the professional society or institution of qualified aeronautical engineers. (2) Organizing discussions and publishing papers on subjects of importance in connection with the various branches of aeronautical science. (3) Encouraging and assisting technical students who desire to adopt the aeronautical profession for their careers. (4) Providing an organization wherein those interested in aeronautics from scientific or other motives, but who are not professionally connected with aviation, may meet together, have opportunity of study, and keep themselves in touch with current aeronautical affairs.

Branches of the Royal Aeronautical Society exist in the following places:—Belfast, Bristol, Brough, Cambridge, Coventry, Derby, Gloucester and Cheltenham, Hatfield, Isle of Wight, Leicester, Luton, Manchester, Portsmouth, Reading, Rochester, Southampton, Weybridge, Yeovil, and overseas at Sydney, Australia; Montreal and Ottawa, Canada; Capetown, S. Africa.

The Royal Aero Club of the United Kingdom. Founded: 1909. Offices: 119, Piccadilly, London, W.1. Affiliated to the *Fédération Aéronautique Internationale.* President: Lord Brabazon of Tara, M.C., P.C. Vice-Presidents: The Duke of Sutherland, K.T., The Marquess of Londonderry, K.G., P.C., M.V.O., Lord Gorell, C.B.E., M.C., Captain Sir Geoffrey de Havilland, O.B.E., Lt-Col. Sir Francis K. McClean, A.F.C., and Sir Frederick Handley Page, C.B.E. Chairman: Lieut. Col. Sir Francis K. McClean, A.F.C. Secretary: Colonel Rupert Preston, C.B.E.

The Club was formed for the association of persons interested in the encouragement and development of the study of aeronautics in all its branches, and for that purpose to provide a centre of information and advice on matters pertaining to aeronautics, to undertake the control of all competitions, sporting events, and trials in connection with aeronautics in the United Kingdom, and generally to do all such acts and things as may be conducive to the encouragement and development of aeronautics. It is the governing body of the sport of flying.

The Royal Air Force Club. Founded: 1918. Offices: 128, Piccadilly, London, W.1. Secretary: Air Cdre. W. H. Dunn, D.S.C., R.A.F. (retired).

This Club exists for the association of officers of the R.A.F., the Fleet Air Arm and the Air Forces of the Dominions and Colonies, and its ordinary membership is confined exclusively to such officers. It was formed originally as the Royal Flying Corps Club. It includes officers of the R.N.A.S., the R.F.C., and all officers who have been attached to these Services.

The Society of British Aircraft Constructors, Ltd. Incorp.: 1916. Offices: 32, Savile Row, London, W.1. President: Arthur Gouge, B.Sc., M.I.Mech.E., F.R.Ae.S., F.I.Ae.S. (U.S.A.). Vice-President: Robert Blackburn, O.B.E., A.M.I.C.E., F.R.Ae.S., M.I.M.E. Solicitor: C. V. Allen. Director: E. C. Bowyer.

The Society is officially recognized as the representative body of the British Aircraft Industry. It acts by agreement in co-operation with the Royal Aeronautical Society and the Royal Aero Club in all matters of common interest.

The Guild of Air Pilots and Air Navigators of the British Empire. Temporary War-time Address: 61, Cheapside, London, E.C.2.

The Guild was founded on October 1, 1929, to further the efficiency of commercial aviation and to uphold the dignity and prestige of air pilots and navigators. Master: The Marquess of Londonderry, K.G., P.C., M.V.O. Deputy Master: Air Vice-Marshal D. C. T. Bennett, C.B., C.B.E., D.S.O. Clerk: Lawrence A. Wingfield, M.C., D.F.C. Treasurer: Norman Holden, Esq., O.B.E. Asisstant Treasurer: Wing Cdr. C. A. Pike, A.F.C., A.F.R.Ae.S.

The Air League of the British Empire. Date of Incorp.: 1909. Offices: Kinnaird House, 1a, Pall Mall East, London, S.W.1. President: His Grace the Duke of Sutherland, K.T. Chairman of the Executive Committee: Air Chief Marshal Sir Philip Joubert de la Ferte, K.C.B., C.M.G., D.S.O. Secretary General: E. Colston Shepard.

The British Gliding Association. Offices: 119. Piccadilly, London, W.1. Chairman: Prof. D. A. Brunt, M.A.

On the Declaration of War on Sept. 3, 1939, gliding came under the general ban imposed on civil flying.

The British Air Line Pilots Association. Founded 1937. Offices: Suites 5 and 6, 9-10, Marble Arch, London, W.1. President: His Grace the Duke of Hamilton and Brandon, A.F.C. Secretary: A. D. Saward, A.C.A.

The principal objects of the Association are to protect, improve and advance the interests of its members and of the profession generally. The business of the Association is done through the Central Board, which is composed of the following members: Capt. J. W. G. James (Chairman), Capts. M. J. R. Alderson, R. Allen, V. A. M. Hunt, E. Rotheram, W. N. C. Griffiths, G. P. Wood and D. Barclay, M.B.E.

Society of Aircraft Engineers. Address 356/366, Oxford Street, London, W.1. Secretary: E. Frank. The object of the Society is to advance the interests of Licensed Aircraft Engineers.

Association of British Aircraft Operators. Address: 60, Haymarket, London, S.W.1.

PUBLICATIONS

Aeronautics. Published monthly, price 2/-, by C. Arthur Pearson, Ltd., Tower House, Southampton Street, Strand, London, W.C.2. Editor: Oliver Stewart, M.C., A.F.C.

The Aeroplane. Published weekly, price 1/-, by Temple Press, Ltd., Bowling Green Lane, London, E.C.1. Founded in 1911 by C. G. Grey. Editor Thurston James.

The Aeroplane Spotter. Incorporating the Bulletin of The National Association of Spotters' Clubs. Published fortnightly, price 3d., by Temple Press, Ltd., Bowling Green Lane, London, E.C.1. Editor: Charles W. Cain.

Air Training Corps Gazette. Journal of the Air Training Corps. Published monthly, price 6d., by the Air League of the British Empire, Kinnaird House, 1a, Pall Mall East, London, S.W.1. Editor: Leonard Taylor.

Air Transport and Airport Engineering. Published monthly, price 1/-, by Temple Press, Ltd., Bowling Green Lane, London, E.C.1. Editor: John Longhurst.

Aircraft Engineering. Published monthly, price 2/-, by Bunhill Publications, Ltd., 12, Bloomsbury Square, London, W.C.1. Editor: Lieut.-Col. W. Lockwood Marsh, O.B.E., F.R.Ae.S., M.S.A.E., F.I.Ae.S.

Aircraft Production. Published monthly by Iliffe & Sons, Ltd., Dorset House, Stamford Street, London, S.E.1.

All the World's Aircraft. Founded in 1909 by the late Fred T. Jane. Published annually, price £3 3s., by Sampson Low, Marston & Company, Ltd., 43, Ludgate Hill, London, E.C.4. Edited and compiled by Leonard Bridgman.

Flight. Founded 1909. (Official Journal of the Royal Aero Club.) Published weekly, price 1/-, by Flight Publishing Company Ltd., Stamford Street, London, S.E.1. Editor: C. M. Poulsen.

The Journal of the Royal Aeronautical Society. The official organ of the Royal Aeronautical Society. Founded 1897, as the Aeronautical Journal. Published monthly, price 7/6, by The Royal Aeronautical Society, 4, Hamilton Place, London, W.1. Editor: Joan Bradbrooke.

Sailplane and Glider. Published monthly, Price 1/-, by the Mendip Press, 231, Strand, London, W.C.2. Joint Editors: Dr. Alan Slater and Vernon Blunt.

FLYING CLUBS

On the outbreak of War on Spetember 3, 1939, all civil flying in Great Britain was banned. All the flying clubs were compelled to close down: their aircraft either being taken over by the Government or put into store and their officials, instructors, ground engineers and many members joining the flying services.

On January 1, 1946, the ban on civil flying was lifted and many flying clubs and schools were planning to begin operations early in the year. Under a fuel rationing scheme introduced concurrently with the lifting of the ban, flying clubs were allocated sufficient fuel to permit 50 hours flying per aircraft per month. Private owners were allocated fuel sufficient for four hours flying per month.

TRANSPORT COMPANIES

The policy of the Socialist Government is that the air transport services of the United Kingdom should be placed under national ownership and control. Under this policy the Government has decided to establish three separate statutory corporations with the following spheres of responsibility: (*a*) routes between the United Kingdom and other Commonwealth countries the United States and the Far East (to be operated by the existing B.O.A.C.); (*b*) internal routes in the United Kingdom and routes to the continent of Europe (British European Airways); and (*c*) routes between the United Kingdom and South America (British South American Airways).

British Overseas Airways Corporation.

Head Office: Airways House, 20, Berkeley Square, London, W.1.

Chairman: Viscount Knollys, K.C.M.G., M.B.E., D.F.C. Deputy Chairman: Sir Harold Howitt, D.S.O., M.C. Other members of the Board are:—Gerard d'Erlanger, John Marchbank, Major K. R. McCrindle, Lord Burghley, G. M. Garro-Jones, Sir Harold Hartley, Major R. H. Thornton and Clement Wakefield Jones.

The British Overseas Airways Corporation, was during the war entirely at the disposal of the Secretary of State for Air. It flew routes which were prescribed for it, and which were in no sense determined by commercial considerations, but purely by war needs; it carried almost exclusively Government passengers and freight, and had no control over its loads. To a preponderating extent its traffic produced no commercial revenue and, moreover, a large proportion of the money paid to it by the Government was not in respect of flying operations at all, but of factories which it operated on behalf of Government Departments, notably the Ministry of Aircraft Production, and of other services it performed.

Regional and Overseas Headquarters Offices.

European Region: H.Q., Airways Terminal, Buckingham Palace Road, London, S.W.1.
West Atlantic Region: H.Q., Marine Terminal, Municipal Airport, Baltimore 22, Md., U.S.A.
Middle East Region: H.Q., 4, Shara Baehler, Cairo, Egypt.
South African Region: H.Q., Devonshire Court, Victoria Embankment, P.O. Box 936, Durban.
India and Burma Region: H.Q., Finlay House, McLeod Road, Karachi, India.
Headquarters, West Africa: Airways House, Marina, Lagos.
Headquarters, Iberian Peninsula: 23-27, Avenida da Libertade, Lisbon, Portugal.
Headquarters, East Africa: Rhodes House, Delamere Avenue, Nairobi, Kenya.
Headquarters, New York: British Empire Building, 620, Fifth Avenue, New York 20, U.S.A.
Headquarters, Scandinavia: Citypalatset, Norrmalstorg 1, Stockholm, Sweden.

Principal Associated and Subsidiary Companies.

Indian Trans-Continental Airways, Ltd.
Qantas-Empire Airways, Ltd.
Tasman Empire-Airways, Ltd.

The Corporations main landplane base in Great Britain in 1945 was Hurn and for flying-boats, at Poole both near Bournemouth. Other landplane bases were Croydon and Prestwick.

Routes Operating at July 31, 1945.

Poole — Foynes — Lisbon — Bathurst — Belem — Trinidad — Bermuda — Baltimore, returning Bermuda — Lisbon — Poole (winter) or Poole — Foynes — Botwood — Baltimore and return (Summer). Four times weekly in Summer of 1945 (Boeing 314A flying-boats).
Prestwick—Montreal (North Atlantic Return Ferry Service). Seven times weekly. (Liberator III landplanes).
Hurn—Lydda—Karachi—Colombo. Twice weekly. (Lancastrian landplanes).
Cairo — Wadi Halfa— —Khartoum — El Fasher — El Geneina — Maiduguri — Kano — Lagos — Accra. Twice weekly. (Dakota landplanes).
Poole — Marignane — Augusta — Cairo — Habbaniyeh — Bahrein — Jiwani — Karachi — Calcutta. Twice weekly to Calcutta, four times weekly to Karachi. (Sunderland flying-boats).
Hurn—Istres—Tripoli—El Adem—cairo. Thrice weekly. (Liberator III landplanes).
Hurn — Rabat — Tripoli — Cairo — Shaibah — Karachi. Twice weekly. (Dakota landplanes).
Cairo — Lydda — Baghdad — Basra — Bahrein — Jiwani — Karachi — Delhi — Allahabad — Calcutta. Connecting with this service at Karachi, Qantas-Empire Airways operates via Ceylon to Australia. Thrice weekly. (Ensign landplanes).
Cairo — Luxor — Port Sudan — Asmara — Kamaran — Aden — Riyan — Salalah — Masirah — Jiwani— Karachi. Once weekly. (Lodestar landplanes).
Great Britain—Eire. Shuttle service as required to meet trans-Atlantic services. (Dakota and Lodestar landplanes).
Great Britain—Lisbon. (Dakota landplanes).
Great Britain—Madrid—Lisbon. Once weekly. (Dakota landplanes).
Great Britain—Lisbon—Gibraltar. Thrice weekly. (Dakota landplanes).
Great Britain — Lisbon — Rabat — Port Etienne — Bathurst — Freetown — Takoradi — Accra — Lagos. Twice weekly. (Dakota landplanes).
Croydon—Stockholm. Daily. (Dakota landplanes).
Cairo — Nicosia — Ankara — Istanbul. Twice weekly. (Lodestar landplanes).
Cairo—Damascus—Baghdad—Teheran. Thrice weekly. (Lodestar landplanes).
Cairo—Lydda—Baghdad—Basra.
Cairo—Port Sudan—Jeddah. Once weekly. (Lodestar landplanes).
Cairo — Luxor — Jeddah — Port Sudan — Asmara — Kamaran—Aden—Addis Ababa. Once weekly. (Lodestar landplanes).
Cairo—Luxor—Port Sudan—Asmara—Aden. Twice weekly. (Lodestar landplanes).
Cairo — Wadi Halfa — Khartoum — Malakal — Juba — Kisumu — Nairobi — Kasama — Gwelo. Twice weekly. (Lodestar landplanes).
Durban — Lourenco Marques — Beira — Diego Saurez — Pamanzi — Mozambique — Lindi — Dar es Salaam — Mombasa — Kisumu — Port Bell — Laropi — Malakal — Khartoum — Wadi Halfa — Luxor — Cairo — Kallia — Habbaniyah — Basra — Bahrein — Dubai — Jiwani — Karachi — Raj Samand — Gwalior — Allahabad — Calcutta. Twice weekly. (Short "C" Class flying-boats).
Kisumu — Mombasa — Dar es Salaam — Lindi — Pamanzi — Diego Suarez (Madagascar). Once weekly. (Short "C" Class flying-boats).
Kisumu — Mombasa — Diego Saurez — Mozambique — Mahé — Addu Atoll — Durban — Kogalla. (Short "C" Class flying-boats).

Statistics

	1944	Percentage increase over 1943
Miles flown	18,813,913	49.6
Passengers carried ..	100,852	51.5
Cargo carried (tons) ..	6,560	69.5
Mail carried (tons) ..	1,980	51.4
Total traffic ton/miles	46,116,424	65.0
Passenger ton/miles ..	17,260,879	45.0

Fleet (as at December 31, 1944):—Landplanes: 123, Flying-boats; 40, Total: 163, of which 15 are used for training and development. Includes the following types:—**Landplanes:** Douglas Dakota (52), Airspeed Oxford (8), Lockheed Hudson I (1), Lockheed Hudson III (3), Lockheed Lodestar (18), Consolidated Liberator II (12), Consolidated Liberator III (5), Avro Lancaster (1), Avro York (5), Vickers Warwick (1), D.H. Mosquito (5), Armstrong Whitworth Ensign (9), Avro Anson (1), D.H.89 Rapide (1), Beechcraft (1). **Flying-boats:** Short Sunderland (22), Short "C" Class (14), Boeing 314A (3), Consolidated Model 28 Catalina amphibian (1).

Allied Airways (Gandar Dower), Ltd., Dyce Airport, Aberdeen. Chairman and Managing Director: E. L. Gandar Dower, M.P.
Routes:—
Aberdeen—Wick—Kirkwall. Thrice weekly.
Aberdeen — Wick — Kirkwall — Sumburgh. Daily, except Sunday.

British South American Airways, Ltd. 19, Grafton Street, London, W.1. Chairman: J. W. Booth, J.P. Managing Director: Air Vice-Marshal D. C. T. Bennett, C.B., C.B.E., D.S.O.

This company was formed by the following shipping companies engaged in South American traffic:—Royal Mail Lines, Booth Steamship Co., Ltd., Blue Star Line, Pacific Steam Navigation Co., Ltd. and Lamport & Holt, Ltd.

The first of six proving flights from Heath Row to Buenos Aires was made in January, 1946.

Channel Island Airways, Ltd. The Airport, Jersey, Channel Islands. London office: 272, Buckingham Palace Road, London, S.W.1. Chairman: K. W. C. Grand. General Manager: Cdr. G. O. Waters.

This company which operated intensive services to the Channel Islands from London, Southampton, Brighton, Exeter and Dinard, ceased its activities in June, 1940 when German forces invaded the islands.

A service from Croydon to Jersey and Guernsey was resumed on June 21, 1945, and the Southampton service was opened later in the year.

Associated Airways Joint Committee. The Grove, Watford, Herts. Members: Sir Harold Hartley, C.B.E., F.R.S. (Chairman)., W. P. Bradbury, O.B.E., John Elliot, K.W.C. Grand, J. W. Ratledge. Manager: Wing Cdr. A. H. Measures, O.B.E., M.I.Mech.E. (Liverpool Airport).

Controls the following Companies:—
Air Commerce, Ltd.
Railway Air Services, Ltd.
Scottish Airways, Ltd.
Western Isles Airways, Ltd.
Olley Air Services, Ltd.

The last mentioned Company, in turn, consists of:
Isle of Man Air Services, Ltd.
Great Western and Southern Air Lines, Ltd.
West Coast Air Services, Ltd.

The routes operated by these Companies, all of which maintain their separate identities, are as follows:—

Air Commerce, Ltd., Speke Airport, Liverpool.

This Company is in charge of the maintenance of the aero-engines of the Railway group of companies operating internal services in Great Britain.

Great Western and Southern Air Lines, Ltd., 88, Kingsway, London, W.C.2.
Route:—
Land's End—Scilly Islands. (Frequent weekday services).

Isle of Man Air Services, Ltd., Isle of Man Airport, Derbyhaven.
Route:—
Isle of Man—Liverpool (Speke). Thrice daily except Sunday.

Railway Air Services, Ltd., Speke Airport, Liverpool.
Routes:—
London—Belfast direct. Daily except Sundays.
London—Liverpool—Isle of Man—Belfast. Daily.
London—Glasgow (for Prestwick). Daily.
Liverpool—Belfast. Four times daily except Sundays.
Glasgow—Belfast. Three times daily except Sundays.

West Coast Air Services, Ltd., Speke Airport, Liverpool.
Route:—
Liverpool—Dublin (Collinstown). A twice daily service is operated in pool with Aer Lingus Teoranta.
London—Dublin (Collinstown). Daily except Sundays. In pool with Aer Lingus Teoranta.

Scottish Airways, Ltd., Renfrew Airport, Glasgow.
Route:—
Inverness—Kirkwall (Orkneys). Twice daily except Sunday.
Inverness—Kirkwall—Lerwick (Shetlands). Daily except Sunday.
Inverness—Stornoway (Hebrides). Thrice weekly.

Western Isles Airways, Ltd.
Routes operated by Scottish Airways, Ltd.:—
Glasgow—Campbeltown—Islay. Twice daily except Sunday.
Glasgow—Tiree—Benbecula—North Uist—Stornoway. Daily except Sunday.

BRITISH OVERSEAS AIRWAYS AT WAR

At the beginning of the war the Secretary of State for Air by virtue of his statutory powers took over the undertakings of Imperial Airways and British Airways, the two constituent companies of the Corporation pending the coming into operation on April 1, 1940, of the British Overseas Airways Act. In effect, the companies were already working under unified control.

Some days before war was declared, all British aircraft on the continent of Europe were recalled, and ordered to assembly aerodromes to be at the disposal of the Secretary of State, for transporting R.A.F. personnel and material to various war stations.

Aircraft overseas were, in the same way, placed under the orders of the Government for the movement of key personnel of all three Services, as required.

On September 2, 1939, Capt. Perry, Imperial Airways, flew the first R.A.F. Officers to France in an Ensign airliner. He made two flights, carrying thirty officers, mechanics and their equipment on each. Three other Ensigns were employed on similar service.

In October 1939, it was decided to re-establish the route to Paris from Heston to Le Bourget; this was operated with "Ensign" landplanes and ran twice each way daily. In 1940 when France was overrun, three of the Ensign aircraft carried food to our troops who were surrounded at Merville. Two of the Ensigns got safely back to this country, one with a damaged tail after an attack in the air, the other was so badly damaged that it crash-landed in Kent. The third was destroyed on the ground by German attack and the crew taken prisoner. Other Corporation machines helped in the evacuation of troops and civilians from France.

It is interesting to note that, of the many British aircraft on the continent of Europe when war was declared, not one fell into enemy hands or had to be destroyed to prevent capture. This was entirely due to the careful measures and planning adopted in the days when the clouds had begun to gather but before the storm actually burst.

The collapse of France in 1940, and the entry of Italy in the war, were severe blows to British Empire air communications, and immediate steps had to be taken to mitigate their effects, so that the vital links with Egypt, South Africa, the Middle and Far East and India could be maintained.

The West African Air Route

Alternative routes had to be found at once, and it was decided to run a service from Britain to West Africa and there link up with the trans-continental African route which had been pioneered some years previously. Imperial Airways had opened a regular service between Khartoum and Lagos in 1936 and this was destined to become the great strategic air route to our armies in Egypt.

No flying-boat had ever before made the voyage from the United Kingdom to the West coast of Africa, and that the over-sea route had never been surveyed. The Corporation's Royal Mail flying-boat "Clyde" was in England and then engaged in the newly-opened Atlantic service to the United States. Her Commander, Capt. A. C. Loraine, was told that he must leave at a few hours notice for Lagos and obtain sufficient operational data for the opening of a West African service. Captain Loraine left next day and flew via Lisbon to Bathurst (Gambia), Freetown and Lagos carrying eight important passengers. The flight from England to Lisbon was approximately 1,000 miles and from Lisbon to Bathurst a further 1,900 miles, the latter journey being equal in length to an Atlantic crossing.

No facilities whatever for flying-boats existed south of Lisbon. On reaching Lagos, Loraine was ordered to proceed to Leopoldville in the Belgian Congo. This meant another flight of 1,200 miles, making a total of some 6,000 miles from the original port of departure. The story of the difficulties encountered and overcome is too long to be told here, and is in itself a tribute to the skill and resource of British Merchant Air Service Captains and crews, and of their ability to rise to any occasion at a moment's notice.

On the return journey, among other troubles, the automatic pilot went out of commission so that Captain Loraine and his second pilot had to fly the aircraft by hand, day and night, for some 3,500 miles on the way back to England. On returning to the home base "Clyde" and her crew had been away 23 days and had flown over 12,000 miles, the return journey from Leopoldville to England taking seven days.

From that flight grew the great air route to West Africa, which has been operated continuously ever since. It was continued across Africa not only by the 2,500-mile landplane route to Khartoum, but by a 3,500-mile flying-boat service up the Congo, also operated by British Overseas Airways. Both services linked up with the Corporation's Empire line from South Africa to Egypt and India, which came into being when the Mediterranean was closed to British air traffic. Known as the "Horseshoe Route" it was made up of the Durban—Cairo section of the former England—South Africa route, and the Cairo—Calcutta section of the former England—India route.

This re-establishing of Empire communications, was only one of the many tasks which the Corporation was called upon to undertake as its part in the war effort. From the outbreak of hostilities very heavy demands were made on the Corporation by the Government, both as regards aircraft and trained personnel.

North Atlantic Ferry Service

One of the most important of all the wartime tasks of the Corporation was the opening and maintenance of the North Atlantic Ferry Service, and it is not an exaggeration to describe this as a great triumph for British civil aviation. In July, 1937, Captains Wilcockson and Powell (now Air Commodore Powell), both of Imperial Airways, had made a series of return flights on the flying-boats "Cambria" and "Caledonia" from Foynes, Ireland, to Botwood, Newfoundland, and through the operational data obtained from these flights, Great Britain was able in August, 1939, to inaugurate her first trans-Atlantic Mail service with two long-range flying-boats, "Cabot" and "Caribou." This mail service operated without a hitch, continuing after the outbreak of war to the advertised closing date, September 30, 1939. The two boats were then required by the Air Council for special duties with the R.A.F. Coastal Command. They were subsequently completely destroyed in a Norwegian fjord while in service with the R.A.F.

Up to 1940 the Atlantic had never been flown in winter at all. The story of the North Atlantic Return Ferry really begins in August, 1940, when the Ministry of Aircraft Production decided that it was necessary to establish an organization for ferrying American military aircraft from Canada to the United Kingdom. Colonel Burchall, formerly an Assistant Director-General of British Overseas Airways, and Captains A. S. Wilcockson, D. C. T. Bennett, I. G. Ross and Humphrey Page, who had been seconded from the Corporation, went over to Canada to assist in the setting up of this ferry service.

In November, 1940, the first American-built bombers were flown to the United Kingdom. Seven Hudsons took off from Newfoundland to fly the Atlantic led by Captain D. C. T. Bennett (now Air Vice-Marshal Bennett, C.B.E., D.S.O., M.P.). They landed in the United Kingdom after a 10½-hour flight.

Next, a much more difficult problem had to be tackled. It was that of organizing a two-way Atlantic Service which would have to function winter and summer. Obviously weeks would by lost if the ferry pilots had to return by sea. Yet the task of flying from east to west across the Atlantic in all weathers was one which some experienced airline operators on both sides of the Atlantic had been wont to declare would not be realised for a long time to come. In winter, temperatures of more than 40° below freezing point are encountered on the route and to avoid icing conditions, aircraft are obliged to fly at a height of 20,000 feet or over. When the pilot flies the Atlantic from America eastward, he has the powerful Atlantic winds behind him. But when he flies the other way, the pilot may have to battle for most of the 2,000 miles with an average headwind of 50 miles per hour. Yet this task was cheerfully faced by the British Overseas Airways Captains and operational staff, who were convinced it could be done at once, and the fact they achieved for Britain the honour of the conquest of the North Atlantic.

The two-way Return Ferry Service was taken over by B.O.A.C. in September, 1941, and was later operated to the requirements of the Royal Air Force Transport Command. Its function has been to take back to Canada the crews who had delivered bombers to the R.A.F., and return with Government passengers and freight.

The service has operated regularly ever since its inception, and has run throughout the year both in winter and in summer. It is the only North Atlantic service to have operated through four winters. When the European war ended a daily service in both directions was being flown.

Flying-boat service to the United States

In May, 1941, three long-range Boeing "Clipper" flying-boats were purchased from Pan American Airways at a cost of £259,250 each—not under Lend/Lease—for the purpose of maintaining the vital route to West Africa via Lisbon at a time when the Mediterranean was closed to us, and these machines would have been equal to the task even if Lisbon had been occupied by the Germans.

Since the Boeings had to be taken across to the United States at frequent intervals for major maintenance work, a regular two-way trans-Atlantic service was instituted, which now operates regularly all the year round between Poole and Baltimore, carrying passengers and freight. In the Summer of 1945 four services weekly were in operation between Poole and Baltimore, with these three Boeing flying-boats.

Other Routes

Another regular service between the United Kingdom and Lisbon was instituted in August, 1940, operated by the Royal Dutch Air Lines (K.L.M.) under Charter to the Corporation.

The line from Leuchars, in Scotland, to Sweden was re-opened, after a very short break, in the early stages of the war, and was operated regularly in spite of enemy fighters, unreliable weather and the absence of normal aids to navigation. Between 1941 and the end of the war in Europe 1,200 flights were made.

At least one British Overseas Airways' aircraft was shot down; others disappeared in the 250-mile area patrolled by German fighters operating from Norwegian bases; and others were damaged, but the service was not only maintained but increased. There were 490 crossings in 1944 alone, compared with 569 in the previous three years.

In the early days the service was maintained by Whitleys, Hudsons, Lodestars and other comparatively slow aircraft which, contrary to normal airline practice, deliberately flew in cloudy conditions. Because of the difficulties and dangers of the route unarmed Mosquitos were introduced on the service in February, 1943.

This service was the principal channel for the interchange of diplomatic correspondence, for the carriage of mail, and for the transport of important personages and technical experts. Lady Mallet, wife of the British Minister in Stockholm, made several adventurous trips in the bomb-bay of the Mosquito, which was fitted with a makeshift seat and provided with oxygen.

The normal time for the hazardous 800-mile journey was a little more than two hours. A number of the Corporation's pilots and crews engaged on the Stockholm service were decorated for meritorious achievements. The crews included Norwegians, wearing B.O.A.C. uniform. Some British crews were decorated by the Norwegian Government for valuable services rendered, which included the flying to Great Britain of many important Norwegians who had escaped to Sweden.

A new service to and from Gibraltar was opened in October, 1942, and has since operated regularly.

Flights to Russia have been made on special occasions, but no regular communications by air have been set up.

A service to Madrid, continuing to Lisbon, was opened in November, 1944.

Norway

It has already been mentioned that the two flying-boats, "Cabot" and "Caribou," which had been on the new trans-Atlantic mail service were at the outbreak of war requisitioned for service with R.A.F. Coastal Command. They were speedily converted for war service at the Corporation's maintenance base at Hythe and each armed with four .303-in. Vickers "K" guns.

The crews were recruited, with one or two exceptions, from personnel of the Corporation who had been on the North Atlantic service. After short intensive courses for the crews at R.A.F. schools, both boats were flown to Invergordon, Scotland, and for two months were used on varying duties, from convoy escort to shadowing suspicious vessels. When the surprise invasion of Norway by the Germans took place, both boats were sent to Harstad, the Allied base for operations against Narvik.

When at anchor the two boats were attacked by enemy aircraft on several occasions and many of the crews became casualties. The vessels had sustained such damage that considerable repairs were necessary and the boats had to be towed to the beach and there stripped. Whilst the stripping operations were in progress the enemy attacked with bombs and machine-guns from the air. "Caribou" was caught by a near hit and burned out almost immediately. "Cabot" was towed out of the harbour and into the open sea up the coast to a sheltered spot under a cliff, but next morning a Dornier flying-boat proceeded to the vessel's hiding place, and an immense column of black smoke announced that "Cabot" had been given a Viking's funeral.

The Western Desert and North African Campaigns

It is not possible to describe here in any detail all the numerous operations carried out by the Corporation's aircraft and ground staff in the Middle East during and after the Western Desert and North African campaigns. As the theatre of operations moved eastward and westward, continuous demands were made by the Commanders-in-Chief for innumerable services from the Corporation. The carrying of urgent despatches, transport of important passengers, munitions, special freight and wounded, were some of the many tasks it was called on to perform.

Flights on highly important missions to Turkey, Iran, Syria, Palestine, Transjordania, Iraq, etc., were almost daily occurrences, to say nothing of the many regular services maintained throughout the Region. Regular services to Teheran and Adana were established; the former still operates, but the terminal of the latter is now at Ankara. There is also a service to Addis Ababa.

The successful conclusion of the North African fighting brought no reduction in the demands for service. Flights which had been made as the situation varied, became regular and fixed, and more calls made for transitory duties to the countries bordering on the shores of the Eastern Mediterranean and beyond.

Southern Arabian Route

The story of the opening of the Hadramaut route along the Southern Coast of Arabia dates from the outbreak in Iraq in 1941. This outbreak threatened the safety of the existing route from Cairo to Karachi via the Persian Gulf, and it was decided by the British and Indian Governments that an alternative route to India must be provided for use in case of emergency. For this reason, and on account of the Japanese threat in the Indian Ocean, the new route had to be kept secret.

Surveys were made by the R.A.F. and the Corporation, by landplanes and seaplanes respectively, and it was quickly found, owing to the wild and waterless nature of the Hadramaut Coast, that landplanes only were suitable for the work, especially in view of the fact that the heavy surf during the monsoon makes alighting and the landing of cargo hazardous and difficult.

Steps were taken by the Government of India, in collaboration with the R.A.F. and the Corporation, to organize speedily a service for use as a supply line, and it was decided to establish bases at Salalah and Masirah. The work entailed was prodigious. Wireless stations and pre-fabricated buildings had to be transported and erected. To build runways, to dig wells, to erect hangers and improvise sleeping quarters for staff and passengers, were some of the tasks that those on the spot were called upon to undertake almost at a moment's notice. Whilst the work was in progress food was an acute problem, and for some time had to be supplied by air.

The whole work was completed at the beginning of 1941, when a monthly service was instituted. To-day the Corporation runs a weekly service.

The Southern Arabian Route, intended as an emergency standby, has become an important strategic link for military reinforcements, much used by the United States Air Transport Command *en route* to the supply line for China, as well as by the R.A.F. and the Corporation.

Heliopolis Workshops

When the Mediterranean was closed to British aircraft and shipping, the campaign in North Africa was in full swing. The Corporation's workshop at Heliopolis, manned originally by a few British engineers and some local labourers, expanded in twelve months until it became one of the main aircraft repair centres for the campaign in the Western Desert. It was originally a maintenance depot for civil aircraft on the African and Indian routes but in its new guise, it repaired and put back into service as many as 250 R.A.F. aircraft in a month. In 1941 fluctuations in the desert campaigns made it advisable to withdraw the purely civil workshop southwards, but the R.A.F. requested that the Corporation staff and much of the equipment might be left behind to continue repair work on Service aircraft.

As an example of the work done by the British Overseas Airways repair unit, figures are given for the month of February, 1943. Aircraft completed and returned for service numbered 142. The total aircraft output to that date was 2,553. In addition a large number of overhauls was completed by the Engine Overhaul Section. Many aircraft of varying types were salved and mobile repair parties were working at widely-scattered points, including a large contingent in Malta and others in Cyrenaica, Tripoli and West Africa.

Evacuation of Crete

To assist in the evacuation from Crete, two Corporation flying-boats "Cambria" and "Coorong" were pressed into service. Thirteen return trips were made between Alexandria and Suda, timed so that alighting was made at sundown and departure at dawn or before. A Sunderland escort was provided at first but, towards the end, due to losses of Sunderlands, the operation was carried out unescorted.

Peace-time passenger accommodation on these boats was for 16, but during the evacuation 469 passengers were carried, giving an average of 36 per trip. On one occasion over 50 passengers were accommodated in one flying-boat.

Malta

For several months when the attacks on Malta were at their height, unarmed aircraft manned by Corporation screws maintained unbroken communication with the besieged island. Aircraft of the Corporation had been calling at Malta since October, 1941, on their way to the near East, running the gauntlet of the German and Italian air bases on both sides of the Mediterranean.

In 1942, when air attacks increased, the maintenance of the service involved still greater risks. Available aircraft were scarce and many were ill adapted for the work, or had only primitive navigation and other equipment.

When the attacks on the island became almost continuous the Corporation aircraft could not wait for the "All Clear" but had to go straight in, or not go in at all. Unloading would be done, often in pitch darkness, while the raids were on and with bombs falling on the aerodrome.

Frequently the aerodrome would be out of action through bomb craters or crashed aircraft when the B.O.A.C. machines arrived, and the Captains would have to circle round the inferno of flak and among the enemy fighters, completely unarmed and defenceless, until the runway was cleared.

Corporation aircraft crews carried many hundreds of

passengers to and from the island, including, on the outward journey, many sick and wounded as well as women and children.

India

Regular services have been and still are being maintained by landplane and flying-boat from the United Kingdom to Cairo and Karachi, there connecting with the Corporation's trans-Indian route to Calcutta.

Ceylon-Australia

After the fall of Singapore and the occupation of the Malay Peninsula and Burma by the Japanese, the services to the Far East ended at Calcutta, and services to Australia and New Zealand stopped for the time being. In July, 1943, under great secrecy, a service was opened between Ceylon and Australia by the Corporation's associate company, Qantas Empire Airways. The route between Ceylon and Western Australia is 3,523 miles, and is the longest non-stop trans-ocean flight in the world. There is no land in a direct line between these two points, with the exception of the Cocos Islands, a possible target for attack by the Japanese.

For this service several Catalina flying-boats were converted and fitted with special fuel and oil tankage in the Corporation's workshops at the United Kingdom Marine Base. The service, later supplemented by Liberator aircraft, linked up with the Tasman Empire Airways, also an associate company of the Corporation, running between Australia and New Zealand. This Service is being augmented by a high-speed mail service also carrying a limited number of passengers, by Lancastrian aircraft which fly through from Great Britain to New Zealand in 86 hours. This is the longest civil air route in the world.

Propeller and Engine Repair Auxiliary (P.E.R.A.)

This auxiliary has formed an integral part of the Corporation with three important units, employing several thousand men and women, under its control. It has worked for the account of the Ministry of Aircraft Production. The largest group of factories is in South Wales, where aeroplane engines of several types have been repaired and re-issued. Other P.E.R.A. factories in the West of England have specialised in the repair and reconstruction of aeroplane propellers.

Supply of Aircraft and Personnel

Until recently the building of civil aircraft in this country ceased entirely. To augment the Corporation's fleet and staff, both much depleted by the demands of H.M. Government, a large number of R.A.F. machines have been converted and adapted for carrying passengers and freight. Pilots and other personnel have been specially seconded from the R.A.F. for duties with the Corporation.

The conversion of these Service aircraft was undertaken by Corporation technicians in its workshops at Hythe and Bramcote; the latter base has now been closed and the plant transferred to Croydon.

When, owing to the closing of the Mediterranean, it became necessary to open a service to West Africa, four Short "Empire" flying-boats from the Corporation's fleet had to be quickly adapted for the 2,000-mile stage from Lisbon to Bathurst (Gambia) an extensive increase in fuel and oil tankage being involved. The work was completed at Hythe and the boats put into service with a minimum of delay.

The Corporation's "Ensign" fleet had to be re-engined and otherwise adapted for the trans-continental African service. This work was done at Bramcote.

Military flying-boats and landplanes, including Catalinas, Hudsons, Liberators, Mosquitos and other types of aircraft, have all been converted in the Corporation's workshops and made available for service on the many routes operated.

In 1944-45 the Corporation received the first new British civil aircraft to be built since before the war. These were of the Avro York and Lancastrian types.

Air Transport Auxiliary (A.T.A.)

Air Transport Auxiliary was formed in 1939 by Mr. Gerard d'Erlanger, who, in March, 1940, was appointed a Member of the Corporation. The purpose of this auxiliary was to ferry aircraft from the manufacturers and repair workshops to the R.A.F. units to which they had been allotted.

It functioned on behalf of the Ministry of Aircraft Production, but for administrative purposes came under the Corporation.

In 1939 and 1940 Corporation staff were seconded to provide personnel for duties with the A.T.A. but as production increased, pilots and crews were recruited from many other sources.

Included in the personnel of A.T.A. were a number of women pilots who rendered much excellent service.

During the five years of its existence, Air Transport Auxiliary delivered over 250,000 aircraft, new and reconditioned, to units of the Royal Air Force.

Some Wartime Statistics

In the five years of war service, ended March 31, 1945, aircraft of British Overseas Airways Corporation flew more than 55,000,000 miles; carried over 271,000 passengers on urgent war journeys, together with nearly 29,120,000 lbs. of cargo and 18,592,000 lbs. of mails.

The number of passengers jumped from 19,800 in 1940/41 to just short of 100,000 in the year ending March 31, 1945, an increase of over 400%.

In 1940/41 the Corporation's aircraft flew 4,874,054 miles. In the same period 1944/45 they flew just on 20,000,000 miles, more than four times as much, and more than twice round the world every day of the year.

Cargo carried in B.O.A.C.'s first year was 1,003,520 lbs. By 1944/45 this figure had grown to 13,037,600 lbs. an increase of over 1,200%. Mails jumped by 306% to 6,097,280 lbs. in the 1944/45 period.

In five years the fleet had more than doubled. On March 31, 1945 there were 160 aircraft in service, including 42 flying-boats. At that date the Corporation had about 20,000 employees, including those working in the engine and propeller overhaul factories which it established and has operated for the Ministry of Aircraft Production.

The Corporation operates more than 55,000 miles of routes. Covering four continents and serving twenty-seven countries.

There have been many casualties among the Corporation's flying crews. Over 80 of its Captains and members of its air-crews have been decorated or have received The King's Commendation for Valuable Service in the Air. Many officials of the Technical and Administrative staffs have also been honoured.

THE BAHAMA ISLANDS

ADMINISTRATION

Civil Administration is under the control of the Bahamas Air Board, Nassau. The Air Board is responsible for advising the Governor and was set up on Nov. 28, 1933, under Article 30 of Air Navigation (Colonies, Protectorates and Mandated Territories) Order, 1927.

Aviation in the Bahamas received an impetus with the opening in January, 1940, of its first aerodrome, two and a half miles south of Nassau, the Capital. Previously the only organized flying facilities in the islands were at the Nassau flying-boat base, which was originally established to serve as a terminal for the Pan American Airways' service from Miami, Florida.

TRANSPORT COMPANIES

Pan American World Airways
Operates a service from Miami to Nassau six times weekly with Douglas DC-3 aircraft.

Bahamas Airways Ltd., Nassau.
Formed in 1936 by the late Sir Harry Oakes, Bart., and began operations in November of that year. It maintained a fleet of three aircraft comprising a Douglas "Dolphin" amphibian, a Grumman "Widgeon" amphibian and a Luscombe seaplane. The first two are used for scheduled and charter flying among the islands and to the American mainland, and the Luscombe seaplane is available for use by the Nassau Flying Club. Charter services are operated to Dunmore Town, Harbour Island, Hatchet Bay and Governor's Harbour, Eleuthera.

In 1944 Pan American Airways acquired a minority interest in Bahamas Airways.

FLYING CLUBS

The Nassau Flying Club, Nassau, Bahamas, was formed in 1940. Operates with one Luscombe seaplane by arrangement with Bahamas Airways Ltd.

AERODROMES AND SEAPLANE STATIONS

OAKES AIRPORT. Customs and Immigration Port. 2½ miles South of Nassau, New Providence Island. Has three runways E/W. 1,000 yds., N.E./S.W. 1,335 yds., N.W./S.E. 1,500 yds. (under construction and was expected to be available for use by August 1, 1941).

The existing passenger station is used by Pan American Airways and plans for a new station are being drawn. No water or power available at present station.

The seaplane base owned by Pan American Airways is situated one mile East of the centre of Nassau, on the North foreshore of New Providence Island. Ramp available on which seaplanes can be hauled up. Customs and Immigration Port.

BARBADOS

ADMINISTRATION

Civil Aviation in Barbados is subject to Air Navigation Directions issued by the Governor under Article 30 of the Air Navigation (Colonies, Protectorates, and Mandated Territories) Order, 1927. The Managing Authority is the Colonial Secretary, Barbados.

TRANSPORT COMPANIES

British West Indian Airways, Ltd. Head Office : Port of Spain, Trinidad.
Services operated :—

Barbados—Trinidad. Direct return service. Eleven times weekly.
Barbados—Trinidad, via Grenada, St. Vincent and St. Lucia. Weekly return.
There is also a weekly round trip from Trinidad serving Barbados, Antigua, St. Christopher, Antigua, St. Christopher, Antigua, Barbados, Trinidad in that order.

Aircraft :—Lockheed 14 and Lockheed Lodestar.

AERODROMES

SEAWELL. Lat. 13°5'N. Long. 59°30'W. 7½ miles E. of Bridgetown. Alt. 167 ft. Runways : No. 1, E./W. 1,000 yds. × 165 yds. No. 2, N.E./S.W. 1,000 yds. × 165 yds. No. 3, N.W./S.E. 800 yds. × 165 yds. No. 4, N./S. 900 yds. × 165 yds. Surface grass. No markings. Radio including telephony available through Cable & Wireless (W. Indies) Ltd. Call sign VPO. Wave length 30-120 m.

CARLISLE BAY has been used on several occasions by Pan American Airways as a seaplane alighting area. It is ¾ mile South of Bridgetown.

BERMUDA

Since the outbreak of War, Bermuda has advanced from being a pleasure resort to a position of some considerable importance from the aviation standpoint, due to its strategic position as an intermediate stop on the Transatlantic air routes.

AIR TRANSPORT COMPANIES

Pan American World Airways
Before this company abandoned the use of flying-boats it operated the following flying-boat services to or through Bermuda :—
New York—Foynes, via Bermuda. Twice weekly in each direction.
New York—Bermuda. Once weekly.
It is now operating a twice-weekly landplane service from New York, using Kindley Field as the Bermuda Terminal

British Overseas Airways Corporation
The Corporation's Boeing 314A flying-boats return from Baltimore to Foynes via Bermuda.

American Export Airlines
The Winter Trans-Atlantic flying-boat service of this Company, before it was absorbed by the American Airlines System, was operated via Bermuda.

FLYING SCHOOLS

Bermuda Flying School, Darrell's Island.
Formed in 1940 and operating two Luscombe seaplanes. Chief Instructor : Mr. E. Stafford, formerly of Port Washington, Long Island. Early in 1941 the School commenced elementary training for pilots for the R.A.F.

AERODROME

In June, 1943, it was announced that KINDLEY FIELD, the U.S.A.A.F. base on St. David's Island, had been completed. A tentative agreement has been reached between the United Kingdom and the United States for this field to be used for commercial air services.

SEAPLANE STATION

DARRELL'S ISLAND, Lat. 32°17'N., Long. 64°48'W., in Great Sound, west of Hamilton. Hangar 150 × 105 ft. Door 150 ft. Control tower in annex on island. Wind sleeve, flare path and N.T. landing beacons, 2 slipways 50 ft. wide. Beaching facilities and six moorings available. Workshops. Radio facilities through Cables & Wireless Ltd. Meteorological data through Bermuda Met. Station.

BRITISH GUIANA

ADMINISTRATION
Civil Aviation is under the control of the Air Board, the principal officials of which are the Commissioner of Police, the Comptroller of Customs and the Harbour Master.

TRANSPORT COMPANIES
British Guiana Airways, Inc., 17, Craol St., Georgetown. Owner: Mr. A. J. Williams.

In October, 1939, British Guiana Airways signed a three-year agreement with the Government by which, in return for an annual subsidy of $21,600, the Government has first call on the services of the company's aircraft and undertakes to take and pay for, at the rate of $60 per hour, a guaranteed minimum of 30 flying hours per year. The company also undertook to run an air service within the colony, to maintain aircraft and provide pilots. The company has operated a passenger and mail service into the gold and diamond fields

of the Mazaruni and into the Rupununi cattle country when occasion demanded, and charter work is undertaken.

In March, 1942 Mr. Williams was commissioned as Major in the U.S. Army and in July, 1942, he was made a service pilot. In October of the same year Major Williams was awarded the Air Medal for meritorious achievement in an aerial flight involving landing and taking off from the confined and dangerous waters of the Orinoco River to rescue the crew of a crashed aeroplane. He has undertaken many other flights of a similar nature from the U.S. Army Air Base at Atkinson Field, British Guiana Base Command.

During Mr. Williams' absence with the U.S. Army Air Forces the activities of British Guiana Airways are carried on by Mr. Wendt, his chief assistant.

Pan American World Airways
Georgetown is a daily stop on the Miami—Beunos Aires

service, which is now flown with landplanes using the new Atkinson Field airport. There are also two weekly services from Miami, one stopping at Georgetown and one going on to Paramaribo, Dutch Guiana.

AERODROME
The ATKINSON FIELD airport was opened in 1942. No details are available.

SEAPLANE STATION
Pan American Airways maintains a seaplane station near Georgetown. Lat. 6°48'N., Long. 58°10'W. Slipway 40 ft. wide. Hangar (wood) 70 ft. × 30 ft. × 16 ft. Wind sleeve on pontoon. Radio call sign: V.R.L. D/F. and telephony.

British Guiana Airways, Inc., owns and maintains a hangar and repair shop on the left bank of the Demarara River.

BRITISH HONDURAS

ADMINISTRATION
Civil Aviation in British Honduras is subject to Air Navigation Directions issued by the Governor under Article 30 of the Air Navigation (Colonies, Protectorates and Mandated Territories) Order 1927.

TRANSPORT COMPANY
The Transportes Aeros Centro Americanos (TACA)
Routes operated into Belize :—

San Pedro—Punta Garda—Belize—El Cayo. Twice weekly.
Belize—Corozal. Weekly.

AERODROMES
COROZAL. Lat. 18°20'N., Long. 88°28'W., Alt. 40 ft. 3 miles S.W. of town. Runs N.E./S.W. 1,400 × 60 ft. Wind cone.
PUNTA GORDA. Lat. 16°06'N., Long. 88°50'W., Alt. 100 ft. ½ mile W. of town. 1,300 × 100 ft. Wind cone.

STANN CREEK. Lat. 16°58'N., Long. 88°14'W. On N.W. edge of town. Runs N.N.W./S.S.E. 1,800 × 100 ft. Wind cone.
BELIZE. (Tillett's Pond). Lat. 17°34'N., Long. 88°22'W., Alt. 12 ft. 10½ mls. N.W. of town. Runs E./W. 2,100 × 350 ft. Hangar marked TACA. Boundary marks and wind cone.
EL CAYO. Lat. 17°11'N., Long. 89°04'W., Alt. 200 ft. On West side of Belize River adjacent to N.E. side of town. Runs N.E./S.W. 2,000 × 300 ft. with runway down centre 2,000 × 80 ft. Wind cone.

CEYLON

Civil Aviation in Ceylon is controlled by the Civil Aviation Directorate.

The Ceylon Government has announced that it intends to operate internal and external airlines, as well as a flying school which will have no connection with either of the two existing flying clubs.

FLYING CLUB
The Aero Club of Ceylon
The activities of this Aero Club were suspended in May, 1942.

The Colombo Flying Club
President - Major M. G. Dover.

Hon. Secretary and Treasurer: Mr. R. A. Tomlinson.
The Club was formed in December, 1942. In 1944 the membership had risen to 152 members. Application has been made to the Secretary of State for the Colonies for the acquisition of training aircraft.

TRANSPORT COMPANIES
British Overseas Airways Corporation
The England-Australia high-speed landplane service operated with Lancastrians in pool with Qantas Empire Airways, calls at Colombo (Ratmalana) thrice weekly in each direction.
Tata Air Lines. The Company maintains a service six times weekly to Colombo from India.

Qantas Empire Airways
In July, 1943, this Australian company, which previously operated the Calcutta-Sydney section of the "Horseshoe" route in pool with B.O.A.C., opened a non-stop service from Perth, Western Australia, to Ceylon, with Catalina flying-boats, later augmented by Liberator landplanes.

AERODROMES
COLOMBO (Ratmalana). Lat. 6°49'N., Long. 79°39'E., Alt. 15 ft. Civil Customs. 5 m. S. of town. 600 × 600 yds. Hangar. No night facilities. Minor repairs.
There are landing grounds at PUTTALAM and JAFFNA.

GAMBIA

ADMINISTRATION
Civil Aviation in Gambia is under Military control during the period of hostilities.

TRANSPORT COMPANIES
British Overseas Airways Corporation
B.O.A.C. operates a landplane service from Great Britain

to Lagos (Nigeria) twice weekly which stops at Bathurst, and the Boeing 314A flying-boats call at Bathurst three times a fortnight en route from the United Kingdom to Baltimore, U.S.A.

AERODROMES
The aerodrome and seaplane base at Bathurst is under military control.

GOLD COAST

ADMINISTRATION
Civil Aviation is under the control of the Military authorities.

TRANSPORT COMPANIES
S.A.B.E.N.A.
This Belgian company is operating a freight service under contract to B.O.A.C. once weekly from Accra to Cairo, via

Lagos, Duala, Libenge, Stanleyville, Entebbe, Juba, Khartoum and Wadi Halfa.

British Overseas Airways Corporation
The B.O.A.C. twice weekly service from Accra to Cairo operates via Lagos, Kano, Maiduguri, El Geneina, El Fasher, Khartoum and Wadi Halfa.

AERODROMES
All aerodromes are under Military Control.

JAMAICA

ADMINISTRATION
Civil Aviation is subject to Air Navigation Directions issued by the Governor under Article 30 of the Air Navigation (Colonies, Protectorates and Mandated Territories) Order 1927.

TRANSPORT COMPANIES
Pan American World Airways
The flying-boat services from Miami to Port au Prince (Haiti) and Miami to Barranquilla (Colombia) stop at Kingston (Harbour Head) weekly and four times weekly respectively.

Royal Dutch Air Lines (K.L.M.)
The weekly service from Curaçao to Miami stops at the new Palisadoes Field at Kingston. The fortnightly shuttle service from Curaçao to Kingston also uses the new airport.

KENYA

ADMINISTRATION
The control of Civil Aviation was taken over for the duration of hostilities by the Military Authorities.

TRANSPORT COMPANIES
British Overseas Airways Corporation
Headquarters, Manager, East Africa, Rhodes House, Delamere Avenue, Nairobi.

The following B.O.A.C. services pass through Kenya Colony :—
Cairo—Gwelo (Southern Rhodesia), calling at Kisumu and Nairobi. Thrice weekly. Lockheed Lodestar landplanes.
Kisumu—Diego Suarez (Madagascar), calling at Mombasa. Once weekly. Short "C" class flying-boats.
Durban—Calcutta, calling at Mombasa and Kisumu. Twice weekly. Short "C" class flying-boats.

Southern Rhodesian Air Services
This organization operates two services weekly into Kenya stopping at Mbeya, Dodoma, Nairobi, one service proceeding on to Kisumu.

AERODROMES
All aerodromes are under Military control.

NIGERIA

ADMINISTRATION
Control of Civil Aviation is normally under the jurisdiction of the Controller of Civil Aviation, but for the duration of the War was subject to Military supervision.

TRANSPORT COMPANIES
British Overseas Airways Corporation
Headquarters, Manager, West Africa, Airways House, Marina, Lagos.

The following B.O.A.C. services serve or pass through Nigeria :—
Cairo—Lagos, via the Nile and the Congo River. Once weekly. Short "C" class flying-boats.
Cairo—Accra, calling at Maiduguri, Kano and Lagos. Twice weekly. Douglas Dakota landplanes.
United Kingdom—Lagos, via the West Coast of Africa. Twice weekly. Douglas Dakota landplanes.

Lignes Aeriennes Militaires
The fortnightly service operated by this French military undertaking between Fort Lamy and Pointe Noire calls at Kano and Lagos. (For further details see under "France").

AERODROMES
All aerodromes are under military control.

NORTHERN RHODESIA

ADMINISTRATION
The officer in charge of aerodromes is the Commissioner of Police, Police Headquarters, P.O. Box 203, Lusaka, but for the duration of the War all flying was subject to Military control.

TRANSPORT COMPANIES
British Overseas Airways Corporation
The B.O.A.C. service from Cairo to Gwelo (Southern Rhodesia) calls at Kasama thrice weekly.

Southern Rhodesian Air Services (formerly R.A.N.A.)
Operates the following services into Northern Rhodesia :—

Salisbury—Lusaka. Twice weekly.
Lusaka—Mumbwa—Mankoya—Mongu. Weekly.
Lusaka—Fort Jameson. Weekly.
A service from Johannesburg to Kisumu stopping weekly at Lusaka, Ndola and Kasama or Mpika.

AERODROMES
LUSAKA. Lat. 15°25′S., Long. 28°18′E. On East side of town. Alt. 4,320 ft. Runways E./W. 1,200 yds. N.E./S.W. 1,100 yds. N./S. 1,100 yds. N.W./S.E. 1,100 yds.
BROKEN HILL. Lat. 14°28′S., Long. 28°27′E. On South side of town. Alt. 3,800 ft. Area 1,250 × 1,000 yds.
FORT JAMESON. Lat. 13 33′S., Long. 32°36′E. 7 miles N.W.

of town. Alt. 3,620 ft. Runways E./W., N./S., N.E./S.W. N.W./S.E. each 1,000 × 150 yds.
M'PIKA. Lat. 11°52′S., Long. 31°27′E. 3½ miles S.S.W. of town. Alt. 4,778 ft. Area 1,450 × 1,250 yds.
LIVINGSTONE. Lat 17°53′S., Long. 25°51′E. 2¼ miles S.S.W. of town. Alt. 2,950 ft. Area 1,160 × 830 yds.
For details of other landing grounds in Northern Rhodesia reference should be made to the *Air Pilot of Northern Rhodesia* obtainable from the Director of Civil Aviation, Salisbury, Southern Rhodesia. Price 12/-.
All aerodromes have been taken over by the Government.

NYASALAND

ADMINISTRATION
Civil Aviation is normally controlled by the Registrar of Aircraft, Directorate of Public Works, Zomba, but for the duration of the War all flying was subject to Military control.

TRANSPORT COMPANY
Southern Rhodesian Air Services (formerly R.A.N.A.)
The following service is operated into Nyasaland :—
Salisbury—Blantyre. Twice weekly.
Lusaka—Blantyre—Lilongwe—Fort Jameson. Weekly.

AERODROMES
CHILEKA. (Blantyre). Lat. 15°42′S., Long. 34°58′E. 7 miles

N.N.W. of Blantyre. Alt. 2,400 ft. Area 1,000 × 600 yds.
ZOMBA. Lat. 15°24′S., Long. 35°23′E. 3 miles E.N.E. of town. Alt. 2,550 ft. Area 1,000 × 900 yds.
LILONGWE. Lat. 13°59′S., Long. 33°47′E. North side of town. Alt. 3,600 ft. Area 1,000 × 1,000 yds.
LUCHENZA. Lat. 16°00′S., Long. 35°20′E. Adjacent to Luchenza Rly. Stn. Alt. 2,300 ft.
There are also landing grounds at :
CHIKWAWA. Lat. 16°03′S., Long. 34°49′E. Alt. 127 ft.
ZOMBWE. Lat. 11°26′S., Long. 33°50′E. Alt. 4,000 ft.
DEDZA. Lat. 14°21′S., Long. 34°21′E. Alt. 5,250 ft.

KOTO KOTO. Lat. 13°00′S., Long. 34°17′E. Alt. 1,800 ft.
MZIMBA. Lat. 11°54′S., Long. 33°56′E. Alt. 4,500 ft.
LIVINGSTONIA. Lat. 10°37′S., Long. 34°08′E. Alt. 3,600 ft.
LODJWA. Lat. 12°21′S., Long. 33°37′E. Alt. 4,800 ft.
FORT HILL. Lat. 9°40′S., Long. 33°08′E. Alt. 4,000 ft.

For further details of aerodromes reference should be made to *Air Pilot of Southern Rhodesia and Nyasaland*, obtainable from the Director of Civil Aviation, Salisbury, Southern Rhodesia. Price 12/6.

All aerodromes are under the control of the Military Authorities.

PALESTINE & TRANS-JORDAN
(British Mandate)

ADMINISTRATION
Civil Aviation in Palestine and Trans-Jordan is controlled by the Directorate of Civil Aviation, Mamillah Road, Jerusalem. The Palestine Government has formed a Palestinian Air Transport Organization, to be run either by the Government or by a local statutory corporation. This organization will enjoy a monopoly in local air services.

TRANSPORT COMPANIES.
The following foreign air transport companies were operating to Palestine in 1943 :—
Misr Airwork S.A.E.
The Company operates a service eleven times weekly to Lydda from Egypt and the Cairo—Beirut and Cairo—Cyprus services also stop at Lydda once daily and once weekly respectively.
British Overseas Airways Corporation
The Corporation's weekly landplane services to Turkey

and India from Egypt both stop at Lydda.
The "Horseshoe" service stops at Kallia.

AERODROMES
There are aerodromes at AMMAN, GAZA, HAIFA, JERICHO, LYDDA, MA'AN, RAMLEH, SEMAKH and seaplane stations at HAIFA and TIBERIAS, but all are under military jurisdiction and no details are therefore given.

SIERRA LEONE

ADMINISTRATION
Civil Aviation is under the control of the Military Authorities.
TRANSPORT COMPANIES
British Overseas Airways Corporation
A landplane service is in operation between Great Britain

and Lagos (Nigeria) which stops at Freetown twice weekly.

Pan American Airways
The Miami—Lagos service stops at Freetown.

AERODROMES
The seaplane base alighting area is in the sea off Freetown. Slipways, W/T. etc. available.

SOUTHERN RHODESIA

ADMINISTRATION
Civil Aviation in Southern Rhodesia is administered by the Department of Defence. Minister for Air : Col. The Hon. E. L. Guest, O.B.E.
On the outbreak of War the Government took over the control of all Civil Aviation activities. The assets of the Rhodesia and Nyasaland Airways (R.A.N.A.) were acquired for the sum of £20,000 and the Company's aircraft and personnel were incorporated in the Southern Rhodesian Air Force.
The services previously assured by R.A.N.A. continue to be operated by the Government under the title of Southern Rhodesian Air Services. The route into Portuguese Colonial territory to Beira is flown with civil aircraft but those serving Northern Rhodesia, Nyasaland and the Union of South Africa are being operated with military aircraft.

TRANSPORT COMPANIES
Southern Rhodesian Air Services, Belvedere Air Station, Salisbury.
Formerly Rhodesia and Nyasaland Airways (R.A.N.A.), which was acquired by the Southern Rhodesian Government on the outbreak of War.
Routes operated :—
Salisbury—Bulawayo—Johannesburg. Twice weekly.
Salisbury—Lusaka. Twice weekly.
Salisbury—Blantyre. Twice weekly.
Salisbury—Beira. Twice weekly.
Lusaka—Mumbwa—Mankoya—Mongu. Weekly.
Lusaka—Blantyre—Lilongwe—Fort Jameson. Weekly.
Johannesburg — Bulawayo — Salisbury—Lusaka—Ndola— (Kasama or Mpika) — Mbeya — Dodoma — Nairobi — Kisumu. Weekly.

Aircraft : D.H. 89 Rapide, D.H. 24 Dragon and D.H. 90 Dragonfly.
British Overseas Airways Corporation
B.O.A.C. operates a thrice-weekly service from Cairo to Gwelo with Lockheed Lodestar landplanes.

S.A.B.E.N.A.
The Company's fortnightly service from Stanleyville to Cape Town stops at Bulawayo.

AERODROMES
All Civil aerodromes in Southern Rhodesia have been taken over by the Department of Defence. For details of aerodromes reference should be made to the *Air Pilot of Southern Rhodesia and Nyasaland*, obtainable from the Director of Civil Aviation, Salisbury. Price 12/6.

TANGANYIKA TERRITORY

ADMINISTRATION

Civil Aviation is normally administered by the Department of Civil Aviation, Dar-es-Salaam, but was subject to Military control for the period of the War.

TRANSPORT COMPANIES

British Overseas Airways Corporation

The B.O.A.C. services from Durban to Calcutta and from

Kisumu to Diego Suarez (Madagascar) both stop at Lindi and Dar-es-Salaam. Both services use Short "C" class flying-boats, the former operating twice weekly and the latter one weekly.

Southern Rhodesian Air Services

The weekly service from Johannesburg to Kisumu stops at Mbeya and Dodoma.

South African Airways Ltd.

A service from Johannesburg to Leopoldville stops weekly at Dodoma.

AERODROMES

All aerodromes are under Military control.

TRINIDAD

ADMINISTRATION

Civil Aviation in Trinidad is under the control of the Director of Civil Aviation, Wing Cdr. Maurice Banks, Port of Spain.

TRANSPORT COMPANIES

British West Indian Airways

Head Office : Port of Spain, Trinidad.
Chairman : Sir Lennox O'Reilly. Managing Director : K. T. Murray.

Since October 12, 1943, the following services have been in operation :—

Port of Spain—Barbados. Eleven times weekly.

Port of Spain—Grenada—St. Lucia. Once weekly.

Port of Spain—Barbados—Antigua—St. Christopher—Antigua—St. Christopher—Antigua—Barbados—Port of Spain (one direction only). Once weekly.

FLYING CLUBS

Light Aeroplane Club of Trinidad and Tobago. Address : P.O. Box 176, Port of Spain, Trinidad. President : Sir Hubert Young, K.C.M.G., D.S.O. Secretary : A. Storey. Instructors : Flt.-Lt. Oliver, R.A.F., Lt. J. F. Carroll, Lt. R. J. Williams. Chief Engineer : R. M. Brown.

In the Summer of 1940 the Club, by agreement with the British Air Ministry, undertook to give initial training to recruits from Trinidad for the Royal Air Force. Equipment : Two D.H. "Tiger-Moths" and one Taylor "Cub."

AERODROMES AND SEAPLANE STATIONS

PIARCO Aerodrome. Lat. 10°36'N. Long. 61°20'W. 11½ miles S.E. of Port of Spain. Alt. 40 ft. 1,000 × 900 yds. Customs airport.

COCORITE. Seaplane Station, situated 2½ miles N.W. of Port of Spain and operated by Pan American Airways.

Port of Spain—Grenada—St. Vincent—St. Lucia—Barbados. Once weekly.
Port of Spain—Tobago. Once weekly.
Aircraft : 1 Lockheed Lodestar, 1 Lockheed 14, 1 Lockheed 12

Pan American Airways

Pan American Airways call at Port of Spain (Trinidad) as follows :—

(a) Once daily in each direction on the Miami—Buenos Aires service with Douglas DC-3 landplanes.

(b) Once weekly in each direction on the Miami—Paramaribo service with Sikorsky S-43 amphibians.

(c) Once weekly in each direction on the Miami—Georgetown service with Sikorsky S-42 flying-boats.

K.L.M.

The Company's service from Curaçao to Dutch Guiana stops six times monthly at Trinidad and there is a six times monthly service between Curaçao and Port of Spain.

UGANDA

ADMINISTRATION

Civil Aviation is normally controlled by the Registrar of Aircraft, Directorate of Public Works, Entebbe, Uganda, but for the period of the War was subject to Military jurisdiction.

TRANSPORT COMPANIES

British Overseas Airways Corporation

Operates through Uganda. The twice-weekly Calcutta—

Durban flying-boat service stops at Port Bell and Laropi, the weekly Cairo—Kisumu landplane service calls at Laropi and the thrice-weekly Cairo—Gwelo landplane service calls at Juba.

South African Airways Ltd.

The weekly service from Johannesburg to Leopoldville stops at Entebbe.

AERODROMES

Aerodrome maps as separate sheets are obtainable from the Government Survey Department, Entebbe. All aerodromes are under the control of the Military Authorities.

INDIA AND BURMA

ADMINISTRATION

Civil Aviation in India is under the control of the Directorate of Civil Aviation.

Director of Civil Aviation : Sir Frederick Tymms, C.I.E., M.C., F.R.Ae.S. (on other duties), Lieut.-Cdr. W. H. Watt, O.B.E., R.N.R. (Retired) (Officiating).

Deputy Director of Civil Aviation : Capt. L. A. Egglestield (on other duties), Air Cdre. A. C. Wright, A.F.C. (officiating).

Administrative Officer : Mr. J. Hamilton (on other duties), P. N. Kapur, B.A. (officiating).

Technical Officers : Mr. K. M. Raha, B.A. (Cantab), D.I.C., A.F.R.Ae.S. (officiating), Capt. A. R. Hasler, Mr. M. L. Sodhi and Mr. B. Bhagat Lal, M.B.E.

Superintendent of Training : Mr. K. L. Puri, B.Sc. (Eng.), A.C.G.I., M.I.B.E., A.F.R.Ae.S., A.M.I.Ae.E.

Chief Aerodrome Officer : Mr. E. M. Rossiter.

Chief Inspector of Aircraft : Mr. J. A. O'Brian, A.M.Inst. C.E., A.F.R.Ae.S.

In order that post-war air transport services in India may proceed on a rational and economic basis, the Indian Aircraft Act, 1934 has been amended. Previously this Act contained no specific provision for controlling and regulating development. In February, 1944 a Bill introducing the Indian Aircraft (Amendment) Act, 1944, takes care of this by the insertion of two clauses, (aa) and (ab) to sub-section (2) of section 5 of the 1934 Act.

A programme of post-war development involving a construction cost of some £12,000,000 is planned for Indian air services. An Air Transport Licensing Board is to be formed and a system of controlled subsidy, probably limited to routes of national importance, will be instituted. Development will be left mainly to private enterprise, although operations will probably be restricted to a limited number of companies.

Twelve main routes are planned, covering some 11,000 miles They are :—

Karachi—Bombay—Madras—Colombo.
Calcutta—Allahabad—Cawnpore—Delhi—Lahore—Peshawar—Kabul.
Delhi—Magpur—Hyderabad—Madras.
Calcutta—Cuttock—Vizagapatam—Madras—Colombo.
Calcutta—Akyab—Mague—Rangoon.
Calcutta—Dacca—Sylhet—Deigau.
Bombay—Nagpur—Calcutta.
Bombay—Indore—Bhopal—Lucknow.
Bombay—Ahmedabad—Delhi.
Karachi—Jodhpur—Delhi.
Karachi—Quetta—Lahore.
Madras—Bangalore—Cochin.

Several of the routes are already operated by Tata Air Lines and Indian National Airways. Development costs will be

for aerodrome construction, runways, administration buildings and air route an aerodrome lighting and equipment. At least four airports for international operations will be provided, at Karachi, Delhi, Calcutta and Bombay. In addition more than 100 other aerodromes and 50 radio stations are to be built.

ASSOCIATION

Aero Club of India and Burma, Ltd. Patron-in-Chief : The Viceroy and Governor-General of India H. E. Field Marshal Lord Wavell, P.C., G.C.B., G.S.C.I., G.C.I.E., C.M.G., M.C. President : H.E. the Commander-in-Chief. Vice-President : The Hon. Sir Maneckji Dababhoy, K.C.I.E., K.C.S.I. Chairman : Mr. P. R. Pinhorn.

FLYING CLUBS

All Flying Clubs have ceased private flying and their equipment and training personnel have been taken over by the R.A.F., India, for other duties.

Bengal Flying Club, Ltd. President : Mr. A. N. Chaudhuri. Hon. Secretary : Mr. S. P. Ray.

Bihar Flying Club. Headquarters : Patna. Patron-in-Chief : H.E. the Governor of Bihar. President : Hon. Mr. Justice H. R. Meredith. Secretary : Mr. Mohammed Yunus.

Bombay Flying Club, Ltd. President : Sir Homi Mehta, K.B.E. Hon. Secretary : Mr. J. R. Taleyarkhan.

Central Provinces and Berar Flying Club. Headquarters : Nagpur. President : Sir Hari Singh Gour. General Hon. Secretary : Mr. E. C. Eduljee.

Delhi Flying Club, Ltd. President : Dr. W. M. Smith.

Hyderabad State Aero Club. General Manager : Mr. J. N. Nanda. Secretary : Mr. Baber Mirza.

Jodhpur Flying Club.

Karachi Aero Club, Ltd. President : Shivji V. Kothari, J.P. Hon. Secretary : G. Grossenbacher.

Madras Flying Club, Ltd. Chairman : K. R. Simpson. Hon. Secretary and Treasurer : Mr. E. G. Kennedy.

Northern India Flying Club. Headquarters : Lahore. President : The Hon. Rai Bahadur Lala Ram Saran Dass. Hon. Secretary : Dr. J. B. Sproull.

The United Provinces Flying Club, Ltd. Headquarters : Cawnpore. Branch : Lucknow. President : R. F. Mudie, Esq., C.S.I., C.I.E., O.B.E., I.C.S. Hon. General Secretary : J. M. Heeramaneck. Cawnpore Committee : Vice President : Mr. C. W. Tosh. Hon. Secretary : Mr. C. O'Malley. Lucknow Committee : Vice-President : M. B. H. Nethersole, D.S.O., I.C.S. Hon. Secretary : B. N. Seth.

FLYING SCHOOLS AND TECHNICAL TRAINING CENTRES

Aeronautical Training School, Jamnagar (No. 5 Civil).
Benares Hindu University, Benares.
Bengal Engineering College, Sibpur (No. 3 Civil).
Calcutta Flying School, Calcutta.
Central Training Workshops, Hyderabad (Deccan).
College of Engineering, Guindy (No. 4 Civil).
College of Engineering, Poona.
Government of India (Civil Aviation) Mechanics Training School, (No. 6 Civil), Juhu, Bombay.
Hyderabad Technical Training Centre, Secunderabad.
Jamshedpur Technical Institute.

On the outbreak of war all Flying Schools ceased private flying training and their equipment and training personnel were taken over by the R.A.F., India, for Army Co-operation and other duties connected with national defence.

GLIDING

Indian Gliding Association, Brabourne Stadium, Churchgate Street, Bombay. President : The Hon. Sir Homi Mehta, K.B.E., J.P. Chairman : Mr. P. M. Kabali. Hon. Secretary : Mr. N. R. Mody.

Owing to lack of equipment and materials this Association has been unable to proceed with the training of glider pilots.

PUBLICATIONS

Indian Aviation. Founded 1925. Published monthly by Thorne's Ltd. Price 8 annas. Editorial Offices : 13, Ezra Mansions. P.O. Box 2361, Calcutta.

TRANSPORT COMPANIES

Indian National Airways, Ltd. Head Office : Scindia House, New Delhi. Chairman : The Hon. Sir Homi Mehta, K.B.E., J.P. Managing Director : Mr. A. F. T. Cambridge.

The Company's original 15 year agreement with the Government of India for the carriage of mails by air has been extended during recent years, and in addition to the scheduled route shown below, it flies Government and private charters.

The Company holds 25% of the share capital of Indian Trans-Continental Airways, Ltd., (at present inactive), and is in charge of the commercial and traffic organization of the British Overseas Airways Corpn. at all trans-Indian stations.

Routes :—

Delhi—Jodhpur—Karachi. Twice weekly.
Delhi—Allahabad—Calcutta. Four times weekly.

Delhi—Bombay. Daily.
Delhi—Madras. Twice weekly.
Delhi—Lahore—Rawalpindi—Peshawar. Daily.

Aircraft used :—Six DC-3, three Beechcraft Traveller and one DH Dragon-Rapide are owned by the company. Other aircraft used are on loan from the Indian Government or the R.A.F.

Tata Air Lines. Head Office : Bombay House, Bruce Street, Fort, Bombay.

Routes :—

Karachi — Bhuj — Ahmedabad — Bombay. Four times weekly.
Bombay — Hyderabad — Madras — Trichinopoly — Colombo. Five times weekly.

(During the S.W. monsoon (June-September) there is a stop at Poona).

Bombay — Indore — Bhopal — Gwalior — Delhi. Twice weekly.
(Seasonal service from November-May).

Aircraft used :—de Havilland D.H. 89, Stinson Model A and Douglas DC-3. The company has bought ten Douglas aircraft from the U.S. disposals authorities.

Air Services of India, Ltd. Head Office : Brabourne Stadium, Churchgate Street, Fort, Bombay.

Routes :—
Bombay — Bhavnagar — Rajkot — Jamnagar — Porbandar.
Jamnagar — Bhuj.
Baroda — Bhavnagar — Amreli.
Bombay — Poona — Kolhapur.

This Company, which ceased operating air services in February, 1941, was taken over in July, 1943, by the Scindia Steam Navigation Co., Ltd.

British Overseas Airways Corporation

Headquarters, India and Burma Region : Finlay House, McLeod Road, Karachi.

The following B.O.A.C. routes serve India :
Great Britain — Mariguane — Augusta — Cairo — Habbaniyeh — Bahrein — Jiwani — Karachi — Calcutta (flying-boat service).
Great Britain — Rabat — Tripoli — Cairo — Shaibah — Karachi (landplane service).
Cairo — Lydda — Baghdad — Basra — Bahrein — Jiwani — Karachi — Delhi — Allahabad — Calcutta.
Cairo — Asmara — Kamaran — Aden — Riyan — Salalah — Masirah — Jiwani — Karachi.

China National Aviation Corporation (C.N.A.C.)

This Company is operating a service, Chungking — Kunming — Dinjang—Calcutta, three times weekly with Douglas DC-2 and DC-3 landplanes.

OTHER OPERATING COMPANIES

Indian Air Survey and Transport Ltd., Jessore Road, Dum Dum, Bengal. Established : 1927. Directors : Col. C. H. D. Ryder, C.B., C.I.E., D.S.O. ; R. C. Kemp, F.R.G.S. ; F. P. Raynham, M.I.A.E.

This Company undertakes aerial survey and kindred work in any part of the World, and over 200 surveys have been completed. Since 1924 the Company has surveyed more than 118,000 square miles of India and Burma.

Is training over 200 mechanics under the Civil Aviation Directorate's Training Scheme.

Indian Aviation Development Co. Ltd., Samudra Bhawan, Juhu, Bombay. Director and Manager : R. Vaughan Fowler, A.M.I.Ae.E.

This Company acts as aeronautical consultants.

Tata Iron & Steel Company Ltd.

This Company operates irregularly between Jamshedpur and Calcutta, using a Waco biplane.

AERODROMES

There are 151 landing grounds in India, including those controlled by the Civil Aviation Directorate, Air Force and Army, Indian States and local governments, and by companies and private individuals. Of these landing grounds there are 23 civil aerodromes for public use by passenger aircraft ; 21 of the latter are controlled by the Civil Aviation Department ; 5 civil landing grounds are open for private use ; 3 aerodromes and 45 landing grounds are maintained in serviceable condition by the units of the R.A.F. stationed in India and by the Indian Air Force ; 59 aerodromes or landing grounds are maintained by the Indian States for the use of civil aircraft.

2—SELF-GOVERNING DOMINIONS

DOMINION OF CANADA

ADMINISTRATION

Amendments were approved and passed by Parliament in 1944 by which the Hon. C. D. Howe was appointed Minister-in-charge of Civil Aviation, and an Air Transport Board was created to administer civil aviation. The members of the Board are : Mr. R. A. C. Henry (Chairman), Air Vice Marshall Alan Ferrier, M.C., J. P. Romeo Vachon, Group Capt. H. S. Rees, Flg. Off. G. A. Scott, and E. J. Bonner.

The Air Transport Board has been designed not only to perform regulatory duties with respect to air traffic in Canada but is also charged with the responsibility on advising the Government on ways and means of bringing about a rapid and well-planned expansion of transport by air. The Board will be in a position to give prompt attention to all matters affecting air transport requiring governmental consideration.

Under the amendments to the Aeronautical Act, the new Board is required to examine the needs for new commercial air services and make recommendations for their establishment and expansion in both the domestic and international fields. Subject to the approval of the Minister, the Board has power to issue licences for the operation of commercial air services and may prescribe the routes to be followed or areas to be served. The Board is likewise required to review all licences now in force respecting commercial air services and may cancel or suspend any such licence as it sees fit. Where any licence is not cancelled or suspended by the Board, the amended Act provides that it shall cease to be valid one year after the termination of the war in Europe.

The regulatory duties of the Board include the establishment of tariffs and the regulating of rates, examination of the ownership, financial structure, operations, and financial position of air carriers ; the making of recommendations for needed financial assistance ; and generally advising the Minister on all matters relating to civil aviation and the performance of such other allied duties as the Minister may direct.

Creation of the Air Transport Board removes from the Board of Transport Commissioners the regulatory duties with respect to air transport which have been under their jurisdiction. The Department of Transport will continue to administer those portions of the Aeronautics Act and The Air Regulations, 1938, which deal with civil aviation and do not come within the scope of the Air Transport Board.

AIR REGULATIONS

The control of Civil Aviation in Canada is provided for by the Aeronautics Act. Under this Act, air regulations have been completely revised and promulgated under Order in Council No. P.C. 1433, dated June 23, 1938, as The Air Regulations 1938. These regulations conform in essentials to the International Convention for Air Navigation. They include a new section providing for the licensing of inter-urban and international scheduled air transport services to provide a measure of control and regulation over such services.

The Air Regulations Section, in charge of the Superintendent, is organized as follows :—

Ottawa.—Headquarters' duties and field work in following areas : Quebec, west of 75th meridian ; Ontario, east of 77th meridian and north of the C.P.R. Montreal and Saulte Ste. Marie line as far west as the 86th meridian.

Montreal.—Quebec, east of the 75th meridian of longitude, and the Maritime Provinces.

Toronto.—That portion of Ontario lying south of the main line of the C.P.R. from Montreal to Saulte St. Marie and west of the 77th meridian of longitude.

Winnipeg.—Manitoba and Northern Ontario west of the 86th meridian of longitude.

Edmonton.—Saskatchewan, Alberta and the North-west Territories.

Vancouver.—British Columbia and Yukon Territory.

The duties include the inspection and registration of aircraft and their certification for airworthiness ; the examination and licensing of pilots and air engineers ; supervision of flying clubs ; prevention of dangerous flying ; inquiries into the cause of aircraft accidents ; and international flying.

AIRWAYS AND AIRPORTS

The duties of this section include the inspection, licensing and registration of airports and seaplane bases ; the licensing of scheduled air transport operations ; the construction and maintenance of airports and intermediate aerodromes, which now includes all the principal municipal airports in Canada, these having been incorporated into the Air Training Scheme ; assistance to municipalities in the designing and constructing of municipal airports ; the lighting of government airports and air routes ; the development and construction of radio range sites and the erection of radio range stations with the exception of the installation of radio equipment ; the construction of buildings and telephone and power lines ; and the calibration and testing of radio aids to air navigation.

This section, in charge of the Superintendent, is organized as follows :—

Headquarters (Ottawa, Ont.).—Headquarters duties.

Western District (Lethbridge, Alta.).—Yukon, North-west Territories, and Provinces of British Columbia and Alberta.

Central District (Winnipeg, Man.).—Provinces of Saskatchewan and Manitoba, and that part of Northern Ontario lying west of the 84th meridian (Nagogami, Ontario).

Southern District (Hamilton, Ont.).—That part of Ontario lying east of the 84th meridian (Hearst, Ontario) and west of the 75th meridian.

Eastern District (Montreal, P.Q.).—That part of Ontario lying east of the 75th meridian and the Provinces of Quebec, New Brunswick, Nova Scotia, and Prince Edward Island.

ASSOCIATIONS

The Canadian Flying Clubs' Association, formed in 1929 at Ottawa. Represents the *Fédération Aéronautique Internationale.* The central organization of the various Light Aeroplane Clubs. Patron : His Excellency the Right Honourable the Earl of Athlone, K.G., P.C., G.C.B., G.C.M.G., G.C.V.O., D.S.O., A.D.C. Hon. President : Air Marshal W. A. Bishop, V.C., C.B., D.S.O., M.C., D.F.C. President : M. A. Seymour, K.C. Treasurer : Dr. J. J. Green. Secretary : Miss Hyacinthe Lambart. Address : Journal Building, Ottawa, Ont.

A total of twenty-two Elementary Flying Training Schools and ten Air Observers' Schools are being operated by the Flying Clubs for the Commonwealth Joint Air Training Plan. A number of clubs have suspended their civil operations, a few are operating on a restricted basis, and those not running schools for the R.C.A.F. are training instructors for the Elementary Schools. The Toronto Flying Club has been helping to train pilots for the Royal Norwegian Air Forces.

Air Industries and Transport Association of Canada. Address : P.O. Box 672, Station B, Ottawa, Ontario. Directors : C. H. Dickins (President), Grant MacDonald (Vice-President), W. F. English (Hon. Secretary), P. C. Garratt (Hon Treasurer), W. N. Deisher, C. R. Troup. Executive Secretary : W. B. Burchall. General Representative : A. J. Veit.

PUBLICATIONS

Canadian Aviation. Address : Journal Building, Ottawa. Published monthly. Subscription : $2 British Empire ; $2.50 U.S.A. ; $3.00 Foreign Countries.

Commercial Aviation. Address : 341, Church Street, Toronto, Ont. Published monthly. Subscription : $2 British Empire ; $3.00 U.S.A. ; $4.00 Foreign Countries.

Air Force Review. Address : 495-517, Wellington Street, W. Toronto. Published monthly. Subscriptions : $1.50 British Empire : $2.00 U.S.A. ; $3.00 Foreign Countries.

Canadian Air Cadet. Address : 122, Wellington Street, Ottawa. Published monthly by the Air Cadet League of Canada. Subscription : $1.00.

TRANSPORT COMPANIES

The Companies operating air services in Canada are as follows :

American Airlines Inc. (U.S. Company), 100, East 42nd Street, New York 17, N.Y.

Routes :
Toronto — Buffalo — New York. Daily.
Windsor — Detroit — Chicago. Twice daily.

Canadian Pacific Air Lines, Limited, 620, Dominion Square Building, Montreal, Quebec.

President : L. B. Unwin.
Vice-President and General Manager : C. H. Dickens.
General Manager — Western Lines : G. W. G. McConachie.
District Offices are located at Toronto, Rimouski, Winnipeg, Regina, Edmonton (Alberta District), Edmonton (Mackenzie District), Whitehorse and Vancouver.

Routes :—
Vancouver—Prince George—Fort St. John—Fort Nelson—Watson Lake—Whitehorse. Daily except Sundays.
Whitehorse—Mayo—Dawson. Twice weekly.
Vancouver—Victoria. Seven times daily.
Vancouver—Zeballos. Weekly.
Vancouver—Port Alice. Twice Weekly.
Edmonton—McMurray—Fort Smith—Hay River—Providence—Fort Simpson. Alternating services nine times weekly.
Fort Smith — Resolution — Hay River — Providence — Fort Simpson—Norman Wells—Yellowknife. Thrice weekly.
Yellowknife—Rae—Port Radium. Weekly.
Fort Smith — Fort Simpson — Wrigley — Norman Wells — Good Hope — Arctic Red River — Fort McPherson — Aklavik. Monthly May to September.
Regina—Moose Jaw — Saskatoon — Prince Albert — North Battleford. Daily.
Regina—Moose Jaw—Saskatoon. Daily except Sunday.
Kenora—Red Lake—McKenzie Island—Favourable Lake—Beresford Lake—Lac du Bonnet—Winnipeg. Daily except Sunday.
Winnipeg—Lac du Bonnet—Beresford Lake—Bissett. Thrice weekly.
Winnipeg—Lac du Bonnet—Little Grande Rapids—Favourable Lake — Island Lake — God's Lake. Alternating services ten times monthly.
Flin Flon—Pelican Narrows—Island Falls—Sherridon—Pukatawagan—South End—Brochet. Alternating services nine times monthly.
Soux Lookout—Goldpines—Red Lake. Twice weekly.
Sioux Lookout—Pickle Lake. Daily except Sunday.
Montreal—Quebec—Saguenay. Daily except Sundays.
Quebec—Rimouski. Once weekly.
Mont Joli—Baie Comeau. Daily except Sundays, with seasonal charter extension to Seven Islands.
Prince George—Fort St. James—Takla Landing—Germanston Landing. Twice monthly.
Prince George—Fort McLeod—Finlay Forks—Fort Graham—Fort Ware. Seasonal only.
Fort Nelson—Nelson Forks—Fort Liard. Seasonal only.

There are also regular and charter services with bases at Senneterre and Roberval in the province of Quebec to the Ontario and Quebec mining areas.

Colonial Airlines (U.S. Company), Mount Royal Hotel, Montreal, Quebec.

Operates a thrice daily service from New York to Montreal via Albany and Burlington.

Maritime Central Airways, Limited, Charlottetown, Prince Edward Island.

President : J. K. Curran.

General Manager : C. F. Burke.
Routes :—
New Glasgow—Charlottetown. Twice daily except Sundays.
Charlottetown—Summerside—Moncton. Three times daily on weekdays, twice on Sundays.
Moncton—St. John. Twice daily except Sundays.
Magdelen Island winter service. Four non-scheduled trips weeekly.

Northeast Airlines (U.S. Company), Mount Royal Hotel, Montreal, Quebec.
Operates a twice daily service from Bangor (Maine) to Moncton.

Northwest Airlines (U.S. Company), 100 McIntyre Building, Winnipeg, Manitoba.
Operates a daily service from Chicago to Winnipeg.

Trans-Canada Air Lines, 203, Portage Avenue, Winnipeg, Manitoba.
President : H. J. Symington.
Routes :—
St. Johns—Gander—Sydney—Moncton. Twice daily.
Halifax—Moncton—Montreal. Thrice daily.
Montreal—Ottawa—Toronto. Thrice daily.
Toronto—London—Windsor. Twice daily.
Toronto—Kapuskasing—Winnipeg. Daily.
Toronto—North Bay—Kapuskasing—Winnipeg—Regina—Lethbridge—Vancouver—Victoria. Twice daily.
Lethbridge—Calgary—Edmonton. Thrice daily.
Toronto—New York—Washington. Thrice daily.
Montreal—Prestwick. Thrice weekly until September 1945, then daily. (Lancastrian landplanes).

United Air Lines (U.S. Company), 723, West Georgia Street, Vancouver, B.C.
Operates a daily service from Seattle to Vancouver.

Western Air Lines (U.S. Company), Burbank, California.
Operates a daily service from Salt Lake City to Lethbridge.

OTHER OPERATING COMPANIES

The following operators, having two or more aircraft, were variously engaged in flying instruction, passenger, freight, and express services, air photography, etc. Several are also operating training schools under the Commonwealth Joint Air Training Plan.

Austin Airways, 73, Adelaide Street W., Toronto, Ont. Charter services from Sudbury, Timagami, Gogama and Biscotasing, serving Northeastern Ontario.

Air Transport & Training Co., Toronto, Ont. Charter service from Island Airport, Toronto, and from North Bay.

Algoma Air Transport, South Porcupine, Ont. Charter services from South Porcupine to Sudbury and Gogama.

Aviation Service Corporation, 60, Front Street W., Toronto, Ont. Charter service from Barker Field.

Fliers Ltd., Barker Airport, Toronto, Ont. Charter services serving Western Ontario.

Leavens Bros. Air Services, Fairbank, P.Q., Toronto, Ont. Charter services serving Western Ontario.

Laurentian Air Services, 239, Queen Street, Ottawa, Ont. Charter services from Ottawa to Ontario and Quebec and from Domaine d'Esterel.

Red Wing Flying Service, Whitby, Ont. Charter service from Whitby, Ont. ; in the Summer from Port Carling.

Savant Airways, Savant Lake, Ont. Charter services from Savant Lake to St. Anthony, Dawson—White, Savant—Sturgeon ; Supreme from Savant Lake South, Central Pat and Pickle Crow North, all in Northern Ontario.

MINING AND EXPLORATION

The following aircraft operators are classified as Commercial Operating Companies, but their activities are distinct from other commercial operators in that there is no direct revenue from the use of their aircraft.

Brett-Trethewey Mines Ltd., 1320, Metropolitan Building, Toronto, Ont.
Consolidated Mining & Smelting Co. of Canada Ltd., Trail, B.C.
Hollinger Consolidated Gold Mines, Timmins, Ont.
McIntyre Porcupine Mines Ltd., Schumacher, Ont.
Prospectors Airways Co. Ltd., 80, King Street W., Toronto, Ont.
Springer, Sturgeon Gold Mines Ltd., 1213-320 Bay Street, Toronto, Ont.

COMMONWEALTH OF AUSTRALIA

ADMINISTRATION

Civil flying in the Commonwealth and Territories is subject to legislative control by the Commonwealth Government. The administration of the Air Navigation Act and Regulations is a function of the Civil Aviation Department under the Minister for Air and Civil Aviation, Mr. A. S. Drakeford. The permanent head of the Department is the Director-General of Civil Aviation, Mr. D. McVey. Assistant Director-General of Civil Aviation : Mr. E. C. Johnston.

A Bill to nationalise Australian Air transport companies was passed in August, 1945.

ASSOCIATIONS

The Royal Aeronautical Society, with which is incorporated the Institution of Aeronautical Engineers, Australasian Branch : "Science House," Gloucester and Essex Streets, Sydney.
Honorary Secretary : P. H. Vyner, A.M.I.Ae.E.

The Institution of Engineers, Australia, Aeronautical Branch, Sydney Division. Address : "Science House," Gloucester and Essex Streets, Sydney.
A branch of the professional engineers' society of Australia.

The Institution of Automotive Engineers (Aust.). Address : 485, Bourke Street, Melbourne, C.1.

The Guild of Aeronautical Engineers. Address : 75, Keaferd Street, Essendon North, Melbourne, W.6.

The Australian Air League. Incorporated Aug. 1, 1934. League Headquarters : Sirius House, 23-25, Macquarie Place, Sydney. General Secretary : K. C. Cameron. Branches : Victorian State Headquarters at Melbourne and Queensland State Headquarters at Brisbane.

The Australian Air League has a membership of over 12,000 and has established 120 branches. On the Declaration of War on Sept. 3, 1939, the League placed the services of its organization at the service of the Federal Government. In response to a suggestion made by the Air Council the League has established Preparatory Training Colleges in the three States in which it operates to give preliminary training to intending recruits for the R.A.A.F. The League is also contributing its services to the operations of the Australian Air Training Corps.

The Model Aeronautical Association of Australia. Address : c/o Box 2489MM., G.P.O., Sydney. Hon. Secretary : L. H. Annesley.

The Australian Women's Flying Club. Address : 221, George Street, Sydney.
The Club gives training in the maintenance of airframes and aero-engines, such as D.H. "Gipsy-Moths" and "Gipsy" engines, signalling and navigation, ambulance and first aid, motor transport, and canteen cookery and stores.

The Australian Flying Corps Association
A body of men who served in the Australian Flying Services during the War, 1914-18. Branches in each State.

The Australian Gliding Association. Address : 28, Princes Street, Footscray, Victoria. Secretary : R. Duckworth

RESEARCH ORGANIZATIONS

Council for Scientific and Industrial Research. Aeronautical Research Laboratory, Fishermen's Bend, Melbourne, S.C.8, Victoria. Division of Forest Products : Yarra Bank Road, Melbourne, S.C.4., Victoria.

Australian Aeronautical Research Committee. Formed in 1941. Co-operation with the Aeronautical Research Committee in Great Britain is one of the defined functions of the new Committee.

FLYING CLUBS

The Agreements between the Commonwealth Government and the Approved Flying Clubs for subsidies expired on Dec. 31, 1939, and all the aeroplanes belonging to the clubs, with the exception of the Tasmanian Aero Club, Broken Hill Aero Club, and Whyalla Aero Club, were taken over and used by the Department of Air, together with the subsidized clubs and most of the private companies, for elementary flying training of Air Force personnel. By 1941 there was practically no Civil flying in Australia, with the exception of the airlines, and most of the former club and flying school instructors were Pilot Officers in the R.A.A.F.

The three flying clubs which were not included in the Air Force Scheme, because of their smallness and their comparative isolation, were given Departmental assistance from Jan. 1, 1940, on the same basis as before the War.

Since the end of the war the subsidy agreement has been renewed whereby the Government undertakes to subsidise two Approved Flying Clubs to the extent of a maintenance grant of £25 for every 50 hours flown by any one aeroplane up to a maximum of 200 hours a year for each aeroplane. In addition a bonus of £50 will be paid to the Clubs for every pupil trained to "A" licence standard from *ab initio*, together with a renewel bonus of £10 for each "A" licence renewed on Club aircraft.

The Subsidized Flying Clubs are :—

The Royal Victorian Aero Club, Government Aerodrome, Essendon, Melbourne.

The Royal Aero Club of New South Wales, Mascot Aerodrome, Sydney.

The Royal Queensland Aero Club, Creek Street, Brisbane.

The Royal Aero Club of South Australia, 112, King William Street, Adelaide.

The Royal Aero Club of Western Australia, Inc., Government Aerodrome, Perth.

The Tasmanian Aero Club, Box 107, P.O., Launceston.

The Newcastle Aero Club, P.O. Box 4, Broadmeadow.

The Spencer's Gulf Aero Club, Whyalla.

The Broken Hill Aero Club, Broken Hill.

Unassisted Training Organizations

Airwork Co., Brisbane.
The Matheson Flying School, Goondiwindi, Queensland.
Kingsford Smith Air Services Ltd., Sydney.
Airflite Ltd., Sydney.
The Macquarie Grove Flying School, Camden, N.S.W.
The Canberra Aero Club, Canberra, A.C.T.
The Australian National Airways Flying School, Melbourne.
C. D. Pratt, Melbourne.
Australian Flying Schools, 18-20, Pelican Street, Sydney.

GLIDING CLUBS

Although the Australian Government suspended the subsidy to gliding clubs on the outbreak of War gliding made rapid progress during 1940 and many new clubs were formed. The Australian Distance Record for Gliders is 105 miles and the Duration Record just over 5 hours.

There is a movement on foot in Australia to give gliding training for recruits to the R.A.A.F. as a preliminary to power training.

Petrol rationing in Australia reduced by half the allowance made to many of the gliding clubs using the towed system of gliding and this seriously curtailed gliding activities.

The position of the clubs continued to deteriorate during 1942. In view of the activities with gliders for war purposes, the Secretary of the Australian Gliding Association, Mr. R. Duckworth, made a plea towards the end of October, 1942, for assistance by the Government to the remaining glider clubs, but apparently without result.

The Australian Air League in Victoria—Geelong Gliding Club.
The New South Wales Gliding Association.
The Gliding Club of Victoria, Melbourne.
The Sydney University Glider Club, Sydney.
The Waikerie Gliding Club, S.A.

PUBLICATIONS

Aircraft. Founded 1918. Published monthly, price 1/- (Overseas subscription : 16/- p.a.), by United Press Pty. Ltd. Editorial Offices : 62-74, Flinders Street, Melbourne, Victoria. London Office : 92, Fleet Street, E.C.4.

The Air Log. Published monthly, price 9d. (Overseas Subscription, British Possessions : 10/- p.a.), by the Proprietors, 75, Pitt Street, Sydney, N.S.W. Edited by Norman J. Tracy. Address : Box 2489 MM., G.P.O., Sydney, N.S.W.

TRANSPORT COMPANIES

In 1945, the Australian Government announced its intention to nationalise all internal inter-state airlines. The commercial airline operators which would have been affected by this action challenged the Commonwealth Government's right to implement the Australian Airlines Act to nationalise all interstate airways before the High Court of Australia. The Court ruled that the Airways Act was ultra vires of the Constitution and therefore invalid.

In retaliation the Commonwealth Government proposes to establish in 1946 an Australian Airlines Commission to operate Government owned inter-state airlines in competition with the privately-owned companies. At the same time the Government is expected to withdraw mail contracts from private contractors, to withdraw all subsidies on such routes and to impose higher charges for the use of aerodromes, radio and meteorological facilities. The Government may also call in all aircraft loaned to the airlines or bought under Government permit.

The domestic Air Transport Companies and their services as at January 1, 1944, were :—

Aircraft Pty. Ltd., 63, Eagle Street, Brisbane.
Routes :—
Brisbane — Maryborough* — Bundaberg* — Rockhampton — Thangool — Monto — Mundubbera* — Kingaroy — Brisbane. Weekly (one direction only).
Brisbane—Kingaroy. Five times weekly.
Brisbane — Kingaroy — Mundubbera** — Monto — Cracow*—Thangool.* Weekly.
Brisbane—Maryborough—Bundaberg*. Twice weekly.
Aircraft used :—D.H. 84, Waco and B.A. Eagle.
*Optional call. **Optional call southbound, regular call northbound.

Airlines of Australia, Ltd.
This Company was absorbed by Australian National Airways Pty. Ltd., on January 1, 1943.

Airlines (W.A.) Ltd., C.M.L. Buildings, St. George's Terrace, Perth.
Routes :—
Perth—Rottnest Island. Twice weekly.
Perth — Norseman — Kalgoorlie — Leonora — Lawlers/Agnew — Mt.Sir Samuel — Wiluna — Meekatharra — Nannine—Reedy—Cue—Mt. Magnet—Perth. Weekly.
Perth—Ravensthorpe*—Esperance*—Norseman. Weekly.
Aircraft used :—Monospar S.T.11 and D.H. 90.
*Optional call.

Ansett Airways Ltd. Aerodrome : Essendon, Melbourne.
Routes :—
Melbourne—Hamilton. Daily except Sunday.
Aircraft used :—Lockheed Electra.

Australian National Airways Pty. Ltd., 390, Flinders Street, Melbourne.
Routes :—
Sydney—Melbourne. Thrice daily.
Sydney—Canberra*—Melbourne. Daily.
Sydney — Wagga — Narrandera — Mildura — Adelaide. Daily on weekdays.
Sydney—Brisbane. Twice daily.
Brisbane — Rockhampton — Mackay — Townsville. Daily.
Townsville—Innisfail**—Cairns. Twice daily.
Cairns—Cooktown. Weekly.
Cairns—Cooktown—Coen—Iron Range. Weekly.

Cairns—Cooktown—Coen—Portland Roads (for Iron Range)—Horn Island (for Thursday Island). Twice weekly.
Cairns — Abingdon — Forest Home — Craydon — Miranda* —Normanton. Weekly.
Normanton — Galbraith — Inkerman — Mitchell River — Rutland Plains — Koolatah — Dunbar — Vanrook — Miranda*—Normanton (one direction only) weekly.
Normanton — Inverleigh — Augustus Downs* — Burketown —Normanton (one direction only). Weekly.
Melbourne — Adelaide — Ceduna — Forrest — Kalgoorlie — Perth. Six times weekly.
Melbourne—Launceston. Twice daily (weekdays) once (Sunday).
Melbourne—Launceston—Hobart. Daily.
Melbourne — Kerang — Mildura — Broken Hill. Daily except Sunday.
Melbourne — King Island — Smithton — Wynyard — Launceston—Flinders Island. Thrice weekly.
Aircraft used :—Lockheed 14, Douglas DC-2 and DC-3 D.H. 89, Stinson Model A, Short S.23 flying-boat and Douglas C-47. Of the total fleet of 25, 16 aircraft were on loan and charter from the Government, R.A.A.F. and U.S. Army.
*Optional call. ** Once daily only.
The Company absorbed Airlines of Australia, Ltd. on January 1, 1943.

Butler Air Transport Co., Kingsford Smith Aerodrome, Mascot, Sydney.
Routes :—
Sydney — Mendooran — Tooraweenah — Coonamble — Bourke—Cunnamulla—Charleville. Twice weekly.
Sydney—Moruya*—Bega. Daily except Sunday.
Aircraft used :—de Havilland D.H.84 and Monospar S.T.12.
* Optional call.

Connellan Airways, c/o C. B. Cantwell, 422, Collins Street, Melbourne.
Routes :—
Alice Springs — Mt. Doreen — The Granites — Tanami — Gordon Downs—Nicholson—Ord River*—Wyndham*— Denham River* — Argyle* — Inveray** — Waterloo — Limbunya—Wave Hill—Victoria River Downs —Katherine. Fortnightly.
Victoria River Downs—Timber Creek—Auvergne—Newry — Ivanhoe—Carlton—Wyndham. Fortnightly.
Alice Springs—Hermansburg—Tempe Downs—Kulgera— Mt. Irwin—Kulgera—Erldunda—Alice Springs (one direction only). Monthly.
Aircraft used :— Percival "Gull."
*Northbound only. **Southbound only.

Guinea Airways Ltd., Adastral Chambers, 16, Currie Street, Adelaide.
Routes :—
Adelaide—Mt. Eba*—Oodnadatta—Alice Springs—Tennent Creek—Daly Waters—Katherine—Batchelor (for Darwin). Thirteen times fortnightly.
Adelaide—Renmark. Twice weekly.
Adelaide—Renmark—Broken Hill. Four times weekly.
Adelaide—Kingscote. Ten times weekly.
Adelaide—Port Lincoln. Nine times weekly.
Adelaide—Cowell—Cleve—Adelaide (one direction only). Four times weekly.
Adelaide—Whyalla. Daily except Sunday.
Adelaide—Port Pirie—Whyalla—Adelaide. Daily except Sunday.
Port Pirie—Whyalla. Twice daily except Sunday.
Aircraft used :—Lockheed 10A and 14, D.H. 89 and Short "Scion."
*Optional call Southbound, no call northbound.

Macrobertson-Miller Aviation Co. Ltd., Pastoral House, 156, St. George's Terrace, Perth.
Routes :—
Perth — Geraldton — Carnarvon — Onslow — Roebourne — Whim Creek*—Port Hedland. Weekly.
Perth — Geraldton — Carnarvon — Onslow — Roebourne — Whim Creek — Port Hedland — Broome — Derby — Noonkanbah — Fitzroy — Hall's Creek — Ord River — Wyndham. Weekly.
Perth — Geraldton — Carnarvon — Onslow — Roebourne — Whim Creek*—Port Hedland—Broome—Derby—Noonkanbah—Fitzroy—Hall's Creek—Wave Hill—Victoria River Downs—Katherine. Weekly.
Aircraft used :—Lockheed 10A.
*Optional call.

Qantas Empire Airways, Shell House, Carrington Street, Sydney.
Routes :—
Sydney—Great Britain (Hurn). Twice weekly. Lancastrian landplanes. Operated jointly with British Overseas Airways.
Perth—Ceylon. Four times weekly. (Liberator landplanes and Catalina flying-boats).
Brisbane — Roma — Blackall* — Longreach — Winton* — Cloncurry — Mt. Isa*** — Camooweal — Alexandria — Brunette Downs — Anthony's Lagoon — Newcastle Waters—Daly Waters—Darwin. Five times weekly.
Cloncurry — Canobie** — Wandoola** — Milgarra** — Normanton. Weekly.
Sydney—Brisbane—Gladstone—Townsville. Daily.
Sydney — Brisbane — Gladstone† — Townsville† — Karumba†—Groote Eylandt†—Darwin. Weekly.
Sydney—New Guinea—Papua. Twice weekly. (Dakota landplanes). Formerly operated by W.R. Carpenter Airlines, which company was absorbed by Qantas in 1944.
Aircraft used :—Lancastrian, Liberator, Dakota, Lockheed 10A, D.H.83 and D.H.86 landplanes, Short S.23 and S.33 flying-boats. 3 Lockheed Lodestars are used for services operated on behalf of the U.S. Army Air Forces.
*Weekly only. **Optional call. ***Twice weekly only.
†Fuel stop.

INTERNATIONAL SERVICES

Tasman Empire Airways (See "New Zealand") operates a weekly service between Sydney and Auckland, New Zealand, with two Short "Empire" flying-boats.

THE AIR AMBULANCE SERVICE

Air Ambulance Services were first established in Australia in 1928 when an agreement was entered into between the Queensland and Northern Territory Aerial Services Ltd. (now Qantas Empire Airways) and the Australian Inland Mission. The Company provided the aircraft and pilot and the Mission Authorities the doctor. The base of the operations at that time was Cloncurry and flights were made to outback centres in Western and Northern Queensland.

The value of the scheme was readily apparent and has resulted in the establishment of other such centres to serve the sparsely populated parts of the Commonwealth not readily accessible by other means of transport. Considerable impetus to the efficiency of the Air Ambulance Service in ameliorating the hardships of settlers in the "outback" was given by the introduction of a system of wireless communication by means of pedal transreceivers. The simplicity of these small wireless units contributed largely to their value, power being supplied by a dynamo operated by bicycle pedals and morse messages may be transmitted by manipulating an automatic keyboard transmitter similar to a typewriter.

Air Ambulance Services, popularly known as the "Flying Doctor" services, were established at the following centres :— Cloncurry, Port Hedland, Wyndham, Kalgoorlie, Broken Hill, Alice Springs. These services were operated by the Australian Aerial Medical Services. A "Flying Doctor" service also operated from Katherine and was controlled by the Department of Health.

The Government recognized the national importance of the scheme in making accessible medical aid to outback settlers and an annual grant of £5,000 (later increased to £7,500) per annum was provided for maintenance and extension of Air Ambulance Services. This grant was administered by the Health, Postmaster-General's and Civil Aviation Departments.

A system whereby daily weather reports were transmitted from outposts to the bases was introduced in 1939. These reports were forwarded to the nearest meteorological or air service station. At the beginning of the War these reports were stopped but they have since been resumed.

The first medical flight from Wyndham was made in August, 1935, and the hundredth on Mar. 9, 1940. These flights covered 35,500 miles, the longest being more than 820 miles. Of the 100 trips, 48 covered an average of 520 miles.

The estimated cost of maintaining the six Flying Doctor Bases for the year ending June 30, 1941, was £22,000.

Although no recent details have been released it is known that the "Flying Doctor" services increased during 1943 and have proved of great value to the community in the remote inland areas.

AERODROMES AND LANDING GROUNDS

No details can be given of aerodromes, since they are under military control. Many new aerodromes were constructed in 1942 and the total number in use is now over 500.

DOMINION OF NEW ZEALAND

ADMINISTRATION

On the 1st April, 1937, an Air Department was established in New Zealand to co-ordinate and administer all matters concerning Civil and Military Aviation. The responsible Minister is the Hon. F. Jones, Minister of Defence.

The New Zealand Government has announced its intention to nationalise civil aviation and to form a single company to operate its air routes.

ASSOCIATIONS

The Royal New Zealand Aero Club, Inc. President : R. I. M. Sutherland. Secretary : T. G. Hull, Box 1527, Wellington.
The objects of the Club are to co-ordinate the efforts of the provincial flying clubs officially recognised by the Government and to foster the development of commercial aviation. It is affiliated with the Royal Aero Club.

The Guild of Air Pilots. Registrar : G. H. Spence, P.O. Box 11, Wellington.

The Guild of Aeronautical Engineers. Registrar : G. H. Spence, P.O. Box 11, Wellington.

PUBLICATION

Whites Aviation. Published monthly, price 1/- by Whites Aviation, Ltd., C.P.O. Box 2040, Auckland. Represented in United Kingdom by Norman Representation Service, 131, Fleet Street, London, E.C.4.

Wings. The official organ of the Royal New Zealand Aero Club, Inc. Published monthly. Address: Box 1527, Wellington. Price : 6/- per annum.

TRANSPORT COMPANIES

Tasman Empire Airways Ltd. Head Office : Wellington.
Capital : £500,000. Subscribers are Union Airways of New Zealand, Ltd., 39 per cent. as representing New Zealand ;
British Overseas Airways Corpn., 38 per cent. as representing the United Kingdom ; and Qantas-Empire Airways, Ltd., 23 per cent. as representing Australia.

Union Airways of New Zealand, Ltd. are Managing Agents in New Zealand, and Qantas-Empire Airways, Ltd. are the Principal Agents in Australia.

The Company operates a thrice weekly air mail and passenger service between Auckland and Sydney with two Short "Empire" flying-boats *Aotearoa* and *Awarua*. Between April 30, 1940 and April, 1945 these two flying-boats carried a total of 14,899 passengers, 601,089 lbs. mail and 225,366 lbs. freight and made 1,000 crossings of the Tasman Sea without injury or loss.

Air Travel (N.Z.) Ltd. Headquarters : Hokitika Aerodrome. Address : P.O. Box 55, Hokitika.
Routes :—
Hokitika—Waiho (for Franz Josef)—Weheka—Bruce Bay— Haast — Okuru (Upper) — Okuru (Mussel Point) — Jackson's Bay. Weekly.
Hokitika—Waiho (for Franz Josef)—Weheka. Eight times weekly.
Greymouth—Hokitika—Waiho (for Franz Josef)—Weheka. Four times weekly.
Aircraft used :—de Havilland D.H.83 and D.H.90.

Cook Strait Airways Ltd. Head Office : Nelson.
Routes :—
Blenheim—Wellington. Eight times weekly.
Wellington—Nelson—West Port—Greymouth — Hokitika. Daily except Sunday.

Union Airways of New Zealand Ltd. Head Office : 36, Custom House Quay, Wellington. Directors : Mr. J. N. Greenland, Mr. C. G. White, Sir A. F. Roberts, K.B.E., Mr. Walter Green. Manager : F. Maurice Clarke, Chief Engineer : Mr. L. Mangham.
Routes :—
Auckland—Palmerston North—Wellington. Six times weekly.
Wellington—Christchurch—Dunedin. Five times weekly return.
Wellington—Christchurch. Five times weekly. (This service commenced in December, 1943).
Aircraft used :—Lockheed Lodestar and Electra.

LIGHT AEROPLANE CLUBS

All private flying ceased in the Dominion on the outbreak of War, the Government taking over the majority of the aircraft and staff from all active Flying Clubs for incorporation in the training organization of the Royal New Zealand Air Force. At the same time the payment due by the Government was allowed to stand over free of interest, and the machines will be replaced after the War. The following is a list of Clubs affiliated to the Royal New Zealand Aero Club, Inc. :—

The Wellington Aero Club, Wellington. President : T. C. A. Hislop. Secretary : E. W. Annand.
The Auckland Aero Club, Auckland. President : F. B. Cadman. Secretary : L. W. Swan.
The Middle Districts Aero Club, Palmerston North. President : P. K. Fowler. Secretary : K. G. Chamberlain.
The Wairarapa and Ruahine Aero Club, Masterton. President : A. McDonald. Secretaries : Dunderdale and Gray.
The Hawke's Bay and East Coast Aero Club, Hastings. President : P. Barker. Secretary : R. D. Brown.
The Marlborough Aero Club, Blenheim. President : A. A. Macnab. Secretary : E. J. Brammall.
The Otago Aero Club, Dunedin. President : J. J. Marlow. Secretary : R. J. Cook.
The Southland Aero Club, Invercargill. President : A. E. W. McDonald. Secretary : J. E. Cuthill.
The West Coast United Aero Club. Greymouth. President : D. F. Gemmill. Secretary : H. J. Wicks.
The Waikato Aero Club, Hamilton. President : T. G. Mullan. Secretary : T. A. Ewan.
The Canterbury Aero Club. President : Sir Bruce Stewart. Secretary : P. R. Climie.
The Wanganui Aero Club, Wanganui. President : A. S. Burgess. Secretary : S. R. McCallum.
The New Plymouth Aero Club, New Plymouth. President : L. M. Moss. Secretary : W. G. Watts.

RADIO SERVICES

The installation of additional navigational aids at aeradio stations has proceeded steadily and during the year D/F. stations have been established at New Plymouth, Blenheim, Hokitika, Harewood and Taieri. Action has also been taken to allow for the remote control of transmission from separately situated receiving stations at these places. The New Plymouth D/F. station, in addition to its use for internal services, is utilised for taking bearings on Trans-Tasman flying-boats when approaching the New Zealand coast.

The aeradio stations, when required, are co-operating in the operations of the Royal New Zealand Air Force.

The aeradio station at Musick Point is now in full operation. This station maintains regular point-to-point services with the air terminal at Rose Bay, Sydney, and with flying-boats crossing the Tasman Sea.

AERODROMES AND LANDING GROUNDS

During the past year, the construction and maintenance of civil aerodromes was largely confined to the extension and improvement of those civil aerodromes and landing grounds which might be used by the Air Force for training and operations. Although much of the work done was primarily of defence importance, the benefit of all these improvements will be available to civil aviation after the War. An extensive programme of improvement was commenced and is in progress on all important aerodromes.

For details regarding aerodromes reference should be made to *"The Air Pilot"* issued by the Air Department (Civil Aviation Branch), New Zealand.

THE UNION OF SOUTH AFRICA

(Die Unie van Suidafrika)

ADMINISTRATION

Civil Aviation is controlled by the Directorate of Civil Aviation, acting under the Minister of Defence. The Directorate is situated at Room 176, Defence H.Q., Potgeiter Street, Pretoria.

Proclamation No. 123 of 1940, gazetted on June 15, 1940, provided for the suspension of all Civil Aviation activities in the Union and the Mandated Territory of South-West Africa. Aircraft exempted from this prohibition were those in the service of the Union Defence Department, those owned by clubs or schools, etc., which were training pilots on behalf of the Union Forces; aircraft owned by the British Overseas Airways Corporation and Southern Rhodesian Air Services while on approved scheduled services; and any other aircraft to which the Secretary for Defence had granted special exemption.

PUBLICATIONS

Wings. The official magazine of the South African Air Force. Published by Wings, London House, 21, Loveday Street, Johannesburg. Price 6d. monthly. Editor: W. T. H. B. Lethbridge.

The Fly Paper. Published by Aviation Publications Ltd., P.O. Box 7105, Johannesburg. After the July, 1940, issue publication was suspended for so long as the Union Government's ban lasts on civil flying.

TRANSPORT COMPANIES

South African Airways (S.A.R. & H.)

Headquarters: Germiston Airport, Johannesburg. General Manager: Brigadier Holthouse (temporarily on overseas service as South African Military Attache, Washington). Acting General Manager: Colonel Leverton.

South African Airways curtailed its commercial operations in September, 1939, when its 18 Junkers Ju 86's were converted for military service. Later its 11 Junkers Ju 52's were formed into a Bomber Transport Brigade and, with the Ju 86's, formed part of the S.A.A.F. unit which participated in the Abyssinian campaign. In June, 1940, S.A.A. ceased all civil operations. In 1941, 28 Lockheed Lodestars, which had been ordered in 1940, were incorporated in the S.A.A.F. and, together with the Ju 52's, were used on military transport services throughout Africa.

In January, 1944, Colonel Leverton, who had commanded the Bomber Transport Brigade, resumed his activities as Acting Manager of South African Airways and ten Lodestars were eventually made available for a resumption of scheduled air services on December 1, 1944.

Routes:—

- Johannesburg (Germiston)—Capetown, via Kimberley or Bloemfontein on alternate days.
- Johannesburg—Capetown, via Durban, Port Elisabeth and East London. Eleven times weekly.
- Johannesburg—East London, via Durban. Thrice weekly.
- Johannesburg—Durban. Four times weekly.
- Johannesburg—Salisbury (Rhodesia). Weekly.
- Johannesburg—Port Elisabeth, via Bloemfontein. Weekly.
- Johannesburg—Hurn (U.K.), via Nairobi, Khartoum, Cairo and Malta. ("Springbok" Service in pool with B.O.A.C.). Weekly.

British Overseas Airways Corporation

Headquarters South African Region: Devonshire Court, Victoria Embankment, P.O. Box. 936, Durban.

The Empire flying-boat headquarters are now established at Durban, where all maintenance work is undertaken.

The Empire service, known as the "Horseshoe" route, continued in operation throughout 1944, from Durban to Calcutta on a twice-weekly basis, with stops at Lorenço Marques, Beira, Mozambique, Lindi, Dar-es-Salaam, Mombasa, Kisumu, Port Bell, Laropi, Malakal, Khartoum, Wadi Halfa, Cairo, Kallia, Habbaniyah, Basra, Bahrein, Dubai, Djwani, Karachi, Raj Samand, Gwalior, Allahabad.

In order to cater for Johannesburg passengers a twice-weekly service is now in operation between Valbank Dam (Durban) and Johannesburg.

The dam is situated seventy miles from Johannesburg and the company operate a training school there for First Officers under the supervision of Capt. M. Gurney.

S.A.B.E.N.A.

This Belgian airline is operating a fortnightly service from Stanleyville to Capetown via Kindu, Manono, Elizabethville, Ndola, Lusaka, Bulawayo, Johannesburg, Bloemfontein and Beaufort West.

Southern Rhodesian Air Services

This Government concern operates a service between Salisbury, Bulawayo and Johannesburg three times weekly.

FLYING CLUBS AND SCHOOLS

Most of the private flying training schools and flying clubs in the Union have been chosen by the Government to train pupils for the South African Air Force. Training is concentrated at four inland centres and equipment from other parts of the country has been transferred to these instructional centres.

AERODROMES

The Railway Administration is undertaking the construction of three large civil airports in the Union, to serve Johannesburg, Durban and Capetown.

The Union's permanent international airport will be established at Kempton Park, between Germiston and Pretoria and about 13 miles from the main railway station at Johannesburg. It will cover an area of more than 6,000 acres and provide three runways, each 66 yards wide. The main runways will be 3,500 yards long, the others 2,750 yards, all built in concrete for aeroplanes of up to 150 tons.

The airport will become the Union's terminal point for aeroplanes bringing passengers, mails, and merchandise from all parts of the world. Such aeroplanes will be permitted to land and depart only at this airport in the Union, unless arrangements are made for them to touch down at other points.

Meanwhile a provisional airport is in preparation at Palmietfontein, south of Johannesburg. This has an area of 700 acres, with a runway of 1,000 yards, and was expected to be completed in the Summer of 1945.

The Durban Airport will be built just north of Isipingo, while the Capetown Airport will be 5 miles W. of Bellville and 11¾ miles by road from the centre of the city.

The Railway estimates include a sum of £3,130,000 for expenditure on the three main civil airports for the Union, of which £500,000 is being spent in the current financial year.

EIRE

ADMINISTRATION

The Department of Industry and Commerce is responsible for the control of Civil Aviation in Eire, and the administration is carried out by the Transport and Marine Branch of the Department of Industry and Commerce, Kildare Street, Dublin. The International Convention on Aerial Navigation is implemented by the Air Navigation and Transport Act, 1936. Matters relating to the control of Civil Flying are dealt with in the Air Navigation (General) Regulations, 1930, as amended by the Air Navigation (Amendment) Regulations of 1934, 1940 and 1943; in the Air Navigation (Investigation of Accidents) Regulations, 1928 (amended 1943) and in The Emergency Powers (Air Navigation Restriction) Orders Nos. 1-8.

TECHNICAL AND RESEARCH ESTABLISHMENT

All technical work is undertaken by the Department of Defence, Air Corps, at Baldonnel Aerodrome, which is under the control of Officer Commanding, Air Corps, Baldonnel Aerodrome.

ASSOCIATION

Irish Aviation Club. Address: 20, Abbey Buildings, Middle Abbey Street, Dublin.

The Executive Committee for 1943-44:—Mr. Sean O'h-Uadhaigh, President; Mr. C. F. Bruton, Hon. Sec.; Mr. J. A. Carrol, Hon. Treas.; Denis M. Greene, Asst. Hon. Sec.; Miss Grainne Scannell, Asst. Hon. Treas.; Committee Members: Messrs. J. McGovern, A. Lokko, W. Phillpots and P. Flynn.

The Club was formed in 1933 as the National Irish Junior Aviation Club with the promotion of aviation amongst minors as its main object. The Club is interested in all branches of aviation and is now open to everyone, but its activities at present are confined to model aeronautics and lectures for members, schools, associations and other bodies.

OPERATING COMPANIES

Aer Lingus Teoranta, 39, Upper O'Connell Street, Dublin. Chairman: John Leydon.

Formed early in 1936. This was the first Air Transport Company to be established in Ireland for the operation of regular services.

Two services per day are operated on week-days between Dublin and Liverpool. These services are operated in pool with West Coast Air Services Ltd., each Company operating one return service daily. Aer Lingus Teoranta uses a Douglas DC-3 and a D.H.86, and West Coast Air Services a D.H.86.

A Dublin—Croydon service was re-opened on November 9, 1945, and is operated with DC-3 airliners daily except Sundays.

The following are the combined statistics of Aer Lingus Teoranta and West Coast Air Services for 1942 and 1943:—

Year	Aircraft Miles Flown	No. of Passengers	Freight (lbs.)
1942	198,181	10,727	36,335
1943	193,481	11,585	41,096

Aer Rianta Teoranta, 39, Upper O'Connell Street, Dublin. Chairman: John Leydon.

This Company was formed in April, 1937, under the provisions of Part VIII of the Air Navigation and Transport Act, 1936, with a registered capital of £500,000, in 500,000 shares of £1 each. The Company, directly or through subsidiaries, will represent Ireland's interest in air services between Ireland and other countries. The Company is also entrusted with the operation of all internal services.

AERODROMES

Dublin Airport, Collinstown. 5⅛ miles N. of Dublin, Civil Customs Airport. All facilities including night-landing equipment. W/T. and D/F. The aerodrome, which is managed on behalf of the Department of Industry and Commerce by Aer Rianta Teoranta, is not open for public use. Applications to use it should be addressed to the Secretary, Aer Rianta Teoranta, 39, Upper O'Connell Street, Dublin.

Baldonnel, Clondalkin, Co. Dublin. 7¾ miles W.S.W. of Dublin. Military aerodrome, controlled by the Army Air Corps. Army Air Corps repair shop available for emergency repairs.

Shannon Airport (Foynes). Flying-boat base 24 miles West of Limerick. This base, which is under the control of the Minister for Industry and Commerce, is of a temporary character and is at present being used for the operation of trans-Atlantic civil air services by the British Overseas Airways Corpn., Pan American Airways and American Export Airlines, pending the completion of a combined flying-boat and landplane airport now under construction at Rineanna, some 8 miles East of Foynes. The airport is not open to public use, and applications to use it should be addressed to the Secretary, Department of Industry and Commerce, Transport and Marine Branch, Kindare Street, Dublin. Customs, Air Traffic Control, W/T., D/F., Meteorological and night landing facilities are available. No hanger and no repair facilities.

Shannon Airport (Rineanna). Proposed combined landplane and flying-boat base approximately 15 miles West of Limerick. The airport is at present in use for landplane services connecting with flying-boat operations from Foynes, and has also been used for a Dublin—Limerick service. The flying-boat base has not yet been completed. A temporary Terminal Building is available and Customs, Air Traffic Control, Radio and Meteorological services are provided. The Airport is not at present open to public use and applications to use it should be addressed to the Secretary, Department of Industry and Commerce, Kildare Street, Dublin. Concrete runways are at present of lengths adequate to meet present demands but are being extended. The flying-boat anchorage within the embankments will be 2,000 ft. in diameter.

CHILE

(The Chilean Republic Republica de Chile)

ADMINISTRATION

Civil Aviation in Chile is under the control of the Direccion de Aeronáutica, which is itself under the direction of the High Command of the Air Force.

Director of Aeronautics: Commander Carlos Montecino A.

ASSOCIATIONS

Club Aéreo de Chile, Casilla 913, Santiago. Aerodrome: "Los Cerrillos." The Club Aéreo de Chile's property on the airport includes a comfortable club house, good tennis courts and sports grounds. The Club receives a subsidy from the Government of one Chilean peso for every gross metric ton of merchandise imported into Chile. 50% of this subsidy is distributed proportionately among the affiliated aero clubs.

PUBLICATION

Chile Aéreo. Official publication of the Club Aéreo de Chile. Published monthly at the Club's Headquarters, Casilla 913,

Santiago, and distributed free of charge among members. Price to the public $2.0 per copy.

The Air Force Review. Edited and published by the General Staff of the Chilean Air Force and published every three months.

TRANSPORT COMPANIES

Linea Aerea Nacional (National Air Line). Terminal Airport: Santiago (Los Cerillos).

Director: Juan del Villar.

The Company receives a Government subsidy which is based on gross weight of imports at the rate of nine Chilean pesos per metric ton.

This airline, which is usually known as the "LAN," began operations in 1930 with a service from Santiago, north and later south, along the coastline of Chile. The Company is partly owned by the Chilean Government, and its operations are confined to Chile, although it still considers the possibility of extending its radius of operation to Lima, La Paz and Buenos Aires.

The principal routes flown are:—

Santiago — Ovalle — Vallenar — La Serena — Copiapo — Antofagasta. Daily both ways except Sundays.

Antofagasta—Tocopilla—Iquiqui—Arica. Alternate days both ways except Sundays.

Santiago — Chillan — Concepcion — Tumeco — Puerto Montt. Unscheduled infrequent service.

Aircraft: Six Lockheed "Electra" and "Lodestar."

Pan American Grace Airways, Inc. (**Panagra**), Santiago.

Operates through Chile under a concession granted by the Government. Services pass through Santiago northward to Antofagasta, Arica and on to the United States five times weekly, and southwards to Buenos Aires five times weekly.

Sociedade Aerea Cruzeiro do Sul (see under Brazil).

Headquarters: Rio de Janeiro, Brazil.

Operates mail and passenger service between Santiago and Rio de Janeiro twice weekly both ways, using Junkers Ju.52 aircraft.

FLYING CLUBS

Aero Clubs are established (December, 1943) at the following centres.

Arica, Chillan, Copiapó, Lauraro, San Felipe, Osorno, Santiago, Castro, Curico, Cauquenes, Antofagasta, Angol, Ovalle, Valdivia, Valparaiso, Ancud. San Fernando, Porvenir, Iquique, Concepción, La Serena, Temuco, Los Andes, Puerto Montt, Rancagua, Punta Arenas, Talca.

Until the war, flying training was given on de Havilland "Gipsy-Moth" and Avro aircraft.

In August, 1941, a well planned campaign sponsored by the President of the Republic was conducted to raise funds for the purchase of further training aircraft to be allotted to the Clubs. As a result ten Aeronca aircraft were distributed to various clubs during 1943. They were the first of thirty trainers to be purchased in the U.S.A. Of these ten, the Club Aéreo de Chile and the University Aviation Club received two each, the others being distributed to clubs at Valparaiso, San Felipe, Los Andes, Chillan, Temuco and Puerto Montt.

AERODROMES

SANTIAGO (Los Cerillos). Lat. 33°13′S. Long. 70°43′W. Alt. 525 m. Principal Customs Airport of Chile. Terminal of the Linea Aerea Nacional. Completely equipped. R/T. and night-flying facilities.

ARICA (El Moro). Lat. 18°28′S. Long. 70°20′W. Alt. 90 m. Principal Customs Airport in the north. Completely equipped. R/T. and night-flying facilities.

The following aerodromes are available for civil flying:—

IQUIQUI. 10 km. S.E. of town. Lat. 20°14′S. Long. 70°07′W. Alt. 350 m.

TOCOPILLA (Barilles). Lat. 22°06′S. Long. 70°05′W. Alt. 1,000 m.

MARIA ELENA. Lat. 22°13′S. Long. 69°43′W. Alt. 1,250 m.

CALAMA. Lat. 22°27′S. Long. 68°56′W. Alt. 2,260 m.

ANTOFAGASTA (Portezuela). 14 km. S.E. of town. Lat. 23°42′S. Long. 70°17′W. Alt. 406 m.

TALTAL. Lat. 25°25′S. Long. 70°35′W. Alt. 20 m.

CHAÑARAL. Lat. 26°21′S. Long. 70°42′W. Alt. 20 m.

PUEBLO HUNDIDO. Lat. 26°23′S. Long. 70°03′W. Alt. 790 m.

COPIAPÓ. On the S.E. outskirts. Lat. 27°21′S. Long. 70°22′W. Alt. 370 m.

VALLENAR. Lat. 28°34′S. Long. 70°48′W. Alt. 403 m.

OVALLE. 9 km. N.E. of the town. Lat. 30°33′S. Long. 71°10′W. Alt. 250 m.

CURICO. Lat. 34°58′S. Long. 71°14′W. Alt. 211 m.

TALCA. Lat. 35°24′S. Long. 71°40′W. Alt. 107 m.

CHILLAN (San Ramon). 6 km. N.E. of the town. Lat. 36°33′S. Long. 72°03′W. Alt. 114 m.

CONCEPCIÓN. Lat. 36°49′S. Long. 73°03′W. Alt. 9 m.

TEMUCO (Maquehua). 5 km. E. of the town. Lat. 38°47′S. Long. 72°44′W. Alt. 75 m.

OSORNO. Lat. 40°35′S. Long. 73°09′W. Alt. 24 m.

PUERTO MONTT (Chamiza). 8 km. S.S.E. of town. Lat. 41°28′S. Long. 72°57′W. Alt. 5 m.

PUNTA ARENAS. Lat. 53°09′S. Long. 70°54′W.

LA SERENA.

EL BELLOTO.

LOS ANGELES.

VALDIVIA.

ANCUD.

CASTRO.

Emergency Landing Grounds are situated at the following places:—ZAPIGA, LA PALMA, BAQUEDANO, CATALINA, POTREILLOS, CARRERA PINTO, ALGARROBAL, CHANAR, COQUIMBO (Cerillos), COMBARBALA, TILAMA, PARRAL, TRAIGUEN.

There are Seaplane Alighting Areas at the following places:—QUINTERO, PUERTO MONTT, RIO PALENA, PUERTO LAGUNAS, PUERTO AYSEN, RIO BAQUER, PUERTO EDEN, PUERTO NATALA, PUNTA ARENAS.

CHINA

(The Great Chinese Republic—Chung-Hua Min-Kuo)

ADMINISTRATION

Civil Aviation in unoccupied China is under the control of the Ministry of Communications of the Central Government of China at Chungking.

ASSOCIATIONS

The Aeronautical Federation of the Chinese Republic and the China Aviation League are at present inactive.

TRANSPORT COMPANIES

China National Aviation Corporation

Associated with Pan American Airways Inc., which holds 45% of the capital.

Routes:—

Chungking—Lanchow.

Chungking—Kunming.

Aircraft used:—Douglas DC-2 and DC-3.

In seven years of the Sino-Japanese War the company had five airliners shot down or forced to land by enemy gunfire.

Since the end of the war in the East the China National Aviation Corpn. has opened many new services. In September, 1945, services were started from Chungking to Shanghai, Peiping and Canton. The Chungking—Kunming service has also been extended to Hanoi, Indo-China, and a service now operates into Hong Kong.

The Sino-Soviet Aviation Corporation (known as "Hamiata")

This Company is a joint Soviet/Ministry of Communications enterprise and operated from Hami to Alma Ata connecting with The Soviet Aeroflot service from Alma Ata to Moscow. The service was irregular but approximated one flight per week.

No information is available on the operations of the Company since June, 1941.

COLOMBIA

(The Republic of Colombia—República de Colombia)

ADMINISTRATION

The general administration of Civil Aviation is controlled by the Ministry of War through the Dirección General de Aeronáutica Civil, which interprets the regulations officially laid down. Director of Civil Aviation: Dr. Pablo Emilio Jurado.

Address: Seventh Street 7-50, Bogotá.

PUBLICATION

Boletin da Aeronautica Civil (Bulletin of Civil Aeronautics). Edited by the General Administration of Civil Aviation. Address: Seventh Street 7-50 (third floor), Bogotá. Distributed free of charge every two months.

TRANSPORT COMPANIES

Aerovias Nacionales de Colombia (**Avianca**). Head Office: Edificio José Joachim Vargos No. 9-23, Bogoto.

President and General Manager: Dr. Martin del Corral.

This Company, an affiliate of Pan American Airways, is controlled by Colombian nationals.

Routes:—

Barranquilla—Medellin. Five times weekly. Twice weekly via Cartagena. Four times weekly variant stops Cartagma, Corozal, Monteria, San Marcos Ayapel, Pato, Otu, Amalfi.

Medellin—Cali. Daily via Cartago.

Barranquilla—Bogota. Five times weekly. Twice weekly via B. Bermeja. Twice weekly via Cartagena. Twice weekly via Cienaga, Cucuta, Bucuramanga.

Cucuta—Bogota. Weekly via Bucuramanga.

Medellin—Bucuramanga. Twice weekly via B. Bermeja.

Bucuramanga—Bogota. Weekly.

K.L.M. Compañia Real Holandesa de Aviación

This Company maintains a weekly service to Barranquilla from Curaçao via Aruba.

COMMERCIAL COMPANY

Aero Fotographia S.A. Head Office: Bogotá.

Formed in 1940 as a subsidiary of the Aero Exploration Co., of Tulsa, Okla., U.S.A., to undertake contracts for the Colombian Government and oil companies.

OTHER COMPANIES OPERATING AIRCRAFT

South American Gulf Oil Company. For oil field service.

Aircraft used:—Ford 5ATC, Lockheed Electra and Stinson Reliant.

Colombian Petroleum Company. For oil field service.

Aircraft used:—Ford 5ATC and Lockheed Electra.

Andean National Corporation. For oilfield service.

Aircraft used:—Barkley-Grow 8T-1.

Alvarez Lopez & Company. For mining service.

Aircraft used:—New Standard biplanes.

FLYING SCHOOLS AND CLUBS

Escuela de Aviacion, A.B.C. Director: Major Camilo Daza.

Address: Banco de la Republica (third floor), Bogotá. Operating Centre: Camalá Aerodrome, Giradot. Aircraft used: Curtiss "Fledgling."

Aero-Club Colombiano. Director: Guillermo Rodriquez Y.

Address: Cali. Operating Centre: At present the "Ernesto Samper" base at Cali, eventually Jamundi Aerodrome. Aircraft used: Bird biplane and Monocoupe monoplanes.

Escuela de Planeadores de Medellin. President: Oscar Botero.

Address: Medellín. Operating Centre: "El Retiro" Field. Uses nationally-built gliders.

AERODROMES

AGUAS CLARAS, ARAUCA, BOGOTÁ, BUCARAMANGA, CALI, CARTAGO, COROZAL, CUCUTA, CABUYARO, CRAVO NORTE, EL MORRO, HATO DE COROZAL, HONDA, IPIALES, MEDELLIN, MORENO NEIVA, NUNCHIA, OROCHE, OTU, POPAYAN, PUERTO CARRENO, SAN MARTIN, SAN MATEO, SAN JOSÉ, LA TRINIDAD, TAME, VALLEDUPAR, VILLAVICENCIO.

SEAPLANE STATIONS

BUENAVENTURA, CHOQUICHOQUI, EL BANCO, GAMARRA, GIRARDOT, GUAPI, LA GLORIA, LORICA, MAGANGUE, PUERTO WILCHES, PUERTO BERRIO, QUIBDO, RIO SUCIO, SANTA MARGARITA, TUMACO.

COMBINED AERODROMES AND SEAPLANE STATIONS

AYAPEL, BARRANQUILLA, BARRANCA BERMEJA, CARTAGENA, CIENAGA, PALANQUERO, PATO, SAN MARCOS, TURBO, MONTERIA.

Medellin—Bogota. Fifteen times weekly either direct or via Honda.

Cali—Ipiales. Weekly. Twice weekly via Popayan.

Medellin—Otu. Thrice weekly. Twice weekly via Amalfi.

Barranquilla—Cienaga. Five times weekly.

Bogota—Cali. Daily.

Bogota—Cartago. Four times weekly.

Barranquilla—B. Bermeja. Twice weekly via Maganque, El Banco, La Gloria, Gamarra, Pto Wilches.

Barranquilla—Buenaventura. Weekly via Cartagena, Lorica, Turbo, Quibdo, Andagoya.

Buenaventura—Tumaco. Weekly via Guapi.

Bogota—Villavicencio. Twice weekly.

A twice-weekly service is available through Ipiales, connecting point between the Avianca Colombian routes and Panagra's service to Quito and Guayaguil for the international network.

From Villavicencio services are operated into the Llanos with flag stops at C. Richmond, Tame, El Morro, H. de Corozal, Moreno, San Mateo, San Martin, Cravo Norte, Arauco, Pto Carreno.

Aircraft:—Douglas DC-3A, Boeing 247-D, Ford Trimotor 5ATC, Ford 8AT, Junkers W-34, Beechcraft 17 and 18, Clark seaplane.

Lineas Aereas Taca de Colombia. Head Office: Edificio Vasquez, Bogotá. Chairman: Edwardo Lopez. Manager: Gomez Picon.

This company, the shares of which are owned partly by Colombian nationals (55%) and by the TACA Company (45%), has a permit to operate scheduled routes and at the time of writing was awaiting the delivery of two Douglas and one Beechcraft twin-engined aircraft.

Pan-American World Airways. Offices: c/o Avianca, Barranquila and Bogotá.

Pan American Airways operates a daily landplane service between Barranquilla and Miami via Camaguey and Kingston. There is also a daily service between Balboa and Port of Spain via Barranquilla.

Pan-American Grace Airways (**Panagra**).

The Company's daily service between Balboa—Buenos Aires stops at Cali.

Urabá Medellin and Central Airways, Inc. Office: Carabobo 320, Medellin. Chairman: Francis S. Adams. Vice-President in charge of operations: Gouzalo Mejia.

This affiliated company of Pan-American Airways operates a thrice-weekly service between Balboa, C.Z., Turbo and Medellin.

COSTA RICA

(The Republic of Costa Rica—República de Costa Rica)

ADMINISTRATION

Civil Aviation is controlled by the Department of Public Safety (Seguridad Publica), through the Inspector-General of Civil Aviation, Coronel Luis Valenzuela.

ASSOCIATION

The Costa Rican Wing of the Inter-American Escadrille was formed in 1941. Officials :—President : Alfredo Volio Mata.

TRANSPORT COMPANIES

Compânia TACA de Costa Rica S.A. Head Office : Tegucigalpa, Honduras. Officials :—President : Modesto Martinez. Vice-President : Porfirio Gongora ; Secretary : Eugene Le Baron ; Treasurer : Raul Zelaya R. ; Manager : Roman Macaya.

International Routes :—

San José—Managua—Tegucigalpa—San Salvador. Five times weekly.
San José—Balboa. Twice weekly.
San José—Puerto Armuelles—Balboa. Weekly.

Domestic Routes :—

San José—Palmar—Golfito. Four times weekly.
San José—San Isidro—Palmar. Weekly.
San José—San Isidro—Palmar—Buenos Aires—Volcan—San Isidro—San José. Weekly.
San José—San Isidro—Buenos Aires—Potrero Grande—La Cuesta. Weekly.
San José—San Isidro. Thrice weekly.
San José—Sixaola—Limón. Weekly.
San José—Parrita. Twelve times weekly.
San José—Rio Cuarto—La Josefina—La Marina—Villa Quesada—San José. Twice weekly.
San José—Puntarenas—Las Juntas—Liberia—Tempate—27 de abril—Santa Cruz—Nicoya—Puntarenas—San José. Weekly.
San José—Puntarenas—Las Juntas—Las Cañas—Liberia—Tempisque—Santa Cruz—Puntarenas—San José. Weekly.
San José—Puntarenas—Las Juntas—Las Cañas—Liberia—Tempisque—Sardinal—Santa Cruz—Nicoya—Puntarenas—San José. Weekly.
Santa Cruz—Tempisque—Sardinal—Liberia—Bagaces—Las Juntas. Weekly.

Aircraft :—3 Lockheed 14's, 1 Curtiss-Wright "Condor," 3 Ford Trimotors, 1 Curtiss-Wright "Kingbird," 2 Travel Airs. The Company has one hangar 170 ft. × 150 ft. at San José with facilities for the overhaul of engines, propellers, instruments and accessories.

Pan American Airways Inc.

Has a through service from Brownsville to Cristobal, C.Z., calling at San José twice daily Southbound and daily Northbound. There is also a daily service between New Orleans and Balboa, stopping at San José in each direction.

AERODROMES

BAGACES. Lat. 10°31'N., 85°16'W. Runway 700 × 150 m.
BUENOS AIRES. Alt. 700 m. Runway 600 × 50 m. W/T. call sign T1F.
CANAS. ½ mile S.W. of Canas. Runway 660 × 95 m.
LA CRUZ. 6 kilos S.E. of La Cruz. Alt. 180 m. Runway 600 × 300 m. W/T. call sign T1Q.
LA CUESTA. ¼ mile from Government Building, Buenos Aires Canton. Runway 675 × 60 m. W/T. call sign T1C.
LIBERIA. Lat. 10°39'N., Long. 85°27'W. Alt. 150 m. Runway 450 × 250 m. W/T. call sign T1D.
LIMON. Lat. 10°00'N., Long. 83°02'W. Alt. 1 m. Runway 1,000 × 75 m. W/T. call sign T1M.
LOS CHILES. North of village of Los Chiles. Runway 700 × 60 m. W/T. call sign T1L.

NICOYA. Lat. 10°05'N., Long. 85°24'W. 1 mile North of Nicoya. Alt. 135 m. Runway 600 × 75 m., soft after rains.
POTRERO GRANDE. ½ mile S.W. of Potrero Grande. Alt. 600 m, Runway 800 × 100 m.
PUERTO JIMENEZ. Lat. 8°34'N., Long. 83°21'W. Alt. 1½ m. Field 700 × 100 m. with landing strip 700 × 30 m., N./S. W/T. call sign T1J.
PUNTARENAS. Lat. 9°58'N., Long. 84°49'W. 6 kilos E. of town. Alt. 2 m. Runway 1,000 × 100 m. W/T. call sign T1P.
SABANA. Customs Airport. Lat. 9°56'N., Long. 84°04'W. 1 mile W. of San José. Alt. 1,180 m. Runway 1,000 × 200 m. Hangars. Radio and weather reports available.
SANTANA. Lat. 9°53'N., Long. 84°15'W. 12 miles W. of San José. Owned by P.A.A. Alt. 850 m. Runway 870 × 60 m. W/T.
URENA DE PEREZ ZELEDON. 4 kilos from Urena. Alt. 800 m. Runway 800 × 150 m. W/T. call sign T1G.
VILLA QUESADA. 1½ miles North of Villa Quesada. Alt. 620 m. Runway 500 × 50 m.
There are private landing grounds at the following places :—
EL JOBO HACIENDA, Guanacaste. Owned by Francisco Hurtado. Alt. 140 m. Runway 700 × 75 m.
EL TEMPISQUE, Guanacaste. Owned by Federico Sobrado. Alt. 90 m. Runway 1,200 × 200 m.
PUERTO CORTES, Puntarenas. Owned by Francisco Olasa Reig. Alt. 15 m. Runway 675 × 85 m.
TABOGA, Hacienda, Guanacaste. Owned by Julio Sachez L. Near town of Canas. Runway 610 × 40 m.
There is an auxiliary field, BARRA DEL COLORADO, at Limon. Lat. 10°47'N., Long. 83°35'W. ½ mile E. of village of La Barra. Runway N.N.W./S.S.E. 900 × 50 yds. W/T. to S.W.

CUBA

(The Republic of Cuba—República de Cuba)

ADMINISTRATION

The Ministry of Communications and Justice controls Civil Aviation. Permits to fly over the island are granted by the Secretary of State and the Ministry of Defence.

ASSOCIATIONS

National Committee for the Development of Aviation

In December, 1943 a group of prominent Cubans formed the above Association to promote civil aviation after the War. Chairman of the group, which includes other educators, and commercial, industrial and civic leaders, is Dr. Pablo Carrera Justiz, Professor at Havana University. A campaign is to be launched in 1944 to induce municipalities to establish air fields for postwar commerce.

TRANSPORT COMPANIES

Cia Nacional Cubana de Aviacion, S.A. (A subsidiary company of Pan American Airways). Head Office : Prado No. 252, Havana. President : Manuel Quevado, Jr. Vice-President and General Manager : G. D. Grossman.

Routes :—

Havana—Cienfugos. Twice daily via Varadero.
Havana—Camaguey. Four times daily.
Santiago—Baracoa. Daily via Antilla, Preston, Cayo Mambi. Flag stop Moa.
Havana—Guantanamo. Twice daily. Variant stops Camaguey, Manzanillo, Antilla, Santiago. Flag stop Preston.

Pan American World Airways

Routes :—

Miami—Havana. Three services daily, including one on to Merida, Yucatan and Mexico City.
A number of Pan American Airway's services to Central and Latin America pass through Cuba (refer under U.S.A.).

Expreso Aereo Inter-Americano. Head Office : Industria No. 508, Havana. President : Dr. Teodoro Johnson.

This newly formed Company opened a cargo service from Havana to Miami on September 3, 1943, with one Sikorsky S-38 amphibian and two Ford Trimotors. Owing to wartime traffic demands, the Company was operating six round trips weekly with substantially full loads at the end of the year.

AERODROMES

The main Aerodromes in Cuba are :—

CIEGO DE AVILA. Lat. 21°47'N. Long. 78°47'W. 1 mile N. of Ciego de Avila. Alt. 20 ft. Landing strip N./S. 700 yds. × 20 yds., N.N.E./S.S.W. 500 yds. × 20 yds. Rest house. No other facilities.
CIENFUEGOS. Lat. 22°09'N. Long. 80°25'W. 1 mile N. of Cienfuegos. Alt. 20 ft. Good grass surface. Rest house. W/T. call sign CMN 99.08 m. Service and minor repairs available.
RANCHO BOYEROS (Havana). Lat. 23°00'N. Long. 82°25'W. 10 miles S. of Havana. Alt. 300 ft. 4,000 ft. paved runway. Administration building and hangar. Obstruction lights. Beacon on top of administration building. W/T. call sign CMI 99.08 m. Service and full repairs available. This is the official airport of entry. Owned by P.A.A.
GUANTANAMO. Lat. 20°09'N. Long. 75°12'W. 2 miles N. of Guantanamo. Alt. 75 ft. Landing strip N./S. 700 yds. × 20 yds. Rest house. No other facilities.
JESUS MARIA. Lat. 20°02'N. Long. 75°47'W. 1 mile N. of Santiago de Cuba. Alt. 20 ft. Field triangular, but rock runway covered with gravel 1,000 yds. × 30 yds. should be used as the rest of the field is very unsafe after rains. Administrative building, hangar and full facilities. W/T. call sign CMH 99.08 m. Minor repairs.
MANZANILLO. Lat. 20°18'N. Long. 77°08'W. 3 miles E.S.E. of Manzanillo. Alt. 150 ft. Landing strips N.W./S.E. 1,120 yds. × 50 yds., N./S. 700 yds. × 33 yds. Rest house. No other facilities.

IGNACIO AGRAMONTE. Lat. 21°25'N. Long. 77°51'W. 5 miles N.E. of Camaguey. Alt. 345 ft. Good grassy surface. Administration building. Minor repairs. W/T. call sign CMM 99.08 m.
ANTILLA. Lat. 20°51'N. Long. 75°44'W. 2 miles N.N.E. of Antilla. Alt. 30 ft. Landing strip 800 yds. × 40 yds. Rest house.
There is a new field Lat. 20°49'N., Long. 75°42'W., ½ mile from the old field. Alt. 30 ft. Landing strip 800 yds. × 50 yds. There are no facilities at either field except W/T. call sign CMG 99.08 m., which can be used for both.
GENERAL ADRIANO GALANO. Lat. 20°20'N. Long. 74°30'W. 5 miles S.E. of Baracoa. Alt. 50 ft. Landing strip N./S. 600 yds. × 20 yds. Rest house. No other facilities. W/T. call sign CMO 44.71 m.
There is a military field at CAMP COLUMBIA (Havana). Lat. 23°06'N., Long. 82°25'W., and a U.S. Navy Base at GUANTANAMO, Lat. 19°55'N., Long. 75°10'W.

There are also the following Landing Grounds :—
FONDEADERO. Lat. 22°00'N. Long. 84°16'W.
PRESIDIO MODELO. Lat. 21°54'N. Long. 80°18'W.
SANTA CLARA. Lat. 22°25'N. Long. 79°59'W.
PINA. Lat. 22°05'N. Long. 78°44'W.
CUAGUA. Lat. 22°05'N. Long. 78°25'W.
CENTRAL JARONU. Lat. 21°50'N. Long. 77°58'W.
SANTA LUCIA. Lat. 22°40'N. Long. 83°58'W.
MACEO. Lat. 22°15'N. Long. 80°38'W.
MORON. Lat. 22°07'N. Long. 78°40'W.
MANATI. Lat. 21°18'N. Long. 76°50'W.
GENERAL MILANES. Lat. 20°25'N. Long. 76°42'W.
ALMEIDA. Lat. 20°12'N. Long. 74°26'W.
PILON. Lat. 19°53'N. Long. 77°18'W.
CAMPO MILLIGAN. Lat. 20°50'N. Long. 76°55'W.
PALMA. Lat. 20°25'N. Long. 76°00'W.
HOLGUIN. Lat. 20°53'N. Long. 76°16'W.
CANADA. Lat. 22°02'N. Long. 78°41'W.
CENTRAL SENADO. Lat. 21°34'N. Long. 77°36'W.

DENMARK

(The Kingdom of Denmark—Kongeriget Danmark)

Civil Aviation in Denmark is under the control of the Minister for Public Works. It is administered by the Director of Civil Aviation (Direktren for Luftfartsvoesenet) and the Aviation Inspection Department (Statens Luftfartstilsyn), both located at Torvegade 45, Copenhagen.

TRANSPORT COMPANY

Det Danske Luftfartselskab A.B. (D.D.L.).

In the Summer of 1945, D.D.L. was operating the following services to Sweden :—

Copenhagen—Malmoe—Stockholm.

Copenhagen—Aalborg—Goteburg.

By the end of 1945 services had also been inaugurated to London, Amsterdam, Paris and Geneva.

D.D.L. is also planning trans-Atlantic services to the United States in co-operation with the other Scandinavian countries.

DOMINICAN REPUBLIC

(Santo Domingo—República Dominicana

ADMINISTRATION

Civil aviation is under the control of the Department of War and Navy. Address : Ciudad Trujillo, Dominican Republic.

TRANSPORT COMPANIES

Compañía Nacional de Aviación, C. por A.

This Company, organized in 1944, operates a passenger, mail and cargo service daily, except Sundays in each direction

between Ciudad Trujillo and Santiago de los Caballeros. The same service is extended to La Romana thrice weekly.

Plans have been formulated and put into effect to expand service of the company to include all of the important cities of the Dominican Republic. At the present time this company operates a Ford Trimotor and a single-engined Stinson Reliant.

The Republic is likewise served by Pan-American Airways System, Royal Dutch Airlines and Taca, as follows :—

Pan American Airways. This company includes the General Andrews Airport, Ciudad Trujillo, in its stops on the following regular daily schedules :—

(1) Miami, Fla.—Venezuela ; (2) Venezuela—Miami, Fla. ; (3) Miami, Fla.—San Juan, P.R. (two sections) ; (4) San Juan, P.R.—Miami, Fla. (two sections) ; (5) Miami, Florida—Rio de Janeiro, Brazil ; and (6) Rio de Janeiro, Brazil—Miami, Fla.

Royal Dutch Airlines (K.L.M.). Operates a fortnightly service from Curaçao to Ciudad Trujillo via Aruba.

TACA Airways System, Inc. Operates an airmail and cargo service between Ciudad Trujillo, Miami and Rio de Janeiro and vice versa twice a month.

AERODROMES

GENERAL ANDREWS AIRPORT, Ciudad Trujillo. Paved runways. There are complete facilities at this airport, for servicing all types of aircraft, both commercial and military. These facilities include aviation gasoline of the proper octane number for use in all types of aero-engines.

In addition to the General Andrews Airport, airports are located at the following cities in the Dominican Repblic :—

CALDERAS, AZUA, BARAHONA, ENRIQUILLO, PEDERNALES, JIMANI, DESCUBIERTA, NEIBA, LAS MATAS, DAJABÓN, MONTE CRISTY, PUERTO PLATA, MONTE LLANO, SANTIAGO DE LOS CABALLEROS, LA VEGA, SAN PEDRO DE MACORIS, LA ROMANA, CONSUELO and SAN JUAN.

SEAPLANE BASES

SAN PEDRO DE MACORIS. Seaplane Station. Pan American Airways' base. Full facilities available.

San Pedro de Macoris is used by the Pan American Airways System as an auxiliary seaplane base on its "Clipper" route between the United States of America and South America.

Seaplane bases are also located at the following places in the Dominican Republic :—

BARAHONA, AZUA, CALDERAS, LA ROMANA, SABANA DE LA MAR, SÁNCHEZ, SAMANÁ, PUERTO PLATA, MONTE CRISTY and CUIDAD TRUJILLO.

Action has been initiated by the Government to improve all existing airports and to construct additional aerodromes.

ECUADOR
(The Republic of El Ecuador—República del Ecuador)

ADMINISTRATION

Civil Aviation in Ecuador is controlled by the Ministry of National Defence and is under the direction of Major Jorge Paez Mena.

In January, 1941, a U.S. Air Mission headed by Colonel Burgess arrived in Ecuador at the Government's invitation to assist in the improvement of air activities.

TRANSPORT COMPANIES

Pan American-Grace Airways, Inc., Guayaquil.

To stress the national character of Panagra's services in Ecuador following the elimination of the German-operated airline SEDTA, the domestic routes set up in March, 1942, are operated under the name of **Aerovias del Ecuador-Panagra.**

Routes :—
Quito-Ipiales (Colombia). Twice weekly.
Quito-Guayaquil. Daily.
Guayaquil-Loja. Thrice weekly, via Cuenca.
Quito-Manta. Twice weekly.
Guayaquil-Manta. Twice weekly.
Guayaquil-Salinas. Twice weekly.
Quito-Esmeraldas. Weekly.
The Balboa—Buenos Aires service stops daily at Guayaquil.
Equipment : Douglas DC-3 landplanes.

GLIDING CLUB
Quito Gliding Club. President : Sr. Juan Muoroz.

AERODROMES

GUAYAQUIL (Simon Bolivar). Lat. 2°10′S., Long. 79°52′W., Alt. 10 ft. 1 mile N. of city. 1,600 × 1,100 yds. Runways N.N.E./S.S.W. 1,094 yds., N.W./S.E. 547 yds. Hangars, beacon and boundary lights. W/T. call sign HCU. Wavelength 3,076 m.

This is a military combined airport and seaplane base but civilian aircraft may land with permission.

QUITO (Mariscal Sucre). 4½ m. N. of town. Alt. 9,400 ft. 2,640 × 492 ft. Floodlight. Minor repairs.

In addition to the above two main airports others are situated at ESMERALDAS, MANTA, SALINAS, CUENCA-LOJA, LATACUNGA, RIOBAMBA and COTOPAXI.

EGYPT
(The Kingdom of Egypt—Misr)

ADMINISTRATION

The Department of Civil Aviation in Egypt comes under H.E. Hussein Sirry Pasha, the Minister of National Defence.

The Director-General of Civil Aviation is Mohamed Roushdy Bey and the Deputy Director is Mustapha Riad Moursi, B.Sc., D.I.C. Mr. A. W. Savage, of the A.I.D., is lent to the Egyptian Government by the Air Ministry.

ASSOCIATION

The Aéro Club d'Egypte. Affiliated with the *Fédération Aéronautique Internationale.*
The Club is at present inactive.

The National Flying Corporation
The Corporation was founded in 1938 to promote aviation and to provide flying facilities in Egypt. It is subsidized by the Government and owns four training aircraft. No recent details are available, but it is presumed activities continue for the training of reserves for the Royal Egyptian Air Force.

TRANSPORT COMPANIES

British Overseas Airways Corporation
Offices : 4, Shara Baehler, Cairo, (Headquarters, Middle East Region).

The Corporation operates numerous services to and through Egypt, both by landplane and flying-boat, as follows :—

Great Britain—Istres—Castel Benito (Tripoli)—Cairo. Fifteen times weekly.
Cairo — Damascus — Baghdad — Teheran. Thrice weekly.
Cairo — Luxor — Jedda — Port Sudan — Asmara — Kamaran—Aden—Addis ababa. Weekly.
Cairo—Aden, via Asmara. Twice weekly.
Cairo—Wadi Halfa—Khartoum—El Fasher—El Geneina—Maiduguri — Kano — Lagos. Twice weekly.
Cairo — Lydda — Baghdad — Basra — Bahrein — Djwani — Karachi — Delhi — Allahabad — Calcutta. Thrice weekly.

Cairo — Asmara — Kamaran — Aden — Rijan — Salalah — Masira—Djwani—Karachi. Weekly.
Cairo—Jeddah. Weekly.
Cairo—Khartoum—Nairobi—Givelo. Thrice weekly.
Cairo—Lydda—Baghdad—Basra. Twice weekly.
The "Horseshoe" Route also passes through Cairo twice weekly.

Misr-Airwork S.A.E.
Head Offices : Almaza Airport, Heliopolis, near Cairo.
Managing Director : H. E. Hassan Sadek Pasha.
Government delegate member of the Board and General Manager : H. E. Mohamed Roushdy Bey.

This first Egyptian Aviation Company, which was formed in association with the British aviation company Airwork, Ltd., holds an authorisation from the Egyptian Government for the establishment and operation, within Egyptian territorial limits, of :—

Civil flying training schools, local passenger-carrying flights, service stations for the provisioning, maintenance, and repair of civil aircraft, regular and occasional civil air transport services for the carriage of passengers, mails and goods, within Egypt and between Egypt and abroad.

The Company is now operating as follows :—
Routes :—
Cairo —Alexandria. Four times daily.
Cairo—Minia—Assuit—Luxor. Thrice weekly.
Cairo—Lydda. Once daily.
Cairo—Beirut. Once daily.
Cairo—Damascus. Twice weekly.
Cairo—Haifa. Twice weekly.
Cairo—Port Said—Alexandria—Cairo. Thrice weekly.
Cairo—Alexandria—Port Said—Cairo. Thrice weekly.
Cairo—Cyprus. Once weekly.
Fleet : Five D.H. 89, four D.H. 86, one D.H. 84, one D.H. 90 and three Avro Anson.

The Company's workshops also undertake the repair and overhaul of service aircraft and provide facilities in their workshops for the British Overseas Airways Corporation.

FLYING SCHOOL
The Misr-Airwork Flying School
Almaza Airport, Cairo.

In addition to flying training for both A and B licences, the school includes Ground Engineering and Radio instructional establishments. There are also branch flying schools at Alexandria and Port Said.

Fleet : Five D.H. Tiger-Moths, two D.H. Gipsy-Moths one D.H. Leopard-Moth, and two Miles Magisters.

AERODROMES

CAIRO (Almaza). Lat. 30°04′N., Long 31°21′E. 5 kms. E. of city. Alt. 262 ft. Full facilities.

ALEXANDRIA (Dekheila). Lat. 31°08′N., Long. 29°48′E. 8 kms S.W. of city. Alt. 7 ft. Full facilities.

The new airport at MARIUT, details of which are not available replaces DEKHEILA, which has been taken over by the Egyptian Air Force.

ASWAN. Lat. 24°03′N., Long. 32°54′E. 2 kms. S.E. of town. Alt. 400 ft. Area 850 × 680 yds. No facilities.

ASSIUT. Lat. 27°13′N., Long. 31°06′E. 8 kms. W. of town. Alt. 150 ft. No facilities.

MINIA. Lat. 28°05′N., Long. 30°44′E. 2 kms. W. of town. Alt. 130 ft. Administration buildings, etc.

LUXOR. Lat. 25°41′N., Long. 32°42′E. 5 kms. E.S.E. of town. Alt. 250 ft.

SOLLUM. Lat. 31°34′N., Long. 25°08′E. 2 kms. W. of town. Alt. 590 ft.

PORT SAID. Lat. 31°17′N., Long. 32°15′E. 4 kms. W. of city. Alt. sea level. Full facilities.

FRANCE

On the liberation of France the first Provisional Government delegated responsibility for all matters concerning air transport to a Minister for Air, who administered air transport through the *Direction des Transports Aériens.*

In order to participate in the war effort all French air transport were militarised. With the object, however, of laying foundations for the future a *Bureau d' Aviation Civil* was formed as an adjoint of the *Direction des Transports Aériens.* This *Direction* had four *Réseaux de Transports Aériens* operating directly under its authority but under military control. These réseaux, or networks, were as follows :—

Réseau Central des Transports Aériens (Central)
Headquarters : Algiers.
Principal routes operated :—
Algiers—Paris—London.
Tunis—Ajaccio—Marseille.
Tunis—Algiers—Casablanca.

Algiers—Casablanca—Dakar.
Algiers—Gao—Fort Lamy—Brazzaville—Pointe Noire.
Algiers—Madagascar, via Cotonou, Loulouabourg and Nairobi.
Algiers—Madagascar, via Bangui and Stanleyville.

Réseau Occidental des Transports Aériens (Western)
Headquarters : Dakar.
Principal routes operated :—
Dakar—Casablanca—Algiers—Paris.
Dakar—Abidjan—Lagos—Pointe Noire.
Dakar—Niamey—Cotonou.

Réseau Oriental des Transports Aériens (Eastern)
Headquarters : Damascus.
Principal routes operated :—
Damascus—Cairo—Algiers—Paris.
Damascus—Baghdad—Teheran.
Damascus—Antananarivo (Madagascar)—La Réunion, via

Khartoum, Djibouti, Nairobi and Lindi.

Réseau Métropolitain des Transports Aériens (Metropolitan).
Headquarters : Paris.
Principal routes operated :—
Paris—Lyon—Marseille.
Paris—Toulouse.
Paris—Bordeaux.
Paris—Rennes.
Paris—Lille.
Bordeaux—Toulouse—Marseille.

As from January 1, 1946, all French military air services assumed the title of Air France. This nationalised concern will be responsible for all internal and external airlines except the trans-Atlantic services, which will be operated by Air France Transatlantique. France has signed an interim agreement with the United States covering the operation of two North Atlantic routes.

GERMANY
(The German Empire—Deutsches Reich)

Under the terms of the Potsdam Agreement drawn up by the United Nations in July, 1945, the production in Germany of arms, ammunition and implements of war, including all types of aircraft and sea-going ships shall be prohibited and prevented. The maintenance of all aircraft, military and civil is also prohibited.

GREECE
(The Kingdom of Greece Hellas)

Greek civil aviation ceased when the Government was forced to capitulate on April 23, 1941. During the Italo-Greek War and the subsequent German invasion the Greek airline Helliniki Eteria Enaerion Synghinonion A.E. was formed into a small Air Transport Command for the Fighting Services. All the aircraft, four Junkers G-24, were lost.

Since the liberation of the country plans have been under consideration for the reorganization of civil aviation.

An Anglo-Greek air transport agreement was signed in November, 1945, providing for reciprocal air services between the two countries to be operated by British Airways Corpn. and presumably a Greek State airline.

GUATEMALA
(The Republic of Guatemala—República de Guatemala)

ADMINISTRATION

The control of air transport in the Republic is vested in the Ministry of Commerce, and is the immediate responsibility of a Director-General of Civil Aviation.

Director-General of Civil Aviation : General José Ovidio Sierra C., La Aurora Airport, Guatemala City.

ASSOCIATIONS

Club Interamericano de Universitarios, 10A, Avenida Sur No. 18, Guatemala City.

A non-profit social organization composed of Guatemalan nationals and U.S. citizens resident in Guatemala. In December, 1944, the Civil Aviation Group of the Club was granted exclusive permission by the Government to develop private flying. Ground classes have been started and the Club hopes to obtain a small number of light aeroplanes for flying instruction.

The Guatemala Wing of the Inter-American Escadrille.

Formed July 5, 1941. Hon. President : General Jorge Ubico, President of Guatemala.

PUBLICATIONS

Alas. Published by the Direccion General de Aeronautica Civil.
Caminos Del Aire. Published monthly by Pan-American Airways.

TRANSPORT COMPANIES

Aerovias de Guatemala S.A., 12, Calle Poniente 6. Guatemala City.
Pan American Airways Inc., 6a, Avenida, Sur No. 26, Guatemala City.

The Brownsville—Balboa service stops twice daily at Guatemala City airport in each direction. There is also a service twice daily from New Orleans.

AERODROMES

Airports of the 1st Category:—
"LA AURORA." The present air centre of the Republic. Situated 7 kms. to the South of the capital. Asphalt runway 5,800 ft.×200 ft. Height above sea level : 1,485 m. Markings : White circle 30 m. dia. and an arrow indicating N.S. No night-markings. Prevailing wind : N. to S. Wireless telephony, telegraph, and telephone. Meteorological information available.

BARRIOS. Situated in the Dept. of Izabhal, Puerto Barrios. 1 km. N.E. of the Port, on the coast. Two landing grounds, 720 and 750 × 125 m. Height above sea level : 1 m. Prevailing winds : N.E. and S.W. Meteorological Office.

Aerodromes of the 2nd Category:—
FLORES (Peten), QUEZALTENANGO (Quezaltenango), COBAN (Alta Verapaz) and BANANERA (Izabal).

Aerodromes of the 3rd Category:—
A Series :—SAN JERONIMO, RABINAL, LOS CERRITOS (Esquintla), MAZATENANGO, JUTIAPA, RETALHULEU, CHIQUIMULA, JALAPA, LA TINTA, ESQUIPULAS, HUEHUETENANGO, QUICHE, PASO CABALLOS (Peten), UAXACTUN (Peten), CARMELITA (Peten), DOS LAGUNAS (Peten), SAN MARCOS and TIQUIZATE.

B Series :—SALAMA, CHAMPERICO, CONCEPCION (Esquintla), MONJAS, SAN PEDRO, PINULA, CHIMALTENANGO, PAJAPITA, YAXHA (Peten), SAN JOSE (Port), ZACAPA, LA LIBERTAD (Peten) and SAN FRANCISCO CHACACLUN (Peten).

Seaplane alighting areas are available in the bays of AMATIQUE and SANTO TOMAS, in the ports of BARRIOS, SAN JOSE, CHAMPERICO and OCOS and on the lakes of FLORES (Peten), IZABAL, AMATITLAN and ATITLAN.

HAITI
(The Republic of Haiti—La Republique de Haiti)

There is no domestic Civil Aviation in Haiti, but due to its geographical position, the airport and seaplane base at Port au Prince have assumed considerable importance in the Caribbean air services.

Pan American Airways have a number of services using the island. The landplane services operated with Douglas DC-3's from Miami to Buenos Aires, San Juan and Venezuela, all stop at Bower Field airport four times weekly, daily and thrice weekly respectively. There are also several Seaplane services to and through the Port au Prince harbour base.

On August 17, 1943, another airline began using the island when the Curaçao-Miami service of K.L.M. was inaugurated. This service is weekly.

The aerodrome, Bowen Field, although primarily military, has been considerably enlarged and improved by Pan American Airways, who have laid an asphalt runway as well as other facilities. W/T. call sign HHD, wave length 37.43 and 50.70 m. Meteorological data is available from the radio station.

HONDURAS
(The Republic of Honduras—República de Honduras)

ADMINISTRATION

Civil Aviation in Honduras is administered by the Department of War, Marine and Aviation with headquarters at Tegucigalpa.

ASSOCIATIONS

The Honduras Wing of the Inter-American Escadrille

Formed on June 29, 1941.

Hon. President : Gral. Tiburcio Carias A. (President of Honduras).

President in Office : Dr. Juan Manuel Galvez (Minister of War).

TRANSPORT COMPANIES

Transportes Aéreos Centro-Americanos, S.A. (TACA), Toncontin Airport, Tegucigalpa.

The headquarters of the Company are situated in Tegucigalpa, and at the Toncontin Airport a complete maintenance and repair department is maintained.

Branch offices are established in British Honduras (Belize), El Salvador (San Salvador), Nicaragua (Managua), Costa Rica (San José) and Panama (Panama City).

In 1943 the Company maintained a regular "International Schedule" serving the above Central American countries, i.e.:—
San Salvador—Tegucigalpa—Managua—San José. Five times weekly.
San José—Balboa. Twice weekly.
San José—Puerto Armuelles—Balboa. Weekly.
In addition to the above the Company maintains services to the various up-country districts. Altogether 118 Airports are served on schedule and 90 Airports are served on charter. The principal airports on these services are as follows :—La Esperanza, Gracias, Sta. Rose, Sta. Barbara, San Pedro, Puerto Cortez, La Union, Tela, Esquias, Yoro, Olanchito, La Ceiba, Talanga, Guiamaca, Manto, S. Fco. Paz, Catacamas, Juticalpa, Agua Fria, Danli, Yuscaran, Guinope, San Marcos, Cholutcca, San Lorenzo, Amapala, Aramecina, Nacaome, Corozal, Belize, Orange Walk, El Cayo, Stann Creek, Punta Gorda, Pto Casina, La Luna, Copan, Sinuapa, Mascala, Esquias, Guimaca, Ocatal, Esteu, Matagalpa, Cumplida, Alamicamba, Siuna, Bonanza, Puerto Casuas, Sewas Carma, Waspan, Olama, La Libertad, Punza Pouca, Bluefields, La Cruz, Los Cheles, Los Anogados, Ubena, Bagaces, Las Canas, Las Juntas, Punta Arenas, Swadelfia, Nicota, Santa Cruz, Tempisque, Sardinal, Villa Quesada, Rio Cuarto, Petal, San Ramon, Parrita, Quepos, Boca Maranjo, San Isisro, Yolcan, Buenos Aires, Potrero Grande, Union, Palmas, Caras Gordas, La Cuesta, Golfito, Puerto Juminez Madrigal, Puerto Armuelles, Altamira, Liberio, Tempate, Pto. Cabezas, Progreso.

The Company maintains thirty-six aircraft, thirty-two licensed pilots, and a ground staff of 319. Thirty-six radio stations are owned by the Company.

Aircraft :—Lockheed 14 aircraft are used on the International Schedule and the other services use Ford Trimotor, Travel Air and other types.

The Company flies approximately 2,000,000 revenue miles, carries over 60,000 passengers and 25,000,000 lbs. of mail, express and freight annually.

Pan American Airways

The Company's "Mexico Flyer" service stops daily in each direction at Tegucigalpa (Toncontin).

AERODROMES

TONCONTIN. Lat. 14°03'N., Long. 87°12'W., Alt. 3,500 ft. 4 miles south of Tegucigalpa. Civil Customs. Runways N.N.W./S.S.E. 1,200 yds., N.E./S.W. 800 yds., N.N.E./S.S.W. 875 yds. Hangars and full night facilities. W/T.

LA LIMA. Lat. 15°23'N., Long. 87°57'W. 7 miles S.S.E. of San Pedro Sula on golf course. Alt. 85 ft. Size 2,000 × 400 ft. Hangar and minor repairs. W/T. call sign HRL.

CATACAMAS. Lat. 14°51'N., Long. 85°56'W. 1 mile S. of town. Alt. 2,000 ft. Size 2,500 × 500 ft. No facilities.

DANLI (Agua Fria). Lat. 14°17'N., Long. 86°33'W. 8 miles N.N.W. of town. Alt. 3,500 ft. Size 2,000 × 150 ft. Nose hangar but no other facilities.

GUINOPE. Lat. 13°53'N., Long. 86°57'W. 1 mile N. of village. Alt. 4,000 ft. Runs E./W. 1,500 × 150 ft. Wind cone. No facilities.

JUTICALPA. Lat. 14°41'N., Long. 86°18'W. 1 mile W. of town. Alt. 2,000 ft. Size 1,800 × 300 ft. No facilities.

PUERTO CORTES. Lat. 15°50'N., Long. 87°56'W. ¾ mile E. of town. Alt. 10 ft. Runs E./W. 3,000 × 300 ft. Limited repairs at Railway shop in town. W/T. call sign HRG.

There are more than fifty other landing fields in addition to the above. All towns of over 500 inhabitants possess a landing ground.

ICELAND

The first aviation company to operate in Iceland was formed in 1938 and was known as the Flugfélag Akureyrar (Akureyri Aviation Company). It was operated from Akureyri on the north coast of the island, maintaining charter services with a seaplane to various points round the coast. The capital of the Company was held by some of the citizens of Akureyri. During the winter 1939/40 the aircraft capsized in taking-off from Skerjafjord and was badly damaged. As a result the Company was reformed in 1940 as Flugfélag Islands H/F. (Iceland Airways, Ltd.) and the capital increased to Kr. 150,000 most of which was taken up by business people in Reykjavik. A new Beechcraft was purchased and the damaged seaplane repaired. The Company also obtained a Government contract during the Summer months for spotting herrings for the herring oil factories on the north coast.

In February, 1944, a new Company known as Loftleidir H/F. (Skyways Ltd.) was formed by three young Icelanders named A. Eliasson, E. K. Olsen and S. Olafsson, who all held Canadian commercial pilot licenses.

TRANSPORT COMPANIES

Flugfélag Islands H/F. (Iceland Airways, Ltd.). Head Office : Bankastraeti 11, Reykjavik. Chairman of the Board : B. G. Gislason. Managing Director and Chief Pilot : Orn O. Johnson
In 1944 this company carried 4,330 passengers, 4,445 kg.

of mail and flew 298,700 kms.
Fleet : two D.H. 89 Rapide, one Beechcraft 18D and one Consolidated Catalina.

Loftleidir H/F. (Skyways, Ltd.). Head Office : Reykjavik. Managing Director : Kristjan J. Kristjansson.
In 1944 Skyways, Ltd., carried 508 passengers, 5,434 kg. of mail and freight and flew 87,750 km. Twenty ambulance flights were made.
Fleet : one Grumman JRF and one Stinson Reliant.

AERODROMES

A number of aerodromes and flying-boat bases have been built in Iceland by the British Government. The two principal aerodromes, built at a cost of £1,500,000, are situated at Reykjavik and Kaldadarnes, on the North and South side respectively of the peninsula at Reykjavik. The Reykjavik aerodrome has four long runways. A number of the flying-boat bases around the island have been provided with extensive hauling-out facilities.

IRAN (PERSIA)
(The Kingdom of Iran—Mamalik-i-mahrousseh-i-iran)

For strategic reasons Iran was occupied by British and Russian Forces on August 20, 1941. These forces are expected to be withdrawn by the end of March, 1946.
The British Overseas Airways Corpn. operated two services to Teheran, one from Cairo and one from Habbaniyah, during the military occupation but these were withdrawn at the end of 1945 in anticipation of the evacuation of all British forces early in 1946.

TRANSPORT COMPANIES

Iranian State Airlines
Before the occupation of Iran by British and Russian Forces the Ministry of Posts and Telegraphs operated several services within the national borders with three D.H. 89 Dragon-Rapide biplanes.
In 1943 the need arose for an air service between Teheran

and Baghdad (Iraq) and the Iranian State Airlines was formed to operate a weekly passenger and mail service between the two capitals, via Kermanshah (Iran).

AERODROMES

TEHERAN (Doshantappeh). Lat. 35°40′N., Long. 51°25′E. 3 kms. E. of city. Customs.
KERMANSHAH. Lat. 34°20′N., Long. 47°00′E. 3.5 kms. E. of city. Customs.
MESHED. Lat. 36°20′N., Long. 59°40′E. 4 kms. S.E. of town. Military and Civil Customs.
TABRIZ. Lat. 38°12′N., Long. 46°20′E. 7 kms. N.W. of town. Military and Civil Customs.
ISPAHAN. Lat. 32°40′N., Long. 51°40′E. 12 kms. S.E. of town.
BUSHIRE. Lat. 29°02′N., Long. 50°42′E. 4 kms. N.E. of town. Customs airport.

JASK. Lat. 25°40′N., Long. 57°45′E. 2.5 kms. N.E. of town. Customs airport.
DJWANI. Lat. 25°03′N., Long. 61°46′E. Alt. 100 ft. Customs.
There are emergency landing grounds at the following places :
KAZVIN. Lat. 36°15′N., Long. 50°00′E. 8 kms. S.E. of town.
HAMADAN. Lat. 34°50′N., Long. 48°20′E. 12 kms. N.W. of town.
SULTANABAD. Lat. 34°10′N., Long. 49°35′E. 12 kms. N. of town.
MAYAMEY. Lat. 36°25′N., Long. 55°40′E. On N.E. edge of town.
SHIRAZ. Lat. 29°35′N., Long. 52°35′E. 1.25 kms. S.S.W. of town.

'IRAQ
(The Kingdom of 'Iraq—Mesopotamia)

During the War Civil Aviation in Iraq was necessarily curtailed and many operating Companies of the various nations involved in the war ceased to function through Iraq. Only two regular airlines, the British Overseas Airways Corporation and the Iranian State Air Lines maintained their services.

The military control and other war restrictions put very little hindrance to commercial traffic and the public availed itself of the facilities of air travel as far as military priority permitted. Among other improvements, the extension of runways at Basrah and Baghdad were completed.

TRANSPORT COMPANIES

British Overseas Airways Corporation

The Corporation operates the following services through Iraq :—
Cairo—Calcutta service, calling at Baghdad and Basrah. Thrice weekly. Ensign landplanes.
Great Britain—Singapore service calling at Habbaniyah only. Twice weekly. Sunderland flying-boats.
Durban—Calcutta service, calling at Habbiniyah and Basrah.

Twice weekly. "C" Class flying-boats.
The Iranian State Air Lines
In 1942, after a break of about 18 months, this Company resumed their weekly service between Teheran and Baghdad, via Kermanshah (Iran), for passengers and mail, using D.H. 89 Dragon-Rapides.

OTHER OPERATING COMPANIES

The Anglo-Iranian Oil Co., Ltd. and the 'Iraq Petroleum Co., Ltd. both own aircraft and operate irregular services within the country for the use of their own personnel, the former between Abadan—Basrah—Baghdad—Khaniqin, and the latter on their pipe-line stations from Kirkuk (Iraq) to Haifa (Palestine) and Tripoli (Syria), using D.H. 89 biplanes.

AERODROMES

BAGHDAD WEST. Customs Airport. 2 miles W. of Baghdad, on right bank of the Tigris. Meteo. Radio. Hangars. Repairs. 875 × 1,560 yds. Runways.

BASRAH (Ma'qil). Combined Landplane and Seaplane Customs Airport. 1 mile N. of Basrah. Meteo. Radio. Hangars. Repairs. 1,000 × 1,000 yds. Runways.
BASRAH (Shaibah). Military Aerodrome. 13 miles S.W. of Basrah. Radio. Hangars. Repairs. 1,000 × 1,000 yds.
AL-RASHID (Hinaidi). Military Aerodrome. 6 miles S.E. of Baghdad. Radio. Hangars. Repairs.
RUTBAH. Customs Aerodrome. Alongside the Fort of Rutbah. Meteo. Radio.
HABBANIYAH LAKE. Seaplane Base. On Lake Habbaniyah, near the Euphrates.
HABBANIYAH (Dhibban). R.A.F. Aerodrome. On the right bank of the Euphrates.

LANDING GROUNDS

Landing Grounds Nos. 1–12 between Trans-Jordan border and Ramadi :—ANAH, HADITHA, HIT, HILLEH, AZIZIA, KUT-EL-AMARA, DIWANIYAH, AMARA, SHATRA, SIMAWA, NASRIYAH, UR. QURNA and over 60 other L.G.'s exist for operational and training purposes.

ITALY
(The Kingdom of Italy—Regno d'Italia)

At the time of writing the status of civil aviation in Italy was undecided, every decision regarding the future being dependent on the terms of peace to be concluded between Italy and the Allies. Signor Gasparetto, the Minister for Aviation in the

provisional government has given his opinion that civil airlines will be in the hands of private industry with the State holding a controlling interest. In the meantime, military aircraft have maintained certain essential air routes for official traffic

only. In the Summer of 1945 these routes were :—Rome—Naples (twice daily) ; Rome—Naples—Bari—Lecce (daily) ; Naples—Sardinia (thrice weekly) and Rome—Sicily (twice weekly).

JAPAN
(The Japanese Empire—Nippon)

On August 10, 1945, Japan accepted the terms of unconditional surrender drawn up by the United Nations at Potsdam in July. These terms include the prohibition and prevention of the

production of arms, ammunition and implements of war, as well as all types of aircraft and sea-going ships. The maintenance of all aircraft, military and civil, is also prohibited.

MEXICO
(The United States of Mexico—Estados Unidos Mexicanos)

ADMINISTRATION

Civil Aviation in Mexico is under the control of the Secretariat of Communication and Public Works. The Secretariat, through its Department of Aerial Communication, regulates and co-ordinates the services of the various aerial transport companies, private pilots and aerial touring.
Director of Civil Aviation : Juan Guillemo Villasana.

ASSOCIATIONS

Asociacion Mexicana de Aeronautica. Address : Edificio del Banco Hipotecario. Jardin del Colegio de Ninas, Mexico City.
Aereo-Club de Tampico. President : Otto B. Stills. Address : Casa Collins, Apartado Postal 21, Tampico. Flying and ground training.
Aereo-Club de Chihuahua. Secretary : Alberto Ruiz de la Peña. Address : Calle 7a, 1220 Chihuahua. Flying and ground training.
Centro Aeronautico de Estudiantes Pilotes Civiles. Address : 927, Galeana-Norte, Monterrey, N.L. Flying school.

PUBLICATIONS

Aviación. Published in Mexico City. Editor : Engineer Fernando Ortiz Monasterio.
El Piloto. Published in Tijuana (Baja California).

TRANSPORT COMPANIES

Mexico's domestic air network increased from 29,390 miles in 1943 to 37,592 miles in 1944.

There are now four American companies which either operate in Mexico or participate in the operation of Mexican airlines. These are Pan American Airways and its subsidiary Cia Mexicana de Aviacion S.A. ; American Airlines ; United Airlines (which has acquired operational control of Lineas Aereas Mineras S.A.) and Braniff Airways (which has formed a Mexican corporation to operate within Mexico).

American Airlines de Mexico, S.A.
Operated two services in Mexico as follows :—
Los Angeles—Phoenix—Tucson—El Paso—Monterrey—Mexico City. Daily.
Forth Worth—Monterrey—Mexico City. Daily.

Aerovias Braniff S.A.
This is a Mexican corporation controlled by T. E. Braniff of Braniff Airways. (See U.S.A.). It has been granted an operating permit by the Mexican Government covering 2,643 miles of air routes. The routes granted are :—
Nuevo Laredo—Ciudad Victorra—Mexico City.
Equipment : Douglas DC-3.

Pan American Airways
Routes to and through Mexico :—

The "Maya Clipper" service :—Miami—Havana—Merida (Mexico). Daily.
The "Mexico Clipper" service :—Brownsville—Mexico City—Tapachula (Mexico) and on to Port of Spain (Trinidad). Daily.
The "Sun Ray" service :—Brownsville—Mexico City direct and on to Balboa. Daily.
Brownsville—Mexico City. Daily.
On June 13, 1943, a new service from New Orleans to Balboa was inaugurated, operating five times weekly and stopping at Merida (Mexico).

Cia Mexicana de Aviacion S.A. (A Subsidiary of Pan American Airways). Address : Bolivar 21, Mexico City, D.F. Manager : E. R. Silliman.
Routes :—
Los Angeles—Mexico City. Daily via Mexicali, Hermosillo, Mazatlan, Guadalajara.
Nuevo Laredo—Mexico City. Daily via Monterrey.
Monterrey—Mexico City. Daily direct and daily via Ciudad Victoria.
Mexico City—Merida. Daily via Veracruz, Minatitlan, Villahermosa, C. del Carmen, Campeche.
Mexico City—Merida. Daily via Veracruz and C. del Carmen.

Mexico City—Chetumal. Thrice weekly via Veracruz, Villahermosa and Campeche.
Monterrey—Veracruz. Daily except Sunday via Cindad Victoria, Tampico and Tuxpan.
Tampico—Mexico City. Daily via Tuxpan.
Mexico City—Tapachula. Thrice weekly via Oaxaca, Ixtepec, Tuxtla, Gutierrez. Three times weekly via Ixtepec.

Lineas Aereas Mineras S.A., Felomena Mata No. 13, Mexico City, D.F.
President : Elmer R. Jones.

In October, 1943, it was announced that United Air Lines of U.S.A. had purchased 3,750 of 5,000 shares of capital stock of the company for £145,750. The examination before the Civil Aeronautics Board disclosed that from January 1, 1938 to March 31, 1943, the company made a loss of 273,328 pesos. However, the airline had a remarkably good safety record and consequent goodwill and estimated profits of 80,000 pesos in 1943 and 128,000 pesos in 1944.

Routes :—
Mazatlán—Durango—Torreón. Daily.
Mexico City—San Luis Potosi—Torreón—Parral—Chihuahua Ciudad Juráez. Daily.
Mazatlán—Tayoltita. Daily except Sundays.
Chihuahua—Cananea—Nogales. Thrice weekly.
Mexico City—Chihuahua—Nogales. Thrice weekly.
Torreón — Cuatro Cienegas — Monclova — Nuevo Laredo. Thrice weekly.

Transportes Aereos Mexicanos S.A. (Tamsa). Head Office : Avenida Madero 29, Mexico City, D.F.
Routes :—
Merida—Cozumel—Chetumal.
Merida—Hopelchen—Chetumal.
Hopelchen—Altamira.
Altamira—Dzibalchen.
Laguna Om—Xpujil.
Peto—Santa Rosa—Chetumal.
Peto—Esmeralda.

Aero-Transportes S.A. Head Office : Balderas 44, Mexico City, D.F. President : Don J. L. Negrete.
Routes :—
Brownsville — Monterrey — Guadalajara — Mazatlán. Daily.
Brownsville—Monterrey—Torreón. Daily.
P. Negros—Rosita—Monclova—Monterrey. Daily.
Equipment : Boeing 247 twin-engined monoplanes.

Communicaciones Aereas de Veracruz (Buch) Calle Lerdi No. 21 Jalapa, Vera Cruz.
Owner : Francisco Buch de Parada.
Routes :—
Jalapa — Gutierrez Zamora — Papantla — Poza Rica — Tuxpan—Tampico. 132 miles. Four times weekly.
Jalapa — Cordoba — Cosamaloápan — Tuxtla — Coatzacoalcos. 211 miles. Twice weekly.
Jalapa—Vega de Alatorre—Misantla. Twice weekly.

Servicio Aereo Panini, Donceles 20, Mexico City, D.F.
President : Carlos Panini.
This Company is reported to be merging with Woodside.
Routes :—
Mexico City—Arcelia—Ajuchitlán—Cuidad Altamirano—Coyuca—Huetamo—Morelia. 243 miles. Thrice weekly.
Morelia — Uruapan — Apatzingán — Coalcoman — Colima Mamzanillo. Thrice weekly.
Mexico City — Huejutla — Platon Sanchez — Tantoyuca — Tempoal—El Higo—Tampico. 228 miles. Thrice weekly.
Colima — Guadalajara — Talpa — Mascata — Pto. Vallaria.

Aeronaves de Mexico S.A., Ave. Juarez 80, Mexico City.
President : Antonio Diaz Lombardo.
Manager : Carlos Ramos.
Pan American Airways has an interest in this Company.
Routes :—
Mexico City—Acapulco. Twice daily.
Mazatlán—La Paz. Twice weekly.
Uruapan—Acapulco. Thrice weekly.
Oaxaca—Acapulco. Twice weekly.
Mazatlán — Culican — Los Mochis Navojoa Cuidad Obregon—Guaymas—Hermosillo. Thrice weekly.
La Paz—Isla Margarita Santa Rosalia Guaymas—Hermosillo. Weekly.
Mazatlán—Los Mochis—Hermosillo. Thrice weekly.

Transportes Aereos de Jalisco, Guadalajara, Jalisco.
Routes :—
Guadalajara — Talpa — Mascota — Puerto Vallarta. 148 miles. Four times weekly.

FLYING SCHOOLS

The Department of Civil Aviation is counting on the assistance of the United States to make available aircraft and technicians in order that a programme for flying schools may be initiated. It is the intention of the Mexican Government to absorb half the cost of the scheme.

At the same time an aircraft factory is to be built at Balbuena for the production of military and civilian types.

The National University de la Plata established a Chair for Aeronautics on March 26, 1943. A course for aeronautical engineering covering six years has been opened.

AIRPORTS

The Department of Civil Aviation has drawn up plans to make the following into first-class airports :—Monterrey, Cuidad Victoria, Cuidad Guerrero, Actopan, Tampico, Veracruz (Las Bajadas), Cuidad,Ixtepec, Tapachula, Merida,Chetumal, Cozumel.

AERODROMES

Agua Caliente (Tijuana). Private. Customs. 3.5 km. S.E. of Agua Caliente, B.C. 32°32′N., 117°32′W. Radio. 700 × 500 m. Alt. : 10 m.

Angangueo. Municipal. 5 km. S.W. of Angangueo, Michoacan. 19°23′N., 100°17′W. Alt. : 2,596 m.

Campeche. Private. S.W. of Campeche. 19°50′N., 90°32′W. 500 × 300 m. Radio. Alt. : 8 m.

Catemaco. Municipal. W. of Catamaco, Vera Cruz. 18°24′N., 95°06′W. Alt. : 338 m.

Cerralvo. Municipal. 1.8 km. S.W. of Cerralvo, Nuevo Leon. 29°06′N., 99°36′W. Alt. : 268 m.

Chihuahua. Military. Customs. 2 km. N.W. of Chihuahua. 28°38′N., 106°05′W. Alt. : 1,430 m.

Cintalapa. Municipal. 1.5 km. S.E. of Cintalapa. 16°44′N., 93°45′W. 450 × 315 m.

Cuidad del Carmen. Private. 2 km. N. of Cuidad del Carmen, Campeche. 18°38′N., 91°50′W. 750 × 500 m. Alt. : 3 m.

Ciudad Obregon. Military. 1.5 km. N.N.E. of Obregon, Sonora. 27°29′N., 109°56′W. 960 × 900 m. Alt. : 110 m.

Comitan. Municipal. 2.1 km. S. of Comitan. 16°15′N., 92°07′W. 900 × 900 m. Alt. : 1,530 m.

Culiacan. Municipal. 3 km. S.W. of Culiacan, Sinaloa. 24°49′N., 107°24′W. 500 × 500 m.

Durango. Military. 4 km. E. of Durango. 24°02′N., 104°40′W., 1,250 × 1,000 m. Alt. : 1,890 m.

El Oro. Private. 2 km. N.E. of El Oro, Mexico. 19°49′N., 100°07′W. 600 × 400 m. Alt. : 1,980 m.

Ensenada. Municipal. Customs. 2 km. N.E. of Ensenada, Baja California. 31°51′N., 116°35′W. 2,000 × 700 m. Alt. : 10 m.

Fresnillo. Private. 2 km. N. of Fresnillo, Zacatecas. 23°10′N., 102°52′W. 700 × 500 m. Alt. : 2,340 m.

Guadalajara. Military. 5.5 km. S.E. of Guadalajara, Jalisco. 20°40′N., 103°20′W. Radio. 1,150 × 650 m. Alt. : 1,556 m.

Guaymas. Municipal. Customs. 6 km. N.W. of Guaymas, Sonora. 27°55′N., 110°53′W. 750 × 450 m. Alt. : 10 m.

Hermosillo. Municipal. Customs. 2.5 km. N. of Hermosillo, Sonora. 29°07′N., 110°56′W. 1,250 × 700 m. Alt. : 230 m. Runways. Airport of Entry.

La Punta. Private. 9.1 km. S. of the Hacienda La Punta, Jalisco. 21°48′N., 101°53′W. 710 × 450 m. Alt. : 2,000 m.

Leon. Private. 1.5 km. W. of Leon, Guana Juato. 21°07′N., 101°41′W. 500 × 300 m. Alt. : 1,786 m.

Los Mochis. Private. 5 km. N.W. of Los Mochis, Sinaloa. 26°45′N., 109°03′W. 475 × 350 m. Runways. Radio. Alt. : 45 m.

Matamoros. Customs. On Texas-Mexican border at Matamoros, Tamaulipas.

Mazatlán. Municipal. Customs. 3.5 km. N.W. of Mazatlan, Sinaloa. 23°14′N., 106°25′W. 750 × 550 m. Radio. Alt. : 10 m.

Merida. Private. Customs. 6 km. S.W. of Merida, Yucatan. 20°58′N., 89°38′W. 1,000 × 650 × 500 m. Runways. Radio. Hangar. Alt. : 20 m.

Mexicali. Municipal. Customs. E. of Mexicali, Baja California. 32°38′N., 115°29′W. 1,100 × 700 m. Runways. Alt. : S.L. Airport of Entry.

Mexico City. Federal Customs. 4 km. E. of Mexico City. 19°25′N., 99°05′W. 810 × 840 × 450. Runways. Radio. Alt. : 2,240 m. Hangars. Repairs. Full night facilities.

Mexico (Valbuena). Military. 19°26′N., 99°05′W. 1,500 × 1,150 m. Radio. Alt. : 2,240 m.

Monterrey. Military. 5 km. N. of Monterrey, Nuevo Leon. 25°43′N., 100°18′W. 1,500 × 600 m. Radio. Alt. : 538 m. Hangars.

Morelia. Municipal. 2 km. S.W. of Morelia, Michoacan. 190°42′N., 101°07′W. 1,800 × 1,400 m. Alt. : 1,940 m.

Nogales. Municipal. 13 km. S. of Nogales, Sonora. 31°19′N., 110°56′W. 1,500 × 1,000 m. Alt. ; 1,120 m.

Nuevo Laredo. Military. Customs. 1.5 km. N.W. of Laredo, Tamaulipas. 27°29′N., 99°31′W. 550 × 515 m. Alt. : 94 m.

Oaxaca. Municipal. 2 km. N.E. of Oaxaca. 17°03′N., 96°43′W. 800 × 150 m. Runways N.W.-S.E. Alt. : 1,546 m.

Panuco. Military. 1 km. S.W. of Panuco, Vera Cruz. 22°03′N., 98°10′W. 400 × 200 m. Alt. : 20 m.

Parral-Hidalgo. Municipal. 8 km. W. of Parral, Chihuahua. 26°56′N., 105° 40W′. Runways : 1,200, 1,400, 1,000 m. Alt. : 1,980 m.

Parras. Municipal. 7 km. N.W. of Parras, Coahuila. 25°25′N., 102°20′W. 1,000 × 400 m. Alt. : 3 m.

Puebla. Municipal. 2 km. S.E. of Puebla. 19°02′N., 98°11′W. 960 × 400 m. Alt. : 2,162 m.

Queretaro. Municipal. 3 km. N.W. of Queretaro. 20°35′N., 100°19′W. 740 × 535 m. Alt. : 1,852 m.

Sabinas Hidalgo. Municipal. 4 km. N.E. of Sabinas Hidalgo, Neuvo Leon. 26°30′N., 100°10′W. 595 × 300 m. Alt. : 313 m.

San Luis de la Paz. Municipal. 0.5 km. S. of San Luis de la Paz, Guanajuato. 21°17′N., 100°30′W. 600 × 500 m. Alt. : 2,020 m.

San Luis Potosi. Municipal. 4 km. S.W. of San Luis Potosi. 22°00′N., 101°05′W. 2,250 × 625 m. Radio. Alt. : 1,877 m.

Santa Rosalia. Municipal. 7 km. N.W. of Santa Rosalia, Baja California. 27°19′N., 112°15′W. 1,000 × 400 m. Alt. : 3 m.

Tampico. Private. Customs. 8.5 km. N. of Tampico, Tamaulipas. 22°17′N., 97°52′W. 760 × 645 m. Radio. Repairs. Alt. : 20 m. Hangar.

Tapachula. Private. Customs. 5 km. S.E. of Tapachula, Chiapas. 14°54′N., 92°15′W. 700 × 680 m. Alt. : 182 m.

Tepic. Municipal. 0.9 km. N. of Tepic, Nayarit. 21°30′N., 104°54′W. 700 × 300 m. Alt. : 182 m.

Toluca. Municipal. 1.5 km.. of Toluca, Mexico. 19°17′N., 99°39′W. 800 × 250 m. Alt. : 2,640 m.

Torreon. Municipal. 4 km. S.E. of Torreon, Coahuila. 25°32′N., 103°28′W. 650 × 800 m. Radio. Alt. : 1,144 m.

In addition to the above list of the more important municipal aerodromes and private aerodromes used for commercial aviation, there are a large number of smaller aerodromes distributed throughout the State, of which details are given in the Bulletin of the Departmento de Communicaciones Aereas of the Secretariat of Communications and Public Works.

NETHERLANDS

(The Kingdom of the Netherlands—Nederland)

TRANSPORT COMPANY

Koninklijke Luchtvaart Maatschappij voor Nederland en Kalonien N.V. (K.L.M.) (Royal Dutch Air Lines).

On the invasion of Holland on May 10, 1940, a number of K.L.M. airliners which survived the bombing of Amsterdam, were flown to Great Britain and headquarters were temporarily established in London. The services of the company were placed at the disposal of the Allies and operating under a charter to the British Overseas Airways Corporation K.L.M. maintained a regular service between Great Britain and Lisbon with outstanding reliability for over five years. By the Spring of 1945, K.L.M. aircraft were operating to Lisbon four times weekly and to Gibraltar once weekly. In Jan., 1946, both these services were taken over by B.O.A.C.

Since the end of the war with Japan K.L.M. has been operating a twice-weekly courier service to Batavia under contract with the Netherlands Government. Shortage of aircraft is delaying the resumption of traffic in Europe, but the Amsterdam Malmoe service has been resumed and the pre-war Lisbon service was due to be re-opened early 1946. Plans are in hand for the establishment of a trans-Atlantic service later in 1946.

NETHERLANDS EAST INDIES

(Nederlandsch-Indië)

TRANSPORT COMPANY

Koninklijke Nederlandsch-Indische Luftvaart Maatschappij (K.N.I.L.M.). (Royal Netherlands Indian Airline Company).

On the occupation of the East Indies by Japan in March, 1942, most of the personnel of K.N.I.L.M. and eleven of its aircraft were evacuated to Australia where they served with the Netherlands Indies Army Transport Service under Allied Command.

Since the defeat of Japan, the political situation in Java has made it impossible for the company to resume any of its activities, and its ambitious plans to extend its pre-war inter-island network as well as to operate international services to India, China, Japan, the U.S.S.R. and the U.S.A. remain in abeyance.

NETHERLANDS WEST INDIES

(The Islands of Curaçao, Aruba and Bonaire)

ADMINISTRATION

Civil Aviation in the Netherlands West Indies was placed under the jurisdiction of an Inspector of Civil Aviation late in 1941. Headquarters : Willemstad, Curaçao, N.W.I.

TRANSPORT COMPANY

K.L.M. Royal Dutch Air Lines (Compañia Real Holandesa de Aviacion), West Indies Section. Address : 3 de Ruy Terkade, Willemstad, Curaçao, N.W.I.

This Company commenced operations in 1934, and in spite of the setbacks occasioned by the invasion of Holland, records a continual increase in traffic since its inception. In 1940 the Company completed a maintenance department at the Hato

Aerodrome, Curaçao, for the overhauling and maintenance of its aircraft.

In May, 1943, permission was granted to the company by the U.S. Civil Aeronautics Board to open a service to Miami and on August 17, the inauguration took place by an extension of the Curaçao—Kingston (Jamaica) route and a new route via Port au Prince (Haiti), both of which unite at Camaguey (Cuba) and proceed to Miami.

Routes :—

Curaçao—Aruba (78 miles). Seventeen times weekly each way.

Curaçao—Aruba—Maracaibo (242 miles). Thrice weekly each way.

Curaçao—Bonaire. Thrice weekly each way.

Curaçao—Port of Spain—Paramaribo. Thrice fortnightly each way.
Curaçao—Port of Spain. Thrice fortnightly each way.
Curaçao—Aruba—C. Trujillo. Fortnightly each way.
Curaçao—La Guaira. Six times weekly each way.
Curaçao—Aruba—Barranquilla. Twice weekly each way.
Curaçao — Aruba — Kingston — Camaguey — Miami. Weekly each way.
Curaçao—Aruba—Port au Prince—Camaguey—Miami. Weekly each way.

Aircraft used :—3 Lockheed 14, 2 Fokker F.XVIII, 2 Lockheed Lodestars (property of the Netherlands Government).

SURINAME
(Dutch Guiana)

There is no internal aviation, but the Colony is served by K.L.M. and Pan American Airways. The former company runs a thrice fortnightly return service between Curaçao and Paramaribo via Port of Spain. The P.A.A. "East Coast Clipper" service from Miami to Buenos Aires makes a stop at Paramaribo. This service is now flown daily in each direction.

During 1942 Pan American Airways completed the improvements begun in 1941 to the Zanderij airport and their own seaplane base at Cobe just below Paramaribo and they are in use on the Buenos Aires and San Juan—Belem services respectively.

AERODROMES

PARAMARIBO (Zanderij). Lat. 5°28′N. Long. 55°12′W. 25 miles S. of Paramaribo alongside E. side of railway. Alt. 10 ft. 1,750 × 875 yds.

SEAPLANE BASE

Pan American Airways base is situated on right bank of the Suriname river just below Paramaribo. There is a slipway and a barge. W/T. by arrangement with P.A.A.

AERODROMES

CURAÇAO (Hato). Lat. 12°11′N. Long 68°58′ W. 4½ miles N.N.W. of Willemstad on coast N.W. of oil refinery at Hato. Alt. 59 ft. Runways : W.N.W./E.S.E. 2,132 × 197 ft. and E.N.E./W.S.W. 2,132 × 197 ft. Hangars and K.L.M. repair shops in S.E. corner. Customs airport of entry.
BONAIRE. Lat. 12°13′N. Long. 68°15′W. 4 miles N.N.E. of Kralendijk. Alt. 147 ft. 1,558 × 1,575 ft.
ARUBA (Oranjestad). Lat. 12°30′N. Long. 70°01′W. 2½ miles S.E. of Oranjestad. Alt. 38 ft. 1,968 × 492 ft. Control tower, hangars. W/T. call sign HHD. Wave length 37.43 and 52.70 m.

NICARAGUA
(The Republic of Nicaragua—República de Nicaragua)

ADMINISTRATION

Civil Aviation in Nicaragua is controlled by the Ministerio de La Guerra, Marina y Aviacion, Managua. The Minister is Capitán Benjamín Argüello.

TRANSPORT COMPANIES

Compania Nacional Taca de Nicaragua

Associated with the Transportes Aereos Centro Americanos (T.A.C.A.) which has its headquarters in Tegucigalpa, Honduras.

Routes :—

Managua—Matagalpa—Jinotega—Managua. Once weekly.
Managua—Bluefields—Puerto Cabezas. Once weekly.
Managua—La Libertad—Managua. Twice weekly.
Puerto Cabezas—Bonanza—Siuna—Managua. Once weekly.
Managua—Ocotal—Matagalpa—Jinotega—Managua. Once weekly.

The Company also engages in many non-scheduled flights serving the goldmines in the interior.

Aircraft operated :—11 Ford Trimotors, 2 Lockheeds, 1 Travel Air, 1 Stinson, 1 Hamilton, 2 "Condors," and 1 "Flamingo."

Transportes Aeros Centro Americanos (T.A.C.A.)

The T.A.C.A. International service stops at Managua five times weekly in each direction.

Pan American Airways

The "Mexico Flyer" service from Brownsville to Balboa stops daily at Managua. The recently opened service from New Orleans to Balboa also stops at Managua five times weekly.

AERODROMES

MANAGUA. Lat. 12°08′N., Long. 86°16′W. Civil Customs. 1½ miles S.E. of town. Alt. 150 ft. Size 2,250 × 1,320 ft. Administrative building and hangars. Minor repairs. W/T. call sign YNP on short wave only.
BLUEFIELDS. Lat. 12°00′N., Long. 83°46′W. ½ mile S. of town. Alt. 50 ft. Runs N.N.E./S.S.W. 2,150 × 180 ft. W/T. call sign YNEI and YNI (TACA). 3° slope to field from S. to N.
SIUNA. Lat. 13°39′N., Long. 84°36′W. 1½ miles S. of mine. Alt. 1,000 ft. Runs N./S. 3,500 × 120 ft.
JINOTEGA. Lat. 13°07′N., Long. 86°00′W. 2½ miles N. of town, at S.W. edge of large plateau. Alt. 3,500 ft. Runs E./W. 1,200 × 150 ft.

LA LIBERTAD. Lat. 12°12′N., Long. 85°06′W. 1½ miles W. of town. Alt. 2,000 ft. Runs N.E./S.W. 1,800 × 150 ft.
OCOTAL. Lat. 13°37′N., Long. 86°31′W. 1¼ miles W.S.W. of town. Customs airport of entry. Two strips N./S. 2,000 × 400 ft. and N.E./S.W. 1,200 × 100 ft.
Other aerodromes are situated at ALAMICAMBA, BILWASKARMA, BONANZA, CUMPLIDA, MATAGALPA, OLAMA, PUERTO CABEZAS, WASPAN.

The following airports have W/T. and telephone :—MANAGUA, PUERTO CABEZAS, SIUNA, BONANZA, BLUEFIELDS, LA LIBERTAD. Pan American Airways operate a meteorological station at Managua, and weather reports are telegraphed to this aerodrome daily from all aerodromes by the Guardia Nacional Radio System.

Landing grounds are situated at LEÓN, GRANADA, APALI, QUILALI, WANK, EL GALLO, BOACO, JUIGALPA, COMALAPA, CORINTO, JALAPA, WANI, SOMOTO, EL SAUCE, CASARES, CONDEGA. Advance notice is required if using these landing grounds in order that cattle may be cleared.

NORWAY
(The Kingdom of Norway—Norge)

In 1945 air transport in Norway was being undertaken by the Norges Luftfartstyre (Royal Norwegian Air Transport), a Government body. This body was established by Royal Decree on December 19, 1943, to operate air lines until Parliament was able to decide how Norwegian civil aviation will function.

The Royal Norwegian Air Force, in co-operation with R.N.A.T. established military air routes to East Finnmark, in the North, before the rest of the country was liberated. After the German defeat R.N.A.T. established military routes linking Oslo, Tromsö Tradjem, Stavanger, London, Copenhagen and Stockholm.

Towards the end of the year it was announced that all R.N.A.T. routes were in process of de-militarisation and that by the Spring of 1946 parallel civil air routes would be established. R.N.A.T. has recommended the formation of a new company to be called Det Norske Luftfartselskap (D.N.L.), the name of the pre-war operating company, which still maintains corporate existence.

PANAMA
(The Republic of Panama—Republica de Panama)

ADMINISTRATION

Civil Aviation is under the control of the Comision Nacional de Aviacion, Palacio Nacional, Panama, R.P. The Technical Adviser in charge of Civil Aviation is Jaime E. Smith Pezet, Ministro de Gobierno y Justicia, Panama.

ASSOCIATIONS

Club Nacional de Aviacion, Aeropuerto Nacional, Panama, R.P. Principal Official : Dr. Adolfo Arias.
Club Americano, Aeropuerto Nacional, Panama, R.P. Principal Official : Mr. J. Hearn.

TRANSPORT COMPANIES

Compania de Transportes Aereos Gelabert, Avenida Central No. 30, Panama, R.P. President : Marcos A. Gelabert.
Operates a service on Mondays, Wednesdays and Fridays from Panama to David, Puerto Armuelles and return. For this service a Vultee monoplane is used. The Company also runs non-scheduled services with 1 Stinson, 1 Lockheed "Vega" and 1 Hamilton monoplane.

Pan American World Airways
Passenger Ticket and Air Express Office, Century Club Building, Calle "L" No. 5, Panama, R.P. Operations Department at Airport, Albrook Field, C.Z. Also offices in Panama

Agencies Building, Cristobal, C.Z.
Routes operated :—
Balboa— Miami, via Kingston. Daily with an additional service thrice weekly.
Balboa—New Orleans, via Mexico. Twice daily.
The Brownsville—Port of Spain service operates daily through Balboa, with one additional service between Brownsville and Balboa.

Pan American-Grace Airways, Inc. (Panagra)
Passenger Ticket and Air Express Office, Century Club Building, Panama, R.P., 203, Terminal Building, Balboa, C.Z. Operations : Airport, Albrook Field, C.Z. Also offices in Grace Line Building, Cristobal.
Routes operated :—
From Balboa to Colombia, Ecuador, etc., to Buenos Aires. Daily.

Uraba, Medellin & Central Airways, Inc. (represented by P.A.A.)
Operates services from Balboa to Medellin (Colombia) (416 miles) on Sundays, Tuesdays, Wednesdays and Saturdays via Turbo, Colombia.

FLYING CLUBS
The Panamanian Wing of the Inter-American Escadrille
Formed on June 20, 1941. President : Dr. Adolfo Arias.

Vice-President : Lt.-Col. Olmedo Fabrega.

There is also a club of owners of light sport-planes banded together to interest the public in flying, who are making efforts to give flying lessons to those interested. They have no official name and are prone to sell their aircraft, which makes for a constant change in the persons identified with this club.

FLYING SCHOOL

Escuela Gelabert, Aeropuerto Nacional, Panama, R.P.
Gives both flying and ground instruction. Planes used :— 2 Piper Cruisers and 1 Piper Cub.

AERODROMES

PAITILLA AIRPORT, Panama City. Customs Airport. 2¼ miles N.E. of Panama City. Altitude 40 ft. Two concrete runways N./S. 2,500 ft. × 450 ft., E./W. 2,100 ft. × 260 ft. and one runway N.E./S.W. 2,500 ft. × 420 ft. in poor condition. Wind cone to North. Boundary lights only. W/T.

DAVID. Lat. 8°23′N., Long. 82°26′W. Customs Airport. Altitude 90 ft. Hangar. W/T. Call sign NEB. Wave length 55.8 m. No runways. No night-landing facilities.

PUERTO ARMUELLES. Golf Course.

PANAMA CANAL ZONE (U.S.)

ADMINISTRATION

The Panama Canal Zone is administered by the United States of America. No private transport companies are established within the Canal Zone. Pan American Airways and Pan American-Grace Airways serving the Zone use the U.S. Army Air Forces aerodrome at Albrook Field, Balboa.

Aeroplanes of the Republic of Panama are not permitted to use the Canal Zone airports. Under present conditions, these aircraft are no longer permitted to fly over the Canal, and upon leaving the Republic of Panama must proceed northwards towards David and make course to Taboga Island and from there back to the mainland.

There are also U.S. Army Air Forces aerodromes at Rio Hato, R.P., and Howard Field and a U.S. Naval Air Base at Coco Solo, C.Z.

PARAGUAY
(The Republic of Paraguay—República del Paraguay)

ADMINISTRATION

Civil Aviation in Paraguay is controlled by the Ministry of War and Marine at Asunción. Director-General of Aeronautics : Lieut.-Col. Atilio Migone.

ASSOCIATION

Aero Club del Paraguay. Formed early in 1938. Its activities are largely promoted by Government officials and Army officers.

Aero Club del Asunción
Address : Artigas No. 280, Asunción.
President : Señor Hermes Gomez Leycano.

TRANSPORT COMPANIES

Linea Aerea de Transporte Nacional (LATN)
This airline was organized in 1944 by the Paraguayan Army Air Force. An experimental flight has been made between Asunción and Buenos Aires, and a once weekly service has been inaugurated over the route Asunción—Arroyas—Esteros—San Raphael—San Estanislao—Irakyu.

Aerovias Paraquayas S.A.
This is a TACA subsidiary. The local operators are Messrs. Navarro and Ladonch, who formerly operated a taxi service with Waco biplanes.

Pan American Airways
This Company's "East Coast Flyer" service deviates once weekly in each direction to call at Asunción.

Panair do Brasil
The Company operates two services weekly to Asunción, one flying in from Iguassu Falls to the east and the other from Corumba to the north. Both services return by the same routes to Rio de Janeiro.

Corporacion Sud Americana de Servicios Aereos
This Argentine airline operates two services weekly from Buenos Aires to Asunción using Macchi MC94 flying-boats. Service commenced on March 26, 1941.

AERODROMES

CAMPO GRANDE (Asunción). Military. 11 kms. E. of city. 1,000 × 1,270 m.

CAMPO PANAIR (Asunción). Private. 11 kms. E. of city. 1,400 × 1,200 m.
AERO CLUB (Asunción). Civil. 11 kms. E. of city. 600 × 500 m.
The above three aerodromes adjoin each other.
CONCEPCION. 4 kms. S. of town. 1,000 × 1,000 m.
ENCARNACION. 8 kms. S.E. of town. 600 × 600 m.
PARAGUARI. 2 kms. S.W. of town. 1,000 × 400 m.
PILAR. 2 kms. N. of town. 800 × 600 m.
PUERTO J. CABALLERO. 3 kms. S.W. of town. 600 × 400 m.
PUERTO PINAZCO. 4 kms. N. of town. 1,000 × 600 m.
PUERTO CASADO. 4 kms. S. of town. 1,000 × 1,000 m.
PUERTO SASTRE. 2 kms. S.W. of town. 600 × 400 m.
PUERTO GUARANI. 5 kms. N. of town. 600 × 550 m.
SAN IGNACIO. 2 kms. S. of town. 500 × 400 m.
SAN ESTANISLAO. 7 kms. S. of town.
SAN JUAN. 4 kms. S.E. of town. 600 × 600 m.
VILLA FLORIDA. 1 km. S. of town.
VILLARRICA. 4 kms. E. of town. 400 × 400 m.
BAHIA NEGRA.

PERU
(The Republic of Peru—Republica del Péru)

ADMINISTRATION

Civil Aviation in Peru is controlled by "Dirección de Aeronáutica," Comandancia General de Aeronáutica, Miraflores, Lima, Peru, through the appropriate Department, i.e., "Dirección de Aviación Comercial y Civil." The Jefe de Aviación Comercial y Civil is General de Aeronautica Carlos A. Gilardi.

At the Council of Ministers held on July 2, 1943, it was announced that in accordance with Law No. 9,577 there would be created the Corporación Peruana de Aeropuertos y Aviación Comercial which would take over airports and commercial air transport services and would undertake the construction of aircraft material in the Republic. Law No. 9,577 was a blanket emergency measure promulgated in March, 1942. It is not known how this will affect the Cia de Aviación Faucett, the only independent national aviation company operating commercial services and manufacturing aircraft in Peru.

A U.S. Aviation Mission assists in the supervision and administration of all matters concerning military, commercial and civil aviation. This Mission is headed by Colonel Ford O. Rogers, U.S.M.C.

ASSOCIATIONS

Aero Club del Peru, Girón de la Unión No. 722, Lima.
President : General de Aeronautica Fernando Melgar C.
Formed September, 1935. The Club has a large membership and operates a flying instruction school for members at Limatambo Aerodrome, Lima. Instruction is given by civil and military pilots, using Aeronca, Waco, Mercury, Taylorcraft and Piper "Cub" aircraft.

Liga Nacional de Aviación (National Aviation League)
Temporary Address : Edificio Piedra, Calle Baguijano No. 722, Lima.
Organized early in 1941 by patriotic citizens and financed by popular subscription, with the support of the President and Cabinet Ministers, the League bought ten Taylorcraft training aeroplanes and launched a Civil Pilot Training Programme. It owns an aerodrome with hangars and workshop, etc., and forms the Reserve of the Peruvian Air Force. Training is given by military personnel and it is hoped to acquire more training aeroplanes in the near future.

PUBLICATIONS

Aviacion. Director : Comandante de Aeronáutica Augusto Correa Santistevan, Real Felipe, Callao. Postal Address : Apartado No. 370, Callao. Published monthly. Price : 0.50 cts.

Boletin de la Direccion de Aviacion Comercial y Civil. A Government bulletin issued free every three months, giving details regarding new regulations and statistics, etc., on Commercial and Civil Aviation.

TRANSPORT COMPANIES

Compañia de Aviación "Faucett" S.A., Lima. Head Office : Hotel Bolivar No. 926, Lima. Headquarters : Santa Cruz Airport, Lima. Managing Director : Mr. Elmer J. Faucett.

Routes : —
Arequipa — Lima — Palamonga — Casma — Niepena — Trujillo — Pacasmayo — Chiclayo — Piura — Talara. Seven times weekly.
Talara—Tumbes. Three times weekly.
Tacna — Moquegua — Ilo — Arequipa—Mollendo—Camana — Atico — Chala — Yauca — Nazca — Lima — Chiclayo — Chachapoyas — Moyobamba — San Martin — Yurimaguas. Twice weekly.
Lima—Trujillo—Cajamarca. Once weekly.
Lima—Puerto Maldonado. Once fortnightly.

The Faucett Company manufactures its own eight-seat single-engined transports (see under "Peru," Section C) and all maintenance and engine overhauls are undertaken by Peruvian labour in the Company's workshops.

The Company has its own airport (Santa Cruz) on the outskirts of Lima—alongside which is located the aircraft factory referred to above.

The Faucett Company also owns the Trujillo Aerodrome.

Since the entry of the United States into the War, the American pilots formerly employed by the Company have gradually been withdrawn with the result that, with one exception, all the pilots now employed by the Company are Peruvians.

Pan American-Grace Airways, Inc. (Panagra), Grace Building, Lima. President : Mr. Harold J. Roig.
The Company's services, which carry Peruvian airmail under authorization of the Governor of Peru, stop seven times weekly in each direction at Lima, Arequipa, Talara and Chiclayo.
Routes : —
The service from Balboa to Buenos Aires stops seven times weekly at Talara, Chiclayo and Lima.
Lima—Arequipa. Ten times weekly.
Arequipa—La Paz. Four times weekly.
Arequipa—Arica. Six times weekly.
Arica—Antofagasta. Five times weekly.
Aircraft :—Douglas DC-3.

Linea Aerea Nacional (LAN), Address : c/o. Commandancia General de Aeronautica, Miraflores, Lima.
This Airline is operated by the Peruvian Air Force as a transport and training service.
Routes :—
Iquitos—Gueppi. Once fortnightly.
Iquitos—Ramon Castilla. Once fortnightly.
Iquitos—Borja. Once fortnightly.
Iquitos—Pucallpa—San Ramon. Twice weekly.
Iquitos—Yurimaguas. Twice weekly.
Passengers, mail and freight are carried to a number of towns in the River Amazon and Madre de Dios districts.
Boeing, Travelair, Fairchild, Keystone and Hamilton aircraft are used.

OTHER OPERATING COMPANIES

Huff-Daland Dusters Inc. (The Peruvian Cotton Dusting Co.). Offices : Hotel Bolivar No. 926, Lima. General Manager : Mr. L. P. Thorndike. General Administrators : Cia de Aviación Faucett S.A.
Aerodrome : Montalban, Cañete.
This company was established in Peru in November, 1926. The machines used for cotton dusting are Keystone biplanes with Wright 220 h.p. "Whirlwind" engines. They carry 600 lbs. of calcium arsenate, and the work calls for skilled flying, owing to the low elevation required to place the dust accurately over the fields and to prevent it being carried away by the wind. American and Peruvian-trained pilots are employed.

AERODROMES

LIMA. "Las Palmas" Peruvian Military Air Base, 8 kms. from the city of Lima, is now closed to all civil and private flying. Heavy penalties are imposed on aircraft landing without special permit.
LIMATAMBO. The chief airport of Peru, is situated only 4 kms. S.S.E. from the city of Lima. It is an up-to-date and modern civil airport, has large hangar, workshops, fuel depôt, customs offices, dispatch section, radio station, hotel, and an excellent car service to the city. It is open day and night.
SANTA CRUZ. Private civil aerodrome belonging to Cia de Aviación Faucett S.A. and situated 4 kms. from Lima. It is very much used by private owners of aircraft. It has modern hangars, workshops, radio and car service directly to offices in Lima. Passengers arriving at Santa Cruz are conveyed directly to passenger residence by Company's private cars.
Coastal Zone:—LIMA (Santa Cruz) 1st Class, LIMA (Limatambo) 1st Class, ICA 1st Class, TALARA (Customs) 1st Class, PIURA 1st Class, CHICLAYO 1st Class, TRUJILLO 1st Class, AREQUIPA 1st Class, TACNA (Customs) 1st Class, TUMBES, 2nd Class, ZORRITOS 2nd Class, PAITA 2nd Class, SULLANA 2nd Class, CHIMBOYE 2nd Class, PACASMAYO 2nd Class, CHINCHA ALTA 2nd Class, PISCO 2nd Class, NAZCA 2nd Class, CAMANÁ 2nd Class, MOLLENDO 2nd Class, MOQUEGUA, LOBITOS, SOMATE, PÁTAPO, CAYALTI, TUMÁN, CASA GRANDE, CARTAVIO, NEPEÑA, CASMA, LAS ZORRAS, LAS PALMAS, HUARMEY, JAQUI, CHALA, ATICO, ILO, VITOR.
On the Plateaux:—CAJAMARCA 1st Class, HUANCAYO 1st Class, CARAZ 1st Class, AYACUCHO 1st Class, CUZCO 1st Class, PUNO (Customs) 1st Class, HUANCABAMBA 2nd Class, CHACHAPOYAS (El Tapial) 2nd Class, SANTA CRUZ (Cajamarca) 2nd Class, PUCRAN (Cerro de Pasco) 2nd Class, JULIACA 2nd Class, PIAZ, CAJABAMBA, HUAMACHUCO, HUANUCO VIEJO, HUANCABAMBA, HUANACOPAMPA, POTO.
In the Mountains:—IQUITOS (Customs) 1st Class, SAN RAMÓN 1st Class, PUCALLPA 1st Class, PUERTO MALDONADO 1st Class, BELLAVISTA 2nd Class, MASISEA 2nd Class, PUERTO BERMUDEZ 2nd Class, MOYOBAMBA 2nd Class, TARAPOTO 2nd Class, YURIMAGUAS 2nd Class, TINGO MARIA 2nd Class, MUANUCO (Huachot) 2nd Class, PUERTO VICTORIA 2nd Class, ATALAYA 2nd Class, RIOJA, LAMAS, JUANJUI, AGUAS CALIENTES, PUERTO INCA, OBENTI, PUERTO OCOPA, SATIPO, SOTZIKE, OXAPAMPA.

POLAND
(The Polish Republic—Rzeczpospolita Polska)

By a decree of the Minister of Communications of the Provisional Polish Government, Polish Air Lines (LOT) passes under State management as from March 6, 1945. This concern started operating regular air services in liberated Poland in the Middle of April with Douglas DC-2 and DC-3 airliners, but details of these services were not available at the time of writing.

In July a delegation from the Polish Air Communications Department opened negotiations with the Director-General of Air Transport of the U.S.S.R. for regular air services between Moscow, Warsaw and Paris. LOT was negotiating for twenty Russian-built DC-3 twin-engined airliners.

PORTUGAL
(The Republic of Portugal—Republica Portuguesa)

ADMINISTRATION

By Decree No. 33,967 dated September 22, 1944, a Secretariat of Civil Aeronautics was established. The new secretariat is responsible for all matters concerning civil aeronautics, except those in connection with the concession and exploitation of airlines and with the aerial services inspection in the Colonies. Until national airlines are formed or authorised to operate, the Secretariat will study and run lines for experimental purposes.

Matters regarding the execution of international agreements and conventions relations with airline companies, problems referring to schools and personnel of civil aeronautics, aviation propaganda and other matters of administration and equipment concern this secretariat.

Lieut.-Col. Humberto de Silva Delgado and Major Humberto Pais Martins dos Santos have been named Director and Sub-Director respectively.

Besides this Secretariat, which has executive powers, there is the Conselho Nacional de Ar, which is the advisory organ on all principal aviation problems. The President is the Prime Minister, and Vice-President is Brigadier Alfredo Sintra, Director of Military Aviation. Other members of the Conselho are the Military Aviation Commanders, a representative of the Lisbon Airport Administrative Council, Chiefs of the Government Departments interested in aerial communications, two representatives of airline companies, and the Director and Sub-Director of the new Secretariat.

ASSOCIATION

Aero Club de Portugal, 226, Avenida da Liberdade, Lisbon. Founded : 1909. Affiliated to the *Fédération Aéronautique Internationale*.

It exercises a certain amount of directive control over other Aero Clubs in the country. The Club has spacious premises and visiting foreign aviators are made welcome.

PUBLICATIONS

Revista do Ar, 226, Avenida da Liberdade, 2nd Floor (same building as Aero Club de Portugal). A high-class monthly having completed its seventh year of existence in its present form.
Director and Editor : Lieut.-Aviator Armando Correira Mera.

TRANSPORT COMPANIES

Aero Portuguesa Limitada. Office : Rua do Alecrim, 33, Lisbon. Manager : Commander J. Judice de Vasconcellos. Operates a frequent (bi, sometimes tri-weekly) service between Lisbon (Portela) and Tangier. This service was extended to Casablanca on January 18, 1944. Has completed ten years operations with a high degree of efficiency. Late in 1943 the greater part of the Capital of this Company was taken over by one of the largest Portuguese Shipping Companies, the Companhia Nacional de Navegação.

British Overseas Airways Corporation. 23/27, Avenida da Liberdade, Lisbon. Local Manager : Cmdr. A.D.S. Murray, R.N. (Retd.). In addition to the regular service U.K.-Lisbon operated by K.L.M. under Charter for B.O.A.C., the Corporation has other services which stop at Lisbon, for which refer under Great Britain.

Pan American Airways. The Lisbon office : c/o. Sociedade Técnica e Maritima, Rua do Comercio, 56, Lisbon, owners (in law) of the Cabo Ruivo aero-marine base. Pan American Airways Atlantic service stops at Lisbon.

Trafico Aéreo Espanol (late Iberia). Local Manager : Senor Jorge Dumlein. Office : 107, Avenida da Liberdade, Lisbon. In April, 1943, the Cia Mercantil Anonima de Linias Aereas (Iberia) cancelled its services due to lack of aircraft and fuel. In August the Spanish Government bought out the German interest in the company and subsequently the name was changed as above. A Barcelona—Madrid—Lisbon service is operated daily.

American Export Air Lines. Local representative : Mr. Johann Beckmann, Rua dos Fanqueiros, 83, Lisbon. In November, 1943 this company commenced using the Cabo Ruivo base at Lisbon on its return Atlantic Service to U.S.A.

Military Service. The Portuguese Military Air Force continued to operate the Terceira—São Miguel (Azores) service which it inaugurated in October, 1942.

AIR SURVEY COMPANIES

Sociedade Portuguesa de Levantamentos Aéreos, Ltda. (S.P.L.A.L.) Rua da Escola Politécnica, 61-63, Lisbon. This Company continues to undertake aerial survey work in various parts of the Portuguese Empire, but principally overseas.

Empresa Nacional de Estudos Tecnicos (E.N.E.T.), Largo do Picadeiro, No. 10, Lisbon. It is not known whether this concern has ever done any aerial survey work.

FLYING CLUBS

Aero Club de Portugal, 226, Avenida da Liberdade, Lisbon. Operates a flying school at the Sintra Military Aerodrome.
Aero Club do Porto, Rua das Flores 6, Oporto. Operates a flying school at Espinho Military Aerodrome.
Aero Club de Braga. Operates at Palmeira Aerodrome, Braga.
Aero Club de Leiria. Operates at an aerodrome at Monte Real.
Aero Club do Ribatejo. Runs a flying school at Tancos, a Military aerodrome.
Aero Club de Figueira da Foz. Gives flying tuition at the Figueira da Foz flying field.

All the provincial clubs are affiliated to and under some measure of control of the Aero Club de Portugal. The Conselho Nacional do Ar keeps a check on their activities.

FLYING SCHOOLS

Soc. Tecnica de Aviação, Avenida da Liberdade, 35, 2nd Floor, Lisbon. Operated at the Alverca Military Aerodrome, but temporarily closed.
The Arraiolos Flying School. Operated at Evora and Arraiolos.
The General "Carmona" School of Civil Aviation. Operates from a flying field at Montemor-o-Novo.
The "Bissaia Barreto" Aviation School. Operates at Coimbra Aerodrome, which belongs to the Administration of the Province of Beira.

AERODROMES

PALMEIRA (Braga). Belongs to the Braga Municipality.
BENALFANGE. Temporary aerodrome of the "General Carmona" School of Civil Aviation.
LEIRIA. The property of the Leiria Municipality. To be turned over to the State to become a Military Air Base.
EVORA }
ARRAIOLOS } Belong to the Arraiolos Flying School.
FIGUEIRA DA FOZ. Belongs to the Municipality.
COIMBRA. Belongs to the Administrations of the Province of Beira.
GAVIÃO. Belongs to Snr. Pequito Rebelo.
CORUCHE (Cascavela Field). Belongs to Snr. C. Patricio.
ESPINHO. (Military Aerodrome). Used by Aero Club de Portugal.
PORTELA (Lisbon). Situated at Portela de Sacavem. Opened to air traffic in October, 1942, and is now in regular use by the airlines. It replaces Sintra which has reverted to Military use.

The Portela airport is 4 miles to the North of the centre of Lisbon and approximately 2 miles from the Cabo Ruivo seaplane base. It has four concrete runways 1,200 metres long and there is ample room for extensions when this becomes necessary.

The airport is still not officially open although it has been in use since October, 1942. Already the need has been felt for extensions to runways and buildings. The Administration building has been enlarged and the Control Tower heightened. Full radio-directional equipment had not been installed at the time of writing.

SEAPLANE BASE

The Cabo Ruivo seaplane base is situated approximately 4 miles N.N.E. of Lisbon. Although still considered provisional, it will probably become the permanent seaplane base, having very adequate equipment and no more suitable site being available.

ANGOLA
(Portuguese West Africa)

ADMINISTRATION

By a Decree issued by the Governor-General of the Colony the Conselho de Aéronautica (Aeronautical Council) was created in 1937.

The Council has a Secretariat which is responsible for the conduct and development of Civil Aviation in the Colony, particularly the organization, establishment and exploitation of airlines and airports, the financing of civil flying schools, of aerodromes and airports and the registration of aircraft.

The Fundo de Fomento Aeronautico (Aeronautical Development Fund) was created in 1927 to intensify the development of Civil Aviation. Funds are obtained from the following contributory sources :—(a) Subsidy from the general budget of the Colony ; (b) Subsidies from the provincial budgets ; (c) Subsidies from the local budgets ; (d) Taxes or additions to existing levies, which by a legal act shall be attributed to the Fund ; and (e) Any eventual receipts.

This Fund is administered by an Aeronautical Development Council, a member of which is the President of the Angola Aero Club.

TRANSPORT COMPANIES

Divisão des Transportes Aereos (Aerial Transport Division). Created in 1938. Headquarters : Luanda.

Personnel consists of five pilots, three mechanics, three radio-telegraphists and the head of the airport at Luanda.

Attached to the Governor-General of Angola, and additional to the personnel already mentioned, is an Air Attaché (an Army pilot).

The following services were believed to be still operating in 1942, but reports received indicate that there has been some curtailment due to the difficulty of obtaining spare parts, etc. at the present time.

Routes :—
Luanda—Ambrizete—Santo Antonio de Zaire—Cabinda. Weekly return.
Luanda—Pôrto Amboin—Novo Redondo—Lobito—Benguela Sa Da Bandeira—Mossamedes. Weekly return.

FLYING CLUBS

The development of Civil Aviation began with the creation of the Aero Club de Angola, and with the organization of a private aerodrome and necessary installations near Luanda. Progress was rapid, and there now exist seven flying schools, functioning at Luanda, Benguela, Nova Lisboa, Mossamedes, Sá da Bandeira, Malange and Lobito.

AERODROMES

BENGUELA, LOBITO, LUANDA, MALANGE, MOSSAMEDES, NOVA LISBOA, PORTO AMBOIM, PORTO ALEXANDRE, SANTO ANTONIO DO ZAIRE, SÁ DE BANDEIRA, CABINDA, HUMPATA, QUIBALA, SILVA PORTO, VILA LUZO AND VILA TEIXEIRA DE SOUZA.

MOÇAMBIQUE
(Portuguese East Africa)

ADMINISTRATION

A Decree issued by the Governor-General of the Colony in 1936 created an Aeronautical Council to superintend all aviation matters in accordance with regulations then laid down. The Council had a Secretariat with functions identical to those of the Angola Secretariat.

TRANSPORT COMPANIES

Divisão de Exploraçao des Transportes Aereos (D.E.T.A.). Lourenço Marques. Manager : Major Pinho da Cunha.

The Company is administered by the Department of Railways, Harbours and Airways. Director : Major Pinto Texeira.

Lourenço Marques—Vila Joa Belo—Inhambane—Mambone

—Beira—Tete—Quelimane—Mozambique. Once weekly.
Lourenço Marques — Inhambane — Beira — Quelimane—Quinga—Mozambique—Porto Amelia—Mocimboa de Praia. Once weekly.
Lourenço Marques—Beira—Quelimane. Once weekly.
Lourenço Marques—Beira—Quelimane—Mozambique. Once weekly.

British Overseas Airways Corporation
The Colony is served by the "Horseshoe" route which stops twice weekly in each direction at Lourenço Marques, Beira and Moçambique.

FLYING CLUBS

Aero Club de Moçambique, Lourenço Marques. President : Manuel Simões Vas. Secretary : Ramiro do Nascimento Coimbra.

The activities of this Club, which were considerable up to 1940 and included free instruction to Members of the Military School are believed to be more or less dormant at present, due to various difficulties and a loss of interest among the local people.
Aero Club da Provincia da Zambézia, Quelimane.
Aero Club de Beira, Beira.

AERODROMES

BEIRA, CHIBUTO, INHAMBANE, INHAMINGA, INHARRIME, LOURENÇO MARQUES, LUMBO, MOCIMBOA DA PRAIA, MAGUDE, MANBONE, M ma, MANHIÇA, MUTARARA, PORTO AMÉLIA, QUELIMANE, QUINGA, TETE, UANETZE, VILA JOÃO BELO, VILAMACHADO VILA PERY, ZEMBO, VILANCULOS AND NOVA LUSITANIA.

PORTUGUESE GUINEA
(West Africa)

Pan American Airways (Africa) Ltd. took over the trans-African route for the delivery of aircraft to the Near East. The operation of the route was taken over by the U.S. Air Transport Command in 1942.

FLYING CLUBS

Aero Club da Guiné

This Club uses the private D.H. "Leopard-Moth" belonging to the Serviços Aereos da Colonia, which was flown out to the Colony from Portugal by Major-Aviator Sérgio da Silva on his appointment as Director in April, 1939.

ADMINISTRATION

Civil Aviation in the Colony is controlled by the Serviços Aereos da Colonia (Aerial Services of the Colony). The Director of the Aerial Services is Major-Aviator Sérgio da Silva.

TRANSPORT COMPANIES

Pan American Airways

The Company's Trans-Atlantic service utilises the seaplane base near Bolama on an alternative E./W. route from Lisbon to Trinidad and thence to the U.S.A.

With the signing of an agreement between the British Government and Pan American Airways, in September, 1941,

AERODROMES

BOLAMA. It would appear certain that this aerodrome has been considerably enlarged to take care of the numerous aircraft using it at present. No details are available.

Emergency Landing Grounds

BAFATÁ, CANCHUNGO, MANŌSA, ILHA DAS GALINAS, ILHA DE BUBAQUE.

AZORES

ADMINISTRATION

The Azores are an integral part of the Republic of Portugal. In September, 1943 the Portuguese Government, in virtue of an ancient alliance, placed the islands at the disposal of Great Britain as a base for the protection of the Atlantic seaways. As a consequence extensive work was immediately undertaken by Britain on the extension of existing, and the building of new aerodromes. These will no doubt be made good use of after the War.

TRANSPORT COMPANIES

Sociedade Acoriana de Estudos Aereos

This Company was formed in the Summer of 1942 with the object of linking the three principal islands, Fayal, San Miguel and Terceira. However, no operations have resulted and it is believed the Company is merely a legal necessity for Pan American Airways.

MILITARY AIR SERVICE

On October 1, 1942, the Military Authorities began a weekly public air service for passengers between Rabo de Peixe (San Miguel) and Lagens (Terceira), using Junkers Ju 52 aircraft. This service was suspended in 1943.

RUSSIA
(The Union of Soviet Socialist Republics—Soyuz Sovietskikh Sotsialistficheskikh Respublik)

ADMINISTRATION

The Director-General of Soviet Air Transport is Marshal of the Red Air Force Astafive. The Vice-Director in charge of civil operations is Lieut.-General Semenov.

Civil Aviation activities in the U.S.S.R. cover Air Transportation, Forestry Patrol, a Flying Medical Service, the sowing and spraying of crops, the latter including the destruction of the malarial mosquito and the locust, Flying and Gliding Schools, the instruction of the population in civil air defence, etc. For these purposes there are certain administrative bodies responsible to the Director-General and through him to the Council of People's Commissars.

Oupravlenie Grajdanskovo Vosdouchnova Flota (Chief Administration of the Civil Air Fleet). Moscow.

This is the chief administrative body in the U.S.S.R. for air transportation, forestry patrol, the flying medical service, the sowing of crops and the extermination of agricultural pests.

Under the name "Aeroflot" the air transport services of the Soviet Union cover a wide network, but details of civil aviation operations are, like all other Soviet air activities, not made available other than in the form of popular propaganda as published in the Soviet press or broadcast over the Moscow radio.

In the Summer of 1945 there were known to be air services between Moscow and the capitals of the fifteen Union Republics, as well as direct air communications with Berlin, Prague, Warsaw, Bucharest, Sofia, Vienna, Budapest, Belgrade and Teheran.

Regular schedules are also maintained between Moscow and Kharbarovsk in Far Eastern Russia. This is the longest route in the U.S.S.R. and hotels have been opened at Novosibirsk, Irkutsk and Nerehinsky, intermediate stops on the route. Radi-ating from Kharbarovsk are many local services. These include routes serving Sakhalin and Kamchatka.

In the Northern Administration more than 100 services had been inaugurated. The main route connects Moscow with Leningrad. Other regular passenger and freight services link Leningrad with Volodga, Murmansk, Kalinin, Novgorod, Velikiye Luki, Archangel and Kolym.

Soviet Russia has held aloof from all attempts to interest her in international co-operation. The U.S.S.R. declined to be represented at the Chicago International Air Conference, but a seat has been reserved for its representative on the Provisional International Civil Aviation Organization established in 1945.

ASSOCIATION

Osoaviakhim (Society for Air and Chemical Defence)

This central Society, with headquarters in Moscow, unites the Osoaviakhim Societies of the Republics forming the U.S.S.R. and is responsible for the activities of the Flying and Gliding Clubs and for the instruction of the civil population in air defence, etc. It is also responsible for pre-military flying training and aerial propaganda.

The Osoaviakhim comprises a large number of Aero Clubs, most of which operate flying schools and have their own aerodromes.

PUBLICATIONS

Westnik Wosdushnowo Flota (News of the Air Fleet). The official organ of the Directorate of the Red Air Force ; chiefly serves the interests of the personnel of the Military Air Fleet.

Samolet (Aircraft). Published by the Union of Osoaviakhim Societies of U.S.S.R. ; deals chiefly with problems of Civil Aviation and airship navigation in U.S.S.R. and abroad, and also with aircraft models and gliders.

Chronika Wosdushnogo Dela (Chronicle of Air Business). Published by the Union of Osoaviakhim Societies ; claims, on the basis of world literature to receive all news of aviation and airship navigation from abroad ; reviews all important foreign articles and books referring to aviation.

Technika Wosdushnowo Flota (Air Fleet Technics). Published by a group of scientific research organizations ; illuminates the problems of aircraft and engine constructions. This journal is chiefly for engineers.

AERODROMES

Customs Aerodromes

Europe :—MOSCOW, LENINGRAD, VELIKIYE LUKI.
Asia :—BAKU, IRKUTSK, VERKUE-UDINSK, KHABAROVSK, TASHKENT, TERMEZ.

Civil Airports are established throughout the Union. Many aerodromes are essentially military, but are used by civil aircraft. The following air routes are known to be equipped with revolving beacons for regular night-flying :—

Moscow—Bologoje—Leningrad.
Moscow — Orel — Kharkov — Rostov — Armavir — Mineralni Vody.
Moscow—Penza—Samara.
Moscow—Nijni Novgorod.
Moscow—Kazan.
Moscow—Novosibirsk—Kharbarovsk.
Sverdlovsk — Shadinsk — Kurgan — Petropavlovsk — Omsk Novosibirsk—Taiga.
Krasnoyarsk—Nishni Udinsk—Irkutsk.
Tshelkar—Kysyl Orda—Tashkent.

SALVADOR
(The Republic of El Salvador—Republica de El Salvador)

ADMINISTRATION

Civil Aviation is controlled by the Department of Aviation acting under the Chief of the Military Aviation Service.

ASSOCIATIONS

Club de Aviacion Civil y de Reserva, Aerodromo de Ilopango, San Salvador.

The Salvadorian Wing of the Inter-American Escadrille. Honorary President : The Minister of National Defence, General Andrés Ignacio Menéndez.

TRANSPORT COMPANIES

Transportes Aéreos Centro Americanos (TACA)

This Company, with headquarters in Tegucigalpa, Honduras, operates five services weekly in each direction to San Salvador on its International Service.

Pan American Airways

San Salvador is a regular stop on the Brownsville—Balboa daily service in each direction.

Transportes Aéreo Salvadoreños

This Company has not begun the operation of regular services. It has, however, operated non-scheduled flights between San Salvador and outlying points. It was last known to own two aircraft of unspecified type.

AERODROMES AND SEAPLANE STATIONS

The chief airport is at SAN SALVADOR (Ilopango). Altitude 2,175 ft. (664 m.). Military and Civil Customs Airport. Runways N./S. and E./W. 1,500 yds. Hangar. Beacon and night-landing facilities. Radio. Call sign YSX. Short wave only. D/F. and Meteorological data available.

There are also aerodromes without service except fuel and oil at the following places :—SAN MIGUEL, AHUACHAPAN, SONSONATE, ZACATECOLUCA, SAN VICENTE, USULUTAN, CHALATENANGO. ILOPANGO LAKE can be used by seaplanes.

Since the German occupation of Norway all national civil aviation has disappeared. The German airline Deutsche Lufthansa is, however, operating certain services into Norway. (See under Germany).

The Royal Norwegian Government in London has established an organization known as Royal Norwegian Air Transport (Norges Luftfartstyre) as a war-time measure, with offices at Kingston House South, 70, Ennismore Gardens, London, S.W.7. The Director-General is Mr. Annaeus Schjodt. The objects of this organization, until the liberation of Norway, are to prepare, by acquisition of rights and equipment and by other means, for the resumption after the war of civil aviation in Norway for the conveyance of passengers and goods both by national and international services. It may also be enjoined by the Norwegian Government to organize civil air lines during the war.

SPAIN
(The Spanish State—España)

ADMINISTRATION

Civil Aviation is under the control of the Directorate of Civil Aviation, Magdalena 12, Madrid, which itself is under the control of the Minister for Air.

The Directorate covers all aspects of Civil Aviation, including gliding.

ASSOCIATIONS

Federación Aeronáutica Nacional de España (F.A.N.E.), Calle Mayor 4, Madrid.

This body is the representative of the *Fédération Aéronautique Internationale* (F.A.I.). President : Don Alfonso de Hoyos Sánchez, Viscount Manzanera. Secretary : Don José Barcala Moreno.

PUBLICATION

Revista de Aeronautica. The official organ of the Air Ministry. Editor : Teniente Coronel Francisco Iglesias. Foreign Editor : Teniente Coronel Ricardo Munaiz. Address : Juan de Mena 8, Madrid. Issued monthly. Price 5.00 ptas.

FLYING CLUBS

The following Aero Clubs are affiliated to the Federación Aernáutica Nacional de España.

Aero Club de Madrid. Airport used : Barajas.
Aero Club de Sevilla. Airport used : San Pablo.
Aero Club de Valencia. Airport used : Manises.
Aero Club de Barcelona. Airport used : Muntadas.
Aero Club de Zaragoza. Airport used : General Sanjurjo.

GLIDING

Several glider schools are operating in Monflorite (Huesca), Somosierra, Cerro del Telegrafo (near Madrid and Santa Colombo de Somoza (León) for the training of youths between 15 and 20 years of age. Hundreds of such pupils receive instruction each year, and surveys are being made by land and air with a view to opening other schools.

For youths between 10 and 15 aero-model schools exist throughout the country to train such pupils in "airmindedness."

TRANSPORT COMPANY

Trafico Aeréo Espanal (late Iberia).

Head Office : Plaza de Cánovas, Madrid.

Director : Cesar Gomez Lucia.

This company holds exclusive rights granted by the Spanish Government for the operation of all commercial air services, both national (including those to the Colonies and Protectorate) and reciprocal international lines. At the present time, apart from having bought from the U.S. Government a few Douglas Dakotas which have landed in Spain, it lacks flying material to extend its interior lines, as well as lines with the Canary Islands and the African colonies.

Routes :—
Barcelona—Madrid. Weekdays.
Lisbon—Madrid. Weekdays.
Madrid—Seville—Tangiers—Tetuan. Weekdays.
Tetuan—Melilla. Weekdays.
Aircraft :—Junkers Ju 52/3m, Douglas DC-2 and DC-3 (Dakota), D.H.84.

OTHER OPERATING COMPANIES

La Compañia Española de Trabajos Fotogramétricos Aéreos S.A. (C.E.T.F.A.). Address : Madera 1, Madrid.

This Company uses a D.H. Tiger Moth for its photographic and survey service.

AERODROMES

Barajas (Madrid). Lat. 40°28′N., Long. 3°36′W. Province of Madrid. 9 miles N.E. of city. Alt. 2,000 ft. 2,200 yds. × 1,800 yds. Full facilities.

San Pablo (Seville). Lat. 37°25′N., Long. 5°55′W. Province of Seville. 4½ miles E.N.E. of city. Alt. 65 ft. 2,700 yds. × 1,100 yds. Full facilities.

Garcia Morato (Málaga). Lat. 36°40′N., Long. 4°27′W. Province of Malaga. 5 miles S.W. of city. Alt. 65 ft. 950 yds. × 950 yds. W/T. and Met. service in Málaga.

Manises (Valencia). Lat. 39°30′N., Long. 0°29′W. Province of Valencia. 5 miles W. of city. Alt. 150 ft. 1,650 yds. × 1,450 yds. W/T.

Muntadas (Barcelona). Lat. 41°18′N., Long. 2°03′E. Province of Barcelona. 9 miles S.W. of city. Alt. 13 ft. 1,300 yds. × 875 yds. W/T. and D/F.

Barcelona (Seaplane Stn.). Lat. 41°22′N., Long. 2°10′E. S.E. side of city. 700 yds. × 550 yds.

Son Bonet (Mallorca Isd.). Lat. 39°35′N., Long. 2°48′E. Province of Baleares. 6 miles N.E. of Palma. Alt. 55 ft. 1,300 yds. × 875 yds.

Pollensa (Seaplane Stn.). Lat. 39°54′N., Long. 3°04′E. Province of Baleares. Close to Pollensa city.

Gando (Las Palmas). Lat. 27°55′N., Long. 15°21′W. 12½ miles S. of Las Palmas in Gando Bay. 1,750 yds. × 600 yds. Full facilities.

SWEDEN

(The Kingdom of Sweden—Sverige)

ADMINISTRATION

Civil Aviation is under the jurisdiction of the :—

Kommunikationsdepartementet, (The Ministry of Communications).
Minister of Communications : F. Domö.
Permanent Secretary : H. Berglund.
Address : Mynttorget 2, Stockholm 2.

The direct control of Civil Aviation and the administration of the state-owned civil airports is exercised by the :—

Väv- och Vattenbyggnadsstyrelsen, Järnvägs- och Luftfartsbyrån, Luftfartsmyndigheten (The Royal Board of Roads and Waterways, The section of private Railways and civil Aviation, The Civil Aviation Authority).
Director-General : N. Bolinder.
Director : C. Ljungberg.
Inspector of Civil aviation : Tord Ångström.
First Secretary : E. Nylund.

ASSOCIATIONS

Kungl. Svenska Aeroklubben (Royal Swedish Aero Club). Founded 1900. Offices : Malmskillnadsgatan 67, Stockholm. President : H. R. H. Prince Gustaf Adolf. Secretary : Colonel H. Enell.

The Club, which is affiliated to *Fédération Aéronautique Internationale*, is the principal organization and the controlling body for the aero clubs in Sweden.

Svenska Flygares Riksförbund (National Guild of Swedish Pilots). 6 Fredsgatan, Stockholm.
Chairman : Carl Trygger.
Vice-Chairman : Colonel K. J. A. Silfverberg (S.A.F.).
General Secretary : Captain G. M. M. Lilliehook.

The aims of the Guild are to serve Swedish aviation and represent the interests of Swedish pilots by promoting the development of aviation and making the Swedish people air-minded. Further to develop comradeship amongst members, to increase the knowledge about aviation matters amongst members and to act in an advisory capacity both within the Guild and outside of it.

Eligible are holders or former holders of civil pilot's licence, civilian/navigators and wireless-operators, pilots, observer, wireless-operators and air-gunners of the Swedish Air Force.

TECHNICAL INSTITUTIONS

Ingeniörsvetenskapsakademiens Flygtekniska Kommitté (The Air Technical Committee of the Academy of Engineering Science).
Address : Grev Turegatan 14, Stockholm.
Members : Edy Velander, President, Karl Lignell, Ivar Malmar, Erik Sjögren, Tord Ångström.

Flygtekniska Föreningen (The Aero Technical Society). Address: AB Aerotransport, Kungsholmstorg 1, Stockholm. President : Tord Ångström.

Kungl. Tekniska Högskolan (The Royal Technical University). Address : Valhallavägen 79, Stockholm.

PUBLICATIONS

Flyg. Published fortnightly at Tegnérgatan 35, Stockholm.

On October 1, 1942, *Flygning*, which was originally the official journal of the Royal Swedish Aero Club, was merged with the Swedish Air Force publication *Flygpost.* Until January 1, 1943, the joint publication bore both names. Now renamed *Flyg.* Managing Editor : Col. W. Kleen. Executive Editor : Lieut. Gunnar Knutsson.

Svensk Flygtidning. Published monthly at Sallerupsvägen 26, Malmö. Editor : H. W. Göst.

Vi Flygare. Published monthly at Fredsgatan 6, Stockholm. Journal of the National Guild of Swedish Pilots. Chief Editor : Hans Ostelius.

TRANSPORT COMPANIES

From about a dozen companies formed between 1919 and 1925 emerged AB. Aerotransport (Swedish Air Lines) as the only company strong enough to survive. Swedish Air Lines was privately-owned during its first five years. Then the Government took over, first a small part and later on, as is the situation at present, 80% of the shares. Although A.B.A. is the only operating Swedish company, no monopolistic legislation exists and several other companies have been formed. They are, however, not yet operating on scheduled lines. Details are given hereunder :—

Aktiebolaget Aerotransport (Swedish Air Lines. A.B.A.). Address : Kungsholmstorg 1, Stockholm. Chairman : Frans Severin. Managing Director : Captain C. Florman.

The following routes were in operation in the Summer of 1945 :—
Stockholm—Turku—Helsinki. Daily.
Stockholm—Visby. Daily.
Stockholm—Göteborg—Croydon.
Stockholm—Amsterdam.
Stockholm—Oslo.
Stockholm—Warsaw (weekly Government courier service only).
Stockholm—Göteborg—Malmö.
Stockholm—Sundsvall—Härnösand—Lulea.

Altogether forty internal services are operated in Sweden with traffic centres at Göteborg, Kopenhamn, Lulea, Malmö, Sundsvall, Härnösand, Visby and Stockholm.

Svensk Interkontinental Lufttrafik A.B. (S.I.L.A.). Chairman : Thorsten Hérnod. Managing Director : P. A. Norlin.

This Company has been formed to permit Sweden to take full advantage of post-war intercontinental air transport. It was formed on February 25, 1943, and at the founders meeting on May 31, 77 representatives of Swedish industry subscribed the fully paid-up capital of Kr. 12,000,000. Participation by the Government was purposely avoided.

During the Summer of 1945 a series of survey flights were made between Stockholm and New York, via Iceland and Labrador, with converted Boeing Fortress monoplanes.

No Government subsidy has been asked for. A close liaison is maintained with A.B.A. who has placed its Administration, Commercial Organization and technical service at the disposal of the new company and will supervise operations. A.B.A. pilots and other staff will be used.

Svenska Aero-Lloyd A.B. Göteborg.

This Company has been formed as a subsidiary of the shipping company, Svenska Lloyd. The Company intends to operate a service from Göteborg to London as soon as conditions permit. The Managing Director of the Company, K. R. Bökman, is also Managing Director of the shipping company, and a member of the Board of Directors of the newly formed S.I.L.A.

Skandinaviska Aero A.B. (Scandinavian Airways, Ltd.). Stockholm. Chairman : K. R. Bökman (Managing Director of Rederi A.B. Svenska Lloyd). Managing Director : A. Forsmark.

This company was formed to take over the taxi and charter flying business formerly operated under the name of A.B. Björkvallsflyg. During the war the company has been mainly occupied with target-towing and other semi-military duties.

In November, 1944, the control of the company was taken over by several shipping owners in Gothenburg and a considerable enlargement of the company's capital at the same time being announced.

The company has applied for Government franchise to operate regular air routes within Sweden.

Svensk Flygtjänst A.B. Arsenalsgatan 4, Stockholm.
Managing Director : Tor Eliasson.

This company has existed for some years and has, until recently, been chiefly occupied with school and taxi flying. It plans to operate feeder lines in connection with A.B.A.'s international lines.

NAVIGATIONAL SERVICES

Radio Services for the use of aviation are in charge of the Radio Department of the Telegraphic Office, the main stations being located at Göteborg (Torslanda), Malmö (Bulltofta), Stockholm (Bromma). In addition there are a number of non-directional radio-beacons put up along the main air routes.

The air routes between Stockholm—Malmö and Malmö—Göteborg are marked with a series of beacons spaced 25 km. apart. These beacons are of the oscillating type, develop about 1,900,000 candle-power and show generally three white flashes every five seconds in the direction of the route.

AERODROMES

Stockholm-Bromma. Lat. 59°23′N. Long. 17°58′E. 8 km. N.W. of city. Landing runs 2,000 × 60 m. N.W./S.E. 950 × 40 m. W./E., 1,000 × 40 m. S.W./N.E., 1,400 × 40 m. N.N.W./S.S.E Hangers. Full repairs. Full night facilities. W/T., D/F. Lorenz. Customs.

Göteborg-Torslanda. Lat. 57°42′N. Long. 11°47′E. 11 km. W. of town Landing runs 1,850 × 60 m. N.E./S.W., 1,150 × 40 m. E. W., 7 0 × 40 m. N.W./S.E. Hanger. Minor repairs Full night facilities W/T., D/F., Lorenz. Customs.

Malmö-Bulltofta. Lat. 53°36′N. Long. 13°04′E. 3.5 km. E. of town. Landing runs 1,200 m. N.W./S.E., 1,100 m. N.E./S.W. Hangars. Full repairs. Full night facilities. W/T., D/F., Lorenz. Customs.

Orebro. Lat. 59°15′N. Long. 15°12′E. 1 km. S. of town. Landing runs 1,200 m. N.E./S.W., 1,150 m. N.W./S.E. Hangar 28 × 18 m. Minor repairs.

Visby. Lat. 57°39′N. Long. 18°20′E. 2 km. N.E. of town. Landing runs 1,350 m. N.E./S.W., 1,000 m. E./W. Hangar 37 × 26 m. Minor repairs. Minor night facilities. W/T., D/F. Customs.

Karlstad. Lat. 59°21′N. Long. 13°28′E. 2 km. S. of town. Landing runs 1,000 m. N./S., 1,000 m. N.E./S.W. No hangar. Minor repairs. W/T., D/F.

Sundsvall-Härnösand. Lat. 62°32′N. Long. 17°27′E. 15 km. N. of town. Landing runs 1,350 m. N.W./S.E., 1,160 m. N.E./S.W. No hangar. Minor repairs.

Norrköping-Kungsängen. Lat. 58°35′N. Long. 16°14′E. 2 km. E. of town. Landing runs 1,000 m. E. W., 700 m. N./S. Hangar 21 × 15 m. Minor repairs. Minor night facilities. W/T., D/F. Customs.

Jönkoping. Lat. 57°46′N. Long. 14°11′E. 2 km. S. of town. Landing runs 750 m. E./W., 650 m. N./S. Hangar 20 × 18 m. Minor repairs. Minor night facilities. W/T., D/F. Customs.

Eslöv. Lat. 55°51′N. Long. 13°20′E. 16 km. N.E. of town, Landing runs 800 m. N.W./S.E., 730 m. N.E. S.W. No hangar. Minor repairs.

SEAPLANE STATIONS

Stockholm-Lindarängen. Lat. 59°21′N. Long. 18°08′E. 3.5 km. N.E. of city. Alighting area 800 × 1,000 × 1,500 m. Hangars. Minor repairs. No night facilities. Customs.

Göteborg-Torslanda. Lat. 57°42′N. Long. 11°47′E. 11 km. W. of town. Alighting area 1,500 × 1,500 × 1,500 m. Hangars. No night facilities. W/T., D/F. Customs.

SWITZERLAND

(The Swiss Confederation—Schweizerische Eidgenossenschaft)

ADMINISTRATION

Civil Aviation is controlled by the Department of Civil Aviation headed by a Delegate for Civil Aviation. This department is part of the Departement des Postes et des Chemins de Fer.

ASSOCIATIONS

Aero Club der Schweiz (Aéro-Club de Suisse). President : Lt.-Col. W. N. Gerber, Sihlquai 55, Zürich. Secretary General : Capt. Rieser, Schanzenstrasse 1, Berne.

The Swiss Aero Club has 22 Sections to which the following groups were attached : 15 power-driven flying groups, 2 free balloon groups ; 51 gliding groups ; and 26 groups for the construction of models.

The Swiss National Office of Transportation

This private organization, which was formed in 1943, has an annual appropriation of about four million Swiss francs of which one million is subscribed by the Government, and the remainder by private commercial interests. The object of the organization, which functions without Government interference, is to promote trade and commerce through publicity.

PUBLICATIONS

Aéro Revue (Official Organ of L'Aéro Club de Suisse). Büchler & Co., Berne, 8. Fortnightly.

Interavia. Aeronautical news from all parts of the globe. Soc. Anon. d'Edition Aéron. Internationales, Cité 20, Geneva, 11. Twice weekly.

AIR TRANSPORT COMPANIES

Swissair. A company formed as the result of the amalgamation of the two firms Ad Astra-Aéro and Balair. Offices: Bahnhofplatz 7, Zürich. Aerodromes: Zürich-Dübendorf.

All civil transport was closed down on August, 1939, owing to mobilisation of the Swiss Army. Swissair resumed operations in March, 1940, with a service from Locarno to Rome but this was interrupted on Italy's entry into the war in June.

On September 30, 1940, Swissair resumed its daily Zurich—Munich service and between November, 1941 and January, 1943, it operated the Zurich—Stuttgart—Berlin route. From January 23, 1943, the service was restricted to the Zurich—Stuttgart section. This reduced service was discontinued on August 17, 1944, following the destruction on Stuttgart aerodrome of a Swissair DC-2, said to have been due to an American air raid in 1944.

In 1944 Swissair, the only Swiss company operating in recent years, covered a mileage of 75,558 km. (46,922 miles) as compared with 146,918 km. (91,236 miles) in 1943, and carried 2,187 passengers, the figure for 1943 being 4,738.

On May 12, 1945, a Swissair DC-3 made the first of several non-scheduled flights to Lisbon in connection with a Swiss exhibition in Oporto. The first Swiss international scheduled service was started on July 16, between Zurich, Geneva and Paris, with one service daily in each direction. It is operated jointly with Air France, each company operating on alternate days.

Before the end of 1945 services were operating between Zurich and London (three weekly) and Zurich and Amsterdam. Future plans include services to Madrid, Cairo and the U.S.A.

In August, 1945, Switzerland signed an agreement with the United States of America which provided for regional rights for trans-Atlantic services between Switzerland and New York.

Aircraft:—Four Douglas DC-3 and three Douglas DC-2, 1 Comte AC.4, 1 D.H. 89, 1 Fokker F.VIIA.

Alpar. Office: Berne Aerodrome.
This Company is at present inoperative.

FLYING SCHOOLS

Swissair. Aerodrome: Zürich-Dubendorf.

Alpar. Aerodrome: Berne-Belpmoos.

Ostschweiz. Aero-Gesellschaft. Aerodrome: Altenrhein - St. Gallen.

Aviatik beider Basle. Aerodrome: Basle-Birsfelden.

Sections of the **Aero Club de Suisse** at:—Basle, Bellinzona, Berne, La Chaux-de-Fonds, Geneva, Grenchen, Lausanne, Neuchâtel, Sion, St. Gall, Thun, Zürich, Locarno.

STATISTICS

A survey from the Swiss Air Office concerning the activities of Swiss civil aviation in 1944 gave these comparative figures for 1941, 1943 and the last full pre-war year of operations:—

	1938	1941	1943	1944
Number of flights ..	82,127	1,880	2,387	2,003
Flying hours	29,112	1,071	974	758
Aggregate distance (km.)	5,398,605	242,266	201,102	142,775
Passengers carried ..	122,937	4,668	5,841	4,152
Mail conveyed (kg.) ..	628,014	36,285	73,322	61,452
Freight conveyed (kg). ..	322,173	45,099	63,331	29,820
Excess luggage (kg.) ..	284,825	22,539	26,662	23,332

The contraction in 1944 was exclusively due to the discontinuance of the Swiss air services, while flying schools had shown intensified activity. There was no private flying in 1944.

AERODROMES

Various plans for new airports in Switzerland have been reported in connection with post-war flying. There is to be a combined land-marine base at LAUSANNE-ECUBLENS on the shore of Lake Geneva at St. Sulpice. The estimated cost is Sw. fr. 7,000,000. Expansion of the airport at COINTRIN is already being proceeded with. The municipality of Berne is sponsoring the construction of a large airport at UTZENSTORF which is intended to be the central Swiss airport for international services.

Aerodromes with Customs facilities:—BASLE-BIRSFELDEN, GENEVA-COINTRIN, ZÜRICH-DÜBENDORF, LOCARNO-MOGADINO, BERNE-BELPMOOS, LAUSANNE-BLÉCHERETTE, ALTENRHEIN-ST. GALLEN, LA CHAUX-DE-FONDS.

Customs Seaplane Stations:—GENEVA (Eaux-Vives), LAUSANNE (Ouchy), LOCARNO, LUGANO, RORSCHACH, ROMANSHORN, ERMATINGEN, KREUZLINGEN, ARBON, ALTENRHEIN (St. Gallen).

Aerodromes for Internal Traffic:—BIENNE, SION, SAMADEN.

Aerodromes available only by special permission:—BELLINZONA, HILFIKON, GLAND, GRENCHEN, PORRENTRUY (Courtedoux), YVERDON.

Winter Aerodrome:—ST. MORITZ (on frozen lake by special permission only).

TURKEY

(The Turkish Republic—Türkiye Cumhuriyeti)

ADMINISTRATION

Civil Aviation in Turkey is under the control of the Ministry of Communications, but the Military General Staff lay down the routes on which aircraft may fly.

ASSOCIATIONS

Türk Hava Kurumu (Air League). A semi-official organization designed to promote and foster the growth of "air-mindedness" in Turkey. It has a considerable income, derived from a tax on all salaries and wages, and from lotteries, subscriptions, and donations. The League runs the only authorized lottery in Turkey.

Every city and town in the country has contributed its quota and many villages have raised sufficient money for one machine. Each machine so added to the National Air Force bears the name of the town or village from which the purchase price was received.

Apart from the purchase of machines the League devotes its energies to the development of flying and gliding schools through its subsidiary organization—the "Türkkusu."

Türkkusu ("Turkish Bird") Association. An offshoot of the Air League. It was inaugurated at Ankara on May 3, 1935, and has since opened branches in the chief provincial towns. Its object is the building up of a reserve of pilots and mechanics for the Government Air Force. Initial training is carried out on gliders and advanced training on powered aircraft. There is a parachute-jumping section and parachute towers have been installed at many places. Since the outbreak of War in Europe, activities have been greatly extended.

GLIDING

Great importance is attached to gliding. Five sections have been established in the provinces of Istanbul, Izmir, Bursa, Adana, and Kaisarieh. An advanced gliding school has been opened at Inonu. The period of training is three months.

AIR TRANSPORT

Devlet Hava Yollari (State Air Lines), Ankara Civil Airport.

Operated by a department of the Ministry of Communications. The State-operation of airlines in Turkey was taken over in 1934.

Ankara—Istanbul. Daily except Sunday.
Ankara—Afyon—Izmir—Istanbul. Thrice weekly.
Ankara—Adana. Daily except Sunday.
Ankara—Elazig—Diyarbakir. Thrice weekly.
Ankara—Gaziantep—Diyarbakir—Van. Thrice weekly.
Ankara—Sivas—Erzurum. Thrice weekly.
Ankara—Konya—Antalya. Thrice weekly.
Ankara—Afyon—Antalya. Thrice weekly.

The equipment owned by the State Air Lines consists of:—One D.H. Tiger Moth, one D.H. Dragonfly, three D.H. Dragon-Rapide, six D.H. Dominie, four D.H. 86B and five Junkers Ju 52/3m.

AERODROMES

ADANA. Lat. 36°58′N. Long. 35°17′E. 1 mile W. of town. Two runways 40 m. × 1,500 m. Hangars. Minor repairs. Military and Civil Customs Aerodrome.

ANKARA. Lat. 39°57′N. Long. 32°52′E. 4 miles W. of town. Alt. 3.000 ft. Three runways 40 m. × 1,200 m. (N.E./S.W.), 40 m. × 1,200 m. (E./W.) and 40 m. × 900 m. (N./S.). Administration building and hangars. W/T.

YESILKÖY (Istanbul). Lat. 40°58′N. Long. 28°50′E. 5 miles S.W. of town. Alt. 50 ft. Three runways 40 m. × 1,200 m. (N.E./S.W., E./W. and N./S.). Administration building and hangars. Full night-landing facilities. Military and Civil Customs Aerodrome.

KONYA. Lat. 37°58′N. Long. 32°34′E. 3 miles E. of town. Alt. 3,500 ft. One runway 40 m. × 2,600 m. (N.N.E./S.S.W.). No facilities.

AFYONKARAHISSAR. Lat. 38°44′N. Long. 30°36′E. Two runways 40 m. × 1,832 m. (N.W./S.E.) and 46 m. × 1,570 m. (N.N.W./S.S.E.). Administrative buildings only. No facilities.

THE UNITED STATES OF AMERICA

ADMINISTRATION

The control of Civil Aviation in the United States is vested in the Civil Aeronautics Authority. Operating under this Authority are the Civil Aeronautics Board and the Administrater of Civil Aeronautics. The Administrator of Civil Aeronautics acts under the direction and supervision of the Secretary of Commerce. The Civil Aeronautics Board exercises its functions of rule making, adjudication and investigation independently of the Secretary of Commerce.

CIVIL AERONAUTICS AUTHORITY, Commerce Building, Washington 25, D.C.
Secretary of Commerce: Henry Wallace.
Assistant Secretary of Commerce: William A. M. Burden.

Civil Aeronautics Administration
Administrator: Theodore P. Wright.
Deputy Administrator: Charles I. Stanton.
Aircraft Control Officer: John P. Morris.
Assistant Administrator for Field Operations: A. S. Koch.
Assistant Administrator for Business Management: A. E. Stockburger.
General Counsel, Aeronautical Legal Staff: Glen D. Woodmansee.
Assistant Administrator for Federal Airways:
Assistant Administrator for Safety Regulation: Fred M. Lanter.
Assistant Administrator for Airports: C. B. Donaldson.
Assistant Administrator for Aviation Training: Bruce Uthus.
Assistant Administrator for Aviation Information: Ben Stern.

Civil Aeronautics Board
Chairman: L. Welch Pogue.
Members: Harllee Branch, Oswald Ryan, Josh Lee.
Secretary: Fred Toombs.
General Counsel: George C. Neal
Director, Economic Bureau: Russell B. Adams.
Director, Safety Bureau: Joseph B. Duckworth.

GOVERNMENT RESEARCH AND TECHNICAL ESTABLISHMENT

The National Advisory Committee for Aeronautics, 3841, Navy Building, Washington, D.C.

An independent Government establishment created by an Act of Congress approved on March 3, 1915, for the supervision and direction of the scientific study of the problems of flight. It consists of fifteen members, appointed by the President, all of whom serve as such without remuneration.

The officials of the Committee are:—
Chairman: Jerome C. Hunsaker, Sc.D.
Vice-Chairman: Lynn J. Briggs, Ph.D.
Director of Aeronautical Research: George W. Lewis, Sc.D.
Secretary: John F. Victory.
Engineer-in-Charge, Langley Memorial Aeronautical Laboratory: Henry J. E. Reid.
Engineer-in-Charge, Ames Aeronautical Laboratory: Smith J. De France.
Manager, Aircraft Engine Research Laboratory: Edward R. Sharp.

ASSOCIATIONS

Aero Medical Association. 5440, Cass Avenue, Detroit 2, Mich.

Aircraft Industries of America, Inc. 610, Shoreham Building, Washington 5, D.C.

Aircraft Owners and Pilots Association. 1003, K Street, N.W., Washington 1, D.C.

Aircraft Parts Manufacturers Association. 540, Chamber of Commerce Building, Los Angeles 15, Cal.

Air Law Institute. 357, E. Chicago Avenue, Chicago, Ill.

Air Line Pilots Association, International. 3145, West Sixty-third Street, Chicago 29, Ill.

Air Transport Association of America. 1515 Massachusetts Avenue, N.W., Washington 5, D.C.

Air Youth (N.A.A.). 1025, Connecticut Avenue, N.W., Washington 6, D.C.

American Association of Airport Executives. Municipal Airport, Peoria, Ill.

American Society of Mechanical Engineers, Aeronautic Division. 29, West Thirty-ninth Street, New York, N.Y.

Aviation Distributors and Manufacturers Association. 505, Arch Street, Philadelphia, Pa.

Aviation Writers Association. P.O. Box 856, Grand Central Annexe, New York 17, N.Y.

Institute of the Aeronautical Sciences. 2, East 64th Street, New York, 21 N.Y.

Manufacturers Aircraft Association, Inc. Suite 726, 30, Rockefeller Plaza, New York 2 0, N.Y.

National Aeronautic Association. 1025, Connecticut Avenue, N.W., Washington 6, D.C.

National Association of State Aviation Officials. 506, Olive Street, S. Louis, Mo.

National Aviation Trades Association. 214, E. Armour Boulevard, Kansas City 2, Mo.

Private Fliers Association. (Inactive for duration of war).

Soaring Society of America. Box 71, Elmira, N.Y.

Society of Automotive Engineers, Inc. 29, West Thirty-ninth Street, New York 18, N.Y.

Sportsman Pilots Association. C/o. Secretary, 372 North Bell Avenue, Chicago 12, Ill.

Wings Club, Inc. 50, Vanderbilt Avenue, New York 17, N.Y.

Women Flyers of America, Inc. 274, Madison Avenue, New York, N.Y.

Women's National Aeronautical Association of the U.S.A., Inc. Tulsa Loan Building, Tulsa 3, Okla.

PUBLICATIONS

Aero Digest, published by the Aeronautical Digest Publishing Corpn., 515, Madison Avenue, New York, N.Y. Monthly.

Aeronautical Engineering Review, published by the Institute of the Aeronautical Sciences, 30, Rockefeller Plaza, New York, N.Y. Editor: George R. Forman.

Aerosphere, published at 370, Lexington Avenue. New York, N.Y. Annual. Editor : Glenn D. Angle.

Air Facts, published at 30, Rockefeller Plaza, New York, N.Y. Editor : Leighton Collins.

The Air Law Review, published at Washington Square East, New York, N.Y. Quarterly.

The Air Line Pilot, published by the International Air Line Pilots Association, 3145, West Sixty-third Street, Chicago, Ill. Editor : David L. Behncke.

The Air Line Mechanic, published by the International Air Line Mechanics Association, 6250 South Kedzie Avenue, Chicago, Ill. Editor : J. L. McFarland.

Air News, published at 545, Fifth Avenue, New York, N.Y. Editor : Phillip Andrews.

Air Trails, published at 79, Seventh Avenue, New York, N.Y. Editor : William Winter.

Air Transport, published by the McGraw-Hill Publishing Co., Inc., 418, West Twenty-fifth Street, New York, N.Y. Monthly Editor : Fowler Barker.

Air Transportation, published by Import Publications, Inc., 10, Bridge Street, New York, N.Y. Monthly. Editor : John F. Budd.

Aircraft Year Book, published by the Aeronautical Chamber of Commerce, 30, Rockefeller Plaza, New York, N.Y. Annual. Editor : Howard Mingos.

American Aviation, published by American Aviation Associates, Inc., American Building, Washington, D.C. Twice monthly. Editor : Wayne W. Parrish.

American Aviation Daily, published by American Aviation Associates, Inc., American Building, Washington, D.C. Daily except Sundays and holidays. Executive Editor : Eric Bramley.

American Aviation Directory, published by American Aviation Associates, Inc., American Building, Washington, D.C. Twice yearly. Managing Editor : Helen L. Walsh.

Aviation, published by the McGraw-Hill Publishing Co., Inc., 330, West Forty-second Street, New York, N.Y. Monthly. Editor : Leslie E. Neville.

Aviation News, published by the McGraw-Hill Publishing Co., Inc., 1252, National Press Building, Washington, D.C. Weekly. Editor : Robert H. Wood.

Aviation Equipment, published at 1170, Broadway, New York, N.Y. Editor : John Regan.

Flying, published by Ziff-Davis Publishing Co., Inc., 185, North Wabash Avenue, Chicago, Ill. Monthly. Managing Editor : Max Karant.

Industrial Aviation, published by Ziff-Davis Publishing Co., Inc., 185, North Wabash Avenue, Chicago, Ill. Monthly.

Journal of the Aeronautical Sciences, published by the Institute of the Aeronautical Sciences, 2, East 64th Street, New York, N.Y. Monthly.

Journal of Aviation Medicine, published by the Aero Medical Association, Detroit, Mich. Quarterly. Editor : Dr. L. H. Bauer.

Model Airplane News, published at 551, Fifth Avenue, New York 17, N.Y. Monthly. $2 per year, 20 cents per copy. Editor : Robert McLarren.

National Aeronautics, published by the National Aeronautic Association, 1025, Connecticut Avenue, N.W., Washington, D.C. Monthly. Editor : Ralph Cohen.

Official Guide of the Airways, published by the Official Aviation Guide Co., Inc., 608, South Dearborn Street, Chicago, Ill. Monthly. Editor : Vincent F. Garvy.

Skyways, published at 444, Madison Avenue, New York, N.Y. Editor : J. Fred Henry.

Southern Flight, published at 1901, McKinley Avenue, Dallas, Texas. Monthly. Editor : George E. Haddaway.

Universal Airline Schedules, published by American Aviation Associates, 139, North Clark Street, Chicago, Ill. Monthly.

U.S. Air Services, published at Transportation Building, Washington, D.C. Monthly. Editor : Earl N. Findley.

Western Flying, published at 304, South Broadway, Los Angeles, Cal. Monthly. Editor : Lawrence Black.

TRANSPORT COMPANIES

Hereafter follows a list of the American airline companies which are operating the Contract Air Mail services listed on a succeeding page. All these companies also contribute to the extensive network of air services which cover the entire territory of the United States. At the time of writing an accurate and up-to-date list of the American domestic air services was not available.

Pan American World Airways, American Overseas Airlines, Inc. and Transcontinental and Western Air Inc. are also engaged in international air traffic but in the transition from war to peace few international services, other than those in Latin America, are as yet fully organized.

All-American Aviation Inc., 210, Greenhill Avenue, Wilmington, 99, Delaware. President : Halsey R. Bazley.

This Company operates an Air Mail Route AM 49 exploiting the "air pick-up" system, for mail and express. Daily services except Sunday are operated on routes 49A, B, D, E and F which include 115 towns in Pennsylvania, New York, Ohio, Delaware, Kentucky and West Virginia.

American Airlines System, New York Municipal Airport, Jackson Heights, L.I., N.Y. President : Ralph S. Damon.

American Overseas Airlines, Inc., (formerly American Export Airlines), 25, Broadway, New York 4, N.Y. President : Sumner Sewall.

Braniff Airways, Inc., Love Field, Dallas 9, Texas. President : T. E. Braniff.

Caribbean-Atlantic Airlines, Inc., 47, Recinto Sur St., San Juan, Porto Rico. President : Dennis Powelson.

Chicago and Southern Air Lines, Inc., Municipal Airport, Memphis, 2, Tenn. President : Carleton Putnam.

Colonial Airlines, New York Municipal Airport, Jackson Heights, Long Island, N.Y. President : Sigmund Janas.

Continental Air Lines, Inc., Municipal Airport, Denver 7, Colo. President : Robert F. Six.

Delta Air Corporation, Municipal Airport, Atlanta, Ga. President : C. E. Faulk.

Eastern Air Lines, Inc., 10, Rockefeller Plaza, New York 20, N.Y. President : E. V. Rickenbacker.

Essair Lines, 3300, Love Field Drive, Dallas 9, Texas. President: W. F. Long.

Hawaiian Airlines, Ltd., 851, Fort Street, Honolulu, Hawaii. President and General Manager : Stanley C. Kennedy.

Inland Air Lines, Inc., 6331, Hollywood Boulevard, Los Angeles 28, Cal. President : William A. Coulter.

Mid-Continent Air Lines, Inc., Waltower Building, Kansas City 6, Mo. President : J. W. Miller.

National Airlines, Inc., Municipal Airport, Jacksonville, Fla. President : G. T. Baker.

Northeast Airlines, Inc., Commonwealth Airport, Boston 28, Mass. President : Paul F. Collins.

Northwest Airlines, Inc., 1885, University Avenue, St. Paul, Minn. President : Croil Hunter.

Pan American World Airways, 135, East 42nd Street, New York 17, N.Y. President : Mr. Juan T. Trippe.

Pan American World Airways is divided into the following operating divisions :—

PACIFIC—ALASKA DIVISION.
LATIN AMERICAN DIVISION.
ATLANTIC DIVISION.
AFRICA—ORIENT DIVISION.

The following companies are subsidiaries of Pan American World Airways :—

AEROVIAS NACIONALES DE COLOMBIA, S.A. (COLOMBIA).
URABA MEDELLIN AND CENTRAL AIRWAYS, INC. (COLOMBIA).
CIA. MEXICANA DE AVIACON, S.A. (MEXICO).
CIA. CUBANA DE AVIACION, S.A. (CUBA).
PANAIR DO BRAZIL, S.A. (BRAZIL).

The following companies are associated with Pan American World Airways :—

PAN AMERICAN-GRACE AIRWAYS, INC.
CHINA NATIONAL AVIATION CORPORATION (CHINA).

For details of the activities of the foreign companies controlled by or subsidiary to Pan American World Airways, see under the countries concerned.

Pan American-Grace Airways, Inc. (Panagra), 135, East 42nd Street 17, New York City, N.Y. President : Harold J. Roig.

Pennsylvania Central Airlines Corpn., Washington National Airport, Washington 25, D.C. President : C. B. Monro.

Transcontinental and Western Air, Inc., 101, West 11th Street, Kansas City 6, Mo. President : Jack Frye.

United Air Lines, Inc., 5959, South Cicero Avenue, Chicago, 28, Ill. President : W. A. Patterson.

Western Air Lines, Lockheed Air Terminal, Burbank, California. President : W. A. Coulter.

AIRPORTS OF ENTRY

On October 30, 1943, there were 39 airports and seaplane bases designated as airports of entry through which aircraft arriving in the United States may clear customs and immigration.

Airports of entry are designated by the Treasury Department after consultation with representatives of other interested Federal agencies and due consideration as to the necessity for such designation. Some are designated without time limit, while others are given temporary designation for the period of one year, as shown in the table below :—

Without Time Limit

Location	Name	Location	Name
Akron, Ohio	Municipal Airport	Miami, Fla.	Dinner Key Seaplane Base
Albany, N.Y.	Municipal Field	Nogales, Ariz.	Nogales International Airport
Brownsville, Tex.	Municipal Airport	Ogdensburg, N.Y.	Ogdensburg Harbor Seaplane Base
Buffalo, N.Y.	Municipal Airport	Pembina, N. Dak.	C.A.A. Intermediate Field
Burlington, Vt.	Burlington Municipal Airport	Port Townsend, Wash.	Fort Townsend Air Field, Army
Caribou, Maine	Caribou Municipal Airport	Put-in-Bay, Ohio	Put-in-Bay Airport
Cleveland, Ohio	Cleveland Municipal Airport	Rochester, N.Y.	Rochester Municipal Airport
Detroit, Mich.	Detroit City Airport	Romulus, Mich.	Romulus Army Air Field
Detroit, Mich.	Ford Airport	Rouses Point, N.Y.	Rouses Point Seaplane Base
Douglas, Ariz.	Douglas International Airport	San Diego, Calif.	Lindbergh Field
Duluth, Minn.	Williamson-Johnson Airport	Seattle, Wash.	Boeing Field, Army
Duluth, Minn.	Duluth Boat Club Seaplane Base	Seattle, Wash.	Lake Union
Eagle Pass, Tex.	Eagle Pass Army Air Field	Swanton, Vt.	Missisquoi Airport
El Paso, Tex.	El Paso Municipal Airport (Ed Anderson Field)	West Palm Beach	Shonnard Seaplane Base (Currie Common Park)
Key West, Fla.	Meacham Outlying Field, Navy		
Miami, Fla.	Miami Army Air Field (Pan American-36th St. Airport)		

Temporary (1 Year)

Location	Name	Date designated
Havre, Mont.	Havre City County Airport	June 2, 1944
Miami, Fla.	Chalks Flying Seaplane Base	Sept. 17, 1944
Ogdensburg, N.Y.	Ogdensburg Municipal Airport	Dec. 10, 1944
Sandusky, Ohio	John G. Hinde Airport	June 1, 1944
Presque Isle, Maine	Presque Isle Army Air Field	Feb. 20, 1945
Watertown, N.Y.	Watertown Municipal Airport	June 2, 1944
Spoken, Wash.	Felts Field	Oct. 1, 1944

OPERATIONS FOR 1944 AS COMPARED WITH 1943

Operator	Revenue Miles Flown Jan./Dec.		Revenue Passengers carried (unduplicated) Jan./Dec.		Revenue Passengers Miles Flown Jan./Dec.	
	1944	1943	1944	1943	1944	1943
All American Aviation, Inc.	1,212,089	1,029,751	0	0	0	0
American Airlines, Inc.	34,582,820	26,397,687	951,269	788,990	572,094,112	435,913,741
Braniff Airways, Inc.	5,412,785	4,057,199	225,007	154,054	94,965,133	66,520,573
Chicago and Southern Air Lines, Inc. ..	2,882,601	2,179,412	104,906	82,017	49,242,103	35,293,185
Continental Air Lines, Inc.	2,371,493	1,543,375	66,808	46,728	23,823,378	14,873,461
Delta Air Corporation	3,499,726	2,339,581	164,257	110,334	65,745,996	43,361,264
Eastern Air Lines, Inc.	17,229,141	13,210,748	487,987	374,419	269,298,050	215,352,713
Inland Air Lines, Inc.	1,229,119	850,449	24,068	12,440	7,610,081	4,011,549
Mid-Continent Airlines, Inc.	2,248,892	1,494,549	74,145	38,439	21,312,458	10,775,481
National Airlines, Inc.	3,363,894	1,923,697	112,756	65,479	40,337,997	23,036,901
Northeast Airlines, Inc.	1,023,104	726,941	53,766	36,263	12,847,261	9,091,388
Northwest Airlines, Inc.	7,405,477	4,475,129	182,528	93,494	120,475,305	63,787,683
Pennsylvania-Central Airlines Corp. ..	5,313,559	3,097,469	413,264	235,196	90,119,936	52,312,234
Transcontinental and Western Air, Inc. ..	21,599,536	16,263,234	393,494	322,697	347,841,327	242,003,432
United Air Lines, Inc.	29,666,110	21,955,194	539,250	430,444	456,514,989	357,196,623
Western Air Lines, Inc.	3,194,491	2,057,028	121,199	75,830	57,342,927	32,589,240
Total	142,234,837	103,601,443	3,914,704	2,866,824	2,229,571,053	1,606,119,468
Index (1943 = 100)	137.29	100.00	136.55	100.00	138.82	100.00
Colonial Airlines, Inc.	1,056,116	691,712	56,032	37,124	17,387,268	11,021,946
Hawaiian Airlines, Ltd.	949,588	909,800	110,242	107,945	15,823,488	15,322,772
Grand Total	144,240,541	105,202,955	4,080,978	3,011,893	2,262,781,809	1,632,464.186
Index (1943 = 100)	137.11	100.00	135.50	100.00	138.61	10,000

Operator	Express carried (pounds) Jan./Dec.		Express pound/miles flown Jan./Dec.		Passenger seat/miles flown Jan./Dec.		Revenue Passenger Load Factor (per cent) Jan./Dec.	
	1943	1943	1944	1943	1944	1943	1944	1943
All American Aviation, Inc. ..	141,377	150,058	21,671,848	20,351,733	0	0	—	—
American Airlines, Inc. ..	23,018,583	21,058,223	10,767,510,676	9,764,229,681	636,211,268	494,320,808	89.92	88.18
Braniff Airways, Inc. ..	1,277,510	1,393,250	638,834,144	703,613,330	106,290,451	72,503,860	89.34	91.75
Chicago & Southern Air Lines, Inc.	1,108,504	859,472	461,043,926	373,296,563	59,653,713	42,057,337	82.55	83.92
Continental Air Lines, Inc. ..	205,854	114,898	82,525,202	40,258,838	27,220,273	17,235,442	87.52	86.30
Delta Air Corporation	953,486	613,972	351,923,300	236,055,752	72,472,175	48,770,186	90.72	88.91
Eastern Air Lines, Inc.	5,888,884	4,519,080	3,492,148,286	2,760,485,818	312,322,409	246,616,267	—	87.32
Inland Air Lines, Inc.	56,176	25,832	11,565,861	5,891,744	11,135,230	6,083,895	68.34	65.94
Mid-Continent Airlines, Inc. ..	257,540	177,929	71,064,191	43,360,732	27,454,494	17,263,216	77.63	62.42
National Airlines, Inc. ..	409,163	343,578	143,351,583	101,817,131	46,028,057	26,701,876	87.64	86.27
Northeast Airlines, Inc. ..	137,199	114,810	26,664,823	23,226,246	21,617,222	15,258,008	59.43	59.58
Northwest Airlines, Inc. ..	2,306,500	1,554,732	1,243,279,753	1,000,534,952	142,509,826	76,038,052	84.54	83.89
Pennsylvania-Central Airlines Corp.	4,889,270	4,257,938	931,700,911	790,484,269	110,140,413	64,420,997	81.82	81.20
Transcontinental & Western Air, Inc.	13,475,633	10,749,067	7,066,035,739	5,997,975,366	379,534,508	271,236,512	91.65	89.22
United Air Lines, Inc. ..	10,895,353	10,553,461	8,445,706,813	7,931,779,115	475,613,300	387,844,653	95.98	92.10
Western Air Lines, Inc. ..	895,805	957,291	433,031,724	442,487,901	64,690,168	38,498,693	87.29	84.65
Total	65,916,837	57,543,591	34,188,058,780	30,235,849,171	2,492,893,507	1,824,849,802	89.40	88.01
Index (1943 = 100)	114.55	100.00	113.07	100.00	136.66	100.00	101.58	100.00
Colonial Airlines, Inc. ..	254,758	216,205	78,880,820	63,113,201	22,036,052	13,720,993	78.90	80.33
Hawaiian Airlines, Ltd. ..	7,269,374	6,064,801	1,123,017,542	958,710,705	16,852,632	16,367,528	93.89	93.62
Grand Total ..	73,440,969	63,824,597	35,389,957,142	31,257,673,077	2,531,782,191	1,854,938,323	89.34	88.01
Index (1943 = 100) ..	115.07	100.00	113.22	100.00	136.54	100.00	101.51	100.00

	January	February	March	April	May	June
Passengers carried (unduplicated) total revenue and non-revenue						
16 domestic airlines	242,683	221,011	251,445	272,273	311,829	326,878
Total airlines	255,001	231,809	262,347	283,899	324,275	340,961
Passenger miles flown (total revenue and non-revenue)						
16 domestic airlines	141,474,106	125,088,611	142,834,165	155,159,351	181,038,023	193,288,705
Total airlines	143,727,253	127,107,076	144,884,424	157,414,978	183,563,374	196,130,812

	July	August	September	October	November	December
Passengers carried (unduplicated) total revenue and non-revenue						
16 domestic airlines	371,972	400,904	394,491	420,839	388,749	364,554
Total airlines	387,674	419,838	409,868	436,934	402,995	379,455
Passenger miles flown (total revenue and non-revenue)						
16 domestic airlines	211,703,804	227,350,700	225,471,943	239,022,033	217,338,262	204,512,740
Total airlines	214,800,861	231,262,843	228,763,362	242,469,884	220,202,530	207,454,248

TOTAL : Passengers carried—16 domestic airlines—3,967,628.   Total airlines : 4,135,056.

TOTAL : Passenger miles flown—16 domestic airlines—2,264,282,443.   Total airlines : 2,297,781,645.

U.S. AIR MAIL SERVICES as at January 1, 1945
Domestic Routes

Air Mail Route No.	Route	Carrier	Miles
1	New York—San Francisco—Seattle	United Air Lines, Inc.	4630
2	New York—Kansas City—Los Angeles	Transcontinental & Western Air, Inc.	2760
3	Chicago—Seattle	Northwest Airlines, Inc.	2490
4	Dallas—Los Angeles ; Oklahoma City—El Paso	American Airlines, Inc.	2057
5	Boston—New York—New Orleans—Houston—Brownsville	Eastern Air Lines, Inc.	2538
6	Boston and Detroit to Miami	Eastern Air Lines, Inc.	2128
7	Boston—Cleveland ; New York—Chicago	American Airlines, Inc.	1472
8	Chicago—St. Louis—New Orleans	Chicago and Southern Air Lines, Inc.	874
9	Chicago—Kansas City—Dallas	Braniff Airways, Inc.	947
10	Chicago—Atlanta—Jacksonville	Eastern Air Lines, Inc.	922
11	Seattle—San Francisco—Los Angeles—San Diego	United Air Lines, Inc.	1544
13	Salt Lake—Los Angeles—San Diego	Western Air Lines, Inc.	799
14	Norfolk—Washington—Cleveland—Detroit	Pennsylvania-Central Airlines Corp.	570
15	Amarillo to Dallas, Memphis and Denver ; Dallas to Galveston—Brownsville	Braniff Airways, Inc.	2248
17	Cheyenne—Denver	United Air Lines, Inc.	96
18	Boston—New York	American Airlines, Inc.	341
19	Salt Lake—Butte—Great Falls	Western Air Lines, Inc.	489
22	Cleveland—Chincinnati—Nashville	American Airlines, Inc.	510
23	New York—Ft. Worth ; Nashville—Oklahoma City	American Air Lines, Inc.	2107
24	Charleston—Augusta—Savannah—Atlanta—Ft. Worth	Delta Air Corp.	1490
25	Washington—Cincinnati—Chicago	American Airlines, Inc.	745
26	Minneapolis—Huron—Omaha—Tulsa—New Orleans	Mid-Continent Airlines, Inc.	1825
27	New York—Burlington ; New York—Presque Isle (Burlington—Montreal and Bangor—Moncton 27-F)	Northeast Airlines	928
		Northeast Airlines	296
28	Great Falls—Billings—Cheyenne—Denver	Western Air Lines, Inc.	669
29	Denver—Albuquerque—El Paso—San Antonio	Continental Airlines, Inc.	1454
30	Chicago—St. Louis—Ft. Worth	American Airlines, Inc.	951
31	New York—Key West via Jacksonville and Miami	National Airlines, Inc.	1513
32	Detroit—Grand Rapids—Chicago—Milwaukee	Pennsylvania—Central Airlines Corp.	407
33	Honolulu—Hilo—Port Allen—Barking Sands Airport	Hawaiian Airways, Ltd.	351
34	Washington—Harrisburg—Buffalo	Pennsylvania—Central Airlines Corp.	376
35	Cheyenne—Pierre—Huron	Inland Air Lines	558
36	Dayton—Chicago	Transcontinental & Western Air, Inc.	243
37	Winslow—Boulder City—Las Vegas—San Francisco	Transcontinental & Western Air, Inc.	855
38	Phoenix—Las Vegas (suspended)	Transcontinental & Western Air, Inc.	277
39	Jacksonville—Tallahassee—New Orleans	National Airlines, Inc.	519
40	Atlanta—Tallahassee—Tampa—Miami	Eastern Air Lines	632
	Memphis and Nashville—Tallahassee	Eastern Air Lines	657
43	Tulsa—Wichita—Pueblo	Continental Air Lines, Inc.	544
44	Kansas City, Chicago—Pittsburgh—New York	Transcontinental & Western Air, Inc.	1552
45	Minneapolis—Duluth	Northwest Airlines, Inc.	147
46	Pittsburgh, Pa.—Buffalo, N.Y.	Pennsylvania-Central Airlines	215
47	Washington and Nashville—St. Louis	Eastern Airlines, Inc.	875
48	Minneapolis—St. Louis	Mid-Continent Airlines, Inc.	523
	Des Moines—Kansas City	Mid-Continent Airlines, Inc.	174
49A	Pittsburgh—Huntington via Elkins and Charleston	All American Aviation, Inc.	333
49B	Pittsburgh, Pa.—Huntington, W. Va., via Parkersburg, W. Va.	All American Aviation, Inc.	338
49D	Pittsburgh—Jamestown	All American Aviation, Inc.	178
49E	Pittsburgh—Williamsport	All American Aviation, Inc.	202
49F	Pittsburgh—Harrisburg—Philadelphia, Pa.	All American Aviation, Inc.	381
50	Houston—Corpus Christi—Houston—San Antonio—Laredo—Nuevo Laredo, Mex.	Braniff Airways	565
51	Norfolk, Va.—Knoxville, Tenn.	Pennsylvania—Central Airlines	500
52	Lethbridge—Great Falls	Western Air Lines, Inc.	163
53	Detroit—Memphis—Houston	Chicago & Southern Airlines	1182
54	Chicago via Cincinnati and Atlanta to Miami	Delta Air Corps.	1468
55	New York—Birmingham via Pittsburgh	Pennsylvania—Central Airlines	958
56	Buffalo—Toronto	American Airlines	69
57	Seattle—Vancouver	United Air Lines, Inc.	128
58	Detroit—St. Louis	Transcontinental & Western Air, Inc.	563
59	San Juan—Mayaguez and Christiansted	Caribbean-Atlantic Airlines, Inc.	206
60	Kansas City—Denver	Continental Air Lines, Inc.	592
61	Washington—Dayton	Transcontinental & Western Air, Inc.	393
62	Washington—Toledo	United Air Lines, Inc.	389
63	Los Angeles—San Francisco	Western Air Lines, Inc.	327
64	Houston—Amarillo	Essair, Inc.	683
66	Cleveland—Boston	United Air Lines, Inc.	570
67	Pittsburgh—Boston	Transcontinental & Western Air, Inc.	504
69	Minneapolis—St. Paul—New York	Northwest Airlines, Inc.	1035

ALASKA

ADMINISTRATION

Civil aviation in Alaska is administered by the U.S. Civil Aeronautics Authority through a Regional Office (Eighth Region) with headquarters in Anchorage.

TRANSPORT COMPANIES

In January, 1943, the Civil Aeronautics Board granted certificates to 21 operators, namely :—Alaska Coastal Airlines, Bristol Bay Air Service, Lon Brennan Air Service, Nat Browne Flying Service, Christensen Air Service, Cordova Air Service, Dillingham Air Service, Jim Dodson Air Service, Ellis Air Transport, Ferguson Airways, Harold Gillam, Lavery Airways, Munz Air Service, Northern Cross, Peck & Rice Airways, Petersburg Air Service, Ray Petersen Flying Service, Pollack Flying Service, Alaska Airlines, Wien Alaska Airlines and Woodley Airways.

Each carrier is privileged to make charter trips to any point in Alaska. The Board also for the first time authorised an "irregular route service" in which areas of operation are defined but in which scheduled service by the irregular route carriers are not permitted if they conflict with the regular route of another carrier.

A separate order issued two certificates to Pan American Airways authorising service between Fairbanks and Nome for persons, property and mail, and between Fairbanks and Bethel for persons and property only.

Alaska Airlines. Offices : Anchorage, Alaska. President : W. N. Cuddy.
Scheduled Routes :—
Anchorage—Fairbanks. Daily.
Fairbanks—Lake Minchumina—McGrath. Twice weekly.
Anchorage—McGrath—Moses Point—Nome. Twice weekly. (Moses Point Sunday only.)
Anchorage—Kenai—Homer. Thrice weekly.
Anchorage—Homer—Kodiak. Four times weekly.
Anchorage—Valdez. Twice weekly.
Anchorage—McGrath. Five times weekly.
Anchorage—McGrath—Flat—Aniak—Bethel. Weekly.
Bethel—Nyac—Flat—McGrath—Anchorage. Weekly.
Fairbanks—Galena—Moses Point—Nome. Weekly.
Anchorage—Cordova—Yakutat—Juneau. Thrice weekly.
Anchorage — Iliamna — Naknek Base — Naknek — Dillingham. Twice weekly.

Anchorage—Seward. Thrice weekly.
In addition frequent services are operated as follow :—
From Bethel to :—Platinum, Mumtrak, Eek, Aklak, Tuluksak, Nunivak Island, Quinhagak, Nelson Island, Crooked Creek, Sleitmute, Napiamute.
From McGrath to :—Ophir, Takotna, Folger, Candle, Medfra, Moore Creek, Cripple Landing, Farewell Lake, Colorado.
From Naknek to :—Kvichak River Points, Koggiung, Dilling, ham, Kanakanak, Ekuk, Clark's Points, Egegik, Pilot Point, Ugashik, Tanalian Point.
From Nome to :—Golovin, Teller, Council Akularak, Solomon, Bluff, White Mountain, Koyuk, Bonanza, Shaktoolik, Egasik, St. Michael.

Pan American World Airways, Pacific-Alaska Division.
Seattle—Juneau—Whitehorse—Fairbanks. Daily with Burwash Landing and Tanacross as flag stops.
Fairbanks—Nome. Three times weekly, with Galena, Tanana and Moses Point as flag stops.
Fairbanks—McGrath—Bethel. Weekly with Lake Minchumina, Flat and Aniak as flag stops.

HAWAIIAN ISLANDS

(Territory of Hawaii)

ADMINISTRATION

Civil Aviation in the Hawaiian Islands is administered by the U.S. Civil Aeronautics Authority, through a Regional office (Ninth Region) with headquarters in Honolulu, T.H.

TRANSPORT COMPANIES

Hawaiian Airlines, Ltd., Inter-Island Building, Honolulu and Rodgers Airport, Honolulu. President: S. C. Kennedy.

This Company is a subsidiary of the Inter-Island Steam Navigation Co., Ltd.

Due to the difficulties of surface transport the Company has entered into a contract with the Post Office Department to carry all classes of regular mail between Honolulu and Hoolehua, operating three round services weekly. This is known as Air Mail Route No. 33.

The Company has offices at 5225, Wilshire Boulevard, Los Angeles, with Vice-President Clarence M. Belinn in charge, as an aid in the expansion of operations.

Pan American World Airways

Pan American World Airways operates a daily service between San Francisco and Honolulu.

AERODROMES

The principle airport in the Hawaiian Islands is the Rodger's Airport at HONOLULU, on the island of Oahu. The marine customs base, used by Pan American Airways, is in Pearl Harbour, HONOLULU. Other aerodromes are situated at PORT ALLEN (Kauai), HILO (Hawaii) and on the islands of MOLOKAI, LANAI, MAUI and HAWAII.

RADIO STATIONS

Radio stations are maintained at Honolulu and on the islands of Hawaii and Maui. Radio beacon stations have been established at Honolulu and on the islands of Hawaii, Kauai and Maui.

URUGUAY

(The Republic of Uruguay—Republica Oriental del Uruguay)

ADMINISTRATION

Civil Aviation is controlled by the Ministry of National Defence and is administered by the Direccion de Aeronáutica Civil. Address: 18 de Julio 2137, Montevideo. Director: Sr. José M. Peña.

An Air Convention exists between the Uruguayan and Argentine Governments regulating the traffic between the two capitals, and the Postal Authorities of the two countries have a close system of co-operation.

The close collaboration between both Governments has had a direct influence on airline transportation, and local services between both countries are operating efficiently in pool.

FLYING CLUBS

Aero-Club del Uruguay, Paysandú 896, Montevideo. Aerodrome: Melilla. President: Sr. Luis A. Castagnola. Affiliated to the *Fédération Aéronautique Internationale* (F.A.I.) and to the *Comision Nacional de Educacion Fisica*.

The Aero Club uses Taylor, Zlin and Aeronca aircraft for training and instruction purposes.

Centro de Aeronautica del Uruguay, Avenida 18 de Julio 968, Montevideo. President: Sr. Leonardo Tuso. Aerodrome: Melilla. Uses Stinson 105 aircraft.

Aero Club de Flores. President: Sr. Arturo Berhouet. Aerodrome: "Carlos Antunez Castellanos." The Club owns a hangar. Aircraft: One Rearwin, one Piper Cub and one Taylorcraft.

Aero Club Mercedes. President: Dr. Salvador Miláns. The Club owns an aerodrome with hangar and uses one Aeronca and one Taylorcraft monoplane.

Aero Club Paysandú. President: Sr. Pedro Harguindegaray. The Club owns an aerodrome with hangar and uses a Taylorcraft monoplane.

Colonia Aero Club. President: Sr. Antonio Ferrando. The Club owns an aerodrome with hangar and uses two Taylorcraft aeroplanes.

Aero Club de Young (Department of Rio Negro). President: Sr. Raymond G. de Boismenu. Owns two Piper "Cub" monoplanes.

Centro de Aviación Civil Salto. President: Sr. Ing. Fernando Silveira Riet.

Possesses an aerodrome with hangar at Salto. Aircraft used: Piper "Cub."

Aero Club de Durazno. The Club owns an aerodrome and hangar and a Taylorcraft monoplane for instruction purposes.

Aero Club Maragato (Department of San José). President: Sr. Ernesto R. Sena. Aircraft used: Piper "Cub."

Centro de Aviación Civil de Florida. President: Sr. José Bide. Aircraft used: Taylorcraft monoplane.

Aero Club de Minas (Department of Lavalleja). President: Sr. Jorge Lombardi. Aircraft used: Taylorcraft monoplane.

Aero Club de Canelones. President: Sr. Juan T. Gonzalez.

Aero Club de Melo (Department Cerro Largo). President: Sr. Olmos Muñoz. Aircraft used: Taylorcraft monoplane.

TRANSPORT COMPANIES

Primeras Lineas Uruguayas de Navegación Aerea S.A. (PLUNA), Avenida 18 de Julio 1000, Montevideo.

This private but Government-subsidised company is being converted in a half private half State-owned organization. The matter has given cause for very long and involved discussions in Parliament and for this reason all services have been suspended for over a year. As soon as possible the old routes will be resumed.

Compañia Aeronautica Uruguaya S.A. (CAUSA), 25 de Mayo 418, Montevideo.

President: Sr. Luis J. Superbielle. Managing Director: Colonel Don Tydeo Larre Borges.

Equipment consists of two Junkers Ju 52 seaplanes which have been arranged to carry 28 passengers.

The routes flown are:—

Daily service to and from Buenos Aires.
Daily service to and from Colonia and Buenos Aires.

Viaçao Aérea Riograndense (Varig).

This Brazilian company operates a twice weekly service between Porto Alegre (Brazil) and Montevideo, with an intermediate landing at Yaguarón.

Pan American Airways System.

On June 16, 1944, Pan American Airways re-established its services to and from Montevideo which are on six days out of the week. This line is using the Melilla Airport.

The Servicios Aereos Cruzeiro do Sul (formerly Condor Syndicate) of Brazil, were planning to resume it service in Uruguay which—as was the case with Pan American Airways—were discontinued some years ago owing to lack of landing facilities.

CIVIL AERODROMES

The CARRASCO Airport, which is being built at a cost of U.S. $5,000,000 and as fast as possible, will be one of the best and most complete in South America and was to have been in operation in 1945. The new airport lies 18 kms. from the centre of the city.

ARTIGAS. Lat. 30°25′S. Long. 56°30′W. 4 kms. W.N.W. of town. Alt. 122 m. Dimensions 1,400 × 600 m.

CARMELO. Lat. 33°59′S. Long. 58°20′W. 3 kms. N. of town. Alt. 10 m. Dimensions 440 × 413 m.

COLONIA. Lat. 34°24′S. Long. 57°48′W. 8½ km. E. of city. Alt. 19 m. Runways W.N.W./E.S.E. 700 m., N./S. 600 m.

DURAZNO. Lat. 33°16′S. Long. 56°17′W. 4½ kms. N.E. of city. Alt. 20 m. Runways N.W./S.E. 1,000 m., N.E./S.W. 800 m. Military aerodrome.

FLORIDA. Lat. 33°55′S. Long. 56°13′W. 4 kms. E.N.E. of city. Alt. 60 m. Runways N./S. 600 m., E.N.E./W.S.W. 450 m.

MELO. Lat. 32°23′S. Long. 54°14′W. N.W. of city. Alt. 97 m. Dimensions 1,049 × 840 × 720 m.

MERCEDES. Lat. 33°15′S. Long. 58°05′W. 6 kms. W. of city. Alt. 15 m. Dimensions 1,100 × 1,000 × 750 m.

MINAS DE CORRALES. Lat. 31°25′S. Long. 55°31′W. 7½ kms. N.N.E. of town. Alt. 150 m. Dimensions 740 × 270 × 560 × 440 m.

MONTEVIDEO ("CAP. BOIZO LANZA"). Lat. 34°49′S. Long. 56°10′W. 12 kms. N.E. of city. Alt. 48 m. Dimensions 841 × 580 × 447 m. Military aerodrome.

MONTEVIDEO (MULILLA). Lat. 34°47′S. Long. 56°17′W. 16 kms. N.W. of city. Alt. 48.5 m. Dimensions 715 × 574 m. Equipped for night flying.

PANDO. Lat. 34°42′S. Long. 55°58′W. 4 kms. S. of town. Alt. 25 m. Runways E./W. 1,000 m., N./S. 800 m. Military aerodrome. Equipped for night landing.

PASO DE LOS TOROS. Lat. 32°49′S. Long. 56°25′W. 9 kms. N.E. of town. Alt. 92 m. Dimensions 1,300 × 800 × 900 m.

PAYSANDU. Lat. 32°22′S. Long. 58°02′W. 6 kms. S.E. of city. Alt. 45 m. Runways E./W. 1,500 m., N./S. 900 m.

PUNTA DEL ESTE. Lat. 34°56′S. Long. 54°55′W. 7 kms. S.E. of town. Alt. 36 m. Dimensions 800 × 600 m.

RIO BRANCO. Lat. 32°36′S. Long. 53°23′W. 5 kms. S.W. of town. Alt. 3 m. Dimensions 800 × 800 m.

RIVERA. Lat. 30°59′S. Long. 55°31′W. 7½ kms. S.E. of city. Alt. 200 m. Runways N./S. 500 m., N.W./S.E. 700 m., E./W. 680 m.

ROCHA. Lat. 34°29′S. Long. 54°15′W. 6 kms. E. of city. Alt. 20 m. Runways N.E./S.W. 800 m., N.W./S.E. 320 m.

SALTO. Lat. 31°26′S. Long. 57°56′W. 5 kms. S.S.W. of city. Alt. 45 m. Runways N.W./S.E. 1,000 m., E./W. 600 m.

SAN JOSE. Lat. 34°20′S. Long. 56°45′W. 3 kms. W. of city. Alt. 60 m. Dimensions 1,000 × 1,000 m.

TACUAREMBO. Lat. 31°47′S. Long. 55°56′W. 14 kms. S.S.W. of city. Alt. 178 m. Dimensions 1,000 × 700 m.

TREINTA Y TRES. Lat. 33°15′S. Long. 54°20′W. 7½ kms. N.E. of city. Alt. 31 m. Runways N./S. 800 m., E./W. 800 m.

TRINIDAD. Lat. 33°29′S. Long. 56°53′W. 1½ kms. N. of city. Alt. 88 m. E./W. 1,000 m., N./S. 600 m.

YOUNG. W. side of town. Dimensions 800 × 400 m.

THE MELILLA AIRPORT, Montevideo. The most important in the country, is equipped for night flying. It has been enlarged considerably and improvements are near completion on the main runway, running N./S., which will be about 1,300 m. long. It is used by Pan American Airways, Varig, Pluna, N.A.T.S (U.S. Navy Air Transport Service); also by the Aero Club del Uruguay and Centro de Aeronáutica del Uruguay. It is expected that the aircraft of the Brazilian airline, Servicios Aereos, Cruzeiro do Sul will also make their landings there when services are resumed. It is the centre of all the Montevideo aeronautical sporting activities.

MILITARY AERODROMES

"CAPITAN BOISO LANZA" (Montevideo). Lat. 34°48′S. Long. 56°11′w. Dimensions: 840 × 580 × 335 × 446 × 293 m.

"GENERAL ARTIGAS" (Pando). Lat. 34°48′S. Long. 55°58, W. Runways 1,100, 1,060, 1,500 and 1,100 m.

VENEZUELA

(United States of Venezuela—Estados Unidos de Venezuela)

ADMINISTRATION

Civil Aviation in Venezuela is controlled by the Ministerio de Guerra y Marina, Direccion de Aviacion, Esquina de Miraflores, Caracas. Director-General of Aviation: Colonel Luis Bruzual Bermudez.

PUBLICATION

Alas. Monthly Magazine. Editor: Pedro Perez Dupouy Apartado 1621, Caracas.

AIR TRANSPORT COMPANIES

Linea Aeropostal Venezolana, Carmelitas a Altagracia, Caracas. Director: Colonel Jose E. Becerra.

All pilots of L.A.V. receive their initial training in the Government School, after which they serve a term with the Army Air Force before being assigned to a position with the company.

Maintenance of the Lockheed aircraft used by the Company is now all performed at the Maracay base, including complete overhaul, instead of in the U.S.A. as previously.

L.A.V. statistics for 1942 (1941 in brackets) were as follows:—

Passengers carried	..	23,371	(16,133)
Flights	..	8,309	(7,072)
Mail carried (lbs.)	..	100,000	
Cargo carried (lbs.)	..	1,000,000	
Net profit approx.	..	$300,000	($221,000)

Routes:—

Maiquetiá — Barcelona — Cumaná — Porlamar — Carúpano—Güiria—Maturín. Thrice weekly.
Maiquetiá—Barcelona — Maturín — Ciudad Bolívar — San Félix—Guasipati—Tumeremo — Luepa — Santa Elena—Tumeremo. Weekly.
Maiquetiá — Barcelona — Cumaná — Maturín — Ciudad Bolívar — Guasipati — Tumeremo — Luepa — Santa Elena—Tumeremo. Weekly.
Maiquetiá — Barcelona — Maturín — Ciudad Bolívar — Guasipati — Tumeremo — Luepa — Santa Elena — Tumeremo. Weekly.
Maiquetiá—Coro—Las Piedras—Maracaibo. Weekly.
Maiquetiá—Barquisimeto—Barinas — Guasdualito — Santo Domingo. Weekly.
Maiquetiá—San Fernando de Apure—Puerto Páez—Puerto Ayacucho. Weekly.
Maiquetiá—Coro—Maracaibo—Santo Domingo. Weekly.
Maiquetiá—Barquisimeto—Valera. Weekly.
Maiquetiá—Barquisimeto—Barinas—Bruzual—Guasdualito Santo Domingo. Weekly.
Maiquetiá—San Fernando—Puerto Páez—Puerto Ayacucho. Weekly.

The Company owns six Lockheed Electra, two Lockheed 14 and one Lockheed Lodestar.

One Howard monoplane is used specially for charter flying.

Aerovias Venezolanas S.A. (Avensa). Apartado 943, Caracas. President: H. L. Boulton. General Manager: C. D. Yaggy.

This company was originally formed to operate a freight-carrying service into the hinterland of Venezuela. More recently, it has been granted a licence to carry passengers and now operates the following scheduled passenger services:—

La Guiara—Ciudad Bolivar, via Barcelona, Anaco and San Tome. Five times weekly.

La Guiara—San Fernando de Apure, via Valencia and Calabozo. Twice weekly.

La Guiara—Cachipo, via Maturin. Four times weekly.

Pan American Airways, Inc., Principal a Santa Capilla, Caracas.

Routes :—

The "Mexico Clipper" daily service, stopping at Maracaibo, Coro, La Guiara, Barcelona and Maturin in each direction, connects at La Guiara with the "West Indies Venezuela Clipper," which operates thrice weekly from Miami.

Cia. Real Holandesa de Aviacion, K.L.M. (Royal Dutch Airlines). Monjas a San Francisco, Caracas.

Routes :—

Curaçao—Aruba—Maracaibo (242 miles). Return service thrice weekly.

Curaçao—La Guiara. Return service five times weekly.

Aircraft used :—Four Lockheed 14 airliners, two Fokker F-XVIII.

OTHER OPERATING COMPANIES

The Standard Oil Company of Venezuela, Sociedad a Traposos, Caracas.

This Company owns one Lockheed 12, one Lockheed "Electra" and one Stinson "Reliant." One of the Lockheeds flies to Maiquetiá once a week. The Stinson "Reliant" and one of the Lockheeds fly regularly three times a week between the oil fields.

Other Oil Companies operating aircraft for their field services are the Texas Company, the Socony-Vacuum Oil Co., Inc., the Shell Oil Company, the Gulf Oil Corporation and the Mene Grande Company.

FLYING SCHOOL

Escuela de Aviacion Civil, Maracay. Director : Captain Leopoldo Vivas González.

Aircraft :—Four Aeronca 65CA, three Piper "Cub" trainers, three Piper "Cub" Coupés, one Fairchild 24, three Fleet 10 and one Fleet 11.

FLYING CLUB

"Ala Venezolana," Escuadrilla Interamericana. Address : Apartado 1621, Mercaderes a Gorda 16, Caracas.

This Club was organized in March, 1941, to develop Civil Aviation in line with the corresponding U.S. Club under the auspices of the "Inter-American Escadrille" and in co-operation with the U.S. Government organization of Mr. Nelson Rockefeller.

AERODROMES

ALTAGRACIA. Lat. 9°51′N. Long. 66°18′W. Alt. 1,080 ft. 5 miles E. of town. Two paved runways 3,300 ft. and 3,000 ft.

ACARIGUA. Lat. 9°33′N. Long. 69°12′W. Alt. 820 ft. 2 miles W. of town. Size : 3,280 × 975 ft. No facilities.

BARQUISIMETO. Lat. 10°04′N. Long. 69°19′W. Alt. 1,715 ft. 1¾ miles W. of town. Size : 3,000 × 3,000 ft. All usable. Boundary marks. No facilities.

BARCELONA. Lat. 10°09′N. Long. 64°42′W. Alt. S.L. N. edge of town. Vee shaped. Runways 2,000 ft. long.

CARACAS. Lat. 10°30′N. Long. 66°56′W. Alt. 2,680 ft. S.W. edge of town. On race track. 1,800 × 550 ft. With runway 1,800 × 150 ft. Obstructions 50 ft. high each end.

CARAPITO (Cachipo). Lat. 9°57′N. Long. 63°10′W. Alt. 210 ft. 13 miles S.S.E. of town. 3 runways graded, oiled and well maintained :—N.E./S.W. 4,395 × 300 ft. E.N.E./W.S.W. 4,257 × 300 ft. N.W./S.E. 1,707 × 145 ft. Two hangars on N. side. Beacon (white) 6 r.p.m. on oil derrick at Quire Quire. Floodlight and boundary lights. W/T. call signs YVA6 and YV8CR. Operated by Standard Oil Co. of Venezuela.

CIUDAD BOLIVAR. Lat. 8°08′N. Long. 63°33′W. Alt. 185 ft. 1½ miles S.E. of town. Size : 3,960 × 3,960 ft. Hangar 75 ft. high N.W. side. Airport of entry.

CUMANA. Lat. 10°27′N. Long. 64°12′W. Alt. S.L. 1¼ miles S.W. of town. Size : 3,500 × 250 ft. Passenger building only.

CUMARIBO. Lat. 11°31′N. Long. 69°18′W. Alt. 100 ft. 2 miles N.E. of town. 2,000 × 2,500 ft. with paved runways N./S. 2,200 × 300 ft., E./W. 2,400 × 300 ft., N.W./S.E. 2,000 × 300 ft.

CORO. Lat. 11°26′N. Long 69°41′W. Alt. 65 ft. N.W. edge of town. 2 runways each 3,200 ft. Hangars. Airport of entry.

EL ROBLE (Anaco). Lat. 9°26′N. Long. 64°28′W. Alt. 738 ft. 43 miles S.S.E. of Barcelona. Graded runway E./W. 3,280 × 130 ft. W/T. call sign YV6CV. Operated by S. O. of Venezuela.

EL SOMBRERO. Lat. 9°23′N. Long. 67°04′W. Alt. 600 ft. 1 mile W. of town. Irregular shape with runway 2,100 ft. long. No facilities.

GUASDUALITO. Lat. 7°15′N. Long. 70°47′W. Alt. 430 ft. 2½ miles W.S.W. of village. Runway 2,500 ft.

GUIRIA. Lat. 10°35′N. Long. 62°18′W. Alt. 43 ft. ½ mile N. of town. Runs N.W./S.E. 3,000 × 500 ft. W/T. call sign YV7CA.

GUASIPATI. Lat. 7°25′N. Long. 61°50′W. Alt. 700 ft. 2 miles S.E. of village. Runway N./S. 3,000 × 150 ft. Rough.

LA POLAMA. Lat. 8°48′N. Long. 72°35′W. Alt. 30 ft. 3½ miles W.N.W. of town. Size : 2,250 × 600 ft.

LAS PIEDRAS. Lat. 11°42′N. Long. 70°12′W. Alt. 50 ft. 3,000 × 2,500 ft. with runway E./W. 3,000 × 150 ft.

LUEPA. Lat. 5°44′N. Long. 61°30′W. Alt. 4,250 ft. Runs E./W. 3,500 ft. × 200 ft. Boundary flags.

MATURIN. Lat. 9°45′N. Long. 63°11′W. Alt. 110 ft. E. side of town. Landing strips N.E./S.W. 2,500 ft., E./W. 1,500 ft. No facilities. Airport of entry for customs.

MARACAIBO (Grano de Oro). Lat. 10°40′N. Long. 71°39′W. Alt. 141 ft. 3 miles N.W. of town. 3 paved runways N./S. 3,727 ft., N.E./S.W. 2,943 ft., N.W./S.E. 2,986 ft. Large hangar. Repairs. W/T. call sign YVAI. Airport of entry.

MARACAY (Boca del Rio). Lat. 10°15′N. Long. 67°38′W. Alt 1,160 ft. 2 miles W. of town. Military and Commercial 3 runways N.N.E./S.S.W. 2,302 × 120 ft., E./W. 3,272 × 120 ft., N.W./S.E. 2,959 × 120 ft. Administration building, hangars, etc. Full repairs. W/T. call sign YVWH.

There is a seaplane base with concrete ramp and hangar on shore of Lake Valencia, ½ mile S. of airport. Taxi strip from airport to S. base. Airport of entry for customs.

MAIQUETIÁ. 1½ miles from town. 1,600 × 600 m. Paved runways.

PORLAMAR. Lat. 10°58′N. Long. 63°52′W. Alt. S.L. N. edge of town. 2 runways each 3,280 ft. Boundary marks. No facilities. Customs airport of entry.

PUERTO PAEZ (El Jobito). Lat. 6°11′N. Long. 67° 24′W. At confluence of Orinoco and Meta rivers. One runway 2,600 ft. Boundary marks.

SAN CARLOS. Lat. 9°39′N. Long. 68°33′W. Alt. 460. ft. E. edge of town. Square shape.

SAN FERNANDO. Lat. 7°52′N. Long. 62°27′ Alt. 230 ft. 1½ miles E. of town. 3,000 × 900 ft. with runway 2,500 ft. Airport of entry.

TEMBLADOR. Lat. 8°57′N. Long. 62°36′W. Alt. 105 ft. Vee shaped. Runways E.N.E./W.S.W. 3,275 × 325 ft. W.N.W./E.S.E. 3,275 × 325 ft. W/T. call sign YV8CC. Operated by S. O. of Venezuela.

PART C

ALL THE
WORLD'S AEROPLANES

(CORRECTED TO SEPTEMBER 1, 1945.)

THE ARGENTINE REPUBLIC

MILITARY AIRCRAFT FACTORY.

FABRICA MILITAR DE AVIONES.

CORDOBA.

Director : Major D. Juan I. San Martin.

The Fábrica Militar de Aviones, which was established at Cordoba on October 10, 1927, forms part of the Instituto Aerotecnico. At the outset the factory only built aeroplanes and aero-engines to various foreign designs under licence, but since 1932 it has built several aeroplanes of its own design.

The first designs were the Ae.C.1 three-seat cabin monoplane and the Ae.C.2 two-seat training monoplane. These were followed, in 1933, by the Ae.T.1, the first commercial aeroplane to be built in the Argentine.

IMPA.

COMPANIA INDUSTRIA METALÚRGICA & PLÁSTICA S.A.

HEAD OFFICE : BUENOS AIRES.

AIRCRAFT WORKS : QUILMES AIRPORT, BUENOS AIRES.

The Compania Industria Metalúrgica & Plástica S.A. was originally formed to take over the firm of Lieneu & Cia, formerly agents for the Fisk Tyre & Rubber Company and Argentine distributors for Chrysler automobiles. It manufactures aluminium, lead and plastic articles and has undertaken the manufacture of munitions for the Argentine Armed Forces.

TUCAN.

SOCIEDAD ANONIMA SFREDDO & PAOLINI.

HEAD OFFICE AND WORKS : M. IRIGOYEN 630, CASTELAR (BUENOS AIRES.)

This concern was originally formed in 1916 by Senores Jorge Sfreddo and Luis Paolini.

It was successful in tendering for the serial manufacture under licence of the "El Boyero" light cabin monoplane designed and built by the Military Aircraft Factory, but owing to the difficulty of obtaining the necessary materials and equipment it has been unable to proceed with its programme.

In has recently built to the designs of Ing. Alfredo Turbay, a light single-seat touring monoplane known as the Tucan T-1.

THE TUCAN T-1.

TYPE.—Single-seat Light monoplane for touring and aerobatics.
WINGS.—High-wing rigidly-braced monoplane. NACA 23012 wing section. Wing in two sections joined on the centre-line and carried above fuselage on a steel tube cabane. Vee bracing struts. Two spar wing structure with piano-wire drag bracing. Leading-edge covered with plywood, remainder with fabric. Slotted flaps inboard of ailerons. Built-in Handley Page wing slots in leading-edge forward of ailerons.
FUSELAGE.—Semi-monocoque structure of spruce and plywood.
TAIL UNIT.—Cantilever monoplane type. Fin built integrally with fuselage. Structure similar to wings.
LANDING GEAR.—Fixed cantilever type. Goodyear low-pressure wheels with brakes. Tail-wheel.
POWER PLANT.—One 65 h.p. Continental A65 four-cylinder horizontally opposed air-cooled engine driving a two-blade Sfreddo y Paolini wood airscrew. Fuel tank in fuselage.
ACCOMMODATION.—Enclosed cockpit aft of trailing-edge of wing. Sliding cockpit cover.
DIMENSIONS.—Span 7.22 m. (23 ft. 8 in.), Length 5.55 m. (18 ft. 2 in.), Height 1.90 m. (6 ft. 2½ in.), Wing area 7.20 sq. m. (77.5 sq. ft.).

During 1934 the Ae.C.3 two-seat light training monoplane and the Ae.M.O.1 two-seat military training monoplane were produced. A number of the former were supplied to several civil flying schools in the Argentine and twelve of the latter were delivered to the Army in July, 1934. All these types have been illustrated and described in previous issues of this Annual. Licences have been held for the manufacture of the Curtiss Hawk 75-O single-seat fighter monoplane and the Focke-Wulf Fw 44 two-seat training biplane.

The factory has also built the Wright Cyclone and the Siemens Sh 14 air-cooled radial engines, as well as metal and wooden airscrews and other equipment. Several sailplanes have also been built for the flying clubs.

In September, 1941, the Company started an aircraft department under the direction of Senor José Mario Sueiro, and in December, 1944, a new factory was opened on the Quilmes Airport.

The first aeroplane built by the Company was a light two-seat cabin monoplane known as the Impa RR-11 which made its first flight at the General Pacheco Airport, near Buenos Aires, on July 25, 1942.

A second prototype, the Impa Tu-Sa-O, made its first flight on April 17, 1943. A small series of this model was built for the

The two-seat light cabin monoplane known as the "El Boyero" was designed and built in 1939-40. The licence for the construction of this aeroplane was granted to the S. A. Sfreddo y Paolini but owing to the international situation it was impossible to obtain the necessary equipment and materials for this programme to proceed. The "El Boyero" has been illustrated and described in previous issues of this Annual.

In 1943 the Factory completed the I.Ae 22-D.L.55 two-seat Advanced Training monoplane which was fitted with the first nationally-designed aero-engine, the El Gaucho nine-cylinder radial. This aeroplane made its first flight on May 25, 1943. No other details are available for publication.

flying-club use but after a number of accidents the type was withdrawn from service.

The Company possesses the exclusive representation in the Argentine for the Continental Motors Corpn. but owing to the political situation it had been unable to import any engines up to the end of 1944.

In addition to development work on a number of projected prototypes the company has built a small quantity of primary training gliders.

The Tucan T-1 Single-seat Light Monoplane (65 h.p. Continental A65 engine).

WEIGHTS.—Weight empty 285 kg. (627 lbs.), Weight loaded (aerobatic factors) 400 kg. (880 lbs.), Maximum loaded weight 450 kg. (990 lbs.)
PERFORMANCE.—Maximum speed 205 km.h. (127.3 m.p.h.), Cruising speed 185 km.h. (115 m.p.h.), Landing speed (with flaps) 72 km.h. (44.7 m.p.h.), Service ceiling 4,200 m. (13,780 ft.), Absolute ceiling 4,700 m. (15,420 ft.), Range 1,100 km. (680 miles) or 6 hours.

BELGIUM

Hereafter follow the names and addresses of those firms which constituted the Belgian Aircraft Industry before the War Details of the activities of these companies have appeared in previous issues of this Annual.

AVIONS TIPSY, Gosselies.
CONSTRUCTIONS AÉRONAUTIQUES G. RENARD, Evère, near Brussels.
SOCIÉTÉ ANONYME BELGE "AVIONS FAIREY," Gosselies.
SOCIÉTÉ ANONYME BELGE DE CONSTRUCTIONS AÉRONAUTIQUES (SABCA), Evère, near Brussels.
SOCIÉTÉ D'ETUDES AÉRONAUTIQUES, Brussels.
J. STAMPE ET M. VERTONGEN, Deurne-Sud, Antwerp.

BRAZIL

CONSTRUCOES AERONAUTICAS S.A.

HEAD OFFICE : RIO DE JANEIRO.

WORKS : LAGÔA SANTA, MINAS GERAES.

President : Dr. Antonio Lartigau Seabra.

Manager : Dr. Edmond d'Oliviera.

In May, 1940, the Brazilian Government signed an agreement guaranteed by the Ministries of War and Marine, for the formation of an aircraft manufacturing company which has erected a factory on a site provided by the Government at Lagôa Santa, in the province of Minas Geraes.

The new firm has been given a concession to manufacture both military and civil aircraft and the Government undertakes to place orders to a predetermined value over a period of 15 years. The first military type to be built is the North American NA-16 (AT-6) advanced training monoplane.

Brazilian materials must be used as far as possible. During the first year of production the company must employ native Brazilians in at least 50 per cent. of the general, administrative and commercial management positions ; 30 per cent. in directional and technical services ; 75 per cent. in commercial and administrative work ; and 30 per cent. in shop work. These percentages will increase in succeeding years.

FABRICA BRASILIERA DE AVIÕES.

WORKS : ILHA DO VIANA, RIO DE JANEIRO.

This is the former Army air workshops. It builds training aeroplanes for the Brazilian Air Force. These have included the M-7 and M-9 two-seat primary training biplanes, designed by Colonel Antonio Muniz.

It is now engaged in the production under licence of a series of Fairchild M-62 (PT-19) two-seat primary training monoplanes for the Army Air Force.

FABRICA DO GALLĒAO.

WORKS : PONTO DO GALLĒAO, ILHA DO GOVERNADOR, RIO DE JANEIRO.

Director : Ten. Col. Av. Eng. Joelmir C. Araripe Macedo.

The Fabrica do Gallēao, the former naval air workshops, builds aircraft for the Brazilian Air Force. The establishment, in addition to its aircraft manufacturing facilities, includes a laboratory of mechanical research with physical and chemical test laboratories etc., an engine test department, an aircraft plywood plant with an electric drier for wood with a capacity of 20 cub. m., a wooden airscrew plant, etc. It has a covered area of over 30,000 sq. m., and employs about 1,500 hands.

It has built two series of Focke-Wulf aircraft, forty Fw 44 two-seat primary trainers and twenty-five Fw 58 twin-engined advanced training monoplanes.

It is now building the Fairchild M-62 (PT-19) primary training monoplane under a licence granted to the Brazilian Government by the Fairchild Engine & Airplane Corporation.

C.N.N.A.

CIA. NACIONAL DE NAVEGAÇÃO AÉREA.

HEAD OFFICE : AVENIDA RODRIGUEZ ALVES 303/331, RIO DE JANEIRO.

WORKS : PRAIA DO CAJÚ No. 68, RIO DE JANEIRO.

The Companhia Nacional de Navegação Aérea is one of the group of companies belonging to the Organização Henrique Lage—Patrimônio Nacional. It undertakes the design and construction of aircraft of original design. These include the HL-1, HL-2 HL-4 and HL-6.

The HL-1 two-seat light cabin monoplane is illustrated herewith. It is of the Piper Cub type, the principal external change being in the use of parallel instead of Vee-type wing-bracing struts. Structure follows standard practice, with welded steel tube fuselage and wooden fabric-covered wings. The landing-gear uses rubber-in-compression springing. The HL-1 has complete dual controls and is fitted with a 65 h.p. Continental A-65-8 four-cylinder horizontally-opposed air-cooled engine, which gives it a speed of 150 km.h. (93 m.p.h.).

The latest product of the company is the HL-6 advanced training monoplane. This aircraft is a low-wing cantilever monoplane. It may be fitted with either the 125 h.p. Continental or 135 h.p. Franklin engine. In 1943 the company was engaged in the production of fifty of this type.

The C.N.N.A. HL-1 Two-seat Light Cabin Monoplane (65 h.p. Continental A-65 engine).

C.A.P.

COMPANHIA AERONÁUTICA PAULISTA.

HEAD OFFICE AND WORKS : RUA DR. FALCÃO FILHO, 56-12, SÃO PAULO.

President : Sr. H. Martini.

The Companhia Aeronáutica Paulista, a subsidiary of the Laminação de Metais S.A., was recently formed to build and repair aircraft, etc. It has so far produced two light aeroplanes of original design, the C.A.P. 1 Planalto and the C.A.P. 4 Paulistinha, and both these types are in production.

The company is also building the Saracura primary and Alcatraz secondary training gliders.

THE C.A.P. 1 PLANALTO.

TYPE.—Two-seat Advanced Training monoplane.

WINGS.—Low-wing cantilever monoplane. Constant taper from roots to tips. Small flat centre-section with outer wings set at dihedral angle. Two-spar wooden wing framework with fabric covering. Split flaps between ailerons and centre-section.

FUSELAGE.—Oval wooden monocoque with plywood skin.

TAIL UNIT.—Cantilever monoplane type. All-wood framework with fabric-covered rudder and elevators.

LANDING GEAR.—Fixed divided type. Cantilever single-leg shock-absorber struts attached to extremities of centre-section front spar. Medium-pressure wheels. Wheel-brakes. Tail-skid.

POWER PLANT.—One 90 h.p. Franklin four-cylinder horizontally-opposed air-cooled engine. Two-bladed wooden airscrew. Fuel capacity 70 litres (15.4 Imp. gallons). Oil capacity 4 litres (0.88 Imp. gallons).

ACCOMMODATION.—Tandem open cockpits with complete dual controls. Turn-over post between cockpits.

DIMENSIONS.—Span 8.6 m. (28 ft. 2⅓ in.), Length 6.5 m. (21 ft. 9⅜ in.), Height 2.15 m. (7 ft. 1 in.), Wing area 12 sq. m. (129.2 sq. ft.).

WEIGHTS AND LOADINGS.—Weight empty 440 kg. (970 lbs.), Weight loaded 670 kg. (1,480 lbs.), Wing loading 55.8 kg./sq. m. (11.4 lbs./sq. ft.), Power loading 7.4 kg./h.p. (16.3 lbs./h.p.).

PERFORMANCE.—Maximum speed 185 km.h. (115.2 m.p.h.), Cruising speed 170 km.h. (106 m.p.h.), Initial rate of climb 192 m./min. (630 ft./min.), Service ceiling 4,000 m. (13,120 ft.), Range 500 km. (312 miles.).

THE C.A.P. 4 PAULISTINHA.

TYPE.—Two-seat Light Primary Training and Touring monoplane.

WINGS.—High-wing braced monoplane. Wings attached direct to built-in centre-section in top of fuselage and braced to lower longerons by streamline steel-tube Vee struts. Two-spar wooden wing structure with fabric covering. Slotted ailerons on under-hung hinges. Fixed slots in leading-edge ahead of ailerons.

FUSELAGE.—Rectangular welded steel-tube framework covered with fabric over light wooden fairing structure.

TAIL UNIT.—Wire-braced monoplane type. Welded steel-tube framework covered with fabric. Tie-rod bracing above and below in plane of main tubular spar of tailplane.

LANDING GEAR.—Divided type. Consists of two side Vees and two inclined half-axles hinged at their inner ends to a Vee cabane beneath the fuselage. Oleo shock-absorber struts form front legs of side Vees. Medium-pressure wheels and brakes.

POWER PLANT.—One 65 h.p. Franklin four-cylinder horizontally-opposed air-cooled engine on welded steel-tube mounting. Two-bladed wooden airscrew. Fuel capacity 58 litres (12.8 Imp. gallons). Oil capacity 4 litres (0.88 Imp. gallons).

ACCOMMODATION.—Enclosed cabin seating two in tandem with dual controls. Entrance door on starboard side. Space for baggage behind rear seat.

DIMENSIONS.—Span 10.1 m. (33 ft. 1½ in.), Length 6.65 m. (21 ft. 9⅞ in.), Height 1.95 m. (6 ft. 4¾ in.), Wing area 17 sq. m. (183 sq. ft.).

WEIGHTS AND LOADINGS.—Weight empty 320 kg. (706 lbs.), Weight loaded 540 kg. (1,190 lbs.), Wing loading 31.8 kg./sq. m. (6.51 lbs./sq. ft.), Power loading 8.3 kg./h.p. (18.3 lbs./h.p.).

PERFORMANCE.—Maximum speed 155 km.h. (96.5 m.p.h.), Cruising speed 140 km.h. (87.2 m.p.h.), Initial rate of climb 185 m./min. (610 ft./min.), Service ceiling 4,000 m. (13,120 ft.), Range 500 km. (312 miles.).

The C.A.P. 1 Planalto Two-seat Advanced Training Monoplane (90 h.p. Franklin engine).

The C.A.P. 4 Paulistinha Two-seat Cabin Monoplane (65 h.p. Franklin engine).

THE C.A.P. 4B AMBULANCIA.

This is a special version of the C.A.P. 4 arranged to carry one stretcher case. The fuselage deck from trailing-edge of wing to tailplane is hinged to open sideways to permit the loading and unloading of the stretcher, the head portion of which extends into the rear portion of the cabin and takes the place of the second seat.

Structural details, specification and performance are the same as for the C.A.P. 4.

THE C.A.P. 4C PAULISTINHA RADIO.

The C.A.P. 4C is a light military observation and liaison monoplane converted from the C.A.P. 4. The fuselage aft of the cabin is cut down in depth, the side windows of the cabin are extended aft, the roof is glazed and the rear end of the upper half of the cabin is provided with a sloping window. The passenger is seated with his back to the pilot and is provided with a radio receiving and transmitting set with a transmitting range of 480 km. (300 miles).

THE BRITISH EMPIRE
GREAT BRITAIN

AIRSPEED.

The Airspeed Oxford II Advanced Training Monoplane (two Armstrong Siddeley Cheetah X engines).

AIRSPEED, LTD.

HEAD OFFICE AND WORKS: THE AIRPORT, PORTSMOUTH, HANTS.

Chairman : A. S. Butler.

Director and General Manager : A. Townsley.

Technical Director and Director of Design : A. E. Hagg.

Directors : G. Wigham Richardson. F. T. Hearle, F. E. N. St. Barbe, W. E. Nixon and J. Liddell, A.C.A. (Secretary).

Airspeed (1934) Ltd., was registered in August, 1934, when Airspeed, Ltd., became associated with the famous Tyneside shipbuilding firm of Swan, Hunter and Wigham Richardson, Ltd.

In 1940 the de Havilland Aircraft Co. Ltd. acquired from Swan, Hunter & Wigham Richardson Ltd. that company's holding of ordinary shares in Airspeed (1934) Ltd. The Company, however, retains its separate identity. On January 25, 1944, the name was changed to Airspeed, Ltd.

An important production of the Company was the Oxford twin-engined training monoplane, large numbers of which were also built by other aircraft manufacturers.

Airspeed Ltd. has also undertaken the design and manufacture of gliders and large transport aircraft. Its first glider is the Horsa, a large transport type for airborne troops and their equipment. The Horsa was used with success in the airborne invasions of Sicily, Italy, Normandy and Germany. Over 500 Horsa gliders were supplied to the U.S. Army under reverse Lease/Lend for the invasion of Europe.

THE AIRSPEED A.S. 10 OXFORD.

The Oxford, built to conform to Air Ministry Specification T.23/26, was evolved from the Airspeed Envoy civil transport. It first went into service in the Royal Air Force as a twin-engined Advanced Trainer in January, 1938.

The 4,411th and last Oxford was delivered to the R.A.F. by Airspeed on July 14, 1945. The Oxford was also built by the de Havilland Aircraft Co., Ltd., Percival Aircraft, Ltd., and the Standard Motor Co., Ltd., the total number produced being over 8,000.

The Oxford was used in Service Flying Training Schools in the United Kingdom, Canada, Australia, New Zealand, Southern Rhodesia and the Middle East, and it was also employed on light transport and communications duties. A small number was made available under reverse Lease/Lend to the U.S.A.A.F. in Great Britain.

The aircraft was produced in the following forms :—

Oxford I. Two 355 h.p. Armstrong Siddeley Cheetah IX or X radial air-cooled engines, the former fitted with Fairey-Reed metal fixed-pitch airscrews and the latter with wood airscrews. Bombing and gunnery trainer. Armstrong Whitworth gun-turret amidships.

Oxford II. Similar to Mk. I but equipped as a navigation and radio trainer. No turret.

Oxford III. Two 425 h.p. Armstrong Siddeley Cheetah XV engines and Rotol two-blade constant-speed airscrews. Navigation and radio trainer.

Oxford IV. Used as a flying test-bed for two D.H. Gipsy-queen IV (Gipsy-Six IIIS) supercharged six-cylinder in-line inverted air-cooled engines.

Oxford V. Two Pratt & Whitney R-985-AN6 Wasp-Junior nine-cylinder radial air-cooled engines and Hamilton Standard two-blade variable-pitch airscrews. Navigation and radio trainer.

TYPE.—Twin-engined Advanced Training monoplane.

WINGS.—Low-wing cantilever monoplane. Centre-section built separately from fuselage. Outer sections, of tapering chord and thickness, attached to centre-section by four bolts and locknuts, one to each spar-joint. Bolts pass through tapered high-tensile steel plugs at each end to take shear. Wing-structure consists of two box-spars of spruce and birch three-ply. Former ribs of normal girder type and in three parts. Special system of inter-spar bracing consists of built-up diagonal struts. Whole wing covered with plywood. Handley Page slotted ailerons. Split trailing-edge flaps.

FUSELAGE.—In two sections. Front section built as a unit and comprises the pilot's cockpit and cabin. It is of semi-monocoque construction. Rear section, also of semi-monocoque construction, has fin built integral with it.

TAIL. UNIT.—Monoplane type. Wooden framework with fabric covering. Cantilever tail-plane and fin. Balanced rudder is hinged to fin only, with hinge-line inclined forward. Trimming-tabs in elevators.

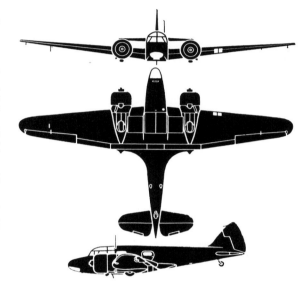

The Airspeed Oxford Advanced Trainer.

LANDING GEAR.—Retractable type. Dunlop type low-pressure wheels and pneumatic wheel-brakes. Dunlop tail-wheel.

POWER PLANT.—Two 355 h.p. Armstrong Siddeley Cheetah X (Oxford I and II) or 425 h.p. Cheetah XV (Oxford III) seven-cylinder air-cooled radial engines on welded steel-tube mountings. Two-bladed fixed pitch wooden airscrews (Oxford I) or two-bladed D.H. constant-speed airscrews (Oxford III). Alternatively two 450 h.p. Pratt & Whitney Wasp-Junior nine-cylinder radial air-cooled engines driving two-bladed two-position variable-pitch airscrews may be fitted (Oxford V). Two main fuel tanks in between spars of centre-section and two auxiliary tanks in outer sections interconnected with main tanks. Combined oil tanks and coolers mounted behind engines.

ACCOMMODATION.—Although crew would not normally exceed three at any one time, stations are provided for pilot, navigator or

WINGS.—High-wing strut-braced semi-cantilever monoplane. Wooden structure with two spruce and plywood box spars, former ribs, and a plywood covering. Sections between the spars watertight to provide buoyancy in the event of a forced-alighting at sea. Wing bracing struts each consist of two steel tubes arranged in Vee formation and faired together to form a single strut. Entire trailing-edge occupied each side by two slotted flaps, the outer flaps also functioning as ailerons. Leading-edge auto slots opposite aileron-flaps. Each wing, complete with two engines and one fuel tank, folds from the root and a jury strut supports the front spar in the folded position.

FUSELAGE.—All-metal stressed-skin monocoque structure built in one unit with the exception of the forward observer's compartment, which is detachable, and the complete tail-unit.

TAIL. UNIT.—Cantilever monoplane type with a fixed fin on the centre-line and a fin and rudder at each extremity. Tailplane has two spruce and plywood box spars, ribs and plywood covering. Elevators and rudders have wood frames and fabric covering, and the fins plywood covering. Tailplane incidence adjustable in flight.

LANDING GEAR.—Fixed divided type. Each unit is a three-member pyramid comprising a forwardly-inclined oleo-pneumatic shock-absorber leg, radius-rod and axle. Wheels fitted with shoe-type pneumatic brakes. Tail-wheel midway between wings and tail has a special long-travel shock-absorber and a powerful self-centering device and steering control.

POWER PLANT.—Four 130 h.p. Pobjoy Niagara V seven-cylinder radial air-cooled geared engines, each driving a two-blade fixed-pitch wooden airscrew 8 ft. (2.4 m.) in diameter. Two fuel tanks (85 Imp. gallons each) mounted in the root ends of the wings between the spars, each tank supplying two engines through dual engine-driven pumps.

ACCOMMODATION.—Crew of three, consisting of pilot, observer and radio-operator. Observer in the nose compartment with clear-vision windows front and sides. Pilot's compartment on separate raised floor offset slightly to port to leave passage-way to radio-operator's compartment. The three compartments together occupy the forward portion of the fuselage from the extreme nose to the rear-spar bulkhead.

DIMENSIONS.—Span 53 ft. 4 in. (16.25 m.), Length 40 ft. (12.2 m.), Height 10 ft. 5 in. (3.17 m.), Width folded 18 ft. (5.5 m.).

WEIGHTS.—Weight empty with fixed military equipment 4,592 lbs. (2,085 kg.), Removable equipment 313 lbs. (142 kg.), Crew (3 with parachutes) 600 lbs. (272 kg.), Fuel and oil 1,430 lbs. (649 kg.), Weight loaded 6,935 lbs. (3,148 kg.).

PERFORMANCE.—Maximum speed 126 m.p.h. (202 km.h.) at 5,000 ft. (1,525 m.), Cruising speed 113 m.p.h. (181 km.h.) at 5,000 ft. (1,525 m.), Stalling speed (full-throttle) at sea level 33 m.p.h. (53 km.h.), Stalling speed at 5,000 ft. (1,525 m.) 37.5 m.p.h. (60 km.h.), Initial rate of climb 865 ft./min. (264 m./min.), Rate of climb at 5,000 ft. (1,525 m.) 630 ft./min. (192 m./min.), Rate of climb at 10,000 ft. (3,050 m.) 365 ft./min. (112 m./min.), Climb to 10,000 ft. (3,050 m.) 18 mins., Service ceiling 14,700 ft. (4,480 m.). Absolute ceiling 16,700 ft. (5,090 m.).

second pilot, bomb-aimer, wireless operator, rear gunner and camera operator. Pilot's cockpit in nose, with seat for second pilot or navigator. Dual controls. When dual control is not in use the space for the prone bombing position is provided by removing the second set of controls. When navigator is carried, he occupies second pilot's seat, which is pushed back in line with chart table. The wireless operator is accommodated on a seat on the rear spar, facing aft, on the starboard side. A rear gunner's station, provided with an Armstrong Whitworth gun-turret may be located amidships (Oxford I only). Equipment can be installed to enable the machine to be used for the following alternative training duties :—(1) Navigational, including night-flying, W/T. and direction-finding ; (2) Bombing, including high-altitude with oxygen supply ; (3) Air gunnery ; (4) Aerial photography ; (5) Ab initio twin-engine training. The Oxford has also been equipped as an air ambulance.

DIMENSIONS.—Span 53 ft. 4 in. (16.25 m.), Length 34 ft. 6 in. (10.5 m.), Height 11 ft. 1 in. (3.3 m.).

WEIGHTS (two Siddeley Cheetah X engines).—Weight empty with fixed military load 5,380 lbs. (2,440 kg.), Removable load varies according to function of aircraft, Fuel and oil 1,305 lbs. (592 kg.), Crew (2-3) 400-600 lbs. (182-272 kg.), Loaded weight 7,600 lbs. (3,450 kg.).

WEIGHTS (two Pratt & Whitney Wasp-Junior engines).—Weight empty 5,670 lbs. (2,575 kg.), Weight loaded 8,000 lbs. (3,632 kg.).

PERFORMANCE (with turret and two Siddeley Cheetah X engines and fixed-pitch airscrews).—Maximum speed 182 m.p.h. (291 km.h.) at 8,300 ft. (2,530 m.), Rate of climb at 6,300 ft. (1,920 m.) 930 ft./min. (284 m./min.), Climb to 10,000 ft. (3,050 m.) 12.5 mins., Service ceiling 19,200 ft. (5,850 m.).

PERFORMANCE (without turret and with two Siddeley Cheetah X engines and fixed-pitch airscrews).—Maximum speed 188 m.p.h. (301 km.h.) at 8,300 ft. (2,530 m.), Rate of climb at 6,300 ft. (1,920 m.) 960 ft./min. (293 m./min.), Climb to 10,000 ft. (3,050 m.) 12 mins., Service ceiling 19,500 ft. (5,945 m.).

PERFORMANCE (without turret and with two Pratt & Whitney Wasp-Junior engines and two-position variable-pitch airscrews).—Maximum speed 202 m.p.h. (324 km.h.) at 4,100 ft. (1,250 m.), Initial rate of climb 2,000 ft./min. (908 m./min.), Climb to 10,000 ft. (3,050 m.) 6 mins., Service ceiling 21,000 ft. (6,400 m.).

THE AIRSPEED A.S.39 FLEET SHADOWER.

The A.S.39 was designed to Air Ministry specification S.23/37 which, in turn, was drawn up to meet the requirements of the Admiralty for a carrier-borne aeroplane capable of shadowing enemy fleets during the hours of darkness. This called for an aircraft combining slow cruising speeds with long duration, possessing an exceptional field of view for pilot and observer,

The Airspeed A.S.39 Fleet Shadower (four 130 h.p. Pobjoy Niagara V engines).

and subject to the dimensional restrictions imposed by the need for shipboard stowage.

TYPE.—Four-engined special Observation monoplane for the Royal Navy.

THE AIRSPEED A.S. 45.

The A.S. 45 was a single-engined Advanced Training monoplane which was designed to meet the requirements of Air Ministry specification T.4/39. Two prototypes were built but the A.S. 45 did not go into production in 1942 as originally planned owing to a change in official policy at that time.

The A.S. 45 was a low-wing cantilever monoplane with inwardly-retracting Dowty oleo-pneumatic landing-gear and accommodation for a crew of two in tandem enclosed cockpits with complete dual controls. It was fitted with a Bristol Mercury VIII nine-cylinder radial air-cooled supercharged engine and either a D.H. or Rotol three-blade constant-speed airscrew. Two fuel tanks, one in each wing, had a total capacity of 130 Imp. gallons.

DIMENSIONS.—Span 42 ft. (12.8 m.), Length 36 ft. 1 in. (11 m.), Height (tail down) 11 ft. 6 in. (3.5 m.), Wing area (including ailerons and flaps) 290 sq. ft. (26.9 sq. m.).

PERFORMANCE.—Maximum economical cruising speeds 228 m.p.h. (365 km.h.) at 12,500 ft. (3,810 m.) and 237 m.p.h. (379 km.h.) at 16,000 ft. (4,880 m.), Climb to 15,000 ft. (4,575 m.) 12½ min., Service ceiling 24,800 ft. (7,565 m.), Range 680 miles (1,090 km.).

THE AIRSPEED A.S. 51 HORSA.

The Horsa was first used in the airborne invasion of Sicily. For the invasion of France Horsas went into action wearing both British and American colours and they played a notable part in the Normandy landings where over 20% of the total material delivered to the beach-heads by air was done by gliders. Horsas also took part in the invasion of Southern France.

The Horsa was available in the following versions:—

Horsa I. Standard troop-carrier as described below. Towable-cable attachment points at upper attachments of main landing-gear legs.

Horsa II. Differs from Mk. I in having a hinged nose to permit the direct loading and unloading of light ordnance and vehicles, a twin nose-wheel and a tow-cable attachment incorporated in the nose-wheel strut.

TYPE.—Military, Troop or Freight-carrying Glider.

WINGS.—High-wing cantilever monoplane. In three sections, a

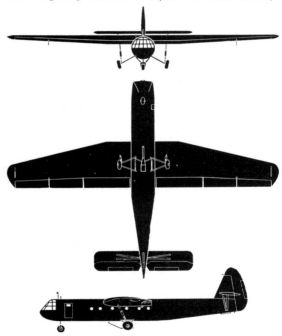

The Airspeed Horsa I Transport Glider.

The Airspeed A.S. 45 Advanced Training Monoplane (Bristol Mercury VIII engine).

The Airspeed Horsa I Troop and Freight-carrying Glider.

centre-section of constant chord and thickness and two tapering outer sections with all taper on leading-edges. All-wood structure. Built-up laminated spruce and plywood main spar, built-up Warren girder ribs and a plywood skin over the leading-edge forms a D-section torsion beam. Aft of the spar Warren girder ribs are covered with fabric which is secured to the rib cap-strips by wires running in troughs in the strips and held in place by split-pins. Fabric strips doped over securing wires. Pneumatically-operated split trailing-edge flaps between ailerons and fuselage.

FUSELAGE.—Circular-section wooden semi-monocoque structure in three-sections bolted together. The nose section includes the pilot's compartment and main freight loading door. The main section encloses the troop or freight compartment. The rear section supports the tail unit. Structure consists of a series of frames and bulkheads interconnected by four longerons and a number of spruce stringers, the whole covered with a plywood skin.

TAIL-UNIT.—Braced monoplane type. Tail plane mounted on fin and braced to fuselage by Vee struts. Two-spar fin with plywood covering. Tailplane elevators and rudder have D-section beams, movable surfaces having fabric covering. Elevators and rudder have aero-dynamic and mass balances and controllable trim-tabs.

LANDING-GEAR.—Tricycle type. Main wheels sprung by oleo shock-absorber legs, the upper ends of which are attached to the centre-section main spar, with the lower ends hinged to the underside of fuselage by Vee struts. Sprung nose-wheel. The main wheels, Vee and oleo struts are droppable. Ash skids under fuselage.

ACCOMMODATION.—Pilot's compartment in extreme nose with side-by-side seats and dual controls. Aft of pilot's compartment on port side is the main freight loading door, the door itself forming a hinged loading ramp. Main compartment seats fifteen fully-armed airborne troops on benches along sides. Further door aft on starboard side. Fuselage joint at rear end of cabin may be broken to permit rapid unloading of compartment in action. Wide variation of military equipment may be carried in main compartment and additional supply containers may be carried on drop fittings under the centre-section of the wing, three on each side of fuselage.

DIMENSIONS.—Span 88 ft. (26.84 m.), Length 66 ft. 11¾ in. (20.43 m.), Height 19 ft. 6 in. (5.9 m.), Wing area 1,104 sq. ft. (102.5 sq. m.).

WEIGHTS.—Weight empty 8,370 lbs. (3,800 kg.), Weight loaded 15,500 lbs. (7,040 kg.), Wing loading 14.05 lbs./sq. ft. (68.56 kg./sq. m.).

THE AIRSPEED A.S.57 AMBASSADOR.

The Ambassador is a twin-engined civil transport which conforms to the No. 2 Specification drawn up by the Brabazon Committee for an aeroplane suitable for European and other medium-range services. It will have a maximum accommodation for 36 passengers and a crew of 3-4 for a range up to 800 miles, or 25 passengers plus additional fuel for ranges up to 1,200 miles.

The Ambassador is a high-wing cantilever monoplane with high aspect-ratio laminar-flow wings, a tricycle landing-gear, a triple-ruddered tail-unit and a power-plant consisting of two 2,580 h.p. Bristol Centaurus 57 two-row radial sleeve-valve engines driving four-blade D.H. Hydromatic constant-speed reversible-pitch airscrews. Landing-gear and flaps are electrically-operated and thermal de-icing is provided for the leading-edges of wings, tailplane, fins and ailerons. Fuel tanks form part of the wing structure.

The main passenger accommodation may seat a maximum of 36 passengers in eight rows of four with a central aisle between pairs of seats. There is a galley and baggage compartment forward of the main cabin and two toilets and a baggage compartment aft. A third baggage compartment is provided in the extreme nose. The aircraft is pressurised to give a cabin pressure equivalent of 8,000 ft. up to 20,000 ft.

DIMENSIONS.—Span 115 ft. (35 m.), Length 80 ft. 3 in. (24.5 m.), Height 18 ft. 9½ in. (5.7 m.), Gross wing area 1,200 sq. ft. (115 sq. m.).

WEIGHTS.—Weight loaded 45,000 lbs. (20,430 kg.), Wing loading 37.5 lb./sq. ft. (183 kg./sq. m.), Power loading 8.7 lb./h.p. (3.9 kg./h.p.).

PERFORMANCE (Estimated).—Maximum weak mixture cruising speed (1,570 h.p. per engine) 300 m.p.h. (480 km.h.) at 18,000 ft. (5,490 m.), Weak mixture cruising speed on one engine 160-190 m.p.h. (256-304 km.h.) at 15,000 ft. (4,575 m.), Initial rate of climb 1,580 ft./min. (482 m./min.), Rate of climb on one engine with landing gear down 240 ft./min. (73 m./min.), Rate of climb on one engine with landing gear retracted 400 ft./min. (122 m./min.).

ARMSTRONG WHITWORTH.

SIR W. G. ARMSTRONG WHITWORTH AIRCRAFT, LTD.

HEAD OFFICE, WORKS AND AERODROME : COVENTRY.

Directors : Sir Frank Spriggs, Hon. F.R.Ae.S. (Chairman), H. K. Jones (Managing), T. O. M. Sopwith, C.B.E., F.R.Ae.S., and H. M. Woodhams, C.B.E.

Chief Designer : J. Lloyd.

Secretary : W. A. Blackler.

Sir W. G. Armstrong Whitworth Aircraft, Ltd., was formed in 1921. In 1935, the Hawker Siddeley Aircraft Co., Ltd., was formed to amalgamate the interests of Hawker Aircraft Ltd. and the Armstrong Siddeley Development Co., Ltd., which latter company controlled Sir W. G. Armstrong Whitworth Aircraft, Ltd., Armstrong Siddeley Motors, Ltd., and A. V. Roe & Co., Ltd.

The Company were pioneers in the development of all-metal aircraft, and it is due to their initiative that the use of high-tensile steel became prominent.

In the pre-1939 era they developed, in addition to the military types then under construction—Siskin, Atlas, etc.—several series of commercial aircraft. These included the Argosy, Atalanta and Ensign classes, all of which gave long and reliable service on the air routes of Imperial Airways. Ten aircraft of the Ensign class are still in operation with the British Overseas Airways Corporation.

Concurrently with the development of these types, the military series of Whitley and Albemarle were in being. The Whitley was the first heavy bomber in production and although it was withdrawn from production in 1942 it was still in service when the war ended. In 1942, a series of Whitley aircraft was converted for use by British Airways as freight-carriers.

The Albemarle was the first British operational aeroplane to be fitted with a tricycle landing-gear. Originally designed as a light bomber-reconnaissance type, it was later converted for bomber-training, glider-towing, troop-carrying, and general transport purposes. As a paratroop carrier and glider-tug the Albemarle took part in the invasions of Sicily and Normandy.

The forward policy of the Company is based upon the development of the large type of aircraft, orthodox and unorthodox, for both civil and military purposes. The unorthodox include jet-propelled flying-wing designs. Successful test of scale models have been made and full-size designs are in course of construction.

THE ARMSTRONG WHITWORTH A.W. 41 ALBEMARLE.

The Albemarle was designed for bomber-reconnaissance duties at a time when the possible shortage of light alloys and other specialised aircraft materials, as well as experienced manu-

facturing facilities, was considered to be a real danger. Consequently, wood and steel were used almost exclusively in the structure of the Albemarle, but in spite of this severe design limitation the percentage structure weight turned out to be very little above the average for this type of aircraft.

During the early production stages, owing to important policy changes made as the result of wartime conditions and experience, the Albemarle was converted to perform a variety of duties, the most important of which were those of special transport, glider-tug and paratroop-carrier.

Operating as a glider-tug and paratroop-carrier, the Albemarle took part in the invasion of Sicily on July 10, 1943, the invasion of France on June 6, 1944, and in the operations at Arnhem in September, 1944. As a special transport it has been used for carrying mail and equipment for the R.A.F. from Great Britain to Gibraltar, North Africa and Malta.

The following are the principal versions of the Albemarle :—

Albemarle I, Series I. Two 1,590 h.p. Bristol Hercules XI fourteen-cylinder air-cooled sleeve-valve radial engines. The original Bomber-Reconnaissance version. Crew consisted of navigator/bomb-aimer, two pilots, radio operator and two gunners. Four-gun Boulton Paul dorsal turret and two-gun power-operated under turret. First delivery to the R.A.F. on October 23, 1941.

Albemarle S.T. I, Series I. Special Transport version. Operational bombing equipment and rear fuselage tank removed, four-gun dorsal turret replaced by hand-operated two-gun installation covered by sliding hood, under-gun turret removed and freight loading door fitted in starboard side of centre fuselage.

Albemarle I, Series II. Fitted with Malcolm glider-towing gear.

Albemarle S.T. I, Series II. Special Transport version with glider-towing gear.

Albemarle II. Paratroop-carrier and Glider-tug. Ten paratroops carried forward of large dropping hole in floor of rear fuselage with rails on each side of fuselage for parachute static strops. Tubular guard under tailplane to prevent free strops fouling elevators. Malcolm glider-towing gear. First deliveries to R.A.F. in January, 1943.

Albemarle IV. Mk. I fitted with two 1,600 h.p. Wright GR-2600-A5B Cyclone 14 radial air-cooled engines. Prototype only.

Albemarle V. Similar to Mk. II with the addition of fuel jettisoning equipment.

Albemarle VI, Series I. Same as Mk. V plus large freight-loading door in fuselage to facilitate loading of bulky articles which may require to be carried on paratroop operations.

Albemarle VI, Series II. Same as Series I, with the addition of special radio equipment for glider towing. Upper gun position deleted.

Type.—Twin-engined Paratroop Transport and Glider-tug.
Wings.—Mid-wing cantilever monoplane. Wing in five sections, comprising centre-section extending back to spar rear face and passing through fuselage, two detachable portions of centre-section aft of spar, and two outer wing sections. Centre-section spar consists of four square steel tubular booms with tubular shear and plan bracing. Two steel-tube ribs at each end of spar carry main power-unit and landing-gear pick-up points. Centre-section covered top and bottom with non-stressed plywood. Outer wing sections have two spars with spruce booms reinforced with light alloy inserts and plywood webs. Standard ribs are of spruce and plywood, special ribs carrying aileron hinge loads of square steel tube aft of spar and spruce and plywood reinforced with steel channels between spars. Steel tubular plan bracing and plywood covering. Frise type ailerons have steel-tube spar, spruce and plywood ribs and plywood covering. Controllable trim-tab in port aileron. Slotted flaps with under-hung hinges between ailerons and fuselage. Same structure as ailerons.
Fuselage.—In three sections. Steel-tube framework with gusseted joints to which fairing panels of spruce and plywood are attached. Sections joined by single pin joints at each of the four longerons.
Tail Unit.—Cantilever monoplane type with twin fins and rudders. Tail-plane and fins have two spruce and plywood spars, spruce and plywood ribs and plywood covering. Elevators and rudders have single steel tubular spars, spruce and plywood ribs and plywood covering. Trim-tab in port elevator, balance tab in starboard elevator. Automatic balance tab in upper part and controllable trim-tab in lower part of each rudder.
Landing Gear.—Retractable tricycle type. Main wheels retract backwards into engine nacelles and are partially enclosed by light alloy doors which at their rear ends fit round the lower halves of the wheels. The nose wheel is raised backwards into front fuselage. Whole landing-gear is hydraulically-operated.
Power Plant.—Two Bristol Hercules XI fourteen-cylinder radial air-cooled sleeve-valve engines mounted in Bristol interchangeable power-units, to which oil-cooler installation and accessory system peculiar to the airframe have been added. Three-bladed D.H. Hydromatic fully-feathering airscrews. Three main fuel tanks between centre-section boom, one in fuselage and one on each side inboard of engine nacelles. Provision for three auxiliary tanks in bomb-bay. Four oil tanks, two in each nacelle.
Accommodation.—Navigator in nose, two pilots side-by-side and radio operator in forward fuselage. As paratroop-carrier accommodation for ten fully-armed troops forward of dropping hole in rear fuselage. Static strop rails on each side of fuselage and guard under tailplane. Large loading door in side of fuselage.
Dimensions.—Span 77 ft. (23.48 m.), Length 59 ft. 11 in. (18.27 m.), Height (to tip of airscrew) 15 ft. 7 in. (4.75 m.), Wing area (including ailerons) 803.5 sq. ft. (74.6 sq. m.).
Weights.—Weight empty (Paratroop-carrier and glider-tug) 22,600 lbs. (10,260 kg.), Maximum overloaded weight 36,500 lbs. (16,570 kg.).
Performance.—Maximum speed over 250 m.p.h. (400 km.h.) at 10,500 ft. (4,575 m.), Normal range 1,350 miles (2,160 km.).

THE ARMSTRONG WHITWORTH A.W. 38 WHITLEY.
Built to Air Ministry Specification B.3/34, the prototype Whitley first flew in March, 1936. It was the first heavy bomber to go into large-scale production for the R.A.F., the first Whitley I being delivered to the service in March, 1937.

The Whitley was withdrawn from production in 1942, after establishing a fine record of operational service. Among some of the major milestones of the war, the Whitley was responsible for the first widespread leaflet raids over Germany in September, 1939; the first bombing raid on Germany in May, 1940; the first bombing raid on Italy in June, 1940; and the first paratroop operation over Southern Italy in February, 1941. After withdrawal from front-line service with Bomber Command the Whitley was converted for use as a General Reconnaissance Bomber and put into service by Coastal Command. In another converted form it was responsible for training the first British airborne troops and taking them into action for the first time in a flight from England to Southern Italy. At the end of the war it was still in service for training and other miscellaneous duties.

The following summarises the stages of development of the Whitley :—
Whitley I. Two Armstrong Siddeley Tiger IX fourteen-cylinder air-cooled radial engines, each rated at 790 h.p. at 6,500 ft. (1,980 m.) and driving D.H. two-position variable-pitch airscrews. Hydraulically-operated nose and ventral turrets and a manually-operated tail turret. Fuel capacity 519 Imp. gallons (normal), 651 Imp. gallons (maximum). Maximum loaded weight 23,300 lbs. (10,569 kg.).
Whitley II. Same as Mk. I except fitted with two Armstrong Siddeley Tiger VIII engines with two-speed superchargers, each rated at 845 h.p. at 6,250 ft. (1,906 m.) and 760 h.p. at 12,750 ft. (3,890 m.). First delivery to R.A.F. in January, 1938.
Whitley III. Similar to Mk. II except increased dihedral to outer wings, improved navigation facilities and provision for carrying larger bombs. Maximum loaded weight 24,430 lbs. (11,081 kg.). First deliveries in August, 1938.

The Armstrong Whitworth Albemarle II Glider-tug and Paratroop Transport (two Bristol Hercules XI engines).

Whitley VII (Naval Conversion). A conversion to Admiralty requirements for training Flight Engineers. Special instructional equipment and seating for pupils provided in rear fuselage.
Whitley IV. Two Rolls-Royce Merlin IV twelve-cylinder Vee liquid-cooled engines, each rated at 990 h.p. at 12,250 ft. (3,740 m.) and driving Rotol constant-speed airscrews. Except for power-plant similar to Mk. III, but fuel capacity increased to 705 Imp. gallons (normal), 837 Imp. gallons (maximum). First deliveries in May, 1939.
Whitley IVA. Same as Mk. IV except for installation of Rolls-Royce Merlin X engines with two-speed superchargers and rated at 1,030 h.p. at 2,250 ft. (685 m.) and 960 h.p. at 13,000 ft. (3,960 m.).
Whitley V. Two Rolls-Royce Merlin X engines driving Rotol constant-speed full-feathering airscrews. Ventral turret deleted and the Armstrong Whitworth two-gun tail turret replaced by a Fraser-Nash four-gun turret in a slightly lengthened stern. Re-designed fins had straight instead of the curved leading-edges of all previous marks. Wing de-icing equipment. Fuel increased to 837 Imp. gallons (normal), 969 Imp. gallons (maximum). Maximum loaded weight 33,500 lbs. (15,196 kg.). First deliveries in August, 1939. Mk. V later modified for use as a paratroop carrier and glider-tug. In 1942, twelve Mk. V's were converted into freight carriers for use by the British Overseas Airways Corpn.
Whitley VII. Same as the Mk. V except specially equipped for service with Coastal Command on general reconnaissance, anti-submarine and convoy protection duties. Crew increased from four to six to include separate navigator and radar operator. Fuel capacity increased to 969 Imp. gallons (normal), 1,101 Imp. gallons (maximum). Normal loaded weight 33,950 lbs. (15,408 kg.).

A full description of the Whitley has appeared in previous issues of this Annual. The performance below refers to the Mk. V.

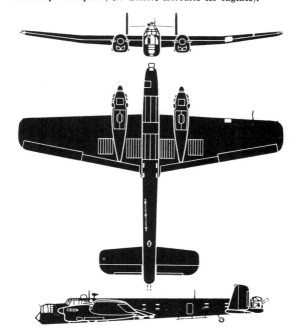
The Armstrong Whitworth Whitley V.

The Armstrong Whitworth Whitley Civil Freight-carrier (two Rolls-Royce Merlin X engines).

Dimensions.—Span 84 ft. (25.6 m.), Length 72 ft. 6 in. (22.1 m.), Height 15 ft. (4.58 m.), Mean chord 14 ft. 4 in. (4.37 m.), Wing area 1,138 sq. ft. (105.7 m.).
Performance (Whitley V).—Maximum speed 230 m.p.h. (370 km.h.) at 16,400 ft. (5,000 m.), Cruising speed 210 m.p.h. (338 km.h.) at 15,000 ft. (4,575 m.), Climb to 12,000 ft. (3,660 m.) 21 mins., Maximum range 2,400 miles (3,860 km.) at 12,000 ft. (3,660 m.), Service ceiling 20,000 ft. (6,100 m.).

THE ARMSTRONG WHITWORTH A.W.27A ENSIGN.
Type.—Four-engined Airliner.
Wings.—High-wing cantilever monoplane, tapering in plan-form and thickness, built on a single box-spar of corrugated light alloy sheet. The leading-edge is metal-covered, and part of it is used for cooling the oil tanks. Aft of the spar the wing consists of a lattice structure of Armstrong Whitworth rolled sections of light alloy, fabric covered, and fitted with split trailing-edge flaps

The Armstrong Whitworth Ensign Commercial Transport in its original form with four Armstrong Siddeley Tiger engines.

extending between ailerons and fuselage. The metal-framed fabric-covered Frise ailerons are mass-balanced and provided with a flap on the port aileron operated from the cockpit for trimming the aircraft laterally.

FUSELAGE.—Oval monocoque structure of light alloy, built of transverse frames, longitudinal stringers and riveted stress-bearing skin.

TAIL UNIT.—Monoplane type. The cantilever tail-plane incorporates a single box-spar of corrugated light-alloy sheet of similar construction to that used in the main wings and is fabric-covered. Fore-and-aft trim by elevator-tabs. The elevators are aerodynamically-balanced automatically by tabs. The elevator controls inside the fuselage are provided with balances of rubber shock-absorber cord. A single cantilever fin and rudder, both metal-framed and fabric-covered, are well faired into the fuselage. As on the elevators, the rudder has an automatic servo-flap which is also fitted with controls for trimming.

WEIGHTS AND LOADINGS.—Weight empty 35,075 lbs. (15,900 kg.), Pay load plus crew 12,000 lbs. (5,450 kg.), Weight loaded 55,500 lbs. (25,200 kg.), Wing loading 22.6 lbs./sq. ft. (110 kg./sq. m.), Power loading (take-off) 11.9 lbs./h.p. (5.4 kg./h.p.).

LANDING GEAR.—Retractable type. Units under the inner engine nacelles, each consisting of one Dunlop wheel and two steel-spring and oleo shock-absorber struts. Wheels are retracted hydraulically by folding the rear struts of each unit. The wheels travel backwards and upwards into the engine fairings and behind the main wing spars. The Dunlop pneumatic brakes are differentially-controlled. Fully-castoring tail-wheel carried on a steel-spring and oleo leg, which is controlled by a self-centering cam.

POWER PLANT.—Four 1,100 h.p. Wright GR-1820-G102A nine-cylinder air-cooled radial engines, in nacelles of welded steel-tube attached to the forward side of the main wing spar. Three-bladed de Havilland constant-speed airscrews. Petrol capacity 670 Imp. gallons. Oil capacity 40 Imp. gallons.

ACCOMMODATION.—The control room for the captain and first officer in the extreme nose has side-by-side dual control with separate columns and handwheels and parallel motion rudder bars. The captain is on the port and the first officer on the starboard side. A radio operator and two stewards complete the crew. Aft of the control room the fuselage is divided up into separate cabins. There may be either four cabins with accommodation for forty passengers, or three cabins with accommodation for twenty-seven passengers by day and twenty by night with sleeping accommodation. In both arrangements there is a steward's pantry and in the former there are three lavatories and in the latter two. Mails and luggage are stowed in the hold on the upper deck of the middle compartment.

DIMENSIONS.—Span 123 ft. (37.5 m.), Length 114 ft. (34.8 m.). Height over airscrews 23 ft. (7.015 m.), Wing area 2,450 sq. ft. (227.6 sq. m.).

PERFORMANCE.—Maximum speed 210 m.p.h. (328 km.h.) at 6,700 ft. (2,045 m.), Maximum cruising speed 180 m.p.h. (290 km.h.) at 5,000 ft. (1,535 m.), Rate of climb at sea level 900 ft./min. (274.5 m./min.), Ceiling (fully loaded) 24,000 ft. (7,320 m.), Ceiling on three engines 18,000 ft. (5,490 m.), Normal range in still air (cruising at 173 m.p.h. = 280 km.h. at 5,000 ft. = 1,525 m.) 1,370 miles (2,200 km.).

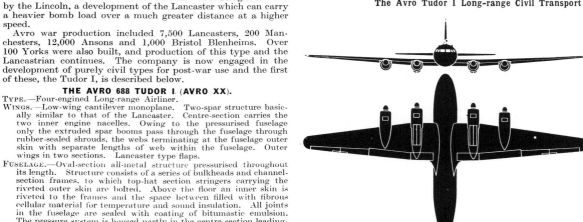

AVRO

A. V. ROE & CO., LTD.

HEAD OFFICE: GREENGATE, MIDDLETON, MANCHESTER.

WORKS: NEWTON HEATH, MANCHESTER, 10, AND IVY WORKS, FAILSWORTH, LANCASHIRE.

Directors: Sir Frank Spriggs, Hon. F.R.Ae.S. (Chairman), T. O. M. Sopwith, C.B.E., F.R.Ae.S., H. K. Jones, Sir Roy Dobson, C.B.E. (Managing), C. E. Fielding and Roy Chadwick, C.B.E. (Chief Designer).

A. V. Roe & Co. was formed in 1909, when the firm advertised itself as constructors of aeroplanes and accessories, and was probably the first firm in Great Britain to do so. The limited company was formed in January, 1913. On the amalgamation of the Hawker and Siddeley interests in 1935, the Avro Company, which formerly was a member of the Siddeley group, became a member of the group of companies controlled by the Hawker Siddeley Aircraft Co., Ltd.

The most notable types produced by the Avro company during the war were the Lancaster, York, Lancastrian and Anson. The most famous of all, the Lancaster, was in service with Bomber Command from 1942 to the end of the war. It is being succeeded by the Lincoln, a development of the Lancaster which can carry a heavier bomb load over a much greater distance at a higher speed.

Avro war production included 7,500 Lancasters, 200 Manchesters, 12,000 Ansons and 1,000 Bristol Blenheims. Over 100 Yorks were also built, and production of this type and the Lancastrian continues. The company is now engaged in the development of purely civil types for post-war use and the first of these, the Tudor I, is described below.

THE AVRO 688 TUDOR I (AVRO XX).

TYPE.—Four-engined Long-range Airliner.

WINGS.—Low-wing cantilever monoplane. Two-spar structure basically similar to that of the Lancaster. Centre-section carries the two inner engine nacelles. Owing to the pressurised fuselage only the extruded spar booms pass through the fuselage through rubber-sealed shrouds, the webs terminating at the fuselage outer skin with separate lengths of web within the fuselage. Outer wings in two sections. Lancaster type flaps.

FUSELAGE.—Oval-section all-metal structure pressurised throughout its length. Structure consists of a series of bulkheads and channel-section frames, to which top-hat section stringers carrying the riveted outer skin are bolted. Above the floor an inner skin is riveted to the frames and the space between filled with fibrous cellular material for temperature and sound insulation. All joints in the fuselage are sealed with coating of bitumastic emulsion. The pressure system is housed partly in the centre-section leading-edge and partly below the fuselage floor. Two Marshall Roots-type blowers driven off inboard engines. Air enters intakes in the leading-edge, passes through filters to blowers, intercooler and silencer before being fed to a non-return valve which is controllable to govern the amount of air admitted to the cabin. The air is then passed through heaters and discharged into the cabin through vents at floor level and louvres above the window posts.

TAIL UNIT.—Cantilever monoplane type. Single fin and rudder. Tailplane same as for Lancaster with extended tips replacing the terminal fins and rudders. Dorsal fin integral with the fuselage but the main fin is a separate structure. Rudder and elevators fitted with servo and trim tabs.

LANDING GEAR.—Same as for Lancaster.

POWER PLANT.—Four Rolls-Royce Merlin 100 twelve-cylinder Vee liquid-cooled engines in circular self-contained and quickly-detachable nacelles. Four-blade Rotol constant-speed airscrews. Fuel carried in wings between main spars in eight Marston crash-proof collapsible bag-type cells, one on each side of the fuselage and three in inner section of each outer wing. Marshall cabin blowers driven off inboard engines.

ACCOMMODATION.—Crew of five, comprising two pilots, flight engineer, radio operator and navigator. Two pilots side-by side with dual controls. Then follows the flight engineer's compartment complete with all engine, fuel and electrical controls; the radio operator's and navigator's compartments. Aft of the flight engineer on the starboard side of the fuselage is a mail and frieght hold, and a further hold follows the navigator's compartment. The combined volume of these two holds is 158 cu. ft. The main cabin is divided into three sub-compartments each seating four passengers, two facing on each side of a central aisle. Each pair of seats is convertible into upper and lower bunks. Aft of the passenger accommodation are dressing rooms and toilets, coatroom and baggage compartment. Main entrance door on the port side, and this door and all escape hatches are sealed by automatically inflatable rubber tubes fed from the pressurisation system. In the tail of the fuselage is a fully-equipped kitchen with seat for steward. The above arrangement is for twelve day and night passengers but an alternative simplified furnishing can be arranged for 24 passengers.

DIMENSIONS.—Span 120 ft. (36.6 m.), Length 79 ft. 6 in. (24.2 m.). Height 22 ft. (6.7 m.), Span of tail 43 ft. (13.1 m.), Wing area 1,421 sq. ft. (132 sq. m.).

WEIGHTS.—Maximum weight 76,000 lbs. (34,500 kg.), Landing weight 66,000 lbs. (30,000 kg.), Wing loading 53.5 lbs./sq. ft. (261 kg./sq. m.).

PERFORMANCE (at 66,000 lbs.—30,000 kg. mean weight).—Maximum speeds 290 m.p.h. (464 km.h.) at sea level, 320 m.p.h. (512 km.h.) at 8,000 ft. (2,440 m.), 346 m.p.h. (554 km.h.) at 20,000 ft. (6,100 m.), Cruising speeds 242 m.p.h. (387 km.h.) at sea level, 283 m.p.h. (453 km.h.) at 12,000 ft. (3,660 m.), 300 m.p.h. (480 km.h.) at 22,500 ft. (6,860 m.), Initial rate of climb 990 ft./min. (302 m./min.), Rate of climb at 20,000 ft. (6,100 m.) 730 ft./min. (223 m./min.), Service ceiling (on 4 engines) 30,100 ft. (9,180 m.), on 3 engines 26,000 ft. (7,930 m.), on 2 engines 10,000 ft. (3,050 m.), Absolute ceiling on 4 engines 31,500 ft. (9,610 m.), on 3 engines 24,300 ft. (7,410 m.), on 2 engines 12,400 ft. (3,780 m.), Maximum range (maximum fuel) 4,660 miles (7,460 km.), Maximum range (maximum payload) 4,100 miles (6,560 km.), Absolute maximum range (500 h.p. per engine) 4,890 miles (7,825 km.) at 10,000 ft. (3,050 m.).

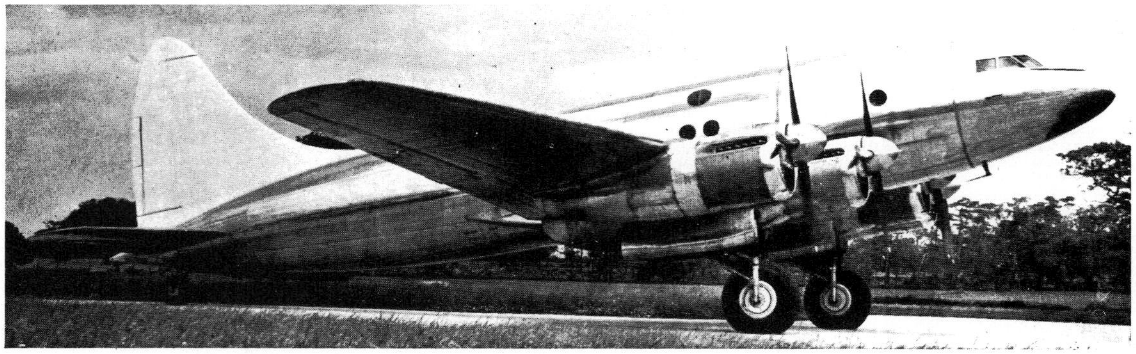

The Avro Tudor I Long-range Civil Transport Monoplane (four Rolls-Royce Merlin 100 engines).

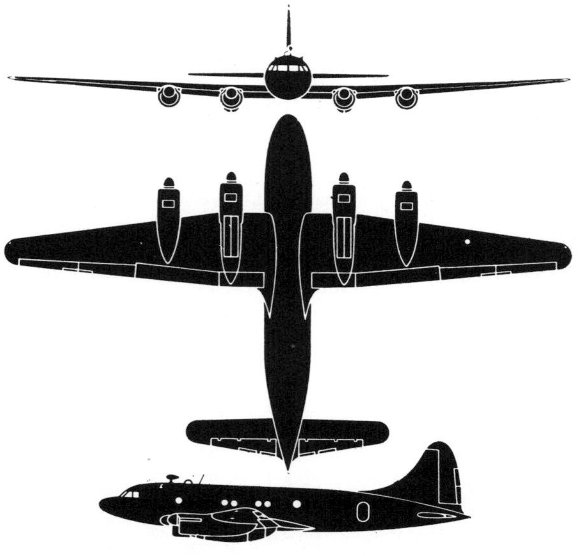

The Avro Tudor I Long-range Transport.

THE AVRO 689 TUDOR II (AVRO XXI).

The Tudor II, a larger version of Mk. I, will be suitable for medium-range flying up to a maximum of 2,000 miles (3,200 km.). Various furnishings will be available with accommodation ranging from 41 passengers by day and 22 by night to 68 passengers for daytime use only. No further details of this aeroplane were available for publication at the time of closing down for press.

THE AVRO 691 LANCASTRIAN.

The Lancastrian is a high-speed long-range transport conversion of the Lancaster bomber. The first conversions were made in Canada by Victory Aircraft, Ltd. for Trans-Canada Air Lines. These aircraft are being operated by this company, on behalf of the Canadian Government, on a trans-Atlantic mail and passenger service between Montreal and Prestwick. The Canadian Lancastrians are fitted with four 1,280 h.p. Packard-built Rolls-Royce Merlin 28 engines and have accommodation for ten passengers, mail and freight.

Production of the Lancastrian is now being undertaken by A. V. Roe & Co., Ltd. and, in addition to deliveries to the R.AF., a fleet of over thirty is being supplied to the British Overseas Airways Corpn. B.O.A.C. Lancastrians are maintaining a high-speed service between the United Kingdom and Australia.

TYPE.—Four-engined Long-range Mail, Freight and Passenger Transport.

WINGS.—Same as for Lancaster.

FUSELAGE.—Main structure as for Lancaster but with new nose and tail fairings.

TAIL UNIT AND LANDING GEAR.—Same as for Lancaster.

POWER PLANT.—Four 1,280 h.p. Rolls-Royce Merlin 24 twelve-cylinder Vee liquid-cooled engines with two-speed superchargers. Three-blade D.H. constant-speed full-feathering airscrews. Fuel tanks in wings (2,154 Imp. gallons) and in fuselage beneath cabin floor (1,020 Imp. gallons).

ACCOMMODATION.—Crew of five and nine passengers. Two pilots side-by-side with dual controls. Navigator and radio-operator behind pilots. Passenger cabin with seats for nine on port side facing inwards. These seats may be converted into three sleeping bunks by lowering seat backs. Three further bunks pull down from the roof above the seats. Sound proofing, ventilation and oxygen equipment. Toilets and galley. Mail and freight carried in nose compartment and beneath floor of cabin. Stowage aft of passenger accommodation for life-saving dinghies.

DIMENSIONS.—Span 102 ft. (31.1 m.), Length 76 ft. 10 in. (23.4 m.), Height 19 ft. 6 in. (5.9 m.), Net wing area 1,205 sq. ft. (112 sq. m.), Gross wing area 1,297 sq. ft. (120.5 sq. m.).

WEIGHTS AND LOADINGS.—Tare weight 30,426 lbs. (13,813 kg.), Fixed and removable equipment (including electrical, instruments, auto-controls, radio, de-icing, dinghies, heating and ventilation, and oxygen) 4,160 lbs. (1,890 kg.), Furnishings (including bunks, mattresses, settees, toilets, upholstery, carpets, sound-proofing, galley, food and water) 1,564 lbs. (710 kg.), Weight fully equipped and furnished 36,150 lbs. (16,413 kg.), Fuel (3,174 Imp. gallons) 22,853 lbs. (10,375 kg.), Oil (150 Imp. gallons) 1,350 lbs. (613 kg.), Crew (5 at 170 lbs.) 850 lbs. (386 kg.), Crew baggage 200 lbs. (91 kg.), Passengers (9 at 170 lbs. each) 1,530 lbs. (695 kg.), Passenger's baggage 495 lbs. (225 kg.), Mail or freight 1,572 lbs. (714 kg.), Payload (passengers, baggage and cargo) 3,597 lbs. (1,633 kg.),

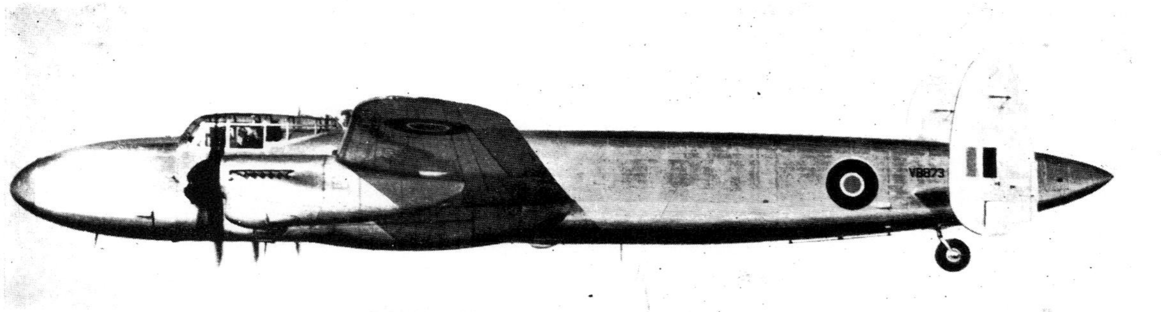

The Avro Lancastrian Long-range Transport (four Rolls-Royce Merlin 24 engines).

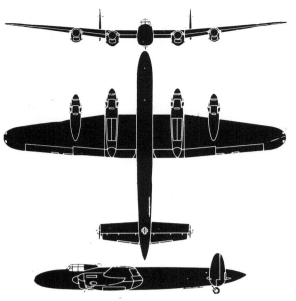

The Avro Lancastrian Long-range Transport.

Maximum payload (with corresponding reduction in fuel) 4,845 lbs. (2,200 kg.), Weight loaded 65,000 lbs. (29,510 kg.), Wing loading 50.10 lbs./sq. ft. (244.5 kg./sq. m.), Power loading 12.7 lbs./h.p. (6.05 kg./h.p.).

PERFORMANCE.—Maximum speed (at 53,000 lbs. = 24,060 kg. mean weight) 295 m.p.h. (472 km.h.) at 3,500 ft. (1,070 m.) and 310 m.p.h.

(496 km.h.) at 12,000 ft. (3,660 m.), Maximum weak mixture cruising speed 275 m.p.h. (440 km.h.) at 11,000 ft. (3,350 m.) and 285 m.p.h. (456 km.h.) at 17,500 ft. (5,340 m.), Rate of climb (at 65,000 lbs. = 29,510 kg.) 750 ft./min. (230 m./min.) at 9,500 ft. (2,900 m.) and 550 ft./min. (168 m./min.) at 16,000 ft. (4,880 m.), Service ceiling 23,000 ft. (7,015 m.).

RANGES (under still air conditions with no allowance for take-off and climb and using 3,174 Imp. gallons of fuel and carrying 3,597 lbs. = 1,633 kg. payload at 15,000 ft. = 4,575 m.). At maximum weak mixture cruising speed (265 m.p.h. = 424 km.h.) 3,570 miles (5,712 km.), At speed between most economical and maximum weak mixture cruising speed (232 m.p.h. = 371 km.h.) 3,950 miles (6,320 km.), At most economical speed (200 m.p.h. = 320 km.h.) 4,501 miles (6,640 km.).

THE AVRO 685 YORK.

TYPE.—Four-engined Transport.

WINGS.—High-wing cantilever monoplane. Wing in five main sections, comprising a centre-section of parallel chord and thickness which is integral with the fuselage centre-section, two tapering outer sections and two semi-circular wing tips. Subsidiary wing units consist of detachable leading and trailing-edge sections of outer wing and centre-section, flaps and ailerons. Two-spar wing structure, each spar consisting of a top and bottom extruded boom bolted to a single thick gauge web-plate. Ribs are aluminium-alloy pressings suitably flanged and swaged for stiffness. The entire wing is covered with a smooth aluminium-alloy skin. Ailerons on outer wing sections have metal noses and are fabric-covered aft of the hinges. The ailerons carry trimming tabs. Split trailing-edge flaps between ailerons and fuselage.

FUSELAGE.—An all-metal structure of roughly rectangular cross-section and built in five main sections. The sections are of semi-monocoque construction. The entire fuselage is covered with a flush-riveted metal skin. The floors and floor structure are reinforced and there are large hatches to enable bulky articles of freight to be loaded.

TAIL UNIT.—Cantilever monoplane type with twin oval fins and rudders. Tail-plane in two sections built up in a similar manner to the wings. The rudders and fins are all metal, but the elevators are fabric-covered. Trimming-tabs are provided on the elevators and rudders. A central stabilising fin is also fitted on top of the fuselage. The tail-unit is mounted on the top surface of the fuselage.

LANDING GEAR.—Retractable main wheels and fixed tail-wheel. Main wheels are hydraulically retracted into the inboard engine nacelles, and hinged doors connected to the retracting gear close

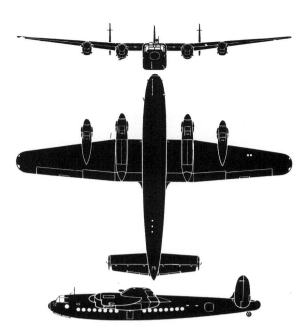

The Avro York Transport.

the apertures when the wheels are raised. Track 23 ft. 9 in. (7.3 m.).

POWER PLANT.—Four 1,280 h.p. Rolls-Royce Merlin 24 twelve-cylinder Vee liquid-cooled engines on welded steel-tube nacelles bolted to the front spar of the centre-section. Three-bladed constant-speed full-feathering airscrews. Seven fuel tanks, three in each outer wing and one in the centre of the wing over the fuselage. Separate oil tanks in each nacelle.

ACCOMMODATION.—The crew depends on whether the aeroplane is arranged to carry passengers or freight. For passenger operation the crew normally consists of one or two pilots, navigator, wireless operator and steward. The flying crew are housed in the front portion of the fuselage. A variety of passenger arrangements can be provided depending on the range and consequent standard of comfort required and the number of people to be carried. The number of passengers can vary from—say—12 for extreme range with the maximum quantity of fuel, to 50 or 56 passengers for a practical range of 1,000 miles (1,600 km.).

DIMENSIONS.—Span 102 ft. (31.1 m.), Length 78 ft. (23.7 m.), Height 20 ft. (6.1 m.), Net wing area 1,190 sq. ft. (110.5 sq. m.), Gross wing area 1,297 sq. ft. (120.5 sq. m.).

WEIGHTS AND LOADINGS (Freighter).—Weight empty 38,000 lbs. (17,250 kg.), Normal loaded weight 65,000 lbs. (29,500 kg.), Wing loading 50.2 lbs./sq. ft. (245 kg./sq. m.), Power loading 12.7 lbs./h.p. (6.05 kg./h.p.).

WEIGHTS AND LOADINGS (Passenger).—Weight empty 40,000 lbs. (18,150 kg.), Normal loaded weight 65,000 lbs. (29,500 kg.), Wing loading 50.2 lbs./sq. ft. (245 kg./sq. m.), Power loading 12.7 lbs./h.p. (6.05 kg./h.p.).

PERFORMANCE.—Maximum speed 290 m.p.h. (467 km.h.), Maximum range approximately 3,100 miles (4,990 km.).

THE AVRO 683 LANCASTER.

The Lancaster owes its origin to Air Ministry specification B.13/36 for a twin-engined medium bomber to be fitted with Rolls-Royce Vulture engines. The first aircraft built to this specification was the Manchester, the prototype of which first flew in July, 1939. About 18 months later the Manchester began to go into squadron service in the R.A.F.

Owing to delays in the development of the Vulture engine the decision was taken in mid-1940 to design a new version of the Manchester to be fitted with four Rolls-Royce Merlin engines. The first conversion made use of about 75 per cent of parts and assemblies of the Manchester, the principal change being the provision of a new centre-section with mountings for four Merlin X engines. This aeroplane became the first prototype of the Lancaster.

A second prototype fitted with four Merlin XX engines and considerably modified in detail was designed, built and flown in some eight months.

The first production Lancasters began to come off the production lines early in 1942 and in the same year the decision was made to produce the Lancaster in Canada. The first Canadian-built Lancaster was delivered by air across the Atlantic in September, 1943. In 1944 Lancaster production was begun in Australia.

The Lancaster is the most versatile of British heavy bombers. It can carry a maximum internal load of 18,000 lbs. without modification to the standard bomb-bay. On a range of 1,000 miles its normal load is 14,000 lbs. With modifications to the bomb-bay it carries both the 12,000 lb. and 22,000 lb. bombs, the only bomber in the World to carry bombs of these sizes.

There have been four basic versions of the Lancaster. These are as follow :—

Lancaster I. Four Rolls-Royce Merlin XX engines.

Lancaster II. Four Bristol Hercules VI air-cooled radial engines.

Lancaster III. Same as the Mk. I but fitted with Packard-built Merlin engines.

Lancaster X. The Canadian-built version of the Mk. III fitted with Packard-built Merlin engines.

TYPE.—Four-engined Heavy Bomber.

WINGS.—Mid-wing cantilever monoplane. Wing in five main sections, comprising a centre-section of parallel chord and thickness which is integral with the fuselage centre-section, two tapering outer sections and two semi-circular wing-tips. Subsidiary wing units consist of detachable leading and trailing-edge sections of outer wings and centre-section, flaps and ailerons. All units are built

The Avro York Four-engined Transport (four Rolls-Royce Merlin 24 engines).

A de-militarised Avro Lancaster I which was supplied to the British Overseas Airways Corporation.

The Avro Lancaster III Heavy Bomber (four Packard-built Merlin engines).

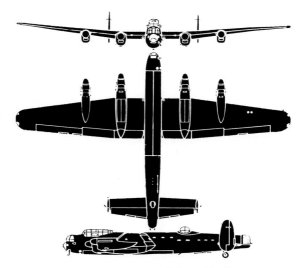

The Avro Lancaster I Heavy Bomber.

The Avro Lancaster II Heavy Bomber (four 1,600 h.p. Bristol Hercules VI engines).

The Avro Anson I Armament and Navigation Trainer (two Armstrong Siddeley IX engines).

up individually with all fittings and equipment before assembly. Two-spar wing structure, each spar consisting of a top and bottom extruded boom bolted on to a single thick gauge web-plate. Ribs are aluminium-alloy pressings suitably flanged and swaged for stiffness. The entire wing is covered with a smooth aluminium-alloy skin. Ailerons on outer wing sections have metal noses and are fabric-covered aft of the hinges. Trimming-tabs in ailerons. Split trailing-edge flaps between ailerons and fuselage.

FUSELAGE.—Oval all-metal structure in five separately-assembled main sections. The fuselage backbone is formed by pairs of extruded longerons located halfway down the cross-section of the three middle sections. Cross beams between these longerons support the floor and form the roof of the bomb compartment. "U"-frames and formers bolted to the longerons carry the smooth skin plating. The remaining sections are built up of oval frames and formers and longitudinal stringers, covered with flush-riveted metal skin. All equipment and fittings are installed before final assembly of the separate units.

TAIL UNIT.—Cantilever monoplane type with twin oval fins and rudders. Tail-plane in two sections built up in similar manner to the wings, the tail-plane spars being joined together within the fuselage on the centre-line. Tailplane, fins and rudders are metal-covered, elevators covered with fabric. Trimming-tabs in elevators and rudders.

LANDING GEAR.—Retractable main wheels and fixed tail-wheel. Main wheels are hydraulically retracted into the inboard engine nacelles and hinged doors close the retracting gear close the apertures when the wheels are raised. Track 23 ft. 9 in. (7.24 m.).

POWER PLANT.—Four 1,280 h.p. Rolls-Royce Merlin XX (Lancaster I), or Packard-built Merlin 28 (Lancaster III) twelve-cylinder Vee liquid-cooled or 1,600 h.p. Bristol Hercules (Lancaster II) fourteen-cylinder two-row radial air-cooled engines in welded steel-tube nacelles cantilevered from the front spar of the wings. Three-bladed constant-speed full-feathering airscrews. Six protected fuel tanks in wings. Separate oil tank in each nacelle.

ACCOMMODATION.—Provision for a crew of seven. Bomb-aimer in the nose below the front gun-turret. Above and behind and to port is the Pilot's position in a raised canopy with good all-round vision. Inside the canopy immediately aft of the pilot's seat is the Fighting Controller's position. Slightly aft of this position is the Navigator's station, with table, chart stowage and astral dome in the roof. At the rear end of the navigator's table and just forward of the front spar is the Radio Operator's station. Within the centre-section is a rest room with bed. Aft of the rear spar are the mid upper and mid lower turrets, together with various equipment stowages for flares, emergency rations, etc. In the extreme tail is the rear turret. A walkway is provided along the entire length of the fuselage and the main entrance door is situated on the starboard side just forward of the tail-plane.

ARMAMENT, BOMBS, ARMOUR AND EQUIPMENT.—Ten Browning .303 machine-guns in four hydraulically-operated Nash & Thompson turrets, one in the nose, two amidships and one in the extreme tail. The tail-turret carries four guns, the remainder two each. The tail-turret is fed by ammunition tracks from boxes in the rear fuselage. The bomb compartment is 33 ft. long and has normal accommodation for a maximum weight of approximately 4 tons in various combinations of bombs. The largest size which can be carried under special conditions is the 22,000 lb. bomb. An armoured bulkhead is fitted across the centre-section portion of the fuselage and is so arranged that it will open up for passage through the fuselage on either side of the centre-line. The back of the pilot's seat is armour-plated and there is armour protection behind his head. Certain other vulnerable parts of the structure and the turrets are armoured. Special bullet-proof glass is provided for the fighting controller's position. Full night-flying equipment, radio, flares, oxygen, de-icing equipment, etc. A dinghy is carried in the centre-section trailing-edge portion of the wing and is automatically released and inflated in a crash alighting in the sea. It can also be operated by hand.

DIMENSIONS.—Span 102 ft. (31.1 m.), Length 69 ft. 4 in. (21.1 m.), Height 20 ft. (6.1 m.), Net wing area 1,205 sq. ft. (112 sq. m.), Gross wing area 1,297 sq. ft. (120.5 sq. m.).

WEIGHTS AND LOADINGS.—Weight empty 37,000 lbs. (16,750 kg.), Maximum bomb load 18,000 lbs. (8,170 kg.), Normal loaded weight 68,000 lbs. (30,800 kg.). Wing loading 52.7 lbs./sq. ft. (258 kg./sq. m.). Power loading 13.3 lbs./h.p. (6.35 kg./h.p.).

PERFORMANCE.—Maximum speed 275 m.p.h. (440 km.h.). Maximum range approximately 3,000 miles (4,800 km.).

THE AVRO 652A ANSON.

The Anson was evolved from the Avro 652 commercial monoplane which was designed and built to the order of Imperial Airways in 1933. The 652A, or Anson I, went into service in the R.A.F. in 1936 as a General Reconnaissance monoplane. It was also adapted for certain specialised training duties.

Before the end of its operational career with Coastal Command the Anson had been earmarked to be the standard twin-engined trainer for the Commonwealth Air Training Plan then being organized in Canada. Production of the trainer was originally

to be undertaken in England but owing to the grave war situation and the shortage of shipping space in 1940 the decision was taken to build the Anson in Canada and to equip it with engines of American design which were then readily available.

A Government-owned company, Federal Aircraft, Ltd. (which see), was set up to handle Anson production in Canada, the Dominion being responsible for the production of the Anson II, III, V and VI. The Mark numbers VII, VIII and IX were also allotted for use in Canada but they were never used. Production continued in England to meet domestic needs, the British versions being the Mk. I, X, XI, and XII.

Hereafter follows brief details of the principal versions of the Anson :—

Anson I. Two 320 h.p. Armstrong Siddeley Cheetah IX engines. Originally built as a General Reconnaissance aircraft and armed with one fixed forward-firing Vickers .303 in. machine-gun in the nose and one Lewis or Vickers K .303 in. gun in an Armstrong Whitworth manually-operated turret amidships. Internal stowage for two 100 lb. bombs and external racks for eight 20 lb. bombs, flares or smoke-floats. Manually-operated landing-gear and flaps. Normal loaded weight 7,663 lbs. (3,476 kg.). Maximum permissible loaded weight 8,000 lbs. (3,627 kg.). On being withdrawn from operational use, the Anson I was converted for navigation or armament training. In former version turret deleted. Production Anson I armament trainers fitted with a Bristol Mk. VI hydraulically-operated turret.

Anson II. Canadian-built under the ægis of Federal Aircraft, Ltd. Two 330 h.p. Jacobs L-6BM engines in new nacelles. Hydraulically-operated Dowty landing-gear retraction. Canadian-built accessories. Moulded plastic-plywood nose. Otherwise similarity in design permitted parts being approximately 75% interchangeable with the British-built Anson. The first Anson II flew in August, 1941. Standard advanced trainer in the Commonwealth Joint Air Training Programme. The Anson II was supplied to the U.S. Army Air Forces under the designation AT-20.

Anson III. British-built airframes converted in Canada by The de Havilland Aircraft of Canada, Ltd. to take two 330 h.p. Jacobs L-6MB engines.

Anson IV. British-built airframes converted in Canada to take two Wright Whirlwind R-975-E3 engines. Only a few converted.

Anson V. Canadian-built under the ægis of Federal Aircraft, Ltd. Two 450 h.p. Pratt & Whitney R-985-AN14B engines. Navigational trainer. New fuselage mainly of plastic-plywood construction. For full constructional details see under "Federal" (Canada). First Anson V flew in November, 1942.

Anson VI. Similar to Anson V except equipped as a bombing and gunnery trainer. Fitted with Bristol Mk. VI hydraulically-operated gun turret.

Anson X. Two 320 h.p. Armstrong Siddeley Cheetah IX engines. Conversion of Anson I for light transport use. Strengthened floor. Loaded weight 9,450 lbs. (4,290 kg.).

Anson XI. Two Armstrong Siddeley Cheetah XIX engines driving Fairey-Reed fixed-pitch metal airscrews. Light transport. Raised cabin roof to give more headroom in cabin. Crew of two and six passengers or light freight. Hydraulically-operated landing-gear and flaps.

Anson XII. Two 420 h.p. Armstrong Siddeley Cheetah XV engines driving Rotol two-blade constant-speed airscrews. Otherwise similar to Anson XI. In civil guise this is the Avro XIX. Loaded weight 9,500 lbs. (4,313 kg.).

TYPE.—Twin-engined Advanced Training monoplane.

WINGS.—Single-piece cantilever monoplane wing, consisting of two box-spars of spruce and plywood construction with plywood and spruce ribs and plywood covering. Portions aft of rear spar and carrying flaps and ailerons are built separately and are detachable for transport. Bakelite plywood, which is stronger than casein plywood and is impervious to water, is used throughout. The wing is let into the fuselage structure so that the underside of the wing is flush with the bottom of the fuselage. Frise-type balanced ailerons. Split trailing-edge flaps between ailerons and fuselage.

The Avro Anson XII Light Transport (two Armstrong Siddeley Cheetah XV engines).

The Avro XIX Six-passenger Transport, the civil version of the Anson XII.

FUSELAGE.—Rectangular welded steel-tube structure, with rigid bracing. Fabric covered over wooden fairings.

TAIL UNIT.—Monoplane type. Fixed tail-plane and rudder of same type of construction as the wing, being built up of spruce frames with plywood covering. Elevators of welded steel-tube construction, fabric covered. Fin, also of fabric-covered welded steel-tube construction, is built integral with fuselage. Trimming-tabs in rudder and elevators.

LANDING GEAR.—Retractable type. Consists of two separate units, one on either side of the fuselage mounted under each engine nacelle, into which they retract. Hand retraction in Anson I. Hydraulic operation in Canadian models. The shock-absorbing units are of compressed-air type. Non-retractable castoring tail-wheel.

POWER PLANT.—Two Armstrong Siddeley Cheetah IX, XIX or XV radial air-cooled engines on welded tubular-steel frames built out from the wing and bolted directly to the front spar. Two entirely independent engine installations, each engine being provided with its own fuel and oil tanks. These are of welded aluminium construction and are mounted in cradles in the wing. Petrol feed by means of duplicated fuel-pumps mounted on the engines. Alternative power plants fitted to the Anson in Canada include two 330 h.p. Jacobs L-6BM (Anson II and III) or two Wright Whirlwind R-975-E3 (Anson IV) or two Pratt & Whitney Wasp-Junior R-985-AN14B (Anson V and VI) radial air-cooled engines.

ACCOMMODATION.—The pilot's seat is in the extreme nose of the fuselage on the left side. Solo controls only are provided but removable dual control can be fitted if desired. Immediately behind the pilot, also on the left side is the navigator/bomb-aimer's seat. A table is provided, also a panel for navigational instruments. An alternative seat for the navigator is provided immediately to the right of the pilot. When not in use this seat can be folded along the side of the fuselage. The bomb-aimer's position is in the extreme nose of the fuselage on the right side. A sliding door in the floor when opened permits the use of a Wimperis course-setting bomb-sight. An adjustable windscreen prevents the entry of air through the aperture. There is provision for the necessary bombing instruments. On the bomber's right hand are the controls for releasing the bombs. Internal stowage is provided for 2—100 lb. and up to 8—20 lb. bombs in the wing. There is alternative external stowage for 2—250 lb. bombs. The pilot is also provided with bomb-release controls. The wireless-operator/gunner's seat is on the left side of the fuselage immediately behind the navigator's. The wireless apparatus is mounted in front of the operator and a table is provided. A fixed aerial is provided but there is also provision for a trailing aerial. At the after end of the cabin is a small door which communicates with the rear gun-station. This may be equipped with either an Armstrong Whitworth totally-enclosed rotating gun-turret armed with one Lewis gun with stowage for five ammunition drums or a Bristol electro-hydraulically-operated gun-turret with two belt-fed Browning guns. Entrance to the cabin and all the crew's stations is through a door on the right side of the fuselage.

DIMENSIONS.—Span 56 ft. 6 in. (17.20 m.), Length 42 ft. 3 in. (12.90 m.), Height 13 ft. 1 in. (4 m.), Wing area 463 sq. ft. (43.1 sq. m.).

WEIGHTS AND LOADINGS.—Weight empty 6,510 lbs. (2,952 kg.), Military load, crew, fuel and oil, 1,990 lbs. (905 kg.), Weight loaded 8,500 lbs. (3,860 kg.), Maximum permissible loaded weight 9,900 lbs. (4,490 kg.), Wing loading 20.7 lbs./sq. ft. (101.5 kg./sq. m.), Power loading 12.15 lbs./h.p. (5.51 kg./h.p.).

PERFORMANCE.—Maximum speed at sea level 170 m.p.h. (272 km.h.), Maximum speed at 7,000 ft. (2,130 m.) 188 m.p.h. (303 km.h.), Maximum speed at 10,000 ft. (3,050 m.) 186 m.p.h. (297.6 km.h.), Maximum speed at 15,000 ft. (4,580 m.) 175 m.p.h. (280 km.h.), Landing speed 57 m.p.h. (92 km.h.), Cruising speed at 6,000 ft. (1,830 m.) 158 m.p.h. (252.8 km.h.), Initial rate of climb 750 ft./min. (229 m./min.), Rate of climb at 6,000 ft. (1,830 m.) 905 ft./min. (276 m./min.), Climb to 5,000 ft. (1,530 m.) 5.2 mins., Climb to 10,000 ft. (3,050 m.) 11.6 mins., Climb to 15,000 ft. (4,580 m.) 21.7 mins., Service ceiling 19,500 ft. (5,948 m.).

THE AVRO XIX.

The Avro XIX is the civil version of the Anson XII which is offered as a light transport suitable for commercial or feeder-line use.

It has accommodation for a crew of two and six passengers. Aft of the passenger cabin, which is more luxuriously furnished than the military Anson XII, there is a lavatory and baggage compartment.

All structural details are as for the Anson. The power-plant consists of two Armstrong Siddeley Cheetah XV engines, each driving a two-blade Rotol constant-speed airscrew.

DIMENSIONS.—Span 56 ft. 6 in. (17.23 m.), Length 42 ft. 3 in. (12.88 m.), Height (tail down) 13 ft. 1 in. (4.0 m.), Nett wing area 410 sq. ft. (38 sq. m.), Gross wing area 463 sq. ft. (43 sq. m.).

WEIGHTS.—Tare weight 6,114 lbs. (2,775 kg.), Fixed and removable equipment (including electrical, instruments and radio) 440 lbs. (200 kg.), Furnishings (including soundproofing, wall panels, carpets, curtains, toilet and passenger seats) 460 lbs. (209 kg.), Crew (two) 350 lbs. (159 kg.), Passengers (six) 1,050 lbs. (477 kg.), Passenger's baggage 180 lbs. (82 kg.), Fuel (140 Imp. gallons) 1,050 lbs. (477 kg.), Oil (14 Imp. gallons) 126 lbs. (57 kg.), Weight loaded 9,770 lbs. (4,432 kg.).

PERFORMANCE.—Maximum speed at sea level 190 m.p.h. (304 km.h.), Cruising speed (rich mixture) 175 m.p.h. (280 km.h.) at 5,000 ft. (1,525 m.), Cruising speed (weak mixture) 167 m.p.h. (267 km.h.) at 7,000 ft. (2,135 m.), Initial rate of climb 1,000 ft./min. (305 m./min.), Rate of climb at 2,320 ft. (710 m.) 900 ft./min. (275 m./min.), Service ceiling 18,750 ft. (5,726 m.), Absolute ceiling on two engines 20,750 ft. (6,330 m.), Absolute ceiling on one engine 5,000 ft. (1,525 m.).

RANGES (in still air, with allowance for warm-up, take off and climb).—600 miles (960 km.) at 160 m.p.h. (256 km.h.) or 660 miles (1,056 km.) at 140 m.p.h. (224 km.h.).

THE AVRO LINCOLN.

The Lincoln is a four-engined Heavy Bomber which is virtually a scaled-up version of the Lancaster. In fact, the Lincoln I and II were originally known as the Lancaster IV and V.

The Lincoln incorporates modifications and improvements suggested as the result of extensive operational experience with the Lancaster in a design which was obviously evolved for the Far Eastern Theatre. Overall dimensions have been increased to permit greater load-carrying capacity and longer range and the aircraft has been completely re-armed with .50 in. guns, two in a nose turret, two in a mid-upper turret, one beneath the fuselage and two in a tail turret. Later aircraft have two 20 m/m. cannon in the mid-upper turret. The normal crew is seven.

Lincoln I. Four 1,750 h.p. Rolls-Royce Merlin 85 engines driving Rotol four-blade constant-speed full-feathering airscrews.

Lincoln II. Four Rolls-Royce Merlin 68 (Packard-built Merlin 66) or Merlin 300 (Packard-built Merlin 100) engines driving D.H. Hydromatic four-blade airscrews.

Lincoln XV. The designation of the version of the Mk. I to be built in Canada by Victory Aircraft, Ltd.

Lincoln 30. The designation of the version of the Mk. I to be built in Australia by the Beaufort Division of the Department of Aircraft Production.

DIMENSIONS.—Span 120 ft. (36.6 m.), Length 78 ft. 3½ in. (23.9 m.), Height 17 ft. 3½ in. (5.3 m.), Wing area 1,421 sq. ft. (132 sq. m.).

LOADED WEIGHT.—About 75,000 lbs. (34,050 kg.).

PERFORMANCE.—Maximum speed over 300 m.p.h. (480 km.h.), Maximum range approximately 3,600 miles (5,760 km.).

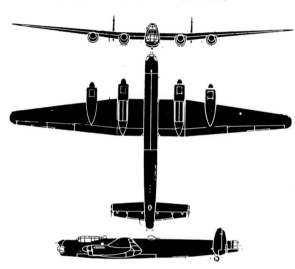

The Avro Lincoln Heavy Bomber.

The Avro Lincoln I Heavy Bomber (four Rolls-Royce Merlin 85 engines).

BLACKBURN.

BLACKBURN AIRCRAFT, LTD.

HEAD OFFICE, WORKS, AERODROME AND SEAPLANE BASE: BROUGH, E. YORKS.

LEEDS WORKS: OLYMPIA, ROUNDAY ROAD, LEEDS, 8.

SCOTTISH WORKS: CASTLE ROAD, DUMBARTON.

LONDON OFFICE: STAFFORD HOUSE, NORFOLK STREET, LONDON, W.C.2.

Chairman and Joint Managing Director: Robert Blackburn, O.B.E., A.M.I.C.E., F.R.Ae.S., M.I.Mech.E.

Directors: Major F. A. Bumpus, B.Sc., A.R.C.S., Wh.Sc., F.R.Ae.S. (Joint Managing Director), Sir Maurice Denny, Bt., C.B.E., B.Sc., M.I.C.E., M.I.N.A., Capt. N. W. Blackburn, R. R. Rhodes, M.I.Ae.E. and Sq. Ldr. J. L. N. Bennett-Baggs.

Chief Designer (Seaplanes): Major J. D. Rennie, F.R.Ae.S., A.R.T.C., A.M.I.C.E.

Chief Designer (Landplanes): G. E. Petty, F.R.Ae.S.

Founded by Mr. Robert Blackburn, who produced his first aeroplane in 1910 and has continued to manufacture aircraft ever since.

Although the Blackburn Company has concentrated mainly on naval types and specialises in torpedo-carrying aircraft, its experience covers a wide range of types, from the single-engined light aeroplane to the multi-engined flying-boat.

In 1936, the Blackburn Company came to an arrangement with the famous Scottish shipbuilding company of William Denny & Bros. Ltd., of Dumbarton, to organise and operate jointly a factory on the Clyde, and Sir Maurice Denny joined the Board of the Blackburn Company.

In 1937, the Blackburn Company received a contract for the production of the Blackburn Skua Fighter Dive-Bomber. In 1938 the Roc was adopted for use by the Fleet Air Arm.

In recent years the Company has, in addition to the develop-ment of aircraft of its own design, devoted a large part of its production facilities to the manufacture of the Fairey Swordfish and Barracuda torpedo-bombers and the Short Sunderland flying-boat. No information may be published concerning the Company's later developments although reference has been made in the press to the Blackburn Firebrand Fleet Fighter.

In 1945 details were released concerning an experimental flying-boat with a retractable planing bottom which was built by the Blackburn company in 1940. An illustrated description of the aircraft follows.

THE BLACKBURN B.20.

One of the problems which the seaplane designer has had to face has been the provision of sufficient clearance for the air-screws above the water, especially in the case of the monoplane where the engines are mounted in or on the wings. A second

The Blackburn B.20 Experimental Flying-boat with planing bottom and wing-tip floats lowered.

difficulty lies in the conflicting requirements for angle of incidence and correct streamlining between the conditions of take-off and level flight. During take-off the wings have to be held at a relatively large angle of incidence, this incidence depending on the running angle of floats or hull. For level flight, however, a much smaller angle of incidence is required and consequently the seaplane often assumes an attitude which gives a higher drag than its form would otherwise have and higher than for a comparative landplane.

Both these problems were attacked several years ago by Major J. D. Rennie, Chief Seaplane Designer of Blackburn Aircraft Ltd., who patented the somewhat novel idea of making the planing bottom of a flying-boat retractable. Details were given in Patent No. 433925. In this patent (which incidentally included the retraction of the wing-tip floats or stabilisers) the planing bottom portion of the hull was to be separated from the main portion on which it was mounted by means of a set of links. The links were so proportioned that in the lower position the hull and wings assumed the best attitude for take-off, while in the retracted position the planing bottom or pontoon fitted snugly to the hull, and the whole formed a good streamline form. The specification gave details of hydraulic operating mechanism for the retraction of the lower pontoon and of the wing-tip floats.

Such a scheme as that outlined seemed to be most suitable for boats of medium size, for with larger boats and multiple engines the height of the wing above the water increased, while the airscrew diameter remained the same. Even with power-units of increasing size, the diameter of the airscrews would not increase so quickly as the size of the hull, so that on very large flying-boats the provision of clearance for the airscrews above the water would not present much difficulty. The retractable planing bottom was actually incorporated in a twin-engined medium-size flying-boat built by the Blackburn company at its Dumbarton works and known as the B.20. This aircraft was completed and flown in 1940.

Work on the prototype was unfortunately brought to an end by an accident and although a second design had been begun embodying similar features to the B.20, further work had to be postoned as wartime demands absorbed all available design and factory capacity.

WINGS.—High-wing cantilever monoplane. Wings of constant taper with the stabilising floats forming the wing-tips when retracted. Three-spar all-metal structure with flush-riveted Alclad skin. Centre-section spars and top skin continuous across top of hull, with front and rear spars attached to strengthened hull frames. Spars have extruded booms and sheet Alclad webs, ribs have stiffened sheet Alclad webs, Alclad skin supported by lateral tubular stringers between spars throughout and in leading-edge outboard of nacelles. Leading-edge between hull and nacelles detachable and stiffened with Z-stringers. Fabric-covered Frise ailerons. Metal-covered Handley Page slotted flaps inboard of ailerons.

HULL.—All-metal stressed-skin structure built up of a series of bulkheads and frames, longitudinal stringers and a flush-riveted Alclad skin. The retractable planing bottom of similar structure and sub-divided into five watertight compartments. Wing-tip floats, of similar structure to hull, carried on single girder-type struts which lay flush with the underside of the wing when floats retracted.

TAIL UNIT.—Cantilever monoplane type. One-piece two-spar tail-plane and vertical fin of all-metal construction. Rudder and elevators have metal frames and fabric-covering.

POWER PLANT.—Two 1,720 h.p. Rolls-Royce Vulture twenty-four-cylinder X-type liquid-cooled engines driving three-blade D.H. Hydromatic constant-speed airscrews. Fuel tanks in retractable portion of hull.

ACCOMMODATION.—Crew of six. Bomb-aimer's compartment in nose, followed by flight deck and main crew compartment accommodating two pilots, seated side-by-side with dual controls, navigator, radio operator, air observer and flight engineer. Then followed the officer's wardroom with sleeping accommodation for two, and crew's sleeping quarters with accommodation for four. Aft of this was the galley, engineer's bench, lavatory, a further rest position, and stowage for dinghies, flares, etc. All mooring equipment stowed on pontoon deck or in underside of hull, all mooring operations being conducted from pontoon.

ARMAMENT.—Provision made for installation of power-operated mid-upper and tail turrets and other defensive gun positions. Bomb cells in centre-section.

DIMENSIONS.—Span (wing-tip floats retracted) 82 ft. (25 m.). Overall length 69 ft. 8 in. (21.2 m.), Height (on beaching chassis and with pontoon down) 25 ft. 2 in. (7.65 m.), Depth of hull (pontoon retracted) 11 ft. 8 in. (3.55 m.), Depth of hull (pontoon lowered) 16 ft. 4½ in. (5 m.), Gross wing area (including floats) 1,066 sq. ft. (99 sq. m.).

WEIGHT LOADED.—35,000 lbs. (15,900 kg.).

PERFORMANCE (Estimated). Maximum speed at sea level 268 m.p.h. (429 km.h.), Maximum speed at 5,750 ft. (1,755 m.) 288 m.p.h. (461 km.h.), Maximum speed at 15,000 ft. (4,575 m.) 306 m.p.h. (490 km.h.), Cruising range 1,500 miles (2,400 km.).

THE BLACKBURN B.37 FIREBRAND.

The Firebrand was originally designed as a single-seat Fleet Fighter around the Napier Sabre III 24-cylinder liquid-cooled H-type engine to Specification N.11/40. The first unarmed prototype flew on February 27, 1942, and the Mk. I prototype with full armament and military equipment five months later. At that time the Sabre engine was just going into production and because the Hawker Typhoon was more fully developed than the Firebrand, the Typhoon received priority for the new engine. It was therefore necessary to find an alternative power-plant for the Firebrand and at the same time it was decided to widen its sphere of usefulness by converting it into what is commonly termed a "strike" aircraft, that is, one capable of striking with torpedoes, heavy bombs or rockets and, after release of its load, of operating as an offensive fighter.

The final production version of the Firebrand is the Mk. IV. The intermediate stages of development are outlined below.

Firebrand F. Mk. I. Napier Sabre III 24-cylinder liquid-cooled H-type engine driving a D.H. Hydromatic three-blade airscrew. Single-seat Fleet Fighter. Armament : four 20 m/m. cannon. Coolant radiators in projections in leading-edge of wing roots. First flew in July, 1942.

Firebrand T.F. Mk. II. The Mk. I arranged as a Torpedo-carrier. Span of wings increased slightly to permit an 18-inch torpedo to be carried under the fuselage between the wheel recess doors. Torpedo gear originally of the fixed type but later a two-position gear as described under T.F. Mk. III was fitted. First flew on March 31, 1943.

Firebrand T.F. Mk. III. Bristol Centaurus VII or XI eighteen-cylinder two-row sleeve-valve radial air-cooled engine driving a Rotol four-blade constant-speed airscrew. Re-designed engine installation with air inlet and oil cooler in wing root extensions. Blackburn two-position torpedo gear under fuselage. With this gear, when the aircraft is on the ground the torpedo is carried with the tail raised to give adequate ground clearance. When the landing-gear is retracted the tail of the torpedo is lowered to the best position for a high-speed release. First flew on December 21, 1943. The Mk. III was found to be unsuitable for deck operation owing to insufficient rudder control at take-off with the new engine.

Firebrand T.F. Mk. IV. Bristol Centaurus IX engine driving a Rotol four-blade constant-speed airscrew. The production version of the Mk. III with larger vertical tail surfaces, horn-balanced rudder and upper and lower wing dive brakes. First flew on May 17, 1945. The description below refers to the Mk. IV.

TYPE.—Single-seat Torpedo-carrier and Fleet Fighter.

WINGS.—Low-wing cantilever monoplane. All-metal two-spar structure consisting of centre-section, two outer panels and detachable tips. Spars composed of hollow extruded booms joined on front and rear faces with plate webs. Spars interconnected by diaphragm ribs, with heavy double frame on centre-line to take main torpedo load. Spanwise tubular stringers on upper surfaces. Stressed skin covering. Outer wing panels fold upwards and backwards round rear spar to lie alongside fuselage. Manual operation. All-metal Frise ailerons with spring servo-tabs. Fowler-type slotted trailing-edge flaps inboard of ailerons and running on rails enclosed completely within wing section. Maximum depression angle 30 degrees. Small automatically-operated supplementary split flap on each main flap depressing 44 degrees. Two small split flaps on centre-section supplement the main flaps. Dive-brakes on upper and lower surfaces of outer wings attached to front spar limit dive to 350 m.p.h. (563.25 km.h.). Main wing root chord 9 ft. 6 ins. (2.9 m.), tip chord 4 ft. 3 in. (1.3 m.). Dihedral (outer wings) 5 degrees (on top surface of front spar).

FUSELAGE.—All-metal structure in two portions jointed at bulkhead behind cockpit. Circular-section forward portion is a tubular structure assembled on a chassis of extruded channel-section members, braced by channel members and plating and covered by detachable metal panels. Rear section is a metal monocoque of oval section.

TAIL UNIT.—Cantilever monoplane type. All-metal structure with smooth metal covering on all surfaces. Forwardly-raked fin and rudder. Trim-tab at top and spring servo-tab at bottom of horn-balanced rudder. Inset one-piece elevator with trim-tabs at outer ends and spring servo-tabs immediately inboard. Fin offset 3 degrees to starboard. Tailplane span 16 ft. 10 ins. (5.1 m.), tail-plane and elevator chord (on c. l.) 5 ft. 10 in. (1.8 m.).

LANDING GEAR.—Retractable type. Lockheed oleo pneumatic legs attached to diagonally-braced cast frames at extremities of centre-section between spars. Inwards retraction. Fairing plates attached to each leg and hinged plates below fuselage completely house undercarriage when retracted. Fully-castoring self-centering tail-wheel carried on oleo-pneumatic shock-absorber strut which retracts forward into fuselage. Automatically-operated enclosure doors. Hydraulic operation, with emergency hand-operated pump. Deck-arrester hook attached aft of tail-wheel.

POWER PLANT.—One 2,500 h.p. Bristol Centaurus IX eighteen-cylinder sleeve-valve air-cooled radial engine driving a Rotol four-blade

The Blackburn Firebrand F. Mk. I Single-seat Fleet Fighter prototype (Napier Sabre III engine).

The Blackburn Firebrand T.F. Mk. II prototype (Napier Sabre III engine) with fixed torpedo gear.

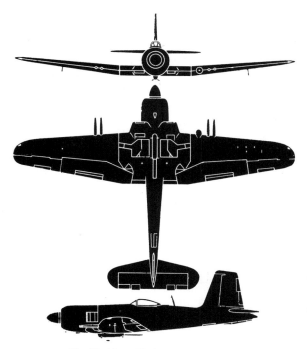

The Blackburn Firebrand T.F. Mk. IV.

The Blackburn Firebrand T.F. Mk. IV Torpedo-carrier (Bristol Centaurus IX engine).

constant-speed airscrew 13 ft. 3 in. (4 m.) diameter. Main and auxiliary self-sealing fuel tanks in fuselage. Oil tank in fuselage behind engine bulkhead. Jettisonable auxiliary fuel tanks of various sizes, up to a maximum capacity of 100 gallons, may be carried on wing bomb-racks and on the torpedo beam. Carburettor intake in port extended centre-section, oil-cooler in similar position to starboard. Jettisonable rocket-assisted take-off gear.

ACCOMMODATION.—Pilot's cockpit over trailing-edge of wing. Sliding blister-type canopy with bullet-proof windscreen. Armour plating behind and below pilot. Metal decking round cockpit of heavy gauge with good deflection qualities.

ARMAMENT.—Four 20 m/m. Hispano cannon, two in each outer wing on hinged mountings for ease of servicing. Access panel in underside of each wing. Ammunition boxes in outer wings and protected from ahead by armour plating. One 1,850 lb. (840 kg.) torpedo on Blackburn two-position mounting below fuselage. Mounting automatically lowers tail of torpedo to horizontal position when landing-gear is retracted. One 1,000 lb. (454 kg.) bomb may be carried under each wing, a rack being fitted on each gun compartment access door. Racks for Rocket Projectiles below outer wings.

EQUIPMENT.—Full equipment includes radar, radio, camera gun, torpedo camera (in leading-edge of port wing), oxygen apparatus, windscreen de-icing, signals and fire-extinguisher. 24-volt electric system.

DIMENSIONS.—Span 51 ft. 3½ in. (15.62 m.), Length 39 ft. 1 in. (12 m.), Gross wing area 381.5 sq. ft. (35.44 sq. m.), Nett wing area 353.6 sq. ft. (32.85 sq. m.).

WEIGHTS AND LOADINGS.—Weight empty 11,357 lbs. (5,152 kg.), Normal take-off weight 15,671 lbs. (7,106 kg.), Maximum weight (maximum fuel) 16,227 lbs. (7,361 kg.), Wing loading 41.7 lbs./sq. ft. (203.6 kg./sq. m.), Power loading 6.37 lbs./h.p. (2.88 kg./h.p.).

PERFORMANCE (at 15,671 lbs.=7,106 kg.).—Maximum level speed (without torpedo) 350 m.p.h. (563.25 km.h.) at 13,000 ft. (3,962 m.), Maximum level speed (with torpedo) 342 m.p.h. (550.37 km.h.) at 13,000 ft. (3,962 m.), Maximum level speed at sea level 320 m.p.h. (515 km.h.), Maximum economic cruising speed at 10,000 ft. (3,050 m.) 289 m.p.h. (465 km.h.), Cruising speed at 75% maximum economic power at 10,000 ft. (3,050 m.) 256 m.p.h. (412 km.h.), Stalling speed (flaps down) 75 m.p.h. (121 km.h.), Initial rate of climb (with torpedo) 2,200 ft./min. (670 m./min.), Initial rate of climb (without torpedo) 2,600 ft./min. (792 m./min.), Range (with torpedo—normal tankage) 745 miles (1,190 km.) at 289 m.p.h. (465 km.h.) at 10,000 ft. (3,050 m.), Maximum range (with torpedo and auxiliary fuel tanks) 1,250 miles (2,000 km.).

BOULTON PAUL.

BOULTON PAUL AIRCRAFT, LTD.

HEAD OFFICE, WORKS AND AERODROME : WOLVERHAMPTON.

Incorporated : June, 1934.

Chairman : R. G. Simpson.

Directors : J. D. North, F.R.Ae.S., M.I.Ae.E., F.R.Met. Soc. and N.R. Adshead (Joint Managing), J. Kissane and R. Beasley.

Boulton Paul Aircraft, Ltd. was formed in 1934 to take over the old-established Aircraft Department of Boulton & Paul, Ltd., together with one-third of the issued capital of A.T.S. Ltd., which company was incorporated in 1931 to hold a large number of patents relating to metal construction pooled by the following aircraft companies :—Boulton & Paul Ltd., Gloster Aircraft Co. Ltd., Sir W. G. Armstrong Whitworth Aircraft Ltd., and the Steel Wing Co.

During 1936 Boulton Paul Aircraft Ltd., moved its works from Norwich to its new factory at Wolverhampton.

The only Boulton Paul aeroplane concerning which information may be published is the Defiant, the first fighter aeroplane to be fitted with an enclosed power-driven gun-turret. It was later adapted for air target towing. In this version the power-turret was replaced by the drogue towing gear.

The Company has also designed and produced large quantities of mechanically-operated gun-turrets of various types. In addition to being engaged in the development of new experimental aircraft, details of which are not yet available for publication, Boulton Paul Aircraft, Ltd. formed part of the Group responsible for the production of the Fairey Barracuda.

THE BOULTON PAUL DEFIANT

The Defiant was designed to conform to the Air Ministry F.9/35 specification and the first flight of the prototype was made on August 11, 1937. The Defiant was the first fighter aeroplane to be fitted with an enclosed Boulton Paul power-driven gun-turret, its entire armament being concentrated therein.

Defiant I. Rolls-Royce Merlin III engine rated at 1,030 h.p. at 16,250 ft. (4,950 m.). Went into production at the end of 1937 and the first production model flew on July 30, 1939.

The Boulton Paul Defiant III Target-tug (Rolls-Royce Merlin III engine).

First used as a day fighter and on May 29, 1940, during the fighting over Dunkirk, one Defiant squadron in action for the first time, destroyed 37 enemy aircraft without loss. Later adapted to night-fighting duties.

Defiant II. Rolls-Royce Merlin XX engine rated at 1,260 h.p. at 12,250 ft. (3,730 m.). Other changes included a new engine-mounting, radiator and cowling, additional fuel tankage, a pressurised fuel system and a slightly enlarged rudder. The prototype Defiant II was flown on July 20, 1940, and deliveries of this mark were made from February 1941 to January 1942.

Defiant III. From the end of January, 1942, Defiants off the production line were delivered as target-tugs and a number of these converted for tropical use were delivered to the Royal Navy for use at training stations in Africa and the Middle and Far East. Later, several of the Mark I fighters were converted to target-tugs for use in Great Britain.

A full structural description and specification of the Defiant has been published in previous editions of this Annual.

BRISTOL.

THE BRISTOL AEROPLANE CO., LTD

HEAD OFFICE, WORKS AND AERODROME : FILTON, BRISTOL.

LONDON OFFICE : 6, ARLINGTON STREET, ST. JAMES'S, S.W.1.

Established : 1910.

Directors : W. G. Verdon Smith, C.B.E., J.P. (Chairman), Sir G. Stanley White, Bt. (Managing Director), H. J. Thomas (Assistant Managing Director), W. R. Verdon Smith, George S. White, N. Rowbotham, K. J. G. Bartlett (Sales Director) and J. S. Daniel (Business Manager).

Chief Engineer (Aircraft) : L. G. Frise.

Chief Designer (Aircraft) : A. E. Russell.

Chief Test Pilot : C. F. Uwins, O.B.E.

Founded in 1910 by the late Sir George White, Bart., pioneer of electric tramways, this company was formerly known as The British and Colonial Aeroplane Co., Ltd.

Throughout the war years Bristol aircraft, powered by Bristol engines, were in constant operational service with the Royal Air Force. With the Blenheim Mk. I in commission with Fighter and Bomber Commands in the early days, the sequence remained unbroken, with the Blenheim Mk. IV and Mk. V versions followed in rapid succession by the Beaufort Mk. I and Mk. II and the Beaufighter Mks. I, II, VI, X and XI.

The Blenheim Mk. IV served with Fighter, Bomber and Coastal Commands and the Blenheim Mk. V was later produced in large numbers for operational duties on the North African and Burma fronts.

The Beaufort Mk. I and Mk. II had meanwhile joined the ranks of Coastal Command and proved to be the most successful torpedo-carrying aircraft of the day.

The Beaufighter, having primarily acquitted itself as a long-range night-fighter was later developed into a long-range day fighter, a reconnaissance aircraft, bomber and torpedo-carrier, large numbers of which were delivered to the Royal Air Force to serve in all theatres of operations.

The total wartime production of Bristol aircraft amounted to over 14,000, including 5,400 Blenheims, 2,200 Beauforts (700 in Australia) and 5,650 Beaufighters (over 250 in Australia). In addition, over 5,000 damaged Bristol aircraft of all types were repaired and put back into service by the company's service engineers. The aircraft division of the company also supplied over 10,000 gun turrets of Bristol design for use in both operational and training aircraft.

For post-war purposes the company is engaged in the development of two main types of civil aircraft—the Type 167 (sometimes referred to as the "Brabazon Type I"), a 110-ton airliner designed for a still-air range of 5,000 miles at a cruising speed of 250 m.p.h., and the Type 170, an economical short-range freight or passenger-carrying aeroplane.

The Bristol company has also formed a Helicopter Department under the direction of Mr. Raoul Hafner, and a prototype four-seat helicopter is under development.

Details of the activities of the Aero-engine Division of the Bristol Aeroplane Co., Ltd. will be found in Section D. In addition to the current production of sleeve-valve radial engines the Division is engaged in an extensive programme of gas-turbine development.

A model of the Bristol Type 167 Long-range Airliner which is under development.

THE BRISTOL 167.

The Bristol Type 167 has been designed as a trans-ocean airliner with a still-air range of 5,000 miles (8,000 km.) and an economical cruising speed of 250 m.p.h. (400 km.h.). The illustration on the previous page shows the general arrangement of the aircraft.

The 167 will be powered by eight Bristol engines totally enclosed in the wings and geared in pairs to drive four contra-rotating tractor airscrews. All engines and accessories will be accessible from within the wing during flight.

The aircraft will have accommodation for a maximum of 224 passengers by day or 80 by night. In addition there will be two holds of 420 cu. ft. capacity for freight, mail and baggage. The flight-deck, crew and passengers, accommodation and cargo holds will be air-conditioned and pressurised to maintain an internal pressure equivalent to that found at 8,000 ft. (2,440 m.) while flying at heights of over 20,000 ft. (6,100 m.).

DIMENSIONS.—Span 230 ft. (70 m.), Length 177 ft. (54 m.), Height over rudder 52 ft. (15.9 m.).

WEIGHTS.—Weight empty 130,000 lbs. (59,020 kg.), Flight crew 2,000 lbs. (910 kg.), Disposable load 117,400 lbs. (53,300 kg.), Normal loaded weight 250,000 lbs. (113,500 kg.).

THE BRISTOL 170 FREIGHTER OR WAYFARER.

The Type 170 has been designed as a simple twin-engined cargo-carrier capable of operating from small landing grounds with a payload of from four to five tons (Freighter) or, alternatively, as an economical transport with accommodation for forty passengers (Wayfarer).

The cargo hold has been specially designed to facilitate rapid loading and unloading through the nose. Large doors opening sideways give unobstructed access to the full width of the hold. A travelling crane of 10 cwt. capacity is provided for handling heavy packages and transporting them the length of the hold. For heavier loads two cranes can be used in tandem. An auxiliary door in the side of the fuselage gives access to a separate compartment for mails or valuable freight, with a doorway into the main hold.

The cargo floor of wood on metal bearers will support a unit load of 200 lbs./sq. ft. but two strips along each side are built to carry wheeled vehicles having a maximum wheel load of 5,000 lbs. Numerous tie-down points are provided in four rows along the floor and can be provided, if necessary, in two rows along the walls.

A fixed non-retractable landing-gear is used for reliability, lightness and ease of maintenance.

TYPE.—Twin-engined Freight or Passenger carrier.

WINGS.—High wing cantilever monoplane. All-metal two-spar structure with stressed-skin covering. Hydraulically-operated split trailing-edge flaps between ailerons and fuselage.

FUSELAGE.—All-metal stressed-skin structure. Lower half of the nose is split vertically to form two doors for direct loading into the main hold.

TAIL UNIT.—Cantilever monoplane type. All-metal framework with metal-covered fixed surfaces and fabric-covered control surfaces.

LANDING GEAR.—Fixed type. Dowty liquid-spring type shock-absorber struts attached at their upper ends to the engine nacelles and hinged at their lower ends by sloping struts to the fuselage. Fixed Dowty tail-wheel with liquid-spring shock-absorber.

POWER PLANT.—Two Bristol Hercules 130 fourteen-cylinder radial air-cooled sleeve-valve engines. Two fuel tanks in wings between main spars. Total capacity 600 Imp. gallons. Fuel system designed for pressure re-fuelling.

ACCOMMODATION.—Crew of two in cabin above cargo hold. Dual control and provision for automatic pilot. Access to crew cabin from inside hold. Cabin heating by combustion heater. Space for radio to suit individual requirements. Main cargo hold extends from nose to aft of trailing-edge of wings. Main entrance to hold through nose doors opening to full width of hold. Travelling crane in roof. Separate compartment aft of hold with internal and external doors for special freight. The main hold is 31 ft. 8 in. (9.65 m.) long, has a floor area of 214 sq. ft. (19.9 sq. m.) and a volume of 2,030 cu. ft. The special compartment has a length of 8 ft. 4 in. (2.54 m.) and has a volume of 340 cu. ft.

DIMENSIONS.—Span 98 ft. (29.8 m.). Length 68 ft. 4 in. (20.8 m.).

WEIGHTS.—Tare weight 21,102 lbs. (9,580 kg.), Crew 400 lbs. (182 kg.), Disposable load 13,498 lbs. (6,128 kg.), Weight loaded 35,000 lbs. (15,890 kg.).

THE BRISTOL 156 BEAUFIGHTER

The Beaufighter was a Private Venture design which in its original form incorporated about 75 per cent. of the airframe of the Beaufort, the only entirely new components being the main fuselage and engine mountings. The wide use of Beaufort components and parts made it possible for the prototype Beaufighter with two Hercules III engines to fly on July 17, 1939, only eight months after the design began.

The Mk. I went into operation as a Home Defence Night Fighter in August, 1940, but by the Spring of 1941 the Beaufighter was serving at home and in the Middle East on long-range escort fighter and ground attack duties. It has since gone into action in the India-Burma and South-west Pacific theatres and has been adapted to many other duties, including those of bomber, torpedo-carrier and rocket fighter.

The first American night fighter squadrons in Europe were trained on and went into action with Beaufighters in the Mediterranean theatre in March, 1944.

The production versions of the Beaufighter were the Marks I, II, VI, X and XI.

Beaufighter I. Two Bristol Hercules III or XI engines. Designed as a night fighter (Mk. IF) with a crew consisting of pilot and radio operator, the latter also serving as observer and cannon loader. Armament : four 20 m/m. cannon and six .303 in. machine-guns, four in starboard wing and two in port wing. Early aircraft had drum-fed cannon with spare racks for drums, but later belt-fed cannon were introduced. Provision made for carrying bombs under the wings. Later adopted for service with Coastal Command (Mk.IC). Extra equipment added for radio-operator/navigator included navigator's table and instruments, D/F radio and Radar, provision for flame and smoke floats, etc.

Beaufighter II. Two Rolls-Royce Merlin XX engines. Owing to the heavy demand for Hercules engines for heavy bombers the Beaufighter was temporarily fitted with Merlin liquid-cooled engines in nacelles identical to those fitted to the Lancaster I. Produced in small numbers only and adapted for Fighter (Mk. IIF) and Coastal Command (Mk. IIC) duties. Same as Mk. I except for power-plant.

Beaufighter III. Two Bristol Hercules III, X or XI engines. This mark number was taken out for a so-called "slim fuselage" type of Beaufighter with twin fins and rudders. It was experimental only.

Beaufighter IV. Two Rolls-Royce Merlin XX engines. Except for power-plant this was the same as the Mk. III.

Beaufighter V. Two Rolls-Royce Merlin XX engines. This mark was allotted to the standard Mk. II fitted with a Boulton Paul four-gun turret immediately behind the pilot's cockpit. The cannon ammunition was reduced to 60 rounds per gun, and the fitting of the turret required approximately 500 watts of additional D.C. supply and the addition of a third member to the crew. Only two Beaufighter II aeroplanes were fitted out experimentally as Mk. V.

Beaufighter VI. Two Bristol Hercules VI or XVI engines. First type to be fitted with one .303 in. Vickers "K" gas-operated machine-gun at the observer's station. First type to be fitted with dihedral tailplane to improve fore and aft stability. This modification was also made retrospective. First type to be fitted with long-range fuel tanks in place of wing guns, a 50 gallon tank in the starboard gun-bay and a 24 gallon tank in the port bay. Two 29 gallon tanks also installed outboard of the engine nacelles. First type to be fitted with rocket projectiles. Various combinations of armament available to suit operational tactics, e.g. (1) four cannon and six wing guns, (2) cannon only with long-range tanks in lieu of wing guns for long-range armed reconnaissance, (3) two 500 lb. bombs with cannon and wing guns, and (4) four cannon and eight rockets, the latter in lieu of wing guns. The Mk. VI was the first to be used by the R.A.F. in India and Burma and the South-west Pacific. Also the first mark to be used by the United States Army Air Forces.

Beaufighter VII. This mark was taken out for an aircraft to be fitted with two Bristol Hercules VIII engines with turbo superchargers and driving four-blade airscrews. This installation required extensive alterations to the standard version, but drawing work was stopped and no aeroplane was produced.

Beaufighter VIII and IX. Two Bristol Hercules XVII engines. These marks were reserved for Beaufighters to be built in Australia but were never allotted.

Beaufighter X. Two Bristol Hercules XVII or XVIII engines. (The Hercules XVII and XVIII have cropped supercharger impellers to give increase in power for take-off and low altitude anti-shipping work. The XVII has the supercharger locked in M gear, the XVIII has two supercharger ratios available). Equipped as a two-seat long-range torpedo and rocket carrier for day and night duties. Armament : four 20 m/m. nose cannon and one .303 in. machine-gun in the observer's station. Six .303 in. wing guns can be installed in

The Bristol Beaufighter X fitted with Rocket Projectile equipment (two Bristol Hercules XVII engines).

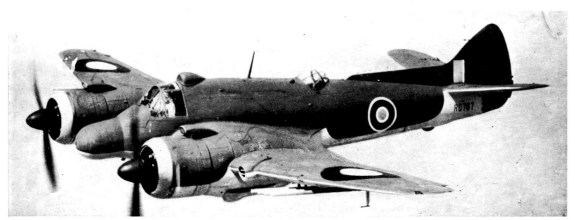

The latest version of the Beaufighter X with extended fin (two Bristol Hercules XVII engines).

The Bristol 170 Freighter or Wayfarer.

place of the long-range tanks which are normally installed. One 18 in. torpedo (1,700 lbs.) carried under fuselage or, alternatively, provision for carrying 2,000 lbs. of bombs under wings. Three cameras and special radio and navigational equipment. All Mk. X aircraft supplied to the R.A.F. fitted with Hercules XVII engines with single-stage blowers, all supplied to the R.A.A.F. fitted with Hercules XVIII with two-speed blowers. At sea level the Mk. X was claimed to be the fastest aircraft of its class in the World.

Beaufighter XI. Two Bristol Hercules XVII engines. Coastal Command fighter similar to Mk. VI except for power-plant. This model preceded the Mk. X and only a small number were built.

Beaufighter XII. This model was to have been similar to the Mk. X but with a different mark of Hercules engine, drop-tank installation and provision for carrying two 1,000 lb. bombs. It did not go into production.

Beaufighter 21. Two Bristol Hercules XVIII engines. Australian Beaufighter based on the Mk. X built by the Beaufort Division of the Australian Government Aircraft Production Department.

TYPE.—Two-seat Long-range Day and Night Fighter, Long-range Reconnaissance Fighter, Torpedo-carrier and Bomber.

WINGS.—Mid-wing cantilever all-metal monoplane. Wing in three sections comprising a nearly rectangular centre-section passing through and bolted to fuselage and two tapering outer sections set at 5° dihedral. Structure consists of two spars having single-sheet webs and extruded flanges, former ribs and stressed-skin covering. Split hydraulically-operated flaps between fuselage and ailerons. Metal-framed ailerons have fabric covering.

FUSELAGE.—All-metal monocoque in three sections. Structure of Z-section frames and L-section stringers, the whole covered with a smooth metal skin.

TAIL UNIT.—Cantilever monoplane type. Tail-plane and fin are separate structures with flush-riveted smooth metal skin, except that tips of tail-plane are of wood. Rudder and elevators have metal frames and fabric covering. Controllable trim-tabs in elevators and rudder.

LANDING GEAR.—Retractable type. Each independent unit is hydraulically raised backwards into the engine nacelle and hinged doors close the aperture. Wheels carried between two oleo-pneumatic shock-absorber legs and have pneumatically-operated twin brakes. Tail-wheel retracts forward into the fuselage.

POWER PLANT.—Two 1,600 h.p. Bristol Hercules XVII fourteen-cylinder sleeve-valve radial air-cooled engines with two-speed superchargers. Constant-speed airscrews. Fuel carried in four self-sealing tanks, two (188 Imp. gallons each) in centre-section and one (87 Imp. gallons) in each outer wing-section. Long-range tanks when fitted include one (29 Imp. gallons) outboard of each engine nacelle and two tanks in lieu of wing guns, i.e. one (24 Imp. gallons) in port gun bay and one (50 Imp. gallons) in starboard gun bay. Separate oil tank for each engine in centre-section with oil cooler in outer section. Electric starters and hand-turning gear.

ACCOMMODATION.—Crew of two with pilot in nose and observer aft of wings. Access to crew positions through hatches in under side of fuselage. These hatches are also intended for emergency exit. By a quick-release each door opens so that part protrudes outwards into airstream to create a dead-air region through which crew can drop without risk of injury even in a 400 m.p.h. (640 km.h.) dive. A knock-out panel on starboard side of pilot, a hinged window above pilot and a hinged hood above the observer provide further emergency exits.

ARMAMENT.—Four 20 m/m. cannon mounted in lower portion of the nose of the fuselage and six 0.303 in. machine-guns in the wings and outboard of the oil-cooler ducts, two in the port wing and four in the starboard wing. In certain aircraft the six wing guns are replaced by four 0.303 in. Vickers gun on manually-operated mounting in observer's station. In bomber version racks are mounted beneath wings outboard of engine nacelles. In torpedo-carrying version 18 in. torpedo carried externally under fuselage. Eight rocket projectiles, four under each wing, may be carried as alternative armament to wing guns.

EQUIPMENT.—Radio equipment mounted in fuselage between centre-section spars on port side and comprise transmitter and receiver operated by pilot by remote controls. Intercommunication telephones and signalling. Navigation, identification and formation keeping lamps, landing-flares, auto-recognition equipment, oxygen, cine-camera unit mounting, fire-extinguishers, first-aid outfit, dinghy, etc. Flying rations, emergency rations and water bottle are carried and provision made for carrying a 4-gallon water tank for desert use.

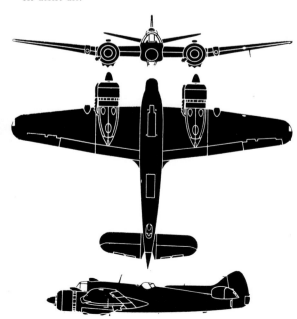

The Beaufighter X with extended fin.

The Bristol Beaufort I Torpedo-Bomber (two Bristol Taurus XII engines).

A Bristol Beaufort II with armament removed and modified for use as a Trainer.

DIMENSIONS.—Span 57 ft. 10 in. (17.65 m.), Length 41 ft. 4 in. (12.6 m.), Height 15 ft. 10 in. (4.84 m.).

WEIGHTS.—(Mks. VI and XI).—Tare weight 14,875 lbs. (6,747 kg.), Disposable load 7,904 lbs. (3,585 kg.), Weight loaded (including two 250 lb. bombs) 22,779 lbs. (10,332 kg.).

WEIGHTS (Mk. X).—Tare weight 15,592 lbs. (7,072 kg.), Disposable load 9,808 lbs. (4,448 kg.), Weight loaded (including one 18 in. torpedo) 25,400 lbs. (11,521 kg.).

PERFORMANCE.—(Mk. VI).—Maximum speed 315 m.p.h. (507 km.h.) at 14,000 ft. (4,420 m.), Rate of climb 2,000 ft./min. (610 m./min.), Service ceiling 26,000 ft. (7,930 m.), Nominal range 1,540 miles (2,480 km.) at 15,000 ft. (4,575 m.).

PERFORMANCE (Mks. X and XI).—Maximum speed 320 m.p.h. (515 km.h.) at 10,000 ft. (3,050 m.), Speed at sea level 305 m.p.h. (491 km.h.), Rate of climb (with torpedo) 1,600 ft./min. (490 m./min.), Service ceiling (without torpedo) 19,000 ft. (5,795 m.), Range (with torpedo and normal tankage) 1,400 miles (2,253 km.), Range (with torpedo and long-range tanks) 1,750 miles (2,816 km.).

THE BRISTOL 152 BEAUFORT

The Beaufort was designed in 1937 to combine the requirements of Air Ministry specifications G.24/35 and M.15/35, the former for a general reconnaissance bomber and the latter for a land-based torpedo-bomber. The prototype flew in October, 1938, and the first production Beaufort I a year later.

In its four years of operational service the Beaufort underwent certain changes, mainly in power-plant and armament. These are detailed hereafter.

Beaufort I. Originally fitted with two Bristol Taurus II or VI fourteen-cylinder two-row radial sleeve-valve engines driving D.H. three-blade Hydromatic airscrews. Later models fitted with Taurus XII or XVI engines. Armament originally consisted of one .303 in. gun in the nose of the fuselage and one .303 in. gun in a Daimler-built dorsal turret. This was later augmented to include two nose guns, two guns in a Bristol power-operated dorsal turret, two side guns and, in some models, one backward-firing gun in a blister under the nose of the fuselage with periscopic sight and remote control.

Beaufort II. Two Pratt & Whitney R-1830-S3C4-G Twin-Wasp engines driving Curtiss Electric constant-speed airscrews. Otherwise as Mk. I.

Beaufort III. Two Rolls-Royce Merlin XX engines in standard nacelles as used in the Beaufighter II and Lancaster I. An installation which did not proceed beyond the experimental stage.

The Beaufort was also manufactured in Australia, over 700 being built before the type was superseded by the Beaufighter on the Australian production lines. The Australian Beaufort was originally to be a replica of Mk. I but owing to the situation in Europe in 1940 it was found impossible to export Taurus engines. The Beaufort was therefore re-designed in Australia to take the Australian-built Pratt & Whitney R-1830-SC3-G Twin-Wasp to become the Mk. IA.

A full structural description and specification of the Beaufort has been published in previous issues of this Annual.

DIMENSIONS.—Span 58 ft. (17.7 m.), Length 44 ft. 7 in. (13.6 m.), Height 12 ft. 5 in. (3.78 m.), Wing area 503 sq. ft. (46.7 sq. m.).

WEIGHTS (Beaufort I).—Tare weight 13,107 lbs. (5,945 kg.), Disposable load 8,121 lbs. (3,683 kg.), Weight loaded (including torpedo) 21,228 lbs. (9,629 kg.).

WEIGHTS (Beaufort II).—Tare weight 14,074 lbs. (6,384 kg.), Disposable load 8,009 lbs. (3,633 kg.), Weight loaded (including torpedo) 22,083 lbs. (10,017 kg.).

PERFORMANCE (Beaufort I).—Maximum speed (with torpedo) 225 m.p.h. (362 km.h.) at sea level, Rate of climb 1,150 ft./min. (350 m./min.), Service ceiling 16,500 ft. (5,032 m.), Nominal range 1,600 miles (2,575 km.).

PERFORMANCE (Beaufort II).—Maximum speed (with torpedo) 230 m.p.h. (370 km.h.) at sea level, Rate of climb 1,400 ft./min. (427 m./min.), Service ceiling 22,500 ft. (6,862 m.), Nominal range 1,450 miles (2,333 km.).

THE BRISTOL 163 BUCKINGHAM.

The Buckingham was produced in 1942 as a medium-range high-speed bomber capable of carrying a crew of four and a bomb-load of 4,000 lbs. Owing to changing strategical requirements and the fact that the D.H. Mosquito had been adapted to carry this load, the Buckingham B.Mk.I did not go into service. Many, however, were converted into military transports as C.Mk.I by the removal of the dorsal turret and other armament and a re-arrangement of the fuselage. The description below refers to the B.Mk.I.

TYPE.—Twin-engined Medium Bomber, later converted for Transport duties.

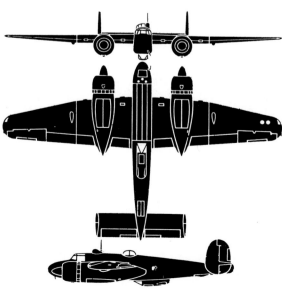

The Bristol Buckingham B. Mk. I Medium Bomber.

The Bristol Buckingham B. Mk. I Medium Bomber (two Bristol Centaurus XI engines).

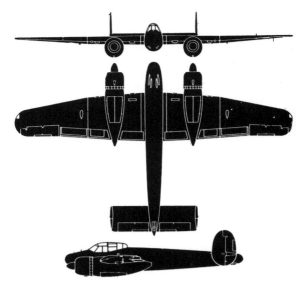

The Bristol Brigand Long-range Attack Monoplane.

The Bristol Buckingham C. Mk. I. Transport (two Bristol Centaurus IV engines).

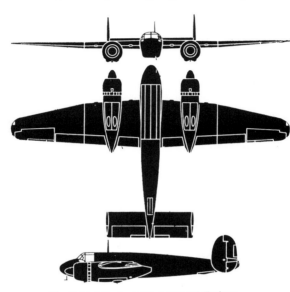

The Bristol Buckmaster Advanced Trainer.

WINGS.—Mid-wing cantilever monoplane. Two-spar all-metal stressed skin structure. Wing in four sections, consisting of two inner sections carrying the engine nacelles and landing-gear and attached to stub roots integral with the fuselage, and two outer sections. Fabric-covered Frise ailerons. Split flaps in six sections between ailerons and nacelles and nacelles and fuselage.

FUSELAGE.—Light alloy semi-monocoque structure in three sections, consisting of front fuselage, rear fuselage and stern frame.

TAIL UNIT.—Cantilever monoplane type with twin fins and rudders. All-metal framework with metal covered fins, tailplane and elevators and fabric-covered rudders. Each rudder in two portions divided by elevators. Spring servo-tabs in upper portion of rudders and in elevators. Gross tailplane and elevator area 119 sq. ft. (11.05 sq. m.).

LANDING GEAR.—Retractable type. Each main unit, consisting of two levered-suspension oleo legs and a single wheel, raised backward into engine nacelle and completely enclosed by doors. Self-centering levered-suspension tailwheel unit retracts forwards into fuselage and enclosed by doors. Hydraulic retraction. Dunlop wheels, tyres and brakes. Cartridge-operated emergency system for lowering landing-gear. Track 20 ft. (6.9 m.).

POWER PLANT.—Two Bristol Centaurus VII or XI eighteen-cylinder sleeve-valve radial air-cooled engines driving Rotol, four-blade constant-speed full-feathering airscrews. Fan-assisted cooling and electrically-operated gills at trailing-edge of cowlings. Internal backswept exhaust-pipes. Self-sealing fuel tanks in wings.

ACCOMMODATION.—Crew of four, consisting of pilot, navigator/bomb-aimer, radio operator and turret gunner. Bomb-aiming and navigating position in gondola beneath fuselage aft of wings. All crew positions provided with armour protection, oxygen and heating.

ARMAMENT.—Total armament of ten .303-in. machine-guns disposed as follows :—four fixed forward-firing in the nose, four (or two .50-in.) in a Bristol hydraulically-operated dorsal turret, and two rearward-firing in the ventral gondola position and operated by a separate hydraulic system. Various bomb loads up to 4,000 lbs. (1,820 kg.) in internal bomb-bay.

EQUIPMENT.—Full equipment includes flotation bags, de-icing equipment, barrage cable cutters, night-flying equipment, etc.

DIMENSIONS.—Span 71 ft. 10 in. (21.9 m.), Length 46 ft. 10 in. (14.3 m.), Height (over radio mast) 17 ft. 6 in. (5.3 m.), Gross wing area 708 sq. ft. (65.7 sq. m.).

WEIGHTS.—Weight empty 24,042 lbs. (10,905 kg.), Disposable load 12,992 lbs. (5,893 kg.), Normal loaded weight 37,034 lbs. (16,779 kg.), Maximum overload weight 38,050 lbs. (17,259 kg.).

PERFORMANCE.—Maximum speed (at 36,600 lbs.=16,602 kg.) 330 m.p.h. (528 km.h.) at 12,000 ft. (3,660 m.), Initial rate of climb 1,700 ft./min. (520 m./min.), Service ceiling 25,000 ft. (7,625 m.), Still-air range (normal tankage=1,055 Imp. gallons) 2,240 miles (3,585 km.) at 15,000 ft. (4,575 m.) at 200 m.p.h. (320 km.h.), Maximum reinforcing range (with wing and two fuselage tanks= 1,455 Imp. gallons) 3,180 miles (5,090 km.) at 200 m.p.h. (320 km.h.).

THE BRISTOL 164 BRIGAND.

The Brigand is a twin-engined three-seat Long-range Attack aircraft capable of fulfilling the duties of a dive-bomber, torpedo-fighter, mine-carrier or day or night fighter, with correspondingly suitable tankage for all operational requirements. But for the sudden end of hostilities the Brigand was destined to take the place of the Beaufighter in the Pacific theatre of war.

A development of the Buckingham, the Brigand uses wings, landing-gear, engine-nacelles and tail-unit which are similar to those of the Buckingham. An entirely new fuselage of smaller cross-sectional area has accommodation for a pilot, navigator/torpedo operator and radio operator/gunner grouped together in the forward fuselage.

The aircraft is built in ten main units comprising the front and rear fuselage, stern frame, inner and outer wings (port and starboard), tail-unit and the two power units. To simplify assembly all controls, hydraulic piping, electrical wiring, etc., have junctions at the ends of the unit into which they are built.

TYPE.—Twin-engined three-seat Long-range Attack monoplane suitable for dive-bombing, torpedo-carrying, mine-laying or day or night fighting.

WINGS.—Mid-wing cantilever monoplane. All-metal two-spar stressed skin structure, similar in arrangement and construction to the Buckingham. Metal-covered Frise type ailerons with pilot-operated trim-tabs. Hydraulically-operated split flaps in six sections, one on each outer and two on each inner wing section and operated by torsional control tubes. Bellows-type dive brakes above the trailing-edge and on the underside of the split flaps. These are maintained closed by venturi valves and ducts in the leading-edge which cause a reduction in pressure within the bellows. To operate brakes valves are closed by hydraulic jacks and ram pressure then builds up to force bellows open.

The Bristol Brigand Long-range Attack Monoplane (two Bristol Centaurus 57 engines).

The Bristol Buckmaster Advanced Trainer (two Bristol Centaurus IV engines).

PERFORMANCE.—Maximum speed 358 m.p.h. (573 km.h.) at 14,000 ft. (4,270 m.), Maximum weak mixture cruising speed 311 m.p.h. (498 km.h.) at 21,300 ft. (6,500 m.), Initial rate of climb 1,500 ft./min. (458 m./min.), Service ceiling 26,000 ft. (7,930 m.), Climb to service ceiling 33 mins., Maximum still-air range 2,100 miles (3,360 km.) at 10,000 ft. (3,050 m.) at 198 m.p.h. (317 km.h.).

THE BRISTOL 166 BUCKMASTER.

The Buckmaster is a three-seat Advanced Trainer version of the Buckingham with the ventral gondola, turret and all armament removed and the fuselage widened at the cockpit to permit side-by-side seating. The structure of the Buckmaster is identical to that of the Buckingham.

The crew of three consists of instructor, pupil-pilot and radio operator. The pilot's cockpit is fitted with complete dual controls, the pupil being seated on the port side. Duplicated controls include those for landing-gear, flaps, airscrews, throttles and brakes. There is an overriding brake control for the instructor's use in an emergency. The radio operator's position is between the main spars with the equipment grouped mainly on the port side. Night and blind flying equipment, fire-extinguishers, emergency signalling and dinghy are fitted.

DIMENSIONS.—Same as for Buckingham.

WEIGHT LOADED.—33,700 lbs. (15,286 kg.).

PERFORMANCE.—Maximum speed 352 m.p.h. (563 km.h.) at 12,000 ft. (3,660 m.), Maximum weak mixture cruising speed 325 m.p.h. (520 km.h.) at 18,000 ft. (5,490 m.), Initial rate of climb 2,245 ft./min. (684 m./min.), Service ceiling 30,000 ft. (9,150 m.).

FUSELAGE.—Oval section semi-monocoque structure in three portions comprising front and rear sections and stern frame. Structure consists of channel-section frames, angle-section stringers and stressed light-alloy skin.

TAIL UNIT.—Cantilever monoplane type with twin fins and rudders. Fixed surfaces of stressed-skin construction. Elevators and rudders have tubular spars, Alclad ribs and are fabric-covered. Elevators and rudders fitted with controllable trim-tabs.

LANDING GEAR.—Retractable type similar to that fitted to the Buckingham. Main and tail-wheel units of levered-suspension type. Electrically-fired cartridge-operated emergency lowering system.

POWER PLANT.—Two 2,585 h.p. Bristol Centaurus 57 eighteen-cylinder two-row sleeve-valve radial air-cooled engines, each driving a Rotol four-blade constant-speed airscrew. Close-fitting low-drag cowlings with Rotol cooling fans and electrically-operated trailing-edge gills. Self-sealing fuel tanks in wings.

ACCOMMODATION.—Crew of three comprising pilot, navigator/torpedo operator, and radio operator/gunner in tandem seats under a continuous transparent canopy.

ARMAMENT.—Four 20 m/m. cannon in underside of fuselage and firing through ports under the nose. One flexible .50-in. machine-gun in rear gunner's position. Torpedo, mine or bombs carried under fuselage, and one bomb or four rocket-projectiles under each wing.

DIMENSIONS.—Span 72 ft. 4 in. (22 m.), Length 46 ft. 5 in. (14.2 m.), Height (over rudder) 17 ft. 5 in. (5.3 m.).

WEIGHTS.—Weight empty 24,627 lb. (11.180 kg.), Disposable load 13,566 lb. (6,160 kg.), Take-off weight 38,193 lb. (17,340 kg.).

CHILTON.

CHILTON AIRCRAFT.

HEAD OFFICE AND WORKS: HUNGERFORD, BERKS.

Partners: The Hon. Andrew Dalrymple, M.A., A.F.R.Ae.S. and A. R. Ward.

Chilton Aircraft was formed in 1936 and its first production was an ultra-light single-seat monoplane fitted with the Carden converted Ford-Ten four-cylinder water-cooled engine of 32 h.p. Chilton Aircraft subsequently took over the stock of Carden Aero-Engines, Ltd., and continued to assemble these engines for their own requirements as well as for various other users.

Another version of the Chilton monoplane fitted with a 40 h.p. Train engine was produced shortly before the outbreak of War and this model won the Folkestone Trophy Race in the Summer of 1939.

Another model which was under construction at the outbreak of War was a two-seat cabin monoplane to be powered with any suitable engine of about 90 h.p. Various other models, including a light five-seat twin-engined cabin monoplane, were under development.

The company was fully engaged on sub-contract work on behalf of the Ministry of Aircraft Production throughout the War, but it is now planning to revive some of its interrupted projects. It will also undertake the manufacture of a comprehensive range of training gliders and high-efficiency sailplanes.

Descriptions of the various Chilton monoplanes and of the Carden engine have appeared in previous issues of this Annual.

CHRISLEA.

CHRISLEA AIRCRAFT CO., LTD.

HEAD OFFICE AND WORKS: HESTON AIRPORT, MIDDLESEX.

Directors: R. C. Christoforides and E. E. Christoforides.

The Chrislea Aircraft Co., Ltd. was formed in 1936 to manufacture light aircraft. Its first prototype L.C.1 was completed in 1938 and this aircraft was undergoing flight tests when the war broke out. The company then abandoned all private work and went over to component manufacture for military aircraft.

In 1944 the company completed a new design, the C.H.3, which it intends to place on the market as soon as possible.

THE CHRISLEA C.H.3.

TYPE.—Four-seat light cabin monoplane.

WINGS.—High-wing rigidly-braced monoplane. Wings attached to top of fuselage and braced to lower longerons by streamline steel-tube Vee struts. Wing structure consists of two wooden box spars, plywood ribs and a plywood skin covering.

FUSELAGE.—Welded steel-tube structure covered with fabric.

TAIL UNIT.—Cantilever monoplane type. Same structure as wings.

LANDING GEAR.—Cantilever tricycle type. Dunlop wheels. Bendix brakes on main wheels.

POWER PLANT.—One 85/90 h.p. Franklin or 100 h.p. Monaco four-cylinder horizontally-opposed air-cooled engine driving a two-blade fixed-pitch wood airscrew. Fuel capacity 17 Imp. gallons. Oil capacity 2 Imp. gallons.

ACCOMMODATION.—Enclosed cabin seating four in two pairs, the front pair with complete dual controls. Door on each side of cabin. Baggage compartment behind rear seats.

DIMENSIONS.—Span 36 ft. (11 m.), Length 20 ft. 6 in. (6.25 m.), Height 7 ft. 6 in. (2.3 m.), Wing area 154 sq. ft. (14.3 sq. m.).

WEIGHTS AND LOADINGS.—Weight empty 850 lbs. (386 kg.), Disposable load 800 lbs. (364 kg.), Pay load 500 lbs. (227 kg.), Weight loaded 1,650 lbs. (750 kg.), Wing loading (maximum) 10.70 lbs./sq. ft. (52.2 kg./sq. m.), Power loading (85 h.p.) 19.40 lbs./h.p. (8.8 kg./h.p.), Power loading (100 h.p.) 16.50 lbs./h.p. (7.5 kg./h.p.).

PERFORMANCE (Estimated).—Maximum speed (full load) 122 m.p.h. (195.2 km.h.), Cruising speed (full load) 110 m.p.h. (176 km.h.), Landing speed (no flaps) 42 m.p.h. (67.2 km.h.), Initial rate of climb (full load) 510 ft./min.(155.5 m./min.), Initial rate of climb (light) 1,450 ft./min. (442 m./min.), Range 360 miles (576 km.).

CUNLIFFE-OWEN.

CUNLIFFE-OWEN AIRCRAFT, LTD.

HEAD OFFICE AND WORKS: SWAYTHLING, SOUTHAMPTON.

Directors: Sir Hugo Cunliffe-Owen, Bt. (Chairman), M. J. H. Bruce, C.B.E., B.Sc., M.I.Mech.E. (Managing Director), J. W. S. Comber, W. Gordon Hill and W. Garrow-Fisher, A.F.R.Ae.S. (Chief Designer).

Secretary: J. R. Ingoldby.

Cunliffe-Owen Aircraft, Ltd., was formed in 1937 to build Flying Wing aircraft based on Burnelli Lifting Fuselage patents. The first machine, known as the O.A. Mk. I, was completed in 1939. It is fitted with two 900 h.p. Bristol Perseus XIIC sleeve-valve engines. This aircraft is now being used by the French authorities for transport purposes in Africa and is probably the first prototype aircraft to go into service. The Company is continuing to develop this type of aircraft and a further model known as the O.A. Mk. II has been designed. Descriptions of both these models were given in the 1940 edition of this Annual. Work is now proceeding on designs for post-war airline work.

Cunliffe-Owen Aircraft Ltd., has handled very extensive contracts in connection with the War programme.

DE HAVILLAND.

THE DE HAVILLAND AIRCRAFT CO., LTD.

HEAD OFFICE, WORKS AND AERODROME: HATFIELD, HERTS.

ENGINE WORKS: STAG LANE, EDGWARE, MIDDLESEX.

AIRSCREW WORKS: EDGWARE, MIDDLESEX, AND BOLTON, LANCASHIRE.

AERONAUTICAL TECHNICAL SCHOOL: HATFIELD.

Chairman: A. S. Butler.

Technical Director: Sir Geoffrey de Havilland, C.B.E., A.F.C., F.R.Ae.S.

Director and Chief Engineer: C. C. Walker, A.M.Inst.C.E., A.F.R.Ae.S.

Managing Director: W. E. Nixon.

Business Director: Francis E. N. St. Barbe.

Director: T. P. Mills.

Associated Companies:—

The de Havilland Aircraft Pty., Ltd., Kingsford Smith Aerodrome, Mascot, N.S.W., Australia.

The de Havilland Aircraft Co. of New Zealand, Ltd., Rongotai, Wellington, New Zealand.

The de Havilland Aircraft of Canada, Ltd., Station L, Toronto, Canada.

The de Havilland Aircraft Co., Ltd., Finlay House, McLeod Road, Karachi, India.

The de Havilland Aircraft Co. of S.A. (Pty.), Ltd., Johannesburg, S. Africa.

The de Havilland Aircraft Co. (Rhodesia) Ltd., Salisbury, S. Rhodesia.

The de Havilland Forge, Ltd., England.

The Hearle-Whitley Engineering Co., Ltd., England.

Airspeed, Ltd., Portsmouth, England.

The de Havilland Aircraft Co., Ltd., which was founded in 1920, has concentrated, to a very large extent, on the development of commercial aircraft of all kinds. Its history up to the outbreak of war was largely a record of the production of successful commercial types. These have given exceptional service all over the World and under the widest possible range of operating conditions.

The most notable aircraft of de Havilland design to go into service in the R.A.F. was the Mosquito twin-engined high-performance military monoplane which was in large-scale production in Great Britain, Canada and Australia. Other types of D.H. aircraft which were used by the R.A.F. include the Tiger-Moth; the Dragon-Rapide communications type and Dominie wireless and navigational trainer.

The 100th D.H. design marks a notable stage in the development of de Havilland military aircraft. The D.H. 100 Vampire single-seat jet-propelled twin-engined fighter was the first aeroplane to exceed 500 m.p.h. in level flight and was, at the time of writing the fastest aeroplane in the World over a considerable altitude range. Another outstanding military type is the D.H. 103 Hornet twin-engined single-seat fighter.

The Company introduced the manufacture and general use of variable-pitch airscrews into Great Britain in 1934-35. De Havilland airscrews were originally based on the Hamilton design and most of the new bomber, fighter and other types now coming into service in the R.A.F. are fitted with de Havilland constant-speed airscrews. The latest developments are a six-bladed contra-rotating constant-speed airscrew and a new Hydromatic airscrew incorporating both feathering and reverse pitch for braking.

Details of de Havilland aero-engines will be found in the appropriate section of this Annual.

THE D.H.104 DOVE.

The D.H.104 is a small twin-engined transport which will be suitable for feeder-line service, charter traffic, executive travel and private ownership. It has been specifically designed for World-wide suitability and for airports of moderate size. It will carry a crew of two with dual controls and eight passengers, with toilet accommodation and fore and aft baggage compartments. Without the toilet the cabin will seat ten passengers, or eleven if the aft baggage compartment is also eliminated.

The D.H.104 is an all-metal low-wing cantilever monoplane with a quick-retracting tricycle landing-gear. It will be powered with two supercharged D.H. Gipsyqueen 71 six-cylinder in-line inverted air-cooled engines, each driving a three-blade D.H. constant-speed feathering and braking airscrew.

TYPE.—Twin-engined eight/eleven-seat Light Transport.

WINGS.—Low-wing cantilever monoplane. Wings in two main sections attached directly to the sides of the fuselage, a built-up box spar

The D.H. Dove Light Commercial Transport (two D.H. Gipsy Queen 71 engines).

member forming part of the fuselage structure interconnecting the main spars of the two wing sections. All-metal stressed-skin wing has an I-section main spar, a built-up false spar carrying the flap and aileron hinges and, between the fuselage and engine nacelle forward of the main spar, a further false spar carrying the attachment points for the engine bearers. Detachable leading-edge to permit installation of wing de-icing equipment. Flaps and ailerons have metal frames and are fabric-covered.

FUSELAGE.—All-metal stressed-skin monocoque structure.

TAIL UNIT.—Cantilever monoplane type. All-metal tailplane and fin with stressed covering. Elevators and rudder have metal frames and fabric covering.

LANDING GEAR.—Retractable tricycle type. Main wheels, below engine nacelles, retract outwardly into wells in the underside of the wings. Nose-wheel raised backwards into fuselage. Pneumatic retraction with mechanical emergency gear. Main wheel units interchangeable. Pneumatic wheel brakes. Fully-castoring self-centering nose wheel with Dunlop-Marstrand non-shimmying tyre.

POWER PLANT.—Two 330 h.p. D.H. Gipsy Queen 71 six-cylinder in-line inverted air-cooled geared and supercharged engines on welded steel-tube mountings and driving D.H. Hydromatic reversible-pitch airscrews. Fuel tanks in wings inboard of nacelles forward and aft of the main spar. Total capacity 130 Imp. gallons. Oil tank (7 Imp. gallons) and oil cooler in each nacelle.

ACCOMMODATION.—Pilot's compartment seats two side-by-side with dual controls. Vee windscreen and frameless moulded blister-type canopy. Cabin may seat eight passengers with toilet and rear baggage compartment ; ten with toilet but without rear baggage compartment ; or eleven if both toilet and baggage compartment are omitted. Further space for light luggage on either side of the nose wheel compartment with door on port side. Individual windows and light luggage racks, heating and ventilation, diffused lighting, &c.

DIMENSIONS.—Span 57 ft. (17.4 m.), Length 39 ft. 4 in. (12 m.), Height 13 ft. (3.9 m.), Wing area 335 sq. ft. (31.1 sq. m.).

WEIGHT LOADED.—8,000 lbs. (3,635 kg.).

PERFORMANCE (Estimated).—Cruising speed (66% power output) 194 m.p.h. (310 km.h.) at 5,000 ft. (1,525 m.), Initial rate of climb 850 ft./min. (260 m./min.), Climb to 5,000 ft. (1,525 m.) 5.8 min., Climb to 10,000 ft. (3,050 m.) 11.7 min., Rate of climb on one engine 120 ft./min. (36.6 m./min.) up to 7,000 ft. (2,135 m.), Service ceiling 21,500 ft. (6,560 m.), Absolute ceiling on one engine 10,000 ft. (3,050 m.).

THE D.H.103 HORNET.

The Hornet twin-engined single-seat monoplane, designed to Specification F.12/43, has been produced in two versions, the F.Mk.I, a long-range single-seat fighter with an armament of four 20 m/m. cannon in the nose and provision for carrying two 1,000 lb. bombs, eight 60-lb. rockets or two 200 gallon drop tanks under the wings, and the P.R. Mk. II, an unarmed photographic-reconnaissance version of the Mk. I. A Mk. XX is now known as the Sea Hornet (see next column).

All versions of the Hornet are fitted with two 2,080 h.p. Rolls-Royce Merlin engines, the port engine a Merlin 130 (right hand rotation) and the starboard engine a Merlin 131 (left hand rotation). The handed airscrews are D.H. Hydromatic four-bladers.

The structure of the Hornet is mixed, the fuselage being all wood and the wings of wood and metal with an upper skin of plywood and a lower skin of light alloy on a framework of composite wood and metal spars.

DIMENSIONS.—Span 45 ft. (13.7 m.), Length 34 ft. 6 in. (10.5 m.), Height (tail down and one airscrew blade vertical) 14 ft. 2 in. (4.3 m.), Wing area 361 sq. ft. (33.5 sq. m.).

LOADED WEIGHT.—17,600 lbs. (7,990 kg.).

PERFORMANCE.—Maximum speed over 470 m.p.h. (752 km.h.), Range (with long-range tanks) over 2,500 miles (4,000 km.), Ceiling over 35,000 ft. (10,675 m.).

THE D.H.103 SEA HORNET XX.

The R.A.F. Hornet previously described has been adapted as a Naval Fighter. The principal modifications consist of folding wings, provision of arrester hook and fittings necessary to permit the aircraft to be accelerated at take-off either by accelerator or

The D.H. Hornet Single-seat Fighter (two Rolls-Royce Merlin 130/131 engines.)

The prototype Sea Hornet landing on an aircraft-carrier during its deck-landing trials.

by rockets. The wing folding is by hydraulic power so that the pilot may undertake this operation without outside assistance while taxying to and from the aircraft-carrier lifts.

A prototype Sea Hornet has completed successful deck-landing trials and the type is now in production by the Heston Aircraft Co., Ltd., which company was responsible for all naval modifications to this aircraft. The Sea Hornet will be the first twin-engined single-seat fighter to go into naval service.

DIMENSIONS.—Same as for Hornet.

WEIGHT LOADED.—18,250 lbs. (8,285 kg.).

PERFORMANCE.—Maximum speed over 450 m.p.h. (720 km.h.), Range (with long range tanks) over 2,000 miles (3,200 km.).

THE D.H. 100 VAMPIRE.

The Vampire is a single-seat twin-boom jet-propelled fighter monoplane with the pilot located in the nose of the central nacelle and the D.H. Goblin turbo-jet unit installed behind the pilot and exhausting between the booms and below the tail-plane. The air inlets are in the wing roots.

The Vampire is all metal except for the forward portion of the nacelle housing the pilot's pressurised cockpit, which is of wooden construction. Armament consists of four 20 m/m. cannon located in the underside of the nacelle and firing through ports beneath the nose.

To test its suitability for deck landing and to obtain general information on the problems involved in operating jet-propelled aircraft in aircraft-carriers, a Vampire has been fitted with an arrester hook. Satisfactory deck-landing trials were completed in December, 1945 in H.M.S. *Ocean*.

Production of the Vampire airframe is being handled by the English Electric Co., Ltd. at Preston, while the power-unit is being produced by the de Havilland Engine Co., Ltd.

DIMENSIONS.—Span 40 ft. (12.2 m.), Length 30 ft. 8 in. (9.4 m.), Height

The D.H. Vampire Jet-propelled Fighter.

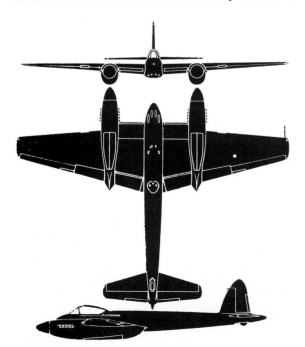

The D.H. Hornet Single-seat Twin-engined Fighter.

The D.H. Vampire Single-seat Jet-propelled Fighter (D.H. Goblin turbo-jet engine).

The D.H. Vampire Single-seat Jet-propelled Fighter (D.H. Goblin turbo-jet engine).

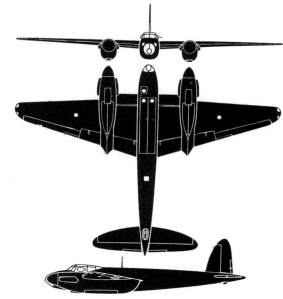

The D.H. Mosquito B. IV Day Bomber.

8 ft. 1 in. (2.4 m.), Wing area 266 sq. ft. (24.7 sq. m.).
WEIGHT LOADED.—8,000 lbs. (3,632 kg.).
PERFORMANCE.—Maximum speed 540 m.p.h. (800 km.h.), Ceiling 45,000-50,000 ft. (13,725-15,250 m.).

THE D.H.98 MOSQUITO.

The Mosquito was originally conceived in 1938 as a small bomber which was to rely for its safety upon speed rather than armament, and was to be built of wood for industrial economy and quickness of production. Capt. de Havilland then envisaged it as having two Rolls-Royce engines and a crew of two. Directly the war was declared the idea was submitted to the Air Ministry and after considerable discussion the D.H. Company was instructed to proceed with the design, aiming at a 1,500 mile range with a 1,000 lb. bomb load and a performance in the fighter class.

The Mosquito prototype unarmed bomber first flew on November 25, 1940, eleven months from the start of the design work. The makers' basic trials were completed in three months and the aircraft was handed over for R.A.F. trials on February 19, 1941. Meanwhile a fighter version was also being developed and the growing importance of long-range photographic reconnaissance also called for an adapted form of the bomber version. The fighter prototype was first flown on May 15, 1941, and the photographic reconnaissance prototype followed on June 10, 1941.

In July, 1941, the first three Mosquitos were delivered to the R.A.F. and in that month a production scheme which included manufacture by the Canadian de Havilland plant was planned. Plans to manufacture the Mosquito in Australia were negotiated nine months later.

Mosquito P.R. Mk. 1. Two Rolls-Royce Merlin 21 engines with two-speed single-stage superchargers and D.H. Hydromatic constant-speed airscrews. Distinguishable by short engine nacelles which did not protrude aft of trailing-edge of wing. The P.R. prototype W.4051 first flew on June 10, 1941. First operational sortie by a Mosquito was a photographic mission by W.4055 on September 20, 1941, to Bordeaux, Brest and La Pallice. Fitted with three vertical and one oblique cameras. Only ten built. Span 54 ft. 2 in. (16.52 m.), Length 40 ft. 9½ in. (12.43 m.), Wing area 420 sq. ft. (39 sq. m.).

Mosquito F. Mk. II. Two Rolls-Royce Merlin 21 or 23 engines. Fighter with armament of four 20 m/m. cannon and four .303 in. Browning machine-guns. Prototype W.4052 first flew on May 15, 1941. The first home defence fighter squadron equipped with the Mk. II became fully operational in May, 1942. A day and night Intruder adaptation, lacking certain equipment normal to the home-defence fighter, went into action over the continent of Europe in June, 1942. The first Mosquito intruder squadron proceeded overseas (Malta) in December, 1942. Length 41 ft. 2 in. (12.55 m.).

Mosquito T. Mk. III. Two-seat Trainer. Modified from Mk. II. Armament removed and dual control fitted. Length 40 ft. 9½ in. (12.43 m.).

Mosquito B. Mk. IV. Two Rolls-Royce Merlin 21 or 23 engines. Unarmed Bomber. First ten were converted from Mk. I airframes. Prototype W.4050 first flew on November 25, 1940. Short engine nacelles. No armament. Fitted to carry four 250 lb. bombs. Later production series, with lengthened engine nacelles, carried four 500 lb. bombs with shortened vanes. First operational sorties made on May 31, 1942, on Cologne at various heights and led to a new technique of low-level attack with 500 lb. bombs, usually fitted with 11-second fuses. Technique developed and perfected during the Summer of 1942. First bombing of Berlin in daylight was by Mk. IV's on January 30, 1943. Many Mk. IV's were converted to carry one 4,000 lb. bomb and some were fitted with strengthened wings to take two 50 gallon drop tanks. The Pathfinder version of the Mk. IV was an R.A.F. modification with special Radar equipment and was in service from 1942.

Mosquito P.R. Mk. IV. Unarmed Photographic-Reconnaissance conversion of the B. Mk. IV with provision for four cameras instead of bomb load.

Mosquito B. Mk. V. Two Rolls-Royce Merlin 21 engines. A prototype development of the B. Mk. IV with the new "Standard Wing" to take two 50 gallon drop tanks or two 500 lb. wing bombs. Not produced in England but formed the basis of the Canadian B. Mk. VII.

Mosquito F.B. Mk. VI. Rolls-Royce Merlin 21, 23 or 25 engines. Developed from the Mk. II as a Fighter-Bomber with the standard fighter armament and accommodation for two 500 lb. bombs in the rear half of the bomb-bay, the front half being taken up by the cannon breeches. Provision for two 50 gallon drop tanks or two 500 lb. bombs under the wings. Total bomb load 2,000 lbs. In action in Europe early in 1943 and in Burma late in 1943. Provision was made in 1944 for carrying four rocket projectiles under each wing in place of tanks or wing bombs. Employed thus by Coastal Command, mainly against shipping, etc. Length 41 ft. 2 in. (12.55 m.).

Mosquito P.R. Mk. VIII. The first high-altitude Mosquito. Converted from Mk. IV by fitting Merlin 61 engines with two-speed two-stage superchargers and providing for two 50 gallon jettisonable wing tanks. Only five built.

Mosquito B. Mk. IX. Two Rolls-Royce Merlin 72 engines with two-speed two-stage superchargers. The first high-altitude Unarmed Bomber. Four 500 lb. bombs in fuselage and two 500 lb. bombs under wings. Extra fuselage tanks and two 50 gallon drop tanks as alternative to bombs. All converted in 1944 to take one 4,000 lb. bomb in fuselage with two 50 gallon drop tanks. 100 gallon drop tanks were substituted later in 1944 subject to a weight limitation of 25,200 lbs. (11,441 kg.). The first daylight raid on Germany by Mosquitos carrying 4,000 lb. bombs made on Duisberg by Mk. IX's on November 29, 1944. Pathfinder version of the Mk. IX with special Radar equipment was an R.A.F. conversion. Length 44 ft. 6 in. (13.57 m.), Wing area 454 sq. ft. (42.2 sq. m.). Maximum speed over 400 m.p.h. (640 km.h.). Still-air range over 1,500 miles (2,400 km.). Ceiling over 36,000 ft. (10,980 m.).

Mosquito P.R. Mk. IX. Photographic-Reconnaissance version of the B. Mk. IX. Range over 2,000 miles (3,600 km.). Used by R.A.F. and U.S. 8th Air Force for meteorological reconnaissance over Europe before all major day and night bombing assaults.

Mosquitos N.F. Mk. X. A proposed Fighter similar to the F. Mk. II but fitted with Rolls-Royce Merlin 61 engines. Never built.

Mosquito F.B. Mk. XI. A proposed Fighter-Bomber similar to the F.B. Mk. VI but fitted with Merlin 61 engines. Never built.

Mosquito N.F. Mk. XII. Two Rolls-Royce Merlin 21 or 23 engines. A four-cannon Night Fighter developed from and similar to the F. Mk. II but with special A.I. (Airborne Interception) Radar equipment in place of the four machine-guns in the nose.

Mosquito N.F. Mk. XIII. Two Rolls-Royce Merlin 21 or 23

The D.H. Mosquito P.R. IX Photographic-Reconnaissance Monoplane (two Rolls-Royce Merlin 72 engines).

The D.H. Mosquito F.B. VI Fighter-Bomber with Rocket Projectile equipment (two Rolls-Royce Merlin 21 engines).

The D.H. Mosquito N.F. XII Night Fighter with A.I. Mk. VII Radar equipment in the nose.

engines. A four-cannon Night Fighter. Replacement of N.F. Mk. XII. Four machine-guns replaced by Radar.

Mosquito N.F. Mk. XIV. A proposed Fighter similar to the N.F. Mk. XIII but with Merlin 72 engines. Never built.

Mosquito N.F. Mk. XV. Two Rolls-Royce Merlin 73 or 77 engines. A special high-altitude Fighter developed urgently in seven days from the prototype P.R. Mk. VIII with pressure cabin, extended wing-tips, reduced fuel tankage, reduced armour and an armament of four .303 in. machine-guns in a blister under the fuselage. Only five built.

Mosquito B. Mk. XVI. Two Rolls-Royce Merlin 72 or 76 (starboard) and 73 or 77 (port) engines, the port engine driving a cabin supercharger. Development of the B. Mk. IX. A Marshall cabin supercharger maintains cabin pressure 2 lb./sq. in. above outside atmosphere, equivalent to about 10,000 ft. less altitude. Original bomb load 3,000 lbs. All converted in 1944 to take one 4,000 lb. bomb with two 50 gallon drop tanks or four 500 lb. bombs with two 100 gallon wing drop tanks. Maximum take-off weight 25,000 lbs. (11,350 kg.). Length 44 ft. 6 in. (13.57 m.).

Mosquito P.R. Mk. XVI. Photographic Reconnaissance version of the B. Mk. XVI. An astro-dome is a distinguishing feature of this model.

Mosquito N.F. Mk. XVII. Two Rolls-Royce Merlin 21 or 23 engines. A Night Fighter version of the N.F. Mk. XII but with American Radar apparatus.

Mosquito F.B. Mk. XVIII. Two Rolls-Royce Merlin 25 engines. A development of the F.B. Mk. VI with the fuselage modified to take an adaptation of the 6-pounder (57 m/m.) anti-tank gun instead of the four 20 m/m. cannon. Crew and engines heavily armoured. Two 500 lb. bombs or eight rocket projectiles, or two 50 gallon or 100 gallon drop tanks, carried under wings. Used by Coastal Command, mainly against shipping, submarines, etc. First into action on November 4, 1943. Length 40 ft. 9½ in. (12.43 m.).

Mosquito N.F. Mk. XIX. Rolls-Royce Merlin 25 engines. Night fighter developed from and similar to N.F. Mk. XIII but with Merlin 25 engines and ability to take either British or American Radar.

Mosquito N.F. Mk. 30. Rolls-Royce Merlin 72 or 76 engines. Replacement of the N.F. Mk. XIX with high-altitude engines. No pressure cabin. Takes either British or American Radar.

Mosquito N.F. Mk. 31. Similar to the N.F. Mk. 30 but fitted with Packard Merlin 69 engines. Not proceeded with.

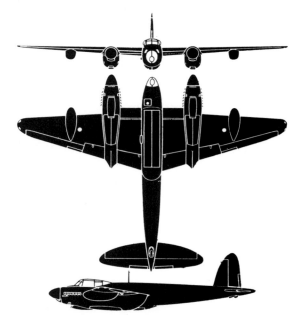

The D.H. Mosquito B. XVI with extended bomb-bay.

Mosquito P.R. Mk. 32. Specially-lightened version of the P.R. Mk. XVI with extended wing-tips for high-altitude operation. No crew armour or fuel tank protection. Reduced photographic equipment.

Mosquito Mk. 33. (See Sea Mosquito below).

Mosquito P.R. Mk. 34. Rolls-Royce Merlin 76 or 113 (starboard) and 77 or 114 (port) engines, the port engine driving a cabin supercharger. A very long-range photographic-reconn-aissance development of the Mk. XVI, with extra tanks in the expanded fuselage and two 200-gallon external wing tanks. Total tankage: 1,267 Imp. gallons. Range in still air at 20,000 ft. (6,100 m.) 3,000 miles (4,800 km.).

Mosquito B. Mk. 35. High-altitude development of the B. Mk. XVI with Rolls-Royce 113/114 engines. Bomb-load: one 4,000-lb. bomb when fitted with two 50-gallon wing tanks, or four 500-lb. bombs with two 100-gallon wing tanks.

Mosquito N.F. Mk. 36. A development of the N.F. Mk. 30 with two Rolls-Royce Merlin 113 engines.

CANADIAN PRODUCTION.

Mosquito B. Mk. VII. Packard Merlin 31 engines. Canadian version of the Unarmed Bomber developed from the B. Mk. V. All remained in Canada.

Mosquito B. Mk. XX. Packard Merlin 31 or 33 engines. Designed from B. Mk. V drawings in Canada and similar to B. Mk. VII except fitted with Canadian-American equipment. First Canadian-built Mosquitos delivered to England flew via Greenland in August, 1943, and went into action from an English R.A.F. base on November 29, 1943, in a raid on Berlin.

Mosquito F.B. Mk. 21. Canadian-built Fighter-Bomber corresponding to Mk. VI, but otherwise as B. Mk. XX. Very few built. Superseded by the F.B. Mk. 26.

Mosquito T. Mk. 22. Canadian-built dual-control Trainer developed from the F.B. Mk. 21 and corresponding to the T. Mk. III. Very few built.

Mosquito B. Mk. 23. Packard Merlin 69 engines. High-altitude unarmed Bomber development of the B. Mk. XX. Not proceeded with.

Mosquito F.B. Mk. 24. High-altitude Fighter-Bomber development of the F.B. Mk. 21 with Packard Merlin 69 engines. Not proceeded with.

Mosquito B. Mk. 25. Canadian-built replacement of the B. Mk. XX fitted with Packard Merlin 225 engines of improved performance (18 lb. boost).

Mosquito F.B. Mk. 26. Fighter-Bomber developed from the F.B. Mk. VI but with Packard Merlin 225 engines and Canadian-American equipment to replace Mk. 21. Armament: four .303 in. machine-guns and four 20 m/m. cannon. Racks for eight 60 lb. rockets.

Mosquito T. Mk. 27. Dual-control Trainer development from the T. Mk. 22 but with Packard Merlin 225 engines.

AUSTRALIAN PRODUCTION.

Mosquito F.B. Mk. 40. First Australian-built Mosquito. A Fighter-Bomber based on the F.B. Mk. VI but fitted with Packard Merlin 31 or 33 engines driving either Hamilton Standard or Australian-built D.H. Hydromatic airscrews. First Australian built Mk. 40 flew at Sydney on July 23, 1943.

Mosquito P.R. Mk. 40. An unarmed photographic conversion of the F.B. Mk. 40 with two 100-gallon wing drop tanks and extra fuel tankage in the fuselage. British or American photographic equipment.

Mosquito F.B. Mk. 41. Similar to the F.B. Mk. 40 but fitted with Packard Merlin 69 two-stage supercharged engines. Automatic pilot.

Mosquito F.B. Mk. 42. Similar to the F.B. Mk. 40 but fitted with Packard Merlin 69 two-stage supercharged engines.

In 1943, Mosquitos with civil markings were put on to special air-line duties by British Airways. They maintained a service to Stockholm over enemy-occupied territory, often in the face of determined efforts at interception by German fighters.

The following general description applies to the basic Mosquito design, specific details of accommodation, armament and equipment of the principal variants being given at the end of the description.

TYPE.—High-performance Military monoplane.

WINGS.—Mid-wing cantilever monoplane. One piece wing with slightly swept-back leading-edge and sharply tapered trailing-edge. Centre portion of wing carries the engine mountings and radiators. All-wood structure comprising two box spars with laminated spruce flanges and plywood webs, spruce and plywood compression ribs, spanwise spruce stringers and a plywood skin which in the case of the upper surface is double with the upper stringers sandwiched between the two skins. A false leading-edge, built up of nose rib formers and a D-skin, is attached to the front spar. The whole wing is screwed, glued and pinned and finally covered with fabric over the plywood. Hydraulically-operated slotted flaps between ailerons and engine nacelles and nacelles and fuselage. Slotted ailerons with controllable trim-tabs.

FUSELAGE.—Oval-section all-wood structure jig-built in two vertical halves, each completely equipped before joining. Seven bulk-heads built up of two plywood skins kept apart by spruce blocks, carry the outer skin which is a sandwich of balsa wood between two layers of plywood. At the points where bulkheads are attached the balsa core is replaced by a spruce ring. Where attachments are made to the skin a bakelite plug is inserted into the balsa, a plywood flange glued to the inner surface distributing the load. The two halves of the fuselage are scarfed together with Vee notches reinforced by ply inserts above and below and an additional overlapping ply strip on the inside of the joint. After assembly the whole fuselage is covered with fabric and doped. The underside of the fuselage is cut out to accommodate the wing, which is attached to four massive pick-up points, the lower portion of the cut-out section being replaced after assembly.

TAIL UNIT.—Cantilever monoplane type. All-wood structure with plywood-covered fixed surfaces and fabric-covered rudder and elevators. Aerodynamically and statically-balanced control surfaces. Automatic rudder bias by spring-loaded telescopic strut link to the trimming-tab. Controllable trim-tabs in elevators.

LANDING GEAR.—Retractable type. Each unit consists of a pair of legs incorporating rubber-in-compression springing and carrying between them one large diameter wheel. The units are retracted hydraulically into the tails of the engine nacelles, hinged doors closing the apertures when the wheels are raised. Hydraulic wheel-brakes. Dunlop-Marstrand non-shimmying retractable tail-wheel.

POWER PLANT.—Two Rolls-Royce Merlin twelve-cylinder Vee liquid-cooled engines on welded steel-tube mountings cantilevered from the wing spars. D.H. three-bladed constant-speed full-feathering airscrews. Radiators housed within the thickness of the wing inboard of the nacelles with the inlets along the leading-edge and the outlets controlled by flaps under the wing surface ahead of the front spar. Each radiator is divided into three parts, the outboard section forming the oil cooler, the middle section the coolant

A Canadian-built Mosquito as supplied to the U.S. Army Air Forces under the designation F-8.

radiator and the inboard section the cabin heater. To accommodate the radiators the leading-edge of the wing between the fuselage and nacelles is set forward 22 inches (0.56 m.). Fuel carried in ten protected tanks, two (68 Imp. gallons each) in the fuselage between the wing spars, two (79 and 65 Imp. gallons each) on either side of the fuselage inboard of the nacelles, and two (32 and 24 Imp. gallons each) outboard of each nacelle. Total normal fuel capacity 536 Imp. gallons. The long-range versions of the Mosquito have three additional tanks, one in the fuselage and two mounted externally under the wing outboard of the nacelles. These latter tanks are of various capacities and are jettisonable.

ACCOMMODATION (Fighter and Fighter-Bomber).—Side-by-side seating for crew of two in nose with pilot on port side. Armoured bulkhead in solid nose and flat bullet-proof windscreen. Entrance to cockpit through door on starboard side.

ACCOMMODATION (Unarmed Bomber and Photographic Reconnaissance).—Accommodation for crew of two as for Fighter. Transparent nose with optically-flat panel for bomb-aimer, Vee windscreen with two layers of glass between which passes constant flow of dried air to prevent misting and icing and spectacle-type control instead of stick-type column in Fighter. Entrance to cabin through hatch in floor. Supercharged and heated cabin in Mk. XVI.

ARMAMENT AND EQUIPMENT (Fighter).—Four 0.303 in. Browning machine-guns in solid nose ahead of armour bulkhead and four 20 m/m. British Hispano cannon in lower portion of fuselage and firing through apertures in underside of nose. In certain marks machine-guns replaced by special radio detection equipment. Full radio and electrical equipment, oxygen, cabin heating, stowage for dinghy in roof of fuselage aft of canopy, etc.

ARMAMENT AND EQUIPMENT (Unarmed Bomber).—No armament. Internal bomb stowage in fuselage and racks beneath outer wings. Maximum bomb load 4,000 lbs. Bomb sights and selector switches in nose. Bomb-aimer's panel has double glass with heated air passing between, as well as an external jet for spraying de-icing fluid thereon. Camera installation in rear fuselage between bulkheads 5 and 6, with remote controls from bomb-aimer's position.

ARMAMENT AND EQUIPMENT (Fighter-Bomber).—Armament as for Fighter. Bomb-bay equal to rear half of Bomber. Internal stowage for 1,000 lbs. Racks under wings for two additional 500 lb. bombs. Total bomb load 2,000 lbs.

ARMAMENT AND EQUIPMENT (Photographic-Reconnaissance).—No armament. Comprehensive camera installation comprising both vertical and oblique cameras. All are electrically-operated and heated. For vertical photography normal bomb sights are used and cameras controlled by observer. For oblique photography pilot is responsible and sighting marks are provided on the side of cockpit canopy and on upper surface of port wing.

DIMENSIONS (Mk. XVI).—Span 54 ft. 2 in. (16.52 m.), Length 44 ft. 6 in. (13.57 m.), Height (over rudder in flying position) 17 ft. 5 in. (5.3 m.), Wing area 454 sq. ft. (42.2 sq. m.).

WEIGHTS.—No data available.

PERFORMANCE (Mk. XVI).—Maximum speed over 400 m.p.h. (640 km.h.), Range with 4,000 lb. bomb over 1,500 miles (2,400 km.), Range (Photographic-Reconnaissance) over 2,000 miles (3,200 km.), Ceiling over 36,000 ft. (10,980 m.).

THE D.H. SEA MOSQUITO.

The Sea Mosquito is the naval adaptation of the R.A.F. Mosquito fighter-bomber, this version being Mk. 33 in the Mosquito Series.

For Naval use a number of modifications have been incorporated. These include folding wings, arrester gear and a new oleo-pneumatic landing-gear in place of the standard rubber-in compression gear which was prone to excessive rebound in landing on carrier decks and liable to cause the arrester hook to bounce over the arrester wires.

The standard armament of the Sea Mosquito consists of four 20 m/m. cannon. The bomb load may consist of two 500-lb. bombs in the rear half of the bomb-bay and two 500-lb. bombs under the wings. Eight 60-lb. rockets, four under each wing, can also be carried. Crutches are fitted under the fuselage for one standard torpedo. Specialised naval Radar equipment is installed in the nose.

The power-plant consists of two 1,635 h.p. Rolls-Royce Merlin 25 engines, each driving a D.H. Hydromatic four-blade constant-speed full-feathering airscrew.

A number of R.A.F. Mosquitos were converted for Naval training pending the development of the Sea Mosquito, and with some of these aircraft satisfactory preliminary deck landing trials were made. Further trials were later completed with the prototype Sea Mosquito.

Rocket-assisted take-off gear is being developed and will be installed in the production aircraft.

DIMENSIONS.—Same as for the Mosquito.

WEIGHT LOADED.—22,500 lbs. (10,216 kg.).

PERFORMANCE.—Maximum speed about 380 m.p.h. (608 km.h.), Range (with drop tanks) 1,680 miles (2,690 km.).

THE D.H.89A DRAGON-RAPIDE.

TYPE.—Twin-engined Passenger or Freight-carrier.

WINGS.—Equal-span braced biplane. Tapered wings. Aspect ratio 11.7. Dihedral 3 deg. Wing section modified R.A.F. 34. Duplicated lift and anti-lift bracing in plane of front spars only. Upper wings, attached directly to top of fuselage, have two wooden spars, wooden girder ribs, tubular drag-struts, internal wire bracing and fabric covering. Lower wing-stubs, out to engines, also have tubular spars and are braced from ends to top of fuselage by parallel struts. Outer sections have wooden spars, wooden ribs, tubular drag-struts and internal wire bracing and fabric covering. Tapered ailerons, on all four wings, interconnected by push-pull rods inside single outer interplane struts. Split trailing-edge flaps.

FUSELAGE.—Box-type structure with spruce longerons and struts inside plywood covering, except for floor which is clear of any projection, the whole faired externally with fabric. Loads from upper front spars taken by tube across fuselage, from upper rear spars by wooden beam, and from lower spars by tubes athwart fuselage beneath floor.

TAIL UNIT.—Monoplane type. Tail-plane, wire-braced to fin and fuselage, is adjustable in the air by screw-jack beneath front spar. Fixed fin. Unbalanced elevator. Rudder has horn-balance and balance flap in trailing-edge. Entire structure of wood with fabric covering.

LANDING GEAR.—Divided type. Single Dunlop wheel under each engine sprung by Dowty shock-absorber legs, one on each side of wheel. Non-moving parts of shock-absorbers braced rigidly to wing structure and fuselage. Bendix wheel-brakes. Tracking and sprung tail-wheel.

The D.H. Sea Mosquito prototype with wings folded. Special Radar equipment is installed in the nose.

The D.H. 89A Dragon-Rapide Light Transport (two D.H. Gipsy-six engines).

POWER PLANT.—Two 200 h.p. D.H. Gipsy-Six air-cooled in-line engines on welded steel mountings in front of lower wings. Anti-freezing controllable induction manifolds. Rotax starters. 38 gall. (173 litres) fuel tank in wing behind each motor, also 3½ gall. (16 litres) oil-tank cooled by scoops in slipstream.

ACCOMMODATION.—Enclosed cabin for pilot in extreme nose. Control column with wheel. Parallel-motion rudder bar. Wheel to tail-incidence gear. Brakes applied by lever, with differential steering by rudder bar. Main cabin, entered by door at back in port side, measures 13 ft. 6 in. long, 4 ft. 6 in. high and 4 ft. wide average (4.1 m. × 1.4 m. × 1.2 m.). Arrangements of seats and freight space to suit requirements.

DIMENSIONS.—Span 48 ft. (14.63 m.), Length 34 ft. 6 in. (10.52 m.), Height 10 ft. 3 in. (3.3 m.), Wing area 336 sq. ft. (31.2 sq. m.).

WEIGHTS AND LOADINGS.—Weight empty (including bonding and screening, starters, navigation and other lighting, landing lights and battery for all purposes) 3,230 lbs. (1,466 kg.), Crew 170 lbs. (77 kg.), Fuel (76 galls.) 585 lbs. (266 kg.), Oil 63 lbs. (28 kg.), Balance for cabin furniture, wireless and pay load 1,452 lbs. (659 kg.), Disposable load 2,290 lbs. (1,040 kg.), Maximum weight 5,550 lbs. (2,520 kg.).

PERFORMANCE.—Maximum speed at sea level 157 m.p.h. (253 km.h.), Cruising speed 132 m.p.h. (212.5 km.h.), Take-off run 290 yds. (265 m.), Landing run 170 yds. (156 m.), Rate of climb at sea level 867 ft./min. (265 m./min.), Time to 5,000 ft. (1,525 m.) 6.75 mins., Ceiling 16,700 ft. (5,100 m.), Ceiling with one engine stopped and full load 3,100 ft. (945 m.), Range in still air at cruising speed 556 miles (895 km.).

THE D.H.89B DOMINIE.

The D.H.89A described above is largely used in the R.A.F. for communications and light service transport work, but a variation known as the D.H. 89B or Dominie has been produced for the R.A.F. as a wireless and navigational trainer, with accommodation for four or five pupils and an instructor.

All structural data for the Dominie are as for the Dragon-Rapide previously described, and although the structure weights are the same as the D.H. Dominie is 5,850 lbs. (2,656 kg.) owing to an increase in loose equipment.

As regards accommodation, the whole of the available floor space of the Dominie is used as one cabin, which is fitted with

Two D.H. 89B Dominie Wireless and Navigational Training biplanes (two D.H. Gipsyqueen III engines).

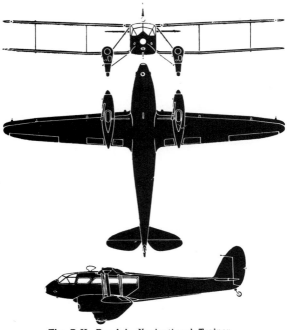

The D.H. Dominie Navigational Trainer.

The D.H. Tiger-Moth II Two-seat Primary Training Biplane (130 h.p. D.H. Gipsy-Major engine).

five forward-facing seats, each having a wireless crate and small table, plus one folding seat for occasional use. The cabin floor is fitted with aerial fairleads and winches and two windmill generators are provided.

For general description and specifications see the Dragon-Rapide on the previous page.

THE D.H.82A TIGER-MOTH II.

TYPE.—Two-seat Primary Training biplane.

WINGS.—Equal-span single-bay biplane. Centre-section, incorporating the petrol tank, is carried above the fuselage on N-struts in front of the front cockpit. Wings are staggered and swept back,

giving maximum visibility and ease of egress from both cockpits. Structure consists of two I-section spruce spars and spruce ribs, the whole covered with fabric. Lower ends of rear flying-wires carried to the front root fitting of the lower wings. Ailerons on lower wings only.

FUSELAGE.—Rectangular steel-tube structure, covered with fabric.

TAIL UNIT.—Monoplane type. Wooden framework, fabric covering, balanced rudder. Elevators have adjustable spring-loading device.

LANDING GEAR.—Split type. Rubber-in-compression springing, low-pressure wheels. Twin long single-step duralumin floats may be fitted in place of land undercarriage, and skis may be interchanged with the wheels.

POWER PLANT.—One 130 h.p. D.H. Gipsy-Major four-cylinder in-line inverted air-cooled engine. Fuel tank (19 Imp. gallons) in centre-section. Extra 10-gallon fuel tank may be installed in front cockpit.

ACCOMMODATION.—Tandem open cockpits with complete dual control. Varied equipment may be installed to suit the machine to various training categories.

DIMENSIONS.—Span 29 ft. 4 in. (8.95 m.), Chord 4 ft. 4¼ in. (1.33 m.), Length (landplane) 23 ft. 11 in. (7.32 m.), Length (seaplane) 25 ft. 5 in. (7.76 m.), Height (landplane) 8 ft. 9½ in. (2.71 m.), Height (seaplane) 10 ft. 4 in. (3.15 m.), Wing area 239 sq. ft. (22.2 sq. m.).

WEIGHTS (Landplane).—Weight empty 1,115 lbs. (506 kg.), Pilot 160 lbs. (73 kg.), Passenger 160 lbs. (73 kg.), Fuel and oil 166 lbs. (75 kg.), Weight loaded (Aerobatic C. of A.) 1,770 lbs. (804 kg.), Maximum loaded weight (Normal C. of A.) 1,825 lbs. (829 kg.).

WEIGHTS (Seaplane).—Weight empty (but including standard removable equipment—not slots) 1,280 lbs. (581 kg.), Crew (2) 320 lbs. (146 kg.), Two parachutes and harness 46 lbs. (21 kg.), Fuel and oil 166 lbs. (75 kg.), Weight loaded (Aerobatic C. of A.) 1,650 lbs. (750 kg.), Maximum loaded weight (Normal C. of A.) 1,825 lbs. (829 kg.).

PERFORMANCE (Landplane—Maximum loaded weight 1,825 lbs.).—Maximum speed at sea level 109 m.p.h. (175 km.h.), Stalling speed 43 m.p.h. (69 km.h.), Initial rate of climb 673 ft./min. (202 m./min.), Climb to 5,000 ft. (1,525 m.) 9 mins., Climb to 10,000 ft. (3,050 m.) 23.5 mins., Service Ceiling 13,600 ft. (4,150 m.).

PERFORMANCE (Seaplane—Maximum loaded weight 1,825 lbs.).—Maximum speed at sea level 104 m.p.h. (167 km.h.), Cruising speed at 1,000 ft. (305 m.) 89 m.p.h. (143 km.h.), Stalling speed 44 m.p.h. (71 km.h.), Initial rate of climb 663 ft./min. (202 m./min.), Time to 5,000 ft. (1,525 m.) 9 mins., Time to 10,000 ft. (3,048 m.) 24.5 mins., Absolute ceiling 15,500 ft. (4,730 m.), Range 285 miles (458 km.).

FAIREY.

THE FAIREY AVIATION CO., LTD.

HEAD OFFICE : HAYES, MIDDLESEX.

WORKS : HAYES, MIDDLESEX; STOCKPORT, CHESHIRE; AND HAMBLE, HANTS.

Chairman : Sir Richard Fairey, M.B.E., F.R.Ae.S.

Directors : M. E. A. Wright, A.F.C., F.R.Ae.S. (Managing-Director), C. H. Chichester Smith, D.S.C., A.F.R.Ae.S. and C. C. Vinson, A.C.A. (Joint Assistant Managing Directors), T. M. Barlow, M.Inst.C.E., M.I.Mech.E., F.R.Ae.S., W. Broadbent, L. M. Hilton, D.F.C., A.F.C., A.F.R.Ae.S. and R. T. Outen.

Established : 1916.

The Fairey Aviation Co., Ltd. is well known as the producer of a wide variety of military aircraft. It has specialised on naval types for many years, although not to the exclusion of aircraft suitable for other purposes.

During 1944 the types of Fairey aircraft in operational use in the Royal Navy were the Swordfish, Albacore, Barracuda and Firefly. The Swordfish, manufactured by Blackburn Aircraft, Ltd. since 1940, was withdrawn from production in mid-1944, although it still continues to be used for a variety of duties by the Royal Navy. The Albacore, the production of which by the parent company in 1940 was responsible for the transfer of Swordfish production to the Blackburn company, has been out of production since 1943, but it was still being used operationally as a land-based aircraft in 1944.

The current production types are the Barracuda and the

Firefly. The Barracuda was produced under a Group production scheme in which the parent company, Blackburn Aircraft, Ltd. and Boulton Paul Aircraft, Ltd. were the major units, and this aeroplane and the Firefly have been in extensive use in the Fleet Air Arm in Home waters and with the Eastern fleets. Both received their baptism of fire in an attack on the German battleship *Tirpitz* in Alten Fjord in April, 1944, and both were reported in action in Far Eastern waters later in the year.

THE FAIREY FIREFLY.

TYPE.—Two-seat Long-Range Naval Reconnaissance Fighter.

WINGS.—Low-wing cantilever monoplane. One-piece centre-section back to rear spar fits into recess in underside of fuselage. Folding outer sections have trailing-edge portions extending inwardly to the fuselage centre-line. Wings, which are folded manually, are turned upward round rear spar universal hinges and swung backward to lie, trailing-edge down, along sides of fuselage. Wings are locked in flying position hydraulically. All-metal wing structure with stressed metal skin. Retractable Youngman aerofoil flaps beneath trailing-edge from ailerons to centre-line of fuselage. Flaps may be swung down and set to give varying positions for take-off, cruising and landing. Hydraulic operation. Trim-tab in port aileron.

FUSELAGE.—Oval section metal semi-monocoque structure with smooth metal skin. Complete engine unit bolts on to front bulkhead, and tubular tail wedge on to rear bulkhead.

TAIL UNIT.—Cantilever monoplane type. Forwardly-placed tailplane.

The Fairey Firefly Two-seat Naval Fighter.

All-metal structure with metal-covered fin, tailplane and elevators and fabric-covered rudder. Trim-tabs in all movable surfaces.

LANDING GEAR.—Retractable type. Wheels and oleo shock-absorber struts, hinged at the extremities of the centre-section front spar, retract inwardly into wells in the underside of the centre-section between the spars, fairing plates on the oleo legs and hinged doors under the centre-section closing the apertures when the gear is raised. Fully-retractable tail-wheel. Hydraulic operation with emergency hydraulic hand pump. Retractable deck arrester hook under rear fuselage. Catapult points in fuselage are retractable at the front station and removable at the rear.

POWER PLANT.—One 2,000 h.p. Rolls-Royce Griffon II twelve-cylinder Vee liquid-cooled engine driving a Rotol three-blade constant-speed airscrew. Main self-sealing fuel tank in fuselage behind pilot's cockpit. Auxiliary fuel tanks in leading-edge of centre-section. Oil tank in centre-section.

ACCOMMODATION.—Pilot's cockpit over leading-edge of wing.

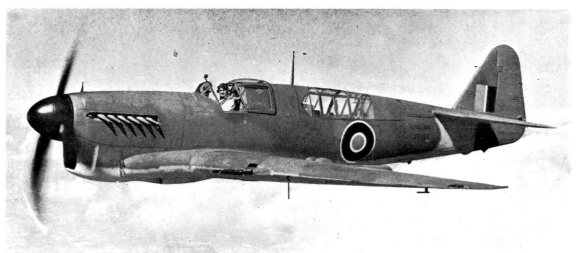

The Fairey Firefly two-seat Naval Reconnaissance Fighter (Rolls-Royce Griffon II engine).

Observer/radio-operator/navigator aft of trailing-edge of wing. Sliding and jettisonable canopies over both cockpits.

ARMAMENT.—Four 20 m/m. British Hispano cannon, two in the leading-edge of each outer wing. Provision for rocket projectile gear. Radio, night flying equipment, etc.

DIMENSIONS.—Span 44 ft. 6 in. (13.6 m.), Length 37 ft. 7 in. (11.4 m.), Height 13 ft. 7 in. (4.45 m.).

WEIGHTS AND PERFORMANCE.—No data available.

Firefly N.F. Mk. II. Rolls-Royce Griffon engine driving a Rotol three-blade airscrew. Night-fighter version of the Mk. I. Fitted with special Radar and flame-damping exhausts. Not built in quantity.

Firefly F.R. Mk. IV and N.F. Mk. IV. Rolls-Royce Griffon 74 engine driving a Rotol four-blade airscrew. Principal external change is the transference of the coolant radiator from under the nose to leading-edge extensions of the centre-section. The wings have also been slightly reduced in span and have square tips. Armament is the same as for the Mk. I. Can also carry a maximum of eight pairs of rocket projectiles or two 1,000-lb. bombs under the wings. Full radio and radar equipment. Provision for assisted take-off either by accelerator or rockets. Production expected to begin early in 1946.

DIMENSIONS.—Span 41 ft. 2 in. (12.55 m.), Length 37 ft. 11 in. (11.56 m.), Height 14 ft. 4 in. (4.37 m.), Wing area 330 sq. ft. (30.65 sq. m.).

WEIGHT LOADED.—13,200 lbs. (6,000 kg.).

PERFORMANCE.—Maximum speed 386 m.p.h. (618 km.h.) at 14,000 ft. (4,270 m.), Climb to 20,000 ft. (6,100 m.) 10.5 mins., Normal range 740 miles (1,185 km.) at 220 m.p.h. (352 km.h.), Maximum range (with auxiliary drop tanks) 1,070 miles (1,720 km.).

THE FAIREY BARRACUDA.

The Barracuda was the first monoplane torpedo-bomber to go into service in the Royal Navy. The original prototype was designed and built with the Rolls-Royce Vulture 24-cylinder X-type engine. When it was decided to discontinue production of the Vulture the Barracuda was redesigned to embody the Merlin, an engine with many entirely different characteristics. The delay this caused was responsible for retarding the initial production programme. The Merlin-engined prototype first flew early in 1941 and the first deck landing with this aeroplane took place on May 18, 1941. The production Barracuda made its first deck landing on September 9, 1942.

The prototype Barracuda had an unbraced tailplane in-line with the top of the fuselage but in the production Barracuda I the tailplane was raised to its present position near the top of the fin clear of air disturbed by the wing flaps. The Mark I was fitted with a Rolls-Royce Merlin 30 engine and a three-bladed Rotol airscrew. The Barracuda II, described hereafter, has the Merlin 32 engine and Rotol four-bladed airscrew.

The Barracuda was first reported in action on April 3, 1944, in a successful bombing attack on the German battleship *Tirpitz* in a Norwegian fjord, although it had been in service in the Fleet Air Arm for over a year previously. It was in action against the Japanese for the first time in an attack on enemy installations at Sabang, in the island of Sumatra, on April 19, 1944.

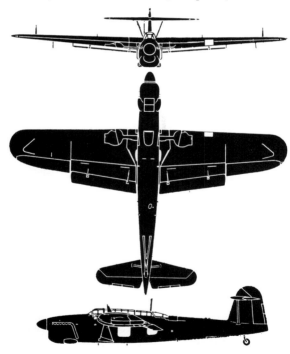

The Fairey Barracuda II Torpedo-Bomber.

TYPE.—Three-seat Naval Torpedo-Bomber.

WINGS.—Shoulder-wing cantilever monoplane. Centre-section stubs built integrally with the fuselage. Outer sections have constant taper and rounded tips. Two-spar all-metal structure with diaphragm ribs, intercostal stringers and a stressed-skin covering. Hydraulically-operated Youngman flaps suspended below and staggered back from trailing-edge of wing, may be partly lowered for take-off, fully lowered for landing and raised to negative angle for retarding speed in a dive. Flaps have metal frames and Alclad sheet covering. Metal-framed ailerons covered with fabric. Wings fold about vertical joint pins at the rear spars, the trailing-edges of the outer wings, complete with flaps, folding up and onto the upper surfaces to give clearance at the fuselage for folding. Retractable wing holds under the wing tips.

FUSELAGE.—Oval all-metal structure with flush-riveted smooth metal skin. Engine-mounting, part of the pilot's cockpit and rear bay of the fuselage are of steel tube. Remainder is a metal monocoque.

The Fairey Firefly IV Two-seat Naval Reconnaissance Fighter (Rolls-Royce Griffon 74 engine).

The Fairey Barracuda II Torpedo-Bomber (Rolls-Royce Merlin 32 engine).

The Fairey Barracuda III Torpedo-Bomber (Rolls-Royce Merlin 32 engine).

The Fairey Barracuda V Torpedo-Bomber (Rolls-Royce Griffon VII engine).

TAIL UNIT.—Braced monoplane type. Tailplane mounted near top of fin and braced to the fuselage by a single strut on each side. All-metal framework with fin and rudder covered with Alclad sheet and the elevators and rudder with fabric. Trim-tabs in elevators and rudder.

LANDING GEAR.—Retractable type. Cantilever oleo legs held at top in torsion boxes at ends of horizontal triangular structures which are hinged to the bottom edges of the fuselage. When retracted the horizontal members of each L-unit hinge up to lie in recesses in the sides of the fuselage and the oleo shock absorber-legs and wheels stow away in the leading-edge of the wings ahead of the front spars. Operation by hydraulic jack located across floor of fuselage between landing-gear units. Hydraulic wheel-brakes. Non-retracting tail-wheel. Deck-arrester hook lies flush in the underside of the fuselage ahead of the tail-wheel. Catapult spools.

POWER PLANT.—One Rolls-Royce Merlin 32 twelve-cylinder Vee liquid-cooled engine driving a Rotol four-blade constant-speed airscrew. Self-sealing fuel tanks in centre-section between spars.

ACCOMMODATION.—Crew of three in tandem cockpits under a continuous transparent hooding. Pilot ahead of the leading-edge of the wing with sliding cockpit canopy. Observer/navigator and rear gunner/radio operator over centre and trailing-edge of wing respectively, with hinged portions of hooding which can be tipped up to form windshields. Navigator and radio operator have alternative positions within the fuselage, the navigator having bay windows beneath the wings for downward vision.

ARMAMENT AND EQUIPMENT.— Two .303 in. Vickers K gas-operated machine-guns on Fairey flexible mounting in rear crew position. One 18 in. torpedo carried externally on crutches under the fuselage. Bombs carried under the wings. Alternatively, depth-charges or sea mines can be carried. For bombing-up, racks are fitted to the bombs on ground or deck and complete assemblies are hoisted up to the wings where the racks are clipped into position. Dinghy and rescue equipment carried in fuselage.

DIMENSIONS.—Span 49 ft. 2 in. (15 m.), Width folded 18 ft. 3 in. (5.56 m.), Length 40 ft. 6 in. (12.35 m.), Height 15 ft. 5 in. (4.7 m.), Wing area 367 sq. ft. (34.1 sq. m.).

WEIGHTS AND PERFORMANCE.—No data available.

Barracuda T.R. Mk. III. Rolls-Royce Merlin 32 engine. Similar to the Mk. II but is fitted with ASV Mk. 10 Radar equipment in a bulge beneath the rear fuselage.

Barracuda T.R. Mk. V. Rolls-Royce Griffon VII engine driving a Rotol four-blade airscrew. Improved version of the Mk. II with greater range and increased speed over a much greater height range. Wings of 4 ft. greater span with squared tips and increased internal fuel capacity. Larger rudder and dorsal fin. Generally strengthened structure to give greater margin of safety in pull-outs from dives. Electrical system completely re-engineered. Radar equipment carried in a quickly removable unit in one wing. Crew consists of a pilot and an observer/telegraphist, the latter carrying out the duties of navigator and radio-operator. Armament consists of one forward-firing .50-in. machine-gun. No rear armament. Carries one 18-in. torpedo or a bomb, depth-charge or mine load up to 2,000 lbs.

DIMENSIONS.— Span 53 ft. 2 in. (16.21 m.), Length 40 ft. 3 in. (12.27 m.), Height 15 ft. 3 in. (4.65 m.), Wing area 425 sq. ft. (39.5 sq. m.).

WEIGHT LOADED.—16,400 lbs. (7,450 kg.).

PERFORMANCE.—Maximum speed 264 m.p.h. (422 km.h.) at 11,000 ft. (3,355 m.), Climb to 5,000 ft. (1,525 m.) 2½ mins., Normal range 735 miles (1,180 km.) at 159 m.p.h. (254 km.h.), Maximum range (with auxiliary drop tank) 1,200 miles (1,920 km.).

THE FAIREY SWORDFISH.

The Swordfish was originally designed to meet Air Ministry specification S.38/34 and the prototype first flew in 1934. Already approaching peacetime obsolescence in 1939, the Swordfish proved to be one of the most versatile aeroplanes under the rigours of modern warfare.

Originally intended to fulfil the requirements of a carrier-borne torpedo-spotter-reconnaissance type, it has served as a torpedo-bomber with the Fleet, as an anti-submarine and

A Fairey Battle fitted with the Fairey P-24 engine and Fairey contra-rotating airscrews.

convoy protection weapon from escort carriers, as a shore-based mine-layer, as a rocket projectile aircraft, as a night-flying flare-dropper, as a trainer and general utility aeroplane throughout five years of war. In the Norwegian and Lowlands campaigns, at Oran, in the naval battle at Taranto, where two Swordfish squadrons crippled the Italian Fleet for negligible losses, in the campaigns in Greece, Crete, Syria and North Africa from Mersa Matruh to Benghazi, in the Battle of Matapan, at Malta, Madagascar, in the trapping and destruction of the German battleship *Bismarck*, in the Battle of the Atlantic, the Swordfish has figured in one or more of its many rôles. As an indication of its sea striking power, during one period of the enemy's attempt to eliminate Malta as a vital factor in the fighting in North Africa and the Mediterranean, Swordfish based on the beleaguered island sank an average of 50,000 tons of enemy shipping per month, 98,000 tons in the peak month.

Production of the Swordfish was transferred from the parent company to Blackburn Aircraft, Ltd. in 1940, by whom it was manufactured under a Group scheme comprising four major production units and hundreds of major and minor sub-contractors. Last of the fully-operational biplanes, the Swordfish was taken out of production in mid-1944.

Swordfish I. Bristol Pegasus III or 30 engine. Three-seat Torpedo-Bomber.

Swordfish II. Bristol Pegasus 30 engine. Similar to the Mk. I but fitted with Rocket Projectile gear under the lower wings.

Swordfish III. Bristol Pegasus 30 engine. Two-seater. Torpedo gear replaced by ASV Mk. 10 Radar equipment mounted under the forward fuselage. Rear cockpit enclosed.

A Blackburn-built Fairey Swordfish with Rocket Projectile equipment (Bristol Pegasus 30 engine).

The Fairey Spearfish Torpedo-Dive-Bomber-Reconnaissance Monoplane (Bristol Centaurus 47 engine).

Swordfish IV. Bristol Pegasus 30 engine. Three-seat Trainer. All cockpits enclosed. Intended for use in Canada. Not proceeded with.

TYPE.—Two/three-seat Torpedo-Bomber-Reconnaissance biplane.

WINGS.—Two-bay unequal-span staggered biplane. Upper centre-section carried on pyramid structure, lower centre-section stubs braced to upper fuselage longerons by inverted Vee struts. Extremities of centre-sections interconnected by pairs of interplane struts. One set of struts to each outer set of wings, which are arranged to fold. Wing structure consists of two built-up steel strip spars, steel drag-struts, and duralumin ribs, the whole covered with fabric. Duralumin-framed ailerons, with fabric covering. Hoisting sling incorporated in upper centre-section. Ailerons on all four wings. Wings fold round rear spar hinges.

FUSELAGE.—Rectangular steel-tube structure, faired to an oval section and covered forward with quickly-detachable metal panels and aft with fabric. Large inspection panels in after covering.

TAIL UNIT.—Monoplane type. Steel and duralumin framework, with fabric covering.

LANDING GEAR.—Divided type. Each unit consists of an oleo shock-absorber leg, the upper end of which is anchored to the extremity of the front spar of the lower centre-section, with the lower end hinged to the fuselage by axle and forwardly-inclined radius-rod. Medium-pressure wheels and pneumatic brakes. Wheel chassis is interchangeable with twin single-step all-metal floats.

POWER PLANT.—One Bristol Pegasus 30 nine-cylinder radial air-cooled engine rated at 750 h.p. at 4,750 ft. (1,450 m.). Townend ring cowling, with leading-edge exhaust-collector. Main fuel tank in centre-section. Gravity tank in top of fuselage. Fairey metal airscrew.

ACCOMMODATION.—Pilot's cockpit aft of wings, with large gunner-observer's cockpit immediately behind. For spotting or reconnaissance crew of three carried, for torpedo work crew of two only. Full range of equipment and instruments for Fleet Air Arm duties. Catapulting points and deck arrester gear.

ARMAMENT.—One 0.303 in. Vickers gun in top deck of fuselage and firing through airscrew and one 0.303 in. Lewis gun on Fairey high-speed gun-mounting at back of rear cockpit. Torpedo crutches beneath fuselage. Bomb racks beneath fuselage and lower wing. Rocket projectile racks beneath wings. One torpedo, sea mine, bombs up to a maximum weight of 1,500 lbs. (680 kg.) or eight 60 lb. (27.2 kg.) H.E. or 25 lb. (11.4 kg.) armour piercing rocket projectiles may be carried.

DIMENSIONS.—Span 45 ft. 6 in. (13.87 m.), Width folded 17 ft. 3 in. (5.26 m.), Length (landplane) 35 ft. 8 in. (10.9 m.), Length (seaplane) 40 ft. 6 in. (12.3 m.), Height (landplane) 12 ft. 4 in. (3.75 m.), Height (seaplane) 14 ft. 7 in. (4.45 m.).

WEIGHTS (landplane).—Weight empty 4,700 lbs. (2,134 kg.), Disposable load (torpedo-bomber) 2,810 lbs. (1,276 kg.), Disposable load (reconnaissance) 2,060 lbs. (935 kg.), Weight loaded (torpedo-bomber) 7,510 lbs. (3,410 kg.), Weight loaded (reconnaissance) 6,750 lbs. (3,065 kg.).

WEIGHTS (seaplane).—Weight empty 5,300 lbs. (2,406 kg.), Disposable load as landplane, Weight loaded (torpedo-bomber) 8,110 lbs. (3,682 kg.), Weight loaded (reconnaissance) 7,360 lbs. (3,541 kg.).

PERFORMANCE (landplane).—Maximum speed (torpedo-bomber) 138 m.p.h. (220.6 km.h.) at 5,000 ft. (1,525 m.), Maximum speed (reconnaissance) 144 m.p.h. (230.4 km.h.) at 5,000 ft. (1,525 m.).

PERFORMANCE (seaplane).—Maximum speed (torpedo-bomber) 128 m.p.h. (204.8 km.h.) at 5,000 ft. (1,525 m.), Maximum speed (reconnaissance) 134 m.p.h. (214.4 km.h.) at 5,000 ft. (1,525 m.).

THE FAIREY BATTLE.

The illustration above shows a Fairey Battle fitted with the Fairey P.24 engine and the Fairey electrically-operated contra-rotating constant-speed airscrews, the first airscrews of this type to be flight-tested in Great Britain. This installation was flying successfully six years ago and between June 13, 1939, and December 5, 1941, it put in about 86 flying hours at the hands of the late Flt. Lieut. Christopher Staniland, Mr. F. H. Dixon, the company's present chief test pilot, and a number of R.A.F. pilots. It was then shipped to the United States of America.

THE FAIREY SPEARFISH.

The Spearfish two-seat Torpedo-Dive Bomber-Reconnaissance Monoplane was designed to Specification O.5/43 and fulfils a role similar to that of the Barracuda. It is a mid-wing monoplane of all-metal construction and is fitted with a 2,585 h.p. Bristol Centaurus 57 two-row radial air-cooled engine driving a Rotol five-blade constant-speed airscrew. Ultimately it is proposed to fit a five-blade reversible-pitch braking airscrew to serve as a dive brake.

A crew of two is carried. The pilot's cockpit with hydraulically-operated canopy is over the leading-edge and the observer's cockpit over the trailing-edge of the wing.

Armament consists of two fixed forward-firing .50-in. machine-guns operated by the pilot and two similar guns in a Nash & Thomson power-operated turret aft. The bomb-bay beneath the wings can accommodate a standard 18-in. torpedo or bombs, mines or depth-charges up to a maximum of 2,000 lbs.

Fairey-Youngman retractable flaps are fitted. The wide-track landing-gear retracts outwardly into the outer wing sections, which are of the power-folding type. There is prov-ision for assisted take-off by accelerator or rockets. Full radio and Radar equipment is carried.

DIMENSIONS.—Span 60 ft. (18.3 m.). Length 45 ft. 4 in. (13.8 m.), Height 16 ft. 6 in. (5 m.). Wing area 530 sq. ft. (49.2 sq. m.).
WEIGHT LOADED.—24,000 lb. (10,000 kg.).

PERFORMANCE.—Maximum speed 301 m.p.h. (482 km.h.) at 16,000 ft. (4,880 m.). Climb to 15,000 ft. (4,575 m.) 9 mins.. Range 900 miles (1,440 km.) at 196 m.p.h. (314 km.h.).

The Folland 43/37 Engine-test Monoplane fitted with Napier-Sabre liquid-cooled power-unit.

FOLLAND.

FOLLAND AIRCRAFT, LTD.

HEAD OFFICE AND WORKS: HAMBLE, SOUTHAMPTON.

Chairman: A. P. Good.

Directors: H. P. Folland, M.B.E., F.R.Ae.S., M.I.Ae.E., F.R.S.A., F.I.Ae.S. (Managing), T. Gilbertson (General Manager), C. L. Hill, E. L. Granville, M.P., and E. N. Egan (Secretary).

Chief Engineer and Technical Director: H. E. Preston, F.R.Ae.S.

Chief Designer: S. H. Evans, F.R.Ae.S., B.Sc., A.F.I.Ae.S.

This Company was originally formed as British Marine Air-craft, Ltd. in February, 1936, primarily to construct civil flying-boats.

In May, 1937, a complete re-organization took place. The Company obtained the services of Mr. H. P. Folland as Managing Director and the name of the company was changed to Folland Aircraft, Ltd. Mr. Folland who had previously served as Chief Designer of the Gloster Aircraft Co., Ltd., was responsible for a long range of successful fighter aircraft, as well as the series of Gloster racing aircraft and Schneider Trophy seaplanes.

The Company has extensive works at Hamble, on Southampton Water. During the war it was almost entirely engaged on sub-contract work, but certain original design work as in hand. One of the company's designs is briefly described below.

THE FOLLAND 43/37.

The 43/37 has been designed for flight-testing large aero-engines. It has accommodation for a pilot and two observers in a roomy cabin fitted with all necessary instruments for observ-ing complete engine performance details in flight. The machine is of mixed construction with a semi-monocoque light alloy fuselage and a plywood-covered wing. Landing flaps and automatic wing-tip slats are fitted.

DIMENSIONS.—Span 58 ft. (17.7 m.), Length 43 ft. 4 in. (13.2 m.), Height 16 ft. 3 in. (4.95 m.), Wing area 588 sq. ft. (54.6 sq. m.).
WEIGHT LOADED.—16,000 lbs. (7,265 kg.).

GENERAL AIRCRAFT.

GENERAL AIRCRAFT LTD.

HEAD OFFICE, WORKS AND AERODROME: THE LONDON AIR PARK, FELTHAM, MIDDLESEX.

Chairman: Sir Maurice Bonham-Carter, K.C.B., K.C.V.O.

Directors: J. M. Ferguson, F.C.A., C. F. Lumb, Sir William Stephenson, M.C., D.F.C. and L. G. Reid (Managing).

Chief Designer: F. F. Crocombe, B.Sc., A.C.G.I., D.I.C., F.R.Ae.S.

There are three wartime products of General Aircraft Limited, of which particulars may now be described. These are the Hotspur eight-seat military glider, which later became the standard glider trainer of Airborne Forces, the Hamilcar heavy glider, which was designed to carry wheeled and tracked armoured vehicles and other heavy or bulky military equipment, and the Fleet Shadower, an experimental aeroplane which was designed to meet Admiralty requirements for a carrier-borne aircraft capable of shadowing enemy fleets at night.

Production of the Hamilcar, which played an important part in two airborne invasions of Europe, was handled entirely by the Birmingham Railway Carriage and Wagon Co., Ltd.

In addition to other activities General Aircraft, Ltd., has been engaged on important experimental contracts and sub-con-tracting work for the Ministry of Aircraft Production.

THE G.A.L. HAMILCAR.

The Hamilcar was originally designed to carry the Tetrarch tank or two Universal carriers. Later, however, it was adapted for the carriage of a great variety of military loads, for which its spacious cabin and load capacity of eight long tons made it particularly suitable. The Hamilcar was towed by Halifax, Lancaster or Stirling four-engined bombers.

TYPE.—Military tank or vehicle carrying glider.

WINGS.—High-wing cantilever monoplane. Wing section RAF.34 modified. Aspect ratio 11.5. Centre-section and two tapering outer sections. Structure comprises two box spars with laminated booms and plywood webs, built-up former ribs and a plywood skin covered with fabric. Attachment of outer wings to centre-section by two fore-and-aft pin-joints per spar. Pneumatically-operated slotted flaps between ailerons and fuselage. Flaps are all wood with single box spar, diaphragm ribs and plywood skin. Dynamically-balanced slotted ailerons have single-spar, former ribs, plywood leading-edge and fabric covering. Trim-tab in starboard aileron.

FUSELAGE.—Rectangular all-wood semi-monocoque structure in two main sections which may be separated for transport purposes. Structure consists of a series of vertical square frames, four corner longerons and a fabric-covered plywood skin supported by inter-costal stringers. Two massive frames reinforced by high-tensile steel gusset plates at their bottom corners transmit lift loads from centre-section spars to the fuselage and a keel beam between the suspension frames acts as the main load anchorage. The nose of the fuselage is hinged to open to starboard for loading. In the roof of the forward portion of the fuselage ahead of the rear centre-section spar is the flight compartment well. This is a separate built-up unit supported on three transverse trusses and is com-pleted by a transparent canopy which stands proud of the fuselage decking. The rear fuselage terminates in two heavy frames which support the fin and tailplane and the tail-wheel.

TAIL UNIT.—Cantilever monoplane type. Fin and tailplane are two-spar structures with a plywood skin. Elevators and rudder are wood-framed and fabric-covered. Trim-tabs in elevators and rudder.

LANDING GEAR.—Divided type. Each unit consists of two Vees hinged to the lower fuselage longerons and a vertical oleo-pneu-matic shock-absorber leg hinged to the centre-section front spar. The Vees are built up of two stainless steel boxes, the rearmost acting as the axle beam. All anchorages are in the form of univ-ersal ball-joints. For loading and unloading the main hold the pressure in the shock-absorber struts is released to permit the aircraft to sink under its own weight on to ash skids mounted on rubber blocks under the lower longerons. Differentially-operated wheel-brakes. Alternative landing-gear without shock-absorbers may be jettisoned in flight when skid landings have to be made. Fully-castoring tail-wheel.

ACCOMMODATION.—Flight compartment in upper portion of forward fuselage seating two in tandem with dual controls. Bullet-proof windshield and armour behind second pilot. Access to compart-ment by ladder on inner starboard side of fuselage, through hatch in roof and along walkway on top of centre-section. Main freight compartment 25 ft. 6 in. (7.78 m.) long, 8 ft. (2.44 m.) wide and 7.5 ft. (2.3 m.) high. A variety of military equipment can be carried up to a maximum of 17,500 lbs. (7,950 kg.). Nose of fuselage hinges to starboard for loading. Cable-operated push-rod assembly opens the nose either manually, or automatically as a vehicle drives forward. Vehicle rails on bottom of fuselage

The G.A.L. Hamilcar Tank or Vehicle-carrying Glider.

can be adjusted to suit tracks of different vehicles. Central load anchorage point on keel beam. Exhaust extractors in sides of fuselage to permit vehicles to start up their engines before landing.

DIMENSIONS.—Span 110 ft. (33.5 m.), Length 68 ft. (20.7 m.), Height (tail down) 20 ft. 3 in. (6.2 m.), Wing area 1,657.5 sq. ft. (154 sq. m.).

WEIGHTS.—Weight empty 18,400 lbs. (8,350 kg.), Military load 17,600 lbs. (7,980 kg.), Weight loaded 36,000 lbs. (16,330 kg.), Wing loading 22.37 lbs./sq. ft. (109.2 kg./sq. m.).

PERFORMANCE (at sea level).—Maximum towing speed 150 m.p.h. (240 km.h.), Maximum diving speed 187 m.p.h. (300 km.h.), Stalling speed 65 m.p.h. (105 km.h.).

THE G. A. HAMILCAR X.

The Hamilcar X is in effect the Hamilcar I Glider strengthened at appropriate points for the installation of two 965 h.p. Bristol Mercury 31 engines. The external appearance excepting for the mounting of these engines ahead of the wing and a minor difference in the ap-plication of the telescopic oleo-pneumatic struts of the main undercarriage is exactly the same as the ordinary glider version. The span, length, height and cubic capacity of the cabin are identical (see p. 37c).

The square-section fuselage comprises an unobstructed hold of internal dimensions sufficient to accommodate a large variety of heavy military freight from a 7¾-ton tank or two Bren gun carriers to a 17-pounder anti-tank gun with its towing vehicle, and engineering equipment loads such as Bulldozers, scrapers and tractors and Bailey bridge equipment.

Single point towing is used in the Hamilcar X as against bi-furcated towing in the case of the Hamilcar I.

The Hamilcar X is capable of solo flight as a normal twin-engined aircraft up to a weight of 32,500 lbs. (14,760 kg.), the disposable load in this condition being 6,990 lbs. (3,175 kg.). In solo flight at full load after release from the tug aircraft the rate of descent is 150 ft./min. (46 m./min.).

DIMENSIONS.—Same as for Hamilcar I.

WEIGHTS.—Weight empty 25,510 lbs. (11,580 kg.), Military Load 17,500 lbs. (7,950 kg.), Normal loaded weight 45,500 lbs. (20,660 kg.), Maximum overloaded weight 47,000 lbs. (21,340 kg.).

PERFORMANCE (as a solo aircraft at 32,500 lbs. = 14,760 kg. all-up weight).—Maximum speed 145 m.p.h. (232 km.h.), Cruising speed 120 m.p.h. (192 km.h.), Ceiling 13,000 ft. (3,970 m.).

PERFORMANCE (in towed flight at full load using a Halifax III as tug).—Towing speed 150 m.p.h. (240 km.h.), Take-off distance to 50 ft. screen 1,040 yds.-1,750 yds. (952 m.-1,600 m.) according to all-up weight of tug dictated by range requirements. Rate of climb at sea level 435 ft./min.-730 ft./min. (133 m./min.-224 m./min.) accord-ing to tug weight.

The G.A.L. Hamilcar Heavy Transport Glider.

The General Aircraft Hamilcar X powered Glider (two Bristol Mercury 31 engines).

The General Aircraft Hamilcar X powered Glider.

The General Aircraft Experimental Twin-Hotspur Troop-transport Glider.

LANDING GEAR.—Two independent units each comprising a single cantilever shock-strut incorporating rubber-in compression springing and a pair of wheels. Units may be jettisoned for landing on rough ground. Long central-skid mounted on rubber blocks.

ACCOMMODATION.—Pilotage compartment in nose with tandem seating and full dual control. Cabins fore and aft of wing structure accommodate six fully-armed troops. Access to pilot's compartment by hinged canopy, to forward cabin by door on starboard side, and to rear cabin by door on port side.

DIMENSIONS.—Span 45 ft. 10¾ in. (14 m.), Length 39 ft. 8¾ in. (12.1 m.), Height 10 ft. 10 in. (3.3 m.), Gross wing area 272 sq. ft. (25.26 sq. m.).

WEIGHTS.—Weight empty 1,755 lbs. (797 kg.), Weight loaded 3,635 lbs. (1,650 kg.).

PERFORMANCE (at sea level).—Maximum towing speed 150 m.p.h. (240 km.h.), Maximum diving speed 170 m.p.h. (273 km.h.), Stalling speed (flaps down) 54 m.p.h. (87 km.h.).

THE G.A.L. HOTSPUR.

The original Hotspur I glider was intended for use as a small troop transport and had a wing span of 61 ft. 6 in. (18.75 m.).

The Hotspur II and III with a reduced span were the standard trainers of the Glider Pilot Regiment. The main difference between the two types was in the flying controls and instruments, the Mk. III aircraft having a complete duplication for each pilot.

TYPE.—Transport and Training Glider.

WINGS.—Mid-wing cantilever monoplane. Rectangular centre-section integral with the fuselage. Tapering outer sections of wooden construction with single spar and plywood covering. Split flaps from ailerons to outer wing root joints.

FUSELAGE.—Oval section wooden structure with stressed plywood-skin. Tow-hook in extreme nose.

TAIL UNIT.—Braced monoplane type. Wooden structure with plywood covering.

THE G. A. TWIN-HOTSPUR.

The purpose of this variation of the Hotspur was to provide a quick solution for a glider capable of carrying an increased number of airborne troops and using as many of the Hotspur standard components as possible.

The Twin-Hotspur consisted of two Hotspur glider fuselages connected together by a special centre-section structure. The outer wings were identical to those of the normal Hotspur and there was a reconstructed tailplane spanning the distance between the twin fuselages. Control was from the port fuselage, where the two pilots were seated in tandem. The total complement was 16 men, 8 in each fuselage.

DIMENSIONS.—Span 58 ft. (17.7 m.), Length 39 ft. 8¾ in. (12.1 m.), Height 10 ft. 6 in. (3.2 m.), Gross wing area 262 sq. ft. (33.6 sq. m.).

WEIGHTS.—Weight empty 3,025 lbs. (1,375 kg.), Military load 3,525 lbs. (1,600 kg.), Normal loaded weight 6,550 lbs. (2,975 kg.).

PERFORMANCE.—Towing speed 150 m.p.h. (240 km.h.), Stalling speed (flaps up) 73 m.p.h. (117 km.h.), Stalling speed (flaps down) 60 m.p.h. (96 km.h.).

THE G.A.L. 38 FLEET SHADOWER.

The G.A.L. 38 was designed to meet Air Ministry specification S.23/27 which, in turn, was drawn up to meet specific Admiralty requirements for a carrier-based aeroplane suitable for the purpose of shadowing, or maintaining contact with, enemy fleets by night. This called for an exceptionally low cruising

speed and a long duration. Flight at a cruising speed of under 40 knots (46 m.p.h.) was obtained by slipstream action on wing flaps spread over a wide area of the main wing by the four-engined installation. Overall dimensions were restricted for shipboard stowage and the wings were made to fold.

TYPE.—Four-engined carrier-based Fleet Shadower.

WINGS.—Sesquiplane wing arrangement with the upper wing braced by single forwardly-inclined struts running from the fuselage to the inboard engine nacelle. Lower wing approximately one third of the span of the upper wing. All-wood structure, with spars of compressed wood and plywood, spruce and plywood ribs and an overall covering of plywood. Upper wing fitted with slotted flaps depressing to 40 degrees and slotted ailerons arranged to droop 15 degrees when the flaps were lowered. Fixed wing-tip slots ahead of the ailerons. The lower wing fitted with split flaps depressing to 60 degrees and continuous across underside of fuselage. Flap operation by a servo-pneumatic hydraulic unit. Upper wings fold from roots, complete with engine installations. Hydraulic folding.

FUSELAGE.—Rectangular cross-section with rounded corners. All-wood structure comprising spruce and plywood frames, spruce longerons and stringers and a plywood covering.

TAIL UNIT.—Cantilever monoplane type. Single fin and rudder. Tailplane and elevators set at slight dihedral. Spruce and plywood spar and ribs, plywood covering. Trim-tabs in rudder and elevator.

LANDING GEAR.—Fixed tricycle type. Main wheels mounted under lower wing extremities. Oleo suspension. Nose unit, fitted with twin wheels, connect to rudder control but could be disconnected in flight. Hydraulic wheel-brakes.

POWER PLANT.—Four 130 h.p. Pobjoy Niagara V seven-cylinder radial air-cooled geared engines driving two-blade fixed-pitch wooden airscrews. Main fuel tanks in fuselage with a hydraulic-motor-driven fuel-pump combination for engine feed. Oil tanks in wings.

ACCOMMODATION.—Crew of three, comprising pilot in enclosed cockpit on top of the fuselage ahead of the main wing and accessible through fuselage ; an observer in the nose of the fuselage ; and a radio operator below and aft of the pilot.

DIMENSIONS.—Span 55 ft. 10 in. (17.02 m.), Width folded 17 ft. 11 in. (5.46 m.), Length 36 ft. 1 in. (11 m.), Height 12 ft. 8 in. (3.86 m.), Wing area 472 sq. ft. (43.85 sq. m.).

WEIGHTS.—Weight empty 6,153 lbs. (2,791 kg.), Normal disposable load 2,438 lbs. (1,106 kg.), Maximum disposable overload 3,305 lbs. (1,499 kg.), Normal loaded weight 8,591 lbs. (3,897 kg.), Maximum overloaded weight 9,458 lbs. (4,290 kg.).

PERFORMANCE (at sea level).—Maximum speed 115 m.p.h. (185 km.h.), Cruising speed 94 m.p.h. (151.3 km.h.), Minimum speed 39 m.p.h. (62.7 km.h.), Landing speed 73 m.p.h. (117.5 km.h.), Initial rate of climb 390 ft./min. (118.8 m./min.), Service ceiling 6,000 ft. (1,830 m.), Endurance 11 hours, Range 990 miles (1,593 km.).

The G.A.L. 38 Fleet Shadower (four Popjoy Niagara engines).

GLOSTER.

GLOSTER AIRCRAFT CO. LTD.

HEAD OFFICE, WORKS AND AERODROME : HUCCLECOTE, GLOS.

Chairman : Sir Frank Spriggs, Hon. F.R.Ae.S.

Managing Director : H. K. Jones.

Director and General Manager : F. McKenna, M.I.Ae.E., F.R.S.A.

Directors : R. V. Atkinson, H. Burroughes, F.R.Ae.S. and T. O. M. Sopwith, C.B.E., F.R.Ae.S.

Chief Designer : W. G. Carter, M.B.E., F.R.Ae.S.

Secretary : E. W. Shambrook.

The Gloster Aircraft Co., Ltd., which now forms part of the Hawker Siddeley Group, was formed in 1917 and since then

has specialised mainly in the production of flight aircraft. The many successful types developed and built by the company, including the Grebe, Gauntlet and Gladiator, have been responsible for the steady expansion of the works organization.

The Gladiator, the last of the biplane fighters, fitted with a Bristol Mercury engine, saw extensive operational service in the early days of the war, including the Norwegian, Abyssinian, Greek and North African campaigns. Four of this type constituted the sole initial fighter defence of Malta. One was shot down, but the other three, now familiarly known as *Faith, Hope* and *Charity*, fought on for two months against all that the Italian Air Force could send against Malta until relief arrived. *Faith*, the only survivor of this famous trio, has now been handed over to the island as a permanent memento.

To the Gloster company belongs the distinction of being the first aircraft manufacturer in either Great Britain or the United States to design, build and fly an aircraft fitted with jet propulsion. Following on the successful development of the Whittle jet engine, the Air Ministry placed an order with the company in 1939 for the design and construction of an aeroplane to be fitted with this power-unit. In May, 1941, the Gloster E.28/39 jet-propelled monoplane made its first flight piloted by the late Flt.-Lt. P. E. G. Sayer, who was then the company's chief test-pilot.

From the experience gained in the design, construction and flight testing of the E.28/39 the Gloster company designed and put into production the Meteor single-seat twin-jet Fighter monoplane, which was the only Allied jet-propelled aircraft to

The Gloster Meteor Jet-propelled Fighter Monoplane (two Rolls-Royce turbo-jet units).

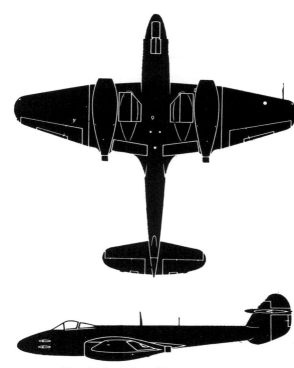

The Gloster Meteor Jet-propelled Fighter.

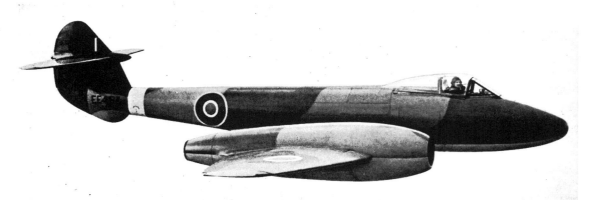

The Gloster Meteor IV (two Rolls-Royce Derwent V turbo-jet engines) which established a new World's speed record of 606 m.p.h. (969.6 km.h.) on November 7, 1945.

go into operational use during the war. The Meteor is fitted with two Rolls-Royce Welland or Derwent jet units.

It is not possible to indicate the full extent of the present activities of the company. During 1944-45, its productive effort was directed mainly towards meeting R.A.F. requirements for Meteor jet fighters and Typhoon rocket fighters and fighter-bombers which, after the invasion of Europe were responsible for so much brilliant work over France, Belgium, Holland and Germany.

Over and above its extensive production commitments, the Company is engaged in a very extensive development and research programme on entirely new projects.

THE GLOSTER METEOR.

The Meteor is a single-seat twin-jet fighter monoplane to which belongs the distinction of being the only Allied jet-propelled aeroplane to go into operational service in the war.

The Meteor first flew in March, 1943, and it shot down its first flying-bomb on August 14, 1944. After being in action against the flying-bomb from bases in Southern England, the Meteor went overseas and served with the 2nd Tactical Air Force in Northern Europe.

On November 7, 1945, a Gloster Meteor IV piloted by Group Capt. H. J. Wilson, A.F.C., R.A.F., broke the World's Speed Record over a 3 km. speed course at Herne Bay, Kent, with a speed of 606 m.p.h. (969.6 km.h.), the average of four runs over the course, two in each direction. A second Meteor IV piloted by Mr. Eric Greenwood, chief test pilot of the Gloster Aircraft Co., Ltd., put up a speed of 603 m.p.h. (964.8 km.h.) over the same course on the same day.

The two Meteor IV aircraft used for these flights were standard production models from which all operational equipment, radio mast, external fuel tank, etc. had been removed, gun ports faired over and a high polish finish applied. They were fitted with two Rolls-Royce Derwent V jet engines which were developing only about 88 to 90 per cent. of their maximum output during the record flights.

TYPE.—Single-seat twin-jet Fighter.
WINGS.—Low-wing cantilever monoplane. Wide centre-section integral with the fuselage centre portion includes the two jet nacelles and landing-gear units. Outer wing sections have increased taper and rounded tips. Upper and lower air-brakes and flaps on centre-section, internally mass-balanced ailerons with automatic balance tabs on outer sections. All-metal stressed-skin wing structure.
FUSELAGE.—Oval section all-metal stressed-skin structure. In four sections comprising the nose, the front fuselage with nose wheel, the centre fuselage embodying the wing centre-section with the two power nacelles and main landing-gear units, and the rear fuselage complete with tail portion.
TAIL UNIT.—Cantilever monoplane type. Tailplane mounted near top of fin splitting the rudder in two parts. Trimming tabs are fitted to each elevator and to lower portion of rudder.
LANDING GEAR.—Retractable tricycle type. Dowty levered-suspension springing. Main wheels raised inwardly, the legs being compressed on retraction to lessen space occupied in the

wings. Nose wheel raised backwards, the wheel itself being housed between the rudder pedals in the front fuselage. In addition to the normal electrical indicators, there is a mechanical down lock indicator for the nose wheel unit showing just forward of the wind-screen. Hydraulic retraction with emergency hand-pump. Pneumatic brakes on main wheels.
POWER PLANT.—Two Rolls-Royce Welland or Derwent turbo-jet units mounted just inboard of the extremities of the centre-section.
ACCOMMODATION.—Pilot's cockpit forward of the leading-edge of the wings. Sliding and jettisonable blister-type cockpit canopy. Pilot armour and bullet-resisting windscreen. Stick type control column with hinged spade grip and parallel-action rudder pedals. Trimming tabs operated by normal hand wheels. Engine-driven hydraulic pump operates the landing-gear, flaps and air brakes. Pneumatic system served by two air containers in rear fuselage operates the gun-cocking gear and wheel brakes.
ARMAMENT.—Four 20 m/m. British Hispano cannon mounted alongside the pilot and firing forward. A camera gun is installed in the fuselage nose fairing and control for this camera is incorporated in the gun-firing button. It may also be used without the guns if required.
DIMENSIONS.—Span 43 ft. (13.1 m.), Length 41 ft. 3 in. (12.6 m.), Height 13 ft. (3.96 m.), Wing area 374 sq. ft. (34 sq. m.).
WEIGHTS AND PERFORMANCE.—No data available.

THE GLOSTER E.28/39.

The first Gloster Whittle jet-propelled aircraft was designed to meet the requirements of Air Ministry specification E.28/39. As a type it could thus be regarded as representing the operational requirements at that time for high-altitude interception. This aspect, however, was not unduly emphasised as the design

proceeded, the main concern being to give special attention to the many novel features associated with the installation of a jet-propulsion unit instead of the usual conventional engine and airscrew.

The E.28/39 is a low-wing cantilever monoplane of all-metal construction with the single turbine unit located in the fuselage aft of the pilot's cockpit. Air is taken in through the nose orifice, the flow being divided to pass on each side of the pilot's cockpit to the gas turbine unit. The products of combustion are ejected through the single jet outlet in the tail of the fuselage.

The cantilever tailplane is mounted above the fuselage with the fin and rudder hinge-line located forward of the leading-edge.

No trimming-tabs are fitted to any of the control surfaces. The low landing-gear permitted by the absence of airscrew is of the tricycle type, the nose wheel retracting backward and the main wheels inward.

From an aerodynamic point of view the E.28/39 is exceptionally clean. No external fitments are carried apart from the radio aerial, the pitot head at its forward extension and a venturi in a small fairing to drive one of the gyroscopic instruments.

The pilot, seated in the forward part of the fuselage, has an excellent view in all directions, particularly forward and downward. The rearward view was not regarded as an item of immediate importance.

The E.28/39, which first flew on May 15, 1941, was the first aeroplane to be fitted with the Whittle power-unit and the first British aeroplane to fly by jet-propulsion.

THE GLOSTER F.9/37.

Information was released during 1944 concerning two experimental single-seat twin-engined fighter monoplanes which were built by the Gloster company to meet the Air Ministry F.9/37 specification, one fitted with two 1,050 h.p. Bristol

The Gloster E.28/39 Monoplane, the first British jet-propelled aircraft to fly.

The Gloster F.9/37 Twin-engined Fighter Monoplane (two Bristol Taurus engines). (*Aeroplane Photograph*).

Taurus TE/1 sleeve-valve air-cooled radial engines and the other with two 885 h.p. Rolls-Royce Peregrine twelve-cylinder Vee liquid-cooled engines.

Although the F.9/37 specification called for a two-seat aircraft, both the Gloster monoplanes were completed as single-seaters.

The Taurus-engined model first flew on April 3, 1939, and was delivered to the R.A.F. for test in the following July. Following a landing accident, it was rebuilt with two 900 h.p. Taurus III engines and trials were finally completed in July, 1940. The Peregrine-engined model first flew in July, 1940.

Both aircraft were of all-metal construction and were fitted with retractable landing-gear and twin-ruddered tail-unit. Armament consisted of two 20 m/m. cannon.

DIMENSIONS.—Span 50 ft. (15.25 m.), Length 37 ft. (11.3 m.), Height 11 ft. 7 in. (3.5 m.), Wing area 386 sq. ft. (35.8 sq. m.).

WEIGHTS AND LOADINGS.—Weight empty 8,828 lbs. (4,008 kg.), Weight loaded 11,615 lbs. (5,273 kg.), Wing loading 30.1 lbs./sq. ft. (146.8 kg./sq. m.), Power loading (Taurus TE/1 engines) 6.5 lbs./h.p. (2.95 kg./h.p.).

PERFORMANCE (two 1,050 h.p. Taurus TE/1 engines).—Maximum speed 360 m.p.h. (576 km.h.) at 15,000 ft. (4,575 m.), Initial rate of climb 2,030 ft./min. (620 m./min.), Service ceiling 30,000 ft. (9,150 m.).

PERFORMANCE (two Taurus III engines).—Maximum speed 332 m.p.h. (531 km.h.) at 15,200 ft. (4,640 m.).

PERFORMANCE (two 885 h.p. Peregrine engines).—Maximum speed 330 m.p.h. (528 km.h.) at 15,000 ft. (4,575 m.).

HANDLEY PAGE.

HANDLEY PAGE, LTD.

HEAD OFFICES AND WORKS : CRICKLEWOOD, LONDON, N.W.2.
AERODROME : COLNEY STREET, RADLETT, HERTFORDSHIRE.
Managing Director : Sir Frederick Handley Page.

The firm of Handley Page, Ltd., has been associated with flying in all its aspects for the past thirty-one years. It thus possesses the proud distinction of being the first limited company incorporated in Great Britain for the purpose of manufacturing aircraft.

The latest military product of the Company is the Halifax four-engined long-range heavy bomber. The first production Halifax flew in October, 1940, and this type made its first operational flight on March 11, 1941.

Manufacture of the Halifax was undertaken by a Production Group consisting of the parent company, which acted as technical advisors and consultants to the Group as a whole ; the English Electric Co. of Preston ; the London Passenger Transport Board ; Rootes Securities, Ltd, Speke ; and the Fairey Aviation Co., Ltd., Stockport. Altogether at the peak of production the Group comprised 41 factories and dispersal units, 600 subcontractors and a total of 51,000 employees. At that peek the Group was producing one complete aircraft every working hour.

In October, 1944, preliminary details of a new four-engined airliner, the H.P.68 Hermes, were released. A summary of these details is given herewith.

THE HANDLEY PAGE H.P.68 HERMES.

In October, 1944, particulars were released of the first civil aeroplane designed by Handley Page, Ltd., since the war began. The H.P.68 is an all-metal low-wing monoplane with retractable landing-gear, single fin and rudder and will be fitted with four 1,650 h.p. Bristol Hercules fourteen-cylinder radial air-cooled sleeve-valve engines, each mounted in a self-contained low-drag nacelle and driving a four-bladed de Havilland Hydromatic full-feathering airscrew. The normal fuel capacity will be 2,574 Imp. gallons.

Two versions of the Hermes will be available, (1) a transport for the carriage of up to 50 passengers in a cabin designed for supercharging, or (2) a freight or cargo carrier capable of carrying a maximum pay load of 17,890 lbs. (8,122 kg.) and with two

large freight-loading doors giving an aperture of 9 ft. 4 in ✕ 5 ft. 9 in. (2.84 ✕ 1.75 m.) aft of the wings. The freight-carrier also has a strengthened floor but no provision for pressurisation is made.

There will be several passenger cabin arrangements, ranging from a maximum of 50 seats for a short range type to a special luxury model for 20 passengers, with an intermediate arrangement for 34 day passengers and 16 sleeping passengers. The crew will consist of two pilots, flight engineer, radio operator, navigator and stewards. There will be 630 cu. ft. of baggage and freight space in four separate compartments, one forward and one aft of the passenger cabin and two beneath the cabin floor. There will be two lavatories and a large steward's galley.

DIMENSIONS.—Span 113 ft. (34.46 m.), Length 81 ft. 8 in. (24.85 m.), Wing area 1,408 sq. ft. (131 sq. m.).

WEIGHTS.—Weight loaded 75,000 lbs. (34,050 km.), Maximum landing weight 70,000 lbs. (31,780 kg.).

PERFORMANCE (estimated).—Maximum speed 340 m.p.h. (544 km.h.), Cruising speed 240 m.p.h. (384 km.h.).

RANGES (Passenger-carrier).—With 15,950 lbs. (7,241 kg.) payload 1,610 miles (2,576 km.) at 240 m.p.h. (384 km.h.) and 1,740 miles (2,784 km.) at 194 m.p.h. (310 km.h.), With 12,000 lbs. (5,448 kg.) payload 2,200 miles (3,520 km.) at 240 m.p.h. (384 km.h.) and 2,450 miles (3,920 km.) at 194 m.p.h. (310 km.h.), Maximum range 3,440 miles (5,504 km.) with 6,350 lbs. (2,883 kg.) payload.

RANGES (Freight-carrier).—With 17,890 lbs. (8,122 kg.) payload 1,600 miles (2,560 km.) at 240 m.p.h. (384 km.h.) and 1,745 miles (2,792 km.) at 194 m.p.h. (310 km.h.), With 16,000 lbs. (7,264 kg.) payload 1,880 miles (3,010 km.) at 240 m.p.h. (384 km.h.) and 2,060 miles (3,296 km.) at 194 m.p.h. (310 km.h.), With 13,000 lbs. (5,902 kg.) payload 2,340 miles (3,744 km.) at 240 m.p.h. (384 km.h.) and 2,600 miles (4,160 km.) at 194 m.p.h. (310 km.h.), With 10,720 lbs. (4,870 kg.) payload 2,700 miles (4,320 km.) at 240 m.p.h. (384 km.h.) and 3,300 miles (4,850 km.) at 194 m.p.h. (310 km.h.), Maximum range 3,445 miles (5,512 km.) with 8,240 lbs. (3,741 kg.) payload.

THE HANDLEY PAGE H.P.57 HALIFAX.

The Halifax owes its origin to the Air Ministry Specification B.13/36 which called for a medium bomber fitted with two of the new Rolls-Royce Vulture twenty-four-cylinder X-type engines then under development. When it was realised that the Vulture engine would not be available in sufficient numbers the design was changed to take four Rolls-Royce Merlin engines

and the designed loaded weight increased from 26,300 lbs. (11,940 kg.) to 40,000 lbs. (18,160 kg.).

The prototype Halifax first flew in October, 1939, twenty-two months after construction began. It was fitted with four Merlin X engines, had a loaded weight of 55,000 lbs. (24,970 kg.), and a maximum speed of 280 m.p.h. (448 km.h.). The production Halifax I flew in October, 1940, delivery to squadrons began in the following month, and the Halifax went into operational service in March, 1941. From then on the Halifax was the subject of steady development and was in continuous service with the R.A.F. in the following forms. :—

Halifax I. Four Rolls-Royce Merlin X engines. Armament originally consisted of eight .303 in. machine-guns, two in a Boulton Paul nose turret, four in a Boulton Paul tail turret and two hand-operated beam-guns. Later a Boulton Paul Hudson-type two-gun turret was introduced in the mid-upper position in place of the beam guns. All-up weight : 60,000 lbs. (27,240 kg.).

Halifax II. Four Rolls-Royce Merlin XX engines. Same armament as Mark I.

Halifax II, Series I. Same as Mark II except nose turret removed and replaced by fairing. This was merely an interim measure before the introduction of the Series IA.

Halifax II, Series IA. Four Rolls-Royce Merlin 22 engines. Greatly cleaned-up version. A new symmetrical transparent plastic nose fitted with one centrally-mounted .303 in. hand-held machine-gun. Hudson-type dorsal turret replaced by Boulton Paul Defiant-type four-gun turret. W/T mast removed and aerial attached directly to top of D/F loop. New type Morris block radiators permitting reduction in cross-section of engine nacelles, improved flame-dampers of better aerodynamic form, lower astro-dome, retractable tail-wheel and smooth-finish paint scheme. All-up weight : 63,000 lbs. (28,600 kg.). The Halifax II, Series IA served as a tug for the Hamilcar tank-carrying glider.

Halifax III. Four Bristol Hercules XVI fourteen-cylinder radial air-cooled sleeve-valve engines. Otherwise same as Mark II, Series IA. A later modification introduced into the Mark III was an increase of wing span from 98 ft. 8 in. (30 m.) to 104 ft. (31.7 m.), which latter dimension became standard in all production Halifaxes.

Halifax IV. One experimental aircraft built for the purpose of testing new engine mountings.

Halifax V. Identical to Mark II, Series IA, but with Dowty landing-gear instead of the Messier gear. Introduced at a time when Messier landing-gear production was insufficient to supply all Halifax production demands.

Halifax VI. Four Bristol Hercules 100 fourteen-cylinder radial sleeve-valve engines in circular self-contained nacelles. Otherwise similar to Mark III but of better performance.

Halifax VII. After production of Mk. VI had begun the supply

A drawing of the Handley Page Hermes Transport monoplane (four Bristol Hercules engines).

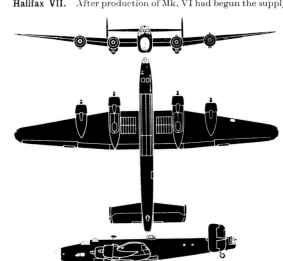

The Handley Page Halifax III with extended span wings.

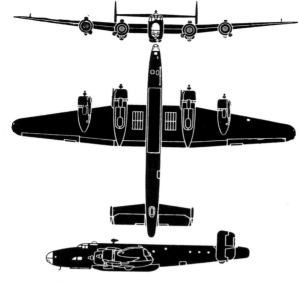

The Handley Page Halifax VI Heavy Bomber (four Bristol Hercules 100 engines).

The Handley Page Halifax VIII Transport.

of Hercules 100 engines was found to be temporarily insufficient and a number of aircraft were fitted with Hercules XVI engines as a stop-gap. This necessitated a change in mark number.

Halifax VIII. A modified version for R.A.F. Transport Command. Standard Mark VI airframe stripped of military equipment, turrets, etc., and fitted for carrying eleven passengers. 24 troops, freight or ambulance equipment. A large boat-shaped pannier fitted in the bomb-bay is capable of carrying some 8,000 lbs. (3,632 kg.) of freight. See also description of Halifax Civil Transport.

TYPE.—Four-engined Heavy Bomber.

WINGS.—Mid-wing cantilever monoplane. Built up of five main sections, consisting of a centre-section carrying the inboard engine-mounting at its extremities, two intermediate sections, and two outer sections which carry the outboard engine mountings at their roots. The centre-section has two spars, the front spar a girder structure built up of channel sections and the rear spar comprising T-section extruded booms and plain sheet web. The intermediate sections, at which the dihedral begins, are built up on two spars which have T-section booms and sheet webs. The outer wings are similar but have L-section booms. All sections have detachable trailing-edge sections aft of the rear spars. The leading-edge of the outer sections is armoured and is provided with balloon cable cutters. The structure of the various sections is completed by former ribs, spanwise stringers and a smooth light alloy skin. Ailerons on the outer sections have aluminium-alloy frames and fabric covering. Handley Page slotted trailing-edge flaps between ailerons and fuselage.

FUSELAGE.—Oval section light alloy monocoque structure in four main sections with L-section and U-section frames, L-section stringers and a stressed-metal skin. Two channel-section longerons run the entire length of the fuselage along the centre-line of the sides, the top flanges forming the floor support.

TAIL UNIT.—Cantilever monoplane type with twin fins and rudders. Two-spar tail-plane. Balanced elevators and rudders. Trimming-tabs in all control surfaces.

LANDING GEAR.—Retractable type. Messier hydraulic units with auxiliary hand pumps. Wheels are retracted backwards into inner engine-nacelles leaving a small portion of each wheel protruding but closely fitted by doors. Retractable tail-wheel.

POWER PLANT.—Four Bristol Hercules fourteen-cylinder radial air-cooled sleeve-valve engines in self-contained units ready to pick up four fixings on the firewalls. Three-blade Rotol constant-speed full-feathering airscrews. Twelve self-sealing fuel tanks, four in each intermediate wing section and two in the inner end of each outer-wing. Normal capacity 1,998 gallons. Oil tanks in outer engine nacelles and in leading-edge of centre-section for inboard engines.

ACCOMMODATION.—Crew of seven normally carried, consisting of two pilots, navigator, radio operator and three gunners. Bomb-aimer's position in extreme nose. Aft of bomb-aimer is the navigator's compartment and chart table. Aft of navigator is the pilot's compartment seating two side-by-side. Pilots have direct communication with the radio operator who is situated below them on the same level as navigator. Behind pilot's compartment is the engineer's station, where there is an astral dome in the roof from which the Fighting Control Officer can direct operations when the aircraft is attacked. In centre-section bunks are fitted for rest quarters for crew. Behind wings there is an upper midships gun-turret and tail-turret. A walkway throughout length of fuselage gives access to all crew stations. Entry to fuselage in rear portion through door in lower port side.

ARMAMENT, BOMBS, ARMOUR AND EQUIPMENT.—Nine Browning 0.303 in. machine-guns, eight in two four-gun Boulton Paul hydraulically-operated turrets, one amidships and one in the extreme tail, and one manually-operated gun in nose. Tail-turret fed by ammunition tracks from magazines aft of the midships turret. Bomb compartments in fuselage and centre-section. Main compartment in lower portion of fuselage is 22 ft. (6.7 m.) long and is closed by eight hydraulically-operated doors. Six bomb compartments in centre-section, three on either side of fuselage. Handley Page loading winches load bombs on their carriers and automatically locates them in correct positions in bomb-bays. Maximum bomb capacity 14,500 lbs. (6,580 kg.). All crew positions are armoured. Full electrical and radio equipment, flares, oxygen, cabin heating, dinghies for emergency use in trailing-edge of port wing, etc.

DIMENSIONS.—Span 104 ft. (31.7 m.), Length 71 ft. 7 in. (21.8 m.), Height 21 ft. 7 in. (6.6 m.), Gross wing area 1,275 sq. ft. (1,184 m.).

WEIGHTS AND LOADINGS.—Weight empty 38,239 lbs. (17,360 kg.), Maximum over-loaded weight 65,000 lbs. (29,510 kg.), Normal wing loading 51 lbs./sq. ft. (248.8 kg./sq. m.), Power loading 12.7 lbs./h.p. (5.76 kg./h.p.).

PERFORMANCE.—Maximum speed over 270 m.p.h. (432 km.h.), Maximum range approximately 3,000 miles (4,800 miles).

THE HANDLEY PAGE HALIFAX CIVIL TRANSPORT

To make available as soon as possible a high-speed long-range civil transport that will serve as an interim type until the Hermes is ready, Handley Page, Ltd. have developed a civil conversion of the Halifax bomber for the use of airline operators.

In a conventional airliner interior arrangement the Halifax

Civil Transport accommodates eleven passengers; nine in adjustable armchair type seats and two in a comfortable compartment which is readily convertible into a two-berth sleeping compartment. If desired additional sleeping berths can be fitted in the main passenger compartment. The whole cabin is upholstered and lined throughout and each passenger seat has a window adjacent thereto. A lavatory is fitted aft of the main compartment.

In addition to the eleven passengers, the Halifax Civil Transport can also carry a large amount of freight and/or mail in a specially-designed pannier of streamline form which fits into the underside of the fuselage where in the military version bombs are carried. This pannier, with a capacity for loads up to 8,000 lbs. (3,632 kg.), has loading hatches fore and aft and can be lowered from and raised up to the aircraft by means of winches. Thus for specific freight-carrying operations, a complete pannier can be detached and replaced by another for rapid "turn-around" flights.

When conditions demand extreme range, with a consequent reduction in payload, additional long-range tanks can be fitted in place of the pannier to give a maximum range of 3,510 miles (5,616 km.).

The general structure of the Civil Transport is identical to that of the Halifax bomber. The power-plant consists of four 1,650 h.p. Bristol Hercules 100 engines, each driving a D.H. three-blade constant-speed full-feathering airscrew.

RANGES (at 65,000 lbs. (29,510 kg.) all-up weight and 55,000 lbs. (24,970 kg.) landing weight).—Range with maximum load of 12,100 lbs. (5,493 kg.) 1,810 miles (2,896 km.), Range with load of 10,000 lbs. (4,540 kg.) 2,150 miles (3,440 km.), Maximum range with normal fuel tanks and load of 7,750 lbs. (3,518 kg.) 2,530 miles (4,050 km.), Maximum range with long-range fuel tanks and load of 2,500 lbs. (1,135 kg.) 3,510 miles (5,616 km.).

RANGES (at 68,000 lbs. (30,870 kg.) all-up weight and 57,000 lbs (25,880 kg.) landing weight).—Range with maximum load of 14,100 lbs. (6,400 kg.) 1,860 miles (2,976 km.), Range with load of 12,500 lbs. (5,675 kg.) 2,120 miles (3,390 km.), Maximum range with normal fuel tanks and load of 10,750 lbs. (4,880 kg.) 2,420 miles (3,872 km.), Maximum range with long-range fuel tanks and load of 5,450 lbs. (2,475 kg.) 3,360 miles (5,376 km.).

DIMENSIONS.—Same as for the Halifax bomber except Length 73 ft. 7 in. (22.45 m.).

WEIGHTS.—Tare weight 37,750 lbs. (17,140 kg.), Removable equipment and crew 2,850 lbs. (1,294 kg.), Basic equipped weight 40,600 lbs. (18,434 kg.).

PERFORMANCE.—Maximum speed 320 m.p.h. (512 km.h.), Maximum weak mixture cruising speed at 10,000 ft. (3,050 m.) 260 m.p.h. (416 km.h.), Maximum weak mixture cruising speed at 15,000 ft. (4,575 m.) 270 m.p.h. (432 km.h.), Economical cruising speed at

The Handley Page Halifax VIII Transport (four Bristol Hercules 100 engines).

Two views of the Handley-Page Manx Experimental tail-less Monoplane. (*Flight Photographs*).

10,000 ft. (3,050 m.) 200 m.p.h. (320 km.h.), Economical cruising speed at 15,000 ft. (4,575 m.) 210 m.p.h. (336 km.h.).

To the various marks of the Halifax enumerated on pages 41-42c should be added the A. Mk. IX. Designed and equipped primarily for duties with the Airborne Forces, although it can be operated as either a bomber or transport, the A. IX normally carries a crew of six, sixteen fully-equipped paratroops and two despatchers, whose duty is to control the dropping of troops.

The main entrance door, which also serves as the paratroop exit, is in the floor of the rear fuselage and opens inwards and backwards. A signalling panel operated by the air bomber and parachute static line rails are fitted in the fuselage.

A streamline pannier may be fitted into the normal bomb-bay for carrying military equipment to a maximum of 8,000 lbs. (3,630 kg.). Alternatively, long-range tanks may be fitted in place of the pannier.

The A. IX has a new Boulton Paul "D" type tail turret armed with two .50-in. machine-guns. No mid upper turret is fitted. The power-plant consists of four 1,675 h.p. Bristol Hercules XVI engines.

PERFORMANCE.—Maximum speed (full load) at 22,000 ft. (6,710 m.) 320 m.p.h. (512 km.h.), Range (full load) 2,080 miles (3,330 km.).

THE HANDLEY PAGE MANX.

The Manx is a light two-seat experimental aeroplane which

was built to carry out flight research on problems connected with tailless aircraft. The backswept wings carry rudders at their tips, these rudders moving outwardly only. The ailerons also act as elevators.

Two 140 h.p. D.H. Gipsy Major engines are installed in the wings and drive variable-pitch pusher propellers through extension shafts.

DIMENSIONS.—Span 40 ft. (12.2 m.), Length of fuselage 18 ft. (5.5 m.), Wing area 246 sq. ft. (22.8 sq. m.).
WEIGHT.—4,000 lbs. (1,820 kg.).
PERFORMANCE.—Cruising speed 150 m.p.h. (240 km.h.), Ceiling 15,000 ft. (4,575 m.).

HAWKER.

HAWKER AIRCRAFT, LTD.

HEAD OFFICE AND WORKS : KINGSTON-ON-THAMES, SURREY.
Established : 1933.
Chairman : Sir Frank Spriggs, Hon. F.R.Ae.S.
Managing Director : H. K. Jones.
Director and Chief Designer : S. Camm, C.B.E., F.R.Ae.S.
Directors : T. O. M. Sopwith, C.B.E., F.R.Ae.S., P. W. S. Bulman, C.B.E., M.C., A.F.C., F.R.Ae.S., P. G. Lucas, G.M., A.F.R.Ae.S. and H. Chandler.
Secretary : M. Robertson.

Hawker Aircraft, Ltd., was incorporated in 1933 as successor to the H. G. Hawker Engineering Co., Ltd., which was formed in 1920 as the outcome of the voluntary liquidation of the famous Sopwith concern.

The Hawker company produced during the war as distinguished a line of single-seater fighters as did their Sopwith ancestors during the 1914-1918 war. By a steady process of evolution during the past 25 years, the Hurricane, the Typhoon, and the Tempest have all been developed from their early Sopwith counterparts, the Pup, the Camel, the Triplane, the Snipe, the Dolphin and the Salamander. In the intervening years between the two wars, such machines as the Hawker Fury and the Hart became the standard equipment in their classes in the Royal Air Force.

It is not possible to cover in a few lines all that has been achieved by Hawker products in the war, but to the credit of each of the three aircraft mentioned above stands an outstanding feat which has had a major effect on the course of the war and of history. Firstly, the Hurricane, which was being produced in large numbers at the outbreak of war in September, 1939, played a far greater part than any other aircraft in winning the Battle of Britain in 1940. Then, while the many versions of the versatile Hurricane were being produced in their thousands for service on more than a score of different battle fronts all over the World, the Typhoon was also put into production. The Hawker Typhoon was the first of the 400 m.p.h. fighters, just as the Hurricane was the first fighter to exceed 300 m.p.h., and the Fury the first to exceed 200 m.p.h. Armed with a battery of four rockets under each wing, in addition to their already formidable armament, Typhoons of the 2nd Tactical Air Force effectively smashed the forces of German armour and transport gathered before the final breakthrough at Avranches, which resulted in the complete liberation of France and Belgium. Finally, the Tempest became operational a few months before the Second Battle of London, during which one Tempest Wing alone, commanded by Wing Cdr. R. P. Beamont, D.S.O., D.F.C., accounted for more flying-bombs than did any other type of aircraft engaged in the defence of the capital.

THE HAWKER TEMPEST.

The Tempest is a progressive development of the Typhoon, the initial design and development of the type being actually undertaken as part of the Typhoon programme. It was in April, 1941, that discussions were opened between the Hawker company and the Ministry of Aircraft Production on the subject of Typhoon development. Proposals for a Typhoon Mk. II included the installation of a Sabre IV engine of higher power and driving a four-blade airscrew, improved view and a cleaned-up tail. Investigation was also to proceed into the possibilities of an improved wing section.

The Hawker proposals, submitted in August, 1941, included the suggestion that the Typhoon Mk. II should have thin elliptical wings of 42 ft. (12.8 m.) span and 300 sq. ft. (27.9 sq. m.) area and with a 15% thickness/chord ratio at the root and 10% at the tip. The introduction of a new thin section wing made it necessary to reduce the amount of fuel carried in the wings and an extra bay was inserted in the fuselage behind the engine to accommodate an additional fuel tank. The lengthening of the fuselage forward called for increased fin area aft.

In April of 1940 the decision had been taken to make a trial installation of the Bristol Centaurus engine in the Tornado and in September, 1941, the Centaurus-Tornado prototype was ready for flight trials at the same time as the introduction of the Typhoon II was under discussion. It was just at this time that production of the Tornado was stopped owing to the limited production of the Rolls-Royce Vulture engine, and thenceforth the Centaurus installation became related to the Typhoon. It was not possible to install a Centaurus engine in a Typhoon I fuselage and it was decided in June, 1942, to fit this engine in the Typhoon II, in which the front spar, because of the additional fuselage bay, was further aft in relation to the engine and no longer in the way. Thus, at that stage there were two possible engine installations for the Typhoon II, so far as production was concerned.

In the meantime, owing to delay in the production of the Sabre IV engine, it was decided to complete the prototype Typhoon II with a Sabre II engine and, to avoid confusion and also because the Mk. II had become a completely different aeroplane both in external appearance and in internal construction, permission was sought to rename it. Eventually the name Tempest was chosen.

The Hawker Tempest V Single-seat Fighter (Napier Sabre IIB engine).

In June, 1942, it was proposed that six Tempest-prototypes should be completed, one with two Sabre IV (Tempest I), two with the Centaurus V (Tempest II), one with a Rolls-Royce Griffon IIB (Tempest III), one with a Griffon 61 (Tempest IV) and one with the Sabre II (Tempest V). Owing to heavy commitments the Hawker company could not undertake to build more than three prototypes at that time and the Marks I, II and V were chosen.

The Tempest V prototype first flew on September 2, 1942, the Tempest I on February 24, 1943, and the Tempest II on June 28, 1943. The Tempest I with Sabre II engine and wing radiators was not proceeded with as the effect of burying the radiators in the wings was negligible except at height whereas the question of their vulnerability was open to argument. As the Sabre II was a well-tried power-unit and available in quantity

the Mk. V was the first Tempest to go into production. The first production Tempest V appeared on June 25, 1943, and this mark was first reported in action early in 1944. It was followed on the production lines by the Tempest II, which was intended for service in the Far East.

TYPE.—Single-seat Fighter and Fighter-Bomber.
WINGS.—Low-wing cantilever monoplane. Thin high-speed laminar-flow wing section with maximum thickness at 37.5% chord. Wings are elliptical in plan form with square-cut tips. No dihedral on inner portions of wings but dihedral outboard of landing-gear pivots. Frise type ailerons with split flaps between ailerons and fuselage.
FUSELAGE.—Engine-mounting and centre fuselage are basically a rectangular rigidly-braced tubular structure assembled with flat plate fittings and machined stampings. The rear fuselage aft

The Hawker Tempest V Single-seat Fighter (2,400 h.p. Napier Sabre IIB engine).

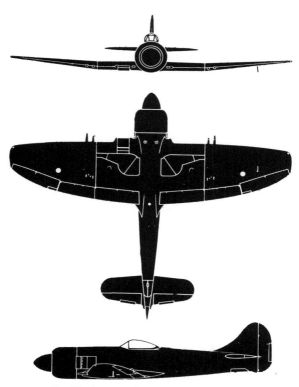

The Hawker Tempest II Single-seat Fighter.

The Hawker Tempest II Single-seat Fighter (Bristol Centaurus V engine).

The Hawker Tempest VI Single-seat Fighter (Napier Sabre V engine).

of the pilot's cockpit is a monocoque structure built up of oval shaped frames, longitudinal stringers and a flush-riveted stressed skin. The forward portion of the fuselage is covered with detachable metal panels.

TAIL UNIT.—Cantilever monoplane type with dorsal fin. Structure similar to that of Typhoon.

LANDING GEAR.—Same as for Typhoon except that main oleo legs are of the Dowty levered-suspension type.

POWER PLANT.—One 2,400 h.p. Napier Sabre IIB twenty-four cylinder H-type liquid-cooled sleeve valve engine. Four-bladed de Havilland Hydromatic constant-speed airscrew. Low-velocity duct beneath engine houses coolant radiator and oil cooler, with the air intake in the centre of the assembly. Main fuel tank and oil tank in fuselage forward of pilot. Additional fuel tanks between main spars of wings and in leading-edge of port wing. Auxiliary fuel tanks may be carried under the wings.

ACCOMMODATION.—Enclosed cockpit over wing. Bullet-proof windscreen and armour forward and aft of pilot. Single-piece moulded "blister" type canopy, which can be jettisoned in an emergency.

ARMAMENT.—Four 20 m/m. British Hispano cannon completely buried in the wings and firing outside the airscrew disc. In addition, eight rocket projectiles or two 500 lb. or 1,000 lb. bombs, may be carried under the wings.

DIMENSIONS.—Span 41 ft. (12.5 m.), Length 33 ft. 8 in. (10.26 m.), Height 16 ft. 1 in. (4.9 m.), Wing area 302 sq. ft. (28.06 sq. m.).

WEIGHT LOADED.—Fighter version 11,400 lbs. (5,176 kg.), Fighter-Bomber with two 500 lb. bombs 12,500 lbs. (5,675 kg.), with two 1,000 lb. bombs 13,500 lbs. (6,130 kg.).

PERFORMANCE.—Maximum speed about 435 m.p.h. (696 km.h.).

THE HAWKER TEMPEST VI.

The third production version of the Tempest was the Mk. VI. On referring to pp. 44-45c it will be seen that of the three original prototypes of the Tempest which were built and flown, two, the Mks. V and II, went into production in that order. The Mk. I was built round the Napier Sabre IV engine and had the coolant radiators built into the centre-section. This aircraft was not proceeded with because the Sabre IV engine did not go into production and also because the effect on performance of positioning the radiators in the wings was negligible except at height, while the vulnerability of the wing cooling system was open to argument.

In the meantime, the Sabre IV was developed into the Mk. V and in October, 1943, it was decided to make a trial installation of the Sabre V in a Tempest with radiator and oil cooler taking up the whole of nose duct and with the air intakes located in the wing leading-edge alongside the fuselage. This version, which, with the original leading-edge radiators, was to have been the Tempest I, became the Tempest VI, the first flight of the prototype taking place in June, 1944. Except for the small intake ducts alongside the fuselage, the Mk. VI is similar in external outline to the Tempest V.

DIMENSIONS.—Span 41 ft. (12.5 m.), Length 34 ft. (10.3 m.), Wing area 302 sq. ft. (28.06 sq. m.).

THE HAWKER FURY AND SEA FURY.

The Fury I is a single-seat R.A.F. fighter which was designed to meet the requirements of the F.2/43 Specification. The Fury is recognisable as belonging to the Hawker family of single-seat fighters for in general appearance it is similar to the Tempest II. It is, however, an entirely new aeroplane with a re-designed fuselage of monocoque construction throughout. Particular attention has been paid to pilot's comfort and view. The cockpit has been raised slightly and the fuselage forward of the cockpit slopes down to the engine cowling to give good forward and downward view.

The wings, of semi-elliptical plan form, are in two sections joined together by a bolted and riveted joint on the fuselage centre-line. The tail-unit has also been re-designed.

The Sea Fury X, which is the naval version of the Fury I, is fitted with power-folding wings, a "sting" type arrester hook, and there is provision for assisted take-off by accelerator or rockets. It is powered with a 2,400 h.p. Bristol Centaurus XVIII two-row radial air-cooled engine which drives a five-blade Rotol constant-speed airscrew. In addition to internal fuel tankage for 200 Imp. gallons, two 45-gallon auxiliary drop tanks may be carried under the wings.

Armament consists of four 20 m/m. cannon and either two 1,000-lb. bombs or six pairs of rockets may be carried under the wings. Equipment includes both Radar and radio.

DIMENSIONS.—Span 38 ft. 5 in. (11.7 m.), Length 34 ft. 6 in. (10.5 m.), Height (tail down and one airscrew blade vertical) 14 ft. 7½ in. (4.4 m.), Height (tail up and wings folded) 16 ft. 3 in. (4.9 m.), Wing area 280 sq. ft. (26 sq. m.).

WEIGHT LOADED.—11,990 lbs. (5,445 kg.).

PERFORMANCE.—Maximum speed about 460 m.p.h. (736 km.h.) at 24,500 ft. (7,470 m.), Climb to 20,000 ft. (6,100 m.) 6.3 mins., Max. Range (with auxiliary drop tanks 1,160 miles (1,860 km.).

THE HAWKER TYPHOON.

The Typhoon, which went into action early in the Summer of 1942, was the first aeroplane to go into operational use with the 2,200 h.p. Napier Sabre twenty-four-cylinder H-type sleeve-valve liquid-cooled engine.

The prototype Typhoon first flew on February 24, 1940, but after the collapse of France in June of that year production was stopped to enable the Hawker company to devote its maximum effort to the production of the Hurricane. This caused

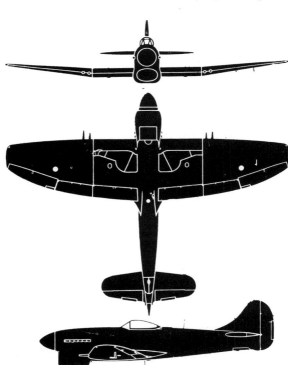

The Hawker Tempest V Single-seat Fighter.

The Hawker Sea Fury Single-seat Naval Fighter (Bristol Centaurus XVIII engine).

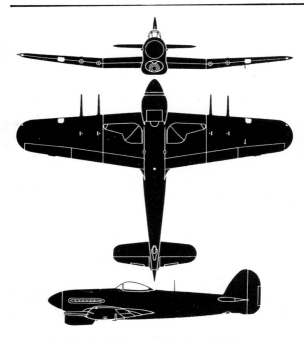

The Hawker Typhoon IB Single-seat Fighter.

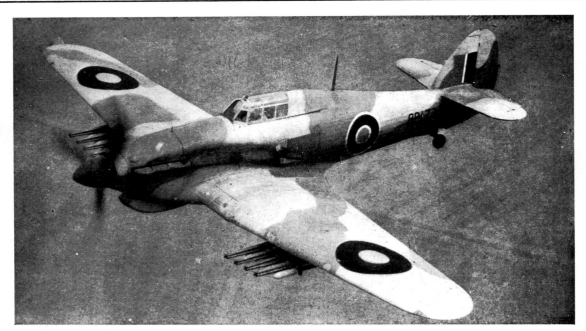

The Hurricane IV Single-seat Fighter with Rocket Projectile equipment (Rolls-Royce Merlin 21 engine).

considerable delay in the introduction of the Typhoon, work on which was not resumed until later in 1940. The first production Typhoon flew on May 26, 1941.

The Typhoon Mk. IA is armed with twelve .303 Browning machine-guns, and the Mk. IB with four 20 m/m. Hispano guns, The Typhoon can also be fitted with racks to carry two 500-lb. or two 1,000-lb. bombs, one under each wing. Alternatively auxiliary drop fuel tanks each of 45 gallons capacity may be fitted under the wings to increase the range.

The rôle in which the Typhoon excelled above all others, however, was that of a rocket-firing ground-attack fighter. With eight rockets, each with a 60-lb. H.E. or 25-lb. armour-piercing head, in addition to its normal four cannon armament, its fire-power has been compared with that of a broadside from a cruiser, and was sufficient to penetrate the most heavily-armoured tanks.

TYPE.—Single-seat Fighter and Fighter-Bomber.

WINGS.—Low-wing cantilever monoplane. Wings have straight taper from roots to semi-circular tips and are attached to the centre fuselage by four pins, two to each spar. There is no centre-section. Two-spar all-metal structure. The two spars are braced together by six main ribs and a number of light ribs. The inner portions of the spars consist of extruded section booms with N-girder webs, the outer portions have extruded T-section booms and single plate webs. In the gun bay a D-section member takes the torsion and provides the stiffness. Aft of the D-spar two large gun doors form the upper surface. Outboard of the gun-bay the wing is of normal stressed-skin construction with two spars and skin reinforced by stringers. Frise ailerons and split flaps are metal-covered. Latter are mechanically interconnected across the fuselage.

FUSELAGE.—Engine-mounting and centre fuselage are basically a rectangular rigidly-braced structure of steel tubes assembled together with flat plate fittings and machined stampings and covered with detachable metal panels. The rear fuselage aft of the pilot's cockpit is a monocoque structure consisting of a stressed skin, flush-riveted to oval-shaped formers and straight longitudinal stringers. The rear end of the rear fuselage carrying the tail-unit and incorporating an integral fin, is a separate unit and is attached to the rear fuselage by a circumferential riveted joint and a number of longitudinal finger plates. The joint between the front and rear sections is by four quickly-removable bolts.

TAIL UNIT.—Cantilever monoplane type. All-metal structure with metal stressed-skin-covered fin and tailplane, metal-covered elevators, and fabric-covered rudder. Adjustable trimming-tabs in movable surfaces.

LANDING GEAR.—Retractable type. Vickers oleo-pneumatic shock-absorber legs and Dunlop wheels and pneumatic brakes. Dowty oleo-pneumatic tail-wheel and shock-absorber and Dunlop-Ecta tail-wheel. Main wheels retract inwardly into wells in the under-side of the inner portion of the wings, tail-wheel forward into fuselage. Doors on the underside of the fuselage close over and seal the wheel wells when the main landing gear is retracted.

POWER PLANT.—One 2,200 h.p. Napier Sabre IIA twenty-four-cylinder H-type liquid-cooled sleeve-valve engine mounted with its rear feet on the front wing spar and its front feet supported by a braced tube structure cantilevered from the front face of the spar. Low-velocity duct beneath engine houses radiator and oil cooler with air intake in the centre of the assembly. Three or four-bladed de Havilland constant-speed airscrew. Four self-sealing fuel tanks in wings, two between wheel wells and rear spar and two forward of front spar at the inboard end of each wing. Oil tank in top of fuselage aft of fireproof bulkhead. Auxiliary fuel tanks may be carried under wings.

ACCOMMODATION.—Enclosed cockpit over trailing-edge of wing. Bullet proof windscreen and armour forward and aft of pilot. Single-piece "blister" type sliding hood. Adjustable seat and rudder-bar. Full electrical equipment, oxygen, radio, etc.

ARMAMENT.—Either twelve 0.303 in. Browning machine-guns (Mk. IA) or four 20 m/m. cannon (Mk. IB) all in the wings and firing outside the airscrew disc. Rack for one 1,000 lb. or 500 lb. bomb under each wing. Alternatively, eight rocket-projectiles can be carried, four under each wing.

DIMENSIONS.—Span 41 ft. 7 in. (12.67 m.), Length 31 ft. 11 in. (9.73 m.), Height 15 ft. 3½ in. (4.66 m.), Wing area 279 sq. ft. (25.92 sq. m.).

WEIGHT LOADED (Fighter version).—11,500 lbs. (5,220 kg.).

PERFORMANCE.—No data available, but stated to exceed 400 m.p.h. (640 km.h.) in level flight.

THE HAWKER HURRICANE.

The Hurricane was designed to Air Ministry Specification F.36/34, the prototype making its first flight on November 6, 1935. Put into production in 1936, the first production Hurricane I flew in October, 1937.

Although it was no longer in production when the war ended the Hurricane was still in service as a first-line aircraft. It served on seventeen different battle fronts—in the British Isles, France, Norway, North Africa, Sicily, Italy, the Middle East, the Far East, Russia, in the Battles of the Atlantic, the Mediterranean and the Northern Convoys, to mention the most important—as a fighter, a fighter-bomber, an R.P. fighter, a "tank-buster," a catapult fighter and carrier fighter. In 1944-55, equipped with rocket projectiles, the Hurricane was used with great effect against enemy shipping in the Adriatic, and as a fighter-bomber it served with distinction in Burma.

Well over 15,000 Hurricanes were built, the last one being delivered from the Hawker factory in September, 1944.

Hurricane I. Rolls-Royce Merlin II or III engine. Armament consisted of eight .303-in. Browning machine-guns, four in each wing. Originally had fabric-covered wings, two-blade wood fixed-pitch airscrew and was without armour or self-sealing tanks. In 1939 the Mk. I was fitted with either the D.H. or Rotol constant-speed airscrew, ejector exhaust stacks, metal-covered wings, armour, etc. In the Battle of Britain the Hurricane I accounted for more enemy aircraft than any other type of aircraft and altogether in the first year of the war Hurricane squadrons accounted for more than 1,500 confirmed victories over the *Luftwaffe*, almost half the total of enemy aircraft destroyed by the R.A.F. in that period. In 1940 the Mk. I was fitted with air cleaner and desert equipment for service in the Middle East.

Hurricane II. Rolls-Royce Merlin XX engine with two-speed supercharger. Except for slight alterations to the wings to cater for increased armament, a new engine mounting for the longer engine and strengthening of the fuselage and landing-gear to take care of the increased power and weight, no other structural changes were necessary. There were four basic versions:—the Mk. IA (1940), with Mk. I metal wings equipped with eight machine-guns; the Mk. IIB (1940), with two additional guns in each wing outboard of the landing-light, to make a total armament of twelve .303-in. guns, six in each wing; Mk. IIC (1941), with an armament of four 20 m m. (.737 in.) British Hispano cannon, the four-cannon wings being initially rebuilt from damaged Mk. I metal wings; and the Mk. IID (1943), which had an armament of two 40 m m. (1.575 in.) Vickers cannon and two .303-in. guns, together with additional armour for low attack. In 1941 both the Mk. IIB and IIC were provided with racks for carrying two 250-lb. or 500-lb. bombs or alternatively two 45 or 90-gallon droppable fuel tanks, and both were equipped with tropical equipment for service overseas. The Mk. IIB fighter-bomber first went into action over occupied France in November, 1941. In both the fighter-bomber and long-range versions, the Mk. II retained all its qualities as a fighter.

Hurricane III. The Mk. III was the British-built Mk. II fitted with the Packard Merlin engine. It was never in production as the Mk. III.

Hurricane IV. Rolls-Royce Merlin 21 or 22 engine. Fitted with wings capable of carrying the following alternative armaments and loads:—(1) two 40 m/m. Vickers cannon and two .303-in. guns; (2) eight Rocket Projectiles and two .303-in. guns; (3) two 250-lb. or 500-lb. bombs and two .303-in. guns; (4) two 45 or 90 gallon drop tanks and two .303-in. guns. Also fitted with 350 lbs. of additional armour. Maximum speed 314 m.p.h. (502.4 km.h.), Range 495 miles (790 km.).

Hurricane V. Rolls-Royce Merlin 27 or 32 engine with increased take-off output. Same alternative armaments and loads as the Mk. IV. Only two built.

Hurricane X. Packard Merlin 28 engine driving a Hamilton Standard Hydromatic airscrew. Built in Canada by Canadian Car and Foundry Co., Ltd. Corresponded to the British-built Mk. I.

Hurricane XII and XIIA. Packard Merlin 29 engine. Built by Canadian Car & Foundry Co., Ltd.

Sea Hurricane I. Rolls-Royce Merlin II or III engine. Conversion from Hurricane I. In three versions:—the Mk. IA (1941), fitted with catapult spools, slinging gear and naval radio for use from C.A.M. ships (catapult-equipped merchantmen) which were introduced in the Spring of 1941 for the air protection of convoys at sea; the Mk. IB (1941) fitted with both catapult spools and deck arrester gear for aircraft-carrier use; and the Mk. IC (1942), with the same airframe as the Mk. IB but with Hurricane Mk. IIC four-cannon wings. The first enemy aircraft to be destroyed by a catapulted Sea Hurricane IA was shot down on August 3, 1941. The Mk. IB was the first single-seat carrier fighter monoplane to be used by the Royal Navy. It first went into operation in the Mediterranean in June, 1942, particularly distinguishing itself in the defence of Malta convoys in the Summer of that year.

Sea Hurricane II. Rolls-Royce Merlin XX engine. Conversion of the Hurricane II. Fitted with deck arrester gear and naval radio, but without catapult points.

Sea Hurricane XIIA. Packard Merlin 29 engine. Canadian-built. A conversion of the Hurricane XIIA.

Hooked Hurricane II. Some Hurricane II's were fitted with arrester hooks in 1943 for use as trainers on dummy carrier

The Hawker Typhoon IB Rocket Fighter (Napier Sabre IIA engine).

Type and Mark No.	Engine	Maximum Power Rating		Weight		Power Loading Lb./B.H.P.	Wing Loading Lb./Sq. Ft.	Performance				
		B.H.P.	Ft.	Fully Loaded Weight Lb.	Service Load Lb.			Max. Level Speed		Max. Rate of Climb Ft./Min.	Time to 20,000 ft. Mins.	Service Ceiling Ft.
								M.P.H.	At			
Hurricane I	Merlin II or III	1,030	16,250	6,666	1,415	6.47	25.9	330	17,500	2,520	9.0	36,000
Hurricane I Tropical	Merlin II or III	1,030	16,250	6,850	1,473	6.65	26.6	317	16,000	2,400	9.5	33,000
Sea-Hurricane IA	Merlin II or III	1,030	16,250	6,780	1,560	6.58	26.3	302	16,400	2,000	11.6	31,000
Sea-Hurricane IB	Merlin II or III	1,030	16,250	6,800	1,580	6.60	26.4	296	16,300	1,950	12.0	30,000
Hurricane IIA	Merlin XX	1,185	21,000	7,014	1,560	5.91	27.2	340	21,500	3,150	7.0	41,000
Hurricane IIB	Merlin XX	1,185	21,000	7,440	1,850	6.23	28.9	340	21,500	2,950	7.5	40,000
Hurricane IIB Fighter-Bomber (2-250lb)	Merlin XX	1,185	21,000	7,970	2,350	6.73	31.0	320	19,700	2,530	9.3	33,000
Hurricane IIB Fighter-Bomber (2-500lb)	Merlin XX	1,185	21,000	8,470	2,850	7.16	32.9	307	19,500	2,280	10.5	30,000
Hurricane IIC	Merlin XX	1,185	21,000	7,670	1,925	6.47	29.8	334	21,500	2,780	7.6	36,000
Hurricane IIC Fighter-Bomber (2-250lb)	Merlin XX	1,185	21,000	8,210	2,425	6.94	31.9	314	19,500	2,400	9.8	32,500
Hurricane IIC Fighter-Bomber (2-500lb)	Merlin XX	1,185	21,000	8,710	2,925	7.35	33.8	301	19,300	2,160	11.5	29,500
Hurricane IIB Tropical	Merlin XX	1,185	21,000	7,540	1,900	6.36	29.3	334	18,200	2,850	7.7	35,500
Hurricane IIC Tropical	Merlin XX	1,185	21,000	7,780	1,980	6.65	30.2	328	18,000	2,650	8.3	34,000
Hurricane IIB Tropical, Long-Range	Merlin XX	1,185	21,000	8,290	2,650	7.00	32.2	312	18,000	2,400	10.4	33,000
Hurricane IIC Tropical, Long-Range	Merlin XX	1,185	21,000	8,530	2,730	7.20	33.1	306	18,000	2,280	11.0	31,500
Sea-Hurricane IIB	Merlin XX	1,185	21,000	7,510	1,890	6.34	29.2	320	19,700	2,780	7.6	35,500
Sea-Hurricane IIC	Merlin XX	1,185	21,000	7,740	1,970	6.53	30.1	314	19,500	2,670	8.0	34,500

The test installation of two D.H. three-blade contra-rotating airscrews on a Hawker Tornado single-seat fighter.

decks ashore. Unlike the Sea Hurricane II they retained standard R.A.F. equipment.

TYPE.—Single-seat Fighter and Fighter-Bomber.

WINGS.—Low-wing cantilever monoplane. Centre-section of parallel chord and thickness and two tapering outer sections. Centre-section in one piece has girder spars, tubular strut drag bracing and a non-stressed metal covering. Outer wings, which are pin-jointed to the centre-section, have two spars with double webs at the inboard ends and single webs toward the tips. The gun-bay at the inboard end is diagonally braced but outboard of this the wing is of the fully stressed-skin type with two light auxiliary spars in addition to the main spars. Remainder of the framework consists of flanged plate ribs and lateral stringers, the whole being covered with a stressed-metal skin, which is flush-riveted over the leading-edge. Fabric-covered ailerons. Hydraulically-operated split flaps between ailerons and fuselage.

FUSELAGE.—Rectangular rigidly-braced structure of steel and aluminium-alloy square-ended tubing assembled by flat-plate fittings and hollow rivets, faired to an oval section and covered forward with detachable metal panels and aft with fabric over light wooden formers.

TAIL UNIT.—Cantilever monoplane type. Fin attached to fuselage by two fin-posts. Fixed tail-plane with adjustable trimming-tabs in each aerodynamically-balanced elevator. Aerodynamically and statically-balanced rudder. All-metal framework with fabric covering.

LANDING GEAR.—Retractable type. Two Vickers shock-absorber struts hinged at the extremities of the centre-section front spar and retracted inwards and slightly backwards by Dowty hydraulic rams to bring wheels between spars when raised. The slight backward motion is imparted by a hinged back strut which slides on a guide at right angles to the span of the wing. Dunlop wheels and pneumatic brakes. Dowty or Lockheed non-retractable tail-wheel unit.

POWER PLANT.—One Rolls-Royce Merlin twelve-cylinder Vee liquid-cooled engine. Rotol or de Havilland three-blade constant-speed airscrew. Main fuel tanks (two) in centre-section between spars with gravity tank in fuselage. Tanks are protected with self-sealing rubber. Ducted radiator under fuselage below cockpit. Oil tank in leading-edge of centre-section on port side. Oil-cooler incorporated in main radiator.

ACCOMMODATION.—Enclosed pilot's cockpit over wing. Sliding canopy with quick-release for emergency exit. Further emergency escape panel in side of fuselage between upper longeron and canopy. Front and rear armour protection and bullet-proof windshield.

ARMAMENT AND EQUIPMENT.—Either eight Browning .303 in. machine-guns; twelve Browning .303 in. machine-guns; four 20 m/m. Hispano cannon; or two 40 m/m. guns and two .303 in. machine-guns, all wing mounted. Wing racks for two 250 or 500 lb. bombs or auxiliary fuel tanks, or rails for eight rocket projectiles. Night-flying equipment with landing-lights in leading-edge of outer wing-sections, navigation lights, oxygen equipment, radio, etc.

DIMENSIONS.—Span 40 ft. (12.2 m.), Length 32 ft. 3 in. (9.84 m.), Height (on wheels) 13 ft. 1½ in. (4 m.), Wing area 257.5 sq. ft. (23.92 sq. m.), Track 7 ft. 10 in. (2.38 m.).

WEIGHTS AND PERFORMANCE. See Table.

HAWKER-SIDDELEY.

HAWKER-SIDDELEY AIRCRAFT CO., LTD.

REGISTERED OFFICE : 55-56, PALL MALL, LONDON, S.W.1.
Directors : T. O. M. Sopwith, C.B.E., F.R.Ae.S. (Chairman), Sir Frank Spriggs, Hon. F.R.Ae.S. (Managing Director), H. K. Jones (General Manager), H. Burroughes, F.R.Ae.S., Sir Roy Dobson, C.B.E., F.R.Ae.S. and H. A. Meredith, O.B.E.

The Hawker-Siddeley Aircraft Co., Ltd., which was formed in 1935, is the controlling organization of Sir W. G. Armstrong Whitworth Aircraft, Ltd., Armstrong Siddeley Motors, Ltd., Gloster Aircraft, Ltd., Hawker Aircraft, Ltd., A. V. Roe & Co., Ltd., and Air Service Training, Ltd.

The component companies of the Hawker-Siddeley Group were responsible for providing approximately 30% of all the equipment supplied by the British Aircraft Industry to the R.A.F. throughout the whole period of the European War. Total deliveries consisted approximately of 40,089 aircraft, inclusive of spares, and 38,564 aero-engines. In addition, the Group repaired 11,010 aircraft and 9,777 aero-engines. Aircraft production in the group rose from 1,753 in 1938-39 to a peak figure of 8,795 in 1943-44, the latter figure not including 2,190 repaired or re-conditioned aircraft. Engine production rose from 2,175 in 1938-39 to 8,008 in 1942-43.

Factory space increased from a floor area of 2,000,000 sq. ft. in 1938 to 15,000,000 sq. ft. in 1944 and the rate of new aircraft production from 60 to 600 per month.

HESTON.

HESTON AIRCRAFT CO., LTD.

HEAD OFFICE : HESTON AIRPORT, MIDDLESEX.
WORKS : HESTON AND SLOUGH, BUCKS.
Chairman : Sir Norman Watson, Bt.
Managing Director : B. R. S. Jones.
Directors : G. A. Lingham, D.F.C. and Lieut. Col. G. C. Golding.
Chief Designer : G. Cornwall, B.A., A.F.R.Ae.S.

This Company was originally formed as the Comper Aircraft Co. Ltd., in 1929 ; the name being changed to the present title in 1934.

The last product of the Company about which details could be published was the Phœnix five-seat cabin monoplane. This machine has been described and illustrated in previous issues of this Annual. In 1938 the Company designed and built two prototype elementary Training monoplanes for the Air Ministry.

The latest activities of the Company may not be specified, but it can be said that it has been fully engaged on large-scale sub-contracting on behalf of the biggest contractors to the Ministry of Aircraft Production as well as in experimental work for the Air Ministry.

MARTIN-BAKER.

MARTIN-BAKER AIRCRAFT CO., LTD.

HEAD OFFICE AND WORKS : HIGHER DENHAM, NEAR UX-BRIDGE, MIDDLESEX.
Directors : James Martin (Managing and Chief Designer) and Francis Francis.

The Martin-Baker Aircraft Co. Ltd. was formed in 1934 to exploit a special system of steel-tube construction evolved by Mr. James Martin. This construction was embodied in the Company's first production, the MB-1, which was described and illustrated in the 1936 edition of this work.

In 1939 details were released concerning an experimental single-seat multi-gun fighter monoplane which the Company built to the order of the Air Ministry. This machine made use of the Martin system of steel-tube construction. Brief details of this aircraft were published in the 1940 issue of this Annual.

Two further prototype Fighter aircraft have been built, one fitted with a Napier Sabre engine and the other with a Rolls-Royce Griffon engine. The latter was, at the time of writing, undergoing test flights and trials.

THE MARTIN-BAKER F.18/49.

The Martin-Baker Aircraft Co., Ltd., designed and built two single-seat fighter aircraft to meet the requirements of the Air Ministry Specification F.18/39. The first was the M.B.3, which was fitted with a 2,020 h.p. Napier Sabre II twenty-four cylinder H-type liquid-cooled engine driving a D.H. Hydromatic three-blade constant-speed airscrew. This aeroplane was designed

The Martin-Baker M.B.5 Single-seat Fighter (Rolls-Royce Griffon 83 engine).

for an armament of six wing-mounted 20 m/m. cannon. It first flew on August 31, 1942. On one of its test flights the M.B.3 was forced to land through engine trouble and in a collision with a tree after touching down the aircraft was destroyed and the pilot, Capt. V. E. Baker, a director of the company, was killed.

A completely new layout was adopted for its successor, the M.B.5, using a Rolls-Royce Griffon 83 twelve-cylinder Vee liquid-cooled engine driving two three-blade D.H. contra-rotating airscrews. This aeroplane first flew on May 23, 1944.

Both these aircraft made use of the Martin-Baker patented system of steel construction, the outstanding features of which are easy servicing and maintenance. The fuselage is a steel tube structure with the covering in the form of quickly-detachable metal panels. The wings employ a D-type torsion box, the main member of which is a steel spar built up of laminated plates. Split flaps and inwardly-retracting landing-gear are pneumatically operated.

The pilot's cockpit is situated over the wing, giving a good view forward and downward. Particular attention has been paid to the layout of the cockpit, with well-designed control and instrument installations. A jettisonable blister-type canopy is fitted.

The power-plant installation is very clean, with the radiator assembly, including coolant and oil radiators and intercooler grouped together, in a laminar-flow duct under the rear fuselage. In the M.B.3 the coolant and oil radiators were in ducts under the wings.

Armament of the M.B.5 consists of four wing-mounted 20 m/m. cannon, two on each side of the fuselage outboard of the landing-gear.

DIMENSIONS.—Span 35 ft. (10.7 m.), Length 37 ft. 9 in. (11.5 m.), Height 15 ft. (4.5 m.), Wing area 262 sq. ft. (24.3 sq. m.).
WEIGHT LOADED.—11,500 lbs. (5,225 kg.).
PERFORMANCE.—Maximum speed over 450 m.p.h. (720 km.h.).

MILES.

MILES AIRCRAFT, LTD.

HEAD OFFICE AND WORKS : READING, BERKS.

Directors : F. G. Miles, F.R.Ae.S., Mrs. M. F. M. Miles, G. H. Miles and W. H. Gatty Saunt.

Miles Aircraft Ltd. was formerly known as Phillips & Powis Aircraft Ltd., which had been formed in March, 1935, as a public company to take over the aircraft manufacturing business previously conducted by Phillips & Powis Aircraft (Reading) Ltd.

The Miles Magister is the only monoplane in Great Britain to be approved by the Air Ministry for *ab initio* instruction of R.A.F. pilots and it is in use in R.A.F. training establishments in England and overseas.

The latest products of the Company concerning which full details may be published are the M-25 Martinet two-seat Target-Tug, the M-18 Light Training monoplane, the M-28 Training and Light Communications monoplane, and the Glider-Tug version of the Master II which was evolved to serve as a tug for the Hotspur III training glider.

Among those products of which only prototypes have been built in recent years are the M-20 all-wood single-seat Fighter, the M-35, a single-engined tandem-wing flying mock-up, the M-39B, a twin-engined tandem-wing flying scale-model, and the M-57 Aerovan, a twin-engined Light Freighter.

In addition, the Company is building the M-60, an all-metal 14-seat Feeder-line transport designed to the Brabazon 5A Specification and powered by four D.H. Gipsyqueen or four Alvis Leonides engines.

THE MILES M-60 MARATHON.

The M-60 is a four-engined medium-range feeder-line aircraft which conforms to the requirements of one of two feeder-line types recommended by the Brabazon Committee. It will be able to carry 14 passengers and baggage, plus 560 lbs. (255 kg.) of mail or freight, over a still-air range of 500 miles (800 km.) at a recommended economical cruising speed of 175 m.p.h. (280 km.h.).

The Marathon will be an all-metal high-wing monoplane with high-lift wings, Miles patent lift flaps, tricycle landing-gear, twin fins and rudders and a power-plant consisting of four 330 h.p. D.H. Gipsyqueen six-cylinder in-line air-cooled engines.

The Miles M-57 Aerovan Light Freight or Passenger-carrying Monoplane (two 150 h.p. Cirrus Major engines).

It is expected that the prototype will be ready to fly by the end of 1945 or early in 1946.
DIMENSIONS.—Span 65 ft. (19.8 m.). Length 51 ft. 6 in. (15.7 m.). Height 13 ft. 3 in. (4.1 m.).
WEIGHTS.—Weight empty 9,914 lbs. (4,500 kg.). Crew (2) 400 lbs. (182 kg.). Fuel and oil (500 miles) 1,040 lbs. (472 kg.). Passengers (14) and baggage 3,080 lbs. (1,398 kg.), Freight and mail 566 lbs. (257 kg.). Total disposable load 5,086 lbs. (2,309 kg.), Weight loaded 15,000 lbs. (6,810 kg.).
PERFORMANCE.—Economical cruising speed 175 m.p.h. (280 km.h.), Initial rate of climb 1,300 ft./mins. (396 m./mins.), Range (still air) 500 miles (800 km.).

THE MILES M-57 AEROVAN.

TYPE.—Light twin-engined Freight or Passenger-carrier.
WINGS.—High-wing cantilever monoplane. All-wood structure with plywood skin. Constant taper from roots to tips. Miles auxiliary aerofoil flaps aft of trailing-edges and inboard of slotted ailerons.
FUSELAGE.—Deep main body enclosing pilot's compartment and main cabin of wooden construction with plywood skin. All-metal tail-boom springing from top of main body carries the cantilever tail-unit.
TAIL UNIT.—Cantilever monoplane type with three fins and horn-balanced rudders. Wooden framework with plywood covering.
LANDING GEAR.—Fixed tricycle type. Main wheels have oleo-pneumatic articulated type suspension units mounted directly on fuselage sides. Steerable cantilever nose wheel mounted under pilot's cabin. Medium-pressure wheels.
POWER PLANT.—Designed for two 140 h.p. D.H. Gipsy-Major or 150 h.p. Cirrus Major four-cylinder in-line inverted air-cooled engines, or any other engines of similar power and weight. Fixed-pitch or constant-speed airscrews. Two flexible crash-proof fuel tanks in wing root leading-edges.
ACCOMMODATION.—Pilot's compartment in nose of fuselage with seats for pilot and one other crew member. Entry to compartment through full-length door on each side. Communicating door to main cabin, which is free of all obstructions and has large freight loading doors at rear end beneath the tail-boom. Can also be arranged to accommodate six passengers. Maximum payload 2,240 lbs. (1,017 kg.).
DIMENSIONS.—Span 50 ft. (15.24 m.), Length 36 ft. (10.97 m.), Height (over rudder) 13 ft. 6 in. (3.5 m.).
WEIGHTS.—Tare weight 3,000 lbs. (1,362 kg.), Maximum payload 2,240 lbs. (1,018 kg.), Weight loaded 5,900 lbs. (2,680 kg.).
PERFORMANCE.—Cruising speed 110 m.p.h. (176 km.h.), Range in still air 450 miles (720 km.).

The prototype Miles M-48 Four-seat Cabin Monoplane (150 h.p. Cirrus Major engine).

The Miles M-39B Experimental Twin-engined Tandem-wing Monoplane (two 130 h.p. D.H. Gipsy-Major engines).

The Miles M-57 Aerovan Light Freighter.

THE MILES M-48.

The M-48 is the commercial post-war development of the M-38 Messenger. It differs from its service counterpart by having Miles retractable auxiliary trailing-edge flaps and suitable furnishings and equipment. A variety of power-plants ranging from 140 to 180 h.p. will be available for installation in the M-48. A prototype fitted with a 150 h.p. Cirrus Major engine was flying early in 1945.

DIMENSIONS.—Same as for M-38.
WEIGHTS.—Weight empty 1,500 lbs. (680 kg.), Weight loaded 2,400 lbs. (1,090 kg.).
PERFORMANCE (150 h.p. Cirrus Major engine).—Cruising speed 115 m.p.h. (184 km.h.), Stalling speed 25 m.p.h. (40 km.h.).

THE MILES M-39B.

The M-39B is a twin-engined tandem-wing monoplane which was built as a flying scale model for a high-speed bomber design.

WINGS.—Tandem wings of all-wood construction. Forward wing attached to underside of fuselage beneath pilot's cockpit. Rear wing mounted at rear end of fuselage. Twin fins and rudders at extremities of rear wing with central stabilising fin on centre-line. Rudders work independently, moving outwards in the direction of the turn, only one rudder being used at a time.
FUSELAGE.—Oval section wooden structure with plywood covering.
LANDING GEAR.—Retractable tricycle type. Main wheels have oleo-pneumatic articulated springing and retract backwards into engine nacelles. Nose wheel retracts into fuselage. Hydraulic wheel-brakes.
POWER PLANT.—Two 130 h.p. D.H. Gipsy-Major four-cylinder in-line inverted air-cooled engines in nacelles mounted on the leading-edge of the rear wing and driving tractor airscrews.
ACCOMMODATION.—Single cockpit in nose of fuselage. Whole cabin hood hinges on starboard side.
DIMENSIONS.—Span of front wing 25 ft. (7.62 m.), Span of rear wing 37 ft. 6 in. (11.43 m.), Length 22 ft. 4 in. (6.7 m.), Height 9 ft. 1½ in. (2.74 m.).
WEIGHTS AND PERFORMANCE.—No data available.

THE MILES M-38 MESSENGER.

The M-38 is a development of the M-28 and was primarily produced to meet the requirements of the Army for use as an Air Observation Post. It has since been adopted as a light communications type by the R.A.F. Basically, the two types are structurally similar but the M-38 incorporates several detail changes. A new wing of thinner section, of slightly wider span and fitted with Miles auxiliary flaps aft of the trailing-edges is employed, the landing-gear is of the fixed type and a third central fin has been added.
TYPE.—Three/four-seat Light Communications and Air Observation Post monoplane.
WINGS.—Low-wing cantilever monoplane. One-piece structure with constant taper and dihedral from fuselage to tips. All-wood construction with plywood covering. Miles auxiliary aerofoil flaps hinged aft of and slightly below trailing-edge between fuselage and ailerons. Slotted ailerons are interconnected with flaps and droop when flaps are lowered.
FUSELAGE.—All-wood structure in two main assemblies, the front or cabin unit and the rear semi-monocoque unit.
TAIL UNIT.—Cantilever monoplane type with triple fins and rudders. All-wood structure with plywood covering. Aerodynamic and mass-balanced rudders.
LANDING GEAR.—Non-retractable type. Miles oleo-pneumatic articulated suspension. Bendix wheel-brakes. Oleo-sprung self-centering tail-wheel.
POWER PLANT.—One 140 h.p. D.H. Gipsy-Major ID four-cylinder in-line inverted air-cooled engine. Two flexible fuel tanks, one in each wing. Maximum fuel capacity 36 Imp. gallons. Oil capacity 2½ Imp. gallons.
ACCOMMODATION.—Enclosed cabin for pilot and two or three passengers. Standard service instrument-flying panel and full instrument equipment. Large clear-view windscreen and Perspex side panels provide unrestricted view forward and on both sides. Cabin doors hinge upwards. Dual control and other features make the aircraft suitable for training purposes. Also adaptable for use as air-taxi, ambulance, light freighter and private-owner aircaft.
DIMENSIONS.—Span 36 ft. 2 in. (11 m.). Length 23 ft. 9 in. (7.24 m.), Height 7 ft. 6 in. (2.28 m.). Wing area 191 sq. ft. (17.7 sq. m.).
WEIGHTS.—Weight empty with standard equipment 1,360 lbs. (617 kg.), Maximum loaded weight 2,400 lbs. (1,090 kg.).

PERFORMANCE. (D.H. Gipsy-Major ID engine).—Maximum speed 120 m.p.h. (193 km.h.), Cruising speed 112 m.p.h. (183 km.h.), Stalling speed at sea level 28 m.p.h. (45 km.h.), Initial rate of climb 1,100 ft./min. (335 m./min.), Service ceiling 17,000 ft. (5,185 m.), Take-off run (5 m.p.h. = 8 km.h. head wind) 60 yards (55 m.), Distance to clear 50 ft. (15 m.) 138 yards (120 m.), Landing-run 5 m.p.h. = 8 km.h. head wind) 60 yards (55 m.).

THE MILES M-35.

The M-35 is a single-engined tandem-wing flying mock-up which was built as an aerodynamic experiment in connection with a design for a shipboard fighter.
WINGS.—Tandem wings of all-wood construction, the forward wing attached to the top of the fuselage aft of the pilot's cockpit and the rear and larger wing attached to the underside of the fuselage ahead of the power-unit. Elevators and flaps hinged to the trailing-edge of the forward wing, the rear wing carrying ailerons and flaps and the two fins and rudders.
FUSELAGE.—Oval section structure of all-wood construction with plywood skin.
LANDING GEAR.—Fixed tricycle type with one wheel mounted beneath the fuselage under the forward wing and two wheels beneath the centre-section of the rear wing. Oleo-pneumatic springing. Wheel-brakes.
POWER PLANT.—One 130 h.p. D.H. Gipsy-Major four-cylinder in-line inverted air-cooled engine mounted at the aft end of the fuselage and driving a pusher airscrew.
ACCOMMODATION.—Single cockpit in nose of fuselage ahead of the forward wing with wide and unobstructed view.
DIMENSIONS.—Span (both wings) 20 ft. (6 m.), Length 20 ft. 3 in. (6.1 m.), Height 6 ft. 9 in. (2.05 m.), Total wing area 135 sq. ft. (12 sq. m.).
WEIGHTS.—Tare weight 1,460 lbs. (662 kg.), Weight loaded 1,850 lbs. (839 kg.).
PERFORMANCE.—No data available.

THE MILES M.33 MONITOR.

The Monitor was designed to Specification Q.9/42 to meet requirements for a high-speed target-tug which would have a

towing speed of not less than 300 m.p.h. (480 km.h.) and an endurance of 3-4 hours. The prototype T.T.Mk.I first flew on April 5, 1944, and proved to be eminently satisfactory, the maximum speed being 360 m.p.h. (576 km.h.). As naval requirements for such an aeroplane, and particularly one which could simulate dive-bombing attacks on ships, were urgent, the R.A.F. relinquished its claim to the Monitor, which was then put into production for the Royal Navy as T.T.Mk.II, with certain modifications, including hydraulically-operated dive-brakes, to suit it to its new duties.

The Mk. II is intended primarily for high-speed Fleet target-towing duties. It can tow sleeve and flag targets as well as special winged targets of 16 and 32 ft. span. A 10 h.p. hydraulic winch is capable of handling all types of targets with 6,000 ft. of towing cable at speeds of over 300 m.p.h. Stowage for spare targets is provided internally and targets can be changed in flight. Winged targets are towed off the ground at the end of a 250-ft. cable, the cable being paid out in the air to anything up to 6,000 ft. according to the type of practice.

Cameras are located in the nose and in the midship cupola for marking Fleet gunnery practices and Radar height-checking equipment is used to determine the accurate heights which are necessary in analysing such practices.

The Monitor is of mixed construction with an all-wood one-piece wing and metal fuselage. To speed up design and production it was originally stipulated that the Monitor should use a standard Beaufighter wing and landing-gear but owing to the increased use of the Beaufighter this decision was abandoned and a new all-wood wing was designed for the aircraft. The Beaufighter landing-gear was, however, standardised. The power-plant consists of two 1,750 h.p. Wright R-2600-31 fourteen-cylinder radial air-cooled engines driving Hamilton Standard Hydromatic airscrews. Hydraulic power for the landing-gear, flaps, dive brakes and towing winch is supplied by pumps driven

The Miles M-38 Messenger Light Communications Monoplane (140 h.p. D.H. Gipsy-Major engine).

The Miles M-35 Experimental Tandem-wing Monoplane (130 h.p. D.H. Gipsy-Major engine).

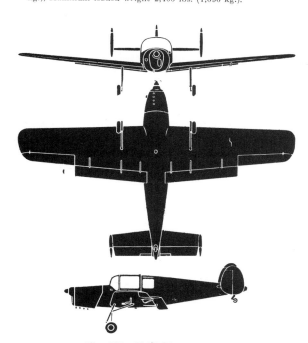

The Miles M-38 Messenger.

The Miles M-35 Experimental Tandem-wing Monoplane (130 h.p. D.H. Gipsy-Major engine).

The Miles M-33 Monitor Target-towing Monoplane (two Wright R-2600-C14AB engines).

off the starboard engine. Wing fuel tanks have a capacity of 480 Imp. gallons.

The crew of two consists of pilot and observer/target-operator. Target operation has been simplified so that the operator merely places a target on an endless belt and, after connecting the target halyard to the towing cable, pulls a lever. By this means the target is automatically ejected from an aperture in the underside of the fuselage, thereby minimising the amount of draught and discomfort usually associated with the opening of doors while flying.

DIMENSIONS.—Span 55 ft. 3 in. (16.85 m.), Length 46 ft. 8 in. (14.23 m.), Height (tail up) 18 ft. 4 in. (5.6 m.), Height (tail down—one airscrew blade vertical) 14 ft. 3 in. (4.35 m.), Wing area 500 sq. ft. (46.5 sq. m.).

WEIGHTS.—Weight empty 15.723 lbs. (7.145 kg.), Petrol and oil 3,744 lbs. (1,700 kg.), Target-towing gear 660 lbs. (300 kg.), Weight loaded 21,056 lbs. (9,560 kg.).

PERFORMANCE.—Maximum speed 360 m.p.h. (576 km.h.), Cruising speed 300 m.p.h. (480 km.h.) at 20,000 ft. (6,100 m.), Stalling speed 90 m.p.h. (144 km.h.), Climb to 25,000 ft. (4,575 m.) 30 mins.

THE MILES M-28.

The M-28 has been built in several versions for experimental purposes. The following are the four main variants, the Mk. IV being that which the company intends to market after the war.

M-28 Mark I. D.H. Gipsy-Major IIA engine and fixed-pitch airscrew. Two-seat dual-control trainer. Mechanically-operated landing-gear and vacuum-operated flaps.

M-28 Mark II. D.H. Gipsy-Major or Cirrus Major engine. Three-seat dual-control trainer. Hydraulically-operated landing-gear.

M-28 Mark III. Cirrus Major III engine. Three-seat triple-control trainer. Vacuum-operated landing-gear, flaps and air-brake.

M-28 Mark IV. D.H. Gipsy-Major III engine with constant-speed airscrew. Four-seat light transport. Single control. Vacuum-operated landing-gear, flaps and air-brake.

TYPE.—Three/four-seat cabin monoplane.

WINGS.—Low-wing cantilever monoplane tapering slightly in chord and with maximum thickness at points where retractable landing gear units are located. All-wood structure. Miles low-drag auxiliary aerofoil flaps between ailerons and fuselage and hinged air-brakes under fuselage. Ailerons droop when flaps are extended.

FUSELAGE.—All-wood plywood-covered structure of characteristic Miles construction.

TAIL UNIT.—Cantilever monoplane type with twin fins and rudders. Wooden framework with plywood skin. Horn-balanced rudders.

LANDING GEAR.—Retractable type. Each main unit comprises a fork incorporating knee-action oleo-pneumatic shock-absorbers and a small-diameter medium-pressure wheel. Wheels retract backwards into wing. Bendix wheel-brakes. Lever-suspension oleo-pneumatic tail-wheel.

POWER PLANT.—Any four-cylinder in-line engine of about 150 h.p may be fitted, including the Cirrus Major or D.H. Gipsy-Major IIA with fixed-pitch airscrew, or the D.H. Gipsy-Major III or IIIS with constant-speed airscrew. Main fuel tanks in wings.

ACCOMMODATION.—Enclosed cabin seating three or four. Full instrument equipment includes standard Service instrument-flying panel. Large clear-view windscreen provides unrestricted view forward on both sides of nose. Sides of cabin hinge upward to give access. Cabin can be adapted for a number of specialised applications, including field ambulance work, army co-operation duties, radio and navigational training, aircrew training, light transport, etc. For freight work the entire cabin roof can be made removable.

DIMENSIONS.—Span 30 ft. 8 in. (9.35 m.), Length 24 ft. (7.32 m.), Height 8 ft. 4 in. (2.54 m.).

WEIGHTS (Gipsy-Major Series III or Cirrus-Major engine).—Weight empty 1,460 lbs. (663 kg.), Fuel (24 Imp. gallons) 180 lbs. (82 kg.), Oil (3 Imp. gallons) 27 lbs. (12.3 kg.), Pilot 170 lbs. (77 kg.), Passengers (two) 340 lbs. (154 kg.), Passengers (three) 510 lbs. (231 kg.), Weight loaded (two-seat Trainer-Aerobatic category) 2,067 lbs. (938 kg.), Weight loaded (three-seater) 2,377 lbs. (1,079 kg.), Weight loaded (four-seater) 2,427 lbs. (1,102 kg.).

WEIGHTS (Gipsy-Major IIIS and constant-speed airscrew).—Weight empty 1,540 lbs. (699 kg.), Weight loaded (two-seat Trainer-Aerobatic category) 2,097 lbs. (952 kg.), Weight loaded (three-seater) 2,457 lbs. (1,115 kg.), Weight loaded (four-seater) 2,497 lbs. (1,134 kg.).

WEIGHTS (Gipsy-Major IC or V engine).—Weight empty 1,400 lbs. (636 kg.), Weight loaded (two-seat Trainer-Aerobatic category) 2,007 lbs. (911 kg.), Weight loaded (three-seater) 2,317 lbs. (1,052 kg.), Weight loaded (four-seater) 2,367 lbs. (1,197 kg.).

PERFORMANCE (Gipsy-Major IIIS with c/s airscrew and at loaded weight of 2,400 lbs. = 1,090 kg.).—Maximum speed 180 m.p.h. (288 km.h.) at 7,000 ft. (2,135 m.), Cruising speed 169 m.p.h. (270.4 km.h.) at 6,400 ft. (1,950 m.), Initial rate of climb 1,080 ft./min. (330 m./min.), Ultimate range (24 Imp. gallons petrol) 480 miles (770 km.).

PERFORMANCE (Gipsy-Major III with c/s airscrew and at loaded weight of 2,400 lbs. = 1,090 kg.).—Maximum speed 160 m.p.h. (256 km.h.) at sea level, Cruising speed 155 m.p.h. (240 km.h.) at 3,600 ft. (1,100 m.), Stalling speed 46 m.p.h. (76.3 km.h.), Initial rate of climb 1,000 ft./min. (305 m./min.), Ultimate range (24 Imp. gallons petrol) 480 miles (770 km.).

PERFORMANCE (Gipsy-Major III or Cirrus Major and fixed-pitch airscrew).—Maximum speed 157 m.p.h. (251.2 km.h.) at sea level, Cruising speed 139 m.p.h. (222.4 km.h.) at sea level, Stalling speed 46 m.p.h. (73.6 km.h.), Initial rate of climb 890 ft./min. (272 m./min.), Ultimate range (24 Imp. gallons petrol) 410 miles (656 km.).

PERFORMANCE (Gipsy-Major IC and fixed-pitch airscrew).—Maximum speed 152 m.p.h. (243.2 km.h.) at sea level, Cruising speed 135 m.p.h. (216 km.h.), Stalling speed 46 m.p.h. (73.6 km.h.), Initial rate of climb 750 ft./min. (230 m./min.), Ultimate range (24 Imp. gallons petrol) 410 miles (656 km.).

THE MILES M-27 MASTER III.

TYPE.—Two-seat Advanced Training Monoplane.

WINGS, FUSELAGE, TAIL UNIT AND LANDING GEAR.—Same as for Master II.

POWER PLANT.—One Pratt & Whitney R-1535-SB4G Twin-Wasp Junior fourteen-cylinder two-row radial air-cooled engine rated at 750 h.p. at 9,000 ft. (2,745 m.) and with 825 h.p. available for take-off. NACA cowling with controllable trailing-edge gills. Fuel tanks in centre-section stubs.

ACCOMMODATION.—Same as for Master II.

DIMENSIONS.—Span 35 ft. 9 in. (10.9 m.), Length 30 ft. 2 in. (10.5 m.), Height (tail down) 9 ft. 3 in. (2.82 m.), Wing area 224 sq. ft. (20.8 sq. m.).

WEIGHTS.—Weight empty 4,210 lbs. (1,911 kg.), Weight loaded 5,400 lbs. (2,452 kg.).

PERFORMANCE.—Speed at 2,000 ft. (610 m.) 214 m.p.h. (342.4 km.h.), Speed at 5,000 ft. (1,525 m.) 221 m.p.h. (353.6 km.h.), Speed at 9,000 ft. (2,745 m.) 231 m.p.h. (369.6 km.h.), Speed at 15,000 ft. (4,575 m.) 227 m.p.h. (363 km.h.), Speed at 20,000 ft. (6,100 m.) 218 m.p.h. (348.8 km.h.), Service ceiling 27,300 ft. (8,350 m.).

THE MILES M-25 MARTINET.

TYPE.—Two-seat Target-Towing monoplane.

WINGS, FUSELAGE AND TAIL UNIT.—Same as for Master II.

LANDING GEAR.—Interchangeable with all Marks of Master aircraft.

POWER PLANT.—One Bristol Mercury XX or 30 nine-cylinder radial air-cooled engine rated at 835/870 h.p. at 4,500 ft. (1,370 m.).

The Miles M-28 Three/four-seat Cabin Monoplane (D.H. Gipsy-Major engine).

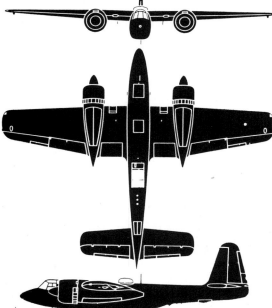

The Miles M-33 Monitor Target-tug.

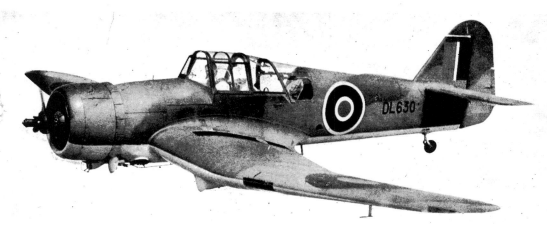

The Miles M-27 Master III Advanced Training Monoplane (Pratt & Whitney Twin-Wasp Junior engine).

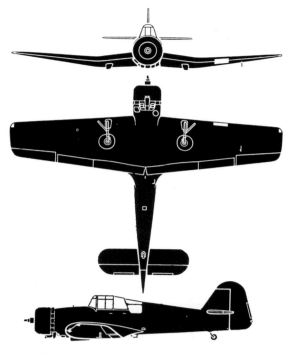

The Miles M-27 Master III Advanced Trainer.

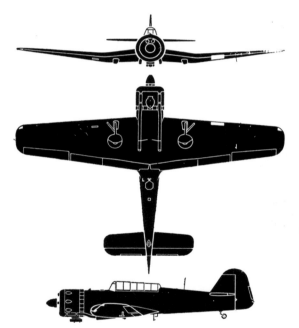

The Miles M-25 Martinet Target-tug.

The Miles M-25 Martinet Target-towing Monoplane (Bristol Mercury engine).

The Miles M-20 Single-seat Fighter (Rolls-Royce Merlin XX engine).

and giving a maximum output of 785/820 h.p. at sea level. NACA cowling with leading-edge exhaust collector ring and trailing-edge controllable gills. Main fuel tanks in centre-section and auxiliary tanks in outer wings. Oil tank in fuselage behind fireproof bulkhead.

ACCOMMODATION.—Enclosed accommodation for two in tandem. The observer occupies the after position. Wind-driven winch for sleeve or flag targets, or electric winch for sleeve target only. Flag targets released from container under fuselage by cockpit control. Sleeve targets stowed in rear cockpit with halyards for attachment to flag target tow-line. Provision is made for the observer to gain access to the end of the winch cable through a hatch in the bottom of the cockpit. A tip-up seat is provided for the observer.

DIMENSIONS.—Span 39 ft. (11.9 m.), Length 30 ft. 11 in. (9.45 m.), Height 11 ft. 7 in. (3.57 m.), Wing area 238 sq. ft. (22.1 sq. m.).

WEIGHTS.—Weight empty 4,600 lbs. (2,090 kg.), Weight loaded 6,600 lbs. (3,000 kg.).

PERFORMANCE.—Maximum speed at sea level 232 m.p.h. (371 km.h.), Speed at 15,000 ft. (4,575 m.) 237 m.p.h. (379 km.h.), Cruising speed at 4,500 ft. (1,370 m.) 225 m.p.h. (360 km.h.).

THE MILES M-20.

The M-20 was designed in 1940 to meet a possible emergency at a time when Great Britain was faced with a shortage of fighters to meet the full strength of the Luftwaffe based in France and the Low Countries.

Nine weeks and two days after authority was received from the Ministry of Aircraft Production to proceed with the design and construction of the M-20, the prototype made its first flight. All-wood construction with plywood and fabric covering was used, hydraulics were eliminated, standard Master training aircraft parts were used wherever possible and a fixed landing gear adopted, all in order to expedite production. A moulded "blister" type cockpit canopy was fitted, one of the first to be provided for a modern fighter.

The power-plant of the M-20 consisted of a standard Rolls-Royce Merlin XX "power-egg" complete with coolant and oil

radiators and all accessories, and interchangeable with the Bristol Beaufighter II.

Armament consisted of eight .303 in. Browning machine-guns, four in each wing, and hinged panels in the upper surface of the wings gave easy access to the guns which were mounted in chassis designed to facilitate rapid servicing and replacement.

The M-20 had a speed comparable with the best fighters at that time, being faster than the Hurricane but slightly slower than the Spitfire. However, it carried considerably more ammunition and had a greater range than either of these two aircraft.

Two prototypes were built, the second being produced to the order of the Ministry of Aircraft Production as a Fleet Fighter. It was equipped with catapult points and embodied other minor modifications.

With the defeat of the Luftwaffe in the Battle of Britain, the need for proceeding with the development and production of the M-20 did not arise.

THE MILES M-19 MASTER II.

TYPE.—Two-seat Advanced Trainer and Glider Tug.

WINGS.—Low-wing cantilever monoplane. NACA Section No. 230 to thickness/chord ratio of 23.8 per cent. Wing-stubs slope down from fuselage, outer sections set at slight dihedral angle. Wooden structure, with plywood covering. Miles hydraulically-operated split trailing-edge flaps, depressable to 25 degrees for take-off and 90 degrees for landing.

FUSELAGE.—Oval wooden semi-monocoque, with stressed plywood skin.

TAIL UNIT.—Cantilever monoplane type. Wooden structure, with plywood and fabric covering.

LANDING GEAR.—Retractable type. Each main wheel unit retracts backwards and upwards, the wheels turning through 90 degrees to lie flush with the underside of the centre-section. Oleo-pneumatic shock-absorbers. Hydraulic wheel brakes. Non-retractable fully-castoring tail-wheel.

POWER PLANT.—One Bristol Mercury XX nine-cylinder radial air-cooled engine rated at 835/870 h.p. at 4,500 ft. (1,370 m.) and giving a maximum output of 785/820 h.p. at sea level. NACA cowling with leading-edge exhaust collector ring and trailing-edge controllable gills. Fuel tanks in centre-section stubs.

ACCOMMODATION.—Enclosed accommodation for two, in tandem, with dual controls. Moulded "Perspex" windscreen. Rear seat adjustable with vertical travel of 12 ins. to bring the occupant's head above the normal fairing line, thus providing excellent view over the centre-section and wing on both sides as well as immediately forward. He is protected while he is in this position by a special design of clear panel windscreen which folds up out of the cabin hooding. Adjustment of rudder-bar may be made simultaneously with seat adjustment.

DIMENSIONS.—Span 35 ft. 9 in. (10.9 m.), Length 29 ft. 6 in. (9 m.), Height 9 ft. 5 in. (2.86 m.), Wing area 224 sq. ft. (20.8 sq. m.).

WEIGHTS.—Weight empty 4,130 lbs. (1,875 kg.), Weight loaded 5,312 lbs. (2,412 kg.).

PERFORMANCE.—Speed at sea level 240 m.p.h. (384 km.h.), Speed at 5,000 ft. (1,525 m.) 260 m.p.h. (416 km.h.), Speed at 10,000 ft. (3,050 m.) 255 m.p.h. (408 km.h.), Speed at 15,000 ft. (4,575 m.) 245 m.p.h. (392 km.h.), Cruising speed at 2/3 power at 5,250 ft. (1,600 m.) 230 m.p.h. (368 km.h.), Service ceiling 28,000 ft. (8,540 m.).

The Miles M-19 Master II Glider-tug. The towing hook is below the cut-away rudder.

The Miles M-18 Two-seat Primary Training Monoplane (150 h.p. D.H. Gipsy-Major III engine).

LANDING GEAR.—Divided type. Lockheed single-strut cantilever legs, with oleo-airdraulic springing and damping. Dunlop low-pressure wheels and tyres. Bendix brakes, with differential rudder-bar control and separate hand-lever.

POWER PLANT.—One 130 h.p. D.H. Gipsy-Major four-cylinder in-line inverted air-cooled engine on welded steel-tube mounting. Fuel tanks of 21 gallons total capacity in centre-section. Oil tank on engine bulkhead.

ACCOMMODATION.—Two open cockpits in tandem, with dual control. A door to each. Parachute seats. Large locker behind rear cockpit. Equipment includes full set of standard instruments in both cockpits, blind-flying instruments and hood and night-flying equipment.

DIMENSIONS.—Span 33 ft. 10 in. (10.3 m.), Length 25 ft. 3 in. (7.7 m.), Height 6 ft. 8 in. (2 m.), Wing area 176 sq. ft. (16.3 sq. m.).

WEIGHTS.—Weight empty (including standard fixed equipment) 1,250 lbs. (568 kg.), Weight loaded 1,863 lbs. (846 kg.).

PERFORMANCE.—Maximum speed at 1,000 ft. (305 m.), 145 m.p.h. (232 km.h.), Stalling speed 45 m.p.h. (72 km.h.), Service ceiling 18,000 ft. (5,490 m.).

THE MILES M-18.

TYPE.—Two-seat Primary Training monoplane.

WINGS.—Low-wing cantilever monoplane. In three sections comprising a rectangular centre-section and two slightly-tapered outer sections with square tips. Structure similar to that of Magister with two spruce and plywood main spars, spruce and plywood ribs and plywood covering. Walnut inserts are used at spar joints instead of ply spreaders. Three portions of wing are joined by large bolts through metal plate fittings bolted to spars. Differentially-operated ailerons of similar structure to wings. Miles patent vacuum-operated split flaps over entire trailing-edge between ailerons and are in five sections, two outer wing flaps, two centre-section flaps and one fuselage flap. Follow-up valve allows flaps to be set in any desired position instead of only two as in the Magister.

FUSELAGE.—Similar to that of Magister but 4 ins. wider internally at cockpits. Spruce framework covered with plywood on bottom and sides. Separate forward and rear semi-circular top decking attached to upper longerons.

TAIL UNIT.—Cantilever monoplane type. Rectangular adjustable tail-plane of similar structure to wings. Fin built into rear end of fuselage, the leading-edge member attaching to sloping bulkhead in fuselage. Both fin and tail-plane are plywood-covered. Elevators of similar structure to tail-plane. Rudder has wooden framework and fabric covering.

LANDING GEAR.—Fixed cantilever type. Top ends of oleo legs attached to front spar of centre-section by light alloy castings. Wheels are interchangeable with those of Magister but are mounted on stub axles to simplify removal. Brake-system similar to that on Magister. Full-swivelling tail-wheel.

POWER PLANT.—One 150 h.p. D.H. Gipsy-Major III or Cirrus Major four-cylinder in-line inverted air-cooled engine on tubular mounting and with cowling similar to that of Magister. Two interchangeable fuel tanks (12 Imp. gallons each) in centre-section,

one on each side of fuselage and accessible through removable panel in under surface. Oil tank (2½ Imp. gallons) in leading-edge of centre-section on port side of fuselage.

ACCOMMODATION.—Tandem open cockpits with complete dual controls. Small doors on starboard side. Locker behind rear cockpit in top decking. Floor of locker removable for access to flap ram and reservoir. Blind-flying hood fitted to rear cockpit. Equipment includes full night-flying and blind-flying equipment, fire extinguishers, map cases, respirator stowage, etc.

DIMENSIONS.—Span 31 ft. (9.45 m.), Length 24 ft. 10 in. (7.57 m.), Height (tail down) 6 ft. 10½ in. (2.10 m.), Wing area 183.2 sq. ft. (17 sq. m.).

WEIGHTS AND LOADINGS.—Weight empty 1,306 lbs. (592.5 kg.), Pilot 200 lbs. (90.5 kg.), Petrol and oil 207 lbs. (94 kg.), Pay load (allowance for pupil and extra equipment) 205 lbs. (93 kg.), Weight loaded 1,918 lbs. (870 kg.), Wing loading 10.48 lbs./sq. ft. (50.8 kg./sq. m.), Power loading 12.76 lbs./h.p. (5.7 kg./h.p.).

PERFORMANCE (150 h.p. Cirrus Major engine).—Maximum speed 130 m.p.h. (208 km.h.), Cruising speed 120 m.p.h. (192 km.h.), Stalling speed 40 m.p.h. (64 km.h.), Initial rate of climb 780 ft./min. (238 m./min.), Service ceiling 12,500 ft. (3,810 m.), Duration 3½ hours.

THE MILES M-14 MAGISTER.

TYPE.—Two-seat Primary Training monoplane.

WINGS.—Low-wing cantilever monoplane. Centre-section let into underside of fuselage. Two built-up wooden box spars. Wooden box-ribs of ring type in centre-section. Wooden girder type in extensions. Whole covered with plywood. Wooden ailerons. Vacuum-operated split trailing-edge flaps.

FUSELAGE.—Box structure of plywood and spruce.

TAIL UNIT.—Cantilever fin with wooden frame covered with fabric. Cantilever tail-plane with wooden frame covered with fabric. Control surfaces of same construction.

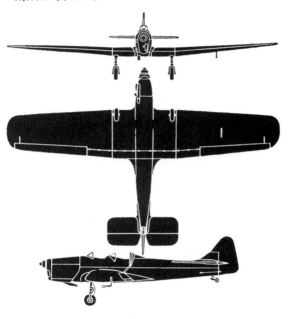

The Miles M-14 Magister Primary Trainer.

PARNALL.

PARNALL AIRCRAFT, LTD.

HEAD OFFICE: 8, SOUTH STREET, LONDON, W.1.

WORKS: YATE, GLOUCESTERSHIRE; NORTH CIRCULAR ROAD, NEASDEN, LONDON; WORMLEY, NEAR BRISTOL; AND TOLWORTH, SURREY.

Directors: The Earl of Limerick, D.S.O. (Chairman), P. C. Crump, O.B.E., F.I.A., Capt. A. G. Frazer-Nash, M.I.A.E.,

M.I.Mech.E., R. Egerton Johnson, R. P. Key, M.Inst.C.E., F.R.Ae.S. (General Manager), F. P. S. Stammers, A.C.A. and Capt. E. Grattan Thompson.

Parnall Aircraft, Ltd., was formed in 1935 to take over the aircraft business previously known as George Parnall & Co.; to acquire the patents, patent rights, designs and existing and pending contracts relating to aircraft and armament of Nash &

Thompson, Ltd., armament engineers; and the patents and patent rights, designs and licences of the Hendy Aircraft Co.

The Company pioneered the power-operated gun turret, and subsequently extended its activities to include the development and production of Radar and other war products. Details of these products still remain on the secret list.

PERCIVAL.

PERCIVAL AIRCRAFT, LTD.

HEAD OFFICE AND WORKS: LUTON AIRPORT, LUTON. BEDFORDSHIRE.

Directors: P. Ll. Hunting (Chairman), Wing Cdr. G. L. Hunting, Capt. C. P. Hunting, W. A. Summers, K. D. Morgan, N. R. Whiteside and R. S. S. Cook.

Chief Designer: A. A. Bage, A.F.R.Ae.S.

Works Manager: W. E. Salmon.

Secretary: J. M. Richards, A.C.A., A.S.A.A.

The Percival Aircraft Company was formed in 1932. It was re-organized as Percival Aircraft Ltd. in 1937, and the works were moved from Gravesend to Luton.

Percival aircraft achieved a number of outstanding performances in the years before the war, details of which have been given in previous issues of this Annual.

When the war came the Percival Vega Gull was chosen by the Air Ministry for conversion to service use. Officially named the Proctor it has been, and still is, serving as a trainer and as a light communications type. It is in use as a navigational, and radio trainer by the R.A.F. and the Royal Navy. It is also serving as a dual control trainer and as a four seat liaison and communications monoplane.

The latest version is the Proctor IV, which is a re-design of the earlier models to conform to an Air Ministry specification for a radio trainer for the R.A.F. and the Fleet Air Arm.

THE PERCIVAL PROCTOR.

The Proctor is in use by the R.A.F., the Royal Navy and Air Transport Auxiliary for training and communications work in the following forms:—

Proctor I. R.A.F. and A.T.A. communications type. Three-seater with side-by-side dual control and one rear seat.

Proctor I. Naval, Radio and Navigational Trainer. Three-seater with radio-operator on rotatable rear seat. D/F loop aerial on top of cabin.

Proctor II. Naval Radio and Navigational Trainer. Three-seater with radio operator beside pilot. D/F loop aerial on top of cabin.

Proctor III. R.A.F. communications type. Three-seater. No dual control. Another version of Mark III has the rear seat on the port side with a small radio set alongside.

Proctor III, Series 2. R.A.F. Radio Trainer. Two-seater

with radio-operator seated beside pilot and facing aft. D/F loop on top of cabin.

Proctor IV. R.A.F. Radio Trainer. A larger, heavier and completely re-designed Proctor which is fully equipped for night flying and carries the largest type of radio transmitter and receiver as used on operational aircraft. Three-seater with radio-operator beside pilot. D/F loop on top of cabin.

Proctor IV. R.A.F. Communications type. Four-seater with dual control and two rear seats.

The following description applies to the Proctor IV.

TYPE.—Three-seat Radio Trainer or Four-seat Communications monoplane.

WINGS.—Low-wing cantilever monoplane. Wing in three sections, a rectangular centre-section and two tapering outer sections. Centre-section located in recess in bottom of fuselage and attached by four bolts. Outer sections hinged at rear spar joints, the portions of the wings aft of rear spars and inboard of ailerons hinging upwards to permit folding. Structure consists of two wooden box spars connected at intervals by bulkheads and spruce diagonal bracing members, former ribs, plywood leading-edge and a fabric covering. Manually-operated all-wood three-position split trailing-edge flaps between ailerons and fuselage.

The Percival Proctor IV Communications and Training Monoplane (208 h.p. D.H. Gipsyqueen II engine).

FUSELAGE.—Rectangular structure with domed top and bottom built up of four spruce longerons, plywood sides and a pre-formed ply bottom skin. Top decking is plywood over laminated spruce frames. Complete structure fabric-covered.

TAIL UNIT.—Cantilever monoplane type. Tailplane and fin built up of two wood box-spars, ribs and plywood covering. Elevators and rudder have single box-spar, spruce and plywood ribs and fabric covering. Trimming-tabs in elevators and rudder operated from cockpit through reversible units on the spars.

LANDING GEAR.—Fixed cantilever type. Track 9 ft. 9 in. (2.97 m.). Each unit consists of a cantilever compression leg, incorporating double steel springs and a hydraulic recoil damper, attached to the centre-section front spar by four bolts. Streamline fairing to leg merges into wheel fairing. Medium-pressure wheels and Bendix mechanical brakes. Full swivelling and self-centering tail-wheel.

POWER PLANT.—One 208 h.p. D.H. Gipsyqueen II six-cylinder inverted air-cooled engine on steel-tube mounting. D.H. constant-speed airscrew. Two fuel tanks (40 Imp. gallons total capacity), one in root of each outer wing section and feeding to three-way cock in the cabin. Oil tank (3.8 Imp. gallons) in leading-edge of centre-section on port side. Oil cooler at inboard end of tank and faired into centre-section with outlet flap adjustable on the ground. Vacuum pump on engine for operation of blind-flying instruments. Large generator with flexible drive from engine.

ACCOMMODATION (Radio Trainer).—Pilot on port side, radio operator further back on starboard side with radio transmitter and receiver in front of him, second radio-operator (who can change places with first operator) in seat at rear of cabin. Fixed and trailing aerials and D/F loop aerial, as well as intercommunication telephones for each member of the crew. A signalling lamp and complete night-flying equipment are installed. Air conditioning is provided by a controllable fresh air inlet and sliding windows.

ACCOMMODATION (Communications).—Two pilots in front, each seat mounted on a standard seat bearer and control unit which can be removed or replaced in a few hours. Two seats side-by-side at back of cabin with room for light luggage behind the seats.

DIMENSIONS.—Span 39 ft. 6 in. (12 m.), Width folded 16 ft. 4 in. (4.98 m.), Length 28 ft. 2 in. (8.6 m.), Height 8 ft. 4 in. (2.54 m.), Wing area 202 sq. ft. (18.76 sq. m.).

WEIGHTS AND LOADINGS.—Weight empty (with full equipment) 2,370 lbs. (1,076 kg.), Disposable load 1,130 lbs. (513 kg.), Weight loaded (max. permissible) 3,500 lbs. (1,589 kg.), Wing loading 17.3 lbs./sq. ft. (84.42 kg./sq. m.), Power loading 16.8 lbs./h.p. (7.62 kg./h.p.).

PERFORMANCE (at max. permissible load).—Maximum speed at sea level 160 m.p.h. (256 km.h.), Maximum cruising speed 148 m.p.h. (237 km.h.), Economical cruising speed (at sea level) 135 m.p.h. (217 km.h.), Economical cruising speed (at 6,000 ft.) 146 m.p.h. (235 km.h.), Stalling speed (flaps down) 55 m.p.h. (88 km.h.), Initial rate of climb 700 ft./min. (213.5 m./min.), Climb to 5,000 ft. (1,525 m.) 9 mins., Ceiling 14,000 ft. (4,270 m.), Range in still air (after allowing for ¼ hour at full throttle) 500 miles (800 km.), Take-off run in still air (from grass) 325 yds. (297 m.), Take-off run in still air (from runway) 285 yds. (261 m.).

THE PERCIVAL PROCTOR V.

The Percival Proctor V is the civil version of the Mark IV (see p. 58c). It is fitted with two adjustable seats in front and one full-width seat across the back of the cabin with a folding central arm-rest. Luggage can be carried in the space behind the back seat and a locker is provided at the rear of the cabin for light articles.

A new instrument panel accommodates all the flying instruments in a single shock-proof panel. Equipment includes full blind-flying and night-flying instruments, landing lamps, navigation, cabin and instrument lights, and provision for radio. Dual controls and long-range tanks can be fitted at extra cost. The Proctor V is priced at £2,900 ex works.

THE PERCIVAL MERGANSER.

The Merganser is a twin-engined all-metal cabin monoplane with accommodation for a crew of two and five passengers. Its features include a cantilever high-wing, a retractable tricycle landing-gear and a power-plant comprising two 296 h.p. D.H. Gipsy Queen 71 engines driving constant-speed airscrews

The passenger cabin has three and two seats respectively on the port and starboard sides of a central gangway. There is a baggage compartment forward and a lavatory aft of the cabin. The pilot's cabin has accommodation for pilot and co-pilot/navigator. Dual controls are standard.

DIMENSIONS.—Span 47 ft. 9 in. (14.56 m.), Length 38 ft. (11.6 m.), Height 14 ft. 5 in. (4.4 m.), Wing area 319 sq. ft. (29.6 sq. m.).

WEIGHTS.—Weight empty 4,232 lbs. (1,921 kg.), Weight loaded 6,532 lbs. (2,965 kg.).

PERFORMANCE (estimated).—Maximum speed at 5,000 ft. (1,525 m.) 194 m.p.h. (310 km.h.), Economical cruising speed at 8,000 ft. (2,440 m.) 170 m.p.h. (272 km.h.), Stalling speed 65 m.p.h. (104 km.h.), Range at 5,000 ft. (1,525 m.) 830 miles (1,330 km.) at 163 m.p.h. (261 km.h.).

POBJOY-SHORT.

POBJOY AIRMOTORS & AIRCRAFT, LTD.

REGISTERED OFFICE: 20, BERKELEY SQUARE, LONDON, W.1.

Formed: June, 1935.

The original firm of Pobjoy Airmotors, Ltd., was founded in 1930 purely as an engine manufacturing company but in 1935 it was converted into a public company with an authorised capital of £250,000, and its scope was enlarged to include aircraft manufacture.

Initially the Pobjoy Company acquired the licence to build the Short Scion light commercial monoplane and this machine became the Pobjoy-Short Scion. In 1937 the licence for the Short Scion-Senior was acquired.

In March, 1938, the firm of Short Bros. (Rochester & Bedford) Ltd. acquired a large proportion of the issued shares of the Pobjoy company and a very close liaison now exists between the two companies.

The recent aircraft activities of the Company have been devoted to the manufacture of parts and sub-assemblies for standard types of service aircraft.

PORTSMOUTH AVIATION.

PORTSMOUTH AVIATION LTD.

HEAD OFFICE AND WORKS: THE AIRPORT, PORTSMOUTH, HANTS.

Chairman: L. M. J. Balfour, B.Sc., A.R.Ae.S.

Directors: L. M. J. Balfour, B.Sc. A.R.Ae.S., Flt. Lt. F. L. Luxmoore, D.F.C. (Director of Design), W. J. Jenks and A. G. Murray.

Portsmouth Aviation under the title of Wight Aviation Ltd. was registered in 1932. The Company operated air services between the Isle of Wight and the Mainland up to the outbreak of War, after which they devoted their resources to the repair of R.A.F. aircraft. They have gained a wide knowledge of constructional practices and operative defects and, as a result, have established a design office and intend to enter the post-war aircraft manufacturing field. Their first design is for a twin-engined twin-boom high-wing cabin monoplane with accommodation for pilot and three or four passengers and suitable for executive, air charter or private owner use. This design will be fitted with either two 100 h.p. Cirrus Minor (Type 109) or 150 h.p. Cirrus Major (Type 110) engines.

SARO.

SAUNDERS-ROE LTD.

REGISTERED OFFICE: COWES, ISLE OF WIGHT.

LONDON OFFICE: 49, PARLIAMENT STREET, S.W.1.

Directors: Sir Alliott Verdon-Roe (President), A. E. Chambers (Chairman), A. Gouge, B.Sc., F.R.Ae.S. (Vice-Chairman), Capt. E. D. Clarke, M.C. (Managing Director), Viscount Cowdray, the Hon. H. N. Morgan-Grenville, O.B.E., J. L. Walsh, R. V. Perfect and H. Knowler, F.R.Ae.S.

Secretary: P. D. Irons, B.Com., A.C.A.

Saunders-Roe Ltd. are designers and builders of all types of aircraft, ground and marine equipment, including trailers, trolleys, beaching chassis, arming and refuelling tenders, ammunition hoists, etc.

The Company is at present engaged on the design, manufacture and repair of aircraft of marine and amphibious types.

Experimental work on modified forms of the Saro 37 scale model flying-boat, previously illustrated and described, is being undertaken to obtain data for the future development of the large flying-boat.

Sanders-Roe, Ltd. were responsible for the detail design and manufacture of the component parts of the wings, including flaps, ailerons, engine-mountings and wing-tip floats, of the Short Shetland flying-boat (see under "Short").

SHORT.

SHORT BROS. (ROCHESTER & BEDFORD), LTD.

HEAD OFFICE AND WORKS: ROCHESTER, KENT.

Honorary Life President: H. O. Short, F.R.Ae.S.

Directors: E. D. A. Herbert, O.B.E., M.A., A.M.I.C.E., M.I. Mech.E., M.I.E.E. (Chairman), S. H. Brown, Sir John S. Buchanan, C.B.E., F.R.Ae.S., C.P.T. Lipscomb, Wh.Ex., F.R.Ae.S., J. Lankester Parker, O.B.E., F.R.Ae.S. and D.E. Wiseman.

Secretary: R. Prentice, C.A.

The firm of Short Bros., which is the oldest established firm of aeroplane designers and producers in the United Kingdom, was founded by two brothers, Eustace and Oswald Short, in the year 1898, their work for some years being the manufacture of spherical balloons.

After the last war Short Bros. concentrated on the development of the all-metal flying-boat, and achieved remarkable success.

In July, 1936, the first "Empire" boat made its preliminary flying tests, and altogether the Company constructed thirty-nine of these boats for Imperial Airways Ltd. The last seven boats were of a modified type, fitted with four Bristol Perseus XIIC sleeve-valve engines.

Three boats of a larger type, the "G" class, intended for a trans-Atlantic service, were taken over by the Air Ministry on the outbreak of war and converted for military uses. One, formerly the "Golden Fleece," was lost on active service but the other two were returned to commercial service late in 1941. One of these has since been lost in commercial service.

For the Royal Air Force, the Sunderland four-engined overseas reconnaissance flying-boat and the Stirling four-engined land-plane bomber have been produced in large numbers. The latest Short product of which details may be published is the Shetland flying-boat, the largest aircraft of its type built in the British Isles.

In June, 1936, Short Bros., Ltd., in collaboration with Harland & Wolff, Ltd., the well-known Belfast shipbuilders, formed a new company known as Short & Harland, Ltd., to build aircraft at Belfast. Further details of this Company will be found under Short & Harland, Ltd.

THE SHORT S-35 SHETLAND.

The Shetland was primarily intended to serve as a long-range patrol and reconnaissance flying-boat for the Royal Air Force, but its layout lends itself admirably to a simple conversion to a civil transport. The prototype has already been so converted and a further example is being built primarily as a commercial aircraft for British Overseas Airways.

The Shetland was designed and constructed by Short Bros., Ltd. with the collaboration of Saunders-Roe, Ltd. The original design was conceived by Short Bros., who were responsible for the manufacture, assembly and flight testing of the aircraft. Saunders-Roe, Ltd. were responsible for the detail design and manufacture of the component parts of the wings, including the flaps, ailerons, engine mountings and wing-tip floats.

In general appearance the Shetland bears a striking resemblance to the "C" and "G" Class flying-boats and with the exception of portions of the control surfaces is entirely of metal construction.

The internal arrangement is of the two-deck type. The lower deck is reserved entirely for passenger accommodation, with dining saloon and cocktail bar situated on the aft upper deck. A fully-equipped kitchen and pantry are included in the layout, together with a coat room, dressing rooms, toilet accommodation, etc., in addition to the special provisions made for the convenience of the crew of eleven.

Mail and freight compartments with external loading hatches are located on the upper deck amidships and aft and have a capacity for the stowage of 6,600 lbs. (3,000 kg.) of freight.

Although a maximum of 70 passengers could be accommodated, the furnishing and equipment of the first Shetland provides for a maximum of 40 day passengers with sleeping facilities for twenty-four. This version is described hereafter.

WINGS.—High-wing cantilever monoplane of all-metal construction. Wing section modified Göttingen 436. Aspect ratio: 8.62. Swept-back leading-edge, straight trailing-edge. Three spar structure, the two front spars forming sides of a torsion box. Spars have reinforced sheet webs and either L or T-section extruded booms.

The Short Shetland Flying-boat (four 2,500 h.p. Bristol Centaurus engines).

The prototype Stirling, fitted with four Bristol Hercules II engines, first flew in May, 1939. This aircraft crashed on landing after its maiden flight, but a second prototype was completed and was flying in the Autumn of 1939.

These two prototypes and the early production aircraft, which were being delivered to the R.A.F. by August, 1940, were built by the parent company, but an organized system of dispersal was soon put into operation whereby the main components were built in more than twenty different factories, in addition to a large sub-contracting scheme for the supply of the smaller components.

Stirling I. Four 1,600 h.p. Bristol Hercules XI fourteen-cylinder radial sleeve-valve engines. No dorsal turret. First into action on the night of February 10-11, 1941.

Stirling II. Four Wright Cyclone R-2600-A5B fourteen-cylinder radial air-cooled engines. A conversion of the Mk. I. Only a few built.

Stirling III. Four 1,650 h.p. Bristol Hercules VI or XVI fourteen-cylinder sleeve-valve engines. Mid-upper turret added. Fitted for glider-towing in 1943.

Stirling IV. A long-range troop transport conversion of the Mk. III. Nose and mid-upper turrets removed and replaced by fairings, but the four-gun tail turret retained. A large opening in the underside of the rear fuselage introduced for the dropping of paratroops. Bomb cells retained and used for the carriage and dropping of airborne supplies. Crew of six, comprising two pilots, navigator, radio operator, flight engineer and tail

The Short Shetland Flying-boat (four 2,500 h.p. Bristol Centaurus engines).

Between two front spars is a series of diagragm bulkheads, a heavy skin supported by lateral stringers completing the box. Remainder of wing is built up of relatively light diaphragm ribs with the skin riveted to Z-section lateral stringers which are, in turn, bolted to the cap extrusions of the ribs. Handley Page slotted flaps of all-metal construction. Fabric-covered Frise type ailerons.

HULL.—All-metal two-step structure of typical Short design and construction. A series of channel-section frames, doubled back-to-back in the midship section, and longitudinal stringers carry the skin plating. Above the window base line the stringers are of open top-hat section and the frames are notched for their passage. Below this line the stringers are of Z-section and are notched for frame passage. Below lower deck level the hull is divided into compartments by shallow stiffened bulkheads which are edged with extrusions to which the floor bearers and hull bottom stringers are attached. Heavy bracing structures enclosed within double solid and reinforced bulkheads are located in the wing spar stations. Upper deck carried on transverse channel section beams at each frame station, with two built-up box-section beams and a series of Z-section stringers running fore-and-aft from mooring compartment bulkhead to the front bulkhead of the after entrance vestibule.

TAIL UNIT.—Cantilever monoplane type. All-metal fixed surfaces, fabric-covered control surfaces. Rudder control has electric boost mechanism to provide three-fourths of the force required to move the rudder.

POWER PLANT.—Four 2,500 h.p. Bristol Centaurus eighteen-cylinder two-row radial air-cooled sleeve-valve engines, each fitted with a Rotol cooling fan and driving a four-blade D.H. Hydromatic constant-speed full-feathering airscrew. The two inboard airscrews are also reversible. Ten fuel tanks in wings. Total fuel capacity: 6,112 Imp. gallons. Oil tanks housed in the wing torsion box immediately aft of each nacelle. Total oil capacity: 280 Imp. gallons.

ACCOMMODATION.—Arranged on two decks. Flight compartment on upper deck forward of leading-edge of wings, accommodates two pilots forward, navigator and radio operator at stations against the starboard wall and the flight engineer facing aft at rear end of compartment. Engineer is provided with all instruments and controls for all mechanical and electrical systems throughout the aircraft except the actual flight controls and services. On the port side of the flight compartment a stairway leads to lower deck. Aft of stairhead is a settee, convertible to two bunks, for off-duty crew. Continuing aft along upper deck to lower deck is the auxiliary engine-room (between wing spars) housing two Rotol generating plants for the supply of all ancilliary services; the main mail compartment (247 cu. ft. capacity) with loading hatch 4 ft. 8 in. × 4 ft. in roof; a fully-equipped kitchen; dining saloon or lounge seating 12; cocktail bar, from which a staircase leads down to rear entry vestibule on lower deck. Vestibule has entrance door on port side and toilet on starboard side. Purser's office beneath stairway.

Opposite stairway is a commodious coat-room and aft of vestibule is the men's dressing-room. In the extreme tail there is stowage space for passenger's hand baggage. Above the dressing room is a second mail or freight compartment (185 cu. ft. capacity). Going forward from vestibule along lower deck are four passenger cabins, each seating two and convertible into two-berth sleeping cabins; four toilets; eight passengers cabins, each seating four and convertible into two-berth sleeping cabins; and forward entrance vestibule, on starboard side of which is a ladies toilet and separate ladies' dressing room. In the nose of the hull are the mooring compartment, crew's toilet and crew entrance door with stairway to flight deck.

EQUIPMENT.—All accommodation is insulated for noise and temperature. Two Rotol auxiliary generating units, each capable of supplying 20 kw. at 110 volts A.C., provide current for all services, including bilging and refuelling. In addition power is available from this plant for lighting, cooking, refrigeration and air-conditioning both in flight and at moorings.

DIMENSIONS.—Span 150 ft. (45.75 m.), Length 108 ft. (32.94 m.), Height (on trolleys) 38 ft. 8 in. (11.8 m.), Maximum beam of hull 12 ft. 6 in. (3.8 m.).

WEIGHTS AND LOADINGS.—Weight empty (including all services and equipment, food and water, etc. and crew of eleven): 75,855 lbs. (34,438 kg.), Fuel and oil (6,112 gals. petrol and 280 gals. oil) 4,6525 lbs. (21,122 kg.), Payload (for maximum range) 7,620 lbs. (3,464 kg.), Weight loaded 130,000 lbs. (59,020 kg.), Wing loading 49.3 lbs./sq. ft. (240 kg./sq. m.).

PERFORMANCE.—Maximum speed 267 m.p.h. (427 km.h.) at 8,000 ft. (2,440 m.), Initial rate of climb at full load 660 ft./min. (200 m/min.).

RANGES.—With 7,620 lbs. (3,464 kg.) pay load 4,650 miles (7,440 km.) at 184 m.p.h. (294 km.h.), With 22,000 lbs. (10,000 kg.) pay load 3,000 miles (4,800 km.) at 185 m.p.h. (295 km.h.), With 30,025 lbs. (13,630 kg.) pay load 2,076 miles (3,322 km.) at 188 m.p.h. (301 km.h.).

THE SHORT S-29 STIRLING.

The Stirling, the design of which was based on Air Ministry Specification B.12/36, was the first of the large four-engined bombers to go into service in the R.A.F. The original layout of the Stirling was tried out by the construction of a half-scale model fitted with four 130 h.p. Pobjoy engines. Flying trials with the model proved the feasibility of the design, which included several novel and previously-untried features.

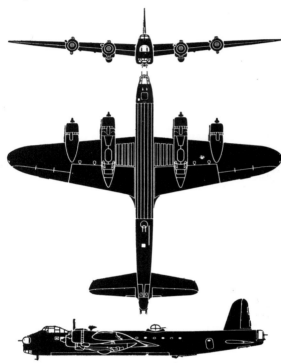

The Stirling III Heavy Bomber.

The Short Stirling IV Troop Transport and Glider-tug (four Bristol Hercules engines).

The Stirling V Transport (four Bristol Hercules engines).

The Short Shetland Flying-boat.

gunner. Aft of rear spar provision for the carriage of 24 paratroops or 34 airborne troops with arms and equipment. Also fitted for glider-towing. Normal loaded weight, wing and power loadings as for Mk. III. Maximum speed 280 m.p.h. (448 km.h.). Normal range in still air 3,000 miles (4,830 km.).

Stirling V. An unarmed military transport and freighter version of the Mk. III, which it resembles in general outline except for a redesigned nose. The forward portion of the nose hinges upwards for loading light freight into the forward compartment, a self-contained beam block and tackle being provided for this purpose. Aft of the rear spar frame fuselage may be adapted to fit the aircraft for a variety of duties, including :— (*a*) military passenger transport with 14 seats ; (*b*) ambulance to carry 12 stretcher cases plus sitting cases ; (*c*) troop transport for 40 fully-armed troops ; (*d*) paratroop transport for 20 paratroops and containers ; (*e*) heavy freighter to carry one Jeep, trailer and 6-pdr. gun complete with ammunition and crew of four, two Jeeps with crew of eight, two Centaurus engines on special stands, 14 standard freight baskets, etc. A large door 9 ft. 6 in. by 5 ft. 1 in. (2.9 m. × 1 53 m.) in rear fuselage complete with portable loading ramps. Normal flight crew of five. Dimensions same as for Mk. III except length 90 ft. 6¾ in. (27.6 m.).

The description below applies to the Stirling III heavy bomber and glider-tug.

Type.—Four-engined Long-range Heavy Bomber and Glider-tug.

Wings.—Mid-wing cantilever monoplane. Two-spar all-metal structure similar to that of Short "Empire" flying-boat. Gouge type trailing-edge flaps with chord equal to 48 per cent. of total wing chord. The leading-edges of the wings are armoured and are provided with barrage-balloon cable cutters.

Fuselage.—Rectangular section with rounded corners. All-metal structure built up of transverse frames covered with aluminium-alloy sheet with intercostal stiffeners and all joints joggled flush and flush-riveted.

Tail Unit.—Cantilever monoplane type. Single fin and rudder similar in form and construction to those of "Empire" boat.

Landing Gear.—Retractable type. Main wheels retract into inner engine nacelles taking part of their fairings with them. Electrical retraction with alternative hand operation. Retractable double tail-wheels.

Power Plant.—Four Bristol Hercules VI or XVI fourteen-cylinder sleeve-valve double-row radial air-cooled engines, each rated at 1,355 h.p. at 2,400 r.p.m. at 4,750 ft. (1,450 m.), developing a maximum output in level flight of 1,640 h.p. at 2,800 r.p.m. at 4,000 ft. (1,220 m.) and with 1,585 h.p. available for take-off Three-bladed de Havilland Hydromatic constant-speed full-feathering airscrews. Self-sealing cylindrical fuel tanks in wings outboard of wing bomb-cells.

Accommodation.—Crew of seven normally carried, comprising two pilots, navigator/bomb-aimer, front gunner/wireless operator, two air-gunners and flight-engineer/air-gunner. Bomb-aimer in nose below pilot's floor and under nose gun-turret. Pilot's coupé gives not only good forward view but is designed to permit fighting controller to operate with minimum of interference during enemy fighter attack. Navigator is also seated within coupé boundary. Retractable astral dome superimposed with escape hatch just aft of back end of coupé. Armoured bulkhead with hinged door separates flight compartment from engineer and wireless-operator. First pilot has additional armour to his back and head and fighting controller has armour protection to his chest when superintending air-gunner's action. Centre-section above bomb floor is braced to allow egress aft and also provides stowage space and rest quarters for any member of crew. Bunk is fitted on starboard side of this compartment. Aft of centre-section is the mid-upper turret and the servo-feed ammunition boxes to the tail turret. Aft of bomb-bay are the multi flare chutes and a walkway to tail-plane spar frames and through them to the tail-turret. Main entrance door to fuselage fitted aft of flare station.

Armament.—Three power-operated gun-turrets, each fitted with armour protection, one in nose, one amidships on top of the fuselage and one in extreme tail. Turrets accommodate a total of eight Browning .303-in. machine-guns. Main bomb-bay in fuselage formed of two main longitudinal girders with arched members to main floor. The bay is 42 ft. 7 in. (13 m.) long and fitted with six hinged doors. Internal stowage for bombs also provided in centre-section inboard of inner engine nacelles. Maximum bomb load 18,000 lbs. (8,170 kg.).

Equipment.—De-icing equipment fitted to leading-edge of wings, tail-plane and fin. Two dinghies carried, one in fuselage and one in wings. Latter dinghy inflates automatically on impact of aircraft with water. Engine maintenance platforms and ladders carried in fuselage. Oxygen equipment for all members of crew.

Dimensions.—Span 99 ft. 1 in. (30.2 m.), Length 87 ft. 3 in. (26.6 m.), Height on ground 22 ft. 9 in. (6.94 m.), Gross wing area 1,460 sq. ft. (135.6 sq. m.).

Weights and Loadings (Stirling III).—Tare weight 44,000 lbs. (19,950 kg.), Typical service load (including crew of 7) 4,230 lbs. (1,923 kg.), Petrol and oil 4,770 lbs. (2,165 kg.), Bomb load 17,000 lbs. (7,720 kg.), Normal loaded weight 70,000 lbs. (31,780 kg.), Wing loading 48 lbs./sq. ft. (234 kg./sq. m.), Power loading 10.6 lbs./h.p. (4.85 kg./h.p.).

Weights and Loadings (Stirling IV).—Tare weight 43,200 lbs. (19,600 kg.), Typical service load (including crew) 8,100 lbs. (3,680 kg.), Petrol and oil 18,700 lbs. (8,490 kg.), Normal loaded weight 70,000 lbs. (31,780 kg.), Wing and power loading as Mk. III.

Weights and Loadings (Stirling V).—Tare weight 43,500 lbs. (19,740 kg.), Typical service load 14,500 lbs. (6,580 kg.), Petrol and oil 12,000 lbs. (5,450 kg.), Normal loaded weight 70,000 lbs. (31,780 kg.), Wing and power loading as Mk. III.

Performance (Stirling IV and V).—Maximum speed 280 m.p.h. (450 km.h.) at 6,000 ft. (1,830 m.), Maximum economical cruising speed 233 m.p.h. (375 km.h.) at 11,000 ft. (3,500 m.), Initial rate of climb 800 ft./mins. (243 m./mins.), Service ceiling 18,000 ft. (5,480 m.), Normal range in still air 3,000 miles (4,830 km.).

THE SHORT S-25 SUNDERLAND.

The Sunderland was designed to meet the requirements of Air Ministry Specification R.2/33 and was virtually a military version of the "Empire" flying-boat. The prototype first flew in 1937, a year after the first "Empire" boat began its trials, and by the outbreak of war there were several squadrons in service and other units were in process of re-equipment or formation. The Sunderland was notable for being the first flying-boat to be equipped with power-operated gun-turrets.

Sunderland I. Four Bristol Pegasus 22 nine-cylinder radial air-cooled medium-supercharged engines. Armament consisted of eight .303 in. machine-guns, two in a Fraser-Nash nose turret, four in a Fraser-Nash tail turret, and two on hand-operated mountings in positions in the upper part of the hull aft of the trailing-edge of the wings.

Sunderland II. Four Bristol Pegasus XVIII nine-cylinder radial air-cooled engines with two-speed superchargers. Otherwise similar to Mk. I in early versions. Late models of Mk. II were fitted with a two-gun dorsal turret in place of the manually-operated guns.

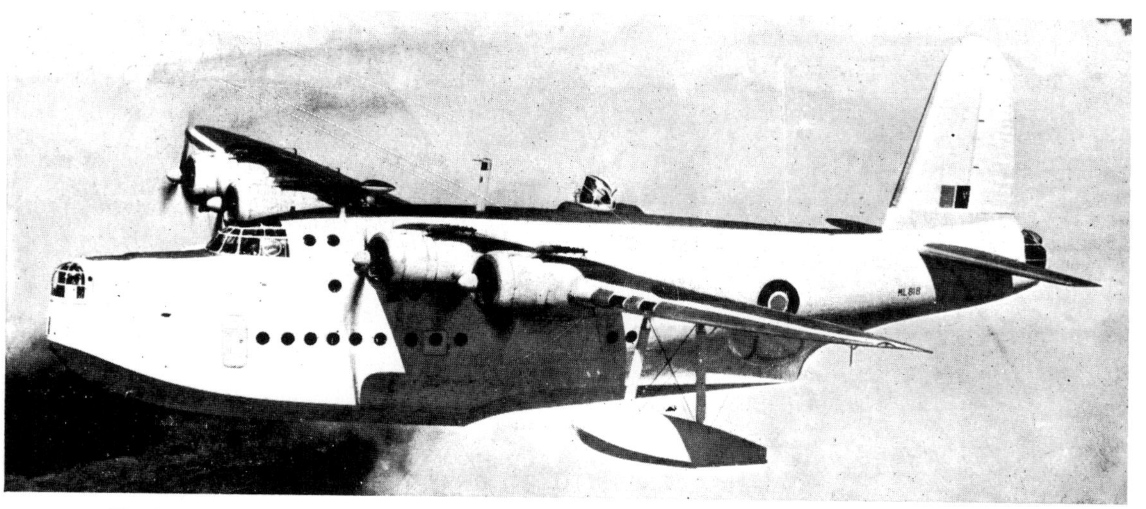

The Short Sunderland III General Reconnaissance Flying-boat (four Bristol Pegasus XVIII engines).

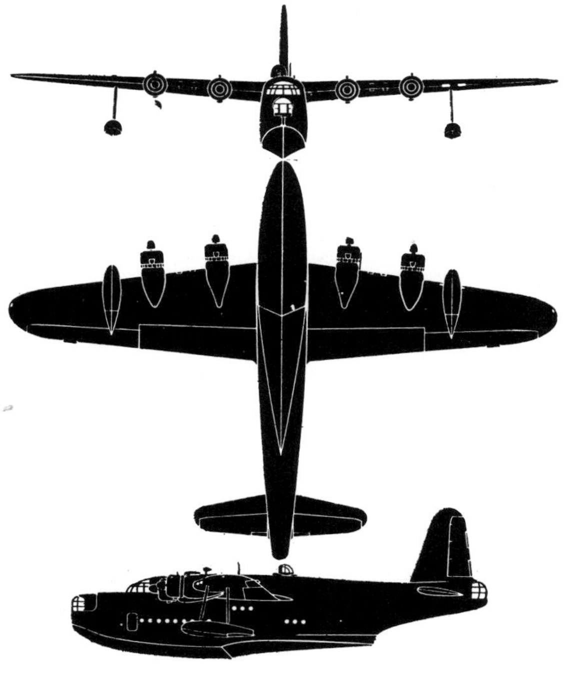

The Short Sunderland III Flying-boat.

Sunderland III. Same power-plant as the Mk. II. Modified hull with streamlined front step. Dorsal turret standard in this mark.

Sunderland V. Four 1,200 h.p. Pratt & Whitney R-1830-90B fourteen-cylinder radial air-cooled engines driving three-blade Hamilton Standard Hydromatic full-feathering airscrews. Otherwise similar to Sunderland III. Armament as Mk. III plus provision for four fixed .303 in. guns in the nose and two .303 in. beam guns.

In 1943 a number of Sunderlands were de-militarised, equipped to carry 20 passengers and turned over to British Airways for commercial use. This version is illustrated and described later.

Type.—Four-engined Reconnaissance Flying-boat.

Wings.—High-wing cantilever monoplane. As on the "Empire" boat the main wing structure consists of four extruded T-sections which form the corners of a box girder. These are braced in the lift bays by tubular struts, and in the drag bays by built-up members. Separate leading and trailing-edge sections. With exception of trailing-edge portion of the ailerons, the whole wing, including the Gouge flap, is metal-covered.

Hull.—The frames are of channel-section, interconnected by Z-section stiffeners. Sheeting is riveted on longitudinally with countersunk rivets.

Tail Unit.—Cantilever monoplane type. Fin and tail-plane metal-covered. The movable surfaces are fabric-covered aft of the leading-edge and have inset trimming-tabs.

Power Plant.—Four Bristol Pegasus XVIII nine-cylinder radial air-cooled engines, each rated at 815 h.p. at 2,250 r.p.m. at 4,750 ft. (1,450 m.), developing a maximum output in level flight of 1,065 h.p. at 2,600 r.p.m. at 1,250 ft. (380 m.) and with 1,050 h.p. available for take-off. NACA type cowling ring with controllable flaps. De Havilland three-bladed metal airscrews.

Accommodation.—The hull is divided into two decks. On the upper deck, there is forward, the control cabin accommodating two pilots side-by-side, a radio operator, a navigator and an engineer. Aft of the spar frames are the reconnaissance flares and stowage for maintenance cradles. In the extreme nose is the bomb-aimer's position and nose gun-turret. This turret slides aft to permit easy mooring. Aft of the turret on the lower deck is the mooring compartment, from which a ladder leads to the upper deck. On the starboard side of the ladder is the lavatory, while on the port side a gangway leads to the officers' wardroom. Further aft is the galley, bomb compartment, and crew's quarters. In the rear end of the hull is the work bench, the collapsible dinghy, flares and sea-markers.

Armament.—Eight 0.303 in. machine-guns in three Fraser-Nash turrets, one in the nose, one amidships and one in the extreme tail, the last-mentioned armed with four guns. Bombs, depth-charges, etc., carried on railed racks which may be wound out from interior of hull to underside of wings inboard of engine nacelles.

Dimensions.—Span 112 ft. 9½ in. (34.39 m.), Length 85 ft. 4 in. (26 m.), Height (to top of fin) 32 ft. 10½ in. (10 m.), Wing area 1,487 sq. ft. (138 sq. m.).

Weights.—Tare empty 34,500 lbs. (15,663 kg.), Service load including crew (eleven) 7,060 lbs. (3,205 kg.), Petrol (2,155 gallons) 15,540 lbs. (7,055 kg.), Oil (100 gallons) 900 lbs. (410 kg.), Weight loaded 58,000 lbs. (26,332 kg.).

Performance (Sunderland III).—Maximum speed 210 m.p.h. (336 km.h.) at 6,500 ft. (1,980 m.), Maximum economical cruising speed 178 m.p.h. (285 km.h.) at 5,000 ft. (1,525 m.), Minimum flying speed 78 m.p.h. (125 km.h.), Rate of climb at sea level 720 ft./min. (220 m./min.), Service ceiling 16,000 ft. (4,880 m.), Take-off time 34 secs., Normal range in still air 1,780 miles (2,848 km.), Overload range in still air 2,900 miles (4,640 km.).

THE SHORT S-25 SUNDERLAND CIVIL TRANSPORT.

A number of Short Sunderlands were supplied to the British Overseas Airways Corpn. during the war to augment their fleet of oversea transports. Gun turrets have been removed and replaced by suitable fairings, all associated military equipment, including reconnaissance flares, etc., have been removed and the interior refitted to meet the requirements of British Airways.

Wings, Hull, Tail Unit, Power Plant and Dimensions.—Same as for Sunderland III.

Accommodation.—Crew's quarters on forward upper deck as for Sunderland. Lower deck adapted to seat a total of twenty passengers, retaining the galley as for the military version. Additional lavatory accommodation is provided, together with washing facilities, etc. Stowages have been added for three extra dinghies and lashing points provided for the carriage of freight.

Weights.—Weight empty 33,190 lbs. (15,070 kg.), Fuel (2,160 gallons)

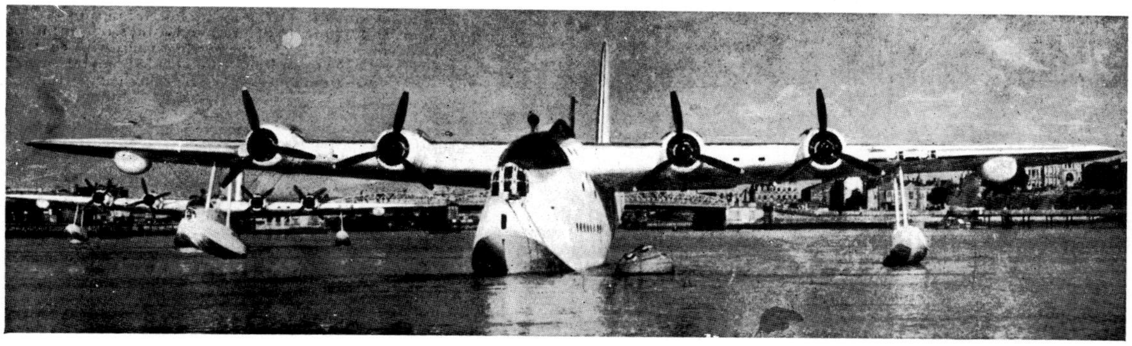

The Short Sunderland V General Reconnaissance Flying-boat* (four Pratt & Whitney Twin-Wasp engines).

15,552 lbs. (7,060 kg.), Oil (120 gallons) 1,080 lbs. (490 kg.), Crew of six 1,020 lbs. (463 kg.), Pay load 4,158 lbs. (1,887 kg.), Weight loaded 55,000 lbs. (24,970 kg.).

PERFORMANCE.—Same as for Sunderland.

THE SHORT S-25/V SANDRINGHAM.

The Sandringham is a four-engined civil flying-boat, the basic airframe of which does not differ from that of the civil conversion of the Sunderland III previously described. The modifications are confined to secondary structural changes and to the complete re-arrangement of the interior to accommodate twenty-four passengers by day and sixteen by night in more luxurious conditions than was provided in the wartime Sunderland conversion.

The bow and tail of the hull have been re-designed, completely eliminating the characteristics associated with the military version, and a mooring compartment has been provided in the bow with equipment closely following that of the "Empire" boat. The passenger accommodation is arranged on two decks, the general furnishings and finish fulfilling the requirements of the British Overseas Airways Corpn.

WINGS, HULL, TAIL UNIT AND DIMENSIONS.—Same as for Sunderland.

POWER PLANT.—Four Bristol Pegasus 38 nine-cylinder radial air-cooled engines each driving a three-blade D.H. Hydromatic constant-speed full-feathering airscrew. Fuel tanks in wings as in Sunderland. Maximum fuel capacity 2,032 Imp. gallons. Maximum oil capacity 138 Imp. gallons.

The Short Sunderland Civil Transport Flying-boat (four Bristol Pegasus engines).

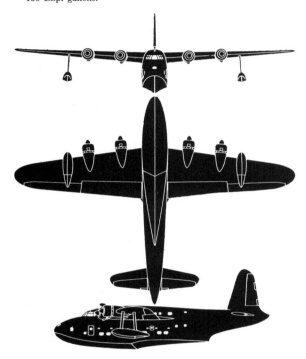

The Short Sandringham Flying-boat.

ACCOMMODATION.—Normal crew of seven, comprising two pilots, navigator, radio operator, flight engineer, purser and steward. Flight deck similar to that of Sunderland civil conversion. Two pilots side-by-side with dual controls. Navigator and radio operator behind pilots, the former facing to starboard and the latter to port. An Alco auxiliary power-unit is located on the flight deck between radio operator and the front spar frame. Flight engineer's position to starboard between spar frames and facing aft. Crew's rest station on port side with two bunks, table for meals, etc. Access to flight deck through hatch between pilot's seats and a hinging ladder providing communication to forward lavatory and purser's office on lower deck. Main passenger entrance on port side forward, with adjacent cloak-room. Three passenger cabins on lower deck seating a total of sixteen passengers or with night accommodation for a total of twelve. Between forward and mid cabins are, on starboard side, two dressing rooms and, on port side, lavatory and stowage for bed-linen. Between mid and after cabin is a thwartship staircase leading to upper deck, on which there is a buffet equipped with refrigerator, steam oven, sink and draining board, service lift to lower deck and snack bar, and a dining room seating eight passengers on settee-type seats. These seats can be converted into four additional bunks. Heating and ventilation, hot and cold running water in dressing rooms, electric lighting, points for electric razors in men's dressing room, etc. Two freight and mail compartments, a forward compartment with a capacity of 137 cu. ft. and an after compartment of 340 cu. ft. capacity. Four dinghies in wings, windows in cabin of push-out type.

WEIGHTS.—Tare weight 34,150 lbs. (15,505 kg.), Removable equipment 2,400 lbs. (1,090 kg.), Fuel and oil (1,115 mile—1,785 km. range) 7,640 lbs. (3,470 kg.), Crew (seven) 1,190 lbs. (540 kg.), Payload 8,197 lbs. (3,720 kg.), Weight loaded 53,577 lbs. (24,325 kg.), Maximum permissible take-off weight 56,000 lbs. (25,425 kg.), Landing weight 46,000 lbs. (20,885 kg.).

PERFORMANCE.—Maximum speed 216 m.p.h. (346 km.h.), Maximum economical cruising speed 184.5 m.p.h. (295 km.h.) at 9,000 ft. (2,745 m.), Initial rate of climb 557 ft./min. (170 m./min.), Service ceiling 14,150 ft. (4,320 m.), Absolute ceiling 16,150 ft. (4,925 m.), Cruising range in still air 1,115 miles (1,785 km.) at 158.5 m.p.h. (254 km.h.) at 10,000 ft. (3,050 m.), Maximum cruising range 1,575 miles (2,520 km.).

THE SHORT S-23 EMPIRE "C" CLASS FLYING-BOAT.

TYPE.—Four-engined Commercial Flying-boat.

WINGS.—High-wing cantilever monoplane. Structure consists of a central girder built-up of two spars of Hiduminium extruded sections braced by tubular struts and interconnected by light former ribs. Separate nose and tail sections of light alloy. Whole of the wings, with the exception of the ailerons, covered with smooth metal sheet with joggled joints and flush riveting. Flaps of the Gouge dragless type which, when open, provide additional wing area in addition to flap effect. When closed these flaps form a continuous surface with the main wing.

HULL.—Two-step type of typical Short construction with closely-spaced rings and continuous longitudinal stringers, the whole covered with smooth metal panels. Countersunk riveting and joggled lap joints used throughout.

TAIL UNIT.—Cantilever monoplane type. Light alloy framework, sheet-metal leading-edges, fabric covering. Movable surfaces on inset hinges. Trimming-tabs in elevators and rudder.

POWER PLANT.—Four Bristol Pegasus XC nine-cylinder radial air-cooled engines each developing a maximum output of 790 h.p. at 2,600 r.p.m. at 5,500 ft. (1,680 m.), a normal output of 740 h.p. at 2,250 r.p.m. at 3,500 ft. (1,070 m.) and a take-off output of 910 h.p. at 2,475 r.p.m. NACA type cowling-rings with controllable flaps. De Havilland two-pitch three-bladed metal airscrews.

ACCOMMODATION.—In extreme nose is the mooring compartment with retracting mooring bollard and landing-light. Immediately aft of this on the lower deck is a forward mail compartment for ½ ton of mail and accommodation for the flight clerk. Next are the buffet and lavatories. Buffet completely equipped for serving meals in the air and has ice-chest, hot-box, wine case, food cupboard, sink, plate-racks, etc. Aft of the buffet are the mid-ship cabin, the promenade cabin and the aft cabin. All cabins are luxuriously furnished, the chairs are adjustable in a number of positions and a table is provided for each seat. Cabins are illuminated with dome lights in the roof, with separate wall lamps for each passenger. Large windows are fitted in all cabins. Passengers enter the boat from the port side by doors in the smoking or promenade compartments. Baggage compartment, aft of the rear cabin, loaded through door on starboard side. On the upper deck there is, forward, the pilot's compartment with the captain and first officer seated side-by-side with dual controls. Immediately behind the pilot is the wireless operator, the navigator's table and the engineer. Also on the upper deck are the mail compartment, with outside door on starboard side, and a compartment for stowing the night equipment during the day time. For day flying the boat carries crew of five, seventeen passengers, baggage and 2 tons of mail. For night flying there is sleeping accommodation for twelve passengers.

DIMENSIONS.—Span 114 ft. (34.77 m.), Length 88 ft. (26.84 m.), Height (to top of fin) 31 ft. 9¾ ins. (9.68 m.), Wing area 1,500 sq. ft. (139.35 sq. m.).

WEIGHTS (Standard Type).—Weight empty 24,820 lbs. (11,268 kg.), Petrol (600 gallons) 4,470 lbs. (2,030 kg.), Oil (44 gallons) 400 lbs. (182 kg.), Equipment 2,810 lbs. (1,276 kg.), Pay load plus crew (5) 8,000 lbs. (3,632 kg.), Weight loaded 40,500 lbs. (18,375 kg.).

PERFORMANCE (Standard Type).—Maximum speed 200 m.p.h. (320 km.h.) at 5,500 ft. (1,680 m.), Maximum cruising speed 164 m.p.h. (265 km.h.), Minimum flying speed 73 m.p.h. (118 km.h.), Rate of climb at sea level (course pitch) 950 ft./min. (290 m./min.), Absolute ceiling 20,000 ft. (6,100 m.), Take-off time (full load) 21 secs., Range in still air 810 miles (1,300 km.).

THE SHORT S-30 EMPIRE MODIFIED "C" CLASS.

This class is generally similar to the standard "C" Class described above except that these boats are fitted with four 1,010 h.p. Bristol Pegasus 22 engines. Their structure has been strengthened to permit a full C. of A. loaded weight of 53,000 lbs. (24,062 kg.).

TYPE, WINGS, HULL, TAIL UNIT.—Same as for "C" Class.

POWER PLANT.—Four Bristol Pegasus 22 nine-cylinder radial air-cooled engines. Maximum power 865 b.h.p. at 2,600 r.p.m. at 6,500 ft. (1,980 m.), Rated power 680 b.h.p. at 2,250 r.p.m. at 8,000 ft. (2,440 m.), Take-off power 1,010 b.h.p. NACA type cowling rings with controllable flaps. De Havilland three-bladed constant-speed metal airscrews.

ACCOMMODATION AND DIMENSIONS.—Same as for "C" Class.

WEIGHTS.—Weight empty 27,825 lbs. (12,632 kg.), Petrol (1,410 gallons) 10,500 lbs. (4,767 kg.), Oil (90 gallons) 810 lbs. (368 kg.), Equipment 2,615 lbs. (1,187 kg.), Pay load and crew 6,250 lbs. (2,838 kg.), Weight loaded 48,000 lbs. (21,792 kg.).

WEIGHTS.—Weight empty 27,180 lbs. (12,340 kg.), Petrol (2,430 gallons) 18,100 lbs. (8,217 kg.), Oil (170 gallons) 1,530 lbs. (695 kg.), Equipment 1,920 lbs. (872 kg.), Pay load and crew 4,270 lbs. (1,938 kg.), Weight loaded 53,000 lbs. (24,062 kg.).

PERFORMANCE.—Same as for "C" Class, except Maximum Range in still air 1,870 miles (2,992 km.).

The Short Empire Modified "C" Class Flying-boat (four Bristol Pegasus engines).

The Short Seaford General Reconnaissance Flying-boat (four Bristol Hercules 100 engines).

THE SHORT S.45 SEAFORD.

The Seaford has been developed from the Sunderland III, the original designation for the S.45 being Sunderland IV. Designed to operate at an all-up weight of 75,000 lbs. (34,020 kg.), the hull has been given a bigger planing bottom with a 1 ft. increase in beam, a 3 ft. increase in length forward of the main step and a corresponding increase in length aft. The wings, of the Sunderland III type, have been strengthened and the tail-unit modified with a dihedral tailplane and a dorsal fin added to the standard Sunderland fin.

The original Sunderland IV power-plant consisted of four Bristol Hercules XVII Engines but in the Seaford these have been replaced by Hercules 100 units. Four-blade D.H. Hydromatic full-feathering airscrews are fitted.

The armament consists of two .50 in. machine-guns in a Brockhouse power turret and four fixed .303 in. guns in the nose of the hull ; two 20 m/m. cannon in a B-17 type mid-upper turret two .50 in. beam guns ; and two .50 in. guns in a Glenn Martin tail turret. Bomb and depth-charge loads and stowage are the same as for the Sunderland III.

DIMENSIONS.—Span as for Sunderland III, Length 88 ft. 6¾ in. (27.1 m.), Height (to top of fin) 34 ft. 3¼ in. (10.45 m.), Wing area as for Sunderland III.

WEIGHTS AND LOADINGS.—Tare weight 45,000 lbs. (20,450 kg.), Typical service load (including crew) 8,200 lbs. (3,730 kg.), Petrol and oil 21,800 lbs. (9,880 kg.), Normal loaded weight 75,000 lbs. (34,020 kg.), Wing loading 44.5 lbs./sq. ft. (217 kg./sq. m.), Power loading 10.9 lbs./h.p. (4.95 kg./h.p.).

PERFORMANCE.—Maximum speed 242 m.p.h. (389 km.h.) at 500 ft. (152 m.), Maximum economical cruising speed 207 m.p.h. (333 km.h.) at 7,000 ft. (2,135 m.), Initial rate of climb 875 ft./min. (267 m./min.), Service ceiling 13,000 ft. (3,960 m.), Normal range in still air 2,800 miles (4,500 km.), Overload range in still air 3,100 miles (4,980 km.).

SHORT & HARLAND.

SHORT & HARLAND, LTD.

HEAD OFFICE AND WORKS : QUEEN'S ISLAND, BELFAST, NORTHERN IRELAND.

General Manager : W. Browning.

Short & Harland, Ltd., was formed in Belfast in June, 1936, as the result of an agreement between Short Bros. (Rochester and Bedford), Ltd., and Harland & Wolff, Ltd. the well-known shipbuilders, to form a new company to build both land and marine aircraft in Belfast.

Since the firm began operating large orders for Hereford, Bombay, Stirling and Sunderland aircraft have been completed.

SUPERMARINE.

VICKERS-ARMSTRONGS, LTD.

SUPERMARINE WORKS : SOUTHAMPTON.
LONDON OFFICE : VICKERS HOUSE, BROADWAY, WESTMINSTER, S.W.1.

Directors : See under "Vickers-Armstrongs."
General Manager : Sq. Cdr. Sir James Bird, O.B.E., R.N.
Chief Designer : J. Smith.

The original Supermarine Company was formed in 1912 and its efforts were chiefly devoted to the production of sea-going aircraft. The firm also specialised in the design and production of high-speed seaplanes and it earned the enviable reputation of winning the Schneider Trophy Contest four times.

The 1922 Contest at Naples was won by the Supermarine Sea Lion Mk. II flying-boat at an average speed of 146 m.p.h. In the 1927 Contest two Supermarine S.5 seaplanes came first and second at average speeds of 281.65 and 273.07 m.p.h. respectively.

The 1929 Contest was won by the Supermarine S.6 at an average speed of 328.63 m.p.h. The S.6 later put the World's Speed Record up to 357.7 m.p.h. and the same type also held the Speed Records over 50 and 100 kilometres.

In the 1931 Contest the Supermarine S.6B won the Schneider Trophy outright for Great Britain at a speed of 340.08 m.p.h. and raised the World's Record for speed over 100 kilometres to 342.7 m.p.h. On the same day another machine of the same type raised the World's Speed Record to 379.05 m.p.h.

On Sept. 29, 1931, the machine which won the Schneider Trophy, but fitted with a special "sprint" engine, raised the World's Speed Record to 407.5 m.p.h.

In November, 1928, Vickers (Aviation), Ltd. took over the control of the Supermarine Aviation Works, Ltd. In October, 1938, the Supermarine Aviation Works (Vickers), Ltd., was, with its parent company Vickers (Aviation), Ltd., taken over by Vickers-Armstrongs, Ltd.

The prototype of the Spitfire, the company's first landplane to go into production, first flew in March, 1936, and since that time it has undergone continuous development to maintain its place in the front rank of the World's fighter aircraft.

In six years of war the power of the Spitfire increased by 100 per cent, its weight by 40 per cent., its maximum speed by 35 per cent and its rate of climb by 80 per cent. Total production of the Spitfire, of which some twenty-nine different versions were built during the war, amounted to 21,000, including naval Seafires and 305 Spitfires built before the war.

The Spitfire has operated in many overseas theatres of war, including Italy, Malta, the Middle East, India and Australia. Apart from being a standard fighter type in the R.A.F. and the Dominion Air Forces, it has also been used by the Air Forces of France, Poland, Norway, the Netherlands, Yugoslavia, Belgium, Russia and the United States. Over 700 Spitfires were supplied to the U.S. Army Air Forces under reverse Lend/Lease.

The naval version of the Spitfire, known as the Seafire, went into service with the Fleet Air Arm in 1942.

The latest Supermarine fighter, which was developed too late

to participate in the war, is the Spiteful, a worthy successor to the Spitfire with a speed in excess of 460 m.p.h. (736 km.h.). Brief details and illustrations were released just before these pages were closed for the press.

On the marine side, the Walrus boat amphibian, which was originally adopted by the Admiralty as standard equipment for all catapult-equipped ships in 1936, was still in production during the first years of the war and was in service throughout the war. Many hundreds of British, American and even German and Italian air crews owe their lives to the Walrus amphibians of the R.A.F. Air/Sea Rescue units serving at home and overseas.

In 1940 the Sea Otter, a development of the Walrus, appeared. This general purpose amphibian was designed for duties similar to those of its predecessor and latterly was also employed on Air/Sea Rescue duties both in home and Far Eastern waters.

THE SUPERMARINE SPITEFUL.

The Spiteful, which was designed to meet the F.1/43 specification, is a direct descendant of the Spitfire. Although it retains something of the general character of its predecessor, the Spiteful is a completely new design with many new and distinctive features. These include wings with straight-tapered leading and trailing-edges and squared tips, larger tailplane and larger fin and rudder, a wide-track landing-gear with the wheels retracting inwardly, wider and shallower radiator ducts under the wings, and a more streamlined fuselage which lacks the straight top line of the Spitfire. With a Rolls-Royce Griffon engine the Spiteful is credited with a maximum level speed of over 460 m.p.h. (736 km.h.). Armament consists of four 20 m/m. cannon.

DIMENSIONS.—Span 35 ft. 6 in. (10.83 m.), Length 32 ft. 4 in. (9.86 m.).

The Supermarine Spiteful Single-seat Fighter (Rolls-Royce Griffon engine).

THE SUPERMARINE SPITFIRE.

The first Supermarine aeroplane to bear the name Spitfire was a single-seat fighter designed to meet the Air Ministry F.7/30 specification. It was a low-wing cantilever monoplane with fixed landing-gear and was fitted with a 600 h.p. Rolls-Royce Goshawk engine. From this type, which was not successful, was evolved as a Private Venture a new prototype to which the name Spitfire was transferred and around which the Air Ministry F.37/34 specification was written. Into this prototype Mr. R. J. Mitchell incorporated the fruitful results of the experience gained in the design of his series of high-speed seaplanes which had previously won three successive Schneider Trophy Contests and established three World's Speed Records.

The prototype F.37/34 Spitfire, which was fitted with one of the first Rolls-Royce Merlin engines, flew in March, 1936. With a fixed-pitch wooden airscrew the prototype had a maximum speed of 342 m.p.h. (547.2 km.h.), which classed it at that time as the fastest military aeroplane in the World.

The soundness of the basic design has been proved in six years of war, throughout which the Rolls-Royce-engined Spitfire has, in its many progressive developments, remained a first-line fighter. Apart from its fighter duties the Spitfire has also been used for the past six years for photographic-reconnaissance. The first photographic mission by an unarmed Spitfire was made on November 18, 1939.

Hereafter are enumerated the successive stages in the development of the Spitfire :—

Spitfire I. Rolls-Royce Merlin III engine. First fitted with a two-blade wood fixed-pitch airscrew. Subsequently replaced by a D.H. three-blade duralumin two-position controllable-pitch airscrew, and later by a D.H. three-blade duralumin bracket-type controllable-pitch airscrew. Armament : (Mk. IA) eight .303 in. machine-guns, or (Mk. IB) two 20 m/m. cannon and four .303 in. guns, all in the wings. First production deliveries to Nos. 19 and 66 (F) Squadrons in 1938. Dimensions : Span 36 ft. 10 in. (11.23 m.), Length 29 ft. 11 in. (9.12 m.).

Spitfire II. Rolls-Royce Merlin XII engine driving a Rotol three-blade constant-speed airscrew. Mks. IIA and IIB otherwise similar to Mks. IA and IB respectively.

Spitfire III. Rolls-Royce Merlin XX engine with two-speed supercharger and driving a three-blade Rotol constant-speed airscrew. Strengthened spar and landing-gear and retractable tail-wheel. Only two built, one with clipped wings and an armament of eight .303 in. machine-guns and the other with "universal" wings permitting the installation of either eight machine-guns, two 20 m/m. cannon and four machine-guns, or four 20 m/m. cannon.

Spitfire P.R. III. Photographic reconnaissance model. Mk. IA airframe modified for additional fuel in the port wing and rear fuselage. Camera mounted in starboard wing. No armament or radio.

Spitfire IV. Rolls-Royce Griffon IIB engine. The first installation of the Griffon engine in the Spitfire. Airframe completely redesigned. Only one built. First flew in 1941. Later redesignated Spitfire XX.

Spitfire P.R. IV. Rolls-Royce Merlin 45 engine. Mk. IA airframe with wings modified for large leading-edge fuel tanks

A Supermarine Spitfire VB with clipped wings as supplied to the U.S.A.A.F. in the British Isles for training purposes.

and wing oil tank. No armament. Extra oxygen. Three F-24 cameras, two vertical and one oblique, all carried in the fuselage.

Spitfire V. Rolls-Royce Merlin 45, 46, 50, 50A, 55 or 56 engine. Rotol or D.H. three-blade constant-speed airscrew. In other respects Mks. VA and VB similar to Mks. IA and IB respectively. Mk. VC fitted with universal wings with a normal armament of two 20 m/m. cannon and four machine-guns. Mk. V went into service in the Summer of 1941 and was the first mark to be fitted with tropical equipment, to carry drop tanks (on VB and VC), and the first to serve outside the British Isles. In 1942 one Mk. VB was modified into a prototype fighter-seaplane with twin floats, a modified upper fin and an additional lower fin. In 1943 the Mk. V was fitted with clipped wings and the Merlin 45M, 50M or 55M engine for service as a low-altitude fighter, and provision was made for carrying a 250 lb. or 500 lb. bomb on the drop tank fittings. Dimensions : Span (standard wing) 36 ft. 10 in. (11.23 m.), Span (clipped wing) 32 ft. 7 in. (9.93 m.), Length 29 ft. 11 in. (9.12 m.).

Spitfire VI. Rolls-Royce Merlin 47 engine driving a Rotol four-blade constant-speed airscrew. Similar to Mk. VB but incorporating a pressure cabin, strengthened spar and extended wing-tips. Dimensions : Span 40 ft. 2 in. (12.24 m.), Length 29 ft. 11 in. (9.12 m.).

Spitfire VII. Rolls-Royce Merlin 61, 64 or 71 engine with two-speed two-stage supercharger. Rotol four-blade constant-speed airscrew. Nose lengthened to take the longer engine, strengthened engine mounting and fuselage, pressure cabin, larger rudder and retractable tail-wheel. Wings with small leading-edge tanks for additional fuel, and extended tips as in Mk. VI. Strengthened spar and landing-gear. Twin radiator ducts, one under each wing, the port duct accommodating a coolant radiator and oil cooler and the starboard duct a coolant radiator and supercharger intercooler. Armament : two 20 m/m. cannon and four machine-guns. Dimensions : Span 40 ft. 2 in. (12.24 m.), Length 31 ft. 3½ in. (9.54 m.).

Spitfire P.R. VII. Rolls-Royce Merlin 45 engine. Mk. IA airframe modified for additional fuel in the rear fuselage. No wing tanks. Three F.24 cameras, two vertical and one oblique. No radio. Armament : eight .303 in. machine-guns.

Spitfire VIII. Rolls-Royce Merlin 61, 63, 63A, 66 or 70 engine. Basically the same as the Mk. VII but without pressure cabin. In three standard versions—the standard fighter F.VIII with Merlin 61, 63 or 63A engine and standard wings ; the low-altitude fighter L.F. VIII with Merlin 66 engine and standard wings ; and the high-altitude fighter H.F. VIII with the Merlin 70 engine and extended span wings. Armament : two 20 m/m. cannon and four machine-guns. All fitted with the new pointed rudder and retractable tail-wheel. Into service in 1943. All fitted with tropical equipment and sent to the Mediterranean, India and the Far East. Dimensions : Span (standard wings) 36 ft. 10 in. (11.23 m.), Span (extended span wings) 40 ft. 2 in. (12.24 m.), Length 31 ft. 3½ in. (9.54 m.).

Spitfire IX. Rolls-Royce Merlin 61, 63, 63A, 66 or 70 engine. Basically similar to the Mk. VC but with the Mk. VII engine and radiator installation. Normal armament : two 20 m/m. cannon and four machine-guns. Tropical equipment. Into service late in 1942, before the Mk. VIII. In three versions—the standard fighter F. IX with the Merlin 61, 63 or 63A engine and standard wings ; the low-altitude fighter L.F. IX with the Merlin 66 engine and clipped wings ; and the high-altitude fighter H.F. IX with the Merlin 70 engine and standard wings. Ultimately Mk. IX versions were adapted to take the new "E" wings with an armament of two 20 m/m. cannon and two .50 in. machine-guns and with wing racks for two 250 lb. bombs. Later aircraft were also fitted with the larger pointed rudder. One Mk. IX was converted into a twin-float seaplane prototype in 1942. Dimensions : Span (standard wings) 36 ft. 10 in. (11.23 m.), Span (clipped wings) 32 ft. 7 in. (9.93 m.), Length 31 ft. 3½ in. (9.54 m.).

Spitfire P.R.X. Rolls-Royce Merlin 64 or 71 engine. Rotol four-blade airscrew. Mk. VII fuselage (pressure cabin) and engine installation and Mk. VC wings modified for large leading-edge tanks for additional fuel. Retractable tail-wheel. All have the larger pointed rudder. No armament. Universal camera installation consisting of either two vertical F.52 or F.8 cameras or two vertical and one oblique F.24 cameras.

Spitfire P.R. XI. Rolls-Royce Merlin 61, 63, 63A or 70 engine. Fuselage as Mk. VC modified for Mk. VII engine installation and wings as for P.R.X. Tropical equipment and universal camera installation.

The Supermarine Spitfire VII High-altitude Fighter, the first to be fitted with a Rolls-Royce Merlin 60 Series engine.

An Experimental Spitfire VIII with a rear-view cockpit canopy, the first to be fitted to a Spitfire.

The Supermarine Spitfire F.R. XIV E Fighter-Reconnaissance Monoplane (Rolls-Royce Griffon 65 engine).

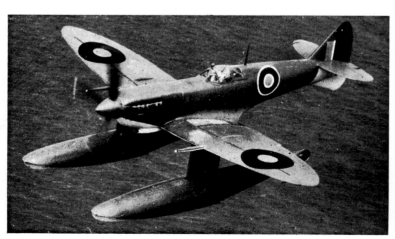

An Experimental Spitfire IX Float Seaplane.

Spitfire XII. Rolls-Royce Griffon III or IV engine. Rotol four-blade constant-speed airscrew. Basically similar to the Mk. VC but with clipped wings, strengthened fuselage, Mk. IV engine-mounting, pointed rudder and, on later aircraft, a retractable tail-wheel. Normal armament : two 20 m/m. cannon and four machine-guns. Dimensions : Span 32 ft. 7 in. (9.93 m.), Length 31 ft. 10 in. (9.7 m.).

Spitfire P.R. XIII. Rolls-Royce Merlin 32 engine. Basically similar to the Mk. VB except for power-plant. Provision for drop tanks. Armament : four .303 in. machine-guns. Three F.24 cameras, two vertical and one oblique.

Spitfire XIV. Rolls-Royce Griffon 65 engine with two-speed two-stage supercharger. Rotol five-blade constant-speed airscrew. Mk. VIII fuselage with new engine mounting and cowling, Mk. VIII wings, and new fin and rudder of larger area. In three versions—the standard fighter F. XIV with armament of two 20 m/m. cannon and four .303 in. machine-guns ; the standard fighter F.XIV E with "E" armament of two 20 m/m. cannon and two .50 in. machine-guns and, on later aircraft, rear-view hood ; and the fighter reconnaissance F.R. XIV E with clipped wings, "E" armament, rear-view hood, additional fuel in the rear fuselage

and one oblique F.24 camera in the fuselage aft of the pilot's cockpit. Provision for one 250 lb. or 500 lb. bomb on fuselage drop tank fittings and, on some aircraft, one 250 lb. bomb under each wing. Into service in 1944. The Mk. XIV was responsible for destroying more than 300 flying-bombs. Length 32 ft. 8 in. (9.96 m.).

Spitfire XVI. Packard-built Merlin 266 engine and four-blade airscrew. The Merlin 266 is the equivalent of the British-built Merlin 66. Low-altitude fighter with clipped wings similar to the L.F. IX E but fitted with the new pointed rudder. Armament : two 20 m/m. cannon and two .50 in. machine-guns. Racks for two 250 lb. bombs under the wings and one 250 lb. or 500 lb. bomb under the fuselage on the drop tank fittings. Some later aircraft fitted with rear-view hood and additional fuel in the rear fuselage. Dimensions : Span 32 ft. 7 in. (9.93 m.), Length 31 ft. 3 in. (9.53 m.).

Spitfire P.R.XIX. Rolls-Royce Griffon 65 or 66 engine driving a Rotol five-blade airscrew. Photographic-reconnaissance version of the Mk. XIV with wings modified for additional fuel. Rear-view hood. Universal camera installation. Maximum speed 460 m.p.h. (736 km.h.), Ceiling over 43,000 ft. (13,120 m.), Range 1,500 miles (2,400 km.).

Spitfire 22. Similar to Mk. 21 but fitted with "blister" type rear-view hood.

Spitfire XX. Rolls-Royce Griffon IIB engine. See Spitfire IV.

Spitfire 21. Rolls-Royce Griffon 61, 64 or 85 engine. Extended span wings of new shape with ailerons extended into tips. Longer oleo legs and wing fairing flaps for wheel wells. Armament : four 20 m/m. cannon, two in each wing. Span : 40 ft. 2 in. (12.24 m.), Wing area : 248 sq. ft. (23 sq. m.).

TYPE.—Single-seat Fighter.

WINGS.—Low-wing cantilever monoplane. Standard wings are elliptical in plan and taper in thickness, but shorter span wings with squared tips or extended span wings with pointed tips may be fitted. Structure is chiefly of light alloy. Single spar with tubular flanges and a plate web. Forward of the spar the wing is covered with heavy-gauge light alloy sheet which forms, with the spar, a stiff and strong torsion box. Aft of the spar a thinner gauge covering is supported by light alloy girder ribs. Standard wings have detachable wing-tips. Split flaps between ailerons and fuselage.

FUSELAGE.—All-metal monocoque. Structure consists of transverse frames, four main longerons, intercostal longitudinals and a flush-riveted "Alclad" skin. Foremost frame forms a fire-proof bulkhead and has built into it the centre-portion of the main wing spar. After portion of fuselage incorporating the fin and tailplane is detachable.

TAIL UNIT.—Cantilever monoplane type. Fin integral with the rear portion of the fuselage. All-metal tailplane with smooth skin covering. Elevators and rudder have light alloy frames and fabric covering. Trimming-tabs in elevators and rudder.

LANDING GEAR.—Retractable type. Consists of two Vickers cantilever oleo-pneumatic shock-absorber legs, which are raised outwardly into the underside of the wings. Hydraulic retraction with emergency device for lowering wheels in case of failure of normal system. Fully-castoring tail-wheel, retractable in some Marks.

POWER PLANT.—One Rolls-Royce Merlin or Griffon twelve-cylinder Vee liquid-cooled engine on steel tube mounting. Three, four or five-blade airscrew (see details above). Two fuel tanks (85 Imp. gallons) in fuselage with direct feed to engine pumps. Some marks have additional fuel in wings or rear fuselage (see above). Auxiliary fuel tank may be carried beneath fuselage.

ACCOMMODATION.—Enclosed cockpit over wing. Sliding canopy and hinged panel in port side of fuselage for entry or exit. Adjustable seat and rudder pedals. Tropical versions have improved cockpit ventilation and stowage for desert equipment, water and emergency rations behind cockpit. Pressure cockpit in certain Marks.

ARMAMENT.—Two 20 m/m. British Hispano cannon and four 0.303 in. or two .50-in. Browning machine-guns, or four 20 m/m. British Hispano cannon, all in wings. Racks under each wing for one 250-lb. bomb and/or under fuselage for one 250 or 500-lb. bomb.

DIMENSIONS.—See descriptions of various Marks.

WEIGHTS AND PERFORMANCE.—See Table.

THE SUPERMARINE SEAFIRE.

The Seafire is the Naval version of the Spitfire specially adapted for operation from aircraft-carriers. It has folding wings and is provided with catapult spools, deck-arrester hook and other specialised equipment. Constructional details are similar to those of the Spitfire previously described.

The following are the four production versions of the Seafire concerning which details were available for publication at the time of closing down for press (for later Marks see Addenda) :—

Seafire I. Rolls-Royce Merlin 32, 45 or 46 engine driving a constant-speed airscrew. Conversion of the Spitfire VA. Fixed wings. Arrester-hook and catapult spools. Armament : eight .303 in. machine-guns.

Seafire II. Rolls-Royce Merlin 32, 45, 46, 48, 50 or 55 engine driving a Rotol constant-speed airscrew. Same as Mk. I except fitted with an armament of two 20 m/m. cannon and four .303 in. machine-guns. May also be fitted with the universal wing permitting the alternative installation of four 20 m/m. cannon and the carriage of wing bombs.

Seafire III. Rolls-Royce Merlin 45, 46, 50, 55 or 56 engine driving a Rotol constant-speed airscrew. Similar to Mk. II except fitted with folding wings. Wings hinge upward inboard of cannon to beyond the vertical and tips hinge outward to a horizontal position.

Seafire XV. Rolls-Royce Griffon VI engine driving a Rotol four-blade airscrew. Fuselage and tail-unit similar to Spitfire XIV. Strengthened Mk. III folding wings. Deck-arrester gear. Standard armament of two 20 m/m. cannon and four .303 in. machine-guns. Can carry one 500 lb. bomb.

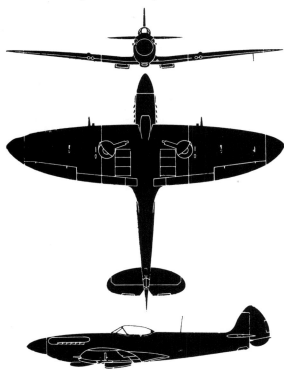

The Supermarine Seafire F. Mk. XVII Naval Fighter.

Mark	Power-plant	Function	Weight loaded (lbs.)	Max. speed (m.p.h.) at operational height	Normal range (miles)	Ceiling (ft.)	Remarks
Spitfire IA	Merlin II or III	Fighter	5,332	367	—	—	
Spitfire IB	Merlin III	Fighter	5,784	—	—	—	
Spitfire IIA	Merlin XII	Fighter	6,317	—	—	—	
Spitfire IIB	Merlin XII	Fighter	6,527	—	—	—	
Spitfire P.R. IV	Merlin 45 or 46	Photo-Reconnaissance	7,178	372	1,460	38,000	Unarmed
Spitfire VA	Merlin 45 or 46	Fighter	6,417		VB { 45=480 46=460 }	{ 45=37,000 46=38,000 }	First to be fitted with fuselage drop tank or bomb
Spitfire VB	Merlin 45 or 46	Fighter	6,622	45=369			
Spitfire VC	Merlin 45 or 46	Fighter	6,785	46=365	VC { 45=470 46=450 }		
Spitfire F. VI	Merlin 47	Fighter	6,797	364	475	40,000	
Spitfire F. VII	Merlin 61 or 64	Fighter	7,875	408	660	43,000	
Spitfire H.F. VII	Merlin 71	High-alt. Fighter	7,875	416	660	44,000	
Spitfire P.R. VII	Merlin 45 or 46	Photo-Reconnaissance	6,585	369	710	37,000	8×.303 in. m.g.
Spitfire F. VIII	Merlin 61, 63 or 63A	Fighter and Fighter-Bomber	7,767	408	660	43,000	
Spitfire L.F. VIII	Merlin 66	Low-alt. Fighter	7,767	404	660	41,500	
Spitfire H.F. VIII	Merlin 70	High-alt. Fighter	7,767	416	660	44,000	
Spitfire F. IX	Merlin 61 or 63	Fighter	7,300	over 400	434	40,000	May be fitted with "E" armament
Spitfire L.F. IX	Merlin 66	Low-alt. Fighter	7,300	404	434	42,500	
Spitfire H.F. IX	Merlin 70	High-alt. Fighter	7,300	416	434	45,000	
Spitfire P.R. X	Merlin 64 or 77	Photo-Reconnaissance	8,159	416	1,370	43,000	Unarmed
Spitfire P.R. XI	Merlin 61, 63, 63A or 70	Photo-Reconnaissance	7,872	422	over 1,200	44,000	Unarmed
Spitfire F. XII	Griffon III or IV	Fighter and Fighter-Bomber	7,280	393	329	40,000	
Spitfire P.R. XIII	Merlin 32	Photo-Reconnaissance	6,364	348	500	38,000	4×.303 in. m.g.
Spitfire F. XIV	Griffon 65	F., F.B. or F. Recco.	8,490	over 450	{ F.XIV=460 FR.XIV=620 }	over 40,000	May be fitted with "E" armament
Spitfire F. XVI	Merlin 266	L.A. Fighter or Fighter-Bomber	7,300	over 400	434	40,000	

The Supermarine Spitfire P.R. Mk. XIX Photographic-Reconnaissance Monoplane (Rolls-Royce Griffon 65 engine).

The Supermarine Spitfire F. Mk. 22 Single-seat Fighter (Rolls-Royce 61 engine).

Mark	Dimensions			Wing Area (sq. ft.)	Weight loaded (lbs.)	Performance	
	Span	Length	Height			Max. Speed (m.p.h.)	Rate of Climb (ft./min.)
SPITFIRE F. XVIII	36 ft. 10 in.	32 ft. 8 in.	12 ft. 8 in.	242	9,320	440	5,012
SPITFIRE F.R. XVIII	36 ft. 10 in.	32 ft. 8 in.	12 ft. 8 in.	242	9,280	440	5,044
SPITFIRE P.R. XIX	36 ft. 10 in.	32 ft. 8 in.	12 ft. 8 in.	242	9,040	446	5,227
SPITFIRE F. 21	36 ft. 11 in.	32 ft. 8 in.	13 ft. 6 in.	244	9,400	450	4,220
SPITFIRE F. 22	36 ft. 11 in.	32 ft. 11 in.	13 ft. 6 in.	244	9,900	450	4,880
SEAFIRE F. XV	36 ft. 10 in.	31 ft. 10 in.	10 ft. 8½ in.	242	8,000	391	4,680
SEAFIRE F.R. XVII	36 ft. 11 in.	32 ft. 3 in.	13 ft. 6 in.	242	8,020	395	4,680
SEAFIRE F. XVIII	36 ft. 11 in.	32 ft. 3 in.	13 ft. 6 in.	242	8,370	411	4,820
SEAFIRE F. 45	36 ft. 11 in.	33 ft. 4 in.	13 ft. 6 in.	243	9,360	446	5,270
SEAFIRE F. 46	36 ft. 11 in.	33 ft. 4 in.	13 ft. 6 in.	243	9,730	449	5,490
SEAFIRE F. 47	36 ft. 11 in.	33 ft. 4 in.	13 ft. 6 in.	243	10,000	453	5,243

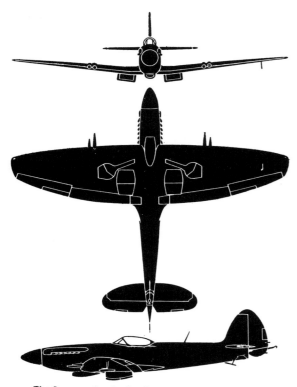

The Supermarine Seafire F. Mk. 47 Naval Fighter.

Seafire XVII. Rolls-Royce Griffon VI engine with increased maximum and take-off boost. Similar to the Mk. XV but fitted with a rear-view hood and "sting" type arrester hook in the lower portion of the rudder. Improved landing gear. The F.Mk.XVII is the standard four-cannon fighter. The F.R.Mk. XVII is similar but is fitted with two cameras, one vertical and one oblique, in the fuselage.

Seafire XVIII. Rolls-Royce Griffon 36 engine. Similar to the Mk. XVII except for engine change.

Seafire 45. Rolls-Royce Griffon 61 engine driving a Rotol five-blade airscrew. Naval adaptation of the Spitfire 21 with the old type cockpit hooding. Fitted with "sting" type hook. Non-folding wings.

Seafire 46. Rolls-Royce Griffon 61 or 64 engine driving a Rotol five-blade airscrew, or a Griffon 85 engine driving two Rotol three-blade contra-rotating airscrews. Similar to Mk. 45 but with Spitfire 22 fuselage and rear-view hood. Non-folding wings.

Seafire 47. Rolls-Royce Griffon 85 engine driving two three-blade contra-rotating airscrews. Similar to Mk. 46 but fitted with folding wings, new flaps and increased fuel tankage. The F.Mk.47 is the standard four-cannon fighter. The F.R.Mk.47 is similar but fitted with two cameras, one vertical and one oblique, in the fuselage. Provision for rockets or three 500 lb. bombs.

DIMENSIONS.—Span 36 ft. 10 in. (11.23 m.), Length 31 ft. 10 in. (9.7 m.), Wing area 242 sq. ft. (22.5 sq. m.).
WEIGHT LOADED.—About 8,000 lbs. (3,632 kg.).
PERFORMANCE.—Maximum speed over 400 m.p.h. (640 km.h.), Ceiling over 35,000 ft. (10,675 m.).

THE SUPERMARINE SEAFANG.

The Seafang is a Naval adaptation of the Spiteful, the necessary modifications being covered by Specification N.5/45.

There are two versions of the Seafang, the F.Mk.31, which is virtually a hooked Spiteful with a Rolls-Royce Griffon 69 engine driving a Rotol five-blade airscrew, and the F.Mk.32, the production version with folding wings, increased tankage, wider landing gear, accelerating equipment and a Rolls-Royce Griffon 89 engine driving two three-blade contra-rotating airscrews.

The general structure of the Seafang is identical to that of the Spiteful. The wings of the Seafang 32 are of the upward-folding type and folding is by hydraulic power under the control of the pilot so that the operation can be undertaken without outside assistance while the aircraft is taxying to and from the aircraft-carrier lifts.

The arrester hook is of the "sting" type in the lower portion of the rudder. This type of hook, which is also fitted to the later marks of Seafire, when it catches in the arrester wires keeps the tail down and avoids the tendency of the V-type hook, which is normally mounted under the fuselage, to let the nose drop after hooking on with consequent risk of damage to the airscrew.

Armament of the Seafang consists of four 20 m/m. cannon, two in each wing.

DIMENSIONS.—Span 35 ft. (10.67 m.), Length 32 ft. 11¼ in. (10 m.). Height (tail down) 13 ft. 5 in. (4.08 m.), Wing area 210 sq. ft, (19.5 sq. m.).
PERFORMANCE.—Maximum speed 450 m.p.h. (720 km.h.) at 21,000 ft. (6,400 m.), Climb to 20,000 ft. (6,100 m.) 6 min., Maximum range 730 miles (1,170 km.).

THE SUPERMARINE SEA OTTER.

The Sea Otter I, which first appeared on 1940, was designed to replace the Walrus on naval spotting, reconnaissance and general purpose duties. It is also being employed on Air/Sea Rescue

The Supermarine Seafire IIC Single-seat Naval Fighter (Rolls-Royce Merlin 48 engine).

The Supermarine Seafire F. Mk. 45 Single-seat Naval Fighter (Rolls-Royce Griffon 61 engine).

The Supermarine Sea Otter Amphibian Flying-boat (870 h.p. Bristol Mercury 30 engine).

duties at home and abroad as the A.S.R. Mk. II.

The Sea Otter is a boat amphibian with an hydraulically retractable landing-gear and catapulting arrangements similar to those used in the Walrus. It has single-bay folding wings and a cantilever tailplane mounted half way up the fin. The structure is mixed, with an all-metal hull, fabric-covered wings with metal spars and wooden ribs, a plywood-covered tailplane and fabric-covered elevators and rudder.

It is fitted with an 870 h.p. Bristol Mercury 30 radial air-cooled engine mounted as a tractor and driving a three-blade Rotol constant-speed airscrew. The two main fuel tanks are located in the roots of the upper wings. An auxiliary fuel tank may be installed in the hull.

Accommodation is provided for a crew of three or four and armament consists of three .303 in. Vickers "K" machine-guns. Bombs or depth-charges may be carried on two universal carriers, one under each lower wing.

DIMENSIONS.—Span 46 ft. (14 m.). Length 39 ft. 4¾ in. (12 m.), Height (on wheels and tail down) 16 ft. 2 in. (4.9 m.), Wing area 610 sq. ft (56.6 sq. m.).
WEIGHT LOADED.—10,000 lbs. (4,540 kg.) approx.
PERFORMANCE.—No data available.

THE SUPERMARINE WALRUS.

The Walrus originally appeared in 1933 under the name Seagull V and was supplied to the Australian Government under that name. In 1935 it was adopted by the Admiralty as the standard A.B.R. (amphibian-boat-reconnaissance) type for employment in all ships equipped with catapults. It was re-named Walrus by the Admiralty.

Apart from service in ships of the Royal Navy, the Walrus has been and is still being used for training, communications duties and on Air/Sea Rescue duties at home and overseas.

There are two versions of the Walrus. The Mk. I is the original metal-hulled version and the Mk. II, built by Saunders-Roe, Ltd., is fitted with a wooden hull. In all other respects both marks are identical.

TYPE.—Single-engined Amphibian Flying-boat.
WINGS.—Equal-span single-bay biplane. Small centre-section carried on engine-mounting struts. Outer wings fold round rear spar hinges on centre-section and hull. One pair of parallel interplane struts on either side. Wing structure consists of two stainless steel spars, with tubular flanges and corrugated webs, and a subsidiary structure of spruce and three-ply. Plywood leading-edge and fabric covering. Inset ailerons on all four wings,

HULL.—Flat-sided single-step hull of anodically-treated aluminium-alloy. Normal Supermarine system of construction. Wing-tip floats of similar construction.

TAIL UNIT.—Monoplane type. Tail-plane carried on top of fin built integral with hull. Tail-plane, elevators and rudder built of steel spars and wooden ribs with fabric covering.

LANDING GEAR.—Retractable type. Each unit consists of an oleo leg and radius-rod hinged to the side of the hull. In raised position wheels are housed in recesses in underside of lower wings. Lifting gear partly compensated and operated manually by hydraulic mechanism. Wheel-brakes.

POWER PLANT.—One 775 h.p. Bristol Pegasus VI nine-cylinder radial air-cooled engine driving pusher airscrew. Monocoque nacelle with manhole to give access to back of engine. Two fuel tanks (each 75 gallons) in upper wings with gravity feed to engine. Oil tank in nose of nacelle. Compressed air-starting with emergency hand-turning gear.

ACCOMMODATION.—Bow cockpit with Scarff ring and stowage for marine gear. Enclosed cockpit with pilot on left side. Detachable controls to right seat. Between pilot's seats and front spar frame is navigator's compartment. Between spar frames wireless compartment. Aft of wings is aft-gunner's cockpit with special gun-mounting.

DIMENSIONS.—Span 45 ft. 10 in. (13.97 m.), Length (on chassis) 37 ft. 7 in. (11.45 m.), Height (on chassis) 15 ft. 3 in. (4.65 m.), Width folded 17 ft. 11 in. (5.46 m.), Wing area 610 sq. ft. (56.67 sq. m.).

WEIGHTS AND LOADINGS.—Weight empty 4,900 lbs. (2,223 kg.), Military load 1,030 lbs. (467 kg.), Disposable load 2,300 lbs. (1,043 kg.), Weight loaded 7,200 lbs. (3,266 kg.), Wing loading 11.8 lbs./sq. ft. (57.61 kg./sq. m.), Power loading 10.6 lbs./h.p. (4.75 kg./h.p.).

PERFORMANCE.—Maximum speed at sea level 124 m.p.h. (200 km.h.), Maximum speed at 4,750 ft. (1,450 m.) 135 m.p.h. (217 km.h.), Cruising speed at 3,500 ft. (1,070 m.) 95 m.p.h. (153 km.h.), Landing speed 57 m.p.h. (92 km.h.), Initial rate of climb 1,050 ft./min. (320 m./min.), Climb to 10,000 ft. (3,050 m.) 12.5 mins., Service ceiling 18,500 ft. (5,640 m.), Cruising range (95 m.p.h. at 3,500 ft.) 600 miles (966 km.).

The Supermarine Walrus Amphibian Flying-boat (775 h.p. Bristol Pegasus VI engine).

TAYLORCRAFT.

TAYLORCRAFT AEROPLANES (ENGLAND) LTD.

HEAD OFFICE AND WORKS: BRITANNIA WORKS, THURMASTON, LEICESTER.

Directors: F. Bates (Managing Director), P. Wykes, A. L. Pickering and K. Sharp.

Taylorcraft Aeroplanes (England) Ltd. was formed to manufacture a cabin monoplane under a licence obtained from the Taylorcraft Aircraft Corpn., of America.

In its service form the British Taylorcraft is known as the Auster. The Auster I (Cirrus Minor engine), Auster III (D.H. Gipsy-Major engine) and Auster IV and V (130 h.p. Lycoming engine) have all seen active service.

The Auster has been progressively modified to meet service requirements and although the structure and the aerodynamic features remain the same as in the original Taylorcraft, the performance in later models has been considerably enhanced by the incorporation of wing flaps and the installation of higher-powered engines.

THE BRITISH TAYLORCRAFT AUSTER III.

TYPE.—Two-seat light Liaison or Observation monoplane.

WINGS.—High-wing braced monoplane. Wings attached to top of fuselage and braced to lower longerons by steel-tube Vee struts. Wing structure consists of spruce spars, ribs formed of drawn sections of Birmabrite steel, drag struts, steel tie-rod bracing, metal leading-edge and an overall fabric covering. Metal split trailing-edge flaps.

FUSELAGE.—Welded steel-tube structure covered with fabric.

TAIL UNIT.—Braced monoplane type. Welded steel-tube framework covered with fabric. Fixed tailplane. Small auxiliary control surface at end of fuselage for fore-and-aft trim. External tie-rod bracing.

LANDING GEAR.—Split-axle type. Two faired steel-tube Vees with half-axles sprung under the centre-line of the fuselage by rubber-cord shock-absorbers. Dunlop wheels and Bendix brakes. Leaf-spring tail-skid.

POWER PLANT.—One 130 h.p. D.H. Gipsy-Major four-cylinder in-verted in-line air-cooled engine. Fixed pitch wooden airscrew. Fuel capacity: 10 Imp. gallons, plus 8 gallons long-range tank.

ACCOMMODATION.—Enclosed cabin seating two side-by-side with complete dual controls. Two large doors, one opening side window and large front, side, upward and rear-view windows. Parachute-type seats. Radio equipment. Armour plate protection for pilot.

DIMENSIONS.—Span 36 ft. (11 m.), Length 23 ft. 5 in. (7.1 m.), Height 6 ft. 8 in. (2 m.), Wing area 167 sq. ft. (15.5 sq. m.).

WEIGHTS AND LOADINGS.—Weight empty 1,050 lbs. (474 kg.), Maximum permissible loaded weight 1,700 lbs. (772 kg.), Wing loading (max.) 9.22 lbs./sq. ft. (45 kg./sq. m.), Power loading 13.1 lbs./h.p. (5.95 kg./h.p.).

PERFORMANCE.—Maximum speed 126 m.p.h. (202.7 km.h.), Cruising speed 96 m.p.h. (154 km.h.), Landing speed (flaps down) 28 m.p.h. (45.1 km.h.), Initial climb 1,075 ft./min. (328 m./min.), Take-off run (with flaps) 70 yds. (64 m.).

THE BRITISH TAYLORCRAFT AUSTER IV.

The Auster IV is a development of the previously described model from which it differs in several respects. The fuselage has been redesigned to give a greatly improved rearward view, made possible by the fitting of a domed Perspex roof-light. Other minor modifications have been made in the wings.

POWER PLANT.—One 130 h.p. Lycoming O-290 four-cylinder horizontally-opposed air-cooled engine. Fixed-pitch wooden airscrew. Fuel capacity: 15 Imp. gallons.

ACCOMMODATION.—Seats for three, two side-by-side with dual controls and third seat immediately behind the second pilot. Two large doors. Both side windows open. Large front windshield, side, upward and rear-view windows. Cabin heating.

DIMENSIONS.—Same as for Auster III except Length: 22 ft. 5 in. (6.83 m.).

WEIGHTS AND LOADINGS.—Weight empty 1,050 lbs. (476 kg.), Maximum permissible loaded weight 1,920 lbs. (827 kg.), Wing loading (max.) 9.87 lbs./sq. ft. (48.2 kg./sq. m.), Power loading 14 lbs./h.p. (6.36 kg./h.p.).

The Taylorcraft Auster V Light Liaison and Observation Monoplane (130 h.p. Lycoming O-290 engine).

The Taylorcraft Auster J.1 Three-seat Light-cabin Monoplane (100 h.p. Cirrus Minor II engine).

PERFORMANCE (at 1,700 lbs. = 772 kg. loaded weight).—Maximum speed 130 m.p.h. (209 km.h.), Normal cruising speed at 1,000 ft. (305 m.) 112 m.p.h. (179 km.h.), Stalling speed (flaps up) 38 m.p.h. (61 km.h.), Stalling speed (flaps fully down) 30 m.p.h. (48 km.h.), Initial rate of climb 800 ft./min. (244 m./min.), Climb to 15,000 ft. (4,575 m.) 46 mins., Service ceiling 15,100 ft. (4,600 m.), Absolute ceiling 18,200 ft. (5,550 m.), Cruising range 220 miles (352 km.), Take-off run (with flaps) 75 yds. (68 m.).

THE BRITISH TAYLORCRAFT AUSTER V.

The Auster V is an improvement of the Auster IV. A full blind-flying panel driven by a mechanised vacuum-pump has been fitted to cater for the bad weather flying done on urgent communication duties. The auxiliary trimming surface below the tailplane has been replaced by a standard elevator trimmer.

The power-plant is a 130 h.p. Lycoming O-290 four-cylinder horizontally-opposed air-cooled engine.

DIMENSIONS, WEIGHTS AND PERFORMANCE.—Same as Auster IV.

THE TAYLORCRAFT AUSTER J.1.

The Auster Series J.1 is a three-seat civil version of the military Auster IV described and illustrated on p. 74c.

The general construction of the civil J.1 is the same as for the military model but cabin furnishing, equipment and finish have been improved. The cabin can seat three, two side-by-side in front with dual controls and one behind. Independently-operated brakes, parking brake, full instrument equipment (less turn-and-bank indicator) and a 100 h.p. Cirrus Minor II four-cylinder inverted air-cooled engine are standard. There is a choice of two external and cabin colour schemes. The standard price (ex works) is £825. Flaps, self-starter and turn-and-bank indicator are extras.

PERFORMANCE.—Maximum speed 125 m.p.h. (200 km.h.), Cruising speed 100 m.p.h. (160 km.h.), Stalling speed (with flaps and two up) 29 m.p.h. (46.4 km.h.), Normal range (still air) 250 miles (400 km.h.), Range with extra tank 550 miles (880 km.).

TIPSY.

TIPSY AIRCRAFT CO., LTD.

Head Office : 20, Elmwood Avenue, Feltham, Middlesex.

Works : Hanworth Air Park, Feltham, Middlesex ; 183-7, Liverpool Road, and 798, Weston Road, Slough, Bucks.

Directors : Major J. E. D. Shaw (Chairman), Flt.-Lt. G. Birkett (Managing Director), Lieut. Cdr. J. Crammond, R.N.V.R., E. O. Tips, Walter Gaskin and C. C. Vinson, A.C.A.

The Tipsy Aircraft Co., Ltd., was formed in 1937 to build Tipsy aircraft under licence from the Fairey Aviation Co., Ltd., the proprietors of the designs.

During the War production of the Tipsy monoplane ceased but the Company has preserved all jigs, tools, etc., so that manufacture may be resumed as soon as circumstances permit. In the meantime the Company has been engaged on important work on behalf of the Ministry of Aircraft Production.

VICKERS-ARMSTRONGS.

VICKERS-ARMSTRONGS, LTD.

Aviation Works : Weybridge.

London Office : Vickers House, Broadway, Westminster S.W.1.

Directors : Sir Frederick Yapp (Chairman), Sir Alexander Dunbar, Major H. R. Kilner, M.C. (Managing-Director, Aircraft), Commander E. R. Micklem, C.B.E., R.N. (Deputy-Chairman and Managing-Director, Engineering Works and Shipyards), J. M. Ormston, M.B.E., A. J. Palmer, C.B.E., F. Pickworth, F.C.I.S., H. Thompson and J. Reid Young, C.A., F.C.I.S.

Chief Designer : R. K. Pierson, C.B.E., B.Sc., A.M.I.C.E., F.R.Ae.S.

Chief of Aeronautical Research and Development : B. N. Wallis, C.B.E., F.R.S., R.D.I., B.Sc., M.Inst.C.E., F.R.Ae.S.

Vickers (Aviation), Ltd. was formed in July, 1928, when Vickers, Ltd. formed their Aviation Department into a separate subsidiary company to take over the manufacture of aircraft, aircraft accessories and equipment. In November, 1928, Vickers (Aviation), Ltd. took over the control of the Supermarine Aviation Works, Ltd.

In October, 1938, Vickers (Aviation), Ltd. and the Supermarine Aviation Works (Vickers), Ltd. were taken over by Vickers-Armstrongs, Ltd.

The most recent Vickers-Armstrongs military product concerning which details may be published is the Warwick General Reconnaissance monoplane and Military Transport. The Warwick is a development of the Wellington which was in continuous service as a bomber from the outbreak of war until early in 1945.

Both the Warwick and the Wellington are built on the Vickers-Wallis "geodetic" system of construction, which is peculiarly suitable for building streamline curvilinear bodies.

The material is put in the most advantageous position for developing the maximum stiffness of structure, and also in the most efficient form for resisting large loads and developing high stress.

Aircraft built on this principle therefore combine in a marked degree great stiffness and strength with a structure weight so low as to give range and load-carrying figures that have hitherto been considered unattainable.

A further advantage inherent in this system of construction is the absence of bulkheads, frames or ribs. The interior of both wings and fuselage is entirely unobstructed, leaving the full volume available for stowage, passenger quarters, tanks, etc.

The exterior surface is preferably covered with fabric, though thin plating or plywood may be substituted if desired. It is found, however, with the novel method of fabric attachment that has been developed in connection with the goedetic bars, that the usual quality of approved linen fabric is capable of withstanding pressures of over 1,000 lbs. per sq. ft., a figure which gives a large reserve factor on the highest wing loadings that are contemplated to-day.

In May, 1945, the preliminary details of the Viking twin-engined commercial monoplane were made available. A description of this aircraft appears hereafter.

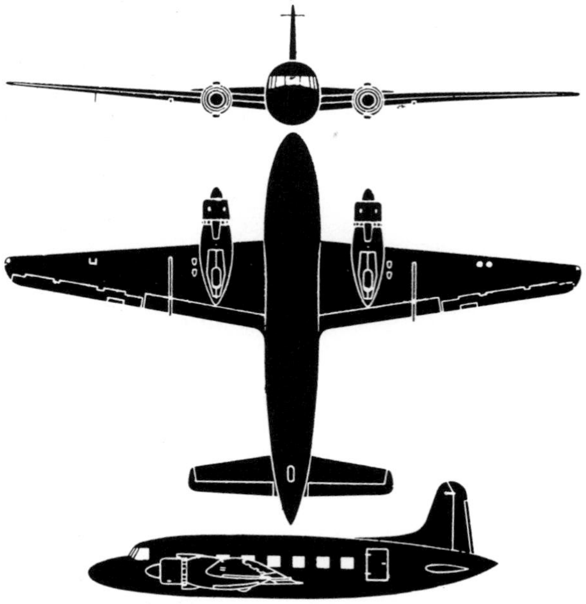

The Vickers-Armstrongs V.C.1. Viking Transport.

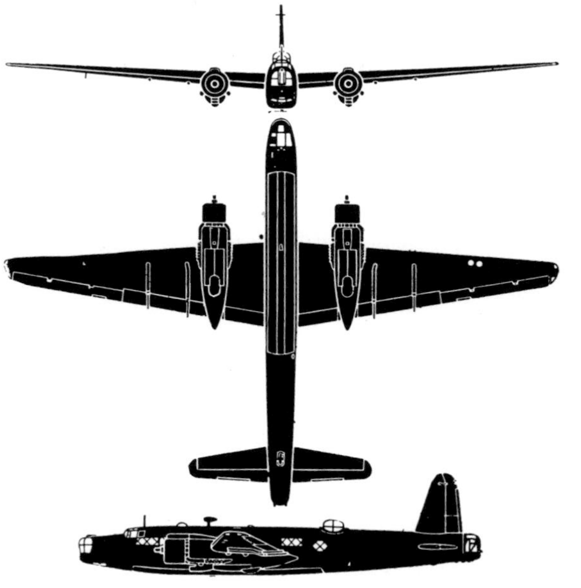

The Vickers-Armstrongs Warwick G.R. Mk. I.

THE VICKERS-ARMSTRONGS V.C.1 VIKING.

Type.—Twin-engined passenger and/or freight transport.

Wings.—Low mid-wing cantilever monoplane. The wing panels, similar to those of the Wellington bomber, are of geodetic construction but are covered entirely with a metal skin. The main spar passes through the fuselage and is free to float vertically although retained fore-and-aft. Attachments to fuselage at leading and trailing-edges by link arms pivoted on pins retained in Silentbloc rubber/metal bushes in the fuselage frames. Drag beams on either side of the fuselage absorb bending loads. Frise type ailerons are mass-balanced and fitted with trimming-tabs. Hydraulically-operated wing flaps between ailerons and fuselage. Tecalemit wet-nose wing de-icing.

Fuselage.—Oval section all-metal structure. A series of channel-section frames carries the longitudinal stringers to which the outer metal skin is riveted. The lower portion of the fuselage is reinforced by heavy sheet corrugated fore-and-aft which, apart from providing a rigid "keel," acts as the floor of the luggage or freight compartment beneath the cabin floor.

Tail Unit.—Cantilever monoplane type. Fin and tailplane of geodetic construction with metal-covering. Rudder and elevators of normal spar and rib construction with fabric covering. Rudder fitted with spring tab.

Landing Gear.—Standard Wellington type hydraulically-operated retractable landing-gear with Vickers oleo-pneumatic shock-absorber legs. Retractable full-castoring tail-wheel. Pneumatic brakes on main wheels with differential action coupled to rudder-bar.

Power Plant.—Two 1,675 h.p. Bristol Hercules 130 fourteen-cylinder radial air-cooled sleeve-valve engines in standard Wellington nacelles and driving four-blade Rotol constant-speed full-feathering airscrews. Power-units easily detachable and interchangeable right and left. Metal fuel tanks in wings and nacelles. Maximum fuel capacity 750 Imp. gallons, of which 630 gals. may be jettisoned in an emergency.

Accommodation.—Flight compartment in nose accommodates pilot, second pilot and radio operator. Main passenger cabin is divided at the main spar frame by a bulkhead and steps over spar. There are two main furnishing schemes, the Standard seating 27 passengers and the De Luxe seating 21 passengers. Seats are arranged in rows of three, two on right and one on left of central aisle. All but two rows face forward. Standard model allows ample leg room for all purposes but De Luxe model permits the use of more luxurious adjustable seats. Controlled heating and ventilation. General lighting by roof lights with individual lamps for each passenger. Main entrance vestibule aft of main cabin with steward's pantry on starboard side facing entrance door. Aft of pantry is a toilet room and hat and coat accommodation. Tip-up seat for steward or air hostess. Space below the cabin floor provides commodious space for freight, mail or passenger's baggage. This hold is provided by wing frames into three separate compartments. External loading doors for each compartment. Capacity of freight hold 300 cu. ft.

Dimensions.—Span 89 ft. 3 in. (27.22 m.), Length 62 ft. 10 in. (19.15 m.), Height (on ground) 19 ft. 7 in. (5.98 m.), Gross wing area 882 sq. ft. (81.9 sq. m.).

Weights (Standard Model—for still air range of 1,190 miles—1,905 km.).—Weight empty 22,116 lbs. (10,040 kg.), Crew (3) 510 lbs. (231 kg.), Stewardess 130 lbs. (59 kg.), Crew's baggage 100 lbs. (45 kg.), Petrol (595 Imp. gals.) 4,281 lbs. (1,944 kg.), Oil (32 Imp. gallons) 288 lbs. (131 kg.), Passengers (27) 4,590 lbs. (2,084 kg.). Passenger's baggage 1,485 lbs. (674 kg.), Total pay-load 6,075 lbs. (2,758 kg.), Weight loaded 33,500 lbs. (14,210 kg.), Wing loading 37.4 lbs./sq. ft. (182.5 kg./sq. m.), T.O. power loading 9.85 lbs./h.p. (4.47 kg./h.p.).

Weights (Standard Model—for still air range of 1,000 miles—1,600 km.).—Same as above except Petrol (500 Imp. gallons) 3,600 lbs. (1,634 kg.), Oil (24 Imp. gallons) 216 lbs. (198 kg.) and addition of freight and mail 753 lbs. (342 kg.) to increase pay-load to 6,828 lbs. (3,100 kg.).

Weights (De Luxe Model—for still air range of 1,500 miles—2,400 km.).—Weight empty 21,918 lbs. (9,951 kg.), Crew (3) 510 lbs. (232 kg.), Stewardess 130 lbs. (59 kg.), Crew's baggage 100 lbs. (45 kg.), Petrol (750 Imp. gallons) 5,400 lbs. (2,452 kg.), Oil (32 Imp. gallons) 288 lbs. (131 kg.), Passengers (21) 3,570 lbs. (1,621 kg.), Passengers' baggage 1,155 lbs. (524 kg.), Freight and mail 360 lbs. (163 kg.), Total pay-load 5,085 lbs. (2,310 kg.), Weight loaded 33,431 lbs. (15,178 kg.).

Weights (De Luxe Model—for still air range of 1,000 miles = 1,600 km.).—Same as for above except Petrol (500 Imp. gallons) 3,600 lbs. (1,634 kg.), Oil (20 Imp. gallons) 216 lbs. (98 kg.), Freight and mail 2,232 lbs. (1,013 kg.), Total pay-load 6,957 lbs. (3,158 kg.), Maximum landing weight of all models 31,000 lbs. (14,074 kg.).

Performance.—Maximum weak-mixture cruising speed at 10,000 ft. (3,050 m.) 210 m.p.h. (336 km.h.), Minimum cruising speed at 10,000 ft. (3,050 m.) 160 m.p.h. (256 km.h.), Climb to 10,000 ft. (3,050 m.) 8 min., Service ceiling 22,500 ft. (6,860 m.), Still air range (500 Imp. gallons fuel) 1,000 miles (1,600 km.), Still air range (750 Imp. gallons fuel) 1,500 miles (2,400 km.).

THE VICKERS-ARMSTRONGS WARWICK.

The Warwick is a slightly enlarged version of the Wellington and embodies the same form of "geodetic" construction. Originally developed as a twin-engined bomber, it has since been adapted to a number of duties, including General Reconnaissance, Air/Sea Rescue, Transport, etc. The following are the principal service versions of the Warwick :—

Warwick G.R. Mk. I. A.S.R. Mk. I and C. Mk. I. Two Pratt & Whitney R-2800-S1A4G or 2SBG eighteen-cylinder radial air-cooled engines. The G.R. Mk. I carries an armament of eight .303 in. machine-guns in three turrets, two in nose turret, two in a mid-upper turret and four in a tail turret. The bomb-bay accommodates either bombs, mines or depth-charges. The A.S.R. Mk. I is similar to the G.R. Mk. I. except for slight modifications to the bomb-bay to permit the carrying of the Mk. IA airborne lifeboat. This lifeboat, which is 23 ft. 6 in. (7.17 m.) long and 5 ft. 6 in. (1.67 m.) wide, is carried under the fuselage by a single central attachment which picks up the ordinary bomb lugs in the Warwick's bomb-bay. The normal bomb sight and bomb release are used for aiming and releasing the lifeboat. The lifeboat weighs 1,700 lbs. (772 kg.) and is dropped on six 32 ft. (9.76 m.) diameter parachutes which are pulled out by a pilot chute attached to the aircraft by a static line. The C. Mk. 1 has no armament and serves as a passenger and freight transport. Several aircraft of this type were handed over to British Airways for civil use, but these are no longer in service.

Warwick G.R. Mk. II. Two Bristol Centaurus VII fourteen-cylinder sleeve-valve radial engines. Except for power-plant similar to G.R. Mk. I. An A.S.R. Mk. II with two Centaurus IV engines was produced in prototype form only.

Warwick C. Mk. III. Transport and Troop-carrier. Generally similar to the C. Mk. I except that a large bulged pannier is arranged to fit into the bomb-bay to increase the freight capacity. No armament.

Warwick C. Mk. IV. Two Bristol Centaurus IV eighteen-cylinder sleeve-valve radial engines. Transport similar to C. Mk. III. Produced in prototype form only.

Warwick G.R. Mk. V. Two Bristol Centaurus VII eighteen-cylinder sleeve-valve radial engines. Generally similar to the G.R. Mk. I except for armament. The nose and mid-upper turrets have been removed and replaced by three .5 in. guns, one in the nose and one on each side of the fuselage midway

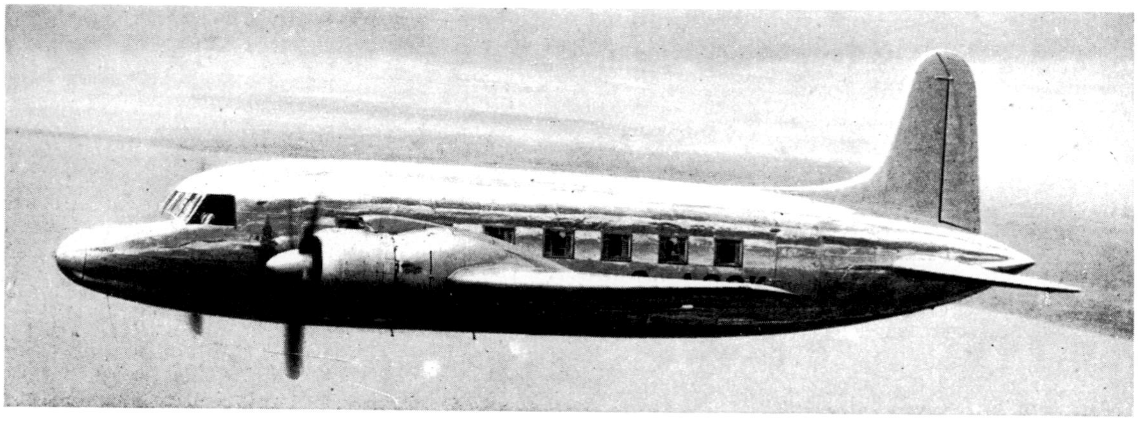

The Vickers-Armstrongs V.C.1. Viking Transport Monoplane (two 1,675 h.p. Bristol Hercules 130 engines).

between the wings and tail. These three guns are manually-operated. The four-gun tail turret is retained. Fitted with Leigh Light. Carries bombs, mines or depth-charges. Later fitted with small dorsal fin, a modification which was also incorporated in other Marks. See silhouette of G.R. Mk. V on prevous page.

DIMENSIONS.—Span 96 ft. 8½ in. (29.5 m.), Length (tail down) 70 ft. 6 in. (21.5 m.), Height 18 ft. 6 in. (5.64 m.), Gross wing area 1,006 sq. ft. (93.45 sq. m.).

MAXIMUM LOADED WEIGHT.—45,000 lbs. (20,430 kg.).

PERFORMANCE.—No data available.

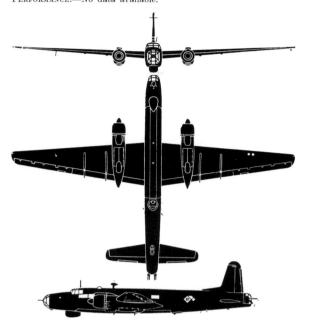

The Vickers-Armstrongs Warwick G.R. Mk. V.

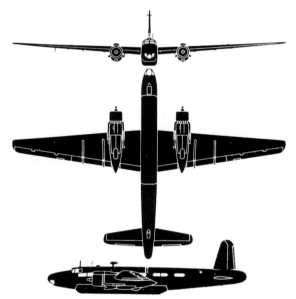

The Vickers-Armstrongs Warwick C. Mk. III.

THE VICKERS-ARMSTRONGS WELLINGTON.

The Wellington was designed to meet the requirements of Air Ministry specification B.9/32 and the prototype first flew on June 15th, 1936. Put into production in 1936, the first production Wellington I flew on December 23, 1937. Delivery to R.A.F. squadrons began in 1939.

The Wellington remained in service as a land bomber for five and a half years, its first operation being an attack on German warships at Wilhelmshafen on the day after war was declared, its last a raid on Previsio in Northern Italy in April, 1945. It operated from bases in Great Britain, India, the Middle East, North Africa and Italy.

The Wellington has also served on convoy protection, oversea reconnaissance, mine-laying and anti-submarine duties in home waters and in the Mediterranean. One of its first duties with Coastal Command was to detect and explode magnetic mines. Later, for oversea duties, the Wellington was fitted to carry depth-charges, mines, two 18 in. torpedoes, Radar, Leigh Light, etc.

The number of Wellingtons built during the war totalled 11,391.

Wellington I. Two 1,050 h.p. Bristol Pegasus XVIII engines. Early production models had Vickers turrets. The Mk. IA had Fraser-Nash two-gun nose and tail turrets and a ventral "dust-bin" turret. The Mk. IC had Fraser-Nash turrets and beam guns in place of the "dustbin."

Wellington II. Two 1,145 h.p. Rolls-Royce Merlin X liquid-cooled engines. Otherwise the same as the Mk. IC.

Wellington III. Two 1,370 h.p. Bristol Hercules III or XI

The Vickers-Armstrongs Warwick Civil Transport (two Pratt & Whitney R-2800 engines).

The Vickers-Armstrongs Warwick A.S.R. Mk. I with the Mk. IA airborne lifeboat under the fuselage.

The Vickers-Armstrongs C. Mk. III Transport (two Pratt & Whitney R-2800 engines).

The Vickers-Armstrongs Wellington X Heavy Bomber (two Bristol Hercules XVI engines).

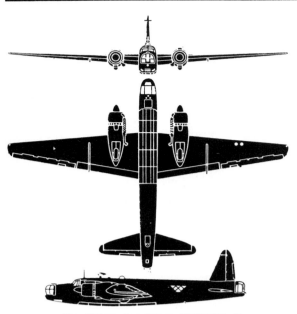

The Vickers-Armstrongs Wellington X.

Mark	Power-plant	Function	Weight loaded (lbs.)	Max. speed (m.p.h.) at operational height	Normal Range (miles)	Max. Range (miles)	Ceiling (ft.)	Bomb load (lbs.)
Wellington IC	2 × Pegasus XVIII	Medium Bomber	25,800	235	1,805	2,550	19,000	4,500
Wellington II	2 × Merlin X	Medium Bomber	27,600	247	1,570	2,220	23,500	4,000
Wellington III	2 × Hercules XI	Medium Bomber	29,500	255	1,470	2,085	22,000	4,500
Wellington IV	2 × Twin-Wasp	Medium Bomber	31,600	229	1,510	2,180	21,250	4,500
Wellington V	2 × Hercules VIII	Ex. High-Alt. Bomber	32,000	292	1,560	2,250	36,800	4,500
Wellington VI	2 × Merlin 60 or 62	Ex. High-Alt. Bomber	31,600	300	1,510	2,180	38,500	4,500
Wellington VIII	2 × Pegasus XVIII	G.R. Bomber	25,800	235	1,805	2,550	19,000	4,500
Wellington X	2 × Hercules VI or XVI	Medium Bomber	29,500	255	1,470	2,085	22,000	4,000
Wellington XI	2 × Hercules VI or XVI	G.R. and Torpedo-Bomber	29,500	255	—	2,020	19,000	4,500
Wellington XII	2 × Hercules VI or XVI	Coastal Recco. Bomber	36,500	256	1,435	1,810	18,500	5,100
Wellington XIII	2 × Hercules XVII	G.R. Bomber	31,000	250	1,390	1,760	16,000	5,000
Wellington XIV	2 × Hercules XVII	G.R. Bomber	31,000	250	1,390	1,760	16,000	5,000

The Vickers-Armstrongs Wellington V Experimental Bomber with pressurised crew accomodation.

The Vickers-Armstrongs Wellington XIV General Reconnaissance Bomber (two Bristol Hercules XVII engines).

sleeve-valve radial air-cooled engines. As Mk. IC but with a larger tailplane and a four-gun instead of a two-gun Fraser-Nash tail turret.

Wellington IV. Two 1,200 h.p. Pratt & Whitney R-1830-S3C4G engines driving Curtiss electric airscrews. Otherwise similar to the Mk. IC with two-gun tail turret.

Wellington V. Two Bristol Hercules VIII engines driving turbo-superchargers. Experimental high-altitude bomber. Circular pressurised compartment built into the upper portion of the fuselage forward of leading-edge to accommodate pilot, navigator and radio operator. Tail turret also pressurised. No nose turret. Only three built.

Wellington VI. Two Rolls-Royce Merlin 60 or 62 liquid cooled engines with two-speed two-stage superchargers. Except for power-plant similar to Mk. V. Only a small number built and did not go into general service.

Wellington VIII. Two Bristol Pegasus XVIII engines. A conversion of the Mk. IC for service as a General Reconnaissance bomber with Coastal Command. Same armament as Mk. IC. Fitted to carry depth-charges, mines or two 18 in. torpedoes, and later to carry a Leigh Light.

Wellington X. Two Bristol Hercules VI or XVI engines. Medium Bomber similar to Mk. III except power-plant.

Wellington XI. Two Bristol Hercules VI or XVI engines. General Reconnaissance and Torpedo-bomber version of the Mk. X. Armament as Mk. III. Fitted to carry 4,500 lbs. of depth-charges, mines or two 18 in. torpedoes. Also carries Leigh Light.

Wellington XII. Two Bristol Hercules VI engines. Coastal Reconnaissance bomber with reduced range and carrying 5,100 lbs. of bombs, mines or depth-charges. Also carries Leigh Light. Armament : six .303 in. machine-guns.

Wellington XIII. Two Bristol Hercules XVII engines. General Reconnaissance bomber. Armament as for Mk. III. Carries 5,000 lbs. of bombs, mines or depth-charges.

Wellington XIV. Two Bristol Hercules XVII engines. General Reconnaissance bomber. No nose turret. Armament : six .303 in. machine-guns, four in tail turret and two in beam positions. Same load as for Mk. XIII.

Wellington XV and XVI. These are transport versions of the bomber. All armament and military equipment removed.

Wellington XVII and XVIII. Two Bristol Hercules VI (Mk. XVII) or XVII (Mk. XVIII) engines. Trainers.

TYPE.—Twin-engined Bomber or General Reconnaissance monoplane.

WINGS.—Middle-wing cantilever monoplane. Wings taper in chord and thickness. Aspect ratio : 8.83 : 1. Wing in three sections consisting of centre-section, main spar of which passes through the fuselage, and two outer sections. Structure consists of main girder spar and two auxiliary spars close to leading and trailing-edges. To these spars are attached a series of geodetic panels which conform to the contour of the upper and lower surfaces. Final covering of fabric is applied to panels before the wings are assembled. Split flaps and Frise ailerons on outer wings.

FUSELAGE.—Oval streamline structure of Vickers "geodetic" construction, covered with fabric. There are six main frames, the geodetic members of the fuselage being built as long panels on longitudinal tubes or longerons. After complete fuselage has been built up, the whole is covered with fabric which is secured to geodetic members by patented wired-on method.

TAIL UNIT.—Cantilever type. Fin and tail-plane are geodetic structures. Elevators and rudder are normal ribbed structures. Fabric covering except tips of fin and tail-plane, which are covered with metal. Trimming-tabs in elevators and rudder.

LANDING GEAR.—Retractable type. Vickers oelo-pneumatic shock-absorbers and brakes. Wheels retract backwards into engine nacelles.

POWER PLANT.—See details of various Marks above. Six fuel tanks fore and aft of main spar in each wing. Normal capacity of 750 gallons. Special long-range tank to carry an additional 250 gallons carried in bomb compartment.

ACCOMMODATION.—Normal crew of six. In nose is the front gunner's station with bomb-aimer's position below. Behind on port side is the single pilot's seat with single controls. On higher level, behind pilot and over bomb compartments are positions for radio operator and navigator. Gun position in tail. May be fitted with tropical equipment.

ARMAMENT.—See Introduction. Maximum bomb load 5,100 lbs.

(2,315 kg.). Can also carry two 18-in. torpedoes, sea mines or depth charges.

DIMENSIONS.—Span 86 ft. 2 in. (26.27 m.), Length 64 ft. 7 in. (19.68 m.), Height 17 ft. 5 in. (5.3 m.), Wing area 840 sq. ft. (78.14 sq. m.).

WEIGHTS AND PERFORMANCE.—See Table.

THE VICKERS-ARMSTRONGS WINDSOR.

The Windsor is an experimental Heavy Bomber fitted with four Rolls-Royce Merlin 85 engines. It is the first four-engined aeroplane to incorporate the Vickers-Wallis Geodetic construction

and is covered throughout with a special woven steel wire/fabric composite material. Certain parts of the aircraft have an additional backing of glass cloth. A further notable feature of this aeroplane is the landing-gear, which consists of four separate units, one under each nacelle. The track of the outer wheels is 50 ft. (15.25 m.).

Details of bomb-load, armament and equipment were not available for publication at the time of closing these pages for press.

DIMENSIONS.—Span 117 ft. 4 in. (35.7 m.), Length 77 ft. 6 in. (23.6 m.),

The Vickers-Armstrong Windsor Heavy Bomber (four Rolls-Royce Merlin 85 engines).

WESTLAND.

WESTLAND AIRCRAFT, LTD.

HEAD OFFICE, WORKS AND AERODROME : YEOVIL, SOMERSET.
LONDON OFFICE : 8, THE SANCTUARY, WESTMINSTER, S.W.1.

Directors : The Rt. Hon. Lord Aberconway, C.B.E. (Chairman), Eric Mensforth, M.A., M.I.Mech.E., M.I.P.E. (Vice-Chairman), John Fearn, M.I.Mech.E. (Managing Director), Arthur Davenport (Technical Director), Edward C. Wheeldon, M.I.P.E. (Works Director), Sir George E. Bailey, C.B.E., Air Vice-Marshal Sir Norman D.K. MacEwen, C.B., C.M.G., D.S.O., Sir Holberry Mensforth, K.C.B., C.B.E., Sir Felix J. C. Pole and S. W. Rawson.

Secretary : W. B. Hickman, A.C.A.

Westland Aircraft Ltd. was formed in July, 1935, to take over the aircraft branch of Petters Ltd., previously known as the Westland Aircraft Works, which had been engaged in aircraft design and construction since 1915.

In July, 1938, Petters' works were acquired and at the same time John Brown & Co. Ltd., the well-known shipbuilding firm, purchased the greater part of Petters' holding in Westland Aircraft, Ltd., the remainder being acquired at a later date by Associated Electrical Industries, Ltd.

The latest Westland type concerning which details may be published is the Welkin twin-engined high-altitude fighter monoplane, particulars of which are given herewith.

THE WESTLAND WELKIN.

The Welkin I is a single-seat high-altitude fighter which was designed to combat possible stratospheric raids by the Luftwaffe over England at heights beyond the range of existing fighters.

In designing this aeroplane the entire emphasis was directed towards the attainment of the highest possible ceiling, at the same time securing the maximum possible speed while carrying an armament of four 20 m/m. cannon. Preliminary investigation of the factors governing the relation between structural weight and aerodynamic efficiency established that a large aspect ratio was essential, and a wing loading of 38 lbs./sq. ft. (185.4 kg./sq. m.) in conjunction with a span of 70 ft. (21.35 m.) gave the maximum ceiling consistent with the specification factors. In view of this medium loading it was found that the required stalling speed and landing runs could be attained by using a normal split flap.

So that full use could be made of the Welkin's ability to fight at great heights, a basic part of the design was a cabin which could be automatically pressurised. This consisted of a relatively small self-contained unit made of extremely heavy gauge bullet-resisting light alloy and bolted to the front face of the main spar, with an armour steel bulkhead at the rear and a special openable bulkhead at the nose.

Concurrently with the development of this cabin, extensive research was necessary to produce a coupé top with a wide field of vision, which not only had to take the abnormal loads of pressurisation but also had to be both slidable for ingress and jettisonable. A sandwich system of glazing was finally evolved, in which the thick inner shell retained the pressure and an outer shell acted as a fairing, leaving a space between through which warm air could be circulated to prevent icing and misting.

The half-cylindrical canopy terminates in a thick laminated glass pressure-retaining bulkhead and abuts on a fixed windscreen similarly composed of a sandwich system of glazing. The de-misting air is drawn through a rain-trap entry and after passing through a glycol heater is led to the space between the inner and outer shells. A Dunlop rubber gasket fitted round the periphery of the hood and automatically inflated when the cabin pressure is on provided the solution to the problem of securing a seal between the sliding and fixed parts of the coupé.

Operational considerations largely dictated the degree of pressurisation required and it was decided that the pilot should be supplied continuously with oxygen and that the cabin pressure should be the equivalent of 24,000 ft. (7,320 m.) for a true height of 45,000 ft. (13,725 m.). To avoid the necessity for the pilot to concentrate on his cabin pressure an ingenious cabin atmosphere control valve was developed which automatically gave the appropriate pressure for any given height, using a differential of 3.5 lbs./sq. in., and employing air supplied to the cabin inlet by a Rotol cabin blower, the valve controlling the exit of air to the atmosphere. These Westland valves are extensively used in every British pressure-cabin military aircraft and developments arising from them have been applied to new long-range high-flying civil aircraft now being designed and constructed.

To reduce as far as possible the necessity for a number of pressure glands to give egress from the cabin to numerous small controls, an electrical system using grouped and pressure-tight junction boxes was adopted and a special remote-control unit devised to operate all trim-tabs and fuel cocks.

The Westland Welkin I High-altitude Fighter.

The Westland Welkin I High-altitude Fighter (two Rolls-Royce Merlin engines).

The Westland Welkin I High-altitude Fighter (two Rolls-Royce Merlin engines).

As enemy high-flying raiders never appeared over England in numbers the Welkin I did not go into operational service. Only a few were built.

A two-seat version known as the Welkin II was developed and two examples were built, but this model did not proceed beyond the experimental stage.

TYPE.—Single-seat High-altitude Fighter.

WINGS.—Mid-wing cantilever monoplane. Wide centre-section extending beyond the engine nacelles with the outer wings set at a greater dihedral. All-metal single-spar stressed-skin structure. Flaps on centre-section, ailerons on outer sections.

FUSELAGE.—Oval section structure in two parts, the forward section comprising the cabin of duralumin and the rear section of magnesium. The cabin section is stressed for pressurisation and is bullet-resisting. It is bolted to the front face of the main wing spar and terminates with a steel armoured bulkhead. The rear fuselage is a monocoque, the skin being longitudinally planked.

TAIL UNIT.—Cantilever monoplane type. The tailplane is mounted about one-third up the fin to ensure good anti-spin qualities at high altitudes. The rudder is in two portions separated by the torpedo-shaped fillet forming the intersection of the tailplane and fin. Electrically-operated trim-tabs in elevators and rudder.

LANDING GEAR.—Retractable type. Main wheels raised backwards into engine nacelles, tail-wheel into fuselage. Lockheed shock-absorbers. Dowty hydraulic retraction. Dunlop wheels and brakes.

POWER PLANT.—Two Rolls-Royce Merlin engines with two-speed two-stage superchargers, Mk. 72 or 76 in the starboard nacelle and 73 or 77 in the port nacelle, the port engine driving the Rotol cabin supercharger. Rotol four-blade constant-speed full-feathering airscrews. Coolant and oil radiators in centre-section between fuselage and nacelles, the air being led to them by a ducted leading-edge entry with a variable exit at the trailing-edge controlled by the angular setting of the main landing flaps. Integral and armoured fuel tanks in centre-section outboard of the nacelles.

ACCOMMODATION.—Pilot's cockpit in line with the leading-edge of the wing. Cockpit is pressurised, a Westland control valve automatically regulating the cabin pressure. Automatic cabin-heating control maintains equable temperature at all heights, thereby eliminating the need for special clothing. At low altitudes either heated or cold air can be admitted at will. The pressure-resisting cockpit canopy and bullet-proof windscreen are double skinned with a space for warm air to be circulated by pump to prevent icing and misting.

ARMAMENT.—Four 20 m/m. British Hispano cannon in the fuselage nose.

DIMENSIONS.—Span 70 ft. (21.35 m.), Length 41 ft. 6 in. (12.6 m.), Height 15 ft. 9 in. (4.8 m.), Wing area 460 sq. ft. (42.7 sq. m.).

WEIGHT LOADED.—17,500 lbs. (7,945 kg.).

PERFORMANCE.—Maximum speed at operational height 385 m.p.h. (616 km.h.), Range about 1,500 miles (2,400 km.).

WICKO.

FOSTER, WIKNER AIRCRAFT CO., LTD.

HEAD OFFICE : COLIN STREET, BROMLEY-BY-BOW, LONDON, E.3.

WORKS : MUNICIPAL AIRPORT, SOUTHAMPTON.

Chairman : J. F. Lusty.

Technical Director (Controlling) : G. N. Wikner.

Directors : N. Edgar, W. K. Lusty and F. A. M. Lusty.

The Foster, Wikner Aircraft Co. Ltd. was formed in 1936 to manufacture the Wicko two-seat cabin monoplane designed by Mr. G. N. Wikner, an Australian. The standard model is fitted with the 130 h.p. D.H. Gipsy-Major engine. Several examples of this type have been used by the R.A.F. for communication work, etc.

A modified version of the two-seat model with accommodation for a third person behind the existing side-by-side seats is known as the Wicko Warferry. The all-up weight and performance of the Warferry remains the same as for the two-seater but the tare weight has been reduced by refinements in design and by the elimination of the dual control and flap mechanism.

AUSTRALIA

The biggest and most important plan for the production of aircraft in Australia was that which concerned the manufacture of the Bristol Beaufort and the Bristol Beaufighter by the Beaufort Division of the Department of Aircraft Production.

This production scheme was designed to secure the greatest degree of decentralisation, whereby parts were manufactured by over four hundred specialised sub-contractors and delivered to the railway workshops in the three States, there to be made up into complete sub-assemblies for delivery to two final assembly plants at Fishermen's Bend, Melbourne, Victoria, and Mascot, Sydney, N.S.W.

In sub-assembly, the works of the New South Wales Government Railways were responsible for the front fuselage, stern frame, landing gear and nacelle structure; the Victorian Railway workshops for the rear fuselage, tail-plane, fin and control surfaces; and the South Australian Government Railway workshops for the centre-section and complete wings. All these sub-assemblies were complete with all equipment and fittings when delivered to the final assembly plants.

It was originally intended that the Bristol Aeroplane Co. Ltd. should supply all drawings, jigs, tools and fixtures, as well as ten sets of fabricated parts and ten sets of raw materials to educate the Australian engineers and operatives in the manufacture of the Beaufort. Conditions brought about by the

War interfered with this programme and it became necessary for the Australian engineers to undertake some of the preliminary work and a large number of jigs and tools had to be manufactured locally. For the same reason Australia was thrown back on its own resources for the development of constant-speed airscrews, oleo landing-gear struts, self-sealing petrol tanks, gunturrets, instruments, as well as aircraft steels, duralumin and Alclad sheet and various other items.

Another big problem arose when it was found that the Bristol Taurus engine for which the Beaufort was designed would not be obtainable in any quantity for the Australian Beaufort owing to home demands and transport difficulties. The Australian Beaufort had therefore to be modified to take the Pratt & Whitney Twin-Wasp engine and a licence for the manufacture of this engine was obtained by the Commonwealth Aircraft Corporation, which was already in production with the Wasp engine.

The first Australian Beaufort, largely assembled from British-made parts but fitted with two Twin-Wasp engines, flew on May 5, 1941. Production reached a "mass" basis in January, 1942, and by the time that the Beaufort was withdrawn from production in 1943 to give place to the Beaufighter, over 700 had been built.

Because of the relationship of the Beaufighter to the Beaufort the change-over was quickly made, the actual production procedure for the two types being identical. The entire airframe and all components of the Beaufighter were manufactured in Australia, only the Bristol Hercules engines being imported from Great Britain.

Production of the Avro Lancaster was also undertaken by the Beaufort Division, but this was later to be superseded by the Lincoln.

In 1945 the Service Department of the Beaufort Division undertook the conversion of the Beaufort into a military personnel and freight transport. Conversion involved the removal of all armament, armour, bomb-racks and other operational fittings, thus reducing the weight by approximately 2,000 lbs. Five seats have been installed and by a re-design of the fuselage and bomb-bay a freight compartment with a capacity of 30 cu. ft. has been provided. With the removal of the dorsal turret, the provision of a fairing eliminating the break in the top line of the fuselage and the cleaner undersurface made possible by the elimination of the bomb-bay, the cruising speed of the Beaufort Transport has been increased by approximately 25 m.p.h.

COMMONWEALTH.

COMMONWEALTH AIRCRAFT CORPORATION PTY., LTD.

HEAD OFFICE : 422, LITTLE COLLINS STREET, MELBOURNE.

AIRCRAFT WORKS : FISHERMEN'S BEND, PORT MELBOURNE, VICTORIA.

AERO-ENGINE WORKS : FISHERMEN'S BEND, PORT MELBOURNE, VICTORIA, AND LIDCOMBE, N.S.W.

General Manager, Aircraft Division : Wing Cdr. L. J. Wackett, D.F.C., A.F.C., B.Sc.

The Commonwealth Aircraft Corpn. Pty., Ltd., was formed in 1936 under a scheme propounded by the Australian Government for the establishment of an aircraft industry to make Australia independent of outside supplies.

The Commonwealth Aircraft Corpn. is financed by some of the most wealthy industrial firms in Australia, and has an authorised capital of £1,000,000. The shareholders include the Broken Hill Pty. Co., the largest iron and steel concern in Australia ; Broken Hill Associated Smelters Pty. and its associate, the Electrolytic Zinc Co. of Australia, the largest producers of lead and zinc in the British Empire ; Imperial Chemical Industries of Australia and New Zealand, said to be the largest individual industrial concern in the Empire ; the Orient Steam Navigation Co. ; and General Motors-Holdens, which is allied to General Motors of the U.S.A.

During 1936, an Air Board Technical Commission visited the United States and began negotiations to acquire the licence for the NA-16 Two-seat General Purposes Monoplane from North American Aviation, Inc.

Negotiations for the manufacturing rights were completed in 1937 and the Corporation took delivery of an American-built NA-16 for submission to official test by the Royal Australian Air Force. The Australian development was known as the Wirraway, and the first of this type was delivered to the R.A.A.F. in July, 1939.

The Commonwealth Aircraft Corpn. has also produced a two-seat trainer designed by Wing Cdr. L. J. Wackett and fitted with the Warner Super-Scarab engine, and a single-seat fighter monoplane known as the Boomerang.

The Corporation is now in production with the North American Mustang single-seat fighter monoplane. Tooling up for the Mustang began in February, 1945, and the first complete aircraft was ready for test in May. The first eighty were to be

A front view of the Commonwealth Boomerang Single-seat Fighter Monoplane.

assembled from imported parts and thereafter it was expected that the aircraft would be entirely of Australian manufacture.

The Commonwealth Aircraft Corpn. also holds the licence to build Pratt & Whitney Wasp and Twin-Wasp and Rolls-Royce Merlin engines.

THE COMMONWEALTH BOOMERANG.

The Boomerang is a single-seat fighter monoplane, the design of which incorporates the principal distinctive features of the Wirraway. These include the rectangular centre-section and tapering outer sections, with all taper on the leading-edge ; continuous flaps between the ailerons ; inwardly retractable landing-gear with the wheel pockets forward of the main spar and protruding ahead of the leading-edge ; and the Wirraway tail-unit.

The pilot's cockpit is over the centre of the wing and is provided with a sliding canopy, bullet-proof windscreen and armour protection. Armament includes two 20 m.m. cannon mounted in the outer wing.

The Boomerang is fitted with a 1,200 h.p. Pratt & Whitney R-1830-S3C4G Twin-Wasp two-row radial air-cooled engine.

DIMENSIONS.—Span 36 ft. 3 in. (10 m.), Length 25 ft. 6 in. (7.77 m.).

WEIGHTS.—Weight empty 5,450 lbs. (2,474 kg.), Normal loaded weight 7,000 lbs. (3,178 kg.), Maximum overloaded weight 7,600 lbs. (3,450 kg.).

PERFORMANCE.—Maximum speed 296 m.p.h. (474 km.h.) at 7,600 ft. (2,320 m.), Speed at sea level 273 m.p.h. (437 km.h.), Service ceiling 29,000 ft. (8,845 m.), Range 930 miles (1,490 km.) at 190 m.p.h. (304 km.h.) at 15,000 ft. (4,575 m.), Endurance 4.9 hours.

THE COMMONWEALTH WIRRAWAY.

TYPE.—Two-seat General-Purposes military monoplane.

WINGS.—Low-wing cantilever monoplane. Wing section varies from NACA 2215 to 2209. In five sections consisting of centre-section, two outer sections and two detachable wing-tips. Centre-section of parallel chord and thickness. Outer sections have swept-back leading-edge and straight trailing-edge and taper in thickness. Single-spar structure with spaced ribs and stressed-skin covering. Dynamically-balanced ailerons with fabric covering. Split trailing-edge flap between ailerons and under fuselage.

FUSELAGE.—Welded chrome-molybdenum steel-tube framework with integrally welded fittings. In four sections all bolted together. Sides covered with fabric over aluminium-alloy frames. Decking and underside are metal-covered.

TAIL UNIT.—Cantilever monoplane type. Fixed surfaces metal-covered and movable surfaces fabric-covered. Right and left side of tail-plane and elevators interchangeable. Non-reversible trimming-tabs in elevators and rudder.

POWER PLANT.—One Australian-built Pratt & Whitney Wasp S1H1-G nine-cylinder radial air-cooled engine rated at 600 h.p. at 7,000 ft. (2,135 m.). Three-bladed D.H. controllable-pitch airscrew. NACA cowling.

ACCOMMODATION.—Tandem cockpits beneath sliding enclosures. Dual controls. Rotating and folding rear seat. Prone bombing position in floor. Special fittings to accommodate full range of equipment for various duties.

DIMENSIONS.—Span 43 ft. (13.11 m.), Wing area 255.75 sq. ft. (23.75 sq. m.).

WEIGHTS.—Weight empty 3,980 lbs. (1,807 kg.), Weight loaded 6,353 lbs. (2,884 kg.).

PERFORMANCE.—No data available.

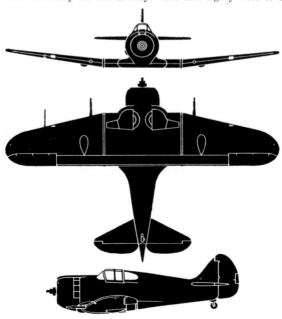

The Commonwealth Boomerang.

The Commonwealth Wackett Two-seat Training Monoplane (165 h.p. Warner Super-Scarab engine).

THE COMMONWEALTH WACKETT TRAINER.

The Wackett Trainer two-seat low-wing cantilever monoplane has been designed by Wing Cdr. L. J. Wackett to fulfil the requirements of a primary trainer suited to Australian conditions.

The prototype was fitted with a D.H. Gipsy-Six engine but owing to the difficulty of obtaining engines of this type under present conditions the American Warner Super-Scarab seven-cylinder radial engine has been adopted and a quantity has been acquired from the United States.

No details of the Wackett Trainer have been released for publication but its general appearance can be gathered from the accompanying illustration.

DE HAVILLAND.

THE DE HAVILLAND AIRCRAFT PROPRIETARY, LTD.

HEAD OFFICE AND WORKS : KINGSFORD SMITH AERODROME, MASCOT, SYDNEY, N.S.W.

AIRSCREW WORKS : ALEXANDRIA, N.S.W.

General Manager : Major A. Murray Jones, A.F.C.

Secretary : Mr. J. J. Byrne.

Early in 1927 the de Havilland Aircraft Co., Ltd. formed the de Havilland Aircraft Proprietary, Ltd., in Melbourne, to act as agents for the parent Company, to build de Havilland aircraft under licence, to assemble new aircraft and to operate service stations for de Havilland products throughout Australia.

In 1929, the Company decided that the amount of work available necessitated an extension of premises, and in March, 1931, it moved to Mascot Aerodrome, where workshops, offices and hangar accommodation had been built.

In 1938-39 the Company began the production of Tiger Moths for the Royal Australian Air Force. In July, 1942, the 1,600th Tiger Moth was completed.

Towards the end of 1941 a £500,000 order for D.H. Dragon-Rapide twin-engined biplanes for use as navigational trainers under the Empire Air Training Scheme was placed with the Aircraft Production Commission by the Air Board. Delivery of these aircraft began in 1942.

In 1942 production of the Mosquito was initiated. All drawings and data were supplied by the parent company in Britain, numerous jigs and tools as well as component samples and supplies were obtained from both the British and Canadian de Havilland organizations, and Packard-built Merlin engines and certain other supplies from the U.S.A. On July 23, 1943, a

The first Australian-built Mosquito F. B. Mk. 40 Fighter-Bomber (two Packard-built Merlin 31 engines).

little over a year after the receipt of the initial batches of data from Britain, the first Australian-built Mosquito was test-flown. Production is now in full swing with the assistance of a host of sub-contractors. For details of the Australian Mosquito production types see under "De Havilland" (Great Britain).

The Company is also assisting, in conjunction with General Motors-Holdens of Melbourne, in the manufacture of D.H. Gipsy engines in Australia. It has also received contracts from the R.A.A.F. for the manufacture of D.H. constant-speed airscrews.

CANADA

BOEING.

BOEING AIRCRAFT OF CANADA LTD.

HEAD OFFICE AND WORKS : VANCOUVER, B.C.

President : Stanley Burke.

Directors : Austin C. Taylor, W. G. Sweny, Jay Morrison and O. W. Tupper.

Boeing Aircraft of Canada Ltd. was formed in 1929 by the Boeing Airplane Company of Seattle, U.S.A.

In 1937 Boeing Aircraft of Canada Ltd. was awarded a contract by the Canadian Department of National Defence for the construction of Blackburn Shark reconnaissance biplanes, to by built under licence from Blackburn Aircraft, Ltd.

In May, 1941, the Company began tooling for the PBY-5 Canso amphibian and between July, 1942, and July, 1943, 55 were delivered to the R.C.A.F. In December, 1942, a contract for the PB2B-1 Catalina flying-boats was received from the U.S. Navy. This contract was to have been completed by the end of 1944.

The Company now has three plants in Vancouver. No. 1 Plant on West Georgia Street is producing Boeing B-29 Super-fortress sub-assemblies. No. 2 Plant is producing the tail-unit for the Mosquito bomber. No. 3 Plant on Sea Island is building the bomb-bay section of the B-29 fuselage. Tooling up for this work began August, 1944, and the first unit was shipped in October.

C.C.F.

CANADIAN CAR & FOUNDRY CO., LTD.

HEAD OFFICE : MONTREAL, P.Q.

AIRCRAFT WORKS : FORT WILLIAM, ONT., POINT ST. CHARLES (MONTREAL), TURCOT (MONTREAL), ST. LAURENT, QUE., AND AMHERST, NOVA SCOTIA.

President : Victor M. Drury.

Executive Vice-President : William Harty.

Vice-President and General Manager : L. McCoy.

The Canadian Car & Foundry Co. Ltd., the largest manu-facturers of railway equipment in the Dominion, entered the Canadian Aircraft Industry by acquiring the licence to construct the Grumman two-seat fighter biplane from the Grumman Aircraft Engineering Corpn., of Bethpage, L.I., N.Y.

The Company has contracts with the Canadian Government for the manufacture and assembly of Avro Ansons and for the overhaul and repair of aircraft of various types, including the maintenance and modification of aircraft of the R.A.F. Transport Command.

The Company also had contracts with the British Ministry of Aircraft Production for the manufacture of the Hawker Hurri-cane for the R.A.F., and with the Departments of Munitions and Supply for the R.C.A.F. The first Canadian-built Hurricane began its flying trials in January, 1940, and the first was delivered in Great Britain in February of that year. Over 1,400 Hurricanes were built. Spares produced were equivalent to well over another 1,000 aircraft.

Canadian Car & Foundry Co. Ltd. has been awarded a contract to build 1,000 Curtiss Helldiver single-engined dive-bomber monoplanes under licence from the Curtiss-Wright Corpn. for the U.S. Navy. The Helldiver built by the Canadian Car and Foundry Co., Ltd. carries the U.S. naval designation SBW-1. It is in production at the Fort William plant. The first SBW-1 flew on July 29, 1943. In 1944, the Company was building the SBW-4 and early in 1945 was going into production with the SBW-5.

The Company has a Dominion Government contract for the large-scale production of hydraulic constant-speed airscrews. These airscrews, designed by the company under licence arrange-ments, cover a wide range of sizes.

CANADAIR.

CANADAIR, LTD.

HEAD OFFICE AND WORKS : CARTIERVILLE, MONTREAL, QUE.

General Manager : Benjamin W. Franklin.

Canadair, Ltd., was formed in December, 1944, by the separ-ation of the Aircraft Division of Canadian Vickers, Ltd. from the parent Company and its formation into a new Company to be solely responsible for the manufacture of aircraft. Canadian Vickers, Ltd. will devote its entire facilities in the future to shipbuilding.

Canadair, Ltd., occupies the Government-built Cartierville

factory formerly operated by the Aircraft Division of Canadian Vickers, Ltd. It also inherits the reputation and wide experience which the parent company, the first to begin the manufacture of aircraft on a commercial scale in the Dominion, has built up over a period of twenty-one years.

In the years before the war Canadian Vickers, Ltd. was engaged in the design and development of special types and the adapt-ation of existing types of aircraft to suit the special requirements of Canada. It made a speciality of winter landing equipment embodying the experience which the long snow period in Canada

afforded and float equipment which is essential for summer operations among the lakes and rivers of Northern Canada.

Since 1939 Canadian Vickers has undertaken extensive contracts in the manufacture of military aircraft for both the Canadian and United States Governments, details of which have been given in previous issues of this Annual. Its latest important contract, awarded in 1944, was for a large number of Douglas DC-4 airliners to be fitted with Rolls-Royce Merlin engines for the Canadian Government.

COCKSHUTT.

COCKSHUTT MOULDED AIRCRAFT, LTD.

HEAD OFFICE AND WORKS : BRANTFORD, ONTARIO.

President : C. Gordon Cockshutt.

Vice-President and Treasurer : W. J. Phillips.

General Manager : Stuart S. Lee.

Secretary : J. A. D. Slemin.

Cockshutt Moulded Aircraft, Ltd. was formed in November, 1942, as a subsidiary of the Cockshutt Plow Co., Ltd. to manu-facture moulded plywood fuselages and other parts for the Anson V (see under "Federal"). The Cockshutt Plow Co., Ltd. had been prominently identified as a sub-contractor in the manufacture of parts and sub-assembles for the Canadian-built Anson under the supervision of Federal Aircraft, Ltd. since 1940.

The new plant of Cockshutt Moulded Aircraft, Ltd. was begun in July 1942, was ready for occupation by December and was in complete operation in July, 1943. It has a floor area of 100,000 sq. ft. and is fully equipped to manufacture parts under the Vidal process.

Tooling for the Anson V contract was begun in November, 1942, and first deliveries were made in the following March. Owing to heavy curtailments in the Canadian training pro-gramme, the Anson contract was terminated in December, 1944. In its place the company is undertaking the manufacture of fuselages for the Mosquito (B. Mk. 25) for the de Havilland Aircraft of Canada, Ltd. and was expected to be in full production by the Spring of 1945.

DE HAVILLAND.

THE DE HAVILLAND AIRCRAFT OF CANADA, LTD.

HEAD OFFICE AND WORKS : POSTAL STATION "L," TORONTO, ONTARIO.

Control Committee : R. A. Laidlaw (Chairman), J. D. Woods, B. L. Smith, G. A. C. Bear (General Manager), G. J. Mickleborough (Secretary and Treasurer) and W. D. Hunter (Director of Engineering).

The de Havilland Aircraft of Canada, Ltd., was established early in 1928 by the de Havilland Aircraft Co., Ltd., as a Canadian constructional plant and service depôt for D.H. aircraft.

The authorised capital of the Company is $500,000, of which $300,000 has been issued and four-fifths is held by Canadian investors.

Considerable experimental work has been done in order to produce components and special accessories to meet all Canadian flying conditions.

The Company has constructed a large number of D.H. Tiger Moths for the Canadian Government. The Tiger Moth has been one of the two standard primary trainers in use by the Commonwealth Joint Air Training Plan since its inception but production of this type has now ceased.

In its place the Company is concentrating on the large-scale production of the D.H. 98 Mosquito twin-engined Bomber monoplane. The Canadian-built Mosquito is fitted with two Packard-built Rolls-Royce Merlin engines and is being supplied to the Royal Air Force, the Royal Canadian Air Force and the U.S. Army Air Forces (under the designation F-8). The first Canadian-built Mosquitos for the R.A.F. were delivered by air across the Atlantic to Great Britain in August, 1943.

Mosquitos on routine delivery flights from Gander Airport, Newfoundland, to the United Kingdom have established many record times for the Atlantic crossing. In October, the 2,200 statute miles were covered in 6 hours 44 mins. at an average ground speed of 322 m.p.h., and by April, 1945, the crossing

D.H. Mosquitos outside the Toronto plant of the de Havilland Aircraft of Canada, Ltd.

time had been reduced to 5 hours 30 mins., representing a speed of 390 m.p.h.

Canadian Mosquitos are now being built on a newly-introduced

mechanised assembly line in which the aircraft are carried throughout the length of their assembly on huge carriages which move forward on a central chain-drive system.

FAIRCHILD.

FAIRCHILD AIRCRAFT, LTD.

HEAD OFFICE AND WORKS : LONGUEUIL, P.Q.

President and Managing Director : H. M. Pasmore.
Executive Vice-President : R. B. Irvine.
Vice-Presidents : Howard Murray, O.B.E. and W. Taylor-Bailey.
Secretary : F. Bindoff.
Treasurer : D. H. Sutherland.

Fairchild Aircraft, Ltd., is a direct outgrowth of the aviation activities of the St. Maurice Valley Protection Association which began operations in 1919 and was the first concern to demonstrate that it was practical to use aircraft for commercial purposes in the Dominion. From the St. Maurice Association was formed Fairchild Aerial Surveys of Canada, Ltd., in 1922, and in 1929 Fairchild Aircraft, Ltd., was formed to act solely as a manufacturing and servicing organization.

The factory built in September, 1930, comprised 38,000 square feet of floor space. Extensions to date now total over 600,000 square feet with machinery and equipment installed valued at approximately $2,000,000. The plant has been in continuous full-time operation since 1930 and in 1944 was employing a total personnel of 9,000 engaged solely on military contracts.

The Company, in association with five other Canadian aircraft manufacturers was awarded a contract by the British Air Ministry for the manufacture of twin-engined Hampden bombers. Certain specific components for the Hampden were built by Fairchild. Manufacture started in June, 1939 and the contract was completed in the early part of 1942.

It has also completed a contract with the Canadian Government for the manufacture of Bristol Bolingbroke twin-engined monoplanes. The Bolingbroke is generally similar to the Bristol Blenheim IV. The landing-gear can be fitted with either wheels, floats or skis. Some are fitted with the Boulton Paul

power-operated gun turret for use as trainers for air-gunners.

In 1943 the Company undertook the work of installing a Wright Cyclone engine in a Fairey Battle. As the result of satisfactory tests further aircraft of this type were similarly modified and converted into target-towing monoplanes.

In addition to the production of Bolingbroke spares, the Company is building the Curtiss Helldiver for the U.S. Navy under licence from the Curtiss-Wright Aircraft Corporation. The Fairchild-built Helldiver carries the United States Navy designation SBF. The U.S. Navy contract was placed in October, 1942, and the first Fairchild-built Helldiver flew on August 28, 1943. It was expected that this contract would be completed in April, 1945.

In 1945 Fairchild Aircraft, Ltd. undertook the production of components and sub-assemblies for the Chance Vought Corsair.

FEDERAL.

FEDERAL AIRCRAFT LTD.

HEAD OFFICE : 276, JAMES STREET WEST, MONTREAL, P.Q.

President : W. A. Newman, B.Sc.
Vice-President and General Manager : D. H. Macfarlane.
Assistant to President : F. T. Smye.
Secretary : G. H. Montgomery, Jr.
Treasurer : A. E. Belcombe.

In connection with the first Empire Air Training Scheme over 1,500 Avro Anson twin-engined trainers had to be provided. Originally, a proportion of these and quantities of components were to have been supplied by the British Government but owing to home needs it eventually fell to the responsibility of Canada to undertake production of the type.

Eleven Canadian aircraft plants were entrusted with the manufacturing or assembling of the major components and in order to co-ordinate the output of Ansons and to expedite production of the complete machines, steps were taken in 1940 to segregate this work from the remainder of the aircraft programme and place it under one management and direction. For this purpose Federal Aircraft, Ltd., a wholly-owned Government Company, was formed with headquarters in Montreal in July, 1940.

The Canadian Anson II was basically the English Avro Anson but had been modified to provide for the installation of two 330 h.p. Jacobs L-6BM engines in place of the Armstrong Siddeley Cheetah engines, which called for new cowlings and nacelles ; the fitting of Dowty hydraulic landing-gear retraction instead of the manually-operated type ; and the use of Canadian-made auxiliaries—controls, instruments, piping, flexible tubing, conduits and all other materials and parts. An interesting feature of the Canadian Anson II was the use of a moulded plastic-plywood nose section made by the Vidal process. Otherwise, similarity in design permitted parts being approximately 75 per cent. interchangeable with the British Anson.

The first Anson II flew in August, 1941, and by the end of August, 1943, Federal Aircraft Ltd. had supervised the construction of over 2,000 aircraft, with a spares replacement varying from 10 to 50 per cent. Federal-built Anson II advanced trainers have been supplied to the U.S. Army Air Forces under the designation AT-20.

Additional requirements under the 1942 Combined Training Plan increased the number of Ansons to be manufactured in Canada under the supervision of Federal Aircraft, Ltd. and two new models, the Anson V navigational trainer and the Anson VI bombing and gunnery trainer were developed.

The Anson V and Anson VI differ in many respects from the Anson II. Major changes include the incorporation of fuselages

A Federal-built Anson II as supplied to the U.S. Army Air Forces under designation AT-20.

The Federal-built Anson V Navigational Trainer (two Pratt & Whitney Wasp-Junior engines).

and numerous sub-components and parts of moulded plastic-bonded plywood, and the use of a different and more powerful type of engine. Production of these new types began early in the last quarter of 1942.

THE FEDERAL ANSON V AND VI.

Type.—Twin-engined Navigational trainer (Mk. V) or Gunnery trainer (Mk. VI).

Wings.—Low-wing cantilever monoplane. Same as for British Anson (see under "Avro").

Fuselage.—In five sections, four of which are of moulded veneer construction made by the Vidal process, the pilot's cabin section being of tubular steel construction similar to that used in the original Anson. The moulded veneer sections are formed on mandrels and bonded by hot-setting urea-formaldehyde resin glues; the skin veneers being bonded together and to frame members longerons and stringers by application of heat and pressure. Longerons and stringers are of solid poplar or pine, transverse frames of laminated construction. All other glued joints such as the longitudinal joints of the fuselage sectional halves, floor framework, reinforcing pads, etc. are made with cold-setting glue and pressure. Before half-sections are spliced and glued together all openings such as doors, windows, escape hatches, etc. are cut out. Half sections of each longitudinal section are joined by gluing before installation of fittings. The five-section design permits the rapid installation of internal fittings prior to the bolting together of the complete sections. The sections are joined by four bolts loaded axially. Final covering of madapolam and one coat of clear and two of aluminium dope.

Tail Unit and Landing Gear.—Same as for British Anson except that landing gear has Dowty hydraulic retraction.

Power Plant.—Two Pratt & Whitney Wasp-Junior R-985AN-12B or 14B nine-cylinder radial air-cooled engines. Four fuel tanks in wing. Total fuel capacity 140 Imp. gallons.

Accommodation.—Crew of five. Pilot's cabin seats two side-by-side with pilot on port side. Three desks on port wall of main cabin for two navigators and radio-operator. Adjustable counter poise lamp to each navigator's desk in addition to overhead illumination. Cabin heating and ventilation. Astro-dome with hot-air de-icing jet. Camera hatch in floor. Entrance door on starboard side aft of wings has quick-release hinges and racks for four crew parachutes grouped round door. Emergency escape hatches are also located centrally above the pilot and co-pilot and at the main cabin window on port side. Sliding windows alongside pilot and co-pilot. Mk. VI differs mainly by introduction of hydraulically-operated Bristol Mk. IV gun-turret and elimination of astro-dome.

Dimensions.—Span 56 ft. 6 in. (17.2 m.), Length 42 ft. 3 in. (12.9 m.), Height 13 ft. 1 in. (4 m.), Wing area (gross) 463 sq. ft. (43.1 sq. m.).

Weights.—Weight empty 6,693 lbs. (3,040 kg.), Normal loaded weight 9,275 lbs. (4,210 kg.), Maximum permissible loaded weight 9,460 lbs. (4,295 kg.).

Performance.—Maximum speed 190 m.p.h. (304 km.h.) at 5,000 ft. (1,525 m.), Cruising speed 145 m.p.h. (232 km.h.), Stalling speed (with flaps) 66 m.p.h. (105.6 km.h.), Stalling speed (without flaps) 73 m.p.h. (116.8 km.h.), Maximum rate of climb 1,500 ft./min. (457.5 m./min.), Average rate of climb to 10,000 ft. (3,050 m.), 1,300 ft./min. (396.5 m./min.), Rate of climb (single engine) 400 ft./min. (122 m./min.), Service ceiling 21,462 ft. (6,546 m.), Single-engine ceiling 7,800 ft. (2,380 m.), Duration 4 hours.

FLEET.

FLEET AIRCRAFT LTD.

Head Office, Works and Airport: Fort Erie, Ontario.

Chairman: E. G. McMillan, K.C.
President: E. G. Smith.
Vice-President and General Manager: W. N. Deisher.
Chief Engineer: G. E. Otter.

Fleet Aircraft, Ltd., is an independent Canadian-owned company and is completely managed by Canadian personnel.

The Company built an up-to-date factory at Fort Erie in 1930 and by 1938-39 this factory had been enlarged to ten times its original size.

The Company took over the complete World's rights from the Consolidated Aircraft Corpn. (U.S.A.), its original parent company, for the Fleet Trainer. It has since developed the Model 50K twin-engined freighter and the Model 60 two-seat advanced training monoplane, now known as the Fleet Fort.

The Fleet Trainer, or Finch, was used for primary training in the Commonwealth Air Training Plan. An original order for 404 was completed in 1940 many months ahead of schedule. A further contract for 202 was completed in 1941.

The Fort was put into production for use as an advanced training type under the Commonwealth Air Training Plan, but on the completion of the 100th machine production ceased on this type in favour of the Fairchild M-62, or Cornell, which had been adopted as the future primary trainer in the R.C.A.F. and was to be manufactured by Fleet Aircraft, Ltd., in place of the Fort and the Finch.

The first Cornell was turned out in the Summer of 1942, one month ahead of schedule. Over 1,000 were produced in the first year of production.

At the end of 1943, owing to a curtailment in the Training Programme, orders were given that the production of the Cornell was to be tapered down, to expire in May, 1944. About the beginning of 1944 the Company began tooling for the manufacture of wings and other components for the Lancaster four-engined bomber being produced by Victory Aircraft, Ltd. By the middle of 1944 the Company's plant was almost entirely turned over to this Lancaster sub-contract.

The Fleet-Fairchild Cornell Two-seat Training Monoplane (200 h.p. Ranger engine).

THE FLEET-FAIRCHILD CORNELL.

R.C.A.F. designation: Cornell II.
U.S. Army Air Forces designations: PT-26A and PT-26B.

The Cornell two-seat primary trainer is basically the American Fairchild PT-26 but has been modified by Fleet Aircraft, Ltd. to meet Canadian requirements. In all some 450 revisions were made from the original design. The principal modifications however concern equipment and include cockpit enclosures, heating, night-flying and blind-flying equipment, etc.

Type.—Two-seat Primary Trainer.

Wings.—Low-wing cantilever monoplane comprising a centre-section and two tapering outer sections. All-wood structure comprising two box-spars with laminated spruce-flanges and two-ply webs, girder type spruce and plywood ribs and a final covering of plywood with spruce or mahogany faces and spruce or poplar core. Tubular-steel compression struts brace centre-section spars at wing joints. Balanced differentially-operated ailerons have aluminium-alloy frames and fabric covering. Split-type flaps of wood or aluminium-alloy construction. Metal tabs in ailerons adjustable on the ground only.

Fuselage.—Rectangular welded chrome-molybdenum steel-tube structure. Four longerons and main members are of squared tube. Bracing members in rear fuselage and stringers are round tubes. Fabric covering over wooden fairing structure, except decking which is of aluminium-alloy construction.

Tail Unit.—Cantilever monoplane type. Fin and tailplane of wood with plywood covering. Rudder and elevators have aluminium-alloy frames with fabric covering. Trim-tab in elevator. Rudder has tab adjustable on ground only.

Landing Gear.—Fixed single-leg cantilever type. Each leg supported by aluminium-alloy casting on front spar of centre-section. Oil-damped steel-spring shock-absorbers. Wheels carried in half forks. Hydraulic brakes of expander tube type. Steerable tail-wheel with release device for full swivelling.

Power Plant.—One 200 h.p. Ranger 6-440-C5 six-cylinder in-line inverted air-cooled engine on welded steel-tube mounting. Two-bladed wooden airscrew. Fuel tanks (two) in centre-section, one on each side of fuselage. Total capacity $37\frac{1}{2}$ Imp. gallons.

Accommodation.—Tandem cockpits with complete dual controls and identical equipment. Continuous transparent canopy with independently-operated sliding sections over each cockpit. Centrally-placed turn-over pylon. Seat height and rudder reach adjustable. Complete blind-flying and navigation instruments in both cockpits. Rear cockpit equipped with blind-flying hood. Cockpit heating and ventilation. Engine-driven generator for electrical equipment.

Dimensions.—Span 36 ft. (11 m.), Length 27 ft. $8\frac{3}{8}$ in. (8.45 m.), Height 7 ft. $7\frac{1}{2}$ in. (2.3 m.), Wing area 200 sq. ft. (18.6 sq. m.).

Weights and Loadings.—Weight empty 2,022 lbs. (918 kg.), Weight loaded 2,736 lbs. (1,242 kg.), Wing loading 13.6 lbs./sq. ft. (66.36 kg./sq. m.), Power loading 13.6 lbs./h.p. (6.17 kg./h.p.).

Performance.—Maximum speed 122 m.p.h. (195.2 km.h.), Cruising speed (60% power) 101 m.p.h. (161.6 km.h.), Climb to 10,000 ft. (3,050 m.) 24 mins., Service ceiling 13,200 ft. (4,025 m.), Endurance at cruising speed 4.25 hours.

MacDONALD.

MacDONALD BROS. AIRCRAFT, LTD.

Head Office and Works: 50, Robinson Street, Winnipeg, Manitoba.

President and General Manager: Grant MacDonald.

MacDonald Bros. Aircraft, Ltd. was formed in 1930 to service and overhaul aircraft. Later it acquired the licence to build Edo floats in Canada and operated an airframe repair depot and general aircraft supply service.

After the outbreak of war the Company erected a new plant on Stevenson Field, just outside Winnipeg, for the assembly and repair of British-built Anson aircraft used in the Commonwealth Joint Air Training Plan.

The original plant at Robinson Street, Winnipeg, undertook the manufacture of metal parts for the Anson, Oxford and Hurricane, and this now operates as the Company's Robinson Street Division. In 1944, this Division was engaged in the manufacture of miscellaneous parts for the Curtiss Helldiver and Boeing-built Catalina, as well as floats for the Noorduyn C 64A Norseman being built for the U.S. Army Air Forces.

The Airport Division in the past assembled the Anson I and II and manufactured wings for the Anson II. It also undertook the repairs and overhaul of the Anson I and II. During 1944, it was assembling the Anson V, including the manufacture of the complete wing and assembly of the fuselage from pressed plywood veneer shells supplied by other contractors. It was also manufacturing components for the D.H. Mosquito.

At the time of writing MacDonald Bros. Aircraft, Ltd. was the only contractor engaged in the final assembly of the Anson V.

The Company has, in its Robinson Street Division and the buildings on Stevenson Field, a total manufacturing floor space of 300,000 sq. ft.

NOORDUYN.

NOORDUYN AVIATION, LTD.

Head Office: 1411, Crescent Street, Montreal, P.Q.

Works: St. Laurent, P.Q., Moreau Street, Montreal, P.Q, and Haig Avenue, Montreal, P.Q.

President: W. L. Bayer.
Vice-President and General Manager: R. B. C. Noorduyn, A.F.R.Ae.S., A.F.I.Ae.S.
Vice-President: Major W. R. G. Holt.
Secretary and Treasurer: L. M. Coughtry.

The expansion of this Company's facilities, personnel and output which set in shortly after the outbreak of war, reached its peak in 1943-44 and has since been declining with the completion of contracts. The Harvard IIB (U.S. designation AT-16) advanced trainer is no longer in production but the Noorduyn Norseman (U.S. designation C-64) was still being produced in 1944 as a general utility cargo and passenger transport for the U.S. Army Air Forces. The Norseman is also used by the R.C.A.F. for the training of wireless operators and for communication duties.

The firm also operates the main repair department in Canada for Harvard and Norseman aircraft, and produces ski equipment for these and several other service types.

THE NOORDUYN NORSEMAN Mk V.

U.S. Army Air Forces designation: C-64A.

Type.—Single-engined Transport monoplane suitable for various military and civil duties.

Wings.—High-wing braced monoplane. Wings attached direct to top of fuselage longerons and braced to stubs by steel tube Vee struts. Structure consists of routed solid spruce spars with walnut packing-pieces under fittings, spruce ribs, steel-tube drag struts and swaged wire bracing, duralumin covered leading-edge, fabric covering. Flaps and ailerons have steel tube frame and fabric covering. Slotted mass-balanced ailerons and flaps. Ailerons droop as flaps with first half of flap movement.

Pilot's seat and rudder pedals fully adjustable. Swing-over type dual control. Below wing is main sound-proofed cabin of 150 cub. ft. capacity. Bench-type seats for eight passengers may be instantly removed. Individual upholstered passenger chairs optional. One passenger door hinged on additional removable section to provide 46 in. opening when required. Fixed front and cabin windows, lowering cockpit and cabin door windows. Additional space for baggage or freight below floor of cabin (33 cub. ft.) and behind cabin (10 cub. ft.) with outside doors. Cabin heater with three controllable outlets. Lower part of back wall of cabin may be removed for stowage of long articles of freight into tail of fuselage.

Dimensions.—Span 51 ft. 8 in. (15.8 m.), Length 31 ft. 9 in. (9.68 m.), Height 10 ft. 1 in. (3 m.), Wing area 325 sq. ft. (30.2 sq. m.).

Weights and Loadings.—Weight empty—Landplane Freighter 4,420 lbs. (2,007 kg.), Seaplane Freighter 4,890 lbs. (2,220 kg.), Skiplane Freighter 4,600 lbs. (2,088 kg.), Additional weight for 6-passenger military cabin equipment 54 lbs. (24.5 kg.), Additional weight for 8-passenger commercial cabin equipment 120 lbs. (54.5 kg.), Weight loaded (Landplane, Seaplane or Skiplane): 7,400 lbs. (3,360 kg.), Wing loading 22.8 lbs./sq. ft. (111.26 kg./sq. m.), Power loading (take-off) 12.3 lbs./h.p. (5.58 kg./h.p.).

Performance.—Cruising speed (75% power)—Landplane: 148 m.p.h. (236.8 km.h.), Seaplane: 130 m.p.h. (208 km.h.), Skiplane: 142 m.p.h. (227.2 km.h.), Landing speed 68 m.p.h. (108.8 km.h.), Climb (Landplane) to 5,000 ft. (1,525 m.) 6.5 min., to 10,000 ft. (3,050 m.) 15.5 min., to 15,000 ft. (4,575 m.) 28.5 min., Service ceiling (Landplane) 17,000 ft. (5,185 m.), Cruising range at 75% power and maximum tankage (Landplane) 1,150 miles (1,840 km.).

Fuselage.—Welded chrome-molybdenum steel-tube framework, faired to an oval section by steel-tube frames and "T" section spruce stringers and covered with fabric.

Tail Unit.—Braced monoplane type. Tail-plane structure same as

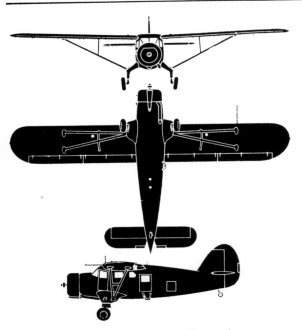

The Noorduyn Norseman Transport.

The Noorduyn C-64 Norseman Transport Monoplane (550 h.p. Pratt & Whitney Wasp engine).

for wings. Fin, rudder and elevators have welded steel-tube frames with fabric covering. Trimming-tabs in elevators and rudder.

LANDING GEAR.—Divided type. Consists of two cantilever oleo legs which may be removed from the fuselage stubs by removing two bolts each for substitution of standard Edo type Yd floats or approved skis of Noorduyn or other design. Tail-wheel strut may carry either wheel or tail-ski.

POWER PLANT.—One Pratt & Whitney Wasp R-1340-AN1 nine-cylinder radial air-cooled engine rated at 550 h.p. at 5,000 ft. (1,525 m.) and with 600 h.p. available for take-off. NACA cowling. Two-bladed Hamilton-Standard constant-speed airscrew. Eclipse direct electric starter with emergency hand-crank. Fuel tanks (two) in wing-roots (100 Imp. gallons = 120 U.S.

gallons) with gravity feed to engine-driven pump. One or two additional tanks of 37 Imp. gallons (45 U.S. gallons) and 64 Imp. gallons (75 U.S. gallons) respectively may be installed in baggage space under floor of cabin, thus providing alternative fuel capacities of 100 Imp. gallons (120 U.S. gallons), 137 Imp. gallons (165 U.S. gallons) or 201 Imp. gallons (242 U.S. gallons). Oil capacity 8-16 Imp. gallons (10-20 U.S. gallons). Equipment includes oil dilution system.

ACCOMMODATION.—Pilot's enclosed and heated cockpit seating two side-by-side in front of wings. Full-size doors on each side.

OTTAWA.

OTTAWA CAR AND AIRCRAFT, LTD.

HEAD OFFICE AND WORKS : SLATER STREET, OTTAWA.

President : H. W. Soper.

Vice-President : A. C. T. Lewis, K.C.

General Manager : E. G. Patterson, B.Sc., M.E.I.C.

Secretary and Treasurer : G. L. Snelling.

This Company, whose principal business is the manufacture of street cars, etc., entered the Canadian Aircraft Industry as the sole Canadian manufacturing and selling agents for Sir W. G. Armstrong Whitworth Aircraft, Ltd., A. V. Roe & Co., Ltd. and Armstrong Siddeley Motors, Ltd.

The Ottawa factory has a floor space of 250,000 sq. ft. and is

well equipped with aircraft and aero-engine erecting shops, doping shops and an aero-engine testing department.

It has been engaged in the manufacture of major components for the Avro Lancaster and machined parts for the Curtiss Helldiver dive-bomber.

VICTORY

VICTORY AIRCRAFT, LTD.

HEAD OFFICE AND WORKS : TORONTO (MALTON), ONT.

President : V. W. Scully.

General Manager : David Boyd.

Victory Aircraft, Ltd., a company wholly-owned by the Crown and responsible to the Minister of Munitions and Supply, was formed in 1942 to take over the ownership and management

of the Malton aircraft plant of the National Steel Car Corporation, Ltd. in order to expedite the production of the Avro Lancaster bomber. The first Victory-built Lancaster bomber was delivered to Great Britain by air across the Atlantic in September, 1943. The 300th was delivered in April, 1945.

In addition to the production of Lancaster X bombers, the company has also built four special Lancaster mail-carriers for

the Canadian Government Trans-Atlantic service which is operated by Trans-Canada Air Lines. The company also manufactured and delivered in 1944 one special Avro York transport.

In July, 1945 it was announced that Victory Aircraft, Ltd. had been acquired from the Canadian Government by the Hawker Siddeley Aircraft Co., Ltd.

INDIA

HINDUSTAN.

HINDUSTAN AIRCRAFT, LTD.

HEAD OFFICE AND WORKS : BANGALORE, MYSORE.

Government Aircraft Inspector : G. M. Randall.

Hindustan Aircraft. Ltd., was formed in 1940 to undertake the manufacture of aircraft for the Indian market. With the financial assistance of the Indian Government, the construction, organization and equipment of the factory at Bangalore was undertaken by Mr. William D. Pawley, President of the Inter-continent Aircraft Corpn. of New York, one of the largest exporters of American aircraft to the Far East.

The Intercontinent Aircraft Corpn. was able to acquire a large quantity of machine-tools before the war emergency shortage

began to be felt and it has obtained further equipment through the co-operation of the American authorities in Washington. A number of Indian and Chinese engineers educated in British and American technical institutions were engaged to occupy key positions in the factory, which is expected to employ over 5,000 workers when in full production.

The first aeroplane to be assembled by the factory was flown in August, 1941. This was a Harlow PC-5 two-seat training monoplane of all-metal construction. The Company is also assembling other aircraft of American design.

On April 2, 1942, it was officially announced that Hindustan Aircraft, Ltd. had been taken over by the Indian Government

and that it would be operated, for the period of the War at least, as a Government concern.

The capital of the Company had formerly been held jointly by the Government of India, the Mysore Government and Mr. Lalchand Hirachand. Mr. Lalchand Hirachand and his associates accepted the offer of the Government for the purchase of their interests. The Mysore Government, while retaining a financial interest in the Company, have agreed to waive the right to share in its active management for the period of the War and for a year to two thereafter, in order to facilitate the operation of the factory as a Government concern.

NEW ZEALAND

DE HAVILLAND.

THE DE HAVILLAND AIRCRAFT CO. OF NEW ZEALAND, LTD.

HEAD OFFICE AND WORKS : RONGOTAI, WELLINGTON.

The New Zealand branch of the de Havilland Aircraft Co., Ltd., was formed towards the end of 1939. An initial order for

100 Tiger Moths was placed with the Company by the New Zealand Government and delivery began in May, 1940.

By 1941 the Company was producing enough Tiger Moths to satisfy the requirements of the Royal New Zealand Air Force, and it had also undertaken the manufacture of parts for

the Airspeed Oxford.

For Tiger Moth production the Company makes all parts except engines, tyres and instruments. Gipsy-Major engines imported from Australia. A subsidiary factory at Rongotai manufactures airscrews from Queensland maple.

CZECHOSLOVAKIA

The former Aircraft Industry of Czechoslovakia consisted of the following Aircraft manufacturing firms:—

AERO TOVARNA LETADEL DR. KABES.	Praha-Vysocany.
"AVIA" AKCIOVA SPOLECNOST PRO PRUMYSL LETECKY (SKODA).	Praha-Cakovice.
BENES-MRAZ TOVARNA NA LETADLA.	Chocen.
VOJENSKA TOVARNA NA LETADLA "LETOV."	Praha-Letnany.
CESKOMORAVSKA KOLBEN DANEK	Praha-Karlin.
RINGHOFFER-TATRA A.S.	Praha-Smichov.
ZLINSKA LETECKA A.S.	Zlin.

Many, if not all, of these firms were at one time absorbed into the German Aircraft Industry and converted to the production of German military aircraft and equipment. The Ceskomoravska Kolben Danek, formerly famous as the manufacturers of "Praga" aircraft and aero-engines, as well as other armaments, was reconstituted as the Böhmisch-Mährische Maschinenfabriken A.G. (Bohemian-Moravian Engineering Works). The Aero, Avia and Letov works were also taken over as shadow factories for German aircraft manufacturers.

DENMARK

Prior to the occupation of Denmark by German Forces on April 9, 1940, the only establishments undertaking the manufacture of aircraft in Denmark were the Royal Army Aircraft Factory (Haerens Flyvertroppernes Vaerkstader) and the Royal Naval Dockyard (Orlogsvaerftet), both situated in Copenhagen.

The Army Aircraft Factory was formed in 1914 and had, since that date, built all service aircraft and had undertaken all repair work for the Royal Army Flying Corps. Aircraft built in the Army Factory were constructed under foreign licences, the most recent types being the Fokker C.V-E reconnaissance biplane, and the Gloster Gauntlet and Fokker D.21 single-seat fighters.

The Naval Dockyard was also formed in 1914. Although the earlier productions of the Dockyard were of original design, later types were built under foreign licences. Types built in the Dockyard included the Heinkel He 8 three-seat reconnaissance seaplane, the Avro Tutor training biplane and the Hawker Nimrod single-seat fighter biplane. The Dockyard also built Fokker monoplanes for Det Danske Luftfartselskabet A.S. (Danish Air Lines).

FINLAND

THE STATE AIRCRAFT FACTORY.

VALTION LENTOKONETÉHDAS (THE STATE AIRCRAFT FACTORY).

WORKS: TAMPERE.

This factory has supplied the Air Force with various types of military aircraft. The Factory-designed Tuisku and Viima II training biplanes and the Pyry advanced training monoplane have been fully illustrated and described in previous issues of this Annual. The last-known original design emanating from the Factory was the Myrsky, a single-seat fighter mono-plane and aero accessories to the Finnish Light Aeroplane Clubs and private owners.

Considerable attention was devoted to the investigation of the qualities of home produced materials, particularly timber. Finnish pine proved to be eminently suitable for aircraft plane fitted with a Pratt & Whitney Twin-Wasp engine, which was designed in 1940.

All reconditioning of aircraft and aero-engines for the Finnish Air Force was done at the Factory, which also supplied aero-use as the result of tests made in the Factory's laboratories show. Finnish bakelite-glued plywood floats also proved themselves to be strong, light, economical and resistent to deterioration.

Other developments were the design and production of skis and adjustable airscrews of bakelite-glued plywood.

No information is available concerning the activities of this establishment since Finland took up arms against Russia in 1941.

FRANCE

(The information below, which was checked and brought up-to-date by the French Air Ministry in Paris in December, 1944, presents a comprehensive picture of the activities of the French Aircraft Industry through the four years of German occupation. Since the liberation of France the Provisional Government has been energetically engaged in a programme of rehabilitation of the Industry under full nationalisation. At the time of writing it was not possible to give more than a brief outline of the initial production programme intended to get existing factories back into production. Nor is it yet possible to give any information on the ultimate composition or disposition of the future industry, the re-organization of which is in the hands of a Government Technical Committee intended to serve as a permanent governing body directly responsible to the Air Ministry.—ED.).

Following on the occupation of Belgium and Holland by Germany, Northern France was overrun and the French Government headed by Marshal Pétain capitulated to the enemy on June 17, 1940. Under the terms of the Armistice France was called upon to store in controlled depôts all military aircraft and to immobilise all factories engaged in the production of military aircraft and equipment. A decree issued by the Petain Government dated July 20, 1940, cancelled all manufacturing contracts for national defence in accordance with the terms of the Armistice.

On the outbreak of War there were six State-controlled groups, which had been formed under the 1936 law for the nationalisation of military industries, and a number of independent undertakings engaged in the manufacture of aircraft.

The following were the six State-owned "Sociétés Nationales," all of which were engaged in the manufacture of military aircraft:—

SOCIÉTÉ NATIONALE DE CONSTRUCTIONS AÉRONAUTIQUES DE L'OUEST (S.N.C.A.O.), Nantes, St. Nazaire and Issy-les-Moulineaux.

SOCIÉTÉ NATIONALE DE CONSTRUCTIONS AÉRONAUTIQUES DE SUD-OUEST (S.N.C.A.S.O.), Courbevoie, Châteauroux, Bordeaux (three factories), Rochefort and Suresnes.

SOCIÉTÉ NATIONALE DE CONSTRUCTIONS AÉRONAUTIQUES DU NORD (S.N.C.A.N.), Meaulte, Sartrouville, Caudebec-en-Caux, Les Mureaux and Havre.

SOCIÉTÉ NATIONALE DE CONSTRUCTIONS AÉRONAUTIQUES DU CENTRE (S.N.C.A.C.), Fourchambault, Bourges and Billancourt.

SOCIÉTÉ NATIONALE DE CONSTRUCTIONS AÉRONAUTIQUES DE SUD-EST (S.N.C.A.S.E.), Clichy, Argenteuil, Berre, Vitrolles, Cannes and Marseille.

SOCIÉTÉ NATIONALE DE CONSTRUCTIONS AÉRONAUTIQUES DU MIDI (S.N.C.A.M.), Toulouse.

At the end of 1940, under the pressure of the Vichy Government and as part of its programme of reorganization, the S.N.C.A. du Sud-Ouest and the S.N.C.A. de Sud-Est took over, respectively, the activities of the S.N.C.A. de l'Ouest and the S.N.C.A. du Midi, which thereupon went into liquidation.

The following companies which had succeeded in retaining their independence were also responsible for the design and/or manufacture of military aircraft:—

AVIONS AMIOT (S.E.C.M.), Colombes.

SOCIÉTÉ ANONYME DES ATELIERS D'AVIATION LOUIS BREGUET, Villacoublay, Bayonne and Toulouse.

SOCIÉTÉ ANONYME DES AVIONS CAUDRON, Issy-les-Moulineaux and Billancourt.

SOCIÉTÉ INDUSTRIELLE D'AVIATION. LATÉCOÈRE, Toulouse.

AVIONS PIERRE LEVASSEUR, Paris.

AÉROPLANES MORANE-SAULNIER, Puteaux.

During 1941 an effort was made by the Vichy Government to revive and consolidate the French aircraft industry. Conforming to the then existing legislation (Law of August 15, 1940) a special committee was created to re-organize the aircraft works in both occupied and unoccupied France. Ingenieur en Chef de l'Aéronautique Roos was appointed Director of this Committee.

In July, 1941, an agreement was concluded between the German authorities and the Vichy Government whereby the aircraft industry in the Occupied Zone would undertake on German account to build more than 2,000 aircraft of the following types:—Caudron Goëland, Arado Ar 196, Focke-Wulf Fw 189, Fieseler Fi 156, Siebel Si 204, Junkers Ju 52 and parts for the Ju 87 and Ju 88. On the other hand factories in the Unoccupied Zone and certain works in the occupied area (Caudron, Issy, S.N.C.A.S.O., Issy and Saint Nazaire) were authorised to build a certain number of military and civil aircraft (1,200 in 2 years) and to build a limited number of prototypes and to undertake certain development work on behalf of the military and civil air services which the Vichy Government was permitted to maintain in the territory which it administrated.

To assist the financing of the German part of the aircraft construction programme a branch of the Bank der Deutschen Luftfahrt was formed in Paris under the name of Aéro-Banque S.A. with a share capital of 200 million francs.

The production of German aircraft was distributed among factories in the Occupied Zone in the following manner:—

Junkers Ju 52. The Junkers group was given control of the Société Amiot (Colombes) as a parent company to handle production under the direction of M. Villard. Manufacture was distributed among the following factories:—

Suresnes (S.N.C.A.S.O.). Outer wings.

Courbevoie (S.N.C.A.S.O.). Tail-unit and landing gear, etc.

Colombes (Amiot). Centre-section, fuselage, equipment.

Villacoublay (Bréguet). Assembly and flight test.

Production in November, 1942, was at the rate of 10 per month.

Junkers Ju 87 and 88. Parts and spares manufactured by several factories in the Paris region.

Messerschmitt Me 108. Production, erection and flight test in the Mureaux factory of the S.N.C.A.N. One Me 208 with tricycle landing-gear was built.

Fieseler Fi 156. Production by the Morane factory at Puteaux. Erection and flight test at Villacoublay.

Siebel Si 204. Outer wings built in the S.N.C.A.C. factory at Fourchambault. All other production, assembly and flight test by S.N.C.A.C. at Bourges. Production in November, 1942, was at the rate of 5 per month.

Arado Ar 196. Entire production in the S.N.C.A.S.O. factory at Bouguenais (St. Nazaire).

Focke-Wulf Fw 189. Production mainly by the S.N.C.A.S.O. factories controlled by Focke-Wulf, but outer wings built by Breguet at Bayonne. The distribution of production was as follows:—

Bordeaux-Bègles (S.N.C.A.S.O.). Small parts.

Bordeaux-Bacalan (S.N.C.A.S.O.). Centre-sections of wings and fuselage.

Rochefort (S.N.C.A.S.O.). Tail-unit and tail booms.

Bayonne (Bréguet). Outer wings.

Bordeaux-Merignac (S.N.C.A.S.O.). Assembly and flight test.

Production in November, 1942, was at the rate of 20 per month.

Focke-Wulf Fw 190. The Brandt factory at Chatillon-sur-Bagneux, in the south-eastern suburbs of Paris, was requisitioned and put onto series production of motor cowlings for the Fw 190. This plant was also allotted to the Groupe Téchnique de Châtillon as a prototype factory. The Groupe Téchnique de Châtillon comprised some 300 French engineers and designers who were under the strict tutelage of technicians of the Focke-Wulf company. Prototypes studied by this group (Fw 206 twin-engined monoplane and Fw 300 four-engined monoplane of 47,000 kg. (103,400 lbs.) loaded weight never saw the light of day.

Except for a very limited amount of Commercial development work provisionally undertaken on French account, from February, 1943, until the liberation of France the Aircraft Industry worked solely for Germany and under the increasingly difficult control of the occupation authorities.

THE AIRCRAFT INDUSTRY DURING THE GERMAN OCCUPATION OF FRANCE.

AVIONS AMIOT.

The Amiot company came under the control of the Junkers group shortly after the Armistice, although still under Amiot direction. It handled production of the Ju 52 transport in the Paris area, the fuselage and centre-section being built in the Colombes factory while other components were built by sub-contractors.

SOCIÉTÉ D'AVIATION LOUIS BREGUET.

Most of the former Breguet factories were incorporated into the nationalised industry in 1936, but in 1937 the Breguet company bought the Latécoère factories at Toulouse-Montaudran and Biscarosse.

The Breguet factory at Villacoublay was occupied by the Junkers company which used it as a repair and assembly plant. The Bayonne factory built outer wings for the Fw 189 under sub-contract from the S.N.C.A.S.O. The Brequet company also built two Blohm & Voss Bv 144 twin-engined transport prototypes for the German authorities.

For the Vichy Government the company was permitted to build a small series of the Latécoère 298 torpedo-seaplane and to undertake the construction of eight Breguet 730 reconnaissance flying-boats. It also developed the Breguet 500 twin-engined commercial monoplane. Two prototypes were built after the Armistice and both were ready to fly by November, 1942.

The Breguet 500 has accommodation for a crew of four, 23 passengers and 1,500 kg. (3,300 lbs.) of freight. It is fitted with two 1,650 h.p. Gnôme-Rhône 14R radial air-cooled engines.

AVIONS CAUDRON-RENAULT.

This concern was very closely linked with the Renault company and a portion of the Renault works at Billancourt was devoted to the series production of Caudron aircraft. This plant, prior to being severely damaged by the R.A.F. in 1943, was in production with the Caudron Goëland twin-engined six-passenger monoplane to both French and German accounts for use as a light communicati ns and transport monoplane. It also undertook considerable sub-contract work for German firms.

S.A. DES AVIONS FARMAN.

The name Farman disappeared from the French Industry when it was nationalised in 1936, but in the Spring of 1941 a new Farman company under the above name was formed. Just prior to the German occupation of the entire country, that is, early in November, 1942, the company acquired the Rosengart motor works in Paris which, before the War, produced a French copy of the Austin Seven automobile. The company undertook sub-contract work for German firms.

SOCIÉTÉ INDUSTRIELLE D'AVIATION LATÉCOÈRE.

This concern, under the direction until his death early in 1944 of M. Latécoère and then under M. Moine, continued the construction of two Laté 631 six-engined trans-Atlantic flying-boats begun before the War. At the beginning of 1942 it received an order for two more of the same type. The first of these boats was transferred in May, 1942, to Marignane where it underwent its flying tests. It was confiscated in 1944 by the German authorities and flown to Lake Constance, where it was destroyed in an attack by allied aircraft.

AVIONS MAUBOUSSIN.

This concern specialised in the design and manufacture of light training and sporting aircraft before the War. After the Armistice it turned its attention to gliders. Later it returned to powered aircraft and prior to the German occupation of France had under development the M.129 two-seat light trainer; the M.202 single-seat advanced trainer; the M.300 light twin-engined trainer and communications type; and the M.400 twin-engined freighter. The M.129 and M.202 were developments of designs produced before the War.

The M.300 was a new design fitted with two 220 h.p. Renault 6Q six-cylinder in-line inverted air-cooled engines, and incorporating a retractable landing-gear and twin-ruddered tail-unit. It was originally designed as a light six-passenger transport but at the request of the Air Ministry it was later converted to a three or four-seat trainer and liaison type.

The M.400 was a biplane generally resembling the D.H. Dragon-Rapide but with two 350 h.p. Béarn six-cylinder in-line inverted engines mounted in nacelles on the lower wing and driving pusher airscrews. The landing wheels retracted into the rear portions of the nacelles beneath the airscrew drive shafts. The M.400 had a freight capacity for 2,500 kg. (5,500 lbs.).

AÉROPLANES MORANE-SAULNIER.

This company was taken over by the Fieseler company after the Armistice and was put onto the production of the Fieseler Storch. The Puteaux factory was entirely devoted to the manufacture of this type, assembly and flight tests being undertaken at Villacoublay.

The Morane company established a technical office and prototype works at Ossun, near Tarbes, both working for French account.

SOCIÉTÉ INDUSTRIELLE POUR L'AVIATION.

This organization was formed by Dewoitine in collaboration with a group formerly representing General Motors in France to undertake aircraft production on behalf of the German authorities. It was engaged exclusively on sub-contracts for the German Arado Ar 199 light trainer and the Ar 196. This concern developed to German account the prototype Ar 296 advanced training monoplane. Five examples of this type were built.

SOCIÉTÉ NATIONALÉ DE CONSTRUCTIONS AÉRONAUTIQUES DE L'OUEST.

This group, which included factories formerly owned by the Breguet and Loire-Nieuport companies, was merged with the S.N.C.A. Sud-Ouest in 1941.

SOCIÉTÉ NATIONALE DE CONSTRUCTIONS AÉRONAUTIQUES DE SUD-OUEST.

The S.N.C.A.S.O. originally embraced factories formerly owned by the Bloch and Blériot companies. After the capitulation of France all the factories in the occupied zone were taken over by the German authorities and placed under the general control of the Focke-Wulf organization.

The activities of the German-controlled S.N.C.A.S.O. factories up to the end of 1942 were as follows :—

Suresnes and Courbevoie. Were working as sub-contractors to the Société Amiot (Junkers group) making parts for the Ju 52. Wings at Suresnes, tail and other parts at Courbevoie.

Issy-les-Moulineaux (formerly S.N.C.A.O.). This factory was permitted to complete about 40 Loire-Nieuport L.N. 40 single-engined naval dive-bombers. When completed in the Summer of 1942 they were flown to Châteauroux (Free France) and eventually delivered to St. Raphael or North Africa. The factory was then put onto repair work for the Ju 87, Me 108 and Do 24.

St. Nazaire-Bouguenais (formerly S.N.C.A.O.). Built to French account a small series (30) of the Loire 130 single-engined reconnaissance flying-boat. It was also engaged in the production of the Heinkel He 111.

Bordeaux (three factories) and Rochefort. Except for outer wings, which were manufactured by Breguet (Bayonne), these factories were producing the Focke-Wulf Fw 189.

The only factory of the Group in Free France, at Châteauroux, undertook the repair of automobiles, lorries, etc. for the French Army after the Armistice, although it was permitted to complete 20-25 Bloch 155 single-engined single-seat twin-cannon fighters (1,100 h.p. Gnôme-Rhône N.49 radial engine) of a series which was in production. These aircraft were subsequently delivered to the Vichy Air Force.

In August, 1940, a technical group composed of S.N.C.A.S.O. engineers and technicians who were unwilling to work in the occupied zone was formed at Châteauroux, but this later moved to Cannes. (See Groupe Téchnique de Cannes).

Châteauroux then undertook the production of the Bloch 175, an order for 300 of which was received from the Vichy French Air Ministry.

The Bloch 175 was a multi-purposes twin-engined monoplane capable of operating as a light bomber (750 kg.= 1,650 lb. bomb load), as a reconnaissance type, as a torpedo-carrier, or as a heavy fighter (4 cannon and 4 machine-guns). The Air Ministry order provided for production of two versions, a light bomber with two Gnôme-Rhône N.48/49 radial engines, and a heavy fighter with two Hispano-Suiza 12Z liquid-cooled engines. The former model had a maximum speed of 540 km.h. (335.3 m.p.h.) at 5,200 m. (17,050 ft.) and the latter 650 km.h. (403.6 m.p.h.) at 8,700 m. (28,500 ft.).

Production was divided between two factories, the Châteauroux plant making the centre-section and the main fuselage section, and the Marignane (S.N.C.A.S.E.) plant the outer wings, tail-unit and front and rear fuselage sections. Châteauroux was responsible for assembly and test.

By November, 1942, production in these two plants was well in hand but on the abolition of the line of demarcation all work on the Bloch 175 was stopped, except on the Gnôme-Rhône-equipped engine nacelles for the light bomber version, which were adapted for use in the Messerschmitt Me 323 six-engined military transport.

SOCIÉTÉ NATIONALE DE CONSTRUCTIONS AÉRONAUTIQUES DU NORD.

This group owned factories which were formerly the property of the Potez-CAMS, Mureaux and Bréguet companies.

The former Potez works at Méaulte, one of the largest in France, was taken over by the Germans as a repair base and was partially destroyed by British and American bombing raids.

The CAMS seaplane works at Sartrouville completed the Potez-CAMS six-engined trans-Atlantic flying-boat (six Hispano-Suiza 12Y engines). This boat, which was built to a French Air Ministry specification issued in 1936 and begun before the War, made its first flight on March 20, 1942, and, wearing German markings, was flown across France to Marseille to complete its flying trials. It was later taken over by the German authorities. A description of this boat appeared in the 1939 edition of this Annual. The Sartrouville works also built a number of Dornier Do 24 three engined flying-boats.

The factory at Les Mureaux was put onto the production of the Messerschmitt Me 108 light single-engined communications monoplane.

SOCIÉTÉ NATIONALE DE CONSTRUCTIONS AÉRONAUTIQUES DE CENTRE.

This group comprised factories formerly belonging to the Farman and Hanriot companies, all in the occupied area.

All were put onto production for the enemy. The former Hanriot factory undertook the production of the Siebel Si 204 light twin-engined communications monoplane.

SOCIÉTÉ NATIONALE DE CONSTRUCTIONS AÉRONAUTIQUES DE SUD-EST.

This group included factories formerly owned by the Lioré-et-Olivier, Potez-CAMS, Romano and S.P.C.A. companies.

At the Marseille-Mariguane works this group worked on an order from the French authorities for two (later four) SE.200 four-engined trans-Atlantic flying-boats. The first two were begun before the War under a programme of technical development drawn up by the French Air Ministry in 1936. The prototype S.E. 200 made its first flight in August, 1942, and early in 1944 it was confiscated by the German authorities and flown to Friedrichshafen, on Lake Constance, where with the Latécoère 631, it was destroyed in an Allied bombing attack.

The Ambérieu (Ain) factory was, at the time of the Armistice, in production with the LeO.45 twin-engined bomber (two Gnôme-Rhône N.48/49 radial air-cooled engines). A considerable number in process of manufacture was completed and delivered to North Africa.

The Toulouse factory (which formerly belonged to Dewoitine and later, the S.N.C.A. du Midi) completed a series order for the Dewoitine D. 520 single-seat fighter and in December, 1941, it began the series production of the S.O. 161 (formerly Bloch 161) on an order from the Vichy Government. The prototype, which had flown in 1939 at Bordeaux, was not allowed to fly to Mariguane to complete its tests until January, 1942. In June, 1942, the S.N.C.A.S.E. received an additional order for 20 aircraft of this type from the Vichy Government, of which 10 were to be delivered to the Deutsche Lufthansa. After the occupation of Southern France, the order was taken over by Deutsche Lufthansa and then abandoned. With the exception of the prototype confiscated by Germany, no other aircraft was delivered.

The S.O. 161 is a four-engined transport suitable for either civil or military use. It is fitted with four Gnôme-Rhône N.44/45 radial air-cooled engines, each rated at 1,100 h.p. at 3,200 m. (10,500 ft.) and has a loaded weight of 22,500 kg. (49,500 lbs.). It has a span of 29.4 m. (96 ft. 6 in.), a length of 24.4 m. (80 ft.), a height of 4.7 m. (15 ft. 5 in.), and a wing area of 111.3 sq. m. (1,198 sq. ft.). The maximum speed of the S.O. 161 is 427 km.h. (267 m.p.h.).

SOCIÉTÉ NATIONALE DE CONSTRUCTIONS AÉRONAUTIQUES DU MIDI.

This organization which operated the factories formerly owned by the Dewoitine company went into liquidation in January, 1941, and its activities were taken over by the S.N.C.A.S.E.

GROUPE TÉCHNIQUE DE CANNES.

This organization owed its origin to a group of 120 engineers and technicians of the S.N.C.A. de Sud-Ouest who, refusing to work for Germany in the occupied zone, proceeded to Châteauroux, where they were joined by volunteers from the technical offices of the S.N.C.A.N., S.N.C.A.O. and S.N.C.A.C., which the Vichy Government had either closed or cut down.

Work was started at Châteauroux in August, 1940, and a move was made to Cannes in May, 1941.

By November, 1942 the Groupe Téchnique de Cannes had achieved the following results :—

S.O. P.1. High-performance sailplane. All test flights completed.

S.O. 800. Twin-engined postal monoplane. Two 375 h.p. Béarn six-cylinder in-line inverted air-cooled engines. Crew of three. Useful load 500 kg. (1,100 lbs.). Maximum speed 460 km.h. (285.6 m.p.h.) at 3,000 m. (9,840 ft.). Range 1,200 km. (745 miles). Development began in September, 1940. First flew in January, 1942.

S.O. 90. Twin-engined commercial monoplane. Two 375 h.p. Béarn six-cylinder in-line inverted air-cooled engines. Crew of three. Useful load 1,200 kg. (2,640 lbs.). Maximum speed 395 km.h. (245 m.p.h.) at 2,800 m. (9,185 ft.). Its first flight was auspicious. Piloted by M. Hurel, chief engineer of the former CAMS company and of the S.N.C.A.N. and designer of the Potez-CAMS 161 six engined flying-boat, it took off under the noses of the Italians and flew to Philippeville in North Africa with nine persons on board. After this episode the flying of all prototypes was forbidden to prevent repitition of further similar escapes.

S.O. 30N. Twin-engined commercial monoplane with pressurised cabin. Two Gnôme-Rhône N.48/49 supercharged radial air-cooled engines. 23 passengers and 1,200 kg. (2,640 lbs.) of freight. Development began in March, 1941. The prototype was ready for test in November, 1942, but test flights were stopped by the Italo-German Armistice Commission.

S.O. 30R. Generally similar to the 30N. Two Gnôme-Rhône 14R engines, each with 1,650 h.p. available for take-off. 30 passengers and 1,500 kg. (3,300 lbs.) of freight. Differed from the 30N by having a wing area of 82 sq. m. (882.3 sq. ft.) instead of 72 sq. m. (774.7 sq. ft.), a tricycle landing-gear instead of the normal type and a single fin and rudder instead of a twin-ruddered tail-unit. It also has hot-air de-icing equipment on wings and tail. The cabins of the two types were designed to maintain pressure conditions equal to 2,500 m. (8,200 ft.) up to a height of 6,000 m. (19,680 ft.). Cabin temperature was also maintained constant at 20°C. (68°F.).

On the abolition of the line of demarcation between the occupied and unoccupied zones the Groupe Téchnique de Cannes ceased all work and its staff were recalled to Paris by the German authorities.

THE AIRCRAFT INDUSTRY SINCE THE LIBERATION OF FRANCE.

During the occupation the French Aircraft Industry suffered damage estimated in value at some 6,500,000,000 francs. Through enemy destruction or Allied air bombardment it lost some half a million square feet of covered manufacturing space and from 3,000 to 4,000 machine-tools. Ten thousand of its best workmen were deported to Germany and confiscation of material reduced its stocks to practically nothing.

Since the end of August, 1944, the French Provisional Government has been engaged in re-establishing the aircraft industry in accordance with a programme drawn up before the liberation of the country. The keystone of this programme is the complete nationalisation of the industry. The Amiot, Caudron and Farman companies have, because of their activities during the German occupation, already been nationalised.

In spite of all present difficulties the industry is progressively resuming work on orders which include :—

(i) German aircraft on which, during a transition period, production is continuing :—
 Junkers Ju 52.
 Siebel Si 204.
 Dornier Do 24.
 Messerschmitt Me 108 and Me 208.
 Fieseler Fi 156.

(ii) French aircraft of old design, on which production is being resumed :—
Caudron C.449 Goëland light twin-engined transport.
S.O. 161 four-engined transport.
Laté 631 trans-Atlantic flying-boat (order increased to 8).
S.E. 200 trans-Atlantic flying-boat.
Breguet 730 flying-boat.

(iii) New French aircraft, for which small series production orders have been placed :—
S.O. 90 twin-engined transport.
Caudron C.800 glider.
Mauboussin glider.

The following is a list of the principal concerns now engaged in the development and manufacture of aircraft :—

ARSENAL DE L'AÉRONAUTIQUE.

HEAD OFFICE AND WORKS : RUE DE LA FILATURE, VILLEUR-BANNE (RHÔNE).

Director : M. Vernisse.

The State-owned Arsenal de l'Aéronautique, apart from undertaking development of military aircraft, engines and equipment, is engaged in the study of an all-wood four-engined high-altitude transoceanic aircraft. No details of this project are available.

The first military design to be completed by the Arsenal is the V.B.10, a single-seat fighter monoplane powered by two Hispano-Suiza 12Y engines mounted in tandem, one in the nose and one behind the pilot's cockpit, and driving co-axial oppositely rotating airscrews through a Vernisse-Waseige transmission. The design for this aeroplane was laid down before the war as the V.G.30 and development continued throughout the occupation. In preliminary tests the V.B.10 achieved a maximum speed of 435 m.p.h. (696 km.h.).

ATELIERS AÉRONAUTIQUES DE COLOMBES (formerly Amiot-S.E.C.M.).

HEAD OFFICE AND WORKS : 171-183, BOULEVARD DU HAVRE, COLOMBES (SEINE).

Director-General : M. Guista.

The former Amiot (S.E.C.M.) company, nationalised under the above name, is building a series of 150 Junkers Ju 52 three-engined monoplanes to French account and is also manufacturing components and parts for the S.O. 161.

ATELIERS AÉRONAUTIQUES D'ISSY-LES-MOULINEAUX (formerly Caudron).

HEAD OFFICE AND WORKS : 52-72, RUE GUYNEMER, ISSY-LES-MOULINEAUX (SEINE).

Director-General : M. Brunet.

The former Caudron concern has been nationalised under the above name because of its collaborationist activities during the German occupation. It is now building in series the Caudron C.449 Goëland twin-engined light transport and training gliders of the Caudron C.800 type.

It has also built a small single-seat Fighter-Training monoplane similar to the C.690 which was produced before the war and is developing a light two-seat monoplane to be fitted with a jet-propulsion unit.

ATELIERS AÉRONAUTIQUES DE SURESNES.

HEAD OFFICE AND WORKS : SURESNES.

This is the former Farman company, which has been nationalised under the above name because of its collaboration with the enemy during the German occupation of France.

SOCIÉTÉ d'ETUDES ET DE CONSTRUCTIONS AERO-NAVALES

(Aircraft Division of the S.A. des Usines Chausson.)

HEAD OFFICE AND WORKS : 35, RUE MALAKOFF, ASNIÈRES (SEINE).

Technical Director : M. Vinsonneau.

This concern is undertaking important studies and investigations concerning the private-owner's aeroplane and its construction. It is engaged in the development of a four-seat civil monoplane to be fitted with two jet-propulsion units.

SOCIÉTÉ DES ATELIERS D'AVIATION LOUIS BREGUET.

HEAD OFFICE : 24, RUE GEORGES BIZET, PARIS (16E).

WORKS : TOULOUSE (HAUTE-GARONNE).

Commercial Director : M. Magnus.

The prototype Breguet 500 Colmar twin-engined commercial transport previously mentioned was, at the time of writing (April, 1945), undergoing flight trials.

Under development are the Breguet 1011, a transport for stratosphere flying and a four-engined trans-Atlantic transport in the Douglas DC-7 class.

SOCIÉTÉ INDUSTRIELLE D'AVIATION LATÉCOÈRE.

HEAD OFFICE : 79, AVENUE MARCEAU, PARIS (8E).

WORKS : TOULOUSE (HAUTE-GARONNE).

Technical Director : M. Jarry.

This concern has under construction eight Laté 631 six-engined trans-Atlantic flying-boats.

SOCIÉTÉ GÉNÉRALE DE MÉCHANIQUE TRACTION (MATRA).

HEAD OFFICE : 49, RUE DE LISBONNE, PARIS.

Technical Director : M. Robert.

This society is engaged in the development of a light aeroplane and in the preliminary studies of a transoceanic mail aeroplane without landing-gear.

MORANE-SAULNIER.

HEAD OFFICE : 3, RUE VOLTA, PUTEAUX (SEINE).

WORKS : PUTEAUX (SEINE) AND OSSUN, NEAR TARBES (TARN-ET-GARONNE).

Commercial Director : M. Sollier.

Morane-Saulnier is continuing to build to French account the Fieseler Fi 156 Storch under the designation MS.500 and fitted with a 200 h.p. Renault 6Q six-cylinder in-line inverted engine.

It also has under development several original designs, including the MS. 472, a two-seat Fighter-Trainer developed from the company's pre-war MS.406 single-seat Fighter ; the MS.560, a light 70 h.p. single-seat touring or training monoplane, and the MS.580, a twelve-seat twin-engined transport.

SOCIÉTÉ INDUSTRIELLE POUR L'AÉRONAUTIQUE (S.I.P.A.)

HEAD OFFICE AND WORKS : NEUILLY, NEAR PARIS.

This company was founded in 1938. From 1938 to 1940 in factories at Neuilly, Asnières and Nantes it manufactured parts and components for the Mureaux 113, 115 and 117 and the Loire 45 military aircraft. After the collapse of France activities were limited to the Neuilly factory and during the occupation the company was engaged in the development of the Arado 296 two-seat advanced trainer for the German authorities. Only a prototype was completed.

Since the liberation the Arado Ar 296, under the French designation S. 10, has been put into production to French account, and further aircraft developments are in hand.

SOCIÉTÉ DES AÉROPLANES G. VOISIN.

HEAD OFFICE AND WORKS : ISSY-LES-MOULINEAU (SIENE).

Technical Director : Maurice Pain.

This company, a successor to one of the pioneer French aircraft manufacturing concerns, is engaged in the development of two tail-first prototypes, the MP. 200 and the MP. 1000, designed by M. Maurice Pain, the company's technical director. It is also developing a 42-cylinder six-row radial engine.

SOCIÉTÉ NATIONALE DE CONSTRUCTIONS AÉRONAUTIQUES DU CENTRE (S.N.C.A.C.).

HEAD OFFICE : 11, RUE PILLET WILL, PARIS.

WORKS : BILLANCOURT (FORMERLY FARMAN), BOURGES (FORMERLY HANRIOT) AND FOURCHAMBAULT.

Technical Director : M. Rocca.

This society is engaged in the development of two aircraft for stratosphere flying, the N.C. 3020 which, at the time of writing was nearly ready to fly, and the N.C. 3030, for trans-Atlantic flying, which has not yet got beyond the project stage.

The Fourchambault factory was, before the liberation of France, engaged in the production of the Siebel Si 204 twin-engined light transport to German account. Production is continuing under French orders, this aircraft now being known as the N.C. 701.

SOCIÉTÉ NATIONALE DE CONSTRUCTIONS AÉRONAUTIQUES DU NORD (S.N.C.A.N.).

HEAD OFFICE : 20, RUE VERNIER, PARIS (17E).

WORKS : LES MUREAUX (FORMERLY A.N.F.), SURESNES (FORMERLY BLÉRIOT) AND SARTROUVILLE (FORMERLY CAMS).

Technical Director : M. Coroller.

The S.N.C.A.N. continues to manufacture the Messerschmitt Me 108 and Me 208, the former under the designation Nord 1000 and the latter as the Nord 1100. Both are fitted with the 220 h.p. Renault Q6 engine. The Nord 1100 differs from the 1000 by having a tricycle landing-gear.

The former CAMS flying-boat factory at Sartrouville is continuing to build the Dornier Do 24 three-engined flying-boat.

The society is also engaged in the manufacture of a large number of single-seat training gliders.

SOCIÉTÉ NATIONALE DE CONSTRUCTIONS AÉRONAUTIQUES DE SUD-EST (S.N.C.A.S.E.).

HEAD OFFICE : 6, AVENUE MARCEAU, PARIS (8E).

WORKS : MARIGNANE-MARSEILLE AND TOULOUSE (BOTH FORMERLY BELONGING TO DEWOITINE).

Technical Director : M. Vautier.

This society has under construction two S.E. 200 four-engined trans-Atlantic flying-boats and a series of 40 S.O. 161 four-engined transport monoplanes. It also has under development the S.E. 1000 for North Atlantic flying, the S.E. 700-A autogiro, and a light private-owner type aeroplane.

SOCIÉTÉ NATIONALE DE CONSTRUCTIONS AÉRONAUTIQUES DE SUD-OUEST (S.N.C.A.S.O.).

HEAD OFFICE : 105, AVENUE RAYMOND POINCARE, PARIS.

WORKS : CHATEAUROUX (S-ET-O) AND COURBEVOIE (SEINE).

Director-General : M. Avenet.

This society is continuing the development of aircraft undertaken by the Groupe Technique de Cannes (see p. 95c).

It has under construction a series of twenty S.O. 90 twin-engined postal monoplanes and tests are proceeding with the S.O. 30N Bellatrix and 30R. In addition, the prototype S.O. 70 four-engined monoplane is being built and a helicopter is under development.

GERMANY

ARADO.

ARADO FLUGZEUGWERKE G.m.b.H.

HEAD OFFICE : BABELSBERG BEI BERLIN.

WORKS : BRANDENBURG (HAVEL), WARNEMÜNDE, ANKLAM, &c.

Managing Directors : F. Wagenführ, Dipl. Ing. W. Blume and Dipl. Ing. R. Heinemann.

Chief Engineer : Dipl. Ing. W. Blume.

Established : 1925.

This Company was the successor of the Werft Warnemünde der Flugzeugbau Friedrichshafen G.m.b.H., which was formed in 1917.

The Ar 96 was adopted in 1940 as a standard training aircraft for the German Air Force. Two models were built, one as a primary trainer and the other as an advanced trainer. Variants of this type were also built in France during the occupation.

The Ar 196 was extensively used during the early part of the war for naval reconnaissance, light bombing and anti-submarine duties. It was also the standard catapult seaplane in ships of the German Navy, up to four being carried in battleships.

Other Arado products which were used on a limited operational scale were the Ar 232 transport, the Ar 234 jet-propelled bomber-reconnaissance monoplane and the Ar 240 high-altitude fighter-reconnaissance monoplane.

THE ARADO Ar 196.

TYPE.—Two-seat Reconnaissance seaplane for shipboard use.

WINGS.—Low-wing semi-cantilever monoplane. Wings have straight leading-edges, slightly swept-forward to trailing-edges and rounded tips. They are attached to the lower fuselage longerons and are braced for about one-third of the half span by inverted Vee struts from the floats. Details of structure unknown.

FUSELAGE.—Welded steel-tube structure. The front part of the fuselage which is circular is covered with a stressed metal skin ; the rear part which is oval, is fabric-covered.

TAIL UNIT.—Cantilever monoplane type with fin located in front of tail-plane. Statically and aerodynamically-balanced rudder and one-piece elevator. All-metal structure with metal-covered tail-plane and fin and fabric-covered rudder and elevator. Trimming-tabs in

elevator adjustable in the air, tab in rudder adjustable on the ground only.

TAIL UNIT.—Cantilever monoplane type. Fin located ahead of tail-plane. Statically and aerodynamically-balanced rudder and one-piece elevator. All-metal structure with metal-covered fixed surfaces and fabric-covered movable surfaces.

FLOATS.—Twin long single-step all-metal floats attached to fuselage by a system of streamline steel-tube struts in the form of an inverted "W" when viewed from the front. Main side struts are cross-braced in the fore-and-aft plane. Floats provided with catapult points. Water-rudders.

POWER PLANT.—One 900 h.p. BMW 132 K nine-cylinder radial

The Arado Ar 196A Two-seat Reconnaissance Seaplane (900 h.p. BMW 132 engine).

air-cooled engine with supercharger and fuel injection pump and driving a three-bladed variable-pitch airscrew with wooden blades. NACA cowling. Two fuel tanks (198 Imp. gallons). one in fuselage and one in starboard float.

ACCOMMODATION.—Tandem cockpits under continuous transparent canopy with sliding sections over the cockpits.

ARMAMENT.—Two MG FF cannon in the wings, one MG 17 machine-gun in the top cowling of the fuselage and twin MG 17 machine-guns on a movable mounting in the rear cockpit. Two 50-kg bombs could be carried under the wings.

DIMENSIONS.—Span 12.4 m. (40 ft. 10½ in.). Span (folded) 4.8 m. (15 ft. 9 in.), Length 11 m. (36 ft. 1 in.), Height 4.4 m. (14 ft. 6 in.), Wing area 28.4 sq. m. (306 sq. ft.).

WEIGHTS.—Weight empty 2,990 kg. (6,580 lbs.). Weight loaded 3,730 kg. (8,200 lbs.).

PERFORMANCE.—Maximum speed 310 km.h. (193 m.p.h.) at 4,000 m. (13,120 ft.), Initial rate of climb 300 m./min. (980 ft./min.), Service ceiling 7,020 m. (23,000 ft.), Range 1,070 km. (670 miles) at 253 km.h. (158 m.p.h.).

THE ARADO Ar 232.

The Ar 232 was a military transport which could be fitted with either two BMW 801 (Ar 232A) or four Bramo 323 (Ar 232B) radial air-cooled engines. Apart from the power-plant there were no major differences between the two sub-types.

TYPE.—Two or four-engined Military Transport.

WINGS.—High-wing cantilever monoplane with rectangular centre-section and tapering outer sections, most taper being on the trailing-edge. Two-spar structure. Ailerons on outer tapering sections. Fowler-type flaps on centre-section.

FUSELAGE.—The shape of the metal fuselage has been governed by the original design as a transport. The forward portion enclosing the crew accommodation and freight compartment is rectangular but aft of the freight-loading ramp the fuselage reduces to a single circular-section boom level with the top of the fuselage which carries the tail-unit.

TAIL UNIT.—Cantilever monoplane type with twin fins and rudders. Divided elevators with trim-tabs.

LANDING GEAR.—Retractable tricycle type. Main wheels raised inwardly to underside of centre-section, nose wheel backwards into fuselage. All oleo legs have knee joints and when at rest the aircraft can be lowered onto eleven pairs of small wheels mounted along the centre-line of the fuselage, thus distributing the load and enabling the aircraft to be taxied on uneven or soft ground.

POWER PLANT.—Two BMW 801 fourteen-cylinder two-row (Ar 232A) or four BMW 323 R-2 nine-cylinder (Ar 232B) radial air-cooled engines in line along the leading-edge of the centre-section. Fuel capacity (Ar 232B) : 595 Imp. gallons.

ACCOMMODATION.—Crew of four in compartment in the nose of the fuselage. Dual controls. The bulkhead aft of the crew accommodation is also the forward wall of the freight compartment. This is rectangular and free from internal obstructions. Loading is through the rear of the compartment by means of a ramp formed by part of the rear wall which, when raised, fairs into the fuselage.

ARMAMENT.—The following armament can be fitted : one MG 131 (500 rounds) in the nose, one MG 151/20 (500 rounds) in dorsal position, and two MG 121 (100 rounds) aft.

DIMENSIONS (Ar 232B).—Span 110 ft. (33.5 m.), Length 77 ft. 2 in. (23.5 m.), Height 18 ft. 8 in. (5.7 m.), Wing area 1,535 sq. ft. (143 sq. m.), Wing area with flaps 1,930 sq. ft. (179 sq. m.).

WEIGHTS (Ar 232B).—Useful load 10,000 lbs. (4,540 kg.), Take-off weight 46,600 lbs. (21,160 kg.).

PERFORMANCE (Ar 232B).—Maximum speed 211 m.p.h. (338 km.h.) at 15,100 ft. (4,605 m.), Maximum cruising speed 180 m.p.h. (288 km.h.) at 6,560 ft. (2,000 m.), Economical cruising speed 161 m.p.h. (258 km.h.), Range at maximum cruising speed 565 miles (905 km.), Range at economical cruising speed 658 miles (1,053 km.).

THE ARADO Ar 233.

The Ar 233 was a twin-engined civil boat amphibian which was under development in France during the occupation. This project was to have been fitted with either two BMW 323 or 801 engines and to have accommodation for ten passengers. The wheeled landing-gear was to have been of a retractable tricycle type. The designed cruising speed was 190 m.p.h. (304 km.h.) and the cruising range some 750 miles (1,200 km.) at 7,000 ft. (2,135 m.).

THE ARADO Ar 234B "BLITZ."

The Ar 234B was the production development of the A sub-type, which was similar but had a jettisonable wheel landing-gear and landing skids under the fuselage and jet nacelles. The B sub-type first flew in December, 1943, and went into production, after very little modification, in June, 1944. It

The Arado Ar 232B Transport (four Bramo 323 engines) with the main oleo legs "broken" to lower the aircraft onto the secondary wheels.

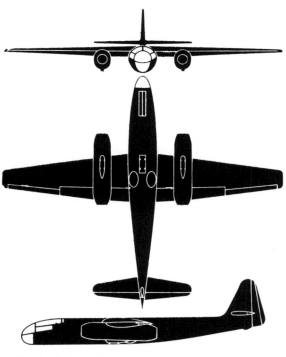

The Arado Ar 234B Bomber-Reconnaissance Monoplane.

was used operationally on a small scale for reconnaissance and tactical bombing. The two principal sub-types were :—

Ar 234B-1. Two Jumo 004 jet units. Reconnaissance model. May be armed with two MG 151/20 cannon fixed to fire aft beneath the fuselage. 200 rounds per gun.

Ar 234B-2. Bomber version. Can carry one 2,200 lb. (1,000 kg.) bomb under the fuselage, and one 1,100 lb. (500 kg.) bomb under each jet nacelle, but a total load of 2,200 lbs. (1,000 kg.) was more representative. The full external bomb load reduced the maximum speed by 60 m.p.h. (96 km.h.). Same armament as the B-1.

TYPE.—Twin-jet Bomber or Reconnaissance monoplane.

WINGS.—Shoulder cantilever monoplane. Wing in one piece. All-metal two-spar structure with flush-riveted stressed skin covering. Narrow-chord Frise-type ailerons have mass-balanced geared tabs on their inner ends. Hydraulically-operated flaps inboard and outboard of jet units. Outboard of jet units are three inset lugs for attachment of assisted take-off units.

FUSELAGE.—Circular-section semi-monocoque structure with flush-riveted stressed skin. Centre section in region of wing and landing-gear attachments is of reinforced box girder construction.

TAIL UNIT.—Cantilever monoplane type. All-metal stressed-skin tailplane is pivoted on self-aligning bearings at the leading-edge, incidence being varied by a screw-jack controlled by lever in the cockpit. Narrow-chord metal elevators have no trim-tabs. Metal fin has a detachable wooden leading-edge, behind which is an aerial. All-metal rudder has tabs along entire trailing-edge, the upper tab being geared and the lower controlled from the cockpit. A single mass-balance weight mounted in the fuselage serves for both the elevators and rudder.

LANDING GEAR.—Retractable tricycle type. Main wheels retract forward and inwards into the fuselage. Nose wheel retracts into a compartment aft of the cockpit, and is fitted with a spring and cam centralising and anti-shimmy device. The fuselage stowage of the main wheels results in an unusually narrow track.

POWER PLANT.—Two Junkers Jumo 004 jet units underslung beneath the wing. Fuel tanks in fuselage, one aft of the cockpit and one aft of the wing attachment fittings. Fuel capacity 836 Imp. gallons. Additional drop tanks may be carried. Rocket-assisted take-off, the rockets being attached to the wings outboard of the jet units.

ACCOMMODATION.—Single-seat cockpit forms the nose of the fuselage. Radio equipment and tail parachute brake stowed in rear fuselage.

The Arado Ar 234A, which had a skid undercarriage, taking off on an auxiliary wheeled chassis.

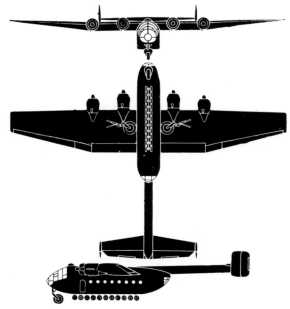

The Arado Ar 232B four-engined Transport.

The Arado Ar 234C fitted with four BMW 003 jet units in two paired units.

ARMAMENT.—Typical armament consists of two 20 m/m. MG 151/20 fixed rearward-firing cannon (200 rounds per gun). Sighting by PV1B periscope with rear field of vision. Some reconnaissance versions were unarmed. Maximum bomb-load 4,400 lbs. (2,000 kg.) carried externally.

DIMENSIONS.—Span 47 ft. 4½ in. (14.5 m.), Length 41 ft. 7½ in. (12.7 m.), Height (on ground over fin) 13 ft. 8½ in. (4.2 m.), Track 6 ft. 6 in. (1.98 m.), Span of tail 16 ft. 5½ in. (5 m.), Gross wing area 298 sq. ft. (27.7 sq. m.).

WEIGHTS.—Normal take-off weight 18,500 lbs. (8,400 kg.), Maximum permissible take-off weight without A.T.O. 19,500 lbs. (8,850 kg.), Maximum permissible take-off weight with A.T.O. 22,000 lbs. (10,000 kg.).

PERFORMANCE.—Maximum speed 470 m.p.h. (752 km.h.) at 19,680 ft. (6,000 m.), Service ceiling 37,700 ft. (11,500 m.), Take-off run with 3,300 lbs. (1,500 kg.) bomb, unassisted 1,950 yds. (1,785 m.), Assisted take-off run with 3,300 lbs. (1,500 kg.) bombs 940 yds. (860 m.).

THE ARADO Ar 234C.

Soon after the Ar 234B first flew, the C sub-type fitted with four BMW 003 jet units was completed for flight trials. Development of this version was slow owing to frequent disruption of the Arado factories by Allied bombing.

The structure of the B series was retained although slight detail modifications were incorporated. The four turbo jets were arranged in pairs in nacelles slung under the wing.

The very high performance, as well as good inherent aerodynamic stability demonstrated in the few flights made, proved the Ar 234C to be an unusually efficient aeroplane.

PERFORMANCE.—Maximum speed 546 m.p.h. (874 km.h.) at 20,000 ft. (6,100 m.), Initial rate of climb 3,600 ft./min. (1,098 m./min.). Service ceiling 37,800 ft. (11,530 m.), Endurance at full thrust and without drop tank 40 min., Endurance at 60% power 1 hour 25 min., Take-off run without A.T.O. 1,550 yds. (1,420 m.).

THE ARADO Ar 240.

The Ar 240 was intended for high-altitude reconnaissance or as a heavy fighter. It saw limited operational service. The earlier sub-types were fitted with DB 601 engines, but later versions had either DB 603 or DB 605 engines.

TYPE.—Twin-engined High-altitude Fighter or Reconnaissance monoplane.

WINGS.—Low-wing cantilever monoplane. Rectangular centre-section. Outer sections have straight leading-edge and swept forward trailing-edge. All-metal structure.

FUSELAGE.—Oval section all-metal monocoque. Fuselage is continued

The Arado Ar 240V-3. One of the prototypes of the Fighter-Reconnaissance Monoplane described above.

to a point beyond the tailplane, the rear extension carrying small stabilisers and a dive-brake.

TAIL UNIT.—Cantilever monoplane type with twin fins and rudders. There is also a third vertical fish-tail fin at the extremity of the fuselage.

LANDING GEAR.—Retractable type. Each main unit, fitted with twin wheels, raised backwards into engine nacelle, hinged doors closing the aperture when wheels are retracted. Retractable tail-wheel.

POWER PLANT.—Two Daimler-Benz DB 603 or DB 605 twelve-cylinder inverted Vee liquid-cooled engines. Engine nacelles extend aft of the trailing-edge of the wings. Eight fuel tanks in wings and one in fuselage. Total fuel capacity 603 Imp. gallons.

ACCOMMODATION.—Crew of two, consisting of pilot and navigator/air-gunner, seated back to back in pressurised cabin in nose of fuselage and ahead of the wings.

ARMAMENT.—Armament varies, the Ar 240C having six MG 151, two in the sides of the fuselage, two in the wing roots and two in a blister below the fuselage, all firing forward ; and four MG 151 in two two-gun remotely-controlled turrets, one above and below the fuselage.

DIMENSIONS.—Span 16.6 m. (54 ft. 6 in.). Length 12.5 m. (41 ft.).

PERFORMANCE.—Maximum speed 528 km.h. (330 m.p.h.) at 7,000 m. (22,960 ft.), Endurance 4-5 hours.

THE ARADO Ar 296

The Ar 432 was identical in appearance to the Ar 232B but was of mixed wood and metal construction instead of being all metal.

direction by the Société Industrielle pour l'Aviation (S.I.P.A.) during the occupation of France. Since the Liberation the aeroplane has flown successfully under the French designation S.10 and production is proceeding to French account.

It is a two-seat dual control monoplane with the crew seated in tandem under a continuous canopy. It is fitted with a 500 h.p. Argus As 411 twelve-cylinder inverted Vee air-cooled engine and a retractable landing-gear.

In general arrangement the Ar 296 closely followed the general lines of the Ar 96 and, to a certain extent, the Ar 196, which was also built in France by the S.N.C.A.S.O. Owing, however, to the shortage of light metals in France the Ar 296 was mainly of wooden construction.

DIMENSIONS.—Span 11 m. (36 ft.). Length 9.3 m. (30 ft. 6 in.).

THE ARADO Ar 432.

The Ar 432 was identical in appearance to the Ar 232B but was of mixed wood and metal construction instead of being all metal.

BACHEM.

In a desperate attempt to arrest the heavy Allied bombing raids over the Reich, the German Air Ministry decided, towards the end of 1944, to produce a cheap, semi-expendable, rocket-propelled and rocket-firing interceptor of very small endurance for defending specific vital targets.

It was to be midway between a directed missile and an interceptor fighter in its method of operation, the sole duty of the pilot being to control the small aircraft during the last few hundred yards of its flight towards a bomber formation. The initial flight was to be directed from the ground according to

information obtained from radar detectors.

Projects to this specification were tendered to the Air Ministry by Heinkel, Junkers, Messerschmitt and Bachem. The Bachem project, designated BP 20 "Natter" (Viper), was selected for development.

With a span of 18 ft. (3.3 m.), a wing area of 1,250 sq. ft. (6.76 sq. m.) and fitted with a Walter HWK 109.509 rocket unit, the latter was intended to have a maximum speed of over 600 m.p.h. (960 km.h.) at 16,000 ft. (4,880 m.). It was to take off vertically with the assistance of auxiliary rockets, climb at

a rate of 37,000 ft./min. (11,290 m./min.) and attack a bomber with a battery of rockets carried in the nose of the fuselage.

This accomplished the pilot was to be ejected and descend by parachute. Simultaneously the rear half of the fuselage containing the liquid-rocket would break off and itself descend by parachute, leaving the remainder of the aircraft to crash.

This project was only in the very early stages of development when Germany collapsed.

BLOHM & VOSS.

BLOHM & VOSS.

HEAD OFFICE : HAMBURG—STEINWÄRDER.
BERLIN OFFICE : TIRPITZÜFER 86-90, BERLIN, W.35.
WORKS : BLOHM & VOSS SHIPYARDS, HAMBURG.
Managing Director : Walthur Blohm.
Chief Engineer : Dr. Ing. Richard Vogt.

Since its foundation in 1933 the Aircraft Division of the Blohm & Voss shipyards at Hamburg has produced a series of aircraft, the most important of which being those of the Ha 139 type. These were used for experimental flights across the South Atlantic, to be followed by the inauguration of a regular service in the Spring of 1938, and for experimental flights across the North Atlantic.

By the end of June, 1939, these three seaplanes had successfully completed 100 trans-Atlantic flights, 40 across the North Atlantic and 60 across the South Atlantic.

After the outbreak of War the Ha 139 was adapted for military usage and for a short time was used for oversea reconnaissance and mine-laying.

All Blohm & Voss aircraft incorporate a novel form of wing construction evolved by Dr. Ing. Richard Vogt. The main supporting member of the wing is represented by one big tubular spar which carries all bending and torsion stresses. It is also used for the stowage of fuel and, in the case of the Bv 144, also acts as a pivot for the variation of wing incidence.

THE BLOHM & VOSS Bv 138.

The prototype of the Bv 138 was built about 1938 and the design was considerably modified to adapt it for service use. As a reconnaissance flying-boat the Bv 138 was in general use throughout the war, operating latterly from Norwegian bases over the North Sea and from German bases over the Baltic.

There were three basic series, as follow :—

Bv 138A-1. The original service version with three Jumo 205 C engines.

Bv 138B-1. A development of the A-1 with modified tail surfaces and armament and fitted with Jumo 205 D engines.

Bv 138C-1. Another version with Jumo 205 D engines and generally similar to the B-1.

TYPE.—Three-engined Reconnaissance flying-boat.

WINGS.—High-wing cantilever monoplane. Wing in three sections with centre-section attached direct to hull. Typical Blohm & Voss tubular spar structure with metal and fabric covering.

HULL.—Short single-step all-metal hull with shallow Vee bottom and

The Blohm & Voss Bv 138 Reconnaissance Flying-boat (three Junkers Jumo 205 engines.

straight sides. All-metal stressed-skin rectangular tail booms attached to roots of centre-section support tail. All-metal stabilising floats under outer wings.

TAIL.—Monoplane tailplane between booms. Each boom terminates in a fin and rudder. All-metal structure with fabric-covered movable surfaces.

POWER PLANT.—Three Junkers Jumo 205 C or D twelve-cylinder compression-ignition engines, one mounted in nacelle above centre-line of wing and two in nacelles at extremities of centre-section and in line with tail-booms. Three-bladed metal controllable-pitch airscrews to outer engines, four-bladed airscrew to centre engine. Fuel carried in tubular spar of centre-section.

ACCOMMODATION.—Mooring compartment in nose. Then follows a gunner's position with gun-turret. Pilot's compartment in front of leading-edge of wing with radio and navigation positions in hull below wings. Two gunner's positions aft of wing, one in tail of central engine nacelle and one in turret in tail of hull to give fields of fire above and below tailplane.

ARMAMENT.—One 20 m/m. MG 151/20 in the nose turret, one 13 m/m. MG 131 in the upper rear position and one 20 m/m. MG 151/20 in the lower rear turret. May carry up to six 110 lb. (50 kg.) bombs, four depth-charges or two sea-mines.

DIMENSIONS.—Span 88 ft. 7 in. (27 m.), Length 72 ft. 3 in. (22 m.), Wing area 1,205 sq. ft. (112 sq. m.).

WEIGHTS.—Normal flying weight 34,100 lbs. (15,480 kg.), Maximum normal take-off weight 36,300 lbs. (16,480 kg.), Maximum take-off weight with rocket-assistance 39,600 lbs. (17,980 kg.), Maximum take-off weight for catapult launch 40,000 lbs. (18,160 kg.).

PERFORMANCE.—Maximum speed at sea level 170 m.p.h. (272 km.h.), Climb to 10,000 ft. (3,050 m.) 24 mins., Range with maximum fuel (825 Imp. gallons) 2,000 miles (3,200 km.).

THE BLOHM & VOSS Bv 141B.

This asymmetric aircraft was developed from the Bv 141A, from which it differed in respect of engine installation and wing, tail and nacelle design. It was intended for reconnaissance and army co-operation duties and the asymmetric layout was adopted to allow maximum field of vision for the crew.

The single BMW 801 engine (BMW 132 in the Bv 141A) was mounted in the nose of the offset fuselage and the crew accommodated in a nacelle alongside and to starboard. The all-metal wing was built in several sections with a spanwise slot in the underside to permit the assembly of the tubular main spar. The asymmetric braced tailplane extended on the port side of the single angular fin, there being only a short stub on the starboard side. The landing-gear retracted outwards into the underside of the outer wings.

Only a few Bv 141B's were built and the type was not used as standard operational equipment.

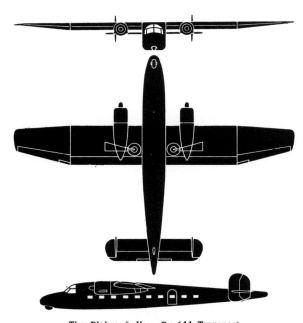

The Blohm & Voss Bv 144 Transport.

THE BLOHM & VOSS Bv 144.

Two prototypes of the Bv 144 were built to German order by the French Société Louis Breguet. The main feature of this commercial design was a wing with a variable incidence linkage for changing the effective angle of attack in flight.

In general arrangement the Bv 144 was a high-wing cantilever monoplane with wide parallel chord centre-section and short tapering outer wings. By tubular spar construction was employed, the spar acting as the pivot for the variation of incidence. Fowler-type flaps were located inboard of the ailerons.

The fuselage in longitudinal section was of roughly aerofoil form in order to provide a flat floor throughout the length of the cabin accommodation. With a tricycle landing-gear the floor was parallel to the ground. The main wheels were retracted inwardly into the underside of the centre-section and the nose wheel was raised partly into the nose of the fuselage. The tail-unit was of the twin-ruddered type.

The power-plant consisted of two BMW 801 two-row radial engines with VDM three-blade constant-speed airscrews.

A crew of three and 18 passengers, as well as 1,000 lbs. (454 kg.) of mail or freight could be carried for a range of 950 miles (1,520 km.). With 420 Imp. gallons of fuel and the above load the all-up weight was 28,900 lbs. (13,120 kg.).

THE BLOHM & VOSS Bv 155.

The Bv 155 high-altitude single-seat fighter was originally of Messerschmitt design but the development was entrusted to Blohm & Voss. Although quantity production was contemplated the aircraft never became operational.

There were two versions, the Bv 155B with a Daimler-Benz DB 603A engine and TKL 15 turbo-supercharger, a wing area of 420 sq. ft. (39 sq. m.) and a fuel capacity of 110 Imp. gallons ; and the Bv 155C with the DB 603U engine and TKL turbo-supercharger, a wing area of 384 sq. ft. (35.6 sq. m.) and a fuel capacity of 264 Imp. gallons.

With the Bv 155B there were four differing armament arrange-

ments—two 20 mm. MG 151/20 and one 30 mm. MK 108 ; two MG 151/20 and one 30 mm. MK 103 ; three 30 mm. MK 108 ; or three 30 mm. MK 103. The Bv 155C was provided with an armament of two MG 151/20 (100 rounds per gun) and one MK 108 (60 rounds).

WEIGHT LOADED (Bv 155B).—12,300 lbs. (5,584 kg.).
WEIGHT LOADED (155C).—13,200 lbs. (5,993 kg.).
PERFORMANCE (Bv 155B).—Maximum speed 428 m.p.h. (685 km.h.) at 54,000 ft. (16,470 m.), Service ceiling 56,000 ft. (17,080 m.).
PERFORMANCE (155C).—Maximum speed 428 m.p.h. (685 km.h.) at 50,000 ft. (15,250 m.), Service ceiling 55,200 ft. (16,840 m.).

THE BLOHM & VOSS Bv 222 "WIKING."

The Bv 222 is a six-engined flying-boat which was designed before the War for a proposed trans-Atlantic service by Deutsche Lufthansa. The first Civil prototype crashed in 1940 but further prototypes were completed as a military freight and personnel transport. The Bv 222 was first reported in service in the Autumn of 1942 in the Mediterranean.

TYPE.—Six-engined Transport flying-boat.

WINGS.—High-wing cantilever monoplane. Centre portion of wing to points just outboard of outer engine nacelles of parallel chord, outer portions tapered. All-metal structure with a single tubular spar 4 ft. 9 in. (1.45 m.) in diameter extending through the hull. The spar is sub-divided by bulkheads within the centre-section to form fuel tanks. A passage inside the wing gives access to the engines in flight. Electric de-icing equipment.

HULL.—All-metal two-step hull covered with corrosion-resisting alloy sheet varying in thickness from 3 to 5 m/m. The all-metal wing-tip stabilising floats are split vertically, each half retracting outwardly flush with the underside of the wing. Electric retraction.

TAIL UNIT.—Cantilever monoplane type. High tapering single fin with tailplane mounted slightly above the top line of the hull. All-metal structure.

POWER PLANT.—Six BMW Bramo 323 R nine-cylinder radial, or Junkers Jumo 207 C twelve-cylinder opposed compression-ignition, engines in-line along the leading-edge of the wings. Fuel carried in tubular wing spar.

ACCOMMODATION.—Crew compartment in nose of hull. Main accommodation on two decks. Two small doors on port side for entry of passengers and crew. For bulky freight two larger doors 5 ft. 7 in. by 6 ft. 8 in. are also provided. In addition to a normal crew of eleven, as many as 110 troops with arms and equipment may be carried. Most of the passengers and freight are accommodated on the lower deck.

ARMAMENT.—Typical armament consists of one 13 m/m MG 131 in a nose turret, one MG 131 in a forward dorsal turret, one MG 811 in the rear dorsal turret, and four MG 81 in lateral mountings in cabin windows.

DIMENSIONS.—Span 157 ft. (48 m.), Length 105 ft. (32 m.), Maximum width of hull 9 ft. 10 in. (3 m.).

WEIGHTS.—Useful load (including fuel) 42,000 lbs. (19,100 kg.), Normal all-up weight 101,000 lbs. (45,900 kg.).

PERFORMANCE.—Maximum speed 210 m.p.h. (336 km.h.), Cruising speed 185 m.p.h. (296 km.h.) at 6,500 ft. (1,980 m.), Ceiling 26,000 ft. (7,930 m.), Endurance 19-20 hours.

THE BLOHM & VOSS Bv 238.

The Bv 238 was generally similar to the Bv 222 but was considerably larger and heavier. Only one or two prototypes were built. It was intended that the production version of this flying-boat would be fitted with six Junkers Jumo 222 engines.

The span of the Bv 238 was 197 ft. (60 m.) and the centre-section carrying the six engines had a constant chord of 23 ft. (7 m.). At the junction between the centre-section and the tapering outer wing panels long nacelles, each with two gun turrets, one forward of the leading-edge and one aft of the trailing-edge, were to be fitted.

The structure was generally similar to that of the Bv 222, with the typical Blohm & Voss tubular spar located at 30 per cent. of the chord. Retractable stabilising floats were fitted under the outer wing sections.

The designed all-up weight of the Bv 238 was 198,000 lbs. (90,000 kg.).

The Blohm & Voss Bv 222 Flying-boat (six Bramo 323 engines).

BÜCKER.

BÜCKER FLUGZEUGBAU G.m.b.H.

HEAD OFFICE : RANGSDORF BEI BERLIN.
WORKS : RANGSDORF AND WERNIGERODE.

Managing Director : Carl Clemens Bücker.

Chief Designer : Anders Andersson.

The formation of this firm was announced early in October, 1933. At the end of 1935 the factory was moved from Johannisthal to Rangsdorf, where a new and enlarged works and main offices were established. The Director and owner of the Company, Carl Cl. Bücker, a former naval pilot, was for more than ten years Managing Director of the Svenska Aero A.B., in Stockholm.

The Bücker Company concentrated on the design and construction of training aircraft.

THE BÜCKER Bü 131 B "JUNGMANN."

TYPE.—Two-seat Primary Training machine.

WINGS.—Single-bay biplane with interchangeable upper and lower wings. Incidence (lower) 0°, (upper) 1°. Dihedral (lower) 4.5°, (upper) 2.5°. Sweep-back 11°. No lift or anti-lift wires attached to lower rear spars. "I"-section wooden spars, wooden ribs, conventional drag bracing. Fabric covering. Steel struts. Ailerons on all four wings.

FUSELAGE. — Welded chrome-molybdenum steel-tube covered with fabric, except for metal sheeting around engine and cockpit.

TAIL UNIT.—Wire-braced. Unbalanced rudder. Divided elevator with trimming-flaps in trailing-edges. Welded structure of chrome-molybdenum steel-tube covered with fabric.

LANDING GEAR.—Divided. Shock-absorbers with steel springs and oil-damping hinged to sides of fuselage, axles hinged to pyramidal structure beneath fuselage. Balloon tyres. Brakes. Sprung tail-wheel.

POWER PLANT.—One 100 h.p. Hirth HM 504 air-cooled four-cylinder inverted in-line engine, on welded steel mounting. Fuel and oil tanks in fuselage.

ACCOMMODATION.—Two open cockpits in tandem.

DIMENSIONS.—Span 7.40 m. (24 ft. 3 in.), Length 6.62 m. (21 ft. 8 in.), Height 2.25 m. (7 ft. 5 in.), Wing area 13.5 sq. m. (145 sq. ft.).

WEIGHTS AND LOADINGS.—Weight empty 380 kg. (836 lbs.), Disposable load 290 kg. (638 lbs.), Weight loaded 670 kg. (1,474 lbs.), Wing loading 46.3 kg./sq. m. (9.49 lbs./sq. ft.), Power loading 6.25 kg./h.p. (13.75 lbs./h.p.).

PERFORMANCE.—Maximum speed 183 km.h. (115 m.p.h.), Cruising speed 170 km.h. (106 m.p.h.), Landing speed 82 km.h. (51 m.p.h.), Climb to 1,000 m. (3,280 ft.) 5.2 mins., Climb to 2,000 m. (6,560 ft.) 12 mins., Climb to 3,000 m. (9,840 ft.) 23 mins., Climb to 4,000 m. (13,120 ft.) 45 mins., Ceiling 4,300 m. (14,000 ft.), Range 650 km. (400 miles).

THE BÜCKER Bü 133C "JUNGMEISTER."

TYPE.—Single-seat Advanced Training biplane.

WINGS.—Single-bay biplane. Centre-section carried above fuselage by "N" struts. Outer sections have 11 degrees sweepback and are interconnected by parallel inter-plane struts with lift and anti-lift wire-bracing attached to front spar fittings only. Wing structure consists of two "I"-section wood spars, wooden ribs, normal drag bracing, the whole covered with fabric. Ailerons on all four wings.

FUSELAGE.—Welded chrome-molybdenum steel-tube framework, covered forward with metal panels and aft with fabric.

TAIL UNIT.—Monoplane type. Wire-braced tail-plane and fin. Trimming-tabs in elevators. Welded chrome-molybdenum steel-tube framework, with fabric covering.

LANDING GEAR.—Split type. Consists of two streamline side Vees incorporating steel spring oil-damped shock-absorbers. Balloon wheels, with brakes, are on bent axles, the inner ends of which are hinged to a steel-tube Vee below the fuselage. Steerable tail-wheel.

POWER PLANT.—One 160 h.p. Siemens Sh 14A-4 seven-cylinder radial air-cooled engine, on a welded chrome-molybdenum steel-tube mounting. Fuel tank in fuselage.

ACCOMMODATION.—Single open cockpit aft of wings.

DIMENSIONS.—Span 6.60 m. (21 ft. 7¼ in.), Length 5.9 m. (19 ft. 4 in.), Height 2.25 m. (7 ft. 4½ in.), Wing area 12 sq. m. (130 sq. ft.).

WEIGHTS AND LOADINGS (Aerobatic Category).—Weight empty 420 kg. (925 lbs.), Weight loaded 586 kg. (1,290 lbs.), Wing loading 48.75 kg./sq. m. (10 lbs./sq. ft.), Power loading 3.6 kg./h.p. (7.29 lbs./h.p.).

PERFORMANCE (Siemens).—Maximum speed 315 km.h. (134 m.p.h.), Cruising speed 200 km.h. (125 m.p.h.), Landing speed 86 km.h. (54 m.p.h.), Climb to 1,000 m. (3,280 ft.) 2.8 mins., Climb to 2,000

Three Bücker Jungmann Two-seat Training Biplanes (100 h.p. Hirth engines).

m. (6,560 ft.) 6.3 mins., Climb to 3,000 m. (9,840 ft.) 10.7 mins., Ceiling 6,100 m. (20,000 ft.), Cruising range 5000 km. (310 miles).

THE BÜCKER Bü 180 "STUDENT."
TYPE.—Two-seat Primary Training monoplane.
WINGS.—Low-wing cantilever monoplane. Wings taper in chord and thickness, leading-edge swept back and trailing-edge straight. Wooden structure with one main and one auxiliary spar and plywood covering back to rear spar and fabric covering thence to trailing-edge. Slotted ailerons.
FUSELAGE.—Oval section structure, the forward section of chrome-molybdenum steel-tube and the after section a wooden monocoque with steel-tube reinforcement aft of pilot's cockpit for protection in case of turn-over. Engine compartment covered with detachable light metal panels and sides of cockpits with fabric.
TAIL UNIT.—Cantilever monoplane type. Wooden framework with tail-plane and fin covered with plywood and the rudder and elevators with fabric. Trimming-tabs in movable surfaces, which are also aerodynamically and statically-balanced.
LANDING GEAR.—Split type. Side Vees incorporate oil-damped spiral steel spring shock-absorbers. Half-axles hinged at their inner ends to a steel-tube Vee beneath the fuselage. Low-pressure wheels and servo brakes. Sprung and oil-damped tail-skid may be either coupled to the rudder or free to swivel through 360 degrees.
POWER PLANT.—One 50-60 h.p. Walter Mikron II or 50 h.p. Zündapp four-cylinder in-line inverted air-cooled engine on steel-tube mounting. Welded aluminium fuel tank (50 litres) in fuselage.
ACCOMMODATION.—Tandem cockpits with dual controls may be either open or closed. Baggage compartment aft of rear cockpit.
DIMENSIONS.—Span 11.5 m. (37 ft. 9 in.), Length 7.1 m. (23 ft 3 in.), Height 1.85 m. (6 ft.), Wing area 15 sq. m. (161.4 sq. ft.).
WEIGHTS AND LOADINGS.—Weight empty 295 kg. (649 lbs.), Disposable load 245 kg. (539 lbs.), Weight loaded 540 kg. (1,188 lbs.), Wing loading 36 kg./sq. m. (8.38 lbs./sq. ft.), Power loading 9 kg./h.p. (19.8 lbs./h.p.).
PERFORMANCE.—Maximum speed 175 km.h. (108.6 m.p.h.), Cruising speed 160 km.h. (99.4 m.p.h.), Landing speed 70 km.h. (43.5 m.p.h.), Climb to 1,000 m. (3,280 ft.) 7.2 mins., Climb to 2,000 m. (6,560 ft.) 16.8 mins., Ceiling 4,500 m. (14,760 ft.), Range 650 km. (404 miles).

THE BÜCKER Bü 181 "BESTMANN."
TYPE.—Two-seat Training monoplane.
WINGS.—Low-wing cantilever monoplane. Wings taper sharply in chord and thickness. All-wood structure with plywood covering over leading-edge to rear spar and fabric covering thence to trailing-edge. Narrow-chord ailerons over half of trailing-edge. Split flaps between ailerons and fuselage.
FUSELAGE.—Oval section structure. Forward portion of chrome-molybdenum steel tubing with metal panels and after portion a wooden monocoque.
TAIL UNIT.—Cantilever monoplane type. Tail-plane and fin have wood framework with plywood covering. Rudder and elevators have wood frames and fabric covering. Trimming-tabs on elevators adjustable in the air. Trimming-tab on rudder adjustable on the ground only.
LANDING GEAR.—Fixed cantilever type. Single legs have steel spring shock-absorbers with oil damping. Fairings on legs and inside and behind wheels. Full-swivelling tail-wheel.
POWER PLANT.—One 105 h.p. Hirth HM 504 four-cylinder in-line inverted air-cooled engine. Fuel tank in fuselage.
ACCOMMODATION.—Enclosed cabin seating two side-by-side with dual controls. Adjustable seats arranged for seat-type parachutes. Large baggage compartment behind cabin.
DIMENSIONS.—Span 10.6 m. (34 ft. 9 in.), Length 7.75 m. (25 ft. 5 in.), Height 2.1 m. (6 ft. 5 in.), Wing area 13.5 sq. m. (145.2 sq. ft.).
WEIGHTS AND LOADINGS.—Weight empty 480 kg. (1,056 lbs.), Disposable load 270 kg. (594 lbs.), Weight loaded 750 kg. (1,650 lbs.), Wing loading 55 kg./sq. m. (11.27 lbs./sq. ft.), Power loading 7.14 kg./h.p. (15.8 lbs./h.p.).
PERFORMANCE.—Maximum speed 215 km.h. (133.5 m.p.h.), Cruising speed 195 km.h. (121 m.p.h.), Landing speed 70 km.h. (43.5 m.p.h.), Climb to 1,000 m. (3,280 ft.) 5.3 mins., Climb to 2,000 m. (6,560 ft.) 12 mins., Climb to 3,000 m. (9,840 ft.) 20.8 mins.,

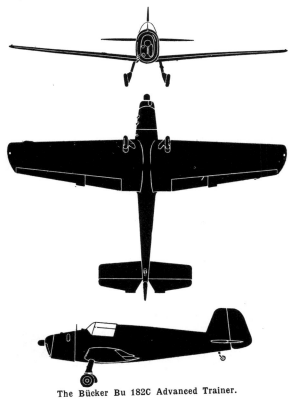

The Bücker Bu 182C Advanced Trainer.

The Bücker Bü 133 Jungmeister Single-seat Advanced Training Biplane (160 h.p. Siemens Sh 14 engine).

The Bücker Bü 180 Student Two-seat Light Training Monoplane (60 h.p. Walter Mikron II engine).

The Bücker Bü 181 Bestmann Two-seat Light Training Monoplane (105 h.p. Hirth HM 504 engine).

The Bücker Bü 182C Kornett Single-seat Advanced Training Monoplane (80 h.p. Bücker M 700 engine).

Service ceiling 5,000 m. (16,400 ft.), Absolute ceiling 5,800 m. (19,025 ft.), Range 800 km. (500 miles), Duration 4 hours.

THE BÜCKER Bü 182C "KORNETT."
TYPE.—Single-seat advanced training monoplane.
WINGS.—Low-wing cantilever monoplane. Wing in one piece and attached to fuselage by three bolts. All-wood monospar structure with plywood covering forward of the spar and fabric aft. There is a short auxiliary spar in the leading-edge of the centre-portion

of the wing to carry the forward attachment point and landing-gear fittings, and an after auxiliary spar to carry the hinges of the flaps and ailerons. The flaps, in two parts, are of light metal and carried on piano-hinges. There are three flap positions, the maximum angle of depression being 50 degrees.
FUSELAGE.—In two sections. The forward section is of metal construction with metal and plywood covering. The rear section is a wooden monocoque and is attached to the forward section at four points.

Tail Unit.—Cantilever monoplane type. All-wood framework, the fixed surfaces covered with plywood and the elevators and rudder with fabric.
Landing Gear.—Fixed type. Cantilever oleo legs attached to the auxiliary spar in the leading-edge of the wing.
Power Plant.—One 80 h.p. Bücker Bü M 700 four-cylinder in-line inverted air-cooled engine. Heine two-blade fixed-pitch wooden airscrew. Fuel capacity 80 litres. Oil capacity 4 litres.
Accommodation.—Single enclosed cockpit with canopy hinged on starboard side. Alternative equipment for gunnery, bombing, dive-bombing or navigation training. For bombing or dive-bombing training four 1.5 kg. practice bombs are carried.
Dimensions.—Span 8.6 m. (28 ft. 2½ in.), Length 6.67 m. (21 ft. 10½ in.), Height 1.85 m. (6 ft. 1 in.), Wing area 9.20 sq. m. (99 sq. ft.).
Weights.—Weight empty 315 kg. (693 lbs.), Weight loaded (S.K.5 load group with limited fuel) 450 kg. (990 lbs.), Weight loaded (P.4 load group—fully loaded) 510 kg. (1,122 lbs.).
Performance (S.K.5 load group).—Maximum speed 205 km.h. (127 m.p.h.), Cruising speed 195 km.h. (121 m.p.h.), Landing speed (with flaps) 80 km.h. (50 m.p.h.), Maximum permissible diving speed 440 km.h. (273 m.p.h.), Climb to 1,000 m. (3,280 ft.) 3.9 min., Climb to 2,000 m. (6,560 ft.) 8.7 min., Service ceiling 5,000 m. (16,400 ft.), Range 740 km. (460 miles) at cruising speed.
Performance (P.4 load group).—As above except maximum permissible diving speed 360 km.h. (224 m.p.h.), Climb to 1,000 m. (3,280 ft.) 5.2 min., Climb to 2,000 m. (6,560 ft.) 11.5 min., Service ceiling 3,900 m. (12,790 ft.).

DFS.

DEUTSCHES FORSCHUNGSINSTITUT fur SEGELFLUG.

Headquarters : Griesheim, near Darmstadt.

The German Research Institute for Sail-flying was responsible for developing a number of military glider and powered-glider designs, of which the DFS 230 "assault" glider was used operationally in Belgium, Crete and North Africa.

THE DFS 228.

This short-range reconnaissance aircraft of a highly-specialised type was still under development at the cessation of hostilities. It had been planned to complete ten during 1945. The DFS 228, which has been described as a powered glider, was intended to be launched at a height of about 32,800 ft. (10,000 m.) after having been towed by or carried up on the back of a Dornier Do 217.

With a Walter 509D liquid rocket unit and approximately 680 gallons of fuel, the launching weight was about 9,000 lbs. (4,090 kg.). The pilot was accommodated in a pressure cockpit and the aircraft was designed to attain a maximum height of about 80,000 ft. (24,400 m.). The total range above 32,800 ft. (10,000 m.) was approximately 450 miles (720 km.). A special Zeiss camera was to be used for high-altitude photography.

THE DFS 230.

The DFS 230 "assault" glider was first reported in Belgium in May, 1940. It was a braced high-wing monoplane with a single-spar wooden wing covered with plywood and fabric, and a steel tube fuselage covered with fabric. Of rectangular section, the fuselage accommodated a crew of two and up to eight fully-armed troops, the latter seated on a central boom. The pilot's cockpit forward of the wings could be fitted with either single or dual control. In operational use the wheel landing-gear was jettisoned after take-off, the landing being made on skids.

The maximum permissible flying weight was 4,600 lbs. (2,090 kg.) including 2,800 lbs. (1,270 kg.) disposable load. Thus, in addition to ten men (including one or two pilots) 600 lbs. (272 kg.) of freight (machine-guns, ammunition, etc.) could be carried.

Various aircraft could be used as tugs, including the He 111, Hs 126, Ju 52, Ju 87 and Me 110. Intercommunication between glider and tug was maintained via the tow-rope. Light machine-guns could be carried for defence.

THE DFS 332.

The DFS 332 glider was developed for testing full-scale wing sections at high speed. The first prototype was nearing completion at the end of the war in Europe. It was a twin-fuselage design with a span of 49 ft. 2 in. (15 m.), the wing section for test being mounted between the fuselages. This central test section was built up from wood around a single duralumin spar and the angle of attack could be varied in flight by an electric motor driving through a torque shaft. Another electric motor permitted the varying of the tailplane incidence to compensate for a large angle of attack of the test section.

The pilot's cockpit was in the starboard fuselage and there was accommodation for an observer in the port fuselage. It was intended that the glider should be towed to a suitable altitude and would then attain the desired testing speed in a sustained glide. The measurements necessary for lift and drag assessment were to be made after levelling out. For higher speeds it was intended to fit some form of reaction propulsion unit of short duration.

THE DFS 346.

This project was still in the design stage at the cessation of hostilities in Europe. It was intended to instal two Walter rocket units with the object of reaching Mach numbers up to 2.6 at an altitude of 100,000 ft. (30,500 m.), representing a speed of about 1,700 m.p.h. (2,720 km.h.).

DORNIER.

DORNIER-WERKE G.m.b.H.

Head Office : Friedrichshafen.
Works : Friedrichshafen, Neuaubing, near Munich, &c.
Associated Company : Norddeutsche Dornierwerke, G.m.b.H., Wismar, Berlin.
Associated Swiss Company : Dornier-Werke A.G., Altenrhein.
Berlin Office : Tirpitzüfer 86-90, Berlin W.35.
Chief Engineer : Dipl. Ing. Pressel.

Dr. Ing. Claude Dornier started the development of metal aircraft in the very early days of the War 1914-18 and his earliest products of this type were giant flying-boats. His efforts in this direction were supported by the Zeppelin interests.

In association with those interests Dornier metal aircraft of various types were produced. During 1922, the firm formerly known as Zeppelin Werk Lindau G.m.b.H., changed its title to the above.

The most widely-used of all pre-war Dornier designs was the Wal flying-boat, originally produced twenty years ago. In addition to its production in Germany, licences for its construction were granted in Switzerland, Italy, Spain, Holland and Japan.

Later the Do 18 was produced as a development of the Wal fitted with Junkers Jumo diesel engines and intended for trans-oceanic flying. The Do 18 was used for the first experimental crossing of the North Atlantic, in 1936, and later went into service across the South Atlantic. It was ultimately produced as a reconnaissance flying-boat for the German Air Force.

The Dornier aeroplane most widely used during the war was the Do 217, which was developed from the pre-war Do 17 through the Do 215, which was one of types standardised for the Luftwaffe before the war, and the Do 17Z. Originally a twin-engined bomber, the Do 217 was later adapted to other duties, including night fighting, torpedo-dropping, mine-laying, etc. Both the Lowenthal and Manzell plants at Friedrichshafen were engaged in the production of the Do 217 in 1944-45.

The Do 335 twin-engined fighter with tractor and pusher airscrews was in limited production at the Dornier Oberpfaffenhofen plant when hostilities ceased. This plant had also been engaged in the production of the Messerschmitt Me 110.

THE DORNIER Do 18.

The Do 18 was originally produced as a trans-Atlantic mail-carrier and used on the South Atlantic service of Deutsche Lufthansa. It was available in two forms, the Do 18 E, with a total loaded weight of 10,000 kg. (22,000 lbs.) and the Do 18 F, with larger wings and a total loaded weight of 11,000 kg. (24,200 lbs.).

During the War the Do 18 was employed mainly as a reconnaissance and air/sea rescue flying-boat by the German Air Force. C, D, G & H sub-types were common.

Type.—Twin-engined flying-boat.
Wings.—High-wing braced monoplane. Centre-section carrying the engine-mountings carried above hull by faired-in structure. Slightly-tapering outer wing-sections braced to lateral sponsons by parallel struts. Wing structure of metal, covered with fabric, except in the slipstream of the airscrew, where the wing is metal-covered. Auxiliary surfaces hinged slightly below trailing-edge of wings act as ailerons and landing-flaps.
Hull.—Semi-circular hull, with characteristic Dornier under-surface and lateral sponsons. Vee bottom forward, becoming flatter at the first step. On both sides of the keel are longitudinal steps running parallel to it. Aft of the main step is a tapering step which carries at its extremity a water-rudder. Rear portion of hull gradually merges into the fin. All-metal structure, with smooth outer skin and flush riveting. Hull specially strengthened for catapulting.
Tail Unit.—Monoplane type. Fin integral with the hull. Tail-plane braced to hull by parallel struts. Aerodynamically-balanced elevators and rudder. Mass-balanced rudder.
Power Plant.—Two 600 h.p. Junkers Jumo 205 six-cylinder double-opposed water-cooled Diesel engines mounted in tandem. Front engine drives a three-bladed metal airscrew direct. Rear engine drives a similar airscrew through shafting. Radiators for both engines in leading-edge of structure connecting hull and centre-section. Fuel tanks in hull.
Accommodation.—Forward gun position and compartment for mooring and stowage of marine gear in nose. Then follows the enclosed pilot's compartment and accommodation for wireless-operator and navigator. Fuel tanks and stowage space for equipment, collapsible rubber dinghy, etc. below wings. An after compartment with second gun position in roof is located aft of trailing-edge of wings.
Armament.—Two machine-guns, one in the nose and one aft of the wings, on flexible unshielded mountings. Bombs carried under wings.
Dimensions.—Span 77 ft. 9 in. (23.7 m.), Length 63 ft. 1 in. (19.25 m.), Height 17 ft. 9 in. (5.45 m.), Wing area 1,054.5 sq. ft. (98 sq. m.).
Weights.—Weight empty 12,265 lbs. (5,575 kg.), Weight loaded 22,000 lbs. (10,000 kg.).
Performance.—Maximum speed 145 m.p.h. (248 km.h.), Service ceiling 17,400 ft. (5,310 m.), Range 2,640 miles (4,225 km.) at 110 m.p.h. (176 km.h.).

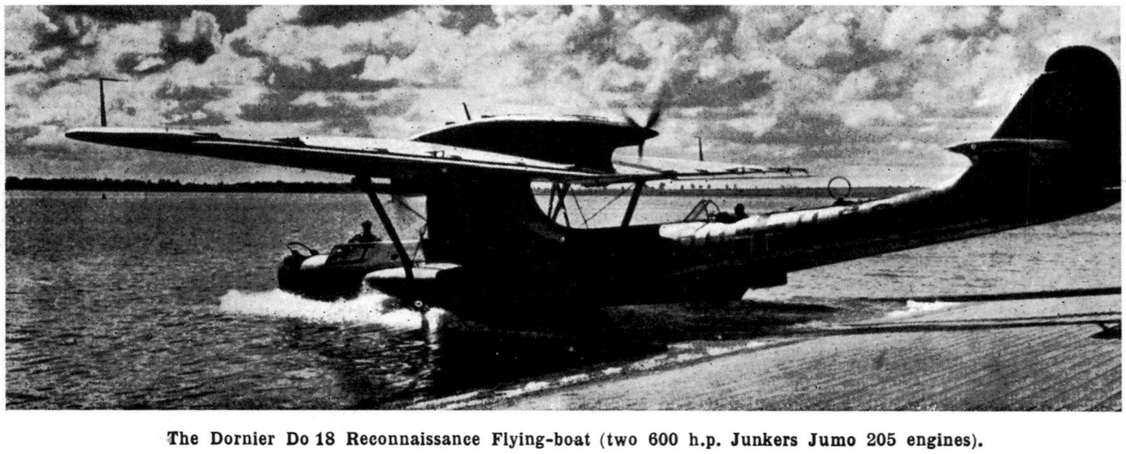

The Dornier Do 18 Reconnaissance Flying-boat (two 600 h.p. Junkers Jumo 205 engines).

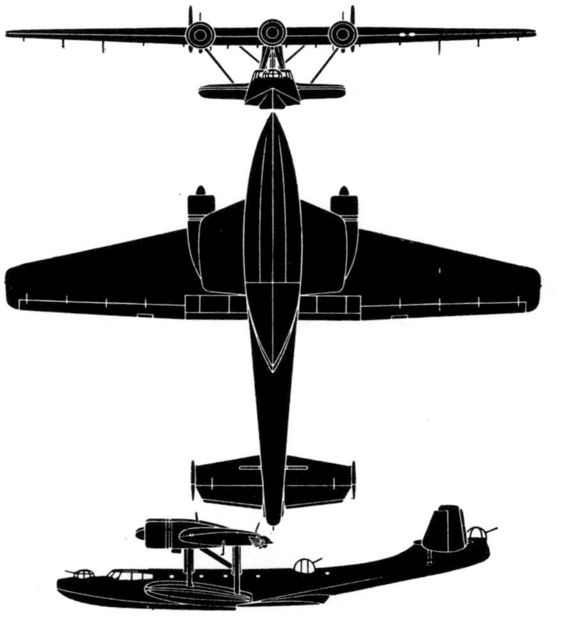

The Dornier Do 24 Flying-boat.

THE DORNIER Do 24.

The Do 24 was designed before the war and a series was built to the order of the Dutch Government for use in the East Indies in 1938. During the war it was used by the Luftwaffe mainly as a reconnaissance and air/sea rescue flying-boat. Sub-types K, N and T were in service.

Type.—Three-engined Reconnaissance flying-boat.
Wings.—High-wing semi-cantilever monoplane. Centre-section carrying the three engines is supported above the hull by inverted Vee struts and braced by sloping parallel struts to the Dornier "stummeln" or sea-wings, which give lateral stability on the water and increase the area of the lifting surface in flight. Cantilever tapering outer wing sections. Wing structure as for Do18. Slotted ailerons on outer wing sections. Split flaps on centre-section.
Hull.—Normal Dornier two-step metal hull. Rear step fairs into a vertical knife-edge. Dornier "sea-wings" for lateral stability on the water.
Tail Unit.—Braced monoplane tail-plane with twin fins and rudders. Metal structure with metal-covered fixed surfaces and fabric-covered movable surfaces. Statically and aerodynamically-balanced rudders with servo flaps. Statically-balanced elevators.
Power Plant.—Three Bramo Fafnir 323 R nine-cylinder radial air-cooled engines mounted in line along the leading-edge of the centre-section. Three-bladed controllable-pitch airscrews. NACA cowlings. Fuel tanks in sea-wings.
Accommodation.—Normal crew of six. Gunner's position in nose with rotatable turret. Pilot's enclosed compartment seating two side-by-side with navigator's and radio operator's positions behind. Within hull below centre-section is the living and sleeping accommodation for crew. Aft of wing is the second gunner's position and in the extreme tail is a third gunner's position, both equipped with rotatable turrets. The boat is fully equipped for extended cruises away from its base.
Armament.—Three machine-guns in rotatable turrets in nose amidships and in the extreme stern. Racks under wings for 12—50 kg. (110 lb.) bombs.

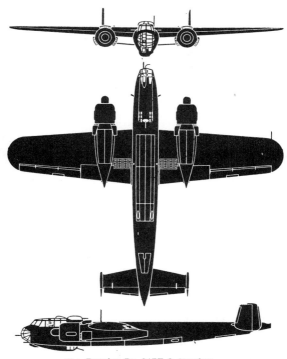

The Dornier Do 217E-2 Bomber.

The Dornier Do 217J Night Fighter (two BMW 801 engines).

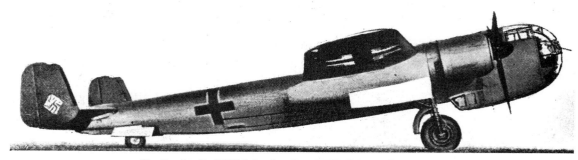

The Dornier Do 217K-1 Bomber (two BMW 801 radial engines).

DIMENSIONS.—Span 88 ft. 7 in. (27 m.), Length 72 ft. 2 in. (22 m.), Height 17 ft. 10 in. (5.45 m.), Wing area 1,162 sq. ft. (108 sq. m.).
WEIGHTS.—Weight loaded 29,700 lbs. (13,500 kg.).
PERFORMANCE.—Maximum speed 190 m.p.h. (304 km.h.), Cruising speed 161 m.p.h. (260 km.h.) at 6,560 ft. (2,000 m.), Alighting speed 67 m.p.h. (109 km.h.), Service ceiling 17,400 ft. (5,310 m.), Range 2,050 miles (3,300 km.).

THE DORNIER Do 214.

The Do 214 was a project for a giant long-range flying-boat suitable for military or civil cargo transport or civil passenger-carrying. It was designed in 1942 but development was later abandoned.

The large two-step hull was of the two-deck type and a hinged nose was envisaged for loading wheeled or tracked vehicles onto the lower deck. In the military version there was provision for eight gun turrets, three dorsal, four in the sides of the hull and one in the tail. The tail turret had triple MG 151 cannon, the remainder having twin MG 151 mountings.

The high monoplane wing with tapered leading-edge and straight trailing-edge carried four tandem engine nacelles, each nacelle having one pusher and one tractor Daimler-Benz DB 613 A, the total power-plant thus consisting of eight double engines, each made up of two DB 603 engines geared together. The total take-off power would thus have been 32,000 h.p.
DIMENSIONS.—Span 197 ft. (60 m.), Length 169 ft. 3 in. (51.6 m.).

THE DORNIER Do 217E.

The earliest operational sub-type of the Do 217 was the E, although sub-types A, C and D are known to have existed. The Do 217 E was used in 1940 and 1941 as a bomber and in attacks on convoys carrying two Hs 293 glider-bombs.

Ro 217E-1. Two BMW 801 A engines. Bomber, dive-bomber with automatic bomb-selection and dive-bombing mechanism, or torpedo-bomber. Armament : one fixed MG 151 and one flexible MG 151/20 in the nose, one MG 131 in a manually-operated dorsal mounting aft of pilot's compartment, one MG 131 in lower rear-firing position, and two MG 15 in lateral firing positions.

Do 217E-2. Same as for E-1 except upper dorsal MG 131 mounted in electrically-operated turret.

Do 217E-3. Similar to E-1 except for minor modifications.
Do 217E-4. Similar to E-2 except for minor modifications.
Do 217E-5. Similar to E-4 but fitted with carriers under the outer wings for two Hs 293 glider bombs for attacking convoys. Special equipment for controlling the bombs installed in the fuselage.

THE DORNIER Do 217J.

The Do 217J was a night fighter developed from the E, to which it was structurally similar except that it was provided with a re-designed solid armoured nose fitted with a forward-firing armament comprising four 20 m/m. MG FF and four 7.92 m/m. MG 17 guns. The upper and lower rear gun positions of the E-2 were retained but the lateral guns were not used. Special night-fighting equipment was installed. For some time the J sub-type was a standard Luftwaffe night fighter.

THE DORNIER Do 217K.

The Do 217K was a further development of the E, the distinguishing feature of this version being a re-designed deeper and more rounded nose. The Do 217K-1 was a bomber, but the K-2 with wings of greater span (80 ft.= 24.4 m.) was equipped to carry two FX 1400 radio-corrected armour-piercing bombs for attacking armoured ships. Another novelty in the K sub-type was the fitting of a battery of four fixed rearward-firing MG 81 machine-guns in the tail-cone. Like the E and J sub-types, the K was fitted with two BMW 801 two-row radial air-cooled engines.

THE DORNIER Do 217M.

The Do 217M-1 was similar to the K-1 except that DB 603 liquid-cooled engines were installed in place of the air-cooled

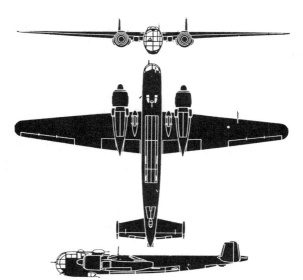

The Dornier Do 217K-2 with wings of increased span.

BMW 801 units. The M sub-type was the latest bomber version of the Do 217 in service at the time of the capitulation of Germany.

TYPE.—Twin-engined Heavy Bomber.
WINGS.—Shoulder-wing cantilever monoplane. Structure in three sections, the centre-section which incorporates a portion of the fuselage, and the two outer sections with semi-circular wing-tips. Two-spar wing structure. All but a few former ribs are girder trusses, solid plate ribs being used at points of stress only. Smooth outer stress-bearing skin riveted to spars and former ribs. Slotted ailerons on outer sections. Electrically-operated split flaps. Maximum flap angles 55°. Ailerons and flaps are linked so that the ailerons droop when the flaps are lowered. Leading-edge of outer wing-sections is doubled-skinned and intervening space fed with hot air from engines through lagged pipes in leading-edge. Air enters at bottom of the sandwich between each nose rib and passes forward and upward around leading-edge and escapes into wing just forward of front spar flange and finally to atmosphere through apertures at the aileron hinges.
FUSELAGE.—All-metal structure in three sections, comprising the nose section accommodating the crew, the section which is integral with the wing centre-section, and the rear fuselage. Main structure built up of a number of formers and stringers to which the stressed skin is riveted. The centre and rear sections of the fuselage are to within a few feet of the tail divided in a horizontal plane, the lower half of the fuselage forming the bomb-cell and the remainder containing transverse bracing frames to support the weight of the bomb loads.
TAIL UNIT.—Cantilever monoplane type with twin fins and rudders. Tail-plane and fins each have two spars and the entire unit, including the movable surfaces, is covered with a metal skin. Fins are fitted with fixed slats, the trailing-edges of the slats being on the inside of the fins. Rudders have very narrow horn balances, used mostly for mass-balancing, and trimming-tabs extending the full length of the trailing-edges. Tailplane incidence is automatically changed when the landing flaps are lowered. It can also be adjusted manually.
LANDING GEAR.—Retractable type. Each unit comprises two oleo legs and a single wheel and is electrically retracted rearwards into the engine nacelle. Electrically-operated retractable tail-wheel.
POWER PLANT.—Two Daimler-Benz DB 603 A twelve-cylinder inverted Vee liquid-cooled engines on welded steel-tube mountings at the extremities of the centre-section. Coolant radiators beneath the engines. Oil radiators in top cowling. Five fuel tanks protected with rubber and leather coverings and two oil tanks in the wings between the spars arranged in the following order :—centre-section tank (230 Imp. gallons), two inner wing tanks inboard of engines (175 Imp. gallons each), two oil tanks outboard of engines (44 Imp. gallons each) and two outer wing tanks out-board of oil tanks (35 Imp. gallons each). CO_2 gas may be released in tank compartments in an emergency. VDM three-bladed fully-feathering airscrews with Schwarz type blades and slinger-ring type de-icing equipment.
ACCOMMODATION.—Crew of four housed in cabin forward of wing. Pilot on port side with spectacle-type control column which slides horizontally into dashboard on rack and pinion for elevator control. Bomb-aimer in nose or seated beside pilot. Radio-operator behind pilot. Rear gunner aft. Cabin heating by exhaust-pipe muffs. Hot-air sprays from cabin heating system are fitted to pilot's windscreen and to all transparent nose panels. Pilot's seat is fully armour-plated and there is armour plate to the sides of the gun-turret. Armoured recess for dinghy stowage in rear fuselage.
ARMAMENT.—One twin MG 81 (1,000 rounds) in the nose, one MG 131 (500 rounds) in dorsal turret, one MG 131 (1,000 rounds) in lower rear position, and two MG 81 (750 rounds per gun) in lateral positions.
BOMB INSTALLATION.—Main bomb cell 14 ft. 10 in. long, with 5 ft. 8 in. extension at after end to take extra length of torpedo. Stowage space for a maximum load of 5,550 lbs. which may be made up of various combinations of bombs, one torpedo or one

The Dornier Do 217M Bomber (two Daimler Benz DB 603 engines).

or two mines. Provision also made for fitting two 550-lb. bomb-racks under wings, one outboard of each engine. Electrical fusing system for level bombing, dive-bombing, mine-laying or torpedo-dropping. Depth-setting and gyro-angling controls provided for torpedo dropping. Heating for bomb compartment when torpedo is carried.

Dimensions.—Span 62 ft. 5 in. (19 m.), Length 56 ft. 6 in. (17 m.), Gross wing area 610 sq. ft. (56.6 sq. m.), Net wing area 522 sq. ft. (48.5 sq. m.).

Weight Loaded.—35,000 lbs. (15,890 kg.).

Performance.—Maximum speed at sea level 290 m.p.h. (464 km.h.), Maximum speed at 22,000 ft. (6,710 m.) 330 m.p.h. (528 km.h.), Service ceiling (fully loaded) 24,000 ft. (7,320 m.), Service ceiling (light) 27,000 ft. (8,235 m.), Range with maximum fuel 2,400 miles (3,840 km.).

THE DORNIER Do 217N.

The Do 217N was the night fighter version of the M and was fitted with two Daimler-Benz DB 603 liquid-cooled engines. The nose was modified and the heavy armament installed could include two or four fixed upward-firing guns.

THE DORNIER Do 317.

The Do 317 was a projected twin-engined bomber which followed the general lines of the Do 217. Two versions were foreseen, one with two DB 603 engines, conventional armament arrangements in the crew compartment in the nose of the fuselage, and a span of 67 ft. 8 in. (20.64 m.). The other version was to have two DB 610 units (each composed of two DB 605 engines coupled together), pressure cabin, remote-control turrets amidships and in the tail and a span of 85 ft. 3 in. (26 m.) permitting the carrying of a bigger bomb load.

The Do 317 embodied the characteristic bulbous nose of the Do 217, equal taper wings with rounded tips and a twin-ruddered tail-unit. The twin fins and rudders were of an unusual triangular shape with rounded corners, the bottom of the fin and trailing-edge of the rudder being at right angles to each other.

Dimensions.—Span 67 ft. 8 in. (20.64 m.) or 85 ft. 3 in. (26 m.), Length 55 ft. 1 in. (16.8 m.), Height 17 ft. 10 in. (5.45 m.).

THE DORNIER Do 335A "PFIEL" (ARROW).

The unusual tandem-engine lay-out employed in the Do 335 was first patented by Dr. Claude Dornier in 1937, when ease of production and interchangeability were claimed as particular virtues of the design, but it was not until the end of 1942 that permission to build the prototype was given. Although available in small numbers towards the end of the war, the Do 335 was not encountered in operations.

There was a project for installing a turbo-jet unit in place of the rear engine.

There were two distinct versions of the Do 335A, a single-seat Day Fighter and Fighter Bomber and a two-seat Night Fighter. These were designated as follow :—

Do 335A-O and A-1. Single-seat Day Fighter and Fighter-Bomber. Armament : three MK 103, two in the wings and one firing through the airscrew hub, and two synchronised MG 151/20 in the top cowling. Fighter-Bomber could carry 1,100 lbs. (500 kg.). of bombs.

Do 335A-6. Two-seat Night Fighter. Second cockpit for radio and radar operator immediately behind pilot and slightly above to give forward vision. Armament : two MG 151/20 (200 rounds per gun) in top cowling and one MK 103 (70 rounds) firing through the airscrew boss. Radar aerials outboard on both wings.

Type.—Twin-engined Day Fighter, Fighter-Bomber or Night Fighter.

Wings.—Low-wing cantilever monoplane. Trapezoidal plan form with 13° sweep-back on leading-edge and blunt wing-tips. Wings are detachable. All-metal stressed-skin structure built round a single box spar. Variable camber flaps inboard of the ailerons. De-icing on leading-edge. Stowage for master compass, hydraulic tanks, oxygen bottles and inner and outer fuel tanks in wings.

Fuselage.—All-metal monocoque structure.

Tail Unit.—Cruciform type with cantilever tailplane and upper and lower fins and rudders. All-metal stressed-skin construction except that leading-edges of fins are of wood and house radio aerials. De-icing on tailplane leading-edges. Rudders and elevators are both aerodynamically and mass-balanced.

Landing Gear.—Retractable tricycle type. Main wheels are raised inwardly into the underside of the wings. Nose wheel retracts backwards and turns through 45° to lie at this angle under the pilot's seat. Hydraulic retraction.

Power Plant.—Two Daimler-Benz DB 603 E twelve-cylinder inverted Vee liquid-cooled engines, one in the nose driving a tractor airscrew and the other in the fuselage amidships and driving a pusher propeller through a long hollow shaft supported by three thrust races. On some versions the front airscrew is of the reversible-pitch type. Annular nose radiator for the front engine and ventral scoop radiator for the rear engine. Fuel tanks in A-O and A-1 entirely in wings and have a total capacity of 407 Imp. gallons.

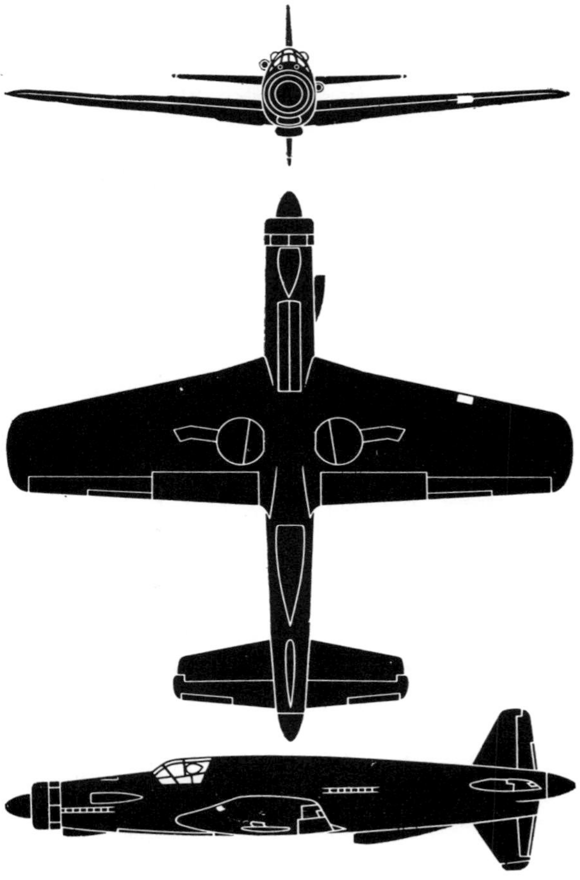

The Dornier Do 335A Tandem-engined Fighter.

Fuel tanks in A-6 are in wings and in fuselage between two cockpits and have a total capacity of 510 Imp. gallons. M 50 tanks (33 Imp. gallons) in wings.

Accommodation.—Pilot's cockpit over leading-edge of wing. In two-seat version, the second cockpit is behind the pilot and slightly above to give forward vision. Cockpit canopy jettisonable and pilot-ejecting seat is fitted. Bullet-proof windscreen and armour protection.

Armament.—Day fighter : three MK 103 and two MG 151/20. Night Fighter : two MG 151/20 in the top cowling and one MK 103 firing through the airscrew shaft.

Dimensions.—Span 45 ft. 4 in. (13.8 m.), Length 45 ft. 6 in. (13.87 m.), Height 16 ft. 3½ in. (5 m.), Wing area 414 sq. ft. (38.5 sq. m.).

Weight Loaded (A-0 and A-1).—21,160 lbs. (9,610 kg.).

Weight Loaded (A-6).—22,230 lbs. (10,090 kg.).

Performance (A-0 and A-1).—Maximum emergency speed 477 m.p.h. (763 km.h.) at 21,000 ft. (6,400 m.), Cruising speed at maximum continuous power 428 m.p.h. (685 km.h.) at 23,300 ft. (7,110 m.), Economical cruising speed at 19,680 ft. (6,000 m.) 295 m.p.h. (472 km.h.), Landing speed 109 m.p.h. (174.4 km.h.), Range and endurance at maximum continuous power 868 miles (1,390 km.) or 2 hours, Range and endurance at economical cruising power 1,280 miles (2,050 km.) or 2 hours 26 mins., Service ceiling at mean weight 37,400 ft. (11,410 m.), Normal landing run 689 yards (630 m.), Landing run with reversible-pitch airscrew in nose 514 yards (470 m.).

Performance (A-6).—Maximum emergency speed 430 m.p.h. (688 km.h.) at 17,700 ft. (5,500 m.), Cruising speed at maximum continuous power 769 m.p.h. (606 km.h.) at 23.300 ft. (7.110 m.). Economical cruising speed at 19,680 ft. (6,000 m.) 275 m.p.h. (440 km.h.), Landing speed 112 m.p.h. (179 km.h.). Range and endurance at maximum continuous power 886 miles (1,420 km.) or 2 hours 26 min., Range and endurance at economical cruising power 1,290 miles (2,065 km.) or 4 hours 46 mins., Service ceiling at mean weight 33,400 ft. (10,190 m.), Landing run 766 yards (700 m.), Landing run with reversible-pitch airscrew in nose 580 yards. (530 m.).

THE DORNIER Do 335B.

A development of the A Series, the Do 335B was equipped specifically for use as a Heavy Fighter and Night Fighter. The following were the principal variants in this series :—

Do 335B-2. Two Daimler-Benz DB 603 E engines. Heavy Fighter.

Do 335B-3. Same as the B-2 but fitted with two DB 603 LA engines with two-stage superchargers.

Do 335B-4. To use more efficiently the high-altitude characteristics of the DB 603 LA engine wings of increased area were fitted on the B-4 sub-types.

Do 335B-6. There were two versions of the B-6 Night Fighter with different wing area. Both fitted with DB 603 E engines.

Do 335B-7. High-altitude Night Fighter with two DB 603 LA engines. Bears the same relationhip to the B-6 as the B-3 bears to the B-2.

Do 335B-8. High-altitude Night Fighter with increased wing area as on the B-4 in the Heavy Fighter series.

THE DORNIER Do 435.

The Do 435 was a projected development of the Do 335 with a roomier fuselage and more powerful engines.

THE DORNIER Do 635.

The Do 635 was a projected twin version of the Do 335, using two standard fuselage and standard port and starboard outer wing sections, the two fuselages being joined by a new centre-section. The power-plant was to consist of four DB 603 engines driving two tractor and two pusher propellers. See 8-635 under "Junkers."

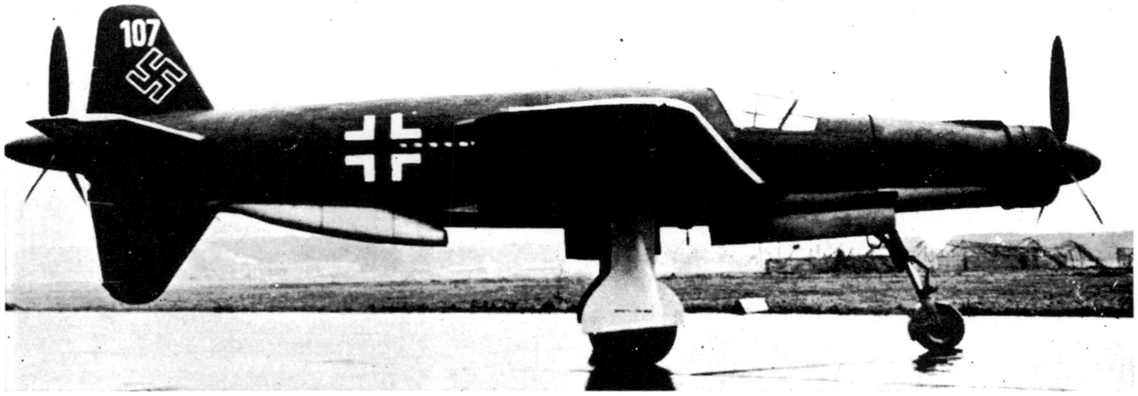

The Dornier Do 335A Tandem-engined Day and Night Fighter.

FIESELER.

GERHARD FIESELER WERKE G.m.b.H.

Works and Head Office : Kassel.

Chairman : Gerhard Fieseler.

Vice-Chairman : Prof. Dr. Ing. K. G. F. Thalau.

Commercial Director : Dr. Goebel.

Technical Director : Dr. Ing. Banzhaf.

Founded in 1930 by Herr Gerhard Fieseler, a famous German aerobatic pilot.

The first type produced was the Fieseler Fi 2 Tiger, of which the first was built for Herr Fieseler's own aerobatic performances. Later types were the Fieseler Fi 5R, a light two-seat monoplane with trailing-edge flaps and cantilever under-carriage, and the Fieseler Fi 97, a four-seat cabin monoplane fitted with slots and flap gear.

The Fi 156, a fully slotted and flapped monoplane which was developed before the war, was used throughout the war as a staff transport, for short-range reconnaissance and army co-operation duties and as an ambulance. It was in production by Morane during the occupation of France.

The Fieseler company was responsible for the design of the Fi 103, the prototype of the FZG 76 Flying-bomb.

The Fieseler plants at Bettenhausen and Waldau, in the Kassel area, were both engaged in the production of the Focke-Wulf Fw 190.

THE FIESELER Fi 156C "STORCH."

The Fi 156 was developed specifically for slow-speed flight and for take-off from and landing in restricted spaces. It was used throughout the war on various military duties, the Fi 156C-1 serving as a Staff transport and the Fi 156C-2 as a short-range reconnaissance aeroplane. Other sub-types were used for general purposes.

During the occupation of France, the Fi 156 was built by the Morane-Saulnier company at its Puteaux factory.

Type.—Three-seat Communications, Army Co-operation, Short-range Reconnaissance or Ambulance monoplane.

Wings.—High-wing braced monoplane. Rectangular outer wings hinged to the upper fuselage longerons and braced to the lower longerons by steel-tube Vee struts. Two-spar wooden construction. Fixed light-metal slot along entire leading-edge. Entire trailing-edge hinged, outer portions acting as statically-balanced and slotted ailerons and inner portions as slotted camber-changing flaps.

Fuselage.—Rectangular welded steel-tube fuselage, covered with fabric.

Tail Unit.—Braced monoplane type. Fin built integral with fuselage. Adjustable tail-plane. Balanced rudder and elevators. Fixed dependent slat below hinge-line of elevators. Tail surfaces have wooden framework with fabric covering.

Landing Gear.—Split type. Consists of two compression legs, incorporating long-stroke steel-spring oil-damped shock-absorbers, the upper ends attached to the apices of two pyramids on the sides of the fuselage, with the lower ends hinged to the centre-line of the underside of the fuselage by steel-tube Vees. Low-pressure wheels with hydraulic brakes. Tail-skid has steel-spring oil-damped shock-absorber.

Power Plant.—One 240 h.p. Argus As10 C eight-cylinder inverted Vee air-cooled engine on welded steel-tube mounting. Two fuel tanks (32 Imp. gallons) in wing-roots. An additional 45 gallon tank may be carried in the fuselage instead of two passengers.

Accommodation.—Enclosed cabin, seating pilot and one or two passengers in tandem. Entire sides and roof of cabin glazed. Side windows are built out with lower panels sloping in acutely to give good downward vision. Door on starboard side. Provision for wireless, camera, and night-flying equipment.

Armament.—Single machine-gun mounted on top of the fuselage at the rear of the cabin.

Dimensions.—Span 46 ft. 9 in. (14.25 m.), Width folded 15 ft. 7 in.

(4.75 m.), Length 32 ft. 6 in. (9.9 m.), Height 10 ft. (3.05 m.), Wing area 279.7 sq. ft. (26 sq. m.).

WEIGHTS.—Weight empty 2,050 lbs. (930 kg.), Weight loaded 2,920 lbs. (1,326 kg.).

PERFORMANCE.—Maximum speed at sea level 109 m.p.h. (175 km.h.), Cruising speed 60-80 m.p.h. (96-128 km.h.), Landing speed 32 m.p.h. (51 km.h.) Climb to 3,000 ft. (915 m.) 4 mins., Service ceiling 16,700 ft. (5,090 m.), Maximum range at sea level (crew of three) 240 miles (385 km.) at 60 m.p.h. (96 km.h.), Maximum range at sea level (crew of one and 77 gals. fuel) 630 miles (1,010 km.) at 60 m.p.h. (96 km.h.).

THE FIESELER Fi 256.

The Fi 256 was basically an enlarged version of the Fi 156. It was under development during the occupation of France by the Fieseler-controlled Morane-Saulnier company. It was intended to carry five passengers and was really a civil project. Development was abandoned.

THE FIESELER Fi 333.

The Fi 333 was a project for a twin-engined general purposes monoplane of novel design. The actual airframe was conventional but a very high fixed helicopter landing-gear permitted the attachment of cabin structure beneath the fuselage to enable the aircraft to be used as a troop-transport, ambulance, freight-carrier, etc. It was to be fitted with two BMW 323 D radial air-cooled engines.

DIMENSIONS.—Span 98 ft. 5 in. (30 m.), Length 72 ft. 2 in. (22 m.), Height 19 ft. (5.8 m.).

The Fieseler Fi 156C "Storch" Three-seat Communications Monoplane (240 h.p. Argus As 410C engine.).

FLETTNER.

The Flettner concern was the second of the two firms engaged during the war in helicopter development.

The Flettner Fl 282 was a small observation helicopter powered by a 150 h.p. Siemens Sh 14 radial engine. It had two rotors which were mounted with axes close together and turning in opposite directions. One or two passengers could be carried in addition to the pilot. The maximum speed of the Fl 282 was about 100 m.p.h. and the ceiling 13,000 ft. The petrol consumption was only about 8.5 gallons an hour.

An improved version of the Fl 282 and known as the Fl 339 was under development at the time of the German capitulation and was to incorporate the results of experience with the earlier model.

FOCKE-ACHGELIS.

FOCKE-ACHGELIS & CO., G.m.b.H.

HEAD OFFICE AND WORKS : HOYKENKAMP BEI DELMENHORST, OLDENBURG.

This Company took over, prior to the War, the development of the Focke Fw 61 experimental helicopter which was invented by Professor H. Focke, of the Focke-Wulf Flugzeugbau G.m.b.H. The Fw 61 had a normal aeroplane fuselage with a 160 h.p. Bramo Sh 14A engine in the nose. On either side of the fuselage forward were two inclined steel-tube pylons, at the apices of which were two three-bladed rotors.

These rotors had a diameter of approximately 7 m. (23 ft.) and a total disc area of 77 sq. m. (828.5 sq. ft.), equal to a loading of 14 kg./sq. m. (2.87 lbs./sq. ft.). The rotors, which turned in opposite directions, had double-articulated blades, the tangential oscillations of which were limited by elastic tension. Their angle of attack varied with the speed of rotation.

The Focke-Achgelis concern was one of two firms which were concerned with helicopter development during the war. The Focke-Achgelis Fa 223, which was first flown in 1940, was a development of the Fw 61. It had two large non-overlapping rotors driven through reduction gearing by a Bramo BMW 323 engine developing about 1,000 h.p. The all-up weight was 8,600 lbs. (3,900 kg.), including a useful load of 1,760 lbs. (800 kg.).

A more ambitious project which was never completed was the Fa 284. This craft was fitted with two BMW 801 engines and the all-up weight was to have been about 33,000 lbs. (15,000 kg.).

Another development of the Focke-Achgelis company was the Fa 330 man-lifting rotor kite. This was specially developed for use by U-boats as an observation post. A free-turning three-blade rotor was mounted on a vertical pylon attached to a simple framework on which there was an unprotected observer's seat. Carried aft on a tubular boom was a rudder and a horizontal stabilising surface. The observer had controls for operating the rudder and for tilting the rotor head. The kite was connected to the U-boat by cable and winch and maintained height when towed by a surfaced submarine. The observer could communicate with the U-boat by telephone.

FOCKE-WULF.

FOCKE-WULF FLUGZEUGBAU G.m.b.H.

WORKS : FLUGHAFEN, BREMEN, AND JOHANNISTHAL, NEAR BERLIN.

BERLIN OFFICE : TIRPITZÜFER 86-90, BERLIN, W.35.

Commercial Director : Dr. Naumann.

Technical Director : Prof. Dipl. Ing. K. Tank.

This firm was founded at the beginning of January, 1924, with a capital of R.M.200,000.

In September, 1931, the Albatros-Flugzeugwerke G.m.b.H. of Berlin was amalgamated with the Company, whose capital was then raised to R.M.285,000. In July, 1937, the Company was converted into a G.m.b.H. and in 1938 the capital was raised to R.M.2,500,000.

The most widely-produced product of the Company was the Fw 190 single-seat fighter. The first radial-engined and most heavily-armed single-seat fighter to be adopted by the German Air Force, it was the subject of continuous development up to the time of the capitulation. New types almost ready for operational service at that time were the Ta 152, a development of the "long-nosed" Fw 190, and the Ta 154 a twin-engined all-wood Day and Night Fighter. These two aircraft, together with several other experimental types described hereafter, carry the new designation "Ta" from the first two letters of the chief designer's name.

The following are some of the principle plants engaged in the production of Focke-Wulf fighter aircraft during 1944-45 :—

Fw 190.

Assembly plants :—Oschersleben (Ago), Kassel-Waldau (Fieseler), Tutow/Mecklenburg, Marienburg (Focke-Wulf), Gydnia-Rahmel, Sorau/Silesia, Cottbus, Halberstadt, Neubrandenburg, Schwerin, Wismer, Einswarden, Eschwege.

Components plants :—Kassel-Bettenhausen (Fieseler), Warnemünde, Anklam (Focke-Wulf), Poznan (Focke-Wulf), Kresinski, Sorau/Silesia, Wismar, Lübeck, Bremen-Hemlingen, Bremen-Hastedt, Bremen-Neuenland (Focke-Wulf), Oranienburg-Annagof (Heinkel), Oranienburg-Harmanndorf (Heinkel), Rathenow (Arado).

Ta 154.

Assembly plants :—Hanover-Langenhagen, Erfurt-Nord and others.

During the German occupation of France, the Fw 189 was manufactured in various plants of the Société Nationale de Constructions Aeronautiqués de Sud-Ouest which were controlled by Focke-Wulf.

THE FOCKE-WULF Ta 152A.

When the so-called "long-nosed Fw 190" (see Focke-Wulf Fw 190D) had been proved to be successful, Professor Kurt Tank redesignated this aircraft the Ta 152A. Structurally there was little difference between the Ta 152A and its predecessor. The wings were of slightly larger area and differed in plan form, from those of the Fw 190, the nose of the aircraft was cleaned up to give a smoother fuselage top-line and hydraulic instead of electrical operation was used for landing-gear and flaps.

The first sub-type of the Ta 152 had a Jumo 213 A engine. It did not go into production.

THE FOCKE-WULF Ta 152B.

After the Ta 152A had been abandoned, the B sub-type appeared but was not produced in any quantity. With the two-stage supercharged Jumo 213 E engine this version had a maximum speed of 428 m.p.h. (685 km.h.) at 36,800 ft. (11,225 m.).

THE FOCKE-WULF Ta 152C.

The Ta 152C was the first series production and operational sub-type of this design. With a Daimler-Benz DB 603 L engine this version was classed as a medium-altitude fighter. A modification was made to the wing structure to carry extra fuel tanks, thus raising the internal fuel capacity to 231 Imp. gallons. Using the MW 50 power-boost, the Ta 152C attained a maximum speed of 467 m.p.h. (747 km.h.) at 35,000 ft. (10,680 m.).

THE FOCKE-WULF Ta 152E.

A conversion of the C sub-type for reconnaissance duties was fitted with a Jumo 213 E engine and designated Ta 152E. The 152E-1 was due to go into production in March, 1945. Using MW 50 injection this version could reach a speed of 463 m.p.h. (741 km.h.) at 31,000 ft. (9,450 m.).

THE FOCKE-WULF Ta 152H.

The Ta 152H was a high-altitude reconnaissance version with extended span wings, a Jumo 213 E engine and pressure cabin.

The wings, of 48 ft. 6 in. (14.8 m.) span, were of unusual construction with the main spar extending outwards each side from a point just outboard of the main landing-gear attachment and with the rear spar extending over the whole span. The necessary structural rigidity was obtained by close-set ribs and numerous lateral stringers reinforcing the stressed skin.

High performance at all altitudes was ensured by carrying 18.6 Imp. gallons of GM 1 as well as 15.4 gallons of MW 50.

The Focke-Wulf Ta 152C Medium-altitude Fighter (Daimler-Benz DB603L engine).

In addition to these quantities of power-boosting chemicals, 216 Imp. gallons of fuel were carried in wing and fuselage tanks. At 30,000 ft. (9,150 m.) the Ta 152H had a maximum speed of 465 m.p.h. (744 km.h.) using MW 50 injection. A speed of 472 m.p.h. (755 km.h.) was possible at 41,000 ft. (12,500 m.) using GM 1.

THE FOCKE-WULF Ta 154A.

(For illustration see Addenda pages).

The Ta 154 was designed to meet a specification for a night fighter and bad-weather day fighter with a high maximum speed and a duration of $2\frac{3}{4}$ hours. Rapid development and quantity production was emphasised, together with extensive use of materials not in short supply : particularly wood, as by the use of the wood-working industry production could be hastened. This aircraft was first publicised over the German radio as the Teuton counterpart of the British Mosquito.

The first experimental prototype was produced in June, 1943. The sub-types of this aeroplane are the A-1 and A-3 two-seat Day Fighters ; the A-2 single-seat Day Fighter ; and the A-4 two-seat Night Fighter.

TYPE.—Single or two-seat Day or Night-Fighter.

WINGS.—Shoulder-wing cantilever monoplane. Single-piece wing of all-wood construction attached to the fuselage by four bolts. Straight leading-edge. Swept-forward trailing-edge carries the ailerons and variable-camber and slotted flaps. The nacelles, which project beyond the trailing-edge are of duralumin, and a lattice bulkhead, located behind the fireproof bulkhead and braced to the rear spar by Vee struts, supports the engine and landing-gear unit.

FUSELAGE.—All-wood oval section structure in one piece from the front bulkhead to the axis of rotation of the rudder. Fin is integral with the fuselage.

TAIL UNIT.—Cantilever monoplane type. One-piece single-spar tailplane of light metal construction. Metal-framed and fabric-covered elevators are interchangeable and are mass-balanced. Horn-balanced rudder is of similar construction and carries a servo tab which also acts as a trimmer. Tailplane is adjustable in flight round the axis of rotation of the elevators.

LANDING GEAR.—Retractable tricycle type. All wheels retract rearwards, the nose wheel turning through 90° to lie flat in the fuselage. Hydraulic retraction.

POWER PLANT.—Two Junkers Jumo 211 N or 211 R twelve-cylinder inverted Vee liquid-cooled engines in underslung nacelles. Annular nose radiators. Two fuel tanks in fuselage aft of the crew accommodation. Total fuel capacity 330 Imp. gallons. Oil tank (25.5 Imp. gallons) in each engine nacelle.

ACCOMMODATION.—Enclosed and armoured cockpit in front of leading-edge of wings. In two-seat version the radio operator sits behind the pilot facing forward. Entrance to cabin is through the jettisonable canopy. Cabin protected in front by 12 m/m. armour plating carried on a bulkhead and small side pieces of 8 m/m. armour plating. The windscreen is of 50 m/m. bullet-proof glass with 30 m/m. side panels.

ARMAMENT.—Two 30 m/m. MK 108 (110 rounds per gun) and two 20 m/m. MG 151/20 (200 rounds per gun) in the fuselage sides below the leading-edge of the wings and firing forward. Alternative armament may consist of four 30 m/m. MK 108 or four 20 m/m. MG 151/20 cannon. Ammunition boxes for the upper guns are in the leading-edge of the wings between the fuselage and nacelles, and those for the lower guns are in the fuselage. In addition to the forward-firing guns, two 30 m/m. MG 108 fixed guns firing forward and obliquely-upward may be installed in the fuselage of the night-fighter.

DIMENSIONS.—Span 52 ft. 6 in. (16 m.), Length 41 ft. 3 in. (12.6 m.), Height 12 ft. $\frac{1}{2}$ in. (3.6 m.), Wing area 349 sq. ft. (32.4 sq. m.).

WEIGHTS.—Weight loaded (A-1) 18,600 lbs. (8,445 kg.), Weight loaded (A-2 with GM 1 installation) 19,480 lbs. (8,845 kg.).

PERFORMANCE (Ta 154A-1 with two Jumo 211 N engines).—Maximum speed 282 m.p.h. (611 km.h.) at 19,000 ft. (5,795 m.), Climb to 26,240 ft. (8,000 m.) 16 mins., Service ceiling 31,200 ft. (9,520 m.), Range at 23,000 ft. (7,020 m.) 890 miles (1,425 km.), Maximum range at 23,000 ft. (7,020 m.) with two 66-gallon drop tanks 1,195 miles (1,912 km.).

PERFORMANCE (Ta 154A-1 with two Jumo 211 R engines).—Maximum speed 394 m.p.h. (630 km.h.) at 26,240 ft. (8,000 m.), Climb to 26,240 ft. (8,000 m.) 14.5 mins., Service ceiling 35,800 ft. (10,920 m.), Normal range at 23,000 ft. (7,020 m.) 855 miles (1,370 km.), Maximum range at 23,000 ft. (7,020 m.) with two 66-gallon drop tanks 1,160 miles (1,860 km.).

PERFORMANCE (Ta 154A-2).—Maximum speed (with GM 1) 388 m.p.h. (621 km.h.) at 32,800 ft. (10,000 m.).

THE FOCKE-WULF Ta 154C.

The outstanding differences between the A and C sub-types of the Ta 154 were, in the latter, the installation of two Jumo 213 A engines, a metal nose and, in the night fighter version, two MK 108 guns in the rear of the fuselage firing forwards and obliquely-upwards at an angle of approximately 70 degrees. In the day-fighter versions the upward-firing guns were omitted but mountings were provided in the sides of the fuselage for six MK 108 guns as an alternative installation to the two MK 103 and two MK 151 cannon.

A noticeable fuselage modification was the introduction of a "bubble" type cockpit canopy, thus altering the otherwise flat

top to the fuselage of the Ta 154A. The Ta 154C-1 night fighter also had a pilot-ejecting seat. Two wing fuel tanks, each with a capacity of 48 Imp. gallons, were fitted.

PERFORMANCE (Ta 154C-3).—Maximum speed (with GM 1) 428 m.p.h. (685 km.h.) at 32,800 ft. (10,000 m.).

THE FOCKE-WULF Ta 183.

The Ta 183 was the last single-seat fighter project of Professor Kurt Tank. At the time of the capitulation it was in an advanced stage of development and was to have been delivered in small quantities to the Luftwaffe during 1945.

It was a single jet fighter with the jet unit mounted in the rear fuselage, the air intake duct passing beneath the pilot's cockpit. A Jumo 004 turbo-jet would have been installed at the outset although the aircraft was designed for the Heinkel-Hirth He S 011 unit. In one version an auxiliary liquid-rocket unit was to be fitted in the rear of the fuselage above the jet tail-pipe for take-off and rapid climb.

One type of wing for the Ta 183 was of wood, the fuel being carried in liquid-tight compartments formed by the actual structure. The wing was very sharply swept-back and was of single-spar construction. The metal fuselage was made in sub-assemblies for ease of production. The tail narrow-chord fin and rudder were sharply swept-back with a Vee-shaped tailplane mounted at the top of the fin.

A maximum speed of 590 m.p.h. (944 km.h.) and an endurance of 3 hours was expected from this aeroplane.

THE FOCKE-WULF Fw 189A.

The Fw 189 was designed and first flown in 1939 and was initially used for Army Co-operation work. Subsequently its use was restricted to less active duties, such as evacuation of wounded, radio training and communications.

The A-1, A-2 and A-3 were common sub-types which differed only in small details.

TYPE.—Twin-engined short-range Reconnaissance monoplane. Also used as an Ambulance or Communications aeroplane.

WINGS.—Low-wing cantilever monoplane. Rectangular centre-section between tail-booms and supporting the crew nacelle on the centre-line. Tapering outer wings outside tail-booms. All-metal

The Focke-Wulf Fw 189A Reconnaissance Monoplane (two 450 h.p. Argus As 410 engines).

The Focke-Wulf Fw 190A-4 Single-seat Fighter-Bomber (BMW 801D engine).

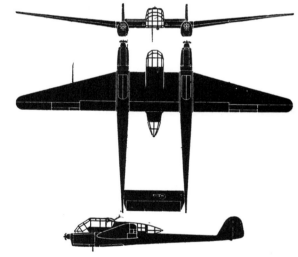

The Focke-Wulf Fw 189A Reconnaissance Monoplane.

structure with stressed-skin covering. Centre-section has three spars, the main and rear spars passing through the nacelle, which is rigidly attached to the centre-section. The undersurface between the main and rear auxiliary spars has detachable inspection panels. Outer sections also have three spars and have detachable leading and trailing-edge sections. They are attached to centre-section by bolts along the wing contour between the main and front spars as well as at the main spar. Electrically-operated fabric-covered split trailing-edge flaps between ailerons and tail-booms and across entire centre-section.

NACELLE.—All-metal structure extensively provided with transparent panels riveted to centre-section.

TAIL-BOOMS.—Two interchangeable oval all-metal booms are attached at the front to extensions of the engine nacelles and at the rear to the fin assembly by circumferential bolts.

TAIL UNIT.—Two fins of stressed-skin construction at ends of booms support between them the all-metal tail-plane. Rudders and elevators have metal frames and fabric covering. Statically and aerodynamically-balanced rudders and elevators. Electrically-controlled trimming tabs.

LANDING GEAR.—Retractable type. Main wheels are raised backwards into engine nacelles and apertures closed by hinged doors when wheels are retracted. Tail-wheel retracted laterally into well in underside of tailplane. Hydraulic retraction, but tail-wheel lowers under its own weight with assistance from rubber "hinges."

POWER PLANT.—Two 450 h.p. Argus As 410A-1 twelve-cylinder inverted Vee air-cooled engines. Two-bladed Argus automatic controllable-pitch airscrews. Two fuel tanks, one in the rear of each engine nacelle.

ACCOMMODATION.—Normal crew of three, but up to five can be accommodated.

DIMENSIONS.—Span 60 ft. 5 in. (18.4 m.), Length 39 ft. 4 in. (12 m.), Wing area 409.7 sq. ft. (38 sq. m.).

WEIGHTS.—Weight empty with equipment 5,930 lbs. (2,690 kg.), Weight loaded 7,500 lbs. (3,410 kg.), Maximum take-off weight 8,700 lbs. (3,950 kg.).

PERFORMANCE.—Maximum speed 215 m.p.h. (344 km.h.) at 8,000 ft.

The Focke-Wulf Ta 154A Twin-engined Day and Night Fighter

The Focke-Wulf Fw 190A-5 Single-seat Fighter (BMW 801D engine).

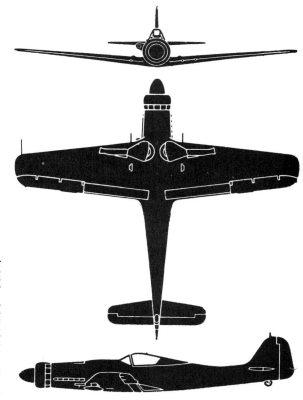

The Focke-Wulf Fw 190D Single-seat Fighter.

(2,440 m.), Maximum cruising speed 198 m.p.h. (317 km.h.) at 8,000 ft. (2,440 m.), Climb to 13,120 ft. (4,000 m.) 8.3 mins., Service ceiling 27,550 ft. (8,400 m.), Range 430 miles (690 km.).

THE FOCKE-WULF Fw 190A.

The first version of the Fw 190 was fitted with a BMW 139 fourteen-cylinder radial air-cooled engine and flew in 1938. The original engine was then replaced by the BMW 801, which was some 200 lbs. (91 kg.) heavier, and several modifications were incorporated in the airframe. At that time the Reichsluftministerium could not be convinced that a successful single-seat fighter could have an air-cooled radial engine and it was intended ultimately to fit a liquid-cooled in-line power-unit. An Fw 190 with a DB 603 engine flew in 1941 and eventually the "long-nosed" 190 with a Jumo 213 engine went into service as the Fw 190D in 1943.

In the meantime, the Fw 190 with the BMW 801 engine became operational in 1941. The first intact specimen was landed in Southern England by a German pilot in June, 1942.

The radial-engined Fw 190 was used extensively until the capitulation and was the subject of continuous development to meet new operational requirements. The performance was increased substantially by the fitting of power-boosting systems and a heavier armament was mounted as new and improved guns became available.

The following are the principal Fw 190A sub-types :—

Fw 190A-1. BMW 801 C engine. Span 34 ft. (10.37 m.). Armament : four 7.9 m/m. MG 17 machine-guns, two in the fuselage top cowling and two in the wing roots, and, optionally, two 20 m/m. MG FF/M cannon in the wings outboard of the main oleo leg attachment. One 550 lb. (250 kg.) or 1,100 lb. (500 kg.) bomb could be carried under the fuselage as an alternative to a jettisonable tank.

Fw 190A-2. Wing span increased to 34 ft. 6 in. (10.5 m.) and new landing-gear linkage. Two 20 m/m. MG 151/20 cannon installed in wing roots in place of the rifle-calibre MG 17 guns. Otherwise as for A-1.

Fw 190A-3. BMW 801 D engine. Otherwise same as for A-2.

Fw 190A-4. As A-3 but with supplementary fuel-injection system, slightly modified fin and revised radio equipment.

Fw 190A-4/U8. Fighter-bomber with racks for jettisonable tanks or bombs under wings as well as provision for bomb load under fuselage.

Fw 190A-5. As A-4 but with redesigned engine mounting resulting in the engine being moved forward 5.9 in. (152.5 m/m.).

Fw 190A-5/U3. Fighter-bomber with wing and fuselage bomb-racks.

Fw 190A-6. Optional outer wing guns changed to MG 151/20. Otherwise as A-5.

Fw 190A-7. Further armament change in that the cowling guns changed to 13 m/m. MG 131. Remaining wing guns as for A-6.

Fw 190A-7/R2. Fitted with two 30 m/m. MG 108, one in each outer wing position instead of MG 151/20.

Fw 190A-8. BMW 801 D engine. Extra 25 gallon fuselage tank. Armament : two 13 m/m. MG 131 in top cowling, two 20 m/m. MG 151/20 in wing roots, and, optionally, two 20 m/m. MG 151/20 or 30 m/m. MK 108 in wings outboard of landing-gear.

Fw 190A-8 D/NL. As A-8 but with BMW 801-2 with higher emergency power rating.

Fw 190A-8/R1. Has four MG 151/20 cannon mounted in pairs, one pair under each wing in a blister, in place of the single outer wing cannon.

Fw 190A-8/R3. Has two MK 103 cannon one under each wing, in place of the outer MK 151/20 wing cannon.

Fw 190A-8 U1. Two-seat trainer.

Fw 190A-8 R11. "Dirty weather" fighter with special radio and automatic pilot.

Fw 190A-9. BMW 801 F engine. Armament as for A-7.

Fw 190A-9 R11. BMW 801 TS engine. "Dirty weather" fighter with special radio and automatic pilot.

TYPE.—Single-seat Fighter or Fighter-Bomber.

WINGS.—Low-wing cantilever monoplane. Wing in one piece, the front spar being continuous and passing through the fuselage, to which it is attached at three points, two on the upper flange and one on the lower. The rear spar is in two sections, the roots being attached to the sides of the fuselage by normal pin-joints. Two-spar wing structure with widely-spaced flanged plate former ribs, spanwise "Z"-section stringers and a stressed-metal skin. The spars are built up of flanged plate which, inboard from the ailerons are reinforced by "L"-section extrusions and progressively thickened cap-strips to form "I"-section members. Outboard of the ailerons the spars have single integral flanges. The front spar from the points of attachment of the landing gear to the upper

attachments to the fuselage is cranked inwards, the landing gear when retracted lying ahead of the front spar. The gun and landing gear bays have specially strengthened ribs. Metal-framed fabric-covered ailerons. Electrically-operated all-metal split trailing-edge flaps between ailerons and fuselage.

FUSELAGE.—All-metal monocoque structure built up of bulkheads, flanged formers, "Z"-section stringers and a smooth stressed-skin covering. The front inverted "U"-shaped bulkhead attaches to the upper flange of the front spar, and on the front face of bulkhead and spar are the five attachments for the engine-mounting, three on the spar and two on the bulkhead. All other bulkheads and frames conform to the full cross-section of the fuselage. Extreme rear section is integral with the fin and is detachable from main structure. Large detachable panel in underside of fuselage extending from engine bay to rear of cockpit, for installation and removal of fuel tanks.

TAIL UNIT.—Cantilever monoplane type. Fin integral with the rear fuselage. Electrically-operated adjustable single-spar tailplane. All-metal framework with metal-covered tail-plane and fin and fabric-covered control surfaces. Fixed perforated trim-tabs in rudder and elevators. Fin-rear fuselage assembly houses the electric tailplane incidence gear and spring for lowering tail-wheel.

LANDING GEAR.—Retractable type. Main cantilever oleo-legs are hinged ahead of the front wing spar and retract inwardly, fairing-plates on legs and wheels and on undersurface of the wings closing the apertures when the wheels are raised. Electrical retraction. The tail-wheel is also partly retractable by cable connected to starboard oleo leg. Tail-wheel has spring-centering and centre-lock, the latter operating when the control-column is pulled hard back.

POWER PLANT.—One BMW 801 fourteen-cylinder two-row radial air-cooled geared and supercharged engine in low-drag cowling with induced fan cooling. The whole engine unit, complete with oil-coolers, is attached to the front bulkhead and spar face by five bolts. Protected fuel tanks beneath the cockpit floor. Oil tank (10 Imp. gallons) in fuselage. Reverse-flow oil-coolers in armoured annular ring which forms the cowl leading-edge. VDM airscrew with electric pitch change and metal blades.

ACCOMMODATION.—Pilot's cockpit over trailing-edge of wing with clear-view canopy and tail fairing, the whole of which slides aft to give access to cockpit and may be jettisoned complete in an emergency. Pilot's seat is armoured and is further backed by an armoured bulkhead and headrest, the latter forming part of the jettisonable cockpit canopy. Bullet-proof windscreen. The radio aerial lead-in is in the roof of the canopy and to keep it taut throughout movement of canopy the aerial is led aft and over a fixed jockey pulley inside the canopy before its final attachment to the fuselage beneath the lead-in. The aerial is ruptured by the explosive charge which jettisons the canopy. The canopy cannot be opened in the air except to be jettisoned.

ARMAMENT.—For details of armament see descriptions of Fw 190A sub-types in introduction.

DIMENSIONS.—Span 34 ft. 6 in. (10.5 m.), Length 29 ft. (8.84 m.), Height 13 ft. (3.96 m.), Wing area 197 sq. ft. (18.3 sq. m.).

WEIGHTS (Fw 190A-8).—Take-off weight with two MG 131, two MG 151/20, ammunition and 141 Imp. gallons of fuel 9,100 lbs. (4,130 kg.), Take-off weight with same armament as above but 272 Imp. gallons of fuel 9,750 lbs. (4,430 kg.), Maximum permissible take-off weight with R.P. equipment, drop tanks and GM 1 10,800 lbs. (4,900 kg.).

PERFORMANCE (Fw 190A-8).—Maximum speed without MW 50 402 m.p.h. (643 km.h.) at 18,000 ft. (5,490 m.), Maximum speed with MW 50 408 m.p.h. (653 km.h.) at 20,600 ft. (6,285 m.), Climb to 32,800 ft. (10,000 m.) without MW 50 26.5 mins., Climb to 32,800 ft. (10,000 m.) with MW 50 16.5 mins., Service ceiling without MW 50 33,800 ft. (10,310 m.), Service ceiling with MW 50 37,400 ft. (11,410 m.), Cruising range with 272 Imp. gallons (including fuel for warm-up, take-off and climb at altitude) 950 miles (5,120 km.) at 298 m.p.h. (477 km.h.) at 23,000 ft. (7,020 m.), Endurance under

above conditions (including time to climb to altitude and time to return to sea level) 3 hours 17 mins.

THE FOCKE-WULF Fw 190D.

The first version of the Fw 190D with a liquid-cooled engine flew in 1941 and towards the end of 1943 Allied pilots reported combats with "long-nosed" Fw 190s. Originally a Daimler-Benz DB 603 was fitted, but the D sub-types all had a Jumo 213. The first operational version was the Fw 190D-9.

Standard Fw 190A, F and G wings and tailplane were fitted but the fuselage was increased in length to 33 ft 11 in. (10.36 m.). The fin was increased in width by $5\frac{1}{4}$ in. (140.3 m/m.), resulting in a $2\frac{1}{2}$ sq. ft. (.23 sq. m.) increase in area over the "short-nosed" version.

The Fw 190D-9 was fitted with the Jumo 213 A-1 liquid-cooled inverted Vee engine and with MW 50 power-boost this version had a maximum speed of 440 m.p.h. (704 km.h.) at 37,000 ft. (11,290 m.).

A later version, the Fw 190D-12, with the Jumo 213 E engine, had a maximum speed with MW 50 of 453 m.p.h. (725 km.h.) at 37,000 ft. (11,290 m.).

In all D sub-types provision was made for the fitting of a 30 m/m. MK 108 cannon in the engine Vee and firing through the airscrew boss.

Ultimately, the Fw 190D was redesignated the Ta 152A (which see).

THE FOCKE-WULF Fw 190F.

Basically identical to the Fw 190A, the F sub-types were developed mainly for ground attack and were provided with additional armour to protect the pilot. The outer wing guns were not fitted.

THE FOCKE-WULF Fw 190G.

A further off-shoot of the Fw 190A, the G was used mainly as a fighter-bomber. It could carry a 3,960 lb. (1,800 kg.) bomb, although the 1,100 lb. (500 kg.) or 2,200 lb. (1,000 kg.) was the more normal load. One sub-type of the Fw 190G had a lengthened tail-wheel strut to give ground clearance for carrying a torpedo.

THE FOCKE-WULF Fw 191.

The Fw 191 was a multi-engined bomber which was under development in 1942. Two versions were projected, one a twin-engined model with Junkers Jumo 222 engines, the other a four-

In this view of the Focke-Wulf Fw 191 Experimental Bomber the rear-firing armament is shown clearly.

engined aircraft with either Jumo 211 or DB 605 engines. Only three or four of the twin-engined version were built and flown.

The Fw 191 followed German practice in concentrating the crew in the nose compartment which, in the case of this aircraft, was pressurised. Aft of the crew compartment was the bomb-bay, above which were the fuselage fuel tanks. Two additional tanks were located in wings, one on each side of the fuselage.

Armament could consist of one MG 151 in a chin turret, twin MG 151 cannon in a remotely-controlled dorsal turret aft of the wings, twin MG 151 cannon in a remotely-controlled ventral turret, and twin MG 131 or one MG 151 in a remotely-controlled tail turret. Sighting stations were provided above and below the nose compartment. Internal stowage was provided for 4,400 lbs. (2,000 kg.) of bombs or two torpedoes could be carried under the wings between the fuselage and engine nacelles.

DIMENSIONS.—Span 85 ft. 3 in. (26 m.), Length 64 ft. 3 in. (19.6 m.), Height 18 ft. 5 in. (5.6 m.).

WEIGHT LOADED.—48,700 lbs. (22,120 kg.).

PERFORMANCE.—Estimated range (with 4,400 lbs.=2,000 kg. bombs) 2,200 miles (3,520 km.) at 270 m.p.h. (432 km.h.) at 19,680 ft. (6,000 m.).

THE FOCKE-WULF Fw 200C.

The original Fw 200 Condor four-engined long-range commercial monoplane was converted for military use in 1940 and the Fw 200C became a standard long-range oversea reconnaissance bomber. It was used extensively against convoys and for U-boat co-operation from 1941 until the Summer of 1944.

In the early stages of the war experiments were made to convert the civil version into a troop transport, a balloon-barrage destroyer, a seaplane and a bomber for the Japanese Army Air Force. Special models were also made and delivered at the outbreak of hostilities for the use of Hitler and his staff.

The early C-1 and C-2 sub-types were fitted with four BMW 132 H-1 engines but subsequent versions had BMW 323 R-2 power-units.

TYPE.—Four-engined long-range Reconnaissance Bomber. Also used for U-boat co-operation.

WINGS.—Low-wing cantilever monoplane. Wing in three portions comprising a centre-section supporting the four engines and two outer sections. All-metal two-spar structure metal covered to rear spar, with fabric covering aft. Two-piece ailerons extend along two-thirds of the outer wing trailing-edges and are mass-balanced. Geared tabs on each aileron. Trim-tab in port aileron is operated by electric motor. Split trailing-edge flaps inboard of ailerons are of two-spar construction and covered with magnesium alloy sheet.

FUSELAGE.—Semi-monocoque structure with flush-riveted smooth metal skin. Bomb-bay beneath main structure and offset slightly to starboard.

TAIL UNIT.—Cantilever monoplane type. Two-spar all-metal tail-plane. Incidence adjustable on the ground. Single-part elevators with forward portion back to spar metal-covered, the remainder covered with fabric. Geared and trim tabs on both elevators. Two-spar fin metal-covered forward of main spar, remainder covered with fabric. All-metal rudder of single-spar design with both geared and trim-tabs.

LANDING GEAR.—Retractable type. Main units have twin wheels and retract forward into inner engine nacelles. Hydraulic retraction with emergency lowering by electric motor. Retractable tail-wheel with shimmy-damping device.

POWER PLANT.—Four BMW 323 R-2 nine-cylinder radial air-cooled engines, each rated at 940 h.p. at 12,000 ft. (3,660 m.). Three-blade VDM metal-blade airscrews.

ACCOMMODATION.—Normal crew of eight, comprising two pilots, radio operator, flight engineer, observer/forward dorsal gunner, rear dorsal gunner, two ventral gunners. The pilot and the rear dorsal gunner are protected by armour plate.

ARMAMENT.—One 20 m/m. MG 151/20 cannon in an electrically-operated turret above the pilot's cabin, one MG 131 in the after dorsal position, two or four MG 81 or 131 guns for lateral fire, one MG 151/20 in the nose of the bomb-bay, and one MG 81, MG 131 or MG 151/20 in the tail of the bomb-bay. Normal bomb-load 3,300 lbs. (1,500 kg.). Maximum bomb-load 11,800 lbs. (5,360 kg.).

The Focke-Wulf Fw 200C Long-range Bomber-Reconnaissance Monoplane (four 940 h.p. Bramo 323 engines).

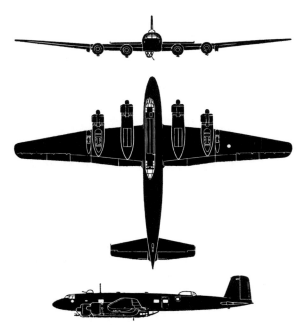

The Focke-Wulf Fw 200C Monoplane.

DIMENSIONS.—Span 108 ft. 3 in. (33 m.), Length 78 ft. 3 in. (23.8 m.), Height 23 ft. 4 in. (7.1 m.), Wing area 1,290 sq. ft. (120 sq. m.).

WEIGHTS (Fw 200C 3).—Maximum take-off weight 50,000 lbs. (22,700 kg.), Landing weight 38,800 lbs. (17,620 kg.).

PERFORMANCE (Fw 200 C-3).—Maximum speed at 13,120 ft. (4,000 m.) 240 m.p.h. (384 km.h.), Maximum cruising speed at 13,120 ft. (4,000 m.) 220 m.p.h. (352 km.h.), Range with 1,770 Imp. gallons of fuel 2,200 miles (3,520 km.), Endurance 9¾ hours.

THE FOCKE-WULF Ta 254.

The Ta 254 was a projected long-span development of the Ta 154C and had a wing area of 453 sq. ft. (42 sq. m.) and an all-up weight of 25,300 lbs. (11,490 kg.). Both day and night fighter versions were planned.

The armament for the night fighter was to be two 20 m/m. MG 151/20 and two 30 m/m. MK 108 cannon, or six MK 108, all firing forward, and two MK 108 cannon in the rear of the fuselage and firing obliquely upwards. The day fighter was to have a fixed forward-firing armament of two MG 151 (200 rounds per gun) and two MK 103 (100 rounds per gun), with the possible alternative of six MK 108 cannon.

The power-plant was to consist of two Jumo 213 E, DB 603 E or DB 603 L engines. The maximum speed of the Ta 254 with two Jumo 213 E engines, using MW 50 boost, was estimated to be 460 m.p.h. (736 km.h.) at 34,500 ft. (10,520 m.).

THE FOCKE-WULF Fw 300.

An improvement of the Fw 200, the Fw 300 did not progress beyond the design stage. The first prototype was projected in 1940. It had a span of 152 ft. (46.4 m.) and a length of 102 ft. (31 m.). It was ultimately to be fitted with four Jumo 222 or four DB 603 engines, both types having turbo-superchargers.

THE FOCKE-WULF Ta 400.

The development of this six-engined project, an alternative designation for which was Fw 300A, was entrusted to the Groupe Téchnique de Châtillon, a group which comprised some 300 French engineers and designers who were under the strict tutelage of technicians of the Focke-Wulf company. This group was located at Châtillon-sur-Bagneux, in the south-eastern suburbs of Paris.

Intended for use as a long-range reconnaissance bomber, it never saw the light of day.

It was to have been a high-wing monoplane with a twin-ruddered tail-unit and four under-carriage landing-gear units, one each under the inner and central engine nacelles. A maximum bomb-load of 22,000 lbs. (10,000 kg.) was provided for, together with a maximum tankage of 5,940 Imp. gallons to give a range of over 3,000 miles (4,800 km.). Sixteen guns were to be provided, of which four were for the tail turret.

One version was to have had two Jumo 004 turbo-jet units, one in each of two engine nacelles behind the engines. This jet-assisted aircraft was expected to have a maximum speed of about 450 m.p.h. (720 km.h.).

GOTHA.

GOTHAER WAGGONFABRIK A.G.

HEAD OFFICE AND WORKS : GOTHA.

This well-known firm inaugurated an aircraft department before the War 1914-18 and then became famous as a producer of multi-engined bombers. It re-entered the German aircraft industry a few years before the present War broke out and at the outset devoted its attention to the design and manufacture of training and light commercial aircraft.

Throughout the war the entire resources of the Company were concentrated on the mass production of military aircraft. It also undertook the development of troop and freight-carrying gliders.

THE GOTHA Go 242.

The Go 242 glider was a high-wing twin-boom monoplane glider with central nacelle accommodating twenty-three fully equipped troops, including two pilots. It was designed with a view to the ultimate installation of engines, the powered version being the Go 244. (See below).

The Go 242 was extensively used from 1942, a typical tug being the Ju 52 or He 111.

The wing was of wooden construction, was strut-braced and was tapered in chord and thickness. Covering was part plywood and part fabric. Flaps and lift-spoilers were fitted.

The nacelle, which was 11.3 m. (37 ft.) long was a tubular metal structure and was hinged at the rear to facilitate loading.

A wheeled landing gear was fitted but was dropped after take-off. Landing was made on three skids, the forward one of which was retractable.

DIMENSIONS.—Span 24 m. (79 ft.), Length 16m. (52 ft. 6 in.).

THE GOTHA Go 244.

The Go 244 was a powered version of the previously described glider. Two French-built Gnôme-Rhône 14M fourteen-cylinder radial air-cooled engines were installed in nacelles which were virtually forward continuations of the tail booms. A and B sub-types, which differed only in detail, were used.

TYPE.—Twin-engined Troop and Freight Transport.

WINGS.—Rigidly-braced high-wing monoplane. Two-spar wooden

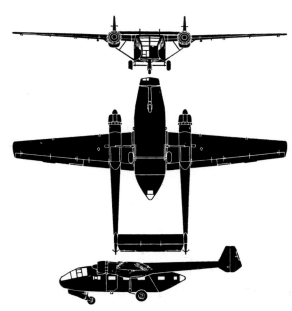

The Gotha Go 244 Transport.

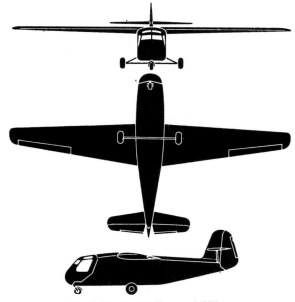

The Gotha Go 345 Transport Glider.

construction with plywood covering from leading-edge to main spar, the remainder, including the control surfaces, being covered with fabric. Ailerons fitted with trimming and geared tabs.

Flaps inboard from ailerons. Lift spoilers on upper surface of wings forward of outer portions of flaps.

FUSELAGE.—Rectangular section structure of welded steel tube covered with fabric. Rear section of fuselage hinged at the top just aft of the trailing-edge of the wings for loading and unloading freight.

Tail Unit.—Monoplane type with twin fins and rudders. One-piece rectangular tailplane is carried between the extremities of the two all-wood booms which extend aft from the engine nacelles. The fins are integral with the boom. Elevator and rudders have geared and trimming tabs.

Landing Gear.—Fixed tricycle type.

Power Plant.—Two Gnôme-Rhône 14M fourteen-cylinder two-row radial air-cooled engines in nacelles forming forward extensions of the tail booms.

Accommodation.—Crew of two in the forward section of the central nacelle or fuselage. The rear section of the fuselage from the bulkhead aft of the crew compartment is available for troops or freight. Entrance doors for troops in sides of fuselage forward of the main landing wheels. For freight loading the rear portion of the fuselage hinges upward to provide an opening the full cross-section of the body.

Dimensions.—Span 79 ft. (24 m.), Length 52 ft. 6 in. (16 m.), Wing area 700 sq. ft. (65 sq. m.).

Weights.—Freight load 4,400 lbs. (2,000 kg.), Take-off weight 17,500 lbs. (7,945 kg.), Landing weight 15,900 lbs. (7,220 kg.).

Performance.—Maximum speed 169 m.p.h. (270 km.h.) at 10,000 ft. (3,050 m.), Cruising speed 100 m.p.h. (160 km.h.) at sea level, Climb to 10,000 ft. (3,050 m.) 21 mins., Maximum range 375 miles (600 km.) at sea level.

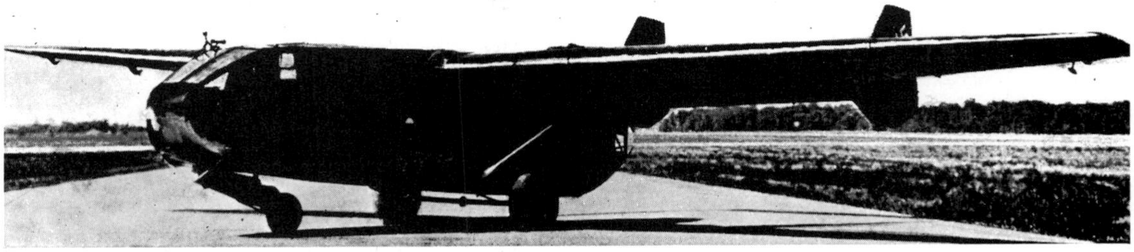

The Gotha Go 242 Transport Glider.

THE GOTHA Go 345.

The Go 345 was designed in 1944 as a transport glider. It was a conventional high-wing cantilever monoplane with single fin and rudder, high-set braced tailplane and a simple fixed tricycle landing-gear. For freight loading the nose and cockpit assembly hinged upward.

Dimensions.—Span 67 ft. (20.4 m.), Length 41 ft. 4 in. (12.6 m.).

HEINKEL.

ERNST HEINKEL A.G.

Head Office and Works: Marienehe, near Rostock.

Associated Establishment: Heinkel-Werke G.m.b.H., Oranienburg, Berlin, and Bärenklau.

Berlin Office: Tirpitzüfer 90, Berlin, W35.

Established: 1922.

President: Prof. Dr. Ing. e. h., Dr. Phil. h. c. Ernst Heinkel.

This Company was formed in 1922 by Dr. Ernst Heinkel, who, as chief designer to the Hansa-Brandenburgische Flugzeugwerke, produced a number of very notable seaplanes during the latter half of the War 1914-18.

The principal types in production in 1944 and 1945 were the He 111, He 219, He 177 and He 162. These aircraft were in production at the following plants:—

He 111.

Assembly plant:—Rostock-Marienehe.

Component plants:—Rostock-Marienehe and Rostock Works I and II.

He 219.

Assembly plants:—Wien-Schwechat and Rostock-Marienehe.

He 177.

Assembly plants:—Oranienberg-Annahof.

Component plants:—Oranienberg-Hermanndorf, Rathenow (Arado) and Wittenberge (Arado).

When the He 177 was withdrawn from production the above plants were turned over to the manufacture of components for the Focke-Wulf Fw 190.

THE HEINKEL He 111H.

The He 111, originally evolved as a camouflaged civil transport in 1935, was in continuous service throughout the war, and was used extensively as a bomber, torpedo-carrier, transport and Glider-tug. The most widely-used production series was the 111H and the best known sub-type was the H-6. This differed little, except in armament and other minor details, from later variants, *e.g.* H-10, 14, 16, 10, 20, and 21.

Type.—Twin-engined Bomber and Torpedo-carrier. Also used as a Transport, Glider-Tug or as a Flying-bomb Carrier.

Wings.—Low-wing cantilever monoplane in three portions comprising a rectangular centre-section built integral with the fuselage and two tapering outer sections. Structure of light metal consisting of two spars and the usual number of ribs, the whole covered with a stressed skin of smooth duralumin sheet. Ailerons on outer sections. Hydraulically-operated slotted flaps in inner sections. Ailerons droop when flaps are lowered.

Fuselage.—Oval section metal structure tapering to a point aft. Structure consists of three main bulkheads, a number of secondary frames, interconnected by longerons and "U" section stringers, the whole covered with smooth metal sheet.

Tail Unit.—Monoplane type. All surfaces elliptical. Cantilever tail-plane and fin. Trimming-tabs in movable surfaces. Metal structure with smooth sheet covering.

Dimensions.—Span 74 ft. 3 in. (22.6 m.), Length 54 ft. 6 in. (16.6 m.), Height 13 ft. 9 in. (4.2 m.), Wing area 942 sq. ft. (87.6 sq. m.).

Weights.—Weight empty 17,000 lbs. (7,720 kg.), Normal loaded weight 26,500 lbs. (12,030 kg.), Maximum permissible overloaded weight 31,000 lbs. (14,075 kg.).

Performance.—Maximum speed 250 m.p.h. (400 km.h.) at 17,000 ft. (5,185 m.), Climb to 17,000 ft. (5,185 m.) 20 mins., Service ceiling 27,500 ft. (8,390 m.), Range with maximum fuel 1,750 miles (2,800 km.).

THE HEINKEL He 111P.

The He 111P was generally similar to the 111H, the main difference being that it was fitted with two Daimler-Benz DB 601 engines in place of the Jumo 211 units. Production was discontinued in favour of the H Series.

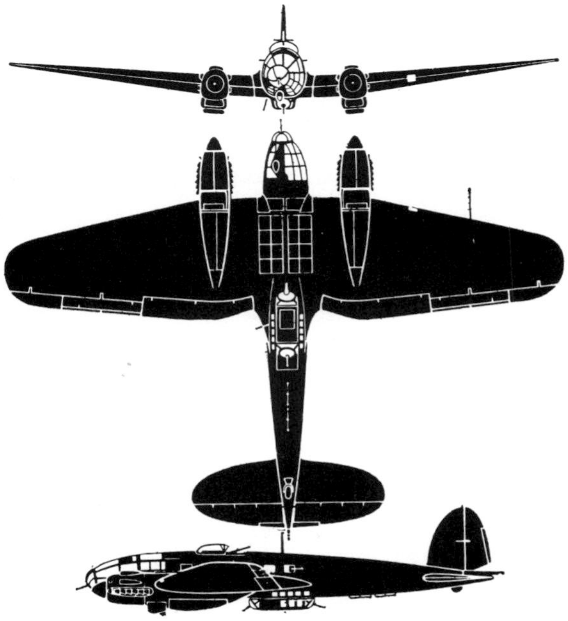

The Heinkel He 111H Heavy Bomber.

THE HEINKEL He 111Z "ZWILLING".

The He 111Z was basically two He 111H airframes, each less one outer wing, joined together outboard of a left and right engine by a length of wing which carried a fifth Jumo 211 engine. The result was a five-engined aircraft with two-separate fuselages and tail-units. The pilot sat in the port fuselage.

The intended function of the He 111Z was that of a glider-tug, although consideration was given to using it as a bomber, to carry four 1,800 kg. bombs; as a reconnaissance aircraft with two 264-gallon jettisonable fuel tanks; or as an anti-shipping aircraft to carry four Hs 293 radio-controlled glider bombs.

Dimensions.—Span 115 ft. 6 in. (35.2 m.), Length 54 ft. 8 in. (16.7 m.), Landing-gear track 32 ft. 10 in. (10 m.).

Take-off Weight.—62,500 lbs. (28,375 kg.).

Performance.—Maximum speed 298 m.p.h. (477 km.h.) at 16,000 ft. (4,880 m.), Range 1,180 miles (1,890 km.).

Landing Gear.—Retractable type. Each unit consists of two oleo legs and two backwardly sloping hinged members which, when broken inwardly, raise the wheels aft into the tails of the engine nacelles. Low-pressure wheels and Cannstadt brakes.

Power Plant.—Two Junkers Jumo 211F twelve-cylinder inverted Vee liquid-cooled engines, each rated at 1,300 h.p. at 3,810 m. (12,500 ft.), in nacelles at extremities of centre-section. Three-bladed VDM controllable-pitch full-feathering airscrews. Four self-sealing fuel tanks, two inboard and two outboard of nacelles. Total fuel capacity 940 Imp. gallons.

Accommodation.—Normal crew of five, three in nose compartment and two aft of wings. Pilot on port side of unsymmetrical nose, which is entirely glazed with transparent panels. Alongside pilot is a tip-up seat for the navigator/bomb-aimer, who also operated the hand-operated machine-gun in a spherical nose mounting offset to starboard. Behind pilot is the bomb compartment located between the wing-spars. Passage between bomb cells leads to after cabin accommodating the radio-operator/gunner operating the upper gun and the gunner operating the lower gun. Pilot's seat and rear upper and lower gun positions are armoured.

Armament.—Differed greatly according to sub-type. The later He 111s were armed with one 13 m/m. MG 131 in the nose, two 7.9 m/m. MG 81 in the lower ventral position firing forward; one 31 m/m. MG 131 in the upper rear-firing position and two 7.9 m/m. MG 81 firing laterally, one on each side of the fuselage.

Bomb Load.—Originally the He 111 had only internal stowage within fuselage for a maximum of eight 250 kg. (550 lb.) bombs suspended vertically. Later, external stowage was provided for bombs of heavier calibre than 250 kg. or for mines, two torpedoes or one FZG 76 flying-bomb. The flying-bomb was carried offset to starboard. Typical alternative bomb loads were:—One 1,000 kg. and one 500 kg.; one 1,400 kg. and one 1,000 kg.; one 1,800 kg. or one 2,500 kg. Two torpedoes carried on crutches under short centre-section roots, one on each side of centre-line

Equipment.—Standard bomber radio equipment comprising long and short wave transmitting and receiving sets, D/F. loop receiver and blind-approach equipment. D/F. loop aerial is housed beneath transparent cover over upper rear gunner. Fixed aerial for Lorenz blind-approach system mounted beneath rear fuselage. Equipment also generally includes an inflatable dinghy.

THE HEINKEL He 119.

The He 119 was a experimental high-performance two-seat bomber-reconnaissance monoplane which was designed around a Daimler-Benz DB 606 or DB 610 double engine. This power-unit was located in the fuselage and drove a single tractor airscrew through shaft-drive. Development was abandoned early in the war.

THE HEINKEL He 162A "SALAMANDER".

Popularly known as the "Volksjäger" (People's Fighter) and code-named "Salamander," the He 162 was designed to employ as little as possible of material which was in short supply.

Design work on the He 162 was started on September 23, 1944, and the first flight took place on December 6, 1944. On the second flight the leading-edge of the wing collapsed and the prototype broke up in the air. This did not seriously hinder the development programme and after modifications were made to the wings the He 162 went into large-scale production in widely-dispersed assembly plants, many of them underground.

The He 162A-1 was the standard service version at the time of Germany's capitulation.

Type.—Single-seat jet-propelled fighter.

Wings.—Shoulder-wing cantilever monoplane. Dihedral 3°. Aspect ratio 4.65. All-wood structure in one piece and attached to the fuselage by four bolts. Straight leading-edge, blunt detachable metal tips and a pronounced sweep forward on trailing-edge. Main and auxiliary T-section spars and plywood covering 5 m/m. thick between spars on upper surface and 4 m/m. elsewhere. Space between spars used as fuel tank. Hydraulically-controlled metal flaps between fuselage and ailerons with maximum depression of 45°. Range of aileron movement 18° either way.

Fuselage.—Semi-monocoque structure of flush-riveted duralumin, except for nose which is of plywood construction. Fittings partly of steel, inspection covers of duralumin or wood. Very clean aerodynamically. Nose of oval section, centre portion pear-shaped with flattened underside, rear portion of circular cross section. Tail cone which carries the empennage may be moved in flight to adjust tailplane incidence, giving a range of movement from + 3° to — 2°.

Tail Unit.—Cantilever monoplane type of mixed construction. Tailplane, elevators and rudders of duralumin construction with steel fittings. Wooden fins bolted to the extremities of the tailplane. Tailplane of constant chord and set at moderate dihedral. Elevators have fixed tabs at their inner ends. Rudders, with three bearings and a 25° range of movement either way, are fully mass-balanced and have fixed tabs above tailplane.

Landing Gear.—Retractable tricycle type. Main wheels of Me 109 type, retract into fuselage. Hydraulic retraction and spring lowering. Fuselage openings covered by mechanically-operated plywood doors. Nose wheel raised backwards into fuselage nose, and has slight castor action and anti-shimmy device.

Power Plant.—One BMW 003 E-1 turbo-jet unit mounted centrally on top of fuselage. With three attachment fittings, the jet being directed above the tailplane and between the rudders. Alternative power-units which could be installed included the BMW 003 E-2, Junkers Jumo 004, or Heinkel-Hirth 011. A quick power-plant change is possible. All joints in pipe lines and leads grouped together. J-2 diesel fuel used. Fuel carried in fuselage and wings. Maximum capacity 168 Imp. gallons in fuselage and 40 gallons in wings.

Accommodation.—Pilot's cockpit in nose forward of wings. Entry and exit through canopy which opens rearwards and can be jettisoned. Pilot-ejecting seat actuated by an explosive cartridge. Plywood instrument panel.

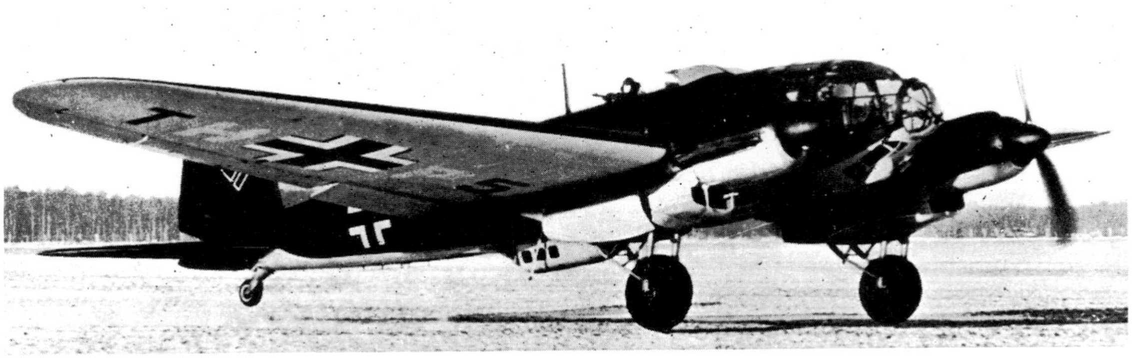

The Heinkel He 111H Heavy Bomber Monoplane (two 1,075 Junkers Jumo 211 F engines).

ARMAMENT.—Either two 30 m/m. MK 108 with 50 rounds per gun, or two 20 m/m. MG 151/20 cannon with 120 rounds per gun, mounted low in the fuselage sides.

DIMENSIONS.—Span 23 ft. 7¾ in. (7.2 m.), Length 29 8½ in. (9 m.), Wing chord (root) 6 ft. 8½ in. (2.06 m.), Span of tailplane 7 ft. 5½ in. (2.3 m.), Tailplane chord 2 ft. 8½ in. (0.84 m.).

WEIGHTS.—Normal loaded weight 5,480 lbs. (2,490 kg.), Weight loaded with maximum fuel 5,940 lbs. (2,700 kg.), Landing weight (with 20% fuel) 4,820 lbs. (2,190 kg.), Wing loading at landing 40 lbs./sq. ft. (18.2 kg./sq. m.).

PERFORMANCE.—Maximum speeds 490 m.p.h. (784 km.h.) at sea level, 522 m.p.h. (835 km.h.) at 19,680 ft. (6,000 m.), and 485 m.p.h. (776 km.h.) at 36,000 ft. (10,980 m.), Rates of climb at mean weight 4,200 ft./min. (1,280 m./min.) at sea level, 2,460 ft./min. (750 m./min.) at 19,680 ft. (6,000 m.), and 690 ft./min. (210 m./min.) at 36,000 ft. (10,980 m.), Climb to 19,680 ft. (6,000 m.) 6.6 min., Climb to 36,000 ft. (10,980 m.) 20 min., Full-throttle ranges (normal fuel) 136 miles (220 km.) at sea level, 267 miles (430 km.) at 19,680 ft. (6,000 m.), 410 miles (656 km.) at 36,000 ft. (10,980 m.) and 434 miles (695 km.) at 38,400 ft. (11,720 m.), Full-throttle ranges (maximum fuel) 242 miles (390 km.) at sea level and 620 miles (1,000 km.) at 36,000 ft. (10,980 m.), Full-throttle endurances (normal fuel) 20 min. at sea level, 33 min. at 19,680 ft. (6,000 m.), and 67 min. at 36,000 ft. (10,980 m.), Full-throttle endurances (maximum fuel) 30 min. at sea level and 85 min. at 36,000 ft. (10,980 m.), Ceiling at mean weight 39,400 ft. (12,020 m.), Take-off run (normal fuel) 710 yards (650 m.) or 350 yards (320 m.) with auxiliary take-off units, Take-off run (maximum fuel) 875 yards (800 m.) or 415 yards (380 m.) with auxiliary take-off units, Landing speed 102 m.p.h. (163 km.h.).

NOTE :—*The above figures are official but were not attained with the early production aircraft.*

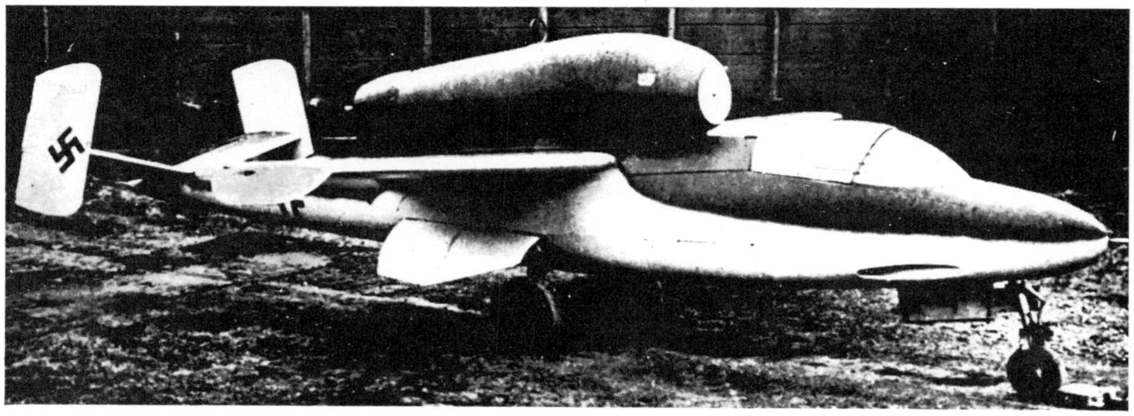

The operational version of the Heinkel He 162A Jet-propelled Fighter

THE HEINKEL He 177A.

Four years of development preceded the placing in production of the He 177 in 1942. The introduction of an entirely new type of power-plant, in which four Daimler-Benz twelve-cylinder inverted Vee liquid-cooled engines were grouped together in pairs, each pair driving a single airscrew, was one of the principal causes of the delays in development. Many prototypes were built, most of which appeared to display some vice or short-coming. There were cases of dangerous diving characteristics, landing-gear and structural weaknesses, as well as troubles associated with the power units, such as persistent crankshaft torsional vibration, lubrication difficulties and airscrew trouble.

In 1943 the He 177 was used for anti-convoy and U-boat co-operation duties. It was used (sub-types A-3 and A-5) in attacks against England in January, 1944. Production was abandoned in October, 1944, after some 200 had gone into service.

The following are the principal A Series sub-types :—

He 177A-0. Pilot production model. Two DB 606 power-units each composed of two DB 601 E engines coupled together and driving a single four-blade airscrew. Armament : two 13 m/m. MG 131, one 20 m/m. MG FF, one 7.9 m/m. MG 81 and twin 7.9 m/m. MG 81.

He 177A-1. Similar to A-O except Armament : three 13 m/m. MG 131, one 7.9 m/m. MG 81, one 20 m/m. MG FF or one 30 m/m. MK 101.

He 177A-3. Two DB 610 power units each, made up of two DB 605 engines. This and previous sub-types fitted with Fowler flaps extending over the entire trailing-edge, including those portions occupied by the ailerons. Each aileron consisted of an upper and lower surface, the lower arranged for relative sliding movement. When the flaps were not extended the two portions were telescoped and locked and the whole hinged to operate in the usual manner. On extension of the flaps the upper portion of each aileron remained as part of the upper surface of the wing, while the lower portion slid aft with the flaps to provide lateral control for take-off and landing. Tail incidence control was coupled with the flap operating-gear. Extension of the flaps increased the lifting surface by 20 per cent. The A-3 could carry two Hs 293 glider bombs. Armament : five MG 131, one MG FF and one MG 81.

He 177A-5. Same power-plant as the A-3 but normal type of ailerons with Fowler flaps between ailerons and fuselage. Could carry three Hs 293, two Hs 294 or two PC 1400 FX (armour-piercing) radio-controlled glider bombs. Armament : four MG 131, one MG 81 and two MG 151/20.

He 177A-7. Similar to A-5 but with wing span increased to 120 ft. (36.6 m.).

Various other sub-types were built, including an experimental heavy fighter.

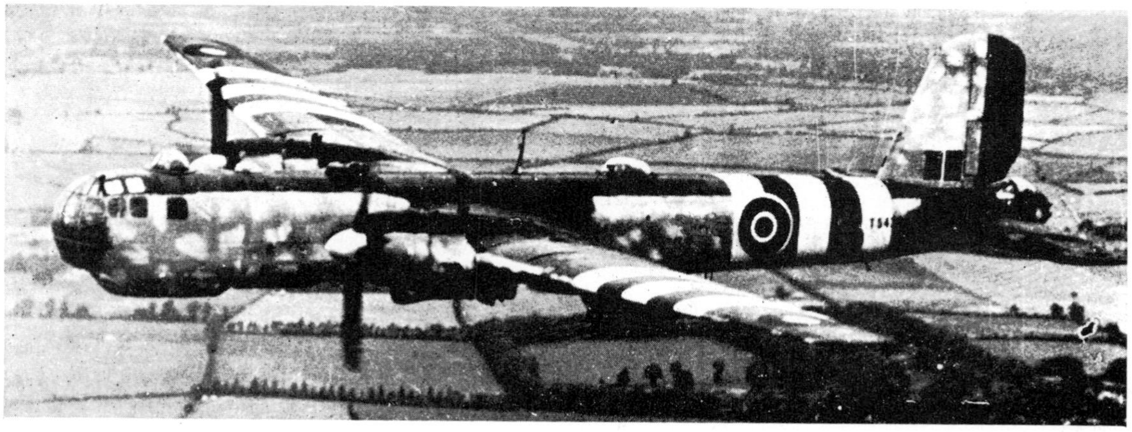

The Heinkel He 177A-5 Bomber or Oversea Reconnaissance Monoplane (two Daimler-Benz DB 610 engines).

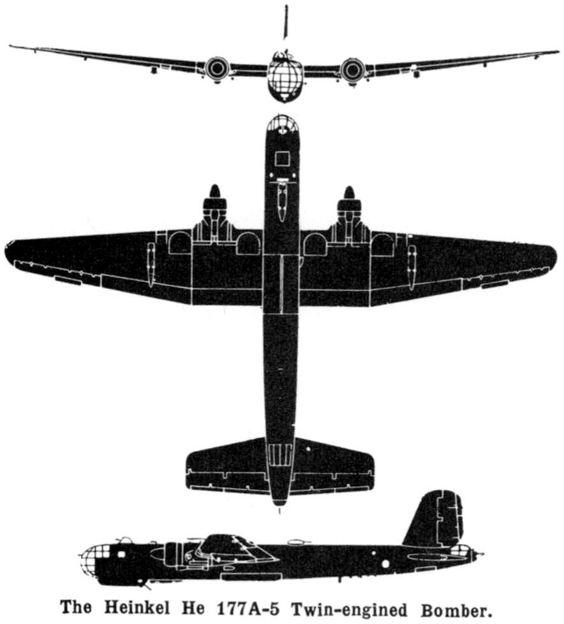

The Heinkel He 177A-5 Twin-engined Bomber.

TYPE.—Twin-engined long, medium or short-range Bomber or Oversea Reconnaissance, Anti-shipping (with glider bombs) or U-boat Co-operation monoplane.

WINGS.—Mid-wing cantilever monoplane. Rectangular centre-section and two tapering outer sections with detachable tips. All-metal single-spar stressed-skin structure. Hydraulically-operated Fowler-type flaps between ailerons and fuselage. (Sub-types up to A-3 had aileron extensions to flaps). Double trim-tabs on ailerons, inner tabs geared and spring-loaded and outer tabs adjustable from cockpit. Cable-cutter housed beneath the leading-edge skin. Heated leading-edge de-icing, hot air being provided by oil-burning heaters.

FUSELAGE.—All-metal stressed-skin structure built in four sections. Framework consists of a series of closely-spaced channel-section formers interconnected by four extruded longerons and a number of Z-section stringers on top and bottom surfaces.

TAIL UNIT.—Cantilever monoplane type. Single-spar tailplane. All surfaces are metal-covered. On sub-types earlier than A-5 the front auxiliary tailplane spar was connected to two screw-jacks which varied the tailplane incidence as the Fowler flaps were operated. All control surfaces have two trim-tabs, one spring-loaded and the other controllable from the cockpit. Hot-air de-icing on tailplane leading-edge.

LANDING GEAR.—Retractable type. Each main unit, located beneath engine nacelle, comprises two independent shock-absorber legs which, when retracted, hinge outwardly, the wheels and struts being accommodated in the wings, one on each side of the engine nacelle and in front of the wing spar. The shock-absorber legs are of the levered type in which grease is used as a damping medium. Hydraulic retraction. Hydraulically-operated doors close apertures in undersurface of wings both when the wheels are retracted and fully extended. Single large tail-wheel retracts into the fuselage and in emergency may be lowered from the tail-gun position by a hand winch.

POWER PLANT.—Two Daimler-Benz DB 610 A (port) or B (starboard) twenty-four-cylinder engines, each rated at 2,700 h.p. at 18,700 ft. (5,700 m.) and with 2,950 h.p. available for take-off. Each engine consists of two modified DB 605 twelve-cylinder inverted Vee liquid-cooled engines mounted side-by-side and inclined so that the inner banks of cylinders are vertical. In place of the normal reduction gear housings, a large single gear casing connects the two crankcases. The two crankshaft pinions drive a single airscrew shaft gear, directly on the starboard unit and indirectly through idler gears on the port unit to give opposite rotation. Two four-blade VDM constant-speed airscrews 14 ft. 10 in. (4.52 m.) in diameter. A clutch permits either one of the two engines of each unit to be uncoupled from the airscrew drive. Annular coolant radiators around each airscrew shaft, the air flow through them being assisted by cuffs on the airscrew blade roots. Fuel tanks in fuselage, centre-section and outer wings. Fuselage and centre-section tanks of metal with self-sealing covering. Outer wing tanks of flexible rubber. Total maximum capacity 2,788 Imp. gallons. Oil, coolant, starting fuel and de-icing fluid tanks in engine nacelles. Slinger-ring airscrew de-icing.

ACCOMMODATION.—Crew of six, four in the forward crew compartment, one in the mid-upper turret and one in the tail-gun position. Forward crew consists of pilot, second pilot/bomb-aimer/front gunner, navigator/radio operator/under gunner, and gunner operating the remote-control dorsal guns. Remainder of the crew consists of the mid-upper gunner and the tail-gunner. A jettisonable entrance hatch is provided in the floor of the fuselage for the mid-upper gunner who, like the tail-gunner, is isolated from the rest of the crew. Equipment includes armour, heating and ventilation, oxygen, 24-volt electrical system, radio, including control for glider bombs, radio altimeter, blind-approach equipment, etc.

ARMAMENT.—Armament disposed in the following positions :—forward dorsal turret (one or two 13 m/m. MG 131) remotely-controlled from sighting station aft of the pilot's cockpits ; rear dorsal turret (one or two 13 m/m. MG 131) ; forward gondola position (one 20 m/m. MG 151/20) ; rear gondola position (one 13 m/m. MG 131) ; observer's position (one 7.9 m/m. MG 81) ; tail position (one 20 m/m. MG 151/20. The rear dorsal turret is electrically rotated but the guns are hand-elevated. The tail gun is on a gimbal mounting and is hand-operated. Normal bomb load carried internally. Typical bomb loads are forty-eight 70 kg., or ten 500 kg., or six 1,000 kg., or two 2,500 kg. bombs. Alternatively carriers for three radio-controlled Hs 293, two Hs 294 or two PC 1400 FX anti-shipping bombs.

DIMENSIONS.—Span 103 ft. 2 in. (31.46 m.), Length 72 ft. (21.9 m.), Height (tail up) 21 ft. 10 in. (6.7 m.), Gross wing area 1,076 sq. ft. (100 sq. m.).

WEIGHTS.—Weight empty 37,000 lbs. (16,800 kg.), Maximum take-off weight 68,500 lbs. (31,100 kg.), Normal landing weight 53,000 lbs. (24,060 kg.), Maximum wing loading 63.7 lbs./sq. ft. (310.8 kg./sq. m.), Power loading 11.4 lbs./h.p. (5.17 kg./h.p.).

PERFORMANCE.—Maximum speed (at 41,000 lbs. = 18,615 kg.) 295 m.p.h. (472 km.h.) at 17,000 ft. (5,185 m.), Climb to 17,000 ft. (5,185 m.) 25 mins., Best climbing speed at maximum loaded weight 171 m.p.h. (274 km.h.), Service ceiling 26,500 ft. (8,080 m.).

THE HEINKEL He 177B.

Mechanical difficulties with the twin-coupled engines in the He 177A resulted in the development of the He 177B with four separate engines. The different power-plant layout constituted the only major modification to the airframe, which was basically that of the A-5 sub-type. Four Daimler-Benz DB 603 A engines were fitted. This version did not progress beyond the prototype stage.

THE HEINKEL He 178.

The He 178, which was test-flown on August 27, 1939, was the first jet-propelled aircraft to fly. It was a shoulder-wing monoplane and was fitted with a large-diameter He S 3 turbo-jet unit which developed a thrust of about 1,000 lbs. Strictly an experimental type, this aircraft was not designed for military purposes.

THE HEINKEL He 219A.

The He 219 was designed in 1940-41 as a high-performance twin-engined fighter. It went into service during 1944-45 as a night fighter.

Representative sub-types are the He 219A-2 with two DB 603 A engines, and the He 219A-5 and A-7 with two DB 603 E engines.

TYPE.—Twin-engined Night Fighter.

WINGS.—Shoulder-wing cantilever monoplane. Wing of single-spar stressed-skin construction built as single unit, the spar being continuous through the fuselage. Straight leading-edge, but sharp sweep-forward on trailing-edge outboard of the nacelles, increasing at the inner ends of the ailerons. Detachable wing-tips. Frise ailerons. Fowler flaps between ailerons and nacelles, and nacelles and fuselage. Ailerons are aerodynamically and mass-balanced and have geared tabs. Part of the tab on the port wing is adjustable for trimming.

FUSELAGE.—Rectangular section with rounded corners. Stressed-skin metal structure in two sections. The front section forms the nose and cockpit, and the rear, or main section houses the three self-sealing tanks. Aft of the rear tank is the electrical and radio equipment, the master compass and emergency seat, access to which is through a trap door under the fuselage. The extreme end of the fuselage has a transparent cone in which the guide for the trailing aerial fits.

TAIL UNIT.—Cantilever monoplane type with twin fins and rudders. Tailplane is one unit and is provided with moderate dihedral. Twin fins and rudders are slightly toed-in.

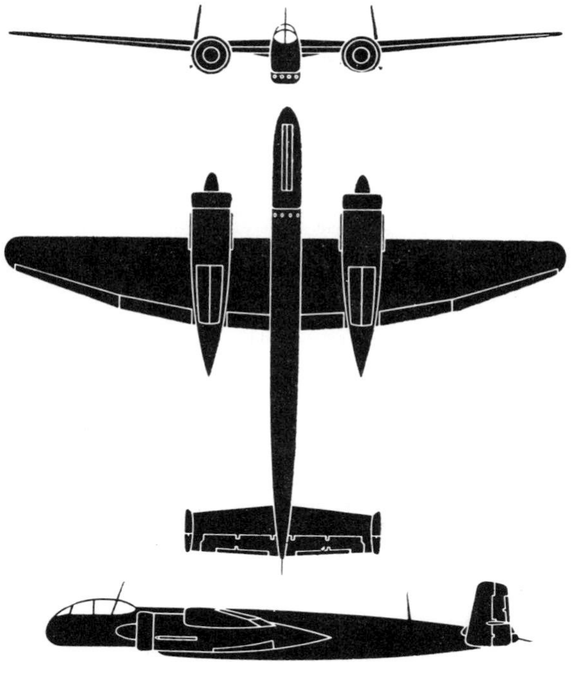

The Heinkel He 219 Twin-engined Night Fighter.

Landing Gear.—Retractable tricycle type. Each main unit consists of a single oleo leg and twin wheels and is raised backwards into the engine nacelle. Nose wheel also retracts backwards and the wheel turns through 90° to lie flat in the fuselage. Hydraulic retraction.

Power Plant.—Two Daimler-Benz DB 603 A or E twelve-cylinder inverted Vee liquid-cooled engines driving VDM three-blade constant-speed airscrews. Annular radiators surround the airscrew shafts. The nacelles are unusually long and are faired to points well aft of the trailing-edge of the wings. Armour plate at the rear of each engine. Three self-sealing fuel tanks in fuselage. The front tank holds 244 Imp. gallons, the centre tank 111 Imp. gallons and the rear tank 222 Imp. gallons.

Accommodation.—Crew of two seated back to back in the nose of the fuselage. Emergency seat in rear fuselage. Entrance to the nose cockpit is through the roof. Full armour plating.

Armament.—Four 20 m/m. MG 151/10 cannon in a detachable fairing under the fuselage, with 300 rounds per gun. Provision for two additional guns in the wing roots. Two fixed 30 m/m. MK 108 cannon behind the cockpit fire forwards and upwards at an angle of 65°. These guns have 100 rounds each.

Dimensions.—Span 60 ft. 8 in. (18.5 m.), Length 51 ft. (15.5 m.), Height 14 ft. 5 in. (4.4 m.), Wing area 478 sq. ft. (44.4 sq. m.).

Weights.—Maximum take-off weight 29,900 lbs. (13,580 kg.).

Performance.—Maximum speed about 385 m.p.h. (616 km.h.) at 21,000 ft. (6,410 m.), Service ceiling 30,500 ft. (9,300 m.), Range at maximum continous speed 960 miles (1,520 km.), Range at economical cruising speed 1,335 miles (2,140 km.).

THE HEINKEL He 219B.

The He 219B was a long-span development of the 219A which did not go into service. Two Junkers Jumo 222 E/F engines were intended for this sub-type. Using the MW 50 power-boost equipment, the estimated speed of the He 219B was 435 m.p.h. (616 km.h.) at 33,000 ft. (10,060 m.). The take-off weight was 32,550 lbs. (14,780 kg.).

THE HEINKEL He 274.

This aircraft was being built in prototype form in France during the occupation by the Société des Avions Farman, under German supervision. Six prototypes were originally ordered but none was completed before the liberation. It is understood that two will be finished by Farman to the order of the French Air Ministry and will be used for high-altitude research flying.

Type.—Four-engined high-altitude Bomber.

Wings.—Mid-wing cantilever monoplane. Centre-section in one piece carries the four engines. Tapered outer wings with dihedral and rounded tips. Split trailing-edge flaps extend outboard as far as the ailerons, which also droop when the flaps are lowered. Hot air leading-edge de-icing.

Fuselage.—All-metal stressed-skin structure built up of four heavy longerons, bulkheads and vertical stiffeners. Nose section houses the pressurised cabin. Behind this are three fuel tanks, one of which is above the bomb-bay. The bomb-bay is comparatively short and is divided down the centre line. The central portion of the fuselage is trapezoidal in section, but changes to rectangular section aft.

Tail Unit.—Cantilever monoplane type with twin fins and rudders. Tailplane has slight taper and dihedral. The trapezoidal-shaped fins and rudders at the extremities have about 40 per cent. of their area below the tailplane.

Landing Gear.—Retractable type. Each main unit consists of a single leg and twin wheels on a levered suspension system. The legs and wheels retract backwards and when raised are completely enclosed in the inboard engine nacelles. Retractable tail-wheel.

Power Plant.—It was intended to fit four Daimler-Benz DB 603 twelve-cylinder inverted Vee liquid-cooled engines with turbo-superchargers. The turbos were to be in the upper part of the nacelles over the wing with the air intakes in the leading-edge. Coolant and oil radiators of the annular type surrounding the reduction gear casings. Seven fuel tanks, four in the wings and three in the fuselage, with total capacity of 1,805 or 2,450 Imp. gallons, depending on the size of the bomb-bay tank. Four 20-gallon oil tanks in the wings. Separate oil tanks for the turbo-superchargers.

Accommodation.—Crew of four, comprising pilot, second pilot/navigator/bomb-aimer, and two gunners, in pressure cabin forming the nose of the fuselage. Cabin pressurisation by two superchargers driven off the inboard engines. Double walls for heat insulation and hot air ducted to windows to prevent misting or icing.

Armament.—Three remotely-controlled turrets outside the pressurised area, one in the nose, one above the fuselage forward of the wings and one below the fuselage aft of the bomb-bay. Sighting stations within the pressurised area, one above and one below the nose of the fuselage. Nose turret had one and the fuselage turrets two 13 m/m. MG 131 machine-guns. The bomb-bay beneath the wings with normal accommodation for about 8,800 lbs. (4,000 kg.).

Dimensions.—Span 145 ft. 1 in. (44.2 m.), Length 73 ft. (22.3 m.), Gross wing area 1,616 sq. ft. (150 sq. m.).

Weights.—Weight empty 46,300 lbs. (21,020 kg.), Weight loaded 79,400 lbs. (36,050 kg.).

Performance (estimated).—Maximum speed 310 m.p.h. (496 km.h.) at 39,360 ft. (12,000 m.).

THE HEINKEL He 280.

The He 280 was a single-seat jet-propelled fighter which was originally under development in the Summer of 1939. It had a typical Heinkel fighter fuselage, elliptically-shaped wings and a dihedral tailplane with twin fins and rudders. The landing-gear was of the retractable tricycle type with very little ground clearance.

It was intended that two He S 8 turbo jet units should be installed, but as the airframe was ready for flight trials before the jet units were available, about twenty take-offs and landings were made, using the aircraft as a glider.

The development of this design was parellel to that of the Messerschmitt Me 262 and continued until late 1944. The aircraft was slower and generally less efficient than the Me 262, and was eventually abandoned. The power-plant of the later versions consisted of two BMW 003A turbo-jet units in nacelles under the wings.

Dimensions.—Span 39 ft. 4 in. (12 m.), Length 34 ft. 1 in. (10.4 m.).

Weight Loaded.—About 9,550 lbs. (4,340 kg.).

Performance.—No data available.

THE HEINKEL He 343.

The He 343 was a project for a monoplane fitted with four turbo-jet units, the development of which was abandoned.

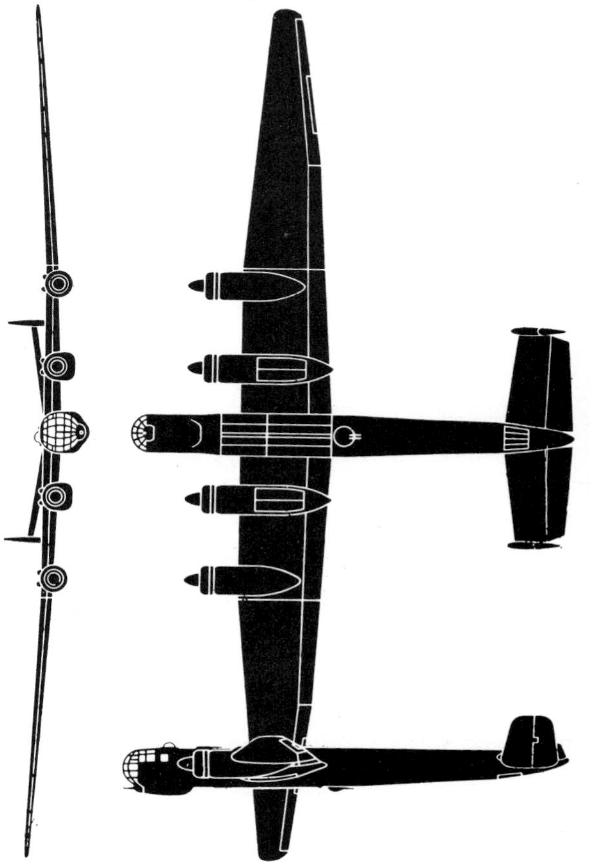

The Heinkel He 274 Four-engined Bomber.

HENSCHEL.

HENSCHEL FLUGZEUG-WERKE A.G.

Head Office: Schönefeld, near Berlin.
Works: Schönefeld, Johannisthal and Vienna.
President: Oscar R. Henschel.
Managing Director: Walter Hormel.
Technical Director: Dipl. Ing. Frydag.
Chief Engineer: Dipl. Ing. Fr. Nicolaus.

In 1933, the well-known builders of locomotives, Henschel & Sohn, G.m.b.H., of Kassel, which had already undertaken the construction of heavy lorries and omnibuses, turned their attention to the building of aeroplanes, so completing the range of transport vehicles. For this purpose a new branch, known as Henschel Flugzeugwerke A.G., was founded.

The only Henschel types used by the Luftwaffe in the European War were the Hs 123 biplane Dive-Bomber and the Hs 126 Army co-operation monoplane, both of which were of pre-war design, and the Hs 129 Ground-Attack monoplane.

THE HENSCHEL Hs 126B.

The Hs 126 was a two-seat parasol monoplane which was originally designed in 1937 as a reconnaissance and Army co-operation aircraft. It was ordered in large numbers by the German Air Ministry and was in service in the Luftwaffe, first as an operational type and latterly as a glider-tug and training aircraft, throughout the European war. It has been fully described in this Annual for the past six years.

THE HENSCHEL Hs 128.

The Hs 128 was an experimental twin-engined mid-wing monoplane with pressure cabin and fixed landing-gear. It was the forerunner of the Hs 130 described later.

THE HENSCHEL Hs 129B.

The Hs 129 was designed solely for ground attack and first went into service on the Russian Front in 1942. The original Hs 129A was fitted with two Argus As 410 twelve-cylinder inverted Vee air-cooled engines driving Argus automatic controllable-pitch airscrews. This was later superseded by the Hs 129B with two French-built Gnôme-Rhône 14M fourteen-cylinder radial air-cooled engines driving French Ratier airscrews.

The Hs 129B-1 and B-2 were the commonest sub-types, the latter fitted to carry a droppable auxiliary fuel tank. Some versions of the B-2 were equipped experimentally with the SG 113 recoil-less gun installation. This consisted of a battery of six 75 m.m smooth-bore tubes, each 5 ft. 3 in. (1.6 m.) long, which was mounted in the fuselage at an angle slightly beyond the vertical to fire downwards and rearwards. The weapon was intended for use against tanks and was triggered automatically when the aircraft flew over a tank at low altitude.

Type.—Single-seat Ground Attack monoplane.

Wings.—Low-wing cantilever monoplane. Centre-section carrying the two engine nacelles is built integrally with the fuselage. Two tapering outer sections. Straight leading-edge and swept forward trailing-edge from roots to tips. Two-spar all-metal construction with stressed skin covering. Entire trailing-edge hinged, the outer sections acting as slotted ailerons and the inner sections as slotted flaps.

Fuselage.—Triangular cross-section structure with the wing centre-section built into the broad base. Nose section of spot-welded 6-12 m/m. armour plate, the remainder of light metal stressed-skin construction. Total weight of nose armour 2,370 lbs. (1,080 kg.).

Tail Unit.—Cantilever monoplane type. All-metal structure. Tailplane incidence adjustable on the ground

Landing Gear.—Retractable type. The single-leg main units retract hydraulically backwards into the engine nacelles, a portion of the wheels protruding slightly from the nacelles when raised. Non-retractable tail-wheel.

Power Plant.—Two Gnôme-Rhône 14M 04/05 fourteen-cylinder radial air-cooled engines, each driving a three-blade Ratier electrically-operated constant-speed airscrew. Self-sealing fuel tanks in wings and fuselage, the two wing tanks having a capacity of 45 Imp. gallons each and the fuselage tank 44 Imp. gallons. Lower halves of the engine nacelles protected by 5 m/m. armour plate.

Accommodation.—Pilot in the armoured nose. Windscreen with bullet-resisting glass 75 m/m. thick in a 6 m/m. armoured frame.

Armament.—One 15 m/m. MG 151 or 20 m/m. MG 151/20 cannon and one 7.9 m/m. MG 17 machine-gun on each side of the fuselage nose and firing forward, and one 30 m/m. MK 101 or 103 cannon under the fuselage. As alternative to the 30 m/m. cannon, a battery of four 7.9 m/m. MG 17 machine-guns or carriers for a total of 770 lbs. (350 kg.) of bombs can be installed.

Dimensions.—Span 44 ft. 6 in. (13.5 m.), Length 33 ft. 3 in. (10.1 m.), Wing area 305 sq. ft. (28.3 sq. m.).

Weights.—Weight empty (according to equipment) 8,770 lbs. to 8,940 lbs. (3,980 to 4,060 kg.), Weight loaded 11,000 to 11,250 lbs. (5,000 to 5,110 kg.).

Performance.—Maximum speed 255 m.p.h. (408 km.h.) at 12,500 ft. (3,810 m.), Climb to 10,000 ft. (3,050 m.) 7 mins., Service ceiling 29,520 ft. (9,000 m.), Range 350 miles (560 km.).

THE HENSCHEL Hs 130A.

The Hs 130A was a high-altitude bomber-reconnaissance development of the experimental Hs 128. It was fitted with two

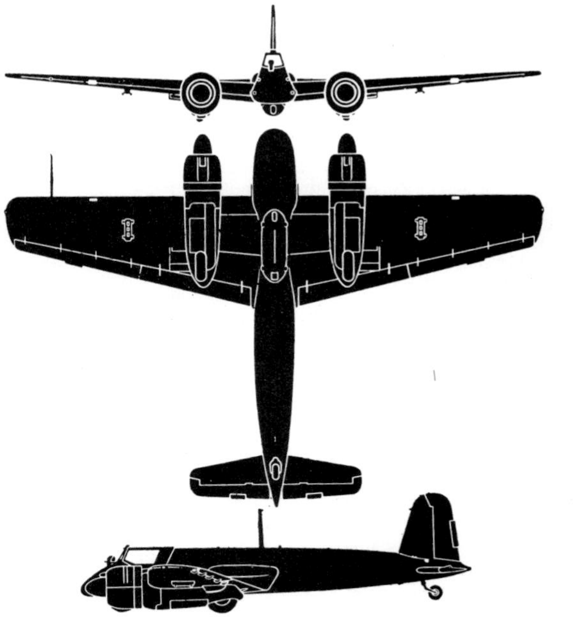

The Henschel Hs 129B Ground-Attack Monoplane.

Daimler-Benz DB 605 engines. No armament was installed.
DIMENSIONS.—Span 85 ft. 3 in. (26 m.), Length 52 ft. 2 in. (15.9 m.).

THE HENSCHEL Hs 130C.

The Hs 130C was a development of the 130A with two BMW 801 J radial air-cooled engines with turbo-superchargers.

THE HENSCHEL Hs 130E.

The HE 130E was developed in 1943 from the Hs 128 and from the earlier Hs 130 sub-types as a high-altitude reconnaissance aircraft or bomber. It was not used operationally.

TYPE.—Twin engined high-altitude Reconnaissance or Bomber monoplane.

WINGS.—Mid-wing cantilever monoplane. Wings of constant taper and with rounded tips. All-metal single-spar stressed-skin construction. Narrow-chord ailerons in two sections. Trailing-edge flaps inboard of ailerons and divided by tails of engine nacelles.

FUSELAGE.—Circular section all-metal stressed-skin structure. Pressure cabin of "hot-wall" type built into the nose of the fuselage. Remotely-controlled photographic equipment aft of the pressure compartment, followed by fuselage fuel tank and one DB 605 engine used to supply supercharged air to the wing engines.

TAIL UNIT.—Cantilever monoplane type. All-metal structure.

LANDING GEAR.—Retractable type. Single oleo legs and main wheels raised backwards into the engine nacelles. Tail-wheel retracts into a lower fin.

POWER PLANT.—Two Daimler-Benz DB 603 S or T twelve-cylinder inverted Vee liquid-cooled engines each driving a four-blade constant-speed airscrew. These engines are fed with supercharged air by a single DB 605 T engine, located in the fuselage amidships, which drives a Roots-type blower. The German designation for this complete blower installation is HZ "Anlage." Radiators for the wing engines are under the wings outboard of the nacelles. Radiators for the blower engine are beneath the fuselage aft of the wings. Supercharger intercoolers are located under the wings between the fuselage and the engine nacelles. Fuel tanks in wings and fuselage, the wing tanks having a combined capacity of 564 Imp. gallons and the fuselage tank 375 Imp. gallons.

ACCOMMODATION.—Crew of four accommodated in a pressurised compartment in the nose of the fuselage.

ARMAMENT.—Two remotely-controlled turrets, each armed with two 13 m/m. MG 131 machine-guns, one above and one below the nose compartment. One 20 m/m. MG 151/20 cannon, remotely-controlled, in tail turret. Periscopic sights. Bombs, when carried, on carriers under the wings outboard of the engine nacelles.

DIMENSIONS.—Span 108 ft. 3 in. (33 m.), Length 64 ft. 7 in. (19.7 m.).

WEIGHT LOADED.—Approximately 38,000 lbs. (17,250 kg.).

PERFORMANCE.—Maximum speed approximately 320 m.p.h. (512 km.h.) at 40,000 ft. (12,200 m.). Service ceiling 45,000 to 50,000 ft. (13,725 to 15,250 m.).

THE HENSCHEL Hs 132.

The Hs 132 was an experimental jet-propelled dive-bomber and ground attack monoplane. It was of mixed construction with a wooden wing and a metal fuselage. The pilot lay prone in the fuselage. The power unit consisted of one Jumo 004 turbo-jet unit. The aircraft had a span of approximately 40 ft. (12.2 m.) and was designed to carry a maximum bomb load of 3,300 lbs. (1,500 kg.). The maximum designed speed (without bombs) was 495 m.p.h. (792 km.h.) at 3,000 ft. (915 m.).

HENSCHEL WINGED MISSILES

The Henschel company was responsible for the development and design of a number of "guided winged missiles" under the direction of Professor Wagner.

Among the many Henschel "winged missiles" were the Hs 293 and its more advanced developments, the Hs 294, 295, 296 and 297 (Hs 117) rocket-propelled and radio-controlled bombs for use against ground, sea or air targets; the Hs 298, a light version of the Hs 293 and designed to be launched from rails fitted to night fighters for combatting night bombers; and the Hs 344, another rocket-propelled missile for use by German aircraft against other aircraft.

The Hs 293 was first used against Allied shipping in the Summer of 1943. It was carried by such aircraft as the Dornier Do 217E-5, the Heinkel He 177 and the Junkers Ju 290 and used for attacks on merchant ships, landing craft and other non-armoured vessels. The Hs 293 is also understood to have been tried as a weapon to combat day bomber attacks on the Reich but it was not successful at height. Also, the advent of powerful fighter cover for U.S. day bomber formations ruled out the use of the comparatively slow and heavy aircraft used as carriers for these missiles.

The Hs 298 was a smaller version of the 293 for use from fighter aircraft. It was fitted with a two-stage rocket motor and could operate successfully up to a height of 20,000 ft. (6,100 m.). It carried a small war-head, believed to be not much more than 150 lbs. (70 kg.), as compared with the 1,100 lbs. (500 kg.) of the Hs 293.

All these missiles were radio controlled and provided with wing and tail surfaces and a rocket device located under the main body to provide initial acceleration after release from the carrier aircraft. In the extreme tail were a number of incandescent candles, the successive glowing of which provided the controller in the carrier aircraft with an aiming guide.

The Hs 293 had a span of 10 ft. 7 in. (3.23 m.) and a length of 13 ft. 4 in. (4.128 m.). It weighed about 1,700 lbs. (770 kg.), of which 1,100 lbs. (500 kg.) was explosive charge.

The Hs 294 had a span of 14 ft. 2 in. (4.326 m.) and a length of 16 ft. 5 in. (6 m.) and the Hs 295 a length of 14 ft. 1 in. (4.3 m.), its span being the same as the 294.

HORTEN.

HORTEN GEBRÜDER.

HEAD OFFICE: BONN.

This concern, which was engaged in the development of tail-less aircraft over a period of years, had under construction and development at the time of the capitulation a jet-propelled tail-less fighter known as the Ho 9.

THE HORTEN Ho 9.

The Ho 9 was an experimental jet-propelled "flying-wing" fighter which was envisaged as both a single-seat Day Fighter and a two-seat Night Fighter. The first prototype was completed as a glider, the second and third prototypes were single-seaters and the fourth was intended to be a two-seater.

The sharply swept-back cantilever wing was of mixed construction with a welded steel-tube centre-section, wood outer sections and metal tips. The crew accommodation was in a swelling on the centre-line which extended aft of the trailing-edge and terminated in a sharp point. Close alongside the central swelling and in the wing were installed the two jet units which passed through the main spar and exhausted over the trailing-edge. The first installation consisted of two Junkers Jumo 004 units, but subsequently two BMW 003 units were to be installed.

All control surfaces were on the outer wings. Divided hinged surfaces were responsible for longitudinal and lateral control and spoilers for directional control.

The landing-gear was of the retractable tricycle type, the main wheels being raised inwardly and the nose wheel backwards.

The proposed armament was to consist of four 30 mm. MK 108 cannon for the Day Fighter, with provision for carrying 2,000 lbs. of bombs when used as a Fighter-Bomber. The Night Fighter would have been fitted with both heavy calibre guns and rockets.

DIMENSIONS.—Span 52 ft. 6 in (16 m.).
WEIGHT.—About 20,000 lbs. (9,080 kg.).
PERFORMANCE.—About 500 m.p.h. (800 km.h.) at 20,000 ft. (6,100 m.).

JUNKERS.

JUNKERS FLUGZEUG UND MOTORENWERKE, A.-G.

HEAD OFFICE AND WORKS: DESSAU.
BRANCH AIRCRAFT FACTORIES: ASCHERSLEBEN, BERNBURG, HALBERSTADT, LEOPOLDSHALL, LEIPZIG, &c.
General Director: Dr. Leo S. Rothe.
Chief Engineer (Military Aircraft): Dipl. Ing. Pohlmann.

The origin of the Junkers Aircraft Factory can be traced back to 1910 when Professor Junkers was granted a patent for an all-wing aeroplane. The idea was to include the engines, fuel system, crew, freight-holds and passenger accommodation within the wing in order to reduce resistance to the minimum.

He adhered to this idea and in 1915 produced the first successful all-metal aeroplane, the Junkers J1, a low-wing cantilever monoplane. Immediately after the end of the War 1914-18, Professor Junkers began the first quantity production of all-metal commercial aircraft with the Junkers F13, for six passengers. Thereafter followed the three-engined G24, for eleven passengers in 1924, the G31 for sixteen passengers in 1926, in 1927 the single-engined Ju 33/34, in 1928 the four-engined G38, for 34 passengers, in 1930/32 the single and three-engined Ju 52, for 15-17 passengers, in 1933 the high-speed Ju 60 and Ju 160, in 1936 the Ju 86, and in 1937 the Ju 90, a high-capacity four-engined monoplane, the last three types being fitted with retractable landing gear.

From 1934 to 1935 the Junkers Ju 52 was produced as a bomber, a conversion which had been provided for in the design and construction of this machine. Later it was produced in large quantities as a troop-carrier.

Similarly the Ju 86, first publically announced as a commercial aircraft, also had a dual function and the military model, known as the Ju 86K, was built in large quantities to equip the first bomber squadrons of the renascent Luftwaffe.

The principal types produced in large numbers during the second World War were the Ju 52/3M, Ju 87 and Ju 88, and all three, but particularly the 88 series, were the subject of continuous development. From the Ju 52 were evolved the Ju 252 and Ju 352, and from the Ju 88 were developed the Ju 188 and Ju 388. From the pre-war commercial Ju 90 were developed the Ju 290 and Ju 390. Considerable experimental work was also done in jet-propulsion, the Junkers company being responsible for the design of the first jet-propelled heavy bomber prototype to fly.

In the latter stages of the war the series production of Junkers aircraft was undertaken in the following plants:—

Ju 88 and Ju 188.
Assembly plants:—Bernburg (Junkers), Leipzig-Schkeuditz (Junkers), Dessau (Junkers), Leipzig-Mockau (A.T.G.), Halle (Siebel).
Component plants:—Aschersleben (Junkers), Halberstadt (Junkers), Dessau (Junkers), Fallersleben (People's Car Works), Rüsselsheim (Opel).

Ju 87.
Assembly plant:—Bremen (Weser).

Ju 52/ 3m.
Assembly plants:—Leipzig-Mockau (A.T.G.), Villacoublay, near Paris (Junkers-controlled).

THE JUNKERS Ju 52/3m.

The original Ju 52 was a single-engined civil transport, the later three engined development being designated the Ju 52/3m. Both these versions appeared as 15-17 passenger transports in the period 1930-32, but from 1934 to 1935 the three-engined Ju 52/3m was produced as a bomber for the Luftwaffe. Later, it was put into production as a military transport, in which category it served throughout the European war. The following are the principal sub-types of the Ju 52/3m.:—

Ju 52/3m g3e. Three BMW 132 A engines. The oldest service sub-type. Maximum flying weight 20,900 lbs. (9,500 kg.).

Ju 52/3m g4e. Landplane transport similar to the g3e but with strengthened landing-gear. Maximum flying weight increased to 23,100 lbs. (10,490 kg.).

Ju 52/3m g5e. Generally similar to the g4e but built as both a landplane and a float seaplane. Fitted with three BMW 132 T engines. Wings fitted with de-icing equipment.

Ju 52/3m g6e. Similar to the g5e but built as a landplane only. Modified radio equipment.

Ju 52/3m g7e. Similar to the g5e but fitted with automatic pilot, wider loading door and certain internal modifications. Maximum flying weight: 24,200 lbs. (10,990 kg.).

Ju 52/3m g8e. Similar to the g6e but available as a landplane transport only.

TYPE.—Three-engined General Purpose Military Transport, Glider-Tug and Paratroop-carrier. Also used as magnetic-mine sweeper.

WINGS.—Low-wing cantilever monoplane. Middle portion built into fuselage, of which it forms the undersurface. Wings joined by typical Junkers screw couplings. Eight duralumin tube spars, arranged in pairs vertically over one another and braced with short struts to each other. The corrugated metal skin stiffens the wing against torsion. Along whole of trailing-edge runs a flap mounted to give double-wing effect. This can be used to vary the camber and so increase the lift of the wing. The outer sections are operated differentially as ailerons and are horn-balanced.

FUSELAGE.—Rectangular section, with domed decking. Duralumin frames and bracing of simple channel section, together with four longerons, compose frame. Stressed skin of corrugated light-alloy sheeting.

TAIL UNIT.—Normal monoplane type, with semi-cantilever tailplane passing through top of fuselage and braced to the underside of same, with single strut on each side. Elevator of double-wing construction like wing and aileron, and horn-balanced. Cantilever fin and horn-balanced rudder. The whole of all-metal construction with corrugated metal covering. Tail-plane adjustable in flight.

LANDING GEAR.—Divided type. Half-axles and radius-rods hinged to fuselage. Oleo-pneumatic shock-absorbers attached to upper wing-root of foremost spar. Compressed-air brakes. Twin single-step floats can replace wheels.

POWER PLANT.—Three BMW 132 A or T nine-cylinder radial air-cooled engines. Fuel capacity 535 Imp. gallons.

ACCOMMODATION.—Totally-enclosed pilot's cockpit above and forward of wing. Side-by-side seats with complete dual controls. Radio operator, when carried, has folding seat in pilots' compartment or is seated near the window gun mountings. Behind cockpit is large cabin for the accommodation of 16-18 fully-armed troops. Cabin may also be fitted to carry twelve stretcher cases.

ARMAMENT.—Guns may be mounted in forward fuselage in dorsal, lateral or ventral positions. A typical armament comprises one dorsal 13 m/m. MG 131 and two lateral 7.9 m/m. MG 15 machine-guns.

DIMENSIONS.—Span 95 ft. 10 in. (29.25 m.), Length 62 ft. (18.9 m.), Height 14 ft. 10 in. (4.5 m.), Wing area 1,190 sq. ft. (110.5 sq. m.),

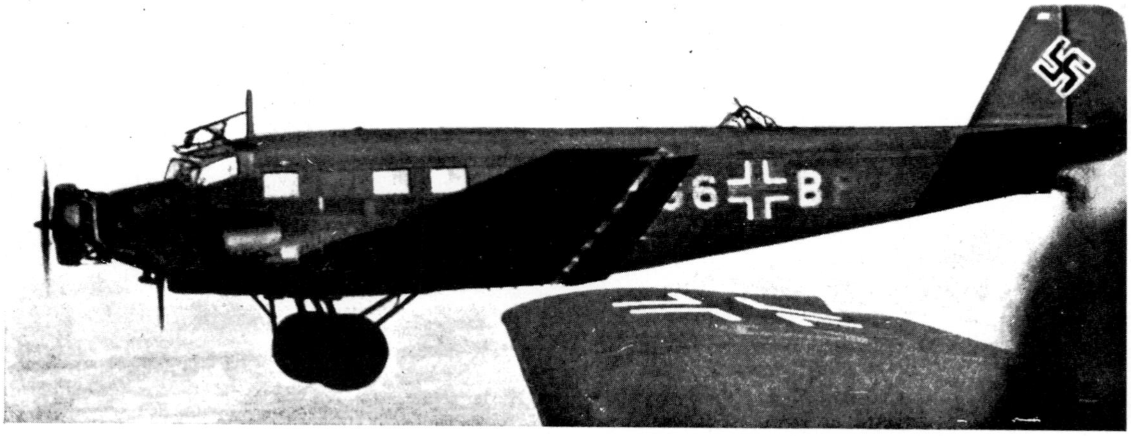

The Junkers Ju 52/3m General Purposes Military Transport (three 830 h.p. BMW 132 engines).

The Junkers Ju 86P High-altitude Reconnaissance Monoplane (two Junkers Jumo 207 engines).

WEIGHTS.—Weight empty 14,325 lbs. (6,510 kg.), Maximum take-off weight 24,200 lbs. (10,990 kg.).
PERFORMANCE.—Maximum speed at sea level 165 m.p.h. (264 km.h.), Cruising speed 132 m.p.h. (211 km.h.), Climb to 10,000 ft. (3,050 m.) 17 mins., Service ceiling at mean weight 18,000 ft. (5,490 m.), Range with maximum fuel 800 miles (1,280 km.).

THE JUNKERS Ju 86P and Ju 86R.

The Ju 86P and Ju 86R were high-altitude reconnaissance or bomber aircraft developed from earlier Ju 86 sub-types. They were used on a few occasions in bombing operations against the British Isles.

Whereas the original Ju 86 had a span of 74 ft. (22.6 m.) for the high-altitude versions this was increased to 84 ft. (25.6 m.) in the Ju 86P and 105 ft. (32 m.) in the Ju 86R. The considerable increase over the original span resulted in a wing plan with a pronounced change of taper at both leading and trailing edges and almost grotesque pointed tips. The usual Junkers "double-wing" construction was employed, with two-flaps and a divided aileron to each wing.

Junkers Jumo 207 or 208 turbo-supercharged compression-ignition engines were fitted, typical installations in the Ju 86P being two Jumo 207A1 and in the Ju 86R two Jumo 207 B-3/V. The Ju 86R could be fitted with GM 1 (nitreous-oxide) power-boosting installation.

Both these aircraft were fitted with pressure cabins and were normally unarmed. The crew consisted of pilot and radio operator.

The maximum flying weight of the bomber version (up to 2,200 lbs.—1,000 kg. bombs) was 25,400 lbs. (11,530 kg.). For reconnaissance three cameras were carried in the fuselage.

The Ju 86R had a maximum speed of about 260 m.p.h. (416 km.h.) at heights above 30,000 ft. (9,150 m.). At these heights an endurance of 7 hours. 10 mins. was obtained with 462 Imp. gallons of fuel. This endurance corresponded to a range of about 980 miles (1,570 km.). The absolute ceiling was about 49,000 ft. (14,950 m.).

THE JUNKERS Ju 87C.

The Ju 87C-1 was an experimental deck-landing development of the Ju 87B-1. Intended for use in the aircraft-carrier *Graf Zeppelin*, which was never completed, the Ju 87C was stressed for catapulting and was fitted with a jettisonable landing-gear for emergency alighting in the sea. Development was abandoned early in the war.

THE JUNKERS Ju 87D.

The Ju 87D was developed from the Ju 87B and R which, in turn, were derived from the Ju 87A. The Ju 87R was similar to the B but had provision for the installation of external fuel tanks under the wings in place of bombs.

The Ju 87D differed considerably from the Ju 87B. The Jumo 211 J engine with induction cooling was installed, cowling and cockpit enclosure were re-designed and provision was made for carrying a bomb up to 3,960 lbs. (1,800 kg.). The coolant radiators were mounted under the wings and additional armour was fitted.

Originally a dive-bomber, the Ju 87D was later used for ground attack, often by night. The following are the principal sub-types of this Series:—

Ju 87D-1. A development of the Ju 87B-2 with the Jumo 211J engine and increased range.
Ju 87D-3. Similar to the D-1 but with increased armour.
Ju 87D-4. Similar to the D-3 with provision for mounting jettisonable weapon containers for service during the Russian campaign.
Ju 87D-5. Developed from the D-3. Span increased to 49 ft. 2¼ in. (15 m.). Increased diving speeds permitted. Jettisonable landing-gear.
Ju 87D-7. Similar to D-1 but with D-5 wings and increased wing armament.
Ju 87D-8. Similar to D-3 but with D-5 wings and increased wing armament.

TYPE.—Two-seat Dive-Bomber and Ground Attack monoplane.
WINGS.—Low-wing cantilever monoplane. Centre-section built integral with the fuselage and set at coarse anhedral. Outer wing-sections, tapering in chord and thickness, set at coarse dihedral. Two-spar all-metal structure with closely-spaced ribs and stressed-skin covering. Entire trailing-edge of wings and centre-section hinged on Junkers "double-wing" principle, outer portions acting as ailerons and inner portions as landing flaps. Diving brakes are fitted beneath front spars and outboard of landing gear legs. They are hinged clear of the under surface of the wings and in normal flight are edge-on to airstream. For dive attack they are turned through 90° to present a flat plate area to airflow.
FUSELAGE.—Oval-section structure of light metal construction. Made in two halves joined on the horizontal centre-line. The smooth metal skin is riveted to "Z"-section frames and open-section stringers. The two halves of the fuselage are joined by two internal angles riveted together.
TAIL UNIT.—Braced monoplane type. Junkers "double-wing" tail-plane and elevators. Tail-plane braced below to fuselage. Cantilever fin and rudder. All-metal structure with smooth sheet covering. Trimming-tabs in movable surfaces.
LANDING GEAR.—Fixed divided type. Each unit incorporates oleo-pneumatic suspension, with legs attached to extremities of centre-section. Legs enclosed in streamline casings. Orientable tail-wheel.

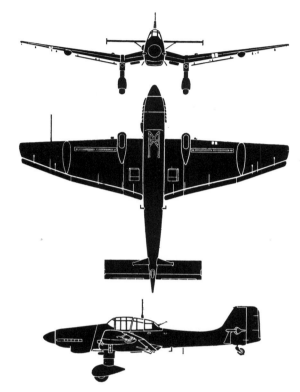

The Junkers Ju 87D Dive-Bomber.

POWER PLANT.—One 1,300 h.p. Junkers Jumo 211 J twelve-cylinder inverted Vee liquid-cooled engine. Three-bladed Junkers wooden-bladed airscrew. Two coolant radiators beneath centre-section, one on each side of fuselage. Oil cooler beneath engine. Fuel tanks in wings have a capacity of 170 Imp. gallons. Two 66 gallon drop tanks can be fitted.
ACCOMMODATION.—Tandem seats over wing and covered by continuous canopy with hinged and sliding sections.
ARMAMENT.—Two 20 m/m. MG 151/20 cannon in wings, one on either side of the fuselage and firing outside area swept by airscrew, and twin 7.9 m/m. MG 81 machine-guns on flexible mounting in rear cockpit. For ground attack two weapon carriers (six MG 81 each) may be mounted under the wings.
BOMB LOAD.—One 550 lb., one 1,100 lb., one 2,200 lb, or one 3,960 lb. bomb may be carried under the fuselage, or four 110 lb., two 550 lb. or two 1,100 lb. bombs under the wings.
DIMENSIONS.—Span 45 ft. 4 in. (13.8 m.), Length 36 ft. 6 in. (11.13 m.), Height 12 ft. 9 in. (3.9 m.), Wing area 335 sq. ft. (31 m.).
WEIGHTS.—Normal flying weight 12,600 lbs. (5,720 kg.), Maximum permissible take-off weight 14,500 lbs. (6,585 kg.).
PERFORMANCE.—Maximum speed 255 m.p.h. (408 km.h.) at 13,500 ft. (4,120 m.), Climb to 15,000 ft. (4,575 m.) 19 mins., Service ceiling at mean weight 24,000 ft. (7,320 m.), Range with maximum fuel 1,200 miles (1,920 km.). Range with maximum bombs (3,960 lbs. =1,800 kg.) 620 miles (1,000 km.).

THE JUNKERS Ju 87G.

Developed from the Ju 87D, the G Series of sub-types carried two 3.7 in. BK (Flak 18) guns under the wings. No dive-brakes were fitted. There were both long and short span versions.

THE JUNKERS Ju 87H.

The Ju 87H was a dual-control trainer. There were versions corresponding to the D-1, D-3, D-5, D-7 and D-8.

THE JUNKERS Ju 88A.

The Ju 88A was first flown as a bomber in 1936 and approximately fifty had been built by the beginning of 1939. This basic design was subsequently adopted for a wide variety of duties, and Ju 88 aircraft in various forms were in operation throughout the entire period of the European war. The Ju 88 was still in production when hostilities ended.

The following were the principal types in the A Series:—

Ju 88A-1. Two Junkers Jumo 211 B-1 or 211 G engines. Armament: four 7.9. m/m. MG 15 machine-guns. Bomb load: 5,500 lbs. (2,500 kg.). Span: 60 ft. 4 in. (18.4 m.). Flying weight: 27,500 lbs. (12,485 kg.).
Ju 88A-2. Similar to the A-1 but with special fittings for catapult-assisted take-off.
Ju 88A-3. Trainer version of A-1 with dual controls and throttles and various instruments duplicated.
Ju 88A-4. Two Junkers Jumo 211 F, 211 J-1 or J-2 engines. Span increased to 65 ft. 10 in. (20 m.) and landing-gear strengthened. Typical armament: one 13 m/m. MG 131, three 7.9 m/m. MG 81 and one twin MG 81. Bomb load increased to 6,600 lbs. (3,000 kg.).
Ju 88A-5. Two Junkers Jumo 211 G engines. Span and bomb load as for A-4 but otherwise similar to A-1. Balloon cable cutter could be fitted.
Ju 88A-6. Similar to A-5. Balloon cable fender and balloon destroying gear fitted. Trimming weight of 130 lbs. (59 kg.) installed in the end of the fuselage to compensate for the weight of the fender. Total weight of fender and trimming weight 840 lbs. (381 kg.) and reduction of speed due to fender about 19 m.p.h. (30.4 km.h.).

The Junkers Ju 87D Two-seat Dive Bomber and Ground Attack Monoplane (Junkers Jumo 211 J engine).

The Junkers Ju 88A-4 Bomber (two Junkers Jumo 211 J engines).

Ju 88A-7. Dual control trainer based on the A-5.

Ju 88A-8. Similar to A-6 but developed from the A-4.

Ju 88A-9. Tropical version of the A-1. Carried water containers, sun-blinds, shot-gun and rifle, rucksacks, sleeping bags, etc., for desert operation.

Ju 88A-10. Two Jumo 211 B or G engines. Tropical version of the A-5.

Ju 88A-11. Tropical version of the A-4.

Ju 88A-12. Trainer similar to the A-5 but with increased cockpit width.

Ju 88A-13. Ground attack aircraft developed from the A-1. Increased armour. No dive-brakes, automatic pull-out device or precision bomb-sight. Fitted with special anti-personnel bomb installation.

Ju 88A-14. Similar to A-4 but with built-in balloon-cable cutters and other refinements.

Ju 88A-16. Dual-control trainer.

Ju 88A-17. Similar to A-4 but equipped for torpedo-carrying.

TYPE.—Twin-engined Bomber, Torpedo-carrier and Reconnaissance monoplane.

WINGS.—Low-wing cantilever monoplane. Wings have constant taper in thickness, but in plan form the portion of the wing between fuselage and engine nacelles is of almost constant chord whereas portions outboard of engines have double taper. All-metal two-spar structure with flush-riveted stressed-skin covering. Entire trailing-edge hinged, the outer portions acting as ailerons and the inner sections as landing flaps. Slatted diving brakes hinged beneath front spar and outboard of engine nacelles. Hot-air leading-edge de-icing.

FUSELAGE.—Oval metal monocoque built up of a number of "Z"-section frames and top hat-section stringers to which is riveted the smooth stress-bearing skin.

TAIL UNIT.—Cantilever monoplane type. All-metal framework with metal-covered fixed surfaces and fabric-covered elevators and rudder. Rubber pulsating overshoe-type de-icers on tailplane leading-edges.

LANDING GEAR.—Retractable type. Wheels are retracted backwards and turn through 90 degrees to lie flat in lower portions of engine nacelles. Fixed tail-wheel.

POWER PLANT.—Two Junkers Jumo 211 J twelve-cylinder inverted Vee liquid-cooled engines in circular nacelles with circular frontal radiators incorporating both water and oil-cooling elements. Controllable gills aft of radiators. There are five petrol tanks, four in the wings, two of 72 gallons (324 litres) inboard of the engine nacelles and two of 90 gallons (405 litres) outboard of the nacelles, all between the wing-spars, and a fifth tank of 250 gallons (1,125 litres) in the fuselage bay between the main spars. Provision is made for fitting another fuselage tank of 152 gallons (690 litres) in the after bomb bay. All tanks are provided with solenoid-operated air-pressure valves and discharge pipes for jettisoning the contents. All tanks are of fibre encased in rubber. VDM or Junkers controllable-pitch full-feathering airscrews with de-icing slinger rings.

ACCOMMODATION.—Provision for crew of four grouped closely together in portion of fuselage forward of front spar. Pilot on left with bomb-aimer alongside, but at lower level. Upper rear gunner's position immediately behind pilot and radio-operator's position behind bomb-aimer but low down to enable him to operate lower rear gun. The fuselage nose is entirely glazed with optically-flat transparent panels. Pilot and rear gunner are beneath short continuous transparent hooding, the after end of which terminates with the upper-gun mounting. Blister beneath fuselage has an armoured gun-mounting aft to fire beneath tail. All crew positions armoured.

ARMAMENT.—One 7.9 m/m. MG 81 (operated by the pilot) and one or two 7.9 m/m. MG 81 (fired by bomb-aimer) in nose, one 7.9 m/m. MG 81 or 13 m/m. MG 131 in upper rear firing position, and one twin MG 81 in lower rear firing position. Two external bomb-carriers under each inner wing suitable for bombs up to 1,000 kg., for larger types of incendiary bomb containers (435 kg. and 900 kg.) or for extra petrol tanks. Normal external bomb load is four 250 kg. bombs, but alternatively the inboard carriers under each wing-root may carry one 1,000 kg. bomb or torpedo and the outboard carriers one 250 or 500 kg. bomb each. Ten bomb-carriers are fitted in the middle fuselage compartment, each capable of taking a 50-kg. bomb, a flare or an incendiary bomb container. The forward bomb bay is no longer used.

DIMENSIONS.—Span 65 ft. 10 in. (20 m.), Length 47 ft. 1 in. (14.4 m.), Height 15 ft. 11 in. (4.8 m.), Wing area 590 sq. ft. (54.5 sq. m.).

WEIGHTS.—Normal loaded weight 26,700 lbs. (12,122 kg.), Maximum permissible take-off weight 31,000 lbs. (14,075 kg.).

PERFORMANCE.—Maximum speed 295 m.p.h. (472 km.h.) at 17,500 ft. (5,340 m.), Climb to 17,500 ft. (5,340 m.) 23 mins., Service ceiling at mean weight 27,000 ft. (8,235 m.), Range with maximum fuel 1,900 miles (3,040 km.), Range with maximum bomb load (6,600 lbs. =3,000 kg.) 650 miles (1,040 km.).

THE JUNKERS Ju 88B.

Only a few aircraft in the B Series (B-1, B-2 and B-3) were built experimentally. All were fitted with BMW 801 radial air-cooled engines and all had a re-designed nose. The Ju 88B may be regarded as one of the forerunners of the Ju 188.

THE JUNKERS Ju 88C.

The Ju-88C Series were day and night fighters developed from the Ju 88 A. A crew of three was carried and the Jumo 211 B, 211 G, 211 J and BMW 801 engines were fitted in the various sub-types.

Ju 88C-1. Also known in the early days as the 88Z, the Z indicating "Zerstörer" (destroyer or heavy fighter). Heavily armoured nose enclosing one MG 151, one MG 15 and three MG 17, all fixed and firing forward. Two further MG 15 guns, one in dorsal and one in ventral positions.

Ju 88C-2. Similar to C-1 but with wider span wing. Sometimes carried an MG FF cannon in place of the MG 151. In addition, two MG FF could be carried under the fuselage.

Ju 88C-3. Similar to C-2 but fitted with BMW engines.

Ju 88C-4. Similar to C-2 but with provision for cameras.

Ju 88C-5. Experimental fighter. No gun blister under the fuselage. Crew of two only.

Ju 88C-6. Two Jumo 211 J engines. Armament : three MG FF cannon and three MG 17 in nose, and two MG 151/20 in a "Schräge Musik" mounting in which the guns are fixed in the fuselage and fire obliquely upward and forward.

Ju 88C-7. Two BMW 801 engines. Special armament installation.

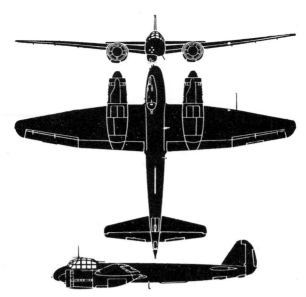

The Junkers Ju 88C-6 Night Fighter.

The following particulars relate to the most commonly-used Ju 88 night fighter (C-6) :—

NORMAL FLYING WEIGHT.—27,500 lbs. (12,485 kg.).

PERFORMANCE.—Maximum speed 300 m.p.h. (480 km.h.) at 17,500 ft. (5,340 m.), Service ceiling at mean weight 27,500 ft. (8,390 m.), Range with maximum fuel 1,250 miles (2,000 km.).

THE JUNKERS Ju 88D.

The Ju 88D Series were specialised long-range reconnaissance aircraft generally similar to the Ju 88A. The D-1 and D-2 were developed from the A-4 and A-5 respectively. The D-3 was a tropical version of the D-1. No dive-brake equipment was fitted, and two cameras with heating installation were mounted in the rear fuselage. Fuel could be carried in both front and rear bomb compartments. The armament for a typical Ju 88D consisted of one MG 131, two MG 81 and a twin MG 81.

NORMAL FLYING WEIGHT.—26,500 lbs. (12,030 kg.).

PERFORMANCE.—Maximum speed 300 m.p.h. (480 km.h.) at 17,500 ft. (5,340 m.), Service ceiling at mean weight 27,000 ft. (8,235 m.), Range with maximum fuel 2,200 miles (3,520 km.).

THE JUNKERS Ju 88G.

All sub-types in the G Series were night fighters developed from the Ju 88C. The G-1 was fitted with BMW 801 D or 2 radial engines, while later sub-types had Jumo 213 A or E liquid-cooled engines. The tail-unit of the Ju 88G was the same as fitted to the Ju 188 and the forward firing guns were in a ventral fairing.

The following particulars relate to the Ju 88G-7, which was distinguished by a long nose fairing which partially enclosed the radar aerial array.

CREW.—Four, consisting of pilot, two observers and radio operator.

POWER PLANT.—Two Junkers Jumo 213 E liquid-cooled engines. Fuel tankage 705 Imp. gallons. One 198-gallon drop tank could be carried.

ARMAMENT.—Four forward-firing MG 151/20 cannon (200 rounds per gun), two MG 151/20 upward-firing cannon (200 rounds per gun) and one rearward-firing 13 m/m. MG 131 (500 rounds).

WEIGHTS.—Normal loaded weight 28,900 lbs. (13,120 kg.), Maximum take-off weight 32,350 lbs. (14,690 kg.).

PERFORMANCE.—Maximum speed (without drop tank or flame-dampers) 402 m.p.h. (643 km.h.) at 29,800 ft. (9,090 m.), Maximum economical endurance (but including one hour at combat rating) 5.2 hours.

THE JUNKERS Ju 88H.

The Ju 88H was characterised by a long fuselage (about 58 ft.= 17.7 m.) resulting from the introduction of two additional bays, one forward and one aft of the main spar. Bomber, fighter and reconnaissance versions were projected but before the end of hostilities the Ju 88H was reserved for use as the lower components of composite aircraft.

THE JUNKERS Ju 88P.

The Ju 88P was a ground attack aircraft and was produced in very limited numbers. It was fitted with a large fairing housing a BK 5 cannon and the airframe was suitably reinforced.

The 75 m/m. BK 7.5 gun originally fitted was not a success and was replaced by the 50 m/m. BK 5. The gun fairing, which was jettisonable, was of sufficient size to accommodate rearward-firing twin MG 81 machine-guns in addition to the large forward-firing cannon, which was inclined downwards at a small angle to the line of flight.

The Jumo 211 J engines were protected by armour and outer wing tanks were not fitted. The all-up weight of the Ju 88P-1 was 24,400 lbs. (11,080 kg.) and the maximum speed at sea level was 244 m.p.h. (390 km.h.). Another version of the Ju 88P was fitted with BMW engines.

THE JUNKERS Ju 88S.

These bomber sub-types were fitted with either BMW 801 G or Jumo 213 A engines. As compared with the A-4, the principal external differences were the provision of a smooth glazed nose, the elimination of the "bola" and lower gun position under the fuselage and the removal of the upper nose guns.

Ju 88S-1. Two BMW 801 G radial engines with GM-1 power-boost installation. The GM-1 tank occupies the rear bomb compartment. Armed with a single rear-firing MG 131. Neither dive-brakes nor automatic pull-out gear were fitted, and there was no provision for de-icing the tail surfaces.

Ju 88S-2. Differed from the S-1 in having a large bomb-bay under the fuselage. Two MG 131 rearward-firing guns were fitted at the rear of the bomb-bay, these guns supplementing the single MG 131 of the S-1. The semi-external bomb stowage left the normal bomb bays free for increased fuel tankage.

Ju 88S-3. Two Jumo 213 A engines. Otherwise similar to the S-1. Loaded weight 23,100 lbs. (10,490 kg.). Maximum speed about 355 m.p.h. (568 km.h.) at combat rating at 20,300 ft. (6,190 m.) and with two 2,200 lb. (1,000 kg.) bombs. The endurance was 7½ hours at maximum economical and 6 hours at maximum continuous rating.

THE JUNKERS Ju 88T.

The Ju 88T was a photographic-reconnaissance type with either BMW 801 G or Jumo 213 A engines.

The Junkers Ju 88G Night Fighter which had a tail similar to that fitted to the Ju 188.

A Junkers Ju 88R Night Fighter (two BMW 801 engines).

Ju 88T-1. Generally similar to the S-1 with BMW 801 G engines. Armament comprised a single rearward-firing MG 131. Either a petrol tank or a GM 1 tank could be housed in the rear bomb-bay.

Ju 88T-3. Two Jumo 213 A engines. Maximum speed 380 m.p.h. (608 km.h.) at 20,500 ft. (6,250 m.). With GM 1 the maximum speed could be boosted to over 400 m.p.h. (640 km.h.) at about 28,000 ft. (8,540 m.).

THE JUNKERS Ju 136.

The Ju 136 was a design for a four-engined development of the Ju 86, achieved by the introduction of a new centre-section carrying two additional engines and a fixed landing-gear between the fuselage and the outer wing panels. This was purely a project, initiated in September, 1942, which never underwent subsequent development.

THE JUNKERS Ju 188A.

The Ju 188 was based on the design of the Ju 88 and was intended to replace it in some of its numerous applications. As compared with the Ju 88, the Ju 188 (all sub-types) had a redesigned nose and a wing of increased span (72 ft. 6 in. = 22.1 m.) with pointed wing-tips.

The Ju 188A, one of the most common sub-types, appeared in service later than the Ju 188E. It was fitted with two Jumo 213 A engines and carried a crew of five.
ARMAMENT.—One 20 m/m. MG 151/20 in the nose, one 20 m/m. MG 151/20 in the dorsal turret, one 13 m/m. MG 131 hand-operated dorsal gun, and one MG 131 or twin 7.9 m/m. MG 81 guns in the lower rear-firing position.
BOMB LOAD.—Maximum 6,600 lbs. (3,000 kg.). Typical loadings twenty 154-lb. (70-kg.), six 550-lb. (250-kg.), four 1,100-lb. (500-kg.) or two 2,200-lb. (1,000-kg.).
DIMENSIONS.—Span 72 ft. 2 in. (22 m.), Length 49 ft. (14.96 m.), Span of tailplane 26 ft. 3 in. (8 m.).
NORMAL LOADED WEIGHT.—32,000 lbs. (14,530 kg.).
PERFORMANCE.—Maximum speed 325 m.p.h. (420 km.h.) at 20,500 ft. (6,250 m.), Climb to 20,000 ft. (6,100 m.) 17 mins., Service ceiling 33,000 ft. (10,060 m.), Range (with 3,000 lbs. = 1,500 kg. bombs) 1,550 miles (2,480 km.).

One version of the Ju 188A was adapted for carrying two torpedoes. At sea level this aircraft had a maximum speed of 267 m.p.h. (427 km.h.).

THE JUNKERS Ju 188C.

A bomber development of the Ju 188A, but fitted with a remotely-controlled tail-turret armed with two MG 131 guns. The rear portion of the fuselage was suitably reinforced. Outer wing tanks were not fitted.

THE JUNKERS Ju 188D.

The Ju 188D was a reconnaissance version of the Ju 188A and was fitted with the same engines and armament. The maximum speed was 330 m.p.h. (528 km.h.) at 20,500 ft. (6,250 m.) and with GM 1 this could be increased to about 350 m.p.h. (560 km.h.) at 25,000—27,000 ft. (7,625—8,235 m.).

The nose of the Junkers Ju 188E showing the radar array.

THE JUNKERS Ju 188E.

Introduced into service before the Ju 188A the E sub-type was fitted with two BMW 801 D engines. The maximum speed was 315 m.p.h. (494 km.h.) at 20,000 ft. (6,100 m.) and the service ceiling 31,000 ft. (9,450 m.).

THE JUNKERS Ju 188F.

The Ju 188F was a reconnaissance version generally similar to the Ju 188D but fitted with BMW 801 D engines. With GM 1 the maximum speed was about 340 m.p.h. (544 km.h.) at 25,000—27,000 ft. (7,625—8,235 m.) and the range with maximum fuel 1,950 miles (3,120 km.).

THE JUNKERS Ju 188G.

The Ju 188G was a projected development of the Ju 188C, with internal bomb stowage in a large faired bay under the fuselage. The fuselage tankage was reduced to provide additional bomb stowage. Armament was the same as on the Ju 188C except that twin MG 131's were to be substituted for the single MG 131 in the ventral position and four MG 131's were visualised as tail armament.

The designed maximum speed was 336 m.p.h. (538 km.h.)

The Junkers Ju 88S twin-engined Bomber with hemispherical nose and no under-gun positions.

The Junkers Ju 188E Bomber (two BMW 801 D engines).

A ground attack version of the Ju 188S had a modified cockpit cover and an armoured nose. It was fitted with a BK 5 or BK 3.7 (Flak 18) gun in a fairing under the nose.

THE JUNKERS Ju 188T.

This was a photographic-reconnaissance aircraft with pressure cabin and either two Jumo 213 A or 801 TM engines. Three cameras were carried.

THE JUNKERS 8-263 (Ju 248).

The development of the Messerschmitt Me 163 was taken over in its later stages by the Junkers company, which designed aircraft of similar characteristics under the designation Ju 248. Later it was given the designation 8-263.

The fuselage of the 8-263 was slimmer and of a better streamline form than the Me 163 and a retractable tricycle landing-gear was fitted to permit the elimination of the landing skid and tail-wheel fairings. The wings of the Me 163 B suitably modified to accommodate larger "C Stoff" tanks were used, the slightly increased span being only due to the wider fuselage. The fin and rudder were standard Me 163 B components.

The power-unit, a 109.509 C rocket unit, differed from that of the Me 163B in having an auxiliary combustion chamber to give more economical cruising performance. A total of 352 gallons of "C Stoff" and 185 gallons of "T Stoff" could be carried.

The pilot's cockpit was pressurised. The armament consisted of two MK 108 cannon mounted in the wing roots.
DIMENSIONS.—Span 31 ft. 2 in. (9.5 m.), Length 26 ft. (7.9 m.), Net wing area 191.5 sq. ft. (17.8 sq. m.).
PERFORMANCE.—Maximum speed 590 m.p.h. (944 km.h.), Climb to 49,000 ft. (14,950 m.), about 3 mins., Endurance at 36,000 ft. (10,980 m.) and at 435 m.p.h. (696 km.h.) 15 mins.

THE JUNKERS Ju 252.

A transport aircraft fitted with three Jumo 211 engines, the Ju 252 was a development of the Ju 52 and the forerunner of the Ju 352. It was produced and operated only on a limited scale.

THE JUNKERS Ju 287.

Although it had not progressed beyond the prototype stage, the Ju 287 was of unusual interest because of its peculiar wing form and the fact that it was the first heavy jet-propelled bomber to fly.

The Ju 287 had wings swept forward approximately 25 degrees, the roots of the wings originating about midway between nose and tail. The crew's cabin in the nose and tail unit were similar to those of the Ju 188. The full crew would have comprised pilot, bomb-aimer/navigator and radio-operator/gunner, although the prototype was flown as a two-seater.

Ultimately the Ju 287 would have been propelled by two large turbo-jet units made by BMW or Junkers and each developing a static thrust of the order of 5,500—7,000 lbs. As these units were not ready various arrangements of four or six units were

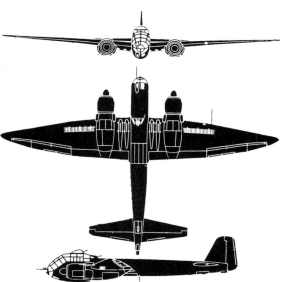

The Junkers 188E Twin-engined Bomber.

at 20,300 ft. (6,190 m.) and the range with 3,300 lbs. (1,500 kg.) of bombs was 1,490 miles (2,385 km.).

THE JUNKERS 188H.

The Ju 188H was a projected reconnaissance sub-type to have the same tail-turret and modified rear fuselage as the Ju 188C. Otherwise it was to be similar to the Ju 188D. The designed maximum speed was 328 m.p.h. (525 km.h.) at 20,300 ft. (6,190 m.) and the range 1,955 miles (3130 km.) at 250 m.p.h. (400 km.h.).

THE JUNKERS Ju 188R.

The Ju 188R was a projected night fighter version which was not produced in quantity. A fairing under the fuselage was designed to take four 20 m/m. MG 151/20 or two 30 m/m. MK 103 cannon.

THE JUNKERS Ju 188S.

The Ju 188S was a bomber with a three-man pressure cabin and was fitted with either two Jumo 213 A or BMW 801 TM engines. The nose fairing was modified as compared with the Ju 188C but the nose glazing was retained. There was a remotely-controlled tail-turret armed with twin MG 131 machine-guns and a large fairing under the bomb-bay.

The Junkers 8-263 Rocket-propelled Interceptor Monoplane (Walter 109.509 C rocket unit).

An interesting view of the Junkers Ju 287 Experimental Jet-propelled Heavy Bomber, showing the layout of the wings and tail-unit.

tried. One prototype was fitted with four Junkers Jumo 004 jet units, one under each wing and one unit on each side of the nose. Another installation consisted of four Heinkel-Hirth 011 units, all mounted under the wings, two on each side of the fuselage, and yet another of six BMW 003 A-1 units, two under each wing and one on each side of the fuselage nose.

Defensive armament was to consist of a remotely-controlled tail-turret similar to that fitted to the Ju 188C and armed with two 13 m/m. MG 131 machine-guns. The designed maximum bomb load was 9,900 lbs. (4,500 kg.).

DIMENSIONS.—Span 66 ft. (20.1 m.), Length 60 ft. (18.3 m.), Wing area 628 sq. ft. (58.3 sq. m.).

NORMAL LOADED WEIGHT.—47,500 lbs. (21,565 kg.).

PERFORMANCE.—Maximum speed at sea level 509 m.p.h. (814 km.h.), Maximum speed at 16,400 ft. (5,000 m.) 527 m.p.h. (859 km.h.), Climb to 19,680 ft. (7,000 m.) 10½ mins., Range with 8,800 lbs. (4,000 kg.) bomb load 985 miles (1,576 km.), Range with 6,600 lbs. (3,000 kg.) bomb load 1,175 miles (1,880 km.), Range with 4,400 lbs. (2,000 kg.) bomb load 1,325 miles (2,120 km.).

THE JUNKERS Ju 288.

In spite of the numerical similarity the Ju 288 was not a development of either the Ju 88 or Ju 188. It was designed as a twin-engined bomber and its later versions were larger, considerably heavier and more powerfully engined than the Ju 88.

It was first test-flown in 1940, after which it was extensively modified. Development was slow but series production was contemplated late in 1944. The Ju 288 was used operationally in very small numbers.

The following particulars relate to the Ju 288 with two Junkers Jumo 222 twenty-four-cylinder engines and arranged to carry a bomb load of 8,800 lbs. (4,000 kg.).

DIMENSIONS.—Span 60 ft. (18.3 m.), Length 52 ft. (15.8 m.), Wing area 582 sq. ft. (54 sq. m.).

WEIGHTS.—Normal loaded weight 33,850 lbs. (15,370 kg.), Maximum take-off weight 38,900 lbs. (17,660 kg.).

PERFORMANCE.—Maximum speed 410 m.p.h. (656 km.h.) at 21,000 ft. (6,405 m.), Range with maximum bomb load 2,235 miles (3,576 km.) at 345 m.p.h. (552 km.h.) at 26,300 ft. (8,020 m.), Range with maximum fuel 3,720 miles (5,950 km.) at 338 m.p.h. (541 km.h.) at 26,300 ft. (8,020 m.).

The Ju 288C, which was the final version intended for product-ion, differed in many respects from the earlier prototypes. A day bomber with a three-man pressure cabin, it was fitted with two Daimler-Benz DB 610 A/B engines. The following are the main characteristics :—

ARMAMENT.—Twin MG 131 or one MG 151 in a remotely-controlled dorsal turret, twin MG 131 or one MG 151 in a remotely-controlled ventral turret aft of the bomb-bay, one MG 151 or two MG 131 in a remotely-controlled tail-turret, and twin MG 131 or one MG 151 in a chin turret. Top and bottom periscope sights were fitted. Internal stowage for the following bomb loads three 2,200 lb. (1,000 kg.), three 1,100 lb. (500 kg.), six 550 lb. (250 kg.) or thirty 110 lb. (50 kg.).

DIMENSIONS.—Span 83 ft. 7 in. (25.5 m.), Length 59 ft. 10 in. (18.25 m.).

WEIGHT LOADED.—50,600 lbs. (22,970 kg.).

PERFORMANCE.—Maximum speed 385 m.p.h. (616 km.h.) at 23,000 ft. (7,015 m.).

The above particulars relate to the day-bomber version. In the night bomber the armament was confined to the ventral turret with twin MG 131 guns. The upper periscope sight was removed.

POWER PLANT.—Four 1,600 h.p. BMW 801 L2 fourteen-cylinder radial air-cooled engines on tubular mountings on the leading-edge of the centre-section. Normal wing fuel tankage 1,580 Imp. gallons. Maximum tankage (including fuselage tanks) 4,620 Imp. gallons.

ACCOMMODATION.—Crew's position in nose seating two side-by-side with dual controls. Then follows the radio-operator's compartment with gun turret in roof and gun blister below. The main cabin may accommodate up to 40 fully-armed troops or a varied freight load, which may include wheeled vehicles. Maximum freight load 22,000 lbs. (10,000 kg.). For freight loading there is a heavy ramp, with wheel troughs on either side of steps, in under-side of the fuselage aft of the wings. It is hinged at the forward end and is lowered and raised by jacks energised by a small auxiliary engine which also operates the winch for hauling heavy loads up the ramp. When the ramp is lowered the tail is jacked up to provide the necessary loading clearance.

ARMAMENT.—Varies considerably according to duty. The most lightly-armed transport version mounts one MG 151/20 in the dorsal turret, one MG 151/20 in the tail and two twin MG 81's in the ventral blister, one pair firing forward and the other aft. The most heavily-armed reconnaissance version carried the following armament : two MG 151/20 in the forward dorsal turret, two MG 151/20 in the rear dorsal turret, one MG 151/20 in the tail, one MG 151/20 in the forward dorsal position, one MG 131 in the rear dorsal position, two MG 151/20 side guns, and one MG 151/20 in the nose.

DIMENSIONS.—Span 138 ft. (42 m.), Length 92 ft. 6 in. (28.2 m.), Wing area 2,210 sq. ft. (205.3 sq. m.).

WEIGHTS.—Loaded weight (transport) 88,000 lbs. (39,950 kg.), Loaded weight (passenger and freight version) 90,500 lbs. (41,090 kg.), Loaded weight (reconnaissance and anti-shipping version) 100,000 lbs. (45,400 kg.).

PERFORMANCE.—Maximum speed 280 m.p.h. (448 km.h.) at 18,000 ft. (5,490 m.), Climb to 6,500 ft. (for 99,000 lbs. = 45,000 kg. take-off weight) 10 mins., Service ceiling 19,700 ft. (6,010 m.), Range at maximum economical cruising speed (with maximum fuel) 3,785 miles (6,060 km.), Range at maximum economical cruising speed (with 17,600 lbs. = 8,000 kg. freight) 2,490 miles (3,985 km.).

One Ju 288 project (G sub-type) was intended to carry a large-calibre recoil-less gun. This was to have been stowed in the bomb-bay and lowered on pivoted arms for firing. The gun calibre was 35.56 cm., the projectile weighed 1,540 lbs. (700 kg.) and the effective velocity (sum of aircraft and muzzle velocities) 1,640 ft./sec. The projectile was designed to penetrate 13.5 to 15.75 inches of armour.

THE JUNKERS Ju 290A.

The Ju 290 was originally designed as a transport and was first test-flown in 1941. Subsequently development was undertaken to enable the Ju 290 ultimately to supersede the Fw 200C for long-range over-sea anti-shipping and U-boat co-operation work. The following are the principal sub-types of the Ju 290A :—

Ju 290A-1. Four BMW 801 D engines. Transport.

Ju 290A-2. Reconnaissance version with additional fuel and oil tanks and much heavier armament.

Ju 290A-5. Another reconnaissance version. As compared with the A-3, the fuselage fuel and oil tanks were modified and the armament further increased.

Ju 290A-6. Transport based on the A-5. The fuselage fuel and oil tanks removed, also part of the armament.

Ju 290A-8. Reconnaissance aircraft with provision for carrying two Hs 293 anti-shipping glider bombs. Armament heavier than on A-5.

TYPE.—Four-engined Military Transport or Anti-shipping and Reconnaissance monoplane.

WINGS.—Low-wing cantilever monoplane. Rectangular centre-section and equally-tapering outer sections. All-metal structure believed to be generally similar to that of the Ju 90. Slotted flaps on centre-section and slotted and divided ailerons on outer-sections.

FUSELAGE.—Rectangular-section structure of all-duralumin construction with transverse bulkheads and frames, longitudinal stringers and a smooth stressed skin.

TAIL UNIT.—Cantilever monoplane type. Tailplane set at slight dihedral. Twin fins and rudders. Duralumin structure with stressed-skin covering.

LANDING GEAR.—Retractable type. Each unit, which includes twin-wheels, is raised backwards into the tails of the inboard engine nacelles. Hydraulic retraction. Fully-retractable tail-wheel.

THE JUNKERS Ju 290B.

The Ju 290B was a projected heavily-armed long-range bomber version of the Ju 290. The fuselage was strengthened as compared with the Ju 290A for a take-off weight of 109,000 lbs. (49,500 kg.) and the design of the nose was modified.

ARMAMENT.—Four MG 131 (1,300 rounds per gun) in the nose, twin MG 151/20 (1,200 rounds each) in both forward and aft dorsal turrets, twin MG 151/20 (800 rounds each) in ventral position, and four MG 131 (1,300 rounds per gun) in tail. The total weight of armament, ammunition and armour 11,100 lbs. (5,045 kg.).

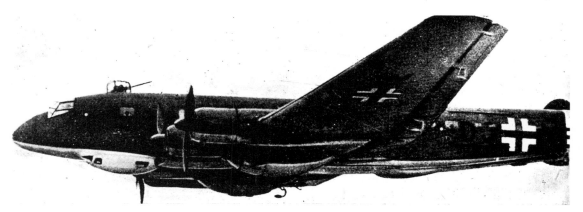

The Junkers Ju 290A Military Transport (four 1,600 h.p. BMW 801 engines).

PERFORMANCE.—Maximum speed 280 m.p.h. (448 km.h.) at 18,000 ft. (5,490 m.), Range with 10,000 lb. (4,540 kg.) bomb load and 4,000 gals. of fuel 3,500 miles (5,600 km.).

THE JUNKERS Ju 290C.

The 290C had the modified nose and strengthened fuselage of the Ju 290B but was fitted with BMW 801 E engines. There were two versions, one for long-range reconnaissance and the other for transport work. The loading-ramp was of new design and, on the reconnaissance model, incorporated a mounting for twin MG 151/20 rearward-firing guns. This version also had an additional large fuselage fuel tank as compared with the Ju 290A-5.

The armament of the Ju 290C (recce.) comprised twin MG 151/20 guns in fore and aft dorsal, tail, loading-ramp and nose positions. On the transport version the rear dorsal turret and the loading-ramp guns were eliminated.

THE JUNKERS Ju 290D.

This long-range bomber, not produced, was similar to the Ju 290C (recce.) except that the second fuselage fuel tank was removed and Hs 293 glider-bomb equipment added.

THE JUNKERS Ju 290E.

The Ju 290E was a projected night bomber based on the Ju 290C (recce.). A large bomb-bay was added under the fuselage and both dorsal turrets and the fuselage fuel and oil tanks removed.

THE JUNKERS Ju 352A.

The Ju 352 was a three-engined military transport which was developed from the Ju 252, to which it bore a superficial resemblance. The Ju 352A was the operational version.

TYPE.—Three-engined Military Transport, Paratroop-carrier, Troop-carrier and Glider-tug.

WINGS.—Low-wing cantilever monoplane. Wing built in one unit, the centre-section passing through the fuselage below the cabin floor. Centre-section attached to fuselage by four self-centering bolts. Each outer wing has a divided aileron and a slotted flap. The inboard portion of the aileron has a tab along its entire length. Half of this tab, on the starboard side, is adjustable in flight for lateral trimming.

FUSELAGE.—Of composite construction and built in units as follows, nose including crew accommodation, main fuselage (stowage space), rear fuselage, tail-cone and loading ramp. The forward fuselage is of duralumin stressed-skin construction. The main fuselage has steel tubular framework with fabric covering. The floor is built on steel girders and the wheel ways are reinforced. The rear fuselage is of duralumin stressed-skin construction and the tail-cone fairing is interchangeable with a 6-ton glider-towing attachment.

TAIL UNIT.—Cantilever monoplane type. Tailplane of symmetrical aerofoil section. Aerodynamically-balanced rudder. All control surfaces and their tabs, apart from the trim-tabs, are collectively mass-balanced. Each elevator has an outboard geared tab and an inboard spring-loaded tab.

LANDING GEAR.—Retractable type. Oleo legs retracted backwards into the engine nacelle fairing, approximately one-third of each wheel projecting from the nacelle. Wheel axles are positively supported in retracted position to take shock of belly landings. Fully-retractable tail-wheel.

POWER PLANT.—Three BMW 323 R-2 nine-cylinder radial air-cooled engines, each driving a VDM wood-blade airscrew. For take-off an auxiliary fuel system supplies 95 octane fuel in place of the normal 87 octane. Normal fuel tanks (two) with a total capacity of 640 Imp. gallons in the wings. For long ranges two 198 gallon wing tanks can be added.

ACCOMMODATION.—Crew of four comprising two pilots, flight mechanic and radio-operator/air gunner. Large cabin may be used for all types of military transport. Large loading ramp beneath fuselage. Capacity of stowage space 1,342 cu. ft.

ARMAMENT.—One dorsal turret armed with one MG 151/20 cannon. Two MG 131 guns may be installed in lateral positions.

DIMENSIONS.—Span 112 ft. (34.2 m.), Length 79 ft. 4 in. (24.2 m.).

WEIGHTS.—Weight empty 27,500 lbs. (12,500 kg.), Normal loaded weight (with 9,500 lbs.=4,320 kg. freight load) 43,000 lbs. (19,520 kg.), Maximum flying weight 43,200 lbs. (19,620 kg.).

PERFORMANCE.—Cruising speed 145-150 m.p.h. (232-240 km.h.), Range (normal fuel) 1,120 miles (1,790 km.), Range (maximum fuel) 1,860 miles (2,980 km.).

The Junkers Ju 388K-1 Bomber (two BMW 801 engines).

THE JUNKERS Ju 388J "STÖRTEBEKER."

The Ju 388, of which the J was the night fighter sub-type, was the last of the Ju 88 Series to reach the production stage. It was test-flown in 1943 and was included in the restricted production programme which was in force when hostilities ended. The Ju 388 was given the code-name "Störtebeker."

All aircraft in the J Series had pressure cabins and pointed nose fairings for the radar aerial arrays. The crew of four consisted of pilot, two observers and radio operator.

POWER PLANT.—Two BMW 801 TJ, or Jumo 213 E or Jumo 222 E/F engines. Normal fuel tankage 720 Imp. gallons. One 95 or 160 gallon drop tank could be carried.

ARMAMENT.—Two MG 151/20 (180 rounds per gun) and two MK 108 (110 rounds per gun) or MK 103 cannon in fairing under fuselage and firing forward, two MG 151/20 (200 rounds per gun) fixed and firing obliquely upward in a "Schräge Musik" mounting.

WEIGHTS.—Normal loaded weight 30,000 to 30,700 lbs. (13,650 to 13,940 kg.) according to engine installation, Maximum take-off weight 32,500 lbs. (14,760 kg.).

MAXIMUM SPEEDS.—362 m.p.h. (580 km.h.) at 40,300 ft. (12,300 m.) with BMW 801 J, 414 m.p.h. (662 km.h.) at 37,000 ft. (11,500 m.) with Jumo 222 E/F (combat rating), 402 m.p.h. (643 km.h.) at 29,600 ft. (9,000 m.) with Jumo 213E.

ENDURANCE.—Maximum economical endurance with BMW J (including one hour at combat rating) 4.45 hours at 26,300 ft. (8,020 m.).

THE JUNKERS Ju 388K.

The Ju 388K is the bomber version and was fitted with a large bulged bomb-bay under the fuselage similar to that of the Ju 88S or Ju 188S.

ARMAMENT.—Twin MG 131 in remote-control tail-turret.

POWER PLANT.—Two BMW 801 G, or Jumo 222 A/B or E/F, or Jumo 213 E engines.

WEIGHT LOADED.—31,400 to 35,200 lbs. (14,260 to 15,980 kg.) depending on engine installation.

PERFORMANCE.—(with BMW 801 G engines) Designed maximum speed 378 m.p.h. (607 km.h.) at 38,000 ft. (11,590 m.), Range 1,100 miles (1,760 km.) at 36,100 ft. (11,000 m.), Service ceiling 42,200 ft. (12,870 m.).

PERFORMANCE (with Jumo 222 A/B engines).—Designed maximum speed 394 m.p.h. (630 km.h.) at 39,400 ft. (12,000 m.), Range 1,290 miles (2,060 km.) at 26,300 ft. (8,020 m.).

PERFORMANCE (with Jumo 222 E/F engines).—Designed maximum speed 432 m.p.h. (690 km.h.) at 37,700 ft. (11,500 m.), Range 1,130 miles (1,700 km.) at 37,700 ft. (11,500 m.).

PERFORMANCE (with Jumo 213 E engines).—Designed maximum speed 368 m.p.h. (590 km.h.) at 33,400 ft. (10,200 m.), Range 1,340 miles (2,140 km.) at 30,200 ft. (9,210 m.).

THE JUNKERS Ju 388L.

The Ju 388L Series covered reconnaissance aircraft which were generally similar to the Ju 388K except that the bomb bulge was omitted. The crew consisted of pilot, observer and radio operator.

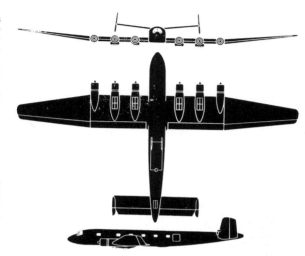

The Junkers Ju 390 Six-engined Transport.

POWER PLANT.—Two BMW 801 TJ or Jumo 213 E engines. Normal fuel tankage 866 Imp. gallons (day) or 656 Imp gallons (night). One 186 or 198 gallon drop tank could be fitted to either version.

ARMAMENT.—Twin MG 131 (600 rounds per gun) in remote-control tail-turret.

WEIGHT LOADED.—30,450 to 30,820 lbs. (13,825 to 14,000 kg.) according to engine installation.

PERFORMANCE (two BMW 801 TJ engines).—Maximum speed 383 m.p.h. (613 km.h.) at 40,300 ft. (12,290 m.), Range at maximum economical cruising speed and with drop tank 2,160 miles (3,460 km.) at 36,000 ft. (10,980 m.).

PERFORMANCE (two Jumo 213 E engines).—Maximum speed 407 m.p.h. (646 km.h.) at 29,800 ft. (9,090 m.), Range at maximum economical cruising speed and with drop tank 2,285 miles (3,660 km.) at 30,200 ft. (9,210 m.).

THE JUNKERS Ju 390.

The Ju 390 was a six-engined development of the Ju 290 with increased span and overall length. An extra panel mounting a BMW 801 E engine was introduced in each wing and a new fuselage centre section increased the length. The landing-gear was duplicated, with twin-wheel units retracting into the two inner engine nacelles on each side of the fuselage.

The Ju 390 was first test-flown in 1943. The following data relates to the transport versions :—

DIMENSIONS.—Span 165 ft. (50 m.), Length 102 ft. (31.1 m.), Wing area 2,728 sq. ft. (254.4 sq. m.).

WEIGHTS.—Loaded weight (with 22,000 lbs.=10,000 kg. useful load and 7,500 gallons of fuel) 161,000 lbs. (73,150 kg.), Loaded weight (with 48 passengers, 4,400 lbs.=2,000 kg. of freight and 6,000 gallons of fuel) 148,300 lbs. (67,420 kg.).

PERFORMANCE.—Maximum speed (transport loading) 280 m.p.h. (448 km.h.) at 18,700 ft. (5,700 m.), Maximum speed (passenger loading) 285 m.p.h. (456 km.h.) at 18,700 ft. (5,700 m.), Initial rate of climb (transport loading) 690 ft./min. (210 m./min.), Initial rate of climb (passenger loading) 788 ft./min. (240 m./min.), Range (7,500 gallons of fuel) 4,970 miles (7,950 km.) at 205 m.p.h. (328 km.h.) at 6,500 ft. (1,980 m.), Range (6,000 gallons of fuel) 4,040 miles (6,460 km.) at 217 m.p.h. (347 km.h.) at 6,500 ft. (1,980 m.).

A long-range reconnaissance version of the Ju 390 was fitted with six built-in fuselage fuel tanks. The armament was identical to that of the Ju 290C (recce.), namely, twin MG 151/20 cannon in the forward dorsal, aft dorsal, tail, ventral and nose positions.

There was also a long-range bomber version. The number of built-in fuselage fuel tanks was reduced to four, and equipment for Hs 293 radio-controlled glider bombs was added.

THE JUNKERS Ju 488.

With the object of developing a four-engined bomber with the minimum of disturbance to existing design and production arrangements, the Junkers company investigated the possibilities of fitting four engines to the basic Ju 88, Ju 188 and Ju 388. None of these developments had proceeded beyond the prototype stage at the conclusion of hostilities and it is uncertain which, if any, would have been finally adopted. It is known, however, that the designation Ju 488 was allocated to a four-engined aircraft based on the 88 Series.

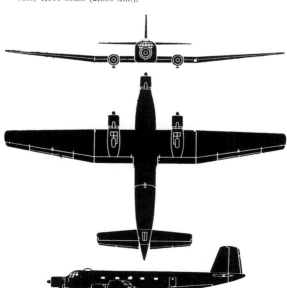

The Junkers Ju 352 Military Transport.

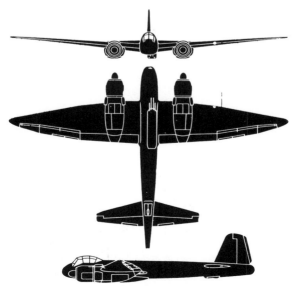

The Junkers Ju 388J twin-engined Night Fighter.

Prototypes based on the Ju 188 were in course of construction during 1944. These incorporated a fuselage lengthened by adding new-sections, Ju 188 outer wings, new inboard wing sections each mounting one extra engine a tail-unit similar to the Ju 288 but with twin fins and rudders, and a landing-gear with single-wheel retractable units under each engine nacelle. The power-plant consisted of four BMW 801 radial engines.

DIMENSIONS.—Span 100ft. (454 m.), Length 66ft. 8in. (20.3 m.), Span of tailplane 22ft. 5in. (6.8 m.).

THE JUNKERS 8-635.

The 8-635 was a project for a long-range reconnaissance air craft to be composed of two Dornier Do 335 twin-engined fighters connected side-by-side by a new centre-section At the capitulation only wind-tunnel experiments had been made and the aircraft had never flown.

Although this aircraft was based on Dornier designs, development Work was allocated to the Junkers company and consequently the development designation 8-635 was applied to this project.

Calculated performance data, based on the use of four Daimler-Benz DB 603 E engines, is given below

DIMENSIONS.—Span 90 ft (275 m), Wing area 866 sq. ft. (80.5 sq. m.).

WEIGHT.—LOADED (With 3,850 gallons of fuel) 72,600 lbs (33,000 kg.).

PERFORMANCE.—Maximum speed (combat rating) 428 mph (685 kmh.) at 23300 ft (7,100 m.), Maximum speed (With MW 50 power-boost in use) 450 m.p.h. (720 km.h.) at 21,300 ft. (6,500 m.), Initial rate of climb 1,180 ft/min. (360 m/min.), Maximum rage 4,720 miles (7,540 km.) at 21,300 ft (6,500 m).

THE JUNKERS COMPOSITE AIRCRAFT ("MISTEL").

Although the Germans had experimented with various composite aircraft combinations and had envisaged others of a more revolutionary type, the comparatively few composites which actually operated had the Ju 88H as the lower component. The upper component was either an Me 109 or Fw 190

Except on training flights no crew was carried in the lower component, all controls being operated by tho pilot of the Me 109 or Fw 190. The Ju 88 was modified to incorporate a large hollow-charge warhead and became in effect a flying-bomb for operation at short ranges. The composite was intended primarily for attacking capital ships and heavily-protected land targets.

The pilot approached his objective with a glide and, at the appropriate distance, released his aircraft from the lower com-

The Junkers/Focke-Wulf Composite Aircraft, the lower component being a Ju 88H with long fuselage.

ponent and climbed away. The Ju88 continued in a glide on its set course. During flight the engines of both upper and lower components were running.

Particularly if fuel for a long range was to be carried, the load on the landing-gear of the Ju 88 was excessive when on the ground. For this reason a third jettisonable oleo-leg was added experimentally under the fuselage of the Ju 88.

MISCELLANEOUS JUNKERS PROJECTS.

"Mistel" 5 Composite Aircraft.   A projected Junkers composite, the upper component of which was to have been an He 162 single-jet fighter. The lower component carrying the warhead and designated Ju 268 was to have been a mid-wing monoplane of wooden construction with twin fins and rudders and a jettisonable tricycle landing-gear. The power-units were to be two BMW 003 jets. The maximum speed was estimated to be over 500 m.p.h. (800 km.h.).

EF 126 Ground Attack Aircraft.   A projected Junkers single-seat mid-wing monoplane of composite construction with a single Argus 004 propulsive duct having a sea-level static thrust of 1,100 lbs. Armament: two MG 151/20 cannon. Span: 20 ft. 10 in. (6.3 m.), Wing area: 95.8 sq.ft. (8.9 sq.m.), Flying weight: 6,160 lbs. (2,800 kg.), Maximum speed: 480 m.p.h. (768 km.h.) at sea level,

EF 128 Jet-propelled Fighter.   A projected Junders single-1 seat single-jet shoulder-wing monoplane of the tail-less type with sharply swept-back wings. Stabilising fins and rudders on the trailing-edge of the wings. Jet unit in the fuselage. Armament: four MG 151/20 cannon. Span: 30 ft. 2 in. (9.2 m.), Loaded weight: 10,780 lbs. (4,900 kg.), Designed maximum speed 590 m.p.h. (944 km.h.) at 19,680 ft. (6,000 m.).

Flying-wing project.   A projected Junkers flying-wing type with stabilising fins and rudders mounted on the trailing-edge of the wings. The wing was of wood and the fuselage of metal. The power-plant was to consist of four jets mounted centrally at the rear. Retractable landing-gear. Span: 78 ft. 10 in. (24 m.), Aspect ration: 4.8, Wing area: 1,290 sq.ft. (120 sq.m.), Loaded weight: 77,000—84,000 lbs. (35,000—38,150 kg.), Designed maximum speed: 620 m.p.h. (990 km.h.), Designed range: 3,700 miles (5,920 km.).

KALKART.

This name was associated with the Ka 430 transport glider, the appearance and aerodynamic form of which had been apparently sacrificed to utility Of medium size, the Ka 430 could carry a useful load of 3,000 lbs. (1,362 kg.).

The High cantilever tapered wing was of wood construction with plywood and fabric covering and had a span of 53 ft. 9 in. (194 m.). The fuselage framework was of welded steel tubing covered with fabric over a light secondary wood structure The forward Portion of the fuselage enclosing the freight hold passenger cabin was rectangular in cross section and forward of the pilots cockpit the section was abruptly reduced, the nose

covering being formed from a single piece of plywood with a small hole giving access to the towing hook.

At the aft end of the hold the lower line of the fuselage swept up, the remainder of the fuselage being a fairly slender boom to carry the angular tailplane and high single fin and rudder. The sloping portion of the fuselage hinged down to form a loading ramp for the hold, which measured 12 ft. (3.66 m.) long, 5 ft. 10 in. (1.77 m.) high (max) and 4 ft. 2 in. (1.25 m.) wide (min.). Doors in the side of the fuselage also gave access to the hold. There were jacking points beneath the aft end of the hold to jack up the tail when additional clearance was needed for loading.

bulky freight.

The tricycle landing-gear was not jettisonable and brakes were fitted to the main wheels only. The nose wheel was self-centering but not steerable.

All controls and flight and navigation instruments in the cockpit were duplicated and provision was made for communicating with the tug.

Experiments were made with this aircraft with rocket braking, but this was not fitted as standard equipment. The solid fuel rockets were mounted under the nose with the venturis pointed forward.

MESSERSCHMITT.

MESSERSCHMITT A.G.

HEAD OFFICE AND WORKS: AUGSBERG

Technical Director: Professor Willy Messerschmitt.

Founded at Augsberg in l926 as the Bayerische Flugzeugwerke, this company was the successor to the Udet Flugzegbau G.m.b.H., of Munchen, which ceased to exist in that year It took over the former works of the Bayerische Rumpler Werke, at Augsberg

In l931, the B.F.W Company found itself in difficulties owing to the prevailing economic depression. The Messerschmitt Flugzeugbau G.m.b.H. of Bamberg was therefore founded to handle the affairs of the former Company and did so with success The firm later reverted to its former style and title, but in 1938 it was reconstituted as the Messerschmitt A.G.

The principal types of operational aircraft in production in 1944 and 1945 were the Me 109G, Me 110G, Me 410A, Me 163B and Me 262A. Among the principal primary plants in which these aircraft were being manufactured were the following:-

Me 109.

Assembly plants :   —Regensburg-Prufening (Messerschmitt), Leipzig-Mockau (Erla), Delitzsch and Wiener-Neustadt (W.N.F.).

Component plants :   —Regensburg-Prufening (Messerschmitt), Leipzig-Heiterblick (Erla) and Kottern.

Me 110.

Assembly plants :   —Gotha (Gothaer Waggonfabrik), Brunswick-Waggum (M.I.A.G.) and Furth (Bachmann, von Blumenfeld).

Component plants :   —Gotha (Gothaer Waggonfabrik), Brunswick-Neupetritor, Brunswick-Wilhelmitor and Furth (Bachmann, von Blumenfeld).

Me 410.

Assembly plants :   —Augsberg (Messerschmitt) and Oberpfaffenhofen (Dornier).

Component plants :   —Augsberg (Messerschmitt) and Neuabing.

Me 262.

Assembly plants :   —Leipheim, Lechfeld, Schwabisch-Hall, Wenzendorf and Giebelstadt.

THE MESSERSCHMITT Me 109.

The design of the 109, originally known as the Bf 109, was begun in 1934, the prototype flying in the following year. The first production version, the Bf 109B, was given an operational try-out in the Spanish Civil War. Many shortcomings were then revealed, including wing flutter and tail buffeting, and although efforts were made to eliminate these failins in subsequent models it was some time before these were eradicated. The Bf 109B had a 20 m/m. cannon firing through the airscrew boss but this cannon siezed badly and in the Bf 109C it was replaced by two machine-guns in the wings. This installation aggravated the wing flutter problem, which was eventually cured by balancing the ailerons and stiffening the leading-edge of the single-spar wing.

With the reconstitution of the company as Messerschmitt A.G. the designation of the 109 was changed to Me 109, the first production version to carry this designation being the Me 109E, with which the Luftwaffe went to war in September, 1939.

The Me 109 was the subject of continuous development throughout the war through the E, F and G Series and their many sub-types. Both the E and F Series have been fully described in previous issues of this Annual. The G Series was very extensively used in all theatres of war from late in 1942 to the final capitulation of Germany in May, 1945. The following are the main sub-types of the G Series, of which the description that follows is representative:-

Me 109G-0.   DB 601 E engine. Armament: two 7.9 m/m. MG 17 machine-guns and one or three 20 m/m. MG 151/20 cannon.

Me 109G-1.   DB 605 A engine. GM 1 (nitreous-oxide) emergency power-boost equipment optional. Pressure cabin. Armament as for G-0.

The Messerschmitt Me 109G-6 Single-seat Fighter with a wooden tail-unit.

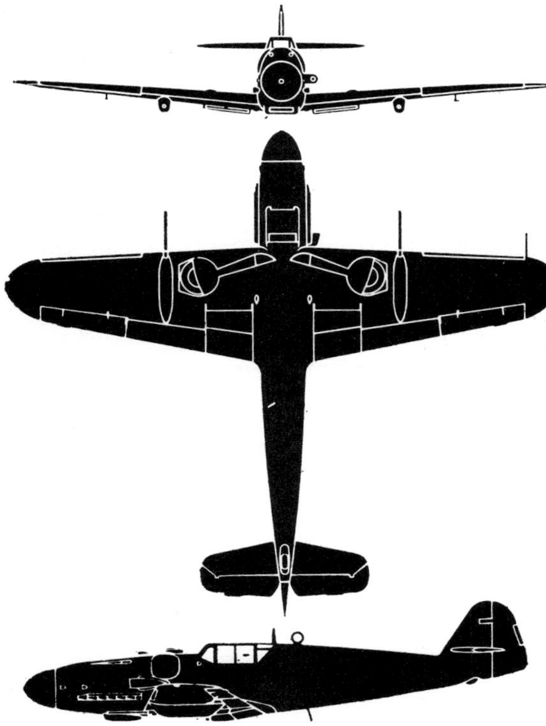

The Messerschmitt Me 109G-6 Single-seat Fighter.

Me 109G-2. Similar to G-1 but without pressure cabin and GM 1 equipment.

Me 109G-3. Similar to G-1 except for radio equipment (FuG 16Z instead of FuG 7A).

Me 109G-4. Similar to G-2 except for radio change as in G-3.

Me 109G-5. DB 605 A or D engine. Similar to G-1 except for cabin blower and the substitution of two 13 m/m. MG 131 for the 7.9 m/m. MG 17 cowling guns.

Me 109G-6. DB 605 A, AS, AM or D engine. As G-5 but no pressure cabin. The G-6/U4 had an armament of one or three 30 m/m. MK 108 cannon and two 13 m/m MG 131 machine-guns. Later production G-6 was fitted with wooden tail-unit to conserve light metal.

Me 109G-8. DB 605 A or D engine. Photographic reconnaissance model fitted with two Rb 12.5/7 or two Rb 32/7 cameras. The MK 108 engine cannon was optional.

Me 109G-10. DB 605 D engine. MK 108 engine cannon optional.

Me 109G-12. Two seat trainer. DB 605 A engine and reduced tankage.

Me 109G-14. DB 605 A, AM AS, ASB, ASM or D engine MK 108 engine cannon optional. Later production G-14 fitted with wooden tail-unit.

Type.—Single-seat monoplane used for fighting, bombing, reconnaissance and ground-attack. Also served as upper component of the Me 109/Ju 88 composite aircraft.

Wings.—Low-wing cantilever monoplane. All-metal single-spar structure, covered with flush-riveted stressed-skin metal covering. Outer wings are attached to the fuselage at three points, two on the flanges of the single spar at right angles to each other and a third at the leading-edge to transmit torsional loads. Entire trailing-edge hinged, the outer portions acting as slotted ailerons and the inner portions as camber-changing flaps. Engine coolant radiators, one on each side of fuselage, partly buried within under surface of wings. Boundary layer beneath wing is picked up in front of each radiator, led over the top and discharged through a double-surfaced flap forming a continuation of the upper wing surface. The section of the main wing flap immediately behind radiator is independent of the rest of the landing flap and is interconnected with the upper flap, which normally moves up when the lower section is depressed, thereby controlling air flow through the radiator and preventing any change in lift. This flap movement is controlled thermostatically but has only two positions. When the main flaps are lowered for landing the upper radiator-flap drops, with the lower one moving progressively ahead of its at a greater angle, thereby maintaining the cooling air flow. Ailerons have external mass-balances. Handley page auto-slots on outer position of leading edges. Attachment points for underslung guns or 21 cm. rocket projectile tubes outboard of wheel wells.

Fuselage.—Oval section light metal monocoque. Made in two halves with longitudinal joints top and bottom. Each half is made up of a number of longitudinal stringers and a series of vertical panels. Every other panel has both its edges flanged to form "Z"-frames and these frames are holed to let the stringers pass through. The flanged panels have their edges "joggled" so that the alternate plain panels may be flush-riveted to give a completely smooth outer surface. The longitudinals have a single row or rivets to the outer skin only. Each half of the fuselage is butt-jointed top and bottom to a double-width longitudinal.

Tail Unit.—Cantilever monoplane type. Balanced rudder and elevators. Normal structure had metal framework with metal-covered fixed surfaces and fabric-covered movable surfaces but various sub-types, notably the G-6 and G-14, were fitted towards the end of the war with wooden tail-units to conserve light metal.

Landing Gear.—Retractable type with narrow track. Wheels raised upwards and outwards by hydraulic jacks. Auxiliary manual raising gear. Hydraulic wheel brakes. Semi-retractable tail-wheel often locked in down position.

Power Plant.—One Daimler-Benz DB 605 A, AS, ASB, AM ASM or D twelve-cylinder inverted Vee liquid-cooled engine on two cantilever magnesium-alloy bearers attached to the fuselage at four points. MW 50 or GM 1 power-boosting equipment, depending on sub-type engine. VDM electrically-operated constant-speed airscrew 9 ft. 10 in. in diameter. Ducted coolant radiators under wings (see "Wings.") Fuel (88 Imp. gallons=400 litres) in a rubber cell in a plywood box behind and under the pilot's seat. An auxiliary drop tank (66 Imp. gallons) may be carried under fuselage. Special long-range variant may have a 66 gallon drop tank under each wing. Oil tank and cooler beneath engine cowling. Water-header tank under reduction-gear housing. Large ramming air-intake scoop on port side of cowling may be fitted with filter for tropical use.

Accommodation.—enclosed cockpit over wing. Cockpit hood hinges to starboard and has sliding panels in sides and roof. Some sub-types have pressurised cockpit in which the fireproof bulkhead, floor and slide walls have been made air-tight. A sloping plate of armour completes the enclosure. Pilot has bullet resisting windscreen and back protection.

Armament.—Typical armament consists of two 13 m/m. MG 131 machine-guns (300 rounds each) in the top cowling and synchronised to fire through the airscrew; one 20 m/m. MG 151/20 cannon (200 rounds) in the engine Vee and firing through the airscrew boss; and two 20 m/m. MG 151/20 cannon (optional), each with 120 rounds, mounted under the outer wings. Revi C12C reflector gun-sight. One 250-kg., four 50 or 70-kg., or ninety-six 2-kg. bombs may be carried under the fuselage. Two 21 c/m. rocket mortar tubes, adapted from the land-service type, are alternatives to the wing guns.

Dimensions.—Span 32ft. 6½in (9.9m.), Length 29 ft 4 in. (8.9 m.), Height (one airscrew blade vertical—tail down) 12 ft. (3.4 m.), Wing area 173 sq.ft. (16.2 sq.m.).

Weights.—Normal loaded weight varies from 7,000 to 7,700 lbs. (3,178 to 3,496 kg.), Maximum permissable flying weight also varies up to 8,100 lbs. (3,678 kg.).

Performance.—(the following figures are for the fastest sub-type (G-10) without wing armament and with DB 605 D engine and MW 50 power boost equipment).—Maximum speed at sea level 344 m.p.h. (550 km.h.), Maximum speed at 24,250 ft. (7,600 m.) 428 m.p.h. (685 km.h.), Climb to 20,000 ft. (6,100 m.) 6 mins., Range 350 miles (569 km.), Endurance 55 mins.

THE MESSERSCHMITT Me 109H.

The Me 109H was a long-span high-altitude development of the Me 109 which did not go into service. The span was increased by the incorporation of a centre-section between the outer wings.

THE MESSERSCHMITT Me 109K.

This development of the Me 109 was essentially similar to the 109G but was fitted as standard with the DB 605 D engine and incorporated minor structural differences. Sub-types included the following:-

Me 109K-4. DB 605 D engine and MW 50 emergency power-boost equipment. The take-off weight was 7,400 lbs. (3,360 kg.). The maximum speed was 440 m.p.h. (704 km.h.) at 24,600 ft. (7,500 m.), the range 365 miles (584 km.) and endurance 50 minutes.

Me 109K-6. DB 605 D engine and MW 50. Maximum armament consisted of two 13 m/m. MG 131 cowling guns, one 30 m/m. MK 108 engine cannon and two 30 m/m. high-velocity Mk 103 cannon under the wings. The take-off weight was 7,920 lbs. (3,596 kg.). Maximum speed 440 m.p.h. (704 km.h.) at 19,700 ft. (6,000 m.).

Me 109K-14. DB 605 L engine and MW 40 power-boost equipment. This model did not go into service. A speed of 455 m.p.h. (728 km.h.) at 37,750 ft. (11,515m.) with an armament of one MK 108 cannon and two MG 131 machine-guns was claimed.

THE MESSERSCHMITT Me 110G.

The 110 was the first twin-engined military aeroplane designed by Prof. Willy Messerschmitt, the original project being drawn up in 1936. The prototype first flew in 1938, too late for the 110 to participate in the Spanish war. It first went into action in Poland on September 1, 1939

The Me 110 was in continuous use throughout the European War and was developed through six series from B to G. The Me 110G was used fairly extensively as a light bomber/attack aircraft and night fighter from early 1943 until the capitulation. Its production was actually increased in the later stages of the war when the short-comings of its intended successors—the Me 210 and 410—became apparent.

The following details distinguish various sub-types in the G Series:—

Me 110G-0. Heavy fighter or bomber. Armament: two 20 m/m. MG FF (Oerlikon) cannon, four 7.9 m/m. MG 17 and one 7.9 MG 15 machine-gun.

Me 110G-2. Heavy fighter or bomber. Armament: two or four 20 m/m. MG 151/20 cannon, four 7.9 m/m. MG 17 and twin MG 81 machine-guns

Me 110G-2/R1. Heavy fighter. Armament: one 37 m/m. Flak 18 cannon with 72 rounds, four 7.9 m/m. MG 17 and twin MG 81 machine-guns.

Me 110G-2/R3. Similar to G-2/R1 except fitted with GM 1 (nitreous-oxide) power-boost equipment.

Me 110G-2/R4. Heavy fighter. Armament: similar to G-2/R1 except the four MG 17 guns replaced by two 30 m/m. MK 108 cannon.

Me 110G-2/R5. Similar to G-2/R4 except fitted with GM 1 power boost system.

Me 110G-3. Long-range Reconnaissance aircraft. Armament same as G-2. Fitted with one Rb. 50/30 and one Rb 75/30 cameras.

Me 110G-3/R3. Long-range Reconnaissance aircraft. Armament same as G-2/R4.

Me 110G-4. Night fighter. Armament: two 20 m/m. MG 151/20 cannon, four 7.9 m/m. MG 17 and twin 7.9 m/m. MG 81 machine guns.

Me 110G-4/U7. Night fighter. Same armament as G-4. Fitted with GM-1.

Me 110G-4/U8. Same as G-4/U7 but with extra tankage instead of GM 1.

Me 110G-4/R3. Night fighter. Armament: two 30 m/m. MK 108 cannon, two 20 m/m. MG 151/20 cannon and twin 7.9 m/m. MG81 machine-guns.

Me 110G-4/R6. Same as G-4/R3 but fitted with GM 1.

Me 110G-4/R7. Same as G-4/R6 but with extra tankage instead of GM 1.

Type.—Twin-engined Day and Night Fighter, Figher-Bomber Reconnaissance and Ground Attack monoplane.

Wings.—Low-wing cantilever monoplane. Wing in two sections, each attached directly to fuselage. Each wing section is tapered throughout its length and has small squared tip. Aspect ration: 7.3 : 1. Ration of root thickness to chord is 0.185. Structure consists of single spar at 39% of chord from leading-edge, former ribs at 10 in. (25.4 cm.) intervals except where nacelle and landing gear gap occurs, and lateral stringers spaced 12 ins. (30.5 cm.) apart, the whole covered with a stressed-metal skin. Wings are attached to the fuselage at three points,—at leading-edge and at top and bottom booms of main spar. Hydraulically-operated slotted flaps (20% of the chord) and slotted ailerons with external mass-balance weights. Landing flaps may be lowered at 250 km.h. (155.25 m.p.h.). The ailerons droop when the flaps are lowered. Flap and tail trimming fear are automatically interconnected. Handley Page automatic slots on leading-edge opposite ailerons.

Fuselage.—Oval all-metal stressed-skin structure in two portions. The construction is similar to that used in the Me 109 (which see).

Tail Unit.—Cantilever monoplane with fins and rudders at extremities. All-metal framework with metal-covered fixed surfaces and fabric-covered control surfaces. Trimming-tabs in elevators and rudders.

Landing Gear.—Retractable type. Wheels are toed-out and retract backwards into tails of engine nacelles. Hinged doors close aperature when wheels are raised. Hydraulic retraction. Fixed tail-wheel.

Power Plant.—Two Daimler-Benz DB 605 B twelve-cylinder inverted Vee liquid-cooled engines, each rated at 1,350 h.p. at 5,700 m. (18,700 ft.) and with 1,500 h.p. available for take-off, on cantilever mountings attached to wing spars. Radiators (50/50 glycol/water) outboard of the nacelles forward of the flaps. They extend upwards into the depth of the wing are are ducted with electrically-operated exit flaps. Oil coolers under noses of nacelles, with manually-operated exit flaps. VDM three-bladed contollable-pitch full-feathering airscrews. Four fuel tanks, two on each side of fuselage fore and aft of the wing spar. Normal fuel capacity 1,270 litres (280 Imp. gallons). There is provision for jettisonable streamline tanks outboard of the nacelles. Oil tank behind each engine holds 43 litres (9.5 Imp. gallons). GM 1 installation when carried is in the fuselage.

Accommodation.—Pilot's cockpit forward of leading-edge, rear gunner over trailing-edge, beneath continuous transparent hooding. Frontal, rear and floor armour.

Armament.—Many different armament schemes have been used. A typical Me 110G night-fighter armament had two 30 m/m. MG 108, and two 20 m/m. MG151/20 cannon in nose of fuselage and firing forward; two 20 m/m. MG FF fixed cannon firing obliquely upward from the rear cockpit and twin 7.9 m/m. MG 81 machine-guns on a flexible mounting and firing aft. For other armament installations see introduction. Four 21 c/m. rocket tubes carried under outer wings for attacking daylight bomber formations. Two bomb-carriers could be fitted under fuselage. A typical load for Me 110 bomber was two 500 kg. (1,100 lbs.) bombs.

Dimensions.—Span 53 ft. 4 in. (16.2 m.), Length 40 ft. 4 in. (12.3 m.). Height 13 ft. 1¼ in. (3.9 m.), Wing area 413 sq. ft. (37.17 sq. m.).

Weights.—Weights varied greatly according to sub-type and equipment. The G-2 with tropical equipment and one 1,000-kg. and one 500-kg. bombs had a flying weight of 22,100 lbs. (10,045 kg.). The empty weight was 11,220 lbs. (5,100 kg.).

Performance.—A typical Me 110G night fighter had the following performance:—Maximum speed at 21,000 ft. (6,404 m.) 340 m.p.h. (544 k.m.h.), Climb to 18,000 ft. (5,490 m.) 8 mins., Range with maximum fuel 1,300 miles (2,080 km.).

THE MESSERSCHMITT Me 163B "KOMET."

The Me 163 was an ultra short-range single-seat tail-less Interceptor Fighter monoplane driven by a rocket propulsion unit. The actual duration of the aircraft under power was only some 8 to 10 minutes, but this could be extended by intermittent periods of gliding. It had a phenomenal rate of climb and a very high driven speed, but its maximum duration was short.

The operational version was the Me 163B-1, which was in service in the defence of the Reich early in 1945. It was developed from the Me 163A, an earlier training version.

Type.—Single-seat Interceptor (developed for the defence of specific targets).

Wings.—Mid-wing cantilever monoplane. Sharply swept-back wings with a marked wash-out of incidence towards the tips. Wooden construction with an 8 m/m. plywood skin covered with doped fabric. The built-up main spar is of laminated wood and is 13 in. deep at the root. A leading-edge slot over 7 ft. long terminated about 12 in. from the wing tip. Lateral and longidutinal control by differentially-operated surfaces which serve the dual function of elevators and ailerons. These "elevons" of composite construction, are mounted in the normal aileron position and inboard of them are large fabric-covered trimming surfaces operated by a screw-jack. Simple split flaps are fitted in the undersurface of the wings forward of the trimming surfaces.

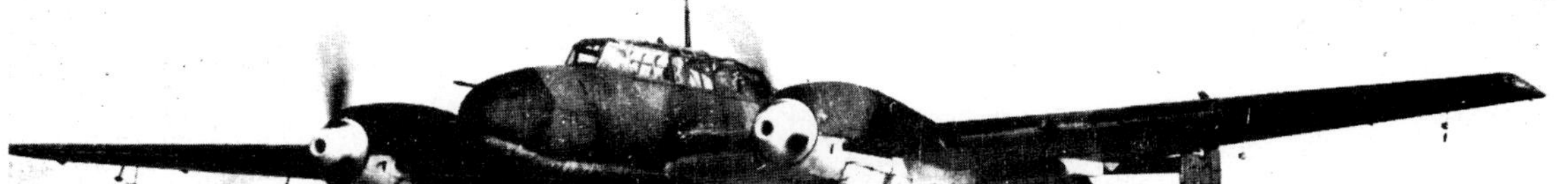

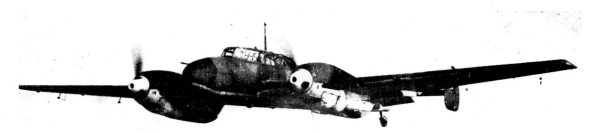

The Messerschmitt Me 110G Twin-engined Fighter (two Daimler-Benz DB 605 engines).

FUSELAGE.—Short symmetrical fuselage of all-metal construction. It is made in halves, the rear half containing the rocket unit being detachable.

TAIL UNIT.—Single vertical fin and rudder but no horizontal tailplane. The rudder is aerodynamically-balanced and is fitted with a plate tab.

LANDING GEAR.—The aircraft normally takes-off under its own power on a jettisonable two-wheel chassis. At the time of take-off, a retractable landing skid is extended. When the skid is retracted the wheels are automatically dropped. A castoring tail-wheel is faired into the lower portion of the fin.

POWER PLANT.—One Walter 109.509 bi-fuel liquid-rocket unit in the fuselage behind the pilot. The unit is just over 7 ft. long and is supplied ready for mounting. It consists of two main assemblies. The forward assembly consists of a housing for the turbine ; two worm-type pumps for delivering the fuel ; a central unit ; pressure-reducing valve ; and an electric starter motor. A small cylindrical unit attached to the forward housing produced steam to drive the turbine by the action of a solid catalyst on the hydrogen-peroxide ("T-Stoff"). The second assembly consists of the combustion chamber unit. The fuels used are concentrated hydrogen-peroxide ("T-Stoff") and a solution of hydrazine-hydrate in methanol ("C-Stoff"). The "T-Stoff" tank holds about 226 gallons and the "C-Stoff" tank about 110 gallons.

ACCOMMODATION.—Pilot's cockpit in front of wings. A mechanical jettisonable hinged Plexiglas moulding forms the cockpit cover. The main instrument panel is hinged to give access to equipment housed in the armoured nose cone. The pilot's seat is of conventional design.

ARMAMENT.—Two 30 m/m. MK 108 guns are normally fitted, one in each wing root. The ammunition, 60 rounds per gun, is carried in two boxes under a detachable fairing in the fuselage.

DIMENSIONS.—Span 30 ft. 7 in. (9.3 m.), Length 19 ft. 5 in. (5.9 m.), Net wing area 186 sq. ft. (17.3 sq. m.).

NORMAL TAKE-OFF WEIGHT.—Approximately 9,500 lbs. (4,313 kg.).

PERFORMANCE.—Maximum speed approximately 550 m.p.h. (880 km.h.) at 20,000 ft. (6,100 m.) and above, Climb to 30,000 ft. (9,150 m.) 2.6 mins.

THE MESSERSCHMITT Me 163C.

The Me 163C was a development of the 163B. It was slightly larger and was fitted with a Walter 109.509 C rocket unit with a smaller auxiliary cruising jet located immediately below the main jet in the tail. The total thrust was thus 3,740+660 lbs. and the power endurance was increased to 12 minutes.

The pressure cabin with blister-type canopy was fitted. The step in the forward "belly" which housed the retractable landing skid was not so pronounced as on the Me 163B.

The armament consisted of two 30 m/m. MK 108 cannon mounted in the nose above the centre-line.

The Me 163C was almost ready for delivery to Luftwaffe squadrons at the time of the German surrender.

DIMENSIONS.—Span 32 ft. 2 ins. (9.8 m.), Length 23 ft. 1 in. (7 m.), Net wing area 197 sq. ft. (18.3 sq. m.).

NORMAL TAKE-OFF WEIGHT.—11,280 lbs. (5,120 kg.).

PERFORMANCE.—Maximum speed 590 m.p.h. (944 km.h.) between 13,120 ft. (4,000 m.) and 39,360 ft. (12,000 m.), Ceiling 52,500 ft. (16,000 m.).

THE MESSERSCHMITT Me 209.

The Me 209 was an experimental development of the Me 109. It was fitted with a Daimler-Benz DB 603 engine and had an inwardly-retracting landing-gear. It was not produced in quantity and was never used operationally.

THE MESSERSCHMITT Me 210.

The Me 210 fighter dive-bomber, which first appeared in service early in 1942, was eventually replaced by the Me 410. It was originally powered with two Daimler-Benz DB 601 F engines (A Series). The later C Series was fitted with two DB 605 B engines. The Me 210 was described in previous editions of this Annual.

THE MESSERSCHMITT Me 261.

The Me 261 was one of the Messerschmitt company's contributions to the 1942 Bomber Programme but it was produced in prototype form only. In general appearance it resembled a scaled-up Me 110.

The roots of the tapered wings were almost as deep as the fuselage and the two Daimler-Benz DB 606 or 610 "double" engines were mounted in nacelles which were nearly as long as the fuselage nose. The single-wheel landing-gear units retracted backwards, the wheels turning through 90° to lie flat in the underside of the wings. The tail-unit was of the twin-ruddered type.

DIMENSIONS.—Span 88 ft. (26.87 m.), Length 54 ft. 8 in. (16.68 m.), Height 15 ft. 6 in. (4.72 m.).

THE MESSERSCHMITT Me 262A.

Designed in 1938, the Me 262 was first flown in 1940 with a Junkers Jumo 211 engine. The airframe proved satisfactory and in 1942 the V-1 and V-2 prototypes (V= prototype) flew with two Jumo 004 A turbo-jet engines. Only limited interest was then displayed by the Reichsluftministerium. The first prototypes had a conventional landing-gear but a tricycle gear was eventually fitted.

In 1943 the V-6 appeared with two Jumo 004 B engines. The V-7 had an experimental pressure cabin. In 1944 the V-9 was completed, and this was the forerunner of the production Me 262A model.

The Me 262A-1 was regarded as a Fighter (armament four 30 m/m. MK 108 guns), and the A-2 as a Bomber (two MK 108 guns), although some A-1's were used for bombing and reconnaissance. A trainer version and a night fighter under development were provided with a crew of two.

TYPE.—Twin-jet Fighter, Fighter-Bomber, Ground Attack or Reconnaissance monoplane.

WINGS.—Low-wing cantilever monoplane. One-piece wing fitted into a recess in the underside of the fuselage. Centre portions between the fuselage and jet nacelles have swept-back leading-edge and swept-forward trailing-edge. Outer portions tapered and swept-back and have square-cut tips. All-metal structure with single built-up I-section main spar in two halves and smooth flush-riveted stressed skin. Detachable wing tips. Frise type ailerons in two sections on each wing. Slotted flaps inboard of ailerons have maximum extension of 60° and a backward movement of about 5 inches. Full-span automatic leading-edge slots.

FUSELAGE.—All-metal semi-monocoque structure of near triangular section with rounded corners, the wing passing through the wide base. Built in four sections : nose cone ; centre-section including cockpit ; rear fuselage and tail section. The nose cone is of steel construction and houses guns and ammunition.

The Messerschmitt Me 163B Rocket-propelled Interceptor (Walter 109-509 liquid-rocket unit.)

The Messerschmitt Me 261 Experimental Twin-engined Bomber (two Daimler-Benz DB 610 engines).

TAIL UNIT.—Cantilever monoplane type. Tailplane mounted half-way up the fin. Rudder and elevators are mass-balanced. A geared tab is fitted to the rudder and is also used for trimming. Trim-tabs in elevators.

LANDING GEAR.—Retractable tricycle type. Main wheels raised inwardly into underside of wings and nose wheel backwards into fuselage. Hydraulic retraction. Hydraulic brakes on all wheels.

POWER PLANT.—Two Junkers Jumo 004 B eight-stage axial-flow gas turbine units in nacelles slung one under each wing. Starting is by a small Riedel two-stroke motor built into each jet unit. Fuel used is J-2 diesel oil. Four fuel tanks in fuselage, two of 198 gallons, one of 38 gallons and one of 132 gallons capacity.

ACCOMMODATION.—Pilot's cockpit over trailing-edge of wing. Sideways-hingeing cockpit canopy. Pilot protected by 15 m/m. armour plate front and rear and by a 90 m/m. bullet-resisting windscreen. In two-seater versions the wireless-operator sits behind the pilot and faces forwards.

ARMAMENT.—Four fixed 30 m/m. MK 108 cannon grouped in the nose and aimed to converge at 400-500 yards. Upper guns have 100 rounds per gun and lower guns 80 rounds per gun. Two external bomb-carriers under the fuselage. Bomb load may consist of either two 250-kg. or one 500-kg. bomb. Drop tanks can be fitted on bomb-carriers.

DIMENSIONS.—Span 41 ft. (12.5 m.), Length 34 ft. 9½ in. (10.6 m.), Height 12 ft. 7 in. (3.8 m.), Wing area 234 sq. ft. (21.7 sq. m.).

WEIGHTS.—Me 262A-1 Fighter, with 522 gallons of fuel and full ammunition, has a take-off weight of 15,500 lbs. (7,045 kg.). Me 262A-2 Bomber, with 528 gallons of fuel, two guns and 160 rounds of ammunition and two 250 kg. bombs, has a take-off weight of 15,400 lbs. (7,000 kg.).

PERFORMANCE (Me 262A-1 Fighter).—Maximum speed about 525 m.p.h. (840 km.h.) at 22,960 ft. (7,000 m.), Climb to 26,240 ft. (8,000 m.) 11 mins., Service ceiling 39,360 ft. (12,000 m.), Take-off run 1,090 yards (1,000 m.), or 655 yards (600 m.) with two auxiliary take-off rockets each with a thrust of 1,100 lbs. (500 kg.).

THE MESSERSCHMITT Me 264.

The Me 264 was designed for bombing and long-range reconnaissance duties and first flew in December, 1942. The prototype

was fitted with four Junkers Jumo 211 engines, but BMW 801 or Jumo 213 were provided for as alternative power-units. Two supplementary BMW 003 turbo-jet units, one under each wing, were also visualised for bursts of high speed.

This aeroplane was evolved with the intention of trying to bomb New York with a bomb load of 4,000 lbs. The attainment of its maximum range was to be made at the expense of armament and other items.

The wings, of exceptionally high aspect ratio, had a backswept leading-edge and straight trailing-edge. The landing-gear was of the tricycle type. Each main oleo leg had a supplementary wheel for take-off with full load and this wheel was jettisoned when the landing-gear was retracted.

Various experiments were carried out with armament, and either one or two dorsal turrets and one ventral turret, as well as beam guns, could be fitted.

DIMENSIONS.—Span 141 ft. (43 m.), Length 69 ft. 9 in. (21.3 m.), Height 14 ft. (4.28 m.).

THE MESSERSCHMITT Me 309.

The Me 309 was an experimental single-seat fighter with a Daimler-Benz DB 603 or Junkers Jumo 213 liquid-cooled engine and tricycle landing-gear.

The armament projected for this model consisted of two 13 m/m. MG 131 cowling guns, one 30 m/m. MK 103 or MK 108 engine cannon, and two 20 m/m. MG 151/20 cannon (inner) and two 13 m/m. MG 131 machine-guns (outer) side-by-side in the wing roots ; all except the engine cannon being synchronised to fire through the airscrew.

The tricycle landing-gear consisted of two main wheels which were raised inwardly and a nose wheel which, on being raised backwards, turned through 90° to lie flat in the nose compartment beneath the engine crankcase.

The Me 309 did not advance beyond the experimental stage.

DIMENSIONS.—Span 36 ft. (11 m.), Length 31 ft. (9.46 m.).

The Messerschmitt Me 262A jet-propelled Single-seat Fighter (two Junkers Jumo 004 jet units.)

The Messerschmitt Me 264 Experimental Long-range Bomber and Reconnaissance Monoplane (four Junkers Jumo 211 engines).

THE MESSERSCHMITT Me 321.

The forerunner of the Me 323, the Me 321 was a large transport glider which was assisted at take-off by rockets under the wings and was towed by a team of three Me 110 twin-engined aircraft. The maximum payload was 21 long tons (21,380 kg.).

THE MESSERSCHMITT Me 323

The Me 323 was a powered development of the Me 321 transport glider. The Gnôme-Rhône 14N radial engine, which was in production in occupied France, was chosen to power this aircraft so as not to interfere with the production of German engines for operational aircraft. The complete engine nacelles were the same as those designed for the Bloch 175 twin-engined military monoplane which was in production before the complete occupation of France in November, 1942. After the abolition of the line of demarcation production of these nacelles was continued by the S.N.C.A.S.O. for installation in the 323.

The latest Series was the Me 323D. The Me 323D-1 and D-6 had metal variable-pitch airscrews. The D-2 had wooden fixed-pitch airscrews.

Type.—Six-engined transport.

Wings.—High-wing semi-cantilever monoplane. Wide-span centre-section, supporting the six engines, is braced by a single strut on each side and tapers in chord and thickness, the upper surface being flat. The outer cantilever sections continue the taper but are set at a dihedral angle. Structure comprises a single rectangular girder spar built up of four steel tube members connected by N-braces, wooden former ribs and plywood and fabric covering. The centre-section is entirely plywood-covered, but the outer sections have plywood over the leading-edge and back to the spar, the remainder being fabric-covered. The entire trailing-edge is hinged, the outer portions acting as ailerons and the inner sections as flaps. Flaps and ailerons carried on steel tube outriggers projecting from the main spar. The ailerons, each in two sections, have combined servo and trim-tabs, movement being assisted by an electric servo-motor in each wing.

Fuselage.—Rectangular framework of welded steel tubing covered with fabric over a secondary wood fairing structure. The main floor in the forward portion of the fuselage is supported on substantial cross girders.

Tail Unit.—Braced monoplane type. All wood structure. The entire unit and the portion of the fuselage to which it is attached is hinged and is operated hydraulically to give a tail incidence change of from +2½ to — 5 degrees.

Landing Gear.—Multi-wheel type comprising ten wheels and designed to overcome ground obstacles like a caterpillar track, all mounted in tandem alongside the lower edge of the fuselage and enclosed in elongated paddle-box type fairings. Wheels attached to girders which are sprung by coil springs, and the disposition of the landing-gear is such that the aircraft remains in a horizontal position irrespective of the loading. When the centre of gravity is correctly placed the aircraft can easily be made to rock about the rear pair of wheels. Six main wheels fitted with pneumatic brakes.

Power Plant.—Six Gnôme-Rhône 14N 48/49 fourteen-cylinder radial air-cooled engines, each rated at 990 h.p. at 12,200 ft. (3,720 m.), in the leading-edge of centre-section. Long-chord cowlings. Variable-pitch metal or fixed pitch wooden airscrews. Port engines L.H. and starboard engines R.H. tractors. Some models were intended to be powered with BMW radial engines. Six self-sealing fuel tanks in wing on each side of fuselage. Total normal fuel capacity (12×197 Imp. gallons), 2,364 Imp. gallons (10,740 litres). Some versions had two 200 Imp. gallon tanks installed in the back of the freight compartment. Engineers' positions within leading-edge of wing-roots, each engineer controlling the three engines on his side of the fuselage. Provision under wings outboard of the outer engines for four rockets, fired electrically by the pilot, to assist take-off.

Accommodation.—Provision for crew of five, comprising two pilots, two flight engineers and one radio operator. Armoured pilots' compartment seating two side-by-side with dual controls in front of the leading-edge of the wing and above the main fuselage structure. Radio operator's cabin inside the main spar on the portside. Engineers' cabins in leading-edge of wing, one on each side of the fuselage. Main hold, 36 ft. long, 10 ft. 3 in. wide and 11 ft. high, occupies the full cross section of the body. Cubic capacity of freight hold

3,530 cu. ft. Access to hold is through the nose of the fuselage which is split vertically to form two outwardly-hingeing doors 11 ft. high. Loading ramps for vehicles and other heavy freight carried in the aircraft. Access to the fuselage may also be had through a door in each side of the main compartment. The makers claim that as alternative loads to two motor trucks, an 88 m/m. flak gun with full equipment ; 8,700 loaves of bread ; fifty-two 250-litre drums of fuel ; or 130 men can be carried. As an ambulance the Me 323 can accommodate 60 stretcher cases.

Armament.—The normal armament scheme provides for five 13 m/m. MG 131 machine-guns, but this may be appreciably increased.

Dimensions.—Span 55.2 m. (181 ft.), Length 28.46 m. (93 ft. 4 in.), Wing area 300 sq. m. (3,230 sq. ft.).

Weights.—Weight empty 61,700 lbs. (28,010 kg.), Crew (five) 1,100 lbs. (500 kg.), Two additional gunners and ammunition 880 lbs. (400 kg.), Fuel 8,800 lbs. (4,000 kg.), Oil 1,100 lbs. (500 kg.), Freight load 21,500 lbs. (9,760 kg.), Weight loaded 99,000 lbs. (45,000 kg.).

Performance (at take-off weight of 96,000 lbs.=43,600 kg.)—Speed at sea level 136 m.p.h. (218 km.h.), Speed at 5,000 ft. (1,525 m.) 129 m.p.h. (206 km.h.) Speed at 10,000 ft. (3,050 m.) 110 m.p.h. (176 km.h.), Rate of climb at sea level 710 ft./min. (216 m./min.), Rate of climb at 10,000 ft. (3,050 m.) 236 ft./min. (72 m./min.).

THE MESSERSCHMITT Me 328.

The Me 328 represented an attempt to produce a cheap and high-performance fighter and ground attack aircraft. The development of this low-wing monoplane, constructed largely of wood, was entrusted to Jacobs Schweyer, glider manufacturers, who began their experimental programme in 1943.

After the 328A sub-type had successfully passed static destruction tests, the Me 328B was completed for flying trials as a glider. In June, 1944, a few prototypes of the powered version of the B sub-type were built. These were fitted with two Argus As 014 propulsive ducts slung beneath the wing. Considerable difficulty arose from vibrations initiated by the pulsation of these "flying-bomb" units, and this project had finally to be abandoned.

A version to be powered by a single Junkers Jumo 004 B-2 turbo-jet unit and designated the Me 328C was foreseen but the project was abandoned soon after its inception.

THE MESSERSCHMITT Me 410A.

The Me 410 was a development of the Me 210, from which it differs mainly in being fitted with Daimler-Benz DB 603 instead of the DB 601 or DB 605 engines.

The main sub-types of the Me 410A are :—

Me 410A-1. High-performance bomber. Armament : two 7.9 m/m. MG 17 machine-guns and two 20 m/m. MG 151/20 cannon in the nose and two 13 m/m. MG 131 machine-guns in barbettes on the sides of the fuselage aft of the wings. Normal bomb load : 500 kg. in bay under nose of fuselage.

Me 410A-1/U2. Fighter conversion of the A-1. In place of bomb load two further 20 m/m. MG 151/20 or one 50 m/m. BK 5 cannon fitted in bomb bay.

Me 410A-3. Reconnaissance model with increased range. Camera equipment carried in bomb-bay.

Type.—Twin-engined Fighter, Fighter Bomber, Reconnaissance or Ground Attack monoplane.

Wings.—Low-wing cantilever monoplane. Wing in three main sections comprising a one-piece centre-section and two tapering outer sections with detachable semi-circular tips. Structure comprises a single "I"-section spar, a secondary false spar carrying the aileron and flap hinges and control brackets, pressed sheet former ribs with narrow turned-over flanges, and a series of lateral top-hat section stringers to which the outer stressed skin is flush-

A view of the Messerschmitt Me 323 Transport (six Gnôme-Rhône 14N engines).

The Messerschmitt Me 323 Transport.

The Messerschmitt Me 410A-3 Reconnaissance Monoplane (two Daimler Benz-DB 603 engines).

riveted. Leading-edge out to slots reinforced by large-diameter tube in both inner and outer wing sections. Main spar built up of extruded light alloy angles riveted to a single plate flange with additional riveted cap strips and vertical web stiffeners. The secondary spar is a flanged plate with an additional angle riveted top and bottom opposite the bent-over flange. Wing joints outboard of engine nacelles by self-aligning joints at main spar with lugs at top and bottom flanges, and Junkers type spherical joint on ends of leading-edge tubes. Hydraulically-operated camber-changing flaps of all-metal construction between fuselage and ailerons. Metal-framed ailerons with "D"-shaped metal nose and fabric-covered trailing-edges. Hydraulically-operated dive-brakes on upper and lower surfaces. These brakes comprise a number of angle slats mounted on parallel link-bars which are hinged to the flanges of the main spar to give sideways motion. When brakes are raised the slats nest together flush with the wing surfaces. The lower brakes have four slats, the upper two. Automatic slots on outer wing sections.

Fuselage.—All-metal structure made in two vertical halves and joined top and bottom. Flush-riveted skin carried by a series of continuous top-hat section stringers supported by widely-spaced frames, some formed by flanging the edges of the vertical skin panels. Skin joints at these points are joggled to give flush external finish. The two halves are joined top and bottom by being riveted to wide channel longerons with lipped flanges.

Tail Unit.—Cantilever monoplane type. Tail-plane has two spars built up from light alloy angles and plate webs, pressed-sheet ribs and stressed skin. Upper and lower surfaces made separately and joined at leading-edge and through flanges on webs of spars. Detachable tips. Elevators have metal frames, metal "D" leading-edge, metal tips, and remainder covered with fabric. All-metal fin and fabric-covered metal-framed rudder. Tail-plane adjustable on the ground only. Trim-tabs in elevators and rudder.

Landing Gear.—Retractable type. Main wheels retracted hydraulically into tails of engine nacelles, the wheels turning through 90 degrees to lie horizontally in wells which are closed by fairing doors. Retractable tail-wheel.

Power Plant.—Two Daimler-Benz DB 603 twelve-cylinder inverted Vee liquid-cooled engines, each rated at 1,720 h.p. at 5,800 m. (19,000 ft.), on hollow welded semi-cantilever mounting beams supported at their mid-points by steel-tube struts. GM-1 emergency power-boost system occasionally fitted. VDM constant-speed airscrews with armour-plate disc behind spinner. Underside of each engine nacelle and radiator armoured. Coolant radiators in ducts under wings outboard of nacelles. Six self-sealing fuel tanks (total capacity 550 Imp. gallons) of rubberised flexible material in wings.

Accommodation.—Crew of two comprising pilot/bomb-aimer and rear-gunner/radio-operator in forward portion of fuselage under continuous transparent fairing. Flat transparent panels in nose for bomb-aiming.

Armament.—Normal bomber version fitted with two 7.9 m/m. MG 17 machine-guns and two MG 151/20 20 m/m. cannon, all fixed, in nose of fuselage and fired by pilot. Two 13 m/m. MG 131 guns in faired blisters, one on each side of the fuselage, remotely sighted and controlled by the rear-gunner. These two blisters are mounted on the ends of a barrel set across the fuselage and carried on annular ball-bearings on inner walls of fuselage. Through a torque multiplier, driven by a small electric motor and trains of gears, this barrel may be revolved to elevate or depress the guns, or further gearing within the barrel may traverse the guns. All movement of the guns is controlled by a pistol grip in gunner's cockpit. The guns may be elevated or depressed through a range of about 70 degrees and traversed independently of each other through about 40 degrees from the sides of the fuselage. The guns may also be fired together towards the rear. A contact-breaker device interrupts firing when the guns, which are electrically fired, are pointing at any part of the aeroplane structure. The heavy fighter versions have two additional MG 151/20 or one 50 m/m. BK 5 cannon in bomb-bay.

Bomb Load.—The bomb compartment is in the nose of the fuselage beneath the pilot's cockpit and provision is made for carrying either two 250 kg. (550 lb.) or one 500 kg. (1,100 lb.) bombs. A special 1,000-kg. (2,200 lb.) bomb may be stowed but loads over 500 kg. count as overloads. For photographic reconnaissance duties cameras are carried in bomb compartment.

Armour.—Armour-plate to a weight of approximately 477 kg. (1,050 lbs.) is fitted. Parts protected include pilot's seat and back, cabin roof, the gunner's position, engines, radiators, coolant pipes, etc.

Equipment.—Radio carried comprises the normal FU.G.10 ground/air set complete with direction-finding and blind approach facilities, and the FU.G.16 air/air set with remote tuning.

Dimensions.—Span 16.4 m. (53 ft. 9 in.), Length 12.4 m. (40 ft. 10 in.), Wing area 36.2 sq. m. (390 sq. ft.).

Weights (Me 410A-1 Bomber).—Weight empty 13,550 lbs. (6,150 kg.), Weight loaded 23,500 lbs. (10,670 kg.).

Performance.—Maximum speed 390 m.p.h. (624 km.h.) at 22,000 ft. (6,710 m.), Climb to 20,000 ft. (6,100 m.) 10.7 mins., Service ceiling 34,000 ft. (1,037 m.).

SIEBEL.

SIEBEL FLUGZEUGWERKE K.G.

Head Office and Works: Halle (Saale).

Managing Director: F. W. Siebel.

This firm, originally known as the Flugzeugwerke Halle G.m.b.H., produced the Fh. 104 light five-passenger cabin monoplane in 1937, and the Si 202 light two-seat sporting monoplane, which appeared in 1938.

The Si 204 light twin-engined monoplane was used on transport and training duties by the German Air Force. During the occupation of France it was built in some numbers by the S.N.C.A.C., thus leaving the Siebel company free to concentrate on the production of trainers (Fw 44) and sub-assemblies for other manufacturers.

This concern also developed the Siebel power-driven ferry or troop and freight-carrying landing craft, large numbers of which were used by the German Army in 1943 in its various evacuations from Africa, Sicily, Corsica and Sardinia.

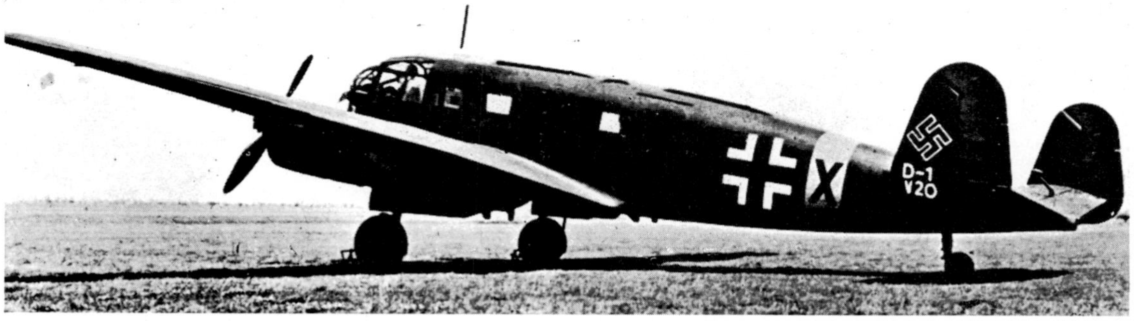

The Siebel Si 204D Light Transport Monoplane (two 600 h.p. Argus As 411 engines).

THE SIEBEL Si 204D.

The Si 204 is a light twin-engined cabin monoplane which was used for communications and light transport, as well as for training twin-engine pilots, navigators and radio operators. During the occupation of France it was in production by the Société Nationale de Constructions Aéronautiques du Centre (S.N.C.A.C.) at Fourchambault and Bourges.

Type.—Twin-engined light Transport and Training monoplane.

Wings.—Low-wing cantilever monoplane with dihedral and taper from roots to tips. All-metal structure with a main spar at 35-40% of the chord and an auxiliary rear spar. Main spar has a duralumin sheet web with flanges built up of L-shaped extrusions. Widely-spaced ribs with intercostal chordwise stiffeners of modified U-section. Frise type ailerons with combined balance and electrically-operated trim-tabs. Flaps between ailerons and fuselage.

Fuselage.—All-metal semi-monocoque structure. Z-section frames are pierced to clear the continuous U-section stringers to which the stressed skin is riveted.

Tail Unit.—Cantilever monoplane type. Dihedral tailplane with fins and rudders at the extremities. Tailplane incidence adjustable on the ground. Elevators have combined trim and balance tabs. Rudders have trim and balance tabs as well as horn balance. Trimming of all control tabs by electric motors incorporated in the tab linkage.

Landing Gear.—Retractable type. Main wheels raised backwards into engine nacelles. Fixed tail-wheel.

Power Plant.—Two Argus As 411 twelve-cylinder inverted Vee air-cooled engines each rated at 600 h.p. at 2,000 ft. (610 m.). Total fuel capacity 240 Imp. gallons.

Accommodation.—Crew of two in glazed nose. As a radio trainer, accommodation provided for five trainees with all equipment.

Dimensions.—Span 69 ft. 9 in. (21.3 m.), Length 39 ft. 2 in. (11.9 m.).

Loaded Weight.—12,300 lbs. (5,590 kg.).

Performance.—Maximum speed 230 m.p.h. (368 km.h.) at 7,600 ft, (2,320 m.), Range 930 miles (1,490 km.).

GERMAN V-WEAPONS

Brief descriptions of the two so-called Vergeltungswaffen (Revenge Weapons) employed by Germany against Southern England in 1944-45 are included in this section of "All the World's Aircraft" for historical reasons. V1, or the FZG 76 flying-bomb, has a legitimate right to appear here as it was actually a pilotless aircraft and, incidentally, the first weapon used offensively to be driven by jet-propulsion.

The prototype of the Flying Bomb was developed by the Gerhard Fieseler Werke G.m.b.H. The Fi 103, as the prototype was designated, differed in several respects from the ultimate production FZG76. The tail unit was of the cruciform type with the vertical fin equally disposed above and below the body. There was also a vertical stabilising surface above the body in line with the wings.

The power unit of the FZG-76 was an Argus development, its full designation being 109.014 or, more generally, As 014.

FZG 76 FLYING BOMB OR "V1."

The general layout of the FZG-76 followed that of a simple mid-wing cantilever monoplane. The streamlined body was divided into six compartments containing, from nose to tail, the magnetic compass; the main explosive charge (about 1,870 lbs.= 850 kg.), the fuel tank (about 150 gals.); compressed air containers; the auto pilot and height and range-setting controls; and, finally, the servo mechanisms controlling the rudder and and elevators. Mounted above the rear portion of the body was the propulsion unit which was supported at its forward end by a crutch and aft by the vertical fin.

The cantilever wing was built round a single tubular spar which passed through the centre of the fuel compartment. The wing was assembled by the spar tube being first passed through the body, after which the outer wings were threaded on the protruding ends and secured to the body at their roots.

The tail-unit consisted of a forwardly-placed tailplane and elevators and a fin and rudder. The elevators and rudder were the only aerodynamic controls, lateral stability being taken care of by the rudder and a balancing couple between the main body and the propulsion unit.

The Automatic Controls.

On the nose of the main body was a small coarse-pitch propeller or anemometer, which drove, through a 60 : 1 reduction gear and electrical contacts, a Veeder-type counter located in the auto-pilot compartment. This counter was the range-setting device, being so set before launching that when a predetermined distance had been covered it fired electrically two detonators which instantaneously locked the elevators and deflected small flaps or spoilers under the elevators to put the bomb in its final dive. Normally, such sudden change in attitude would cause precession of the gyros, the effect of which would be to apply full rudder. To forestall such movement a small guillotine interconnected with the spoiler severed the air leads from the auto-pilot to the rudder servo-motor so that the rudder remained in a neutral position for the dive. The sudden change in attitude also cut the fuel supply by uncovering the outlet from the petrol tank.

The compressed air supply for operating the automatic pilot and various relays and servos, as well as for pressurising the fuel was contained in two light-gauge steel spheres, each covered by a series of reinforcing steel bands which were gripped in place by the internal air pressure of about 2,000 lbs./sq. in. Air was fed to the various services and into the top of the petrol tank through pressure-reducing valves at about 56 lbs./sq. in.

The control compartment contained the automatic pilot, height and range-setting controls and a 42-cell dry battery for the various electrical services, including the transmission from the magnetic compass and anemometer, warhead fuses and dive detonators. The auto-pilot had three air-driven gyros, one for longitudinal and directional stability, the other two functioning as dampeners; the bomb itself being aerodynamically unstable.

The magnetic compass in the nose compartment was provided with an air pick-up device which recorded any deviation, thereby closing electrical contacts to energise magnets in the directional gyro and to correct both deviation and precession. This ensured the maintainance of a magnetic course to within a ½ degree.

There was provision for including a clockwork device which could cause the course of the bomb to be changed once at a certain elapsed time after launching.

The Propulsion Unit.

The propulsion unit, called an impulse duct engine, consisted of a welded steel tube "stove-pipe" about 11 ft. (3.35 m.) long in the front end of which was a bank of spring air valves and nine backward-facing fuel nozzles. The forward speed of the flying-bomb opened the spring valves and forced air into the combustion space, into which the fuel was injected. Pressure of combustion closed the one-way spring valves so that the only outlet for the heated and expanded gas was out of the rear end of the propulsion unit. Inertia of the escaping gas reduced pressure chamber were fed from an external source with Butane, which was ignited by the single spark-plug, also energised externally, until the walls of the combustion chamber became hot enough for auto-ignition. When the engine was sufficiently warmed-up and the gyros had reached their operating speed, the bomb's in the combustion chamber below atmospheric, permitting the valves to re-open. This process was repeated 40-45 times per second to give the flying-bomb a forward speed of about 390-410 m.p.h. (624-656 km.h.). The fuel feed was regulated to maintain a correct mixture strength according to forward speed and altitude through compensating mechanism controlled by a pitot head and diaphragm. A single sparking-plug in the top of the combustion chamber was used for starting but thereafter the unit was self-igniting. The thrust of the propulsion unit at normal speed was estimated to be equivalent to something of the order of 750 h.p.

The structure of the flying-bomb was of the simplest. Except for the light metal nose cone enclosing the magnetic compass, it was entirely of welded steel sheet.

Fusing and Launching.

All flying-bombs when leaving the assembly plants were fitted with a time-fuse so that should it have been necessary to abandon any bomb before launching the fuse could be set to explode the war-head within any predetermined period up to 2 hours. When the bomb was ready for launching the time fuse was removed and two others were installed. One was electrically-operated from the bomb's battery system and had contacts in the nose and belly. The other was an all-way fuse which, after the bomb had travelled approximately 40 miles, was primed to go off upon the bomb receiving any sharp jar.

The flying-bomb was launched from a ramp about 180 ft. (55 m.) long and inclined at about 6 degrees. The ramp was a steel truss topped by two rails between which and at the same level was a steel pipe about 12 inches in diameter and with a slot cut through its top over its entire length. A dumb-bell-shaped piston weighing about 300 lbs. (136 kg.) was fitted with a hook which protruded through the slot and engaged in the underside of the bomb casing.

The bomb was lowered by a gantry onto the ramp and connected up to the piston hook. When in position, a breech in the rear end of the launching tube was closed, the bomb propulsion unit was started up and the gyros were put into operation. For starting the engine three auxiliary nozzles in the combustion main fuel supply was opened and at the same time hydrogen-peroxide and calcium permanganate was forced into the launching tube behind the piston by compressed air. The expansion of this mixture generated enormous thrust which, combined with that of the bomb's jet unit, shot the missile up and off the ramp, which it left under its own power. The piston was shot out of the end of the tube, but was recoverable for further use.

The slot in the tube was sealed by a small diameter continuous pipe which was suspended below the slot by fine wires. These wires were severed by the piston hook as it progressed along the slot and internal pressure behind the piston forced the pipe up into the slot and prevented the escape of gas.

Dimensions.—Span 17 ft. 6 in. (5.3 m.), Overall length 26 ft. (7.9 m.). Diameter of body 2 ft. 7 in. (0.8 m.), Wing chord 3 ft. 5 in. (1.03 m.). Weights.—Weight loaded 4,800 lbs. (2,180 kg.), Wing loading 85 lbs./sq. ft. (414.8 kg./sq, m.). Performance.—Maximum speed 390-410 m.p.h. (624-656 km.h.), Launching speed 200 m.p.h. (320 km.), Stalling speed 150 m.p.h. (240 km.), Normal range 150 miles (240 km.), Average ceiling 2,500 ft. (760 m.), Maximum ceiling 10,000 ft. (3,050 m.).

THE A 4 ROCKET OR "V2."

V2 was a long-range rocket projectile which weighed fully loaded about 12 tons (of which only about 2,000 lbs. was explosive) and had a range of about 200 miles.

It was a wingless streamlined projectile 46 ft. (14 m.) long, 5 ft. 6 in. (1.67 m.) in diameter and fitted with four large external stablising fins at right-angles to each other at the rear end. It comprised the following main assemblies, all contained in a shell-like structure which followed in construction the same general form as an aircraft fuselage : (a) the nose, which contains the explosive warhead of 2,000 lbs. (910 kg.) ; (b) a compartment containing control equipment ; (c) two large aluminium fuel tanks, one holding about 7,500 lbs. (3,410 kg.) of alcohol and the other about 11,000 lbs. (5,000 kg.) of liquid oxygen ; (d) a turbine and pump assembly with a gas generator to drive the turbine ; and (f) two sets of control vanes, one operating internally in the jet stream and the other externally on the edges of the four stabilising fins.

For launching, the rocket was stood on its fins in a vertical position on a concrete platform or hard level surface. The turbine, which was driven by superheated steam produced by mixing very concentrated hydrogen-peroxide with a calcium permanganate solution, was started up to drive the alcohol and liquid oxygen into the combustion chamber. This mixture was then ignited electrically from some distance away and the rocket took off.

Once ignited, the mixture of alcohol and oxygen continued to burn violently and the products of combustion were forced out at a high speed through the orifice in the rear end of the venturi as a jet of very hot gases. The energy so liberated created a thrust of about 26 tons. All the fuel was expended in about 65 seconds and thereafter, the rocket having lost about three-quarters of its weight, proceeded on the rest of its journey on the stored energy of its initial velocity, following the normal trajectory of a shell to its target.

The rocket was launched vertically and, initially, it travelled comparatively slowly. As height increased and the rocket began to lose weight, it gained speed very rapidly, gradually turning away from the vertical towards its target. When the fuel was either cut off or completely expended it was pointing upward at an angle of about 40° or less, depending upon the range required, to the horizontal. The change of direction from the vertical was achieved automatically by gyroscope controls within the rocket which governed four graphite controllers symmetrically placed around the nozzle of the jet. The rocket action was cut off when the velocity reached corresponded to the required range.

After the fuel was expended or the jet action stopped the rocket continued on its way, describing a curved parabolic path typical of any shell. Eventually a height of about 60 miles (96 km.) above the earth's surface was reached. A range of about 220 miles (352 km.) was possible which, in conjunction with a total time of flight of about 5 minutes, meant that the rocket reached a maximum speed of about 3,600 m.p.h. (5,760 km.h.), or one mile per second, or five times the speed of sound. As it was travelling so much faster than sound, the noise of its passage was not heard until after it had exploded.

The weight of explosive was only a little more than was carried by V1. The amount of damage caused was generally about the same. Neither V1 nor V2 was reliable in either launching or flight control and numbers of both weapons failed to leave the launching areas or went off course. Although London was specified as the target by the enemy, and was frequently described as being in flames or in ruins, the British term "Southern England" was, in its vagueness, more descriptive of the area in which these missiles fell. Many V2's aimed at London actually fell in the Rhineland cities, at least six coming to earth in the Wiesbaden area.

The following is a brief description of the main assemblies of the V2 rocket :—

Nose of Warhead.

Of truncated conical shape and attached to the forward end of the control compartment. The casing was of mild steel just under a quarter of an inch thick and contained a ton of explosive which was of a kind that is insensitive to a considerable degree

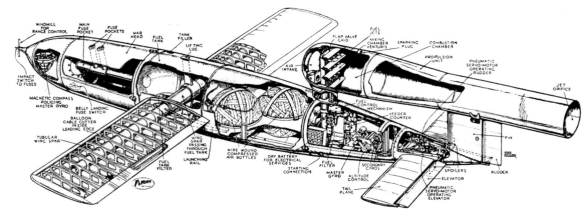

A cut-away diagram of the FZG 76 Flying-bomb. This diagram is reproduced by courtesy of "Flight."

of heat. This was necessary since the casing of the rocket attained a temperature of about 600°C. through air friction. Three fuses, two of which were situated at the front and one at the rear of the charge, were used.

Control Compartment.

In the first rockets fired against Great Britain radio control from the ground was used to cut off the fuel when the necessary speed to give the desired range was attained. In later specimens radio control was superseded by a unit known as an integrating accelerometer which was capable of measuring the velocity of the rocket and shutting off the fuel for any predetermined range. The accelerometer also provided for reducing the thrust for control purposes. Gyroscopic controls were employed for turning the projectile from the vertical during its upwards flight, and keeping it steady on its passage to the target.

Fuel Tanks.

Two large fuel tanks which together carried about eight tons of fuel were supported within the main framework of the rocket. The mounting was specially designed to allow for the large degree of expansion and contraction that occurs. The front tank contained alcohol, and the rear tank liquid oxygen. Flexible pipes to provide for expansion and contraction connected the tanks to their respective fuel pumps.

Turbine and Fuel Pumps Unit.

A steam turbine and fuel pump unit was situated between the rear of the liquid oxygen tank and the combustion chamber and venturi unit, and was used for driving the separate alcohol and liquid oxygen fuel pumps, by means of which the fuel mixture was delivered in correct proportions to the combustion chamber. The two pumps were driven at the same speed as the turbine, and were of approximately equal capacities to provide the correct proportions of the two main fuels required in the final mixture. The steam supply for operating the turbine was supplied by the mixing of two additional fuels ; hydrogen peroxide and calcium permanganate.

Combustion Chamber and Venturi.

This unit was made of sheet steel about a quarter of an inch thick. It was built into the rear end of the rocket, so that the swelled portion or combustion chamber was adjacent to the fuel pumps unit, and the tapered or jet portion projected from the rear end of the rocket. The alcohol was circulated first of all through a jacket which enshrouded both the combustion chamber and venturi for the double purpose of cooling the unit and preheating the alcohol to promote a greater efficiency when burning. The alcohol then entered the combustion chamber through a series of burner cups located in the end cover of the chamber ; this supply was governed by valves for starting and for operation at reduced thrust. A small proportion of the alcohol was also supplied to four annuli formed around the venturi ; series of small orifices conveyed the alcohol from these annuli into the venturi to form a cool protective envelope over the interior of the venturi that served to shield the walls from the high combustion temperature of 3000°C. The liquid oxygen was conveyed from the pump through a system of distributors and individual feed pipes to each of the above-mentioned burners. The two fuels were thus mixed and burnt, resulting in the hot, high velocity gas jet already mentioned which, issuing from the open end of the venturi jet, provided the propulsive power of the rocket.

Control Surfaces.

Four large stabilising fins, spaced at right angles to each other and each incorporating a movable control tab, were mounted on the rear end of the rocket casing. In addition, four graphite tabs or controllers were placed symmetrically around the nozzle of the jet. All these eight control surfaces were governed by the gyroscopes already mentioned through the agency of servo motors. The graphite tabs controlled the rocket during its initial flight and were of course only operative when the jet was in action. The fin tabs controlled the rocket during its subsequent journey to the target.

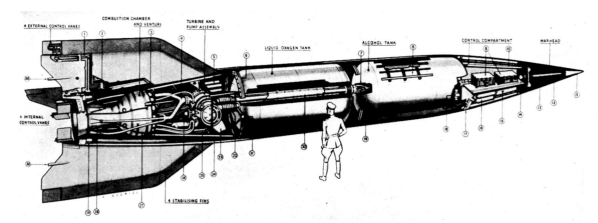

The official diagram of the A4 Long-range Rocket. The numbered references indicate the following :—1. Chain drive to control tabs on external fins from 2. electric motor. 3. Injection nozzles on main combustion chamber. 4. Alcohol delivery piping. 5. Compressed-air bottles. 6. Rear joint ring and lifting point. 7. Servo-controlled alcohol valve. 8. Shell casing support structure. 9. Radio control equipment. 10. Pipe from warhead to alcohol tank. 11. Nose with fusing switch. 12. Conduit for fuse wiring. 13. Exploder tube. 14. Electric fuse for warhead. 15. Plywood support for radio. 16. Nitrogen bottles. 17. Front joint ring and lifting point. 18. Gyros for pitch and azimuth. 19. Alcohol tank filling point. 20. Insulated alcohol feed pipe. 21. Oxygen tank filling point. 22. Expansible bellows connections to alcohol and oxygen pumps. 23. Hydrogen peroxide tank. 24. Tubular support frame for turbine and pumps assembly. 25. Calcium permanganate tank—hydrogen/permanganate steam generator for turbine is located behind this tank. 26. Oxygen distributor unit. 27. Alcohol pipes for subsidiary cooling. 28. Alcohol inlet to double wall of rocket motor. 29. Electro-hydraulic servo motors.

ITALY

BREDA.

SOCIETA ITALIANA ERNESTO BREDA.

Head Office : Milan.

This enormous Milanese concern began building aircraft in 1917. From 1919 onwards, when the production of aircraft was at a standstill, the Breda Works carried on research work and built experimental machines. The construction of all-metal aircraft was begun in 1922.

In the years between the two wars it built both military and civil aircraft. Its best known products were the Breda 25 and 28 two-seat training biplanes, the Breda 65 single-engined Fighter-Reconnaissance monoplane and the Breda 88 twin-engined Bomber. The last-mentioned aeroplane put up a number of "prestige" speed records carrying various loads in 1937 but it achieved little success in action, and only the trainers were used in any quantity by the *Regia Aeronautica*.

CANT.

CANTIERI RIUNITI DELL'ADRIATICO.

HEAD OFFICE AND WORKS : MONFALCONE, TRIESTE.

The famous naval construction firm Cantiere Monfalcone entered the aircraft industry late in 1923. The aircraft branch, which was known as the Cantiere Riuniti dell'Adriatico, specialised in seagoing aircraft.

Of the many types of military and civil aircraft built by this Company, the Z.506B and Z.1007*bis* were used by the *Regia Aeronautica* during the war. Some of these aircraft survived to serve with that part of the Italian Air Force owing allegiance to the Italian Government which was recognised as a co-belligerent by the Allies on October 14, 1943.

THE CANT Z.506 B.

TYPE.—Three-engined Bomber-torpedo Reconnaissance seaplane.

WINGS.—Low-wing cantilever monoplane. Wings taper in chord and thickness, elliptical wing-tips. Wooden structure consists of three spars, former ribs and plywood covering. Solid ribs divide wing into a number of watertight compartments. Hinged trailing-edges, inner sections acting as camber-changing flaps and outer sections as ailerons.

FUSELAGE.—Wooden structure of elliptical cross-section. Longitudinal system of construction with one main keel member, one main deck member and four side members. These are interconnected by three main bulkheads at the main wing-spar points and a series of reinforced transverse panels and formers, the whole covered with plywood.

TAIL UNIT.—Monoplane type. Tail-plane mounted on fin, clear of fuselage. Wooden framework, with plywood covering. Trimming-tabs in elevators. Balanced rudder and elevators.

FLOATS.—Two long single-step duralumin floats attached to the wing engine-mountings and fuselage by Vee struts, which are wire-braced in their lateral planes. Each float is divided into two watertight compartments. Total buoyancy of floats equal to twice the total loaded weight of machine, to conform to Italian requirements.

POWER PLANT.—Three 770 h.p. Alfa-Romeo 126 RC34 nine-cylinder radial air-cooled supercharged engines, one in the nose and two on lateral mountings in the leading-edge of the wings. Fuel tanks in wings.

ACCOMMODATION.—Pilot's compartment, seating two side-by-side, with dual controls, behind nose engine. Bomb-aimer's position in nose of swelling beneath fuselage, which also accommodates bomb load or torpedo amidships. At the tail of this swelling is the rear lower gun position. An upper position provided with rotatable turret is located above trailing-edge of wing, the gun being operated by the radio-operator. Equipment includes an inflatable rubber boat.

ARMAMENT.—One Breda-Safat 12.7 m/m. machine-gun in dorsal position, two 7.7 m/m. machine-guns in lateral positions and one 7.7 m/m. machine-gun in the lower gun position. Bombs or torpedo carried in lower portion of fuselage with hydraulically-operated doors closing the compartment.

DIMENSIONS.—Span 26.5 m. (86 ft. 11 in.), Length 18.92 m. (62 ft.), Height 6.77 m. (22 ft. 2¼ in.), Wing area 85 sq. m. (914.6 sq. ft.).

WEIGHTS.—Weight empty 8,200 kg. (18,040 lbs.), Weight loaded 12,210 kg. (26,860 lbs.).

PERFORMANCE.—Maximum speed at sea level 312 km.h. (195 m.p.h.),

The Cant Z.506 B Torpedo-carrying Seaplane.

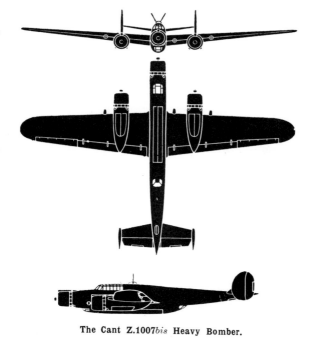

The Cant Z.1007*bis* Heavy Bomber.

Maximum speed at 4,000 m. (13,120 ft.) 366 km.h. (229 m.p.h.), Climb to 4,000 m. (13,120 ft.) 14 mins., Service ceiling 7,320 m. (24,000 ft.), Absolute ceiling 8,500 m. (27,880 ft.), Cruising range 1,600 km. (1,000 miles) or 5 hours.

THE CANT Z.1007*bis*.

TYPE.—Three-engined Torpedo-Bomber.

WINGS.—Mid-wing cantilever monoplane. Wing in three sections with centre-section passing through fuselage. All-wood structure comprising two box-spars and usual former ribs and plywood skin with final covering of fabric. Camber-changing flaps between ailerons and fuselage.

FUSELAGE.—All-wood semi-monocoque structure built up of a frame-work of longitudinals and transverse frames and stiffeners, the whole covered with a plywood skin.

TAIL UNIT.—Strut-braced monoplane tail-plane mounted on fin slightly above fuselage. Rudder and elevators statically and aerodynamically balanced. All-wood structure, with fabric-covered movable surfaces.

LANDING GEAR.—Retractable type. Wheels are raised backwards into tails of engine nacelles. Hydraulic operation.

POWER PLANT.—Three Piaggio P.XI RC.40 radial air-cooled engines

each rated at 1,000 h.p. at 4,000 m. (13,120 ft.). Alfa-Romeo three-bladed controllable-pitch airscrews. Fuel tanks between spars in centre-section.

ACCOMMODATION.—Two pilots in tandem aft of nose engine with rotatable turret over second pilot. Then follows radio and D/F. compartment, second gunner's position, photographic equipment and rear gunner. In protruberance beneath fuselage there is a bomb-aimer's position forward and a gunner's position aft. Between these two positions is space for the internal stowage of bombs.

ARMAMENT.—One 12.7 m/m. machine-gun in dorsal turret, one 12.7 m/m. gun under fuselage, and two 7.7 m/m. guns on lateral mountings. Normal bomb load 1,180 kg. (2,600 lbs.). Alternatively two 450 kg. (1,000 lb.) torpedoes may be carried.

DIMENSIONS.—Span 24.8 m. (81 ft. 4 in.), Length 18.4 m. (60 ft. 4 in.), Height 5.2 m. (17 ft.).

WEIGHTS.—Weight empty 8,630 kg. (19,000 lbs.), Disposable load 4,210 kg. (9,260 lbs.), Weight loaded 12,840 kg. (28,260 lbs.).

PERFORMANCE.—Maximum speed 448 km.h. (280 m.p.h.) at 4,575 m. (15,000 ft.), Cruising speed 376 km.h. (235 m.p.h.) at 4,575 m. (15,000 ft.), Service ceiling 8,100 m. (26,500 ft.), Cruising range 1,280 km. (800 miles) or 3.4 hours.

CAPRONI.

SOCIETA ITALIANA CAPRONI.

HEAD OFFICE AND WORKS : MILAN (TALIEDO).

The group of companies controlled by Count Gianni Caproni was the largest in Italy. It included the following :—Aeroplani Caproni S.A. ; Compagnia Commerciale Caproni S.A. ; S.A. Caproni Africa Orientale Italiana ; S.A. Officine Meccaniche Ceruti ; S.A. Construzioni Elettromechaniche Saranno ; S.A. Officine Reatine - Lavorazioni Aeronautiche ; S.A. Caproni-Vizzola ; Compania Aeronautica Bergamasca ; S.A. Aeronautica Predappio ; Officine Meccaniche "Reggiane" ; Avio Industrie Stabiensi C. Coppola ; S.A. Fabbrica Nazionale d'Armi ; Compania Nazionale Aeronautica ; S.A. Castelli ; Aeroplani Caproni Trento ; Aeronautica Sicula S.A. ; S.A. Capodimente ; Societa Romana Gassogeni ; Manganesifera Italiana S.A ; Officine Romagnole S.A. ; S.A. Armamenti Caproni ; as well as the famous Isotta-Fraschini Company and its subsidiaries.

Of the large number of Caproni military aircraft most of them designed for "Colonial" use, produced before the war, only one

survives to be worthy of mention. The Ca 313 was adopted for service as a light liaison aeroplane by the German Air Force. A number of aircraft of this type was also acquired by the Swedish Government at a time when Sweden was cut off from the outside world.

THE CAPRONI Ca 313.

TYPE.—Twin-engined Light Reconnaissance Bomber.

WINGS.—Low-wing cantilever monoplane. Comprises centre-section and two tapering outer sections. Wing structure of wood with two box spars, former ribs and plywood covering. The main portion of the wing between the spars is watertight and is divided into a number of compartments for emergency flotation.

FUSELAGE.—Jig-built welded steel-tube framework in two sections and bolted together. Fabric covering over light fairing structure.

TAIL UNIT.—Cantilever monoplane type. Wooden structure with plywood and fabric covering. Aerodynamically and statically-balanced elevators and rudder.

LANDING GEAR.—Retractable type. Wheels are raised backwards into tails of engine nacelles. Hydraulic retraction with emergency hand-operated gear.

POWER PLANT.—Two 650 h.p. Isotta-Fraschini Betta R.C.35 twelve-cylinder inverted Vee air-cooled engines. Fuel tanks in centre-section.

ACCOMMODATION.—Enclosed accommodation for crew of three or four. Observer or bomb-aimer in transparent nose. Pilot and second pilot or navigator seated side-by-side with dual controls, consisting of throw-over wheel and two rudder bars. Upper gunner's position aft of pilots.

ARMAMENT AND EQUIPMENT.—Armament consists of two machine-guns, one fixed and firing forward in port wing and one flexible gun in cupola in roof of cabin. Equipment includes two-way radio, full night-flying equipment, camera, etc. External bomb stowage.

DIMENSIONS.—Span 16.3 m. (53 ft. 6 in.), Length 11.8 m. (38 ft. 9 in.), Height 4.37 m. (14 ft. 4 in.).

WEIGHT LOADED.—5,652 kg. (12,450 lbs.).

PERFORMANCE.—Maximum speed 397 km.h. (248 m.p.h.), Stalling speed 129.6 km.h. (81 m.p.h.), Service ceiling 6,800 m. (22,300 ft.).

FIAT.

AERONAUTICA D'ITALIA S.A. (FIAT).

HEAD OFFICE AND WORKS : TURIN.

This concern was formed in January, 1916, under the name Societa Anonima per Construzione Ing. O. Pomilio & Co. On April 24, 1920, it changed its name to Aeronautica Ansaldo S.A. and in the Summer of 1925 began the construction of Fiat aircraft. On March 30, 1926, it was incorporated in the Fiat Group under its present name.

Of the many aircraft products of the great Fiat organization most of which have been described and illustrated in earlier issues of this Annual only one survived to serve with the co-belligerent Italian Air Force in small numbers. This was the R.S.14 seaplane described below.

THE FIAT R.S.14.

TYPE.—Twin-engined multi-seat Torpedo-Bomber-Reconnaissance seaplane.

WINGS.—Mid-wing cantilever monoplane. Wings taper in chord and thickness and have dihedral from roots to tips. All-metal structure.

FUSELAGE.—Oval section all-metal structure with stressed-skin covering.

TAIL UNIT.—Cantilever monoplane type. All-metal framework with metal covered fixed surfaces and fabric-covered elevators and rudder.

FLOATS.—Two long single-step all-metal floats attached to the engine nacelles by pairs of vertical struts and braced to the fuselage by parallel sloping struts.

POWER PLANT.—Two Fiat A.74 RC.38 fourteen-cylinder radial air-cooled engines, each rated at 840 h.p. at 3,800 m. (12,500 ft.). Three-bladed Fiat-Hamilton constant-speed airscrews. Fuel tanks in wings.

ACCOMMODATION.—Crew of four or five. Pilot's compartment over leading-edge of the wing. Bomb-aimers position in nose. Further details of accommodation unknown.

DIMENSIONS.—Span 19.6 m. (64 ft. 3 in.), Length 13.8 m. (45 ft. 6 in.), Height 5.4 m. (17 ft. 9 in.), Wing area 51.5 sq. m. (555 sq. ft.).

WEIGHT LOADED.—7,264 kg. (16,000 lbs.).

PERFORMANCE.—Maximum speed 379 km.h. (237 m.p.h.) at 4,000 m. (13,120 ft.).

MACCHI.

AERONAUTICA MACCHI.

HEAD OFFICE : VARESE.

WORKS : VARESE-SCHIRANNA AND LONATE POZZOLO.

The Macchi Company was founded in 1912 and since then devoted its entire energies to the construction of aircraft. Its

first aeroplane was produced in 1913 and this was followed during the war 1915-18 and since by many other types of aircraft, particularly flying-boats and seaplanes, in which this firm specialised for many years.

After successfully developing a number of racing seaplanes,

the firm turned its attention to the production of fighter aircraft. The Macchi C.202 was one of the best fighters used by the *Regia Aeronautica* and after the surrender of the Italian Government it continued to be standard equipment in some squadrons of the Fascist Republican Air Force.

The Macchi C.202 Single-seat Fighter wearing the colours of the Italian Co-belligerent Air Force.

THE MACCHI C.202.

TYPE.—Single-seat Fighter monoplane.

WINGS.—Low-wing cantilever monoplane. In three sections, comprising a centre-section built integral with the wing and two tapering outer sections. All-metal structure with smooth stressed skin. Nose section detachable for inspection of interior and controls. Entire trailing-edge hinged, the outer sections acting as ailerons and the inner sections as hydraulically-operated landing-flaps. Flaps and ailerons are interconnected and when flaps are lowered the ailerons are also drooped.

FUSELAGE.—Oval section all-metal monocoque.

TAIL UNIT.—Cantilever monoplane type. All-metal framework, with fixed surfaces metal-covered and movable surfaces fabric-covered. Adjustable tail-plane.

LANDING GEAR.—Retractable type. Wheels raised inwards into underside of centre-section and apertures closed by fairing plates on landing gear legs and wheels. Hydraulic retraction.

POWER PLANT.—One Daimler-Benz DB 601N twelve-cylinder inverted Vee liquid-cooled engine rated at 1,200 h.p. at 4,880 m. (16,000 ft.). Three-bladed controllable-pitch airscrew. Ventral radiator beneath pilot's cockpit.

ACCOMMODATION.—Enclosed cockpit over trailing-edge of wing. Pilot armour.

ARMAMENT.—Four fixed machine-guns, two 12.7 m/m. in fuselage and firing through airscrew and two 7.7 m/m. in wings.

DIMENSIONS.—Span 10.58 m. (34 ft. 8 in.), Length 8.87 m. (29 ft. 1 in.), Height 3 m. (9 ft. 10 in.), Wing area 16.8 sq. m. (180.7 sq. ft.).

NORMAL LOADED WEIGHT.—2,860 kg. (6,300 lbs.).

PERFORMANCE.—Maximum speed 528 km.h. (330 m.p.h.) at 5,490 m. (18,000 ft.), Cruising speed 480 km.h. (300 m.p.h.) at 5,490 m. (18,000 ft.), Service ceiling 10,520 m. (34,500 ft.).

MERIDIONALI.

S.A. INDUSTRIE MECCANICHE E AERONAUTICHE MERIDIONALI (BREDA).

HEAD OFFICE AND WORKS : NAPLES.

This concern was, up to 1936, known as the Societa Anonima Industrie Aeronautiche Romeo, which was formed in 1934 to take over the aeronautical activities of the Officine Ferroviarie Meridionali.

The Officine Ferroviarie Meridionali entered the Italian Aircraft Industry in 1923 and two years later this concern acquired the rights to build Fokker aeroplanes under licence.

In 1936, the Societa Anonima Industrie Aeronautiche Romeo absorbed the industrial activities of the Officine Ferroviarie Meridionali and changed its name to Industrie Meccaniche e Aeronautiche Meridionali.

PIAGGIO.

SOCIETA ANONIMA PIAGGIO & C.

HEAD OFFICE : GENOA.

The famous firm of engineers and shipbuilders entered the aircraft industry in 1916. Some years later the firm began aero-engine manufacture at their Pontedera factory while aircraft construction was concentrated at the Sestri and Finale works.

At the Finale-Ligure works the firm built aeroplanes, sea planes and flying-boats, both in wood and metal.

The only Piaggio type known to be in use with the *Regia Aeronautica* during the war was the P.108 four-engined bomber. This aircraft was in service in very small numbers and was described in the last issue of this Annual.

REGGIANE.

OFFICINE MECCANICHE "REGGIANE" S.A. (CAPRONI).

HEAD OFFICE AND WORKS : REGGIO EMILIA.

This concern built Caproni aeroplanes during the war 1915-18, but abandoned its aircraft department after the War. Later it resumed aircraft manufacture, and during 1937 produced the Ca.405, Procellaria, high performance twin-engined bomber. Its most recent products were the Re 2000 single-seat interceptor fighter monoplane, which appeared in 1940, the Re 2001, which was developed in 1941 and the Re 2005, which appeared in 1943. The Re 201 and 2005 were in service in small numbers in the Fascist Republican Air Force.

THE REGGIANE Re 2001.

TYPE.—Single-seat Fighter monoplane.

WINGS.—Low-wing cantilever monoplane. In three sections comprising centre-section and two tapering outer sections. Multi-spar structure with a stressed-skin covering. Wing flaps extend from ailerons to fuselage.

FUSELAGE.—Oval metal monocoque structure with stressed-skin covering reinforced with "Z"-type longitudinal stiffeners.

TAIL UNIT.—Cantilever monoplane type. All-metal framework with fixed surfaces covered with metal and movable surfaces with fabric. Trimming-tabs in elevators and rudder.

LANDING GEAR.—Retractable type. Cantilever compression legs raised backwards, the whole being turned through 90 degrees to lie flush with the underside of the centre-section when raised. Steerable tail-wheel is retracted electrically.

POWER PLANT.—One 1,150 h.p. Daimler-Benz DB 601 twelve-cylinder inverted Vee liquid-cooled engine on welded steel-tube mounting. Three-bladed constant-speed airscrew. Main fuel tank in fuselage with additional tanks in centre-section.

ACCOMMODATION.—Enclosed pilot's cockpit over centre of wing.

ARMAMENT.—Two 12.7 m/m. machine-guns in fuselage firing forward through airscrew and two 7.7 m/m. machine-guns in wings. Bomb-rack under fuselage for one 250-kg. bomb. Equipment includes compressed-air starter, fire-extinguisher, radio, etc.

The Reggiane Re.2001 Single-seat Fighter Monoplane (1,150 h.p. Daimler-Benz DB.601 engine).

DIMENSIONS.—Span 11.2 m. (36 ft. 9 in.), Length 8.9 m. (29 ft. 3 in.), Height 3.6 m. (12 ft.), Wing area 20.4 sq. m. (220 sq. ft.).

WEIGHT LOADED.—3,178 kg. (7,000 lbs.).

PERFORMANCE.—Maximum speed 557 km.h. (348 m.p.h.) at 6,710 m. (22,000 ft.).

THE REGGIANE Re 2005.

The Re 2005 was similar to the Re 2001 except that it was fitted with the higher-powered DB 605 engine with the radiator beneath the fuselage instead of under the wings and had an outwardly retracting landing gear.

SAIMAN.

SOCIETA ANONIMA INDUSTRIE MECCANICHE AERONAUTICHE NAVALI (SAIMAN).

HEAD OFFICE : ROME.

This firm was founded in 1934 in order to take over the works formerly belonging to the S.A. Navigazione Aerea, at the seaplane base at the Lido di Roma.

The Company undertook the construction, repair and maintenance of aircraft, aero-engines and motor-boats.

It produced several light aircraft of its own design. These included the Saiman 200 two-seat training biplane (200 h.p. Alfa 115 engine), the Saiman 202/1 two-seat cabin monoplane (120 h.p. Alfa 110 engine) and the Saiman 204/R four-seat cabin monoplane (180 h.p. Alfa 115 engine). These types have been described in previous issues of this Annual.

SAVOIA-MARCHETTI.

SOCIETA ITALIANA AEROPLANI IDROVOLANTI "SAVOIA-MARCHETTI."

HEAD OFFICE : SESTO CALENDE.

WORKS : SESTO CALENDE AND BORGOMANERO.

The Savoia-Marchetti Company built a large number of commercial and military aircraft, both landplanes and seaplanes.

The military products of this concern were mainly conversions of its three-engined airliners, the SM.79 and SM.82 being the types most used by the *Regia Aeronautica* during the war. Both were also employed as transports by the German Air Force. After Italy's defeat in 1943 the SM.79 continued in service in both the co-belligerent and Fascist Republican Air Forces.

THE SAVOIA-MARCHETTI SM.79.

TYPE.—Three-engined Bomber and Reconnaissance monoplane.

WINGS.—Low-wing cantilever one-piece monoplane. All-wood structure. Whole trailing-edge from wing-tips to wing engine-mountings hinged, inner portions acting as camber-changing flaps and outer sections as ailerons and flaps. Handley Page slots on leading-edge from engine nacelles to tips.

FUSELAGE.—Welded steel-tube structure. Front portion covered with duralumin sheet, top partly with duralumin sheet and partly with plywood ; sides and bottom with fabric.

TAIL UNIT.—Monoplane type. Steel-tube framework covered with fabric. Rudder and elevators aerodynamically and statically balanced.

LANDING GEAR.—Retractable type.

POWER PLANT.—Three Alfa-Romeo 126 RC.34 nine-cylinder radial air-cooled geared and supercharged engines each rated at 750 h.p. at 3,400 m. (11,150 ft.) on welded steel-tube mountings with S.I.A.I. vibration dampers. Savoia-Marchetti two-position variable-pitch airscrews. Main fuel tanks in wing. Two auxiliary fuel tanks behind engines. In some cases the fuel tanks are provided with armour protection.

ACCOMMODATION.—Pilots' compartment, with two seats side-by-side, behind nose engine. The pilots' seats provided with armour back-plates 9.5 m/m. thick. Wireless operator and engineer accommodated aft of pilots. The bomb compartment is in the centre portion of the fuselage, and behind is the bomber's position, with duplicate rudder control, flight instruments, bomb-sights and releases and automatic camera. All compartments are interconnected.

ARMAMENT AND EQUIPMENT.—Armament consists of four machine-guns, one on a fixed mounting firing forward, and two on movable mountings aft of the wings, one above and one below the fuselage. A fourth machine-gun is installed on a sliding mounting inside the rear portion of the fuselage for defence on both sides. The bomb compartment is provided with racks for a total load of 1,000 kg. (2,200 lbs.). Alternatively two torpedoes can be carried under the fuselage. Equipment includes complete electrical installation, retractable landing-light, wireless, etc. Direction-finding equipment and telephonic intercommunication may be installed.

DIMENSIONS.—Span 21.2 m. (66 ft. 3 in.), Length 16.2 m. (53 ft. 2 in.), Height 4.1 m. (13 ft. 6 in.), Wing area 61 sq. m. (656.3 sq. ft.).

WEIGHTS AND LOADINGS (Alfa-Romeo 126 RC.34 engines).—Weight empty 6,800 kg. (14,960 lbs.), Crew (four) 320 kg. (704 lbs.), Guns and ammunition 246 kg. (541 lbs.), Radio 144 kg. (317 lbs.), Camera 38 kg. (84 lbs.), Fuel and oil 2,430 kg. (5,346 lbs.), Bombs 1,200 kg. (2,640 lbs.), Weight loaded 10,500 kg. (23,100 lbs.), Wing loading 172 kg./sq. m. (35.26 lbs./sq. ft.), Power loading 4.47 kg./h.p. (9.83 lbs./h.p.).

PERFORMANCE.—Maximum speed at 3,500 m. (11,500 ft.) 416 km.h. (260 m.p.h.), Cruising speed (60% output) at 5,000 m. (16,400 ft.) 360 km.h. (225 m.p.h.), Climb to 1,000 m. (3,280 ft.) 3 min. 10 sec., Climb to 2,000 m. (6,560 ft.) 6 min. 20 sec., Climb to 3,000 m. (9,840

ft.) 9 min., Climb to 4,000 m. (13,120 ft.) 13 min. 15 sec., Climb to 5,000 m. (16,400 ft.) 19 min. 45 sec., Service ceiling 7,000 m. (22,960 ft.), Range 1,600 km. (1,000 miles) or 4.5 hours.

THE SAVOIA-MARCHETTI SM.82.

The SM.82 was a development of the SM 75, from which it differed by having a deeper fuselage, greater loaded weight, redesigned fin and rudder and the addition of a hydraulically-operated retractable gun-turret with one 12.7 m/m. machine-gun on top of the fuselage to the rear of the pilot's cockpit. The remainder of the armament consisted of one 7.7 m/m. machine-gun in the nose and two guns of similar calibre mounted in lateral positions.

The deep fuselage was provided with overhead runway and block and tackle for the loading and movement of heavy freight and provision was made for the transportation of troops, supplies of petrol, aero-engines and even complete single-seat fighter aircraft in their dismantled state. Either 40 fully-armed troops or 600 gallons of petrol could be carried.

The SM.82 was fitted with three 950 h.p. Alfa Romeo 128 RC.21 nine-cylinder radial air-cooled engines. Structure followed standard Savoia-Marchetti practice with wood wings and welded steel-tube fuselage. The landing-gear retracted backwards into the wing engine nacelles.

The Savoia-Marchetti SM.79 Bomber (three 750 h.p. Alfa-Romeo 126 RC.34 engines).

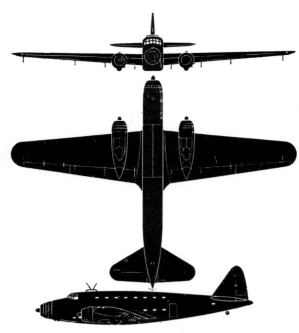

The Savoia-Marchetti SM.82 Transport.

DIMENSIONS.—Span 29.5 m. (97 ft. 5 in.), Length 22.5 m. (73 ft. 10 in.), Height 5.5 m. (18 ft.), Wing area 118.5 sq. m. (1,276 sq. ft.).

WEIGHTS.—Weight empty 12,000 kg. (26,400 lbs.), Weight loaded 18,020 kg. (39,700 lbs.).

PERFORMANCE.—Maximum speed 328 km.h. (205 m.p.h.) at 2,500 m. (8,200 ft.), Initial rate of climb 198 m./min. (650 ft./min.), Service ceiling 6,100 m. (20,000 ft.), Range 3,970 km. (2,480 miles) at 320 km.h. (200 m.p.h.).

JAPAN

AICHI.

AICHI TOKEI DENKI KABUSHIKI KAISHA (The Aichi Watch & Electric Machinery Co., Ltd.).

HEAD OFFICE AND WORKS : 15, CHITOSE FUNAKATACHO, NAGOYA.

BRANCH WORKS : 3, HORITADORI, MINAMIKU, NAGOYA. Established : 1899.

This company had supplied a number of different types of aircraft to the Japanese Naval Air Service. These included training aeroplanes and reconnaissance, torpedo and dive-bomber landplanes and seaplanes. The company also built aero-engines of both water and air-cooled types.

In addition to the types described below, the Aichi company was responsible for the production of the Yokosuka-designed "Suisei" carrier-borne Dive-Bomber and Reconnaissance monoplane.

THE AICHI B7A1 "GRACE."

Japanese Navy designation : "Ryusei" (Shooting Star) Carrier-borne Attack Plane, Model 11.

TYPE.—Two-seat Naval Torpedo-Bomber or Dive-Bomber.

WINGS.—Low-mid inverted gull-wing cantilever monoplane. Inner portion of each wing set at anhedral for about 20 per cent. of half span, remainder at fairly coarse dihedral. Outer wings at about 20 per cent. from knuckle fold upwards for stowage in aircraft-carriers. All-metal structure with flush-riveted stressed metal skin. Ailerons on outer folding sections, flaps inboard of ailerons to fuselage.

FUSELAGE.—Oval all-metal semi-monocoque structure with flush-riveted stressed skin.

TAIL UNIT.—Cantilever monoplane type. All-metal framework with metal-covered fixed surfaces and fabric-covered elevators and rudder. Controllable trim-tabs in all control surfaces.

LANDING GEAR.—Retractable type. Oleo shock-absorber struts hinged at wing knuckles and are raised inwardly into underside of wings. Fully-retractable tail-wheel.

POWER PLANT.—One Nakajima Homare 11 fourteen-cylinder radial air-cooled engine rated at 1,500 h.p. at 16,400 ft. (5,000 m.) and with 1,800 h.p. for take-off. Four-blade Hamilton type hydraulic constant-speed airscrew. Fuel tanks in wings.

ACCOMMODATION.—Crew of two in tandem under continuous transparent canopy with sliding sections over cockpits.

ARMAMENT.—Two forward-firing 7.7 m/m. machine-guns in fuselage cowling and one 7.7 m/m. gun operated by rear gunner. Provision for carrying one 1,760 lb. (880 kg.) torpedo or armour-piercing bomb of the same weight, or combinations of smaller bombs to a maximum of 1,100 lbs. (500 kg.) for dive-bombing.

DIMENSIONS.—Span 47 ft. 3 in. (14.4 m.), Length 37 ft. 7 in. (11.5 m.).

WEIGHTS.—Weight empty 6,820 lbs. (3,100 kg.), Normal loaded weight 10,780 lbs. (4,900 kg.), Maximum overloaded weight 11,792 lbs. (5,360 kg.).

PERFORMANCE.—Maximum speed 350 m.p.h. (560 km.h.) at 19,680 ft. (6,000 m.), Cruising speed 230 m.p.h. (368 km.h.) at 13,120 ft. (4,000 m.), Landing speed 75 m.p.h. (120 km.h.), Climb to 13,120 ft. (4,000 m.) 7.5 min., Range 1,200 miles (1,920 km.).

THE AICHI E13A1 "JAKE."

Japanese Navy designation : Type O Reconnaissance Seaplane, Model 11.

TYPE.—Three-seat Reconnaissance Seaplane.

WINGS.—Low-wing cantilever monoplane. Wing in three sections, comprising wide-span almost rectangular centre-section and two elliptical outer sections. Dihedral on outer sections only. All-metal structure. Flaps on centre-section, ailerons on outer sections.

FUSELAGE.—Oval all-metal structure with stressed skin covering.

TAIL UNIT.—Cantilever monoplane type. All-metal framework with metal-covered fixed surfaces and fabric-covered rudder and elevators. Trim-tabs in rudder and elevators.

FLOATS.—Two long single-step all-metal floats, each attached to the centre-section by two pairs of struts, one pair vertical and the other pair sloping inwardly to the centre-section spar root fittings. Steerable water rudders.

POWER PLANT.—One Mitsubishi Kinsei 43 or 44 fourteen-cylinder two-row radial air-cooled engine.

ACCOMMODATION.—Crew of two or three in tandem cockpits beneath a continuous transparent canopy.

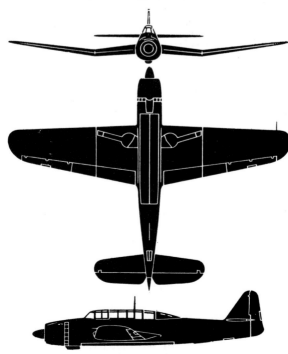

The Aichi "Grace" 11 Carrier-borne Attack Plane.

ARMAMENT.—Two 7.7 m/m. machine-guns in engine cowling and synchronised to fire through the airscrew, and one or two 7.7 m/m. guns on a flexible mounting in the rear cockpit.

DIMENSIONS.—Span 47 ft. 6 in. (14.5 m.), Length 36 ft. 11 in. (11.2 m.).

WEIGHTS AND PERFORMANCE.—No data available.

AICHI E16A1 "PAUL."

Japanese Navy designation : "Zuiun" (Auspicious Cloud) Reconnaissance Seaplane, Model 11.

TYPE.—Two-seat Naval Reconnaissance and Dive-Bomber Seaplane.

WINGS.—Low-wing cantilever monoplane. Constant taper from roots to tips with most taper on the trailing-edge. All-metal structure with detachable wood wing-tips. Double-acting Fowler type flaps between ailerons and fuselage. Trim-tabs in ailerons.

FUSELAGE.—All-metal structure with flush-riveted smooth stressed skin.

TAIL UNIT.—Cantilever monoplane type. All-wood tailplane. Metal fin and metal-framed fabric-covered elevators and rudder. Controllable trim-tabs in all movable surfaces.

FLOATS.—Twin single-step all-metal floats attached to the wings by vertical N-struts, the rear struts being braced to the underside of the fuselage by inclined struts. Hinged to the trailing-edges of the front vertical struts are hydraulically-operated double-acting dive-brakes. Water-rudder on stern of each float.

POWER PLANT.—One Mitsubishi Kinsei 54 fourteen-cylinder radial air-cooled engine rated at 1,080 h.p. at 20,000 ft. (6,100 m.). Three-bladed Mitsubishi-Hamilton constant-speed airscrew.

ACCOMMODATION.—Tandem cockpits under continuous transparent canopy with sliding sections over each cockpit.

ARMAMENT.—One 20 m/m. cannon in each wing and one 7.7 m/m. machine-gun on a flexible mounting in rear cockpit. For dive-bombing provision for two 550 lb. (250 kg.) bombs on special swinging racks under the fuselage.

DIMENSIONS.—Span 42 ft. (12.8 m.), Length 35 ft. 7 in. (11.5 m.).

WEIGHTS.—Weight empty 5,960 lbs. (2,710 kg.), Weight loaded 8,360 lbs. (3,800 kg.).

PERFORMANCE.—Maximum speed 278 m.p.h. (445 km.h.) at 19,680 ft. (6,000 m.), Cruising speed 178 m.p.h. (285 km.h.), Climb to 16,400 ft. (5,000 m.) 8 min., Range (Reconnaissance) 1,200 miles (1,920 km.), Range (Dive-bomber) 580 miles (930 km.).

THE AICHI D3A2 "VAL."

Japanese Navy designation: Type 99 Carrier-borne Bomber, Model 22.

TYPE.—Single-engined Naval Dive-Bomber, also being converted for training purposes.

WINGS.—Low-wing cantilever monoplane. Wing in three sections. Flat rectangular centre-section. Elliptical outer sections with dihedral. The outer sections of the wings hinge up about 6 ft. from each tip in order to save space on carriers. Flaps and the ailerons have inset trim-tabs. The structure is all-metal. Single slat-type dive-brakes are attached under the main spar.

FUSELAGE.—Oval section metal structure with metal covering.

TAIL UNIT.—Cantilever monoplane type with straight taper on leading edges of tailplane. High aspect-ratio elevators with curved trailing edges. Balanced rudder mounted completely above fuselage. Fin swept forward to just behind cockpit. Trim-tabs on elevators and rudder.

LANDING GEAR.—Fixed single leg cantilever type. Spats are fitted.

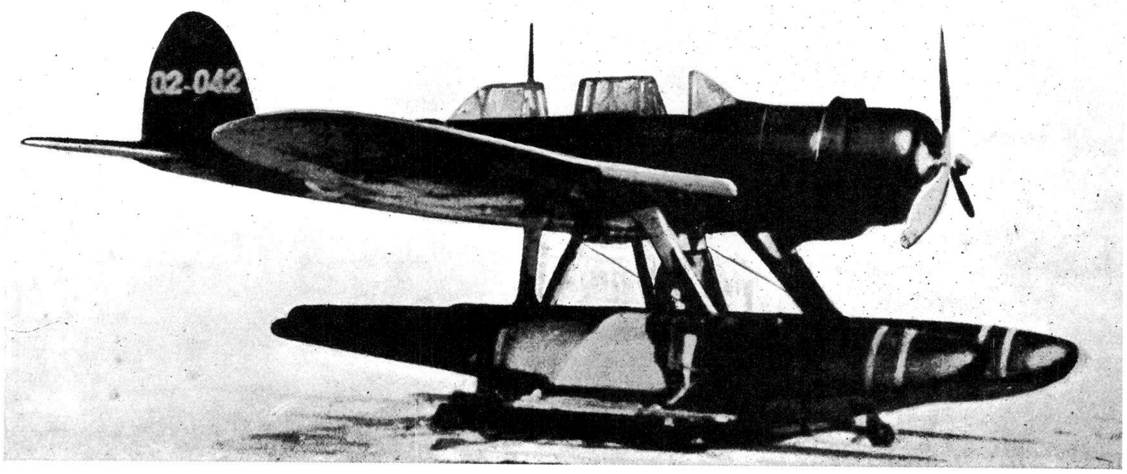

The Aichi "Jake" 11 Naval Reconnaissance Seaplane (Mitsubishi Kinsei 43 engine).

Fixed tail-wheel. Deck arrester-hook fitted just forward of tail-wheel.

Power Plant.—One 1,280 h.p. Mitsubishi Kinsei 54 fourteen-cylinder air-cooled radial engine. Fuel capacity 206 Imp. gallons.

Accommodation.—Enclosed transparent raised cockpit for crew of two starting over main spar and running back to aft of the trailing-edge.

Armament and Equipment.—Two 7.7 m/m. synchronised machine-guns mounted over the engine and one or two 7.7 m/m. flexible machine-guns in rear cockpit. One 250 kg. (550 lb.) bomb is carried under the fuselage and is swung down and forward on arms before release. In addition one 60 kg. (132 lb.) bomb can be carried on external rack under each wing outboard of the dive-brakes.

Dimensions.—Span 47 ft. 8 in. (14.53 m.), Length 34 ft. 9 in. (11.5 m.), Wing area 389 sq. ft. (36.2 sq. m.).

Weights and Loadings.—No data available.

Performance.—Maximum speed 281 m.p.h. (450 km.h.) at 20,300 ft. (6,100 m.), Range of 874 miles (1,400 km.) at 205 m.p.h. (328 km.h.), Ceiling of 30,000 ft. (9,180 m.).

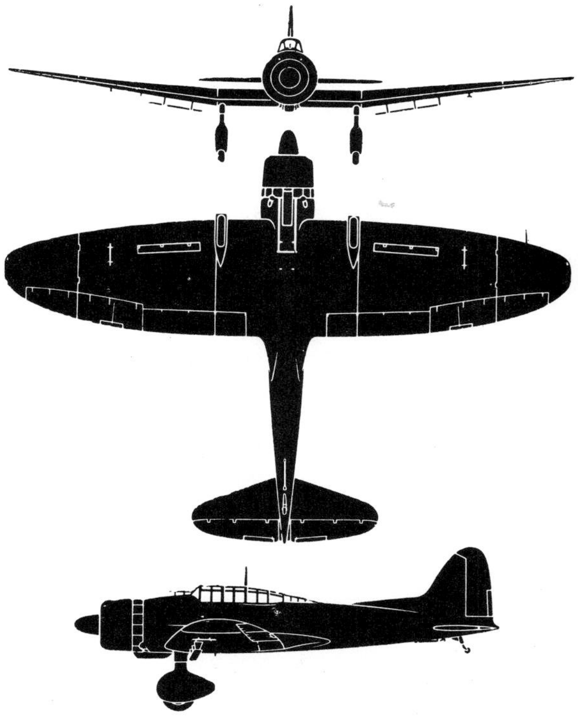

The Aichi "Val" 22 Navy Dive-bomber.

HITACHI.

HITACHI KOKUKI KABUSHIKI KAISHA (Hitachi Aircraft Co., Ltd.).

Head Office and Works: Ohmori, Nr. Tokyo.

Branch Works: Tatchikawa, Kawasaki and Haneda, near Tokyo.

Established: May, 1939.

This Company was formed in May, 1939, by the separation of the aircraft department of the Tokyo Gasu Denki K.K., which latter firm then concentrated its aeronautical activities solely in aero-engine construction.

Apart from the T.R.1 transport monoplane and the T.2 training sesquiplane described in previous editions, the Hitachi concern had under development the H.T.3 eight-passenger all-metal transport fitted with two 450 h.p. inverted Vee air-cooled (Hirth or Argus) engines. No details of this machine, which was being developed with financial assistance from the Japanese Government, are available.

KAWANISHI.

KAWANISHI KOKUKI KABUSHIKI KAISHA (The Kawanishi Aircraft Co., Ltd.).

Head Office and Works: Naruo Mukogun Hyogoken, near Kobe.

Established: November 5, 1928.

This Company was founded in November, 1928, and took over the aircraft works and wind-tunnel of the Kawanishi Machine Works. It was engaged in supplying aeroplanes, aircraft parts and accessories to the Japanese Navy.

Owing to the ever-increasing demand for such aeroplanes, the Company removed its works at the end of 1930 to the newly-built up-to-date works in Naruo, on the coast between Osaka and Kobe.

THE KAWANISHI H6K5 "MAVIS."

Japanese Navy designation : Type 97 Flying-boat, Model 23.

Type.—Four-engined Bomber-Reconnaissance flying-boat.

Wings.—Parasol strut-braced monoplane. Parallel leading and trailing edges to well outboard of outer engines and taper on outer wing sections. Dihedral from centre line of hull. All-metal structure. Flaps and ailerons take up the complete length of the trailing-edge. The wing is mounted above the hull on inverted V-struts and braced by two struts each side running from low down on the hull to half way along the span.

Hull.—All-metal shallow but wide two-step hull swept up to tailplane. Braced wing-tip floats are fitted rather far in from the tips.

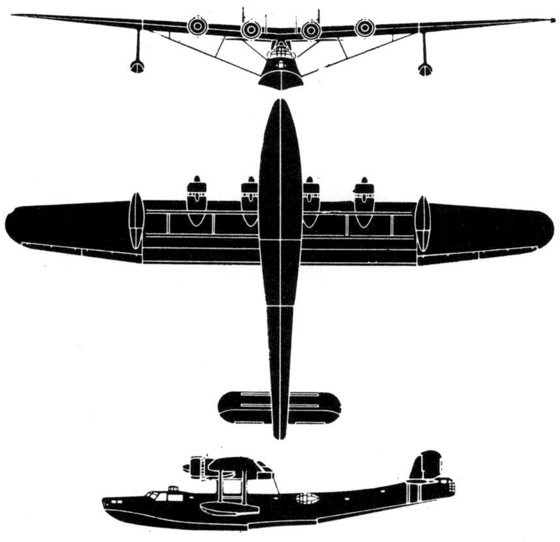

The Kawanishi "Mavis" 23 Flying-boat.

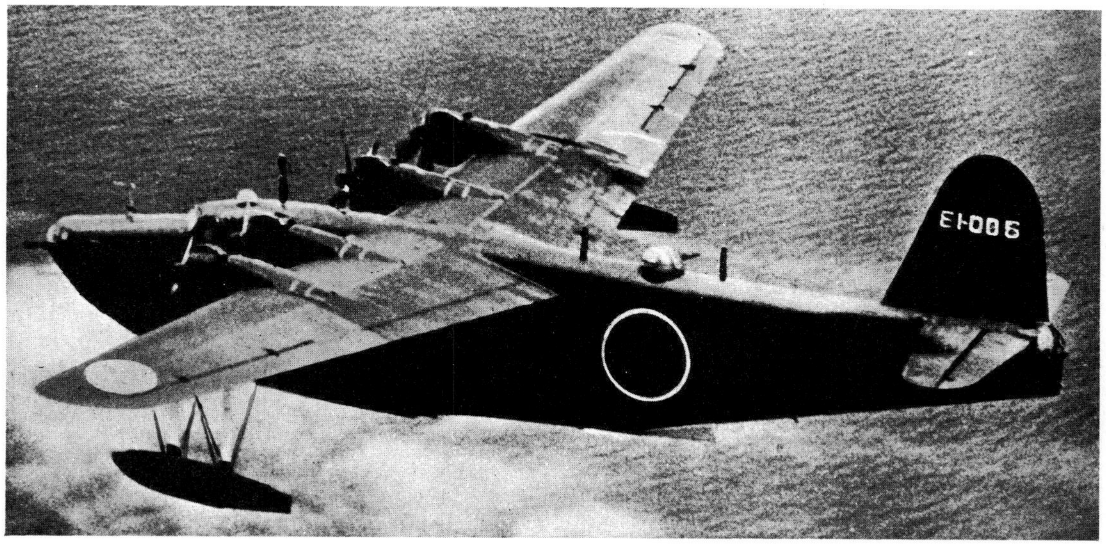

The Kawanishi "Emily" 22 Flying-boat (four Mitsubishi Kasei 22 engines).

Tail Unit.—Braced tailplane with two strut-braced fins and rudder mounted on the tailplane and inset.

Power Plant.—Four 900 h.p. Mitsubishi Kinsei 51 or 53 fourteen-cylinder radial air-cooled engines. Three-bladed metal airscrews. Fuel capacity 1,950 Imp. gallons.

Accommodation.—The crew are accommodated in a raised covered cockpit forward of the leading-edge of the wing. Designed as a civil flying-boat, the original accommodation was for twenty day passengers or a smaller number on night journeys with bunks. The service crew is ten.

Armament and Equipment.—Uncertain but believed to include two 20 m/m. cannon and several 7.7 m/m. machine-guns. Bomb load reported to be 3,500 lb. (1,590 kg.), externally slung.

Dimensions.—Span 131 ft. 4 in. (40 m.), Length 84 ft. (25.6 m.), Height 20 ft. (6.1 m.).

Weights.—Loaded 45,000 lbs. (20,430 kg.).

Performance.—Maximum speed 190 m.p.h. (304 km.h.) at 8,000 ft. (2,440 m.), Speed at sea level 170 m.p.h. (272 km.h.), Operational radius about 1,000 miles (1,600 km.), Service ceiling 26,000 ft. (4,880 m.).

THE KAWANISHI H8K2 "EMILY."

Japanese Navy designation : Type 2 Flying-boat, Model 12.

"Emily" was mainly used for long-range reconnaissance, but it was also in service as a transport flying-boat. The latter version carried the Japanese Navy designation "Seiku" (Clear Sky) Transport Flying-boat, Model 32. The type/model symbol was H8K1-L.

Type.—Four-engined Bomber-Reconnaissance flying-boat.

Wings.—High-wing cantilever monoplane. Straight taper on leading and trailing edges. Dihedral from roots. Structure of metal with metal covering. High aspect ratio ailerons. No information on flaps.

Hull.—All-metal deep two-step hull. Long nose with high bows. Almost slab-sided at centre-section and oval section aft. Large strut-braced wing-tip floats.

Tail Unit.—High cantilever tailplane with slight taper on both leading and trailing-edges. Large single fin and balanced rudder.

Power Plant.—Four 1,825 h.p. Mitsubishi Kasei 22 fourteen-cylinder radial air-cooled engines driving four-blade Hamilton type constant-speed airscrews. Protected fuel tanks in wings.

Accommodation.—Crew of ten to twelve. Armour protection.

Armament.—Has nose, dorsal and tail gun turrets and beam gun positions. Armament includes both 20 m/m. cannon and 7.9 m/m. machine-guns.

Dimensions.—Span 124 ft. 7 in. (38 m.), Length 92 ft. 3 in. (28.1 m.).

Weights.—Weight empty 34,000 lbs. (15,440 kg.), Weight loaded 68,000 lbs. (30,870 kg.).

Performance.—Maximum speed 296 m.p.h. (472 km.h.) at 19,680 ft. (6,000 m.), Cruising speed 172 m.p.h. (275 km.h.), Climb to 20,000 ft. (6,100 m.) 20 min., Service ceiling 28,000 ft. (8,540 m.), Maximum range 3,000 miles (4,800 km.).

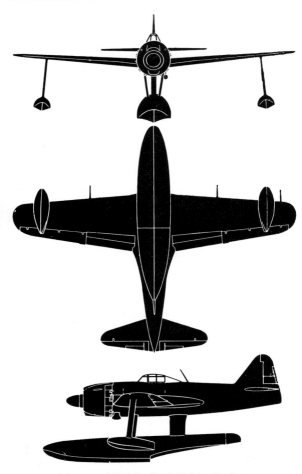

The Kawanishi "Rex" 11 Fighter Seaplane.

The Kawanishi "George" 11 Single-seat Naval Fighter (Nakajima Homare 21 engine).

THE KAWANISHI N1K1 "REX."
Japanese Navy designation : "Kyofu" (Mighty Wind) Fighter-Seaplane, Model 11.
TYPE.—Single-seat Fighter-Seaplane.
WINGS.—Mid-wing cantilever monoplane. Wings of equal taper and with rounded tips. All-metal structure with flush-riveted stressed-skin covering. Flaps inboard of ailerons.
FUSELAGE.—Almost circular section all-metal structure with flush-riveted stressed-skin covering.
TAIL UNIT.—Cantilever monoplane type. All-metal framework with metal-covered tailplane and fin and fabric-covered elevators and rudder. Rudder has shielded horn balance and is entirely above rear end of fuselage.
FLOATS.—Central single-step all-metal float and two stabilising wing-tip floats, all on cantilever struts.
POWER PLANT.—One 1,550 h.p. Mitsubishi Kasei fourteen-cylinder two-row air-cooled radial engine.
ACCOMMODATION.—Enclosed cockpit over trailing-edge of wing. Blister-type canopy. Pilot armour.
ARMAMENT.—No data available.
DIMENSIONS.—Span 39 ft. 4 in. (12 m.), Length 35 ft. 4 in. (10.8 m.).
WEIGHTS AND PERFORMANCE.—No data available.

THE KAWANISHI N1K2-J "GEORGE."
Japanese Navy designation : "Shiden" (Violet Lightning) Fighter, Model 11.
"George" was a single-seat landplane fighter development of the Kawanishi N1K1 single-seat fighter seaplane.
TYPE.—Single-seat Fighter.
WINGS.—Low mid-wing monoplane. Structure as for "Rex."
FUSELAGE AND TAIL UNIT.—Same as for "Rex."
LANDING GEAR.—Retractable type. Wide track with main wheels and oleo legs raised inwardly into recesses in underside of wings. Hydraulic retraction. Retractable tail-wheel.
POWER PLANT.—One 2,000 h.p. Nakajima Homare 21 eighteen-cylinder two-row radial air-cooled engine with ejector exhausts. Four-blade constant-speed airscrew.
ACCOMMODATION.—Same as for "Rex".
ARMAMENT.—Four 20 m/m. wing cannon and two 7.7 m/m. machine-guns in fuselage and synchronised to fire through the airscrew. Wing cannon are in pairs.
DIMENSIONS.—Span 39 ft. 4 in. (12 m.), Length 29 ft. 4 in. (8.9 m.).
WEIGHTS.—No data available.
PERFORMANCE.—Maximum speed over 400 m.p.h. (640 km.h.) at 20,000 ft. (6,100 m.).

THE KAWANISHI E15K1 "NORM."
Japanese Navy designation : "Shiun" (Violet Cloud) High-speed Reconnaissance Seaplane, Model 11.
"Norm" was a single-engined two-seat Reconnaissance single-float seaplane. It was fitted with a Mitsubishi Kasei 24 fourteen-cylinder two-row radial engine. Armament consisted of one 7.7 m/m. machine-gun on a flexible mounting in the rear cockpit.
DIMENSIONS.—Span 45 ft. 9 in. (13.9 m.), Length 37 ft. 7 in. (11.5 m.), Height 16 ft. 4 in. (4.9 m.).
WEIGHTS.—No data available.
PERFORMANCE.—Maximum speed 300 m.p.h. (480 km.h.) at 19,680 ft. (6,000 m.).

KAWASAKI.
KAWASAKI KOKUKU KOGYO KABUSHIKI KAISHA (The Kawasaki Aircraft Engineering Co., Ltd.).
HEAD OFFICE AND WORKS : HIGASHI-KAWASAKI-CHO, HYOGO, KOBE.
A famous firm of shipbuilders which entered the Aircraft Industry by constructing, under licence, the Salmson biplane and the Salmson engine, large numbers of which were supplied to the Japanese Army. From 1923 to 1933 the Chief Designer of the Company was Doctor Richard Vogt.

THE KAWASAKI ARMY 99 LIGHT BOMBER "LILY."
Japanese Army Designation : Type 99 Light Bomber, Model 2.
TYPE.—Twin-engined Light Bomber.
WINGS.—Mid-wing cantilever monoplane with straight taper on leading and trailing-edges and dihedral from roots. Metal structure with flaps between fuselage and engine nacelles and between nacelles and ailerons. The ailerons are fabric-covered. Landing-light in leading-edge of both wings. Small fillet on trailing-edge roots.
FUSELAGE.—Deep metal structure to aft of trailing-edge. Slender rear fuselage. Metal covering. Bomb stowage in centre-section.
TAIL UNIT.—High cantilever tailplane with metal covering. Fabric-covered elevators. Single metal fin. Fabric-covered rudder. The trim-tabs on rudder and elevators are metal.
LANDING GEAR.—Retracts backwards into engine nacelles leaving part of each wheel exposed. Tail-wheel semi-retractable.
POWER PLANT.—Two 1,150 h.p. Nakajima Type 2 (Ha 115) fourteen-cylinder radial air-cooled engines. Underslung nacelles extend to trailing-edge. Controllable cooling gills are fitted to the cowlings. Three-bladed metal airscrews.
ACCOMMODATION.—Transparent bomb-aiming and gun position in nose. Covered cockpit just forward of leading-edge and another covered position over trailing-edge. Crew of four or five.
ARMAMENT AND EQUIPMENT.—Believed one forward 7.7 m/m. machine-gun, two 7.7 m/m. dorsal machine-guns, and one 7.7 m/m. machine-gun in the fuselage step aft of the wing. All armament is movable. Internally-stowed bomb load 1,500 lbs. (680 kg.).
DIMENSIONS.—Span 57 ft. 9 in. (17.6 m.), Length 40 ft. 6 in. (12.35 m.).
WEIGHTS AND LOADINGS.—No data available.
PERFORMANCE.—Maximum speed 285 m.p.h. (456 km.h.) at 14,000 ft. (4,270 m.), Speed at sea level 255 m.p.h. (408 km.h.), Maximum operational radius 500-600 miles (800-960 km.).

THE KAWASAKI Ki 45 "NICK."
Japanese Army designation : Type 2 Heavy Fighter, Model 1.
Popular name : "Toryu" (Dragon Slayer).
TYPE.—Twin-engined Fighter.
WINGS.—Mid-wing cantilever monoplane. Wings of equal taper with rounded tips. All-metal structure with flush-riveted smooth stressed skin. Split trailing-edge flaps between ailerons and fuselage.
FUSELAGE.—Oval section all-metal semi-monocoque structure with smooth stressed-skin covering.
TAIL UNIT.—Cantilever monoplane type. All-metal framework with metal-covered tailplane and fin and fabric-covered elevators and rudder. Rudder has shielded horn balance and hinge-line does not extend below top of fuselage.
LANDING GEAR.—Retractable type. Hydraulic retraction. Main wheels raised backwards into engine nacelles and hinged doors enclose wheels within contours of nacelles. Retractable tail-wheel.
POWER PLANT.—Two 1,050 h.p. Mitsubishi Type 1 (Ha 102) fourteen-

The Kawasaki "Lily" 2 Light Bomber (two Nakajima Type 2 engines).

The Kawasaki "Nick" 1 Two-seat Fighter (two 1,050 h.p. Mitsubishi Type 1 engines).

cylinder two-row radial air-cooled engines with two-speed super-chargers and driving three-blade Hamilton type constant-speed airscrews. Fuel tanks in wings.
ACCOMMODATION.—Crew of two. Pilot's cockpit over leading-edge and rear gunner over trailing-edge.
ARMAMENT.—Two 12.7 m/m. machine-guns in nose of fuselage and two 7.7 m/m. machine-guns on flexible mounting in rear cockpit. Armament may also consist of either a 20 m/m. or 37 m/m. cannon in the nose and two 20 m/m. fixed guns behind the pilot's cockpit

and inclined to fire upwards.
DIMENSIONS.—Span 49 ft. 6 in. (15 m.), Length 34 ft. 5 in. (10.5 m.), Wing area 365 sq. ft. (34 sq. m.).
WEIGHTS.—Weight empty 8,340 lbs. (3,790 kg.), Weight loaded 12,000 lbs. (5,450 kg.).
PERFORMANCE.—Maximum speed 355 m.p.h. (568 km.h.) at 16,400 ft. 5,000 m., Climb to 10,000 ft. (3,050 m.) 4 mins., Climb to 20,000 ft. (6,100 m.) 9 mins., Service ceiling 35,000 ft. (10,680 m.), Range 640 miles (1,025 km.).

THE KAWASAKI Ki 61 "TONY."

Japanese Army designation : Type 3 Fighter, Model 1.

TYPE.—Single-seat Fighter.

WINGS.—Low-wing cantilever monoplane. Wings of equal taper and rounded tips. All-metal structure with flush-riveted smooth stressed skin. Split flaps between ailerons and fuselage.

FUSELAGE.—Oval section all-metal structure with flush-riveted stressed skin covering.

TAIL UNIT.—Cantilever monoplane type. All-metal framework with metal-covered fixed surfaces and fabric-covered elevators and rudder.

LANDING GEAR.—Retractable type. Main wheels raised inwardly into underside of wings. Hydraulic retraction. Retractable tail-wheel.

POWER PLANT.—One 1,100 h.p. Kawasaki Type 2 (DB 601A licence) twelve-cylinder inverted Vee liquid-cooled engine driving a three-blade constant-speed airscrew. Ventral radiator beneath pilot's cockpit. Protected fuel tanks in wings.

ACCOMMODATION.—Pilot's cockpit over rear spar of wing. Sliding cockpit canopy.

ARMAMENT.—Two 20 m/m. cannon or 12.7 m/m. machine-guns, one in each wing and firing outside airscrew disc, and two 12.7 or 7.7 m/m. machine-guns in cowling above engine and synchronised to fire through the airscrew. Bomb-racks beneath wings outboard of wing guns.

DIMENSIONS.—Span 39 ft. 4 in. (12 m.). Length 30 ft. 1 in. (9.2 m.).

WEIGHTS.—No data available.

PERFORMANCE.—Maximum speed 356 m.p.h. (570 km.h.) at 16,400 ft. (5,000 m.).

The Kawasaki "Tony" 1 Single-seat Fighter (1,100 h.p. Kawasaki Type 2 engine).

MITSUBISHI.

MITSUBISHI JUKOGYO KABUSHIKI KAISHA (Mitsubishi Heavy Industries, Ltd.).

HEAD OFFICE : No. 4, NICHOME, MARUNOUCHI, KOJIMACHI-KU, TOKYO.

NAGOYA AIRCRAFT WORKS : OE-MACHI, MINAMI-KU, NAGOYA.

TOKYO ENGINEERING WORKS : OI-MORIMAE-CHO, SHINAGAWA-KU, TOKYO.

Established : October, 1917.

The Aircraft Branch of the Mitsubishi Combine had, since its inauguration supplied to the Imperial Japanese Navy and Army a great number of Fighters and Bombers, Deck Fighters, Deck Reconnaissance machines, Deck Bombers and Training machines.

The Nagoya Works was the largest of its kind in Japan, and its equipment comprised the most up-to-date machinery and apparatus for the production of aircraft and aero-engines.

The Tokyo Engineering Works were located at Oimachi, within the limits of the Capital and here were manufactured aeronautical armament, various classes of instruments and vehicles.

THE MITSUBISHI A7M1 "SAM."

Japanese Navy designation : "Reppu" (Hurricane) Carrier-based Fighter, Model 11.

"Sam" is believed to be a development of "Zeke" but no details of structure, power-plant, armament or performance were available at the time of closing for press.

THE MITSUBISHI J4M1 "LUKE."

Japanese Navy designation : "Jinrai" (Thunderclap) Fighter, Model 11.

"Luke" is believed to be a single-engined twin-boom Intercepter Fighter Monoplane. No further details were available at the time of closing for press.

THE MITSUBISHI J2M2 "JACK."

Japanese Navy designation : "Raiden" (Thunderbolt) Fighter, Model 11.

"Jack" was a single-seat land-based Fighter of the type which falls into the Japanese Kyokuchi or Kyoku (Interceptor) Class. J2M2 was the production development of the J2M1 experimental prototype.

TYPE.—Single-seat Interceptor Fighter.

WINGS.—Low-wing cantilever monoplane. One-piece wing has equal taper and dihedral from roots to rounded tips and is built integral with the forward section of the fuselage. All-metal structure with flush-riveted smooth stressed skin covering. Flaps between ailerons and fuselage.

FUSELAGE.—Oval section all-metal semi-monocoque structure with flush-riveted smooth stressed skin covering.

TAIL UNIT.—Cantilever monoplane type. Tailplane and elevators forward of rudder hinge-line. All-metal framework with metal-covered fixed surfaces and fabric-covered rudder and elevators. Trim-tabs in all control surfaces.

LANDING-GEAR.—Retractable type. Main wheels and oleo legs retracted hydraulically inward into recesses in underside of wings. Retractable tail-wheel.

POWER PLANT.—One 1,850 h.p. Mitsubishi Kasei 23 fourteen-cylinder two-row radial air-cooled engine with two-speed supercharger. Ejector exhaust stacks. Four-blade Hamilton type constant-speed airscrew. Protected fuel tanks in wings. Auxiliary fuel tanks may be carried under the fuselage.

ACCOMMODATION.—Enclosed cockpit over trailing-edge of wing. Sliding canopy of the rear-view type in Model 31. Pilot armour.

ARMAMENT.—Two 7.7 m/m. machine-guns in fuselage and synchronised to fire through the airscrew, and two 20 m/m. cannon, one in each wing outboard of the airscrew disc.

DIMENSIONS.—Span 35 ft. 5 in. (10.8 m.), Length 31 ft. 10 in. (9.7 m.).

WEIGHTS.—No data available.

PERFORMANCE.—Maximum speed over 400 m.p.h. (640 km.h.) at 20,000 ft. (6,100 m.).

THE MITSUBISHI A6M5 "ZEKE."

Japanese Navy designation : Type O Carrier-borne Fighter, Model 52.

There were five stages in the development of "Zeke". The original Zero, or "Zeke" 11, was the standard carrier-borne fighter in the Japanese Navy when Pearl Harbour was attacked. It was fitted with a Nakajima "Sakae" (Prosperity) 12 engine and wings of 39 ft. 5 in. (12 m.) span.

"Zeke" 21, built by Nakajima, had the same engine and wing span, but the wing-tips were arranged to fold upwards to facilitate stowage in aircraft-carriers. Normal fuel capacity was 142 U.S. gallons.

"Zeke" 22 was fitted with the Nakajima Sakae 21 engine with two-speed supercharger and downdraught carburetter and had a normal fuel capacity of 156 U.S. gallons.

"Zeke" 32, which was originally given the code name of "Hamp", was fitted with clipped square-tipped wings of 36 ft.

The Mitsubishi "Jack" 11 Single-seat Naval Fighter (1,850 h.p. Mitsubishi Kasei 23 engine).

2 in. (11 m.) span, a modification achieved by the removal of the folding wing-tips, and had a reduced fuel capacity of 134 U.S. gallons.

"Zeke" 52, the latest standard carrier-borne version described below, had round-tipped wings of the same span as the Model 32. The "Zeke" 53 was fitted with the improved Nakajima Sakae 31 engine with individual ejector exhaust stacks.

TYPE.—Single-seat Naval Carrier-borne or Land-based Fighter.

WINGS.—Low-wing cantilever monoplane. One-piece wing built integrally with the forward section of the fuselage. All-metal two-spar structure, the spars being continuous from tip to tip. Spars have extruded booms and sheet webs. Stressed skin covering. Hydraulically-operated split trailing-edge flaps between ailerons and fuselage.

FUSELAGE.—Oval section light alloy semi-monocoque structure in two sections divided at a vertical bulkhead aft of the pilot's cockpit. Forward section built integrally with the wing, the upper surface of which forms the floor of the cockpit. Front and rear sections butt-jointed and secured by 80 bolts.

TAIL UNIT.—Cantilever monoplane type. All-metal framework with the fixed surfaces metal-covered and the control surfaces covered with fabric. Controllable trim-tabs in elevators. Trim-tab in rudder adjustable on the ground only.

LANDING GEAR.—Retractable type. Hydraulic retraction, the main wheels being raised inwardly. Fairing plates on oleo legs and hinged doors under wing close apertures when wheels raised. Partly retractable tail-wheel. Deck-arrester hook flush with fuselage just forward of tail wheel.

POWER PLANT.—One Nakajima Sakae 21 fourteen-cylinder radial air-cooled engine with two-speed supercharger and downdraught carburettor. Rated at 1,020 h.p. at 6,400 ft. (1,950 m.), 885 h.p. at 15,700 ft. (4,790 m.) and with 950 h.p. available for take-off. Mitsubishi-Hamilton three-blade constant-speed airscrew 10 ft. (3.05 m.) diameter. Three unprotected fuel tanks, one in fuselage just forward of cockpit and two in wing, one on each side of the fuselage. Maximum internal fuel capacity 156 U.S. gallons. Permanent faired fitting on centre-line of fuselage to support metal or wood stream-line jettisonable fuel tank of 94 U.S. gallons capacity. Small wing tank ventilators in underside of each wing to help to prevent vapour-lock at altitude. Oil tank (13 U.S. gallons) in engine compartment.

ACCOMMODATION.—Pilot's enclosed cockpit over centre of wing. No pilot armour, bulletproof windscreen nor emergency release for canopy.

ARMAMENT AND EQUIPMENT.—Two 7.7 m/m. machine-guns (similar to .303 in. Vickers Mk. V) in cowling and synchronised to fire through the airscrew, and two 20 m/m. Japanese-built Oerlikon cannon in wings. 600 rounds per machine-gun and 100 rounds per cannon. Provision for carrying one 132 lb. (60 kg.) bomb under each wing, mainly for air-to-air bombing attacks. Two watertight compartments in each wing and canvas bag in rear fuselage for flotation.

The Mitsubishi "Zeke" 52 Single-seat Naval Fighter (1,200 h.p. Nakajima Sakae 21 engine).

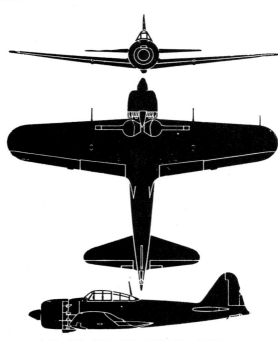

The Mitsubishi "Zeke" 52 Naval Fighter.

Valve in cockpit (normally open) is closed in emergency to trap air at atmospheric pressure in entire flotation system.
DIMENSIONS.—Span 36 ft. 2 in. (11 m.), Length 29 ft. 9 in. (9 m.), Height 9 ft. 2 in. (2.8 m.), Wing area 238 sq. ft. (22.1 sq. m.).
WEIGHTS AND LOADINGS.—Weight empty 3,920 lbs. (1,780 kg.), Normal loaded weight 5,750 lbs. (2.610 kg.), Maximum permissable weight 6,330 lbs. (2,874 kg.), Wing loading 24.2 lbs./sq. ft. (118 kg./sq. m.), Power loading 5.63 lbs./h.p. (2.55 kg./h.p.).
PERFORMANCE.—Maximum speed 340 m.p.h. (544 km.h.) at 19,700 ft. (6,000 m.), Maximum rate of climb 3,020 ft./min. (920 m./min.) at 8,000 ft. (2,440 m.).

THE MITSUBISHI A6M2-N "RUFE."

Japanese Navy designation : Type 2 Fighter Seaplane, Model 11.
TYPE.—Single-seat Fighter Seaplane.

The Mitsubishi "Rufe" 11 Single-seat Fighter Seaplane (Nakajima Sakae 12 engine).

The Mitsubishi "Pete" 11 Observation Seaplane (900 h.p. Mitsubishi Zuisei 13 engine).

WINGS AND FUSELAGE.—As for "Zeke" 11.
TAIL UNIT.—Tailplane, elevators and fin as for "Zeke" 11. The rudder has been given increased area and extends to the bottom line of the fuselage. Two small fins have been added under rear fuselage and rudder base.
FLOAT GEAR.—Large central single-step float strut-braced to centre-section. Two stabilising floats near wing-tips, each suspended by a single strut.
POWER PLANT, ACCOMMODATION AND ARMAMENT.—As for "Zeke" 11.
DIMENSIONS.—Span 39 ft. 5 in. (12 m.), Length 33 ft. 9 in. (10.3 m.).
WEIGHTS AND LOADINGS.—No data available.
PERFORMANCE.—Maximum speed 265 m.p.h. (424 km.h.).

THE MITSUBISHI F1M2 "PETE."

Japanese Navy designation : Type O Observation Seaplane, Model 11.
TYPE.—Single-engined Naval Reconnaissance catapult seaplane.
WINGS.—Unequal-span braced single-bay staggered biplane. Each wing in three sections comprising flat centre-section and dihedral outer sections. Taper on leading and trailing edges. Ailerons on upper and lower wings. Flaps on lower wing. "N" centre-section struts and single interplane struts. Wire-bracing.
FUSELAGE.—Construction uncertain.
TAIL UNIT.—Cantilever monoplane type. Elliptical tailplane. Balanced elevators. Single fin and rudder. Trim-tabs in rudder and elevators.
FLOAT GEAR.—Large central float with pylon mounting forward of lower wing and two side-by-side struts under centre-section trailing-edge. Stabilizing floats strut-braced to lower wing-tips.
POWER PLANT.—One 900 h.p. Mitsubishi Zuisei 13 fourteen-cylinder radial air-cooled engine. Three-bladed metal airscrew.
ACCOMMODATION.—Open cockpit for pilot under cut-away in upper wing. Rear cockpit at lower level. Front half with transparent canopy.
ARMAMENT.—Two fixed 7.7 m/m. machine-guns in engine cowling and one 7.7 m/m. movable machine-gun in rear cockpit.
DIMENSIONS.—Span 37 ft. (11.28 m.), Length 34 ft. 6 in. (10.5 m.).
WEIGHTS AND LOADINGS.—No data available.
PERFORMANCE.—Maximum speed 200 m.p.h. (320 km.h.) at 5,000 ft. (1,525 m.), Speed at sea level 185 m.p.h. (296 km.h.), Operating radius 225 miles (260 km.).

THE MITSUBISHI Ki 462 "DINAH."

Japanese Army designation : Type 100 H.Q. Reconnaissance Plane, Model 2.
TYPE.—Twin-engined Reconnaissance monoplane.
WINGS.—Low-wing cantilever monoplane with straight taper on leading and trailing-edges. Dihedral outboard of narrow centre-section. Flaps extend from centre-section to ailerons.
FUSELAGE.—Oval section all-metal structure.
TAIL UNIT.—Cantilever tailplane placed well forward. Single fin and rudder. Trim-tabs on elevators and rudder.
LANDING GEAR.—Backwardly-retracting into engine nacelles. Retractable tail-wheel.
POWER PLANT.—Two 1,050 h.p. Mitsubishi Type 1 (Ha 102) fourteen-cylinder radial air-cooled engines. Nacelles extend to trailing-edge. Three-bladed controllable-pitch airscrews.

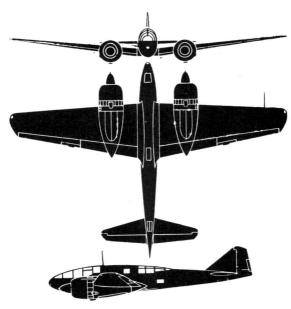

The Mitsubishi "Dinah" 3 Reconnaissance Monoplane which differs from Model 2 in the shape of the forward cockpit canopy.

ACCOMMODATION.—Pilot's cockpit above leading-edge with another covered position aft of the trailing-edge.
ARMAMENT.—Normally as armament is carried.
DIMENSIONS.—Span 48 ft. 3 in. (14.7 m.), Length 36 ft. 1 in. (10.9 m.).
WEIGHTS AND LOADINGS.—No data available.
PERFORMANCE.—Maximum speed 370 m.p.h. (592 km.h.) at 20,000 ft. (6,100 m.), Speed at sea level 310 m.p.h. (496 km.h.), Maximum operational range 1,800 miles (2,880 km.).

THE MITSUBISHI Ki 67 "PEGGY."

Japanese Army designation : Type 4 Heavy Bomber, Model 1.
There were two versions of "Peggy" 1, the standard Bomber carrying a crew of seven, a bomb load of about 3,500 lbs. and with an armament of one 20 m/m. cannon and four 12.7 m/m. machine-guns ; and a Special Attack model which was used for suicide attacks on Allied shipping. This latter version was un-armed, had faired-in nose and tail, no side blisters, and carried a crew of three. A long rod projecting from the nose tripped a switch to explode two 1,760 lb. bombs on impact with the target. Both versions carried their bombs internally. The Bomber version was fitted with crutches to carry one standard naval torpedo instead of bombs.

TYPE.—Twin-engined Bomber.
WINGS.—Mid-wing cantilever monoplane. Equal taper and dihedral from roots to tips. All-metal structure with flush-riveted smooth metal skin. Hydraulically-operated split trailing-edge flaps inboard of ailerons.
FUSELAGE.—Oval section all-metal semi-monocoque structure covered with a flush-riveted stressed skin.
TAIL UNIT.—Cantilever monoplane type. All-metal structure with stressed-skin covering. Trim-tabs in elevators and rudder.
LANDING-GEAR.—Retractable type. Main wheels raised backwards into engine nacelles. Tail-wheel partly retractable. Hydraulic retraction.
POWER PLANT.—Two 1,920 h.p. Mitsubishi Ha 42 eighteen-cylinder two-row radial air-cooled engines with multi-blade cooling fans

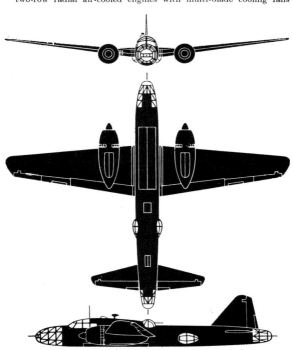

The Mitsubishi "Peggy" 1 Heavy Bomber.

The Mitsubishi "Dinah" 2 Army Reconnaissance Monoplane (two 1,050 h.p. Mitsubishi Type 1 engines).

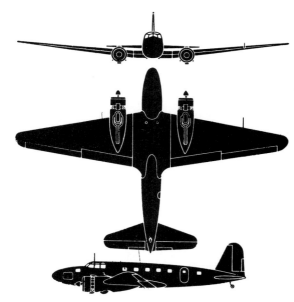

The Mitsubishi "Topsy" 1 Transport.

The Mitsubishi "Betty" 11 Naval Bomber (two Mitsubishi Kasei 15 engines).

All tanks except outboard wing tanks have rubber protection. Protected oil tank in leading-edge of wings. Fuel capacity 810 Imp. gallons.

ACCOMMODATION.—Normal crew of five to seven.

ARMAMENT AND EQUIPMENT.—Two 7.7 m/m. movable machine-guns in nose, dorsal and lateral positions, two 7.7 m/m. ventral machine-guns, and remote-controlled fixed machine-gun in extreme tail of fuselage. Maximum internal bomb load 4,400 lbs. (2,000 kg.).

DIMENSIONS.—Span 74 ft. 8 in. (22.8 m.), Length 52 ft. (15.86 m.), Height 11 ft. 11 in. (36.6 m.), Wing area 675 sq. ft. (62.7 sq. m.).

WEIGHTS.—Weight empty 10,450 lbs. (4,750 kg.), Weight loaded 22,000 lbs. (10,000 kg.).

PERFORMANCE.—Maximum speed 248 m.p.h. (397 km.h.) at 8,000 ft. (2,440 m.), Speed at sea level 225 m.p.h. (360 km.h.), Operational range 600-700 miles (960-1,120 km.), Service ceiling 22,000 ft. (6,710 m.).

THE MITSUBISHI Ki 57 "TOPSY."
Japanese Army designation : Type 100 Transport Plane, Model 1.

TYPE.—Twin-engined Military Transport evolved from the M.C. 20 civil transport.

WINGS.—Low-wing cantilever monoplane. In three sections, comprising a narrow centre-section attached to the underside of the fuselage and two tapering outer sections. Dihedral on outer sections. All-metal construction with stressed-skin covering.

FUSELAGE.—Oval metal monocoque structure.

TAIL UNIT.—Cantilever monoplane type. Metal framework with metal covered fixed surfaces and fabric-covered movable surfaces. Trimming-tabs in elevators and rudder.

LANDING GEAR.—Retractable type. Each unit comprises two oleo shock-absorber legs and a backwardly-inclined forked strut. Wheels are raised upwards and forwards round the hinge-points of the forked struts into the engine nacelles. Hydraulic retraction. Non-retractable tail-wheel.

POWER PLANT.—Two 850 h.p. Mitsubishi Type 97 (Ha 5) fourteen-cylinder radial air-cooled engines. Three-bladed controllable-pitch airscrews. Fuel tanks in the wings.

ACCOMMODATION.—Crew of four, comprising pilot, second pilot, navigator and radio operator. Cabin can accommodate from 12 to 20 passengers or troops according to mission. Equipment includes automatic pilot, full radio equipment, etc.

DIMENSIONS.—Span 74 ft. (22.6 m.), Length 52 ft. 8 in. (16 m.), Height 16 ft. (4.9 m.), Wing area 755 sq. ft. (70 sq. m.).

WEIGHTS AND LOADINGS.—Weight empty 11,900 lbs. (5,400 kg.), Disposable load 6,400 lbs. (2,900 kg.), Weight loaded 18,300 lbs. (8,300 kg.), Wing loading 24.2 lbs./sq. ft. (118 kg./sq. m.), Power loading 8.8 lbs./h.p. (4 kg./h.p.).

PERFORMANCE.—Maximum speed 266 m.p.h. (426 km.h.), Cruising speed 193 m.p.h. (309 km.h.) at 7,000 ft. (2,135 m.), Landing speed 75 m.p.h. (120 km.h.), Service ceiling 23,000 ft. (7,020 m.), Normal cruising range 1,240 miles (1,985 km.), Maximum range (with fuel overload) 1,865 miles (2,985 km.).

---

in the cowling openings and driving four-blade VDM type hydraulically-operated constant-speed full-feathering airscrew. Protected fuel tanks in wings and fuselage. Protected oil tank in leading-edge of each wing.

ACCOMMODATION.—Normal crew of seven, comprising nose gunner, two pilots, radio operator, turret gunner, waist gunner and tail gunner. Armour protection for pilot and co-pilot.

ARMAMENT.—One 20 m/m. cannon in dorsal power-operated turret and four flexibly-mounted 12.7 m/m. machine-guns, one in nose, one in each waist blister and one on tail mounting. Internal bomb stowage.

DIMENSIONS.—Span 73 ft. 5 in. (22.4 m.), Length 63 ft. 10 in. (19.4 m.).

WEIGHT LOADED.—30,500 lbs. (13,850 kg.).

PERFORMANCE.—Maximum speed 346 m.p.h. (554 km.h.) at 18,700 ft. (5,700 m.).

THE MITSUBISHI G4M2 "BETTY."
Japanese Navy designation : Type 1 Land Attack Plane, Model 22.

In addition to "Betty" 22 described below, a later "Betty" 24 had slightly bulged bomb-bay doors and an armament of one 7.7 m/m. gun in the nose and four 20 m/m. cannon, one each in the dorsal and tail turret and one in each waist position.

TYPE.—Twin-engined Naval Land-based Bomber or Reconnaissance monoplane. Also used as carrier for "Baka" suicide bomb.

WINGS.—Mid-wing cantilever monoplane of constant taper and thickness from roots to tips. Structure comprises centre-section, two outer sections and two detachable tips. All-metal two-spar structure with flush-riveted smooth stressed skin. Electrically-operated all-metal flaps between ailerons and fuselage. Statically-balanced Frise type ailerons with controllable trim-tabs.

FUSELAGE.—Elliptical section semi-monocoque of aluminium-alloy construction.

TAIL UNIT.—Cantilever monoplane type. Aluminium-alloy framework with metal-covered fixed surfaces and fabric-covered elevators and rudder. Aerodynamically-balanced control surfaces fitted with trim-tabs.

LANDING GEAR.—Retractable type. Main wheels raised forward into engine nacelles. Electrical retraction, with separate motor for tail-wheel retraction.

POWER PLANT.—Two Mitsubishi Kasei 21 fourteen-cylinder radial air-cooled engines with two-speed superchargers and water injection system. Engines rated at 1,350 h.p. at 10,000 ft. (3,500 m.) 1,260 h.p. at 20,000 ft. (6,100 m.) and with 1,500 h.p. available for take-off. Four-blade Mitsubishi-Hamilton constant-speed airscrews. Ten fuel tanks, five in each wing. Oil tanks in leading-edge of centre-section inboard of nacelles.

ACCOMMODATION.—Crew of six/seven. Navigator/bomb aimer in nose, two pilots side-by-side in cockpit forward of leading-edge, upper turret gunner, one or two waist gunners and tail gunner.

ARMAMENT.—One 7.7 m/m. machine-gun in nose, one 20 m/m. cannon in upper turret, two 7.7 m/m. guns in side ports, one on each side of fuselage aft of wings, and one 20 m/m. cannon in tail. The nose gun is in a ball mount in a section of the nose which revolves electrically through 360 degrees. The upper turret is electrically-operated but the gunner is on a fixed platform and must follow movements of turret. The waist guns and tail cannon are on slide mounts and are manually operated. Bomb-bay beneath wings can accommodate one 1,760 lb. (800 kg.) torpedo or bombs to a maximum weight of 4,840 lbs. (2,200 kg.). When bombs or torpedo are carried no bomb doors are fitted. When bombs are carried a deflector is fitted at the rear end of the bay to reduce turbulence. The bomb-bay is closed by a fairing when no bombs are carried and aircraft is used for reconnaissance.

DIMENSIONS.—Span 81 ft. 10½ in. (25 m.), Length 65 ft. 7 in. (20 m.), Wing area 841 sq. ft. (78.1 sq. m.).

WEIGHTS.—Weight empty 17,600 lbs. (8,000 kg.), Weight loaded 27,500 lbs. (12,500 kg.), Maximum permissible loaded weight 33,100 lbs. (15,030 kg.).

PERFORMANCE.—Maximum speed 325 m.p.h. (520 km.h.) at 20,000 ft. (6,100 m.), Cruising speed 250 m.p.h. (400 km.h.) at 19,680 ft. (6,000 m.), Climb to 10,000 ft. (3,500 m.) 7.5 mins., Climb to 20,000 ft. (6,100 m.) 16.6 mins., Service ceiling 30,800 ft. (9,400 m.).

THE MITSUBISHI Ki 213 "SALLY."
Japanese Army designation : Type 97 Heavy Bomber, Model 3.

TYPE.—Twin-engined Army Bomber.

WINGS.—Mid-wing cantilever monoplane. In three sections, comprising a narrow centre-section and two tapering outer sections. Dihedral on outer sections. All-metal structure with stressed-skin covering. Flaps run from centre-section to ailerons.

FUSELAGE.—Oval metal semi-monocoque structure.

TAIL UNIT.—Cantilever monoplane type of high aspect ratio with straight taper on leading-edge of tailplane and trailing-edges of elevators. Tall single-fin and rudder. Trim-tabs on elevators and rudder.

LANDING GEAR.—Retractable type. Each unit comprises two oleo shock-absorber legs and a backwardly-inclined forked strut. Wheels are raised upwards and forwards round the hinge-points of the forked struts into the engine nacelles. Hydraulic retraction. Tail wheel non-retractable.

POWER PLANT.—Two 1,450 h.p. Mitsubishi Type 100 (Ha 101) fourteen-cylinder two-row radial air-cooled engines. Three-bladed hydraulic or electric controllable-pitch airscrews. Fuel tanks in wings inboard and outboard of nacelles and in fuselage over centre-section.

The Mitsubishi "Sally" 2 Army Bomber (two 1,450 h.p. Mitsubishi Type 100 engines).

N.K.K.
NIPPON KOKUSAI KOKUKI KOGYU KABUSHIKI KAISHA (Japanese International Aeroplane Industry Co., Ltd.).

HEAD OFFICE : KITAKYUTAROCHO, HIGASHIKU, OSAKA.
BRANCH OFFICE : TOKYO.
WORKS : HIRATSUKA, KANAGAWA PREFECTURE.

This Company was originally formed in May, 1937, as the Nippon Koku Kogyo Kabushiki Kaisha (Japan Aviation Engineering Co., Ltd.). In 1940 it was merged with the Nichii Koku Kogyo Kabushiki Kaisha, which had been formed in 1939 by the Kanegafuchi Cotton Mills and the Italian Fiat Company to manufacture Fiat aircraft, in particular the Fiat BR. 20, and aero-engines under licence. On Italy's entry into the War the Italian personnel in this latter company returned home. The result of the merger was the formation of the Nippon Kokusai Kokuku Kogyu Kabushiki Kaisha.

THE N.K.K. Ki 59 "THERESA."
Japanese Army designation : Type 1 Transport, Model 1.

TYPE.—Twin-engined Military Transport evolved from the T.K.3 civil transport.
WINGS.—High-wing cantilever monoplane. All-wood structure, comprising two box-spars, plywood ribs and plywood covering.
FUSELAGE.—Rectangular structure of mixed wood and metal construction.
TAIL UNIT.—Cantilever monoplane type. Tail-plane situated forward of fin. All-wood framework with plywood-covered tailplane and fin and fabric-covered elevators and rudder.
LANDING GEAR.—Fixed cantilever type. Consists of two vertical forked members cantilevered from the wing engine-nacelles and incorporating oleo-pneumatic shock-absorbers. Legs and wheels enclosed in streamlined fairings. Fixed tail-wheel.
POWER PLANT.—Two 450 h.p. Nakajima Kotobuki nine-cylinder radial air-cooled engines on steel-tube mountings. Long-chord cowlings. Two-bladed metal airscrews.
ACCOMMODATION.—Pilot's compartment in front of wing seats two side-by-side with dual controls. Cabin beneath wing can accommodate 8 to 10 fully-armed troops.
DIMENSIONS.—Span 55 ft. 8½ in. (17 m.), Length 39 ft. 6 in. (12 m.), Height 10 ft. (3 m.).
WEIGHTS.—Weight empty 5,940 lbs. (2,700 kg.), Weight loaded 9,020 lbs. (4,100 kg.).
PERFORMANCE.—Maximum speed 205 m.p.h. (330 km.h.), Cruising speed 174 m.p.h. (280 km.h.), Range 527 miles (845 km.).

NAKAJIMA.
NAKAJIMA HIKOKI KABUSHIKI KAISHA (Nakajima Aircraft Co., Ltd.).

HEAD OFFICE : YURUKUKAN, MARUNOUCHI, TOKYO.
AEROPLANE WORKS : OHTA, GUMMA-KEN.
ENGINE WORKS : OGIKUBO, TOKYO-FU.
AERODROME : OJIMA, GUMMA-KEN.
Established : December, 1917.

This company supplied the Japanese Army and Navy with aeroplanes and engines, and in addition to building machines of its own design, it manufactured the Douglas DC-2 airliner under licence for commercial use.

THE NAKAJIMA Ki 84 "FRANK."
Japanese Army designation : Type 4 Fighter, Model 1.
Popular name : "Hien" (Flying Swallow).

TYPE.—Single-seat Fighter.
WINGS.—Low-wing cantilever monoplane. Wings taper in chord and thickness, the chord taper being mainly on the trailing-edge. All-metal structure with flush-riveted stressed metal skin. Metal-framed fabric-covered ailerons. Hydraulically-operated Fowler type flaps inboard of ailerons.
FUSELAGE.—Oval section structure of all-metal construction and covered with a flush-riveted stressed skin.
TAIL UNIT.—Cantilever monoplane type. Tailplane and elevators forward of rudder hinge-line. All-metal fin and tailplane, metal fabric-covered rudder and elevators.
LANDING-GEAR.—Retractable type. Hydraulic operation. Main legs and wheels raised inwardly into recesses in the underside of the wing.
POWER PLANT.—One 1,900 h.p. Nakajima Ha 45 eighteen-cylinder two-row radial air-cooled engine driving a Japanese-built Ratier type electrically-operated constant-speed airscrew. Fuel tanks in fuselage and wings, oil tank in fuselage. All tanks have self-sealing protection.
ACCOMMODATION.—Pilot's cockpit over trailing-edge of wings. Sliding "blister" type canopy. Pilot armour.
ARMAMENT.—Two 12.7 m/m. machine-guns in fuselage and synchronised to fire through the airscrew and two 20 m/m. cannon in the wings outboard of the airscrew disc. Racks for light bombs or jettisonable fuel tanks.
DIMENSIONS.—Span 37 ft. (11.3 m.), Length 32 ft. 3 in. (9.8 m.), Height 11 ft. 2 in. (3.4 m.), Wing area 226 sq. ft. (21 sq. m.).
WEIGHT LOADED.—7,940 lbs. (3,600 kg.).
PERFORMANCE.—Maximum speed 426 m.p.h. (682 km.h.) at 23,000 ft. (7,020 m.), Range 1,000 miles (1,600 km.).

THE NAKAJIMA Ki 44 "TOJO."
Japanese Army designation : Type 2 Fighter, Model 2.
Popular name : "Shoki" (Formidable).

TYPE.—Single-seat Fighter.
WINGS.—Low-wing cantilever monoplane. Wings taper in chord and thickness, with leading-edge nearly straight, a slightly curved trailing-edge and rounded tips. Wide centre-section built integrally with fuselage. Landing-flaps on centre-section, ailerons on outer sections. All-metal structure with smooth stressed skin.
FUSELAGE.—Oval all-metal structure with flush-riveted stressed skin.
TAIL UNIT.—Cantilever monoplane type. Tailplane and elevators forward of the rudder hinge line. Fixed surfaces are all metal, movable surfaces have metal frames and fabric-covering.
LANDING GEAR.—Retractable type. Wheels and oleo legs raised inwardly into underside of fuselage. Hydraulic retraction. Retractable tail-wheel.
POWER PLANT.—One 1,500 h.p. Nakajima Type 2 (Ha 109) fourteen-cylinder two-row radial air-cooled engine with two-speed supercharger. Three-blade Hamilton type constant-speed airscrew. Fuel tanks in wings and fuselage. One or two jettisonable fuel tanks may be carried under fuselage or wings.
ACCOMMODATION.—Pilot's cockpit over the trailing-edge of the wing. Sliding "blister" type canopy.
ARMAMENT.—Two 7.7 m/m. machine-guns in the fuselage and synchronised to fire through the airscrew and two 20 m/m. cannon, one in each wing and firing outside the airscrew disc. "Tojo" was also found fitted with a new type of automatic cannon firing a 40 m/m. mortar-type caseless H.E. shell. Rate of fire 400 rounds per min.
DIMENSIONS.—Span 31 ft. (9.45 m.), Length 29 ft. 2½ in. (9 m.), Wing area 169 sq. ft. (15.7 sq. m.).
WEIGHTS.—Weight empty 4,300 lbs. (1,950 kg.), Weight loaded 6,100 lbs. (2,770 kg.).
PERFORMANCE.—Maximum speed 383 m.p.h. (652 km.h.) at 17,000 ft. (5,185 m.), Cruising speed 268 m.p.h. (430 km.h.), Initial rate of climb 3,940 ft./min. (1,100 m./min.), Climb to 10,000 ft. (3,050 m.) 2½ mins., Climb to 20,000 ft. (6,100 m.) 5½ mins., Service ceiling 36,000 ft. (10,980 m.).

THE NAKAJIMA Ki 43 "OSCAR."
Japanese Army designation : Type 1 Fighter, Model 2.
Popular name : "Hayabusa" (Peregrine Falcon).

TYPE.—Single-seat Fighter.
WINGS.—Low-wing cantilever monoplane. Wings taper in chord and thickness. All-metal three-spar structure built integrally with centre-section of fuselage. Remainder of structure consists of former ribs, transverse stringers and a flush-riveted stressed metal skin. Detachable wing-tips. Metal-framed fabric-covered ailerons. Hydraulically-operated Fowler type flaps inboard of ailerons.
FUSELAGE.—Oval section all-metal semi-monocoque structure with a flush-riveted stressed metal skin.
TAIL UNIT.—Cantilever monoplane type. One-piece tailplane and fin are all metal. Rudder and elevators have metal frames and fabric covering.
LANDING GEAR.—Retractable type. Wheels and oleo legs raised inwardly into recesses in the underside of the wings. Hydraulic retraction. Non-retracting tail-wheel.
POWER PLANT.—One 1,150 h.p. Nakajima Type 2 (Ha 115) fourteen-cylinder two-row radial air-cooled engine with two-speed supercharger and driving a three-blade Hamilton type constant-speed airscrew. Fuel tanks in wings have rubber self-sealing protection. Unprotected oil tank. Jettisonable fuel tanks may be carried under the wings.
ACCOMMODATION.—Pilot's cockpit over the wings. Sliding "blister" type canopy. Armour at back of pilot.
ARMAMENT.—Two 12.7 m/m. machine-guns in the fuselage and synchronised to fire through the airscrew.
DIMENSIONS.—Span 35 ft. 7 in. (10.86 m.), Length 29 ft. 3 in. (9 m.).
WEIGHT LOADED.—5,500 lbs. (2,500 kg.).
PERFORMANCE.—Maximum speed 333 m.p.h. (533 km.h.) at 19,680 ft. (6,000 m.), Range 1,000 miles (1,600 km.).

THE NAKAJIMA J1N1 AND J1N1-S "IRVING."
Japanese Navy designation : Type 2 Land Reconnaissance Plane, Model 11 (J1N1), or "Gekko" (Moon Light) Night Fighter, Model 11 (J1N1-S).

This aeroplane was originally developed as a reconnaissance type. In mid-1943 it was modified as a night fighter, re-designated J1N1-S and named "Gekko" (Moon Light).
TYPE.—Twin-engined Naval Reconnaissance (J1N1) or Night Fighting (J1N1-S) monoplane.
WINGS.—Low-wing cantilever monoplane with constant taper and dihedral from roots to tips. All-metal structure comprising one main and two auxiliary spars, former ribs and a flush-riveted smooth metal skin. Fowler-type hydraulically-operated trailing-edge flaps between fuselage and ailerons, the operating arms forming the trailing-edges of the engine nacelles. Leading-edge Handley Page type slots interconnected with the flaps. Metal-framed fabric-covered ailerons with controllable trim-tabs.
FUSELAGE.—Oval section all-metal structure with flush-riveted smooth metal skin.
TAIL UNIT.—Cantilever monoplane type. All-metal framework. Fin and tailplane covered with metal, rudder and elevators with fabric. Trim-tabs in all control surfaces.
LANDING GEAR.—Retractable type. Main wheels raised backwards into engine nacelles, tail-wheel into fuselage. Hydraulic retraction.
POWER PLANT.—Two Nakajima Sakae (Prosperity) 21 fourteen-cylinder radial air-cooled engines with two-speed superchargers and down-draught carburettors, rated at 1,020 h.p. at 6,400 ft. (1,950 m.), 835 h.p. at 15,700 ft. (4,790 m.) and with 950 h.p. available for take-off. Three-blade Mitsubishi-Hamilton constant-speed airscrews 10 ft. (3.05 m.) diameter. Flame-damping exhaust stacks in night-fighter version. Self-sealing fuel tanks in wings. Provision for jettisonable tanks under outer wings.
ACCOMMODATION.—Crew of two, pilot and navigator/radio-operator.
ARMAMENT (Reconnaissance).—One 20 m/m. cannon and two 7.7 m/m. machine-guns in nose fired by pilot, and two tandem dorsal turret mountings each fitted with two 7.7 m/m. guns and remotely controlled by the radio-operator. Provision for one 7.7 m/m. tunnel

The Nakajima "Frank" 1 Single-seat Army Fighter (1,900 h.p. Nakajima Ha 45 engine).

The Nakajima "Oscar" 2 Single-seat Army Fighter (1,150 h.p. Nakajima Type 2 engine).

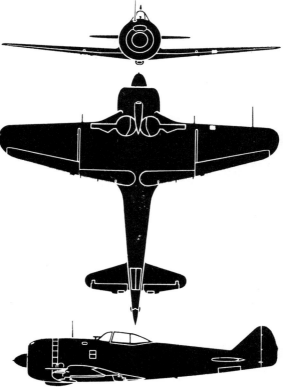

The Nakajima "Tojo" 2 Army Fighter.

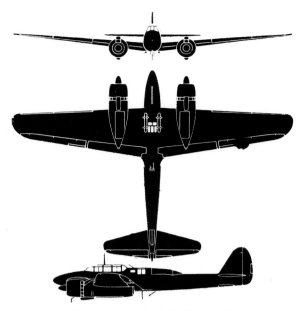

The Nakajima "Irving" 11 Night Fighter.

gun beneath radio-operators' compartment. Two vertical cameras amidships.

ARMAMENT (Night-Fighter).—Four 20 m/m. cannon mounted in pairs, one pair above and one below fuselage amidships. Upper pair fires upward at angle of 30 degrees, lower pair at same angle downward. Provision for one 20 m/m. or 30 m/m. fixed nose gun. Racks under wing-roots for two 550 lb. (250 kg.) bombs and under outer wings for two smaller bombs or droppable fuel tanks. Equipment includes Radar, D/F homing radio, automatic pilot, etc.

DIMENSIONS.—Span 55 ft. 9 in. (17 m.), Length 40 ft. (12.2 m.), Height 15 ft. 5 in. (4.7 m.), Wing area 430 sq. ft. (40 sq. m.).

WEIGHTS.—Weight empty 10,700 lbs. (4,860 kg.), Weight loaded 15,320 lbs. (6,955 kg.).

PERFORMANCE.—Maximum speed 333 m.p.h. (533 km.h.) at 19,700 ft. (6,010 m.), Cruising speed 186 m.p.h. (300 km.h.), Initial rate of climb 1,780 ft./min. (543 m./min.), Climb to 10,000 ft. (3,050 m.) 5.5 mins., Climb to 20,000 ft. (6,100 m.) 12 mins., Service ceiling 32,740 ft. (9,990 m.), Range (75% power) 1,360 miles (2,176 km.).

THE NAKAJIMA C6N1 "MYRT."

Japanese Navy designation : "Saiun" (Painted Cloud) Carrier-borne Reconnaissance Plane, Model 12.

TYPE.—Two/three-seat Long-range Reconnaissance monoplane. May also be used as a torpedo-carrier.

WINGS.—Low-wing cantilever monoplane. Wings of equal taper and with rounded tips. All-metal structure with flush-riveted smooth metal skin. Flaps inboard of ailerons.

FUSELAGE.—Oval section all-metal structure with flush-riveted smooth metal skin.

TAIL UNIT.—Cantilever monoplane type. Tailplane and elevators forward of rudder hinge-line, which slopes forward. All-metal framework with metal-covered tailplane and fin and fabric-covered elevators and rudder. Trim-tabs in elevators and rudder.

LANDING GEAR.—Retractable type. Wide track. Main wheels and cantilever oleo legs raised inwardly into wells in the underside of the wings. Tail-wheel retracts into fuselage.

POWER PLANT.—One Nakajima Homare 21 eighteen-cylinder two-row radial air-cooled engine rated at 1,700 h.p. at 19,680 ft. (6,000 m.) and with 2,000 h.p. available for take-off. Fuel tanks in wings have self-sealing covers.

ACCOMMODATION.—Crew of three for reconnaissance duties, or two when used as torpedo-carrier. Tandem cockpits under continuous canopy. No armour protection.

ARMAMENT.—One 7.9 m/m. machine-gun on flexible mounting in rear cockpit. Cameras in middle cockpit. When carried, torpedo is mounted externally beneath fuselage and to starboard of centre-line.

DIMENSIONS.—Span 41 ft. 1 in. (12.5 m.), Length 36 ft. 6 in. (11.1 m.).

WEIGHTS.—No data available.

PERFORMANCE (Reconnaissance version).—Maximum speed 390 m.p.h. (624 km.h.) at 19,680 ft. (6,000 m.), Cruising speed 240 m.p.h. (384 km.h.), Normal range 1,840 miles (2,940 km.), Maximum range (with overload fuel) 2,900 miles (4,640 km.).

THE NAKAJIMA B6N2 "JILL."

Japanese Navy designation : "Tenzan" (Heavenly Mountain) Carrier-borne Attack Plane, Model 12.

TYPE.—Two-seat Naval Carrier-borne Torpedo-Bomber and Reconnaissance monoplane.

WINGS.—Low-wing cantilever monoplane. Constant taper from roots to rounded detachable tips. Wide centre-section with outer half of each wing arranged to fold upwards for stowage in aircraft-carriers. All-metal two-spar structure with flush-riveted stressed metal skin. Fowler type flaps on centre-section, ailerons on outer sections.

FUSELAGE.—Oval section all-metal structure with flush-riveted smooth metal skin.

TAIL UNIT.—Cantilever monoplane type. All-metal structure. Controllable trim-tabs in all control surfaces.

LANDING GEAR.—Wide-track retractable type. Wheels raised inwardly into wells in the underside of the centre-section. Fully-retractable tail-wheel. Retractable arrester hook.

POWER PLANT.—One Mitsubishi Kasei 25 fourteen-cylinder radial air-cooled engine rated at 1,540 h.p. at 18,040 ft. (5,500 m.). Four-blade Hamilton type constant-speed airscrew. Six fuel tanks, three on each side of the fuselage, in the centre-section.

ACCOMMODATION.—Crew of two in tandem under continuous transparent canopy with sliding sections over cockpits.

ARMAMENT.—One 7.7 m/m. machine-gun in port wing firing outside airscrew disc, one 7.7 m/m. gun on swing mount in rear cockpit, and one 7.7 m/m. gun in floor hatch. Torpedo or bomb carrier beneath fuselage off-set to starboard from centre-line.

DIMENSIONS.—Span 48 ft. 6 in. (14.8 m.), Length 35 ft. (10.7 m.), Height 14 ft. (4.3 m.), Wing area 400 sq. ft. (37.2 sq. m.).

WEIGHTS AND LOADINGS.—Weight empty 6,797 lbs. (3,090 kg.),

The Najakima "Myrt" 12 Naval Reconnaissance Monoplane (1,700 h.p. Najakima Homare 21 engine).

The Nakajima "Jill" 12 Naval Torpedo-Bomber (1,540 h.p. Mitsubishi Kasei 25 engine).

The Nakajima "Kate" 12 Naval Torpedo-Bomber (1,020 h.p. Nakajima Sakae 11 engine).

Weight loaded (Torpedo-Bomber) 11,464 lbs. (5,210 kg.), Weight loaded (Reconnaissance) 10,740 lbs. (4,880 kg.), Wing loading 28.6 lbs./sq. ft. (139.5 kg./sq. m.), Power loading 6.8 lbs./h.p. (3.08 kg./h.p.).

PERFORMANCE.—Maximum speed 300 m.p.h. (480 km.h.) at 16,080 ft. (4,900 m.), Landing speed 82.5 m.p.h. (132 km.h.), Climb to 16,400 ft. (5,000 m.) 10.5 mins., Service ceiling 26,660 ft. (9,050 m.), Range (Torpedo-Bomber) 1,080 miles (1,728 km.) at 209 m.p.h. (334 km.h.) at 13,120 ft. (4,000 m.), Range (Reconnaissance) 2,300 miles (3,680 km.) at 209 m.p.h. (334 km.h.) at 13,120 ft. (4,000 m.).

THE NAKAJIMA B5N2 "KATE."

Japanese Navy designation : Type 97 Carrier-borne Attack Plane, Model 12.

TYPE.—Single-engined Torpedo-Bomber.

WINGS.—Low-wing cantilever monoplane. Taper on leading and trailing-edges. Dihedral on outer sections only. Flaps are quite short. Metal structure and covering.

FUSELAGE.—Metal monocoque structure.

TAIL UNIT.—Cantilever tailplane and single fin and rudder. Trim-tabs on elevators and rudder.

LANDING GEAR.—Inward retracting type. Non-retracting tail-wheel.

POWER PLANT.—One Nakajima Sakae 11 fourteen-cylinder two-row radial air-cooled engine.

ACCOMMODATION.—Crew of two or three in tandem under a continuous raised canopy.

ARMAMENT.—Two 7.7 m/m. fixed machine-guns mounted on cowling and one or two movable 7.7 m/m. machine-guns in rear cockpit. One 18 in. torpedo or up to 1,100 lb. (500 kg.) bomb load.

DIMENSIONS.—Span 52 ft. 5 in. (15.9 m.), Length 33 ft. 9 in. (10.3 m.).

WEIGHTS AND LOADINGS.—No data available.

PERFORMANCE.—Maximum speed 225 m.p.h. (360 km.h.) at 8,000 ft. (2,440 m.), Speed at sea level 205 m.p.h. (328 km.h.), Operational radius 300 miles (480 km.).

THE NAKAJIMA Ki 49 "HELEN."

Japanese Army designation : Type 100 Heavy Bomber, Model 2. Popular name : "Donryu" (Dragon Swallower).

TYPE.—Twin-engined Heavy Bomber.

WINGS.—Mid-wing cantilever monoplane. Wing in three sections, comprising centre-section with straight leading-edge well in front of outer section leading-edge. Slight taper on trailing-edge. Normal outer sections with most of taper on trailing-edge. Dihedral from roots. Structure is all metal with three main and one auxiliary spars and a flush-riveted stressed skin. Flaps extend from ailerons to fuselage. Trailing-edges of ailerons are further aft than the trailing-edges of inner wing section.

FUSELAGE.—Deep oval-section metal structure.

TAIL UNIT.—Cantilever tailplane. Single fin and rudder.

LANDING GEAR.—Retractable type. Non-retracting tail-wheel.

POWER PLANT.—Two 1,450 h.p. Nakajima Type 2 (Ha 109) fourteen-cylinder radial air-cooled engines. Protected fuel tanks in wings.

ACCOMMODATION.—Cockpit over centre-section leading-edge. Bomb-aimer's position in nose, midship gun position and tail-turret. Armour for pilots, turret gunner and tail gunner.

ARMAMENT.—Consists of one 20 m/m. cannon in dorsal turret, two 12.7 m/m. machine-guns, one in nose and one in tail turret, and three 7.9 m/m. machine-guns, two in waist positions and one in aft-firing ventral position. Internal bomb-bay may accommodate up to 2,200 lbs. (1,000 kg.) of bombs in various combinations.

DIMENSIONS.—Span 66 ft. 7 in. (20.3 m.), Length 53 ft. (16.2 m.).

WEIGHT LOADED.—23,520 lbs. (10,680 kg.).

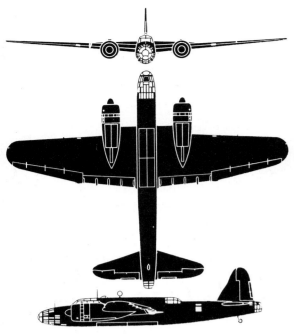

The Nakajima "Helen" 2 Army Bomber.

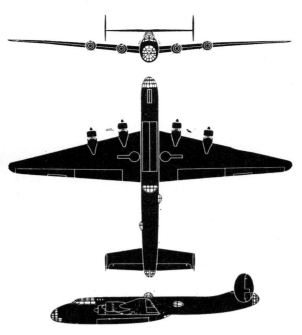

The Nakajima "Liz" 2 Heavy Bomber.

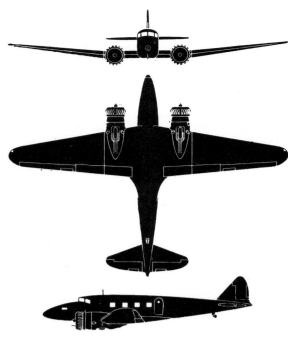

The Nakajima "Thora" 2 Army Transport.

PERFORMANCE.—Maximum speed 312 m.p.h. (510 km.h.) at 16,400 ft. (5,000 m.), Range 1,500 miles (2,400 km.).

THE NAKAJIMA G8N1 "RITA."

Japanese Navy designation : "Renzan" (Mountain Range) Land Attack Plane, Model 11.

The code-name "Rita" was given to a new four-engined land-based bomber designed by Nakajima. No details of this aircraft were known at the time of closing for press.

THE NAKAJIMA G5N1 "LIZ."

Japanese Navy designation : "Shinzan" (Mountain Recess) Type 2 Land Attack Plane, Model 11.

This aircraft, the first Japanese four-engined operational type, was originally designed by the Mitsubishi company as the G5M1 but was not successful. It was modified by the Nakajima company and put into production as the G5N1. Although designed as a heavy bomber it was never used as such.

TYPE.—Four-engined Heavy Bomber, now used as a Transport.

WINGS.—Low-wing cantilever monoplane. Sharply tapered wings with most taper on the leading-edge. All-metal structure with a smooth external skin reinforced with an inner corrugated skin with the corrugations running spanwise. Landing flaps inboard of ailerons.

FUSELAGE.—Oval all-metal semi-monocoque structure with a flush-riveted stressed skin.

TAIL UNIT.—Cantilever monoplane type with twin fins and rudders. All-metal structure.

LANDING GEAR.—Retractable tricycle type. Main wheels retract outwardly into underside of wings. Hydraulic retraction.

POWER PLANT.—Four Nakajima Mamoru fourteen-cylinder two-row radial air-cooled engines each driving a four-blade Hamilton type constant-speed airscrew. Main fuel tanks in wings. Oil tanks in engine nacelles.

ACCOMMODATION.—In Bomber version provision for a crew of eight/nine. Other details not available. As a Transport can carry from twenty to twenty-five paratroops or airborne troops, or varied loads of freight.

ARMAMENT.—Gun positions in nose, above power-operated turret and below fuselage, in staggered waist positions and in extreme tail. Internal bomb-bay designed to accommodate an approximate maximum of 6,000-7,000 lbs. No further details available.

DIMENSIONS.—Span 138 ft. 3 in. (42.2 m.), Length 101 ft. 9 in. (31 m.).

WEIGHTS AND PERFORMANCE.—No data available.

THE NAKAJIMA Ki 34 "THORA."

Japanese Army designation : Type 97 Transport, Model 2.

TYPE.—Twin-engine Military Transport evolved from the Nakajima AT civil transport.

WINGS.—Low-wing cantilever monoplane. All-metal structure. Taper on leading and trailing-edges. Dihedral outboard of engine. Flaps extend between ailerons and centre-line of fuselage.

FUSELAGE.—All-metal structure.

TAIL UNIT.—Cantilever monoplane type. Single fin and rudder.

LANDING GEAR.—Retracts forward into engine nacelles. Non-retracting tail-wheel.

POWER PLANT.—Two 650 h.p. Nakajima Type 97 (Ha 1B) nine-cylinder radial air-cooled engines. Two-bladed controllable-pitch metal airscrews.

ACCOMMODATION.—Crew of two with dual controls. Cabin can accommodate from five to eight fully-armed troops.

DIMENSIONS.—Span 65 ft. 4 in. (19.9 m.), Length 50 ft. (15.25 m.), Height 13 ft. 7 in. (4.15 m.).

WEIGHTS.—Weight empty 7,656 lbs. (3,475 kg.), Weight loaded 10,736 lbs. (4,875 kg.).

PERFORMANCE.—Maximum speed 230 m.p.h. (368 km.h.), Cruising speed 217 m.p.h. (347 km.h.), Landing speed 59 m.p.h. (94.4 km.h.), Climb to 9,840 ft. (3,000 m.) 5 mins. 39 secs., Range 1,520 miles 2,430 km.).

NIPPON.

NIPPON HIKOKI KABUSHIKI KAISHA (Japan Aeroplane Co., Ltd.).

HEAD OFFICE : TOKYO.

WORKS : YOKOHAMA.

Established : October, 1934.

The Japan Areoplane Co. Ltd. was responsible for the design and construction of two military gliders, the Ku. 7 (Code name : "Buzzard") and Ku. 8 (Code-name : "Gander"). The first known example of a Japanese Military cargo glider, the "Gander" was first discovered on Luzon after the invasion of the Philippines.

The "Gander" could carry approximately 14 men or a variety of vehicles and freight. It had a span of 71 ft. 2 in. (21.7 m.) and was 43 ft. 9 in. (13.3 m.) long. It was a rigidly-braced high-wing monoplane of all-wood construction.

SHOWA.

SHOWA HIKOKI KOGYO KABUSHIKI KAISHA (Showa Aeroplane Engineering Co., Ltd.).

HEAD OFFICE : 2, CHOME-KOBUNE-CHO NIHONBASHI-KU, TOKYO.

WORKS : TOKYO-SEISAKUSHO (NEAR TOKYO) AND HEIJO-SEISAKUSHO (HEIJO, CHOSEN).

Established : 1924.

This company was founded in 1924 as the Ishikawajima Aircraft Co., Ltd., but in 1936 it changed its name to the Tatikawa Aircraft Co. Ltd. It was engaged in supplying aeroplanes, aircraft parts and accessories to the Japanese Government. These included reconnaissance, fighting and training aeroplanes

and aero-engines. Its principal production was, however, in training aircraft.

TATIKAWA

TATIKAWA HIKOKI KABUSHIKI KAISHA (Tatikawa Aircraft Co., Ltd.).

HEAD OFFICE : NEW KAIJO BUILDING, 6, MARUNOUCHI, 1-CHOME, TOKYO.

WORKS : TATIKAWA-MACHI, TOKYO.

Established : June, 1937.

This concern was formed in June, 1937, with a capital of

Y.30,000,000 to build aeroplanes and aero-engines. The works, which covered 5 acres, were completed early in 1939.

The Showa organization built the Japanese version of the Douglas DC-3 which was used by the Japanese Navy as a transport and was identified under the Allied code-name system as "Tabby." The Japanese DC-3 was fitted with two Mitsubishi Kinsei 53 fourteen-cylinder air-cooled engines. It had accommodation for from 22 to 24 fully-armed troops.

WATANABE.

WATANABE TEKKOSHO KABUSHIKI KAISHA (Watanabe Iron Works, Ltd.).

HEAD OFFICE AND WORKS : ZATSUSHONOKUMA, FUKOAKA.

Established : January, 1886.

The Aircraft Branch of the Watanabe Iron Works supplied aeroplanes, parts and accessories to the Imperial Japanese Navy. It designed and built the E9W1 Type 96 reconnaissance seaplane (S.W. Pacific Code name, "Slim") for use from submarines, and it also built the Aichi-designed "Jake" reconnaissance seaplane. The latest known product of this company was the "Tokai" twin-engined anti-submarine patrol monoplane.

THE WATANABE Q1W1 "LORNA."

Japanese Navy designation : "Tokai" (Eastern Sea) Patrol Plane, Model 11.

"Lorna" was a twin-engined anti-submarine patrol monoplane of conventional design. It was fitted with two 480 h.p. Tokyo Gasu Denki "Amikaze" radial air-cooled engines and had a retractable landing-gear. The bomb load could consist of either two 550 lb. bombs or four 132 lb. depth-charges. No further details are available.

DIMENSIONS.—Span 52 ft. 6 in. (16 m.), Length 39 ft. 4½ in. (12 m.).

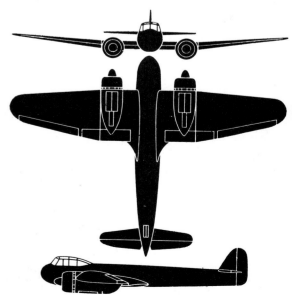

The Watanabe "Lorna" 11 Patrol Monoplane.

YOKOSUKA.
YOKOSUKA NAVAL AIR DEPOT.

The principal Naval Depot in Japan. Undertook research and development and designed and built aircraft and aero-engines.

Hereunder are described three designs which originated at this Depot. Production of "Judy" was handled by the Aichi company and "Frances" was manufactured by the Nakajima company.

THE YOKOSUKA D4Y2 AND D4Y2-R "JUDY."
Japanese Navy designation : "Suisei" (Comet) Carrier-borne Bomber (D4Y2) or Reconnaissance Plane (D4Y2-R).

"Judy" was designed by the Yokosuka Naval Air Depot as No. 13 Experimental Carrier-borne Bomber and was accepted for production in 1942 as Type 2 Reconnaissance plane, Model 11. In mid-1943 "Judy" was reconverted to a carrier-borne bomber and designated "Suisei" Model 11. It was later adapted for catapult launching. The Model 11 versions of "Judy" were fitted with the 1,180 h.p. Aichi Atsuta 21 engine, the Japanese version of the German Daimler-Benz DB 601A. "Suisei" Model 12, described below, had the higher-powered Atsuta 31 engine.

There was also a radial-engined version of "Judy." The Model 33 was fitted with the Mitsubishi Kinsei 62 fourteen-cylinder radial and except for the change in power-plant was identical to the Model 12 described below. Benefitting from a slight increase in horse-power, Model 33 had a maximum speed of about 390 m.p.h. (624 km.h.) at 18,500 ft. (5,640 m.). Both the in-line and radial-engined versions of "Judy" were used for suicide attacks on Allied shipping.

The production of "Judy" was handled by the Aichi company.

TYPE.—Two-seat Naval Carrier-borne Dive-Bomber or Reconnaissance monoplane.
WINGS.—Low mid-wing cantilever monoplane. One-piece all-metal wing structure with two continuous I-section spars extending from tip to tip, and a stressed-skin covering. Metal-framed fabric-covered ailerons with trim-tabs. Electrically-operated Fowler type flaps between ailerons and fuselage. Dive brakes hinged to rear spar ahead of flaps are raised in recess when flaps are lowered to create slot effect.
FUSELAGE.—Oval section all-metal structure with a flush-riveted smooth metal skin.
TAIL UNIT.—Cantilever monoplane type. All-metal framework with fabric-covered elevators and rudder. Controllable trim-tabs in all movable surfaces.
LANDING GEAR.—Retractable type. Wheels raised inwardly into underside of leading-edge of wing. Solid tail-wheel retracts in conjunction with the main wheels. Electrical retraction. Hydraulic wheel-brakes. Retractable arrester hook beneath rear portion of fuselage.
POWER PLANT.—One Aichi Atsuta 31 (D.B.601E) twelve-cylinder inverted Vee liquid-cooled engine rated at 1,265 h.p. at 16,400 ft. (5,000 m.) and with 1,380 h.p. available for take-off. Three-blade Mitsubishi-Hamilton constant-speed airscrew. Four fuel tanks in wing, two on each side of fuselage, and one in the fuselage over the bomb-bay. Two jettisonable tanks may be carried on bomb-racks under wings outboard of the landing-gear. Tunnel coolant radiator under engine.
ACCOMMODATION.—Crew of two—pilot and navigator/radio-operator—in tandem under continuous transparent canopy with sliding sections over cockpits.
ARMAMENT.—Two fixed 7.7 m/m. machine-guns in forward fuselage and one 7.7 m/m. gun on flexible mounting in rear cockpit. Internal bomb-bay with displacement gear for one 550 lb. (250 kg.) or one 1,100 lb. (500 kg.) bomb. Light bombs may also be carried on wing racks. In reconnaissance version (D4Y2-R) one vertical camera installed in floor of rear cockpit.
DIMENSIONS.—Span 37 ft. 10 in. (11.5 m.), Length 33 ft. 7 in. (10.2 m.), Wing area 254 sq. ft. (23.6 sq. m.).
WEIGHTS.—Weight empty 5,420 lbs. (2,460 kg.), Weight loaded 8,610 lbs. (3,910 kg.).
PERFORMANCE.—Maximum speed 361 m.p.h. (578 km.h.) at 19,680 ft. (6,000 m.), Cruising speed (75% power) 205 m.p.h. (328 km.h.), Initial rate of climb 2,270 ft./min. (690 m./min.), Climb to 20,000 ft. (6,100 m.) 9.2 mins., Service ceiling 32,400 ft. (9,880 m.), Range 1,320 miles (2,110 km.) at 205 m.p.h. (328 km.h.).

THE YOKOSUKA P1Y1 AND P1Y1-S "FRANCES."
Japanese Navy designation : "Ginka" (Milky Way) Land-based Bomber, Model 11 (P1Y1) or "Hakko" (White Light) Night Fighter, Model 11 (P1Y1-S).

"Frances" was designed by the Yokosuka Naval Air Depot and was built by the Nakajima company. The basic 1940 design was for a land-based bomber, but it was later adapted for night fighting duties with a different power-plant and specialised armament and equipment.
TYPE.—Twin-engined Naval land-based Horizontal Bomber, Torpedo-Bomber or Dive-Bomber (P1Y1) or Night Fighter (P1Y1-S).

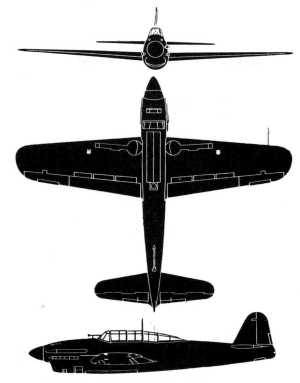

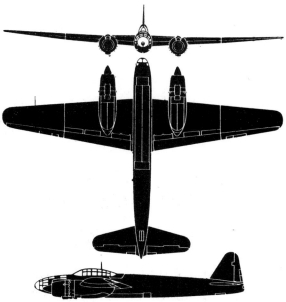

The Yokosuka "Judy" 22 Naval Dive-Bomber.

The Yokosuka "Frances" 11 Naval Bomber.

WINGS.—Mid-wing cantilever monoplane. Constant taper from roots to tips with most taper on trailing-edges. Wing in three main sections comprising wide centre-section with flat upper surface and two outer sections with dihedral on upper surfaces and with detachable tips. All-metal structure with one main and two auxiliary spars, former ribs and a smooth metal skin. Metal-

framed fabric-covered Frise type ailerons with both fixed and controllable trim-tabs. All-metal Fowler type flaps on centre-section. Dive brakes forward of landing flaps.
FUSELAGE.—Oval section all-metal monocoque with flush-riveted smooth metal skin.
TAIL UNIT.—Cantilever monoplane type. All-metal tailplane and fin, metal-framed fabric-covered elevators and rudder. Controllable trim-tabs in all control surfaces.
LANDING GEAR.—Retractable type. Main wheels raised backwards into engine nacelles. Fully-retractable tail-wheel.
POWER PLANT (P1Y1 "Ginka").—Two Nakajima Homare 11 eighteen-cylinder radial air-cooled engines with two-speed superchargers and water injection, each rated at 1,130 h.p. at 19,680 ft. (6,000 m.) and with 1,795 h.p. for take-off. Three-blade Hamilton type hydraulic constant-speed airscrews. Fuel tanks with some leak-proof protection in wings and fuselage, and provision for auxiliary tanks in bomb-bay and under wings.
POWER PLANT (P1Y1-S "Hakko").—Two Mitsubishi Kasei 25 fourteen-cylinder radial air-cooled engines, each rated at 1,540 h.p. at 5,500 m. (18,040 ft.).
ACCOMMODATION (P1Y1 "Ginka").—Crew of three—front gunner in transparent nose, and pilot and radio-operator/rear-gunner under transparent canopy over the wing. Armour protection for pilot.
ARMAMENT (P1Y1 "Ginka").—Two 20 m/m. Japanese-built Oerlikon cannon, one in section of symmetrical transparent nose which revolves through 360 degrees, and one on flexible mounting in rear cockpit. Bomb-bay under cockpit floor with accommodation for one 1,760 lb. (880 kg.) torpedo, or two 1,100 lb. (500 kg.) or two 550 lb. (250 kg.) bombs. Provision for carrying small calibre anti-personnel bombs under wings.
DIMENSIONS.—Span 65 ft. 7 in. (20 m.), Length 49 ft. 2½ in. (29.75 m.), Height 17 ft. 5 in. (5.3 m.), Wing area 592 sq. ft. (55 sq. m.).
WEIGHTS.—Weight empty 14,652 lbs. (6,660 kg.), Weight loaded 23,100 lbs. (10,500 kg.).
PERFORMANCE.—Maximum speed 354 m.p.h. (570 km.h.) at 20,600 ft. (6,280 m.), Cruising speed 210 m.p.h. (336 km.h.), Climb to 10,000 ft. (3,050 m.) 5 mins., Climb to 20,000 ft. (6,100 m.) 12 mins., Service ceiling 30,000 ft. (9,150 m.).

THE YOKOSUKA E14Y1 "GLEN."
Japanese Navy designation : Type O Small Seaplane, Model 11.

TYPE.—Two-seat Light Reconnaissance Seaplane for use from sub-marines.
WINGS.—Low-wing rigidly-braced monoplane with slight sweep-back. Wings of mixed construction with light metal spars, wood ribs and fabric covering. Entire trailing-edge hinged, inner portions acting as flaps and outer portions as ailerons. Wings detach from fuselage at spar fittings, flaps and ailerons fold under wings and Vee struts hinged at wing attachments and fold up against lower surface of wings for stowage.
FUSELAGE.—Welded steel-tube structure, covered forward with light metal panels, aft with fabric over light wooden formers and on the underside with metal sheet.
TAIL UNIT.—Braced monoplane type. Top section of fin and vertical stabilising surface below fuselage detachable. Tailplane braced to fin. Outer sections of tailplane fold up for stowage.
FLOATS.—Twin long single-step floats attached to fuselage by transverse inverted W-struts. Floats and struts detachable from fuselage and struts from floats for stowage. Catapult points.
POWER PLANT.—One 360 h.p. Tokyo Gasu Denki Amikaze 11 nine-cylinder radial air-cooled engine driving a two-blade fixed-pitch airscrew. Complete engine unit quickly detachable. Two fuel tanks in fuselage.
ACCOMMODATION.—Crew of two in tandem under a continuous transparent canopy with sliding sections over cockpits.
ARMAMENT.—One 7.7 m/m. machine-gun on flexible mounting in rear cockpit.
DIMENSIONS.—Span 36 ft. (10.96 m.), Length 22 ft. (8.54 m.), Height 9 ft. (3.68 m.).
WEIGHTS.—Weight empty 2,390 lbs. (1,085 kg.), Weight loaded 3,190 lbs. (1,450 kg.), Maximum catapult loaded weight 3,520 lbs. (1,600 kg.).
PERFORMANCE.—No data available.

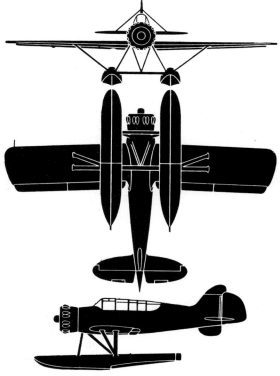

The Yokosuka "Glen" 11 Light Seaplane.

The Yokosuka "Judy" 33 Naval Dive Bomber (Mitsubishi Kinsei 62 engine).

SUICIDE AIRCRAFT

A supplementary use to which the Japanese put powered aircraft was the suicide attack, in which many types of combat aeroplanes were used in attempts to crash dive into Allied ships. Suicide bombing became a regular tactic late in 1944, the first reported attacks of this kind being made in October soon after the successful American landings in the Phillipines.

Although no British or U.S. capital ship was sunk, a number of smaller ships were lost and many ships of all kinds were damaged. Off the Phillipines in October, H.M.A.S. *Australia* was seriously damaged by this form of attack. In February, 1945, the U.S. aircraft-carrier *Saratoga* was hit by seven suicide bombers. In a two month's combat period off the Sakashima

Islands in April-May seven Japanese aircraft crash-dived into ships of the British Pacific Fleet but none was out of action for more than a few hours. On May 4, the U.S. escort-carrier *Sangamon* was damaged, and on May 11 the aircraft-carrier *Bunker Hill* was put out of action by two suicide bombers. There were many other such incidents.

Most suicide bombers were of the single-engined types—"Zeke," "Judy," "Jill," "Kate," "Val" and "Oscar," although some twin-engined aircraft, notably "Frances," "Irving," "Lily," "Sally" and "Peggy," were also employed. Usually bombs were carried and sometimes extra fuel tanks with detonators were used to add to the destruction. In some cases entire

reliance was placed on the incendiary effect of exploding petrol.

A "Kamikaze" Special Air Corps was formed to perform these attacks. This suicide unit was named after a timely typhoon that frustrated a Mongolian invasion of Japan in the year 1280, a storm which came to be revered as the Divine Wing ("Kamikaze"). Membership of this corps was first believed to be voluntary and pilots were reported to have performed their final rites in flowing ceremonial funeral robes before diving to eternal glory. Much play was made of this corps on the Japanese radio. Latterly, however, far from being the prerogative of any select corps suicide attacks became part of the duty of ordinary pilots, some of whom had to be forcibly secured in their cockpits before taking off.

The "Baka" Flying Bomb

Seemingly inspired by the German flying-bomb, the Japanese evolved a somewhat similar rocket-propelled winged and piloted bomb for suicide attacks. This projectile, known by the Japanese as "Jinrai" (Thunderclap), was given the Allied code-name "Baka," the Japanese for idiot or fool.

"Baka" consisted of a cylindrical fuselage 19 ft. 10 in. (6 m.) long, a mid-wing cantilever monoplane wing of 16 ft. 5 in. (5 m.) span, and a twin-ruddered tail-unit. The nose of the fuselage consisted of a warhead of some 2,640 lbs. (1,200 kg.) of tri-

nitro-aminol and was provided with a nose fuse and four base fuses. Behind the warhead was the pilot's cockpit with blister canopy and simple controls. The propulsion unit consisted of three rocket tubes, the rockets being ignited electrically by the pilot.

"Baka" was carried under the belly of a "Betty" bomber and was launched at about 27,000 ft. (8,240 m.) and at a speed of about 175-200 m.p.h. (280-320 km.h.) some 55 miles (88 km.) from the target. The first 52 miles (83.2 km.) to the target

were covered at a gliding speed of about 230 m.p.h. (368 km.h.) and at a gliding angle of about 5 degrees. The rockets were then ignited, which increased the level speed to about 535 m.p.h. (856 km.h.). In the final dive to the target the maximum speed reached about 620 m.p.h. (990 km.h.). Although the pilot was provided with some light armour for protection from behind, he had no means of getting out of the projectile once it was secured to the shackles of the carrier aircraft before taking-off.

MEXICO

NATIONAL AIRCRAFT FACTORY.

TALLERES NACIONALES DE CONSTRUCCIONES AERONAUTICAS.
VALBUENA, MEXICO CITY.

The Mexican National Aircraft Factory was established at Valbuena, near Mexico City, in November, 1915, and from then

until 1929 the factory designed and produced a number of different types of aeroplanes and aero-engines.

In 1930, the Mexican Government decided to discontinue the design and manufacture of aircraft at the National Aircraft

Factory, in order to encourage private enterprise, but later the Government acquired a licence to construct the Vought Corsair from the American Chance Vought Corporation, and a number of machines of this type were built at this Factory.

NETHERLANDS

The following is a list of the firms which constituted the Netherlands Aircraft Industry before the invasion of Holland. Details of the products of these companies have been given in previous issues of this Annual.

KONINKLIJKE MAATSCHAPPIJ "DE SCHELDE," Flushing.
MAATSCHAPPIJ VOOR VLIEGTUIGBOUW N.V. "AVIOLANDA," Papendrecht, near Doordrecht.
N.V. KOOLHOVEN VLIEGTUIGEN, Rotterdam.
N.V. NEDERLANDSCHE VLIEGTUIGENFABRIEK FOKKER, Amsterdam-Noord.

NORWAY

The only aircraft manufacturing establishments in Norway prior to its occupation by Germany were the Army Aircraft Factory at Kjeller, and the Naval Aircraft Factory at Horten, both of which were bombed in the initial stages of the invasion.

The Army Aircraft Factory built aircraft of foreign design under licence and was responsible for all repair and maintenance of Army aircraft. The Naval Aircraft Factory, which was established in 1915, built seaplanes of original design and also undertook all repair and overhaul of Naval aircraft. Both these establishments were later operated by the Germans as repair bases for the *Luftwaffe* stationed in Norway.

PERU

NATIONAL AIRCRAFT FACTORY.

FABRICA NACIONAL DE AVIONES.
LAS PARMAS AIRPORT, LIMA.

The Peruvian Government Aircraft Factory was established in May, 1937, for the construction and repair of military and naval service aircraft. It was established under a Government contract with the Societa Italiana Caproni, of Milan, Italy, which company agreed to supply all the necessary plant and equipment, as well as six technical experts to supervise and operate the factory.

The agreement, which gave the Caproni Company a ten-year

monopoly in the construction and repair of military aircraft, stipulated that the factory should produce twenty-five aircraft in the first two years. In this period only twelve Caproni Ca 100 light trainers, the engines for which were obtained in the United States, were produced at a cost far in excess of that for which similar aircraft could be bought elsewhere, in spite of the fact that the factory was permitted to import from Italy free of duty all material and instruments needed.

At that time an Italian Air Mission was in Peru and on its advice a number of military aircraft were bought in Italy.

These gave considerable trouble and the factory was mainly engaged on the repair and reconstruction of these aircraft.

After the outbreak of the European War the Italian Mission was withdrawn and the factory, which is said to be the largest of its kind in South America, remained inactive, except for minor repair work, until the middle of 1941.

On June 1, 1941, the Peruvian Government took the plant over at a valuation of $550,000 and now operates it as a repair and maintenance plant.

FAUCETT.

CIA. DE AVIACION FAUCETT S.A.
HEAD OFFICE: EDIFICIO HOTEL BOLIVAR No. 926, LIMA.
Managing Director: Elmer Faucett.

This is the oldest aeronautical concern in Peru and apart from operating airlines and engaging in all phases of civil and commercial flying (details of which will be found in the Civil Aviation Section of this annual), it conducts an aircraft factory for the manufacture, repair and maintenance of all types of aircraft.

It has built a number of Faucett eight-seat cabin monoplanes for use on its own airlines. Its latest productions are the F-19 landplane fitted with the 875 h.p. Pratt & Whitney Hornet engine and the F-19 seaplane fitted with the 600 h.p. Pratt & Whitney Wasp engine. Both these types have also been supplied to the Peruvian Government.

No recent constructional work has been undertaken by the company owing to the difficulty of obtaining the necessary materials from the United States.

THE FAUCETT F-19.

The F-19 is an eight-seat transport monoplane. It is of

The Faucett F-19 Eight-passenger Commercial Monoplane (875 h.p. Pratt & Whitney "Hornet" engine).

mixed construction with wooden wings and welded steel-tube fuselage and tail unit, the whole being covered with fabric.

The latest model of the F-19 is fitted with a Pratt & Whitney Hornet S1E3-G radial air-cooled geared engine and Hamilton-Standard constant-speed airscrew.

DIMENSIONS.—Span 17.7 m. (58 ft.), Length 11.79 m. (38 ft. 8 in.), Height 4.37 m. (14 ft. 4 in.), Wing area 40.5 sq. m. (435.8 sq. ft.).
WEIGHTS AND LOADINGS (Landplane—875 h.p. Pratt & Whitney Hornet S1E3-G engine).—Weight empty 2,581 kg. (5,690 lbs.), Pay load 850 kg. (1,874 lbs.), Disposable load 1,527 kg. (3,366 lbs.).

Weight loaded 4,108 kg. (9,056 lbs.). Wing loading 109.8 kg./sq. m. (22.5 lbs./sq. ft.). Power loading 4.7 kg. h.p. (10.34 lbs. h.p.).
WEIGHTS AND LOADINGS (Seaplane—600 h.p. Pratt & Whitney Wasp S1H1-G engine).—Weight empty 2,622 kg. (5,775 lbs.). Pay load 747 kg. (1,645 lbs.), Disposable load 1,350 kg. (2,975 lbs.), Weight loaded 3,972 kg. (8,750 lbs.). Wing loading 106.38 kg. sq. m. (21.8 lbs./sq. ft.). Power loading 6.62 kg. h.p. (14.58 lbs. h.p.).
PERFORMANCE (Landplane—875 h.p. Pratt & Whitney Hornet S1E3-G engine).—Speed at sea level 264 km.h. (165 m.p.h.), Maximum speed 288 km.h. (180 m.p.h.) at 2,440 m. (8,000 ft.). Cruising speed 224 km.h. (140 m.p.h.) at 3,355 m. (11,000 ft.).

Landing speed (without flaps) 112.6 km.h. (70 m.p.h.), Initial rate of climb 305 m./min. (1,000 ft./min.), Service ceiling 6,710 m. (22,000 ft.).
PERFORMANCE (Seaplane—600 h.p. Pratt & Whitney Wasp S1H1-G engine).—Speed at sea level 232 km.h. (145 m.p.h.), Maximum speed 256 km.h. (160 m.p.h.) at 2,440 m. (8,000 ft.), Cruising speed at sea level 216 km.h. (135 m.p.h.), Cruising speed at 3,050 m. (10,000 ft.) 240 km.h. (150 m.p.h.), Alighting speed (without flaps) 112.6 km.h. (70 m.p.h.), Service ceiling 5,490 m. (18,000 ft.).

POLAND

On September 1, 1939, Germany invaded Poland. On the first day one-fifth of the Polish Air Force had been destroyed and aircraft production was brought almost to a standstill by air operations alone. Within a week the principal aircraft factories had been destroyed by bombing attacks and the Polish industry ceased to exist.

Hereafter follows a list of the firms which constituted the Polish Aircraft Industry prior to September 1, 1939 :—

DOSWIADCZALNE WARSZTATY LOTNICZE (R.W.D.), Warsaw.
LUBELSKA WYTWORNIA SAMOLOTOW (L.W.S.), Lublin.
PANSTWOWE ZAKLADY LOTNICZE (P.Z.L.), Warsaw and Mielec.
PODLASKA WYTWORNIA SAMOLOTOW (P.W.S.), Biala Podlaska.

The products of all these companies have been fully illustrated and described in previous issues of this Annual.

PORTUGAL

GOVERNMENT WORKSHOPS.

OFICINAS GERAIS DE MATERIAL AERONAUTICO (GENERAL AERONAUTICAL MATERIAL WORKSHOPS).
ALVERCA DO RIBATEJO.

Director : Lieut. Col. Engineer Henrique Mora.
Sub-Director and Chief Engineer : Lieut. Col. Jorge Metelo de Napoles Manuel.

This is the only establishment in Portugal manufacturing aircraft, and it belongs to the Ministry for War. Manufacture of aircraft, aero-engines and equipment is by licence. The following types have been built for the Military Aeronautical Corps :—Vickers Valparaiso, Potez XXV, and Morane-Saulnier 233. The Jupiter and Titan engines which were

fitted to the above types were also manufactured in this factory.

The types of aircraft at present in production are the Avro 626 and D.H. Tiger Moth, which are used in the Military Aviation Schools. All repair and overhaul work on aeroplanes of the Air Force is done at this factory.

RUMANIA

Rumania signed the Axis Tripartite Pact on November 23, 1940, and assisted Germany in the invasions of the Balkans and Russia.

After having its territory overrun by the Russian forces, Rumania accepted a peace offer from the Allies on August 24, 1944 and declared war on Germany on the following day. Before the invasion of Rumania the undermentioned aircraft manufacturers built aircraft for the Rumanian Air Force which served under German command in Russia.

REGIA AUTONOMA INDUSTRIA AERONAUTICA ROMANA, Brasov.
This was a State-owned establishment controlled by the Ministry of Air and Marine. It built both aircraft and aero-engines of domestic and foreign design.

FABRICA DE AVIONE S.E.T., Bucharest.
This concern manufactured aircraft of its own design to the order of the Rumanian Government.

The products of these two concerns have been fully described and illustrated in previous volumes of this Annual.

RUSSIA

(Union of Socialist Soviet Republics)

SINGLE-ENGINED FIGHTER MONOPLANES.
THE LA-5.

DESIGNER.—Lavochkin.
TYPE.—Single-seat Fighter.
WINGS.—Low-wing cantilever monoplane. Wing in three sections comprising normal centre-section with two outer sections having taper on leading and trailing-edges. Structure consists of two wooden box section spars with flanges of vertically laminated plastic-bonded veneer strips. Webs and spar sheathing of three-ply birch. Plastic-bonded diagonal plywood strips form covering. Split-flaps of duralumin sheet are fitted.
FUSELAGE.—Triangular section wooden longerons and birch frames with skin of diagonal plywood strips. Plastic bonding used as adhesive and as impregnating medium.
TAIL UNIT.—Cantilever monoplane type. Tailplane of similar construction to wing. Fin integral with fuselage. Control surfaces have metal frames and fabric-covering. Trim-tabs on elevators.
LANDING GEAR.—Retractable type. Hydraulically-operated and re-tracting inward and upward into recesses in front of the main spar. Oleo-pneumatic shock-absorbers. The tail-wheel is not always retracted.
POWER PLANT.—One 1,600 h.p. M.82 two-row radial engine. Bullet-proof fuel tanks, three in centre-section and one in each outer wing panel.
ACCOMMODATION.—Enclosed pilot's cockpit over trailing-edge of wing. Transparent cover slides.
ARMAMENT.—Two 20 m/m. cannon mounted above the engine. Four 110-lb. (50 kg.) bombs can be carried under the wings.
DIMENSIONS.—Span 9.8 m. (32 ft. 2 in.), Length 8.46 m. (27 ft. 9 in.), Wing area 17.4 sq. m. (188 sq. ft.).
WEIGHTS.—No data available.
PERFORMANCE.—Maximum speed 592 km.h. (370 m.p.h.) at 5,000 m. (16,400 ft.), Cruising speed 400 km.h. (250 m.p.h.), Range 640 km. (400 miles).
REMARKS.—A later version of this aeroplane, known as the LA-7, has a 2,000 h.p. engine and an additional 37 m/m. cannon mounted beneath the engine. No further details are available.

THE LAGG-3.
DESIGNERS.—Lavochkin, Gorbunov and Gudkov.
TYPE.—Single-seat Fighter and Fighter-bomber.
WINGS.—Low-wing cantilever monoplane. Wing in three sections comprising normal centre-section with two outer sections having taper on leading and trailing-edges. Structure consists of two wooden box section spars with flanges of vertically-laminated,

plastic-bonded veneer strips. Webs and spar sheathing of three-ply birch. Plastic-bonded diagonal plywood strips form covering. Split-flaps of duralumin sheet are fitted.
FUSELAGE.—Triangular section wooden longerons and birch frames with skin of diagonal plywood strips. Plastic bonding used as adhesive and as impregnating medium.
TAIL UNIT.—Cantilever monoplane type. Tailplane of similar construction to wing. Fin integral with fuselage. Control surfaces have metal frames and fabric covering. Trim-tabs on elevators. Three types of rudder balance are known to exist.
LANDING GEAR.—Retractable type. Hydraulically-operated and re-tracting inward and upward into recesses in front of the main spar. Oleo-pneumatic shock absorbers. The tail-wheel is not always retracted.
POWER PLANT.—One 1,100 h.p. M-105P (cannon) twelve-cylinder 60 degree Vee liquid-cooled engine. Three-bladed all-metal Wisch-61P airscrew with hydraulic pitch control and constant-speed governor. Radiator under fuselage aft of trailing-edge. Oil

radiator under front end of engine crankcase. Induction airscoops near leading-edge wing-root fillets. Bullet-proof fuel tanks, three in centre-section and one in each outer wing panel.
ACCOMMODATION.—Enclosed pilot's cockpit over trailing-edge of wing. Cockpit canopy slides and has three positions. No emergency release. Armour-plate behind seat.
ARMAMENT AND EQUIPMENT.—One 20 m/m. Shpitalny-Vladimirov motor-cannon and two 12.7 m/m. Beresin synchronised machine-guns mounted over the engine. Six 56 lb. (25 kg.) rocket-impelled fragmentation bombs can be carried on special guide-rail type racks, three under each wing.
DIMENSIONS.—Span 9.8 m. (32 ft. 2¼ in.), Length 8.79 m. (28 ft. 10 in.), Wing area 17.4 sq. m. (188 sq. ft.).
WEIGHTS AND LOADINGS.—Weight empty 2,620 kg. (5,764 lb.), Weight loaded 3,200 kg. (7,040 lb.), Wing loading 181.5 kg./sq. m. (37.2 lb./sq. ft.), Power loading 2.9 kg./h.p. (6.37 lb./h.p.).
PERFORMANCE.—Cruising speed at 5,000 m. (16,400 ft.) 446 km.h. (279 m.p.h.), Maximum speed at 5,000 m. (16,400 ft.) 556.6 km.h. (348

The LAGG-3 Single-seat Fighter (1,100 h.p. M-105P engine).

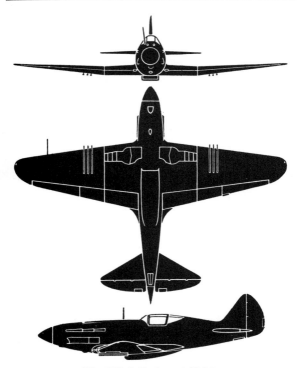

The MIG-3 Single-seat Fighter.

The YAK-1 Single-seat Fighter (1,100 h.p. M-105P engine).

IL-2 two-seat "Stormovik" Assault Bombers of the Red Air Force.

m.p.h.), Landing speed 139 km.h. (87 m.p.h.), Climb 3,000 m. (9,840 ft.) in 5 min., Service ceiling 9,000 m. (29,520 ft.), Range 640 km. (400 miles) at 446 km.h. (279 m.p.h.), Endurance 2½ hours.

THE MIG-3.
DESIGNERS.—Mikoyan and Gurevich.
TYPE.—Single-seat Fighter and Fighter-bomber.
WINGS.—Low-wing cantilever monoplane. Wing in three sections comprising normal centre-section with slight anhedral and large trailing-edge fillets and tapering outer sections with dihedral. The centre-section is of metal construction with metal covering and the outer sections are of wood construction with wood covering.
FUSELAGE.—Centre and forward sections of metal with light metal covering. Rear fuselage section of wood with ply covering.
TAIL UNIT.—Cantilever monoplane type. Tail-plane of metal construction with metal covering. Fin integral with fuselage. Fin and rudder of wood with wood covering. Trim-tabs on rudder and elevators.
LANDING GEAR.—Retractable type. Retracting inward and upward into recesses in front of the main spar. Hinged flaps attached to the underside of the centre-section completely cover the wheels when retracted. Retractable tail-wheel only fitted to small number of aircraft.
POWER PLANT.—One 1,200 h.p. AM-35A twelve-cylinder Vee liquid-cooled engine. Three-bladed all-metal controllable-pitch airscrew. Radiator under fuselage amidships. Induction air-scoops in leading edge roots.
ACCOMMODATION.—Enclosed pilot's cockpit over trailing-edge of wing. Transparent cover slides.
ARMAMENT AND EQUIPMENT.—According to German reports one 12.7 m/m. and two 7.7 m/m. machine-guns mounted in the nose. Six 56 lb. (25 kg.) rocket-impelled fragmentation bombs can be carried on special guide-rail type racks, three under each wing.
DIMENSIONS.—Span 11.4 m. (37 ft. 6 in.), Length 9.5 m. (31 ft. 2 in.).
WEIGHT LOADED.—About 2,820 kg. (6,200 lb.).
PERFORMANCE.—Maximum speed about 576 km.h. (360 m.p.h.), Range 800 km. (500 miles).
REMARKS.—There is a later version of this aeroplane known as the MIG-5, but no details are available.

THE YAK-1.
DESIGNER.—Alexander Yakovlev.
TYPE.—Single-seat Fighter.
WINGS.—Low-wing cantilever monoplane. Wood structure with ply covering and fabric-covered ailerons. Sharp taper on leading and trailing-edges. Dihedral from roots. Flaps extend between fuselage and ailerons.
FUSELAGE.—Mixed construction with metal covering forward of cockpit and ply covering aft.
TAIL UNIT.—High cantilever tailplane with taper on leading-edge. Single fin and rudder. Fixed surfaces have plywood covering. Control surfaces fabric-covered. Trim-tabs in rudder and elevators.
LANDING GEAR.—Inwardly retracting. Tail-wheel retracts on some versions.
POWER PLANT.—One 1,100 h.p. M-105P (cannon) twelve-cylinder Vee liquid-cooled engine. Three-bladed metal airscrew with hydraulic pitch-control and constant-speed governor. Radiator under fuselage placed far back. Oil radiator under front end of engine crankcase. Induction air-scoops in leading-edge of wing-root fillets.
ACCOMMODATION.—Enclosed pilot's cockpit over wing. Sliding cover.
ARMAMENT AND EQUIPMENT.—One 20 m/m. motor cannon and two 12.7 m/m. synchronised machine-guns mounted over the engine. Six 56 lb. (25 kg.) rocket-impelled fragmentation-bombs can be carried on special guide-rail type racks, three under each wing.
DIMENSIONS.—Span 10 m. (32 ft. 10 in.), Length 8.5 m. (27 ft. 10 in.).
WEIGHTS AND LOADINGS.—No data available.
PERFORMANCE.—Maximum speed 536 km.h. (335 m.p.h.).

THE YAK-9.
DESIGNER.—Alexander Yakovlev.
TYPE.—Single-seat Fighter.
WINGS.—Same as for YAK-1.
FUSELAGE.—Same as for YAK-1, but is shallower aft of cockpit.
TAIL UNIT.—Same as for YAK-1, but has modified trim tab in rudder.
LANDING GEAR.—Inward retracting. Retractable tail-wheel.
POWER PLANT.—One M-107 twelve-cylinder Vee liquid-cooled engine.
ACCOMMODATION.—Raised enclosed pilot's cockpit. Faired into fuselage. Sliding cover.
ARMAMENT AND EQUIPMENT.—Believed to be as for YAK-1.

DIMENSIONS.—Span 10 m. (32 ft. 10 in.), Length about 8.5 m. (28 ft.).
WEIGHTS.—No data available.
PERFORMANCE.—Maximum speed 592 km.h. (370 m.p.h.), Cruising speed 368 km.h. (230 m.p.h.), Service ceiling 9,760 m. (32,000 ft.), Range 1,040 km. (650 miles).
REMARKS.—There are two sub-types of this aeroplane. The YAK-9D is fitted with one motor cannon and two synchronised 0.50-in. machine-guns. The YAK-9T is a low attack model fitted with a 37 m/m. cannon in place of the 20 m/m. weapon.

SINGLE-ENGINED BOMBERS.
THE IL-2.
DESIGNER.—Sergei Iliuchin.
TYPE.—Two-seat Assault Bomber ("Stormovik").
WINGS.—Low-wing cantilever monoplane. Centre-section has no taper on leading-edge. Outer sections and trailing edges of centre-section have taper. Very slight dihedral from roots. Metal structure and covering. Flaps between ailerons and fuselage. Trim tabs in ailerons. Landing-light in leading-edge of port wing.
FUSELAGE.—Oval section, forward part of metal construction with metal covering. Rear fuselage of wood.
TAIL UNIT.—Cantilever tailplane with sharp taper on leading edge. Single fin and mass balanced rudder. Trim-tabs in elevators and rudder. Fixed surfaces believed to be metal-covered and movable surfaces fabric-covered.

The YAK-9 Single-seat Fighter.

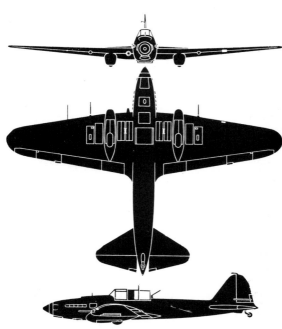

The IL-2 "Stormovik" Assault-Bomber.

LANDING GEAR.—Retracts backwards into large bulge under each wing leaving part of each wheel exposed. Non-retracting tail-wheel.

POWER PLANT.—One 1,300 h.p. M-38 twelve-cylinder Vee liquid-cooled engine. Three-bladed controllable-pitch metal airscrew. Radiator under fuselage. Engine has armour-plate on underside.

ACCOMMODATION.—Pilot's cockpit with raised canopy above wing with partly open cockpit for rear gunner. Armour-plate beneath and behind seat and on sides and top of cockpit cover.

ARMAMENT AND EQUIPMENT.—Two 23 m/m. cannon and two 7.6 m/m. machine-guns in the leading edge of the wing. Eight 56 lb. rocket-impelled fragmentation-bombs are carried an special guide-rail type racks, four under each wing. For special low attack missions two 37 m/m. cannon may be carried.

DIMENSIONS.—Span 14.58 m. (47 ft. 10 in.), Length 11.6 m. (38 ft.).

WEIGHTS AND LOADINGS.—No data available.

PERFORMANCE.—Maximum speed about 448 km.h. (280 m.p.h.).

TWIN-ENGINED BOMBERS.
THE DB-3F.

DESIGNER.—Sergei Iliuchin.

TYPE.—Twin-engined long-range Bomber and Torpedo-carrier.

WINGS.—Low-wing cantilever monoplane. Taper on leading and trailing-edges. Flat centre-section. Dihedral on outer sections. All-metal structure and covering. Flaps extend from ailerons to fuselage. Landing-light in leading-edge of port wing.

FUSELAGE.—Oval-section metal structure with metal covering.

TAIL UNIT.—Cantilever tailplane. Single fin and mass-balanced rudder. Trim-tabs in rudder and elevators.

LANDING GEAR.—Retracts backwards into engine nacelles leaving part of each wheel exposed. Non-retracting tail-wheel.

POWER PLANT.—Two 1,100 h.p. M.88 fourteen-cylinder radial air-cooled engines. Three-bladed metal airscrews.

ACCOMMODATION.—Pilot's enclosed cockpit above leading-edge with sliding cover. Navigator/bomb-aimer and radio-operator in glazed nose and fourth member of crew in dorsal gun-turret.

ARMAMENT AND EQUIPMENT.—Movable machine-gun in nose, movable machine-gun in dorsal turret and one in ventral position. Maximum bomb-load believed to be 2,000 kg. (4,400 lb.) stowed in fuselage and carried on racks under wings both inboard and outboard of engines.

DIMENSIONS.—Span 21.4 m. (70 ft. 2 in.), Length 14.5 m. (47 ft. 6 in.).

WEIGHT LOADED.—15,000 kg. (33,000 lb.).

PERFORMANCE.—Maximum speed 424 km.h. (265 m.p.h.), Range 4,000 km. (2,500 miles).

THE IL-4.

The IL-4 is an improved version of the DB-3F. It is fitted with two 1,600 h.p. M-82 two-row radial air-cooled engines. The armament consists of two machine-guns and a bomb load of 2,700 kg. (5,950 lbs.) can be carried. No other details are available.

PERFORMANCE.—Maximum speed 368 km.h. (230 m.p.h.), Cruising speed 298 km.h. (186 m.p.h.), at 7,000 m. (22,960 ft.), Service ceiling 9,000 m. (29,520 ft.), Normal Range 1,200 km. (750 miles), Maximum range (with auxiliary fuel tanks) 1,640 km. (1,025 miles).

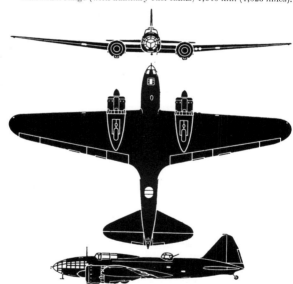

The DB-3F Long-Range Bomber.

THE PE-2.

DESIGNER.—Petlyakov.

TYPE.—Long-range Fighter, Low-level Attack and Dive-Bomber monoplane.

WINGS.—Low-wing cantilever monoplane. Wings taper in chord and thickness from roots to tips. All-metal two-spar structure. Ailerons have servo-operated trim-tabs. Electrically-operated dive-brakes between ailerons and nacelles and nacelles and fuselage.

FUSELAGE.—Oval all-metal monocoque structure in three sections, bolted together.

TAIL-UNIT.—Cantilever monoplane type with slight dihedral and twin fins and rudders. All-metal framework with metal-covered fixed surfaces and fabric-covered elevators and rudders. Electric servo-operated trim-tabs in all movable surfaces.

LANDING GEAR.—Retractable type. Electro-hydraulic retraction for main wheels and tail-wheel, the former being raised backwards into the tails of the engine nacelles and the latter into the fuselage. Hinged doors close all apertures.

POWER PLANT.—Two M-105R twelve-cylinder Vee liquid-cooled engines with electrically-operated two-speed superchargers, each rated at 1,100 h.p. at 2,000 m. (6,560 ft.) and 1,050 h.p. at 4,000 m. (13,120 ft.) and with 1,100 h.p. available for take-off. Wisch-61 three-blade electrically-operated constant-speed airscrews. Eleven self-sealing fuel tanks in wings and fuselage. Total capacity 1,500 litres (330 Imp. gallons). Tanks are interconnected and feed to small header tank behind each engine. Inert gas fed under pressure into air spaces above fuel in tanks as a precaution against fire. Self-sealing oil tank in each engine nacelle ahead of fireproof bulkhead. Oil coolers in lower portion of each nacelle with servo-controlled exit shutters. Coolant radiators, two per engine, between wing spars with air ducts in leading-edge and air outlets in upper

The PE-3 Fighter-Reconnaissance Monoplane, a solid-nose version of the PE-2.

The PE-2 Low Attack and Dive-Bomber Monoplane (two 1,100 h.p. M-105R engines).

surface of wings. Passage of air through radiators controlled by electric servo-operated shutters.

ACCOMMODATION.—Crew of three, pilot, radio-operator and rear gunner. Pilot and radio-operator seated back to back under continuous canopy over leading-edge of wing. Radio-operator may obtain access to prone bombing position under pilot's seat. Rear gunner aft of trailing-edge of wing. All positions armoured.

ARMAMENT.—Varies according to function of aircraft. May consist of four 7.62 m/m. machine-guns, two fixed in nose of fuselage, one upper gun operated by radio-operator and one lower retractable gun aft of wings; or two 7.62 m/m. and two 12.7 m/m. machine-guns. The lower retractable gun is remotely-controlled and sighted by periscope. Bomb-bay beneath wing with accommodation for a maximum load of 1,000 kg. (2,200 lbs.). External racks under wing inboard of nacelles.

DIMENSIONS.—Span 17.16 m. (56 ft. 3 in.), Length 12.6 m. (41 ft. 6 in.), Wing area 40.5 sq. m. (436 sq. ft.).

WEIGHTS AND LOADINGS.—Weight empty 5,870 kg. (12,900 lbs.), Normal loaded weight 7,700 kg. (16,930 lbs.), Maximum permissible loaded weight 8,520 kg. (18,730 lbs.), Normal wing loading 190.3 kg./sq. m. (39 lbs./sq. ft.), Maximum wing loading 210 kg./sq. m. (43 lbs./sq. ft.).

PERFORMANCE.—Maximum speed at 5,000 m. (16,400 ft.) 540 km.h. (335 m.p.h.), Maximum speed at 2,000 m. (6,560 ft.) 506 km.h. (314 m.p.h.), Maximum speed at ground level 460 km.h. (286 m.p.h.), Cruising speed 428 km.h. (226 m.p.h.), Climb to 3,000 m. (9,840 ft.) 3.5 min., Climb to 5,000 m. (16,400 ft.) 7 min., Service ceiling 9,000 m. (29,520 ft.).

THE TU-2.

DESIGNER.—Andreas Nikolaievitch Tupolev.

The TU-2 is a three/four-seat Attack Bomber designed to replace the PE-2. It is fitted with two 1,750 h.p. M-82 liquid-cooled engines each with one 20 m/m. motor cannon firing through the airscrew shaft. Other armament consists of four .50 in. machine-guns, one fixed in the extreme tail, and the other three on hand-operated mountings above and below the fuselage.

DIMENSIONS.—Span 21.3 m. (69 ft. 10 in.), Length 13.8 m. (45 ft. 4 in.).

WEIGHT LOADED.—12,812 kg. (28,220 lbs.).

PERFORMANCE.—Maximum speed 557 km.h. (348 m.p.h.), Cruising speed 416 km.h. (260 m.p.h.), Service ceiling 10,980 m. (36,000 ft.).

FOUR-ENGINED BOMBER.
THE TB-7.

DESIGNER.—Andreas Nikolaievitch Tupolev.

TYPE.—Four-engined Heavy-bomber.

WINGS.—Thick mid-wing cantilever monoplane. All-metal structure with taper on leading and trailing-edges. Flat centre-section between fuselage and inner engines. Marked dihedral outboard of inner engines. High aspect ratio ailerons with trim tabs. Flaps extend from fuselage to ailerons. Landing-lights in leading-edge of both wings.

FUSELAGE.—All-metal structure.

TAIL UNIT.—Cantilever tailplane with sharp taper on leading-edge. Large single fin and rudder. Trim-tabs in rudder and elevators.

LANDING GEAR.—Retracts backwards into engine nacelles leaving wheels partly exposed. Castoring non-retracting tail-wheel.

POWER PLANT.—Early version has four 1,100 h.p. M-105 twelve-cylinder upright Vee liquid-cooled engines. Later version has four 1,300 h.p. AM-38 twelve-cylinder upright Vee liquid-cooled engines. Three-bladed controllable-pitch metal airscrews. Radiators for inner and outer engines are combined in the inner nacelles.

A close-up view of the nose and power-units of the TB-7 Heavy Bomber.

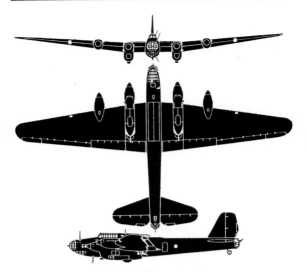

The TB-7 Heavy Bomber.

ACCOMMODATION.—Enclosed cockpit offset to port above wing with accommodation for first and second pilots in tandem. Radio-operator believed to be behind second pilot. Dorsal gun-turret at rear of cockpit fairing. Navigator's and bomb-aimer's positions in nose. Other members of crew in gun positions.

ARMAMENT AND EQUIPMENT.—Two machine-guns in spherical turret in nose, two machine-guns in dorsal turret, 20 m/m. cannon in tail turret and one hand-operated movable machine-gun in the rear of each inboard engine nacelle under trailing-edge. Maximum bomb load of about 3,630 kg. (8,000 lb.) stowed internally in fuselage.

DIMENSIONS.—Span 40 m. (131 ft. 3 in.), Length 24.5 m. (80 ft. 6 in.).

WEIGHT LOADED.—About 22,250 kg. (49,000 lb.).

PERFORMANCE.—Maximum speed 448 km.h. (280 m.p.h.) at 7,260 m. (25,000 ft.), Range 4,000 km. (2,500 miles) with 2,000 kg. (4,400 lb.) bomb load.

REMARKS.—Also fitted with four 1,600 h.p. two-row radial air-cooled engines, but further details of this, the latest, version are not available.

FLYING BOATS.
THE GST.

DESIGNER.—(Russian version of Consolidated PBY with modifications). Built in State Factories.

TYPE.—Twin-engined long-range Patrol-Bomber Flying-boat.

WINGS.—Semi-cantilever high-wing monoplane. Wing in three sections, the centre-section supported above the hull by a streamline superstructure and braced by two pairs of parallel streamline struts to the sides of the hull. Wing structure is of the beam bulkhead and stressed-skin type, the skin being reinforced with "Z"-section extruded stiffeners. The trailing-edge section consists of aluminium alloy ribs cantilevered from the main beam and covered with fabric. Aluminium-alloy-framed balanced ailerons covered with fabric. An adjustable camber device is installed on the upper surface of the ailerons.

HULL.—Two-step semi-circular-topped hull of all-metal construction. Aluminium-alloy bulkheads, framing, stringers and skin. All-metal retractable wing-tip floats. When the floats are retracted they form tips to the wings and the float struts and bracing structure are recessed flush with the lower surface of the wings. Electrical and mechanically-operated retracting mechanism. Automatic locks and warning lights.

TAIL UNIT.—Cantilever monoplane type. Lower fin built integral with the hull. Tail-plane and upper section of fin covered with smooth metal sheet reinforced with extruded sections. Elevators and rudder are aluminium-alloy structures with fabric covering. Trimming-tabs in elevators and rudder.

POWER PLANT.—Two 1,000 h.p. Pratt & Whitney Twin-Wasp fourteen-cylinder radial air-cooled engines on welded steel-tube mountings in the leading-edge of the centre-section. Shuttered cowlings for Arctic use. Three-bladed metal airscrews. Fuel tanks are integral with the structure of the centre-section.

ACCOMMODATION.—Enclosed pilot's compartment seating two side-by-side with dual controls. Engineer's station in hull below centre-section. Bow gun-turret.

The GST Patrol-Bomber Flying-boat.

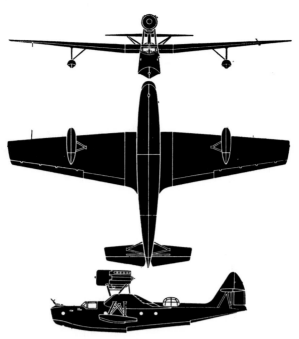

The MBR-2 Reconnaissance Flying-boat.

ARMAMENT.—Machine-gun in bow turret and probably two movable beam machine-guns, one on each side of hull aft of wing.

DIMENSIONS.—Span 31.7 m. (104 ft.), Length 19 m. (62 ft. 6 in.), Height 5.64 m. (18 ft. 6 in.), Wing area 130 sq. m. (1,400 sq. ft.).

WEIGHT LOADED.—12,300 kg. (27,080 lb.).

PERFORMANCE.—Maximum speed 304 km.h. (190 m.p.h.), at 3,200 m. (10,500 ft.), Range 6,400 km. (4,000 miles), Climb to 1,525 m. (5,000 ft.) 4½ mins., Service ceiling 7,690 m. (25,200 ft.).

THE MBR-2.

DESIGNER.—Blochavindin.

TYPE.—Single-engined Short-range Reconnaissance flying-boat.

WINGS.—High-wing cantilever monoplane. Taper on leading and trailing-edges. Dihedral from roots. Square tips. Construction appears to be all-metal. Flaps are fitted. Trim-tabs in ailerons.

HULL.—Two-step all-metal hull. Braced single-step stabilizing floats are attached about halfway between the hull and wing tips.

TAIL UNIT.—Strut-braced tailplane. Single fin and rudder. Trim-tab in rudder.

POWER PLANT.—One 680 h.p. M-17 twelve-cylinder Vee water-cooled engine mounted above the hull on two sets of "N" struts. The radiator is immediately in front of the engine.

ACCOMMODATION.—Crew of five accommodated in enclosed cockpit forward of wing, midship cabin in hull, open bow gun position and dorsal gun-turret.

ARMAMENT AND EQUIPMENT.—Movable hand-operated machine-gun in open bow position and one movable machine-gun in dorsal turret.

DIMENSIONS.—Span 13.4 m. (44 ft.).

WEIGHTS AND LOADINGS.—No data available.

PERFORMANCE.—Maximum speed 217.6 km.h. (136 m.p.h.), Range 1,200 km. (745 miles).

THE MDR-6.

DESIGNER.—Believed Blochavindin.

TYPE.—Twin-engined Long-range Reconnaissance flying-boat.

WINGS.—High wing cantilever monoplane. Taper on leading and

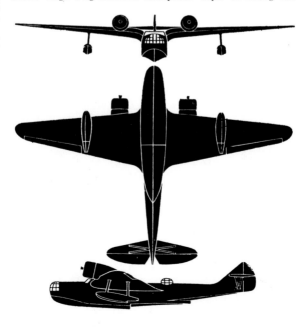

The MDR-6 Reconnaissance Flying-boat.

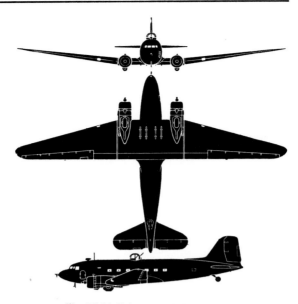

The PS-84 Twin-engined Transport.

trailing-edges. Sharp dihedral on centre-section. Less dihedral on outer sections. Believed to be all-metal structure.

HULL.—Two-step all-metal structure. Braced single-step stabilizing floats are attached about halfway between the hull and the wing tips.

POWER PLANT.—Two air-cooled radial engines mounted on the leading-edge of the wing.

ACCOMMODATION.—Enclosed cockpit forward of leading-edge, bow gun-turret and dorsal gun-turret.

ARMAMENT.—No definite information but bow and dorsal-gun turrets are known to exist.

DIMENSIONS, WEIGHTS AND PERFORMANCE.—No data available.

TWIN-ENGINED TRANSPORT.
THE PS-84.

DESIGNERS.—The Douglas Aircraft Company, Inc. (Russian-built Douglas DC-3 with modifications by Musalo).

TYPE.—Twin-engined Transport.

WINGS.—Low-wing cantilever monoplane with straight trailing-edge and pronounced sweep-back to leading-edge. Dihedral on outer sections. Douglas cellular multi-web construction. Fabric-covered ailerons. Hydraulically-operated trailing-edge flaps. Detachable wing-tips. Landing-light in leading-edge of both wings.

FUSELAGE.—Oval-section structure built of transverse frames of formed sheet, longitudinal members of extruded bulb angles and covered with a smooth stressed skin.

TAIL UNIT.—Cantilever monoplane type. Tail-plane and fin of multi-cellular construction. Rudder and elevators have aluminium-alloy frames and fabric covering.

LANDING GEAR.—Retracts forward into engine nacelles, leaving part of each wheel exposed. Non-retracting tail-wheel.

POWER PLANT.—Believed to be two 1,000 h.p. M-63 air-cooled radial engines. Three-bladed metal airscrews.

ACCOMMODATION.—Enclosed pilot's compartment forward of wing. Main cabin 6 ft. 6 in. high, 7 ft. 8 in. wide and 27 ft. 8 in. long.

ARMAMENT.—Fixed machine-gun in nose, machine-gun in turret above the main cabin and two beam guns, one in each side of rear fuselage.

DIMENSIONS.—Span 28.9 m. (95 ft.), Length 19.6 m. (64 ft. 5½ in.), Height 5.2 m. (16 ft. 11⅛ in.), Wing area 91.7 sq. m. (987 sq. ft.).

WEIGHTS AND PERFORMANCE.—No data available but about the same as American-built DC-3.

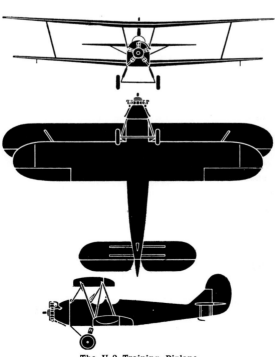

The U-2 Training Biplane.

SINGLE-ENGINED TRAINERS.
THE U-2.

DESIGNER.—N. N. Polikarpov.

TYPE.—Single-engined Training and Ambulance biplane.

WINGS.—Single-bay braced staggered unequal-span biplane. Dihedral on both wings. Ailerons on both upper and lower wings. Wood structure fabric-covered.

FUSELAGE.—Wood construction with wood and fabric covering.

TAIL UNIT.—Strut-braced tailplane. Single fin and balanced rudder.

LANDING GEAR.—Normal non-retracting cross-axle type. Tail-skid. Can be operated on skis.

POWER PLANT.—One 110 h.p. M-11 five-cylinder radial air-cooled engine. Two-bladed fixed-pitch wooden airscrew. Fuel tank in centre-section of upper wing.

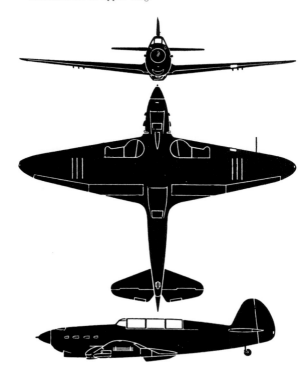

The YAK-7 Advanced Training Monoplane.

The UT-2 Two-seat Training Monoplane (110 h.p. M-11 engine).

ACCOMMODATION.—Trainer : Tandem open cockpits with dual controls. Ambulance : Open pilot's cockpit and two stretcher containers on top of fuselage aft of cockpit. Some aircraft have three open cockpits.

ARMAMENT AND EQUIPMENT.—Light bombs have been slung on racks under the lower wing.

DIMENSIONS.—Span 11.4 m. (37 ft. 5 in.), Length 8.1 m. (26 ft. 8 in.), Height 2.9 m. (9 ft. 6 in.), Wing area 33.1 sq. m. (356.8 sq. ft.).

WEIGHTS AND LOADINGS.—Weight empty 605 kg. (1,331 lb.), Weight loaded 860 kg. (1,892 lb.), Wing loading 25.8 kg./sq. m. (5.3 lb./sq. ft.), Power loading 8.6 kg./h.p. (18.9 lb./h.p.).

PERFORMANCE.—Maximum speed 150 km.h. (93 m.p.h.) at sea level, Landing speed 69 km.h. (43 m.p.h.), Service ceiling 4,000 m. (13,120 ft.).

THE YAK-7.

DESIGNER.—Alexander Yakovlev.

TYPE.—Two-seat Advanced Training monoplane.

WINGS.—Low-wing cantilever monoplane. Wood structure with ply covering. Fabric-covered ailerons. Sharp taper on leading and trailing-edges. Dihedral from roots. Flaps extend between fuselage and ailerons with hinges at right angles to line of flight.

FUSELAGE.—Mixed construction with metal covering forward of cockpit and ply covering aft.

TAIL UNIT.—Cantilever tailplane with taper on leading-edge. Single fin and rudder. Fixed surfaces have plywood-covering. Control surfaces fabric-covered. Trim-tabs in rudder and elevators.

LANDING GEAR.—Inwardly retracting. Non-retractable tail-wheel.

POWER PLANT.—One 1,100 h.p. M-105 twelve-cylinder Vee liquid-cooled engine. Three-bladed metal airscrew. Radiator under fuselage placed amidships. Oil radiator under front end of engine crankcase.

ACCOMMODATION.—Enclosed cockpit over wing. Sliding covers above seats.

DIMENSIONS.—Span 10 m. (32 ft. 10 in.), Length about 8.5 m. (27 ft. 10 in.).

WEIGHTS AND PERFORMANCE.—No data available.

THE UT-2.

DESIGNER.—Alexander Yakovlev.

TYPE.—Two-seat Training monoplane.

WINGS.—Low-wing cantilever monoplane. Taper on leading and trailing-edges. Flat centre-section. Dihedral on outer sections. Wood structure with plywood or fabric covering.

FUSELAGE.—Wood structure with mixed plywood and fabric covering.

TAIL UNIT.—Braced monoplane type. Single fin and balanced rudder. Trim-tab on rudder.

LANDING GEAR.—Non-retracting split type. Tail-skid.

POWER PLANT.—One 110 h.p. M-11 five-cylinder radial air-cooled engine. Two-bladed fixed-pitch wooden airscrew.

ACCOMMODATION.—Tandem open cockpits with dual controls.

DIMENSIONS AND WEIGHTS.—No data available.

PERFORMANCE.—Maximum speed 192 km.h. (120 m.p.h.) at sea level.

REMARKS.—The UT-1 is generally similar but has only a single open cockpit for the pilot.

SPAIN

A.I.S.A.
AERONAUTICA INDUSTRIAL S.A.

HEAD OFFICE AND WORKS : CARABANCHEL ALTO, MADRID.

This Company, with fully-equipped works and adjoining aerodrome at Carabanchel Alto (Madrid), has for some years been engaged in the design and manufacture of aircraft of mixed construction. It has been responsible for the production of several national prototypes.

In 1943, three new types were produced and put into service, the H.M.1 and H.M.5 trainers and H.M.9 glider-tug.

THE A.I.S.A. H.M.1.

TYPE.—Two-seat Primary Training monoplane.

WINGS.—Low-wing cantilever monoplane. Wings have constant taper and dihedral from root to rounded tip. All-wood structure

FUSELAGE.—Welded steel tube structure covered forward with detachable metal panels and aft with fabric.

TAIL UNIT.—Monoplane type. Braced tailplane and cantilever fin. Wood framework with plywood-covered fixed surfaces and fabric-covered rudder and elevators. Adjustable trimming-tabs in central surfaces.

LANDING GEAR.—Fixed type. Consists of two cantilever legs incorporating steel spring oil-damped shock-absorbers. Swivelling tail-wheel may be interconnected with rudder pedals by clutch when desired.

POWER PLANT.—One 150 h.p. Hirth HM 506 four-cylinder inverted air-cooled engine on welded steel-tube mounting. Two-bladed wooden fixed-pitch airscrew. Fuel tanks in wings.

ACCOMMODATION.—Tandem open cockpits with conventional dual controls and instrument equipment.

DIMENSIONS.—Span 9.65 m. (31 ft. 8 in.), Length 7.65 m. (25 ft.), Height 2.20 m. (7 ft. 2½ in.), Wing area 14 sq. m. (150.6 sq. ft.).

WEIGHTS AND LOADINGS.—Weight empty 620 kg. (1,364 lbs.), Weight loaded 850 kg. (1,870 lbs.), Wing loading 60 kg./sq. m. (12.3 lbs./sq. ft.). Power loading 5.2 kg./h.p. (11.4 lbs./h.p.).

PERFORMANCE.—Maximum speed 230 km.h. (142.8 m.p.h.), Cruising speed 195 km.h. (121 m.p.h.), Minimum speed 70 km.h. (43.5 m.p.h.), Climb to 1,000 m. (3,280 ft.) 3 min., Climb to 4,000 m. (13,120 ft.) 20 min., Service ceiling 5,000 m. (16,400 ft.), Duration 3.5 hours.

THE A.I.S.A. H.M.5.

TYPE.—Single-seat Advanced Training monoplane.

WINGS, FUSELAGE, TAIL UNIT, LANDING GEAR AND POWER PLANT.—Same as for H.M.1. except that no flaps fitted.

ACCOMMODATION.—Single open cockpit with conventional controls and instrument equipment.

DIMENSIONS.—Span 8.2 m. (26 ft. 10 in.), Length 7 m. (22 ft. 11 in.), Height 2.06 m. (6 ft. 9 in.), Wing area 11.5 sq. m. (123.7 sq. ft.).

THE A.I.S.A. H.M.9.

TYPE.—Two-seat Glider-Towing monoplane.

WINGS, FUSELAGE, TAIL UNIT, POWER PLANT AND ACCOMMODATION.—Same as for H.M.1.

LANDING GEAR.—Fixed type. Consists of two tripod units, the main struts with steel-spring oil-damped shock-absorbers.

DIMENSIONS.—Span 10.65 m. (24 ft. 11 in.), Length 7.60 m. (24 ft. 11 in.), Height 2.12 m. (7 ft.), Wing area 18 sq. m. (193.6 sq. ft.).

WEIGHTS AND LOADINGS.—Weight empty 700 kg. (1,540 lbs.), Weight loaded 920 kg. (2,025 lbs.), Wing loading 51.1 kg./sq. m. (10.47 lbs./sq. ft.), Power loading 5.7 kg./h.p. (12.5 lbs./h.p.).

PERFORMANCE.—Maximum speed 175 km.h. (108.6 m.p.h.), Cruising speed 140 km.h. (87 m.p.h.), Minimum speed 60 km.h. (37.3 m.p.h.), Climb to 1,000 m. (3,280 ft.) 3 min. 20 sec., Climb to 4,000 m. (13,120 ft.) 24 min., Service ceiling 4,500 m. (14,760 ft.), Duration 2 hours.

C.A.S.A.
CONSTRUCCIONES AERONAUTICAS S.A.

HEAD OFFICE : CALLE DE COVARRUBIAS No. 4, MADRID.

WORKS : MADRID, SEVILLE AND CADIZ.

This important firm has three factories wherein are built various types of all-metal military aircraft of national and foreign design for the Spanish Air Force.

Prior to the Civil War this Company, in the two factories it then possessed at Getafe and Cadiz, built 400 Breguet XIX reconnaissance biplanes, 27 Vickers "Vildebeest" torpedo-carrying seaplanes and 40 Dornier "Wal" twin-engined flying-boats for the Spanish Government.

Since the Civil War C.A.S.A. has expanded its Madrid and Cadiz factories and has built a new plant at Seville.

In 1942 this Company was successful in being awarded a contract to manufacture a large number of bomber aircraft.

HISPANO-SUIZA.
LA HISPANO AVIACIÓN, FÁBRICA DE AVIONES.

HEAD OFFICE : AVENIDA DE JOSÉ ANTONIO No. 7, MADRID.

AIRCRAFT WORKS : SEVILLE.

This concern, which is a branch of La Hispano Suiza, Fabrica de Automoviles S.A., is devoted to the construction of aircraft. The parent company manufactures Hispano-Suiza aero-engines of both liquid and air-cooled types at its Barcelona works.

The latest original production of the Company of which details may be published is the H.S.42, a two-seat training monoplane suitable for combat or observer training. Having successfully passed all its tests the H.S.42 has been adopted by the Spanish Air Force and it is now in production in series by Hispano-Suiza.

The prototype was fitted with the 430 h.p. Piaggio P.VIIC.16 engine but this will ultimately be replaced by the new Hispano-Suiza H.S.93 engine.

In 1942 La Hispano Aviación was awarded a contract to manufacture a large number of fighter aircraft.

THE HISPANO-SUIZA H.S.42.

TYPE.—Two-seat advanced Training monoplane.

WINGS.—Low-wing cantilever monoplane. In three sections and of all-wood construction with plywood covering. Hydraulically-operated split trailing-edge flaps. Flap and ailerons have welded steel-tube frames and fabric covering.

FUSELAGE.—Oval section structure of welded steel-tube covered forward with detachable metal panels and aft with fabric.

TAIL UNIT.—Monoplane type. Metal framework with fabric covering. Adjustable tail-plane.

LANDING GEAR.—Retractable type. Wheels raised inwardly into underside of centre-section. Hydraulic retraction.
POWER PLANT.—One 430 h.p. Piaggio P.VIIC.16 seven-cylinder radial air-cooled engine driving an Alfa-Romeo electrically-operated variable-pitch airscrew. This engine will be replaced later by the new Hispano-Suiza H.S.93 engine.
ACCOMMODATION.—Tandem enclosed cockpits under continuous

canopy with sliding portions over the two seats. May be equipped with fixed forward-firing gun in cowling and flexible gun in the rear cockpit.
DIMENSIONS.—Span 10 m. (32 ft. 9½ in.), Length 7.88 m. (25 ft. 10 in.), Wing area 16.3 sq. m. (175.4 sq. ft.).
WEIGHTS AND LOADINGS.—Weight empty 1,000 kg. (2,200 lbs.), Disposable load 500 kg. (1,100 lbs.), Weight loaded 1,500 kg

(3,300 lbs.), Wing loading 92 kg./sq. m. (18.86 lbs./sq. ft.), Power loading 3.5 kg./h.p. (7.7 lbs./h.p.).
PERFORMANCE.—Maximum speed 310 km.h. (192.5 m.p.h.), Cruising speed 280 km.h. (173.8 m.p.h.), Minimum speed 107 km.h. (66.4 m.p.h.), Climb to 3,000 m. (9,840 ft.) 10 mins., Service ceiling 6,100 m. (20,000 ft.), Duration 3 hours.

SWEDEN

KUNGL. FLYGFÖRVALTNINGENS FLYGVERKSTAD.
ULVSUNDA.

Owing to the difficulty of purchasing aircraft abroad and the fact that the small Swedish aircraft industry is fully engaged. the Swedish Air Board has undertaken the design and construction of a single-seat fighter. The design of the new fighter, designated J 22, was supervised by Mr. Bo Lundberg. Its production is being handled by the Kungl. Flygförvaltningens Flygverkstad at Ulvsunda.

THE J 22.

TYPE.—Single-seat Fighter.
WINGS.—Low mid-wing cantilever monoplane. Wings have constant taper and almost square tips. Stainless steel structure with a plywood skin. Entire trailing-edge hinged, the inner sections acting as camber-changing flaps and the outer sections as ailerons. Flaps and ailerons have spot-welded stainless steel frame and fabric-covering.
FUSELAGE.—Oval section structure having a welded steel-tube primary structure covered with birch plywood.
TAIL UNIT.—Cantilever monoplane type. Stainless steel framework with the tail-plane and fin covered with plywood and the rudder and elevators covered with fabric.
LANDING GEAR.—Retractable type. The shock-absorber legs are hinged to the lower fuselage members and retract backward into the fuselage, the hinged doors covering the apertures closing both while the landing gear is fully lowered as well as when retracted. Retractable tail-wheel.
POWER PLANT.—One 1,050 h.p. Swedish-built Pratt & Whitney Twin-Wasp two-row radial air-cooled engine enclosed in long-chord cowling with trailing-edge controllable gills. Air intake and oil cooler apertures in leading-edge of wing roots. Three-bladed controllable-pitch airscrew.

The J 22 Single-seat Fighter Monoplane (Swedish-built Pratt & Whitney Twin-Wasp engine).

ACCOMMODATION.—Enclosed cockpit over wing.
ARMAMENT.—Two 13.2 m/m. and two 7.9 m/m. machine-guns (J 22A) or four 13.2 m/m. machine-guns (J 22B), all in the wings.
DIMEESIONS.—Span 10 m. (32 ft. 10 in.), Length 7.8 m. (25 ft. 7 in.),

Height 2.9 m. (9 ft. 6 in.).
WEIGHTS.—No data available.
PERFORMANCE.—Maximum speed about 575 km.h. (360 m.p.h.), Cruising speed 450 km.h. (280 m.p.h.)

BA.
BJORN ANDREASSON.

Mr. Bjorn Andreasson, an engineer at the former sailplane factory A. B. Flygindustri, Halmstad, has designed the ultra-light experimental single-seat advanced training and touring biplane described below.

THE BA-4.

TYPE.—Single-seat experimental advanced training and touring biplane.
WINGS.—Single-bay rigidly-braced staggered biplane. Dihedral 2° upper and 4° lower. Centre-section carried above fuselage on N-struts in front of cockpit. Single I-type interplane strut on either side of fuselage with sloping I strut from upper attachment of interplane strut to bottom of fuselage. Wing structure consists of two I-section plywood spars, pine and plywood ribs and plywood and fabric covering. Slotted ailerons on lower wings have their leading-edges covered with plywood and the remainder with fabric.

The BA-4 Single-seat Light Biplane.

FUSELAGE.—Rectangular structure with domed roof. Wood (pine) framework with plywood stressed skin covering.
TAIL UNIT.—Cantilever monoplane type. Wooden framework with plywood-covered tailplane and fin and fabric-covered elevators and rudder.
LANDING GEAR.—Cantilever split type of chrome-molybdenum steel tube. Leaf-spring tail-skid.
POWER PLANT.—One 28 h.p. Scott Flying Squirrel four-cylinder air-cooled two-stroke engine. Fuel tank (6 Imp. gallons) in fuselage behind engine.
ACCOMMODATION.—Open cockpit aft of upper wing centre-section.
DIMENSIONS.—Span 5 m. (16 ft. 5 in.), Length 4.6 m. (15 ft.), Wing area 7.2 sq. m. (77.2 sq. ft.).
WEIGHTS.—Weight empty 143 kg. (315 lbs.), Weight loaded 260 kg. (572 lbs.).
PERFORMANCE.—Maximum speed 150-160 km.h. (93-99 m.p.h.), Landing speed 70 km.h. (43.5 m.p.h.).

BHT.
SKANDINAVISKA AERO A.B. (SCANDINAVIAN AIRWAYS, LTD.).
HEAD OFFICE : MÄSTER SAMUELSGATAN 18, STOCKHOLM.
WORKS : NORRTÄLJE.
Chairman : K. R. Bökman (Managing Director of Rederi A.B. Svenska Lloyd).
Managing Director : Åke Forsmark.
Chief Designer and Chief Test Pilot : Erik Bratt.
This Company has been formed to take over the taxi-flying business formerly operated under the name of A. B. Björkvallsflyg. During the war the company has been mainly occupied with target-towing and other semi-military duties.
In November, 1944, the control of the Company was taken over by several shipowners in Gothenburg, a considerable enlargement of the Company's funds at the same time being announced. The Company has applied for Government franchise to operate

a number of regular domestic air routes details of which will be found in Section B.
Twin-engined aircraft are proposed to be used for these lines, which will be opened as soon as the aircraft required can be obtained and Government permission is granted.
In December, 1944, the Company completed the construction of its new single-seater BHT-1 Beauty, designed by E. Bratt, K. E. Hilfing and B. Törnblom.

THE BHT-1 BEAUTY.

TYPE.—Single-seat High-speed Fighter-Training, Target-towing and Long-Range Light monoplane.
WINGS.—Low-wing cantilever monoplane. Tapering wing in three sections. Wooden two-spar structure with plywood covering. Slotted flaps and ailerons.

FUSELAGE.—Wooden monocoque structure with a stressed plywood skin.
TAIL UNIT.—Cantilever monoplane type with aerodynamically and mass-balanced rudder and elevator—trimming tabs, adjustable in air, on both. Tailplane and elevator are halfway up the fin, and the rudder therefore is divided. The hinges of elevator and rudder consist of plywood-tubes, at the same time functioning as spars.
LANDING GEAR.—Retractable type with springing and oleo damping. Wheels raised backwards, at the same time turned 90 degrees, and retracted completely into centre-section of the wing. Hand-operating gear. Metal fairings follow the legs. Wheel-brakes. Full-swivelling tail-wheel.
POWER PLANT.—One 60 h.p. Walter Mikron 4, four-cylinder in-line inverted air-cooled engine on a duralumin and steel-tube mounting. The 90 h.p. Cirrus-Minor or the 105 h.p. Hirth HM 504A-2 engine can also be installed with only slight alterations. Wooden airscrew, but provision made for controllable-pitch airscrew. Oil tank in fuselage. Fuel tanks in fuselage (38 litres) and wings (two of 25 litres each). Special reserve fuel tank (127 litres) can be installed behind the pilot in luggage compartment. Maximum capacity 215 litres, sufficient for 3,000 km. (1,860 miles) range.
ACCOMMODATION.—Enclosed cabin of "Astralon" over centre-section, opening to starboard. Adjustable seat designed for seat-type parachute. Adjustable rudder-pedals. Cabin-roof jettisonable. Turn-over post behind pilot's seat.
DIMENSIONS.—Span 6.82 m. (22 ft. 4½ in.), Length 5.80 m. (19 ft.), Height 1.90 m. (6 ft. 3 in.), Wing area 7 sq. m. (75.3 sq. ft.).
WEIGHTS AND LOADINGS.—Weight empty 240 kg. (528 lbs.), Weight loaded (aerobatic factors) 365 kg. (803 lbs.), Maximum weight loaded (for long-range flights) 420 kg. (924 lbs.), Wing loading (aerobatic factors) 52 kg./sq. m. (10.6 lbs./sq. ft.), Power loading 6.10 kg./h.p. (13.42 lbs./h.p.).
PERFORMANCE (60 h.p. Walter Mikron 4 engine).—Maximum speed 250 km.h. (155 m.p.h.), Cruising speed 210 km.h. (130 m.p.h.), Landing speed with flaps down 75 km.h. (46.5 m.p.h.) without flaps 95 km.h. (59 m.p.h.), Initial rate of climb 312 m./min. (1,024 ft./min.) with 105 h.p. Hirth H.M. 504A-2 engine 540 m./min. (1,770 ft./min.), Maximum permissable diving speed (with controllable pitch airscrew) 580 km.h. (335 m.p.h.), Service ceiling 7,500 m. (24,600 ft.), Take-off run 100 m. (98.4 yds.), Landing run 80-90 m. (78-88 yds.), Range with standard fuel capacity 1,700 km. (1,056 miles), Range with special reserve fuel 3,000 km. (1,860 miles).

THE BHT-2.

The BHT-2 is a two-seat development of the BHT-1. A new and wider fuselage accommodates the pilot and passenger in side-by-side staggered seats and the wings are of greater span

The BHT-1 Beauty Single-seat Light Monoplane.

and area. The standard power-plant will be a 90 h.p. Cirrus Minor. Except for these details the BHT-1 and 2 are similar in general arrangement and construction.

SAAB.
SVENSKA AEROPLAN A.B. (SAAB).

HEAD OFFICE : LINKÖPING.
WORKS : LINKÖPING AND TROLLHÄTTAN.
Managing Director : R. Wahrgren.
Deputy Managing Director : S. Otterbeck.
Technical Manager : E. Nordquist.
Works Manager (Linköping) : H. Bertler.
Works Manager (Trollhätten) : E. Rydberg.
Chief Design Engineer : B. Bjurströmer.

This Company which was formed in 1937, has emerged from a concern with the same name which originally included in its organization the Svenska Flygmotor A.B. (now an independent firm), the Svenska Aeroplan A.B. at Trollhättan and the Aeroplane Division of the A.B. Svenska Järnvägsverkstaderna at Linköping.

This Trollhättan factory has built the Junkers Ju 86 twin-engined bomber under licence as well as air-cooled aero-engines and Hamilton-Standard variable-pitch airscrews. The Linköping factory has produced both the NA-16 trainer and the Douglas (Northrop) 8A-1 single-engined light bomber under licence.

Since 1940 the Company, whose share capital has been increased to Kr. 21,000,000, engaged in the production of all-metal military aircraft of its own design. The first of these was the two-seat single-engined SAAB-17 Dive-Bomber (Air Force designation B17) or Reconnaissance (Air Force designation S17) monoplane, and this has been followed by the SAAB-18 twin-engined Light-Bomber (Air Force designation B18) or Long-Range Reconnaissance (Air Force designation S18) monoplane, and the SAAB-21A (J21A) single-seat Fighter monoplane.

THE SAAB-21A.
Royal Swedish Air Force designation : J 21 A.

TYPE.—Single-seat Fighter.
WINGS.—Mid-wing cantilever monoplane. All-metal flush-riveted stressed-skin construction. Surfaces covered with a smooth putty layer to reduce drag. Trimming-tab in right aileron.
FUSELAGE.—Central nacelle enclosing cockpit and engine and two tail-booms terminating in vertical fins. Flush-riveted all-metal construction. Similar surface finish as on wings.
TAIL UNIT.—Tailplane mounted between extremities of tail booms. All-metal structure with flush-riveted metal-covered fixed surfaces and fabric-covered movable surfaces. Trimming-tabs in elevator and right rudder.
LANDING GEAR.—Retractable tricycle type. All wheels raised backwards, the nose wheel into the central nacelle and the main wheels into the tail booms. Apertures closed by hinged panels when wheels retracted.
POWER PLANT.—One SFA (Svenska Flygmotor A.B.) licence-built DB 605B twelve-cylinder inverted Vee liquid-cooled engine in rear end of central nacelle and driving a three-blade VDM constant-speed full-feathering propeller. Coolant and oil radiators located in wings between the central nacelle and tail booms with the cooling air entering through ducts in the leading-edge of the wings.
ACCOMMODATION.—Pilot's cockpit in central nacelle above leading-edge of wing with unobstructed forward and side views. The sides of the cockpit canopy are bulged to improve downward and backward views. Pilot's seat mounted on a powder-driven catapult to be thrown clear of the airscrew disc after release of canopy for emergency exit.
ARMAMENT.—One 20 m/m. cannon and two 13 m/m. machine-guns in the nose of the central nacelle.
DIMENSIONS.—Span 11.6 m. (38 ft. 1 in.), Length 10.45 m. (34 ft. 3 in.), Height (one propeller blade vertical) 3.97 m. (13 ft.), Wing area 22.2 sq. m. (232.6 sq. ft.).
WEIGHTS AND LOADINGS.—Weight empty 3,250 kg. (7,150 lbs.), Weight loaded 4,150 kg. (9,130 lbs.), Wing loading 190 kg./sq. m. (39 lbs./sq. ft.).
PERFORMANCE.—Maximum speed about 650 km.h. (403.6 m.p.h.).

THE SAAB-18.
Royal Swedish Air Force designations : B 18 and S 18.

TYPE.—Twin-engined Light Horizontal and Dive-Bomber (B18) or Long-range Reconnaissance (S18) monoplane.
WINGS.—Mid-wing cantilever monoplane. Wings have constant taper from fuselage to tips with all of taper on trailing-edge. All-metal structure, centre-section with three, outer sections with two spars. Entire trailing-edge hinged, inner portions acting as camber-changing flaps and outer sections as ailerons. Slotted type dive-brakes hinged under wings outboard of engine nacelles. These brakes lie flush with the under surface of the wings when retracted.
FUSELAGE.—Oval section all-metal monocoque structure stepped up beneath the leading-edge of the wings to provide a ventral rear-firing gun position.
PERFORMANCE (SAAB-18B).—Maximum speed about 550 km.h. (342 m.p.h.).

PERFORMANCE.—Maximum speed 260 km.h. (161 m.p.h.), Cruising speed 228 km.h. (141.5 m.p.h.), Landing speed 86 km.h. (53.4 m.p.h.). Initial rate of climb 288 m./min. (995 ft./min.), Service ceiling 6,500 m. (21,320 ft.).

TAIL UNIT.—Cantilever monoplane type with twin fins and rudders. Tailplane has 80 dihedral and vertical surfaces at the extremities are toed-in. All-metal structure with metal-covered fixed surfaces and fabric-covered elevators and rudders. Movable surfaces have trimming-tabs.
LANDING GEAR.—Retractable type. Single cantilever shock-absorber legs retract backwards into tail of engine nacelles. Retractable tail-wheel.
POWER PLANT.—Two 1,050-1,200 h.p. Swedish-built Pratt & Whitney R-1830-S1C3G fourteen-cylinder radial air-cooled engines driving Hamilton-SFA controllable-pitch full-feathering airscrews (SAAB-18A) or two Swedish-built Daimler-Benz DB-605B twelve-cylinder inverted-vee liquid-cooled engines driving VDM-SFA full-feathering airscrews (SAAB-18B).
ACCOMMODATION.—Bomb-aimer's position in glazed nose of the fuselage. Pilot and radio-operator/rear-gunner in tandem under a continuous transparent canopy offset to the port side of the centre-line. Armament consists of one fixed forward-firing gun in the starboard side of the fuselage and upper and lower gun positions at the after end of the crew accommodation. Internal bomb stowage in fuselage and beneath wings.
DIMENSIONS.—Span 17 m. (55 ft. 9 in.), Length 13.23 m. (43 ft. 5 in.), Height 4.35 m. (14 ft. 3 in.), Wing area 43.8 sq. m. (471.3 sq. ft.).
WEIGHTS AND LOADINGS.—Weight empty 6,100 kg. (13,420 lbs.), Weight loaded 8,800 kg. (19,360 lbs.), Wing loading 200 kg./sq. m. (41 lbs./sq. ft.).

DIMENSIONS.—Span 7.92 m. (26 ft.), Length 5.8 m. (19 ft.), Height 1.75 m. (5 ft. 9 in.), Wing area 8.71 sq. m. (93.7 sq. ft.).
WEIGHTS.—Weight empty 315 kg. (693 lbs.), Weight loaded 600 kg. (1,320 lbs.).

The SAAB-21A Single-seat Fighter Monoplane (Swedish-built DB 605B engine).

The SAAB-17B Three-seat Reconnaissance Seaplane (Swedish-built Pegasus engine).

THE SAAB-17.
Royal Swedish Air Force designation: B 17 or S 17.

TYPE.—Two-seat Dive-Bomber (B17) or Reconnaissance (S17) monoplane.
WINGS.—Cantilever mid-wing monoplane. Rectangular centre-section with tapering outer sections. All-metal two-spar structure with flush-riveted smooth metal skin. Centre-section spars pass through the fuselage one in front and one behind the pilot. Split trailing-edge flaps. Frise-type ailerons with trimming-tabs.
FUSELAGE.—Oval section metal monocoque with flush-riveted smooth metal skin.
TAIL UNIT.—Cantilever monoplane type. Fin built integral with the fuselage. Metal structure with metal-covered fixed surfaces and fabric-covered control surfaces. Trimming-tabs in right elevator and rudder.
LANDING GEAR.—Retractable type. Wheels are raised backwards and when in raised position each landing gear unit is completely enclosed forward of the wheel by a fairing attached to the landing gear leg and aft of the wheel by a fixed fairing under the trailing-edge of the centre-section. Oleo shock-absorbers. Low-pressure wheels and brakes. Retractable ski landing-gear may be fitted. Tail-wheel or tail-skid is also retractable. Retractable landing-gear may be replaced by a twin-float installation.
POWER PLANT.—One 1,050-1,200 h.p. Swedish-built Pratt & Whitney R-1830-S1C3G fourteen-cylinder radial air-cooled engine driving a Hamilton-SFA controllable-pitch airscrew (SAAB-17A), or 800-1,000 h.p. Swedish-built Bristol Pegasus 24 nine-cylinder radial air-cooled engine driving a Hamilton-SFA controllable-pitch airscrew (SAAB-17B) or 1,000 h.p. Piaggio P. XI bis R.C.40 fourteen-cylinder radial air-cooled engine driving a Piaggio P.1001 controllable-pitch airscrews (SAAB-17C). NACA-type cowling with trailing-edge gills.
ACCOMMODATION.—Crew accommodation under continuous canopy with hinged and sliding sections over seats and gun positions.
ARMAMENT.—Bomb-load carried in internal bomb-bay, under fuselage and under wings. Heavy bombs carried under fuselage on special racks which swing down to enable them to be dropped clear of the airscrew in a dive. No dive-brakes fitted but landing-gear may be lowered in a dive to increase drag, the wheel landing-gear fairings being specially designed for this purpose. Ski landing-gear has dive-brake plates attached to the legs.
DIMENSIONS, WEIGHTS AND PERFORMANCE.—No data available.

THE SAAB-91.

The SAAB-91 is a three-seat light civil monoplane. the prototype of which was due to fly in 1945. It is a low-wing cantilever monoplane of all-metal construction, mainly aluminium-alloy although steel plate will be used to cover the underside of the fuselage to ensure the maximum safety for the occupants in

The SAAB-18A Three-seat Light Bomber (two Swedish-built Pratt & Whitney engines).

the event of a belly landing. The landing-gear is of the retractable tricycle type.

Originally designed as a two-seater, the prototype is being completed as a three-seater with the third seat behind the starboard front seat, making it possible to convert the two passenger seats into a bed so that the aircraft may be used as an ambulance.

The prototype is being fitted with a 130 h.p. D.H. Gipsy-Major engine. It will have a basic designed weight of 550-575 kg. (1,210-1,270 lbs.) and a loaded weight of 900 kg. (1,980 lbs.). The estimated cruising speed will be 200 km.h. (125 m.p.h.) and the range will be 1,000 km. (625 miles.).

THE SAAB FORTRESS CONVERSION.

In 1944 the Svenska Aeroplan A.B. converted five Boeing B-17 Fortress bombers into 14-passenger transports for A.B. Aerotransport (Swedish Air Lines). These aircraft had been forced to land in Sweden while engaged on operations against Germany and they were allocated to Swedish Air Lines by the Swedish Government under a loan arrangement with the U.S. Government.

The conversion, planned by A.B.A. engineers, involved a lengthening of the nose of the fuselage by some 3 ft. and the complete re-fitting of the rear fuselage with comfortable accommodation for fourteen passengers with windows for each seat, entrance door aft, toilet, etc. The whole of the interior of the fuselage has been sound-proofed and heated. The bomb-bay has been converted into a freight compartment, the former bomb-hoist gear being used as a freight hoist.

A close-up of the converted Fortress showing the lengthened nose.

The converted Fortresses have been used by A.B.A. on its service to Great Britain, and by S.I.L.A. on its experimental trans-Atlantic service from Sweden to New York. Illustrations of one of the converted Fortresses are given herewith.

SWITZERLAND

THE FEDERAL FACTORY.

FABRIQUE FÉDÉRALE D'AVIONS EMMEN (EIDG. FLUGZEUG-WERK EMMEN).

HEAD OFFICE AND WORKS : EMMEN, LUCERNE.
Director : M. Buri.

This official Government establishment manufactures aircraft for the Swiss Army Air Corps. Its most recent original production is the C. 3603 illustrated and described herewith.

THE C.3603.

TYPE.—Single-engined Fighter, Short-range Reconnaissance and Bomber monoplane.
WINGS.—Low-wing cantilever monoplane. Wing panels taper from roots to tips. All-metal structure with flush-riveted smooth stressed-skin. Split flaps between ailerons and fuselage.
FUSELAGE.—Rectangular section all-metal structure.
TAIL UNIT.—Cantilever monoplane with twin fins and rudders. All-metal framework with metal-covered tailplane and fins and fabric-covered single-piece elevator and rudders.
LANDING GEAR.—Retractable type. Each unit hinged in a shallow fairing under the wings, the shock-absorber legs being retracted backwards and turned through 90° so that the wheels lie flush with the underside of the wings while the legs are enclosed in the fixed fairing beforementioned. Non-retractable tail-wheel.
POWER PLANT.—One 1,000 h.p. Hispano-Suiza 12Y twelve-cylinder Vee liquid-cooled engine driving a three-blade Escher-Wyss constant-speed airscrew with hollow shaft for a 20 m/m. cannon mounted in the Vee of the engine cylinders.
ACCOMMODATION.—Tandem cockpits under a continuous transparent canopy with a sliding section over the pilot and a tip-up section over the rear gunner's cockpit.
ARMAMENT.—One 20 m/m. Oerlikon cannon firing through the airscrew shaft and two machine-guns on a flexible mounting in the rear cockpit.
DIMENSIONS.—Span 13.74 m. (45 ft. 1½ in.), Length 10.23 m. (36 ft. 9½ in.), Height (tail down and over airscrew with one blade vertical) 4.07 m. (13 ft. 1 in.), Wing area 28.7 sq. m. (309.9 sq. ft.)
WEIGHTS AND LOADINGS.—Weight empty 2,272 kg. (5,009 lbs.), Useful load and standard equipment 1,185 kg. (2,391 lbs.), Weight loaded (Fighter) 3,450 kg. (7,600 lbs.), Wing loading 120 kg./sq. m. (24.6 lbs./sq. ft.), Power loading 3.4 kg./h.p. (7.5 lbs./h.p.).
PERFORMANCE.—No data available.

The C.3603 Two-seat General Purposes Military Monoplane (1,000 h.p. Hispano-Suiza 12Y engine).

FARNER.

FLUGZEUGBAU FARNER A.G.

HEAD OFFICE AND WORKS : GRENCHEN (SOLEURE).

This concern was originally engaged in aero-service, re-building, overhauling and repairs, &c. In 1934 it produced a small two-seat light biplane which was exhibited for the first time at the International Aero Show held at Geneva in that year.

In 1935 it produced, to the designs of M. Weber, a four-seat cabin monoplane known as the WF.21/C4. This model was illustrated and described in the 1936 edition of this Annual.

The latest production of the company is the WF.12, the prototype of which was completed in 1943. This is a two-seat light cabin monoplane with the 90 h.p. Cirrus-Minor engine installed aft of the cabin and driving the tractor airscrew through shafts over the top of the cabin. A non-retracting tricycle landing-gear is provided. The cabin seats two side-by-side with dual controls.

The structure comprises a steel-tube fuselage with metal and fabric covering and a single-spar wooden wing with plywood and fabric covering.

DIMENSIONS.—Span 11 m. (36 ft.), Length 7.45 m. (24 ft. 5 in.), Height 2.6 m. (8 ft. 6 in.), Wing area 16 sq. m. (172 sq. ft.).
WEIGHTS AND LOADINGS.—Weight empty 560 kg. (1,232 lbs.), Weight loaded 800 kg. (1,760 lbs.), Wing loading 50 kg./sq. m. (10.25 lbs./sq. m.), Power loading 8.9 kg./h.p. (19.58 lbs./h.p.).
PERFORMANCE.—Maximum speed 175 km.h. (108.6 m.p.h.), Landing speed with flaps 75 km.h. (36.7 m.p.h.).

DORNIER.

DORNIER-WERKE A.G.

HEAD OFFICE : ZÜRICH.
WORKS, AERODROME AND SEAPLANE STATION : ALTENRHEIN

Dornier-Werke A.G. was a branch of the German Dornier company, and was originally formed at the time when the building of military aircraft was forbidden in Germany by the Treaty of Versailles. A large number of Dornier aeroplanes of various types were built for experimental purposes and for export by the Swiss company. It also built the Bücker Jungmann training biplane under licence for the Swiss Government.

PILATUS.

PILATUS FLUGZEUGWERKE A.G.

HEAD OFFICE AND WORKS : STANS, NEAR LUCERNE.
Managing Direc or : H. F. Alioth.
Chief Engineer : Dipl. Ing. H. Fierz.

Pilatus Flugzeugwerke A.G. was formed in December, 1939, with a capital of two million Swiss francs and it began work in September, 1941. A founder's syndicate was formed in 1938 under the leadership of M. E. Bührle, the Swiss industrialist and owner of the Oerlikon Company, of which the Pilatus Company is now a subsidiary.

The Chief Engineer of the Pilatus Flugzeugwerke was formerly with the firm known as Alfred Comte (Schweizerische Flugzeug-fabrik), which operated a flying school at Zürich (Dübendorf) for several years and also built a number of aircraft of original design in its workshops. When this Company abandoned aircraft manufacture in 1936, Dipl. Ing. Fierz became Chief of the Technical Services of Swissair.

The first product of the company is the Pelican light transport monoplane.

THE PILATUS SB.2 PELICAN.

TYPE.—Five-seat cabin monoplane.

WINGS.—High-wing braced monoplane. Forwardly-swept wings attached to roots built integrally with the fuselage roof and braced to the bottom of the fuselage by single struts. All-wood single-spar structure. Auto slots along entire leading-edges of wings. Trailing-edge flaps between ailerons and fuselage.

FUSELAGE.—All-metal monocoque structure.

TAIL UNIT.—Cantilever monoplane type with twin fins and rudders.

LANDING GEAR.—Fixed tricycle-type. Main shock-absorber struts cantilevered from the apices of two rigid pyramids, each of which consists of a vertical strut attached at its upper end to the wing spar and a down-sloping Vee, the inner ends of which are attached to the lower sides of the fuselage. Cantilever nose wheel strut. Steerable nose wheel interconnected with the rudder control.

POWER PLANT.—One 450 h.p. Pratt & Whitney Wasp-Junior nine-cylinder radial air-cooled engine. Fuel tanks in wings.

ACCOMMODATION.—Enclosed accommodation for crew of two and three passengers. Pilot's compartment forward of leading-edge of wings. Passenger cabin beneath wings. Baggage compartment aft of cabin. Partition between cabin and baggage room may be removed to provide space for bulky freight, which can be loaded through a hatch in the floor.

DIMENSIONS.—Span 15.5 m. (51 ft.), Wing area 29 sq. m. (313 sq. ft.).

WEIGHTS.—Weight empty 1,600 kg. (3,528 lbs.), Weight loaded 2,400 kg. (5,290 lbs.).

PERFORMANCE.—Maximum speed 250 km.h. (156 m.p.h.), Stalling speed 70 km.h. (43.5 m.p.h.), Service ceiling 6,100 m. (20,000 ft.).

TURKEY

NURI DEMIRAG.

NURI DEMIRAG TAYYARE FABRIKASI (Nuri Demirag Aircraft Works).

HEAD OFFICE : BESIKTAS (ISTANBUL).

WORKS : BESIKTAS AND YESILKÖY (ISTANBUL).

AERODROME : YESILKÖY (ISTANBUL).

This factory was established in 1937 by Nuri Demirag. The Nu.D.36 type two-seat training biplane and a Nu.D.38 type, six-seat passenger prototype monoplane described and illustrated in previous editions, have been built from original designs.

The Nu.D.36 type biplane has been produced in quantities. In addition, gliders of different types have been constructed under licence.

THE Nu.D.36.

TYPE.—Two-seat training biplane.

WINGS.—Unequal-span single-bay staggered biplane. Centre-section attached to fuselage by splayed-out "N"-struts. One "N"-type interplane strut on either side

The Nu.D.36 Two-seat Training Biplane (150 h.p. Walter Gemma engine).

of fuselage. Interplane bracing-wires in plane of rear spar of upper wing and front spar of lower wing. Duplicated flying-wires and single landing-wires. Wood structure with fabric covering. Ailerons on upper wings only.

FUSELAGE.—Rectangular structure of riveted steel tubes, covered with fabric.

TAIL UNIT.—Normal monoplane type with steel-tube frames and fabric covering.

LANDING GEAR.—Divided type. Comprises two long-stroke shock-absorber struts, the upper ends of which are attached to the upper fuselage longerons with the lower ends hinged to the underside of the fuselage by steel-tube Vees. Wheel-brakes.

POWER PLANT.—One 150 h.p. Walter Gemma I nine-cylinder radial air-cooled engine on steel-tube mounting. Small fuel tank in centre-section with direct gravity feed. Large fuel tank in fuselage behind fireproof bulkhead feeding the small tank by hand pump.

ACCOMMODATION.—Tandem open cockpits with dual controls.

DIMENSIONS.—Span 9.74 m. (31 ft. 11 in.), Height 2.44 m. (8 ft.), Length 7.30 m. (24 ft.), Wing area 21.8 sq. m. (234.5 sq. ft.).

WEIGHTS.—Weight empty 650 kg. (1,430 lbs.), Petrol and oil 160 kg. (352 lbs.), Maximum loaded weight 1,000 kg. (2,200 lbs.).

PERFORMANCE.—Maximum speed with maximum load 182 km.h. (113 m.p.h.), Landing speed 85 km.h. (52.7 m.p.h.), Climb to 500 m. (1,640 ft.) 2 mins., Climb to 1,000 m. (3,280 ft.) 5.26 mins., Climb to 1,500 m. (4,920 ft.) 10 mins., Service ceiling 3,350 m. (11,000 ft.), Range 500 km. (310.5 miles) or 3.5 hours.

THE UNITED STATES OF AMERICA

AERONAUTICAL PRODUCTS.

AERONAUTICAL PRODUCTS, INC.

HEAD OFFICE : 18100, RYAN ROAD, DETROIT 12, MICH.

WORKS : DETROIT, MICH. AND WASHINGTON COURT HOUSE, OHIO.

President : Charles C. Layman.

Vice-President in Charge of Sales : Edward C. Jonke.

Chief Engineer : Frank Dobson.

Treasurer : Byron Layman.

Aeronautical Products, Inc. was formed in 1935 in Detroit and manufactures precision aircraft parts.

In 1942, Mr. Alfred Jackson, the President of the Company, became interested in the possibilities of a helicopter designed and built to be sold in the $3,000 field. On April 17, 1944, the Company's first helicopter, designated the NX-1270, made its first successful flight.

Within the short span of six months, this helicopter made a number of demonstration flights in Detroit, including a daily flight during the 14-day Army Air Show. In Boston, it made the first commercial helicopter delivery for William Filene's Sons Company, flying package freight from the firm's warehouse to a suburban store 12 miles away.

In October, 1944, the NX-1270 was removed from active service and a new and improved two-seat dual-control model was flight tested. This model, designated the A-3 or NX-1272, was, at the time of writing, undergoing tests in order to receive a CAA certificate. A third model of "tear-drop" design and with a vertically-mounted engine, was also nearing completion.

The company's post war plans call for continued production of precision aircraft and other precision parts, with the organization of a subsidiary company to manufacture and distribute helicopters.

THE AERONAUTICAL PRODUCTS MODEL A-3 HELICOPTER.

The Model A-3 is a single-rotor helicopter with a vertically-mounted torque-compensating variable-pitch rotor at the rear end of the fuselage and the power-unit mounted in the nose instead of being buried amidships as in most designs. The forward mounting of the engine allows the passengers to be accommodated near the C.G., makes possible a simple and easily-serviced engine installation and simplifies engine cooling.

The power-plant is a Franklin 6AC-298 six-cylinder opposed air-cooled engine mounted horizontally and with a fan above it directing air down around the cylinders. Drive from the engine is by belts to a horizontal shaft and then through a bevel gear drive to the main rotor shaft, which rotates at about 250 r.p.m.

The main rotor is 30 ft. (9.15 m.) in diameter and has three blades which are mounted so that they may flap freely in both vertical and horizontal planes. The position of the blades is determined by the balance between lift, centrifugal force and engine torque.

Movement of the normal control column varies the incidence of the blades during each revolution, the incidence being controlled by a system of linkages which balance completely all loads in the control system. When the column is moved forward the blades on the right side are turned to a larger angle of incidence while those of the left side are given a lesser angle. The blades rise as they travel towards the rear on the right side, reaching their highest point directly aft, and fall on the left side to their lowest point directly forward ; the effect being to tip the rotor forward, or in whatever direction the control column is moved.

A secondary lever varies the angle of all three blades in unison to control lift. This lever is interconnected with the throttle to keep the engine r.p.m. approximately constant as the lift is changed.

Directional control is by means of the vertically-disposed variable-pitch propeller or rotor at the tail, which rotates at about 1,200 r.p.m. The pitch is controlled by foot pedals. In forward or hovering flight the pitch of the tail rotor is adjusted to counteract exactly the torque required to turn the main rotor. Movement to right or left is by depressing the appropriate pedal.

In case of engine failure an automatic free-wheeling mechanism permits auto-rotation.

AERONCA.

THE AERONCA AIRCRAFT CORPORATION.

HEAD OFFICE AND WORKS : MIDDLETOWN MUNICIPAL AIRPORT, MIDDLETOWN, OHIO.

President : Carl I. Friedlander.

Executive Vice-President : John W. Friedlander.

Vice-President : Elmer L. Sutherland.

Vice-President and Director of Purchases : E. H. Wideman.

Sales Manager and Executive Assistant : R. L. Davison.

Chief Engineer : W. D. Hall.

Treasurer : Albert Helmers.

Secretary : G. L. Hoffman.

This Company was incorporated as the Aeronautical Corporation of America in November, 1928, and was the first American company to build and market a truly light aeroplane. The name was changed to its present title in 1941.

The contracts for the production of the L-3 light liaison-observation monoplane and the PT-19 and PT-23 primary trainers built under Fairchild licence ceased in 1944, and a contract for the manufacture of the C-64 Norseman under Noorduyn licence was cancelled before production was started.

For post-war production the Aeronca company is developing three civil aircraft, the Champion, a 65 h.p. two-seat tandem trainer developed from the Defender ; the Chief, a 65 h.p. de Luxe two-seat side-by-side cabin monoplane ; and the Arrow, a 90 h.p. two-seat low-wing cabin monoplane with retractable landing-gear.

The Aeronca Aircraft Corpn. has signed a contract with the Engineering and Research Corpn. granting it the right to build on a royalty basis aircraft embodying the "two-control" system originated by Erco and used by the latter concern in the Ercoupe monoplane.

THE AERONCA GRASSHOPPER.

U.S. Army Air Forces designation : L-3.

The description below applies to the L-3, L-3A, L-3B and L-3C, all of which are generally similar, differing mainly in details of equipment.

TYPE.—Two-seat Light Liaison and Observation monoplane.

WINGS.—High-wing rigidly braced monoplane. NACA 4412 wing section. Wings in two sections attached to top longerons of fuselage and braced to lower longerons by Vee struts. Structure consists of two solid spruce spars, aluminium-alloy ribs, steel-tube compression struts and single-wire drag bracing, the whole being covered with fabric. Ailerons have metal frames with fabric covering.

FUSELAGE.—Welded steel-tube structure covered with fabric over spruce fairing stringers.

TAIL UNIT.—Braced monoplane type. Welded steel-tube framework covered with fabric. Fin built integral with fuselage. Trimming tab in starboard elevator adjustable from cockpit.

LANDING GEAR.—Divided type. Faired-in side Vees hinged to lower

The Aeronca L-3H Light Liaison and Observation Monoplane (65 h.p. Lycoming O-145-B1 engine).

The Aeronca Super-Chief (Model 65LB) Two-seat Light Monoplane (65 h.p. Lycoming engine).

fuselage longerons and half-axles hinged to Vee cabane beneath fuselage. Oleo-spring shock-absorber struts incorporated in side Vees. Full swivelling tail-wheel. Mechanical wheel-brakes.

POWER PLANT.—One 65 h.p. Continental O-170-3 four-cylinder horizontally-opposed air-cooled engine on detachable welded steel-tube mounting. Fuel tanks (12 U.S. gallons) in roof of cabin and conforming to curvature of wings.

ACCOMMODATION.—Enclosed cabin seating two in tandem. Dual controls provided but L-3 usually flown from front seat. Observer's seat may face forward or aft and when in latter position a folding table may be brought into use for maps etc. Radio equipment.

DIMENSIONS.—Span 35 ft. (10.67 m.), Length 21 ft. 10 in. (6.67 m.), Height 9 ft. 1 in. (2.74 m.), Wing area (including ailerons) 169 sq. ft. (15.6 sq. m.).

WEIGHTS AND LOADINGS.—Weight empty 835 lbs. (379 kg.), Weight loaded 1,260 lbs. (572 kg.), Wing loading 7.45 lbs./sq. ft. (36.1 kg./sq. m.), Power loading 19.39 lbs./h.p. (8.8 kg./h.p.).

PERFORMANCE.—Maximum speed 87 m.p.h. (139 km.h.), Cruising speed 79 m.p.h. (126.4 km.h.), Stalling speed 46 m.p.h. (73.6 km.h.), Initial rate of climb 404 ft/min. (123 m./min.), Service ceiling 10,000 ft. (3,050 m.), Normal range 218 miles (350 km.).

The U.S. Army also acquired secondhand a number of Aeronca two-seat cabin monoplanes of various models for pre-glider training purposes. These were given designations in the L-3 Series as follow :—

L-3D	Model 65TAF Defender. Franklin 4AC-176-B2 engine.
L-3E	Model 65TAC Defender. Continental A65-8 engine.
L-3F	Model 65CA Super-Chief. Continental A65-8 engine.
L-3G	Model 65LB Super-Chief. Lycoming O-145-B1 engine.
L-3H	Model 65TL Defender. Lycoming O-145-B1 engine.
L-3J	Model 65TC Defender. Continental A65-7 engine.

These are all standard dual control civil models without service modifications.

THE AERONCA SUPER-CHIEF MODELS 65CA AND 65LB.

TYPE.—Two-seat light monoplane.

WINGS.—High-wing rigidly-braced monoplane. Wings, of Clark "Y" section, in two sections, attached to the top longerons of the fuselage and braced to the bottom fuselage longerons by duralumin-tube Vee struts. Structure consists of two solid spruce spars, spruce truss type ribs, steel compression members and single wire drag-bracing, the whole being covered with fabric. The ailerons of duralumin with fabric covering.

FUSELAGE.—Welded steel-tube structure, with four nearly-parallel longerons forward and three from the back of seat aft to the tail-post. The two top longerons act as the anchorage for the wings forward and forms the apex of the triangular-sectioned fuselage aft. The two upper longerons which form the top of the forward section in the region of the cockpit terminate aft of the cockpit.

TAIL UNIT.—Normal monoplane type. Welded steel-tube framework covered with fabric. The fin is built integral with the fuselage. The left elevator has trimming-tab adjustable from cockpit.

LANDING GEAR.—Divided type. Consists of two streamline side Vees incorporating oleo shock-absorber struts and two half-axles hinged to centre-line of fuselage. Airwheels and spring tail-skid are standard, but mechanical brakes and full-swivelling and steerable tail-wheel are available as special equipment.

POWER PLANT.—One 65 h.p. Lycoming or Continental four-cylinder horizontally-opposed air-cooled engine on welded steel-tube mounting. Main fuel tank holds 17 U.S. gallons and an auxiliary tank (8 U.S. gallons) may be installed aft of baggage compartment as special equipment.

ACCOMMODATION.—Closed cockpit under the wings, seating two side-by-side. Doors on both sides. Luggage compartment behind seat.

DIMENSIONS.—Span 36 ft. (10.9 m.), Length 21 ft. (6.3 m.), Height 6 ft. 7 in. (2 m.), Wing area 169 sq. ft. (15.7 sq. m.).

WEIGHTS AND LOADINGS.—Weight empty 750 lbs. (340 kg.), Pilot 170 lbs. (77 kg.), Passenger 170 lbs. (77 kg.), Baggage 70 lbs. (32 kg.), Fuel and oil 110 lbs. (50 kg.), Disposable load 500 lbs. (225 kg.), Weight loaded 1,250 lbs. (567 kg.), Wing loading 7.4 lbs./sq. ft. (36.1 kg./sq. m.), Power loading 19.23 lbs./h.p. (8.37 kg./h.p.).

PERFORMANCE.—Maximum speed 109 m.p.h. (174.4 km.h.), Cruising speed 100 m.p.h. (160 km.h.), Landing speed 38 m.p.h. (61 km.h.), Initial rate of climb 600 ft./min. (183 m./min.), Service ceiling 15,000 ft. (4,575 m.), Cruising range 400-500 miles (640-800 km.).

THE AERONCA DEFENDER.

TYPE.—Two-seat light Training monoplane.

WINGS.—Same as for Super-Chief except that the wing section is NACA 4412 and ribs are of aluminium-alloy.

FUSELAGE.—Normal welded steel-tube four-longeron structure covered with fabric over spruce fairing stringers.

TAIL UNIT AND LANDING GEAR.—Same as for Super-Chief.

POWER PLANT.—One 65 h.p. Lycoming, Continental or Franklin four-cylinder horizontally-opposed air-cooled engine on detachable welded steel-tube mounting. Main fuel tank (12 U.S. gallons) in roof of cabin and conforming to curvature of wings. Small auxiliary tank (1 U.S. gallon) in front of instrument panel.

ACCOMMODATION.—Enclosed cabin seating two in tandem with dual controls. Large door on right side. Luggage compartment aft of rear seat.

DIMENSIONS.—Span 35 ft. (10.67 m.), Length 21 ft. 10 in. (6.7 m.), Height 9 ft. 1 in. (2.75 m.), Wing area 169 sq. ft. (15.7 sq. m.).

WEIGHTS AND LOADINGS.—Weight empty 750 lbs. (340 kg.), Pilot and passenger 340 lbs. (154 kg.), Baggage 40 lbs. (18 kg.), Weight loaded 1,200 lbs. (545 kg.), Wing loading 7.1 lbs./sq. ft. (34.6 kg./sq. m.), Power loading 18.5 lbs./h.p. (8.4 kg./h.p.).

PERFORMANCE.—Maximum speed 95 m.p.h. (152 km.h.), Cruising speed 87 m.p.h. (139 km.h.), Landing speed 38 m.p.h. (61 km.h.), Initial rate of climb 450 ft./min. (137 m./min.), Service ceiling 12,000 ft. (3,660 m.), Cruising range 225 miles (360 km.).

ALLIED.

ALLIED AVIATION CORPORATION.

HEAD OFFICE AND WORKS : COCKEYSVILLE, MARYLAND.
President : Richard E. Breed, 3rd.
Executive Vice-President : Charles J. MacGatvey.
Superintendent : Judson C. Richardson.
Chief Engineer : Linn L. Collins.
Comptroller : Elwood C. Hewitt.

The Allied Aviation Corporation was organized in January, 1941, to produce moulded plywood aircraft structures. The Company has manufactured aircraft components, such as wings, fuselages, fins, flaps, tail-surfaces, landing-gear doors and fairings for military aircraft.

In 1943 the Company undertook the production of a twelve-seat troop transport amphibious glider under contract from the U.S. Navy Department. Only one glider, the LRA-1, was built before the Navy cancelled its glider programme.

Since then the Company has developed and built a three-seat twin-engined light amphibian flying-boat which, in prototype form, has given very satisfactory results. The manufacturing rights for this aircraft have been acquired by Commonwealth Aircraft, Inc. of Kansas City, Mo.

THE ALLIED TRIMMER.

TYPE.—Three-seat Light Amphibian flying-boat.

WINGS.—High-wing cantilever monoplane. Rectangular centre-section, incorporating the two engine nacelles, all engine instruments, throttles, switches, battery, flaps and flap-controls, are attached to a steel tube cabane in the hull and can be completely removed by the loosening of four fittings and the disconnection of aileron controls and fuel lines. Tapering outer wings have built-in leading-edge slots and carry ailerons and wing-tip floats. Structure entirely of plastic bonded plywood.

HULL.—Two-step structure of plastic bonded plywood.

TAIL UNIT.—Braced monoplane type. Fin built integrally with hull with tailplane mounted above hull and braced by single struts. Plastic bonded plywood construction.

The Allied Trimmer Light Amphibian Flying-boat (two Continental C75 engines).

LANDING GEAR.—Rectractable type. Oleo-sprung wheels raised into faired recesses in sides of hull. Landing-gear detachable and when dismounted auxiliary drum-shaped tanks may be carried in wheel recesses to increase range. Leaf-spring tail-wheel on second step.

POWER PLANT.—Two 75 h.p. Continental C75 four-cylinder horizontally-opposed air-cooled engines in nacelles in the leading-edge of the centre-section. Laminated wood airscrews with pitch adjustable on the ground. Airscrew diameter 6 ft. 6 in. (2 m.). Normal fuel capacity 40 U.S. gallons. Two 10 U.S. gallon auxiliary drum tanks may be installed in wheel recesses when amphibian-gear not fitted.

ACCOMMODATION.—Enclosed cabin seating three, two seats side-by-side with dual controls in front of cabin and one aft. Entrance hatch aft of wing with second hatch in nose.

DIMENSIONS.—Span 35 ft. 8 in. (10.87 m.), Length 24 ft. 9 in. (7.5 m.), Height 7 ft. 4 in. (2.24 in.), Wing area 164 sq. ft. (15.23 sq. m.).

WEIGHTS AND LOADINGS.—Weight empty 1,470 lbs. (667 kg.), Weight loaded 2,150 lbs. (976 kg.), Wing loading 13 lbs./sq. ft. (63.4 kg/sq. m.), Power loading 14.3 lbs./h.p. (6.5 kg./h.p.).

PERFORMANCE.—Maximum speed 140 m.p.h. (224 km.h.), Cruising speed 115 m.p.h. (184 km.h.), Landing speed (with flaps) 45 m.p.h. (72 km.h.), Service ceiling 12,000 ft. (3,660 m.), Range (as amphibian with three occupants) 350 miles (560 km.).

AVION

AVION, INC.

HEAD OFFICE AND WORKS : LOS ANGELES, CALIFORNIA.
President : Richard W. Millar.
Vice-Presidents : Don I. Carroll and Richard W. Palmer.
Secretary and Treasurer : Morgan W. Lowery.

Avion, Inc. was formed in 1942 to concentrate on research, engineering and the production of military aircraft. Its principal executives were formerly associated with Vultee Aircraft, Inc., Richard Millar being President, Don Carrill Vice-President in charge of Production, and Richard Palmer Vice-President in charge of Engineering. All three resigned from Vultee in 1942.

The main production plant of Avion, Inc. is in Los Angeles. Several substantial orders, including sub-assembly contracts for the Northrop and Lockheed companies, have been fulfilled.

BEECHCRAFT.

BEECH AIRCRAFT CORPORATION.

HEAD OFFICE AND WORKS : EAST CENTRAL AVENUE, WICHITA, KANSAS.
Established : April, 1932.
President : Walter H. Beech.
Vice-President : R. K. Beech.
Vice-President and General Manager : J. P. Gaty.

Vice-President and Chief Engineer : T. A. Wells.
Secretary and Treasurer : O. A. Beech.

The Beech Aircraft Corpn. was formed in 1932 by Mr. Walter Beech, one of the pioneers of light commercial aeroplanes in the United States.

In 1942, he helped to form the Travel Air Manufacturing Co. and developed a notable range of commercial and training

aeroplanes. In 1929, the Travel Air Company was merged with the Curtiss-Wright group, and Mr. Walter Beech was placed in charge of sales and continued in this capacity until he resigned to form the Beech Aircraft Corporation.

The Beech Aircraft Corporation has supplied large numbers of training and liaison aircraft for the U.S. Army Air Forces and Navy Bureau of Aeronautics. Types produced have been adaptations of the Corporation's former single and twin-engined commercial aircraft.

In 1944–45 the company undertook the large-scale production of wings and other parts for the Douglas A-26 Invader.

THE BEECHCRAFT MODEL 28.
U.S. Army Air Force designation: XA 38.

The XA-38 is a twin-engined Attack monoplane which was designed to carry, in addition to defensive armament, one 75 m/m. cannon. It is a low-wing monoplane with a monoplane tail and twin fins and rudders. The power-plant consists of two Wright R-3350 radial air-cooled engines. This aircraft did not proceed beyond the experimental stage.

THE BEECHCRAFT TRAVELLER.
U.S. Army Air Forces designation: UC-43.
U.S. Navy designation : GB.
British name : Traveller.

The UC-43 has been supplied to the U.S. Army Air Forces as a light personnel transport.

The GB-1 and GB-2 perform similar functions in the U.S. Naval Air Service as the UC-43 does in the Army Air Forces.

TYPE.—Five-seat Light Personnel Transport.

WINGS.—Equal-span single-bay biplane with back stagger. Upper wing attached direct to the top of the fuselage with one "I"-type heat-treated steel interplane strut on either side of the fuselage. Duplicated flying-wires attached to front spar in upper wing and to fuselage at rear spar attachment of lower wing. Landing wires are attached to fuselage at front spar fitting of upper wing and to rear spar in lower wing. Wing structure consists of two wooden spars, wooden ribs and fabric covering. Statically and aerodynamically-balanced ailerons on upper wings and electrically-operated lift-flaps on lower wings.

FUSELAGE.—Oval structure of metal with two heat-treated steel trusses below lower longerons to carry all main loads. These trusses eliminate cross tubes in cabin and luggage compartments.

TAIL UNIT.—Cantilever monoplane type. Welded steel-tube framework for elevators and rudder, wood framework for tail-plane and fin, all fabric-covered.

LANDING GEAR.—Retractable type. Hydraulic shock-absorbers, semi-balloon wheels and brakes. Electrical retraction. Retractable tail-wheel.

POWER PLANT.—One 450 h.p. Pratt & Whitney R-985-AN-1 or 3 nine-cylinder radial air-cooled engine, driving a two-blade Hamilton Standard constant-speed airscrew. Engine-driven fuel pump with auxiliary hand-pump operated by remote control.

ACCOMMODATION.—Enclosed cabin to accommodate pilot and three passengers, 125 lbs. of baggage and full load of fuel, or pilot and four passengers with reduced fuel load. Adjustable front seats and wide seat across back of cabin. Full vision windows, ventilators and heaters. Large door on left side of cabin to give easy access to both front and back seats.

DIMENSIONS.—Span 32 ft. (9.76 m.), Length 26 ft. 2 in. (7.98 m.), Height 10 ft. 3 in. (3.12 m.), Wing area 296 sq. ft. (27.5 sq. m.).

WEIGHTS.—Weight empty 3,085 lbs. (1,400 kg.), Weight loaded 4,250 lbs. (1,928 kg.).

PERFORMANCE.—Cruising speed 195 m.p.h. (312 km.h.) at 5,000 ft. (1,525 m.), Landing-speed 60 m.p.h. (96 km.h.), Initial rate of climb 1,500 ft./min. (455 m./min.), Service ceiling 20,000 ft. (6,100 m.), Range 500 miles (800 km.) at 5,000 ft. (1,525 m.) at 170 m.p.h. (272 km.h.).

The Army Air Forces also acquired a number of second-hand Beechcraft Model 17 biplanes and these were given designations in the UC-43 Series as follow :—

UC-43A	Model D-17R	Wright R-975.
UC-43B	Model D-17S	Pratt & Whitney R-985.
UC-43C	Model D-17D	Jacobs R-915.
UC-43D	Model E-17B	Jacobs L-5.
UC-43E	Model C-17R	Wright R-975.
UC-43F	Model D-17A	Wright R-760E-2.
UC-43G	Model C-17B	Jacobs L-5.
UC-43H	Model B-17R	Wright R-975.
UC-43J	Model C-17L	Jacobs L-4.

Most of these models have been described and illustrated in previous issues of this Annual.

THE BEECHCRAFT EXPEDITOR.
U.S. Army Air Forces designation : C-45.
U.S. Navy designation : JRB.
British name : Expeditor.

The C-45 is a military utility transport version of the earlier civil Model 18S. The variants of the C-45, all of which are fitted with two Pratt & Whitney R-985 engines, are the C-45 (JRB-1), C-45A (JRB-2), C-45B (JRB-3 and Expeditor I), C-45C (Commercial model 18-S) C-45D, C-45E and C-45F (JRB-4 and Expeditor II).

TYPE.—Twin-engined Light Personnel or Utility Transport.

WINGS.—Low-wing cantilever monoplane. Centre-section integral with the fuselage. Tapering outer wing sections. Structure consists primarily of a single beam, in the form of a welded tube monospar, which at approximately half-way to the tip is spliced

The Beechcraft GB-2 Traveller Light Transport Biplane (Pratt & Whitney R-985 engine). (*Photograph by Peter Bowers*)

The Beechcraft SNB-2 Navigator Navigational Training Monoplane (two Pratt & Whitney R-985 engines).

to a duralumin girder. Continuous duralumin ribs are anchored at their ends by a light spar, which carries the aileron and flap hinges. Extruded duralumin stringers extend spanwise, and the whole is covered with a smooth skin riveted to all parts. Duralumin-framed ailerons and flaps, with fabric covering. Trimming-tab in left aileron. Electrical flap operation.

FUSELAGE.—Oval metal structure, comprising built-up bulkheads and extruded section stringers, the whole covered with a smooth skin riveted to bulkheads and stringers. Single steel-tube spar built into the fuselage to carry engine, landing-gear and wing loads. Remainder of centre-section built up as wings.

TAIL UNIT.—Monoplane, with twin fins and rudders. Stressed-skin tail-plane and fins. Rudder and elevators have welded steel-tube frames with fabric covering. Trimming-tab on port rudder and others on each half of elevator.

LANDING GEAR.—Retractable type. Wheels carried in forks and are electrically retracted backwards into engine nacelles. Air-oil shock-absorbers. Low-pressure wheels and hydraulic brakes.

POWER PLANT.—Two 450 h.p. Pratt & Whitney R-8985-AN-1 or 3 radial air-cooled engines. Hamilton-Standard constant-speed airscrews.

ACCOMMODATION.—Pilot's compartment in nose, seating two side-by-side, with dual controls. Passenger cabin seats six passengers. Baggage compartments in extreme nose and behind cabin. Sound-proofing, controlled ventilation and heating.

DIMENSIONS.—Span 47 ft. 8 in. (14.5 m.), Length 34 ft. 3 in. (10.4 m.), Height 9 ft. 9 in. (2.8 m.), Wing area 349 sq. ft. (32.4 sq. m.).

WEIGHTS.—Weight empty 5,420 lbs. (2,460 kg.), Weight loaded 7,500 lbs. (3,405 kg.).

PERFORMANCE.—Maximum speed 225 m.p.h. (360 km.h.), Landing speed 61 m.p.h. (98 km.h.), Initial rate of climb 1,850 ft./min. (564 m./min.), Service ceiling 26,000 ft. (7,930 m.), Single-engine ceiling (at 50 ft./min. climb) 12,300 ft. (3,752 m.), Range 1,200 miles at 5,000 ft. (1,525 m.) at 160 m.p.h. (256 km.h.).

THE BEECHCRAFT NAVIGATOR.
U.S. Army Air Forces designation: AT-7.
U.S. Navy designation: SNB-2.

The AT-7 was the first type of aircraft supplied to the Army Air Forces purely for navigational training. It carries a crew of

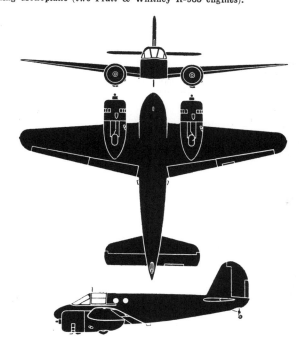

The Beechcraft AT-10 Wichita Advanced Trainer.

five and is equipped with individual chart tables, aperiodic compasses and stabilised drift signals for each of three navigational students. It is also provided with a rotatable celestial dome for sextant readings.

DIMENSIONS.—Span 47 ft. 8 in. (14.5 m.), Length 34 ft. 3 in. (10.4 m.), Height 9 ft. 9 in. (2.8 m.), Wing area 349 sq. ft. (32.4 sq. m.).

WEIGHTS.—Weight empty 5,800 lbs. (2,633 kg.), Weight loaded 7,850 lbs. (3,564 kg.).

PERFORMANCE.—Maximum speed 224 m.p.h. (358.4 km.h.) at 5,000 ft. (1,525 m.), Landing speed 67 m.p.h. (107 km.h.), Climb to 10,000 ft. (3,050 m.) 6.8 min., Service ceiling 24,000 ft. (7,320 m.), Range 730 miles (1,170 km.) at 5,000 ft. (1,525 m.) at 190 m.p.h. (304 km.h.).

THE BEECHCRAFT WICHITA.
U.S. Army Air Forces designation: AT-10.

The AT-10 is a twin-engined advanced training monoplane intended for the first step in training pilots to operate twin-engined aircraft. Accommodation is provided for two pilots seated side-by-side with dual controls and full instrument equipment is provided, including automatic pilot. The AT-10 is fitted with two 280 h.p. Lycoming R-680-9 radial air-cooled engines driving two-bladed constant-speed airscrews.

The AT-10 was the first all-wood aeroplane designed by the

The Beechcraft C-45A Expediter Light Personnel Transport (two Pratt & Whitney R-985 engines).

A Beechcraft AT-10 Wichita fitted with an experimental Vee tail-unit.

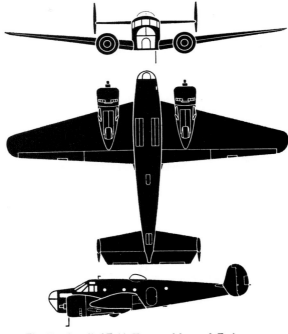

The Beechcraft AT-11 Kansan Advanced Trainer.

Company and was the first all-wood type to be accepted as an advanced trainer by the U.S. Army.

Although when the AT-10 was designed there was no shortage of light metals, the Beech Company foresaw the difficulties that such a shortage might present and from the outset planned in wood with a view to making as much use of sub-contracting as possible.

One of the most interesting innovations was the use of wooden petrol tanks lined with special synthetic rubber which is unaffected by the fuel. No double-curvature sections were used and no hot-moulding processes were necessary in the forming of the various wooden parts. For this reason it was possible for furniture manufacturers and similar wood-working organizations to undertake the building of major sub-assemblies and 85 per cent. of these parts were built by sub-contractors.

The principal production and assembly of the AT-10 was undertaken by the Beech Aircraft Corpn. and the Globe Aircraft Corpn., but all contracts ceased in 1944.

One AT-10 has been experimentally fitted with a Vee, or "Butterfly", tail-unit. This aircraft is illustrated on this page.

DIMENSIONS.—Span 44 ft. (13.4 m.), Length 34 ft. 4 in. (10.4 m.), Wing area 298 sq. ft. (27.68 sq. m.).
WEIGHTS.—Weight empty 4,750 lbs. (2,156 kg.), Weight loaded 6,130 lbs. (2,783 kg.).
PERFORMANCE.—Maximum speed 198 m.p.h. (317 km.h.), Landing speed 80 m.p.h. (128 km.h.), Climb to 10,000 ft. (3,050 m.) 12.7 min., Service ceiling 16,900 ft. (5,155 m.), Range 770 miles (1,232 km.) at 177 m.p.h. (283 km.h.).

THE BEECHCRAFT KANSAN.

U.S. Army Air Forces designation: AT-11.
U.S. Navy designation: SNB-1.

The AT-11 is intended for the specialised training of bombardiers and air-gunners. It is equipped with flexible guns and bomb-racks for the instruction of a crew of three or four, depending upon the instructional mission.

In general design it is similar to the C-45 but has a modified fuselage with transparent nose. Wings, tail-unit and landing gear are the same as for the C-45. The AT-11 is fitted with two 450 h.p. Pratt & Whitney R-985-AN-1 engines.

DIMENSIONS.—Same as AT-7.
WEIGHTS.—Weight empty 6,160 lbs. (2,796 kg.), Weight loaded 8,730 lbs. (3,963 kg.).
PERFORMANCE.—Maximum speed 215 m.p.h. (344 km.h.) at 5,000 ft. (1,525 m.), Landing speed 86 m.p.h. (137.6 km.h.), Climb to 10,000 ft. (3,050 m.) 10 min., Service ceiling 20,000 ft. (6,100 m.), Range 870 miles (1,390 km.) at 5,000 ft. (1,525 m.) at 142 m.p.h. (227 km.h.).

BELL.

BELL AIRCRAFT CORPORATION.

HEAD OFFICE : 2050, ELMWOOD AVENUE, BUFFALO, N.Y.
WORKS : BUFFALO AND NIAGARA FALLS, N.Y., MARIETTA, GEORGIA AND BURLINGTON, VT.

President : Lawrence D. Bell.
Vice-President and Manager, Niagara Falls Division : Ray P. Whitman.
Vice-President and Manager, Georgia Division : James V. Carmichael.
Vice-President and Secretary : Charles L. Beard.
Vice-President and Treasurer : Louis Fenn Sperry.
Vice-President in charge of Washington office : Harry E. Collins.
Manager of the Ordnance Division : Julius J. Domonkos.
Chief Design Engineer : Robert J. Woods.

The Bell Aircraft Corpn. was formed in 1935 by Lawrence D. Bell, formerly Vice-President and General Manager of the Consolidated Aircraft Corpn., R. P. Whitman, who was Assistant General Manager of Consolidated, and Robert J. Woods, Consolidated's Chief Engineer. When Consolidated moved its factory from Buffalo to San Diego, Cal., these three men remained in Buffalo to form the new company.

Most of the company's early business was in the nature of sub-contracting, but in July, 1937, it completed its first original design, the XFM-1 twin-engined long-distance escort monoplane which incorporated many radical departures from conventional military aircraft, including twin shaft-driven pusher airscrews and an armament which included two 37 m/m. cannon and several 50 cal. machine-guns. Thirteen Airacudas were built for the U.S. Army and before the last one was delivered the Bell company was ready with a new single-seat fighter, the P-39 Airacobra. This aeroplane also incorporated interesting innovations, includ-ing an Allison engine located aft of the cockpit and driving a tractor airscrew through an 8 foot extension shaft and remote gear-box.

While the P-39 was still in production, the Bell Corpn. introduced its third new Army fighter, the P-63 Kingcobra. This aeroplane incorporates many of the basic features of the P-39, including the tricycle landing-gear, cannon in the nose and engine behind the pilot. When the P-63 completely supplanted the P-39 on the Bell assembly lines in July, 1944, 9,584 Airacobras had been produced, more than half of which were delivered to Russia under Lend/Lease.

During the preliminary stages of the transition from P-39 to P-63, Bell was also engaged in the design, building and testing of the first American jet-propelled fighter, the P-59A Airacomet. This aeroplane, fitted with two jet units built by the General Electric Company to British designs, made its first flight on October 1, 1942, seventeen months after the first successful flight had been made in Great Britain with the Whittle jet engine, the prototype of the American power unit.

In addition to the production of fighter aircraft, the Bell Corpn. was also engaged in the manufacture of the Boeing B-29 Superfortress at its bomber plant in Marietta, Georgia, just outside Atlanta, the State capital. Following the surrender of Japan production at this plant ceased.

As part of its overall war programme, the Bell Aircraft Corpn., also developed a helicopter which incorporates important stability principles.

THE BELL XP-83.

The XP-83 is an experimental single-seat fighter monoplane fitted with two General Electric I-40 axial-flow jet units. It has a span of 53 ft. (16.2 m.) and a loaded weight of 18,600 lbs. (8,450 kg.). No further details were available at the time of closing down for press.

THE BELL AIRACOMET.

U.S. Army Air Forces designation : P-59A.

The Bell Aircraft Corpn. was requested on September 5, 1941, to design a fighter aeroplane to be equipped with thermal jet propulsion units of British Whittle design and before the end of that month the preliminary drawings had been submitted to and approved by the U.S. Army. To maintain secrecy this project was given the designation XP-59A, the XP-59 being a totally different fighter project with a pusher radial engine and twin-tail booms. In six months the design was completed and work started on parts for the first XP-59A. In September, 1942, the prototype was shipped to a secret base at Muroc, California, for flight testing and on September 26 the turbine engines were run up for the first time. Taxying trials took place on September 30 and on the following day the first flight of 30 minutes duration was made. On October 2, two flights were made, one to 6,000 ft. and the other to 10,000 ft., and the pilot reported that he had less trouble and fewer mechanical inter-ruptions than on any other prototype he had ever flown.

In the Spring of 1942 the original order for three XP-59A experimental prototypes was supplemented by a contract for twelve YP-59A's for service trials and most of these were delivered in 1943. The first production P-59A was accepted by the U.S. Army in August, 1944. The P-59A is now classified as a fighter trainer.

TYPE.—Single-seat jet-propelled Fighter Trainer.
WINGS.—Mid-wing cantilever monoplane. Laminar flow wing section with a 2° geometric twist from root to tip chord, 3½° dihedral, 2° incidence and 7° leading-edge sweep-back. Structure comprises two main spars, an auxiliary spar, a nose beam, ribs, stringers and transverse bulkheads, the whole being covered with a flush-riveted smooth metal skin with a glazed finish. Each outer wing is attached to a centre-section by eight bolts, the front and rear spars being continuous across the centre-section. Detachable wing-tips. Aerodynamically-balanced flaps between ailerons and wing roots. Ailerons of the pressure-balance type with pressure seals.
FUSELAGE.—In two sections. The forward section comprises the armament bay and centre section, including the cabin, and is constructed with two built-up longitudinal beams with transverse bulkhead frames and stringers to reinforce the outer skin. The centre-section also includes the two main centre-section spars, the twin engine nacelles and the radio compartment. The rear fuselage is a semi-monocoque built up of vertical frames, longerons and stringers and covered with a stressed skin.
TAIL UNIT.—Cantilever monoplane type. All-metal framework with metal covered fixed surfaces. Trim-tabs in elevators.
LAND GEAR.—Retractable tricycle type. Self-castoring non-steerable nose wheel retracts backwards into the bottom of the fuselage and the main wheels are raised inwardly into the underside of the outer wings. Retracting mechanism is operated by a 1½ h.p. electric motor through a series of torque tubes, universal joints, gear boxes and enclosed chain drive.
POWER PLANT.—Two General Electric I-16 Whittle-type turbine jet units in nacelles beneath the wing roots and as close to the fuselage as their dimensions permit. Each unit is supported at three points to allow for normal expansion due to the heat of the engine. Each has a centrifugal compressor and a single-stage turbine wheel mounted on a central rotor assembly. The turbine is driven by burning a liquid hydrocarbon fuel (kerosene) in combustion chambers. Oxygen to support combustion is obtained from the compressor. The speed of the rotor and thereby the flow through the compressor is controlled by varying the flow of hot gas past the turbine wheel. This is accomplished by the throttle which

The Bell P-59A Airacomet Single-seat Fighter Trainer (two General Electric I-16 turbo-jet units).

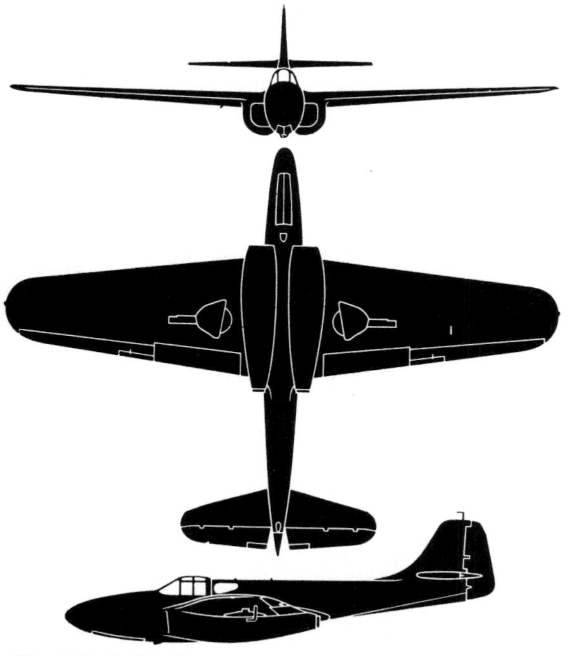

The Bell P-59A Airacomet Jet-propelled Fighter Trainer.

governs the supply of fuel to the burners. Four interconnected self-sealing fuel cells in each wing. A shackle-type bomb-rack under each wing outboard of the landing-gear provides for the installation of an auxiliary fuel tank.

Accommodation.—Pilot's cockpit just forward of the engine compartment. Canopy is a rigid structure and flush when closed. Doors in the fuselage behind the canopy swing in to allow the cover to slide back by mechanism actuated by the same crank which operates the canopy. The entire canopy may be jettisoned by a separate handle for emergency exit. Fume-tight bulkheads between engine compartment and pilot's cockpit and between the cockpit and armament compartment.

Armament.—Varying combinations of forward-firing armament may be installed in the nose compartment. One arrangement consists of one 37 m/m. cannon and three 50 cal. machine guns. Bomb-racks under each outer wing.

Dimensions.—Span 45 ft. 6 in. (13.87 m.), Length 38 ft. 1½ in. (11.63 m.), Height over canopy 7 ft. 9 in. (2.36 m.), Height over tail 12 ft. (3.66 m.), Wing area 385.8 sq. ft. (35.8 sq. m.).

Weights and Loadings.—Weight empty 7,950 lbs. (3,610 kg.), Weight loaded 10,822 lbs. (4,915 kg.), Wing loading 28.05 lbs./sq. ft. (136.88 kg./sq. m.).

Performance.—Maximum speed over 400 m.p.h. (640 km.h.), Service ceiling over 40,000 ft. (12,200 m.).

THE BELL KINGCOBRA.

U.S. Army Air Forces designation : P-63A.

The P-63, the prototype of which first flew on December 7, 1942, is a development of the P-39, which it resembles in all its general features.

The P-63 was never used operationally by the U.S.A.A.F., the greater proportion of the output being delivered to Russia under Lend/Lease.

A special modification of the P-63 was, however, evolved to serve as a target in the U.S. Army's live ammunition training programme. This model, which carried the designation RP-63, was covered with more than a ton of special duralumin-alloy armour plate against which 30-cal. lead and plastic frangible machine-gun bullets disintegrated harmlessly. Under the armour were special instruments which, when bullets struck the armour, transmitted impulses to a spot-light in the centre of the airscrew hub, causing it to flash brightly.

The armour was heaviest round the cockpit and varied from ⅛ to ¼ in. in thickness. The windshield and cockpit side windows were of bulletproof glass, a steel grille covered the air intake and a steel guard the exhaust stacks. A special thick-walled hollow-blade airscrew was used.

In spite of the greatly increased weight of the RP-63 target, it had a maximum speed of over 300 m.p.h. (480 km.h.) at 25,000 ft. (7,625 m.).

Type.—Single-seat Fighter.

Wings.—Low-wing cantilever monoplane. Low drag laminar-flow wing section. Structure similar to that of P-39. Electrically-operated landing-flaps between ailerons and fuselage.

Fuselage.—Similar to P-39.

Tail Unit.—Cantilever monoplane type. Tailplane and elevators located forward of rudder hinge-line. Structure similar to P-39.

Landing Gear.—Same as for P-39. Re-designed nose-wheel. Electric retraction, with emergency hand-gear. Hydraulic wheel-brakes.

Power Plant.—One Allison V-1710-93 (-E11) twelve-cylinder Vee liquid-cooled engine with both a built-in and a separate auxiliary-stage supercharger and driving a four-bladed Aeroproducts hydraulic constant-speed airscrew through an extension shaft and remote gearbox. Engine rated at 1,000 h.p. at 20,000 ft. (6,100 m.) and with 1,325 h.p. available for take-off. Self-sealing fuel tanks (two) in wings. Total capacity 136 U.S. gallons. Provision for self-sealing droppable belly tank (75 U.S. gallons) on bomb shackles under fuselage. Auxiliary fuel tanks may also be carried under wings. Oil tank in fuselage aft of engine. Armoured bulkhead at aft end of engine compartment. Coolant radiator and oil cooler installations as for P-39.

Accommodation.—Same as for P-39. Bullet-proof windscreen and bullet-proof glass panel behind pilot's head. Armour plate in nose to protect reduction gear-box, on bulkhead forward of pilot and at pilot's back. Cabin heating and ventilation.

Armament.—One 37 m/m. cannon and two 50 cal. machine-guns in gun compartment in the nose of the fuselage, the 37 m/m. cannon firing through the gear-box and airscrew hub. Fume-proof armoured bulkhead separates the gun compartment from the pilot's cockpit. Two additional 50 cal. guns in fairings under the wings and firing outside the airscrew disc. One 500 lb. bomb may be carried under the fuselage.

Dimensions.—Span 38 ft. 4 in. (1.69 m.), Length 32 ft. 8⅜ in. (10 m.), Height to top of airscrew disc. 12 ft. 7 in. (3.84 m.), Wing area 248 sq. ft. (23 sq. m.).

Weights and Loadings.—Weight empty 6,694 lbs. (3,040 kg.), Weight loaded 8,442 lbs. (3,833 kg.), Wing loading 34.04 lbs./sq. ft. (166.1 kg./sq. m.).

Performance.—Maximum speed 410 m.p.h. (655 km.h.) at 25,000 ft. (7,625 m.).

THE BELL AIRACOBRA.

U.S. Army Air Forces designation: P-39.
British name : Aircobra.

The first contract for the P-39 was awarded by the U.S. Army on September 13, 1939. The original XP-39 was fitted with the Allison V-1710-17 engine and a turbo-supercharger but this aeroplane was modified at Wright Field and Langley Field to become the XP-39B. In this model the turbo-supercharger was removed, the cabin was lowered and a turn-over beam and numerous minor changes were added. Thirteen YB-39B's were ordered for service trials.

P-39C. One Allison V-1710-35 (E4) engine rated at 1,150 h.p. at 12,000 ft. (3,660 m.) and with the same power available for take-off. The first combat model and essentially the same as the YP-39B. First flew in 1941. Armament consisted of one 37 m/m. cannon (15 rounds) and two 50 cal. (200 rounds each) and two 30 cal. machine-guns (500 rounds each), all in the fuselage and synchronised to fire through the airscrew. Leakproof fuel tanks and pilot armour added.

Airacobra I and IA. The P-400 export version contracted for by the French Government and taken over by the British Government on the fall of France. Substantially the same as the P-39C except that a 20 m/m. cannon (60 rounds) was substituted for the 37 m/m. weapon and the two 30 cal. fuselage guns were replaced by two unsychronised 30 cal. guns (1,000 rounds each) in the wings. The Airacobra I first went in action with the R.A.F. in October, 1941, but was withdrawn from service after a few missions. When the United States entered the war the undelivered balance of the British contracts was taken over by the U.S. Army and these aircraft were given the U.S. Army designation P-400 and used for training. A total of 336 of this model was delivered.

P-39D. One Allison V-1710-35 engine. The first of the P-39 Series to go into quantity production for the U.S. Army Air Forces. Except that the P-39D had a 37 m/m. cannon (30 rounds) instead of the 20 m/m. weapon, it was substantially the same as the R.A.F. Airacobra. The first model to carry an auxiliary fuel tank (75 U.S. gallons) under the fuselage. 429 were built. A later contract for 158 of the same type but with an Allison V-1710-63 (E6) with a 2 : 1 airscrew reduction gear ratio was designated the P-39D-2.

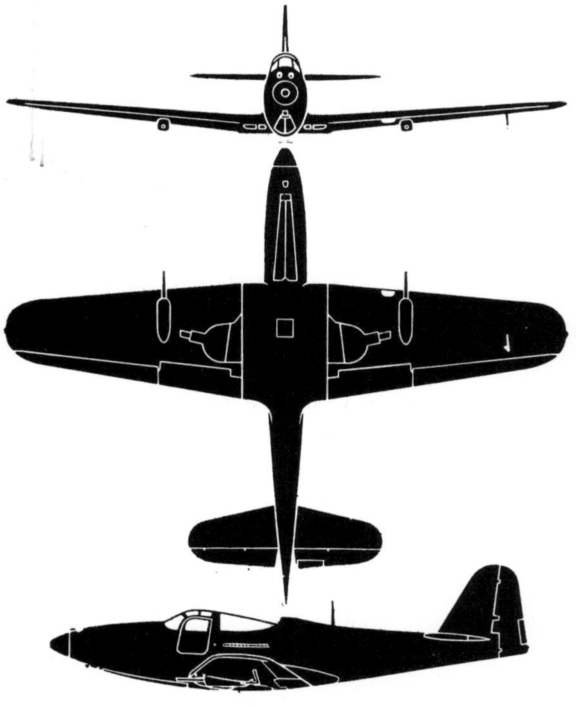

The Bell P-63A Kingcobra Single-seat Fighter.

XP-39E. One Allison V-1710-47 (E9) engine. An experimental model with re-designed square-cut wings and tail surfaces. Span 35 ft. 10 in. (10.91 m.).

P-39F. Similar to the P-39D but fitted with an Aeroproducts hydraulically-operated constant-speed airscrew instead of a Curtiss Electric airscrew. 229 were built.

P-39K. One Allison V-1710-63 (E6) single-stage low-altitude engine rated at 1,150 h.p. at 12,000 ft. (3,660 m.) and with 1,325 h.p. available for take-off. Aeroproducts airscrew. An additional 15 rounds of 50 cal. ammunition for each of the sychronised fuselage guns. 210 were built.

P-39L. Similar to the P-39K except that a Curtiss Electric airscrew was used and a new low-profile nose wheel was introduced. 250 were delivered.

P-39M. One Allison V-1710-83 (E18) single-stage high-altitude engine rated at 1,125 h.p. at 15,500 ft. (4,730 m.) and with 1,200 h.p. available for take-off. Curtiss Electric airscrew 10 ft. 4½ in. (3.14 m.) diameter. 240 were built.

P-39N. One Allison V-1710-85 (E19) engine with different airscrew reduction gear ratio. Same rating as E18. Aeroproducts airscrew 11 ft. 7 in. (3.52 m.) diameter. At the request of the A.A.F. certain fuel cells were removed to lighten the aeroplane, leaving a fuel capacity of 86 U.S. gallons instead of the former standard 120 U.S. gallons. 500 P-39N-0, 900 P-39N-1, which incorporated several minor changes, and 695 P-39N-5, which had a curved armour head plate in place of the bullet-proof glass behind the pilot, were built.

P-39Q. One Allison V-1710-85 engine and Aeroproducts airscrew. This model carried the first armament change since the P-39D. The 30 cal. wing guns were replaced by two 50 cal. guns mounted in external blisters, one under each wing. Later minor revisions of equipment carried the P-39Q through the Q-5, Q-10, Q-20, Q-21, Q-25 and Q-30 sub-series. A four-bladed Aeroproducts airscrew replaced the three-blader in the Q-21 and Q-25. The internal fuel capacity was increased from 86 to 110 U.S. gallons in the P-39Q-5 and further increased to 120 U.S. gallons in the Q-10. Various other models were provided with different auxiliary fuel tanks for ferrying purposes, the largest having a capacity of 250 U.S. gallons. The description that follows refers to the P-39Q, of which over 4,900 were built.

Production of the Airacobra ceased in July, 1944. Of a total of 9,584 built, approximately 5,000 were supplied to Russia under Lend/Lease.

Type.—Single-seat Fighter.

Wings.—Low-wing cantilever monoplane. Wing section NACA 0015 at root and modified NACA 23009 at tip. Centre-section integral with forward fuselage. Tapering outer-sections have three spars, front, rear and auxiliary, the front and rear spars having extended aluminium booms and sheet webs and the auxiliary spar formed cap strips and solid web. Pressed and beaded aluminium ribs and bulkheads, Z-section spanwise stringers and a flush-riveted smooth aluminium skin. Ailerons, which have metal frames with fabric covering, are differentially-controlled and have modified Frise type nose balance and Venturi-shaped slot. Controllable trimming-tabs in ailerons. These tabs also act as a servo control through a mechanical linkage which automatically rotates them to an angle opposite to the movement of the ailerons. Additional servo tabs not controlled by the pilot are located just outboard of the controllable tabs. Electrically-operated trailing-edge flaps between ailerons and fuselage.

Fuselage.—Oval all-metal structure in two sections. Forward section consists primarily of two main longitudinal beams with a horizontal upper deck between and extends from the nose to the bulkhead aft of the engine which is installed inside the fuselage aft of the pilot's cockpit. The fuselage covering above the main beams is in the form of detachable cowling to give easy access to engine, cockpit, armament and radio equipment. The aft section is a metal monocoque.

Tail Unit.—Cantilever monoplane type. Fixed surfaces are all-metal and movable surfaces have metal frames and fabric covering. Trimming-tabs in all movable surfaces controllable from cockpit.

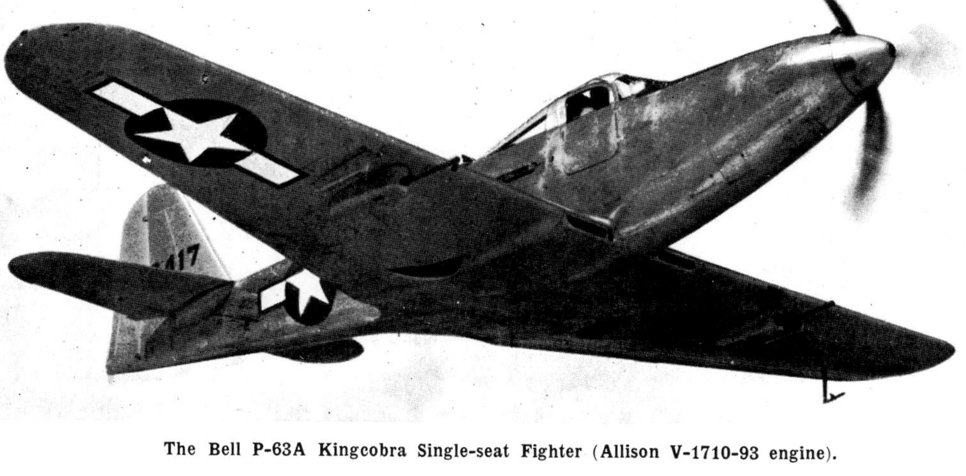

The Bell P-63A Kingcobra Single-seat Fighter (Allison V-1710-93 engine).

The Bell P-39Q Airacobra Single-seat Fighter (Allison V-1710-85 engine).

The Bell XP-77 Light Single-seat Fighter (Ranger V-770-7 engine).

The Bell Experimental Two-seat Helicopter (160 h.p. Franklin engine).

ARMAMENT AND EQUIPMENT.—One 37 m/m. cannon on fuselage centre-line and firing through gear box and airscrew hub, two 50 cal. machine-guns in forward fuselage and synchronised to fire through airscrew and two 50 cal. guns in fairings under the outer wings and firing outside the airscrew disc. All guns electrically fired. One 500 lb. bomb may be carried under the fuselage on the same shackles as the auxiliary fuel tank. Remotely-controlled two-way radio and storage battery in aft section of fuselage. Radio antenna enclosed in transparent plastic leading-edge of the vertical fin. Full electrical and oxygen equipment.

DIMENSIONS.—Span 34 ft. (10.37 m.), Length 30 ft. 2 in. (9.2 m.), Height to top of airscrew (one blade vertical) 11 ft. 10 in. (3.63 m.), Wing area 213 sq. ft. (19.8 sq. m.).

WEIGHTS AND LOADINGS.—Weight empty 5,968 lbs. (2,709 kg.), Weight loaded 8,052 lbs. (3,656 kg.), Wing loading 37.76 lbs./sq. ft. (184.26 kg./sq. m.).

PERFORMANCE (P-39Q).—Maximum speed 385 m.p.h. (606 km.h.) at 11,000 ft. (3,355 m.), Climb to 15,000 ft. (4,575 m.) 4.5 min., Service ceiling 35,000 ft. (10,670 m.), Range (with external auxiliary tank) 675 miles (1,080 km.) at 240 m.p.h. (384 km.h.). or 1,475 miles (2,360 km.) at 160 m.p.h. (256 km.h.).

THE BELL XP-77.

The XP-77 is an experimental all-wood lightweight single-seat fighter which was designed at a time when a shortage of aluminium alloy metals for aircraft appeared imminent.

TYPE.—Single-seat lightweight Fighter.

WINGS.—Low-wing cantilever monoplane. All-wood structure. Main spar has wide spruce flanges and moulded plywood webs, rear auxiliary spar of moulded plywood, ribs at 7½ in. centres and a plywood skin. Manually-operated trailing-edge flaps between ailerons and fuselage.

FUSELAGE.—All-wood structure. Laminated frames and a laminated moulded plywood skin. There are no stringers, but four longerons in the region of the cockpit.

TAIL UNIT.—Cantilever monoplane type. Fin built integral with the fuselage. All-wood structure with plywood covering.

LANDING GEAR.—Retractable tricycle type. Manual operation.

POWER PLANT.—One 575 h.p. Ranger V-770-7 twelve-cylinder inverted Vee air-cooled supercharged engine. Large upward offset of the spur reduction gear permits the installation of a 20 m/m. cannon above the crankcase to fire through the airscrew hub. Self-sealing fuel tank in fuselage in front of cockpit.

ACCOMMODATION.—Pilot's enclosed cockpit aft of trailing-edge of wing. Armour protection.

ARMAMENT.—One 20 m/m. cannon firing through the airscrew hub and two 50 cal. machine-guns, one on each side of the cannon and synchronised to fire through the airscrew.

DIMENSIONS.—Span 27 ft. 6 in. (8.38 m.), Length 22 ft. 10½ in. (6.9 m.), Wing area 100 sq. ft. (9.29 sq. m.).

WEIGHT LOADED.—3,650 lbs. (1,657 kg.).

PERFORMANCE.—Maximum speed over 400 m.p.h. (640 km.h.).

THE BELL HELICOPTER.

The Bell Aircraft Corpn. has had an experimental helicopter flying since the middle of 1943. A feature of this helicopter is the stabilising system. The position of the rotor, which is mounted on the mast by a cardan universal joint, is governed by a stabilising bar mounted just below the rotor hub and set at right angles to the two rotor blades. This stabilising bar, which is about 5 ft. long and weighted at the ends, is linked to the rotor in such a way that it tends to determine the plane of the rotor and maintain it generally horizontal irrespective of the angle of the mast. The rotor blades are not articulated but are rigidly connected to the hub, which is rocked about its longitudinal axis to control the rotor.

TYPE.—Two-seat Experimental Helicopter.

ROTORS.—Two-blade main rotor and auxiliary two-blade controllable-pitch anti-torque propeller. Main rotor hub mounted on transmission mast by universal joint and provided with a stabilising bar below and at right angles to the blades. A wobble plate revolving with the mast but free to move up and down provides cyclical pitch control. Lower half of wobble plate which does not revolve alters pitch of the blades differentially for directional control. Main rotor drive through a centrifugal clutch and a two-stage planetary transmission with a 9 : 1 reduction ratio. Free-wheeling mechanism incorporated in the transmission. Anti-torque propeller driven by a tubular shaft and controlled by cables and pulleys. Main rotor blades, of symmetrical aerofoil section, of solid wood with a steel insert in leading-edge for mass-balance. Anti-torque propeller blades also of solid wood.

FUSELAGE.—In two sections. Forward section built up on two rigid longitudinal beams which support the cabin and engine mounting. Rear section is a metal semi-monocoque of aerofoil section, with the leading-edge upward to offer minimum obstruction to the downward slipstream of the main rotor.

LANDING-GEAR.—Three-wheel type with two forwardly-placed castoring main wheels and a single wheel under the rear fuselage.

POWER PLANT.—One vertically-mounted 160 h.p. Franklin six-cylinder horizontally-opposed air-cooled engine, clutch, drive-shaft and rotor assembly in an integral unit in a steel tube framework with the engine mounting ring at the top and supporting legs attaching the unit to the longitudinal beams of the forward fuselage. The engine-mounting structure has three attachment points for the rear fuselage. Engine is fan-cooled with cooling air ducted from the nose and exhausted through vents in the side of the fuselage.

ACCOMMODATION.—Enclosed cabin seating two side-by-side. Pilot's controls include stick which tilts the main rotor to control the horizontal direction of flight, and a left-hand lever for pitch control—up and down for main rotor blades and right and left for tail rotor. Twist-grip engine throttle control on top of stick, and control for governor which regulates engine power to maintain constant r.p.m. of rotor in spite of variations in pitch on pitch-control lever.

DIMENSIONS.—Diameter of main rotor 33 ft. (10 m.), Diameter of anti-torque rotor 5 ft. (1.525 m.).

WEIGHTS AND PERFORMANCE.—No data available.

LANDING GEAR.—Retractable tricycle type. Electrical retraction with emergency hand gear. Main wheels are raised inwardly into wells in underside of wings aft of the main spar structure. Castoring nose wheel is raised aft into fuselage. Hydraulic suspension to all wheels. Hydraulic multiple disc brakes to main wheels.

POWER PLANT.—One 1,200 h.p. Allison V-1710-85 twelve-cylinder Vee Prestone-cooled engine mounted within the fuselage aft of the pilot's cockpit and driving a tractor airscrew through an extension shaft and remote 2.23 : 1 reduction gear box. Aeroproducts three or four-blade hydraulically controlled constant-speed airscrew 11 ft. 7 in. (3.54 m.) diameter. Coolant radiator in centre-section beneath engine, with two separate air ducts in leading-edge of centre-section and single controllable exit beneath fuselage. Two oil coolers in after portion of centre-section, one on each side of fuselage, with air ducts in leading-edge outboard of coolant air

ducts. Two fuel tanks (60 U.S. gallons each), each comprising six leak-proof bags, integrally built in outer wing sections. Droppable auxiliary fuel tank of either 75 or 175 U.S. gallons capacity may be carried beneath centre-section. Engine oil tank (13.8 U.S. gallons) in fuselage aft of engine. Separate reduction-gear oil system in nose of fuselage.

ACCOMMODATION.—Enclosed cockpit over leading-edge of wing. Two outward-swinging doors, one on each side of cabin, the one on the starboard side for normal entrance and exit. Both doors have quickly-releasable hinge-pins operated either inside or out for emergency use. Both doors have roll-down windows. Fume-proof bulkheads between armament compartment and pilot's cabin and between cabin and engine compartment. Cabin heating and ventilation. Armour in nose ahead of airscrew gear-box, on bulkhead ahead of pilot, at pilot's back, ahead of engine accessory compartment and aft of oil tank. Bullet-proof windscreen.

BELLANCA.

THE BELLANCA AIRCRAFT CORPORATION.

HEAD OFFICE, WORKS AND AERODROME: NEW CASTLE, DELAWARE.

Established : December 30, 1927.
Chairman of Board of Directors : E. M. Bellanca.
President : N. F. Vanderlipp.
Vice-President and Acting General Manager : I. I. Islamoff.
Vice-President and Treasurer : S. Samuel Arsht.

Chief Engineer : Andrew F. Haiduck
Secretary : James R. Morford.
Treasurer : H. L. Thompson.
Assistant Secretary and Assistant Treasurer : L. J. Koenig.

The Bellanca Aircraft Corpn. was incorporated on Dec. 30, 1927, taking over the old Bellanca Aircraft Corporation of America.

During 1941 the manufacture of commercial aircraft was suspended, and all facilities were fully converted to war production. In 1944 a contract for the construction of a large number of Fairchild AT-21 twin-engined gunnery-training aircraft for the U.S. Army Air Forces was completed. The Sub-Contract Division of the Corporation expanded rapidly and was mainly engaged in the production of aircraft components and armament equipment.

BOEING.

THE BOEING AIRCRAFT COMPANY.

Head Office : Seattle 14, Wash.

Aircraft Manufacturing Divisions : Seattle, Wash., Renton, Wash., and Wichita, Kansas.

Established : July, 1916.

Chairman : C. L. Egtvedt.

President : William M. Allen.

Assistants to President : O. W. Tupper, A. F. Logan and R. P. Holman.

Executive Vice-President : H. Oliver West.

Assistant to Executive Vice-President : T. J. Emmert.

Vice-President and Eastern Representative : J. P. Murray.

Vice-President in charge of Engineering : Wellwood E. Beall.

Chief Engineer : Edward C. Wells.

Assistant Chief Engineer : L. A. Wood.

Secretary and Treasurer : H. E. Bowman.

Renton Division.

Vice-President and Division Manager : F. P. Laudan.

Assistant Division Manager : W. F. Flanley.

Division Comptroller : Ralph Teig.

Wichita Division.

Vice-President and Division Manager : J. E. Schaefer.

Executive Assistant to Division Manager : L. M. Divinia.

Chief Engineer : H. W. Zipp.

Assistant Secretary and Treasurer : Clif Barron.

The Boeing Aircraft Company is the wholly-owned manufacturing subsidiary in Seattle of the Boeing Airplane Company, the parent corporation. Boeing Aircraft Company of Canada, Ltd., is a direct subsidiary of the Boeing Aircraft Company. The Boeing Aircraft Company also has a Renton Division at Renton, Washington, some ten miles from the Seattle plant. In addition, there is the Wichita Division of the Boeing Airplane Company in Wichita, Kan.

The bulk of all Boeing facilities at the end of the war were devoted to the manufacture of the B-29 Superfortress. During 1944, the Seattle plant of the Boeing Aircraft Company began the process of conversion to all-out B-29 production. While this conversion work was carried on, the Company continued to turn out the B-17 Fortress in large quantities.

In April, 1945, the Boeing Seattle plant completed its 6,891st and last B-17 and thereafter turned over completely to B-29 production. Production of the B-17 continued in the Douglas and Lockheed plants in California, which had been manufacturing the B-17 under a pool agreement since 1941.

The B-29 was produced by one of the most wide-spread manufacturing pools ever established in American industry. The Renton Division served as a final assembly factory, with the Seattle plant and its branch factories supplying sub-assemblies for the Renton plant. This made it possible for more B-29's to be built than if Seattle and Renton separately made complete aircraft. The Boeing Wichita Division where the first production models of the B-29 were built, the Martin plant in Omaha, Neb., and the Bell Plant in Marietta, Ga., were also building the B-29 complete. Following the surrender of Japan production of the B-29 was heavily curtailed, only the Boeing Seattle-Renton plants remaining in production to a greatly reduced programme.

During 1944, the company completed and successfully tested the C-97, a transport counterpart of the B-29. Early in January, 1945, this aeroplane, broke all existing transcontinental records by flying from Seattle to Washington, D.C., a distance of 2,323 miles (3,720 km.), in 6 hrs. 3 mins. 50 secs. The flight was made at an altitude of 30,000 ft. (9,150 m.), and the ground speed at times reached 448 m.p.h. (717 km.h.).

The C-97 is the prototype of a post-war transport to be known as the Stratocruiser. It will be capable of carrying up to 100 passengers in luxurious comfort for operating ranges up to 3,500 miles with ample fuel reserves.

The Wichita Division produced its 10,346th and last Kaydet trainer in February, 1945.

THE BOEING XB-39.

This designation covered an experimental modification of the B-29 Superfortress fitted with four Allison V-3420-11 twenty-four-cylinder liquid-cooled engines in place of the Wright R-3350 air-cooled units. The new power-plant installation was designed and built by the Power-plant Development Division of the General Motors Corporation.

THE BOEING XB-38.

The XB-38 was an experimental modification of a Vega-built B-17E fitted with four Allison V-1710-89 twelve-cylinder Vee liquid-cooled engines in place of the standard radial air-cooled units. Except for the engine installation this aircraft was identical to the B-17E Fortress.

THE BOEING MODEL 345 SUPERFORTRESS.

U.S. Army Air Forces designation : B-29 and F-13.

The original specification for a large four-engined bomber to succeed the B-17 Fortress was issued by the U.S. War Department in January, 1940, but it was considerably modified some months later to incorporate increased armament and load requirements. To meet the original specification the Boeing company designed the Model 341, and this was modified into the Model 345 to incorporate the later requirements.

The contract for three XB-29 prototypes was placed with the Boeing company on August 24, 1940, and a service development order for 13 YB-29's followed in the following May. With America's entry into the war a vast production programme for the B-29 was initiated, involving five main production plants and hundreds of sub-contractors.

The first XB-29 prototype built at Seattle flew on September 21, 1942. The first YB-29 built at Wichita flew on April 15, 1943, and the first Renton-built B-29 was delivered in December, 1943.

The B-29 was first reported in action on June 5, 1944, in an attack on railway yards at Bangkok, Siam, and on June 15 the first raid was made on Japan from bases in China. Since that

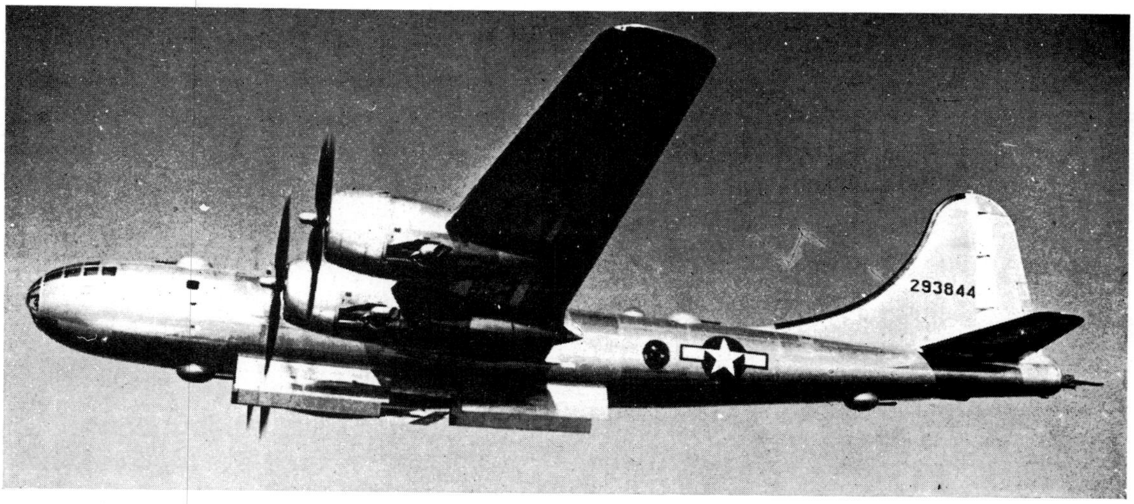

The Boeing B-29 Superfortress Heavy Bomber (four Wright R-3350-23 engines).

date attacks on the Japanese mainland were steadily stepped up, mainly from bases in the Marianas and on Guam, with forces of up to 450 and 500 Superfortresses. A B-29 dropped the first atomic bomb on Hiroshima, Japan, on August 6, 1945.

The B-29 was also modified into a photographic reconnaissance aeroplane and given the designation F-13. Development of this model was undertaken by the Air Technical Service Command, 20th Air Force, the Boeing Aircraft Co., and the Continental Air Lines Modification Center at Denver, Colo., the last-mentioned being responsible for the actual modifications. Equipped with more camera equipment than ever before installed in an aeroplane, the F-13 was responsible, from bases 1,500 miles away, for all reconnaissance work which preceded the bombing of Japan.

Type.—Four-engined Heavy Bomber.

Wings.—Mid-wing cantilever monoplane. Boeing 117 wing-section. Aspect ratio 11.5/1. Dihedral $4\frac{1}{2}$ degrees. 7 degrees sweep-back on leading-edge, straight trailing-edge. Centre-section and two outer sections with detachable wing-tips. All-metal web-type structure covered with a flush-riveted butt-jointed metal skin. Detachable leading-edge to give access to controls, etc. Electrically-operated flaps of the extensible type and when fully extended increase the wing area by 19 per cent. The trailing-edge of the flaps between the inboard nacelles and fuselage extend aft of the normal wing trailing-edge line and hook downward to decrease aerodynamic interference between wings and body and over tail when flaps extended. Statically and aerodynamically-balanced ailerons fitted with combination trim and servo tabs.

Fuselage.—Circular section semi-monocoque structure in five sections. Built up of a series of circumferential bulkheads and frames, extruded longerons and stringers and a flush-riveted and butt-jointed stressed metal skin. The stringers are riveted to the skin and the circumferentials are attached to the stringers by means of slips. Three pressurised compartments, one forward and one aft of the bomb-bay and one in the extreme tail. Crawl tunnel over the bomb-bays interconnects the two forward compartments but the tail compartment is isolated.

Tail Unit.—Cantilever monoplane type with single fin and rudder. All-metal fixed surfaces, and metal-framed fabric-covered aerodynamically and statically-balanced control surfaces. Controllable trim-tabs.

Landing Gear.—Retractable tricycle type. Main gear has two oleo-pneumatic shock-struts and twin wheels. Double nose wheel has single strut. Electrical retraction, the main wheels being raised backwards into the inboard engine nacelles and the nose wheel into a well in the fuselage below the flight deck. Hydraulic wheel-brakes. Retractable tail bumper skid.

Power Plant.—Four 2,200 h.p. Wright R-3350-23 eighteen-cylinder radial air-cooled engines, each engine with two General Electric exhaust-driven turbo-superchargers mounted vertically, one on each side of the nacelle. Hamilton-Standard Hydromatic four-blade constant-speed full-feathering airscrews 16 ft. 7 in. (5m.)

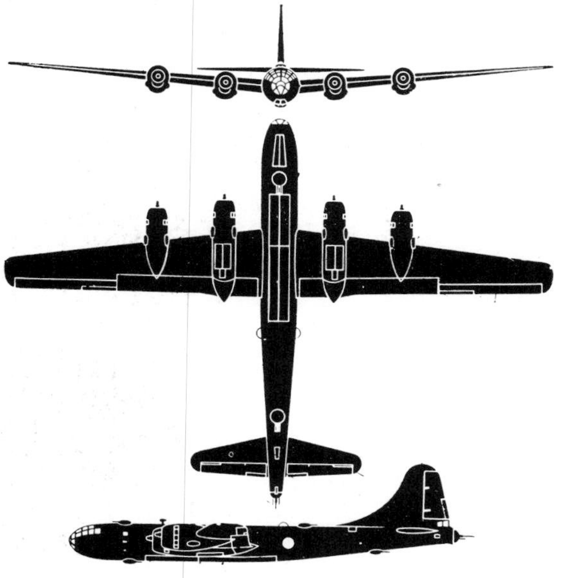

The Boeing B-29 Superfortress Heavy Bomber.

diameter. Self-sealing fuel cells integral with wing structure. Maximum capacity over 8,000 U.S. gallons. Self-sealing oil tank in each nacelle.

Accommodation.—Crew of ten to fourteen. Normal crew consists of pilot, co-pilot, navigator, bombardier, engineer, radio-operator and four gun-control operators. Forward pressurised compartment accommodates bombardier, pilot and co-pilot side-by-side with aisle in between, navigator facing forward behind pilot, engineer facing aft behind co-pilot and radio-operator behind engineer. Engineer's station has all power-plant controls and instruments but pilot's master throttle controls may override engineer's throttles. Crawl-tunnel over bomb-bays connects with second pressurised compartment which contains three gun-sighting stations in transparent blisters, one on top and one on each side of the fuselage. Pressurised tail-gunner's compartment in extreme tail of fuselage. All crew positions armoured or protected with armoured flak curtains. The three pressurised compartments are served by two superchargers driven off two inboard engines.

Armament.—Four General Electric remotely-controlled and electrically-operated turrets, each armed with two 50 cal. machine-guns, two above and two below the fuselage. Bell electrically-operated tail turret with one 20 m/m. cannon and two 50 cal. guns. Five sighting stations, one in the nose, three in the middle pressurised compartment and one in tail compartment. Mid-upper station controls either or both upper turrets, side sighting stations control lower rear turret, nose sighting station controls lower front turret and tail station controls tail turret. Some stations have secondary control over certain other turrets but only one sight may be in control of a given turret at one time. Two bomb-bays, one forward and one aft of the wing centre-portion which passes through the fuselage, and in order that the balance of the aircraft is preserved during bomb-dropping a system is used whereby bombs are dropped alternately from the two bays. Total maximum bomb load 20,000 lbs. (9,080 kg.). Electrically-operated bomb-bay doors.

Dimensions.—Span 141 ft. 3 in. (43.1 m.), Length 99 ft. (30.2 m.), Height (over tail) 27 ft. 9 in. (8.46 m.), Wing area 1,739 sq. ft. (161.5 sq. m.).

Weight Loaded.—135,000 lbs. (61,290 kg.).

Performance.—Maximum speed over 350 m.p.h. (560 km.h.), Landing speed about 100 m.p.h. (160 km.h.), Ceiling over 35,000 ft. (10,680 m.), Longest range so far announced 4,100 miles (6,560 km.).

THE BOEING MODEL 377.

U.S. Army Air Forces designation : C-97.

The Model 377 is a transport development of the B-29 Superfortress which, although built and flown as a military prototype, has been announced as the first of the post-war commercial transports to be built by the Boeing company.

The military prototype, carrying the designation C-97, was designed and built under contract from the Air Service Technical Command of the A.A.F. It is fitted with the same engine installation as the B-29, whereas the commercial version, to be known as the Stratocruiser, will be equipped with four engines of a different type and each expected to develop a maximum of 3,500 h.p.

The Model 377 has the same wings, tail surfaces and landing-gear as the B-29 but has a fuselage which has twice the volume and is 12 ft. (3.66 m.) longer than that of the Superfortress. The new fuselage is of the two-deck type and in cross-section resembles an inverted figure "8," achieved, in effect, by building one fuselage section on top of another, the lower and shorter section being faired into the upper. The lower section is of the same diameter as the B-29 whereas the upper section has a width of about 11 ft. (3.35 m.). The two-deck arrangement with two separate cabins below and a main cabin 78 ft. (23.8 m.) long above permits unusual versatility in using the aircraft for military transport purposes.

Under the rear fuselage large loading doors and a ramp permit the loading of wheeled or tracked vehicles, and an electrically-powered cargo-hoist running along the entire length of the fuselage can pick up loads from the trucks or from the ground through the loading doors. Two fully-loaded $1\frac{1}{2}$ ton trucks or two light tanks can be driven into the fuselage, the drive-up ramp being raised and lowered by the cargo hoist. Adequate cargo handling and tie-down equipment is provided. The cabins can also be arranged to accommodate more than 100 fully-equipped troops, or be fitted out as a hospital transport.

The standard crew for the C-97 is composed of pilot, co-pilot, flight engineer, radio operator and navigator. The entire fuselage, except for the tail storage section, is pressurised for operation at high altitudes.

On January 9, 1945, the prototype C-97, carrying a payload of more than 20,000 lbs. (9,080 kg.) flew across the American

The Boeing Model 377 Transport.

The Boeing Model 377 Transport Monoplane (four Wright R-3350-23 engines).

continent from Seattle to Washington, D.C., a distance of 2,323 miles (3,720 km.) in 6 hours 3 mins., representing an average speed of 383 m.p.h. (615 km.h.). The flight was made at a height of 30,000 ft. (9,150 m.).

The commercial version of the Model 377, which has been named the Stratocruiser, will not be available until after the war. The two-deck arrangement will permit great flexibility in furnishing and equipment. For day use 100 passengers can be carried. For long-range trans-ocean transport accommodation can be provided for 72 day seats and 36 sleeping berths in the main cabin, with the rear lower cabin fitted as an observation, dining and cocktail lounge seating 14 persons and the lower forward cabin used for cargo, galley and crew's quarters. As a purely cargo transport, using the loading facilities found in the C-97, a maximum cargo payload of 35,000 lbs. (15,890 kg.) can be carried. In the last-mentioned version a total of 3,000 cub. ft. (90 cub. m.) of usable cargo space will be available.

The general structure of the Stratocruiser is similar to that of the B-29 already described.

DIMENSIONS.—Span 141 ft. 3 in. (43.1 m.). Length 110 ft. 4 in. (33.64 m.), Height 33 ft. 3 in. (10.14 m.).

WEIGHTS.—Weight empty 70,000 lbs. (31,780 kg.). Weight loaded 130,000 lbs. (59,020 kg.), Landing weight 105,000 lbs. (47,670 kg.).

PERFORMANCE (Estimated).—Maximum speed 400 m.p.h. (640 km.h.), Cruising speed 340 m.p.h. (544 km.h.), Operating range 3,5000 miles (5,600 km.), Operating ceiling 30,000 ft. (9,150 m.).

THE BOEING MODEL 299 FORTRESS.
U.S. Army Air Forces designations : B-17, F-9 and YC-108.
British name : Fortress.

The Fortress was originally designed to meet a bomber specification issued by the U.S. Army Air Corps in 1934. The prototype first flew on July 28, 1935 and the first Y1B-17 of a production order of thirteen was delivered to the Air Corps in March, 1937. In January, 1939 an experimental Y1B-17A fitted with turbo-supercharged engines was delivered to the Army Air Corps. Following successful trials with this aircraft an order for 39 was placed for this model under the designation B-17B.

B-17B. Four 1,000 h.p. Wright R-1820-51 engines with exhaust driven superchargers. First B-17B delivered to the Army in June, 1939.

B-17C (Fortress I). Four 1,200 h.p. Wright R-1820-65 engines. Similar to B-17B except armament increased from five to seven 30 cal. guns. Side gun blisters abandoned in favour of plain openings. Twelve B-17C's ferried across the Atlantic in the Spring of 1944 for service with the R.A.F. These were the first Fortresses to go into combat operations in a daylight raid on Brest on July 24, 1941.

B-17D. Similar to B-17C but incorporating self-sealing tanks and armour protection for the crew. Later all B-17C's were converted to B-17D's.

B-17E (Fortress IIA). Major re-design and put into large-scale production by Boeing, Douglas and Vega. First Fortress to incorporate power-driven turrets and a tail-gun position. The total armament consisted of eleven 50 cal. machine-guns. Enlarged horizontal and vertical tail-surfaces. First B-17E flew in September, 1941.

B-17F (Fortress II). Similar to the B-17E. Fitted with additional wing fuel tanks and with external racks under inner wings for a maximum of two 4,000 lb. bombs. Later models fitted with four R-1820-97 engines.

B-17G (Fortress III.) Four 1,200 h.p. R-1820-97 engines. Similar to B-17F. Various armament changes. Fitted with a remotely controlled two-gun Bendix chin turret in place of hand-operated nose guns. In later versions the two 50 cal. side nose guns were reinstated, the open waist guns were replaced by staggered enclosed waist guns, and a new tail gun mounting with increased angles of fire and a reflector sight instead of ring and bead was installed. The B-17G was modified experimentally to carry two JB-2 American-built Flying-bombs, one under each wing. A control panel in the bombardier's compartment governed the starting and launching of the bombs, which were released at a speed of about 200 m.p.h.

F-9. A photographic reconnaissance version of the B-17F Fortress bomber. Three cameras were installed in the nose and extra fuel tanks accommodated in the bomb-bay. The first conversion was made by the United Air Lines Modification Center at Cheyenne, Ohio, in January, 1942.

YC-108. A special executive transport version of the B-17F. De-luxe furnishings. Some defensive armament retained.

CB-17. B-17G's withdrawn from operations were stripped of armament and used for general utility transport duties in the European Theatre under the CB-17 designation.

TYPE.—Four-engined Bomber.

WINGS.—All-metal midwing cantilever monoplane. Wing section varies from NACA 0018 at root to NACA 0010 at tip. Aspect ratio 7.58/1. Taper ratio 2.4/1. Incidence 3½°. Dihedral 4½°. Sweepback on leading-edge 8¼°. Structure, consisting of two inner sections carrying the engine nacelles, two outer sections and two detachable tips, chiefly of aluminium-alloy, with two spars, ribs and stressed-skin covering. Electrically-operated split trailing-edge flaps on inner wing sections, ailerons on outer sections. Flaps and ailerons covered with fabric. Ailerons fitted with control trimming-tabs.

FUSELAGE.—Semi-monocoque structure, consisting of bulkheads and circumferential stiffeners, tied together with longerons and longitudinal stiffeners, the whole covered with a smooth metal stressed skin.

TAIL UNIT.—Cantilever monoplane type. Aluminium-alloy framework, with fixed surfaces covered with smooth metal sheet and movable surfaces covered with fabric. Elevators and rudder fitted with control and trimming-tabs.

LANDING GEAR.—Retractable type. Air-oil shock-absorber units. Hydraulic wheel-brakes. Electrical retraction. Retractable tail-wheel.

POWER PLANT.—Four 1,200 h.p. Wright R-1820-97 nine-cylinder radial air-cooled engines with General Electric Type B-22 exhaust-driven turbo-superchargers installed in the undersides of the engine nacelles. Hamilton-Standard three-bladed constant-speed full-feathering airscrews 11 ft. 7 in. (3.54 m.) diameter. Self-sealing fuel tanks in wings. Normal fuel capacity carried in six tanks in the inner wing sections 1,700 U.S. gallons (1,510 Imp.

gallons). Nine self-sealing auxiliary feeder tanks in outer wings. Two self-sealing droppable ferry tanks may be carried in bomb-bay. Maximum capacity of all wing tanks 2,780 U.S. gallons (2,316 Imp. gallons). Self-sealing hopper oil tank in each nacelle. Oil capacity 148 U.S. gallons (124 Imp gallons).

ACCOMMODATION.—Normal crew of six to ten. Bomb-aimer's compartment in extreme nose. Pilot's compartment seating two side-by-side with dual controls in front of leading-edge of wing. Aft of pilot's position is an upper electrically-operated two-gun turret. Radio-operator's position amidships. Two gun positions aft of the wings, one two-gun electrically-operated turret beneath the fuselage and one position in the extreme tail. Equipment includes automatic pilot, two-way radio and radio "homing" equipment. Oxygen equipment with points of supply for each member of the crew, de-icers on leading-edges of wings, tail-plane and fin, two collapsible dinghies, etc.

ARMAMENT.—Thirteen 50 cal. machine-guns. From nose to tail these are : two, remotely-controlled, in a "chin" turret beneath the plastic bomb-aimer's nose ; two in "cheek" mountings, one on either side of the plastic nose ; two in an electrically-operated turret on top of the fuselage just aft of the pilot's cockpit ; one manually-operated firing through the top of the fuselage above the radio-operator's compartment ; two in a Sperry electrically-operated "ball" turret below the fuselage ; two on hand-operated mountings and firing through side ports, one on each side of the fuselage midway between wings and tail ; and two in the extreme tail. Internal bomb stowage in fuselage between the main spar frames, the bomb-bay occupying the full cross-section of the fuselage. Normal capacity of bomb-bay is 6,000 lbs. (2,724 kg.). Largest bomb which can be carried internally is the 2,000 lb. (908 kg.). External racks no longer fitted.

DIMENSIONS.—Span 103 ft. 9 in. (31.6 m.), Length 74 ft. 9 in. (22.8 m.), Height 19 ft. 1 in. (5.8 m.), Wing area 1,420 sq. ft. (132 sq. m.).

WEIGHTS.—Weight empty 32,720 lbs. (14,855 kg.), Normal weight loaded 49,500 lbs. (22,475 kg.), Maximum overloaded weight 60,000 lbs. (27,240 kg.).

PERFORMANCE.—Maximum speed 295 m.p.h. (472 km.h.) at 25,000 ft. (7,625 m.), Climb to 25,000 ft. (7,625 m.) 41 min., Service ceiling 35,000 ft. (10,670 m.), Normal range (maximum bomb load and normal fuel) 1,100 miles (1,760 km.) at 220 m.p.h. (352 km.h.) at 25,000 ft. (7 625 m.).

A Boeing B-17G, the 5,000th Fortress built by the Boeing Company, which went into service with the 8th Air Force covered with the signatures of employees of the company.

The Boeing 307-B Stratoliner as supplied to Transcontinental and Western Air, Inc.

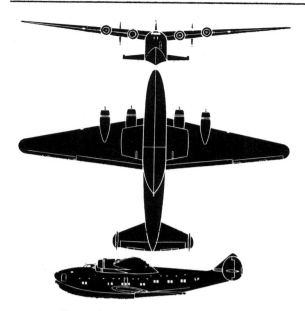

The Boeing 314-A Clipper Flying-boat.

THE BOEING 314-A CLIPPER.

TYPE.—Four-engined Trans-oceanic flying-boat.

WINGS.—High-wing cantilever monoplane. Structure same as for Model 307 (which see).

HULL.—Semi-monocoque structure, divided into eleven sections by truss-type bulkheads. Hull includes an upper or control deck, a main or passenger deck, and a series of watertight compartments below the floor structure, with flush riveting on the bottom skin. Cantilever two-spar hydro-stabilisers.

TAIL UNIT.—Cantilever monoplane type with three fins and rudders. Aluminium-alloy framework, with smooth sheet covering on fixed surfaces and fabric covering on movable surfaces. Trimming-tabs in elevators and rudders.

POWER PLANT.—Four 1,600 h.p. (take-off rating) Wright Cyclone 709C-14AC1 double-row fourteen-cylinder radial air-cooled geared engines, in semi-monocoque nacelles in the leading-edges of the wings. Engines accessible during flight through wing companion-way. Hamilton-Standard full-feathering constant-speed airscrews. Fuel tanks in wings and hydro-stabilisers. Fuel capacity 5,408 U.S. gallons.

ACCOMMODATION.—On two decks, upper, or control, deck and main, or passenger, deck, providing accommodation for crew of eleven (including two stewards) and sixty-eight day passengers and 36 sleeping passengers. Aft of the control cabin on the upper deck are the main cargo, mail and baggage holds with combination cargo-loading hatch and navigator's observatory above. Additional cargo space is provided in the bow of the hull. Mail and cargo holds have a total capacity of approximately 5 tons. The passenger deck is divided into nine sections, including a lounge or recreation room seating twelve passengers, six separate passenger compartments, a specially furnished de-luxe compartment, galley and rest rooms and lavatories for men and women. The two decks are interconnected by staircase. Complete radio, interphone and signal light systems. Soundproofing, controlled heating and ventilation.

DIMENSIONS.—Span 152 ft. (46.36 m.), Length 106 ft. (32.33 m.), Height 20 ft. 4½ in. (6.22 m.).

WEIGHTS.—Weight empty 48,400 lbs. (21,930 kg.), Weight loaded 84,000 lbs. (38,136 kg.).

PERFORMANCE.—Maximum speed 210 m.p.h. (336 km.h.) at 6,200 ft. (1,890 m.), Cruising speed at 66½% rated output 188 m.p.h. (301 km.h.) at 11,000 ft. (3,355 m.), Normal cruising range 3,685 miles (5,896 km.), Maximum cruising range at maximum loaded weight 4,900 miles (7,840 km.).

THE BOEING 307 STRATOLINER.

Eight Stratoliners were delivered to commercial operators, three Model 307 to Pan American Airways and five Model 307-B to Transcontinental and Western Air, Inc.

In January, 1942, the five 307-B Stratoliners were converted for military use and given the Army designation C-75. In February of the same year they initiated the first transocean services on behalf of Air Transport Command, firstly to Cairo across the South Atlantic and Africa and later across the North Atlantic to Great Britain. These services were operated by TWA under contract to A.T.C. In the Summer of 1944 the five C-75's were returned to Boeing for reconversion and return to TWA. In 2½ years as military transports they flew nearly 45,000 hours and covered 7½ million miles without trouble or casualty.

In the process of reconversion the 307-B's were fitted with B-17G wings, power-units, landing-gear and tailplane. The cabin was also completely re-designed, only the forward of the four former separate compartments, which can be used for freight or cargo when necessary, being retained. The seating capacity has been increased from 33 to 38 with the seats arranged in pairs on each side of a central aisle. Cabin supercharging has been removed. The re-built TWA Stratoliners carry the designation SA-307-B1.

TYPE.—Four-engined Air-liner.

WINGS.—All-metal low-wing monoplane. Wing in six sections, consisting of two inner sections, two outer sections, and two tips. Structure mainly of aluminium-alloy, built up of two spars, ribs, and stressed-skin covering. Split trailing-edge flaps. Trimming-tabs in ailerons. Flaps and ailerons are fabric-covered.

FUSELAGE.—Semi-monocoque structure of circular cross-section. Structure consists of aluminium-alloy ring and partition bulkheads, longitudinal stiffeners and circumferentials, the whole covered with smooth "Alclad" skin. In original design the fuselage was sealed for high-altitude operation with moderate supercharging. Automatically-controlled supercharging and pressure-regulating equipment provided for operation at altitudes of 14,000-20,000 ft. (4,270-6,100 m.), with a pressure differential of 2½ lbs./sq. in. between outside atmospheric pressure and inside pressure. At an

The Boeing 314-A Clipper Trans-Atlantic Flying-boat (four Wright Cyclone 709C-14AC1 engines).

The Boeing PT-17 Kaydet Two-seat Primary Training Biplane (220 h.p. Continental engine).

actual height of 14,700 ft. (4,480 m.) cabin conditions designed to be equivalent to a height of 8,000 ft. (2,440 m.). This equipment has now been removed.

TAIL UNIT.—Cantilever monoplane type. Aluminium-alloy framework, fixed surfaces covered with smooth metal skin and movable surfaces with fabric. Trimming-tabs in elevators and rudder.

LANDING GEAR.—Retractable type. Electrically-operated, with auxiliary manual control. Hydraulic brakes. Retractable tail-wheel.

POWER PLANT.—Four 1,100 h.p. Wright Cyclone GR-1820-G102 (Model 307) or 1,200 h.p. GR-1820-G666 (Model SA-307-B1) radial air-cooled engines in semi-monocoque nacelles in the leading-edge of the wings. Hamilton-Standard three-bladed constant-speed full-feathering airscrews. Fuel tanks in inner wing sections. No tanks in fuselage.

ACCOMMODATION.—Crew of five and thirty-three (Model 307) or thirty-eight (Model SA-307-B1) passengers. Main passenger cabin of Model 307 divided into four compartments, each accommodating six day passengers or four night passengers in transverse bunks, on right side of central aisle, with nine individual reclining chairs on left side of aisle. Separate dressing-rooms for men and women. Fully-equipped galley. Cargo compartments with capacity for 6,590 lbs. (2,990 kg.) beneath floor of cabin and accessible from inside or out. The rebuilt SA-307-B1 accommodates thirty-eight passengers in the main cabin, which is not compartmented like the Model 307.

DIMENSIONS.—Span 107 ft. (32.63 m.), Length 74 ft. 4 in. (22.6 m.), Height 20 ft. 9½ in. (6.33 m.).

WEIGHTS.—Weight empty 30,000 lbs. (13,620 kgs.), Weight loaded 45,000 lbs. (20,430 kg.).

PERFORMANCE.—Maximum speed at 6,000 ft. (1,830 m.) 241 m.p.h. (385.6 km.h.), Cruising speed at 10,000 ft. (3,050 m.) on 2,500 h.p. 215 m.p.h. (344 km.h.), Service ceiling 23,300 ft. (7,110 m.), Service ceiling on three engines 18,200 ft. (5,550 m.), Absolute ceiling with any two engines 10,500 ft. (3,200 m.), Maximum range at 10,000 ft. (3,050 m.) at 50 per cent. power 1,750 miles (2,815 km.) at 184 m.p.h. (294.4 km.h.).

THE BOEING (STEARMAN 75) KAYDET.

U.S. Army Air Forces designations : PT-13, PT-17, PT-18 and PT-27.
U.S. Navy designation : N2S.

The first service training version of the Stearman Model 75 was the PT-13 (Lycoming R-680-5 engine) which was ordered by the Army in 1935. Then followed the PT-17 (Continental R-670-5 engine) in 1940, the PT-18 (Jacobs R-755-7 engine) and the PT-27. All were similar, except for the engines fitted and certain minor equipment charges, with the exception of the PT-27 which was built for use in Canada. The PT-27 had the same airframe and power-plant as the PT-17 but was fitted with cockpit enclosures and heating, night-flying equipment, blind-flying hood and instruments, etc.

Of the U.S. Navy versions, the N2S-1 and N2S-4 (Continental R-670-4 engine) are similar to the PT-17, the N2S-2 (Lycoming R-680-8 engine) is similar to the PT-13A, the N2S-3 (Continental R-670-4 engine) is similar to the PT-17A, and the N-2S-5 (Lycoming R-680 engine) is identical to the PT-13D, these last two aircraft eventually being standardised for unified production for both services.

Production of the Kaydet was completed in February, 1945, after 10,346 had been built.

TYPE.—Two-seat Primary Training biplane.

WINGS.—Single-bay unequal-span staggered biplane. NACA 2213 wing-section. Centre-section carried above the fuselage by splayed-out wire-braced streamline steel-tube struts. One "N"-type streamline steel-tube interplane strut on each side of the fuselage. Wing structure consists of spruce laminated spars and ribs, duralumin channel compression struts and steel tie-rod bracing, the whole covered with fabric. Ailerons, of duralumin construction, on lower wings only.

FUSELAGE.—Rectangular welded chrome-molybdenum steel-tube, covered forward with metal panels and aft with fabric.

TAIL UNIT.—Monoplane type. Wire-braced tail-plane and fin.

Welded chrome-molybdenum steel-tube framework and fabric covering. Trimming-tab in elevator.
LANDING GEAR.—Divided cantilever type. Each leg incorporates a torque-resisting oleo-spring shock-absorber, enclosed in a metal fairing. Hydraulic wheel-brakes. Steerable tail-wheel.
POWER PLANT.—One 220 h.p. Lycoming R-680 (PT-13 or N2S-2) or 220 h.p. Continental R-670 (PT-17, PT-27, N2S-1, N2S-3 or N2S-4) or 225 h.p. Jacobs R-755 (PT-18) radial air-cooled engine, on steel-tube mounting. Two-bladed adjustable-pitch metal airscrew. Petrol tank (43 U.S. gallons = 162.75 litres) in centre-section. Oil tank (4 U.S. gallons = 15.14 litres) in engine compartment.
ACCOMMODATION.—Tandem open cockpits, with complete dual controls. Baggage compartment aft of rear cockpit.
DIMENSIONS.—Span 32 ft. 2 in. (9.8 m.), Length 25 ft. ¼ in. (7.63 m.), Height 9 ft. 2 in. (2.79 m.), Wing area 297.4 sq. ft. (27.6 sq. m.).
WEIGHTS AND LOADINGS.—Weight empty 1,936 lbs. (878 kg.), Weight loaded 2,717 lbs. (1,232 kg.), Wing loading 10.94 lbs./sq. ft. (44.6 kg./sq. m.), Power loading 12 lbs./h.p. (3.85 kg./h.p.).
PERFORMANCE.—Maximum speed 124 m.p.h. (199.5 km.h.), Cruising speed at sea level at 65 per cent. power 106 m.p.h. (171 km.h.), Landing speed 52 m.p.h. (83.6 km.h.), Initial rate of climb 840 ft./min. (256 m./min.), Service ceiling 11,200 ft. (3,413 m.), Range 505 miles (812 km.), Endurance at cruising speed (65 per cent. output) 4.75 hours.

BREWSTER.

BREWSTER AERONAUTICAL CORPORATION.

HEAD OFFICE AND WORKS: LONG ISLAND CITY, N.Y.
President: Preston Lockwood.
Vice-Presidents: Zeus Soucek, Dan C. Peacock, Jr. and Lamond C. Henshaw.
Controller: Alfred B. Cipriani.

The Brewster Aeronautical Corpn., formed in 1932, took over the equipment, plant, designs and goodwill of the Aircraft Division of Brewster & Co., Inc., a company which had been manufacturing carriages and, later, automobile bodies since 1810.

At the outset the Company concentrated on the manufacture of seaplane floats, wings and tail surfaces, but later it undertook the design and construction of complete aircraft.

It has specialised in the design of Naval shipboard aircraft. Its first design was the SBA-1 two-seat Scout-Bomber, a quantity of which was built for the U.S. Navy by the Naval Aircraft Factory under the designation SBN-1.

This was followed by the F2A-1 single-seat fighter, a production order for which was placed by the U.S. Navy in the Summer of 1938, and the F2A-2 which was ordered by the U.S. Navy, the British Government and the Netherlands East Indies Government in 1940. This model was known in both the American and British services as the Buffalo.

In 1941 production was started on a new dive-bomber designated by the U.S. Navy as the SB2A-1, and by the Royal Air Force as the Bermuda. The manufacture of this aeroplane was abandoned after two deliveries to the U.S. Navy and R.A.F.

On April 18, 1942, the control of the Brewster factories was taken over by the U.S. Navy Department and Capt. G. C. Westervelt of the Navy Construction Corps (Ret.) was placed in charge. The Company was restored to private ownership a month later.

In 1943, the Company undertook the manufacture of the Vought Corsair single-seat fighter for the U.S. Navy under the designation F3A-1. The contract for this aircraft was terminated by the Navy Department on July 1, 1944.

BUDD.

EDWARD G. BUDD MANUFACTURING COMPANY.

HEAD OFFICE AND WORKS: PHILADELPHIA, PA.
President: Edward G. Budd.
Vice-Presidents: Edward G. Budd, Jr. and Donald Alexander.
Chief Aircraft Engineer: Dr. Michael Watter.
Secretary: H. A. Coward.
Treasurer: Paul Zens.

The Edward G. Budd Manufacturing Co. has specialised in the development of welded stainless steel products and is probably best known for its production of spot-welded stainless steel streamline railroad cars. In the aeronautical field it has concentrated mainly on the production of component parts under sub-contract with most of the aircraft manufacturers, although it has also devoted considerable research into the design and manufacture of spot-welded stainless steel aircraft.

In August, 1942 the Company was awarded a contract by the U.S. Navy Department for the manufacture of a number of transport aircraft of stainless steel construction. This aircraft, carrying the Naval designation RB-1, was later adopted by the U.S. Army as the C-93.

THE BUDD CONESTOGA.

U.S. Navy designation: RB-1.
U.S. Army Air Forces designation: C-93.

The Conestoga was the first aircraft of original design to be fabricated entirely of shotwelded stainless steel. It was developed under the sponsorship of the U.S. Navy Bureau of Aeronautics and was designed to meet a U.S. Navy specification for a twin-engined cargo carrier and troop transport.

The design of the RB-1 was accepted by the Navy early in 1942 and a contract for 200 was awarded in August of that year. The U.S. Army also showed interest in the design and subsequently a military contract was awarded to the Budd company for 600 Conestogas to carry the A.A.F. designation C-93.

Static tests and the first test flight with the prototype were made in October, 1943.

Owing to manufacturing problems associated with a completely new type of construction there were delays in production and costs turned out to be substantially greater than the original estimates. These difficulties, taken in conjunction with the fast-changing situation in service requirements, resulted, in 1944, in the Army cancelling its contract for the C-93 and the Navy cutting its original contract for the RB-1 from 200 to twenty-five. These have since been sold out of the service.

TYPE.—Twin-engined Cargo-carrier and Troop Transport.
WINGS.—High-wing cantilever monoplane. Stainless steel structure fabricated by the Budd "Shotweld" method. Wings consist of two inner sections, which are welded to special fuselage bulkheads, two readily-detachable and interchangeable outer sections and two wing-tips. Structure of stressed-skin D-spar type with shear web located at 40% of the chord line, except for portions of inner sections from nacelles to fuselage, which are of the two-spar box type with removable leading-edges. In addition to the spars the inboard ends of the inner sections incorporate three sets of top and bottom members to transmit wing loads to the fuselage frames. Aft of rear spar or D-spar, former ribs carry metal skin on inner wing sections and fabric covering on outer sections. Electrically-operated split flaps, of D-spar type construction with fabric covering over former ribs aft of spar, on inner wing sections. Ailerons, of similar structure to flaps, on outer sections.
FUSELAGE.—Stressed-skin shot-welded stainless steel structure built up of a series of channel-type bulkhead rings spaced 18 in. apart and closed-hat type longitudinal stringers, the whole covered with a smooth skin. There are only two solid bulkheads throughout the length of the fuselage, a crash bulkhead at the forward end of the cargo hold and an end bulkhead to which the fin spar is attached.
TAIL UNIT.—Cantilever monoplane type with dihedral tailplane. Fixed surfaces are all-metal of D-spar design with former ribs aft of spar covered with a steel skin which is reinforced with chordwise top-hat section stiffeners between ribs. Movable surfaces have D-spar structure with fabric covering aft of spar. All control surfaces balanced dynamically, aerodynamically and statically.
LANDING GEAR.—Retractable tricycle type. Cleveland pneumatic shock-absorbers. Main wheels retract into engine nacelles, leaving about half of each wheel in airstream. Non-steerable nose wheel retracts into fuselage. Electric retraction.
POWER PLANT.—Two 1,200 h.p. Pratt & Whitney R-1830-92 Twin-Wasp fourteen-cylinder radial air-cooled engines in semi-monocoque stressed-skin stainless steel nacelles. Forward nacelle bulkhead acts as fireproof bulkhead and attaches to the front spar. Landing-gear bulkhead mounted on rear spar. Between these bulkheads is a fuel tank (259 U.S. gallons = 215 Imp. gallons) with access door below. Further fuel tank (238 U.S. gallons = 198 Imp. gallons) in each wing outboard of nacelle, also with access panel below. All tanks of stainless steel. Total fuel capacity: 994 U.S. gallons. Hopper oil tank (30 U.S. gallons) in each nacelle. Hamilton Standard Hydromatic three-bladed constant-speed full-feathering airscrews. Diameter: 11 ft. 7 in. (3.54 m.). Complete power-unit assembly, including cowled engine, airscrew, engine-mounting, oil tank and cooler, direct-cranking starter and accessories, is quickly detachable at the main fireproof bulkhead and is interchangeable from left to right side or vice-versa.
ACCOMMODATION.—Normal crew of two. Flight deck accommodates pilot and co-pilot side-by side with dual controls. Navigating position with table and stool behind pilot's seat. Remotely-controlled radio is accessible to both pilot and co-pilot. Below flight deck is an access compartment with entrance door on port side. Stairs lead to flight deck. There is also stowage in this compartment for miscellaneous equipment. Cargo compartment aft of crash bulkhead is 25 ft. (7.625 m.) long with an unobstructed cross-section 8 ft. × 8 ft. (2.44 × 2.44 m.) throughout its length. At the beginning of the upsweep of the lower fuselage lines is hinged an electrically-operated ramp 10 ft. (3.05 m.) long and 8 ft. (2.44 m.) wide for loading. Manually-operated clam-shell doors aft of ramp retract upward into the sides of the fuselage to maintain the 8 ft. × 8 ft. cross-section throughout travel from the ground. The ramp when closed can be used for additional cargo space and is capable of supporting substantially the same load as the main cargo floor. The largest military ambulance or a 1½ ton truck can be driven up the ramp into the body. In addition to the ramp there are two 40 in × 60 in. doors, one on each side of the compartment. For cargo handling there is an overhead manually-operated 2 ton hoist for unloading trucks and a 1 ton winch for skidding cargo up the ramp. Tie-down rings in floor and sides of cargo compartment for lashing down cargo. Along the sides of the compartment removable seats may be provided for 24 fully-armed airborne or parachute troops, together with carriers for six parachute containers. The containers are released through the opening aft of the cargo ramp. Twenty-four stretcher cases and sixteen sitting cases can also be accommodated. Heating, lighting and ventilation of cargo space. 42 volt electrical system provides power for engine starting, radio, interphone system, lighting circuits, heaters, hydraulic wheel brakes, cowl flaps, ramp door, wing flaps and landing-gear retraction. Emergency hand gear for landing-gear, wing flaps, cowl flaps and ramp.
DIMENSIONS.—Span 100 ft. (30.5 m.), Overall length 68 ft. (20.7 m.), Height 31 ft. 9 in. (9.68 m.), Wing area 1,400 sq. ft. (130 sq. m.).
WEIGHTS.—Weight empty 20,156 lbs. (9,150 kg.), Cargo load (with 390 U.S. gallons fuel) 9,600 lbs. (4,358 kg.), Disposable load 13,704 lbs. (6,222 kg.), Weight loaded 33,860 lbs. (15,372 kg.).
PERFORMANCE.—Maximum speed 197 m.p.h. (315.2 km.h.) at 7,500 ft. (2,290 m.), Cruising speed 165 m.p.h. (264 km.h.), Stalling speed (with full load) 78 m.p.h. (125 km.h.), Normal range 700 miles (1,120 km.), Maximum cruising range (normal tankage) 1,620 miles (2,590 km.).

The Budd RB-1 Conestoga All-steel Transport (two Pratt & Whitney R-1830-92 engines).

CALL.

CALL AIRCRAFT COMPANY.

HEAD OFFICE AND WORKS: AFTON, WYO.
General Manager: Reuel Call.
Chief Engineer: Ivan Call.
Acting Chief Engineer: Spencer Call.

The Call Aircraft Company has developed a light two-seat cabin monoplane known as the Call-Air, a description of which follows.

In July, 1944, the Call-Air Model A fitted with a 100 h.p. engine received Approved Type Certificate No. 758.

THE CALL-AIR MODEL A.

TYPE.—Two-seat light cabin monoplane.
WINGS.—Rigidly-braced low-wing monoplane. Structure comprises

The Call-Air Model A Two-seat Light Monoplane (100 h.p. Lycoming engine).

two laminated reinforced spruce spars, built-up spruce ribs, duralumin leading-edge and fabric covering. Wing bracing by Vee
struts from upper longerons of fuselage. An additional strut
each side to point of attachment of landing-gear shock-strut.

FUSELAGE.—Welded chrome-molybdenum steel-tube framework
covered with fabric over light secondary structure.

TAIL UNIT.—Braced monoplane type. Welded steel-tube framework
covered with fabric.

LANDING GEAR.—Divided type. Comprises hydraulic shock-
absorber legs the upper ends of which are attached to the front
wing-spars with the lower ends hinged to the lower fuselage

longerons by faired-in steel-tube Vees. Hayes low-pressure wheels
and hydraulic brakes. Full-swivelling tail-wheel.

POWER PLANT.—One 100 h.p. Lycoming O-235 four-cylinder horizontally-opposed air-cooled engine on welded steel-tube mounting.

Sensenich airscrew. Fuel capacity : 25 U.S. gallons. Oil capacity:
2 U.S. gallons.

ACCOMMODATION.—Enclosed cabin seating two side-by-side with dual
controls. Door on each side of cabin. Baggage space behind
seats.

DIMENSIONS. – Span 35 ft. 9⅜ in. (10.9 m.), Length 23 ft. 7⅜ in. (7.25

m.), Height (tail down) 7 ft. (2.135 m.), Wing area 181.6 sq. ft. (16.8
sq. m.).

WEIGHTS AND LOADINGS.—Weight empty 1,050 lbs. (477 kg.), Disposable load 500 lbs. (227 kg.), Weight loaded 1,550 lbs. (704 kg.),
Wing loading 8.53 lbs./sq. ft. (41.7 kg./sq. m.), Power loading
15.5 lbs./h.p. (67.0 kg./h.p.).

PERFORMANCE.—Maximum speed 115 m.p.h. (184 km.h.), Cruising
speed 101 m.p.h. (162 km.h.), Stalling speed 45 m.p.h. (72 km.h.),
Initial rate of climb 710 ft./min. (216.5 m./min.), Service ceiling
13,000 ft. (3,965 m.), Cruising range 342 miles (550 km.).

CESSNA.

THE CESSNA AIRCRAFT CO., INC.

HEAD OFFICE : WICHITA, KANSAS.
WORKS : WITCHITA AND HUTCHINSON, KANSAS.

Established : August 22, 1927.
President and General Manager : Dwane L. Wallace.
Executive Vice-President and Treasurer : Dwight S. Wallace.
Secretary and Controller : Frank Boettger.
Chief Engineer : Tom Salter.
Factory Superintendent, Wichita Plant : Arthur Sheldon.
Factory Manager, Hutchinson Plant : C. R. Larkin.

During 1944, the Cessna Aircraft Company continued the
production of the service version of its pre-war T-50 commercial
cabin monoplane, concentrating only on the UC-78 (JRC-1)
light personnel transport version. All AT-17 advanced training
models accepted for delivery after January 1, 1943, were re-
designated UC-78.

THE CESSNA BOBCAT.

U.S. Army Air Forces designations: AT-17 and UC-78.
U.S. Navy designation: JRC-1.
R.C.A.F. name: Crane.

The Bobcat is a military adaptation of the T-50 five-seat
commercial monoplane which appeared in 1940. It was first
built in military form in 1941 as an advanced trainer for the
R.C.A.F. as the Crane (two Jacobs engines) and for the U.S.
Army Air Forces as the AT-8 (two Lycoming R-680-9 engines).
Later the Jacobs power-plant was standardised for both models,
the U.S.A.A.F. version being re-designated AT-17. In 1942-3
the aircraft was adopted for light personnel transport use as
the C-78 (later UC-78) and JRC-1.

Both the AT-17 and UC-78 were fitted with Hamilton Standard
constant-speed airscrews, but subsequent series of both models
have had two-blade fixed-pitch wooden airscrews. Otherwise
only minor variations in equipment distinguish the various
series models.

With the reduction in U.S.A.A.F. training requirements,
all AT-17B and AT-17D trainers delivered after January 1,
1943, were re-designated UC-78B and UC-78C respectively.

TYPE.—Twin-engined Advanced Training monoplane (AT-17 Bobcat
or Crane) or light Personnel Transport (UC-78 or JRC-1).

The Cessna UC-78 Bobcat Light Personnel Transport two 225 h.p. Jacobs engines).

WINGS.—Low-wing cantilever monoplane. NACA 23012 wing-
section. Wing in one piece with laminated spruce spars, spruce
ribs, plywood-covered leading-edge and wing-tips, the whole
covered with fabric. Spruce compression members and stainless-
steel drag wire internal bracing. Trailing-edge flaps between
ailerons and fuselage. Flaps are of wooden construction and
electrically-operated. Statically and aerodynamically-balanced
ailerons of similar construction to flaps. Trim-tab in starboard
aileron adjustable on ground only.

FUSELAGE.—Rigidly-braced welded steel-tube structure covered with
fabric over a light wooden secondary framework.

TAIL UNIT.—Cantilever monoplane type. Tail-plane and fin of
wooden construction. Rudder and elevators have welded steel-
tube frames. The whole unit is covered with fabric. Both rudder
and elevators incorporate metal remotely-controllable balanced
type twin-tabs.

LANDING GEAR.—Retractable type. Two independent units,
incorporating Bendix air-oil shock-absorbers beneath each engine
nacelle. Wheels retracted backwards into engine nacelles by
single electric motor, roller chains and screw-jack arrangement.

Hydraulic expander-type wheel brakes.

POWER PLANT.—Two Jacobs R-755-9 seven-cylinder radial air-cooled
engines each rated at 225 h.p. at sea level and with 245 h.p. available
for take-off. Engine mountings are attached to welded steel
front nacelle truss through four vibration-absorber bushings.
NACA cowlings. Hamilton-Standard constant-speed or Hartzell
fixed-pitch wood airscrews. Fuel tanks in wing. Normal fuel
capacity 120 U.S. gallons (454 litres). Maximum capacity 160
U.S. gallons (605 litres).

ACCOMMODATION.—Enclosed cabin seating four or five. Front pair
of seats have dual controls.

DIMENSIONS.—Span 41 ft. 11 in. (12.8 m.), Length 32 ft. 9 in. (10 m.),
Height 9 ft. 11 in. (3.03 m.), Wing area 295 sq. ft. (27.5 sq. m.).

WEIGHTS.—Weight empty 4,050 lbs. (1,839 kg.), Weight loaded 5,700
lbs. (2,588 kg.).

PERFORMANCE.—Maximum speed at sea level 179 m.p.h. (286.4 km.h.),
Landing speed with flaps 65 m.p.h. (104 km.h.), Initial rate of
climb 1,525 ft./min. (460 m./min.), Service ceiling 15,000 ft. (4,575
m.), Cruising range 750 miles (1,200 km.).

CHANCE VOUGHT.

CHANCE VOUGHT AIRCRAFT DIVISION OF THE UNITED AIRCRAFT CORPORATION.

HEAD OFFICE AND WORKS : STRATFORD, CONNECTICUT.
General Manager : Rex B. Beisel.
Assistant General Manager : J. M. Barr.
Assistant General Manager—Assistant Secretary : James J.
Gafney.
Engineering Manager : Paul S. Baker.
Chief Engineer : James M. Shoemaker.
Factory Superintendent : J. W. Palmer.

In January, 1943, the Chance Vought and Sikorsky Aircraft
Divisions of the former Vought-Sikorsky Division of the United
Aircraft Corpn. were reconstituted as separate manufacturing
divisions to enable Chance Vought to devote all its energies to
the development and production of combat aircraft, while the
Sikorsky Division will work solely on the development of the
helicopter for both military and civil purposes.

During 1944-45 production of the Chance Vought Division was
devoted entirely to the F4U Corsair single-seat shipboard fighter
for the U.S. Navy and the Royal Navy. The Corsair was also in
production by the Goodyear Aircraft Corpn.

THE CHANCE VOUGHT CORSAIR

U.S. Navy designation : F4U (Also F3A when built by Brewster and
FG when built by Goodyear).
British name : Corsair.

The Prototype XF4U-1 was delivered to the U.S. Navy in
1940 and after protracted tests the Corsair was ordered in

quantity in the Autumn of 1941. The first production F4U-1
flew in June, 1942.

Up to the end of 1944 the U.S. Corsair had been used exclusively by the U.S. Navy and Marine Corps as a land-based fighter
in the Pacific, being first reported in action in the Solomon Islands
area on February 15, 1943. It has, however, been under constant
development and has now been revised to meet all U.S. deck-
landing requirements.

Since the first deliveries of the F4U-1 over 500 major and
2,500 minor engineering and production changes were made
in this aircraft, the version known as the F4U-1D being fitted
with clipped wing-tips, a twin-pylon rack under the fuselage
for carrying two 1,000 lb. bombs or auxiliary fuel tanks, a new
clear-view sliding hood, night-fighting and rocket-projectile
equipment, water injection, etc.

The latest version of the Corsair, the F4U-4, is fitted with a
two-stage turbo-supercharged R-2800-18 engine and incorporates several other detail changes.

The Corsair was also put into production by the Brewster
Aeronautical Corpn. and the Goodyear Aircraft Corpn. The
Brewster production programme failed to meet requirements
and the contract was cancelled by the U.S. Navy in July, 1944.

By mid-1945 over 10,000 Corsairs had been delivered, over
6,000 by Chance Vought, 3,000 by Goodyear and 735 by Brewster.

TYPE.—Single-seat Fighter.

WINGS.—Low-wing cantilever monoplane with inverted "gull"-type
roots and the outer wing-sections set at a coarse dihedral angle.

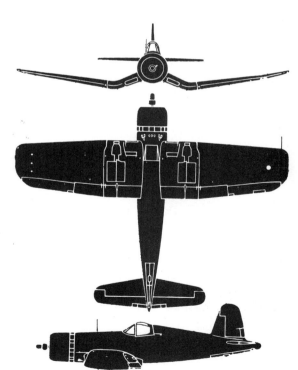

The Chance Vought Corsair Naval Fighter.

Single-spar all-metal construction with spot-welded smooth skin.
Outer wings fold upward for stowage in aircraft carriers.

FUSELAGE.—All-metal monocoque structure with smooth spot-welded
skin.

TAIL UNIT.—Cantilever monoplane type. All-metal monocoque
construction similar to that of wings. Balanced rudder.
Trimming-tabs in elevators.

LANDING GEAR.—Retractable type. Wheels are raised backwards
into underside of wings and apertures are closed by hinged doors
and strut fairings after wheels are retracted.

POWER PLANT.—One 2,000 h.p. Pratt & Whitney R-2800-8 double-row

The Chance Vought F4U-4 Corsair Single-seat Naval Fighter (Pratt & Whitney R-2800-18 engine).

radial air-cooled engine. Three-bladed Hamilton-Standard Hydromatic constant-speed airscrew. Water-injection system. Droppable long-range fuel-tank may be carried beneath fuselage.

ACCOMMODATION.—Enclosed pilot's cockpit over wing.

ARMAMENT.—Six 50 cal. machine-guns, all mounted in outer wings. Two 1,000 lb. bombs may be carried under the fuselage. Eight rockets may be installed, four under each wing.

DIMENSIONS.—Span 41 ft. (12.5 m.), Length 33 ft. 4 in. (10.15 m.).

WEIGHTS AND PERFORMANCE.—No data available.

THE CHANCE VOUGHT KINGFISHER.

U.S. Navy designation : OS2U (also OS2N when built by Naval Aircraft Factory).

Fleet Air Arm name : Kingfisher.

The XOS2U-1 protype was delivered to the U.S. Navy in 1938 and the first production OS2U-1's went into service in 1940. Two further and generally similar series, the OS2-U2 and OS2U-3 followed, the latter model also going into production at the Naval Aircraft Factory as the OS2N-1. The British Kingfisher I was a counterpart of the OS2U-3.

The Kingfisher is no longer in production, but it was still in service at the end of 1944.

TYPE.—Two-seat Observation-Scout seaplane or landplane.

WINGS.—Mid-wing cantilever monoplane. Centre-section integral with fuselage. Two tapering outer panels. Structure comprises a single-spar with a D-shaped torque-resisting metal leading-edge. Aft of spar wing is covered with fabric. The trailing-edge includes deflector-plate type flaps and drooping ailerons. Spoilers are built into the upper wing surfaces to provide lateral control when the ailerons are drooped.

FUSELAGE.—All-metal monocoque of riveted and spot-welded construction. The skin panels, reinforced by spot-welded stiffeners or channels, are riveted to two upper longerons and one keel member.

TAIL UNIT.—Cantilever monoplane type. Fixed surfaces are all-metal. Movable surfaces have fabric-covered metal frames. The movable surfaces are equipped with trimming-tabs controllable in flight by the pilot.

LANDING GEAR.—Split type. Each oleo shock-absorbing strut forms one leg of a tripod bolted to fuselage fittings. Duo-servo hydraulic brakes and high pressure tyres. Free swivelling lockable tail-wheel equipped with smooth-contour pneumatic tyre. The tail-wheel shock-strut is of the oleo-air cushion type. As a seaplane, a single main float is attached to the fuselage by two centre-line struts and bracing wires. Wing-tip floats are connected to the wing by five aluminium-alloy streamline struts.

The Chance Vought OS2U-3 Kingfisher Two-seat Observation Scout Seaplane (Pratt & Whitney R-985-AN-2 engine).

POWER PLANT.—One Pratt & Whitney Wasp-Junior R-985-AN-2 radial air-cooled engine rated at 400 h.p. at 5,000 ft. (1,525 m.) and at 450 h.p. for take-off. NACA cowling, adjustable trailing-edge gills, Hamilton-Standard constant-speed airscrew. Cartridge starter. The fuel tank is built integral with the centre-section of the wing and has a capacity of 144 U.S. gallons. The oil tank is of welded aluminium-alloy construction mounted in the engine compartment and has an oil capacity of 10 U.S. gallons. An oil-cooler, and automatic oil-temperature control-unit are included in the lubricating system.

ACCOMMODATION.—Pilot and gunner in enclosed cockpits. Complete flying, engine, and navigation instruments.

ARMAMENT.—One fixed 30-cal. synchronized machine-gun firing through the airscrew, 500 rounds of ammunition ; and one flexible machine-gun in rear cockpit mounted on a rotating and tilting seat, 600 rounds of ammunition. Bomb-racks in the outer panels, for carrying two 100-lb. bombs or eight 30-lb. bombs. Provision

for camera-gun, radio, smoke-tank and other equipment for special missions.

DIMENSIONS (Seaplane).—Span 35 ft. 10¼ in. (10.96 m.), Length 33 ft. 7⅞ in. (10.25 m.), Height 14 ft. 8 in. (4.47 m.), Wing area 261.9 sq. ft. (24.4 sq. m.).

WEIGHTS AND LOADINGS (Observation Seaplane).—Weight empty 3,335 lbs. (1,514 kg.), Weight loaded 4,980 lbs. (2,260.8 kg.), Wing loading 19.0 lbs./sq. ft. (92.6 kg./sq. m.), Power loading 12.45 lbs./h.p. (5.63 kg./h.p.).

PERFORMANCE (Observation Seaplane).—Maximum speed at 5,000 ft. (1,525 m.) 171 m.p.h. (275 km.h.), Cruising speed at 75% power at 6,000 ft. (1,830 m.) 152 m.p.h. (244.7 km.h.), Landing speed 55 m.p.h. (88.5 km.h.), Rate of climb at 4,000 ft. (1,220 m.) 960 ft./min. (292.8 m./min.), Service ceiling 18,200 ft. (5,550 m.), Cruising range at 6,000 ft. (1,830 m.) at 75% power 908 miles (1,460 km.).

COLGATE.

COLGATE AIRCRAFT CORPORATION.

HEAD OFFICE AND WORKS : AMITYVILLE, LONG ISLAND, N.Y.
President and General Manager : Gilbert Colgate.
Secretary and Treasurer : E. H. Fulton.

The Colgate Aircraft Corpn. is the successor to the Spencer-Larsen Aircraft Corpn. which was formed to develop an amphibian flying-boat with several novel features.

During 1941 the company continued with the development work on the Colgate-Larsen CL-15 amphibian and in addition undertook sub-contract work on behalf of other aircraft companies

in connection with the Air Defence Programme.

After America's entry into the War all development work was suspended and the Company devoted itself solely to work of national importance.

COMMONWEALTH.

COMMONWEALTH AIRCRAFT, INC.

HEAD OFFICE AND WORKS : KANSAS CITY, KANSAS
President and General Manager : Charles H. Dolan.

Commonwealth Aircraft, Inc., came into being in October, 1942, when Rearwin Aircraft & Engines Inc., was acquired by New York interests headed by Mr. Charles H. Dolan, and was reconstituted under its new name.

The original Rearwin Company was formed in May, 1929 and was operated as a partnership by R. A. Rearwin, Royce S. Rearwin and Kenneth R. Rearwin. In December, 1937, Rearwin Airplanes bought the assets, including patents, machinery, fixtures, patterns, etc., of the Le Blond Aircraft Corpn. of Cincinnati, Ohio, and the name of the concern was changed to Rearwin Aircraft & Engines, Inc. The products of the Rearwin and Le Blond Companies and of Rearwin Aircraft & Engines, Inc., have been fully described in earlier editions of this Annual.

During 1944 Commonwealth Aircraft, Inc., was engaged in the production of Waco troop-carrying gliders for the U.S. Army Air Forces.

In 1945 Commonwealth Aircraft, Inc. acquired the manufacturing rights of the Trimmer three-seat twin-engined Amphibian (see under "Allied"). It is also engaged on the development of several other post-war aircraft, one of which will be an enlarged version of the Trimmer with increased power and capacity.

CONSOLIDATED VULTEE.

THE CONSOLIDATED VULTEE AIRCRAFT CORPORATION.

HEAD OFFICE : SAN DIEGO, CAL.

WORKS : SAN DIEGO AND VULTEE FIELD, CAL.; FORTH WORTH TEX.; NASHVILLE, TENN.; WAYNE, MICH.; NEW ORLEANS, LA.; MIAMI, FLA.; ALLENTOWN, PA.

MODIFICATION CENTERS : TUCSON, ARIZ.; ELIZABETH CITY, N.C. AND LOUISVILLE, KY.

President : Harry Woodhead.
Executive Vice-President : I. M. Laddon.
Vice-President : C. T. Leigh.
Vice-President in Charge of Finance : F. A. Callery.
Secretary and Treasurer : W. M. Shanahan.

The Consolidated Vultee Aircraft Corpn. was formed in March, 1943, by the merging of the Consolidated Aircraft Corpn. and Vultee Aircraft, Inc.

The first step towards the merger occurred in December, 1941, when Vultee Aircraft, Inc. acquired 34 per cent of the common stock of the Consolidated Aircraft Corpn. and although the final merger did not take place until March, 1943, the two concerns were linked closely in management by January, 1942.

The Consolidated Vultee Aircraft Corpn. has manufactured a wide variety of military aircraft ranging from the four-engined Dominator B-32, Liberator B-24 and Liberator Express C-87 landplanes, the Catalina PBY twin-engined flying-boat down to the Valiant single-engined Basic Trainer, and the Sentinel light liaison monoplane.

Consolidated Vultee co-operated with the U.S. Government in facilitating the production of its aircraft by other companies. At the request of the Army authorities it made its designs available to the Ford Motor Company, the Douglas Aircraft Company and North American Aviation, Inc., all of which were engaged in the manufacture and assembly of Liberator bombers to augment the production in the Company's own plants.

The Catalina was re-designed by the Naval Aircraft Factory in a slightly modified form as the PBN-1 and, during 1944, it was also in production by the Boeing Aircraft of Canada, Ltd. and Canadian Vickers, Ltd.

The Consolidated Vultee B-32 Dominator Heavy Bomber (four Wright R-3350-23 engines).

In 1943 the corporation acquired the resources of the Stout Research Division in Dearborn, Mich., where projects for post-war development are in progress.

THE CONSOLIDATED VULTEE MODEL 33 DOMINATOR.

U.S. Army Air Forces designation : B-32.

The B-32 was the last U.S. heavy bomber to go into action in the war, aircraft of this type flying a score or so of sorties before Japan surrendered.

Although the B-32 was designed to the same specification as the B-29 Super-fortress and the prototypes of both aircraft were flying at the same time, considerably more development was necessary with the B-32. Pressurisation and remote control

of gun turrets were abandoned and the twin-ruddered B-24 type tail used in the three XB-24 prototypes was replaced by the gigantic single fin and rudder shown in the accompanying illustrations.

With the end of the war production of the B-32, which was undertaken as possible insurance against tactical or production failure of the B-29, was cancelled.

The power-plant consisted of four Wright R-3350-23 engines driving four-blade Curtiss Electric reversible-pitch airscrews.

The B-32 carried a normal crew of eight and was provided with an armament of ten 50 cal. guns in five turrets. The tandem bomb-bays had a maximum capacity for 20,000 lb. (9,080 kg.) of bombs.

The Consolidated Vultee B-32 Dominator.

DIMENSIONS.—Span 135 ft. (41.2 m.), Length 83 ft. 1 in. (25.3 m.), Height 32 ft. 2 in. (9.8 m.), Wing area 1,422 sq. ft. (132 sq. m.).
WEIGHTS.—Weight empty 60,272 lbs. (27,365 kg.), Weight loaded 100,000 lbs. (45,400 kg.), Maximum overloaded weight 120,000 lbs. (54,480 kg.).
PERFORMANCE.—Maximum speed over 360 m.p.h. (576 km.h.) at 25,000 ft. (7,625 m.), Ceiling over 35,000 ft. (10,680 m.), Range with maximum bomb load 800 miles (1,280 km.), Maximum range 3,800 miles (6,080 km.).

THE CONSOLIDATED VULTEE MODEL 32 LIBERATOR.
U.S. Army Air Forces designations : B-24, TB-24, C-109, F-7.
U.S. Navy designation : PB4Y.
British name : Liberator.

The contract for the construction of the first Model 32 was signed with the U.S. Army on March 30, 1939. The prototype XB-24 flew nine months later, on December 29, 1939. It was put into production in the Autumn of 1940, for the U.S., French and British Governments, and when France fell the French contracts were taken over by the British authorities. Development of the B-24 progressed through several stages before it went into large scale use in the U.S. Army Air Forces, the early production Liberators being mainly delivered under British contracts.

The Liberator was finally withdrawn from production on May 31, 1945, after a total of over 19,000 had been built, over 10,000 by Consolidated Vultee at San Diego and Fort Worth, and a further 9,000 by Ford, Douglas and North American.

B-24 (LB-30A). The first twenty-six Liberators off the production lines at San Diego were released to the British Government and delivered by air to Great Britain. They were found to be unsuitable for European combat conditions and were converted into unarmed transports for use on the trans-Atlantic Return Ferry service.

B-24A (Liberator I). As with the B-24, fitted with four Pratt & Whitney R-1830-33 engines with two-speed superchargers and driving Hamilton Standard Hydromatic full-feathering airscrews. The B-24A had an armament of six 50 cal. and two 30 cal. flexible guns, the latter in the tail position. The Liberator I was put into service with R.A.F. Coastal Command and was armed with four 20 m/m. cannon in a fairing beneath the forward fuselage, two .303 in. waist guns, one .303 in. tunnel gun and two .303 in. tail guns.

Liberator II (LB-30). Had no B-24 counterpart (LB-30 designation signifies Liberator built to British specifications. Four Pratt & Whitney R-1830-S3C4G engines with two-speed superchargers and driving Curtiss Electric full-feathering airscrews. Armed with eleven .303 in. guns, eight in two Boulton

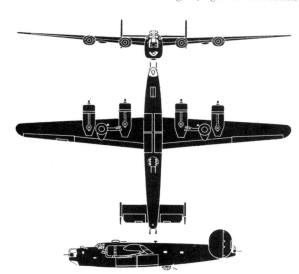

The Consolidated Vultee B-24J Liberator.

Paul power turrets, one dorsal and one tail, one in the nose and two in waist positions.

XB-24B. The first B-24 to be fitted with turbo-supercharged engines, self-sealing tanks, armour, and other modern refinements.

B-24C. Four Pratt & Whitney R-1830-41 engines with exhaust-driven turbo-superchargers. Armament augmented to include two power-driven turrets, one dorsal and one tail, each fitted with two 50 cal. guns. In addition, there was one 50 cal. nose gun and two similar guns in waist positions.

B-24D (PB4Y-1 and Liberator B.III and G.R.V.). Four Pratt & Whitney R-1830-43 engines. Armament further increased by the addition of two further nose guns and one tunnel gun, making a total of ten 50 cal. guns. Fuel capacity increased by the addition of auxiliary self-sealing fuel cells in the outer wings and there was provision for long-range tanks in the bomb-bay. The first model to be equipped to carry two 4,000 lb. bombs on external racks, one under each inner wing. The Liberator G.R.V. was used as a long-range general reconnaissance type by R.A.F. Coastal Command. Fuel capacity was increased at the expense of armour and tank protection. Armament consisted of one .303 in. or 50 cal. gun in the nose, two 50 cal. guns in the upper turret, four .303 in. or two 50 cal. guns in waist positions and four .303 in. guns in a Boulton Paul tail turret. Bombs or depth charges 5,400 lbs.

B-24E (Liberator IV). Similar to B-24D except for minor equipment details. Built by Consolidated (Forth Worth), Ford (Willow Run) and Douglas (Tulsa).

B-24F. An experimental version of the B-24E fitted with exhaust-heated surface anti-icing equipment on wings and tail surfaces.

B-24G, B-24H and B-24J (PB4Y-1 and Liberator B.VI and G.R.VI). Similar except for details of equipment and minor differences associated with different manufacturing methods. B-24G built by North American (Dallas). B-24H built by Consolidated (Forth Worth), Ford (Willow Run) and Douglas (Tulsa). B-24J built by Consolidated (San Diego and Fort Worth), Ford, Douglas and North American (Dallas). Four Pratt & Whitney R-1830-43 or 65 engines. Armament further improved to include four two-gun turrets, in nose and tail and above and below the fuselage (details below). Later models of the B-24J were fitted with exhaust-heated anti-icing equipment. The Liberator G.R.VI was used as a long-range general reconnaissance type by R.A.F. Coastal Command. Armament consisted of six 50 cal. guns, two each in nose and dorsal turrets and in waist positions, and four .303 in. guns in a Boulton Paul tail turret. Bombs or depth charges 4,500 lbs. (2,045 kg.).

XB-24K. The first Liberator to be fitted with a single fin and rudder. An experimental model only.

B-24L. Similar to the B-24J but fitted with a new tail turret with two manually-operated 50 cal. guns. The two guns had a wider field of fire and the new turret, which was designed by the Consolidated Vultee Modification Center at Tucson, permitted a saving of 200 lbs. (91 kg.) in weight.

B-24M. Same as the B-24L except fitted with a new Motor Products two-gun power-operated tail turret. A B-24M was the 6,725th and last Liberator built by Consolidated Vultee at San Diego.

B-24N. The first production single-tail Liberator. Fitted with new nose and tail gun mountings. Only a few were built before the Liberator was withdrawn from production on May 31, 1945.

CB-24. Numbers of B-24 bombers withdrawn from operational flying in the European Theatre of Operations were stripped of all armament and adapted to various duties, including utility transport, etc. Painted in distinctive colours and patterns, they were also used as Group Identity. Aircraft to facilitate the assembly of large numbers of bombers into their battle

The Consolidated Vultee B-24J Liberator Long-range Bomber (four Pratt & Whitney R-1830-65 engines).

formations through and above overcast weather. All these carried the designation CB-24.

TB-24 (formerly AT-22). A conversion of the B-24D for specialised advanced training duties. All bombing equipment and armament removed and six stations provided in the fuselage for the instruction of air engineers in power-plant operation, essentially for such aircraft as the Boeing B-29 and the Consolidated Vultee B-32, which are the first large combat aircraft in the U.S.A.A.F. to have separate completely-equipped engineer's stations.

C-109. A conversion of the B-24 into a fuel-carrying aircraft. The first version, modified by the U.S.A.A.F., had metal tanks in the nose, above the bomb-bay and in the bomb-bay holding a total of 2,900 U.S. gallons. Standard fuel transfer system for loading and unloading through single hose union in side of fuselage. Inert gas injected into tanks as fuel pumped out to eliminate danger of explosion. Developed for transporting fuel from India to China to supply the needs of the B-29's operating therefrom. Later version, modified by the Glenn L. Martin Company, fitted with collapsible Mareng fuel cells.

F-7. A long-range photographic reconnaissance version of the Liberator bomber. The first conversion was made at the Northwest Airlines Modification Center at St. Paul, Minn., in the Autumn of 1943. Bomb racks and other structural obstructions in the fuselage were removed and extra fuel tanks installed in the front section of the bomb-bay to give increased range. The crawl deck over the former bomb compartment was raised to permit head clearance and an upholstered cabin built in aft of the fuel tanks and provided with five windows for the cameras. Photographic equipment of eleven cameras includes a tri-metrogon camera which takes three photographs simultaneously, one vertically downward and two at angles of 30 degrees from the horizontal, to cover an area of 40 square miles from a height of 20,000 ft. The standard Liberator armour and armament of ten 50 cal. machine-guns are retained.

The description below applies specifically to the B-24J Liberator bomber.

TYPE.—Four-engined Long-range Bomber.
WINGS.—High-wing cantilever monoplane. Davis wing of high aspect ratio and constant taper from roots to tips. Wing in three sections comprising centre-section and two outer sections with detachable tips. All-metal two-spar structure. Spars have angle-section booms and reinforced sheet webs. Pressed or built-up former ribs. Spanwise stringers support the flush-riveted smooth metal skin. Statically-balanced ailerons have metal frames and fabric covering. Hydraulically-operated Fowler flaps between ailerons and fuselage.
FUSELAGE.—Aluminium-alloy monocoque structure. Five main bulkheads and intermediate secondary frames, longitudinal Z-section stringers, and a smooth stressed Alclad skin.
TAIL UNIT.—Cantilever monoplane type with twin fins and rudders. Light-alloy framework, the fixed surfaces being metal-covered. The rudders have metal leading-edges, the remainder being covered with fabric. The elevators are fabric-covered.
LANDING GEAR.—Retractable tricycle type. Main wheels retract outwards into wells in the underside of the wings just inboard of the outer engine nacelles. Nose wheel retracts backwards into the fuselage. Hydraulic retracting mechanism and wheel-brakes.
POWER PLANT.—Four 1,200 h.p. Pratt & Whitney Twin-Wasp R-1830-65 fourteen-cylinder two-row radial air-cooled engines with single-stage engine-driven superchargers and exhaust-driven turbo-superchargers. Hamilton-Standard Hydromatic constant-speed full-feathering airscrews 11 ft. 7 in. (3.54 m.) diameter. Twelve self-sealing fuel cells in centre-section between spars, and three auxiliary self-sealing fuel cells in each outer wing outboard of the wheel wells. Two further long-range ferrying tanks may be installed in the bomb-bay. Normal fuel capacity : 2,344 U.S. gallons. Each engine has independent oil system. Hopper type self-sealing oil tank (32.9 U.S. gallons) in each engine nacelle.
ACCOMMODATION.—Crew of ten. Power-driven turret in nose with bombardier's prone position below. Aft of the navigator's compartment, with astro-dome in roof, is the pilot's compartment, seating two side-by-side with dual controls. Then follows the

The Consolidated Vultee B-24J Liberator Long-range Bomber (four Pratt & Whitney R-1830-43 engines).

radio operator's compartment with turret in roof. A cat-walk through the bomb-bay leads to the after fuselage, which contains the lower retractable "ball" turret, two side gun positions and the tail turret. All crew positions are armoured.

ARMAMENT AND EQUIPMENT.—Ten 0.5 in. machine-guns. One Consolidated or Emerson electrically-operated two-gun turret in nose. One Martin two-gun electrically-operated dorsal turret in the roof of the radio operator's compartment. One retractable Briggs-Sperry two-gun electrically-operated "ball" turret aft of the bomb-bay. Two "waist" guns on manually-operated mountings firing through side ports, one on each side of the fuselage midway between wings and tail. One Consolidated or Motor Products two-gun electrically-operated turret in extreme tail. Tail turret has ammunition feed tracks from magazines amidships. Tandem bomb-bays in fuselage beneath wings, each containing two vertical racks accommodating bombs of from 100 to 1,600 lbs. Special carriers may be installed for four 2,000 lb. bombs. Maximum internal bomb load : 8,000 lbs. Bomb doors of "roll-top desk" type are hydraulically operated, the doors sliding outwards and upwards from the centre-line. Emergency hand operation is provided. Two 4,000 lb. bombs may be carried on external racks, one under each inner wing. Equipment includes two inflatable dinghies, high-pressure oxygen system, full radio and intercommunication equipment, automatic pilot, cameras in rear fuselage, sound-proofing and heating of bombardier's position and flight deck forward of wings, etc. Heating system provides warm-air sprays for pilot's windscreen and bombardier's sighting panel.

DIMENSIONS.—Span 110 ft. (33.5 m.), Length 67 ft. 2 in. (20.5 m.), Height 17 ft. 7½ in. (5.4 m.), Wing area 1,048 sq. ft. (97.4 sq. m.).

WEIGHT LOADED.—Over 60,000 lbs. (27,240 kg.).

PERFORMANCE.—Maximum speed 297 m.p.h. (475.2 km.h.) at 25,000 ft. (7,625 m.), Normal range 1,540 miles (2,465 km.) at 237 m.p.h. (379 km.h.) at 25,000 ft. (7,625 m.) with normal fuel and maximum internal bomb load, Service ceiling 28,000 ft. (8,540 m.).

THE CONSOLIDATED VULTEE MODEL 32 LIBERATOR TRANSPORT.

U.S. Army Air Forces designation : C-87.
U.S. Navy designation : RY.
British Name : Liberator.

The C-87 Liberator is a military transport version of the B-24 and is in service in both the U.S. Army Air Forces and the U.S. Navy, as well as in the R.A.F.

During the Battle of Java the B-24, because of its capacious fuselage, was used to carry personnel and cargo in the evacuation to Australia. The adaptability of the B-24 to this work and the growing need for air transport to the spreading theatres of war led the U.S. Army to order Consolidated to produce a special transport version of the bomber.

The bomb-bay and rear fuselage were replaced by a passenger or freight compartment, the nose and tail gun positions were closed in and a 6 ft. square door was cut in the rear fuselage for loading purposes. Production of the C-87 Liberator Express was begun at Fort Worth in April, 1942, and moved to San Diego in 1944.

There are also certain freight and passenger-carrying versions of the Liberator bomber which have been converted in Great Britain and Canada for use by R.A.F. Transport Command and the British Overseas Airways Corporation. These have no equivalents in the C-87 Series.

The following are the principal versions of the standard U.S. Liberator Express :—

C-87 (RY-2 and Liberator C.VII). General transport to carry cargo, personnel and their equipment, or both. Tie-down

The Consolidated Vultee B-24N Liberator Long-range Bomber (four Pratt & Whitney R-1830-75 engines).

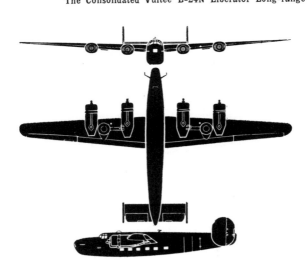

The Consolidated Vultee C-87 Liberator Transport.

fittings in the floor and sides of the main compartment and 20 easily-removable seats. Originally fitted with one 50 cal. tail gun, but later replaced by a faired tail-cone.

C-87A (RY-1). De luxe passenger transport with seats for 16 passengers by day or five folding berths and four single seats by night. There is a galley aft. Only a few were so equipped.

C-87B. This was an armed version of the C-87. It was fitted with two fixed nose guns fired by the pilot, a top turret and a ventral rear-firing tunnel gun. All crew positions were armoured. Only a few were so equipped.

C-87C (RY-3 and Liberator C.IX). A modified version of the Liberator Express with single fin and rudder, dihedral tailplane and a lengthened forward fuselage.

TYPE.—Four-engined military transport.

WINGS, FUSELAGE, TAIL UNIT AND LANDING GEAR.—Same as B-24.

POWER PLANT.—Four 1,200 h.p. Pratt & Whitney R-1830-43 fourteen-cylinder radial air-cooled engines with General Electric exhaust-driven turbo superchargers. Hamilton-Standard Hydromatic airscrews 11 ft. 7 in. (3.54 m.) diameter. Fuel tanks in wings, either self-sealing or non-self-sealing cells or integral with structure. Total fuel capacity : 2,910 U.S. (2,425 Imp.) gallons.

ACCOMMODATION.—Crew of four—pilot, co-pilot, navigator and radio-operator, with provision for fifth crew member—on flight deck above nose-wheel well. Nose compartment used for baggage and equipment stowage, and can also accommodate two extra passengers. Main compartment with large loading door, 70 × 70 inches (1.8 × 1.8 m.) on port side aft and smaller hatch opposite. Dimensions of main compartment : length 33 ft. (10 m.), width 4 ft. (1.22 m.) and maximum height 8 ft. (2.44 m.). Alternative fittings and furnishings as detailed above. Rear compartment includes lavatory and is used for further equipment stowage. Heating and ventilation. Oxygen for crew and occupants of main compartment. Life-rafts stowed in top and fuselage, with two additional rafts in main compartment. For range of 1,000 miles (1,600 km.) average cargo capacity of 10,000 lbs. (4,540 kg.) or on trans-ocean routes 6,000 lbs. (2,725 kg.).

DIMENSIONS.—Span 110 ft. (33.55 m.), Length 66 ft. 4 in. (20.23 m.), Height 17 ft. 11 in. (5.47 m.).

WEIGHTS.—Weight empty 30,645 lbs. (13,913 kg.), Normal loaded weight 56,000 lbs. (25,424 kg.).

PERFORMANCE.—Maximum speed 300 m.p.h. (480 km.h.) at 25,000 ft. (7,625 m.), Climb to 20,000 ft. (6,100 m.) 60 min., Service ceiling 30,000 ft. (9,150 m.), Normal range (60% power) 1,400 miles (2,240 km.) at 215 m.p.h. (344 km.h.) at 10,000 ft. (3,050 m.), Maximum range 3,300 miles (5,280 km.) at 188 m.p.h. (300 km.h.) at 10,000 ft. (3,050 m.).

THE CONSOLIDATED VULTEE MODEL 37.

The Model 37 is a six-engined landplane which exists in three projected forms, as the XB-36, a heavy bomber ; as the C-99, the transport conversion of the XB-36 with a new fuselage ; and as a civil transport. Pan American World Airways has placed an order for fifteen of the last-mentioned type for construction after wartime restrictions have been removed.

The Model 37 is a mid-wing cantilever monoplane of all-metal construction. To take advantage of laminar air flow the six 3,000 h.p. Pratt & Whitney R-4360 twenty-eight-cylinder four-row radial turbo-supercharged engines will be mounted on the trailing-edge and drive pusher airscrews.

The fuselage of the civil transport version ordered by Pan American World Airways will be of the two-deck type and accommodation will be provided for 204 passengers, together

The Consolidated Vultee C-87 Liberator Transport (four Pratt & Whitney R-1830-43 engines).

The Consolidated Vultee RY-3 Transport.

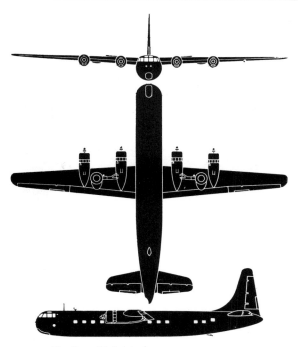

The Consolidated Vultee Model 39 Transport.

The Consolidated Vultee RY-3 Liberator Naval Transport (four Pratt & Whitney R-1830-94 engines).

with 15,300 lbs. (6,950 kg.) of baggage, freight and mail. The cabins will be conditioned for operation at a height of 30,000 ft. (9,150 m.). The tail-unit is of the single fin and rudder type and both wings and tail surfaces will be protected by a thermal anti-icing system.

DIMENSIONS.—Span 230 ft. (70.15 m.), Length 182 ft. (55.5 m.).
WEIGHTS.—Payload 50,000 lbs. (22,700 kg.), Estimated loaded weight 320,000 lbs. (145,280 kg.).
PERFORMANCE (Estimated).—Cruising speed 310 to 342 m.p.h. (496 to 547 km.h.) according to altitude and power output, Range 4,200 miles (6,720 km.).

THE CONSOLIDATED VULTEE MODEL 39.
U.S. Navy designation : R2Y-1.

The Model 39 was evolved by applying to a new fuselage the wings, power-plant and landing-gear of the Model 32 Liberator. The tail-unit is similar to that of the PB4Y-2 Privateer.

The Model 39 was intended for long-range operations and could carry 48 passengers with baggage and 1,200 lbs. (545 kg.) of mail on flights up to 2,500 miles (4,000 km.). A cargo version would be able to carry a load of 12,000 lbs. (5,450 kg.).

The prototype was built as a military aeroplane but it has since been converted for civil use and has been loaned to American Airlines, Inc. for experimental air-freight operations. It will not be reproduced.

DIMENSIONS.—Span 110 ft. (33.55 m.), Length 90 ft. (27.45 m.)
WEIGHTS.—Normal loaded weight 56,000 lbs. (24,960 kg.), Maximum loaded weight 62,000-64,000 lbs. (28,150-29,100 kg.).
PERFORMANCE.—Normal cruising speed 240 m.p.h. (384 km.h.) at 60% power, Stalling speed 88 m.p.h. (141 km.h.), Maximum range 4,000 miles (6,400 km.) at 200 m.p.h. (320 km.h.).

THE CONSOLIDATED VULTEE PRIVATEER.
U.S. Navy designation : PB4Y-2.

The PB4Y-2 is a long-range oversea Bomber-Reconnaissance development of the PB4Y-1 Liberator. The original contract for the PB4Y-2 was placed with the Consolidated Vultee Corpn. by the U.S. Navy in May, 1943, and work on three prototypes

The Consolidated Vultee Model 39 Transport (four Pratt & Whitney R-1830-94 engines).

was begun almost immediately. Four months later, on September 20, the first prototype flew, followed on October 30 and December 15 by the second and third respectively.

The PB4Y-2 uses the same Davis wing and landing-gear as the Liberator. Otherwise it is a new design embodying most of the structural features of its predecessor.

The fuselage forward of the wings has been lengthened by 7 ft. (2.135 m.) and the armament has been rearranged to include a Consolidated nose-turret, two Martin dorsal turrets, one forward and one aft of the wings, a Consolidated tail-turret and

two Erco "blister" type waist turrets, one on each side of the fuselage midway between the wings and tail. Each turret is armed with two 50 cal. Browning machine-guns. The fuselage bomb-bay is similar to that of the Liberator and can accommodate on normal missions 6,000 lbs. (2,725 kg.) of bombs or depth charges.

The tail-unit is of the single rudder type with the tailplane set at a slight dihedral angle. The fixed surfaces are of stressed-skin construction, the movable surfaces having metal frames and fabric covering.

The Consolidated Vultee PB4Y-2 Privateer.

The Consolidated Vultee PB4Y-2 Privateer (four Pratt & Whitney R-1830-94 engines).

The Consolidated Vultee PBY-5 Catalina Patrol Bomber Flying-boat (two Pratt & Whitney R-1830-92 engines).

The power-plant consists of four 1,200 h.p. Pratt & Whitney R-1830-94 fourteen-cylinder radials, each driving a three-blade Hamilton Standard Hydromatic airscrew with slinger-ring anti-icing equipment. The engines are enclosed in oval cowlings with the larger diameter vertical instead of horizontal as in the Liberator.

Accommodation is provided for a crew of eleven, comprising pilot and co-pilot, navigator, bombardier, five gunners and two radio-operators. The Convair hot-air system employing exhaust heat exchangers is used for cabin heating and for heated-surface de-icing for wings and tail-unit.

DIMENSIONS.—Span 110 ft. (33.5 m.), Length 74 ft. (22.6 m.), Height 26 ft. (7.9 m.), Wing area 1,048 sq. ft. (97.4 sq. m.).

WEIGHT LOADED.—62,000-65,000 lbs. (28,250-29,510 kg.).

PERFORMANCE.—Maximum speed over 250 m.p.h. (400 km.h.), Maximum range over 3,000 miles (4,800 km.).

THE CONSOLIDATED VULTEE MODEL 28 CATALINA.
U.S. Navy designation : PBY.
R.A.F. name: Catalina.

The prototype XPBY-1 made its first flight in the Spring of 1935 and the type has been in continuous service in the U.S. Navy since 1936. The PBY-5 went into service in 1939-40 and this was the model which was adopted by the R.A.F. and named the Catalina. This name was recognised by the U.S. Navy in 1941.

Apart from its primary rôle as a patrol bomber, the Catalina has been used as a torpedo-carrier, as a night bomber, as a convoy protection and anti-submarine weapon, for long-range reconnaissance and air/sea rescue duties, and as a glider-tug. The U.S. Navy has also used the Catalina as a mail and freight transport. On an empty weight of 17,500 lbs. (7,945 kg.) the modified Catalina has a cargo capacity of up to 15,000 lbs. (6,810 kg.).

The Catalina has also been built by the Naval Aircraft Factory (PBN-1), Boeing Aircraft of Canada, Ltd. (PB2B-1) and by Canadian Vickers, Ltd. (PBV-1).

The last version built by Consolidated Vultee—the PBY-6A —embodied the modifications incorporated in the PBN-1 (see under "Naval Aircraft Factory").

TYPE.—Twin-engined Long-range Patrol-Bomber flying-boat.

WINGS.—Semi-cantilever high-wing monoplane. Wing in three sections, the centre-section supported above the hull by a streamline superstructure and braced by two pairs of parallel streamline struts to the sides of the hull. Wing structure is of the beam bulkhead and stressed-skin type, the skin being reinforced with "Z" section extruded stiffeners. The trailing-edge section consists of aluminium alloy ribs cantilevered from the main beam and covered with fabric. Aluminium-alloy-framed balanced ailerons covered with fabric.

HULL.—Two-step semi-circular topped hull, of all-metal construction. Aluminium-alloy bulkheads, framing stringers and skin. All-metal retractable wing-tip floats. When the floats are retracted they form tips to the wings and the float struts and bracing structure are recessed flush with the lower surface of the wings. Electrical and mechanically-operated retracting mechanism. Automatic locks and warning lights.

TAIL UNIT.—Monoplane cantilever type. Lower fin built integral with the hull. Tail-plane and upper section of fin covered with smooth metal sheet reinforced with extruded sections. Elevators and rudder are aluminium-alloy structures with fabric covering. Trimming-tabs in elevators and rudder.

POWER PLANT.—Two 1,200 h.p. Pratt & Whitney Twin-Wasp R-1830-92 radial air-cooled engines on welded steel-tube mountings in the leading-edge of the centre-section. NACA cowling. Hamilton-Standard Hydromatic constant-speed airscrews. Protected fuel tanks (1,750 U.S. gallons) in centre-section.

ACCOMMODATION.—Bow compartment for mooring gear, etc. Enclosed pilot's compartment seating two side-by-side with dual controls. Engineer's station in hull below centre-section. Two large

The Consolidated Vultee PBY-5A Catalina Amphibian (two Pratt & Whitney R-1830-92 engines).

The Consolidated Vultee PB2Y-3R Naval Transport (four Pratt & Whitney R-1830-92 engines).

transparent gun-blisters each with one Browning gun on the sides of the hull aft of the wings. Details of military equipment not available.

DIMENSIONS.—Span 104 ft. (31.72 m.), Length 63 ft. 10 in. (19.52 m.), Height 18 ft. 10 in. (5.65 m.), Wing area 1,400 sq. ft. (130 sq. m.).

WEIGHTS AND LOADINGS.—Weight empty 17,564 lbs. (7,974 kg.), Weight loaded 34,000 lbs. (15,436 kg.), Wing loading 24.3 lbs./sq. ft. (118.5 kg./sq. m.), Power loading 14.1 lbs./h.p. (6.4 kg./h.p.).

PERFORMANCE.—Maximum speed at 7,500 ft. (2,290 m.) 196 m.p.h. (314 km.h.), Cruising speed 130 m.p.h. (208 km.h.) at 10,000 ft. (3,050 m.), Stalling speed at sea level 76 m.p.h. (112 km.h.), Climb to 5,000 ft. (1,525 m.) 4.5 mins., Climb to 15,000 ft. (4,755 m.) 16 mins., Service ceiling 18,200 ft. (5,550 m.), Maximum range (1,570 U.S. gallons of fuel) at critical altitude 3,100 miles (4,960 km.).

THE CONSOLIDATED VULTEE MODEL 28-5A CATALINA AMPHIBIAN.
U.S. Navy designation: PBY-5A.
U.S. Army Air Forces designation: OA-10.
R.A.F. name: Catalina III.
R.C.A.F. name: Canso.

The Model 28-5A is an amphibian version of the previously-described flying-boat.

It is fitted with a tricycle landing gear, with single wheel under the nose and two aft. The side wheels and supporting mechanism, complete with oleo shock-absorbers, retract into wells in the sides of the hull. The nose wheel in the bow is completely enclosed in the retracted position by automatically-operated hatches.

All three wheels are operated by a central hydraulic power drive and the operations are carried out in sequence automatically. A single lever controls both the extension and retraction of the landing gear. Hydraulic power is derived from the main power plant or from an auxiliary engine, but the landing-gear can be manually-operated if necessary.

PERFORMANCE.—Same as for Catalina flying boat except, Cruising speed 125 m.p.h. (200 km.h.) at 10,000 ft. (3,050 m.), Service ceiling 15,800 ft. (4,820 m.), Range 2,520 miles (4,030 km.).

THE CONSOLIDATED VULTEE MODEL 29 CORONADO.
U.S. Navy designation : PB2Y-3 and 5 and PB2Y-3R.

The XPB2Y-1 prototype of the Coronado, ordered in 1936, was delivered to the U.S. Navy in August, 1938. After service trials it served for some time as Flagship of Aircraft, Scouting Force, U.S. Navy. The first PB2Y-2, the production development of the XPB2Y-1, went into service in January, 1941. The PB2Y-3 was ordered in quantity in 1941 and remained in production until 1944.

Following on the successful power-plant modification in the PB2Y-3R (see below), the PB2Y-3 was submitted to the same change, the Patrol-Bomber conversion with R-1830-92 engines being designated the PB2Y-5.

The PB2Y-5H is fitted as a naval ambulance with accommodation for 25 stretcher cases.

Many Coronado flying-boats were converted into transports under the designation PB2Y-3R. Conversion was undertaken by the Rohr Aircraft Corpn. of Chula Vista, Cal.

In the process of conversion all military equipment has been removed and the nose and tail turret positions faired over. All control cables within the hull have been re-routed and the interior accommodation completely redesigned.

On C deck over the crew's quarters, formerly used as stowage for life-rafts, etc., have been installed a galley, auxiliary power-plant, main cabin heater and emergency water-still. Below the flight deck is the forward sound-proofed sleeping compartment equipped with bunks which let down to form seats for day use.

The main cabin and rear portion of the hull has been provided with a smooth wood and duralumin floor (stepped-up towards the tail) and cargo tie-down rings have been fitted in the floor and sides of the hull. A large cargo loading hatch replaces the former small entrance door beneath the wing and hoisting eyes have been fitted both inside and outside the hull. All seats in the main cabin and tail space are easily removable.

The PB2Y-3R can be used for either passenger or cargo transport. Without cargo there is accommodation for a crew of five and 44 passengers. With 8,600 lbs. (3,905 kg.) of cargo, 24 passengers may be carried. With no passengers 16,000 lbs. (7,264 kg.) of cargo can be transported on a range of 1,000 miles (1,600 km.).

The former standard Coronado power-plant units (Pratt & Whitney R-1830-88 engines with two-speed superchargers) have been replaced by modified Catalina units (Pratt & Whitney R-1830-92 single-stage low-altitude engines) complete with accessories and oil tanks. Airscrews on the inboard engines are four-bladed, and those on the outer engines three-bladed. The outer wings have been strengthened to carry larger wing-tip floats.

The modified PB2Y-3R in its unladen state weighs 8,000 lbs. (3,624 kg.) less than the former PB2Y-3 Patrol-Bomber flying-boat.

TYPE.—Four-engined Patrol (PB2Y-3) or Transport (PB2Y-3R) flying-boat.

WINGS.—High-wing cantilever monoplane. Wings mounted direct to top of hull and taper in chord and thickness, with a swept-back leading-edge and a straight trailing-edge. All-metal structure with stressed aluminium-alloy skin. Entire trailing-edge hinged, the outer portions acting as ailerons and inner portions between ailerons and hull as flaps. Ailerons and flaps have metal frames with fabric covering.

HULL.—Two-step semi-circular-topped hull of all-metal construction. The after step terminates in a vertical knife-edge. Hull treated inside and out with anti-corrosion finishes. Stabilising floats retract to form wing-tips, the supporting struts being recessed flush with the underside of the wings.

TAIL UNIT.—Cantilever monoplane type with twin fins and rudders. All-metal structure with fabric-covered elevators and rudders. Statically and aerodynamically-balanced movable surfaces, which are also fitted with trimming-tabs.

POWER PLANT.—Four 1,200 h.p. Pratt & Whitney R-1830-88 (PB2Y-3) or R-1830-92 (PB2Y-5 and PB2Y-3R) radial air-cooled engines in line along the leading-edge of the wings. NACA cowlings. Hamilton-Standard Hydromatic full-feathering airscrews.

ACCOMMODATION.—Patrol-Bomber version (PB2Y-3 and 5) accommodates crew of ten. Internal arrangements include sleeping quarters, galley with electric range and refrigerator, workshop, independent electric generating system, intercommunication telephone system, etc. Equipment includes breaching gear, lifting slings for engines etc. The Transport version (PB2Y-3R) has a maximum capacity for 16,000 lbs. (7,264 kg.) with strengthened flooring, large loading door and facilities for handling cargo (see above).

ARMAMENT.—Three power-operated turrets armed with 50 cal. machine guns. Stowage for bombs or depth-charges in wings.

DIMENSIONS.—Span 115 ft. (35 m.), Length 79 ft. 3 in. (24.2 m.), Height 27 ft. 6 in. (8.4 m.), Wing area 1,780 sq. ft. (175.4 sq. m.).

WEIGHTS.—Maximum cargo capacity 16,000 lbs. (7,264 kg.), Weight loaded 66,000 lbs. (29,964 kg.).

PERFORMANCE.—Maximum speed 194 m.p.h. (310.4 km.h.), Cruising speed 170 m.p.h. (272 km.h.), Maximum range 1,070 miles (1,710 km.) at 131 m.p.h. (210 km.h.).

THE CONSOLIDATED VULTEE SEAWOLF.
U.S. Navy designation : TBV-2.

The TBV-2 was the production development of the Vought-designed XTBU-1 Torpedo-Bomber monoplane. It was fitted with a Pratt & Whitney R-2800 engine and had accommodation for a crew of three. The loaded weight was about 16,000 lbs. (7,260 kg.). Production of the Seawolf was cancelled before any aircraft could be delivered to the U.S. Navy.

THE CONSOLIDATED VULTEE (VULTEE 70) XP-54.

The XP-54 was an experimental single-seat twin-boom fighter with a Lycoming R-2470 engine driving a four-blade pusher propeller. The original design made provision for the installation of contra-rotating propellers but these were not fitted in the prototype.

The pilot's cockpit, well forward of the wings, was provided with an emergency pilot-ejection device. The general arrangement of the XP-54 can be gathered from the accompanying photograph.

THE CONSOLIDATED VULTEE (VULTEE 72) VENGEANCE.
U.S. Army Air Forces designations : A-31 and A-35.
British name : Vengeance.

The Vultee Model 72 was designed to a British specification by Vultee Aircraft, Inc. and was put into production by both the Vultee company and Northrop Aircraft, Inc. When the United States entered the War, the Vengeance was given the U.S. Army designation A-31.

Vengeance I, II and III (A-31). Fitted with the 1,600 h.p. Wright R-2600-A5B5 (R-2600-19) engine. British armament and equipment, the armament consisting of four .303 in. machine-guns in the wings and two .303 in. guns on a flexible mounting in the rear cockpit. The Vengeance I was built by Northrop, the others by Consolidated Vultee.

Vengeance IV (A-35). One 1,700 h.p. Wright R-2600-13 engine. Fitted with American armament and equipment and built to American contracts for the U.S.A.A.F. and for delivery to the British under Lend/Lease. Early models fitted with four 50 cal. guns in the wings, but on later versions six wing guns were installed. One 50 cal. gun in the rear cockpit. The Vengeance was only used operationally by the R.A.F. and the Royal Indian Air Force in the India-Burma theatre. The U.S.A.A.F. was mainly used as a high-speed target-tug. Production of the Vengeance ceased at the Nashville plant of Consolidated Vultee in the Autumn of 1944, after 1,528 had been built. The last batch off the production lines was delivered to the Brazilian Government.

TYPE.—Two-seat Dive-Bomber.

WINGS.—Mid-wing cantilever monoplane. Flat centre-section with swept-back leading-edge and straight trailing-edge. Outer sections have straight leading-edges and swept forward trailing-edges. All-metal single-spar structure with stressed skin covering. Hydraulically-operated dive-brakes on both upper and lower surfaces of outer sections hinge upwards and backwards and forward and downward respectively. Differentially-operated and statically, and aerodynamically-balanced ailerons have metal frames and smooth sheet covering. Electrically-operated trim-tabs in both ailerons. Hydraulically-operated slotted trailing-edge flaps between ailerons and fuselage.

FUSELAGE.—Oval all-metal structure in two sections, the forward section a semi-monocoque and the rear section a monocoque. Entire skin is flush-riveted and lap-jointed.

TAIL UNIT.—Cantilever monoplane type. Fin forward of the tail-plane. Fin and tailplane are all-metal structures. Elevators have metal frames and metal and fabric covering. Statically and aerodynamically-balanced control surfaces. Rudder has a metal frame and fabric covering. Controllable trim-tabs in rudder and port elevator.

LANDING GEAR.—Retractable type. Cantilever oleo legs retract backward and rotate through 90 degrees for wheels to lie flat in undersurface of centre section. Legs are enclosed by hinged fairings. Partially retractable non-steerable tail-wheel. Hydraulic retraction.

POWER PLANT.—One Wright Cyclone R-2600-13 fourteen-cylinder radial air-cooled engine on welded steel-tube mounting. Hamilton-Standard Hydromatic constant-speed airscrew. Ten self-sealing fuel cells in the wings and fuselage interconnected to form three separate tanks, with a total capacity of 275 U.S. gallons. Electrically-driven booster pumps for use in power dives.

ACCOMMODATION.—Crew of two. Tandem cockpits under continuous

The Consolidated Vultee Vengeance IV Dive Bomber (Wright R-2600-13 engine).

transparent canopy with sliding sections over each seat. Armour protection for pilot and rear gunner.

ARMAMENT.—Four or six 50 cal. machine-guns in wings, two or three in each extremity of the centre-section. One 50 cal. machine-gun on flexible mounting in rear cockpit. Internal bomb-bay in fuselage can accommodate two 500 lb. bombs. As overload two further 250 lb. bombs may be carried on external wing racks.

DIMENSIONS.—Span 48 ft. (14.64 m.), Length 39 ft. 9 in. (12.12 m.), Height 14 ft. 6 in. (4.4 m.), Wing area 332 sq. ft. (30.8 sq. m.).

WEIGHT LOADED.—13,500 lbs. (6,130 kg.).

PERFORMANCE.—Maximum speed 279 m.p.h. (446.4 km.h.), Service ceiling 27,000 ft. (8,235 m.).

THE CONSOLIDATED VULTEE (VULTEE 74D) VALIANT.
U.S. Army Air Forces designations : BT-13 and BT-15.
U.S. Navy designation : SNV.

The original contract for the BT-13 was awarded in September 1939. Production ceased in the Summer of 1944 after 11,537 Valiants had been delivered to the U.S. Army Air Forces and the U.S. Navy.

There have been several variants of the Valiant. These include the BT-13, BT-13A (SNV-1) and BT-13B (SNV-2), all with the Pratt & Whitney R-985 Wasp Junior engine, and the BT-15 with the Wright R-975-11 engine. The differences between the various models have been mainly in matters of equipment.

TYPE.—Two-seat Basic Trainer.

WINGS.—Low-wing cantilever monoplane. Wing section NACA Symmetrical 18% at root tapering to NACA Symmetrical 9% at tips. Wide centre-section, two outer sections and detachable and interchangeable semi-circular wing-tips. All-metal structure

with flush-riveted stressed-skin covering. Ailerons on three-quarters of span of outer wing sections. Slotted flaps with hydraulic operation between ailerons and fuselage. Ailerons and flaps have metal frames and fabric covering.

FUSELAGE.—Oval all-metal structure of composite construction. Forward section including cockpits of welded steel tubing covered with detachable metal panels. Rear section is a semi-monocoque with flush-riveted stressed-skin covering.

TAIL UNIT.—Cantilever monoplane type. All-metal structure with metal-covered fixed surfaces and fabric-covered movable surfaces. Trimming-tabs in elevators and rudder.

LANDING GEAR.—Fixed type. Cantilever units provided with air-oil shock-absorbers. Wheels carried at extremities in cranked extensions on stub-axles to permit easy removal of wheels. Hydraulic brakes and parking brake. Steerable tail-wheel.

POWER PLANT.—One 450 h.p. Pratt & Whitney Wasp-Junior R-985-AN-1 or AN-3 nine-cylinder radial air-cooled engine. NACA cowling. Hamilton-Standard two-position variable-pitch airscrew. Fuel tanks in wings. Total capacity 120 U.S. gallons.

ACCOMMODATION.—Tandem cockpits beneath continuous transparent hooding. Dual controls. Full navigation and night-flying equipment.

DIMENSIONS.—Span 42 ft. 2 in. (12.86 m.), Length 28 ft. 8½ in. (8.76 m.), Height 12 ft. 4⅜ in. (3.75 m.), Wing area 238 sq. ft. (22.2 sq. m.).

WEIGHTS AND LOADINGS.—Weight empty 3,345 lbs. (1,520 kg.), Disposable load 1,015 lbs. (460 kg.), Weight loaded 4,360 lbs. (1,980 kg.), Wing loading 18.3 lbs./sq. ft. (89.3 kg./sq. m.), Power loading 9.7 lbs./h.p. (4.4. kg./h.p.).

PERFORMANCE.—Maximum speed at sea level 164 m.p.h. (293 km.h.), Maximum speed at 1,400 ft. (425 m.) 166 m.p.h. (265.6 km.h.), Cruising speed at 5,500 ft. (1,675 m.) 140 m.p.h. (224 km.h.), Stalling speed 75 m.p.h. (120 km.h.), Climb to 10,000 ft. (3,050 m.) 13 mins., Service ceiling 16,500 ft. (5,030 m.), Maximum range 516 miles (826 km.).

The Consolidated Vultee SNV-2 Valiant Two-seat Basic Trainer (Pratt & Whitney R-985 engine).

CULVER.

CULVER AIRCRAFT CORPORATION.

HEAD OFFICE AND WORKS : 600, E. 35TH STREET, WICHITA, KANSAS.

President : Charles G. Yankey.
Vice-President and General Manager : T. Bowring Woodbury.
Chief Designer : Albert W. Mooney.
Treasurer : Felix M. Farrell.
Secretary : Verne M. Laing.

The Culver Aircraft Corpn. was formed in 1939 to take over from the Dart Manufacturing Corpn. the manufacturing and sales rights of the Dart Model G two-seat light cabin monoplane.

In the following year the Company produced the Culver light cabin monoplane with retractable landing-gear. This was marketed in two versions, the Model LFA fitted with the 80 h.p. Franklin engine, and the Model LCA with the 75 h.p. Continental engine. These two models were described and illustrated in the previous issues of this Annual. They are no longer in production although many are still being used in C.A.P. service and on other civilian duties.

In November, 1941, control and management of the Culver Aircraft Corporation was acquired by Mr. Walter Beech and Mr. Charles G. Yankey, the latter becoming President of the company.

During the war the company devoted its resources to the production of radio-controlled aircraft for use as targets for gunnery practice. The PQ-8 (TDC-1) and PQ-14 (TD2C-1) are based on the LFA light cabin monoplane. No details were available for publication at the time of going to press.

Immediately on release from Government work the Culver Aircraft Corpn. is prepared to produce for civilian use a light two-seat cabin monoplane based on the design to which it has devoted considerable attention since 1940.

CUNNINGHAM-HALL.

THE CUNNINGHAM-HALL AIRCRAFT CORPORATION.

HEAD OFFICE AND WORKS : 13, CANAL STREET, ROCHESTER 8, N.Y.

President and General Manager : F. E. Cunningham.
Vice-President : A. J. Cunningham.
Chief Engineer : David Fergusson.

Secretary : R. Morgan.
Treasurer : J. W. Fulreader.

The Cunningham-Hall Aircraft Corpn. was formed in 1928, in close association with the firm of James Cunningham, Son & Company. The firm has produced several aircraft, the most recent type being the PT-6F freight-carrying biplane, which was described in the 1940 edition of this Annual.

During the past three years the Company has been almost entirely engaged on work in connection with the War Programme, either directly for the U.S. Air Forces or on sub-contract work for other firms in the aircraft industry. It is not now actively engaged in the production of complete aircraft.

CURTISS.

THE CURTISS-WRIGHT CORPORATION, AIRPLANE DIVISION.

HEAD OFFICE : 30, ROCKEFELLER PLAZA, NEW YORK, N.Y.
Established : 1910.
President : Guy Vaughan.
Vice-President in Charge of the Airplane Division : Burdette S. Wright.
Executive Assistant to Vice-President : A. W. Smith.
Director of Production : P. N. Jansen.
Director of Finance : G. M. Ebert.
Director of Contracts : W. J. Crosswell.
Director of Engineering : G. A. Page, Jr.
Executive Engineer : N. F. Vanderlipp.
Director of Sales : G. J. Brandewiede.
Director of Public and Internal Relations : A. D. Palmer, Jr.
Director of Research : Dr. C. C. Furnas.

During the war the Curtiss-Wright Corporation, Airplane Division was wholly engaged in the production of various types of military aircraft for the U.S. Army and Navy.

Plants at Buffalo and Kenmore, N.Y., Columbus, Ohio, St. Louis, Mo., and Louisville, Ky. were all engaged in the mass production of various types of fighter aircraft, dive-bombers and transports for both the U.S. Army and Navy. Production of the P-40 fighter was maintained at two of the Division plants throughout 1944, the last Warhawk being delivered to the U.S. Army in December. Other units were turning out the SC Seahawk scouting seaplane ; the SB-2C Helldiver Navy dive-bomber and its Marine counterpart the A-25, and the C-46 Commando Army transport.

During the war the Curtiss-Wright Corpn. Airplane Division built 27,000 aircraft, and other divisions produced 139,000 engines representing a total of 280,000,000 h.p., and 146,250 airscrews.

With the surrender of Japan production of aircraft was drastically curtailed, but both the Helldiver and Seahawk continued in limited production, and production at the Buffalo plant was converted to the commercial CW-20 version of the C-46 Commando.

Few details of Curtiss experimental types built during the war were available at the time of writing. These included the XF14C-1 and XF15C-1 Naval fighters, the latter with both airscrew and jet power-units ; the XBTC-1 and XBT2C-1 Naval torpedo-bombers ; the XA-40 and XA-43 Army attack bombers ; and the XF-71 twin-engined Army fighter.

THE CURTISS XP-62.

The XP-62 was a single-seat Fighter-Bomber development from the XP-60 Series. It was fitted with a Wright R-3350-17 radial air-cooled engine with a single-stage variable-speed turbo-supercharger and driving two three-blade contra-rotating airscrews. It was provided with a pressure-cabin and apart from a heavy cannon armament, it had provision for carrying a 1,000 lb. bomb load. The XP-62 was the largest and heaviest single-seat fighter built by Curtiss.

THE CURTISS XP-60 SERIES.

The XP-60 was designed as an improved version of the P-40 Warhawk but a number of variations were produced under this designation to test different power-plant installations with the result that five distinct prototypes were evolved.

The original XP-60 had a modified P-40 fuselage, laminar-flow wings, an inwardly-retracting landing-gear and was fitted with a Packard Merlin V-1650-1 engine driving a Curtiss three-blade airscrew. The armament originally projected for this aeroplane was to consist of eight .50 cal. machine-guns, all mounted in the wings. This armament was reduced to four guns in subsequent models. The XP-60 was later fitted with a Merlin V-1650-3 two-speed two-stage supercharged engine driving a four-blade airscrew and was re-designated the XP-60D.

The XP-60A was fitted with an Allison V-1710-75 engine and turbo supercharger. This installation resulted in the provision of a bulkier fuselage with the radiator scoop moved forward under the engine crankcase. A YP-60A was projected with a Pratt & Whitney R-2800 two-stage supercharged radial air-cooled engine but this version was eventually completed as the XP-60E.

The XP-60B was to have been a modification of the Allison-engined XP-60A with a different type of turbine supercharger but it was never built.

The XP-60C had the same airframe as the 60A but was fitted with a Pratt & Whitney R-2800 two-row radial engine driving two three-blade co-axial contra-rotating airscrews.

The XP-60E signalised a return to the single-rotation four-blade airscrew, this model being the re-designated YP-60A mentioned above. It was followed by the YP-60E, which was fitted with a blister-type canopy.

DIMENSIONS.—Span 41 ft. 5 in. (12.6 m.), Wing area 275 sq. ft. (25.5 sq. m.).
WEIGHT LOADED.—Over 10,000 lbs. (4,542 kg.).
PERFORMANCE.—No data available.

THE CURTISS ASCENDER.

U.S. Army Air Forces designation : XP-55.

The XP-55 was an experimental tail-first single-seat fighter monoplane, the development of which began at the St. Louis plant in the Spring of 1939. It was first flown at Scott Field, Illinois, on July 13, 1943. The Ascender was one of a number of fighter types built experimentally for the Army Air Forces which did not go into quantity production.

The Curtiss XP-55 Ascender Experimental Single-seat Fighter (Allison V-1710-95 engine).

TYPE.—Single-seat Experimental Fighter.

WINGS.—Low-wing cantilever monoplane. Sharply swept-back wings of thin laminar-flow section with the roots originating between pilot's cockpit and pusher engine installation. Fins and rudders near outer extremities of wings. Trailing-edge inboard of fins hinged, the inner sections acting as flaps and the outer sections as ailerons. All-metal structure with flush-riveted smooth metal skin.

FUSELAGE.—Symmetrical oval section structure of all metal construction.

CONTROL SURFACES.—Fins and rudders at extremities of wings. Small horizontal stabilising surface and elevators mounted on the nose of the fuselage.

LANDING GEAR.—Retractable tricycle type. Main wheels raised inwardly into underside of wings. Nose wheel raised backwards into fuselage.

POWER PLANT.—One 1,275 h.p. Allison V-1710-95 (F23R) twelve-cylinder Vee liquid-cooled engine mounted at the aft end of the fuselage and driving a three-blade Curtiss Electric pusher airscrew. The airscrew may be jettisoned in an emergency. Air intake above and coolant radiator duct below engine, both being incorporated in rectangular vertical stabilising surfaces. Main fuel tanks in fuselage.

ACCOMMODATION.—Pilot's cockpit over leading-edge of wing roots. Jettisonable cockpit canopy.

ARMAMENT.—Two 20 m/m. cannon and four 50 cal. machine-guns in the nose of the fuselage.

DIMENSIONS, WEIGHTS AND PERFORMANCE.—No data available.

THE CURTISS XP-46.

The XP-46 was designed as a possible successor to the P-40, from which it was developed. It was fitted with an Allison V-1710-39 engine and carried an armament of two 50 cal. machine guns in the fuselage and eight 30 cal. guns in the wings. It also had armour protection for the pilot, a bullet-proof windscreen and protected fuel tanks.

Among the most noticeable design features by which the XP-46 differed from the P-40 were an inwardly-retracting landing-gear in which wheels and legs when raised were flush with the underside of the wings, a lower cockpit canopy, and a ventral ducted radiator located beneath the pilot's cockpit.

Only two prototypes were built and tests with this design did not justify further development.

THE CURTISS XP-42.

The XP-42 was the basis of experiments carried out by the Army Air Corps, the Curtiss and Pratt & Whitney companies and the N.A.C.A. in connection with the cowling of air-cooled radial engines. Basically, it was a P-36A fitted with a 1,000 h.p. Pratt & Whitney R-1830-31 engine with extended airscrew shaft and completely enclosed in a long-nosed streamline cowling.

The XP-42 was first flown on May 31, 1941, and at 15,500 ft. (4,730 m.) it showed a maximum speed of 340 m.p.h. (544 km.h.). As the result of experiments conducted with this aeroplane the N.A.C.A. developed the D-type cowling for high-speed radial engine installations.

On the conclusion of the tests no further development of the XP-42 was made. It was eventually converted back into a P-36A.

THE CURTISS WARHAWK.

U.S. Army Air Forces designation : P-40.
British names : Tomahawk and Kittyhawk.

The Curtiss Warhawk went into production in the Summer of 1939 and from then until December, 1944, when the Warhawk was withdrawn from production, it has been the subject of continuous development and has served in the Air Forces of the Allies in practically every theatre of war. In all, the Warhawk has worn the insignia of twenty-eight Allied and friendly nations.

On November 22, 1944, the Curtiss Airplane Division delivered

The Curtiss XP-46 Experimental Single-seat Fighter (Allison V-1710-39 engine).

to the Army Air Forces the 15,000th fighter built for service in the present war. This aeroplane was a P-40N Warhawk.

Hereafter follows a brief outline of the development of the Warhawk.

XP-40. The prototype, evolved from the radial-engined P-36A by the installation of the Allison V-1710-19 (C-13) engine, the first altitude-rated Allison with built-in supercharger, and a liquid-cooling system with the radiator mounted under the fuselage aft of the trailing-edge of the wings. Standard P-36 wings, fuselage, tail-unit and landing-gear. Won a U.S. Army Pursuit Competition at Wright Field, Dayton, Ohio, in 1939, as the result of which the largest peacetime order for fighter aircraft, valued at nearly $13,000,000, was placed for the P-40.

P-40 (Tomahawk I, IA and IB). Fitted with the Allison V-1710-33 (C15) engine. Considerably revised in structure of both wings and fuselage and stressed to take the increased horse-power of the new engine. Landing-gear and other structural members strengthened to take care of the increased gross weight. Radiators moved forward under the nose. Armament consisted of two 50 cal. machine-guns in the engine cowling and two 30 cal. guns, one in each wing. The Tomahawk I had British .303 in. machine-guns and equipment.

P-40B (Tomahawk IIA and IIB). Same as P-40 but fitted with pilot armour, bulletproof windscreen and leakproof fuel tanks. Wing armament increased to four 30 cal. guns, two in each wing. The Tomahawk II retained the U.S. armament, the IIA having British radio and the IIB American radio.

P-40C. Same as the P-40B but fitted with improved self-sealing tanks.

P-40D (Kittyhawk I). Fitted with the Allison V-1710-39 (F3R) engine, which differed from the V-1710-33 by having an external spur airscrew reduction gear. This resulted in a shorter reduction gear casing and a higher airscrew thrust-line which, in turn, permitted the fuselage to be shortened by 6 in., the cross-section to be reduced, the cowling to be redesigned and the landing-gear to be reduced in height. The synchronised fuselage guns were abandoned, the entire armament of four 50 cal. guns being mounted in the wings. Shackles under the fuselage for a 52 U.S. gallon drop tank or a 300-500 lb. bomb. Racks under the outer wings for six 20 lb. bombs.

P-40E (Kittyhawk IA). Similar to the P-40D but fitted with six 50 cal. guns, three in each wing. A few P-40E's were converted into two-seat trainers by having the fuselage fuel tank removed and a second seat and dual controls added.

P-40F (Kittyhawk II). The P-40F was the first in the P-40 Series to be fitted with the Packard V-1650-1 (Rolls-Royce Merlin 28 engine) engine rated at 1,240 h.p. at 11,500 ft. (3,510 m.), 1,120 h.p. at 18,500 ft. (5,640 m.) and with 1,300 h.p. available for take-off. With this engine the air intake was removed from the top of the cowling and incorporated in the cooling scoop beneath the engine. Armament consisted of six 50 cal. machine-guns, three in each wing, with 235 rounds per gun. A rack under the fuselage could accommodate an auxiliary fuel tank (75 U.S. gallons) or a single bomb (100 to 600 lbs.). Racks for three light fragmentation or practice bombs mounted under each wing outboard of the guns. Later models of the F had a lengthened fuselage. This moved the rudder hinge aft of the elevator hinges and gave increased manœuvrability and improved control characteristics.

P-40G. The same as the P-40 except fitted with pilot armour, self-sealing fuel tanks, bullet-proof windscreen and P-40B wings and wing armament.

P-40K (Kittyhawk III). Fitted with the Allison V-1710-73 (F4R) engine, rated at 1,150 h.p. at 12,000 ft. (3,660 m.) and with 1,325 h.p. available for take-off. This production ran through the production lines simultaneously with the P-40F and as with that version the lengthened fuselage was introduced in the later models. Later P-40K's were winterised and many saw service in Alaska and the Aleutians.

P-40L (Kittyhawk II). Fitted with the Packard V-1650-1 (Merlin 28) engine. A development of the P-40F but much lighter. Saving in weight achieved by the elimination of head armour and the removal of the Prestone tank and the front portions of the multiple wing fuel tanks. All had the long fuselage.

P-40M (Kittyhawk III and IV). Fitted with the Allison V-1710-81 (F20R) engine rated at 1,000 h.p. at 16,400 ft. (5,000 m.) and with 1,200 h.p. available for take-off. A development of the P-40L.

P-40N (Kittyhawk III). Fitted successively with the Allison V-1710-81 (F20R), V-1710-99 (F26R) and V-1710-115 (F31R) engine. A further development of the P-40L. The first production models were further lightened by the removal of two of the six machine-guns, and smaller and lighter landing wheels and aluminium radiators and oil coolers were installed. The head armour, however, was reintroduced, together with improved rear vision panels. After the first few hundred had come off the production lines the two machine-guns and the front portions of the wing multiple fuel tanks were reinstated. In 1943 the P-40N was fitted with two additional bomb racks under the wings, each capable of carrying a bomb of from 100 to 500 lbs. or a droppable "ferry" tank. Other new features included improved non-metallic self-sealing fuel tanks, new radio and oxygen equipment, flame-damping exhaust stacks, etc.

XP-40Q. Fitted with the Allison V-1710-121 engine. A greatly cleaned-up version of the Warhawk. Re-designed fuselage with the coolant radiators removed to the wings, "blister" type sliding cockpit hood and a shallower rear fuselage. Clipped wings with squared tips. The Allison engine fitted with water-injection and driving a four-blade airscrew. Only one built.

P-40R. Several hundred P-40F and P-40L Warhawks were modified by having their Merlin engines replaced by the Allison V-1710-81 (F20R) engine. This conversion was given the designation P-40R. All had the lengthened fuselage.

TYPE.—Single-seat Fighter and Fighter-Bomber.

WINGS.—Low-wing cantilever monoplane. Aerofoil section NACA 2215 at root, 2209 at tip. Wing in two panels joined at the centre-line of the fuselage. Structure consists of longitudinal stringers

The Curtiss P-40N-40 Warhawk Single-seat Fighter (Allison V-1710-115 engine).

The Curtiss P-40K-1 Warhawk Single-seat Fighter with modified fin introduced before the fuselage was lengthened in later models. (*Photograph by Peter Bowers*).

and shear beams of aluminium-alloy, Alclad bulkheads and flush-riveted Alclad skin. Ailerons have Alclad frames and fabric covering. Hydraulically-operated split trailing-edge flaps extend between ailerons and fuselage.

FUSELAGE.—Semi-monocoque structure made up of Alclad bulkheads, aluminium-alloy stringers and a flush-riveted Alclad skin.

TAIL UNIT.—Cantilever monoplane type. All-metal framework. Fixed surfaces have smooth metal covering, movable surfaces covered with fabric. Adjustable trim-tabs in rudder and elevators.

LANDING GEAR.—Retractable type. Curtiss oleo-pneumatic shock-absorber legs and wheels are retracted hydraulically aft and up, rotating about bevel gears until the wheels in raised position lie flush within the wing. In both lowered and retracted positions landing-gear main wheels are automatically locked by hydraulically-operated mechanical locks. Fully-retractable steerable tail-wheel has positive-action hinged fairing which smoothly cover the aperture after the wheel is retracted.

POWER PLANT.—One Allison V-1710 or Packard V-1650-1 (Merlin 28) twelve-cylinder Vee liquid-cooled engine driving a three-bladed Curtiss electrically-controlled multi-position constant-speed airscrew. Ducted coolant and oil radiators beneath engine with controllable air exit. Fuel carried in two wing tanks, a fuselage tank and an auxiliary "belly" tank. Each wing tank and the fuselage tank consists of a multiple self-sealing fuel cell contained in an aluminium-alloy shell. Auxiliary tank carried on bomb-rack beneath the fuselage. Oil system incorporates provision for oil dilution for cold weather starting.

ACCOMMODATION.—Enclosed pilot's cockpit over trailing-edge of wing. Bullet-proof windscreen with glycol spray and warm air de-frosting. Sliding cockpit cover with rear vision side panels in fuselage aft of cockpit. Armour plate forward of the instrument panel and aft of the pilot's seat and head. Cockpit heating and ventilating system. Heat may also be ducted to gun compartments in wings. 24-volt electrical system. Radio equipment.

ARMAMENT.—Three .50-cal. machine-guns in each wing and firing outside the airscrew disc. 235 rounds of ammunition per gun. Bomb rack beneath fuselage may carry a single bomb ranging from 100 to 600 lbs. Racks under wing to carry two 100-500 lb. bombs or two auxiliary "belly" fuel tanks.

DIMENSIONS.—Span 37 ft. 3½ in. (11.36 m.), Length (short fuselage) 31 ft. 8¾ in. (9.68 m.), Length (long fuselage) 33 ft. 3¾ in. (10.14 m.), Height (thrust-line horizontal) 12 ft. 2 in. (3.7 m.), Wing area 236 sq. ft. (21.9 sq. m.).

WEIGHTS (P-40F).—Weight empty 6,550 lbs. (2,974 kg.), Weight loaded 8,720 lbs. (3,960 kg.).

PERFORMANCE (P-40F—Packard V-1650-1 engine).—Maximum speed 364 m.p.h. (582 km.h.) at 20,000 ft. (6,100 m.), Cruising speed 300 m.p.h. (480 km.h.) at critical height, Economical cruising speed 220-245 m.p.h. (352-392 km.h.) according to mission, Climb to 15,000 ft. (4,575 m.) 7.5 mins., Climb to 20,000 ft. (6,100 m.) 10 mins. Service ceiling 33,000 ft. (10,060 m.), Normal range 610 miles (976 km.) at 310 m.p.h. (496 km.h.), Maximum range (with auxiliary fuel tank) 1,200 miles (1,920 km.) at 210 m.p.h. (336 km.h.).

THE CURTISS SEAHAWK.

U.S. Navy designation : SC-1.

The development of the Seahawk began in June, 1942, when the U.S. Navy Bureau of Aeronautics invited the Curtiss company to submit proposals for an improved scout seaplane to replace

The Curtiss XP-40Q Warhawk Single-seat Fighter (Allison V-1710-121 engine).

The Curtiss SC-1 Seahawk Single-seat Shipborne Scout (Wright R-1820-62 engine).

A Curtiss C-46E Commando with the stepped windscreen and revised side windows to be introduced in the post-war CW-20E.

the Kingfisher and Seamew. The Curtiss proposals were submitted on August 1 and on the 25th of that month a contract was placed with the company for seven aircraft, two experimental models for flight testing and five additional aircraft for equipment and service testing.

The first XSC-1 flew on February 16, 1944, and by April 28 all seven experimental aircraft had flown. The Seahawk was developed by and is in production at the Curtiss Columbus plant.

It was first reported in action with the U.S. Fleet in the pre-invasion bombardment of Borneo in June, 1945.

TYPE.—Single-seat Shipborne Scout.
WINGS.—Low-wing cantilever monoplane. Rectangular centre-section with dihedral. Outer sections have taper and dihedral with square detachable wing-tips. Wings fold back for shipboard stowage. All-metal stressed-skin structure. Full-span automatic leading-edge slots. Slotted flaps inboard of ailerons.
FUSELAGE.—All-metal stressed-skin structure of circular section forward and changing to oval section aft.
TAIL UNIT.—Cantilever monoplane type. All-metal structure. Trim-tabs in elevators and rudder.
FLOATS.—Central single-step float on streamline pedestal mounting and two wing-tip stabilising floats on single cantilever struts. Main float accommodates bomb load or auxiliary fuel tanks. Wheel landing-gear for ferrying operations may replace float gear, the same attachments points being used for both gears. Catapult points and hook under nose of main float for net pick-up.
POWER PLANT.—One Wright R-1820-62 nine-cylinder radial air-cooled engine driving a Curtiss electrically-operated airscrew with four hollow steel paddle-type blades. Fuel tanks in centre-section. Auxiliary tanks may be carried in the main float.
ACCOMMODATION.—Pilot's cockpit over wing with sliding blister-type canopy. For sea-rescue work a bunk can be fitted in the fuselage aft of the pilot's seat into which a man can crawl.
ARMAMENT.—Two 50-cal. machine-guns in the centre-section, one on each side of the fuselage. Bombs or depth-charges may be carried in the central float, which has bomb-doors controllable from the pilot's cockpit.
DIMENSIONS.—Span 41 ft. (12.5 m.), Length 36 ft. 5 in. (11.1 m.).
WEIGHTS AND PERFORMANCE.—No data available.

THE CURTISS CW-20E COMMANDO AIRLINER.

Profiting from the experience gained with the large-scale production of the C-46 Commando military transport, the Curtiss company in 1944 prepared designs and mock-up of a commercial version of the Commando for immediate post-war production. At least two American air-line companies placed orders for the CW-20E before the end of 1944.

The CW-20E will accommodate 36 passengers. Among the major changes in the new model are the re-designed nose with a stepped windscreen and deeper side-windows to the pilot's compartment already incorporated in the later models in the C-46A Series, all-metal control surfaces, the introduction of welded easily-removable fuel tanks, and the fitting of two 2,100 h.p. Wright R-3350 (C18B2) eighteen-cylinder engines in place of the Pratt & Whitney R-2800 eighteen-cylinder radials fitted to the C-46.

The following is a provisional specification of the new commercial version of the Commando :—

DIMENSIONS.—Span 108 ft. 1 in. (32.9 m.), Length 76 ft. 4 in. (23.3 m.), Height (tail down) 21 ft. 9 in. (6.6 m.), Wing area 1,360 sq. ft. (126.3 sq. m.).
WEIGHTS.—Weight empty 32,100 lbs. (14,573 kg.), Maximum Pay-load 12,430 lbs. (5,643 kg.), Design disposable load 15,900 lbs. (7,219 kg.), Normal take-off loaded weight 48,000 lbs. (21,792 kg.), Maximum gross landing weight 46,400 lbs. (21,066 kg.).
PERFORMANCE.—Maximum cruising speed 242 m.p.h. (387 km.h.) at 10,000 ft. (3,050 m.).

CURTISS-WRIGHT.
THE CURTISS-WRIGHT CORPORATION.

GENERAL OFFICES : 30, ROCKEFELLER PLAZA, NEW YORK 20, N.Y.
President : G. W. Vaughan.
Senior Vice-President : G. M. Williams.
Secretary and Treasurer : E. S. Cramer.

The Curtiss-Wright Corporation operates four Divisions, the Curtiss-Wright Airplane Division (Aircraft), the Wright Aeronautical Corporation (Aero-engines), the Curtiss-Wright Propeller Division (Propellers) and the Curtiss-Wright Development Division (Special Research). Details of the products of the Curtiss-Wright Airplane Division will be found under "Curtiss" in this section. Full details of the products of the Wright Aeronautical Corporation will be found under "Wright" in the Aero-engine Section (D).

DOUGLAS.
THE DOUGLAS AIRCRAFT COMPANY, INC.

HEAD OFFICE AND WORKS : SANTA MONICA, CALIFORNIA.
OTHER WORKS : EL SEGUNDO AND LONG BEACH, CAL., CHICAGO, ILL., OKLAHOMA CITY, OKLA., AND TULSA, OKLA.
Established : 1920. (Reorganized : 1928.)
President : Donald W. Douglas.
Vice-President—Manufacturing : Frederick W. Conant.
Vice-President—Engineering : A. E. Raymond.
Vice-President—Comptrolling : R. V. Hunt.
Vice President—Contract Administration : J. M. Rogers.
Executive Secretary : T. C. McMahon.
Treasurer : H. P. Grube.

The Douglas Aircraft Company has occupied the present factory site at Clover Field, Santa Monica, Cal., since 1928. It also operates plants at El Segundo, Cal., nine miles from the main plant, Long Beach, Cal., Tulsa, Okla., Chicago, Ill., and Oklahoma City, Okla.

The main production during 1944-45 was devoted to two and four-engined transports and twin-engined bombers for the U.S. Army and Navy. During 1944 manufacture of the Havoc

(20-9-44) and Dauntless (22-7-44) ceased, but production of the C-47 Skytrain, C-54 Skymaster and A-26 Invader was stepped up to meet the increased demands of the services. After the surrender of Japan production of the C-47 was discontinued but the C-54 and A-26 remained in limited production.

The Company has also co-operated in the production of Boeing B-17 long-range bombers and of the first 10,000 B-17's built under the joint Boeing-Douglas-Lockheed production scheme, Douglas built 1,982. The Long Beach plant was responsible for the Douglas share in this programme.

At its production peak the Douglas company employed some 150,000 hands, half of them women, and, based on total structure weight, produced during 1943-44 one-sixth of the total national production of military aircraft.

The company has prepared a number of post-war projects for commercial aircraft, including the DC-4, DC-6, DC-7 and DC-8.

THE DOUGLAS DC-3.

TYPE.—Twin-engined Commercial Transport.
WINGS.—Low-wing cantilever monoplane. Rectangular centre-section and tapering outer sections with detachable wing-tips. Douglas cellular multo-web construction. Fabric-covered ailerons, with controllable trim-tabs in the starboard aileron. Hydraulically-operated all-metal split trailing-edge flaps. Detachable wing-tips.
FUSELAGE.—Almost circular-section structure built up of transverse frames of formed sheet longitudinal members of extruded bulb angles, with a covering of smooth sheet.
TAIL UNIT.—Cantilever monoplane type. Tail-plane and fin of multi-cellular construction. Rudder and elevators have aluminium-alloy frames and fabric covering and are aerodynamically and statically balanced. Trim-tabs in all control surfaces.
LANDING GEAR.—Retractable type. Each unit comprises two air-oil shock-absorber legs. Wheels are retracted forward and upward into engine nacelles and can be raised or lowered in 15 secs. by engine-driven hydraulic system. Hydraulic wheel-brakes. Non-retractable steerable tail-wheel.
POWER PLANT.—Two 1,000 h.p. Wright Cyclone GR-1820-G102A or 1,100 h.p. GR-1820-G202A nine-cylinder, or 1,200 h.p. Pratt & Whitney Twin-Wasp R-1830-S1C3G fourteen-cylinder radial air-cooled engines with two-speed superchargers. Three-bladed Hamilton-Standard constant-speed airscrews. Two main fuel

The Douglas DC-3 Commercial Airliner, the progenitor of the most widely-used military transport of the war,—the C-47 Skytrain or Dakota.

tanks (210 U.S. gallons = 794 litres) located forward of centre-section spar. Two auxiliary tanks (201 U.S. gallons = 760 litres) aft of spar. One oil tank (29¼ U.S. gallons = 109 litres) in each engine nacelle.

ACCOMMODATION.—The pilot's compartment is forward of the wing and is reached through a corridor from the passenger cabin. Emergency exit is provided in the ceiling of the pilot's compartment. Dual controls. The cabin accommodates up to twenty-eight passengers. A sleeper (DST) version with separate compartments which can be made up with upper and lower bunks can accommodate sixteen passengers for day and night travel. The cabin is completely sound-insulated and ventilation and steam heating systems are provided. There are four mail cargo compartments forward of the main cabin, two on each side of the centre aisle. The right forward compartment has a capacity of 35 cub. ft. (.991 cub. m.), and the compartment directly aft has a capacity of 50 cub. ft. (1.42 cub. m.). The left forward compartment has a capacity of 13.5 cub. ft. (.38 cub. m.), and is connected to a 50 cub. ft. (1.42 cub. m.) compartment directly aft. With these two compartments connected, it is possible to accommodate extra large parcels. An outside cargo loading door is located on the left side, just aft of the pilot's seat. A baggage compartment of 103 cub. ft. (2.9 cub. m.) capacity is provided aft of the buffet and lavatory and has an outside loading door on the left side. The equipment for night-flying and radio telephone communication is provided.

DIMENSIONS.—Span 95 ft. (28.9 m.), Length 64 ft. 5½ in. (19.63 m.), Height 16 ft. 11¼ in. (5.2 m.), Wing area 987 sq. ft. (91.7 sq. m.).

WEIGHTS AND LOADINGS (Wright Cyclone GR-1820-G102A engines).—Weight empty 16,480 lbs. (7,482 kg.), Disposable load 8,720 lbs. (3,960 kg.), Weight loaded 25,200 lbs. (11,411 kg.), Wing loading 25.5 lbs./sq. m. (124.4 kg./sq. m.), Power loading 11.45 lbs./h.p. (5.2 kg./h.p.).

WEIGHTS AND LOADINGS (Wright Cyclone GR-1820-G202A engines).—Weight empty 16,600 lbs. (7,536 kg.), Disposable load 8,600 lbs. (3,905 kg.), Weight loaded 25,200 lbs. (11,411 kg.), Wing loading 25.5 lbs./sq. ft. (124.4 kg./sq. m.), Power loading 10.5 lbs./h.p. (4.76 kg./h.p.).

WEIGHTS AND LOADINGS (Pratt & Whitney Twin-Wasp R-1830-S1C3G engines).—Weight empty 16,865 lbs. (7,657 kg.), Disposable load 8,335 lbs. (3,784 kg.), Weight loaded 25,200 lbs. (11,441 kg.), Wing loading 25.5 lbs./sq. ft. (124.4 kg./sq. m.), Power loading 10.5 lbs./h.p. (4.76 kg./h.p.).

PERFORMANCE (Wright Cyclone GR-1820-G102A engines).—Maximum speed 216 m.p.h. (346 km.h.) at 7,700 ft. (2,350 m.), Cruising speed (maximum cruise power) 191 m.p.h. (306 km.h.), Initial rate of climb 1,080 ft./mins. (329.4 m./mins.), Service ceiling 21,700 ft. (6,620 m.), Normal range (maximum fuel and most economical speed) 1,565 miles (2,504 km.).

PERFORMANCE (Wright Cyclone GR-1820-G202A engines).—Maximum speed 220 m.p.h. (352 km.h.) at 7,900 ft. (2,410 m.), Cruising speed (maximum cruising power) 194 m.p.h. (310.4 km.h.) at 11,200 ft. (3,415 m.), Stalling speed 67 m.p.h. (107.8 km.h.), Initial rate of climb 1,070 ft./min. (326.3 m./min.), Service ceiling 21,900 ft. (6,680 m.), Normal range (maximum fuel and most economical speed) 2,125 miles (3,400 km.).

PERFORMANCE (Pratt & Whitney Twin-Wasp R-1830-S1C3G engines).—Maximum speed 230 m.p.h. (368 km.h.) at 8,500 ft. (2,590 m.), Cruising speed 207 m.p.h. (331.2 km.h.), Stalling speed 67 m.p.h. (107.8 km.h.), Initial rate of climb 1,130 ft./min. (345 m./min.), Service ceiling 23,200 ft. (7,076 m.), Normal range (maximum fuel and most economical cruising speed) 2,125 miles (3,400 km.).

The description above applies to the civil versions of the DC-3 (21 passengers) and the DC-3A and DC-3B (28 passengers). Of the 300 aircraft operated by the U.S. domestic airlines at the end of 1944, 275 were DC-3's. Apart from being the most used commercial transport, the DC-3 in military guise is used more than any other type for troop and cargo transport and as a glider-tug.

There are many service versions of the DC-3, the two principal models being the C-47 Skytrain and the C-53 Skytrooper, both of which have been produced in very large numbers for the Army Air Forces and the U.S. Navy, as well as for the Royal Air Force. Since January, 1943, these have been the two principal military versions produced by the Douglas Company.

The 10,000th DC-3 was delivered to the U.S. Army Air Forces on May 5, 1945, all but 500 of which had been built since Pearl Harbour.

The following list details the various military versions of the DC-3, some of which are conversions from civil models taken over from the airlines by the military authorities early in 1942.

C-47 (R4D and Dakota). Two Pratt & Whitney R-1830-92 engines. A cargo re-design of the DC-3 for large-scale military production. Large loading door, reinforced floor, strengthened landing-gear, etc. For further details see Skytrain description.

C-48. Two Pratt & Whitney R-1830 engines. DC-3's taken over from the airlines for use as personnel transports. Furnishings retained but accommodation provided for extra crew member. Some were DTS sleeper transports and used as such.

C-49. Two Wright R-1820-71 engines. DC-3 commercial design modified for military use. Crew of 3 and 21 passengers. Reinforced floor for light cargo and astro-hatch for navigator. This series also included some Wright-engined DC-3's taken over from the airlines, including some DST sleeper transports.

C-50. Two Wright R-1820-85 engines. Some 21-passenger transports and some troop-carriers.

C-51. Two Wright R-1820-83 engines. Paratroop transport. Only one built.

C-52. Two Pratt & Whitney R-1830-51 engines. DC-3's taken over on the production lines before delivery to commercial customers and fitted as paratroop transports.

C-53 (R4D and Dakota). Two Pratt & Whitney R-1830-92 engines. Troop-carrying version of the C-47. No heavy cargo facilities, only small door and no reinforced floor. Supply dropper and glider-tug. For further details see Skytrooper description.

C-68. Two Pratt & Whitney R-1830 engines. DC-3A's taken over from the airlines.

C-84. Two Wright R-1820-G202A engines. DC-3B's taken over from the airlines.

C-117A. Two 1,200 h.p. Pratt & Whitney R-1830-90C engines. Combines the original features of the standard 21-seat commercial DC-3 with the latest improvements developed for the C-47 Series, including C-47 wing flaps and landing gear, hot-air cabin heating system and many internal changes. Produced for the A.A.F. at the Oklahoma City plant but production cancelled after surrender of Japan. Many released for sale to the airlines.

By the end of 1944 all surviving civil DC-3's taken over by the U.S. Army Air Forces in 1942 had been returned to the airlines. In addition numbers of C-47's and C-53's have been released for conversion to civil use.

THE DOUGLAS SKYTRAIN.

U.S. Army Air Forces designation: C-47.
U.S. Navy designation: R4D.
British name: Dakota.

The C-47 Skytrain is the most commonly-used transport in the Allied Air Forces and has operated in every theatre of war. It exists in the following forms:—

C-47 (R4D-1 and Dakota I). Two Pratt & Whitney R-1830-92 engines. All-purpose transport. Large cargo loading doors, reinforced metal floor and tie-down fittings, wood seats folding against sides of cabin, etc. Glider towing-cleat, formerly exclusive to the C-53, is now a standard fitting on the C-47.

C-47A (R4D-5 and Dakota III). Same as C-47 except fitted with a 24-volt instead of a 12-volt electrical system. Description below refers to the C-47A.

C-47B (R4D-6 and Dakota IV). Same as C-47A except fitted with two Pratt & Whitney R-1830-90C engines with two-stage blowers and provision for carrying increased fuel in the cabin. Evolved for use in the India-China Theatre.

TC-47B (R4D-7). Navigational trainer version of the C-47B.

C-47C. Fitted with an Edo twin-float amphibian installation. The floats are of the all-metal single-step type and each is fitted with two retractable wheels, one under the nose and one aft of the step. The space between the two midship bulkheads in each float is used as an auxiliary fuel tank with a capacity of 300 U.S. gallons.

TYPE.—Twin-engined Military Transport.
WINGS, FUSELAGE, TAIL UNIT AND LANDING GEAR.—Same as DC-3.
POWER PLANT.—Two Pratt & Whitney R-1830-92 Twin-Wasp fourteen-cylinder radial air-cooled geared and supercharged engines each

The Douglas C-47A Skytrain Military Transport (two Pratt & Whitney R-1830-92 engines).

The Douglas C-47B Skytrain Military Transport (two Pratt & Whitney R-1830-90C engines).

The Douglas C-47C Skytrain Transport fitted with Edo amphibian float gear.

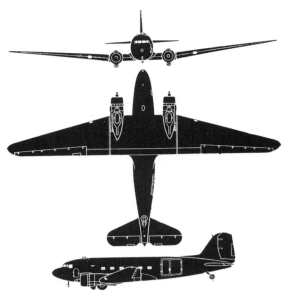

The Douglas C-47 Skytrain Military Transport.

The Douglas C-53 Skytrooper Troop-carrier and Glider-tug (two Pratt & Whitney R-1830-92 engines).

rated at 1,050 h.p. at 7,500 ft. (2,207 m.) and with 1,200 h.p. available for take-off. Three-bladed Hamilton-Standard constant-speed airscrews. Two main fuel tanks (202 U.S. gallons each) located forward of centre-section spar. Two auxiliary tanks (200 U.S. gallons each) aft of spar. Each engine is served by a separate fuel system but cross-feed permits both engines to be supplied by either set of tanks in case of emergency. Oil dilution system. One oil tank (29 U.S. gallons) in each engine nacelle.

ACCOMMODATION.—Crew of three consisting of pilot, co-pilot and radio operator. Fuselage divided into six compartments—pilot's compartment; port and starboard baggage compartment; radio operator's compartment; main cargo hold and lavatory. Pilot's compartment seats two side-by-side with dual controls. Automatic pilot. Full radio equipment includes radio compass, marker beacon receiver and receivers for localised and glide-path reception for the instrument-landing equipment. Steam or hot air heating and ventilation. Main cargo hold equipped with snatch block, idler pulley and tie-down fittings for cargo handling. Large freight door on port side. Cargo load of 6,000 lbs. (2,725 kg.) may include three aero-engines on transport cradles, or two light trucks. Folding seats down sides of cabin for 28 fully-armed airborne or parachute troops. Alternatively fittings for carrying two three-bladed airscrews. Glider-towing cleat in tail. De-icing equipment includes airscrew anti-icing system, rubber de-icer shoes on outer wings, tailplane and fin leading-edges and alcohol-type windscreen de-icer. Oxygen equipment.

DIMENSIONS.—Span 95 ft. (28.9 m.), Length 64 ft. 5½ in. (19.63 m.), Height 16 ft. 11⅜ in. (5.2 m.), Wing area 987 sq. ft. (91.7 sq. m.).

WEIGHTS AND LOADINGS.—Weight empty 16,970 lbs. (7,705 kg.), Useful load 8,600 lbs. (3,904 kg.), Weight loaded 26,000 lbs. (11,805 kg.), Wing loading 25.3 lbs./sq. ft. (123.5 kg./sq. m.), Power loading 12 lbs./h.p. (5.45 kg./h.p.).

PERFORMANCE.—Maximum speed 229 m.p.h. (368 km.h.) at 7,500 ft. (2,290 m.), Cruising speed 185 m.p.h. (296 km.h.) at 10,000 ft. (3,050 m.), Stalling speed 67 m.p.h. (107.8 km.h.), Initial rate of climb 1,130 ft./min. (345 m./min.), Service ceiling 23,200 ft. (7,076 m.), Normal range 1,500 miles (2,400 km.).

THE DOUGLAS SKYTRAIN GLIDER.
U.S. Army Air Forces designation : XCG-17.

As an experiment a standard C-47A was converted at Wright Field into a glider suitable for towing behind the C-54. The engines and airscrews were replaced by hemispherical fairings, all excess weight and unnecessary fittings were removed and a towing cleat was fitted under the front spar of the centre-section. The result was a clean and efficient glider with which a towing speed of 290 m.p.h. (464 km.h.) was possible as compared with the previous maximum speed of 200 m.p.h. (320 km.h.). The XCG-17 had a gliding angle of 14/1 and a stalling speed of 35 m.p.h. (56 km.h.).

On a gross weight of 26,000 lbs. (11,805 kg.) the XCG-17 could carry a maximum pay-load of 14,000 lbs. (6,356 kg.) and could accommodate up to 40 fully-armed troops. No ballast was required for flying at minimum weight conditions.

Successful trials were made with the XCG-17 using two tandem-coupled tugs to give assisted take-off, the leading tug casting off on reaching a certain height.

THE DOUGLAS SKYTROOPER.
U.S. Army Air Forces designation: C-53.
U.S. Navy designations : R4D-3 (C-53) and R4D-4 (C-53C).
British name : Dakota II.

The Douglas C-53 Skytrooper is similar to the C-47 but it has not the facilities for carrying heavy cargo. It has a normal wooden floor, fixed metal seats for twenty-eight fully-armed airborne or parachute-troops and a towing cleat for use as a glider-tug. It has no large loading door. Power-plant, dimensions and other general particulars are the same as for the C-47.

THE DOUGLAS SKYMASTER.
U.S. Army Air Forces designation: C-54.
U.S. Navy designation : R5D.

The design of the original DC-4 was developed by the Douglas Company in collaboration with the technical departments of five of the biggest airline companies in the United States. The prototype received its Approved Type Certificate in May, 1939, and it was then submitted to prolonged service tests under the supervision of United Air Lines. The first model was fitted with four 1,150 h.p. Pratt & Whitney R-2180 Twin-Hornet engines and had accommodation for 52 passengers. It was eventually sold to Japan and subsequently crashed.

On the basis of service tests a new and slightly scaled-down design was prepared for production with accommodation for 40-42 passengers and fitted with four 1,100 h.p. Pratt & Whitney R-2000 Twin-Wasp engines. In 1941 production of provisional orders for sixty aircraft of this type was slowed down owing to defence needs but later in the year the DC-4 design was converted to meet U.S. Army specifications, redesignated C-54, and ordered in large quantities as a long-range military transport.

The first production C-54 flew early in 1942 without experimental prototype.

C-54. Four 1,100 h.p. Pratt & Whitney R-2000-3 radial engines. The original military conversion of the DC-4. Does not have the heavy-duty floor and floor support structure found in the later models in the C-54 Series. No large cargo door or facilities for handling military cargo. Main cabin has seats for 26 passengers. Fuel compartment in fuselage houses four fuel tanks to augment the standard wing tanks. Fuel capacity 3,580 U.S. gallons.

C-54A (R5D-1). Four 1,100 h.p. Pratt & Whitney R-2000-7 engines. Structurally re-designed to provide for carrying heavy cargo. Large cargo-loading door cut in fuselage aft of wings, floor and floor supporting structure strengthened to support heavy items of freight and twin-boom hoist and winch installed to load and unload cargo and ordnance. Provision for suspension beneath fuselage of items of heavy equipment the size and weight of which would prevent them from being loaded in the cabin. Cabin designed to be rapidly converted for carrying cargo or troops, or for the evacuation or transport of wounded. Fuel capacity 3,620 U.S. gallons.

C-54B (R5D-2). Four 1,100 h.p. Pratt & Whitney R-2000-7 engines. Development of C-54A. Chief structural change consists of the removal of two fuselage fuel tanks and installation of integral fuel tanks of comparable capacity in outer wings. Standardisation of cabin interior fittings to permit rapid conversion from cargo transport or troop carrier. Removable stretcher fittings and individual oxygen outlets throughout the cabin. Fuel capacity, 3,720 U.S. gallons.

C-54C. One special Skymaster equipped for the personal use of the late President Roosevelt. Fitted with electrically-operated elevator, Presidential state-room, three other state-rooms, main cabin with conference table, etc. Crew of seven and fifteen passengers with sleeping accommodation for six.

C-54D (R5D-3). Cargo model with cabin interior similar to C-54B. Many improvements introduced in C-54E progressively incorporated in C-54D, including later installation of R-2000-11 engines. Produced in Chicago plant only.

C-54E (R5D-4). Four Pratt & Whitney R-2000-11 engines with better altitude performance. Combines passenger features of original C-54 with cargo facilities of C-54A and B. Remaining two fuselage tanks removed and additional collapsible tanks installed in wings. Twenty double passenger seats, ten on each side of central aisle, fit on combination seat and cargo tie-down fittings. Detachable full-length baggage racks above windows. Buffet, toilet, lavatory and coat-room at aft end of cabin. Sound-proofing, heating and individual oxygen outlets. For cargo carrying, seats, carpets, baggage racks, etc. removed and floor covered with plywood covering. Fuel capacity 3,540 U.S. gallons. Produced in Santa Monica plant only.

The Douglas C-54B Skymaster Long-range Military Transport (four Pratt & Whitney R-2000-7 engines).

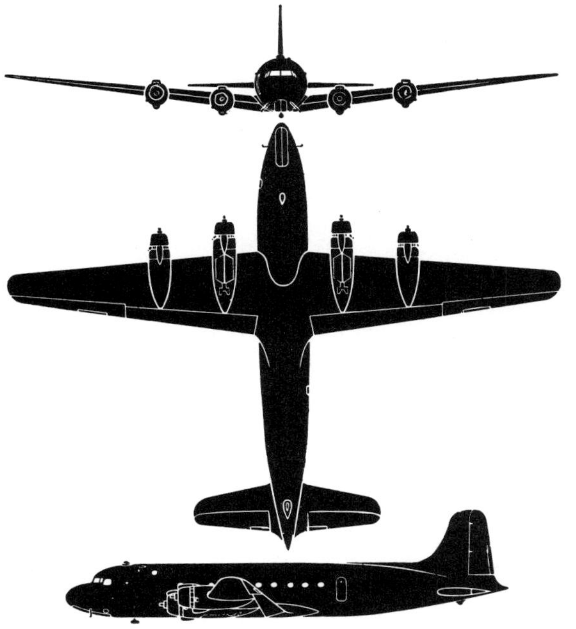

The Douglas C-54 Skymaster Military Transport.

C-54F. A modification of the C-54B incorporating special requirements of Troop Carrier Command.

C-54G (R5D-5). Four Pratt & Whitney R-2000-9 engines. Except for power-plant similar to C-54E.

C-54J (R5D-6). Same power-plant as C-54G. Personnel transport with full airline furnishings. No cargo facilities.

Type.—Four-engined medium and long-range Troop or Cargo Transport.

Wings.—Low-wing cantilever monoplane with constant taper from roots to tips. Wing section NACA 23016/23012. Incidence at root 4 degrees. Dihedral 7 degrees. Centre-section of three-spar construction, spars passing through the fuselage to which they are permanently attached. Self-sealing fuel tanks built integrally with structure. Outer wings have single main spar. Structure of centre-section and outer wings completed by former ribs, span-wise stringers and a smooth Alclad skin. NACA slotted flaps from fuselage to ailerons. Flap doors on wing undersurface are automatically retracted to permit smooth flow of air through slot when flaps are down. Both flaps and ailerons are single-spar metal structures. Controllable tab in starboard aileron.

Fuselage.—Semi-monocoque all-metal structure made up of a series of transverse frames, longitudinal stringers and a flush-riveted smooth Alclad skin.

Tail Unit.—Cantilever monoplane type. Fin and tailplane have two-spar frames and are covered with smooth Alclad sheet. Tail-plane units have removable leading-edges and detachable tips, and are interchangeable from right to left or vice-versa. Rudder which is statically, aerodynamically and dynamically balanced by lead weights, has single channel spar and fabric covering. Elevators, with similar balances to rudder, have single-spar frames, metal leading-edges and overall fabric covering.

Landing Gear.—Retractable tricycle type. Each unit of main gear has twin-wheels and single shock-strut. Steerable nose wheel has single wheel. Hydraulic retraction, the main wheels being raised forward into inboard engine nacelles and the nose wheel backward into fuselage. Manual emergency gear. Automatic devices provided to prevent retraction while any load remains on the landing-gear. Dual hydraulic brakes on each main wheel.

Power Plant.—Four Pratt & Whitney R-2000-7 or 11 fourteen-cylinder radial air-cooled engines with two-speed superchargers, each rated at 1,100 h.p. to 7,000 ft. (2,135 m.), 1,000 h.p. from 7,000 to 14,000 ft. (4,270 m.) and with 1,350 h.p. available for take-off. Four-bladed Hamilton-Standard Hydromatic constant-speed full-feathering airscrews 13 ft. 2 in. (4 m.) diameter. Fuel tanks in fuselage and wings. Oil tank in each engine nacelle behind fireproof bulkhead. Auxiliary oil tank in fuselage.

Accommodation.—Crew of six, comprising pilot, co-pilot, navigator, radio-operator and two relief crew members. Flight compartment accommodates pilot and co-pilot side-by-side with dual controls, and navigator and radio-operator behind. Crew compartment aft of flight compartment provides accommodation for two relief crew members, and is provided with rest bunks, toilet, water tank and stowage for parachutes, life-raft, etc. Both these compartments are sound-proofed. In C-54 fuel compartment housing four fuel tanks follows crew compartment and is separated from main compartment by removable partition. Main compartment equipped with 26 seats, overhead baggage racks and stowage for four life-raft. Coatroom, buffet and food storage unit and lavatory and wash-room aft of main compartment. In C-54A main compartment re-arranged to provide troop benches instead of passenger seats. Flooring and floor beams strengthened to withstand heavy concentrated loads. Tie-down fittings for engines, ordnance and cargo installed throughout length of main cabin. Large loading door on starboard side 94 in. (2.38 m.) wide × 67 in. (1.7 m.) high, with provisions for attaching a platform and ramp for loading wheeled vehicles. Built-in twin-boom hoist capable of supporting 4,000 lbs. (1,820 kg.). Provision for removable stretcher installation and for stowage space for sea rescue equipment. Low-pressure continuous-flow oxygen system for pilot's and crew's compartments. In C-54B two of four tanks removed from fuselage and tanks of comparable capacity installed in outer wings. In C-54E remaining two tanks removed. Additional all-purpose floor fittings for passenger seats or troop benches. A demand-type oxygen supply system with individual outlets installed throughout main cabin. Improved hoist permits greater clearance and outreach for handling cargo or stretchers. Emergency exit doors in sides of fuselage over wings. Front (125 cub. ft.) and rear (165 cub. ft.) belly compartments beneath cabin floor with access from outside. Provision for carrying external loads under fuselage, such as airscrews, etc. Glider tow cleat and release in aft end of tail-cone. Heating and ventilating system, full radio equipment, including marker beacon and radio compass, etc.

Dimensions.—Span 117 ft. 6 in. (35.8 m.), Length 93 ft. 11 in. (28.6 m.), Height 27 ft. 6$\frac{5}{16}$ in. (8.4 m.), Wing area 1,462 sq. ft. (135.8 sq. m.).

Weights (C-54).—Weight empty 36,400 lbs. (16,526 kg.), Weight loaded 62,000 lbs. (28,150 kg.).

Weights (C-54A).—Weight empty 37,300 lbs. (16,934 kg.), Maximum loaded weight 65,000 lbs. (29,510 kg.), Maximum landing weight 62,000 lbs. (28,150 kg.).

Weights (C-54B).—Weight empty 38,200 lbs. (17,343 kg.), Maximum loaded weight 73,000 lbs. (33,142 kg.), Maximum landing weight 62,000 lbs. (28,150 kg.).

Performance—Maximum speed 274 m.p.h. (438 km.h.) at 14,000 ft. (4,270 m.). Cruising speed (maximum cruising power) 239 m.p.h. (382 km.h.) at 15,200 ft. (4,640 m.), Stalling speed (flaps in landing position) 88 m.p.h. (141 km.h.), Initial rate of climb 1,070 ft./min. (326 m./min.), Service ceiling 22,500 ft. (6,860 m.), Service ceiling (on three engines) 17,300 ft. (5,280 m.), Normal range (16,500 = 7,490 kg. cargo) 1,500 miles (2,480 km.) at 220 m.p.h. (352 km.h.) at 10,000 ft. (3,050 m.), Maximum range (5,400 lbs. = 2,450 kg. cargo) 3,900 miles (6,240 km.) at 190 m.p.h. (304 km.h.) at 10,000 ft. (3,050 m.).

THE DOUGLAS DC-4.

The DC-4 for post-war delivery will be based on the C-54 Skymaster and will incorporate many of the design features introduced into the military model.

Accommodation will be provided for a crew of five and 44 passengers, baggage and freight for day use and 22 passengers, baggage and freight as a sleeper. Freight will be carried in three compartments, one (135 cu. ft.) forward of the passenger compartment on the right side with a 5 ft. (1.52 m.) wide loading door, and two beneath the cabin floor (120 and 165 cu. ft.) with 30 in. × 36 in. (.76 × .915 m.) loading doors.

The basic design of the new DC-4 will be such that cabin supercharging may be installed if desired. The general structure will be the same as the Skymaster.

Dimensions.—Same as the Skymaster.

Weights and Loadings.—Weight empty 39,000 lbs. (17,710 kg.), Weight loaded 65,000 lbs. (29,510 kg.), Wing loading 44.5 lbs./sq. ft. (217.7 kg./sq. m.), Power loading 12.05 lbs./h.p. (5.47 kg./h.p.).

Performance.—Maximum cruising speed 280 m.p.h. (448 km.h.) at 23,200 ft. (7,080 m.), Normal cruising speed (60% power) 239 m.p.h. (382 km.h.) at 10,000 ft. (3,050 m.), Stalling speed 80 m.p.h. (128 km.h.), Initial rate of climb 1,200 ft./min. (366 m./min.), Range (with normal 20,000 lbs. = 9,080 kg. pay load) 1,500 miles (2,400 km.).

THE DOUGLAS DC-6.

U.S. Army Air Forces designation : XC-112.

The DC-6 will be a larger and slightly more powerful version of the DC-4. The chief differences will be in overall length of fuselage and in power-plant with, in consequence, an increase in load capacity and gross weight. DC-4 wings will be used but the vertical and horizontal tail surfaces will be larger. It will be fitted with four Pratt & Whitney R-2000-C engines, each having 2,100 h.p. available for take-off.

The DC-6 is designed to carry a flight crew of four and 50 passengers by day or 24 sleepers plus 2 sitting passengers by night. It will have a supercharged cabin divided into two by a central entrance vestibule with coat-room, wash-room, etc.

Dimensions.—Span 117 ft. 6 in. (35.8 m.), Length 100 ft. 7 in. (30.68 m.), Height 28 ft. 5 in. (8.66 m.), Wing area 1,457 sq. ft. (135.35 sq. m.).

Weights.—Maximum gross take-off weight 80,500 lbs. (36,550 kg.), Landing gross weight 63,500 lbs. (28,830 kg.), Wing loading 55.2 lbs./sq. ft. (269.4 kg./sq. m.), Power loading 9.6 lbs./h.p. (4.35 kg./h.p.).

Performance (at 63,500 lbs. = 28,830 kg.).—Maximum cruising speed 334 m.p.h. (534 km.h.) at 23,800 ft. (7,260 m.), Normal cruising speed (60% power) 278 m.p.h. (445 km.h.), Absolute range 2,715 miles (4,345 km.).

THE DOUGLAS DC-7 GLOBEMASTER.

U.S. Army Air Forces designation : XC-74.

The DC-7 is a greatly enlarged version of the DC-4 for trans-oceanic flying. Twenty-six have been ordered by Pan American Airways for post-war trans-Atlantic operations. A military prototype—the XC-74—first flew in September, 1945.

The civil model will have accommodation for a crew of ten and a maximum of 108 passengers for day flying or 76 for night flying. The passenger accommodation will be supercharged and will include chair and compartment sections, lounge bar and dining area, sleeping cabins, cloakroom, four lavatories, stewardess' and crew quarters. Cargo holds will be below the main floor, and will have a total capacity of 1,169 cu. ft.

In general arrangement the DC-7 is characteristically Douglas with equal-tapered wings set well back along the circular fuselage, DC-4 type tail and tricycle landing-gear with dual wheels throughout. The nose of the fuselage is symmetrical with separate blister-type transparent cockpit fairings for the two pilots. The power-plant consists of four 3,500 h.p. Wright R-4360 four-row radial air-cooled engines.

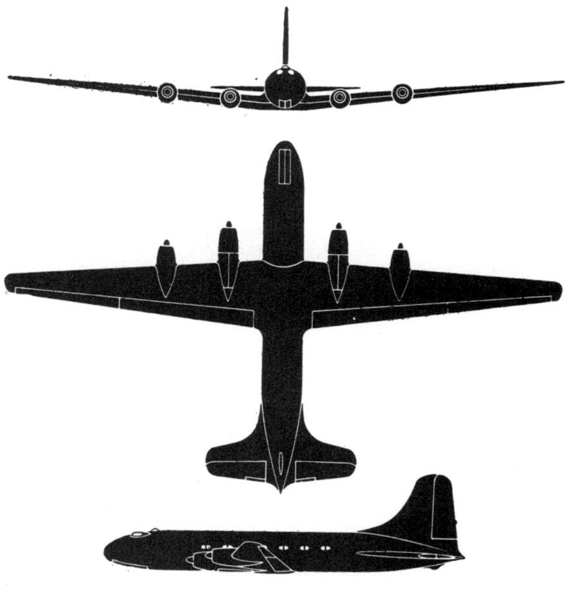

The Douglas C-74 (DC-7) Transport.

Dimensions.—Span 173 ft. 3 in. (52.8 m.), Length 123 ft. 4 in. (37.6 m.), Height 43 ft. (13.1 m.).

Weights.—Weight empty 86,000 lbs. (39,045 kg.), Weight loaded 145,000 lbs. (65,830 kg.).

Performance.—Cruising speed (64.3% power) 296 m.p.h. (474 km.h.) at 20,000 ft. (6,100 m.), Maximum range 3,500 miles (5,600 km.)

THE DOUGLAS DC-8.

The DC-8 will be a twin-engined transport monoplane incorporating the novel engine installation originally designed for the XA-42. This consists of two Allison V-1710 liquid-cooled engines located in the fuselage forward and driving contra-rotating propellers aft of the tail-unit through shafting passing beneath the passenger cabin. The DC-8 will have normal accommodation for 38 passengers.

Dimensions.—Span 110 ft. 2 in. (33.6 m.), Length 77 ft. 10 in. (23.7 m.), Height 25 ft. 9 in. (7.8 m.).

Weights.—Weight empty 23,920 lbs. (10,860 kg.), Weight loaded 39,500 lbs. (17,935 kg.).

Performance.—Maximum speed 270 m.p.h. (432 km.h.) at 10,000 ft. (3,050 m.), Range 2,680 miles (4,290 km.) at 176 m.p.h. (282 km.h.).

THE DOUGLAS INVADER.

U.S. Army Air Forces designation : A-26.
U.S. Navy designation : JD-1.

The contract for the prototype XA-26 was placed in June, 1941. Actually three experimental models were produced to the basic design, the XA-26 light bombardment and attack aeroplane, the XA-26A, a modification for use as a night fighter, and the XA-26B attack-bomber, mounting a large calibre cannon.

The XA-26 was flown for the first time on July 10, 1942, and it is interesting to note that this aeroplane carried approximately twice the bomb load required by the original specification and exceeded every performance guarantee. It was also 700 lbs. (318 kg.) under the designed weight. Tests with these three experimental models culminated in the design of the production A-26B which carried additional armour protection for the pilot and a closed-in nose armed with six 50 cal. machine-guns. The A-26C which serves as a lead ship, is fitted with a transparent bombardier nose and two forward-firing 50 cal. guns.

The JD-1 is a stripped version of the Invader used by the U.S. Navy as a target-tug.

The Invader first went into action with the 9th Air Force in the European Theatre of Operations on November 19, 1944.

Type.—Twin-engined Attack Bomber.

Wings.—Shoulder-wing cantilever monoplane. NACA low-drag laminar-flow wing section. Complete left and right-hand wing panels attach directly to fuselage without centre-section. Two-spar structure, the spars being built up of unspliced spar caps having integral end fittings. Chordwise stiffeners and flush-riveted flush metal skin. Electrically-operated slotted trailing-edge flaps.

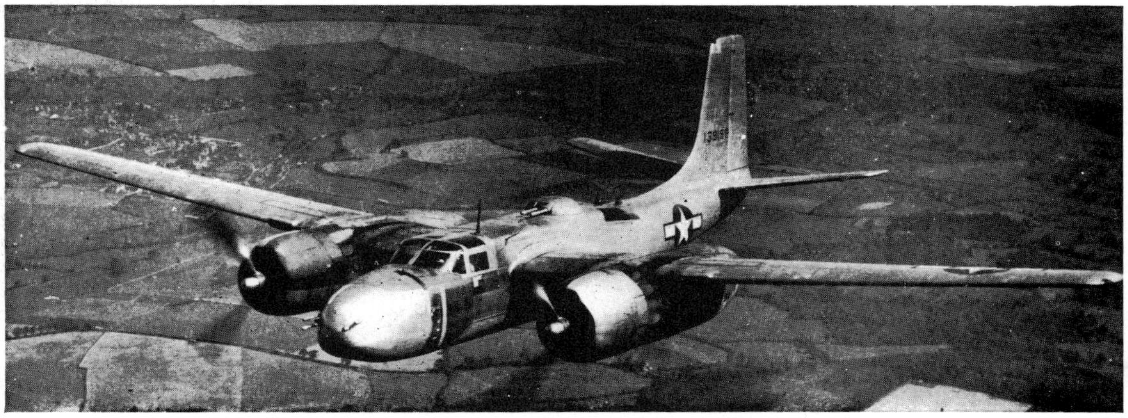

The Douglas A-26B Invader Three-seat Attack Bomber (two Pratt & Whitney R-2800-71 engines).

The Douglas A-26 Invader.

FUSELAGE.—All-metal semi-monocoque structure, practically square with rounded corners in cross section.

TAIL UNIT.—Cantilever monoplane type. Dihedral tailplane. All-metal structure. Trim-tabs in all control surfaces.

LANDING GEAR.—Retractable tricycle type. Hydraulic operation. Main wheels retract into engine nacelles and nose wheel rotates through 90° to lie flat in the bottom of the fuselage.

POWER PLANT.—Two 2,000 h.p. Pratt & Whitney R-2800-71 eighteen-cylinder radial air-cooled engines with two-speed superchargers. Three-blade Hamilton-Standard Hydromatic constant-speed quick-feathering airscrews. Engine mountings, interchangeable right to left or vice-versa, built up of a large metal spinning forward and a stainless steel rear part, tied together by six identical forgings. The six engine attachment points pick up the front of the forgings and the bolts for removing the whole power-plant installation tie the aft end of the forgings and the engine mounting to the nacelle. All lines, pipes and wiring grouped together inside skin of mounting and fitted with quick release fittings. Access door in two halves, upper and lower, and quickly removable. Quick-release access panels and doors in mounting. Access door in fire-wall permits mechanic to enter nacelle to work on engine accessory section. Self-sealing fuel tanks in wings and oil tanks in nacelles.

ACCOMMODATION.—Crew of three. All positions armoured.

ARMAMENT.—Several types of fuselage nose for different armament installations, as well as a transparent bombardier nose. A-26B has a fixed forward-firing armament of six machine-guns in the nose and provision for eight paired 50-cal. "package" guns under the wings, two pairs outboard of each engine nacelle. A-26C has transparent bombardier nose and fixed nose armament of two 50-cal. guns. Defensive armament comprises two two-gun electrically-operated turrets one above and one below the fuselage, and both remotely-controlled from a gun-sighting station aft of the wings, aiming being by periscopic sights. Upper turret when locked in forward position may be fired by pilot in conjunction with nose armament. External bomb racks under wings.

DIMENSIONS.—Span 70 ft. (21.35 m.), Length 50 ft. 9 in. (15.47 m.), Height 18 ft. 6 in. (5.64 m.), Wing area 540 sq. ft. (50 sq. m.).

WEIGHTS.—Normal loaded weight 27,000 lbs. (12,247 kg.), Maximum overloaded weight 32,000 lbs. (14,515 kg.).

PERFORMANCE.—Maximum speed 345 m.p.h. (552 k.m.h.) at 5,000 ft. (1,525 m.).

THE DOUGLAS HAVOC.

U.S. Army Air Forces designations : A-20, P-70 and F-3.
U.S. Navy designation : BD.
British name : Boston.

The original DB-7 was a private venture and was first produced to the order of the French Government. The first production DB-7 flew at El Segundo on August 17, 1939. When France fell the undelivered portions of the French contracts was taken over by the British Government and the DB-7 was given the type name Boston. The following briefly traces the development of this aeroplane from the Boston I to the A-20K (Boston V), the production of which ceased on September 20, 1944, after 7,097 had been built for the U.S., British and Russian Air Forces. Russia received twice as many as the R.A.F. and only some 800 less than the U.S. Army.

Boston I. Two Pratt & Whitney Twin-Wasp R-1830-S3C4G engines. The undelivered portion of the French contract. Mainly used for training but some experimentally converted for night fighting and given the British name Havoc I.

A-20 (Boston II). This was the first of the DB-7 series to be built to a U.S. Army Specification. The A-20 was fitted with two 1,500 h.p. Wright Cyclone R-2600-7 engines with exhaust-driven turbo-superchargers, and American armament and equipment. The Boston II had R-2600-A5B engines and British armament. Was later converted into a Night Fighter under the British name Havoc. The nose was lengthened and fitted with twelve forward-firing .303 in. guns. Operated as a night fighter without bomb-load but with special radar equipment, or as an intruder fighter-bomber with full armament and bombs. The British name Havoc has now been abandoned.

A-20A (BD-1). Two 1,600 h.p. Wright R-2600-11 engines with integral two-speed superchargers. Crew of three. American armament and bombing equipment.

A-20B (BD-2). Development of the A-20A. Armament consisted of two 50 cal. guns firing forward, one 50 cal. upper flexible gun, one 30 cal. lower flexible gun and one 30 cal. gun in the tail of each engine nacelle and firing aft. Nacelle guns

The Douglas Boston III Medium Bomber (two Wright R-2600-A5BO engines).

remotely-controlled by foot trigger in rear compartment. Provision for temporary auxiliary fuel tanks to permit flight delivery to various war theatres.

A-20C (Boston III and IIIA). Two 1,600 h.p. Wright R-2600-23 engines. Armament consists of four fixed guns, two on either side of the transparent nose firing forward, two on a flexible mounting in the rear cockpit and one in the lower rear-firing position, all .30 cal. in A-20C or .303 in. in Boston III. Ejector-type exhaust stacks replaced the collector rings used on the earlier models and increased fuel capacity by use of a self-sealing fuel tank in the forward and rear bomb-bay compartments. Provision for carrying one 2,000 lb. naval torpedo. The Boston III was fitted with R-2600-A5BO engines, the light-bomber version accommodating a crew of four ; pilot, bomb-aimer, upper gunner and lower gunner. Boston IIIA same but built by the Boeing Aircraft Company. Some Boston III's and IIIA's fitted as Intruder fighters with four 20 m/m. cannon under forward fuselage, four .303 in. guns in the nose and two .303 in. guns in the upper flexible position. Overall length 47 ft. (14.33 m.).

XA-20E. An experimental model developed from the A-20A. Fitted with a 37 m/m. nose cannon and upper and lower General Electric turrets, each armed with two 50 cal. machine-guns. Only one built.

A-20G. Similar to A-20C except that the transparent bombardier nose replaced by a closed-in nose fitted, in the case of earlier versions of the A-20G, with four 20 m/m. cannon and two 50 cal. machine-guns, and ultimately with six 50 cal. guns. A few A-20G's had a single 50 cal. upper flexible gun, but this was soon replaced by a power-driven turret armed with two 50 cal. guns. One flexible 50 cal. gun in the rear-firing lower position. Thicker armour for increased crew protection on ground attack missions. Fuel capacity augmented by use of one self-sealing fuel-tank in the forward bomb-bay compartment and two in the rear compartment. Droppable streamline "belly" fuel tank also provided for long-range missions or ferrying. Later versions of the A-20G incorporated improved exhaust ejector stacks and fuel system. Wing racks provided for additional bombs or chemical tanks for smoke-screen laying. Contrary to previous models all auxiliary flight controls removed from rear compartment and provisions for photographic equipment deleted. Overall length increased to 48 ft. (14.64 m.).

A-20H. Two 1,700 h.p. Wright R-2600-29 engines. A later model of the A-20G. Various minor improvements incorporated.

A-20J (Boston IV). Identical to the later version of the A-20G except that the attack nose is replaced by a moulded

plastic bombardier's nose incorporating bombing controls and flight navigation instruments. One in ten A-20G's completed as A-20J's to serve as squadron lead planes. Armament consists of two 50 cal. machine-guns, one on each side of the transparent nose, two in the dorsal power-operated turret and one in the lower rear-firing position. Overall length, 48 ft. 4 in. (14.7 m.).

A-20K (Boston V). Identical to the A-20H except that the attack nose is replaced by a bombardier's nose, as with the A-20J.

P-70. The P-70 is the night fighter version of the A-20 Havoc. The first P-70 was a conversion of the A-20A, with two 1,600 h.p. Wright R-2600-11 engines. The crew consisted of a pilot and radio-operator, and the armament four 20 m/m. cannon mounted in a fairing beneath the fuselage bomb-bay. The major portion of the radio equipment was installed in the nose.

P-70A. A conversion of the A-20G, with two 1,600 h.p. R-2600-23 engines. Armament consists of six 50 cal. machine-guns in the solid nose, a flexible 50 cal. gun in the upper rear position and a similar gun in the lower tunnel position.

P-70B. A development of the P-70A with six 50 cal. "package" guns, three on each side of the fuselage, and one 50 cal. gun in the lower tunnel position. The nose accommodates the special radar equipment.

F-3. A photographic reconnaissance version of the A-20A. A crew of two, pilot and photographer/rear-gunner, was carried. Photographic equipment was installed in the after portion of the bomb-bay. Armament consisted of two 30 cal. machine-guns, one on each side of the standard A-20 transparent nose, two flexible 30 cal. guns in the upper gunner's position, one flexible 30 cal. gun in the lower tunnel position, and two remotely-controlled fixed 30 cal. guns, one in the tail of each engine nacelle and firing directly aft.

Another Havoc project, the XO-53, with provision for photographic equipment in the bomb-bay was cancelled.

TYPE.—Twin-engined Attack Bomber.

WINGS.—Mid-wing cantilever monoplane. Each wing comprises an inner section with integral engine nacelle, an outer section and a wing-tip. Inboard section attached to fuselage at five points, one at leading-edge, two at main spar and two at rear shear web. Five similar attachment points between inner and outer sections. Single-spar aluminium-alloy structure with stressed Alclad skin. Trailing-edge flaps on inner wing sections, ailerons on outer sections. Trimming-tabs in both ailerons, interconnected and operated by single control in pilot's compartments.

FUSELAGE.—Aluminium-alloy monocoque structure with smooth flush-riveted Alclad skin. Detachable nose and tail cone.

TAIL UNIT.—Cantilever monoplane type. Tailplane set at 10 degrees dihedral. Fixed surfaces all metal with stressed-skin covering. Movable surfaces have metal frames with fabric covering.

The Douglas A-20G Havoc Attack Bomber (two Wright R-2600-23 engines).

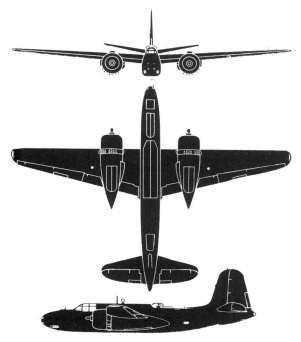

The Douglas A-20G Havoc Attack Bomber.

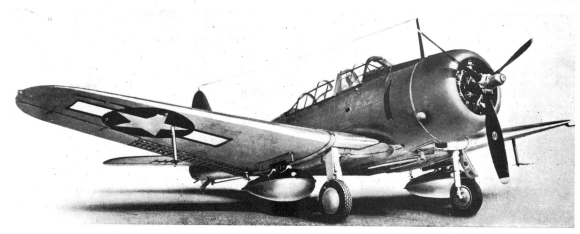

The Douglas SBD-6 Dauntless Naval Scout Bomber (Wright R-1830-66 engine).

Trimming-tabs in both elevators and rudder controllable from pilot's cockpit.

LANDING GEAR.— Retractable tricycle type. Main wheels retract backwards into tails of engine nacelles, nose-wheel into fuselage. Hydraulic retraction with provision for emergency hand operation. Oleo-pneumatic shock-absorber struts. Goodyear wheels and hydraulic brakes.

POWER PLANT.—Two 1,700 h.p. Wright R-2600-29 fourteen-cylinder radial air-cooled engines with two-speed superchargers on welded steel-tube mountings attached to fireproof bulkheads at four points. Hamilton-Standard Hydromatic three-blade constant-speed full-feathering airscrews. Diameter : 11 ft. 3 in. (3.43 m.). Four main self-sealing fuel tanks in wings, two inboard (136 U.S. gallons each) and two outboard (64 U.S. gallons each) of engine nacelles. Total normal fuel capacity : 400 U.S. gallons. Three auxiliary long-range tanks may be installed in bomb-bay and used in combat. One external long-range tank (374 U.S. gallons) may be carried under fuselage for long-range bombing missions, but must be dropped before bomb-doors can be opened. This tank is boat-shaped with flat top and is of Duramold plywood construction. For long-range ferrying four easily-removable tanks (676 U.S. gallons) may be carried in the bomb-bay.

ACCOMMODATION.—Bomb-aimer's compartment in A-20J and K has moulded transparent plastic nose with optically-flat section for bomb sighting. Replaced by closed-in attack nose in A-20G and H. Pilot's cockpit in front of leading-edge of wings. Entrance through side-hinged hatch in roof, the hinge-pins of which can be withdrawn for emergency exit. Aft of cockpit is the main internal bomb compartment with hydraulically-operated doors. Rear gunner's compartment aft of wings with gun positions above and below fuselage. A door in the floor is used for entry and exit and for the lower flexible gun. Upper emergency hatches are provided for two front and rear view positions for exit in case of descent on water. All crew positions are armoured.

ARMAMENT.—See above.

DIMENSIONS.—Span 61 ft. 3½ in. (17.8 m.), Length 48 ft. 4 in. (14.74 m.), Height 18 ft. 1½ in. (5.5 m.), Wing area 465 sq. ft. (43.2 sq. m.).

WEIGHTS AND LOADINGS.—Weight loaded 20,000 lbs. (9,080 kg.), Wing loading 43.01 lbs./sq. ft. (209.88 kg./sq. m.), Power loading 7.4 lbs./h.p. (3.36 kg./h.p.).

PERFORMANCE.—Maximum speed 325 m.p.h. (520 km.h.) at 14,500 ft. (4,420 m.), Cruising speed 280 m.p.h. (448 km.h.) at 14,000 ft. (4,270 m.), Stalling speed 98 m.p.h. (157 km.h.), Initial rate of climb 2,000 ft./min. (610 m./min.), Service ceiling 25,300 ft. (7,720 m.).

THE DOUGLAS DAUNTLESS.
U.S. Navy designation : SBD.
U.S. Army Air Forces designation : A-24.

The Dauntless went into production in June, 1940, as the SBD-1, the first deliveries being to the U.S. Marine Corps. By December, 1941, the SBD-3 was the standard carrier-borne dive-bomber with the U.S. Fleet and for two years the Dauntless fulfilled the entire Scout Dive-Bomber requirements of the naval forces operating in the Pacific.

In 1941 the U.S. Army took delivery of a military version

of the Dauntless designated the A-24. This was a counterpart of the SBD-3 and differed from it in only minor equipment details and by the elimination of deck-landing gear. The A-24A (SBD-4) and A-24B (SBD-5) followed. While all SBD models were built at El Segundo, the A-24 versions emanated from the Douglas Tulsa plant. Production of the A-24 ceased in November, 1943.

With the completion of the 5,936th Dauntless on July 22, 1944, production of the SBD ceased. Although the type was still in operational service at the end of 1944 it was gradually being replaced by aircraft of more recent design.

The following information details briefly the development of the Dauntless :—

SBD-1. Wright R-1820-32 engine with two-speed supercharger, rated at 950 h.p. at 5,000 ft. (1,525 m.), 800 h.p. at 16,000 ft. (4,880 m.) and with 1,000 h.p. available for take-off. Welded fuel tanks, all in centre-section. Total capacity 210 U.S. gallons. Armament consisted of two 50 cal. guns in fuselage and one 30 cal. flexible gun in rear cockpit. Delivered to U.S. Marine Corps.

SBD-2. Similar to SBD-1 except for revision of fuel system to two tanks in centre-section (90 U.S. gallons each) and two in outer wings (65 U.S. gallons each). Total capacity 310 U.S. gallons. Armament consisted of one 50 cal. fuselage gun and one 30 cal. flexible gun. Automatic pilot installed. Delivered to U.S. Navy.

SBD-3 (A-24). Wright R-1820-52 engine with same output as previous power-unit. Aluminium-alloy fuel tanks with self-sealing liners. Two centre-section tanks (75 U.S. gallons each) and two outer wing tanks (55 U.S. gallons each). Total capacity 260 U.S. gallons. Same armament as SBD-1, but flexible armament revised in service to two 30 cal. guns to agree with later models. Armour protection and bullet-proof windscreen.

SBD-4 (A-24A). Similar to SBD-3 except Hydromatic airscrew, installation of 24-volt electrical system in place of former 12-volt, and other minor equipment changes.

SBD-5 (A-24B). Wright R-1820-60 engine rated at 1,000 h.p. at 4,500 ft. (1,370 m.), 900 h.p. at 14,000 ft. (4,270 m.) and with 1,200 h.p. available for take-off. Illuminated Mk. VIII sight for fixed guns and Mk. IX for flexible guns in place of former telescopic and ring sights respectively. Ammunition capacity increased. Radar installed. Otherwise as for SBD-4.

SBD-6. Wright R-1820-66 engine rated at 1,200 h.p. at 5,500 ft. (1,680 m.), 900 h.p. at 18,500 ft. (5,640 m.) and with 1,350 h.p. available for take-off. Non-metallic self-sealing

The Douglas Boston IV Medium Bomber, the R.A.F. equivalent of the U.S.A.A.F. A-20J Havoc.

The Douglas A-20K Havoc Attack Bomber (two Wright R-2600-29 engines).

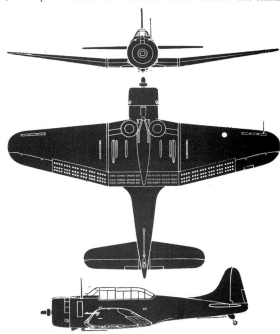

The Douglas Dauntless Naval Scout Bomber.

fuel cells of increased capacity. Total fuel, 284 U.S. gallons. Otherwise as for SBD-5.

Type.—Two-seat Scout Bomber (SBD) or Dive-Bomber (A-24).

Wings.—Low-wing cantilever monoplane. Rectangular centre-section with outer sections tapering in chord and thickness and with detachable wing-tips. Duralumin multi-cellular structure with flush-riveted stressed-skin covering. Metal-framed ailerons with fabric-covering. Trim-tab in port aileron. Slots in wings ahead of ailerons. Hydraulically-operated perforated metal dive-brakes above and below trailing-edges of outer wings and below trailing-edge only of centre-section beneath fuselage.

Fuselage.—Oval duralumin monocoque structure. For manufacture fuselage split longitudinally, the upper half in one piece and lower in three, plus a tail cone. Forward lower section includes built-in centre-section. Fuselage structure built up of channel-section transverse frames, extruded stringers and 24ST Alclad skin. Aft of rear cockpit solid bulkheads divided the rear fuselage into a series of watertight compartments.

Tail Unit.—Cantilever monoplane type. Fin built integral with fuselage. All-metal tailplane with stressed-skin covering. Rudder and elevators have metal frames and fabric covering. Trimming-tabs in movable surfaces.

Landing Gear.—Retractable type. The two cantilever oleo shock-absorber legs are hinged at the extremities of the centre-section and are raised inwardly, the wheels being buried in wells in the underside of the centre-section. Hydraulic retraction with emergency hand-operated mechanical gear. Locked or free swivelling solid-tyre tail-wheel. Deck-landing hook under rear fuselage.

Power Plant.—One Wright R-1820-66 Cyclone nine-cylinder radial air-cooled engine rated at 1,200 h.p. at 5,500 ft. (1,680 m.) 900 h.p. at 18,500 ft. (5,640 m.) and with 1,350 h.p. available for take-off. NACA cowling. Hamilton-Standard Hydromatic full-feathering airscrew, 10 ft. 10 in. (3.3 m.) diameter. Fuel tanks (4) in centre-section and roots of outer wings. Total capacity: 284 U.S. gallons. Oil tank (15.5 U.S. gallons) in engine compartment with oil cooler below. Controllable air scoop for oil cooler at bottom of cowling with fixed exit louvres on either side of cowling.

Accommodation.—Tandem cockpits beneath continuous transparent canopy. Bullet-proof windscreen. Sliding hood over pilot's and gunner's cockpits. Armour protection for crew. Duplicate set of controls in rear cockpit. Equipment includes Sperry automatic pilot, full radio equipment, automatically inflatable two-seat dinghy, oxygen, 24 volt electrical system, etc.

Armament.—Two 0.50 in. Browning machine-guns in fuselage firing through the airscrew. Two 0.30 in. machine-guns on flexible mounting in rear cockpit. Swinging bomb cradle beneath fuselage and bomb-racks mounted under roots of outer wing sections. For dive-bombing one 1,000 lb. is carried beneath fuselage, and two 100 lb. bombs, may be carried beneath wings. On scout-bombing missions, with increased fuel, one 500 lb. and two 100 lb. can be carried. Certain versions of the SBD are equipped for long-range photographic reconnaissance duties.

Dimensions.—Span 41 ft. (12.5 m.), Length 32 ft. (9.76 m.), Height 13 ft. (3.96 m.), Wing area 325 sq. ft. (30.2 sq. m.).

Weights and Loadings.—Weight empty 6,535 lbs. (2,970 kg.), Weight loaded (Dive-bomber) 9,519 lbs. (4,320 kg.), Wing loading 29.3 lbs./sq. ft. (142.9 kg./sq. m.), Power loading 9.5 lbs./h.p. (4.3 kg./h.p.).

Performance.—Maximum speed 255 m.p.h. (408 km.h.) at 14,000 ft. (4,270 m.), Cruising speed 185 m.p.h. (296 km.h.) at 14,000 ft. (4,270 m.), Stalling speed 78 m.p.h. (125 km.h.), Climb to 10,000 ft. (3,050 m.) 7 mins., Service ceiling 25,200 ft. (7,690 m.), Range (Dive-bomber) 456 miles (730 km.), Range (Scout-bomber) 773 miles (1,240 km.).

EASTERN AIRCRAFT.

EASTERN AIRCRAFT DIVISION, GENERAL MOTORS CORPORATION.

Head Office : Linden, N.J.
General Manager : L. C. Goad.
Assistant to General Manager : H. L. Jennings.
Divisional Controller : W. G. Kileen.

The Eastern Aircraft Division of the General Motors Corpn. was formed in January, 1942, to utilise the production facilities of five General Motors plants on the Eastern seaboard of the United States for aircraft production. These plants were at Baltimore, Md., Tarrytown, N.Y., Linden, N.J., Bloomfield, N.J., and Trenton, N.J., and all were formerly engaged in various branches of the automotive industry.

They were converted for the production of aircraft and built the Wildcat fighter and Avenger torpedo-bomber under licence from the Grumman Aircraft Engineering Corpn. to leave that company free to devote its entire facilities to the production of the F6F Hellcat, the F7F Tigercat and the F8F Bearcat. The General Motors versions of these two Naval aircraft were designated FM and TBM respectively. The first FM-1, assembled from parts supplied by the Grumman Company, flew on September 1, 1942. On December 5, 1943, the company produced its 1,000th Avenger and on April 11, 1944, its 2,500th Wildcat.

The last version of the Wildcat built by the Eastern Motors Division was the FM-2 (see under "Grumman"). General Motors was also going into production with the Grumman Bearcat under the designation F3M-1.

Following the final surrender of Japan all aircraft contracts with this concern were cancelled and all plants were due for reconversion to automobile production.

ERCO.

ENGINEERING & RESEARCH CORPORATION.

Head Office and Works : Riverdale, Md.
Chairman of the Board of Directors : H. A. Berliner.
President : L. A. Wells.
Chief Engineer : Fred E. Weick.
Sales Manager, Aircraft Division : Harry Agerter.

The Engineering and Research Corporation manufactures various types of machinery used in aircraft and airscrew production and it has recently begun the manufacture of controllable-pitch airscrews. It has also undertaken the design and manufacture of light aircraft.

The first aircraft produced by the Company was designed by Mr. Weick and was a two-seat all-metal low-wing cantilever monoplane incorporating a control system which eliminated the necessity for rudder pedals, the aeroplane being flown entirely by the control wheel. This aeroplane, known as the Ercoupe Model 415-C, was introduced on the market in 1940, but production ceased on America's entry into the war. In 1944 it was said that over 100 Ercoupes were still in use.

The Company has been fully engaged on defence contracts, but the Ercoupe Model 415-C was ready to go into production as soon as the situation permitted.

THE ERCOUPE MODEL 415-C.

U.S. Army Air Forces designation : YO-55.

Type.—Two-seat light monoplane.

Wings.—Low-wing cantilever monoplane. Wings of constant chord and thickness and with marked dihedral. Centre-section built integrally with fuselage. Structure consists of extruded duralumin spars and ribs, the centre-section metal-covered and the outer sections fabric-covered.

Fuselage.—All-metal structure with stressed skin covering.

Tail Unit.—Cantilever monoplane type with twin fins and rudders. All-metal structure with metal covering throughout.

Landing Gear.—Tricycle type. Nose wheel has an Erco oleo shock-absorber unit which permits taxying on air admitted at atmospheric pressure. Main wheels also have Erco shock-absorbers. 12 in. travel on all shock-absorbers. All wheels have low-pressure tyres and main wheels have internally-expanding hydraulic brakes.

Power Plant.—One 65 h.p. Continental A65 four-cylinder horizontally-opposed air-cooled engine. Fuel capacity 23 U.S. gallons.

Accommodation.—Enclosed cockpit seating two side-by-side. Ailerons, rudder and nose wheel are mechanically co-ordinated so that turning in the air and on the ground is accomplished by single wheel control. Rudder pedals may be installed and aileron-rudder connection removed to enable three controls to be used independently if desired. Large luggage compartment aft of cockpit.

Dimensions.—Span 30 ft. (9.15 m.), Length 20 ft. 9 in. (6.32 m.), Height 5 ft. 11 in. (1.82 m.), Wing area 142.6 sq. ft. (13.2 sq. m.).

Weights and Loadings.—Weight empty 725 lbs. (329 kg.), Disposable load 535 lbs. (243 kg.), Weight loaded 1,260 lbs. (572 kg.), Wing loading 8.8 lbs./sq. ft. (42.9 kg./sq. m.), Power loading 19.4 lbs./h.p. (8.8 kg./h.p.).

Performance.—Maximum speed 117 m.p.h. (187.2 km.h.), Cruising speed 105 m.p.h. (168 km.h.), Minimum speed (power on) 42 m.p.h. (67.2 km.h.), Initial rate of climb 700 ft./min. (352 m./min.), Service ceiling 13,000 ft. (3,955 m.), Cruising range 525 miles (840 km.).

The Ercoupe Model 415-C Two-seat "Two-control" Light Monoplane (65 h.p. Continental A65 engine).

ESHELMAN.

THE CHESTON L. ESHELMAN COMPANY.

Head Office : P.O. Box 4091, Dundalk, Md.
President and Secretary : Cheston L. Eshelman.
Vice-President : Sidney S. Zell.
Treasurer : Frank K. Kriz.

The Cheston L. Eshelman Company was formed on January 19, 1942, to undertake the development of aircraft. It has built five experimental aeroplanes of unconventional design, the latest of which, known as the FW-5, has been subjected to protracted tests at Logan Field, Dundalk. At the time of writing application was being made for an Approved Type Certificate.

The Company has also produced a conventional type three-seat low-wing cabin monoplane known as the Winglet. The only novelty about this aircraft is a tubular steel spar which serves as the fuel tank. The spar is baffled and the aircraft is fuelled at both wing-tips. The prototype has been submitted for A.T.C. approval.

THE ESHELMAN FW-5.

Type.—Four-seat cabin monoplane.

Wings.—Low-wing cantilever monoplane. Centre-section, which is built integrally with the fuselage, has a maximum chord of 15 ft. (4.6 m.) and tapers in span and chord to the points of attachment of the normal outer wings. Structure consists of steel-tube spars and ribs, plywood leading-edge and fabric covering.

Fuselage.—Steel-tube framework covered with fabric.

Tail Unit.—Fin built integrally with fuselage. Tailplane aft of fin with one-piece elevator. Steel-tube framework covered with fabric.

Landing Gear.—Temporarily fixed type, to be replaced by retractable gear. Hydraulic wheel-brakes. Full swivelling tail-wheel.

Power Plant.—One 325 h.p. Lycoming six-cylinder horizontally-opposed air-cooled engine on a welded steel-tube mounting. Two-blade Aeromatic constant-speed airscrew. Two aluminium fuel tanks (25 U.S. gallons each) in wing roots.

Accommodation.—Enclosed cabin seating four in two pairs, the front pair with dual controls. Four doors, with quick-release hinges for emergency exit. Framework of cabin stressed to support the weight of the aircraft in case it should turn upside down.

Dimensions.—Span 30 ft. (9.15 m.), Length 23 ft. (7 m.), Height 7 ft. 7 in. (2.3 m.), Wing area 232 sq. ft. (21.55 sq. m.).

Weights and Loadings.—Weight empty 1,507 lbs. (684 kg.), Disposable load 1,143 lbs. (520 kg.), Weight loaded 2,650 lbs. (1,203 kg.), Wing loading 11.4 lbs./sq. ft. (55.6 kg./sq. m.), Power loading 113 lbs./h.p. (5.13 kg./h.p.).

Performance.—Maximum speed 180 m.p.h. (288 km.h.) Cruising speed 165 m.p.h. (264 km.h.), Landing speed 50 m.p.h. (80 km.h.), Initial rate of climb 1,200 ft./min. (366 m./min.), Service ceiling 18,000 ft. (5,490 m.), Range 700 miles (1,120 km.).

The Eshelman FW-5 "The Wing" Four-seat Cabin Monoplane (325 h.p. Lycoming engine).

FAIRCHILD.

THE FAIRCHILD AIRCRAFT DIVISION OF THE FAIRCHILD ENGINE AND AIRPLANE CORPORATION.

EXECUTIVE OFFICE : 30, ROCKEFELLER PLAZA, NEW YORK CITY, N.Y.

WORKS : HAGERSTOWN, MARYLAND.

Incorporated : 1935.

Chairman of the Board : Sherman M. Fairchild.

President : J. Carlton Ward, Jr.

Vice-President and General Manager : R. S. Boutelle.

Chief Engineer : Armand Thieblot.

Secretary-Treasurer : W. H. Schwebel.

The Fairchild Aircraft Division dates back to 1925 when two groups interested in aircraft manufacture began separate activities which later were to merge and finally become the present organization. In that year the Fairchild Airplane Manufacturing Corpn. and the Kreider-Reisner Aircraft Co. were formed.

The Fairchild Aviation Corpn. of which the Fairchild Airplane Manufacturing Corpn. was a unit, took over the Kreider-Reisner Company in 1929 and when Mr. Sherman Fairchild re-purchased his interest from The Aviation Corpn. in 1931, his interests included the Kreider-Reisner Company. The name of the concern was changed to the Fairchild Aircraft Corpn. in 1935.

In 1936 the Fairchild Engine & Airplane Corpn. was formed to acquire from the Fairchild Aircraft Corpn. its aeroplane and aero-engine manufacturing subsidiaries and in 1939 the Fairchild Aircraft Corpn. became the Fairchild Aircraft Division of the Fairchild Engine and Airplane Corpn.

In 1941 the Fairchild Aircraft Division changed over to full-time military production, and plant facilities were doubled to increase the output of the Fairchild primary trainer. This type, now known by the type name Cornell, was produced in three versions by five aircraft manufacturers, the Fairchild Aircraft Division, the Aeronca Aircraft Corporation, the Howard Aircraft Corporation, the St. Louis Aircraft Corporation, and Fleet Aircraft, Ltd. (Canada). Between February, 1940, and May, 1944, when production of the Cornell ceased, over 8,000 were built, 5,000 by the Fairchild Aircraft Division.

The Fairchild 24 cabin monoplane has been supplied to the U.S. Army Air Forces, the U.S. Navy and the Royal Air Force as a light transport and communications type and is known by the Army as the UC-61, the U.S. Navy as the GK-1 and the R.A.F. as the Argus. The last model, the UC-61K (Argus III) was developed early in 1944 and was in production from April to November.

The latest product of the company is the C-82 Packet twin-engined Cargo Transport. Although this aeroplane was designed for military use its possibilities as a commercial passenger or freight carrier have not been lost sight of, and a civil conversion of the Packet is included in the company's post-war programme. This programme also includes the M-82, a development of the Cornell ; the F-24, a revision of the UC-61K Forwarder with either the 200 h.p. Ranger or 165 h.p. Warner engine ; and the M-84, a new four-seat low-wing cabin monoplane with retractable landing-gear and a 225 h.p. Ranger engine.

THE FAIRCHILD PACKET.

U.S. Army Air Forces designation : C-82.

The original design of the C-82 was begun in 1941 and the design and mock-up were approved by the U.S. Army in 1942. The actual detailed development and engineering, including the construction and preliminary testing of the prototype, which first flew on September 10, 1944, took less than 21 months.

The C-82 was put into production by both Fairchild and North American Aviation, Inc. but at the end of the war military production was reduced by 80 per cent. and the North American contract was cancelled.

TYPE.—Twin-engined Cargo and Troop Transport.

WINGS.—High-wing cantilever monoplane. Centre-section passes through top of fuselage at its point of maximum depth and slopes downward on either side of the fuselage to the points where outer wings are attached. All-metal two-spar structure with Alclad spars, ribs and outer covering. The outer wings are reinforced above and below by corrugated sheet beneath the smooth outer skin. The corrugated reinforcement is used on the undersurface only

The Fairchild C-82 Packet Cargo and Troop Transport (two Pratt & Whitney R-2800-22 engines).

The Fairchild UC-61A Forwarder Light Utility Transport (165 h.p. Warner R-500-7 Super-Scarab engine).

of the centre-section. Metal-framed fabric-covered ailerons. Electrically-operated slotted flaps between ailerons and tail-booms and booms and central fuselage.

FUSELAGE AND TAIL-BOOMS.— Metal monocoque structures. Central fuselage built up of Alclad frames, formed longitudinal stringers and a smooth Alclad skin. Seven longitudinal beams take the floor and tie-down loads beneath a plywood-covered floor. Aft end of fuselage is split vertically, the halves hinging outwards for direct loading into cargo hold.

TAIL UNIT.—Monoplane type with tailplane between extremities of tail-booms. Fins and tailplane have metal frames and metal covering. Elevator and rudders have fabric covering. Statically and aerodynamically-balanced elevator and rudders.

LANDING GEAR.—Retractable tricycle type. Main wheels raised into undersides of engine nacelle extensions, nose wheel into nose of central fuselage. Single main wheels each sprung by two oleo shock-absorber units, nose wheel by half fork unit. Electric retraction. Hydraulic wheel-brakes.

POWER PLANT.—Two 2,100 h.p. Pratt & Whitney R-2800-22 eighteen-cylinder radial air-cooled engines in nacelles at extremities of centre-section. Nacelles extended aft for attachment of tail-booms. Three-bladed Hamilton Standard constant-speed full-feathering airscrews. Fuel tanks in wings.

ACCOMMODATION.—Pilot's compartment seats two side-by-side in nose of central fuselage. Radio operator's position behind pilots. Main hold, which will carry loads up to 10 short tons, has unobstructed cargo space for its entire length. Main loading doors at rear of compartment, hinge outward to full cross-section of hold. Smaller doors for personnel use at front and rear of hold. Adjustable ramps permit vehicles, tanks, ordnance, etc., to be driven directly into hold. Floor is parallel to ground and is same height as that of standard truck floor to permit rapid loading operations under all conditions. Tie-down fittings located at centre of 20-in. squares over the entire floor area. Provision for troop transportation and for glider towing.

DIMENSIONS.—Span 106 ft. (32.1 m.), Length 75 ft. 10¼ in., (23.1 m.), Height 26 ft. 4 in. (8 m.), Wing area 1,400 sq. ft. (130.9 sq. m.).

WEIGHTS.—Weight empty 26,530 lbs. (12,045 kg.), Weight loaded 42,000 lbs. (19,050 kg.).

PERFORMANCE.—No data available.

THE FAIRCHILD FORWARDER.

U.S. Army Air Forces designation: UC-61.

U.S. Navy designation: GK-1.

British name: Argus.

The Forwarder was an adaptation of the Model 24 four-seat commercial monoplane and was originally produced as a light military utility transport in 1942 for the Royal Air Force, under the name Argus I. The Argus I, later adopted by the U.S. Army under the designation C-61, was fitted with the 145 h.p. Warner R-500-1 Super Scarab engine. This was followed by the UC-61A (Argus II) with the more powerful 165 h.p. R-500-7 Super-Scarab engine. Early in 1944 the UC-61K (Argus III), fitted with the 200 h.p. Ranger L-440-7 six-cylinder in-line inverted engine, was developed and was in production from April to November of that year.

The sub-types between UC-61A and K were various commercial models of the Model 24 bought secondhand for various military duties and given designations in the UC-61 Series. These were :—

UC-61B Model 24J (Warner Super-Scarab).

UC-61C Model 24R (Ranger 6-410-B1).

UC-61D Model 51A (Pratt & Whitney R-985).

UC-61E Model 24K (Ranger 6-410-B1).

UC-61F Model 24R (Ranger 6-410-B1).

UC-61G Model 24W (Warner Super-Scarab).

UC-61H Model 24G (Warner Super-Scarab).

UC-61J Model 24C (Ranger 6-390-D3).

A small number of the commercial Model 24R-40 (Ranger engine) was also given the designation UC-86.

Most of these have been illustrated and described in previous issues of this Annual. The description which follows refers to the UC-61K.

TYPE.—Four-seat utility-cargo monoplane.

WINGS.—High-wing braced monoplane. Wing in two sections, each attached to the top fuselage longerons and braced to the bottom longerons by parallel steel-tube struts. No. 22 wing section. Wings taper in plan and section where they join the fuselage. Structure consists of spruce spars and ribs, duralumin and steel-tube compression struts and wire drag bracing, plywood leading-

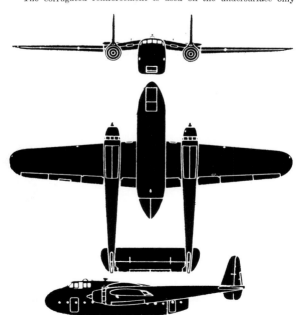

The Fairchild C-82 Packet Transport.

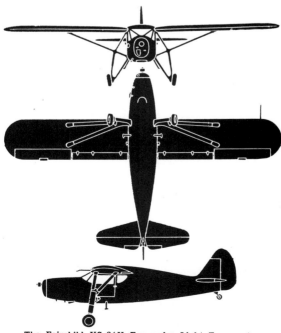

The Fairchild UC-61K Forwarder Light Transport.

The Fairchild UC-61K Forwarder Light Utility Transport (200 h.p. Ranger L-440-7 engine).

The Fairchild PT-19 "Cornell" Two-seat Primary Training Monoplane (175 h.p. Ranger engine).

edge, fabric covering. Frise-type statically-balanced ailerons have built-up aluminium-alloy frames and fabric covering. Flaps have aluminium-alloy and wood frames and are covered with aluminium sheet.

FUSELAGE.—Rectangular welded steel-tube structure, covered with fabric.

TAIL UNIT.—Normal monoplane type. Tail-plane and fin have wood spars and plywood covering, rudder and elevators welded steel-tube frames and fabric covering. Adjustable trimming-tabs on elevators.

LANDING GEAR.—Divided type. Each unit consists of a Fairchild oleo leg with 8 in. travel, the top end attached to the front wing-bracing strut, with the bottom end hinged to the bottom fuselage longerons by steel-tube axle and backwardly-inclined radius-rod. Medium-pressure tyres and wheel-brakes. Steerable-automatic swivel oleo-spring tail-wheel.

POWER PLANT.—One 200 h.p. Ranger L-440-7 six-cylinder in-line inverted air-cooled engine on steel-tube mounting. Fuel tanks (two) in wing roots, with a total capacity of 60 U.S. gallons.

ACCOMMODATION.—Enclosed cabin, seating four in two pairs with dual controls for the front pair. Sloping windshield and side windows. Two doors, one on either side, give access to either front seat. Seat cushions may be removed to accommodate seat-type parachutes. Dual controls may be disconnected and removed.

DIMENSIONS.—Span 36 ft. 4 in. (11.7 m.), Length 23 ft. 10¼ in. (7.24 m.), Height 7 ft. 7½ in. (2.3 m.), Wing area 193.3 sq. ft. (18.5 sq. m.).

WEIGHTS AND LOADINGS.—Weight empty 1,813 lbs. (823 kg.), Weight loaded 2,882 lbs. (1,308 kg.)., Wing loading 14.9 lbs./sq. ft. (72.7 kg./sq. m.), Power loading 14.4 lbs./h.p. (6.5 kg./h.p.).

PERFORMANCE.—Maximum speed 124 m.p.h. (198.4 km.h.), Cruising speed 112 m.p.h. (179.2 km.h.), Landing speed 57 m.p.h. (91.2 km.h.), Service ceiling 12,700 ft. (3,873 m.), Normal range 465 miles (745 km.).

THE FAIRCHILD CORNELL.

U.S. Army Air Forces designations: PT-19, PT-23 and PT-26.
R.C.A.F name: Cornell (PT-26).

There were three production versions of the Cornell, the PT-19, the PT-23 and the PT-26.

PT-19A. Fitted with the 175 h.p. Ranger 6-440C-2 six-cylinder in-line inverted engine. Built by the Fairchild Aircraft Division and the Aeronca Aircraft Corpn. Production ceased late in 1943.

PT-23. Built by the Howard Aircraft Corpn., the Aeronca Aircraft Corpn. and the St. Louis Aircraft Corpn. Identical in construction to the PT-19 but fitted with the 220 h.p. Continental R-670-11 seven-cylinder radial air-cooled engine. Production ceased in May, 1944. The PT-23 has been modified to carry two stretcher cases and was the first trainer to be re-designed for overseas duties.

PT-26. Adopted by the Canadian Government as the standard primary trainer for the Commonwealth Joint Air Training Plan and built by Fleet Aircraft, Ltd., Toronto, Canada (which see). Production ceased in May, 1944.

The following general description applies to all three training versions mentioned above.

TYPE.—Two-seat Primary Trainer.

WINGS.—Low-wing cantilever monoplane in three portions, consisting of centre-section and two tapering outer sections. Conventional two-spar construction with spruce spars and girder ribs and formed plywood covering. End ribs, landing gear ribs and those at the fuselage attachment points are of chrome-molybdenum steel. Built-in slots. Manually-controlled split flaps on centre-section. Statically and aerodynamically-balanced ailerons have aluminium-alloy frames and fabric covering.

FUSELAGE.—Welded chrome-molybdenum steel-tube framework. Fabric covering over wooden stringers except on top of fuselage aft of cockpits, which is of Duramold plywood.

TAIL UNIT.—Monoplane type. Fixed surfaces have wooden frames and plywood covering. Movable surfaces have welded steel-tube frames and fabric covering. Cockpit-controlled tabs on elevators.

LANDING GEAR.—Fixed single-leg cantilever type. Streamline wheels and hydraulic brakes. Steerable tail-wheel, which may be disconnected to become full-swivelling for ground manœuvring.

POWER PLANT.—One 175 h.p. Ranger L-440-1 (PT-19A) or 200 h.p. L-440-7 (PT-26) six-cylinder in-line inverted, or 220 h.p. Continental R-670-11 (PT-23) seven-cylinder radial air-cooled engine. Two fuel tanks (22½ U.S. gallons each) in each wing.

ACCOMMODATION.—Tandem cockpits, open (PT-19 and PT-23) or under continuous canopy (PT-26). Seats have vertical adjustment and are designed for seat-type parachutes. Dual controls. In PT-26 equipment includes cockpit heating, blind and night-flying instruments, etc.

DIMENSIONS.—Span 36 ft. 11 3/16 in. (11.2 m.), Length (PT-19A and PT-36) 27 ft. 11⅜ in. (8.5 m.), Length (PT-23) 25 ft. 10⅞ in. (7.9 m.), Height 7 ft. 6 in. (2.2 m.), Wing area 200 sq. ft. (18.6 sq. m.).

WEIGHTS AND LOADINGS (PT-19A—175 h.p. Ranger engine).—Weight empty 1,851 lbs. (840 kg.), Weight loaded 2,518 lbs. (1,143 kg.), Wing loading 12.6 lbs./sq. ft. (61.5 kg./sq. m.), Power loading 14.4 lbs./h.p. (6.53 kg./h.p.).

WEIGHTS AND LOADINGS (PT-23—220 h.p. Continental engine).—Weight empty 2,046 lbs. (928.8 kg.), Weight loaded 2,747 lbs. (1,247 kg.), Wing loading 13.7 lbs./sq. ft. (66.8 kg./sq. m.), Power loading 12.5 lbs./h.p. (5.67 kg./h.p.).

WEIGHTS AND LOADINGS (PT-26—200 h.p. Ranger engine).—Weight empty 2,022 lbs. (918 kg.), Weight loaded 2,741 lbs. (1,244 kg.), Wing loading 13.7 lbs./sq. ft. (66.8 kg./sq. m.), Power loading 13.7 lbs./h.p. (6.2 kg./h.p.).

PERFORMANCE (PT-19A—175 h.p. Ranger engine).—Maximum speed 125 m.p.h. (200 km.h.), Cruising speed 113 m.p.h. (181 km.h.), Stalling speed (with flaps) 52 m.p.h. (83.2 km.h.), Initial rate of climb 655 ft./min. (200 m./min.), Service ceiling 13,000 ft. (3,965 m.), Normal range 430 miles (690 km.).

PERFORMANCE (PT-23—220 h.p. Continental engine).—Maximum speed 131 m.p.h. (209.6 km.h.), Cruising speed 109 m.p.h. (174.4 km.h.), Stalling speed (with flaps) 54 m.p.h. (86.4 km.h.), Initial rate of climb 965 ft./min. (294 m./min.), Service ceiling 13,250 ft. (4,040 m.), Normal range 370 miles (592 km.).

PERFORMANCE (PT-26—200 h.p. Ranger engine).—Maximum speed 126 m.p.h. (201.6 km.h.), Cruising speed 114 m.p.h. (182 km.h.), Stalling speed (with flaps) 53 m.p.h. (85 km.h.), Initial rate of climb 675 ft./min. (206 m./min.), Service ceiling 17,300 ft. (5,276 m.), Normal range 450 miles (720 km.).

THE FAIRCHILD GUNNER.

U.S. Army Air Forces designation: AT-21.

The AT-21 was developed from two previous models, the XAT-13 and XAT-14. It was manufactured by Fairchild and under licence by the Bellanca Aircraft Corpn. and the McDonnell Aircraft Corpn. It was withdrawn from production in October, 1944.

TYPE.—Twin-engined five-seat Advanced Gunnery Crew Trainer.

WINGS.—Mid-wing cantilever monoplane. Centre-section has dihedral, outer sections flat. Wing structure comprises two wooden box spars and girder type former ribs, the whole covered with a Duramold skin, in which thin strips of veneer are bonded together and moulded to the requisite form under heat and pressure before assembly. Split flaps on centre-section are of wood and plywood construction. Ailerons on outer-sections have aluminium-alloy frames and fabric covering.

FUSELAGE.—Oval section structure. Forward portion has welded steel-tube framework with Duramold pre-formed skin. After portion from wings to tail is a pure wood monocoque with wood bulkheads and Duramold covering.

TAIL UNIT.—Cantilever monoplane type with twin fins and rudders. Fixed surfaces have wood spars and ribs and Duramold covering. Rudders and elevator have aluminium-alloy frames and fabric covering.

LANDING GEAR.—Retractable tricycle type. Unit under each engine nacelle comprising single air-oleo shock strut braced fore and aft by retracting strut and torque arms to resist torsional motion. Nose-wheel is free swivelling with air-oleo shock absorber unit. Hydraulic brakes on main wheels. Hydraulic wheel retraction with auxiliary hand gear.

POWER PLANT.—Two Ranger V-770-15 twelve-cylinder inverted Vee air-cooled engines, each rated at 450 h.p. at 12,000 ft. (3,660 m.) and with 520 h.p. available for take-off. Welded steel-tube mountings. Two-bladed Hamilton Standard constant-speed airscrews. Four fuel tanks in wings with a total capacity of 225 U.S. gallons.

ACCOMMODATION.—Crew of five comprising pilot, co-pilot (instructor), turret-gunner, nose-gunner and relief gunner.

ARMAMENT AND EQUIPMENT.—One flexible .30-cal. machine-gun in Plexiglas nose and two .30 cal. machine-guns in power-operated turret aft of wings. Equipment includes oxygen supply system, night-flying equipment, radio, radio compass, marker beacon receiver, cabin heaters, interphone system, etc.

DIMENSIONS.—Span 52 ft. 8 in. (16 m.), Length 37 ft. 11 15/16 in. (11.6 m.), Height 13 ft. 1⅝ in. (4 m.), Wing area 378 sq. ft. (35.1 sq. m.).

WEIGHTS AND LOADINGS.—Weight empty 8,654 lbs. (3,930 kg.), Weight loaded 11,288 lbs. (5,124 kg.), Wing loading 30.1 lbs./sq. ft. (146.8 kg./sq. m.), Power loading 12.5 lbs./h.p. (5.67 kg./h.p.).

PERFORMANCE.—Maximum speed 225 m.p.h. (360 km.h.) at 12,000 ft. (3,660 m.), Cruising speed 196 m.p.h. (313.6 km.h.) at 67% power at 12,000 ft. (3,660 m.), Initial rate of climb 930 ft./min. (284 m./min.), Service ceiling 22,150 ft. (6,760 m.), Normal range 910 miles (1,460 km.).

The Fairchild AT-21 Gunner Gunnery Crew Trainer (two Ranger V-770-15 engines).

FISHER.

FISHER BODY DIVISION, GENERAL MOTORS CORPORATION.

HEAD OFFICE : DETROIT, MICH.

AIRCRAFT WORKS : CLEVELAND, OHIO.

In 1942, the U.S. Army approved the construction of a prototype and probable mass production of a single-seat fighter designated the XP-75 and designed by General Motors' engineers under the supervision of Mr. Don Berlin, who was formerly Chief Engineer of the Curtiss Airplane Division of the Curtiss-Wright Corporation. Because of changes in military requirements the contract for the manufacture in quantity of the P-75 was cancelled in 1944.

The Fisher Body Division played a major rôle in the B-29 Superfortress production programme in a new aircraft plant under its management at Cleveland, Ohio. It was responsible for the production of most of the nacelles for the entire B-29 programme. Each nacelle is composed of more than 3,000 parts and four nacelles represented about 18 per cent of the production of each B-29.

At the end of 1944 the Aircraft Development Section of the Fisher Body Division was transferred to the Allison Division at Indianapolis in order to consolidate the aeronautical activities of the General Motors Corpn.

THE FISHER EAGLE.

U.S. Army Air Forces designation : P-75A.

The XP-75 was originally designed in 1942 to make use of parts and components already in production for other standard types of aircraft. For example, the design and first prototype incorporated Curtiss P-40 outer wings, Vought F4U landing-gear and Douglas A-24 tail-unit. The general layout of the design followed that of the Bell P-39 with the engine located amidships and shaft drive to an airscrew reduction gear-box in the nose. The power-plant consisted of a 2,600 h.p. Allison V-3420-19 twenty-four-cylinder engine driving co-axial contra-rotating tractor airscrews.

Development of the prototype resulted in a complete re-design of the wings and tail-unit, a lengthening of the forward fuselage, and several other changes, the final development model emerging in 1944 as a completely new design. A production order was placed for this version as the P-75A, but was later cancelled owing to the Army decision to limit the number of combat types in production and not to embark on the manufacture of new types of aircraft which might not be available in effective numbers before the war ended.

DIMENSIONS.—Span 49 ft. 1 in. (15 m.), Length 41 ft. 4 in. (12.6 m.), Wing area 342 sq. ft. (31.8 sq. m.).

WEIGHT LOADED.—17,200 lbs. (7,810 kg.).

PERFORMANCE.—Maximum speed 430 m.p.h. (688 km.h.) at 20,000 ft. (6,100 m.). Landing speed 88 m.p.h. (141 km.h.), Climb to 20,000 ft. (6,100 m.) 7 mins. Service ceiling 36,000 ft. (10,980 m.).

The prototype Fisher XP-75 Single-seat Fighter with P-40 outer wings and A-24 tail-unit.

The final version of the Fisher P-75A Single-seat Fighter (Allison V-3420-19 engine).

FLEETWINGS.

FLEETWINGS DIVISION OF KAISER CARGO, INC.

HEAD OFFICE AND WORKS : BRISTOL, PENNSYLVANIA.

President : E. E. Trefethen, Jr.

Vice-President and General Manager : S. D. Hackley.

Operations Division Manager and Assistant Secretary : S. H. Wilde.

Executive Assistant to the Vice-President and Assistant Treasurer : F. R. Browning.

Controller : W. E. Lucie.

Chief Engineer : G. G. Cudhea.

Research Engineer : C. de Ganahl.

Fleetwings, Inc., was organized in 1929 and has been engaged continuously in design and research work in stainless-steel construction. In 1934, the firm acquired its present works, formerly belonging to the Keystone Aircraft Corporation.

Up to 1939 the Company devoted its efforts largely to research work but since that time it has actively entered the manufacturing field and has executed contracts for the U.S. Army and Navy and sub-contracts for such firms as the Curtiss-Wright Corpn., the Republic Aviation Corpn., the Douglas Aircraft Company, the Vought and Sikorsky Divisions of the United Aircraft Corpn., the Brewster Aeronautical Corpn., Grumman Aircraft Engineering Corpn. and others.

The Company is doing an increasing amount of business in the manufacture of stainless steel and aluminium alloy aircraft parts and with its large line of hydraulic equipment. In addition, it has developed several experimental aircraft for the U.S. Army and Navy. The Fleetwings BT-12 trainer of stainless-steel construction has been described in previous issues.

In March, 1943 Mr. Henry J. Kaiser, the famous shipbuilder, acquired Fleetwings Inc., which is now operating as a Division of Kaiser Cargo Inc. of Oakland, Cal. Kaiser Cargo, Inc. was formed in November, 1942, as a subsidiary of the Henry J. Kaiser Company, the shipbuilding organization.

FLETCHER.

FLETCHER AVIATION CORPORATION.

HEAD OFFICE AND WORKS : PASADENA, CAL.

President and Chief Engineer : Wendell S. Fletcher.

Vice-President : Frank P. Fletcher.

Secretary and Treasurer : Maurice C. Fletcher.

The Fletcher Aviation Corpn. entered the aircraft manufacturing field in 1941 with a two-seat primary trainer employing a plastic-plywood construction and incorporating symmetrical wings and control surfaces to provide complete interchangeability of wings, flaps, ailerons and tail-surfaces. This aircraft, the FBT-2, has been described in previous issues of this Annual.

The Company was also developing a seven-cylinder radial air-cooled engine.

The Fletcher Aviation Corpn. was almost exclusively engaged in the manufacture of plastic plywood aircraft, components, parts and assemblies for various aspects of the War effort.

FORD.

THE FORD MOTOR COMPANY.

HEAD OFFICE AND WORKS : DEARBORN, MICH.

AIRCRAFT WORKS : WILLOW RUN, MICH.

GLIDER WORKS : IRON MOUNTAIN, MICH.

President and Founder : Henry Ford.

Executive Vice-President : Henry Ford II.

Vice-President and Treasurer : B. J. Craig.

Secretary and Assistant Treasurer : H. L. Moekle.

In April, 1941, the Ford Motor Company began the construction of an aircraft factory at Willow Run, 21 miles from the Ford main plant at Dearborn and 2 miles from Ypsilanti, to undertake the manufacture of bombers for the U.S. Government. This plant included its own airport, hangars, assembly building one mile long, machine shop, power plant and offices. The total manufacturing floor area of the Willow Run plant was 2,547,000 sq. ft.

Originally designed to produce only sub-assemblies and parts for the Consolidated B-24 bomber, the plant was later extended to include facilities for the final assembly of bombers as well as the production of complete sub-assemblies and parts.

The first Ford-built B-24 was accepted by the U.S. Army on September 30, 1942. By the time that Willow Run had ceased production on August 1, 1945, 8,809 B-24's had been produced, of which 6,915 were completed and flown away and 1,894 were shipped in parts for assembly elsewhere.

The Company's plant at Iron Mountain produced Waco troop-carrying gliders for the U.S. Army Air Forces.

FRANKFORT.

THE GLOBE CORPORATION, AIRCRAFT DIVISION (formerly Frankfort Sailplane Company).

HEAD OFFICE AND WORKS : Box 922, TOLIET, ILL.

President : George F. Getz, Jr.

Vice-President and General Manager : Russell E. Gage.

Secretary : Robert N. Little.

Treasurer : Bruce C. Hightower.

Before the war the Frankfort Sailplane Co., now the Aircraft Division of the Globe Corpn., built gliders, its most successful product being the Cinema two-seat model which proved its efficiency in various national competitions. As the TG-1 it has since been used by the U.S. Army as a training glider.

The Frankfort TG-1A Two-seat Training Glider.

THE FRANKFORT GLIDER.

U.S. Army Air Forces designation : TG-1A.

TYPE.—Two-seat training glider.

WINGS.—High-wing braced monoplane. No taper on braced portion of wing, outer portions taper to rounded tips. Single steel-tube bracing struts. Single spar structure of spruce and plywood with fabric covering. Spoilers on upper surface of wings inboard of ailerons.

FUSELAGE.—Welded steel-tube structure covered with fabric.

TAIL UNIT.—Cantilever monoplane type. Spruce and plywood structure covered with fabric. Horn-balanced elevators and rudder.

LANDING GEAR.—Single wheel on centre-line of fuselage with central skid sprung by rubber blocks ahead of the wheel.

ACCOMMODATION.—Tandem seats with dual controls under transparent canopy.

DIMENSIONS.—Span 46 ft. 3¼ in. (14.1 m.), Length 23 ft. 2¼ in. (7 m.), Height 8 ft. 3 in. (2.5 m.).

WEIGHTS.—Weight empty 500 lbs. (227 kg.), Weight loaded 920 lbs. (418 kg.).

PERFORMANCE.—Placard speed 80 m.p.h. (128 km.h.), Stalling speed 37 m.p.h. (59 km.h.), Gliding angle 20 : 1, Sinking speed 3.2 ft./sec. (.976 m./sec.).

G & A.

G & A AIRCRAFT, INC.

HEAD OFFICE AND WORKS : WILLOW GROVE, PA.

President : Virgil H. Frazier.
Vice-Presidents : J. L. Cohill and R. H. Isbrandt.
Production Manager : A. W. Keiser.
Chief Engineer : J. P. Perry.
Secretary : H. S. Brainard.
Treasurer : C. A. Pauley.

G & A Aircraft, Inc. (formerly the AGA Aviation Corporation) is the successor to the Pitcairn-Larsen Autogiro Co., Inc., which,

in 1940, took over the plant and all existing contracts of the original Pitcairn Autogiro Company.

In 1943 G & A Aircraft, Inc., was acquired by the Firestone Aircraft Company of Akron, Ohio, a subsidiary of the Firestone Tire and Rubber Company. Nearly 200 patents concerned with developments in rotary wing aircraft, covering both Autogiros for which the Company holds manufacturing rights from the Autogiro Corporation of America, and helicopters, were included in the transfer.

Details were released early in 1945 of an experimental Autogiro

which was developed for the U.S.A.A.F. Materiel Command by the AGA Corpn. before it was reconstituted as G. & A. The XO-61 is a two-seat aircraft with a central nacelle, twin tail-booms, tricycle landing-gear, a Jacobs R-915 engine driving a pusher airscrew, and a three-blade "direct take-off" rotor.

During the War G & A Aircraft Inc. produced cargo-carrying gliders and experimental rotary wing aircraft for the U.S. Government. It also undertook extensive sub-contract work for other aircraft manufacturers.

GENERAL.

THE GENERAL AIRCRAFT CORPORATION.

HEAD OFFICE : 4302, DITMARS BOULEVARD, ASTORIA, LONG ISLAND, N.Y.

President and Treasurer : E. S. Gremse.
Vice-President and General Manager : Lawrence W. Mattson, Sr.
Secretary : K. I. Deane.

The General Aircraft Corpn. entered the aircraft industry in 1941 with the production of the Skyfarer, a two-seat cabin

monoplane with simplified controls which had been designed and developed by Dr. Otto C. Koppen, Professor of Aeronautical Engineering at the Massachussets Institute of Technology. The Skyfarer was only the second aeroplane to be certified by the U.S. Civil Aeronautics Board as "characteristically incapable of spinning."

On America's entry into the War the Company discontinued the manufacture of the Skyfarer. In 1943 it granted non-

exclusive licences for the use of all patents associated with the design of the Skyfarer to Grand Rapids Industries, Inc.

During the war the Corporation maintained a small experimental department but devoted its main resources to the war effort. It completed large contracts for the manufacture of the Waco CG-4A troop-carrying glider for the U.S. Army Air Forces.

With the end of the war the General Aircraft Corpn. will now resume the manufacture of civil aircraft.

GENERAL AIRBORNE.

GENERAL AIRBORNE TRANSPORT, INC.

HEAD OFFICE AND WORKS : LOS ANGELES, CAL.

General Airborne Transport, Inc., was responsible for the construction of the XCG-16A military transport glider, brief details of which were released towards the end of 1944.

The XCG-16A, which was designed by Mr. Hawley Bowlus, is an all-wood twin-boom craft of 91 ft. 10 in. (28 m.) span, with an aerofoil "flying-wing" centre-section between the booms in which there are two cargo compartments 15 ft. (4.57 m.) long, 7 ft. (2.135 m.) wide and from 5 to 2⅓ ft. (1.5 to .76 m.) high, the two compartments being separated by a structural bulkhead. The loading or access doors in the leading-edge are opened upwards by hand-jacks, the forward sections of the floor hingeing downwards to provide loading ramps.

The crew's compartment is on top of the centre-section with seats for two in tandem under a continuous canopy.

The tailplane is carried between the booms and mounted on the centre-line is the single fin and rudder. The landing-gear is retractable.

The XCG-16A can carry 40 troops or a cargo payload of 4 short tons (3,635 kg.). It has a loaded weight of 19,600 lbs. (8,900 kg.).

The General Airborne XCG-16A "Flying-wing" type Military Troop and Cargo-carrying Glider.

GLOBE.

THE GLOBE AIRCRAFT CORPORATION.

HEAD OFFICE AND WORKS : NORTH SIDE STATION, FORT WORTH, TEXAS.

President : John Kennedy.
Vice-Presidents : William Viner and C. D. Reimers.
Works Manager : E. J. Rivers.
Chief Engineer : K. H. Knox.
Secretary : Edwin H. Jackson.
Treasurer : George P. Hill.

This Company was originally formed as the Bennett Aircraft Corporation to manufacture aircraft employing the use of Duraloid, a new phenol-formaldehyde bakelite-bonded plywood. In 1941 the Company was reorganized and the name was changed to the Globe Aircraft Corporation.

The first product of the re-constituted company was a small

two-seat low-wing cabin monoplane known as the Swift. The Swift Model GC-1 was awarded an Approved Type Certificate in the Spring of 1942 but it never went into production owing to the restriction of materials. A description of the Model GC-1 appeared in the 1942 edition of this Annual.

In 1942 a licence agreement was concluded between the Beech Aircraft Corpn. and the Globe Aircraft Corpn. under which the latter undertook to manufacture 600 Beechcraft AT-10 twin-engined training monoplanes for the US. Army Air Forces. This contract was completed in 1944 and to replace it the company undertook sub-contract work for the Curtiss C-46 and other aircraft.

The Company now plans to go into production with a new version of the Swift. The prototype GC-1A began flying tests in January, 1945.

The post-war Swift will have an all-metal fuselage and wooden wing, a hydraulically-operated retractable landing-gear and slots and flaps. The standard model will be fitted with an 85 h.p. Continental engine but a special model will be available with the 100 h.p. Lycoming engine.

The following is the provisional specification of the Model GC-1A.

DIMENSIONS.—Span 29 ft. (8.84 m.), Length 20 ft. 4 in. (6.2 m.), Height 6 ft. 2 in. (1.87 m.), Wing area 130 sq. ft. (12 sq. m.).

WEIGHTS AND LOADINGS.—Weight empty 1,030 lbs. (468 kg.), Weight loaded 1,569 lbs. (712 kg.), Wing loading 12.07 lbs. /sq. ft. (59 kg./sq. m.), Power loading 18.45 lbs./h.p. (8.4 kg./h.p.).

PERFORMANCE.—Maximum speed 135 m.p.h. (216 km.h.), Cruising speed 125 m.p.h. (200 km.h.), Landing speed 42 m.p.h. (67.2 km.h.), Range 600 miles (960 km.).

GOODYEAR.

THE GOODYEAR AIRCRAFT CORPORATION.

HEAD OFFICE AND WORKS : AKRON, OHIO.

President : P. W. Litchfield.
Vice-President and General Manager : Harry E. Blythe.
Vice-President in charge of Production : Russell DeYoung.
Vice-President in charge of Engineering : Dr. Karl Arnstein.
Vice-Presidents : E. J. Thomas, P. E. H. Leroy and J. M. Linforth.
Secretary : H. L. Hyde.
Treasurer : Zimri C. Oseland.
Comptroller : C. H. Brook.

The Goodyear Aircraft Corpn. was formed on December 5, 1939, to take over from the parent Goodyear organization its principal manufacturing operations in the field of aeronautics, with the exception of tyres, inner tubes, bullet-proof fuel tanks and other rubber accessories. This also included the activities of

the former Goodyear-Zeppelin Corpn., then mainly devoted to lighter-than-air craft. Since then the Corporation has undertaken the manufacture of aircraft, aircraft parts and sub-assemblies.

The Goodyear airship dock at Akron was first converted into a plant for the manufacture of tail-surfaces, outer wings and similar metal sub-assemblies for the Martin, Consolidated, Grumman and Northrop Companies.

Three additional plants were added as the war approached the United States, increasing the Akron floor space from 450,000 sq. ft. to over 3,000,000 sq. ft. The first of these, Plant B, was responsible for the manufacture of aeroplane wheels and brakes and also for the huge lighter-than-air programme of upwards of 200 airships ranging from the L type trainers of 125,000 cu. ft. capacity to the K and M patrol ships having a helium gas capacity of 425,000 and 725,000 cu. ft. respectively. With the completion of the airship programme in April, 1944, the manufacture of Lockheed P-38 tail-units took up the available floor space.

Plant C was erected to build wing and tail assemblies for the Martin B-26 and with the winding-up of that contract in February, 1944, another for the centre-section and tail of the Boeing B-29 Superfortress took its place. First B-29 assemblies were shipped away in the following month. Parts for the Northrop P-61 Black Widow were also built in this plant.

Plant D was built to house the complete production of the FG-1 Corsair, built to Chance Vought design. The Corsair contract was received in February, 1942, and the first Corsair was accepted by the U.S. Navy in April, 1943. On March 14, 1944, the 1,000th Corsair was delivered, and by mid-1945 production had passed the 3,000 mark. Late in 1945 details of the F2G-1, a Goodyear development of the Corsair, were made known. This incorporated a redesigned fuselage with blister-type cockpit canopy and a new power section fitted with a Pratt & Whitney R-4360 twenty-four cylinder four-row radial engine.

GRAND RAPIDS.

GRAND RAPIDS INDUSTRIES, INC.

HEAD OFFICE : MONUMENT SQUARE BUILDING, GRAND RAPIDS, MICHIGAN.

President : Frederick H. Mueller.

Grand Rapids Industries, Inc. embraces a group of furniture manufacturing plants which, during the war, was in production on wing and other wood sub-assemblies for trainers, troop-carrying gliders and other types of military aircraft.

This concern has also concluded agreements with the General Aircraft Corporation for the right to manufacture the Skyfarer two-seat light cabin monoplane with simplified controls, and for a non-exclusive licence to use all General Aircraft patents, including the two-control system embodied in the Skyfarer, whereby Grand Rapids Industries may develop and manufacture any aircraft of its own design incorporating these patents. The

acquisition of the licence to build the Skyfarer included the transference of a number of completed aircraft, all partially finished parts and material, and all jigs used in its production.

In 1944, the company transferred its Skyfarer licence to the Le Mars Manufacturing Co., of Le Mars, Iowa. It still retains the licence from the General Aircraft Corpn. to manufacture the two-control type of aeroplane.

GRUMMAN.

THE GRUMMAN AIRCRAFT ENGINEERING CORPORATION.

HEAD OFFICE AND WORKS : BETHPAGE, LONG ISLAND, N.Y.

Incorporated : December 6, 1929.

President : Leroy R. Grumman.
Executive Vice-President : Leon A. Swirbul.
Vice-President and Chief Engineer : William T. Schwendler.
Vice-President : E. Clinton Towl.
Secretary : Joseph A. Stamm.
Treasurer : Edmund W. Poor.

Since the beginning of 1942 the manufacturing floor space of the Grumman Company has been more than trebled and production was solely devoted to aircraft construction and experimental development for the U.S. Navy.

During 1944-45 the Grumman Aircraft Engineering Corpn. was in production with the F6F Hellcat, the F7F Tigercat, a twin-engined carrier fighter, and the F8F Bearcat.

The Grumman Company ceased production of the F4F Wildcat and TBF Avenger in 1943 but both types continued to be built in the five plants of the Eastern Aircraft Division of the General Motors Corpn.

The J4F Widgeon was in production for the U.S. Navy and Coast Guard until early 1945. With the approval of the War Production Board the company has continued to produce this model commercially for agencies or companies with a high priority rating. The Widgeon was at the time of writing the company's only product which is available for immediate post-war commercial use.

THE GRUMMAN BEARCAT.

U.S. Naval designation: F8F (F3M when built by Eastern Aircraft Division, General Motors Corpn.).

The Bearcat is a smaller, faster and more powerful development of the Hellcat. It is fitted with a Pratt & Whitney R-2800-22W engine. Further details and an illustration will be found in the Addenda pages.

THE GRUMMAN TIGERCAT.

U.S. Naval designation : F7F.

The Tigercat is a twin-engined Carrier Fighter Monoplane which is in service in two versions,—as the F7F-2 single-seat Day Fighter and the F7F-2N two-seat Night Fighter. Outwardly, the two versions are indistinguishable, as the Day Fighter uses the second cockpit to carry additional fuel tanks and no change is made in the canopy. Initially, the Tigercat was used by land-based Marine fighter squadrons, but ultimately it will form part of the equipment of the new 45,000 ton aircraft carriers of the "Midway" Class.

The F7F is a mid-wing monoplane with tricycle landing-gear and is fitted with two Pratt & Whitney R-2800-22W engines with water-injection equipment. For carrier use the wings outboard of the engine nacelles fold upwards, and deck arrester-gear is fitted.

The Tigercat can carry 4,000 lbs. of bombs, a full-size naval torpedo, rocket projectiles, etc. The heavy cannon armament is concentrated in the nose of the fuselage.

DIMENSIONS.—Span 51 ft. 6 in. (15.7 m.), Length 45 ft. 4 in. (13.8 m.).

THE GRUMMAN HELLCAT.

U.S. Naval designation : F6F.
British name : Hellcat.

The Hellcat was designed in the Spring of 1942, the prototype XF6F-1 first flew in August and it was in large-scale production as the F6F-3 by the end of the same year. The Hellcat was first reported in action with a U.S. Carrier Task Force in an attack on Marcus Island on September 1, 1943.

The F6F-5 differs from its predecessor by having a redesigned engine cowling, improved windshield, new ailerons, strengthened tail surfaces, additional armour behind the pilot and a waxed high-gloss skin finish. The F6F-5 can also carry two 1,000 lb. bombs under the centre-section, drop tanks in place of bombs and can be equipped with rocket projectile equipment.

TYPE.—Single-seat Fighter.

WINGS.—Mid-wing cantilever monoplane. Centre-section is flat and of constant thickness but has same constant taper as outer wing sections. Outer sections have dihedral angle and are arranged to fold. All-metal structure with flush-riveted metal skin. Split-flaps between ailerons and fuselage.

FUSELAGE.—All-metal monocoque structure with integral fin.

TAIL UNIT.—Cantilever monoplane type. Fin built integral with the fuselage. All-metal structure.

LANDING GEAR.—Retractable type. Shock-absorber units hinged at extremities of centre-section and are raised backwards, the wheels being turned through 90° to lie flush in wells in underside of centre-section. Hydraulic retraction. Retractable tail-wheel and arrester-hook.

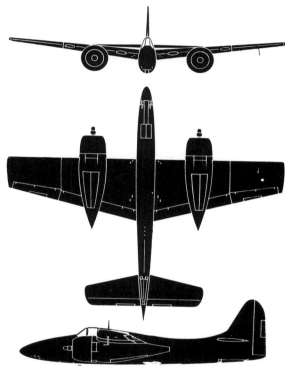

The Grumman F7F-2 Tigercat Twin-engined Fighter.

The Grumman F7F-2N Tigercat Two-seat Night Fighter (two Pratt & Whitney R-2800-22 engines).

The Grumman F6F-5 Hellcat Single-seat Naval Fighter Pratt & Whitney R-2800-10 engine).

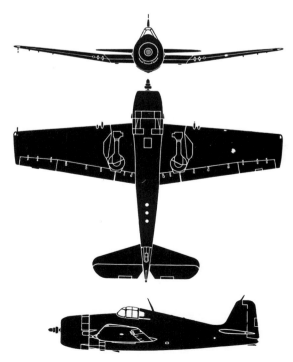

The Grumman F6F-3 Hellcat Single-seat Fighter.

The Grumman TBF-1 Avenger Three-seat Torpedo Bomber (Wright R-2600-8 engine).

The Avenger II Torpedo Bomber, the Royal Navy version of the TBM-1 built by the Eastern Aircraft Division of General Motors.

POWER PLANT.—One 2,000 h.p. Pratt & Whitney R-2800-10W eighteen-cylinder double-row radial air-cooled engine driving a three-blade Hamilton Standard Hydromatic constant-speed airscrew 13 ft. 1 in. (4 m.) diameter. Bullet-proof fuel tanks in wings. An auxiliary droppable belly-tank may be fitted.

ACCOMMODATION.—Enclosed cockpit over wing with sliding canopy. Bullet-proof windscreen and armour behind pilot.

ARMAMENT.—Six 50 cal. machine-guns, three in each outer wing.

DIMENSIONS.—Span 42 ft. 10 in. (13 m.), Width folded 16 ft. 2 in. (4.9 m.), Length 33 ft. 6⅝ in. (10.2 m.), Height 13 ft. (3.96 m.), Wing area 334 sq. ft. (31 sq. m.).

PERFORMANCE.—Maximum speed over 400 m.p.h. (640 km.h.), Rate of climb 3,000 ft./min. (915 m./min.), Service ceiling 37,800 ft. (11,530 m.), Maximum range 1,800 miles (2,880 km.).

THE GRUMMAN AVENGER.

U.S. Navy designation : TBF. (TBM when built by Eastern Aircraft Division, General Motors Corpn.).
British name : Avenger.

The XTBF-1 prototype of the Avenger was ordered by the U.S. Navy in 1940 and was delivered in 1941. The TBF-1 went into production in the same year and it began to go into service as a replacement for the TBD early in 1942. It was first reported in action in the Battle of Midway in June, 1942.

The Avenger was latterly in production solely by the Eastern Aircraft Division, General Motors Corpn., under the designation TBM. The first TBM-1 assembled from parts supplied by Grumman flew on November 11, 1942, and by December, 1943, all production of the Avenger by Grumman had ceased.

The last model of the Avenger was the TBM-4. This version was fitted with a Wright R-2600-20 engine, and had a strengthened airframe.

TYPE.—Three-seat Torpedo-Bomber.

WINGS.—Mid-wing cantilever monoplane. Rectangular centre-section and equally-tapered folding outer wing-sections. All-metal single-spar structure with flush-riveted smooth metal skin. Split trailing-edge flaps between ailerons and centre-section. Outer wings fold. Hydraulic folding and unfolding, the locking-pins being operated in the proper sequence by one motion of the hydraulic control lever.

FUSELAGE.—Oval section semi-monocoque structure built up of a series of angle frames and stamped bulk-heads and covered with a smooth metal skin which is reinforced internally by longitudinal Z and channel type stringers, with suitable stiffening at highly-stressed points.

TAIL UNIT.—Cantilever monoplane type. Integral fin with the cantilever tail-plane mounted above fuselage. All-metal structure with metal-covered fixed surfaces and fabric-covered rudder and elevators. Trimming-tabs in control surfaces.

LANDING GEAR.—Retractable type. Cantilever oleo legs hinged at extremities of centre-section and are raised outwardly into recesses in underside of outer wing-sections. Fully-retractable tail-wheel. Catapult points and electrically-operated retractable arrester hook. Provision for "Jato" rocket boost take-off.

POWER PLANT.—One 1,700 h.p. Wright R-2600-8 fourteen cylinder radial air-cooled engine with two-speed supercharger. Three-blade Hamilton-Standard Hydromatic constant-speed airscrew. Three main fuel tanks built integral with centre-section, centre tank (150 U.S. gallons) within fuselage and outer tanks (90 U.S. gallons each) in centre-section stubs. Auxiliary streamline droppable tanks (58 U.S. gallons each) under outer wings. Droppable long-range ferry tank (275 U.S. gallons) in bomb-bay. Oil tank (32 U.S. gallons) in engine compartment.

ACCOMMODATION.—Crew of three—pilot, bomb-aimer and radio-operator. Pilot's cockpit over leading-edge of wing. Pilot fires forward fixed guns and releases torpedo. Bomb-aimer's position in lower fuselage aft of bomb-bay. Bomb-aimer also operates ventral gun. Radio-operator aft of pilot serves as turret-gunner.

ARMAMENT.—One 30 cal. machine-gun in cowling and synchronised to fire through airscrew, one fixed 50 cal. gun in each outer wing, one 50 cal. gun in power operated-turret, and one 30 cal. gun in ventral hatch at aft end of bomb or torpedo bay. Bomb-bay can accommodate one U.S.N. short air torpedo, one 2,000 lb. or one 1,600 lb. armour-piercing bomb, four 500 lb. bombs or equivalent load of bombs of smaller calibre, a smoke-screen tank, droppable fuel tank or tow target and equipment. Hydraulically-operated bomb doors controlled by pilot or bomb-aimer.

DIMENSIONS.—Span 54 ft. 2 in. (16.5 m.), Width folded 19 ft. (5.8 m.), Length 40 ft. 0⅛ in. (12.2 m.), Height 16 ft. 5 in. (5 m.), Wing area 490 sq. ft. (45.5 sq. m.).

NORMAL LOADED WEIGHT.—15,536 lbs. (7,053 kg.).

PERFORMANCE.—Maximum speed 278 m.p.h. (445 km.h.), Rate of climb 1,075 ft./min. (376 m./min.), Service ceiling 22,600 ft. (6,890 m.), Normal range 905 miles (1,450 km.) at 215 m.p.h. (344 km.h.).

THE GRUMMAN WILDCAT.

U.S. Naval designation : F4F. (Also FM when built by Eastern Aircraft Division, General Motors Corpn.).
British name : Wildcat.

The Wildcat was first ordered by the U.S. Navy in 1940 and the F4F-3, F4F-4 and F4F-7, the last mentioned a special long-range photographic reconnaissance version of the F4F-4, were all built by the Grumman company. Concurrently, the British Martlet (later renamed Wildcat) Mks. I to IV were Grumman-built.

In 1942 the manufacture of the Wildcat was transferred to the Eastern Aircraft Division, General Motors Corpn. The first FM-1 Wildcat, assembled from parts supplied by Grumman, flew on September 1, 1942. By April 11, 1944, the Eastern Aircraft Division had produced its 2,500th Wildcat.

The FM-1 (Wildcat V) fitted with the Pratt & Whitney R-1830-86 engine, was virtually the same as the F4F-4 (Wildcat IV). The FM-2 (Wildcat VI), which went into production in 1943, is fitted with a Wright R-1820-56 engine of greater output but less weight than the previous power-unit, has a re-designed tail-unit with taller fin and rudder and has the oil-coolers removed from the under-surface of the centre-section to the cowling, which has been revised in shape. The removal of the oil-coolers permits the installation of universal racks under the inner wings for bombs or auxiliary fuel tanks.

The FM-2 and Wildcat VI have served as light escort-carrier fighters.

TYPE.—Single-seat Fighter.

WINGS.—Mid-wing cantilever monoplane. NACA 23015 wing section. Wings attach directly to sides of fuselage. All-metal structure with single aluminium-alloy spar and butt-jointed and flush-riveted smooth metal skin. All-metal vacuum-operated split trailing-edge flaps. Folding wings.

FUSELAGE.—Oval section monocoque structure of aluminium-alloy construction.

The FM-2 Wildcat Single-seat Naval Fighter.

TAIL UNIT.—Cantilever monoplane type. Aluminium-alloy construction with metal-covered fin and tail-plane and fabric-covered rudder and elevators.

LANDING GEAR.—Grumman type with wheel retracting into sides of fuselage. Fixed tail-wheel.

POWER PLANT.—One Pratt & Whitney R-1830-86 (FM-1 or Wildcat V) or Wright R-1820-56 (FM-2 or Wildcat VI) radial air-cooled engine. NACA cowling. Curtiss Electric or Hamilton-Standard Hydromatic constant-speed airscrew. Fuel capacity 160 U.S. gallons in self-sealing tanks in wings. Droppable fuel tanks may be carried on wing bomb-racks.

ACCOMMODATION.—Enclosed cockpit with sliding transparent canopy top over centre of wing. Bullet-proof windshield and armour behind pilot.

ARMAMENT AND EQUIPMENT.—Armament consists of six 50 cal. machine guns, three in each wing. Racks for two 250 lb. bombs, one under each wing. Versions of the F4F and FM are equipped for long-range photographic reconnaissance. These have comprehensive camera equipment but no armour or tank protection.

DIMENSIONS.—Span 38 ft. (11.6 m.), Width folded 14 ft. 6 in. (4.4 m.), Length 28 ft. 10 in. (8.5 m.), Height 11 ft. 11 in. (3.6 m.), Wing area 260 sq. ft. (24.2 sq. m.).

NORMAL LOADED WEIGHT (FM-1).—7,412 lbs. (3,365 kg.).

PERFORMANCE (FM-1).—Maximum speed 318 m.p.h. (509 km.h.), Rate of climb 1,920 ft./min. (586 m./min.), Service ceiling 34,800 ft. (10,615 m.), Maximum range 925 miles (1,480 km.).

The FM-2 Wildcat Single-seat Naval Fighter (Wright R-1830-56 engine).

THE GRUMMAN GOOSE.

U.S. Navy designation : JRF.
U.S. Army Air Forces designation : OA-9 and OA-13.
British name : Goose.

The Goose is a military adaptation of the commercial Model G-21A. It was first put into service in the U.S. Navy as the JRF-1 and the U.S. Coast Guard as the JRF-2 in 1939-40. Further series included the JRF-1A, fitted for target-towing and photography ; the JRF-3 (Coast Guard) fitted with anti-icing equipment and auto-pilot for use in Northern waters ; the JRF-4, a development of the JRF-1 ; the JRF-5, similar to the JRF-4 but fitted for photography ; and the JRF-6B, which was equipped as a navigational trainer.

The JRF-1 and 1A are in service in the U.S. Army Air Forces as the OA-13 and the JRF-6B as the OA-9. The British Goose is similar to the JRF-6B.

TYPE.—Twin-engined General Utility amphibian.

WINGS.—High-wing cantilever monoplane. Centre-section and detachable tapering outer sections. Metal structure consists of a tapering box-spar with its rear face at 36% of the chord from the leading-edge. Elementary rib structure and metal skin plating complete the leading-edge. The rear 66% of both centre-section and outer sections is fabric-covered over duralumin ribs cantilevered from the rear face of the spar. Vacuum-operated split trailing-edge flaps from hull to ailerons.

HULL.—Two-step all-metal hull. Rectangular section forward, but aft of second step the section is oval and fairs into fin. Six water-tight bulkheads.

TAIL UNIT.—Monoplane type. Cantilever fin built integral with hull. Tail-plane strut-braced to hull. All-metal framework with sheet covering. Movable surfaces have duralumin frames and are covered with fabric. Trimming-tabs in elevators and rudder.

LANDING GEAR.—Grumman type with parallelogram linkage mechanically retracted by worm and gear. Wheels withdrawn into recesses in sides of hull. Retractable tail-wheel, with centering lock.

POWER PLANT.—Two Pratt & Whitney Wasp-Junior R-985-AN6 radial air-cooled engines, each rated at 400 h.p. at 5,000 ft (1,525 m.). Steel-tube mountings bolted to lower flanges of box-spar and to upper edges of duralumin anchors built into upper surface of wing-spar at extremities of centre-section. Fuel tanks integral with box-spars. Total fuel capacity 220 U.S. gallons. Oil tanks in engine-mountings. Total oil capacity 15 U.S. gallons. Hamilton-Standard controllable-pitch airscrews.

ACCOMMODATION.—In the nose is a mooring compartment with stowage for anchor and marine gear, vacuum storage tank, radio units and excess baggage. Pilot's compartment seats two side-by-side, with dual controls and wide aisle between. Thereafter follows cabin, to which access is gained through a wide hatch at the trailing-edge of the wing on the port side. Emergency hatch on

The Grumman JRF-5 Goose General Utility Amphibian (two Pratt & Whitney R-985-AN6 engines).

The Grumman J4F-1 Widgeon General Utility Amphibian (two 200 h.p. Ranger L-440-5 engines).

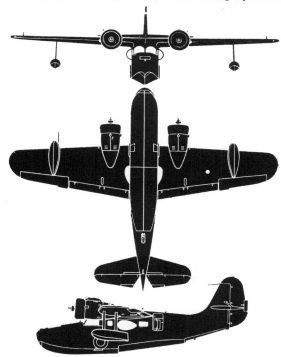

The Grumman JRF-6B Goose Amphibian.

starboard side, opposite main hatch. Equipment varies according to function of aircraft. JRF-5 and earlier models still in service are for general utility work, which includes personnel transport, ambulance duties, photographic work, target towing, etc. JRF-6B is a navigational trainer and general utility amphibian.

DIMENSIONS.—Span 49 ft. (14.95 m.), Length 38 ft. 4 in. (11.7 m.), Height (on wheels) 15 ft. (4.57 m.), Wing area 375 sq. ft. (34.8 sq. m.).

WEIGHTS AND LOADINGS.—Weight empty 5,425 lbs. (2,461 kg.), Disposable load (standard equipment) 2,575 lbs. (1,168 kg.), Weight loaded 8,000 lbs. (3,629 kg.), Wing loading 21.3 lbs./sq. ft. (103.9 kg./sq. m., Power loading 8.9 lbs./h.p. (4 kg./h.p.).

PERFORMANCE.—Maximum speed at 5,000 ft. (1,525 m.) 201 m.p.h. (323 km.h.), Cruising speed at 5,000 ft. (1,525 m.) 191 m.p.h. (307 km.h.), Rate of climb at sea level 1,100 ft./min. (335 m./min.), Service ceiling 21,000 ft. (6,405 m.), Maximum range 640 miles (1,287 km.).

THE GRUMMAN WIDGEON.

U.S. Navy designation : J4F.
U.S. Army Air Forces designation: OA-14.
British name : Gosling.

The Widgeon is a service utility version of the commercial Model G-44. It first went into service in the U.S. Coast Guard as the J4F-1 in 1941 and the U.S. Navy as the J4F-2 in 1942. It has also served in the U.S. Army Air Forces as the OA-14 and

in the R.C.A.F. and the Royal Navy as the Gosling.

Its principal functions are coastal patrol, air/sea rescue, light personnel transport and instrument flying training.

TYPE.—Twin-engined light General Utility amphibian.

WINGS.—High-wing cantilever monoplane. All-metal structure with large single box-spar containing integral fuel tanks. Centre-section metal-covered, outer sections metal-covered to rear of spar with fabric aft to trailing-edge. Slotted trailing-edge flaps from hull to ailerons. Flaps pulled down hydraulically but returned to up position by springs within the operating cylinders. Fixed trim-tab in port aileron. Flaps and ailerons fabric-covered.

HULL.—Two-step all-metal structure divided into five watertight compartments. No bulkheads in cabin.

TAIL UNIT.—Cantilever monoplane type. Tail-plane mounted half-way up fin built integral with hull. All-metal construction with metal-covered fixed surfaces and fabric-covered rudder and elevators. Trimming-tabs in movable surfaces.

LANDING GEAR.—Standard Grumman type with wheels fitting nearly flush in sides of hull. Retractable tail-wheel with directional lock. Windows in wheel pockets to check location of gear. Hydraulic retraction with emergency hand-gear.

POWER PLANT.—Two 200 h.p. Ranger L-440-5 six-cylinder in-line inverted air-cooled engines on cantilever mountings from wing spar. Nacelles accessible from upper surface of wing. Fuel capacity 108 U.S. gallons. Each tank normally supplies its own engine but cross-flow valve permits both engines to operate from either tank. Oil tank (3½ U.S. gallons) in each nacelle.

ACCOMMODATION.—Enclosed cabin seating four or five. Anchor compartment and entrance hatch in nose. Main entrance door behind wing on port side. Side-by-side seats with throw-over type control wheel in front of wheel pockets with sliding side windows. One fixed auxiliary seat behind left wheel pocket. Two seats ahead of door. Four fixed windows in cabin.

DIMENSIONS.—Span 40 ft. (12.2 m.), Length 31 ft. 1 in. (9.45 m.), Height 11 ft. 5 in. (3.48 m.), Wing area 245 sq. ft. (22.76 sq. m.).

NORMAL LOADED WEIGHT.—4,500 lbs. (2,043 kg.).

PERFORMANCE.—Maximum speed 153 m.p.h. (245 km.h.), Cruising speed at 62.5% power 138 m.p.h. (221 km.h.), Initial rate of climb 700 ft./min. (2,135 m./min.), Service ceiling 14,600 ft. (4,453 m.), Absolute ceiling 17,500 ft. (5,340 m.), Maximum cruising range 920 miles (1,472 km.).

THE GRUMMAN DUCK.

U.S. Navy designation : J2F-6.

Nine series of this particular aeroplane, which first appeared in 1933, have been built for the U.S. Navy and Coast Guard. The latest J2F-6 series was in production in 1944 by the Columbia Aircraft Corpn. of Valley Stream, Long Island, N.J. under licence from the Grumman Company.

TYPE.—General Utility amphibian for photographic, target-towing, rescue, ambulance and other similar duties.

WINGS.—Equal-span single-bay staggered biplane. Upper wing in two sections joined at the centre-line and carried above the fuselage on splayed-out struts and braced to the lower wings by N-type interplane struts. No transverse bracing in centre-section struts but vertical wires from strut attachments on wings to bottom of fuselage. Lift and anti-lift wires in plane of upper rear and lower front wing spars. Wing structure of metal with fabric covering. Spars have two extruded channel section booms with a wandering web riveted alternately to front and rear faces of channels. Shot-welded steel girder ribs. Frise ailerons on all four wings.

HULL AND FUSELAGE.—Single-step hull is a metal monocoque of aluminium alloy. Internal bracing of cross-floor type with longitudinal stresses taken by skin, with reinforcement from chines and keel and from inverted U-members riveted to deck in forward section. The fuselage is of stressed skin construction. The hull is stressed to catapult launching and deck arresting.

TAIL UNIT.—Braced monoplane type. All-metal fin and tailplane. Rudder and elevators have aluminium-alloy frames and fabric covering. Trim-tabs in rudder and elevators.

The Grumman J2F-6 Duck General Utility Amphibian built by Columbia Aircraft Corpn.

LANDING-GEAR.—Retractable type. Consists of two oleo shock-absorber struts with their upper ends hinged to extensions on two fore-and-aft revolving tubes and with their lower ends attached to axle-blocks which are hinged to the chines of the hull by steel-tube Vees. Wheels are raised into recesses in the sides of the hull. Retraction by chains and sprockets. Combined tail-wheel and water-rudder has self-centering lock.

POWER PLANT.—One 900 h.p. Wright R-1820-54 nine-cylinder radial air-cooled engine driving a three-blade Hamilton-Standard constant-speed airscrew. NACA cowling. Fuel tanks in fuselage. Capacities : main tank 150 U.S. gallons, auxiliary tank 65 U.S. gallons.

ACCOMMODATION.—Tandem cockpits under a continuous transparent canopy with opening sections over each cockpit. Folding door in rear cockpit gives access to lower compartment in which two persons may sit side-by-side. External doors on each side of lower compartment, which may also accommodate one stretcher case, target-towing gear, etc.

DIMENSIONS.—Span 39 ft. (11.9 m.), Length 34 ft. (10.37 m.), Height on wheels 13 ft. 11 in. (4.25 m.), Wing area 409 sq. ft. (38 sq. m.).

WEIGHT LOADED 7,700 lbs. (3,496 kg.).

PERFORMANCE.—Maximum speed 190 m.p.h. (304 km.h.), Cruising speed 155 m.p.h. (248 km.h.), Stalling speed 70 m.p.h. (112 km.h.), Service ceiling 20,000 ft. (6,100 m.).

HARLOW.

HARLOW AIRCRAFT COMPANY.

HEAD OFFICE AND WORKS : ALHAMBRA AIRPORT, ALHAMBRA, CALIFORNIA.

President : H. F. Keenan.
Vice-President and General Manager : Frank Der Yuen.
Vice-President and Secretary : J. E. Addicott, Jr.
Chief Engineer : D. Mendenhall.

The Harlow Aircraft Company was formed in 1939 to manufacture all-metal aircraft. Its first two products were the PJC-2 and PC5A. Both these types have been illustrated and described in previous issues of this Annual. Examples of the PJC-2 taken over by the U.S. Army Air Forces were given the designation UC-80.

On America's entry into the War in December, 1941, the entire manufacturing facilities of the Company were turned over to the production of standard requirements of the aircraft industry.

In 1945 Harlow bought the aircraft designs and production equipment of the Interstate Aircraft & Engineering Corpn.

HIGGINS.

HIGGINS AIRCRAFT, INC.

HEAD OFFICE AND WORKS : P.O. BOX 32, NEW ORLEANS 6, LOUISIANA.

President : Andrew J. Higgins.
Vice-President : Frank O. Higgins.
Director of Engineering : George A. Allward.
Secretary : Charles P. Fenner, Jr.
Treasurer : Morris Gotteswan.

Higgins Aircraft, Inc., was formed in 1942 to undertake the construction of transport aircraft for the U.S. Army Air Forces.

Higgins Aircraft, Inc., is a subsidiary of Higgins Industries, Inc., which, in turn, is owned by Mr. Andrew Higgins who has earned world-wide fame as a builder of ships.

Towards the end of 1942, Mr. Andrew J. Higgins was awarded a contract to build 500 Curtiss C-76 Caravan all-wood twin-engined transport for the U.S. Army Air Forces. In September, 1943, the C-76 contract was cancelled and replaced by another to build the same number of Curtiss C-46 Commando twin-engined all-metal transports.

On August 17, 1944, the Army, as part of a national cut-back programme on certain types of aircraft, cancelled the Commando contract but took delivery of two which were in an advanced stage of construction. After the completion of the second aircraft in November, the company undertook the manufacture of C-46 outer wings under sub-contract to the Curtiss Wright Corporation.

HELICOPTER DIVISION, HIGGINS INDUSTRIES, INC.

HEAD OFFICE AND WORKS : NEW ORLEANS, LOUISIANA.

President : Andrew J. Higgins.
Consulting Helicopter Engineer : Enea Bossi.

In 1943 Higgins Industries, Inc. began development of a helicopter under the direction of Mr. Enea Bossi in part of the Isaac Delgado Trade School, New Orleans, which was taken over by the Higgins organization for the purpose. This work was quite independent of the activities of Higgins Aircraft, Inc.

THE HIGGINS HELICOPTER.

The Higgins Helicopter is a two-seat single-rotor craft with

The Higgins Experimental Two-seat Helicopter (180 h.p. Warner engine).

a small vertical torque rotor at the rear end of the fuselage.

The power-plant consists of a 180 h.p. pressure-cooled Warner seven-cylinder radial mounted flat on the floor of the fuselage behind the pilot's cabin and driving the four-blade rotor through a clutch transmission and free-wheeling unit.

The four-blade rotor tilts as a unit and the direction of tilt determines the direction of flight. The pitch of the four blades is changed in unison, as opposed to the cyclical pitch-change in which the pitch is different for each blade depending on its position in the disc area.

For longitudinal or lateral control a normal control column is used, fore-and-aft or lateral movement rocking a swash-plate in the rotor head which causes the blades to tilt as a unit, the fuselage remaining on an even keel regardless of the pitch of the blades or the positions of their axes with respect to the axis of the fuselage. Pitch control for ascent or descent is by a separate lever operating a shaft within the main drive shaft which, in sliding up or down, changes the rotor pitch uniformly through a series of levers within the head acting on the rotor

spars. Blade pitch may be varied from 5 to 15 degrees. At a predetermined pitch control position hovering is achieved. In the event of engine failure a free-wheeling unit permits auto-rotation.

Directional control, by the usual foot pedals, is through the power-driven vertical tail rotor which consists of a two-blade variable-pitch propeller normally set, with pedals in the neutral position, to act as a torque compensator. Movement of the pedals varies the pitch. There is a small fixed stabilising surface opposite the hub of the torque or directional control rotor.

Structurally, the Higgins Helicopter has a metal-framed fuselage with a metal-covered cabin and engine compartment. The rear half is covered with fabric over a light fairing structure. The tricycle landing-gear has oleo-sprung main wheels and a steerable nose wheel. The enclosed cabin seats two side-by-side with the controls opposite the left seat. There are two doors, one on each side of the cabin.

HILLER.

HILLER INDUSTRIES, AIRCRAFT DIVISION.

HEAD OFFICE : 5TH AND ALLSTON WAY, BERKELEY, CALIFORNIA.

Partners : Stanley Hiller, Sr., Stanley Hiller, Jr. and Patricia Hiller Chadwick.

The Aircraft Division of Hiller Industries was established in 1942 for the development and production of co-axial helicopters. Entirely new principles of control and operation were incorporated in the first Hiller-copter model, which was publicly demonstrated in San Francisco in August, 1944.

Patent rights for this first successful co-axial helicopter were leased to the Hiller-copter Division of Kaiser Cargo, Inc. in September, 1944, for the production of Hiller-copters in the United States.

The Hiller-copter Division is engaged in further experimentation and development of a two-seat model. It is also producing for the U.S. Navy experimental Hiller-copter units of the co-axial type similar to those used on the prototype.

The prototype Hx-44 Hiller-copter, which is illustrated herewith, has an aerofoil-shaped fuselage of fabric-covered steel-tube construction, above which are mounted two two-blade oppositely-rotating rotors 25 ft. (7.625 m.) in diameter and driven by a 125 h.p. vertically-mounted Lycoming engine. No details of the transmission are available for publication.

The first experimental Hx-44 Hiller-copter (125 h.p. Lycoming engine).

WEIGHTS.—Weight empty 1,200 lbs. (545 kg.), Weight loaded 1,410 lbs. (640 kg.).

PERFORMANCE (Estimated).—Cruising speed 70 m.p.h. (112 km.h.),

Direct-lift ceiling 500 ft. (152.5 m.), Forward lift ceiling 8,000 ft. (2,440 m.), Cruising range 130 miles (178 km.).

HOCKADAY.

HOCKADAY AIRCRAFT CORPORATION.

HEAD OFFICE AND WORKS : 60, EAST ORANGE GROVE AVENUE, BURBANK, CAL.

President : Noel R. Hockaday.
Secretary and Treasurer : R. I. Hockaday.

The Hockaday Aircraft Corpn. was formed in October, 1937, and at that time the engineering and design of the Hockaday Comet two-seat light cabin monoplane was begun. This proceeded until 1940, when all experimental work was set aside

to enable the company to undertake sub-contract work for other aircraft companies.

In the Spring of 1944, work was resumed on the Comet and in June the prototype was test-flown.

THE HOCKADAY COMET.

TYPE.—Two-seat light cabin monoplane.

WINGS.—High-wing externally-braced monoplane. NACA M-6 wing-section. Wing structure consists of spruce spars, spruce and plywood ribs, plywood leading-edge, internal wire bracing and an overall covering of fabric. Parallel streamline steel-tube bracing struts with intermediate jury struts.

FUSELAGE.—Welded steel-tube framework covered with fabric over a light wood superstructure.

TAIL UNIT.—Braced monoplane type. Welded steel-tube framework covered with fabric. Streamline wire bracing.

LANDING GEAR.—Fixed cantilever type. Steerable tail-wheel.

POWER PLANT.—One 130 h.p. Franklin six-cylinder horizontally-opposed air-cooled engine. Fuel capacity : 24 U.S. gallons.

ACCOMMODATION.—Enclosed cabin seating two side-by-side with dual wheel controls. Equipment includes engine-driven generator,

electric starter, radio, complete blind-flying equipment, etc.
DIMENSIONS.—Span 33 ft. (10 m.), Length 22 ft. 2 in. (6.75 m.), Wing area 156 sq. ft. (14.5 sq. m.).
WEIGHTS AND LOADINGS.—Weight empty 953 lbs. (433 kg.), Disposable

load 647 lbs. (294 kg.), Weight loaded 1,600 lbs. (727 kg.), Wing loading 10.25 lbs./sq. ft. (50 kg./sq. m.), Power loading 12.8 lbs./h.p. (5.8 kg./h.p.).
PERFORMANCE.—Maximum speed 140 m.p.h. (224 km.h.), Cruising

speed 130 m.p.h. (208 km.h.), Landing speed 50 m.p.h. (80 km.h.), Initial rate of climb 1,150 ft./min. (351 m./min.), Service ceiling 19,000 ft. (5,795 m.), Cruising range 500 miles (800 km.).

HOWARD.

HOWARD AIRCRAFT CORPORATION.

HEAD OFFICE : 116, W. MAIN STREET, ST. CHARLES, ILL.
President : Daniel Peterkin, Jr.
Executive Vice-President and General Manager : Kenneth W. Rowe.
Secretary : F. B. Evans.
Treasurer : L. M. McBride.

The Howard Aircraft Corpn. was formed on January 1, 1937, to manufacture a four-seat cabin monoplane designed by Mr. Ben O. Howard.

On America's entry into the war the company discontinued the manufacture of commercial aircraft, and devoted its entire facilities to work of national importance.

The Howard DGA-15 was converted for service use and supplied to the U.S. Navy as a four-seat personnel transport under the designation GH-1, as an Ambulance as the GH-2 and GH-3 and as an Instrument Trainer as the NH-1. The company also undertook the manufacture of the Fairchild PT-23 primary trainer under licence.

In mid-1944 all Government contracts were terminated and the production of aircraft ceased. The company was unable to engage in the construction of non-military aircraft until the material situation was resolved.

THE HOWARD NIGHTINGALE.

U.S. Navy designations: GH-1, GH-2, GH-3 and NH-1.
TYPE.—Four-seat Personnel Transport (GH-1) Ambulance (GH-2 and GH-3) or Instrument Trainer (NH-1).
WINGS.—High-wing braced monoplane. Wings attached direct to upper fuselage longerons and braced to lower longerons by Vee struts. Wing structure consists of two rectangular spruce spars, built-up wooden ribs, and a covering of mahogany plywood, and finally fabric. Ailerons on the outer portions of the wings and landing-flaps between the ailerons and the fuselage. The flaps are electrically-operated and may be stopped in any position between neutral and fully deflected.
FUSELAGE.—Rectangular welded chrome-molybdenum steel-tube structure, with the cabin covered with aluminium sheet and the remainder with fabric over a light aluminium and wood fairing structure. The top and sides of the fuselage are flat and underneath is semi-circular.
TAIL UNIT.—Monoplane type. Wire-braced tail-plane and fin. Welded steel-tube framework, covered with fabric. Adjustable tail-plane.
LANDING GEAR.—Divided type. Consists of two fixed tripods of welded chrome-molybdenum round and streamline steel-tube, with the front and drag struts enclosed in streamline fairing. Front struts incorporate oleo shock-absorbers and spring dampers.

Hydraulic wheel-brakes. Steerable or swivelling tail-wheel, with spring-damped oleo shock-absorber.
POWER PLANT.—One 450 h.p. Pratt & Whitney R-985-AN-12 Wasp-Junior radial air-cooled engine. Hamilton-Standard Hydromatic constant-speed airscrew. NACA cowling. Fuel tanks below floor of cabin. Normal fuel capacity 152 U.S. gallons.
ACCOMMODATION.—The cabin arrangement in NH-1 is two pairs of two individual seats. Dual controls to front seat with third set of controls and instruments provided for left rear seat for instrument training. Arrangement for GH-2 is two front seats, two standard U.S. Navy litters or stretchers one above the other on left side of cabin and third seat on right side. Stretchers are inserted into and removed from cabin through specially enlarged baggage door on right side. Main cabin door, also on right side, is quickly detachable in flight. Stretchers can be replaced by fourth seat for conversion to personnel transport. Baggage compartment behind cabin.
DIMENSIONS.—Span 38 ft. (11.6 m.), Length 26 ft. (7.9 m.), Height 8 ft. 4 in. (2.5 m.), Wing area 210 sq. ft. (19.5 sq. m.).

WEIGHTS AND LOADINGS.—Weight empty 3,050 lbs. (1,385 kg.), Weight loaded 4,500 lbs. (2,040 kg.), Wing loading 21.4 lbs./sq. ft. (104.4 kg./sq. m.), Power loading 11.3 lbs./h.p. (5.1 kg./h.p.).
PERFORMANCE.—Speed at sea level 165 m.p.h. (265 km.h.), Maximum speed 175 m.p.h. (282 km.h.) at 6,100 ft. (1,860 m.), Cruising speed 154 m.p.h. (248 km.h.) at 15,000 ft. (4,880 m.), Service ceiling 20,000 ft. (6,100 m.), Cruising range at 6,100 ft. (1,860 m.) 700 miles (1,130 km.) for NH-1 or 875 miles (1,410 km.) for GH-2.

The description above applies to the service adaptations of the DGA-16 which have been supplied to the U.S. Navy. The U.S. Army also acquired a number of Howard cabin monoplanes of various models from private sources for use as utility or light personnel transports. These were given designations in the UC-70 Series as follow :—

UC-70A Model DGA-12 (Jacobs L-6).
UC-70B Model DGA-15J (Jacobs L-6MB).
UC-70C Model DGA-8 (Wright R-760-E2).
UC-70D Model DGA-9 (Jacobs L-5).

The Howard GH-2 Light Personnel Transport (Pratt & Whitney R-985-AN12 engine).

HUGHES.

HUGHES AIRCRAFT COMPANY.

HEAD OFFICE AND WORKS : FLORENCE AVENUE AT TEALE STREET, CULVER CITY, CAL.
President : Howard R. Hughes.
Vice-President and General Manager : C. W. Perelle.
Chief Engineer : K. F. Ridley.

The Hughes Aircraft Company was formed in 1936 by Mr. Howard Hughes, a young American sportsman and film producer,

to develop a racing monoplane with which he had established the International Landplane Speed Record of 352.46 m.p.h. (563.2 km.h.) on September 12, 1935. With a modified version of this monoplane Mr. Hughes flew non-stop across the United States, a distance of 2,490 miles in 7 hrs. 28 mins., representing an average speed of 332 m.p.h. In July, 1938 he flew round the World in 3 days 19 hrs. 8 mins. in a Lockheed 14 twin-engined monoplane.

The Company's most recent development was a high-speed

twin-engined twin-boom experimental monoplane known as the D-2, which Mr. Howard Hughes had under test in 1944. From this aircraft was evolved a military photographic reconnaissance monoplane which carried the U.S. Army designation XF-11. A contract for the production of this type was cancelled in 1945.

The Hughes Hercules eight-engined all-wood transport flying-boat mentioned in previous issues of this Annual was nearing completion early in 1945.

INTERSTATE.

INTERSTATE AIRCRAFT & ENGINEERING CORPORATION.

HEAD OFFICE AND WORKS : EL SEGUNDO, CAL.
President : Don P. Smith.
Executive Vice-President : W. E. Hirtensteiner.
Vice-President : Lawrence J. Lay.
Secretary : L. A. Kavanagh.
Treasurer : W. C. Barnett.

The Interstate Aircraft and Engineering Corpn. was organized in April, 1937, and the present management took over the corporation on August 29, 1938. The corporation designs and manufactures hydraulic units, bomb-shackles, gun-chargers both hydraulic and mechanical, and other precision units and mechanical assemblies for various major aircraft plants.

In 1940 the company produced the Cadet two-seat light cabin monoplane and since America's entry into the war Model S-1B, was, at the request of the U.S. Army authorities, developed into a light liaison and observation monoplane of the Grasshopper class. It was originally given the designation XO-63, later altered to XL-6. Several Interstate Models S-1A Cadets acquired

secondhand by the U.S. Army authorities were given the designation L-8.

In 1945 Interstate abandoned the manufacture of complete aircraft, all production equipment being sold to the Harlow Aircraft Company.

THE INTERSTATE S-1B.

U.S. Army Air Forces designation : XL-6.
TYPE.—Two-seat light cabin monoplane.
WINGS.—High-wing braced monoplane. Wing section NACA 23012. Structure consists of solid spruce spars, girder type ribs, metal leading-edge, steel compression struts and internal bracing, the whole covered with fabric. Steel-tube bracing struts with intermediate jury struts. Mass-balanced ailerons and split flaps.
FUSELAGE.—Welded steel-tube monoplane. Faired with a light super-structure and covered with fabric.
TAIL UNIT.—Braced monoplane type. Metal frames with fabric covering. Fin integral with fuselage. Trimming-tab in port elevator.
LANDING GEAR.—Semi-cantilever type with one oleo-spring shock-

absorbing unit mounted within the fuselage serving both legs. Low-pressure wheels and hydraulic brakes. Steerable tail-wheel.
POWER PLANT.—One 115 h.p. Franklin O-200-5 four-cylinder horizontally-opposed geared air-cooled engine.
ACCOMMODATION.—Enclosed cabin seating two in tandem with dual controls. Roof and sides of cabin to a point some way aft of the trailing-edge of the wings provided with Plexiglas panels. The side panels in the region of the seats slope outwards to give downward vision. Rear seat is reversible to enable observer to use collapsible table for maps, etc. Equipment includes engine-driven generator, electric starter, radio, complete blind-flying equipment, etc.
DIMENSIONS.—Span 35 ft. 6 in. (10.9 m.), Length 23 ft. 5½ in. (7.16 m.), Height 7 ft. 3 in. (2.6 m.), Wing area 173.8 sq. ft. (16.1 sq. m.).
WEIGHTS AND LOADINGS.—Weight empty 1,103 lbs. (500 kg.), Disposable load 547 lbs. (248 kg.), Weight loaded 1,650 lbs. (748 kg.), Wing loading 9.47 lbs./sq. ft. (46.2 kg./sq. m.), Power loading 14.3 lbs./h.p. (6.5 kg./h.p.).
PERFORMANCE.—No data available except Stalling speed (without flaps) 44 m.p.h. (70.4 km.h.), Stalling speed (with flaps) 39 m.p.h. (62.4 km.h.), Range 540 miles (864 km.).

KELLETT.

THE KELLETT AIRCRAFT CORPORATION.

HEAD OFFICE AND PLANT NO. 2 : LANSDOWNE AVENUE AND STATE ROAD, UPPER DARBY, PA.
PLANT NO. 1 : 58TH STREET AND GRAYS AVENUE, PHILADELPHIA, PA.
President : W. Wallace Kellett.
Executive Vice-President : R. G. Kellett.
Vice-President in Charge of Engineering : R. H. Prewitt.
Assistant to the President : William L. Wilson.
Factory Manager : W. V. Trelease.
Secretary and Treasurer : W. R. Yarnall.

The Kellett Aircraft Corpn., formerly the Kellett Autogiro Corpn., resumed its former name in June 1943, because of the larger scope of the aviation activities in which it is at present engaged. It is still, however, undertaking the development and manufacture of rotary-wing aircraft, in which it has been engaged since 1929.

In 1943 the Company completed the delivery of a small service development order for the YO-60 Autogiro to the U.S. Army Air Forces.

The YO-60 is a development of the Kellett KD-1A Autogiro

with jump take-off rotor head and a large transparent "bubble" canopy over the tandem cockpits. It is fitted with a 300 h.p. Jacobs R-915-3 radial air-cooled engine.

Kellett has been engaged in helicopter development work for several years and during 1944 the XR-8 helicopter developed for the U.S. Army Air Forces was successfully flown. The Kellet Company is no longer engaged in the production of Autogiros.

During the war the company was also engaged in the production of parts for other aircraft manufacturers.

LAISTER-KAUFFMANN.

LAISTER-KAUFFMANN AIRCRAFT CORPORATION.

HEAD OFFICE : 6376, CLAYTON ROAD, ST. LOUIS 17, MO.
President and Chief Engineer : John W. Laister.
Vice-President : M. Nanson Whitehead.
Secretary and Treasurer : John R. Kauffmann.
Assistant Secretary : William F. Nesbit.

During 1944 production at the main plant of the Laister-Kauffman Aircraft Corpn., was mainly devoted to the Waco CG-4A troop-carrying and cargo glider. When the original contract was completed shortly after the middle of the year, the company initiated an extensive repair and re-building pro-gramme on gliders of this same model which had been damaged in training.

During the year the company's experimental department completed two XCG-10A cargo gliders. In addition, Civil Aeronautics Authority approval was obtained on a civil version of the Army TG-4A two-seat training glider to be known as the LK-10B Yankee-Doodle Two.

In January, 1944, the Laister-Kauffman Aircraft Corpn. acquired the Bowlus Sailplane Co., Inc., by an exchange of shares and thereby acquired manufacturing facilities on the Pacific coast. Bowlus types taken over by Laister-Kauffmann included the experimental XCG-7 eight-seat military glider and the Baby Albatross, a light single-seat glider which will be marketed complete or in kit form for home building.

THE LAISTER-KAUFFMANN XCG-10A.

The XCG-10A is a large military glider capable of accommo-dating 30 troops or a freight load of 5 short tons. It is a high-wing cantilever monoplane with deep forward fuselage tapering aft to a tadpole boom which supports the tail-unit. At the break in the bottom lines of the fuselage clam-shell doors give access to the main hold 30 ft. (9.15 m.) long, 7 ft. (2.14 m.) wide and 8 ft. 6 in. (2.59 m.) high, which can accommodate a 155 m/m. howitzer or a 2½ ton truck.

Structure is entirely of wood with plywood covering. The main landing-gear wheels are fixed but the nose wheel is retract-able. The wings, which are fitted with Fowler type landing flaps, have an overall span of 105 ft. (32 m.). No other details are available.

THE LAISTER-KAUFFMANN XCG-7.

The XCG-7 is of similar general arrangement to the XCG-10A but is considerably smaller. The cabin provides accommo-dation for one pilot and seven passengers or troops. Access to the cabin is through doors on each side just aft of the pilot's cockpit.

The cantilever wing is of single-spar construction and incor-porates ailerons, landing flaps and spoilers.

The Laister-Kauffman LK-10B (TG-4A) Two-seat Training Glider.

FUSELAGE.—Welded seamless steel-tube framework covered with fabric over a light wood fairing structure. Centre-section spar and adjacent structure is heat-treated as a separate unit and welded into the fuselage truss.
TAIL UNIT.—Cantilever monoplane type. All-wood framework with fabric covering. Statically-balanced movable surfaces. Trimming-tabs in both elevators and in rudder.
LANDING GEAR.—Single wheel built into fuselage on centre-line.
ACCOMMODATION.—Tandem cockpits fore and aft of the centre-section spar. Dual controls. Sliding canopy over each cockpit.
DIMENSIONS.—Span 50 ft. (15.25 m.), Length 21 ft. 3 in. (6.48 m.), Height 4 ft. (1.22 m.), Wing area 166 sq. ft. (15.42 sq. m.).
WEIGHTS AND LOADINGS.—Weight empty 475 lbs. Weight loaded 875 lbs. (397 kg.), Wing loading 5.27 lbs./sq. ft. (25.7 kg./sq. m.).

THE LAISTER-KAUFFMANN BABY ALBATROSS.

The Baby Albatross is a single-seat glider of all wood con-struction which the Laister-Kauffmann Aircraft Corpn. intends to market after the war either complete or in kit form for home construction.
DIMENSIONS.—Span 44 ft. 4 in. (13.52 m.), Length 19 ft. 2 in. (5.84 m.).
WEIGHTS AND LOADINGS.— Weight empty 250 lbs. (113.5 kg.), Weight loaded 450 lbs. (204.3 kg.), Wing loading 3.5 lbs./sq. ft. (17 kg./sq.m.).
PERFORMANCE.—Aircraft towing speed up to 65 m.p.h. (104 km.h.), Sinking speed 2.25 ft./sec. (.68 m./sec.), Gliding angle 20 : 1.

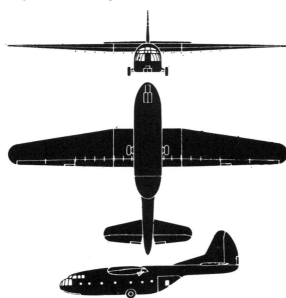

The Laister-Kauffmann XCG-10A Glider.

The Laister-Kauffmann XCG-10A Military Troop or Cargo-carrying Glider.

The fuselage, which tapers to a large tubular boom aft of the cabin, is a semi-monocoque built up of a series of laminated spruce frames with a plywood skin. It is divided into three sections to facilitate transport.

The landing-gear is of the conventional type with two main wheels and tail-wheel. The main wheels and the framework which attaches them to the fuselage may be jettisoned as a complete unit.
DIMENSIONS.—Span 65 ft. (19.82 m.), Length 53 ft. 4 in. (16.26 m.), Height (tail down) 13 ft. 9 in. (4.2 m.).
WEIGHT LOADED.—4,675 lbs. (2,122 kg.).

THE LAISTER-KAUFFMANN LK-10B.

U.S. Army Air Forces designation: TG-4A.

TYPE.—Two-seat Training glider.
WINGS.—Mid-wing cantilever monoplane. NACA 4418-12 wing section. Welded steel-tube centre-section integral with fuselage structure. Outer wing sections have single wooden box-spar, a stressed plywood leading-edge and a normal ribbed structure aft of the spar. The whole wing is covered with fabric. Ailerons hinged to false spar and are statically-balanced. Spoilers on upper surface inboard of the ailerons and are linked to operate with the wheel brake.

A line-up of three Laister-Kauffmann Baby Albatross Single-seat Gliders.

LANGLEY.

ANDOVER KENT AVIATION CORPORATION.

HEAD OFFICE and WORKS : NEW BRUNSWICK, N.J.
President : John J. Brooks.
Vice-President and General Manager : Lee E. Sherrod.
Vice-President and Sales Manager : William L. Smith.

Chief Engineer : Lawrence Smithline.
Secretary and Treasurer : Irving C. Schaefer.

The Andover Kent Aviation Corpn. specialises in the manu-facture of moulded plastic plywood aircraft, and with the most modern equipment it undertakes the mass-production of plastic

bonded aircraft parts and assemblies for the aircraft industry.
It also holds the manufacturing rights for the Langley twin-engined cabin monoplane, originally developed by the Langley Aircraft Corpn. This aircraft has been illustrated and described in previous issues of this Annual.

LANDGRAF.

THE LANDGRAF HELICOPTER COMPANY.

HEAD OFFICE AND WORKS : 8024, SOUTH WESTERN AVENUE, LOS ANGELES 44, CALIFORNIA.

President and Treasurer : Fred Landgraf.

Vice-President and Treasurer : James S. Ricklefs.

The Landgraf Helicopter Company was incorporated on September 20, 1943. The Model H-2 helicopter had been under development for some years previous to that date under the guidance of its inventor-designer Mr. Fred Landgraf. This experimental model was first flown on November 2, 1944. In 1945 the Landgraf Company received an experimental contract from the U.S. Army for development of the H-2.

The Landgraf Model H-2 helicopter has a number of revolutionary design features, among which are a cyclically-controlled aileron system on the tips of the rotor blades; automatic col- lective pitch control ; a centre of gravity ahead of the rotor axes ; a tricycle retractable landing-gear designed to withstand a vertical power-off landing ; and rotors which are overlapping and sychronised.

THE LANDGRAF MODEL H-2 HELICOPTER.

TYPE.—Single-seat twin-rotor experimental helicopter.

ROTORS.—Two three-bladed overlapping rotors rigidly attached to hubs which are carried on sloping booms springing from the sides of the fuselage. NACA 0015 aerofoil section faired to oval section at the root. Solid birch leading-edge spar with plywood covered trailing-edge. Metal hub. Ailerons on blade tips give attitude control. Pitch of all blades is the same and is automatically controlled through a centrifugally-operated spring-loaded device. Rotor speed 485 r.p.m.

FUSELAGE AND BOOMS.—All of plywood monocoque construction.

The Landgraf Model H-2 Twin-rotor Helicopter

The Landgraf Model H-2 Twin-Rotor Helicopter (85 h.p. Pobjoy Type R engine).

Vertical stabilising fin built integrally with the fuselage.

LANDING GEAR.—Retractable tricycle type. Air-oil shock-absorbers. 20 in. travel on main units to take a vertical power-off landing.

POWER PLANT.—One 85 h.p. Popjoy Type R seven-cylinder radial blower-cooled engine on a steel tube mounting aft of the pilot's cockpit. Fuel capacity 6½ U.S. gallons.

ACCOMMODATION.—Enclosed pilot's cockpit in nose of fuselage. Simplified controls require only a stick and throttle.

DIMENSIONS.—Two 16 ft. (4.88 m.) diameter rotors spaced on 11 ft. (3.35 m.) centres, giving an overall width of 27 ft. (8.23 m.), Length of fuselage 15 ft. (4.57 m.), Disc area (effective) 360 sq. ft. (33.4 sq. m.), Blade area 32.4 sq. ft. (3 sq. m.).

WEIGHTS AND LOADINGS.—Weight empty 636 lbs. (290 kg.), Weight loaded 850 lbs. (386 kg.), Disc loading 2.36 lbs./sq. ft. (11.5 kg./ sq. m.), Blade loading 26.2 lbs./sq. ft. (127.8 kg./sq. m.), Power loading 10 lbs./h.p. (4.54 kg./h.p.).

PERFORMANCE.—Maximum speed over 100 m.p.h. (160 km.h.). Other data confidential.

LEMARS.

THE LEMARS MANUFACTURING COMPANY.

HEAD OFFICE AND WORKS : LEMARS, OHIO.

The LeMars Manufacturing Company has purchased the manufacturing rights of the pre-war General Skyfarer G1-80 (See under "General" in the 1941 edition of this Annual). It will build this aeroplane after the war under the name LeMars Skycoupe.

The LeMars company acquired the rights from the Grand Rapids Industries, Inc. which, in turn, had bought the manufacturing licence of this aeroplane from the General Aircraft Corpn. in 1943.

LOCKHEED.

THE LOCKHEED AIRCRAFT CORPORATION.

HEAD OFFICE AND WORKS : BURBANK, CALIFORNIA.

Incorporated : 1932.

President : Robert E. Gross.

Vice-President and General Manager : Courtland S. Gross.

Vice-President in charge of Administration : Cyril Chappellet.

Vice-President in charge of Sales : Carl B. Squier.

Vice-President in charge of Engineering on Special Navy Projects : Mac Short.

Vice-President and Chief Engineer : Hall L. Hibbard.

Vice-President in charge of Materiel : H. E. Ryker.

Vice-President in charge of Finance and Treasurer : Charles A. Barker, Jr.

Secretary : L. W. Wulfekuhler.

Controller : Dudley E. Browne.

The original Lockheed Aircraft Co. dates from 1916 when the brothers Allen and Malcolm Loughead, the founders, began with what was the forerunner of the true streamline aeroplane. The factory was moved to Burbank, Cal., the present site, in 1926, and the name changed to Lockheed.

On November 30, 1943, the Vega Aircraft Corporation, which had been formed in 1937 as an affiliate, and in 1941 became a wholly-owned subsidiary of the Lockheed Aircraft Corpn., was absorbed and the name Vega has now been abandoned.

In 1945 Lockheed was employing approximately 100,000 men and women working in more than 100 geographical locations in 18 nations on five Continents. It operated 18 manufacturing plants in Southern California ; service bases and modification centres in California, Texas, Northern Ireland and England ; and liaison offices in Washington, New York City, Rio de Janeiro, Cleveland, Detroit and Chicago.

The main Lockheed Factory B has produced the P-38 Lightning and also handles the final assembly of the C-69 Constellation. Production of the P-38 was due to be terminated in October, 1945.

In 1944 preparations were made to go into large-scale production of the P-80A Shooting Star, the first jet-propelled combat aircraft to be ordered by the U.S.A.A.F. Four Lockheed plants were to be turned over to P-80A production, and manufacture was also to be undertaken in the Kansas City plant of North American Aviation, Inc. With the termination of the European War considerable cut-backs in military contracts were ordered and the North American P-80A programme was cancelled.

Factory A (the former Vega plant) undertakes the fabrication and sub-assembly of the Constellation and has also built the PV-1 Ventura and PV-2 Harpoon for the U.S. Navy. Lockheed production of the B-17 Fortress was also handled at this plant.

The Constellation, which has been in production as an Army transport, forms part of the company's post-war constructional programme. There is also under development a large 120,000 lb. airliner know as the Constitution and a medium-sized twin-engined feeder line type known as the Saturn.

THE LOCKHEED SHOOTING STAR.
U.S. Army Air Forces designation : P-80A.

The Shooting Star was the first jet-propelled combat aircraft to be accepted by the U.S. Army Air Forces. The XP-80 was designed round a British de Havilland H-1 jet-unit which was supplied to the American authorities in July, 1943, and turned over by Wright Field to the Lockheed company to power the prototype. In 143 days Lockheed had designed, built and flown the XP-80. Later, a General Electric power-unit was adopted for the YP-80 and the production P-80A.

TYPE.—Single-seat jet-propelled Fighter.

WINGS.—Low-wing cantilever monoplane. Laminar-flow wing section with knife-sharp leading-edge. Centre-line of wing 2 in. behind the midpoint of the fuselage. Wings of equal taper and no dihedral. One-piece wing of aluminium-alloy construction. Normal ailerons with hydraulic boost control. Electrically-operated split flaps inboard of ailerons with separate fuselage flap interconnecting the wing flaps. Fuselage flap may be operated with or independently of the wing flaps.

FUSELAGE.—All-metal semi-monocoque structure in three sections,— nose, centre and aft. Nose section contains either armament or photographic equipment, and oxygen, radio equipment and adjustable landing-light. Centre-section houses cockpit, fuel tanks and power-plant, with space below cockpit for hydraulic, fuel and radio equipment. Aft section incorporates the jet tail pipe and tail unit.

TAIL UNIT.—Cantilever monoplane type. All-metal construction. Balanced control surfaces.

LANDING GEAR.—Retractable tricycle type. Main wheels raised inwardly into underside of wings. Nose wheel raised into fuselage. Hydraulic retraction.

POWER PLANT.—One General Electric I-40 centrifugal-flow jet unit in centre-section of fuselage with air intakes on either side of the fuselage forward of the wing leading-edges. Aft section of fuselage, including the jet nozzle, removed by detaching three fittings and tail pipe clamp for servicing and maintenance of jet unit. Complete unit may be changed in 20 minutes. Self-sealing fuel tanks in fuselage and wings. Streamline drop tanks may be carried at the wing-tips.

ACCOMMODATION.—Pressurised cockpit over leading-edge of wings.

The Lockheed P-80A Shooting Star Single-seat Fighter (General Electric I-40 turbo-jet unit).

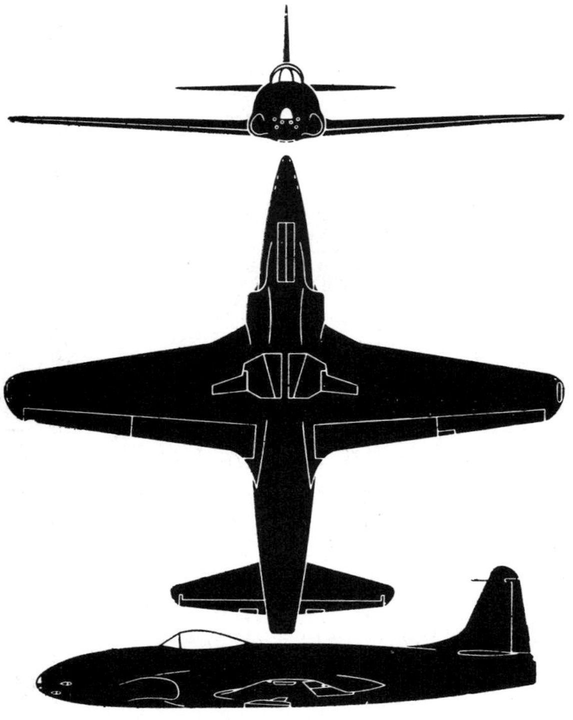

The Lockheed P-80A Shooting Star.

Sliding moulded cockpit canopy. Armoured windscreen. Steel armour plate on upper forward side of front bulkhead and behind pilot's seat and head, with duralumin armour plate aft of front bulkhead. Cockpit pressure is automatically reduced when the combat gun switch is turned to prevent physical injury to pilot from explosive decompression should the canopy be pierced. Provision for use of G-suit.

ARMAMENT.—Six 50-cal. machine-guns (300 rounds per gun) in lower portion of nose. Electric gyro-lead computing gun sight with reflex optical system. Guns and magazines may be removed and replaced in 15 min. without use of platforms or ladders. Complete gun nose can be replaced by nose containing camera equipment for photographic-reconnaissance duties. Gun camera in slight bulge in starboard air-intake duct. Bombs may be carried on wing-tip shackles.

FINISH.—Glass-smooth external finish. To attain this surface, rivets are cut and surface-ground. A zinc-chromate primer is applied, all butt-joints are cement-filled and flexible joints covered with organdy mesh tape. An undercoat is then applied and final paint coat is baked on in special ovens big enough to hold entire aircraft. Light sanding and buffing follow. Finally, a specially-developed wax is sprayed on and polished.

DIMENSIONS.—Span 38 ft. 10½ in. (11.8 m.), Length 34 ft. 6 in. (10.5 m.), Height 11 ft. 4 in. (3.45 m.), Wing area 237 sq. ft. (22 sq. m.), Total area of control surfaces 31.6 sq. ft. (2.93 sq. m.).

WEIGHTS.—Weight empty 8,000 lbs. (3,630 kg.), Maximum take-off weight (maximum fuel) 14,000 lbs. (6,360 kg.).

PERFORMANCE.—Maximum speed over 550 m.p.h. (880 km.h.), Ceiling over 45,000 ft. (13,720 m.).

THE LOCKHEED XP-58.

The XP-58 was an experimental two-seat fighter monoplane similar in general arrangement to the P-38 but fitted with a flexible rear-firing armament of four 50-cal. guns in addition to the fixed nose armament of two 20 m/m. cannon and four 50-cal. guns

The power-plant of the XP-58 consisted of two Wright R-2160 Tornado 42-cylinder seven-bank liquid-cooled engines driving handed airscrews.

THE LOCKHEED XP-49.

The XP-49 was an experimental prototype which resembled the P-38 except for the engine installation. This consisted of two Continental I-1430 inverted twelve-cylinder Vee liquid-cooled engines driving handed airscrews. Armament was similar to that of the P-38.

THE LOCKHEED LIGHTNING.

U.S. Army Air Forces designation: P-38 and F-5.

The Lightning was the first military type developed by the Lockheed Aircraft Corpn. It was designed to meet an Air Corps specification issued in 1936 for a twin-engined interceptor fighter a specification which called for, among many other stringent requirements, a minimum speed of 360 m.p.h. (576 km.h.) at 20,000 ft. (6,100 m.). The design was accepted by the Air Corps on June 23, 1937, and the XP-38 prototype was delivered in January 1939. It made its first flight on January 27, 1939, but crashed at the end of a record transcontinental flight from California to New York on February 11. The XP-38 was fitted with two 1,040 h.p. Allison V-1710-33 (C15) engines with exhaust-driven G.E. turbo-superchargers and driving Curtiss electric inwardly-rotating airscrews. The armament consisted of one 23 m/m. Madsen cannon and four 50 cal. machine-guns.

YP-38. A Limited Procurement order for 13 YP-38's followed. Complete structural re-design lightened this model by 1,300 lbs. It was fitted with two 1,150 h.p. Allison V-1710-27/29 (F2R/F2L) engines driving outwardly-rotating airscrews. (*Note*: V-1710-27 (F2R) righthand rotation, V-1710-29 (F2L) lefthand rotation, both from rear end). The turbo and coolant installations were improved. The armament compartment was re-designed to house one 37 m/m. cannon, two 50 cal. and two 30 cal. machine-guns. The YP-38 first flew on September 18, 1940, and first delivery to the Air Corps was made in March, 1941.

P-38. Deliveries were begun in July, 1941. The 30 cal. guns were replaced by two 50 cal. guns and pilot armour was added. Thirty were built.

P-38D. In this model self-sealing tanks were introduced. A change in angle of incidence of the tailplane and redistribution of elevator balance weights improved elevator control, facilitated dive recoveries and eliminated tail-buffeting. Deliveries began in August, 1941.

P-38E. Principal change in this model was in armament. The 37 m/m. cannon was replaced by one of 20 m/m., the standard cannon on all subsequent models. The armament compartment and nose landing gear section were also completely re-designed to accommodate double the quantity of ammunition previously carried. Deliveries began in November, 1941.

P-38F. Power-plant changed to two 1,325 h.p. Allison V-1710-49/53 (F5R/F5L) engines. The P-38F was the first model to be equipped with brackets for 150 gal. auxiliary fuel tanks or 1,000 lb. bombs, one under each inner wing section. The P-38F was also the first model to be converted for training by the removal of all radio equipment and the substitution of a second seat behind the pilot for a trainee to get air experience in the P-38 before taking off alone. Dual control was not fitted. Deliveries began in March, 1942.

P-38G. A further power-plant change to two 1,325 h.p. Allison V-1710-51/55 (F10R/F10L) engines, each giving an additional 100 h.p. for cruising. The first version to use the so-called "manoeuvring" flaps, a feature of all subsequent models. The Fowler-type flaps are given a special combat setting which permits a small extension and droop to provide greatly increased lift for very little drag. The result is a very high degree of manoeuvrability over a wide speed range. The capacity of the auxiliary fuel tanks was doubled and, fitted with two 300 gal. auxiliary fuel tanks, the P-38G was the first American fighter to be ferried across the Atlantic by way of Labrador, Greenland and Iceland. The first trans-ocean flight was made early in 1943 by more than 100 Lightnings, escorted by Boeing Fortresses for navigational purposes. Deliveries began in August, 1942.

P-38H. This model was essentially the same as the P-38G except for the installation of two Allison V-1710-89/91 (F17R/F17L) engines, each developing 1,425 h.p. for take-off and, when needed, 1,600 "war emergency" h.p. Automatic control of coolant radiator shutters was introduced and the electrical system was modified. The P-38H, operating in the Pacific theatre, was the first model to carry two 1,600 lb. bombs. Deliveries began in the Summer of 1943.

P-38J. Fitted with the same engines as the P-38H but with increased take-off and altitude ratings, and driving new airscrews to give improved speed and climb at altitude. The former leading-edge type intercoolers replaced by core-type intercoolers and re-located with the oil radiators in scoops beneath each engine. The engine coolant radiators on the tail booms given greater capacity. Additional fuel tanks installed in the leading-edges of the outer wing sections. An optically-flat bullet-proof windscreen replaced the former curved screen. Late models in the J series were fitted with electrically-operated dive-flaps and an aileron boost system.

To serve as bombing formation leaders a number of P-38J fighters were converted into two-seaters to carry a bombardier and Norden bomb-sight. The first conversion, carried out by Lockheed engineers at Langford Lodge, England, had a typical Boston-type transparent nose and carried instruments for both navigation and bombing. These aircraft, without armament or bombs, led formations of Lightning fighter-bombers, each carrying 3,200 lbs. of bombs, on high-altitude precision bombing missions and were responsible for navigation to the target and for supervising the dropping of all bombs of the formation.

This first version was later superseded by the "Pathfinder" P-38, which had a new elongated cylindrical nacelle with blunt hemispherical nose. This model was developed at the Lockheed Modification Center at Dallas, Texas. The "Pathfinder" was fitted with more advanced instruments than its predecessor, including "Gee" radar equipment for bombing through cloud.

P-38K. This was an experimental model with an improved power-plant but the P-38L was developed so quickly that the K model was never put into production.

P-38L. A development of the P-38J. Fitted with two Allison V-1710-111/113 (F30R/F30L) engines, each with a rated output of 1,475 h.p. and a considerably higher war emergency horsepower than in previous models. A new General Electric turbo regulator replaced the hydraulic regulator used in the P-38J. Some P-38L's were also fitted with bombardier noses introduced in the P-38J (which see).

Two photographs on this page show the rocket projectile installation used on the P-39L Lightning in the closing stages of the war. The upper illustration shows the first installation of the American 5-inch rocket-projectile in two batteries of seven on free flight launchers which released their projectiles after one inch of forward motion. The fitting of seven of these launchers under each wing necessitated changes in the Lightning's wing structure and this arrangement was abandoned in favour of the inverted pyramid mounting shown in the lower illustration. This mounting was installed as standard equipment during the last few months of Lightning production, and it was also issued to squadrons for installation in the field.

F-4. The first unarmed photographic-reconnaissance version of the Lightning. It was a conversion of the P-38E (F-4) and P-38F (F-4A) and was fitted with four cameras. Deliveries began in March, 1942.

F-5. A development of the F-4. From three to five cameras in any one of four different installations may be carried in the nacelle nose. Cameras are remotely controlled by an electrical impulse unit and may be operated either separately or collectively. A shutterless continuous-strip camera is used for low altitude photography. The Sperry A-4 automatic pilot is standard equipment. The photographic Lightning was several hundred pounds lighter than its fighter counterpart and was some 10 m.p.h. faster.

TYPE.—Twin-engined single-seat Fighter or Fighter-Bomber.

WINGS.—Mid-wing cantilever monoplane. Wings taper in chord and thickness and are set at 5°40′ dihedral throughout span. In five sections, comprising centre-section, two outer sections and two tips. All-metal construction, mainly 24ST Alclad. Structure of centre-section consists of a main box spar and front and rear shear members, the whole tied together with corrugated and flat sheet to form a box section in which space is provided for the fuel cells. Outer sections built up of single-web spar, rear shear member, sheet ribs and upper and lower stressed skins. At the rear of shear members and inboard of the ailerons are the trailing-edge ribs which support the rear upper skin and the Lockheed-Fowler flaps. The leading-edge is separate and is built up of upper and lower halves joined at the leading-edge with piano-type hinges. All-metal hydraulically-operated Fowler-type trailing-edge flaps. Separate electrically-operated dive flaps outboard of engine nacelles and hinged to under surface of wings beneath main spar. All-metal statically and aerodynamically-balanced ailerons on piano-type hinges. Hydraulically-operated aileron "booster" system so that the pilot retains feel but supplies only 17 per cent of the force required to operate ailerons.

NACELLE.—All-metal structure built of bulkheads and covered with flush-riveted smooth metal skin.

TAIL BOOMS.—Booms extend from the fireproof bulkheads to the tail-unit attachments, and are in two portions, front portions accommodating the turbo-superchargers and main landing gear units, and the rear portions the coolant radiators. Semi-monocoque structures built up of bulkheads and rolled sheet covering reinforced internally with extruded bulb angles. Mainly of 24ST Alclad but stainless steel used in region of superchargers in front sections.

TAIL UNIT.—Monoplane type with fins and rudders at extremities of tail booms and single-piece tailplane and elevator between booms. Tailplane built of two spars and smooth flush-riveted skin reinforced internally with extruded bulb angles. Elevator, of similar construction, statically balanced by three weights, one in each boom and one on the centre-line. Elevator attached to tailplane by piano-type hinges. Centrally-placed controllable trim-tab. Fins, including tail-cones of booms, made up of multiple shear webs, ribs and smooth skin covering. Rudders, of similar construction, are statically and aerodynamically-balanced and provided with trim-tabs. Entire tail-unit quickly detachable.

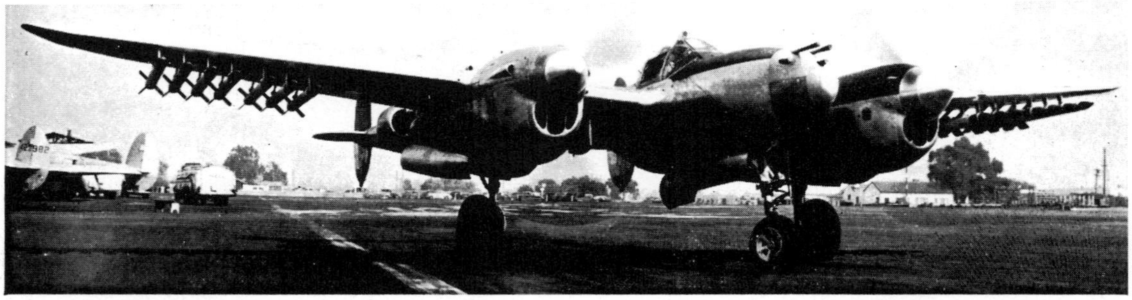

The Lockheed P-38L Lightning with the original 14-rocket installation referred to on this page.

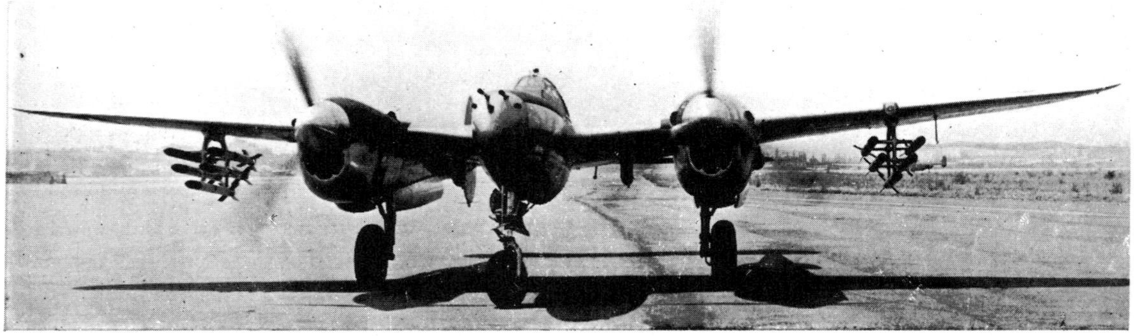

The Lockheed P-38L Lightning with the final standard rocket-cluster installation in use when the war ended.

LANDING GEAR.—Retractable tricycle type. All wheels have single oleo struts and retract backwards, the main wheels into the forward portions of the tail booms and the nose wheel into the central nacelle. Hydraulic retraction. Automatically opening and closing wheel-well doors. Brakes on main wheels.

POWER PLANT.—Two 1,520 h.p. Allison V-1710 twelve-cylinder Vee liquid-cooled engines driving oppositely-rotating Curtiss Electric constant-speed full-feathering airscrews. Airscrew diameter: 11 ft. 6 in. (3.5 m.). General Electric turbo-superchargers in upper portions of booms aft of rear shear member of centre-section. Air scoops on outboard sides of booms below trailing-edge of wings feed air to the turbo compressors. Air is then ducted forward to intercoolers beneath engine and thence to engine induction system. Engine coolant radiators on sides of after sections of tail booms with controllable exit flaps. Separate fuel system for each engine, each consisting of three self-sealing tanks or cells, two (main and auxiliary) in the centre-section and one in outer wing leading-edge. Systems are interconnected so that fuel from any tank, except outer wing tanks, is available for either engine. Droppable fuel tanks may be carried under centre-section midway between central and engine nacelles. Drop tanks are of streamline form and are made from two steel pressings welded together. They are of two capacities, either 150 or 300 U.S. gallons. Electrically-driven fuel boost pumps assist engine-driven pumps. Oil tank in each engine nacelle with two oil coolers, one on each side of intercooler air duct beneath nose of engine, and with thermostatically-controlled temperature regulator and exit flap.

ACCOMMODATION.—Pilot's cockpit in central nacelle over leading-edge of wing. Centre panel of windshield optically-flat bullet-proof glass. Side windows may be lowered and top centre panel is hinged at aft edge for entrance and exit. Quick release hinges for emergency exit. Pilot armour on front bulkhead, back and bottom of seat and behind seat and head. Armour plate on inboard sides of turbo-superchargers to protect pilot against possible fragmentation of turbo blades. Oxygen equipment. Cockpit heating and canopy de-frosting by hot air.

ARMAMENT.—One 20 m/m. cannon and four 50 cal. machine-guns in compartment in nose of central nacelle. All guns fire straight ahead without converging. Racks under centre-section can carry either bombs ranging from 100 to 1,600 lbs. (45.4 to 726 kg.), drop tanks or chemical tanks for smoke-screen laying. Gun camera installed in fairing of port rack. In photographic-reconnaissance model (F-5) armament removed and compartment redesigned to accommodate varying camera installations.

DIMENSIONS.—Span 52 ft. (15.86 m.), Length 37 ft. 10 in. (11.53 m.), Height 12 ft. 10 im. (3.9 m.). Wing area 327.5 sq. ft. (30.4 sq. m.).

WEIGHTS.—Weight empty (with fixed equipment) 12,700 lbs. (5,766 kg.), Normal loaded weight 15,341 lbs. (6,865 kg.), Designed loaded weight 15,500 lbs. (7,040 kg.), Alternate loaded weight (No. 1) 16,376 lbs. (7,435 kg.), Alternate loaded weight (No. 2) 18,000 lbs. (8,172 kg.).

PERFORMANCE.—Maximum speed over 414 m.p.h. (662 km.h.) at 25,000 ft. (7,625 m.), Service ceiling over 35,000 ft. (10,680 m.). Normal without drop tanks 460 miles (736 km.).

THE LOCKHEED (VEGA 37) VENTURA.

U.S. Navy designations : PV-1 and PV-3.
U.S. Army Air Forces designations : B-34 and B-37.
British name : Ventura.

The Ventura, a military development of the Lockheed Lodestar transport, was originally designed and built to the order of the British Government.

Ventura I. Two 1,850 h.p. Pratt & Whitney R-2800-S1A4G engines. First British contracts placed with the Vega Aircraft Corpn. in 1940. Armament consisted of two fixed 50 cal. and two .303 in. machine-guns in the nose, two or four .303 in. guns in a Boulton Paul dorsal turret, and two .303 in. guns in a rear-firing ventral position. First went into service with the R.A.F. as a medium bomber in 1942.

B-34 (Ventura II and IIA). Two 2,000 h.p. Pratt & Whitney R-2800-31 engines. Also built by Vega but under American contracts. Various detail changes, mainly in armament and equipment. B-34 used for coastal patrol, advanced training and as a target tug.

B-37 (Ventura G.R. III). Two 2,000 h.p. Wright R-2600-13 engines. Built by the Lockheed Aircraft Corpn. Originally O-56 but re-designated B-37.

PV-1 (Ventura IV and G.R.V). U.S. Navy Patrol Bomber version of the B-34. Closed-in nose with two fixed forward-firing 50 cal. machine-guns. Remainder of armament same as B-34. Bomb-bay adapted to accommodate bombs, depth-charges or one torpedo. Increased fuel capacity. The description below applies to the PV-1 which was still in production in 1944. The PV-3 is similar to the PV-1 but had British equipment and is obsolete.

TYPE.—Twin-engined Oversea Patrol monoplane.

WINGS.—Mid-wing cantilever monoplane. Centre-section integral with fuselage. Outer sections have detachable wing-tips. Centre-section has one main spar and front and rear shear beams, the main spar passing through fuselage and secondary beams attaching to fuselage sides. Upper smooth Alclad skin reinforced with corrugated sheet, lower skin by stringers. Outer wings have one spar and auxiliary rear beam sheet ribs and Alclad skin. Skin upper surface reinforced by corrugations and stringers, lower surface by stringers only. All-metal ailerons on piano-type hinges, Trim-tabs in ailerons, port tab controllable. Fixed slots in leading-edge ahead of ailerons. Fowler flaps over 34% of trailing-edge between ailerons and fuselage.

FUSELAGE.—All-metal elliptical-section monocoque structure built up of bulkheads and frames, longitudinal members and stringers and a flush-riveted Alclad skin, butt-jointed ahead of pilot's compartment and lapped aft.

TAIL UNIT.—Cantilever monoplane type with twin fins and rudders. All-metal structure. Tailplane comprises centre-section, two outer-sections and two semi-circular tips outboard of fins. Fin and rudder assemblies interchangeable right or left. Trim-tabs in elevators and rudders.

LANDING GEAR.—Retractable type. Aerol shock-absorber units retract backwards into tails of engine nacelles. Units interchangeable right or left with minor adjustments. Hydraulic retraction. Goodyear wheels and hydraulic brakes. Retractable tail-wheel.

POWER PLANT.—Two 2,000 h.p. Pratt & Whitney R-2800-31 eighteen-cylinder radial air-cooled engines with two-speed superchargers, on welded steel-tube mountings. Three-blade Hamilton-Standard Hydromatic broad-blade constant-speed airscrews, 10 ft. 7 in. (3.23 m.) diameter. Main fuel system comprises four tanks in centre-section, two in outer sections, and two cabin tanks, all self-sealing. Two external droppable tanks under outer wings. Provision for long-range ferry tanks in bomb-bay. Main oil tank in each nacelle with reserve tank in fuselage.

The Lockheed P-38J Lightning Single-seat Fighter (two Allison V-1710-89/91 engines).

A Lockheed P-38L Lightning with bombardier nose in place of the fighter armament. *(Photograph by Peter Bowers).*

The Lockheed F-5B Photographic-Reconnaissance Monoplane (two Allison V-1710-89/91 engines).

The Lockheed PV-1 Ventura Naval Patrol Monoplane (two Pratt & Whitney R-2800-31 engines).

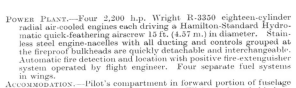

POWER PLANT.—Four 2,200 h.p. Wright R-3350 eighteen-cylinder radial air-cooled engines each driving a Hamilton-Standard Hydromatic quick-feathering airscrew 15 ft. (4.57 m.) in diameter. Stainless steel engine-nacelles with all ducting and controls grouped at the fireproof bulkheads are quickly detachable and interchangeable. Automatic fire detection and location with positive fire-extinguisher system operated by flight engineer. Four separate fuel systems in wings.

ACCOMMODATION.—Pilot's compartment in forward portion of fuselage with pilot on left and co-pilot on right. Flight engineer behind co-pilot facing outboard. Radio-operator behind pilot facing forward. Aft of pilot's compartment and separated therefrom by bulkhead are navigator's cabin and accommodation for crew. Through a further bulkhead access is given to space for cargo on right and communicating equipment on left of central passage. Then follows the main compartment which may be furnished in any one of several day and night arrangements for from 30 to 64 passengers. Food lockers, cloakroom, lavatory, etc. are aft of main compartment. Additional cargo space beneath floor. Access to main compartment on port side aft and to crew accommodation on starboard side forward. All cabin space is pressurised to permit operation up to 30,000 ft. (9.150 m.). Sea level conditions will be maintained in the fuselage up to 10,000 ft. (3,050 m.), and between 25,000 ft. (7,625 m.) and 30,000 ft. (9,150 m.) the relative conditions in the fuselage will be equivalent to those found between 8,000 ft. (2,440 m.) and 12,000 ft. (3,660 m.). Two cabin superchargers, fully automatic with manual override control. Thermostatically-controlled heating and cooling. Full cabin insulation

The Lockheed PV-2 Harpoon Naval Patrol Monoplane (two Pratt & Whitney R-2800-31 engines).

ACCOMMODATION.—Crew of four, comprising pilot, navigator/bomb-aimer, radio operator/gunner and turret gunner.

ARMAMENT.—Two fixed 50 cal. machine-guns in nose, two 50 cal. guns in Martin electrically-operated dorsal turret and two 30 cal. tunnel-guns. Internal bomb-bay may accommodate up to 2,500 lbs. of bombs, six 325 lb. depth-charges or one standard 22 in. short aircraft torpedo. Two 500 lb. bombs or two depth-charges may replace external wing tanks.

DIMENSIONS.—Span 65 ft. 6 in. (19.96 m.), Length 51 ft. 7½ in. (15.74 m.), Height 14 ft. 1⅜ in. (4.31 m.), Wing area (with flaps retracted) 551 sq. ft. (51.2 sq. m.), Wing area (with flaps fully lowered) 619 sq. ft. (57.5 sq. m.).

WEIGHTS.—Weight empty 19,373 lbs. (8,795 kg.), Normal loaded weight 26,500 lbs. (12,030 kg.), Maximum permissable overloaded weight 31,000 lbs. (14,075 kg.).

PERFORMANCE.—Maximum speed over 300 m.p.h. (480 km.h.), Service ceiling over 25,000 ft. (7,625 m.), Normal range over 1,000 miles (1,600 km.).

THE LOCKHEED HARPOON.

U.S. Navy designation : PV-2.

The Harpoon is a development of the Ventura PV-1. It has wings of greater span (75 ft. = 22.8 m.), constant taper and with rounded wing-tips, a new rectangular tailplane with new fins and rudders at the outer extremities, a bigger bomb-bay and a heavier armament. The power-plant consists of two Pratt & Whitney R-2800-31 engines, the same as fitted to the PV-1 Ventura.

The armament consists of five fixed 50 cal. machine-guns in the nose, two 50 cal. guns in the dorsal Martin turret, and two 50 cal. guns in a power-operated mounting in the break in the underside of the fuselage. The larger bomb-bay completely encloses the torpedo, which in the PV-1 partly protruded between the bomb-bay doors.

LOCKHEED MODEL 49 CONSTELLATION.

U.S. Army Air Forces designation: C-69.

The Constellation is a four-engined transport monoplane which was originally designed to the requirements of Trans-Continental and Western Air, Inc. During its development and after consultation with TWA, Pan American Airways also ordered a number of Constellations, but on the entry of the United States into the war both companies waived their rights in favour of the Army Air Forces, and production was devoted solely to the C-69 military transport version.

Since the end of the war military contracts have been cut down and production converted for civil purposes. First deliveries of commercial Constellations were due to be made in November, 1945.

As a commercial aeroplane the Constellation will carry from 30 to 64 passengers in several different cabin arrangements, in addition to a crew of six, and baggage, mail and express.

The Lockheed C-69 Constellation Military Transport (four Wright R-3350-31 engines).

provision is made for a crew of five, plus a relief crew of four, and 60 seats or 22 sleeping berths.

The provisional description below refers to the commercial Constellation, which is now in production.

TYPE.—Four-engined Airliner.

WINGS.—Low-wing cantilever monoplane. All-metal structure with flush-riveted smooth stressed skin. Lockheed-Fowler flaps with take-off, manoeuvring and landing positions. Hot air de-icing.

FUSELAGE.—All-metal semi-monocoque structure. Circular cross-section throughout length and with centre-line cambered to give longitudinal aerofoil section and maximum width of level floor particularly in nose and tail sections.

TAIL UNIT.—Cantilever monoplane type with triple fins and rudders. All-metal structure. Hydraulic power-boost controls reducing pilot effort and assuring positive control without fatigue. Manual override for auxiliary use.

LANDING-GEAR.—Retractable tricycle type with dual main wheels and steerable nose wheel. Dual hydraulic brake systems on main wheels with auxiliary manual override.

against sound, vibration and temperature. Infra-red windshield de-icers.

DIMENSIONS.—Span 123 ft. (37.5 m.), Length 95 ft. 1⅜ in. (29 m.), Height over fuselage from ground 18 ft. 8⅝ in. (5.7 m.), Height overall from ground 23 ft. 8 in. (7.2 m.).

WEIGHTS.—Weight empty (depending on interior arrangements) 50,100-51,400 lbs. (22,745-23,335 kg.), Operating weight empty (including crew and all passenger service equipment) 53,500-55,500 lbs. (24,290-25,200 kg.), Maximum take-off gross weight 86,250 lbs. (39,160 kg.), Maximum landing gross weight 75,000 lbs. (34,050 kg.).

PERFORMANCE.—Maximum speed (fully loaded) 340 m.p.h. (544 km.h.), Cruising speed (65% power) over 300 m.p.h. (480 km.h.), Landing speed 80 m.p.h. (128 km.h.), Service ceiling over 25,000 ft. (7,625 m.), Range (with 20,000 lbs. = 9,080 kg. pay load) over 2,000 miles (3,200 km.), Take-off run (at sea level—fully loaded) 1,600 ft. (488 m.), Take-off run to clear 50 ft. obstacle (fully loaded) 2,800 ft. (854 m.), Landing-run (to full stop after clearing 50 ft. obstacle) 2,300 ft. (700 m.).

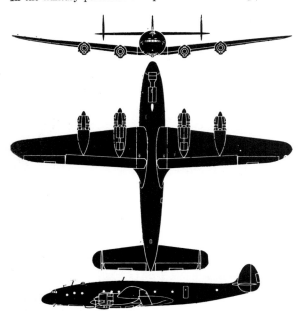

The Lockheed Model 49 Constellation.

The Lockheed Constellation Four-engined Commercial Airliner.

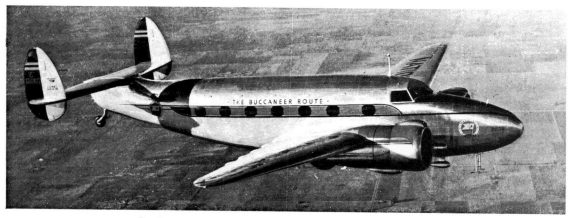

The Lockheed Lodestar Twin-engined Fourteen-passenger Airliner.

THE LOCKHEED MODEL 75 SATURN.

This is a design for a feeder-line monoplane which will be built when military production permits. It is a twin-engined all-metal high-wing monoplane with accommodation for a crew of two, fourteen passengers, baggage and cargo. It will be fitted with two 525 h.p. Continental-built Wright Whirlwind engines and will have a retractable bicycle landing-gear. One of the features of the Saturn will be interchangeability of its parts, including the dual wheels of the main landing-gear, the horizontal and vertical tail surfaces and the power-units. The passenger seats will be quickly removable and a movable bulkhead will permit quick cargo conversion where conditions require it.

DIMENSIONS.—Not available.
WEIGHT LOADED.—13,500 lbs. (6,130 kg.).
PERFORMANCE (Estimated).—Maximum speed 240 m.p.h. (384 km.h.), Cruising speed 200 m.p.h. (320 km.h.), Landing speed 73 m.p.h. (117 km.h.), Initial rate of climb 1,230 ft./min. (375 m./min.), Service ceiling 26,000 ft. (7,930 m.), Maximum range 1,600 miles (2,560 km.).

THE LOCKHEED MODEL 18 LODESTAR.

U.S. Army Air Forces designations : C-56, C-57, C-59, C-60 and C-66.
U.S. Navy designation : R50.
British name : Lodestar.

The Lodestar commercial transport, which is still flying for more than a dozen airlines on four continents, normally has accommodation for a crew of three and fourteen passengers. It has also been widely adapted for service transport use by the U.S. Army Air Forces and the U.S. Navy. The following are the various service versions of the Lodestar, of which the C-60 is the most used model.

C-56 (R50-1). Both Army and Navy models equivalent to the civil Model 18-40 and fitted with two Wright GR-1820-G102A Cyclone engines, with the exception of the C-56D which has two Pratt & Whitney R-1830-S1C3G Twin-Wasp engines. Some are fitted with furnishings of the executive type and others for general personnel transportation.

C-57. Similar to the C-56 except for cabin installations and the power-plant. Two Pratt & Whitney R-1830-51 Twin-Wasp engines.

C-59 (R50-2 and Lodestar IA). A military adaptation of the civil Model 18-07 with two Pratt & Whitney R-1690 Hornet engines. Carries a crew of 4 and 14 passengers.

R50-3. A naval executive transport with accommodation for a crew of 4 and four passengers. Similar to the civil Model 18-10 with two Wright R-1820-84 Cyclone engines.

C-60 (R50-4, R50-5, R50-6 and Lodestar II). Developed from the civil Model 18-56 and fitted with two Wright R-1820-87 Cyclone engines. The C-60 (R50-5) has accommodation for 12 passengers ; the R50-4 is an executive version with seats for 7 passengers ; and the C-60A (R50-6 and Lodestar II) is provided with benches for 18 fully-armed troops. The C-60 has also been used to train glider-tug pilots.

C-66. An adaptation of the civil Model 18-10 to carry a crew of 2 and eleven passengers. Fitted with two Wright R-1820 Cyclone engines.

TYPE.—Twin-engined Transport.
WINGS.—Mid-wing cantilever monoplane of single-spar construction. Wing in three sections. Fuel tanks integral with centre-section. Fowler flaps. Ailerons are inter-connected to droop with flaps.
FUSELAGE.—Elliptical cross-section monocoque of all-metal construction.
TAIL UNIT.—Cantilever monoplane type with twin fins and rudders.
LANDING GEAR.—Hydraulically-operated retractable type. May be lowered in six seconds at 250 m.p.h. Low-pressure tyres and hydraulic disc brakes. Pneumatic hydraulic shock-absorbers.
POWER PLANT (C-60A).—Two Wright R-1820-87 nine-cylinder radial air-cooled engines each rated at 1,000 h.p. at 14,200 ft. (4,330 m.) and with 1,200 h.p. available for take-off. Hamilton-Standard constant-speed hydromatic airscrews. Fuel tanks have total maximum capacity of 644 U.S. gallons (536 Imp. gallons = 2,438 litres). Maximum oil capacity 44 U.S. gallons (36.6 Imp. gallons = 166.5 litres).
ACCOMMODATION (C-60A).—Crew of three, pilot, co-pilot and radio operator. Benches in cabin for eighteen troops or other personnel. Dimensions of cabin : 28 ft. (8.54 m.) long × 5 ft. 5½ in. (1.7 m.) wide × 6 ft. 3 in. (1.9 m.) high.
DIMENSIONS.—Span 65 ft. 8 in. (19.96 m.), Length 49 ft. 9⅞ in. (15.19 m.), Height 11 ft. 10½ in. (3.6 m.), Wing area 551 sq. ft. (51.2 sq. m.).
WEIGHTS (C-60A).—Weight empty 12,075 lbs. (5,480 kg.), Normal loaded weight 18,500 lbs. (8,400 kg.), Maximum overloaded weight 21,500 lbs. (9,760 kg.).
PERFORMANCE (C-60A).—Maximum speed 266 m.p.h. (425.6 km.h.) at 17,000 ft. (5,185 m.). Cruising speed 200 m.p.h. (320 km.h.), Climb to 10,000 ft. (3,050 m.) 6.6 min., Service ceiling 30,000 ft. (9,150 m.), Range with full complement and maximum fuel 1,660 miles (2,660 km.).

THE LOCKHEED MODEL 414 HUDSON.

British name : Hudson.
U.S. Army Air Forces designations: A-28 and A-29.
U.S. Navy designation: PBO-1.

The Hudson was originally built to the order of the British Government as a military conversion of the Type 14 transport. It was in production from 1939 to June, 1943, and thousands were built and delivered to the British, Australian, New Zealand, Canadian, Netherlands, Chinese and American flying services.

In all, six versions were delivered to the British Government, the majority of which were delivered by air across the Atlantic.

Hudson I. Two Wright GR-1820-G102A engines driving Hamilton-Standard two-position airscrews.

Hudson II. Similar to Mk. I but fitted with Hamilton-Standard Hydromatic constant-speed airscrews.

Hudson III (A-29 and PBO-1). Two Wright GR-1820-G205A engines driving Hamilton-Standard Hydromatic constant-speed airscrews. Retractable rear firing under-gun position. A-29 fitted with Wright R-1820-87 engines. A-29A similar to A-29 except fitted with benches for troop-carrying. The latter was originally given the designation C-63.

Hudson IV. Two Pratt & Whitney R-1830-SC3G engines. Originally supplied to Australia but a small batch was delivered to the R.A.F. No under-gun position. D/F loop aerial in transparent blister.

Hudson V. Two Pratt & Whitney R-1830-S3C4G engines driving Hamilton-Standard two-position airscrews. Retractable under-gun position as on Mk. III.

Hudson VI (A-28). Two Pratt & Whitney R-1830-67 engines driving Hamilton-Standard Hydromatic constant-speed airscrews. External D/F loop aerial (no blister). Convertible to troop transport or cargo-carrier when turret removed.

After withdrawal from combatant service with the R.A.F., U.S. Army or Navy, the Hudson continued to be used for miscellaneous duties, including transport, air/sea rescue, training, target-towing, etc.

The Hudson III was the first aeroplane to be fitted to carry the British-developed Mk. I airborne lifeboat. This lifeboat was first used operationally in May, 1943, by an R.A.F. Air/Sea Rescue Squadron equipped with Hudsons to rescue the crew of an R.A.F. bomber forced down in the North Sea, 50 miles from the British coast.

TYPE.—Twin-engined General Purposes monoplane.
WINGS.—Mid-wing cantilever monoplane. Wing in three sections with single spar and stressed-skin covering. Built-in fuel tanks in centre-section. Lockheed-Fowler flaps, between ailerons and fuselage, slide back 42 in. in streamline guides. Ailerons are interconnected to droop with flaps. Low-drag slots in each wingtip in front of ailerons.
FUSELAGE.—Elliptical cross-section monocoque fuselage of all-metal flush-riveted construction.
TAIL UNIT.—Cantilever monoplane type with twin fins and rudders. All-metal construction.
LANDING GEAR.—Retractable type with wheels retracting backwards into engine nacelles. Hydraulic retraction with emergency hand operation.

The Lockheed C-60 Lodestar Military Transport (two Wright R-1820-87 engines).

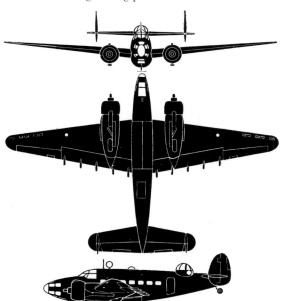

The Lockheed Hudson III.

A Lockheed Hudson III carrying the British Mk. I Airborne lifeboat.

Power Plant.—Two Wright Cyclone (Hudson I, II and III) or Pratt & Whitney Twin-Wasp (Hudson IV and V) radial air-cooled engines. Hamilton-Standard constant-speed airscrews. NACA cowlings. Built-in fuel tanks in centre-section.

Accommodation.—Normal crew of five. Bomb-aimer's position in nose. Pilot and navigator over leading-edg~ of wing. Radio operator and rear gunner in cabin over wing.

Armament.—Two fixed 0.303 in. Browning machine-guns in top of fuselage in front of pilot. Boulton Paul turret with two 0.303 in. Browning guns at after end of fuselage near tailplane ; two 0.303 in. Browning guns on beam mountings one on each side of fuselage ; and one 0.303 in. Browning gun in retractable prone position beneath fuselage. Internal stowage for bombs or depth-charges (total load : 1,400 lbs.) in fuselage beneath floor of cabin.

Dimensions.—Span 65 ft. 6 in. (19.95 m.), Length 44 ft. 4 in. (13.4 m.), Height 11 ft. $10\frac{1}{2}$ in. (3.63 m.), Wing area 551 sq. ft. (51.2 sq. m.).

Weights.—Weight empty 12,536 lbs. (5,690 kg.), Weight loaded 18,500 lbs. (8,400 kg.).

Performance.—Maximum speed 275 m.p.h. (440 km.h.), Cruising speed 223 m.p.h. (356.8 km.h.) at 8,000 ft. (2,440 m.), Landing speed 72 m.p.h. (115.2 km.h.), Service Ceiling 24,500 ft. (7,470 m.).

LUSCOMBE.

LUSCOMBE AIRPLANE CORPORATION.

Head Office and Works : Trenton 7, New Jersey.
President : Leopold H. P. Klotz.
Vice-President in charge of Engineering : Frederick J. Knack.
Secretary and Treasurer : Clarence L. Riegel.

The Luscombe Airplane Corpn. pioneered the development of die-cut metal construction and worked out methods that made this type of production with interchangeable parts a reality.

It produced its first all-metal aeroplane in 1934 and in 1937 introduced the first of the Silvaire series of light two-seat all-metal cabin monoplanes. Production of the Silvaire ceased shortly after America's entry into the War owing to priority restrictions on the use of metal for non-military aircraft, after about 1,200 had been built.

The company's plant was enlarged and converted for the production of metal parts and assemblies for several types of American combat aircraft, on which work it has been wholly engaged since 1942.

As soon as the military situation permits the Luscombe Airplane Corpn. will reintroduce the Silvaire with a number of minor improvements. Three alternate engines will be offered, one of which—the 75 h.p. Continental—has direct fuel injection.

The Luscombe Silvaire Two-seat All-metal Monoplane (75 h.p. Continental A75 engine). *(Photograph by Peter Bowers)*

THE LUSCOMBE SILVAIRE.

Type.—Two-seat all-metal cabin monoplane.

Wings.—High-wing externally-braced monoplane. Wings attached to top sides of cabin and braced by streamline steel-tube Vee struts. Structure consists of two I-type spars of extruded duralumin, ribs of riveted T-section Alclad extrusions, and on Alclad skin. Ailerons covered with beaded Alclad sheet riveted to a single duralumin spar.

Fuselage.—Monocoque structure using curved Alclad pre-drilled sheets riveted to oval duralumin bulkhead stampings. Wing struts and landing-gear attached to aluminium forgings riveted to forward section of metal seat bottom on either side. Standard size pre-drilled skin sections are easily replaceable.

Tail Unit.—Cantilever monoplane type. Duralumin spars and ribs with Alclad sheet covering. Tip sections of tailplane and fin are interchangeable. Fixed surfaces bolted to rear of fuselage.

Landing Gear.—Divided type. Heat-treated steel tube-legs and struts. Main legs hinged at sides of fuselage with springing by single oleo-sprung unit mounted within fuselage. Wheels may by replaced by twin Edo floats.

Power Plant.—One 75 h.p. Continental A-75 four-cylinder horizontally-opposed air-cooled engine. Fuel capacity : 23 U.S. gallons. 65 h.p. Continental or Lycoming engines are alternative power-units.

Accommodation.—Enclosed cabin seating two side-by-side with dual controls. Large door on each side. Baggage compartment behind seats.

Dimensions.—Span 35 ft. (10.7 m.), Length 20 ft. (6.1 m.), Height 5 ft. 10 in. (1.79 m.), Wing area 140 sq. ft. (13 sq. m.).

Weights and Loadings.—Weight empty 710 lbs. (322 kg.), Disposable load 600 lbs. (272 kg.), Weight loaded 1,310 lbs. (594 kg.), Wing loading 9.3 lbs./sq. ft. (45.4 kg./sq. m.), Power loading 17.4 lbs./h.p. (7.9 kg./h.p.).

Performance.—Maximum speed 115 m.p.h. (185 km.h.), Cruising speed 110 m.p.h. (176.3 km.h.), Landing speed 42 m.p.h. (67.3 km.h.), Initial rate of climb 900 ft./min. (274 m./min.), Service ceiling 15,000 ft. (4,575 m.), Cruising range 500 miles (800 km.).

McDONNELL.

McDONNELL AIRCRAFT CORPORATION.

Head Office and Works : St. Louis, Mo.
Branch Works : Memphis, Tenn.
President : James S. McDonnell.
Executive Vice-President : Gardner W. Carr.
Chief Engineer : Garrett C. Covington.
Vice-President and Treasurer : L. A. Smith.
Manager, Memphis Division : Fred G. Essig.
Manager, Plastics Division : Charles F. Marschner.

The McDonnell Aircraft Corpn. was incorporated on July 6, 1939, to undertake the manufacture of military aircraft and aircraft parts. In 1942 the Company received contracts for the construction of a series of Fairchild AT-21 advanced training monoplanes for the U.S. Army Air Forces. The AT-21 was withdrawn from production in October, 1944.

In addition to primary production and experimental contracts with the U.S. Government, the Company has manufactured parts and sub-assemblies for other aircraft manufacturers. It is also engaged in the production and use of plastics in aircraft manufacture. It has developed a laminated paper plastic for use instead of aluminium in the fabrication of some aircraft shapes, using a strong paper made of special wood pulp impregnated with phenol-formaldehyde.

Information was released early in 1945 concerning one of the experimental aircraft designed and built by the McDonnell Corpn. This was the XP-67 single-seat twin-engined interceptor fighter, two examples of which were built.

THE McDONNELL XP-67.

The XP-67 was a twin-engined monoplane which was developed for the U.S. Army Air Forces to test out a "flying-wing" design. The middle portion of the fuselage and the rear portions of the engine nacelles merged into each other, the outer wings, forward portions of the nacelles and the dihedral tail-unit being of conventional design. The landing-gear was of the tricycle type.

The power-plant consisted of two 1,250 h.p. Continental I-1430 twelve-cylinder inverted Vee liquid-cooled supercharged engines each driving a four-bladed tractor airscrew, the turbo exhaust being ejected through an annular aperture in the tail of each nacelle to give additional jet thrust.

The pilot's cabin was pressurised and an armament of six 37 m/m. cannon was provided for. The XP-67 had a span of 55 ft. (16.8 m.) and a designed loaded weight of 21,000 lbs. (9,535 kg.).

McFARLAND.

McFARLAND AIRCRAFT COMPANY.

Head Office and Works : Greenville, Ohio.
Sailplane Division : Spring Valley, California.
President and Treasurer : Walter D. McFarland.
Vice-President and Chief Design Engineer, Sailplane Division : James B. Neiswonger.
Chief Design Engineer (Greenville) : C. L. Ofenstein.
Executive Secretary : C. E. Snyder.

This company was founded under the name Neiswonger-McFarland Aeronautical Co., in May, 1934, but in October of that year the name was changed to McFarland Aircraft Company. In December, 1943, the Sailplane Division of the company was established in Spring Valley, Cal.

From its inception the company's activities have been devoted mainly to the research, development, design, production and marketing of aircraft for the private market, specialising for the most part in training gliders and sailplanes and, more recently, in the production of primary training glider construction kits.

The Sailplane Division has for several years concentrated on the development of the single-seat high-performance advanced training sailplane.

MARTIN.

THE GLENN L. MARTIN COMPANY.

Head Office and Works : Middle River, Baltimore, Md. and Omaha, Nebraska.
Established : 1909.
President and Manager : Glenn L. Martin.
Executive Vice-President and President of Glenn L. Martin Nebraska Company : J. T. Hartson.
Vice-President in Charge of Manufacturing : H. F. Vollmer.
Vice-President in Charge of Engineering : William K. Ebel.
Vice-President in Charge of Contract Administration : H. T. Rowland.
Secretary : T. H. Jones.
Treasurer : M. G. Shook.

The Martin plant group in the Baltimore area is one of the largest in the United States. A subsidiary known as the Glenn L. Martin Nebraska Company operated a Government-constructed bomber assembly plant at Omaha, Nebraska. Production in these plants was concentrated on the production of the B-26 Medium Bomber for the U.S. Army Air Forces, the PBM-3 Mariner twin-engined Patrol-Bomber or Cargo Transport, and the JRM-1 four-engined Cargo Transport flying-boats for the U.S. Navy.

Although the Martin Company has in the past years been engaged entirely on the manufacture of military aircraft, the Company's policy and plans for the future envisage a bold entry into the air transport field.

THE MARTIN MODEL 170 MARS.

U.S. Navy designation : XPB2M-1 and JRM-1.

The Mars was originally built as an experimental Patrol Bomber with the designation XPB2M-1. It was subsequently modified to serve as a cargo transport with reinforced floors, larger hatches and loading equipment and re-designated XPB 2M-1R.

In December, 1943, the XPB2M-1R made its first service flight as a naval transport, flying from the Patuxent River Naval Air Station, Md. to Natal, Brazil, a distance of 4,375 miles non-stop with 13,000 lbs. of mail and freight. The take-off weight for this flight was 148,500 lbs. On part of the return journey a load of 35,000 lbs. was carried. Early in 1944 the Mars completed a 4,700 mile round trip to Hawaii in 27 hours 26 min. and delivered 20,500 lbs. of cargo.

The JRM-1 is the production development of the XPB2M-1R. An order for 20 was placed as the result of the successful performance of the prototype with the U.S. Naval Air Transport Service. The first of the new boats was completed in the Summer of 1945, but it foundered after one of its early test flights. The U.S. Navy contract for the JRM-1 was later reduced to five aircraft.

The principal external changes in the JRM-1 include the substitution of a single fin and rudder for the former twin-ruddered tail ; the lengthening of both the bow and the rear step by about 4 ft. to provide additional cargo space ; and a re-design of both main and cargo hatches.

Internally, the hull has been stripped of all equipment and fittings, one bulkhead has been removed and frames with openings wide enough to permit the passage of vehicles, ordnance, aircraft engines, etc. substituted for the remaining bulkheads on the main cargo deck. The main deck is provided with cargo tie-down fittings running fore-and-aft and athwartships on 30 in. centres, metal skid strips for sliding heavy cargo and tracks fore-and-aft and athwartships for handling engine dollies.

A 5,000 lb. capacity cargo hoist on an overhead track runs out 20 ft. under both wings through the main loading hatches, each of which is 99 in. wide × 92 in. high (2.52 m. × 2.34 m.) with doors divided vertically and opening outwards. Two further hatches 50 in. wide × 62 in. high (1.27 m. × 1.5m). are located just forward of the second step and have doors which slide up inside the hull.

Aft of the main cargo hold and in the space provided by moving the second step aft is a stairway leading to the upper deck where, as on the main deck, all bulkheads have been replaced by open frames. Trap doors 50 in. long × 24 in. wide (1.27 m. × 0.6 m.) in the upper deck floor and immediately above the after loading doors are for loading low density freight onto the upper deck. The stairway already mentioned has been provided to permit the loading of stretcher cases onto the upper deck.

The flight deck forward accommodates a duty crew of four and aft of the pilot's compartment there are four bunks for the use of off-duty officers on long flights. Four further bunks are provided on the upper rear deck aft of the auxiliary power-plant compartment. Washroom facilities are right aft in the tail section which is reached from the upper deck. In the nose ahead of the flight deck is the stowage for anchors and the anchor windlass, and aft of this and ahead of the main cargo hold is a combined galley and entrance to the flight deck.

While primarily designed as a cargo transport, the JRM-1 has built-in fittings which will permit rapid conversion into an ambulance to carry 84 stretcher cases and 25 medical attendants; a passenger transport to carry fifty in reclining chairs all on the main deck; or a troop-carrier to accommodate 132 troops, all seated. As a cargo-carrier the JRM-1 will have ample space for seven Jeeps or other bulky military equipment.

The JRM-1, which has a span of 200 ft. (61 m.), an overall length of 117 ft. 3 in. (35.7 m.), and a wing area of 3,686 sq. ft. (342.4 sq. m.), is fitted with four 2,200 h.p. Wright R-3350-18 eighteen-cylinder radial air-cooled engines, each driving a three-blade Curtiss Electric airscrew 16 ft. 6 in. (5 m.) in diameter. The four airscrews will be controlled by an electric automatic synchroniser. It has been designed to fly at weights up to 145,000 lbs. (65,830 kg.), as compared with a design weight of 140,000 lbs. (63,560 kg.) for the prototype.

The Martin company has prepared designs for several commercial applications of the Mars for post-war development. These include the Model 170-21A passenger flying-boat, the Model 170-22A commercial cargo flying-boat, the Model 170-23A combination cargo and passenger-carrying flying-boat and the Model 170-24 passenger flying-boat.

The 170-21A will carry a crew of 11 for flights under 1,500 miles (2,400 km.) or 14 for longer ranges, and 58 passengers with sleeping facilities or 79 for day travel.

The 170-23A will carry 23 sleeper passengers or 65 day passengers. The 170-24 will have accommodation for 105 passengers. In the wings of all but the 170-22A there will be cargo-bays with a total capacity of 1,880 cu. ft.

The major portion of the hull of the commercial 170 below the main deck will consist of six integral fuel tanks, with a total capacity of 12,000 U.S. gallons. Auxiliary tanks in the wings will increase the total to 13,220 U.S. gallons.

For commercial use the Mars is expected to be fitted with four Pratt & Whitney R-4360 twenty-eight-cylinder radial air-cooled engines. The airscrews of the two inboard engines will be reversible to serve as brakes and to facilitate manoeuvability on the water.

THE MARTIN MODEL 162 MARINER.
U.S. Navy designations : PBM-3 and PBM-5.

The XPBM-1 was originally ordered by the U.S. Navy in 1936. Before it was built a quarter-scale flying prototype (Model 162A) was built and flown. The full-size prototype was delivered to the U.S. Navy in 1938.

The PBM-1, fitted with two Wright R-2600-6 radial air-cooled engines, a dihedral tail and retractable wing-tip floats, was ordered in 1938, and was followed in 1939 by an experimental XPBM-2, a long-range model specially strengthened for catapult take-off.

The PBM-3, with two Wright R-2600-12 engines, was ordered in quantity in 1941 and deliveries began in 1942. In the PBM-3 the crew was increased from seven to nine, the armament was revised and fuel capacity increased. The retractable wing-tip floats of the PBM-1 were replaced by fixed floats.

In 1942 the PBM-3 was adopted as a naval transport and given the designation PBM-3R. Structural changes included the removal of all military equipment, turrets, etc., and the provision of a strengthened floor, cargo-loading door and facilities for loading and handling cargo. The PBM-3R will carry 40 passengers or 8,000-9,000 lbs. (3,630-4,090 kg.) in freight and cargo. At an all-up weight of 48,000 lbs. (21,800 kg.) it has a range of 1,200 miles (1,920 km.) at a cruising speed of 150 m.p.h. (240 km.h.).

The PBM-5 is fitted with two Pratt & Whitney R-2800 engines in redesigned nacelles and has certain internal design changes to give greater capacity and longer range.

TYPE.—Twin-engined Patrol-Bomber or Naval transport.

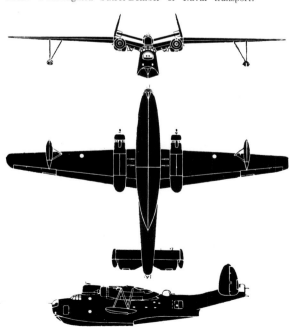

The Martin PBM-3 Mariner Flying-boat.

The Martin XPB2M-1R Mars Transport Flying-boat (four Wright R-3350 engines.)

The Martin PBM-3 Mariner Patrol-Bomber Flying-boat (two Wright R-2600-12 engines).

WINGS.—High-wing cantilever monoplane. Inner sections of wing set at coarse dihedral and outer wing at no dihedral. Constant taper and rounded wing-tips. All-metal structure with flush-riveted smooth metal skin. Entire trailing-edge hinged, outer sections acting as ailerons and inner sections as flaps.

HULL.—All-metal two-step structure, the rear step terminating in a vertical knife-edge. Details of structure not released. Fixed stabilising floats attached to wings by "N" struts.

TAIL UNIT.—Cantilever monoplane type with twin-fins and rudders. Dihedral tail-plane with fins and rudders mounted at right angles to the tail-plane surfaces. All-metal structure with metal-covered fixed surfaces and fabric-covered elevators and rudders. Statically and aerodynamically-balanced control surfaces.

POWER PLANT.—Two 1,700 h.p. Wright Cyclone R-2600-12 fourteen-cylinder two-row radial air-cooled engines on mountings at the extremities of the centre-section. Three or four-bladed Curtiss Electric constant-speed full-feathering airscrews. Self-sealing fuel cells in wings.

ACCOMMODATION.—Provision for crew of seven. Details of interior arrangements not released but equipment includes galley, sleeping accommodation, sound-proofing, heating and ventilation.

ARMAMENT.—Details not released. Turrets in nose, amidships and in extreme tail and beam gun positions in the sides of the hull midway between wings and tail. Internal stowage for bombs or depth-charges in each engine nacelle beneath wings. Crutches for 21 in. torpedo inboard of each nacelle.

DIMENSIONS.—Span 118 ft. (36 m.), Length 77 ft. 2 in. (23.5 m.), Height 17 ft. 6 in. (5.33 m.).

WEIGHT LOADED.—56,000 lbs. (25,425 kg.).

PERFORMANCE.—Maximum speed over 200 m.p.h. (320 km.h.), Maximum range 3,000 miles (4,800 km.).

THE MARTIN MODEL 179 MARAUDER.
U.S. Army Air Forces designation : B-26.
U.S. Navy designation : JM-1 and JM-2.
British name : Marauder.

The projected design data for the Model 179 Medium Bomber were accepted by the U.S. Army on July 5, 1939 and the first Marauder flew on November 25, 1940. The flow of production Marauders began on February 25, 1941, and by the end of 1944, over 5,000 had been delivered. The Marauder first went into action in the Australian Theatre in April, 1942.

The following briefly outlines the stages of development of the Marauder.

B-26. Two 1,850 h.p. Pratt & Whitney R-2800-5 eighteen-cylinder radial air-cooled engines. Crew of five. Armament consisted of five 50 cal. machine-guns, two in the nose, two in a Martin dorsal turret and one in the extreme tail. Normal bomb load 2,000 lbs., maximum 5,800 lbs. in tandem bomb-bays.

B-26A (Marauder I). Two 2,000 h.p. Pratt & Whitney

The Martin B-26F Marauder Medium Bomber (two Pratt & Whitney R-2800-43 engines).

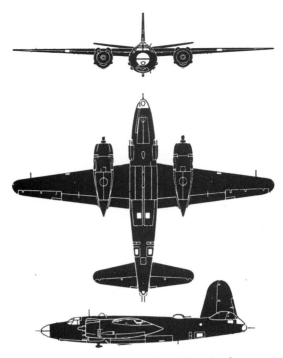

The Martin B-26C Marauder Medium Bomber.

R-2800-39 engines. Same as B-26 except for minor changes.

B-26B (Mararder IA and II). Two 2,000 h.p. Pratt & Whitney R-2800-43 engines. Span increased from 65 ft. (19.8 m.) to 71 ft. (21.6 m.). Two 50 cal. guns in the tail position. From B-26B-10 (Marauder II) the area of the vertical tail surfaces was increased and armament was raised to include one fixed and one flexible gun in the nose, four "package" guns on the sides of the forward fuselage, two in the Martin dorsal turret, two flexible "waist" guns, one tunnel gun and two tail guns. Crew increased to seven. Maximum bomb load 4,000 lbs. Front bay could carry two 2,000 lb. bombs on special carriers. Use of rear bomb-bay later discontinued.

B-26C (Marauder II). Same as B-26B-10 but built at the Martin Omaha plant.

B-26D. Same as B-26C but fitted experimentally with exhaust-heated surface de-icing equipment. Only one.

B-26E. A special stripped model with the weight reduced by about 2,000 lbs. Upper turret moved forward to the roof of the navigator's compartment. One only.

B-26F and G (Marauder III). Similar to the B-26C except that the incidence of the wing was increased by 3½ degrees. Rear bomb-bay eliminated and no provision for torpedo. Eleven 50 cal. guns, one in the nose, four "package" guns, two in the Martin turret, two waist guns and two tail guns.

TB-26. Certain examples of the earlier versions of the Marauder were stripped of armament and adapted for training and general utility duties, particularly for high-speed target-towing. These were originally given the designation AT-23 but they are now known as TB-26.

JM-1 and JM-2. Stripped versions of the B-26C and B-26G respectively, and used by the U.S. Navy for target-towing and other general utility duties. The JM-1P was equipped for photographic reconnaissance.

TYPE.—Twin-engined Medium Bomber.

WINGS.—Cantilever shoulder-wing monoplane. Wings have equal taper, rounded tips and a flat upper surface. Wings in four sections consisting of two inner sections forming the centre-section and two outer sections with detachable tips. All-metal two-spar corrugated-box-type structure, the whole covered with flush-riveted stressed skin. Ailerons, on outer wing sections, have metal frames and fabric covering. Slotted flaps on inner sections are divided by extensions of engine nacelles.

FUSELAGE.—Circular section all-metal monocoque structure. Built in three sections and bolted together.

A Martin TB-26B Marauder, a stripped version of the B-26B used for training and target towing.

TAIL UNIT.—Cantilever monoplane type. Dihedral tailplane. Metal framework with metal-covered fixed surfaces and fabric-covered rudder and elevators. Trimming-tabs in control surfaces.

LANDING GEAR.—Tricycle type. All wheels fully retractable. Main wheels retract into engine nacelles by parallel linkage system. Each main oleo leg hinged about one-third from the top by a "W" strut and by a pair of drag struts attached near lower end and extending forward and upward at about 60 degrees. Hydraulic retracting jacks operating on "W" strut swing, this strut and drag struts through an arc towards rear end of the nacelle. The shock strut moves aft and upward into the horizontal, bringing the wheel slightly forward and up into the well. Gear held in raised position by lock which hooks onto wheel axle. When lowered the wheel moves aft and down and is held in landing position by down-lock hooking onto a "steeple" extension of shock strut. Gear is balanced so that should hydraulic system fail it will drop by gravity, airstream locking it in landing position. Hinged doors closed when gear fully raised by strut linkage attached to oleo strut. Nose wheel retracts aft into fuselage well. Dual brakes on main wheels.

POWER PLANT.—Two Pratt & Whitney R-2800-43 eighteen-cylinder double-row radial air-cooled engines on welded steel-tube mountings. Four-bladed hollow-steel Curtiss Electric constant-speed full-feathering airscrews. Airscrew diameter : 13 ft. 6 in. (4.12 m.). Fuel tanks in wings. Main tanks, each made up of three Mareng self-sealing cells, inboard of engine nacelles. Two auxiliary tanks, each of two interconnected cells, outboard on nacelles. Long-range ferry tanks may be carried in the bomb-bay.

ACCOMMODATION.—Normal crew of seven. Bombardier in nose ; pilot and co-pilot side-by-side ; navigator-radio-operator behind pilot, waist-gunner ; upper turret gunner or tail gunner. Armour plate protects all crew positions, as well as vital aircraft parts. Life-raft stowed in roof of fuselage aft of pilot's compartment. Main entrance to fuselage in nose wheel well. Pilot's escape hatches in roof of canopy. For rest of crew astro-hatch is used.

ARMAMENT.—Eleven 50 cal. machine-guns, one flexible in nose ; four "package" guns in pairs, one pair on each side of the fuselage forward of the wings ; two in Martin electrically-operated turret on top of fuselage aft of wings ; two in waist positions, one on each side of the fuselage aft of the turret ; and two in a Bell tail turret. Tail-gun position has remote-feed ammunition tracks from mid fuselage. Internal bomb-bay with maximum accommodation for two 2,000 lbs. or four 1,000 lb. bombs, latter carried in pairs one above each other on each side of central catwalk. Hydraulically-operated bomb-doors.

DIMENSIONS.—Span 71 ft. (21.65 m.), Length 56 ft. 6 in. (17.23 m.), Height 21 ft. 2 in. (6.45 m.), Wing area 658 sq. ft. (61.1 sq. m.).

WEIGHTS.—Weight empty 25,300 lbs. (11,490 kg.), Maximun loaded weight (with 4,000-lb. bomb load) 38,200 lbs. (17,340 kg.).

PERFORMANCE.—Maximum speed 287 m.p.h. (459.2 km.h.) at 5,000 ft. (1,525 m.), Landing speed 104 m.p.h. (166.4 km.h.), Service ceiling 19,800 ft. (6,040 m.).

THE MARTIN MODEL 187 BALTIMORE.
U.S. Army Air Forces designation : A-30.
British name : Baltimore.

The Model 187 was designed in 1940 to meet the tactical requirements of the British and French Governments as a medium bomber to supersede the Model 167 Maryland, which was then being built for the French. When France fell the British Government took over the French contracts for both types.

Six versions of the Model 187 Baltimore have been supplied to the Royal Air Force. Until Lease/Lend was introduced

The Martin Baltimore V Light Bomber (two Wright GR-2600-A5B5 engines).

the Baltimore was built to British contracts. Thereafter it was ordered by the U.S. Government as a light Attack-Bomber under the designation A-30 and production was shared with the British Government.

The Baltimore was engaged exclusively on operations in the Mediterranean area by the Royal Air Force and Allied Air Forces operating under R.A.F. Command. It was never used operationally by the U.S. Army Air Forces. Production ceased in May, 1944.

The following are the six versions of the Baltimore as delivered to the R.A.F. :—

Baltimore I and II. Two 1,600 h.p. Wright GR-2600-A5B radial air-cooled engines. Armament consisted of four .30 in. machine-guns in the wings firing forward ; four in the lower portion of the fuselage aft of the wings firing aft ; two on a flexible mounting in the rear cockpit and two on a flexible mounting in the lower rear-firing position. Internal stowage for 2,000 lbs. bombs.

Baltimore III and IIIA. Similar to Mk. II except that the upper flexible guns were replaced by a four-gun Boulton Paul power-operated turret.

Baltimore IV. Similar to Mk. III except that a Martin electrically-operated turret armed with two 50 cal. guns replaced the Boulton Paul turret.

Baltimore V. Two 1,700 h.p. Wright GR-2600-A5B5 engines. Light bomber model. Armament consisted of four 50 cal. machine-guns in the wings ; two 50 cal. guns in Martin turret and one flexible 50 cal. gun in the lower rear-firing position.

Baltimore VI. Similar to Mk. V except equipped for General Reconnaissance duties.

TYPE.—Twin-engined Light Bomber and General Reconnaissance monoplane.

WINGS.—Mid-wing cantilever monoplane. Wing in four sections, comprising two inner and two outer sections, the latter with detachable tips. All-metal structure with smooth stressed-skin covering.

FUSELAGE.—All-metal monocoque structure. Very deep forward and with the underside tapering aft of wing to provide rear-firing gun-position.

TAIL UNIT.—Cantilever monoplane type. Fin built integral with fuselage. All-metal framework with metal-covered fixed surfaces and fabric-covered rudder and elevators. Trimming tabs in control surfaces, which are aerodynamically and statically balanced.

LANDING GEAR.—Retractable type. Main wheels raised into engine nacelles, hinged doors closing apertures when gear fully retracted. Hydraulic retraction. Non-retracting tail-wheel.

POWER PLANT.—Two Wright Cyclone GR-2600-A5B5 fourteen-cylinder radial air-cooled engines with two-speed superchargers each rated at 1,600 h.p. at 2,200 ft. (670 m.) and 1,400 h.p. at 10,800 ft. (3,295 m.). Three-bladed Hamilton-Standard constant-speed airscrews 12 ft. 1 in. (3.6 m.) diameter. Self-sealing Mareng fuel cells (507 Imp. gallons total capacity) in wings. Long-range reserve tank (800 Imp. gallons) may be carried in bomb-bay.

ACCOMMODATION.—Crew of four, comprising pilot, navigator/bomb-aimer, radio-operator and rear-gunner. All positions armoured.

ARMAMENT.—Seven 50 cal. machine-guns, four in wings firing forward ; two in Martin power-operated turret on top of fuselage over trailing-edge of wing ; and one on flexible mounting in position in break in underside of fuselage. Internal stowage for a bomb load of 2,000 lbs. (908 kg.).

DIMENSIONS.—Span 61 ft. 4 in. (18.7 m.), Length 48 ft. 6 in. (14.8 m.), Height 14 ft. 2 in. (4.32 m.), Wing area 538.5 sq. ft. (50 sq. m.).

WEIGHT LOADED.—About 24,000 lbs. (10,900 kg.).

PERFORMANCE.—Maximum speed 305 m.p.h. (488 km.h.) at 11,600 ft. (3,540 m.).

THE MARTIN MODEL 202.

The Model 202 is a proposed twin-engined short-range civil transport which has been designed for post-war service.

There are several versions of the basic design, including the 202-11 low-wing monoplane and 202-12 high-wing version, both designed for two Wright R-2600 engines ; and the 202-15 low-wing model with Pratt & Whitney R-2800 engines. Cabins of all versions will be convertible to passenger, cargo or combined passenger/cargo operation. Normal accommodation will be provided for 30 passengers, mail and freight.

Preliminary data on the several versions have been submitted to the airlines for study. The following covers information included in the provisional specifications.

WEIGHTS (Model 202-11).—Weight empty 21,460 lbs. (9,743 kg.), Designed disposable load 11,040 lbs. (5,022 kg.), remainder as for Model 202-12 below.

WEIGHTS (Model 202-12).—Weight empty 21,842 lbs. (9,916 kg.), Designed disposable load 10,658 lbs. (4,840-kg.), Normal loaded weight 32,500 lbs. (14,756 kg.), Wing loading 44 lbs./sq. ft. (214.7 kg./sq. m.).

PERFORMANCE.—Cruising speed (at 60% power) 250 m.p.h. (400 km.h.) at 10,000 ft. (3,050 m.), Operating range (with 50% fuel reserve) 500 miles (800 km.).

MEYERS.

MEYERS AIRCRAFT COMPANY.

HEAD OFFICE AND WORKS : TECUMSEH, MICH.

President and Chief Engineer : A. H. Meyers.

The Meyers Aircraft Company was formed in 1936. It specialises in the design and manufacture of light training and touring aircraft, aircraft wheels and shock-absorber struts.

In 1944 production was concentrated on the Model OTW-160, the entire output of which was delivered to flying schools.

THE MEYERS OTW-160.

TYPE.—Two-seat light training biplane.

WINGS.—Equal-span single-bay staggered biplane. Centre-section carried above fuselage on splayed-out "N"-struts, with one set of "N" interplane struts on each side of fuselage. Lower wings attached to stubs built integral with fuselage. Structure consists of solid spruce spars, spruce and plywood ribs and fabric covering. Metal ailerons on lower wings only.

FUSELAGE.—Oval metal structure of semi-monocoque construction to rear cockpit and full monocoque thence to tail. Structure of 24ST "Alclad."

TAIL UNIT.—Braced monoplane type. Vertical surfaces are of riveted 24ST "Alclad" including the covering. Horizontal surfaces have metal frames and fabric covering. Adjustable tail-plane.

LANDING GEAR.—Divided type. Upper ends of main compression legs attached to upper fuselage longerons with the lower ends hinged by interchangeable Vee struts to the centre-line of the underside of the fuselage. Swivelling tail-wheel.

POWER PLANT.—One 160 h.p. Kinner R-56 seven-cylinder radial air-cooled engine on welded steel-tube mounting. Fuel tank (26 U.S. gallons) in fuselage aft of fireproof bulkhead.

ACCOMMODATION.—Tandem open cockpits with dual controls. Baggage compartment aft of rear seat.

The Meyers OTW-160 Light Training Monoplane (160 h.p. Kinner R-56 engine).

DIMENSIONS.—Span 30 ft. (6.1 m.), Length 22 ft. 8 in. (4.7 m.), Height 8 ft. 6 in. (1.8 m.), Wing area 262 sq. ft. (24.3 sq. m.).

WEIGHTS AND LOADINGS.—Weight empty 1,340 lbs. (608 kg.), Pay load 200 lbs. (91 kg.), Disposable load 570 lbs. (259 kg.), Weight loaded 1,910 lbs. (867 kg.), Wing loading 7.3 lbs./sq. ft. (35.6 kg./sq. m.), Power loading 11.9 lbs./h.p. (5.4 kg./h.p.).

PERFORMANCE.—Maximum speed 120 m.p.h. (193 km.h.), Cruising speed 105 m.p.h. (169 km.h.), Landing speed 40 m.p.h. (64 km.h.), Initial rate of climb 1,200 ft./min. (366 m./min.), Service ceiling 17.500 ft. (5,334 m.), Cruising range 400 miles (640 km.).

NAVAL AIRCRAFT FACTORY.

THE NAVAL AIR MATERIAL CENTER.

U.S. NAVY YARD, PHILADELPHIA 12, PA.

With the expanding activities of war the Naval Aircraft Factory has undergone a complete reorganization and is now established as the Naval Air Material Center. The Center includes the following (a) The Naval Aircraft Factory ; (b) The Naval Aircraft Modification Unit ; (c) The Naval Air Experimental Station and (d) The Naval Auxiliary Air Station, Mustin Field. The former supply depot functions have been completely detached from this organization.

The Naval Aircraft Factory, the manufacturing branch of the Center, builds complete aircraft of both Factory or external design.

The Naval Aircraft Modification Unit is engaged in prototype and production modification of Naval aircraft and in special aeronautical development work. This unit has been moved from the Navy Yard, Philadelphia, into the plant at Johnsville, Pennsylvania, formerly occupied by the Brewster Aeronautical Corporation.

The Naval Air Experimental Station includes : (1) The Aeronautical Engine Laboratory, handling the test and development of engines and power plant accessories ; (2) The Aeronautical Materials Laboratory, handling test and development of metals, fabrics, paints, dopes, finishes, etc., as well as numerous accessories and articles of equipment ; also the test and development of aircraft structures, static destruction tests and vibration tests on complete aircraft structures and components ; (3) The Aeronautical Instrument Laboratory, which handles development and test of specialized aeronautical instruments ; (4) The Radio and Radar Laboratory, which handles special developments and tests of radio and radar, and specialized electronics equipment ; (5) The Aero Medical Department, engaged in the

The Naval Aircraft Factory PBN-1 Catalina Flying-boat (two Pratt & Whitney R-1830-92 engines).

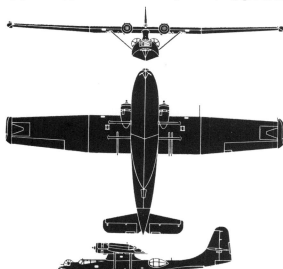

The Naval Aircraft Factory PBN-1 Catalina.

The Naval Aircraft Factory PBN-1 Catalina Flying-boat (two 1,200 h.p. Pratt & Whitney R-1830-92 engines).

development and test of oxygen equipment and personal flying equipment ; (6) The Aeronautical Photographic Experimental Laboratory, which designs, modifies, and tests specialized photographic equipment.

The Naval Auxiliary Air Station, Mustin Field, handles all flight test and other flying activities of the Naval Air Material Center and is designated a military airport and seaplane base.

THE NAVAL AIRCRAFT FACTORY CATALINA.

U.S. Naval designation : PBN-1.

The Naval Aircraft Factory has produced a modified version of the Catalina to incorporate changes which, if undertaken by plants already in full production, would have seriously interfered with deliveries to the U.S. Navy. These changes, which resulted in improved take-off with heavy load and increased range, were later introduced into the design of the Consolidated Vultee PBY-6A Catalina.

The modifications made in the PBN may be summarised as follows :—

HULL.—Bow extended 2ft and sharpened ; 20° taper step amidships ; after step extended aft some 5 ft ; and shallow breaker step added just forward of the tail.

WINGS.—Strengthened to meet a 28,000 lb. (12,710 kg.) gross load (2,000 lbs. = 908 kg. more than PBY). Shape and size of wing-tip floats changed to provide improved lift and planing characteristics.

TAIL UNIT.—Re-designed with new upper fin and horn-balanced rudder of greater aspect ratio.

FUEL TANKS.—Two additional integral fuel tanks in centre-section to raise total capacity from 1,495 to 2,095 U.S. gallons. Tanks equipped with vapour-dilution system and dump valves. Range increased by ⅓ over PBY.

ARMAMENT.—Increased fire-power at all stations and guns equipped with continuous-feed mechanisms.

EQUIPMENT.—Modernised electrical system with greater load capacity. Auxiliary power-plant installed. Storage batteries re-located in hull instead of leading-edge of centre-section.

NORTH AMERICAN.

NORTH AMERICAN AVIATION, INC.

HEAD OFFICE AND WORKS : LOS ANGELES MUNICIPAL AIRPORT, INGLEWOOD, CAL.

NEW YORK OFFICE : 1775, BROADWAY, NEW YORK.

President and General Manager : J. H. Kindelberger.

First Vice-President : J. L. Atwood.

Vice-President and Treasurer : R. A. Lambeth.

Vice-President in charge of Engineering : R. H. Rice.

North American Aviation, Inc., was incorporated in Delaware in 1928 and has been engaged solely in the design and manufacture

of military aircraft since 1934. Manufacturing facilities were established at Inglewood, California, in 1935, where a modern production plant was erected on the Los Angeles Municipal Airport. Early types of aircraft built under contract included the BT-9, NJ-1, BC-1, BT-14, AT-6, SNJ-1 and O-47 for the United States Army and Navy, Harvards for the R.A.F. and

The North American P-51B Mustang Single-seat Fighter (Packard Merlin V-1650-3 engine).

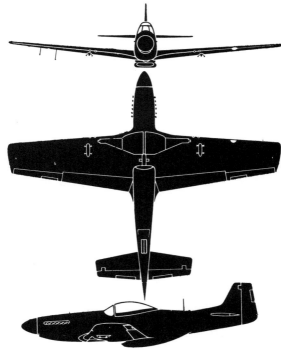

The North American P-51D Mustang.

R.C.A.F., and trainers for nine other foreign nations.

North American Aviation, Inc. began production of the B-25 Mitchell bomber and the Mustang in 1940.

When the company erected a new plant in Dallas, Texas, in 1941, production of the entire trainer series was moved to that site. The Dallas plant later took over part of the production of the P-51 Mustang, and in November, 1944, completed a contract to build B-24 Liberator bombers.

Another plant in Kansas City, owned by the U.S. Government and operated by North American Aviation, Inc., began production of B-25 Mitchell bombers in December, 1941. In July, 1944, the entire production of Mitchells was transferred to Kansas City, permitting the Inglewood plant to devote its entire facilities to the output of P-51 Mustangs.

Soon after the end of the war all remaining B-25 contracts were cancelled, resulting in the closing of the Kansas City plant and its return to the Government. At the same time all contracts at the Dallas plant were cancelled, including one for the Fairchild C-82 Packet. Manufacture of the P-51 Mustang at Inglewood, was cut back by 85 per cent.

THE NORTH AMERICAN MUSTANG.
U.S. Army Air Forces designations : P-51, A-36 and F-6.
British name : Mustang.

The N.A. 73 Mustang was designed and built to a British specification and order. The prototype was actually designed, built and flown in 100 days, its first flight taking place in October, 1940. Passing all tests satisfactorily it was put into production before the end of 1940. The first production Mustang I was delivered to the R.A.F. in Great Britain in November, 1941.

The 5th and 10th aircraft off the production lines were taken over by the American Army for experimental test at Wright Field, Dayton, Ohio, and these two aircraft were given the designation XP-51. The first two batches of Mustangs, amounting to over 600 aircraft, were supplied under British contracts but after the passing of the Lease-Lend Act the aircraft were ordered by the American authorities as the P-51 and allotted to Great Britain. On the entry of America into the war a proportion of the P-51 contracts was diverted to the U.S. Army Air Forces.

Mustang I (P-51). The Mustang I was fitted with the Allison V-1710-F3R engine rated at 1,000 h.p. at 12,000 ft. (3,660 m.) and with 1,150 h.p. available for take-off. Its armament consisted of four 50 cal. and four 30 cal. machine-guns, two of the 50 cal. guns being mounted in the fuselage, one on each side of the engine crankcase and synchronised to fire through the airscrew. All the other guns were in the wings.

Owing to poor performance at height the Mustang I was re-mustered as a low-altitude reconnaissance fighter and posted to the R.A.F. Army Co-operation Command. An oblique camera for tactical photographic reconnaissance was installed in the port backward-vision panel behind the pilot, together with a vertical camera in the rear fuselage. The Mustang I made its first operational sortie with Army Co-operation Command on July 27, 1942.

Mustang IA (P-51). This was the Mustang I with an armament of four 20 m/m. cannon mounted in the wings.

Mustang II (P-51A). Initially the new designation covered solely a change in armament to four 50 cal. machine-guns, all in the wings. Later series were fitted with the Allison V-1710-81 (F20R) engine rated at 1,125 h.p. at 15,500 ft. (4,700 m.) and with 1,200 h.p. available for take-off.

The contracts for this model were equally divided between Great Britain and America. From the American P-51A were developed the A-36A dive-bomber and the F-6A photographic-reconnaissance model (see later).

P-51B and P-51C (Mustang III). These were the first models to be fitted with the Merlin engine and four-bladed airscrew. The original conversion was made in Great Britain by Rolls-Royce, Ltd. by the installation of the Merlin 61 engine in the Mustang II. The success of the conversion was such that steps were immediately taken by N.A.A. to re-design the P-51 to take the 1,520 h.p. Packard V-1650-3 (Packard-built Merlin 68 with two-speed two stage supercharger and aftercooler) which was at that time going into production in the United States. The airframe was strengthened to take the new engine, the radiator installation was re-designed, new ailerons were installed and streamline racks for long-range tanks or two 500

lb. bombs were provided under the wings. The bomb load was later increased to two 1,000 lb. bombs. The new design was originally given the designation XP-78 but this was later changed to P-51B.

The P-51B and P-51C were put into production in 1943, the P-51C at the Dallas plant of North American Aviation, Inc. of Texas. The first Merlin-engined Mustangs were delivered to a U.S. Combat Group of the 8th Air Force in Great Britain, on December 1 of that year. The P-51B first went into action as a fighter on December 17, and on January 15, 1944, P-51B's with drop tanks made their first long-range mission as fighter escort to heavy bombers of the 8th Air Force over Germany.

A modification which had no bearing on the designation was the introduction of the Malcolm backward-sliding bulged cockpit hood on examples of the P-51B, P-51C and F-6A. This modification was undertaken in the British Isles.

P-51D (Mustang IV). A development of the P-51B with the armament increased to six 50 cal. machine-guns, all in the wings. Fitted with a moulded plastic "blister" type sliding hood and a modified rear fuselage. A later modification was the introduction of a small dorsal extension to the fin. This modification was made retrospective for the P-51B, C and earlier D models.

XP-51F. A complete structural redesign of the Mustang as a pure interceptor, to a combination of the optimum British and American strength requirements. No single structural part interchangeable with earlier P-51 models. New low-drag laminar-flow wing section, new wing plan, improved fuselage and radiator fairing contours, new lightened engine-mounting and landing-gear, substitution of heat exchanger for oil radiator, simplified hydraulic system and cockpit layout, etc. Structural weight reduced by 1,600 lbs. (726 kg.). Armament reduced to four 50-cal. guns. Reduced petrol capacity.

XP-51G. A redesign of the XP-51H into a long-range escort fighter. Higher powered Packard Merlin V-1650-9 engine, which called for a longer fuselage (12 in.) and increase in area and aspect ratio of tail surfaces. Armament reverted to six 50 cal. guns and internal fuel capacity increased with additional fuselage tank behind pilot.

A North American Mustang III Single-seat Fighter with the Malcolm bulged cockpit hood.

A North American P-51D Single-seat Fighter fitted with Bazooka-type rocket projectile equipment.

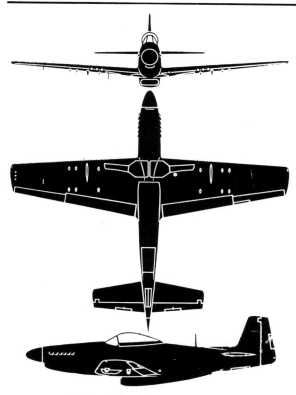

The North American P-51H Mustang.

P-51H. Production version of XP-51G with further improvements including a new Merlin V-1650-11 engine developing a maximum of over 2,000 h.p. with water injection and 150 grade fuel, changes in control surfaces, etc. 700 lbs. (318 kg.) lighter than P-51D. Armament six 50-cal. guns. Can also carry ten 5-in. rockets or maximum of two 1,000 lb. bombs or two 110 gallon drop tanks.

P-51K. Similar to the P-51D except fitted with the Aeroproducts instead of the Hamilton Standard Hydromatic four-bladed constant-speed airscrew. All built at the Dallas plant of North American Aviation, Inc.

XP-82. Consists of two P-51 H fuselages and port and starboard outer wings joined together by rectangular centre-section and tailplane between the fuselages. Pilot in the port fuselage, co-pilot in starboard. Evolved as possible long-range escort fighter. Span 50 ft. 9 in. (15.5 in.), Length 33 ft. 4 in. (10.16 m.), Weight loaded 21,210 lbs. (9 630 kg.).

A-36A. This was an attack or dive-bomber version of the P-51A. Development began in June, 1942 and the first model flew in September of that year.

It was fitted with the 1,325 Allison V-1710-87 (F21R) engine, and had hydraulically-operated dive-brakes and a rack under each wing to carry either a bomb (250, 300 or 500 lb.), or a droppable fuel tank. Armament comprised six 50 cal. machine-guns, two in the fuselage and two in each outer wing.

The A-36 went into service with the U.S.A.A.F. in the Mediterranean just prior to the invasion of Sicily. Production was completed in March, 1943.

F-6. This is a photographic-reconnaissance version of the P-51. Photographic equipment replaced all armament. The P-51A was fitted with the 1,200 h.p. Allison V-1710-81 (F20R) engine. For improved vision certain aircraft of this model were fitted with the Malcolm bulged sliding hood as shown in the accompanying illustration. The F-6D was similar to the P-51D and the F-6K was similar to the P-51K.

TYPE.—Single-seat Fighter and Fighter Bomber.

WINGS.—Low-wing cantilever monoplane. N.A.A.-NACA laminar-flow wing section. Wing in two sections bolted together on the centre line of the fuselage, the upper surface of the wing forming the floor of the cockpit. Two-spar all-metal structure with smooth Alclad skin. Spars have single plate flanges and extruded top and bottom booms. Remaining structure consists of pressed ribs with flanged lightening holes and extruded spanwise stringers. Space between spars on each side of centre-line accommodates the self-sealing non-metallic fuel cells. A structural door is provided in the undersurface of each wing section to facilitate fuel cell installation and removal. The rear spar carries the hinges for the ailerons and slotted flaps. Metal-covered ailerons, the port aileron having a controllable trim-tab. Hydraulically-operated trailing-edge flaps between ailerons and fuselage.

FUSELAGE.—Oval all-metal structure in three sections, the engine section, the main section and the tail section. With the exception of cockpit armour the fuselage is constructed entirely of Alclad and aluminium-alloy extrusions. The engine section consists of two V-type cantilever engine-bearers built up of plate webs and top and bottom extruded numbers, each attached at two points to the front fireproof bulkhead of the main section. The main section consists of two beams, each side beam comprising two longerons, which form the caps, and the skin, reinforced by vertical frames, forming the webs. Aft of the cockpit the longerons extend into a semi-monocoque structure reinforced by vertical frames. The detachable tail-section continues structure of rear portion of main section.

TAIL UNIT.—Cantilever monoplane type. One-piece tailplane with detachable tips. Structure of tailplane and fin comprises two spars, pressed ribs and extruded stringers, the whole covered with stressed Alclad skin. Rudder and elevators have aluminium-alloy frames and fabric covering. Control surfaces are dynamically balanced and have trimming-tabs controllable from cockpit.

LANDING GEAR.—Retractable type. Cantilever air-oil shock-absorber legs hinged to large forged fittings bolted to reinforced ribs and retracted inwardly, the wheels and legs being accommodated forward of main spar. Hydraulic retraction. Fairing plates on legs and doors forming part of wing contour cover main landing gear when retracted. Hydraulic wheel-brakes. Retractable tail-wheel is full swivelling and steerable within range of rudder pedal travel.

POWER PLANT.—One 1,590 h.p. Packard V-1650-7 (Rolls-Royce Merlin 69) twelve-cylinder Vee liquid-cooled engine on built-up cantilever mounting. Four-bladed Hamilton-Standard Hydromatic or Aeroproducts automatic constant-speed airscrew. Coolant (30/70 ethylene-glycol/water) and oil radiators in scoop under fuselage and aft of cockpit with thermostatically-controlled exit-flaps. Self-sealing fuel cells (184 gallons total capacity) in wings and self-sealing tank (85 U.S. gallons) in fuselage behind pilot. Oil tank (12 U.S. gallons) in engine compartment. Droppable ferrying or combat tanks may be installed on bomb racks.

ACCOMMODATION.—Enclosed cockpit over centre of wing. Windshield incorporates an optically-flat 5 ply laminated glass bullet-proof front panel with side panels of safety glass. Moulded "bister" type sliding cockpit cover. Stainless steel sheet and armour plate, fireproof bulkhead in front of cockpit and two plates of face-hardened steel armour behind seat. Cockpit heating and ventilation. Equipment includes 24 volt electrical system, radio, oxygen, etc.

ARMAMENT.—Six 0.50 in. machine-guns, three in each wing outside the area swept by the airscrew. Guns are adjusted to converge at 300 yds. range. Removable streamlined bomb-rack under each wing for bombs up to 1,000 lbs., auxiliary fuel tank or chemical container for smoke making. Fusing of bombs is electrically-controlled from cockpit and bombs may be dropped in a dive, in level flight or a 30 degree climb.

DIMENSIONS.—Span 37 ft. $\frac{5}{16}$ in. (11.27 m.), Length 32 ft. 3¼ in. (9.75 m.), Height 13 ft. 8 in. (4.16 m.), Wing area 233.19 sq. ft. (21.66 sq. m.).

WEIGHT LOADED.—10,000 lbs. (4,540 kg.) approx.

PERFORMANCE (Packard V-1650-7 engine).—Maximum speed 445 m.p.h. (712 km.h.) at 24,000 ft. (7,320 m.), Climb to 20,000 ft. (6,100 m.) 6.5 min., Service ceiling over 40,000 ft. (12,200 m.).

The North American P-51H Mustang Single-seat Fighter (Packard V-1650-11 Merlin engine).

THE NORTH AMERICAN MITCHELL.

U.S. Army Air Forces designations : B-25, F-10.

U.S. Navy designation : PBJ.

British name : Mitchell.

The design of the XB-25 was approved in September, 1939, and the prototype flew on August 19, 1940. The XB-25 and the first few B-25's had wings with constant dihedral from roots to tips but from the 10th aircraft off the production line the outer wings were re-rigged flat to give the characteristic "gull-wing" arrangement which has since been such a distinctive feature of the Mitchell. The armament consisted of four 30 cal. machine-guns, one in the nose and three amidships, and one 50 cal. gun in the tail. The normal bomb load was 2,000 lbs. (910 kg.) with a maximum permissible overload of 3,600 lbs. (1,635 kg.). A crew of five was carried. The power-plant consisted of two 1,700 h.p. Wright R-2600-9 fourteen-cylinder radial engines each driving a Hamilton-Standard airscrew, 12 ft. 7 in. (3.84 m.) diameter.

B-25A. Similar to the B-25 except that self-sealing fuel tanks and armour for the pilot were added.

B-25B (Mitchell I). This model had a completely revised armament. The nose gun remained but the midship and tail guns were replaced by two Bendix electrically-operated turrets each with two 50 cal. machine-guns. The lower turret was retractable and remotely controlled. The former tail gun position became a prone observation post. A separate photographic station was located between the upper turret and the tail. Overall length, 54 ft. 1 in. (16.49 m.). Aircraft of this model were used on the Tokyo raid on April 18, 1942.

B-25C and B-25D (PBJ-1C and D and Mitchell II). These models were virtually the same as the B-25B but were equipped with automatic flight control equipment. Wright R-2600-13

The North American F-6A Mustang Photographic-reconnaissance Monoplane (Allison V-1710-81 engine).

The North American F-6D Mustang Photographic-Reconnaissance Monoplane (Packard V-1650-9 Merlin engine).

(Photograph by Peter Bowers)

engines with 1,700 h.p. available for take-off were substituted for the earlier power-units. B-25C built in the Inglewood, Cal., plant, B-25D built in the Kansas City plant. The Mitchell II was first reported in action with the R.A.F. on January 22, 1943.

B-25E and F. One only of each model. Both fitted experimentally with heated-surface anti-icing equipment to wings and tail surfaces, a different system being used for each model.

B-25G (PBJ-IG). The first aircraft to be fitted with a 75 m/m. cannon. This cannon is installed in a new armoured nose which also includes two 50 cal. machine-guns. The 75 m/m. (2.953 in.) M-4 aircraft cannon is 9 ft. 6 in. (2.9 m.) long and weighs about 900 lbs. (410 kg.). It is mounted in a cradle extending aft under the pilot's seat where a hydro-spring mechanism takes care of the 21 in. (53 cm.) recoil. Each shell is 23 in. (58 cm.) long and weighs 15 lbs. (6.8 kg.). Aft of the nose the armament is the same as for the B-25C. The standard bomb-bay is retained but is modified to permit the installation of a standard aircraft torpedo. The crew is reduced to four, comprising the pilot (who fires the nose armament and releases the bombs or torpedo); navigator (who also hand-loads the cannon); gunner (who mans the upper turret and operates the camera); and radio operator (who also mans the lower turret). Overall length, 50 ft. 10 in. (15.50 m.).

B-25H (PBJ-1H). A development of the B-25H but with a greatly enhanced armament. The forward firing-guns are increased to include four 50 cal. machine-guns in the armoured nose and two pairs of 50 cal. "package" guns, one pair on each side of the fuselage in line with the pilot's cockpit.

The top turret is moved forward into the roof of the navigator's compartment. Between the wings and tail are two new waist positions, each armed with one 50 cal. gun. Finally, there is a new tail gun position armed with two 50 cal. guns. The crew is increased to five and their duties rearranged as follows :—pilot (who fires forward-firing armament and releases bombs or torpedo); navigator-radio operator (who also loads the cannon); flight engineer (who also mans the top turret); midship gunner (responsible for guns in both waist positions and also operates camera); and tail gunner. Overall length, 51 ft. 3¾ in. (15.63 m.).

B-25J (PBJ-IJ and Mitchell III). This is the precision bomber version of the B-25H. A glazed nose of the B-25C type replaces the armoured nose and the nose armament is reduced to one fixed and one flexible 50 cal. machine-guns. Aft of the nose the armament remains the same as for the B-25H. The crew is increased to six to include a bombardier. Internal bomb load increased to from 2,000 to 6,000 lbs. (2,720 m.) for short range operations. Overall length, 53 ft. 5¾ in. (16.3 m.).

TB-25 (formerly AT-24). A number of earlier Mitchells were de-militarised and converted into training aircraft. These were originally given the designation AT-24. This was later cancelled and they are now known by the classification TB-25.

F-10. A specially-equipped photographic reconnaissance version of the B-25. All armament was removed and a variety of cameras installed, including a tri-metrogon camera in the nose.

TYPE.—Twin-engined Medium Bomber.

WINGS.—Mid-wing cantilever monoplane of all-metal construction. Wing in five sections consisting of a two-spar centre-section permanently attached to the fuselage, two outer single-spar sections and two detachable wing-tips. Fuel and oil tanks integral with the centre-section structure. Outer wings have sealed compartments for flotation purposes. Ailerons of sealed type and are fitted with fixed and controllable trimming-tabs. Hydraulically operated slotted trailing-edge flaps inboard of ailerons and divided by tails of engine nacelles. Flaps have fairings which hinge upward into the wings to form a continuous slot opening when the flaps are lowered.

FUSELAGE.—Semi-monocoque four-longeron structure of aluminium-alloy with covering of same material. That portion of the fuselage above the bottom surface of the centre-section and between the front spar and trailing-edge is permanently attached to and removable with the centre-section.

TAIL UNIT.—Cantilever monoplane type with twin fins and rudders. Elevators and rudders have fixed and controllable trimming-tabs.

LANDING GEAR.—Tricycle type with all wheels fully retractable. All wheels retract aft, the main wheels into the engine nacelles and

The North American B-25H Mitchell Medium Bomber armed with a 75 m/m. cannon and fourteen 50-cal. machine-guns.

The North American B-25J Mitchell Medium Bomber (two Wright R-2600-29 engines).

A North American B-25J Medium Bomber with a special nose armament of eight 50-cal. machine-guns.

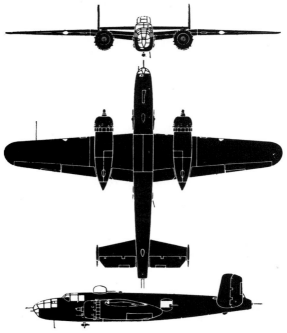

The North American B-25J Mitchell Bomber.

The North American F-10 Mitchell, an unarmed Photographic-Reconnaissance version of the B-25 Medium Bomber.

the nose wheel and tail-skid into the fuselage. Doors cover all openings in both the retracted and extended positions. Hydraulic retraction, with a mechanically-operated emergency system. The swivelling nose-wheel has shimmy damper and centering device and lock. Main wheels have hydraulic brakes.

POWER PLANT.—Two Wright Cyclone R-2600-13 two-row radial air-cooled engines with two-speed superchargers in semi-monocoque nacelles mounted below the extremities of the centre-section. Three-bladed Hamilton-Standard constant-speed full-feathering airscrews with anti-icers. Each engine fitted with independent fuel system consisting of two interconnected fore and aft compartments equipped with bullet-proof self-sealing fuel cells located between fuselage and nacelles. Three auxiliary fuel cells in centre-section outboard of each engine nacelle together with a self-sealing tank in fuselage above bomb-bay. All fuel lines in wings and fuselage are of self-sealing type. Additional droppable long-range ferry tank may be installed in bomb-bay. Each engine has independent oil system,

ACCOMMODATION.—Provision for crew of from four to six. (See above). All crew positions are armoured. Heating and ventilation systems, radio equipment, oxygen etc.

ARMAMENT.—For various models see introduction. Bomb-bay in fuselage beneath wings may accommodate bombs, depth-charges or a torpedo. Maximum internal bomb-load 3,000 lbs. Provision for 2,400 lb. bombs on external wing racks. 2,150 lb. torpedo only partly enclosed in bomb-bay.

DIMENSIONS.—Span 67 ft. 7 in. (20.6 m.), Length 53 ft. 5¾ in. (16.13 m.), Height 16 ft. 4¾ in. (4.6 m.), Wing area 609.8 sq. ft. (56.6 sq. m.).

WEIGHTS—Weight empty 21,100 lbs. (9,580 kg.), Weight loaded 33,500 lbs (15,210 kg.).

PERFORMANCE.—Maximum speed 303 m.p.h. (485 km.h.) at 13,000 ft. (3,965 m.), Landing speed 95 m.p.h. (152 km.h.), Climb to 15,000 ft. (4,575 m.), 11.3 min., Service ceiling 24,200 ft. (7,380 m.)

THE NORTH AMERICAN TEXAN.

U.S. Army Air Forces designation : AT-6.
U.S. Navy designation : SNJ.
British name : Harvard.

The AT-6 was first produced in 1939 and was similar to and eventually replaced the BC-1A basic combat trainer when the Basic Combat classification was abandoned. The BC-1A was a development of the BC-1 (SNJ-1 and Harvard I). Both were fitted with the Pratt & Whitney R-1340-47 engine, the BC-1 having a steel tube fabric-covered fuselage while the BC-1A had a semi-monocoque rear fuselage and a re-designed tail-unit.

Since then several series of AT-6 Advanced Trainers have been built, the various sub-types varying mainly in matters of equipment. These may be summarised as follows :—

AT-6 (Harvard II). Pratt & Whitney R-1340-47 engine. Integral fuel tanks in centre-section.

AT-6A (SNJ-3). Pratt & Whitney R-1340-49 engine. Removable aluminum fuel tanks. The AT-6A built in Canada under licence by Noorduyn Aviation, Ltd. was the Harvard IIB. Canadian-built Harvards were also delivered to the U.S. Army and because of manufacturing and equipment differences these were given the designation AT-16.

AT-6B. Pratt & Whitney R-1340-AN1 engine.

AT-6C (SNJ-4 and Harvard IIA). Pratt & Whitney R-1340-AN1 engine. In 1941, owing to possible shortages in strategic materials, the structure of the AT-6C was re-designed to eliminate the use of aluminium-alloy and high-alloy steels. The wings, centre-section, fin, rudder, elevators, ailerons, flaps, etc. were made of spot-welded low-alloy steel, and the side panels of the forward fuselage, the entire rear fuselage tailplane, floor boards, etc. were of plywood. A saving of 1,246 lbs. (566 kg.) of aluminimum-alloy per aircraft was achieved. The fear of material shortages having been found to be groundless, the standard structure was later reverted to.

AT-6D (SNJ-5 and Harvard III). Pratt & Whitney R-1340-AN1 engine. Standard structure as described below. 24-volt electrical system. No photographic equipment.

The British Harvard versions of the AT-6 carried no armament and were fitted with British instruments, radio, shoulder harness, etc.

The North American AT-6C Texan Two-seat Advanced Trainer (Pratt & Whitney R-1340-AN1 engine).

TYPE.—Two-seat Advanced Training (AT-6) or Scout Training (SNJ) monoplane.

WINGS.—Low-wing cantilever monoplane. Two spar rectangular centre-section and two single-spar tapered outer sections with detachable wing-tips. All-metal structure with aluminium-alloy spars and ribs and a smooth Alclad skin. Aerodynamically and statically-balanced ailerons have metal frames and fabric covering. Split trailing-edge flaps between ailerons.

FUSELAGE.—Welded chrome-molybdenum steel-tube structure from fireproof bulkhead to rear cockpit, remainder of aluminium-alloy semi-monocoque construction. Side panels of the forward section are of aluminium-alloy and are removable.

TAIL UNIT.—Cantilever monoplane type. Aluminium-alloy framework, fixed surfaces covered with Alclad sheet and movable surfaces with fabric. Elevators and rudder have trim-tabs controllable from both cockpits.

LANDING GEAR.—Retractable cantilever type, with wheels folding inwards. Retraction by engine-driven hydraulic pump. Hydraulic wheel-brakes. Full-swivelling tail-wheel.

POWER PLANT.—One 550 h.p. Pratt & Whitney R-1340-AN1 radial air-cooled engine. Two-bladed Hamilton-Standard constant-speed airscrew. Fuel tanks (111 U.S. gallons capacity) in centre-section. Oil tank (9.5 U.S. gallons) in engine compartment.

ACCOMMODATION.—Tandem cockpits with individually-operated sliding enclosures. Complete dual flight and engine controls in each cockpit. Adjustable seat in front cockpit, rotating and adjustable gunner's seat in back cockpit.

ARMAMENT.—One 0.30 in. machine-gun in starboard side of fuselage forward of pilot's cockpit, one 0.30 in. machine-gun in leading-edge starboard outer wing, and one 0.30 in. machine-gun on flexible mounting in rear cockpit.

DIMENSIONS.—Span 42 ft. 0¼ in. (12.9 m.), Length 28 ft. 11⅞ in. (8.8 m.), Height 11 ft. 8½ in. (3.5 m.), Wing area 253.7 sq. ft. (23.6 sq. m.).

WEIGHTS AND LOADINGS.—Weight empty 4,158 lbs. (1,888 kg.), Disposable load 1,142 lbs. (518 kg.), Normal loaded weight 5,300 lbs. (2,406 kg.), Wing loading 20.8 lbs./sq. ft. (101.5 kg./sq. m.), Power loading 9.6 lbs./h.p. (4.35 kg./h.p.).

PERFORMANCE.—Maximum speed at 5,000 ft. (1,525 m.) 205 m.p.h. (331.2 km.h.), Cruising speed at 5,000 ft. (1,525 m.) 170 m.p.h. (272 km.h.), Landing speed 63 m.p.h. (101 km.h.), Service ceiling 21,500 ft. (6,560 m.), Normal range 750 miles (1,200 km.).

THE NORTH AMERICAN N.A. 63.

U.S. Army Air Forces designation : XB-28.

The XB-28 was ordered by the U.S. Army Air Forces Materiel Command as part of the experimental programme on the development of pressurised cabins for military aircraft.

It was a twin-engined Medium Bomber monoplane with a tricycle landing-gear, single rudder tail-unit and pressurised crew accommodation fed by a mechanical engine-driven supercharger to maintain a cabin pressure equivalent to that found at 8,000 ft. (2,440 m.) up to a height of 33,000 ft. (10,060 m.). Cabin heating was by auxiliary heaters in the ducting that circulated air through the cabin. To seal the cabin section rubber strips were sandwiched between all riveted joints and a plastic compound was sprayed throughout the interior.

Armament was carried in three two-gun turrets, all placed outside the pressurised area and remotely-controlled from sighting stations within the cabin.

The XB-28 was fitted with two Pratt & Whitney R-2800 eighteen-cylinder radial air-cooled engines with turbo-superchargers, one of the engines being responsible for driving the cabin supercharger.

The XB-28, which first flew in 1942, played an important part in the development of the B-29, the first American tactical aircraft incorporating pressurisation to go into operational service.

NORTHROP.

NORTHROP AIRCRAFT, INC.

HEAD OFFICE AND WORKS : NORTHROP FIELD, HAWTHORNE, CALIFORNIA.

President and Chief Engineer : John K. Northrop.
General Manager and Chairman of the Board : LaMotte T. Cohu.
Vice-President in Charge of Production : Gage H. Irving.
Vice-President and General Counsel : Graham L. Sterling, Jr.
Vice-President in charge of Sales : Theodore C. Coleman.
Secretary : Moye W. Stephens.

This concern was formed in 1939 by Mr. John K. Northrop to undertake the manufacture of military aircraft. Mr. Northrop, who has long been associated with the design of high-performance all-metal military aircraft, was latterly associated with the Douglas Aircraft Company. He resigned from the Douglas Company in 1939 to form his new company.

The Company's first contract was for the supply of twenty-four single-engined high-performance Patrol-Bomber seaplanes for the Norwegian Government. These aircraft were delivered early in 1941.

In 1944-45 the Company was in production for the U.S. Army Air Forces with the P-61 Black Widow, the first American aeroplane specifically built as a Night Fighter.

Northrop Aircraft, Inc. is also engaged in the development of "flying-wing" aircraft under Army and Navy direction. Northrop "flying-wing" types include the XB-35, a four-engined Bomber of 178 ft. (54.3 m.) span, originally intended to be fitted with four pusher-mounted 3,000 h.p. Pratt & Whitney R-4360 engines but also being engineered for jet propulsion; the XP-56 single-seat Fighter described overleaf; and the XP-79 a single-seat jet-propelled Fighter, which crashed on its first flight.

The company is also interested in the Northrop-Hendy Company, which was formed to develop turbo-jet power units.

THE NORTHROP BLACK WIDOW.

U.S. Army Air Forces designation : P-61 and F-15.
U.S. Navy designation : FT-1.

The Black Widow was built to an Army specification issued in 1940. Development began in 1940, an order for two XP-61's was placed in January, 1941, and the first prototype flew on May 26, 1942.

P-61A and P-61B. Generally similar, the earlier P-61A being fitted with two Pratt & Whitney R-2800-10 (B Series) and the later P-61A and P-61B with the R-2800-65 (C Series) engines, all with two-stage superchargers.

P-61C. Two Pratt & Whitney R-2800-57 engines with single-stage superchargers and new Curtiss Electric airscrews with paddle-type blades. Aircraft fitted with slatted air-brakes on upper and lower surfaces of outer wings.

F-15. A photographic reconnaissance version of the P-61E.

TYPE.—Twin-engined Night Fighter.

WINGS.—Shoulder-wing cantilever monoplane. Centre-section panels between central nacelle and points outboard of engine nacelles set a coarser dihedral than outer wings. Two-spar all-metal structure. Landing flaps extend over most of trailing-edge. Aileron system consists of two small conventional ailerons, each with a trim-tab, four retractable aileron panels, all mechanically connected and

The Northrop P-61A Black Widow Night Fighter (two Pratt & Whitney R-2800-10 engines).

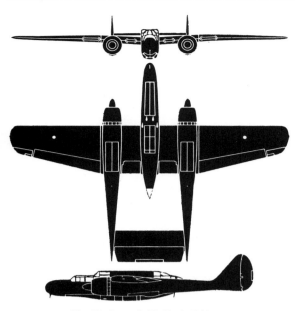

The Northrop P-61 Black Widow.

constant-speed full-feathering airscrews, 12 ft. 2 in. (3.7 m.) diameter. Self-sealing fuel tanks in wings. Streamline auxiliary drop tanks may be carried under wings outboard of engine nacelles.

ACCOMMODATION.—Crew of three, comprising pilot, gunner and radar operator, in central nacelle. All crew positions armoured.

ARMAMENT.—Four forward firing 20 m/m. cannon in underside of fuselage aft of nose-wheel well and four 50 cal. machine-guns in a 360-degree electrically-operated General Electric dorsal turret. Turret is remotely controlled and fired by the pilot or from either one of two gun-sighting stations, one forward and one aft. Full Radar equipment.

DIMENSIONS.—Span 66 ft. (20.13 m.), Length 48 ft. 11 in. (13.72 m.), Height 14 ft. 2 in. (4.3 m.), Wing area 664 sq. ft. (61.7 sq. m.).

WEIGHT LOADED.—27,000 lbs. (12,260 kg.).

PERFORMANCE.—Maximum speed 375 m.p.h. (600 km.h.) at 17,000 ft. (5,190 m.), Climb to 25,000 ft. (4,575 m.) 13 min., Service ceiling 33,000 ft. (10,070 m.).

THE NORTHROP N-2B.
U.S. Army Air Forces designation : XP-56.

The XP-56 is one of several types of fighter aircraft which have been developed experimentally for the Army Air Forces to investigate possible future aircraft design projects.

It is a tail-less mid-wing monoplane of all-metal construction. The Pratt & Whitney R-2800 eighteen-cylinder air-cooled radial engine is buried in the short symmetrical fuselage amidships and drives two co-axial contra-rotating three-bladed pusher propellers. The ducted cooling air intakes are in the leading-edge of the wings.

Lateral and directional control are by spoilers hinged flush with the upper and lower surfaces of the drooping wing tips. Elevators are hinged at the trailing-edge inboard of the droop.

The landing-gear is of the retractable tricycle type, with the main wheels being raised into the undersurface of the wings and the nose wheel into the fuselage.

The pilot's cockpit is in front of the leading-edge of the wings and in front of the cockpit is the armament compartment in which there are two 20 m/m. cannon and four 50 cal. machine-guns.

No further details of this interesting aeroplane are available for publication.

The Northrop XP-56 Experimental Single-seat Tail-less Fighter (Pratt & Whitney R-2800 engine).

linked to control system. The retractable panels are perforated metal scoop-shaped strips and when not in use are retracted into slots near trailing-edge. When raised they spoil airflow and reduce lift on one wing.

NACELLE AND TAIL BOOMS.—All-metal structures. The tail booms are metal monocoques extending aft from engine nacelles.

TAIL UNIT.—Monoplane type. Fins built integral with tail booms, the tailplane being located between the fins and above centre-line of bombs. Single-piece elevator with centrally-located trim-tabs. Statically and aerodynamically-balanced rudders.

LANDING GEAR.—Retractable tricycle type. Main wheels raise aft into booms and nose wheel into central nacelle.

POWER PLANT.—Two 2,000 h.p. Pratt & Whitney R-2800-10 eighteen-cylinder radial air-cooled engines. Curtiss Electric four-blade

NORTHWESTERN.
NORTHWESTERN AERONAUTICAL CORPORATION.

HEAD OFFICE AND WORKS : MINNEAPOLIS MUNICIPAL AIRPORT AND 1902, MINNEHAHA AVENUE, SAINT PAUL, MINN.

Chairman of the Board, President and General Manager : John E. Parker.

Vice-President and Treasurer : George H. Plufka.

Secretary and Production Manager : R. W. Whittingham.

Assistant Secretary and General Counsel : Jack Foote.

Chief Engineer : B. H. T. Lindquist.
Comptroller : T. W. Pallister.
Planning Director : Lynn J. Lubins.

This company was formed in February, 1942, to manufacture the Waco CG-4A fifteen-seat troop-transport and cargo-glider for the U.S. Army Air Forces. The Company delivered the first CG-4A glider to the Army Air Forces in September, 1942.

In May, 1943 the Company under an experimental contract with the Army Air Forces designed a detachable engine installation for the CG-4A and flew the first glider of this type under its own power. This model, designated the XPG-1, was fitted with two 120 h.p. Franklin 6AC-298 horizontally-opposed engines in nacelles mounted on the bracing struts below the wings.

The Northwestern Aeronautical Corpn. is also manufacturing the Waco CG-13 thirty-seat troop transport and cargo glider.

P-V.
P-V ENGINEERING FORUM, INC.

HEAD OFFICE AND WORKS : ELMWOOD AVE. BELOW CALCON HOOK ROAD, SHARON HILL, PENNA.

President : Frank N. Piasecki.

Vice-President and Chief Engineer : Elliot Daland.

Secretary and Treasurer : Wesley R. Frysztacki.

The P-V Engineering Forum was organized in 1941 and incorporated in the State of Pennsylvania in 1943.

It is engaged in the design, engineering and construction of rotary wing aircraft, specialising in helicopters. Its first helicopter—the PV-2—demonstrated for the first time in September, 1943, at the Washington National Airport, was the second American helicopter to be flown publicly.

Under a confidential contract with the U.S. Navy Department, Bureau of Aeronautics, it has built the PV-3 experimental helicopter, and, during the war, was also engaged as a sub-contractor for the manufacture of PBY Catalina and radar parts.

THE P-V 2.

The PV-2 is an experimental single-seat single-rotor helicopter which has been flying since the middle of 1943. The power-plant is a 90 h.p. four-cylinder Franklin vertically mounted aft of the pilot's compartment and driving through a universally-jointed shaft, the three-blade 25 ft. (7.6 m.) diameter rotor. The rotor blades have a constant chord of 9½ in. except at root and tip and are built round a steel-tube spar, with wood ribs, leading and trailing edges and fabric covering. The two-blade anti-torque, or directional, control rotor mounted aft on the right side of the fuselage is 5 ft. in diameter and is geared to maintain a constant speed relationship to the main rotor. With the main rotor turning at approximately 350 r.p.m. in normal horizontal cruising flight the anti-torque rotor turns at 1,600-1,700 r.p.m.

The column for fore-and-aft and lateral control is suspended from the roof of the cabin, with conventional foot pedals changing the pitch of the anti-torque rotor for directional control.

The rotor controls, of which no details are available, are housed in the fabric-covered faired "discus" some 3 ft. in diameter which encloses the roots of the rotor blades. The PV-2 differs from other helicopters in that pitch can be set and the craft flown with the throttle. For take-off, the pitch control is set in the forward position and the throttle opened until the craft ascends vertically. To change from vertical to forward motion the control column is pushed forward and then eased back to neutral as the craft gains speed. The throttle can then be eased back to maintain cruising speed.

The fuselage is of normal welded steel tube construction, faired up over the rotor mount to the rotor hub and covered with fabric. The landing gear is of the normal two-wheel and tail-skid type. The rotor blades may be grouped aft over the fuselage to allow the craft to be housed in an ordinary garage.

Specification.

Rotor blade diameter	25 ft. (7.62 m.).
Rotor blade chord	9½ in. (0.24 m.).
Anti-torque rotor diameter	5 ft. (1.525 m.).
Main Rotor speed (cruising)	350 r.p.m.
Anti-torque rotor speed (cruising)	1,600 r.p.m.
Weight loaded	1,000 lbs. (454 kg.).
Maximum speed	90-100 m.p.h. (144-160 km.h.).
Cruising speed	65 m.p.h. (104 km.h.).

THE PV-3.
U.S. Navy designation : XHRP-1.

The PV-3 is a large helicopter with accommodation for a crew of two and ten passengers. It has two large rotors, one at each end of the fuselage, which is 48 ft. (14.6 m.) long.

The PV-3 has flown successfully but at the time of closing for press no further details were available for publication.

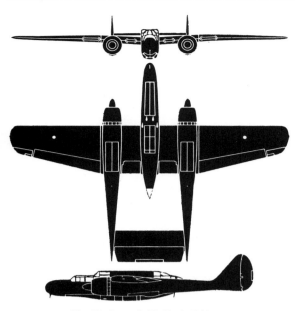

The Piasecki P-V2 Experimental Single-seat Helicopter (90 h.p. Franklin engine).

PIPER.

THE PIPER AIRCRAFT CORPORATION.

HEAD OFFICE AND WORKS : LOCK HAVEN, PENNSYLVANIA.
President, General Manager and Treasurer : W. T. Piper, Sr.
Vice-President : T. V. Weld.
Chief Engineer : Walter Jamouneau.
Secretary and Assistant Treasurer : W. T. Piper, Jr.

Originally the Taylor Aircraft Co., this firm was reorganised and renamed the Piper Aircraft Corpn. in 1937.

In 1938, the Company's first full year of production, 737 "Cubs" were built. The 1939 production totalled 1,806 and in 1940 3,016 Cubs were delivered. Production was further stepped up in 1941 and before the end of year the 10,000th Cub had been completed.

During the War the Piper Company produced the L-4 Grasshopper light liaison and observation monoplane.

For post-war use the Company has under development several new designs, including the 55 h.p. single-seat Skycycle, the 113 h.p. two-seat Skycoupe and the 165 h.p. four-seat Skysedan.

THE PIPER GRASSHOPPER.

U.S. Army Air Forces designation : L-4.
U.S. Navy designation : NE-1.
British name : Piper Cub.

The Piper Grasshopper is a light observation and liaison monoplane which has been developed from the Cub Trainer. It is basically similar to the civil model except that the rear of the cabin has been provided with greater window area. This aircraft was originally given the Army designation O-59 but was subsequently transferred to the liaison category and re-designated the L-4.

The L-4A, L-4B and L-4H were all manufactured under Army contracts and differ from each other only in minor details. Other models in the L-4 Series were civil models which were bought secondhand for pre-glider training and other miscellaneous duties. These civil models are identified as follow :—

L-4C. J3L-65 Cub Trainer. Lycoming O-145-B1 engine.
L-4D. J3F-65 Cub Trainer. Franklin 4AC-176-B2 engine.
L-4E. J4 Coupe. Continental A75-9 engine.
L-4F. (originally UC-83). J5A Cruiser. Continental A75-8 engine.
L-4G. J5B Cruiser. Lycoming GO-145-C2 engine.

The following description applies to the L-4A, L-4B and L-4H models.

TYPE.—Two-seat Light Liaison and Reconnaissance monoplane.
WING, FUSELAGE, TAIL UNIT AND LANDING GEAR.—Same as for Cub J3 Trainer.
POWER PLANT.—One 65 h.p. Continental O-170-3 four-cylinder horizontally-opposed air-cooled engine. Fuel tank (12 U.S. gallons) in fuselage behind fireproof bulkhead.
ACCOMMODATION.—Enclosed cabin seating two in tandem with dual controls. Observer's seat may face forward or aft and when in latter position a small table for maps, etc. is provided. In L-4H two-way radio is standard equipment. No radio in L-4B and L-4A.
DIMENSIONS.—Span 35 ft. 2½ in. (10.7 m.), Length 22 ft. 4½ in. (6.83 m.), Height 6 ft. 8 in. (1.9 m.), Wing area 178.5 sq. ft. (16.5 sq. m.).
WEIGHTS.—Weight empty (L-4A with radio) 740 lbs. (336 kg.), Weight empty (without radio) 695 lbs. (315.5 kg.), Weight loaded 1,220 lbs. (554 kg.).
PERFORMANCE.—Maximum speed 87 m.p.h. (139 km.h.), Cruising speed 75 m.p.h. (120 km.h.), Stalling speed 39 m.p.h. (60.8 km.h.), Initial rate of climb 450 ft./min. (140 m./min.), Service ceiling 11,500 ft. (3,510 m.), Range 260 miles (416 km.).

THE PIPER CUB J-3 TRAINER.

TYPE.—Two-seat light training monoplane.
WINGS.—High-wing braced monoplane. Wings attached direct to built-in centre-section on top of the fuselage and braced to the lower longerons by steel-tube Vee struts. Wing structure consists of spruce spars and aluminium-alloy ribs, the whole being covered with fabric. Frise-type ailerons operated by cables.
FUSELAGE.—Rectangular structure of welded steel tubes, with fabric covering.
TAIL UNIT.—Normal monoplane type. Welded steel-tube framework, covered with fabric.
LANDING GEAR.—Divided type. Consists of two side Vees and two half-axles hinged to cabane below fuselage. Rubber-cord springing at top anchorages of axles. Wheel landing-gear may be replaced by twin Edo all-metal floats.
POWER PLANT.—One 65 h.p. Continental, Lycoming or Franklin four-cylinder horizontally-opposed air-cooled engine. Main fuel tank in fuselage.
ACCOMMODATION.—Cabin seating two in tandem under the wing. Dual control, with front control detachable. Baggage compartment at back of cabin.

The Piper L-4H Grasshopper Light Observation and Liaison Monoplane (65 h.p. Continental O-170-3 engine).

The Piper J4 Coupe Two-seat Light Cabin Monoplane (75 h.p. Continental engine).

DIMENSIONS.—Span 35 ft. 2½ in. (10.7 m.), Length 22 ft. 4½ in. (6.83 m.), Height 6 ft. 8 in. (1.9 m.), Wing area 178.5 sq. ft. (16.5 sq. m.).
WEIGHTS AND LOADINGS.—Weight empty 680 lbs. (309 kg.), Pay load 360 lbs. (163 kg.), Disposable load 540 lbs. (245 kg.), Weight loaded 1,220 lbs. (554 kg.), Wing loading 6.7 lbs./sq. ft. (32.7 kg./sq.m.), Power loading 18.7 lbs./h.p. (8.5 kg./h.p.).
PERFORMANCE.—Maximum speed 87 m.p.h. (139 km.h.), Cruising speed 75 m.p.h. (120 km.h.), Stalling speed 38 m.p.h. (60.8 km.h.), Initial rate of climb 450 ft./min. (140 m./min.), Service ceiling 11,500 ft. (3,510 m.), Cruising range 206 miles (330 km.).

THE PIPER J4 COUPÉ.

TYPE.—Two-seat light cabin monoplane.
WINGS AND FUSELAGE.—Same as for Cub Trainer.
TAIL UNIT.—Braced monoplane type. Welded steel-tube framework covered with fabric. Self-aligning streamline wire bracing. Elevator tab adjustable in flight.
LANDING GEAR.—Divided type. Faired-in side Vees incorporate oleo-springing. Hayes wheels and hydraulic brakes. Wheels enclosed in streamline fairings. Full-swivelling tail-wheel. Wheel landing gear may be replaced by twin metal floats.
POWER PLANT.—One 75 h.p. Continental A-75-8 four-cylinder horizontally-opposed air-cooled engine on welded steel-tube mounting. Engine completely enclosed in hinged cowling. Fuel tank (16 U.S. gallons) in fuselage.
ACCOMMODATION.—Enclosed cabin seating two side-by-side with dual controls. Doors on each side of cabin. Luggage compartment aft of cabin. Cabin heater.
DIMENSIONS.—Span 36 ft. 2 in. (11.5 m.), Length 22 ft. 6 in. (6.9 m.), Height 6 ft. 10 in. (2.1 m.), Wing area 183 sq. ft. (17 sq. m.).
WEIGHTS AND LOADINGS.—Weight empty 865 lbs. (392 kg.), Pay load 275 lbs. (125 kg.), Disposable load 535 lbs. (242 kg.), Weight loaded 1,400 lbs. (637 kg.), Wing loading 7.64 lbs./sq. ft. (37.3 kg./sq.m.), Power loading 18.7 lbs./h.p. (8.5 kg./h.p.).
PERFORMANCE.—Maximum speed 100 m.p.h. (160 km.h.), Cruising speed 96 m.p.h. (150 km.h.), Landing speed 40 m.p.h. (64 km.h.), Initial rate of climb 450 ft./min. (138 m./min.), Service ceiling 12,000 ft. (3,660 m.), Cruising range 455 miles (735 km.).

THE PIPER J5B CRUISER.

TYPE.—Three-seat light cabin monoplane.
WINGS, FUSELAGE AND TAIL UNIT.—Same type and structure as for Cub Coupe.
LANDING GEAR.—Same as for Cub Trainer.
POWER PLANT.—One 75 h.p. Continental A-75-8 four-cylinder horizontally-opposed air-cooled engine. Fuel tank (25 U.S. gallons) in fuselage. Also available with 75 h.p. Lycoming geared engine.
ACCOMMODATION.—Enclosed cabin with single seat forward and side-by-side seat behind. Dual controls.
DIMENSIONS.—Span 35 ft. 5¼ in. (10.8 m.), Length 22 ft. 6 in. (6.9 m.), Height 6 ft. 10 in. (2.1 m.), Wing area 179 sq. ft. (16.6 sq. m.).
WEIGHTS AND LOADINGS.—Weight empty 830 lbs. (377 kg.), Pay load 380 lbs. (172 kg.), Disposable load 620 lbs. (281 kg.), Weight loaded 1,450 lbs. (658 kg.), Wing loading 8.1 lbs./sq. ft. (39.5 kg./sq.m.), Power loading 18 lbs./h.p. (8.8 kg./h.p.).
PERFORMANCE.—Maximum speed 100 m.p.h. (160 km.h.), Cruising speed 85 m.p.h. (136.8 km.h.), Landing speed 39 m.p.h. (52.4 km.h.), Initial rate of climb 450 ft./min. (138 m./min.), Service ceiling 10,000 ft. (3,050 m.), Cruising range 450 miles (720 km.).

THE PIPER J5C SUPER-CRUISER.

The Super-Cruiser is similar to the Cruiser but is fitted with the 100 h.p. Lycoming engine and has a fuel capacity of 25 U.S. gallons.

DIMENSIONS.—Same as for J5B Cruiser.
WEIGHTS AND LOADINGS.—Weight empty 860 lbs. (390 kg.), Disposable load 690 lbs. (313 kg.), Weight loaded 1,550 lbs. (703 kg.), Wing loading 8.5 lbs./sq. ft. (41.5 kg./sq.m.), Power loading 15.5 lbs./h.p. (7 kg./h.p.).
PERFORMANCE.—Maximum speed 110 m.p.h. (176 km.h.), Cruising speed 90 m.p.h. (144 km.h.), Landing speed 42 m.p.h. (67.2 km.h.), Initial rate of climb 650 ft./min. (198 m./min.), Service ceiling 15,000 ft. (4,575 m.), Range 300 miles (480 km.).

THE PIPER AMBULANCE.

U.S. Navy designation: AE-1 (formerly HE-1).

The AE-1 is an ambulance conversion of the J5C Super-Cruiser which has been specially developed for the U.S. Navy. Accommodation is provided for a pilot and one stretcher case. The deck of the fuselage from the trailing-edge of the wing to the fin is arranged to hinge up to permit the loading and unloading of a U.S. Navy standard stretcher.

DIMENSIONS.—Same as for Super-Cruiser.
WEIGHTS.—Weight empty 906 lbs. (411 kg.), Weight loaded 14,26 lbs. (647 kg.).
PERFORMANCE.—Same as for Super-Cruiser except Landing speed 45 m.p.h. (72 km.h.), Initial rate of climb 600 ft./min. (183 m./min.), Range 264 miles (422 km.).

The Piper AE-1 Light Naval Ambulance (100 h.p. Lycoming engine).

PLATT-LE PAGE.

PLATT-LEPAGE AIRCRAFT COMPANY.

HEAD OFFICE AND WORKS : EDDYSTONE, PA.
President : W. Laurence Le Page.
Vice-President : Haviland H. Platt.
Vice-President and Treasurer : J. Brooks B. Parker.
Secretary : H. F. A. Sessions.

This company is devoting its attention to rotary wing aircraft. Its entire resources are at present devoted to confidential work for the U.S. Government, including the development and production of experimental rotary wing aircraft for the Army Air Forces.

Only brief details may be given concerning the Platt-Le Page XR-1 and XR-1A helicopters which, after successful trials by the Rotary Wing Branch of the Air Technical Service Command at Wright Field, Dayton, Ohio, have been accepted by the U.S. Army.

Both are fitted with one Pratt & Whitney R-985-AN1 engine mounted within the fuselage and driving two 30 ft. 6 in. (9.3 m.) oppositely-rotating three-blade rotors carried on faired outriggers, one on each side of the fuselage. The crew of two is seated in tandem in the nose of the fuselage, the only difference between the XR-1 and XR-1A being in the amount of transparent panelling provided. In the XR-1 only the continuous canopy over the two seats and the lower half of the pilot's compartment is glazed, whereas in the XR-1A the entire compartment including the sides and nose is fitted with transparent panels for maximum visibility. The loaded weight of the XR-1 is about 4,800 lbs. (2,180 kg.).

The Platt-Le Page XR-1A Experimental Twin-rotor Helicopter (Pratt & Whitney R-985-AN1 engine).

REPUBLIC.

THE REPUBLIC AVIATION CORPORATION.

HEAD OFFICE AND WORKS : FARMINGDALE, LONG ISLAND, N.Y.
President : Alfred Marchev.
Vice-President and Manager of the Farmingdale Division : C. Hart Miller.
Vice-President and Manager of the Evansville Division : Mundy I. Peale.
Vice-President in Charge of Engineering : Alexander Kartveli.
Vice-President and Director of Exports : Harrison W. Flickinger.
Vice-President and Counsel : John J. Ryan.
Secretary and Treasurer : Thomas Davis.

During 1943 the Republic Aviation Corpn. was in large-scale production of the P-47 Thunderbolt interceptor fighter monoplane for the U.S. Army Air Forces and, through Lend/Lease, for the Air Forces of Great Britain, Russia, France and Brazil. Increased contracts placed with the Company during 1943-44 for the P.47 made necessary further expansion of the Farmingdale plant and the establishment of new production facilities in Indiana. Thunderbolt production passed the 10,000 mark in September, 1944.

A standard high-altitude fighter in the U.S. Army Air Forces, the Thunderbolt was employed primarily as a long-range bomber escort over Germany and enemy-occupied territory. Early in 1944 it went into service as a dive-bomber and ground-attack fighter in Italy and it became a foremost factor in the ground operations in the European invasion and subsequent operations on the Western Front. It was also in the Pacific theatre of operations both as a high-altitude bomber escort and as a low-altitude ground attack fighter.

During the War the Company was engaged in the development of a large four-engined photographic-reconnaissance monoplane under the designation XF-12. Fitted with four Pratt & Whitney R-4360 engines this aeroplane had a range of 4,500 miles (7,200 km.). This design forms the basis of the RD-2 Rainbow high-performance transport which the company is building to the order of Pan American Airways.

THE REPUBLIC THUNDERBOLT.

U.S. Army Air Forces designation : P-47.
British name : Thunderbolt.

The specification to which the P-47 was designed was drawn up at Wright Field in June, 1940. The original XP-47 design was for a lightweight interceptor fighter fitted with an Allison

The Republic P-47D Thunderbolt Single-seat Fighter with three auxiliary fuel tanks.

V-1710 liquid-cooled engine and an armament of one 50 cal. and one 30 cal. guns and provision for two additional 30 cal. wing guns. This was not proceeded with.

The first experimental prototype of the Thunderbolt as it is known to-day was the XP-47B which was flown from Farmingdale to Mitchel Field on May 6, 1941. Production got under way in the following November. The first production P-47B was delivered on March 18, 1942.

P-47's began to arrive in Britain in November, 1942, and the first operational mission with the 8th Air Force was made on April 8, 1943. The first mission with auxiliary fuel tanks took place in July and during the last few weeks of 1943 the first fighter-bomber missions with two 500 lb. bombs were made. The first pairs of 1,000 lb. bombs were carried by P-47's in Italy early in 1944.

The Thunderbolt, in addition to being a standard fighter in the U.S. Army Air Forces, was also supplied, under Lend/Lease, to Great Britain, Russia, France and Brazil. The R.A.F. used the Thunderbolt in India and Burma. The Brazilian fighter squadron which served in Italy was equipped with Thunderbolts.

The 10,000th Thunderbolt came off the assembly lines at Farmingdale on September 20, 1944, just two and a half years after the first P-47B was delivered to the U.S. Army Air Forces.

The following are the principal production and development versions of the Thunderbolt :—

P-47B. 2,000 h.p. Wright R-2800-21 eighteen-cylinder radial air-cooled engine with exhaust-driven turbo-supercharger. Curtiss Electric four-blade constant-speed airscrew 12 ft. 2 in. (3.7 m.) diameter. Self-sealing fuel tanks (307 U.S. gallons capacity). Armour protection for pilot. Eight 50 cal. machine-guns. Length, 34 ft. 10 in. (10.6 m.).

P-47C. Similar to P-47B but fitted with special shackles to carry one 200 U.S. gallon auxiliary fuel tank under the fuselage. Overall, length, 35 ft. 7 in. (10.8 m.).

P-47D (Thunderbolt I and II). First models similar to the P-47C but fitted with universal shackles under fuselage for either droppable fuel tank or 500 lb. bomb, and similar wing racks. Later models fitted with water injection, which added several hundred horse-power for emergency use ; improved turbos ; wide-blade airscrews 13 ft. (3.96 m.) diameter, which added 400 ft. per minute to the climb ; increased fuel capacity, which increased the radius of action to 637 miles (920 km.) ; jettisonable standard canopy and, later, a new jettisonable "blister" hood and flat bulletproof windscreen. The bomb load was increased from two 500 lb. to two 1,000 lb. and one 500 lb. bombs, and three auxiliary fuel tanks could be carried externally on the same racks. Various combinations of bombs and tanks could be carried to suit tactical requirements. After the introduction of the "blister hood" in the P-47D-25 a dorsal fin was added. Overall length 36 ft. 1 9/16 in. (11 m.).

XP-47E. An experimental version of the P-47B fitted with a pressure cabin. Only one aircraft was so fitted.

XP-47F. Another experimental version of the P47B fitted with laminar flow wings.

P-47G. Similar to P-47C and early D but built by Curtiss Airplane Division at Buffalo, N.Y. Progressive developments introduced in P-47D, including water-injection and racks for bombs or auxiliary fuel tanks, also incorporated in P-47G.

XP-47H. A modification of the P-47B to test the experi-

The Republic P-47D Thunderbolt Single-seat Fighter (Pratt & Whitney R-2800-21 engine).

mental Chrysler XIV-2220 inverted Vee liquid-cooled engine.

XP-47J. Similar to the P-47D but with many engineering changes. Weight reduced by 1,000 lbs. (454 kg.). Reduced diameter engine cowling with cooling fan. Redesigned wings. Many features of this experimental model were incorporated in the production P-47M and N.

P-47M. A special model which went into service in Europe early in 1945. Fitted with a P-47D wing. P-47N fuselage and a 2,100 h.p. Pratt & Whitney R-2800-57 engine with larger supercharger and improved water-injection system. Was claimed to be the fastest airscrew-driven aeroplane in service at that time and to be successful in combatting German jet-propelled fighters.

P-47N. A long-range fighter developed for bomber escort duties in the Pacific theatre. Same fuselage and power-unit as the P-47M but fitted with re-designed wings of 18 in. greater span and 22 sq. ft. increased area and with squared wing-tips and larger ailerons; increased petrol capacity with eight additional tanks, one in the leading-edge of each wing and three near each wheel well; and a strengthened landing-gear with wider tread. Armament the same as for previous P-47's but provision for two 500 lb. bombs and ten 5 in. rockets under the wings. Maximum weight over 20,000 lbs. (9,080 kg.).

TYPE.—Single-seat Long-range Fighter or Fighter-Bomber.

WINGS.—Low-wing cantilever monoplane. Republic S-3 wing section. Aspect ratio 5.61 Incidence + 1°. Dihedral (upper surface) 4°. Wings taper in chord and thickness, the leading-edge having a straight taper of 3° and the trailing-edge a curved taper, terminating in rounded detachable wing-tips. Ailerons on skew hinges. Hydraulically-operated NACA slotted trailing-edge flaps between ailerons and fuselage. The flaps are on trapezoidal linkage hinges which permit them, when lowered, to move first aft then down and, when retracted, first up and then forward. Later P-47's have electrically-operated dive-recovery flaps just forward of the main flaps. When in retracted position these lie flush with underside of wing.

FUSELAGE.—Oval-section all-metal monocoque structure.

TAIL UNIT.—Cantilever monoplane type. All-metal structure with metal-covered fixed surfaces, rudder and elevators. Control surfaces statically and aerodynamically balanced and provided with trimming-tabs.

LANDING GEAR.—Retractable type. Cantilever shock-absorber struts retract inwardly, the wheels being raised into wells in the underside of the wings. Fairing plates on legs and wheels and hinged fairings on inner edges of wells close apertures when wheels are raised. Retractable tail-wheel.

POWER PLANT (P-47D).—One Pratt & Whitney R-2800-59 Double-Wasp eighteen-cylinder air-cooled supercharged engine rated at 1,625 h.p. at 30,000 ft. (9,150 m.) and with 2,300 h.p. available for take-off. Water-injection equipment provides an emergency increase in power to 2,535 h.p. G.E. turbo supercharger located in rear fuselage. Air fed to impeller through scoop in lower portion of cowling and compressed air led forward to carburetter through intercoolers in side of fuselage. Exhaust gases are ducted aft to supercharger through throttles which control speed of turbine and after passing through turbine are ejected through large diameter pipe near tail-wheel. Four-bladed Curtiss Electric constant-speed full-feathering airscrew. Two self-sealing and armoured fuel tanks in fuselage, the main tank (270 U.S. gallons) aft of the fireproof bulkhead and auxiliary tank (100 U.S. gallons), beneath pilot's seat. Auxiliary droppable fuel tanks of various capacities may be carried beneath fuselage and/or wings. In P-40N greatly increased fuel capacity in eight additional wing tanks, nearly doubling the former total internal capacity. Oil tank in front of firewall and two oil coolers in lower portion of engine cowling, one on each side of main air duct to supercharger.

ACCOMMODATION.—Enclosed cockpit over trailing-edge of wing. Sliding moulded plastic "blister" type canopy. Bullet-proof windscreen and front and rear armour protection for pilot. Cockpit and other vulnerable points armoured.

ARMAMENT.—Eight 50 cal. machine-guns, four in each wing outboard of landing-gear. Guns electrically-fired. Combat cine-camera in port wing root. Bombs may be carried under fuselage or wings. Maximum bomb load : two 1,000 lb. bombs, one under each wing,

An R.A.F. Republic Thunderbolt II fitted with two auxiliary long-range tanks.

The Republic P-47N Thunderbolt Long-range Fighter (Pratt & Whitney R-2800-57 engine).

and one 500 lb. bomb under the fuselage. Ten 5 in. velocity aircraft rockets may be carried, the latest type of rocket needing neither launching-rails or tracks.

DIMENSIONS.—Span 40 ft. 9 9/16 in. (12.4 m.), Length 36 ft. 1 3/16 in. (11 m.), Height 14 ft. 2 in. (4.3 m.), Wing area 300 sq. ft. (27.9 sq. m.).

WEIGHT LOADED (P-47D).—12,500 lbs. (5,675 kg.).

PERFORMANCE (P-47D).—Maximum speed 440 m.p.h. (704 km.h.) at 29,000 ft. (8,850 m.), Landing speed 100 m.p.h. (160 km.h.), Climb to 15,000 ft. (4,575 m.) 5.1 min., Service ceiling 40,000 ft. (12,200 m.).

THE REPUBLIC SEABEE AMPHIBIAN.

The C-1 amphibian was designed by Mr. P. H. Spencer and has been developed and built by the Republic Aviation Corpn. as a prototype for post-war production.

In 1945 the U.S. Army placed an order for a modified version of this aircraft for Air/Sea Rescue duties.

TYPE.—Three-seat Amphibian flying-boat.

WINGS.—High-wing cantilever monoplane. Wings taper in chord and thickness with dihedral on lower surface only. Attached directly to the top of the hull superstructure. All-metal stressed-skin construction. Ailerons and vacuum-operated slotted flaps have metal frames and fabric covering.

HULL.—Basic structure is a shallow two-step boat hull with the cabin structure built up forward and the rear portion swept up to carry the tail-unit. All-metal structure covered with Alclad. All-metal stabilising floats attached to wings by single fabricated streamline tubular struts.

TAIL UNIT.—Cantilever monoplane type. Lower fin integral with the hull. Upper fin and tailplane of all-metal stressed skin construction. Elevators and rudder have metal frames and fabric covering.

LANDING GEAR.—Retractable type. Main struts hinged to chines of hull. Struts and wheels are raised electrically into recesses in sides of hull superstructure. Tail-wheel at rear step. Water-rudder aft of tail-wheel.

POWER PLANT.—One 175 h.p. Franklin 6ALG-315 six-cylinder horizontally-opposed air-cooled engine driving a two-blade fixed-pitch wood propeller aft of the wings and cabin. Fuel tanks in wing.

ACCOMMODATION.—Enclosed cabin seating three, two side-by-side in front and one behind. Centrally-mounted wheel may be swung in front of either seat. Dual rudder pedals. Two side doors give access to front seats. Back of righthand front seat folds forward to give access to rear seat. Door on starboard side of nose for mooring, etc.

DIMENSIONS.—Span 36 ft. (11 m.), Length 26 ft. 6 in. (8 m.), Height (on wheels) 8 ft. 7 in. (2.62 m.), Wing area 170 sq. ft. (15.8 sq. m.).

WEIGHTS AND LOADINGS.—Weight empty 1,775 lbs. (805 kg.), Disposable load 825 lbs. (375 kg.), Weight loaded 2,600 lbs. (1,180 kg.), Wing loading 15.2 lbs./sq. ft. (74.2 kg./sq. m.), Power loading 14.9 lbs./h.p. (6.7 kg./h.p.).

PERFORMANCE.—Maximum speed 125 m.p.h. (200 km.h.), Cruising speed 105 m.p.h. (68 km.h.), Landing speed (with flaps) 53 m.p.h. (85 km.h.), Initial rate of climb 750 ft./min. (230 m./min.), Service ceiling 12,000 ft. (3,660 m.), Cruising range 420 miles (672 km.).

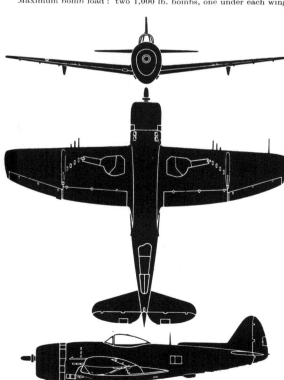

The Republic P-47N Thunderbolt Long-range Fighter.

The Republic Seabee Light Amphibian Flying-boat (175 h.p. Franklin engine).

RYAN.

THE RYAN AERONAUTICAL COMPANY.

Head Office and Works: Lindbergh Field, San Diego, California.

President and Treasurer: T. Claude Ryan.

Vice-Presidents: Earl D. Prudden, Eddie Molloy and George Woodward (and Secretary).

Chief Engineer: Benjamin T. Salmon.

The Ryan Aeronautical Company is a successor to the old Ryan Company which produced the aeroplane in which Mr. Charles Lindbergh made the first non-stop flight from New York to Paris in 1927. Mr. T. Claude Ryan severed his connections with the original Ryan Company in 1927 but he continued to operate the Ryan School of Aeronautics which he had established at San Diego in 1922.

In 1933 he saw an opportunity to re-enter the manufacturing field and consequently began the development of the Ryan S-T series of low-wing training monoplanes.

The Ryan Company was one of three firms selected by the Government for the mass-production of military training aircraft under a type standardisation programme and was the first company to manufacture in quantity an all-metal low-wing primary trainer. The S-T (PT-16 and PT-20) was the first low-wing monoplane trainer to satisfy Army requirements, and this model was followed by the ST-3 (PT-21 and PT-22). Both these models were produced in large quantities. Large numbers of Ryan trainers were also supplied to the Air Forces of the Netherlands East Indies, Guatemala, China, Honduras, Mexico, etc.

The ST-3 (PT-22) was in production until 1942 when the Ryan Company, as the result of a request to undertake studies towards the conversion of the PT-22 all-metal trainer to non-strategic materials in order to release essential metals for more urgent purposes, produced the ST-4 (PT-25) a new two-seat trainer built almost entirely of plastic-bonded wood. Aluminium alloys and all strategic materials were eliminated with the exception of the cowling, firewall and certain simple metal fittings which represent less than 2 per cent. of the total weight of the aircraft. No forgings, castings or extrusions were used, nor any critical steels for any of the fittings or structural parts. The PT-25 did not go into production.

The aircraft production facilities of the company were later concentrated on the design and quantity production of a new fighter aircraft for the U.S. Navy known as the FR-1 Fireball.

The Fireball is fitted with two power units,—a normal Wright R-1820 radial in the nose and a General Electric I-16 turbo-jet engine in the rear fuselage and exhausting aft of the tail-unit.

ST. LOUIS.

ST. LOUIS AIRCRAFT CORPORATION (DIVISION OF THE ST. LOUIS CAR COMPANY).

Head Office and Works: St. Louis, Mo.

President and General Manager: E. B. Meissner.

Vice-Presidents: N. L. Rehnquist and H. M. McKay.

Chief Engineer: L. S. Lutton.

Secretary: J. F. Tringl.

Treasurer: E. Augustine.

During 1940 the St. Louis Aircraft Corpn. delivered a small number of PT-15 training biplanes to the U.S. Army Air Forces.

In 1942-43 the Corporation was engaged on the production of the Fairchild PT-23 two-seat primary training monoplane (see Fairchild) and was manufacturing parts and sub-assemblies for other aircraft manufacturers.

It also produced for the U.S. Army Air Forces a quantity of other aeronautical equipment, including cars for motor balloons, centrifugal blowers for observation balloons, bombing trainers and targets, ammunition mount assemblies, retractable skis, etc.

SCHWEIZER.

SCHWEIZER AIRCRAFT CORPORATION.

Head Office and Works: Chemung County Airport, Elimra, N.Y.

President and Chief Engineer: Ernest Schweizer.

Vice-President and General Manager: Paul A. Schweizer.

Secretary: Robert P. McDowell.

The Schweizer Aircraft Corpn. specialises in the design and construction of gliders and sailplanes for military and civilian use. It also manufactures parts and assemblies for other aircraft companies under sub-contract. The company furthermore maintains a complete aircraft and glider overhaul and repair service and does work in the heat-treatment and processing of aluminium and in magnaflux inspection.

The Schweizer SGU 1-19 Single-seat Glider.

THE SCHWEIZER SGS 2-8 SAILPLANE.

U.S. Army Air Forces designation: TG-2.

U.S. Navy designation: LNS-1.

Type.—Two-seat high-performance all-metal Sailplane.

Wings.—Semi-cantilever shoulder-wing monoplane. Single-strut bracing. Braced portion of wings rectangular, outer cantilever portions tapered with rounded tips. Single aluminium-alloy spar, with metal D leading edge. Aluminium-alloy pressed ribs cantilevered from rear face of spar with fabric covering to trailing edge. Metal-framed fabric-covered ailerons.

Fuselage.—Welded chrome-molybdenum steel-tube structure covered with fabric.

Tail Unit.—Cantilever monoplane type. Framework of formed steel and aluminium-alloy parts and covered with fabric.

Landing-Gear.—Single wheel with friction-type brake rigidly mounted on centre-line with single skid on rubber blocks forward of wheel. Rubber-mounted tail-skid.

Accommodation.—Tandem seats under continuous transparent canopy. Dual controls.

Dimensions.—Span 52 ft. (15.86 m.), Length 25 ft. 3 in. (7.7 m.), Height 6 ft. 10 in. (2.1 m.), Wing area 214 sq. ft. (19.9 sq. m.).

Weights and Loading.—Weight empty 460 lbs. (208.8 kg.), Weight loaded 860 lbs. (390.4 kg.), Wing loading 4.01 lbs./sq. ft. (1.95 kg./sq. m.).

Performance.—Maximum glide, dive or aeroplane tow speed 72 m.p.h. (115.2 km.h.), Maximum Auto or winch tow speed 54 m.p.h. (86.4 km.h.), Stalling speed 34 m.p.h. (54.4 km.h.).

THE SCHWEIZER SGS 2-12 SAILPLANE.

U.S. Army Air Forces designation: TG-3A.

Type.—Two-seat high-performance Sailplane.

Wings.—Cantilever low mid-wing monoplane. Middle half of wing of rectangular plan form, outer portions tapered with rounded tips. Single cantilever spruce spar, spruce and mahogany plywood ribs, plywood D-tube leading-edge ahead of spar, fabric covering over entire wing. Wooden-framed fabric-covered ailerons. Spoilers above and below wing inboard of ailerons.

Fuselage.—Welded chrome-molybdenum steel-tube structure covered with fabric.

Tail Unit.—Cantilever monoplane type. Spruce framework mahogany plywood leading-edges to fin and tailplane and fabric covering over all. Trim-tabs in rudder and port elevator.

Landing Gear.—Unsprung single wheel with mechanical disc-type brake on centre-line with rubber-mounted single skid forward of wheel. Rubber-mounted tail-skid.

Accommodation.—Tandem seats beneath continuous transparent canopy. Dual controls.

Dimensions.—Span 54 ft. (16.47 m.), Length 27 ft. 7 in. (8.4 m.), Height 8 ft. (2.44 m.), Wing area 237 sq. ft. (22 sq. m.).

Weights and Loadings.—Weight empty 820 lbs. (372 kg.), Weight loaded 1,200 lbs. (545 kg.), Wing loading 5.15 lbs./sq. ft. (2.51 kg./sq. m.).

Performance.—Maximum glide, dive or tow speed 100 m.p.h. (160 km.h.), Stalling speed 38 m.p.h. (61 km.h.).

THE SCHWEIZER SGU 1-19 GLIDER.

Type.—Single-seat utility training Glider.

Wings.—High-wing braced monoplane. Wing of parallel chord and constant thickness with parallel bracing struts. All-wood structure with two spruce spars, spruce and mahogany plywood ribs, plywood leading-edge and fabric-covering overall.

Fuselage.—Welded chrome-molybdenum steel-tube framework covered with fabric.

Tail Unit.—Braced monoplane type. Horizontal surfaces of welded steel-tube covered with fabric. Vertical surfaces may be of fabric-covered wooden construction (when supplied in kit form for schools) or of fabric-covered steel and aluminium-alloy construction (when completed in factory).

Landing Gear.—Single unsprung wheel with mechanical disc-type brake mounted on centre-line with single skid on rubber blocks ahead of the wheel. Rubber-mounted tail-skid.

Accommodation.—Single open cockpit with optional transparent enclosure.

Dimensions.—Span 36 ft. 8 in. (11.2 m.), Length 20 ft. 7½ in. (6.3 m.), Height 10 ft. 4½ in. (3.2 m.), Wing area 170 sq. ft. (15.8 sq. m.).

Weights and Loadings.—Weight empty 320 lbs. (145.3 kg.), Weight loaded 550 lbs. (250 kg.), Wing loading 3.23 lbs./sq. ft. (1.58 kg./sq. m.).

Performance.—Maximum tow speed 75 m.p.h. (120 km.h.), Maximum gliding speed 75 m.p.h. (120 km.h.), Stalling speed 28 m.p.h. (45 km.h.).

The Schweizer SGS 2-12 Two-seat Sailplane which was used as a training glider by the U.S. Army.

SIKORSKY.

SIKORSKY AIRCRAFT DIVISION OF THE UNITED AIRCRAFT CORPORATION.

Head Office and Works: South Avenue, Bridgeport, Conn.

General Manager: B. L. Whelan.

Engineering Manager: Igor I. Sikorsky.

Chief Engineer: Michael E. Gluhareff.

Assistant Engineering Manager: Serge E. Gluhareff.

Factory Manager: John L. Brown, Jr.

Assistant Secretary: Richard T. Horner.

Assistant Treasurer: J. H. Spade.

In January, 1943 the Chance Vought and Sikorsky Divisions of the former Vought-Sikorsky Division of the United Aircraft Corpn. were reconstituted as separate manufacturing divisions to enable Chance Vought to devote all its energies to the development and production of combat aircraft, while the Sikorsky Division concentrates on the development of the helicopter for both military and civil purposes.

Sikorsky Aircraft moved from Stratford to Bridgeport Conn., where a leased factory was occupied, tooled-up and put into production. One of the features of the new plant was "the smallest airport in the World," an area just outside the factory about the size of an automobile park from which the products of the company were flown.

The original Sikorsky helicopter—the experimental VS-300—was placed in the Edison Museum in Dearborn, Mich., in 1943.

The first helicopter built for military service—the experimental XR-4—first flew on January 14, 1942, and was delivered by air from Stratford, Conn., to Wright Field, Dayton, Ohio, a distance of 760 miles, by easy stages and under widely-varying weather conditions without any trouble whatsoever.

On the basis of successful tests with the XR-4, a limited production order for a progressive development known as the YR-4 was placed with Sikorsky Aircraft.

These craft were intended for training and service trials. One was sent to Burma and another to Alaska. Others were allocated to the U.S. Navy, Coast Guard and the Royal Navy. Subsequently a production order for 100 R-4B's was placed.

In May, 1943, tests were conducted, through the co-operation of the Army Air Forces, the War Shipping Administration and the Coast Guard, to prove the feasibility of operating the YR-4 from a platform on a ship. These tests were conducted in Long Island Sound from a tanker. The deck used was not specially built but was one which had been used for cargo-carrying purposes and had a clear space only 14 ft. greater than the diameter of the main rotor of the YR-4. Under relatively calm water conditions 24 take-offs and landings were made while the ship was at anchor, while steaming up to 16 knots in a wind of more than 20 m.p.h. and while steaming with the wind and across wind.

Two other Sikorsky designs are now in production. The R-5A is being built by Sikorsky Aircraft, and the R-6A by the Nash-Kelvinator Corpn. under Sikorsky licence.

THE SIKORSKY VS-316A.

U.S. Army Air Forces designation: R-4B.

U.S. Navy designation: HNS-1.

British name: Hoverfly I.

Type.—Two-seat Training Helicopter.

Rotors.—One three-blade main rotor 38 ft. (11.6 m.) dia. and one three-blade vertical controllable-pitch anti-torque and steering rotor 7 ft. 8 in. (2.30 m.) dia. carried on an outrigger extension of the fuselage, both rotors driven through transmission shafts and gear boxes by a single engine. Transmission for the main rotor is through a single plate clutch and double reduction gear. Rotor brake, free-wheel and emergency rotor release to permit auto-rotation in case of transmission seizure provided. Fixed rotor

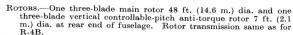

The Sikorsky R-4B Two-seat Training Helicopter (185 h.p. Warner R-550-1 engine).

The Sikorsky R-5A Two-seat Observation Helicopter (450 h.p. Pratt & Whitney R-985-AN1 engine).

head with cyclic pitch control mounted on a welded steel tube pylon forming integral part of fuselage structure.

FUSELAGE.—Welded steel tube structure covered with detachable metal panels forward and fabric aft.

LANDING GEAR.—Three wheel type. Two main wheels forward have vertical shock-absorber struts supported by steel tube pyramids built into the sides of the fuselage. Tail-wheel mounted under rear fuselage. Wheel gear may be replaced by two low-pressure rubberised floats.

POWER PLANT.—One 185 h.p. Warner R-550-1 seven-cylinder radial fan-cooled engine mounted within fuselage aft of cockpit. Cooling air drawn through louvres in forward face of the rotor pylon casing blown by large-diameter engine-driven fan onto engine and exhausted through openings in underside of fuselage. Cylindrical fuel and oil tanks in fuselage aft of transmission compartment.

ACCOMMODATION.—Enclosed cabin in nose of fuselage seating two side-by-side with dual controls. Two central control columns operate cyclical pitch for forward, sideways and reverse movements. Second lever between seats controls blade pitch in unison for vertical movement. Rudder pedals operate on tail rotor for directional control. Radio equipment originally fitted has been removed. One litter may be carried externally.

DIMENSIONS.—Rotor diameter 38 ft. (11.6 m.), Overall length (including rotor) 48 ft. 1 in. (14.65 m.), Overall height 12 ft. 5 in. (3.78 m.),

Wheel track 10 ft. (3.05 m.), Rotor disc area 1,134 sq. ft. (105.3 sq. m.).

WEIGHTS.—Weight empty 2,011 lbs. (913 kg.), Weight loaded 2,540 lbs. (1,153 kg.).

PERFORMANCE.—Maximum speed 75 m.p.h. (120 km.h.), Climb to 8,000 ft. (2,440 m.) 45 min., Service ceiling 8,000 ft. (2,440 m.).

THE SIKORSKY R-5A.
U.S. Navy designation: HO2S-1.

TYPE.—Two-seat Observation Helicopter.

ROTORS.—One three-blade main rotor 48 ft. (14.6 m.) dia. and one three-blade vertical controllable-pitch anti-torque rotor 7 ft. (2.1 m.) dia. at rear end of fuselage. Rotor transmission same as for R-4B.

FUSELAGE.—In three sections. Centre-section enclosing power-unit and rotor pylon of welded steel tube and cowled with plastic-impregnated moulded plywood. The nose section enclosing the crew compartment has as a foundation an aluminium monocoque floor on which is built an aluminium-alloy channel superstructure panelled with Plexiglas windows. The tail section is a light wooden monocoque.

LANDING GEAR.—Conventional three-wheel type with the two main wheels sprung at the extremities of two cantilever side members. Tail wheel on steel tube pylon aft of the engine housing at the root of the rear fuselage.

POWER PLANT.—One 450 h.p. Pratt & Whitney R-985-AN-1 radial fan-cooled engine modified for installation within the fuselage with crankshaft vertical. Main rotor drive through conventional reduction gear, with take-off drive in main gear box for auxiliary tail rotor drive. Tail rotor drive shaft runs externally along top of rear fuselage. Cooling air for engine drawn in through aperture in front of face of rotor pylon housing and exhausted through openings in underside of fuselage. Fuel and oil tanks in fuselage aft of transmission compartment.

ACCOMMODATION.—Enclosed compartment in nose seats two in tandem with dual controls. Observer in front. Provision for cameras, radio and other auxiliary equipment. Four litters, two on each side of the fuselage, may be carried.

DIMENSIONS.—Rotor diameter 48 ft. (14.6 m.), Overall length 57 ft. 1 in. (17.4 m.), Wheel track 12 ft. (3.6 m.), Rotor disc area 1,810 sq. ft. (168 sq. m.).

WEIGHT LOADED.—5,000 lbs. (2,270 kg.).

PERFORMANCE.—Maximum speed 90 m.p.h. (144 km.h.).

THE SIKORSKY R-6A.
U.S. Navy designation: HOS-1.
British name : Hoverfly II.

TYPE.—Two-seat Observation Helicopter.

ROTORS.—Rotor system and transmission similar to R-4B.

FUSELAGE.—All-metal framework. The cabin section has an aluminium floor and is covered with moulded plastic-impregnated glass fibre cloth and Plexiglas transparent moulded nose and side and roof windows. Paper-based moulded plastic cowling encloses the engine compartment and rotor pylon. The rear fuselage carrying the tail rotor is a light metal monocoque.

LANDING GEAR.—Conventional landing-gear with the main wheels on cantilever oleo struts, a tail-wheel on a steel tube pyramid midway between nose and tail and a small nose wheel to guard against a nose over. Hydraulic wheel brakes on main wheels. Landing-gear may be replaced by flotation gear.

POWER PLANT.—One 245 h.p. Franklin O-405-9 six-cylinder horizontally-opposed fan-cooled engine mounted with crankshaft vertical within the fuselage aft of the cabin. Planetary gear transmission to rotor. Fuel and oil tanks in fuselage aft of transmission compartment.

ACCOMMODATION.—Enclosed cabin seating two side-by-side with dual controls. Equipment includes high-frequency radio communication set. An evacuation litter may be installed on each side of fuselage.

DIMENSIONS.—Rotor diameter 38 ft. (11.6 m.), Overall length 47 ft. 11 in. (14.6 m.), Wheel track 9 ft. (2.7 m.), Rotor disc area 1,134 sq. ft. (105.3 sq. m.).

WEIGHT LOADED.—2,600 lbs. (1,180 kg.).

PERFORMANCE.—Maximum speed 100 m.p.h. (160 km.h.), Climb to 5,900 ft. (1,800 m.) 7 min., Service ceiling 10,000 ft. (3,050 m.), Maximum duration 5 hours.

The Sikorsky R-6A Two-seat Observation Helicopter (245 h.p. Franklin O-405-9 engine).

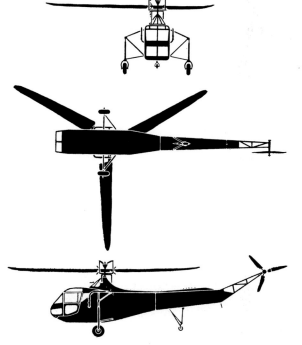

The Sikorsky R-4B Training Helicopter.

The Sikorsky R-6A Two-seat Observation Helicopter (245 h.p. Franklin O-405-9 engine).

SOUTHERN.

SOUTHERN AIRCRAFT CORPORATION.

HEAD OFFICE AND WORKS : GARLAND, TEXAS.
President and General Manager : Willis C. Brown.
Vice-President and Treasurer : A. E. Pattison.
Comptroller and Assistant Treasurer : Hugh G. Humphreys.
Secretary : Frances H. Brown.

In 1940 the Southern Aircraft Corpn. completed the BM-10 two-seat training biplane which was designed to conform to the requirements of the U.S. Army Air Forces. This type has not been proceeded with.

In the latter part of 1940 the Company began the construction of a new works and aerodrome at Garland and the first part of the plant was ready for occupation early in 1941.

The manufacturing facilities of the Company were then devoted to the production of aircraft components for the leading types of U.S. combat aircraft, including the Consolidated-Vultee B-24 Liberator, and the Grumman Avenger and Hellcat. By the end of 1944 the plant of the Southern Aircraft Corpn. was five times its original size.

SPARTAN.

THE SPARTAN AIRCRAFT COMPANY.

HEAD OFFICE AND WORKS : TULSA, OKLAHOMA.
President : J. Paul Getty.
Vice-President : Capt. M. W. Balfour.
Chief Engineer : W. Fred Stewart.
Secretary and Treasurer : F. T. Hopp.

The Spartan Aircraft Company, which was incorporated in 1928, originally devoted itself to the design of commercial aircraft, of which the Spartan Executive four/five-seat low-wing cantilever monoplane with retractable landing gear and the 450 h.p. Pratt & Whitney Wasp-Junior engine, was the most recent type produced before the United States entered the war. This model was originally designed and built in 1935.

Several examples of the Executive taken over by the U.S. Army Air Forces for light personnel transport use after the outbreak of war were given the designation UC-71.

In 1940 the Company produced its first military design, the NS-1 primary training biplane. This model when ordered by the U.S. Navy was designated NP-1.

For the past two years the company has been engaged solely in the manufacture of aircraft parts and assemblies under subcontracts from other manufacturers. The factory has been greatly enlarged and now has a floor area of 350,000 sq. ft.

The post-war plans of the company envisage the production of two all-metal commercial aircraft. One will be a faster and more economical version of the Executive, a four/five-seat single-engined monoplane with fully-retractable landing-gear. The other will be a twin-engined six/eight-seat monoplane, to be known as the Skyway Traveler, which will be suitable for feeder airline services and business use.

STINSON.

THE STINSON DIVISION OF THE CONSOLIDATED VULTEE AIRCRAFT CORPORATION.

HEAD OFFICE : SAN DIEGO, CAL.
WORKS : WAYNE, MICH.
Manager of the Stinson Division : T. Y. Smith.

In the Summer of 1940 the Stinson Aircraft Division of the Aviation Manufacturing Corpn. was taken over by Vultee and became the Stinson Aircraft Division of Vultee Aircraft, Inc. Early in 1943 the Vultee Company merged with the Consolidated Aircraft Corpn. to form the Consolidated Vultee Aircraft Corpn.

The Stinson Division of Consolidated Vultee is still located at Wayne but the original Stinson factory has been greatly extended and during the war was engaged solely in the manufacture of military aircraft and parts.

The principal wartime products of the Division were the L-5 Sentinel and the AT-19 Reliant, both directly descended from pre-war Stinson civil aeroplanes. The predecessor of the Sentinel, the Stinson Voyager, and the pre-war Reliant are both being revived for post-war use and details are given hereafter of the new Stinson Voyager 125, which is now in production.

THE STINSON 125 VOYAGER.

Production of the original three-seat Stinson 105 Voyager was discontinued by the Stinson Division when America entered the War, but preparations were made in 1944-45 to resume production as soon as possible after the war.

The prototype of the post-war Voyager was test flown in December, 1944. It was fitted with a 125 h.p. Lycoming engine. The following is a provisional specification of the aircraft with this power-plant.

DIMENSIONS.—Span 34 ft. (10.37 m.). Length 23 ft. 6 in. (7.2 m.).
WEIGHTS.—Weight empty 1,088 lbs. (494 kg.), Disposable load 757 lbs. (344 kg.), Weight loaded 1,875 lbs. (838 kg.).
PERFORMANCE.—Cruising speed (at 83% power) 112 m.p.h. (179 km.h.), Stalling speed 51.5 m.p.h. (82.4 km.h.), Service ceiling 14,000 ft. (4,270 m.), Range 470 miles (752 km.).

THE STINSON 76 SENTINEL.

U.S. Army Air Forces designation : L-5.
U.S. Navy designation: OY-1.
British name : Sentinel.

The Sentinel, which was originally designated the O-56, is a product of the Stinson Division of the Consolidated Vultee Aircraft Corpn. There are three Army versions of the Sentinel, as detailed below.

L-5 and L-5A (OY-1 and Sentinel I). Standard two-seat short-range Liaison and Observation monoplane. The L-5A is identical to the L-5 except that it is fitted with a 24-volt electrical system. The landing gear fairings have been removed from all L-5's.

L-5B (Sentinel II). Adaptation of the L-5 to carry one stretcher case or light cargo up to a maximum of 200 lbs. Fuselage aft of the rear wing spar is deeper and retains its rectangular cross-section to the fin. A large door aft of the observer's door opens downwards to permit the loading of a stretcher. When a stretcher is carried the back of the observer's seat is folded forward and the rear panel of the observer's compartment hinges down to form the front portion of the floor of the stretcher or cargo compartment. Tie-down fittings for light cargo. The L-5B may be fitted with twin-float gear.

TYPE.—Two-seat Liaison/Observation or Ambulance monoplane.
WINGS.—High-wing braced monoplane. Structure consists of spruce-spars and ribs, steel tube compression struts and wire bracing, and fabric covering. Vee type steel or duralumin tube bracing struts. Manually-operated trailing-edge flaps between ailerons and fuselage. Flaps have light metal frames and fabric covering.
FUSELAGE.—Welded steel tube structure covered with fabric.
TAIL UNIT.—Cantilever monoplane type. All wood framework with fabric covering. Fin built integral with the fuselage. Fixed tailplane. Horn-balanced control surfaces.
LANDING GEAR.—Single-leg cantilever fixed type. Long-stroke oleo-spring shock absorber units. Hydraulically operated wheel brakes. Steerable tail-wheel with leaf-spring shock-absorber.
POWER PLANT.—One 190 h.p. Lycoming O-435-1 six-cylinder horizontally opposed air-cooled engine. Two fuel tanks, one in root of each wing. Gravity feed. Total maximum fuel capacity : 36 U.S. gallons (30 Imp. gallons). Sesenich fixed-pitch wood airscrew, 7 ft 1 in. (2.16 m.) diameter.
ACCOMMODATION.—Enclosed cockpit seating two in tandem with dual controls. Entire roof of cabin glazed. Side windows inclined slightly outwards to improve downward vision. Doors on starboard side of cabin, pilot's door hinging forward and observers' door downward. In L-5B further stretcher-loading door swings downwards. Normal equipment includes radio, night-flying equipment, fire extinguisher, first-aid kit, etc.
DIMENSIONS.—Span 34 ft. (10.37 m.), Length 24 ft. 1¼ in. (7.33 m.), Height 7 ft. 1 in. (2.13 m.).
WEIGHTS.—Weight empty 1,472 lbs. (668 kg.), Weight loaded 2,158 lbs. (980 kg.).
PERFORMANCE.—Maximum speed 129 m.p.h. (206.4 km.h.), Service ceiling 15,800 ft. (4,820 m.).

The Stinson L-5A Sentinel Two-seat Light Liaison and Observation Monoplane (190 h.p. Lycoming O-435-1 engine).

THE STINSON RELIANT.

U.S. Army Air Forces designations : AT-19 and UC-81.
British name : Reliant.

The Reliant was originally a four/five-seat commercial monoplane which was in wide use in the United States by sportsmen and business executives.

Although commercial production ceased on America's entry in the War, the Reliant was built in 1942-43 in a modified form as the AT-19, for assignment to the British Government as a navigation trainer for use by the Royal Navy.

TYPE.—Three-seat Navigation Trainer.

The Stinson L-5 Sentinel.

The Stinson 125 Voyager Three-seat Light Cabin Monoplane (125 h.p. Lycoming engine).

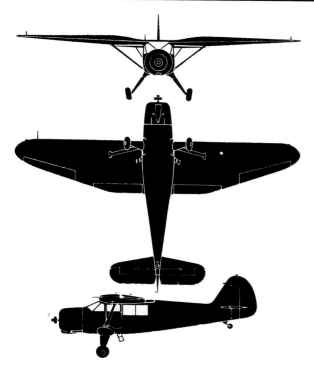

The Stinson AT-19 Reliant Navigational Trainer.

WINGS.—High-wing braced monoplane. Wings attached to top longerons and braced to the bottom of the fuselage by single struts. Clark "Y" wing section. Structure consists of a single steel-tube main spar, steel-tube drag bracing, duralumin auxiliary spar, riveted square duralumin tube ribs, duralumin sheet leading-edge and an overall fabric covering. Vacuum-operated trailing-edge flaps between ailerons and fuselage.

FUSELAGE.—Welded steel-tube structure covered with fabric.

TAIL UNIT.—Braced monoplane type. Welded steel-tube framework covered with fabric.

LANDING GEAR.—Divided type. Cantilever legs incorporating spring shock-absorbers. Hydraulic wheel-brakes. Castoring tail-wheel.

POWER PLANT.—One 290 h.p. Lycoming R-680-13 nine-cylinder radial air-cooled engine on welded steel-tube mounting. Fuel tanks in wing roots.

ACCOMMODATION.—Enclosed cabin seating three, two in front side-by-side with dual controls. Specialised equipment for navigational training.

DIMENSIONS.—Span 41 ft. 10½ in. (12.8 m.), Length 29 ft. 4¼ in. (8.9 m.), Height 8 ft. 7 in. (2.59 m.), Wing area 258.5 sq. ft. (24 sq. m.).

WEIGHTS.—Weight empty 2,810 lbs. (1,276 kg.), Weight loaded 4,000 lbs. (1,816 kg.).

PERFORMANCE.—Maximum speed 141 m.p.h. (226 km.h.), Service ceiling 14,000 ft. (4,270 m.).

The U.S. Army also acquired a number of secondhand five-seat commercial Reliants for general utility transport duties and gave them designations in the UC-81 Series. These were as follow :—

UC-81   Model SR-8B (Lycoming R-680-B6 engine).
UC-81A Model SR-10G (Lycoming R-680-E1 engine).
UC-81B Model SR-8D (Wright R-760-E2 engine)
UC-81C Model SR-9C (Lycoming R-680-D5 engine).
UC-81D Model SR-10F (Pratt & Whitney R-985 engine).
UC-81E Model SR-9F (Pratt & Whitney R-985 engine).
UC-81F Model SR-10F (Pratt & Whitney R-985 engine).
UC-81G Model SR-9D (Wright R-760-E1 engine).
UC-81H Model SR-10E (Wright R-760-E2 engine).
UC-81J Model SR-9E (Wright R-760-E2 engine).
UC-81K Model SR-10C (Lycoming R-680-D5 engine).
UC-81L Model SR-8C (Lycoming R-680-B5 engine).
UC-81N Model SR-9B (Lycoming R-680-B6 engine).

The Stinson L-5B Sentinel Light Ambulance (190 h.p. Lycoming O-435-1 engine).

The commercial Stinson SR-10 Reliant Four/five-seat Cabin Monoplane.

The Stinson AT-19 Reliant Navigational Training Monoplane (290 h.p. Lycoming R-680-13 engine).

STRICKLAND.

STRICKLAND AIRCRAFT CORPORATION.

HEAD OFFICE AND WORKS : HIGH POINT, NORTH CAROLINA.
President and General Manager : C. Kenneth Strickland.
Vice-President : H. Winton Strickland.
Chief Engineer : Bion S. Hutchins, Jr.

Secretary and Treasurer : O. H. Moore.

The Strickland Aircraft Corpn. is engaged in the manufacture of aircraft parts and sub-assemblies under sub-contract to other aircraft manufacturers.

For post-war production it has designed a twin-engined mid-wing monoplane, the principal feature will be an engine installation in which the power-units will be buried within the wings and drive tractor airscrews. It will be offered in two models, one accommodating pilot and four or five passengers and the other from twelve to fifteen persons.

SUMMIT.

SUMMIT AERONAUTICAL CORPORATION.

HEAD OFFICE : 30, Broad Street, New York 4, N.Y.
President and Treasurer : M. V. D. Towt.
Vice-President : Joseph R. Reilly.
Consulting Engineer : Harris S. Campbell.

The Summit Aeronautical Corpn. holds a licence to build aircraft by the Vidal Process, as developed by the Aircraft Research Corporation.

Primarily the "Vidal Process" is a method of moulding under fluid pressure and heat plastic impregnated sheets of veneer which have been placed on properly contoured and slotted wood formers. The "cooking" process welds and presses skin, ribs, stringers, pads and other members into a single homogeneously-bonded unit. Sub-assemblies may be pre-moulded, trimmed and fitted, and again moulded as an integral part of larger complex structures.

The first product of the Company built under this process was the HM-5 two-seat light cabin monoplane, which was described and illustrated in the 1941 edition of this work.

Engineering and flight test work was conducted on the HM-5 during 1941 and this work was nearing completion at the time America entered the War. Owing to restrictions on the manufacture of civil aircraft, plans for production have been temporarily suspended and Bendix Airport, where the Summit plant was located, has been diverted to other uses. As a result no active manufacturing work is being done by the Company.

SWALLOW.

SWALLOW AIRCRAFT COMPANY, INC.

HEAD OFFICE AND WORKS : WICHITA, KANSAS.
President and Chief Engineer : S. Bloomfield.
Vice-President : Leland R. Wilson.
Secretary and Treasurer : M. H. Cundiff.

The Swallow Aircraft Company is the successor to the Swallow Airplane Company, one of the oldest producers of light commercial aircraft in the United States.

In 1941 the Company completed the development of the LT-65 two-seat low-wing cabin monoplane, a description of which was included in the 1941 edition of this Annual. Production of this type could not be proceeded with owing to priority restrictions on constructional materials. Development of a high-wing tandem training monoplane fitted with either a 50 h.p. or 65 h.p. Continental engine has been similarly restricted. In the meantime the Company is operating a training school for aircraft hands.

TAYLORCRAFT.

TAYLORCRAFT AVIATION CORPORATION.

HEAD OFFICE AND WORKS : ALLIANCE, OHIO.

President : James C. Hart.

Assistant to President : Richard G. King.

Vice-President in charge of Production : Kenneth W. Tibbits.

The Taylorcraft Aviation Corpn. was formed to take over the Taylorcraft Aviation Co., which was formed in 1936 by Mr. C. G. Taylor. Mr. Taylor had previously been President and Chief Engineer of the Taylor Aircraft Co., which produced the original "Cub" light cabin monoplane, the forerunner of the modern popular-priced American light aeroplane. The present company produced the Taylorcraft side-by-side two-seat cabin monoplane in various forms, as well as a tandem trainer which was specially developed for the Civilian Pilot Training Programme.

On September 1, 1941, the Taylorcraft Aviation Corpn. turned over its entire production of light aircraft to manufacture for specific defence needs, such as for civilian pilot training programme schools, airline instrument training schools, other C.A.A. approved flying schools, Home Guard units, forest fire patrol, State and city police, etc.

In the Spring of 1944 the company completed its contracts with the U.S. Army Air Forces for the manufacture of the L-2 Series light liaison-observation monoplanes and for the remainder of the year it concentrated on the production of parts under sub-contract from another company.

In the meantime it has designed and built prototypes of two new civil aircraft for post-war production. One is the Model B-12B, a two-seat side-by-side cabin monoplane developed from the 1941 B-12, and the other is the Model 15, a new four-seat cabin monoplane which the company intends to place on the market after the war at a price of $4,000. A third post-war model is also in the development stage. This will be the Model 12, a two-seat side-by-side high-wing monoplane of all-metal construction.

THE TAYLORCRAFT MODEL 15.

The Model 15 is one of three new prototypes which have been developed for post-war production. It is a high-wing rigidly-braced monoplane of similar outline and structure to the standard Taylorcraft Model B monoplane, but the wings have slots and flaps and the landing-gear has hydraulic shock-absorbers. It has an engine of 125 h.p.

The cabin seats four in two pairs, the front pair with dual wheel control. There are front and rear doors and there is a large baggage compartment behind the two back seats. These two seats and the baggage compartment are easily removable so that the cabin may be used for light freight-carrying.

DIMENSIONS.—Span 36 ft. 6 in. (11.1 m.), Length 23 ft. (7 m.), Height 7 ft. (2.1 m.).

WEIGHTS.—Weight empty 1,275 lbs. (560 kg.), Weight loaded 2,250 lbs. (1,020 kg.).

PERFORMANCE.—Maximum speed 125 m.p.h. (200 km.h.), Cruising speed 112 m.p.h. (179 km.h.), Landing speed 40 m.p.h. (64 km.h.), Duration 5.5 hours.

THE TAYLORCRAFT MODEL B TRAINER.

TYPE.—Two-seat light cabin monoplane.

WINGS.—High-wing braced monoplane. Wings attached to top of fuselage and braced to lower longerons by steel-tube Vee struts, which have vertical intermediate struts located at their centres. Wing structure consists of two wood spars, wood ribs, and fabric covering.

FUSELAGE.—Welded steel-tube structure, covered with fabric.

TAIL UNIT.—Wire-braced monoplane type. Welded steel-tube framework, covered with fabric.

LANDING GEAR.—Split type. Consists of two faired side Vees hinged to the lower fuselage longerons, with bent half-axles sprung on the centre-line of the underside of the fuselage by rubber shock-absorber cord. Welded steel-tube swivelling tail-wheel.

POWER PLANT.—One 65 h.p. Lycoming O-145-B2, Continental A-65 or Franklin 4AC-176 four-cylinder opposed air-cooled engine. Fuel capacity 12 U.S. gallons. Auxiliary tank (6 U.S. gallons capacity) may be installed.

The Taylorcraft Model 15 Four-seat Cabin Monoplane.

The Taylorcraft L-2 Grasshopper Light Liaison and Observation Monoplane (65 h.p. Continental engine).

ACCOMMODATION.—Enclosed cabin, seating two side-by-side, with dual control. Interchangeable wheel or stick type controls. Door on each side of cabin.

DIMENSIONS.—Span 36 ft. (11 m.), Length 22 ft. (6.7 m.), Height 6 ft. 8 in. (2.1 m.), Wing area 183.5 sq. ft. (17 sq. m.).

WEIGHTS AND LOADINGS (65 h.p. Lycoming engine).—Weight empty 670 lbs. (287 kg.), Disposable load 480 lbs. (235 kg.), Weight loaded 1,150 lbs. (522 kg.), Wing loading 6.88 lbs./sq. ft. (33.6 kg./sq. m.), Power loading 22 lbs./h.p. (10 kg./h.p.).

PERFORMANCE (65 h.p. Lycoming engine).—Maximum speed 105 m.p.h. (155 km.h.), Cruising speed 95 m.p.h. (142 km.h.), Landing speed 35 m.p.h. (46.3 km.h.), Initial rate of climb 450 ft./min. (137 m./min.), Absolute ceiling 17,000 ft. (3,660 m.), Cruising range 250 miles (400 km.).

THE TAYLORCRAFT MODEL D TANDEM TRAINER.

The Tandem Trainer is similar in general arrangement and construction to the Model B Trainer and differs mainly by having a narrower fuselage and a cabin seating two in tandem with complete dual controls. This model may be fitted with either the 65 h.p. Lycoming, Continental or Franklin engine.

THE TAYLORCRAFT "GRASSHOPPER."

U.S. Army Air Forces designation: L-2.

The L-2 is a special version of the Tandem Trainer, a large number of which has been supplied to the U.S. Army Air Forces for observation and light liaison duties. It has been supplied in four versions, the L-2, L-2A, L-2B and L-2M, all fitted with the 65 h.p. Continental O-170-3 engine and equipped with two-way radio.

To provide increased vision for the pilot and observer, the

fabric formerly covering the cabin roof and the rear deck of the fuselage to a point about midway to the tail has been replaced by transparent "Vinylite" panels. For the same reason, the root ends of the wings have been cut away at the trailing-edge.

The observer has a two-way seat and a table is provided at the rear of the cabin for use by the observer when facing aft.

The latest version in the L-2 Series—the L-2M—has a closed engine cowling and "spoilers" have been fitted to the wings to facilitate landing in small areas. Operation of these "spoilers" has the effect of doubling the rate of descent.

In addition to the versions mentioned above, the U.S. Army also purchased secondhand a number of civil Taylorcraft Model B and Model D monoplanes. These were given designations in the L-2 Series as follows :—

L-2C	Model DC-65	Continental A-65-8 engine.
L-2D	Model DL-65	Lycoming O-145-B2 engine.
L-2E	Model DF-65	Franklin 4AC-150 engine.
L-2F	Model BF-65	Franklin 4AC-150 engine.
L-2G	Model BFT-65	Franklin 4AC-150 engine.
L-2H	Model BC-12	Continental A-65-7 engine.
L-2J	Model BI-12	Lycoming O-145-B1 engine.
L-2K	Model BF-12	Franklin 4AC-150 engine.
L-2L	Model BF-50	Franklin 4AC-150 engine.

The Taylorcraft Model D Two-seat Light Training Monoplane (65 h.p. Continental engine).   (Photograph by Peter Bowers)

The Taylorcraft L-2 Grasshopper.

TIMM.

TIMM AIRCRAFT CORPORATION.

HEAD OFFICE AND WORKS : 8055, WOODLEY AVENUE, VAN NUYS, CAL.

President and Chief Engineer : O. W. Timm.

Executive Vice-President : J. P. Davies

Vice-President : F. E. Dent.

Secretary and Treasurer : G. Shrader.

The Timm Aircraft Company is specialising in the development of a system of plastic construction based on its patented "Aero-mold" process. Its first product built by this process was the S-160-K, a two-seat primary training monoplane.

On April 2, 1941, the S-160-K was awarded the first Approved Type Certificate ever given to a trainer built entirely of plastic-bonded plywood. The S-160-K was then submitted to tests by the Army and the Navy and as a result the U.S. Navy placed a contract for aircraft of this type fitted with the 220 h.p. Continental W-670 radial engine under the designation N2T-1.

UNITED AIRCRAFT.

THE UNITED AIRCRAFT CORPORATION.

HEAD OFFICE : 400, SOUTH MAIN STREET, EAST HARTFORD 8, CONN.

Chairman of the Board : F. B. Rentschler.
Vice-Chairmen : Eugene E. Wilson and Raycroft Walsh.
President : H. Mansfield Horner.
Vice-Presidents : S. A. Stewart and C. J. McCarthy.
Controller : Joseph F. McCarthy.
Secretary : Charles H. Chatfield.

Treasurer : Carroll L. Gault.

The United Aircraft Corpn., founded in 1934, includes four divisions engaged in the manufacture of aircraft, engines and airscrews. These are the Chance Vought Aircraft Division (Aircraft), the Sikorsky Aircraft Division (Helicopters), the Pratt & Whitney Aircraft Division (Engines), and the Hamilton Standard Propeller Division (Airscrews).

After America's entry into the War the United Aircraft Corpn. enlisted the assistance of a number of independent manufacturing organizations to help in the production of aircraft, aero-engines and airscrews.

Jacobs, Continental, Ford, Buick, Chevrolet and Nash-Kelvinator have built Pratt & Whitney engines ; Goodyear has built Chance Vought aircraft ; and Nash-Kelvinator Sikorsky helicopters. Frigidaire, Remington-Rand and Nash-Kelvinator have manufactured Hamilton Standard airscrews. All these concerns have built United Aircraft products on a nominal licence basis without profit to the United Aircraft Corpn.

WACO.

THE WACO AIRCRAFT COMPANY.

HEAD OFFICE AND WORKS : TROY, OHIO.
Established : 1921.
President : Clayton J. Brukner.
Vice-President : H. R. Perry.
Vice-President in charge of Engineering : A. Francis Arcier.
Secretary : L. E. St. John.
Treasurer : R. E. Hoefflin.

The Waco Aircraft Co. is the oldest and, before America entered the War, was one of the largest producers of civil aircraft in the U.S.A. It specialised in the production of training and touring aircraft and has always adhered faithfully to the biplane.

Since August, 1941, the Company has devoted its entire efforts to war contracts. Its most important contribution to the war programme has been in the troop and cargo-carrying glider field. Four gliders have been produced, the CG-3A troop training glider and the CG-4A, CG-13A and CG-15A troop and cargo-carrying gliders. The CG-4A was mass-produced by fifteen American manufacturers and by the end of 1944 over 20,000 had been delivered. The CG-3A was never built in quantity.

The CG-13A forty-two-seat troop and cargo-carrying glider of Waco design was built by the Northwestern Aeronautical Corpn. and by the Ford Motor Co.

THE WACO CG-15A.

The CG-15A is a development of the CG-4A and, compared with it, has a reduced span, a strongly-reinforced nose, improved landing-gear shock-absorbers, and the addition of flaps to counteract the effect of the shortened span. With these changes the maximum permissible towing speed was increased to 180 m.p.h. (288 km.h.), which permitted the CG-15A to be towed by fighters.

It has a capacity for 16 men, including two pilots, or 4,000 lbs. (1,816 kg.) of equipment. The loaded weight is 8,000 lbs. (3,632 kg.).

DIMENSIONS.—Span 62 ft. 2¼ in. (18.9 m.), Length 48 ft. 9⅞ in. (14.8 m.).

THE WACO CG-13A.

The CG-13A is a large glider capable of carrying a maximum of forty-two airborne troops and their equipment or their equivalent weight in military vehicles, ordnance, etc. The first experimental XCG-13 was delivered by the Waco Company to the

The Waco CG-13A Military Transport Glider.

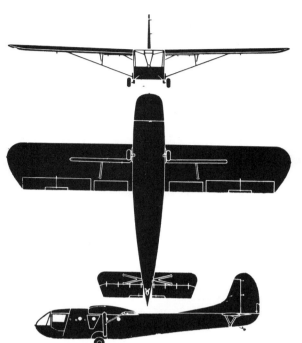

The Waco CG-15A Military Transport Glider.

Army in March, 1942, and as the result of extensive trials with the prototype a small production order was placed with the North-western Aeronautical Corpn. for the YCG-13, the first of which was towed off the ground on December 2, 1943. Production orders for the CG-13A, were handled by the North-western Aeronautical Corpn. and the Ford Motor Company.

TYPE.—Forty-two-seat Troop or Freight-carrying Glider.
WINGS.—High-wing rigidly-braced monoplane. General arrangement and structure similar to CG-4A. All-wood structure covered with plywood and fabric. Hydraulically-operated flaps.
FUSELAGE.—Rectangular welded steel-tube structure covered with fabric.
TAIL UNIT.—Rigidly-braced monoplane type. All-wood framework covered with plywood and fabric.
LANDING GEAR.—Fixed tricycle-type. Oleo-pneumatic shock-absorbers.
ACCOMMODATION.—Pilot's compartment in nose with side-by-side seating and dual controls. The entire nose hinges up hydraulically to give direct access to the main hold which can accommodate up to forty-two fully-armed airborne troops, or varying loads of ordnance, military vehicles or freight. Typical loads may consist of one 105 m/m. howitzer, towing vehicle and gun crew (6) ; two ¼ ton trucks and eight troops ; 75 m/m. howitzer, towing vehicle, ammunition and eight troops, etc. All mobile units drive up a rampway into the hold. Two doors, one on each side at the aft end of the hold, for troop loading. Equipment similar to CG-4A.
DIMENSIONS.—Span 85 ft. 8 in. (26.13 m.), Length 54 ft. 4 in. (16.57 m.), Height 20 ft. 3 in. (6.2 m.), Wing area 873 sq. ft. (80 sq. m.).
WEIGHTS (Approximate).—Weight empty 8,900 lbs. (4,040 kg.), Weight loaded 18,900 lbs. (8,580 kg.).
PERFORMANCE.—Maximum towing speed 190 m.p.h. (304 km.h.), Landing speed 80 m.p.h. (148 km.h.).

THE WACO CG-4A.

British name : Hadrian.

The CG-4A was the only American built troop-carrying glider to be used by the Allied forces in the airborne invasion of Sicily and France. It has been the subject of a widespread production programme. Apart from its manufacture by the parent company by whom it was put into production in April, 1941, it was also built by Cessna, Commonwealth, Ford, G & A., the Gibson Radiator Company, the Ridgefield Manufacturing Corpn., Laister-Kauffman, Northwestern, Pratt Read, Robertson Aircraft Corpn., etc.

TYPE.—Fifteen-seat Troop or Cargo-carrying Glider.
WINGS.—High-wing rigidly-braced monoplane. Two-spar wood structure with plywood covering over leading-edge to rear spar and a final overall covering of fabric. Vee bracing struts are of steel-tube faired with fabric over wood formers. Unbalanced ailerons with controllable trim-tabs. Spoilers on upper surfaces of wings to steepen gliding angle and increase sinking speed.
FUSELAGE.—Rigidly-braced welded steel-tube framework covered with fabric over wooden formers and longitudinal stringers.
TAIL UNIT.—Braced monoplane type. Wooden framework covered with plywood and fabric. Tailplane braced to fin and fuselage by streamline wires. Trim-tabs in elevators and rudder.
LANDING GEAR.—Of two types, training and operational. Training gear consists of two tripods, each consisting of an axle and radius-rod hinged to the lower fuselage longeron and an oleo-spring shock-absorber leg attached to the fuselage at the point of attachment of the front wing spar. Hydraulic wheel-brakes. Operational gear is jettisonable and consists of a cross axle and brake-less wheels. Non-steerable tail-wheel.
ACCOMMODATION.—Pilot's compartment in the hinged nose seats two side-by-side with dual controls. Control wheels on inverted Vee frame suspended from the roof of the compartment. Starboard wheel may be removed, when port wheel may then be swung across to starboard seat if necessary. Dual rudder-pedals. Main compartment may seat 13 fully-armed airborne troops on benches along sides, or may carry varying loads of cargo or ordnance. Typical loads may consist of one Army ¼ ton Jeep with its crew of four and extra equipment to make up the full disposable load, or one standard Army 75 m/m. howitzer and carriage with gun-crew of three, ammunition and supplies to make up full load. Normal troop entrance through doors at aft end of compartment,

The Waco CG-15A Sixteen-seat Troop and Cargo-carrying Glider.

The Waco CG-13A 42-seat Troop or Cargo-carrying Glider.

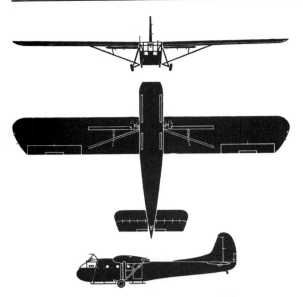

The Waco CG-4A Troop-carrying Glider.

The Waco CG-4A Fifteen-seat Troop or Cargo-carrying Glider.

one on each side. Nose of fuselage hinged to fold upward to give direct entry into main hold for loading truck, howitzer or other heavy equipment. Tackle provided to enable truck to raise nose automatically when being driven out. Equipment includes inter-communication system for use between glider and tug, landing-light, night-flying equipment, etc.

DIMENSIONS.—Span 83 ft. 8 in. (25.5 m.), Length 48 ft. 3¾ in. (14.7 m.), Height 12 ft. 7⁷⁄₁₆ in. (3.84 m.), Wing area 851.5 sq. ft. (79.1 sq. m.).

WEIGHTS AND LOADINGS.—Weight empty 3,790 lbs. (1,721 kg.), Disposable load 3,710 lbs. (1,684 kg.), Normal loaded weight 7,500 lbs. (3,405 kg.), Maximum permissible overloaded weight 9,000 lbs. (4,086 kg.), Normal wing loading 8.81 lbs./sq. ft. (43 kg./sq. m.), Maximum permissible wing loading 10.56 lbs./sq. ft. (51.53 kg./sq. m.).

PERFORMANCE.—Normal towed speed 125 m.p.h. (200 km.h.), Minimum gliding speed 38 m.p.h. (61 km.h.).

THE WACO CG-3A.

The CG-3A is an externally braced high-wing monoplane of fabric-covered wood and steel-tube construction. It carries nine fully armed men each carrying 40 lbs. (18 kg.) of equipment. Two of the troops act as pilot and co-pilot.

The CG-3A was originally designed as a troop transport. One hundred were built and delivered to the U.S. Army Air Forces by Commonwealth Aircraft, Inc. It was later used for training glider pilots.

DIMENSIONS.—Span 73 ft. 1 in. (22.2 m.), Length 48 ft.5¹⁹⁄₁₆ in. (14.8 m.).

WEIGHT LOADED.—4,000 lbs. (1,816 kg.) approx.

PERFORMANCE.—Maximum towed speed 120 m.p.h. (192 km.h.), Normal towed speed 100 m.p.h. (160 km.h.), Minimum gliding speed 28 m.p.h. (61 km.h.).

THE WACO CABIN BIPLANES.
U.S. Army Air Forces designation : UC-72 Series.

Since the Model VKS-7F four-seat cabin biplane was specially evolved to meet the requirements for a cross-country navigational trainer for the civilian training programme early in 1942, all production of this type of aircraft has ceased.

A large number of Waco cabin biplanes in the C, E, N and S Series which were in use at the outbreak of war were acquired by the U.S. Army Air Forces from private owners or commercial operators and given designations in the UC-72 Series.

The following is a full list of these aircraft :—

UC-72	Model SRE (Pratt & Whitney R-985).
UC-72A	Model ARE (Jacobs L-6).
UC-72B	Model EGC-8 (Wright R-760-E2).
UC-72C	Model HRE (Lycoming R-680).
UC-72D	Model VKS-7 (Continental W-670).
UC-72E	Model ZGC-7 (Jacobs L-5).
UC-72F	Model CUC-1 (Wright R-760-E).
UC-72G	Model AQC-6 (Jacobs L-6).
UC-72H	Model ZQC-6 (Jacobs L-5).
UC-72J	Model AVN-8 (Jacobs L-6).
UC-72K	Model YKS-7 (Jacobs L-4).
UC-72L	Model ZVN-8 (Jacobs L-5).
UC-72M	Model ZKS-7 (Jacobs L-5).
UC-72N	Model YOC-1 (Jacobs L-5 or L-6).
UC-72O	Model AGC-1 (Jacobs L-6).

The Waco CG-3A Training Glider.

ALL THE
WORLD'S AERO-ENGINES

(CORRECTED TO NOVEMBER 30th, 1945)

ARRANGED IN ALPHABETICAL ORDER OF

NATIONALITY

THE BRITISH EMPIRE
GREAT BRITAIN
GAS TURBINE ENGINES

ARMSTRONG SIDDELEY.

ARMSTRONG SIDDELEY MOTORS, LTD.

HEAD OFFICE AND WORKS : COVENTRY.

Directors : See p. 10d.

Armstrong Siddeley Motors, Ltd. have been engaged in the development of gas turbines for aircraft propulsion for several years, but the only engine of this company's design of which details may be published is the ASX axial-flow jet unit. The first tests with this engine were run in April, 1943.

THE ARMSTRONG SIDDELEY ASX.

The ASX engine consists of a 14-stage axial-flow compressor driven by a two-stage turbine which is fed by eleven combustion chambers disposed axially around the compressor casing and parallel to the axis of the unit. The compressor is of the reverse flow type, the intake air entering through a series of ports situated midway along the engine between the rear ends of the combustion chambers.

The rotor runs at a maximum speed of 8,000 r.p.m. and gives a static sea level thrust of 2,600 lb. (1,180 kg.) at take-off and combat ratings. Under cruising conditions a thrust of 2,050 lbs. (931 kg.) is obtained at 7,500 r.p.m. The fuel consumptions are 1.03 lb./hr./lb. thrust at 8,000 r.p.m. and 1.0 lb./hr./lb. thrust at 7,500 r.p.m.

NET DRY WEIGHT.—1,900 lbs. (865 kg.).

DIMENSIONS.—Maximum diameter 42 in. (1,068 mm.), Overall length (including exhaust cone and propelling nozzle) 13 ft. 11 in. (4,240 m/m.).

THE ARMSTRONG SIDDELEY ASP.

The ASP is the ASX engine arranged to drive an airscrew. This engine develops 3,600 shaft horse-power and 1,100 lbs. (500 kg.) thrust.

The Armstrong Siddeley ASX axial-flow turbo-jet engine. *(Flight Photograph)*

BRISTOL.

BRISTOL AEROPLANE CO., LTD.

HEAD OFFICE AND WORKS : FILTON, NR. BRISTOL.

Directors : See p. 12d.

For many years the Bristol Aeroplane Co. Ltd. has been interested in the gas turbine in its various forms.

As far back as 1924-25 the company was actually flying a Bristol exhaust turbo-supercharger on an adapted Jupiter engine. It was flown successfully at over 30,000 feet and proved very promising, but the state of engine development then made it necessary to concentrate on gear-driven superchargers from 1926 onwards.

Work was resumed on exhaust-turbos in 1937, when the line of development envisaged by the company was a turbo-blown version of the sleeve-valve engine—the idea being that boost and back-pressure could be progressively increased, as the sleeve-valve was very well suited to operate at high back-pressure. Thus a state of affairs would ultimately be reached where the powers of the engine and of the exhaust-turbo were equal and it would so be possible to interchange airscrew and compressor, thereby making the engine and compressor virtually a gas generator unit, the airscrew being driven by the exhaust turbine.

By the outbreak of war, Bristol had a general plan for entry into the gas turbine field. The primary aim was the production of a compound unit of low fuel consumption, a feature which would make it peculiarly applicable to long-range aircraft. Long-term research of this kind had to be closed down however, and the project was discontinued so that attention could be concentrated on sleeve-valve engines for war purposes.

A little later, the design staff became aware of the extent to which Group Captain Whittle's research had progressed, and later still, the Bristol project team accordingly tackled the job of designing a turbine for long-range aircraft. The target set them was to produce a turbine which would have an overall fuel consumption comparable with that of a piston engine at 300 m.p.h. (480 km.h.) at a height of 20,000 ft. (6,100 m.). These conditions were postulated as the lowest speed and altitude at which the turbine could compete with conventional engines ; at higher speeds and altitudes turbine efficiency increases. The Bristol company did not believe that civil aircraft speeds would be less than 300 m.p.h. and the height of 20,000 ft. was chosen because pressure cabins were thought to be inevitable and they would not be worth while at lower altitudes.

As gas turbines have no cooling systems other than a small oil-cooler for the reduction-gear, it was concluded that, if the designers could get down to within 5-10 per cent. above piston engine consumption, they could compete successfully with such engines. This was fixed as the full load condition, as turbines are most efficient at full power and it was not necessary to provide for any other condition except that of cruising speed.

A careful study was made of every form of prime-mover, including piston engines, turbines and jets, and every form of coupling. The result was to strengthen the opinion that the idea projected was fundamentally the best for the particular purpose envisaged. The decision was then taken to concentrate work on the scheme, and the design was settled for a unit in which the greater proportion of the output would be taken to

drive an air-screw and only residual thrust utilised in the form of a jet.

The Theseus I, the first unit to satisfactorily pass its tests, is only the first of a family of Bristol gas-turbine units in which the primary objective is the attainment of the highest possible thermal efficiency consistent with reasonable weight and bulk and, in this connection the company, having initiated development in this direction, intend to pursue it in a variety of designs, not all of which will necessarily include airscrews and/or heat exchangers.

THE BRISTOL THESEUS.

The Theseus, which has a dry weight of 2,310 lbs. (1,049 kg.), consists of a multi-stage axial-cum-centrifugal compressor which aspires air through an annular entry around the reduction gear.

The Bristol Theseus Gas Turbine engine.

The compressed air is delivered (via a heat-exchanger) to a number of combustion chambers, where its temperature is further raised by the burning of injected fuel. The products of compression pass to a turbine which is directly coupled to the compressor, and thence to a further separate turbine stage which drives, via a forward extension shaft, the airscrew reduction gearing. After leaving this turbine, the gases pass through the heat exchanger, where they give up some heat to the compressed air on its way to the combustion chambers. From the heat exchanger the exhaust gases are finally discharged through a controllable nozzle, thus producing forward thrust. About 80 per cent. of the power is absorbed by the airscrew, the remainder being used for jet reaction.

DE HAVILLAND.

THE DE HAVILLAND ENGINE CO., LTD.

HEAD OFFICE : HATFIELD, HERTS.
ENGINE WORKS : STONEGROVE, EDGWARE, MIDDLESEX.
Directors : See p. 20d.

The de Havilland Engine Co, Ltd. entered the jet-propulsion field in the Spring of 1941, as soon as concentration on the grave National dangers of 1940-41 would permit. Design of the first D.H. jet engine—the H-1 or Goblin—began in April, 1941, and within a year the prototype was running on the Hatfield test-beds. Within two months the engine was giving its designed thrust, by March 5, 1943, it was flying in a Gloster Meteor, and by September 20, 1943, it was taking the D.H.100 Vampire single-seat single-jet fighter monoplane on its initial flights.

A D.H. H-1 was supplied to the American authorities in July, 1943, and this engine was turned over by the U.S. Air Technical Service Command to the Lockheed Aircraft Corporation to form the power unit of the XP-80 Shooting Star single-seat fighter monoplane. This aircraft was designed, built and flown in 143 days. A D.H. H-1 engine was also installed in the Curtiss XF15C-1 single-seat naval fighter, a dual-powered aircraft with a normal R-2800 radial engine driving a tractor airscrew and a turbo-jet exhausting beneath the tail-unit.

The Goblin I engine was the first British jet to pass the official type-test in the new Gas Turbine category and holds Approval Certificate No. 1.

THE D.H. H-1 GOBLIN.

The Goblin engine consists of a single-sided centrifugal compressor feeding sixteen straight-flow combustion chambers, a single-stage turbine, exhaust case and propelling nozzle.

The combination of a single-sided impeller and straight-through combustion eliminates the third bearing. The larger impeller has a slower rotational speed and generates less centrifugal stress, while the ducting of air to the single-sided impeller is less complicated than to a double-sided impeller.

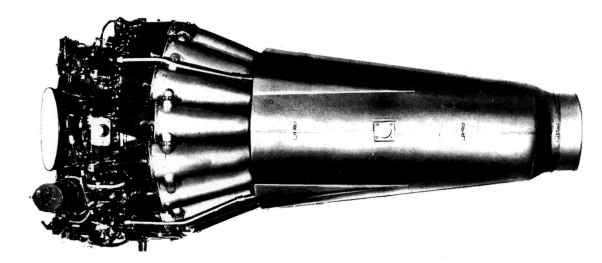

The de Havilland H-1 Goblin centrifugal-flow gas turbine, the first to pass the British official type test for engines of this class.

The production Goblin is rated at 3,000 lbs. (1,362 kg.) thrust at 10,200 r.p.m. and this unit gives the standard R.A.F. Vampire fighter a normal level top speed of 540 m.p.h. (864 km.h.) over a wide altitude range. Development Goblins are running at considerably higher powers and Vampire aircraft are flying with special category approval at 3,400 lbs. (1,544 kg.) thrust.

NET DRY WEIGHT.—1,500 lbs. (681 kg.).

DIMENSIONS.—Maximum diameter 50 in. (1,270 mm.), Overall length to rear flange of exhaust cone 8 ft. 4½ in. (2,553 mm.).

METROPOLITAN-VICKERS.

METROPOLITAN-VICKERS ELECTRICAL CO., LTD.

REGISTERED OFFICE : 1, KINGSWAY, LONDON, W.C.2.
WORKS : TRAFFORD PARK, MANCHESTER, 17.

Metropolitan-Vickers started development work on gas turbines for aircraft propulsion in 1938, and in 1940 designed the F2 jet propulsion engine with axial-flow compressor. The first engine was run on bench test in 1941 and, after modification passed a Special Category Test for flight clearance in 1942. The earliest flights with engines of this type took place in a Lancaster flying test-bed on June 29, 1943, and in a Gloster F.9/40 Meteor prototype on November 13, 1943.

This first engine, known as the F2/1, had a thrust rating of 1,800 lbs. (817 kg.) on a weight of 1,525 lbs. (692 kg.). It had a maximum diameter of 32.9 in. (835 mm.) and a length of 10 ft. 8 in. (3,251 mm.).

This was followed by an engine of a new design known as the F2/4. The first engine of this type was run in 1945.

Metropolitan-Vickers also designed the first ducted fan augmenter. Combined with an F2 engine this augmenter, known as the F3, has given most promising results. Bench tests began with it in August, 1943.

THE METROPOLITAN-VICKERS F.2/4.

The F2/4 consists of a multi-stage axial-flow compressor, an annular combustion chamber, a turbine coupled to the compressor an exhaust cone and a propelling nozzle ; all arranged axially in line. Excluding certain accessories which project locally at the front where the air inlet is situated, the F2/4 has a maximum diameter of 36.75 in. (933 mm.). It can be mounted within a nacelle of 42 in. (1,067 mm.) diameter. At the time of writing the F2/4 had run a 100-hour endurance test under type-test conditions.

The following are the leading particulars of the F2/4 :—Thrust rating in static conditions, Maximum take-off 3,500 lbs. (1,590 kg.), Maximum climb 3,300 lbs. (1,500 kg.), Maximum cruising 3,000 lbs. (1,362 kg.) ; Net dry weight 1,750 lbs. (795 kg.) ; Fuel consumption 1.05 lbs./hr./lbs. thrust at maximum static thrust ; Overall length (including exhaust cone and propelling nozzle) 13 ft. 3 in. (4,041 mm.) ; Maximum diameter 36.75 in. (933 mm.).

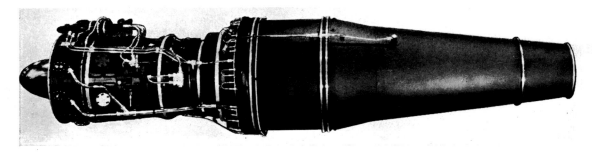

The Metropolitan-Vickers F2/4 axial flow turbo-jet engine which has a maximum thrust rating of 3,500 lbs. (1,590 kg.).

POWER JETS.

POWER JETS (RESEARCH AND DEVELOPMENT), LTD.

REGISTERED OFFICE : 8, HAMILTON PLACE, LONDON, W.1.
OTHER ESTABLISHMENTS : WHETSTONE, LEICESTER AND PYESTOCK ESTATE, COVE, FARNBOROUGH, HANTS.

Directors : Dr. H. Roxbee Cox (Chairman and Managing Director), H. R. Ricardo, F.R.S., Sir William Stanier, F.R.S., J. W. Stephenson, C.B.E., J. C. B. Tinling, Air Cdre. F. Whittle, C.B.E., and R. D. Williams.

Power Jets (Research & Development) Ltd. was formed in 1944 as an entirely State-owned organization to acquire the whole voluntarily-sold assets of the foundation Company, Power Jets, Ltd., of which the major shareholding was private. The Directors were appointed by the Minister of Aircraft Production. The Company does not engage in production, and has for its object to foster the gas turbine industry as a whole, primarily by technical contribution to the art, and to exploit Government-owned rights in inventions, etc. The following brief note gives an indication of some of the work of the organization from 1936 through the war period.

The first Whittle gas turbine engine was built by the British Thomson-Houston Company at Rugby, under contract to Power Jets, Ltd., and ran first in April, 1937. It was intended to form the design basis of a stratospheric trans-Atlantic mailplane. It appears in Fig. 1. Between then and 1938 there were various modifications and reconstructions, and the engine first ran in the form shown in Fig. 2 in October, 1938. This engine, known as WU, was the only one in existence until December, 1940, and with it alone was done the whole of the development leading up to the first run of the W1X in that month.

The officially unairworthy W1X was the first engine to be airborne ; this was an "unofficial" occurrence which arose during taxying trials of the Gloster E.28/39 in April, 1941. The W1 engine (Fig. 3), the airworthy twin of the W1X, had a water-cooling system, and was the first official flight engine. It was flown in the E.28/39 by P. E. G. Sayer at Cranwell on May 14, 1941, and thereafter for its permitted time of ten hours without anything more than routine attention.

It is noteworthy that this highly experimental engine and hardly less revolutionary aircraft completed the whole of their initial proving trials without modification, and not one minute of flying time was lost by defect of either airframe or engine. Within 46 days the engine ran a 25-hour Special Category Test and was installed and flew ten hours in the aircraft. All the engines up to this stage had been built by B.T.H.

In October, 1941, a Whittle engine, a set of manufacturing drawings and a number of engineers from PowerJets, Ltd. were flown to America to assist the General Electric Company to initiate manufacture in the United States. Within a year the Bell XP-59A fitted with two G.E. Whittle-type units had been built and flown, to become the second Allied jet-propelled aeroplane to take the air.

The trend of events had now forced the decision that the first use of the engine was for fighter aircraft propulsion—the extreme opposite of its original purpose. The fundamental adaptability of the class is well illustrated by the fact that the development programme was hardly affected by the change of objective.

Among the detailed achievements of the Company and its collaborators may be mentioned, by way of example, the development of a single-stage centrifugal compressor delivering 47 lbs. (21.3 kg.) air./sec. with a compression ratio of over 4 : 1 ;

Fig. 1.—The first Whittle gas-turbine engine.

the development of a single-stage turbine of 54 blades and a mean blade diameter of 15.127 in. (384 mm.), delivering over 5,400 shaft h.p. ; the development of a combustion system evolving approximately 10,000,000 B.T.Us/cu. ft. of volume/hour ; and the development in four years of the W1 to the latest model without significant change of dimension, in the following approximate values :—W1, Weight 700 lbs. (318 kg.), Air consumption 20.6 lb./sec. (9.35 kg./sec.), Fuel consumption 1,170 lbs./hour (531 kg./hour), Thrust 850 lbs. (386 kg.). W2/850, Weight 950 lbs. (471 kg.), Air consumption 47 lbs./sec. (21.34

Fig. 2.—The Whittle WU experimental engine which first ran in October, 1938.

Fig. 4.—The W2/700 jet-propulsion engine. This unit was designed for a static thrust of 2,000 lbs. (908 kg.) at 16,700 r.p.m.

kg./sec.), Fuel consumption 2,610 lbs./hour (1,185 kg./hour), Thrust 2,485 lbs. (1,128 kg.).

In an aircraft flying at 500 m.p.h. (800 km.h.) the latter engine weighs about 0.25 lbs. (0.11 kg.) equivalent thrust h.p.

In the course of further development, Whittle and Power Jets, Ltd. evolved many projects, and constructed and tested a proportion of them. Typical of these was the W2/700 (Fig. 4) of which various experimental Marks have flown in various aircraft, including the Gloster E.28/39 and F.9/40 Meteor. The then very limited resources of the Company and the exigencies of war required that practical development should be confined strictly to the lines of accumulated experience so that such projects as the W2Y (Fig. 5) though attractive when laid out by Power Jets, Ltd. in May, 1940, had to be left unpursued by the Company. Fortunately other collaborating firms such as Rolls-Royce and de Havilland, with their great facilities and enterprise, were able to explore in such wider fields with results which

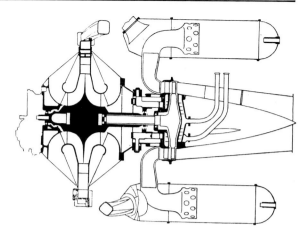

Fig. 3.—The Whittle W1, the first jet-propulsion engine to fly in Great Britain. It was cleared for flight at a static thrust of 850 lbs. (386 kg.).

are well renowned, the Derwent and Nene of Rolls-Royce and the Goblin of de Havilland all having their places in the genealogy.

A result of the acquisition of the organization by the State was its amalgamation with the Turbine Section of the Royal Aircraft Establishment, where earlier Dr. Griffith and later Mr. H. Constant had made valuable contributions both to theory and practice, more especially on the basis of axial-flow compressor units. As a result, the Company is now closely interested in both species of engine, and extends its activities into the fields of industrial power-plant for marine, locomotive and general shaft-power purposes.

In relation to aircraft propulsion, much is done in regard to methods of thrust augmentation, airscrew drive, innumerable ancilliary problems of installation and operation, and constant study of supersonic and other aspects of aerodynamics and thermodynamics. The Company engages in special machine-tool design, metallurgy, fuel chemistry, and, indeed, almost any line of research, experiment or development which may be thought to contribute basically to the gas turbine art. The Company's services are available to Industry by way of general advice, or private consultancy, as well as to all Government Departments.

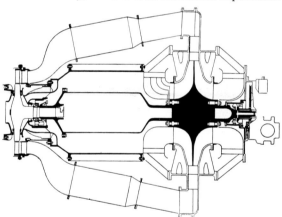

Fig. 5.—The W2Y direct-flow jet-unit which did not proceed beyond the drawing stage.

ROLLS-ROYCE.

ROLLS-ROYCE, LTD.

HEAD OFFICE: DERBY.

JET ENGINE DIVISION: BARNOLDSWICK.

Assistant Chief Engineer in charge of the Jet Engine Division: Dr. S. G. Hooker.

Development Engineer: J. P. Herriot.

It was in 1938 that Rolls-Royce first took an interest in jet-propulsion units for aircraft, and in 1939 the first design projects were made. In 1940 test work was begun on various components; facilities for manufacture at Derby were lent to Power Jets, Ltd., the producers of Air Commodore Whittle's type of jet-propulsion

engine; and the machining of such parts as supercharger casings and wheelcase, and the manufacture of turbine blades and all pumps were undertaken.

In June, 1941, a test plant was set up by Rolls-Royce at Derby for development work on compressors. At the end of 1941, under instructions from the Ministry of Aircraft Production, Rolls-Royce undertook the development and manufacture of the Whittle-type engine in conjunction with Power Jets, Ltd. and the Rover Company.

The first Rolls-Royce jet-propulsion engine known as the WR1 was designed for experimental test purposes, with low turbine blade stresses, i.e., a comparatively big engine for a given

thrust. Its diameter was 54 inches (1,376 m/m.) and the design thrust was 2,000 lb. (910 kg.). It only weighed 1,100 lb. (500 kg.) and the first engine ran for some 35 hours. Two of these were built, but trouble was experienced with the combustion equipment, so extensive development work on combustion chambers and turbine blades was carried out.

The restricting factor at the time was the construction of the turbine blades, due to limitations of temperature and r.p.m., but so much progress was made that Rolls-Royce was asked to take over the development and manufacture of the Whittle units

Meanwhile Rolls-Royce had converted a Vickers Wellington twin-engined bomber into a flying test-bed for the W2B/23 Whittle engine, which was mounted in the tail in place of the gun turret. The instrument panel was mounted forward in the aircraft, with remote control to the engine. Twenty-five hours flying was carried out with the first engine giving 1,250 lb. (565 kg.) thrust. A second Wellington was adapted for high altitude work at 35,000 ft. (10,675 m.) and this aircraft is still flying.

The first Rolls-Royce version of the Whittle W2B/23 jet-propulsion engine passed its 100-hour type test in April, 1943. It was 43 ins. (1,098 m/m.) in diameter and gave a thrust of 1,700 lb. (772 kg.) for a weight of 850 lb. (386 kg.). It was named the Welland, being the first of the Rolls-Royce "River" class of jet-propulsion engines, this name being chosen to give the idea of flow associated with jet-propulsion. Production deliveries of the Welland to the R.A.F. began in May, 1944, when this engine also passed its first 500-hour type test and went into service with 180 hours between overhauls.

Meanwhile the Gloster E.28/39 experimental jet-propelled monoplane was fitted with the Rolls-Royce engine in 1943 and the F9/40, the prototype of the Meteor, was fitted with two Welland engines.

In March, 1942, the Rover Company ran its prototype W2B/26 engine which was based on a Power Jets' design for a "direct-flow" combustion engine. The development of this engine was pursued by the Rover Company until Rolls-Royce took over the Rover factory at Barnoldswick in April, 1943. The W2B/26 served as the prototype for the Derwent I and the first Rolls-Royce engine of this type, completed in three and a half months, was on test in July, 1943. It passed its 100-hour type test at 2,000 lb. (910 kg.) in November, 1943, and in April, 1944, completed its first flight test. This engine was intended as a replacement for the Welland engine in the Gloster Meteor twin-jet fighter. The Meteor first flew with two Series I Derwent engines in March, 1944, each unit developing a thrust of 2,000 lb. (910 kg.) for a weight of 920 lb. (418 kg.).

The satisfactory performance of this new engine gave great promise for further development. A continuous programme, involving many 100-hour tests to a type-test schedule, was carried out, culminating in a successful 500-hour type-test without strip or major replacement of any kind.

The Derwent Series II engine gave a 10% improvement in thrust, delivering 2,200 lb. (1,000 kg.). The Series III was an experimental engine to provide suction on the wing surfaces for boundary layer removal. Series IV gave another 10% increase up to 2,400 lb. (1,090 kg.) thrust; and the Series V Derwent engine, which is fitted in the Gloster Meteor IV, is rated at 3,500 lbs. (1,590 kg.) thrust.

THE ROLLS-ROYCE DERWENT.

COMPRESSOR.—Single-stage double-entry centrifugal compressor with double-sided impeller 20.68 in. (525 mm.) in diameter. A 20-vane diffuser has a throat area of 38 sq. in. (245 sq. cm.) Compression ratio 3.9 : 1 static, at take-off. The compressor is mounted on the forward end of the shaft carrying the single-stage axial-flow turbine. The main shaft is carried on three bearings and is surrounded by the ten combustion chambers.

TURBINE.—Single-stage axial-flow turbine with 54 blades. Direction of rotation anti-clockwise (viewed from rear).

COMBUSTION CHAMBERS.—Ten straight flow-combustion chambers with internal concentrically-mounted domed colander flame tubes. Balance pipes are provided between the chambers to equalise pressure and to allow flames to ignite the fuel in adjoining flame tubes when starting up. Two igniter plugs (in chambers 3 and 10). Combustion is complete before the gases enter the turbine guide vane ring at the rear of the chambers.

FUEL SYSTEM.—An engine-driven positive-displacement multi-plunger swashplate pump, with built-in overspeed governor, draws fuel through a fabric-element low-pressure filter and delivers it to fixed orifice type burners, one in each combustion chamber, via a throttle control valve and ring manifold. The pump delivery pressure is controlled by a barostat relief valve, with setting dependent on atmospheric pressure, excess fuel from the barostat being delivered directly back to the aircraft tank. A combined shut-off cock accumulator and dump valve unit is fitted at the lowest point (inlet) of the fuel manifold, for stopping the engine. The accumulator supplies a metered quantity of fuel, at controlled pressure,

The Rolls-Royce Welland jet-propulsion engine. This engine, of the "reverse-flow" type, was originally designed by Power Jets, Ltd. After development by the Rover and Rolls-Royce companies, it was put into production by Rolls-Royce, Ltd.

to the burners during the starting cycle. The dump valve spills unwanted fuel to the atmosphere when the engine is being stopped and prevents the combustion chambers becoming flooded.

FUEL.—Aviation Kerosene (paraffin) to which has been added 1% of lubricating oil.

LUBRICATION SYSTEM.—The oil tank (22 pints capacity) is mounted on the engine wheelcase and its internal construction allows 15 seconds inverted flight without interruption of oil supply. The nominal oil circulation rate at maximum r.p.m. is 215 gallons (976 litres) per hour (minimum) and the nominal flow rates to front, centre and rear main bearings are 30, 50 and 70 gallons per hour respectively.

A gear-pump supplies pressure oil to the main bearings and wheel-case. The front bearings drain into the wheel-case, which is scavenged by the upper unit of a twin gear-type scavenge pump. The lower unit scavenges directly the centre and rear main bearings. The combined delivery from the twin scavenge pump is discharged into the tank, via an oil cooler, which is mounted on the engine compressor casing.

ACCESSORIES.—Engine accessories, including fuel and oil pumps, generator and accessory gear-boxes, are mounted on the wheelcase at the front of the engine, together with an electric starter motor.

MOUNTING.—Two trunnions are mounted on the horizontal centre-line of the compressor casing, and a torsionally-free diamond frame with link connections and two aircraft pick-up points is located 40 in. (1,006 mm.) aft of the two main trunnions.

HOUSING.—The whole engine is housed in a streamline cowling which has a large air intake in front and a projecting jet-pipe or propelling nozzle at the rear.

DIMENSIONS.—Maximum diameter 41.5 in. (1,055 mm.). Length over exhaust cone flange 84 in. (2,135 mm.), Length of jet pipe 38.5 in. (976 mm.), Diameter of propelling nozzle (internal) 13.08 in. (332 mm.).

WEIGHT.—Dry (including oil tank and cooler) 975 lbs. (442.6 kg.).

PERFORMANCE.—The following ratings were established in the official 100-hour Type Test of the Derwent engine I :—Take-off rating : Static thrust at sea-level 1,920-2,000 lbs. (870-910 kg.), Maximum r.p.m. 16,400-16,600. Cruising Rating : Static thrust at sea level 1,550 lbs. (705 kg.), Maximum r.p.m. 15,000. Idling Rating : Maximum static thrust at sea level 120 lbs. (55 kg.), r.p.m. 5,000-6,000.

FUEL CONSUMPTIONS.—At maximum static thrust (2,000 lbs. at 16,500 r.p.m.) 2,360 lbs./hr. (1,070 kg./hr.), Cruising (1,550 lbs., thrust at 15,400 r.p.m.) 1,820 lb./hr. (830 kg./hr.), Idling (120 lb. thrust at 5,500 r.p.m.) 470 lb./hr. (215 kg./hr.).

OIL CONSUMPTION.—Maximum, all conditions 1 pint/hr. (.568 litres/hr.).

THE ROLLS-ROYCE NENE.

The Nene, a parallel development of the Derwent which it resembles in general features and layout, was designed and built in 5½ months and was first run in October, 1944. This engine has flown in the Lockheed P-80 Shooting Star.

As with the Derwent, it has a double-entry centrifugal compressor, nine straight-through combustion chambers and a single-stage turbine.

Designed for a static thrust of 4,000 lbs. (1,820 kg.) at 12,300 r.p.m., performance was later improved and cleared for flight at 5,000 lbs. (2,270 kg.) at 12,400 r.p.m.

NET DRY WEIGHT.—1,600 lbs. (726 kg.).

DIMENSIONS.—Maximum diameter 49.5 in. (1,258 mm.), Overall length to exhaust cone flange 8 ft. 1 in. (2,960 mm.).

THE ROLLS-ROYCE TRENT.

The Trent is a modification of the Derwent arranged to drive a five-blade airscrew. It is being used for experimental work.

Two engines of this type have been flown in a Gloster Meteor, each developing 1,250 lbs. (570 kg.) thrust and 750 shaft horse-power.

The Rolls-Royce Derwent V Jet-propulsion engine. The Gloster Meteor IV fitted with two engines of this type holds the World's Speed Record with a speed of 606 m.p.h. (969.6 km.h.).

INTERNAL COMBUSTION ENGINES

A.B.C.

A.B.C. MOTORS, LTD.

HEAD OFFICE AND WORKS : A.B.C. WORKS, WALTON-ON-THAMES.
Established : 1910.
Managing Director : T. A. Dennis.

The first A.B.C. aircraft engines were produced in 1911 and were of the vertical and Vee type water-cooled. During the War 1914-18 the firm was responsible for the design of the A.B.C. Wasp and Dragonfly seven and fourteen-cylinder radials of 180 and 350 h.p. respectively, the first serious attempt to produce high-powered engines of this type.

In the inter-war period the company produced a series of horizontally-opposed air-cooled engines, of which the 34 h.p. Scorpion two-cylinder and the 75 h.p. Hornet four-cylinder engines were typical.

For some years the company has, at the request of the Air Ministry, been engaged in the development of auxiliary power-units. The latest unit of this type is described below.

THE A.B.C. TYPE II AUXILIARY POWER-UNIT.

The A.B.C. Auxiliary Power-Unit, Type II, comprises a horizontally-opposed twin-cylinder air-cooled four-stroke engine, driving a dynamotor and a gear-box by which the drive may be engaged with a re-fuelling pump, bilge-pump, and two air-compressors.

The unit is designed for installation in flying-boats, the generator being employed to maintain the accumulators in a charged condition, the re-fuelling pump to replenish the fuel tanks from an outside source of supply, the bilge-pump to remove any bilge water that may accumulate in the hull or floats, and the air-compressors to charge air-bottles for use with a gas-starter system.

The unit is fitted with a pulley starter, but the engine may also be started electrically be means of the dynamotor. The fuel supply may be taken from the main tanks, or from an independant source of supply, while the oil supplies for both the engine and pumps are contained in the base of the unit. Each cylinder of the engine is cooled by a fan, which blows air through a duct to a cowl covering the cylinder and cylinder-head fins. The unit may thus be installed in flying-boats fitted with air-cooled or liquid-cooled engines.

The engine is of the horizontally-opposed type and uses a three-throw crankshaft, which entirely avoids the rocking couple so prevalent in normally designed horizontally-opposed engines.

The engine speed is controlled within specified limits by a governor of the centrifugal type. Careful design and the use of light alloys where practicable, has produced a unit which is very compact, and of exceptionally light weight.

LEADING PARTICULARS.

ENGINE.—Bore 54 m/m., Stroke 38 m/m., Capacity 174 c.c., Compression Ratio 7 to 1, Normal R.P.M., 4,000, B.H.P. at Normal R.P.M. 5. Carburetter, Zenith Type 24UH. (Modified), Magneto B.T.H. Type MC.2-S1.

DYNAMOTOR.—A.M. Type 5U/824. Output 12 volts, 350 watts, or A.M. Type 5U/784. Output 24 volts, 350 watts. In addition to the above types, a 24-volt 1,000 watt dynamotor is now available.

AIR COMPRESSORS.—B.T.H. Type AW-1A or 1B. The two compressors are together capable of charging air bottles of 400 cu. in. capacity to a pressure of 200 lbs./sq. in. in 2.5 minutes.

REFUELLING PUMP.—Type: Eccentric rotor and vane. Duty: 2,000 gallons per hour with suction lift of 16 ft. and discharge head of 10 ft. through 1½ in. diameter pipes. Relief Valves set for 30 lbs./sq. in.

BILGE-PUMP.—Type: Eccentric rotor and vane. Duty: 2,500 gallons per hour with suction lift of 16 ft. through 1½ in. diameter pipes.

WEIGHT OF UNIT COMPLETE.—146 lbs. (66.3 kg.).

ALVIS.

ALVIS LTD.

HEAD OFFICE AND WORKS: COVENTRY.

Managing Director: A. E. Nicholson, J.P.

Chief Engineer: Capt. G. Smith-Clarke, M.I.Mech.E., M.I.A.E., M.S.A.E., A.F.R.Ae.S., M.S.I.A.

Alvis Limited, who are pioneers in the production of high-class motor cars, entered the aero-engine industry towards the end of 1935.

Its first products were the 1,060 h.p. Pelides fourteen-cylinder two-row radial, the Pelides-Major supercharged for medium and high-altitude respectively, and the 450 h.p. Leonides nine-cylinder radial supercharged for medium altitude. Both the Pelides and Leonides passed the British Air Ministry Civil Type Test. These three engines have been illustrated and described in previous issues of this Annual.

The Alvis company has been fully engaged on other aeronautical work of national importance throughout the war period, but further development of the Leonides engine is now recognised as an important part of the company's programme.

ASPIN.

F. M. ASPIN & CO., LTD.

HEAD OFFICE AND WORKS: ELTON, BURY, LANCASHIRE.

Managing Director: F. M. Aspin, M.S.A.E., M.Inst.B.E.

Directors: T. B. Aspin, W. R. Chown, L. Clough, E. Riddel and G. E. Varley.

This Company was formed during 1936 to build a new type of internal combustion engine, the departure from orthodox lines being primarily the valve gear. This new type of valve gear takes the form of a rotating cone-shaped valve for each cylinder. The valve embodies the combustion chamber, which is coupled to the periphery of the cone by a determined size of port which, as the valve rotates, uncovers in the cylinder head, the sparking plug, exhaust valve and inlet valve in rotation.

The Company has three engines in course of development, but work on them was interrupted during the war. The works were largely engaged on products of national importance and the development of engines for heavy transport.

THE ASPIN FLAT-FOUR.

TYPE.—Four-cylinder horizontally-opposed air-cooled, incorporating the Aspin patent rotary combustion chamber.

CYLINDERS.—Bore 4⅝ in. (117.5 m/m.), Stroke 3 in. (76.2 m/m.), Capacity 201.6 cub. ins. (3.26 litres), Compression Ratio 10 : 1. Machined from alloy-steel forgings, heat treated.

CYLINDER HEADS.—The steel heads house the rotary combustion chambers, or rotors, which also function as inlet and exhaust valves. The combustion chambers run on lead-bronze bearing faces. Uniting each pair of heads is a gear case, housing the skew gears which drive each rotor. The skew gear driving shafts are driven through a train of spur gears from the crankshaft and provide driving points for magneto and generator, etc.

PISTONS.—Aluminium-alloy, with three compression rings and one scraper ring. Fully-floating gudgeon-pin retained by circlips.

CONNECTING RODS.—Light alloy rods have pressure-fed bronze bushes in little-ends and split lead-bronze-lined bearings in big-ends.

CRANKSHAFT.—Machined from a one-piece forging in alloy steel with four throws and three main bearings. All journals hard chrome-plated. Spur gear to drive generator, magneto and rotary combustion chambers is attached to rear of crankshaft. Front end extends to take the airscrew-hub.

CRANKCASE.—Aluminium-alloy, split down its vertical centre. Internal webbing supports the three lead-bronze-lined main bearings.

CARBURATION.—One up-draught carburetter is attached to the base of sump. The induction system for the first part is cast integral with the sump and rises vertically to a central distribution point under oil level, where it branches four ways to sump walls and is picked up here by pipes to inlet point on each head.

IGNITION.—B.T.H. type CSE4-4.V Duplex magneto with impulse starter. Screened ignition is optional. Two 14 m/m. sparking-plugs per cylinder.

LUBRICATION.—Full pressure lubrication is provided to main bearings and connecting-rod bearings, also all plain bearings in auxiliary drives. The head lubrication is covered by a special control unit governed by engine running conditions. An oil baffle is provided between crankcase and sump, which has a capacity of 12 pints.

ACCESSORIES.—Standard equipment includes fuel-pump and tachometer drive. Provision is also made for the fitting of a generator and a starter which operates directly on the crankshaft. A further drive-point is provided for the fitting of a hydraulic pump, vacuum pump, or air-compressor.

DIMENSIONS.—Overall length 33 in. (839 m/m.), Width 32 in. (811 m/m.), Overall height 24½ in. (612 m/m.).

WEIGHT.—200 lbs. (90.8 kg.).

PERFORMANCE.—Normal output 100 h.p. at 2,500 r.p.m., Maximum power 114 h.p. at 2,800 r.p.m.

ARMSTRONG SIDDELEY.

ARMSTRONG SIDDELEY MOTORS LIMITED.

HEAD OFFICE AND WORKS: COVENTRY.

Directors: Sir Frank Spencer Spriggs, F.R.Ae.S. (Chairman), T. O. M. Sopwith, C.B.E., F.R.Ae.S., H. K. Jones (Managing), and Lt.-Col. The Hon. C. D. Siddeley.

Secretary: W. T. Johnson.

This Company, which forms part of the Hawker Siddeley Group, has over a period of years produced a comprehensive range of air-cooled aero-engines ranging in output from 85 to over 1,000 h.p.

During the war the company concentrated on the development and large-scale production of the Cheetah range, which has powered the majority of aircraft used in the advanced training of thousands of R.A.F. and R.C.A.F. aircrews in England and overseas. Over 35,000 Cheetah engines were built up to the end of the war in Europe and during these years the output of the Cheetah was increased from 375 h.p. to 475 h.p.

In spite of the arduous conditions imposed on engines used in training aircraft, the Cheetah was the first engine of its type to be approved by the Air Ministry to run 1,200 hours between overhauls, which put it in the forefront of its class for reliability and low operational costs.

Apart from aero-engine production Armstrong-Siddeley Motors, Ltd. manufactured during the war large quantities of tank gear boxes and torpedo propulsion units.

THE ARMSTRONG SIDDELEY COUGAR.

The Cougar is a nine-cylinder geared and moderately-supercharged radial air-cooled engine with an international rating of 690 h.p. at 2,500 r.p.m. at 6,000 ft. (1,830 m.) and a take-off output of 850 h.p. It has a bore and stroke of 5.5 in. × 5.5 in. (140 mm. × 140 mm.) and a capacity of 1,176 cu. in. (19.28 litres). The net dry weight is 1,050 lbs. (478 kg.)

THE ARMSTRONG SIDDELEY CHEETAH 25.

This, the latest version of the Cheetah is basically the same as the Mk. XV described hereunder, but has a higher take-off rating of 475 h.p. at 2,700 r.p.m. at sea level.

THE ARMSTRONG SIDDELEY CHEETAH XV.

TYPE.—Seven-cylinder medium-supercharged air-cooled radial.

CYLINDERS.—Bore 5.25 in. (133 m/m.), Stroke 5.5 in. (140 m/m.), Compression ratio 6.35/1. Swept volume 834 cub. in. (13.65 litres). Barrel machined from steel forging. Forged aluminium-alloy head shrunk and locked in position.

PISTONS.—One compression ring nearest crown, two 1° angle rings above gudgeon pin and double scraper ring nearest skirt. Fully-floating gudgeon pins retained in position by circlips.

CONNECTING RODS.—One master rod and six auxiliary rods are air-hardened steel stampings. Master-rod lined with lead-bronze and held on crankpin by four bolts, which also position four grooved anchor pins securing four auxiliary rods. Other two auxiliary rods secured by plain anchor pins pressed into master-rod caps and located by circlips. Auxiliary rods and gudgeon pin end of master rod have fixed bronze bushes.

CRANKSHAFT.—One-piece single-throw steel forging, with pendulum type damper fitted to each crank-web.

CRANKCASE.—Hiduminium R.R.50 casting or forging of barrel type, consisting of front cover, main case, induction case and rear cover. Rear cover carries magnetos and auxiliaries.

SUPERCHARGER.—Unit-mounted on rear crankcase flange. Impeller driven at 6.52 times crankshaft speed through spring-drive and centrifugal clutch gears mounted on diaphragm plate on rear of crankcase.

VALVE GEAR.—Fully-enclosed. One inlet and one sodium-cooled exhaust valve per cylinder. Valve-seats, of nickel-chrome-manganese steel with exhaust seat stellited on face, shrunk and screwed into head. Compensated rocket brackets on heads.

CARBURATION.—One Claudel-Hobson A.V. 70ME. master-control carburetter incorporating delayed-action acceleration pump, variable datum boost and mixture controls and slow-running cut-out. Hot oil circulates around chokes.

IGNITION.—Completely screened ignition system. Two B.T.H. SC7-2 magnetos mounted at 40 degrees on rear cover. Vernier adjustment for timing of each magneto incorporated on drives.

LUBRICATION.—Two-stage pump mounted on reduction-gear casing, incorporating pressure relief valve and filter of the fine mesh disc type. Crankcase oil jet supplies additional oil for cold starting.

AIRSCREW DRIVE.—Epicyclic reduction gear .732 : 1 ratio. Provision for Hydromatic constant-speed airscrew.

STARTER.—Hand/Electric.

ACCESSORY DRIVES.—Provision for 750 watt generator, hydraulic pump, air compressor and vacuum pump on auxiliary-drive box mounted on rear cover, which also incorporates two diaphragm fuel pumps.

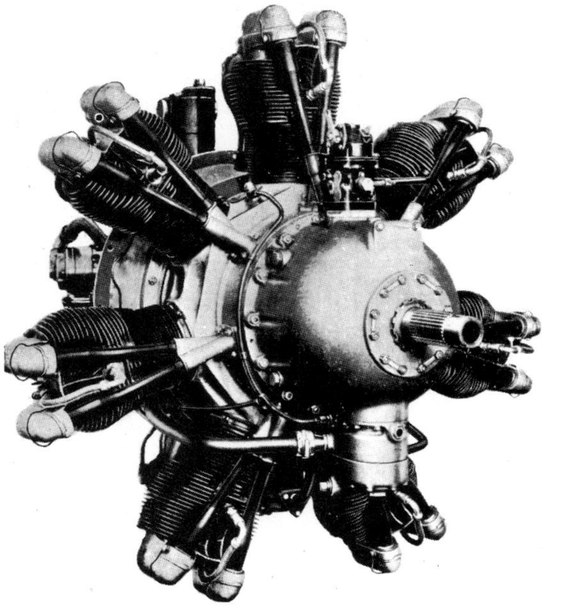

The 420 h.p. Armstrong Siddeley Cheetah XV engine.

A rear view of the 420 h.p. Armstrong Siddeley Cheetah XV engine.

DIMENSIONS.—Diameter overall 47.7 in. (1,210 m/m.), Length overall 49.6 in. (1,261 m/m.).

WEIGHT (Bare and dry).—805 lbs. (365.5 kg.) including carburetter, two magnetos, ignition harness and two fuel pumps.

PERFORMANCE.—Take-off output 420 h.p. at 2,550 r.p.m. at sea level, Maximum climb output 370 h.p. at 2,300 r.p.m. at 3,600 ft. (1,098 m.), Maximum power 400 h.p. at 2,425 r.p.m. at 4,000 ft. (1,220 m.), Economical cruising fuel consumption (87 Octane) 16/17 gallons/hr. Oil consumption 2¼-8 pints per hour.

THE ARMSTRONG SIDDELEY CHEETAH X.

AIRSCREW DRIVE.—Direct. Left-hand tractor. Fixed pitch or controllable-pitch airscrew may be used.

DIMENSIONS.—Diameter overall 47.7 in. (1.210 m.), Length overall 47.425 in. (1.204 m.).

WEIGHT (Bare and dry).—663 lbs. (301 kg.) including carburettor, two magnetos, ignition harness and two fuel pumps.

PERFORMANCE (with controllable-pitch airscrew).—Take-off output, 375 h.p. at 2,300 r.p.m., Rated power 325-340 h.p. at 2,300 r.p.m. at 6,750 ft. (2,058 m.), Maximum power 355 h.p. at 2,425 r.p.m. at 7,000 ft. (2,135 m.).

THE ARMSTRONG SIDDELEY CHEETAH IX.

AIRSCREW DRIVE.—Direct. Left-hand tractor.

DIMENSIONS.—Diameter overall 47.7 in. (1,210 m/m.), Length 52.9 in. (1,342 m/m.), Diameter of pitch circle of mounting bolt holes 25 in. (635 m/m.), 16 holes 13/32 in. diameter.

WEIGHT (Bare and dry).—635 lbs. (298 kg.) including carburettor, two magnetos, ignition harness and two fuel pumps.

PERFORMANCE.—Take-off 340 h.p., Rated power 310 h.p. at 2,100 r.p.m. at 6,000 ft. (1,829 m.), Maximum power 355 h.p. at 2,425 r.p.m. at 7,000 ft. (2,135 m.).

BRISTOL.

THE BRISTOL AEROPLANE CO., LTD.

HEAD OFFICE AND WORKS : FILTON, BRISTOL.

LONDON OFFICE : 6, ARLINGTON STREET, ST. JAMES'S, S.W.1.
Directors : W. G. Verdon Smith, C.B.E., J.P., (Chairman) ; Sir G. Stanley White, Bt., (Managing Director) ; H. J. Thomas, (Assistant Managing Director) ; George S. White ; N. R. Rowbotham, C.B.E., B.Sc. (Chief Engineer, Aero-Engine Division) and K. J. G. Bartlett (Sales Director).

The Bristol Aeroplane Co., Ltd. was originally founded in 1910 but it did not enter the aero-engine field until 1920, when an Aero-engine Department was established to design and manufacture radial air-cooled engines.

Its first engine was the famous Jupiter nine-cylinder radial which quickly established for the company a world-wide reputation. It was used in all types of military and civil aircraft and was built under licence in almost every country possessing suitable manufacturing facilities.

The Jupiter, a nine-cylinder air-cooled radial with compensated rocker mechanism, was developed through a long series. The Jupiter VII was the first model with mechanically driven supercharger and the Jupiter VIII the first model with reduction gear. The Jupiter was the first air-cooled engine to pass the Air Ministry full-throttle test, the first to employ automatic boost control and the first to be installed in air-liners. The Jupiter captured the World's Height Record in 1929.

The Jupiter was followed in 1927 by the Mercury and in 1932 by the Pegasus. The Mercury, developed for fighter aircraft, was similar to the supercharged Jupiter but was fitted with a reduction gear and had a shorter stroke. It was the first British aero-engine to be approved for controllable-pitch airscrews.

The Pegasus was also a development of the Jupiter. It progressed through many series, all fitted with superchargers and reduction gears. The Pegasus XVIII was the first Bristol engine to be fitted with a two-speed single-stage supercharger. The Pegasus gained three Height Records (1932-1936-1937), it was used for the first flight over Mt. Everest (1933) and attained the World's Long-Distance Record in 1938. The latest models have an output of over 1,000 h.p. as compared with the 450 h.p. of the original Jupiter of the same capacity. Pegasus and Perseus engines are the standard power units in the four-engined flying-boat fleet of the British Overseas Airways Corporation.

Concurrently with the steady development of poppet-valve engines, the Bristol company began research in 1926 with sleeve-valves and the first complete Bristol sleeve-valve engine—the Perseus was built in 1932. The Perseus was followed by the Aquila, Taurus, Hercules and Centaurus and development still proceeds. The Hercules has been in large scale production not only by the parent Company but also in various shadow factories, some operated under Bristol supervision.

The Perseus, a nine-cylinder radial with single-speed supercharger and reduction gear, initiated the use of an auxiliary gear-box for accessories. The Taurus, a fourteen-cylinder two-row radial with single-speed supercharger, has a smaller bore and stroke than the Perseus.

The Hercules has been developed through many series. In eight years its output has been increased from 1,375 h.p. to 1,800 h.p., a gain in power of over 30% which has been obtained at the expense of only about 10% increase in engine weight.

The Bristol Taurus fourteen-cylinder sleeve-valve engine.

The latest product of the company is the eighteen-cylinder Centaurus engine which covers the 2,500-3,500 h.p. range.

The company will later offer a development of the nine-cylinder Perseus engine using Centaurus instead of Hercules type cylinders and with a power of around 1,200 h.p., compared with the pre-war version which developed rather less than 1,000 h.p. A few details of this engine are included in the Table relating to sleeve-valve engines.

From the beginning of the re-armament programme in 1936 to the end of the European war, the Bristol company, its dispersal plants and shadow factories built over 101,000 engines, of which 57,400 were Hercules, 2,500 Centaurus, 20,700 Mercury and 14,400 Pegasus. In addition the company's service engineers repaired and put back into service during the war over 21,000 salvaged engines.

In the gas-turbine field the Bristol Aeroplane Co., Ltd. has concentrated on the evolution of a type of turbine in which the bulk of the power is used to drive a variable-pitch airscrew, while means are provided for the recuperation of heat energy which would otherwise be lost in the jet discharge. For details of this branch of the company's activities see pages 3-4d.

THE BRISTOL SLEEVE-VALVE ENGINES.

So long ago as 1926, the Bristol Aeroplane Co. foresaw the speed and load limitations which would eventually be met in high-performance engines which have push-rod operated over-head valves. The increasing seriousness of maintenance problems with this mechanism was also foreseen. With the encouragement and support of the British Air Ministry, the Company therefore decided to develop the single sleeve-valve.

The first complete Bristol sleeve-valve engine, a nine-cylinder air-cooled radial of 24.9 litres capacity, was designed and built in 1932. It completed its official trials with great success soon afterwards. This was the Perseus. With further development it was the first sleeve-valve aero-engine in the World to be put into large quantity manufacture.

The potential advantages of the sleeve-valve for high-output two-row radial engine design were also apparent. In 1936, the Bristol Hercules fourteen-cylinder radial sleeve-valve engine of 38.7 litres capacity appeared and this was followed by the Taurus, a similar but much smaller engine of 25.4 litres. The latest type is the Centaurus, an eighteen-cylinder development of the Hercules.

After the most thorough endurance and overload testing, which make up many thousands of hours on the dynamometer and in flight, and nearly six years of operational service in the Royal Air Force, Bristol sleeve-valve aero-engines have now definitely achieved a leading position.

Externally, the most impressive characteristics of these engines is the extreme cleanness and simplicity, which is the result of the entire absence of outside valve-gear, together with valve-maintenance routine.

All Bristol sleeve-valve engines have high-speed, centrifugal, gear-driven superchargers, either single or two-speed. The supercharger is associated with a carburetter of the latest fully automatic type, incorporating variable-datum servo devices for the control of both boost-pressure and mixture strength. Later production types employ pressure injection carburettors enabling a closer control of mixture strength under varying conditions and greater freedom from ice formation.

An installation feature of great importance is the arrangement of engine-driven accessories. The crankcase rear cover carries only those accessories which serve the engine unit itself, namely the engine oil pump, the dual fuel pump, the magnetos and the constant-speed airscrew governor unit. All other accessories are carried by a separate accessory gear-box mounted on the bulkhead and driven by the engine through an enclosed flexibly-jointed shaft.

Several alternative arrangements of the gear-box drives are available to provide for the full range of accessories involved in modern aircraft equipment. This arrangement considerably simplifies installation work, and also lends itself to the adoption of standardized, interchangeable power units—a policy long recommended by the Bristol Company.

THE BRISTOL CENTAURUS.

The Centaurus is the most powerful of the officially approved and issued types of British aero-engines. Originally type-tested in 1938, the Centaurus is capable of further development well beyond the present nominal power of 2,500 h.p. for take-off. With a swept volume of 53.6 litres, it has nearly 40% greater cylinder capacity than the Hercules although the overall diameter is only just over 6% greater.

The latest model in the Centaurus Series of which details

The Bristol Perseus nine-cylinder sleeve-valve engine.

The 2,500 h.p. Bristol Centaurus fourteen-cylinder two-row sleeve-valve engine.

were available at the time of writing was the CE.22 SM. This engine is a forward development of the Centaurus XVIII and 57 Series and is the prototype of the Centaurus 130 which will power the Airspeed Ambassador and other British civil transport aircraft.

The Centaurus 57 has a maximum power rating on 130 grade fuel of 2,475 h.p. for take-off, 2,560 h.p. at 4,250 ft. (1,300 m.) and 2,300 h.p. at 17,000 ft. (5,185 m.). With methanol-water injection the take-off power is increased to 2,800 h.p. and a corresponding increase is available for emergency level flight.

The Centaurus CE.22 SM, although type-tested initially at a rating corresponding to that of the 57, is designed for immediate development to 3,500 h.p. It has a single-stage two-speed supercharger and direct fuel-injection.

The Centaurus 130 will normally have a single-stage super-charger but the two-speed version will be available, and the engine is designed to facilitate the application of other develop-ments in supercharging and fuel systems. The airscrew reduction gear will be suitable for reversing airscrews and an alternative reduction gear can be provided for counter-rotating airscrews if required.

Particular attention has been paid to obtaining the cleanest possible cowl lines, both externally and internally, and with this object a rear-swept exhaust system of individual pipes has been introduced, thereby doing away with the parasitic drag of the conventional large external exhaust manifold.

The nose cowl has been designed to reduce entry loss to a minimum and the airscrew spinner line is carried rearward to the cylinder base by means of a fairing over the reduction gear, so as to permit the use of a cooling-fan if required.

In accordance with Bristol practice, provision is made to drive a number of aircraft accessories by means of a separate gear-box of varying capacity.

TYPE.—Eighteen-cylinder two-row air-cooled sleeve-valve radial with two-speed supercharger.

CYLINDER ASSEMBLY.—Bore 5.75 in. (146 m/m.), Stroke 7 in. (178 m/m.), Swept Volume 3,270 cu. in. (53.6 litres). Open-ended barrels, with deep closely-pitched fins, machined from solid. Each barrel retained by sixteen large-diameter securing studs, the nuts for which are locked by spring locking plates. Cylinder heads of two-piece type, with screwed-in spark plug adaptors and provision for fitting of thermocouples.

SLEEVE-DRIVE.— See Hercules.

PISTONS.—Each piston is fitted with two wedge-section gas rings, a channel section scraper-ring, and a normal type bottom scraper ring. Fully-floating gudgeon pins retained by circlips.

CRANKCASE.—The main case is in three sections of forged aluminium-alloy. The front, centre and rear sections are bolted together, the joints being on the vertical centre-line of the cylinders. The bolts for the rear section are made long enough also to secure the blower casing. Each section carries a housing for a crankshaft main bearing, and the front and rear sections also contain roller bearings for the front and rear sleeve-cranks. These sections also carry the sleeve crank gear-trains for their respective cylinder banks. The front cover encloses the front bank sleeve-drive mechanism, carrying nine plain bearings for the forward ends of the sleeve cranks, and locating the three layshafts for the inter-mediate wheels of the sleeve crank gear-trains. A pressure oil supply to the sleeve cranks is provided through integral passages to the plain bearings. A crankshaft main bearing of the parellel roller-type is fitted in the centre bore of the casting. An airscrew constant-speed unit is mounted at the top of the front cover, and driven through an auxiliary gear train off the sleeve-valve train. Oil passages drilled in the casting supply oil to the unit, and also lead the high-pressure delivery oil to the reduction-gear case. The rear cover carries drives for the magnetos and auxiliary drive. The starter, which is arranged in a vertical position, drives the crankshaft through bevel gears. An auxiliary-drive facing to supply power for a separate accessory gearbox is provided and has a capacity of 30 h.p.

CRANKSHAFT.—Built-up in three sections, the front and rear portions being attached to the centre section by maneton joints, each secured by two bolts. The shaft runs in three high-capacity main bearings of the spherical roller, self-aligning pattern. Shrunk on to the two crankpins are white-metalled sleeves which form the big-end bearings. They are lubricated by pressure oil through drilled passages in the crankshaft. Each of the two balance weights contain two vibrations damping units of the Salomon pattern. Three oil jets are also provided in the crankshaft, one in each balance-weight and one in the centre section. This latter sprays oil on to the centre main bearing, while the other two lubricate the pistons and sleeves of their respective cylinder banks.

CONNECTING RODS.—An articulated connecting-rod system is employed for each bank of cylinders. Pressure lubrication of the wrist-pin bearings is provided through an oil retainer, while the small ends are supplied by splash lubrication and the balance-weight oil jets. Oil retainers are fitted at each side of the big-end assemblies to control the rate of leakage and to ensure that full oil pressure is maintained in the bearings.

REDUCTION GEAR.—Epicyclic bevel unit with a ratio of 0.44 to 1. Power from the crankshaft is transmitted to the rear bevel wheel through a toothed coupling, and the wheel is positioned by a ball thrust-bearing located in a spherical seating. The airscrew shaft has three trunnion arms, which carry the bevel pinions. Lead bronze bushes are pressed into the bores of the pinions and longitud-inal location is achieved by ball thrust-bearings secured on the ends of the trunnion arms. The front bevel wheel is stationary, being secured to the reduction gear case by a toothed coupling, and located on a spherical seating. As both front and rear wheels are able to tip slightly, the load is distributed evenly over the three pinions regardless of manufacturing tolerances. The airscrew shaft runs on two bearings, the rear comprising a lead-bronze sleeve pressed into the end of the crankshaft, and the front a large ball bearing which also takes airscrew thrust. An oil transfer sleeve is arranged on the airscrew shaft to transmit oil from the constant-speed unit to the airscrew through the hollow forward end of the shaft. The supercharger gear-ratio control valve is located in the top of the crankcase rear cover and is supplied, and delivers, through internal oil passages in the casting.

SUPERCHARGER.—The centrifugal supercharger uses a double-shrouded light alloy impeller which is carried on a shaft supported by two ball bearings, of which the front is self-aligning and the rear of normal pattern. Two blower gear ratios available, selection being by two compound hydraulic clutches. The oil for clutch actuation passes through two centrifuges. The units are located at the top of the blower casing and are readily accessible for cleaning. The clutches are driven by a spring-drive gear on the crankshaft, this unit protecting the drive from cyclic torque variations.

OIL SUMP.—The oil sump is a large capacity casting bolted on to the underside of the supercharger. It has an easily accessible oil

filter, and carries the petrol and oil pumps which are driven by shafts powered from the rear-cover gear trains. This arrangement ensures that the scavenge oil pump is always submerged. A small gear-driven scavenge oil pump is fitted in the base of the front cover casting and is driven off the sleeve-crank train. Its purpose is to remove surplus oil from the forward end of the engine, and return it to the sump through an external pipe.

WEIGHTS AND PERFORMANCE.—See Table.

THE BRISTOL HERCULES.

The most widely-used versions of the Hercules during the war were the VI and XVI Series which powered the Stirling III and

IV, Halifax III and VII and Lancaster II four-engined bombers, the Wellington X twin-engined bomber and the Beaufighter VI twin-engined fighter.

The Hercules XVII and XVIII engines differ from the XVI in having cropped supercharger-impellers, giving an increase in power for take-off and low-altitude work, and were installed in Beaufighter and Wellington aircraft serving with Coastal Command.

The Hercules 100, the successor to the Hercules XVI and XVII Series, embodies a number of technical improvements, of which the chief is a two-speed supercharger of greater efficiency, whereby the maximum power rating has been increased by

Two views of the 1,675 h.p. Bristol Hercules XVI fourteen-cylinder two-row sleeve-valve engine.

Two views of the 1,800 h.p. Bristol Hercules 100 fourteen-cylinder two-row sleeve-valve engine.

The Bristol Hercules 100 low-drag Power-unit ready for installation in an aeroplane.

BRISTOL SLEEVE-VALVE ENGINES.

	Bore and Stroke	Capacity	Gear Ratio	Diameter	Weight (dry)	Take-off Power	Maximum Power for all-out level flight for 5 mins.	Normal Climb	Maximum Economical Cruising	Octane No. and Grade
Hercules XI	5¾ in. × 6½ in. (146 m/m. × 165 m/m.)	2,360 cu. in. (38.7 litres)	0.44 : 1	52 in. (1.32 m.)	1,870 lbs. (849 kg.)	1,590 h.p. at 2,900 r.p.m.	1,315 h.p. at 2,800 r.p.m. at S/L and 1,460 h.p. at 2,800 r.p.m. at 9,500 ft. (2,900 m.)	1,315 h.p. at 2,500 r.p.m. at 2,000 ft. (610 m.) and 1,185 h.p. at 2,500 r.p.m. at 12,750 ft. (3,890 m.)	1,020 h.p. at 2,500 r.p.m. at 7,500 ft. (2,290 m.) and 920 h.p. at 2,500 r.p.m. at 17,750 ft. (5,260 m.)	100/130
Hercules VI and XVI	5¾ in. × 6½ in. (146 m/m. × 165 m/m.)	2,360 cu. in. (38.7 litres)	0.44 : 1	52 in. (1.32 m.)	1,930 lbs. (875 kg.)	1,615 h.p. at 2,900 r.p.m.	1,675 h.p. at 2,900 r.p.m. at 4,500 ft. (1,370 m.) and 1,445 h.p. at 2,900 r.p.m. at 12,000 ft. (3,660 m.)	1,355 h.p. at 2,400 r.p.m. at 4,750 ft. (1,450 m.) and 1,240 h.p. at 2,400 r.p.m. at 12,000 ft. (3,660 m.)	1,050 h.p. at 2,400 r.p.m. at 10,250 ft. (3,130 m.) and 955 h.p. at 2,400 r.p.m. at 17,750 ft. (5,260 m.)	100/130
Hercules VII and XVII	5¾ in. × 6½ in. (146 m/m. × 165 m/m.)	2,360 cu. in. (38.7 litres)	0.44 : 1	52 in. (1.32 m.)	1,915 lbs. (868 kg.)	1,725 h.p. at 2,900 r.p.m.	1,735 h.p. at 2,900 r.p.m. at 500 ft. (152 m.)	1,395 h.p. at 2,400 r.p.m. at 1,500 ft. (460 m.)	1,085 h.p. at 2,400 r.p.m. at 7,000 ft. (2,135 m.)	100/130
Hercules XVIII	5¾ in. × 6½ in. (146 m/m. × 165 m/m.)	2,360 cu. in. (38.7 litres)	0.44 : 1	52 in. (1.32 m.)	1,930 lbs. (875 kg.)	1,725 h.p. at 2,900 r.p.m.	1,735 h.p. at 2,900 r.p.m. at 500 ft. (152 m.)	1,395 h.p. at 2,400 r.p.m. at 1,500 ft. (460 m.) and 1,300 h.p. at 2,400 r.p.m. at 8,250 ft. (2,520 m.)	1,085 h.p: at 2,400 r.p.m. at 7,000 ft. (2,135 m.) and 1,010 h.p. at 2,400 r.p.m. at 13,500 ft. (4,120 m.)	100/130
Hercules 100	5¾ in. × 6½ in. (146 m/m. × 165 m/m.)	2,360 cu. in. (38.7 litres)	0.44 : 1	52 in. (1.32 m.)	1,990 lbs. (903 kg.)	1,675 h.p. at 2,800 r.p.m.	1,800 h.p. at 2,800 r.p.m. at 9,000 ft. (2,745 m.) and 1,625 h.p. at 2,800 r.p.m. at 19,500 ft. (5,950 m.)	1,515 h.p. at 2,400 r.p.m. at 7,750 ft. (2,365 m.) and 1,415 h.p. at 2,400 r.p.m. at 16,500 ft. (5,030 m.)	1,215 h.p. at 2,400 r.p.m. at 12,250 ft. (3,740 m.) and 1,125 h.p. at 2,400 r.p.m. at 21,000 ft. (6,405 m.)	100/130
Hercules 120	5¾ in. × 6½ in. (146 m/m. × 165 m/m.)	2,360 cu. in. (38.7 litres)	0.44 : 1	52 in. (1.32 m.)	1,970 lbs. (894 kg.)	1,675 h.p. at 2,800 r.p.m.	1,775 h.p. at 2,800 r.p.m. at 6,750 ft. (2,060 m.) and 1,330 h.p. at 2,800 r.p.m. at 27,500 ft. (8,390 m.)	—	*1,015 h.p. at 2,000 r.p.m. at 7,250 ft. (2,210 m.) and 915 h.p. at 2,000 r.p.m. at 18,250 ft. (5,570 m.)	100/130
Hercules 130	5¾ in. × 6½ in. (146 m/m. 165 m/m.)	2,360 cu. in. (38.7 litres)	0.44 : 1	52 in. (1.32 m.)	1,870 lbs. (849 kg.)	1,675 h.p. at 2,800 r.p.m.	1,775 h.p. at 2,800 r.p.m. at 7,250 ft. (2,210 m.)	1,550 h.p. at 2,400 r.p.m. at 4,750 ft. (1,450 m.)	*1,040 h.p. at 2,000 r.p.m. at 6,750 ft. (2,060 m.)	100/130
Taurus XII and XVII	5 in. × 5⅝ in. (127 m/m. × 143 m/m.)	1,550 cu. in. (25.4 litres)	0.44 : 1	46¼ in. (1.175 m.	1,335 lbs. (606 kg.)	1,085 h.p. at 3,100 r.p.m.	1,130 h.p. at 3,100 r.p.m. at 3,500 ft. (1,070 m.)	980 h.p. at 2,800 r.p.m. at 3,750 ft. (1,145 m.)	700 h.p. at 2,500 r.p.m. at 7,250 ft. (2,210 m.)	100/130
Perseus XII	5¾ in. × 6½ in. (146 m/m. × 165 m/m.)	1,520 cu. in. (24.9 litres)	0.5 : 1	52 in. (1.32 m.)	1,105 lbs. (501 kg.)	830 h.p. at 2,650 r.p.m.	905 h.p. at 2,750 r.p.m. at 6,500 ft. (1,980 m.)	745 h.p. at 2,400 r.p.m. at 6,500 ft. (1,980 m.)	620 h.p. at 2,400 r.p.m. at 10,000 ft. (3,050 m.)	87
Perseus XIIC	5¾ in. × 6½ in. (146 m/m. × 165 m/m.)	1,520 cu. in. (24.9 litres)	0.5 : 1	52 in. (1.32 m.)	1,110 lbs. (503 kg.)	855 h.p. at 2,700 r.p.m.	815 h.p. at 2,600 r.p.m. at 6,000 ft. (1,830 m.)	680 h.p. at 2,250 r.p.m. at 4,000 ft. (1,220 m.)	* 550 h.p. at 2,200 r.p.m. at 8,750 ft. (2,670 m.)	87
Perseus XVI	5¾ in. × 6½ in. (146 m/m. × 165 m/m.)	1,520 cu. in. (24.9 litres)	0.5 : 1	52 in. (1.32 m.)	1,140 lbs. (517.5 kg.)	905 h.p. at 2,750 r.p.m.	955 h.p. at 2,750 r.p.m. at 5,000 ft. (1,525 m.)	745 h.p. at 2,400 r.p.m. at 6,500 ft. (1,980 m.)	560 h.p. at 2,200 r.p.m. at 9,000 ft. (2,745 m.)	87
Perseus 100	5¾ in. × 7 in. (146 m/m. × 178 m/m.)	1,635 cu. in. (26.8 litres)	0.5 : 1	55.3 in. (1.405 m.)	1,380 lbs. (626 kg.)	1,175 h.p. at 2,700 r.p.m.	1,200 h.p. at 2,700 r.p.m. at 4,250 ft. (1,296 m.)	1,025 h.p. at 2,400 r.p.m. at 7,500 ft. (2,290 m.)	* 650 h.p. at 2,000 r.p.m. at 10,000 ft. (3,050 m.)	100/130
Centaurus XI	5¾ in. × 7 in. (146 m/m. × 178 m/m.)	3,270 cu. in. (53.6 litres)	0.4 : 1	55.3 in. (1.405 m.)	2,695 lbs. (1222.5 kg.)	2,520 h.p at 2,700 r.p.m.	2,520 h.p. at 2,700 r.p.m. at 1,000 ft. (305 m.) and 2,225 h.p. at 2,700 r.p.m. at 11,000 ft. (3,355 m.)	2,150 h.p. at 2,400 r.p.m. at 3,000 ft. (915 m.) and 1,975 h.p. at 2,400 r.p.m. at 12,750 ft. (3,890 m.)	1,670 h.p. at 2,400 r.p.m. at 8,500 ft. (2,590 m.) and 1,530 h.p. at 2,400 r.p.m. at 18,000 ft. (5,490 m.)	100/130

* Recommended maximum continuous cruising for civil operation.

Note :—1. Mark numbers of Bristol engines up to XX are distinguished by Roman numbers. All marks above XX are in Arabic numerals.
2. Hercules XVII and XVIII engines differ from the XVI in having a cropped supercharger impeller, giving an increase in power for take-off and low-altitude work. Moreover, as the Hercules XVII is intended only for operation at comparatively low altitudes the two-speed supercharger is locked in the "M" gear and the centrifuges are consequently removed. In the Hercules XVIII both ratios are available and centrifugers are fitted as usual.

over 10% B.H.P. and 60% in altitude at the same boost pressure compared with the previous series. The Hercules 100 also introduces the rear-swept exhaust system of individual pipes, thus replacing the leading-edge exhaust collector ring which was standard on earlier Hercules engines. This engine develops 1,625 B.H.P. at 19,500 ft. (5,950 m.), combined with a take-off power of 1,675 B.H.P. and a maximum power of 1,800 B.H.P. at 9,000 ft. (2,745 m.).

The Hercules 120, a civil engine, is similar to the 100 in general design, but the drive provided in the back of the engine for coupling to an auxiliary gear box for the aircraft accessory services is, in this case, of specially large power capacity to cater for driving cabin superchargers in aircraft to be operated at very high altitudes. At the same time, the engine supercharger itself has been modified so that the optimum altitude for continuous economic cruising is over 25,000 ft. (7.625 m.), compared with 21,000 ft. (6,405 m.), for the Hercules 100, while retaining the same power for take-off.

The Hercules 130, also a civil engine, is intended for aircraft operating mainly at moderate altitudes, for which a single-speed supercharger is sufficient, with consequent simplification in design and appreciable saving in weight. Otherwise, it is the same as Hercules 100 and maintains substantially the same power up to 7,250 ft. (2,210 m.).

The Hercules HE.20 SM is a forward development of the Hercules 100, 120 and 130 Series and is the prototype of the Hercules 200 and 230 engines. The HE.20 SM has been type-tested at more than 2,500 h.p. This engine has direct-fuel injection and is equipped for methanol-water injection.

TYPE.—Fourteen-cylinder sleeve-valve two-row radial air-cooled.

CYLINDERS.—Bore 5¾ in. (146 m/m.), Stroke 6½ in. (165 m/m.), Capacity 2,360 cub. in. (38.7 litres). Open-ended barrel machined from a light alloy forging with deep-pitch fins, extra deep at exhaust zone. Barrel attached to crankcase by twelve studs. Cylinder, or junk, head is a heavily-finned Y-alloy die-casting and is recessed into the barrel with clearance between head and inner surface of cylinder for upward movement of sleeve. Recessed portion of head provided with oil reservoir grooves and wedge-section scraper rings with interlocking joints. Relief valve for release of oil trapped by sleeve. Head attached to barrel by twelve studs.

SLEEVE AND SLEEVE DRIVE.—Nitrided steel sleeve with four ports to admit and expel charge as they register with corresponding ports in cylinder barrel. Sleeves driven at half engine speed by system of cranks and gears off forward end of main crankshaft. Each sleeve provided, at its lower end, with a spherically-seated phosphor-bronze bearing in which crankpin of sleeve drive is free to slide and rotate. Ball bearings for sleeve cranks housed seven in each front and centre section of crankcase. Pressure-lubricated sleeve crank journals and ball-joints. Sludge trap in hollow crankpins.

PISTONS.—Light alloy, with flat crown and short skirts. Two compression rings and two scraper rings, one above and one below gudgeon-pin. Fully-floating gudgeon-pins retained by circlips.

CONNECTING RODS.—One-piece master-rod and six identical articulated rods in each cylinder bank. All machined and polished high-tensile stampings. Big-end bushes are white-metalled sleeves shrunk on crankpins. Pressure-lubricated case-hardened wrist-pins secured and located in master-rod by circlips and locating flanges.

CRANKSHAFT.—Three-piece two-row shaft with torsional and flexural vibration eliminators, on three main self-aligning roller bearings, the centre-bearing split-sleeve mounted and threaded on to shaft. Twin-bolt clamp at front end for torque transmission to airscrew. Piston temperature-control oil spray jets in each balance-weight.

CRANKCASE.—Forged light alloy, in three main sections split on centre-lines of each bank of cylinders. Crankshaft main bearings in each section. Ball bearings for sleeve cranks in front and centre sections.

SUPERCHARGER.—Centrifugal two-speed type, gear-driven through three hydraulically-operated clutches from a torsion shaft splined into the rear of the crankshaft. Dynamically-balanced forged light alloy shrouded impeller in aluminium-alloy casing with intregral diffuser vanes.

INDUCTION.—Downdraught carburetter with variable-datum servos for control of both boost pressure and mixture strength. Latest production types employ pressure-injection carburation enabling a closer control of mixture strength under varying operating conditions and greater freedom from ice formation.

IGNITION.—Completely screened dual ignition by two transversely-mounted magnetos firing two plugs in each cylinder head. Magneto drive incorporates variable timing device interconnected with carburetter to ensure automatically best ignition setting for every throttle position.

LUBRICATION.—Main pressure feed at 80 lbs./sq. in. with device to

The Bristol Hercules 130 civil-rated engine. The rear-swept exhaust system employed in the 100 Series is well-shown in this uncowled view.

permit increase to 200 lbs./sq. in. for rapid opening to full power and automatically returning to normal when warmed up. Feed and scavenge pump combined in one unit. Scavenge pump 25% oversize and pressure-primed by feed pump.

AIRSCREW DRIVE.—Bevel epicyclic type reduction gear concentric with airscrew shaft. For reduction gear ratios see Table. Provision for constant speed airscrews of Hydromatic or electrically-operated type.

ACCESSORY DRIVES.—Rear cover carries main engine accessories only. Drive to gearbox carrying aircraft accessories.

MOUNTING.—Special complete power-unit mounting may be provided. This includes circular fireproof bulkhead rigidly supported in mounting structure forward of the four main airframe pick-up points. On bulkhead, carried in standard position to ensure

interchangeability of power-units, are union connections for fuel pipes, oil supply and return pipes, oil tank vent, primer boost gauge, fire-extinguisher system and cabin heater supply and return pipes. Electric junction boxes for starter, ignition cut-out, fuel pressure transmitter and pyrometer cable. Provision in main box for connections of electric circuits of cowling gill motor, tacho-meter and other variable items such as fully-feathering or constant-speed airscrews, cowling gill position indicator and booster coil. Standard positions used for connections of Worth oil-dilution system and thermometer and pressure gauge capillaries. Opening on starboard side of bulkhead for hydraulic and pneumatic accessories panel to be supplied by airframe manufacturer. Mounted on port side of bulkhead is engine control box to which all control rods from cockpit are connected. The complete unit includes

BRISTOL POPPET-VALVE ENGINES

	PEGASUS XC	PEGASUS 22	PEGASUS XVIII	PEGASUS XVIII	MERCURY XV and 25	MERCURY XV and 25	MERCURY XX and 30
No. of Cylinders ..	9	9	9	9	9	9	9
Bore	5¾ in. (146 m/m.)	5¾ in. (146 m/m.)	5¾ in. (146 m/m.)	5¾ in. (146 m/m.)	5¾ in. (146 m/m.)	5¾ in. (146 m/m.)	5¾ in. (146 m/m.)
Stroke ..	7½ in. (190.5 m/m.)	7½ in. (190.5 m/m.)	7½ in. (190.5 m/m.)	7½ in. (190.5 m/m.)	6½ in. (165 m/m.)	6½ in. (165 m/m.)	6½ in. (165 m/m.)
Capacity	1,753 cu. in. (28.7 litres)	1,753 cu. in. (28.7 litres)	1,753 cu. in. (28.7 litres)	1,753 cu. in. (28.7 litres)	1,520 cu. in. (24.9 litres)	1,520 cu. in. (24.9 litres)	1,520 cu. in. (24.9 litres)
Gear Ratio ..	0.5 : 1	0.5 : 1	0.5 : 1	0.5 : 1	0.5 : 1	0.5 : 1	0.5 : 1
Diameter ..	55.3 in. (1.405 m.)	55.3 in. (1.405 m.)	55.3 in. (1.405 m.)	55.3 in. (1.405 m.)	51.5 in. (1.307 m.)	51.5 in. (1.307 m.)	51.5 in. (1.307 m.)
Weight (Bare Dry) ..	1,050 lbs. (476.7 kg.)	1,105 lbs. (501.6 kg.)	1,180 lbs. (535.7 kg.)	1,180 lbs. (535.7 kg.)	1,065 lbs. (483.5 kg.)	1,065 lbs. (483.5 kg.)	1,065 lbs. (483.5 kg.)
Octane No. ..	87	87	87	100	87	100	87
Take-off Power ..	920 h.p. at 2,475 r.p.m.	1,010 h.p. at 2,600 r.p.m.	965 h.p. at 2,475 r.p.m.	1,050 h.p. at 2,600 r.p.m.	725 h.p. at 2,650 r.p.m.	905 h.p. at 2,650 r.p.m.	820 h.p. at 2,650 r.p.m.
Maximum Power (all-out level flight for 5 mins.)	830 h.p. at 2,600 r.p.m. at 5,250 ft. (1,600 m.)	865 h.p. at 2,600 r.p.m. at 6,500 ft. (1,980 m.)	1,000 h.p. at 2,600 r.p.m. at 3,000 ft. (915 m.) and 885 h.p. at 2,600 r.p.m. at 15,500 ft. (4,730 m.)	1,065 h.p. at 2,600 r.p.m. at 1,250 ft. (380 m.) and 965 h.p. at 2,600 r.p.m. at 13,000 ft. (3,965 m.)	840 h.p. at 2,750 r.p.m. at 14,000 ft. (4,270 m.)	995 h.p. at 2,750 r.p.m. at 9,250 ft. (2,820 m.)	870 h.p. at 2,650 r.p.m. at 4,500 ft. (1,370 m.)
Normal Climb ..	815 h.p. at 2,475 r.p.m. at 4,500 ft. (1,370 m.)	825 h.p. at 2,250 r.p.m. at 4,000 ft. (1,220 m.)	815 h.p. at 2,250 r.p.m. at 4,750 ft. (1,450 m.) and 750 h.p. at 2,250 r.p.m. at 14,750 ft. (4,500 m.)	815 h.p. at 2,250 r.p.m. at 4,750 ft. (1,450 m.) and 750 h.p. at 2,250 r.p.m. at 14,750 ft. (4,500 m.)	825 h.p. at 2,650 r.p.m. at 13,000 ft. (3,965 m.)	825 h.p. at 2,650 r.p.m. at 13,000 ft. (3,965 m.)	810 h.p. at 2,400 r.p.m. at 2,500 ft. (760 m.)
Maximum Economical Cruising ..	575 h.p. at 2,200 r.p.m. at 9,250 ft. (2,820 m.)	680 h.p. at 2,250 r.p.m. at 8,000 ft. (2,440 m.)	645 h.p. at 2,250 r.p.m. at 9,500 ft. (2,900 m.) and 585 h.p. at 2,250 r.p.m. at 20,000 ft. (6,100 m.)	645 h.p. at 2,250 r.p.m. at 9,500 ft. (2,900 m.) and 585 h.p. at 2,250 r.p.m. at 20,000 ft. (6,100 m.)	590 h.p. at 2,400 r.p.m. at 16,000 ft. (4,880 m.)	590 h.p. at 2,400 r.p.m. at 16,000 ft. (4,880 m.)	605 h.p. at 2,400 r.p.m. at 9,250 ft. (2,820 m.)

NOTE.—Mark numbers of Bristol engines up to XX are distinguished by Roman numbers. All marks above XX are in Arabic numerals.

Front and rear views of the 1,000 h.p. Bristol Pegasus nine-cylinder radial air-cooled engine.

The Bristol Mercury nine-cylinder radial engine.

cowling, exhaust system, air intakes, etc., ready for installation in airframe. Provision for complete shrouding of exhaust system for night flying.

DIMENSIONS, WEIGHT AND PERFORMANCE.—See Table.

THE BRISTOL PEGASUS AND MERCURY ENGINES.

The latest types of this famous series of Bristol poppet-valve radial air-cooled engines are given in the table on the next page. The Mercury types have shorter stroke than the Pegasus types, and are therefore more compact and of less overall diameter. (Where more than one type number is shown under one heading, the only difference between the engines concerned is in the airscrew reduction gear ratio.)

The following general description is common to all types.

CYLINDERS.—Open-ended barrel machined from an alloy steel forging. Bores surface-hardened. Forged aluminium-alloy heads shrunk and locked in position.

PISTONS.—Full-skirted type. Machined inside and outside from aluminium-alloy forgings. One single and one double scraper ring and two gas rings. Robust fully-floating, case-hardened gudgeon pins.

CONNECTING RODS.—I-section, machined from alloy steel stampings.

CRANKSHAFT.—Two-piece, machined from alloy steel stampings. Front half, which incorporates large-diameter crank-pin, is surface-hardened all over. Separate tail-shaft for auxiliary drives. Carried on two main roller-bearings, with a deep-groove journal-bearing at the reduction end and steadying bearing in rear.

CRANKCASE.—Machined from aluminium-alloy forgings, split on centre-line of cylinders and held with nine through-bolts.

VALVE GEAR.—Two inlet and two sodium-cooled stellited exhaust valves and stellited seats per cylinder. Clearances between rockers and valves automatically compensated for expansion. A two-row cam runs concentric with the crankshaft in front of the crank at one-eighth engine speed in an anti-crank direction. It operates the tappets through rollers on floating bronze bushes, and thence by push-rods enclosed in oval tubes.

CARBURATION.—Claudel-Hobson carburettor, with delayed action acceleration pump, variable datum automatic boost and mixture control and slow-running cut-out. Controllable hot and cold air-intakes. Hot oil circulated round chokes.

SUPERCHARGER.—High-speed centrifugal type. Driven off crankshaft through spring-drive and automatic centrifugal clutches. Aluminium-alloy supercharger casing with integral diffuser vanes. Aluminium-alloy volute casing. Whole unit mounted behind rear wall of crankcase on nine crankcase bolts. The two-speed supercharger fitted to the Pegasus XVIII embodies a change-speed gear, which comprises three hydraulic clutch units, actuated by oil from the main pressure lubrication system.

IGNITION.—Dual ignition by two B.T.H. or Rotax magnetos transversely mounted on rear cover and driven by bevel gearing from crankshaft. Variable-timing device interconnected with carburetter to give best setting for various throttle openings. Completely screened ignition system.

LUBRICATION.—Dry sump, with pressure feed. Duplex gear pump incorporates pressure and scavenge units in one assembly. Separate feed and scavenge filters. Special device provides high initial oil pressure for rapid opening to full power.

AIRSCREW DRIVE.—For reduction ratios see Table. Self-centralising bevel-epicycle gear. All bearings pressure-lubricated. Airscrew shafts suitable for either fixed or controllable-pitch hubs. Oil-transfer housing and internal oil-seal provided for Hamilton pitch-control mechanism.

ACCESSORY DRIVES.—Provision for single or dual fuel pump, high and low pressure air-compressors, shaft-driven electric generator, hydraulic pump, vacuum pump; also for constant-speed airscrew governor and pump unit on Pegasus XVIII.

STARTER SYSTEM.—Combined electric and hand turning gear.

EXHAUST SYSTEM AND COWLING.—Complete standardised units, combining ring-type exhaust manifold and long or short-chord cowlings, are available. Long-chord cowlings embody controllable gills.

DIMENSIONS, WEIGHTS AND PERFORMANCE.—See Table.

COVENTRY CLIMAX.

COVENTRY CLIMAX ENGINES, LTD.

HEAD OFFICE : MOUNT SION, OSWESTRY, SHROPSHIRE.

Directors : H. P. Lee, M.I. Mech.E., Leonard P. Lee, L. Hathaway, M.I.A.E. and N. Magson.

Secretary : P. W. Cooper, A.I.A.C.

This Company has specialised in internal combustion engines since 1903. Before the outbreak of War the Company had acquired the manufacturing licence for the American Continental four-cylinder horizontally-opposed air-cooled aero-engine from the Continental Motors Corporation, of Detroit, Mich., but production of this engine was suspended for the duration of the War.

During the war the company manufactured engines for light marine craft, large quantities of light engines for generating sets for aerodrome use, special purpose generating sets to very advanced specifications, as well as other units and component parts.

COVENTRY VICTOR.

THE COVENTRY VICTOR MOTOR CO. LTD.

HEAD OFFICE AND WORKS : COVENTRY.

Managing Director : W. A. Weaver.

Director and Secretary : S. J. Cordery.

The Coventry Victor Motor Company has been engaged since 1911 in the design and manufacture of horizontally-opposed engines for land, sea and air purposes. Two, four and eight-cylinder opposed engines have been built with outputs ranging from 2¾ to 50 h.p.

During the war the activities of the Company were devoted entirely to the requirements of the British Government and production of the Company's small four and eight-cylinder horizontally-opposed air-cooled aero-engines was suspended.

CIRRUS.

THE CIRRUS ENGINE SECTION OF BLACKBURN AIRCRAFT LTD.

HEAD OFFICE AND WORKS : ENGINE DEPT., BROUGH, E. YORKS.

Managing Directors : R. Blackburn, O.B.E., A.M.I.C.E., F.R.Ae.S., M.I.Mech.E. ; Major F. A. Bumpus, B.Sc., A.R.C.S., Wh.Sc., F.R.Ae.S.

Directors : Sir Maurice Denny, Bt., C.B.E., B.Sc., M.I.C.E., M.I.M.A. ; Captain N. W. G. Blackburn ; R. R. Rhodes, M.I.Ae.E. ; and Sqdn. Ldr. J. L. N. Bennett-Baggs.

The Cirrus aero-engine, the pioneer light four-cylinder in-line air-cooled engine, made possible the "light aeroplane" of today, and its long list of successes in light aircraft of many types dates back to 1925.

In 1934 the manufacture of these engines was taken over by Blackburn Aircraft Ltd., and a new series of engines was produced which achieved further excellent results in many different aircraft.

The first of these, the Cirrus Minor of 90 h.p., in the Auster I Army observation monoplane, saw active service in France, Libya, Tripoli and Tunisia with marked success and a fine record for reliability. The R.A.F. type, which embodies a number of alterations from the pre-war civilian model, is known as the Cirrus Minor Series I.

A new engine, the Cirrus Minor Series II of 100 h.p. is now added to the Cirrus range, which also includes the Major Series II of 150 h.p. and the Major Series III of 155 h.p. The four types are described below.

THE 90 h.p. CIRRUS MINOR SERIES I.

TYPE.—Four-cylinder in-line air-cooled inverted.

CYLINDERS.—Bore 95 m/m. (3.73 in.), Stroke 127 m/m. (5 in.). Capacity 3,605 c.c. Compression ratio 5.87 : 1. The high-grade carbon steel cylinders with machined fins have detachable "Y" alloy heads attached by eight studs to a flange on the barrels. A gas-tight joint is ensured by a laminated copper washer. The valve operating gear is enclosed by an electron cover which also acts as an oil bath for the valve mechanism. The cylinders are located by short anchoring studs in the crankcase.

PISTONS.—Y-alloy of slipper type. Fully floating gudgeon pins One scraper and two compression rings.

CONNECTING RODS.—Hiduminium forgings with steel-backed white metal bearings.

CRANKSHAFT.—Steel forging carried in five plain white-metal bearings with a ball thrust bearing at the front end and fitted at the rear with a gear wheel for driving the two vertical magneto drive-shafts, which also operate the fuel pumps.

CRANKCASE.—Electron casting with all oilways carried internally and fitted with an electron top-cover which carries a one-piece cast breather at the rear, and lifting eyes fore and aft.

VALVE GEAR.—One inlet and one exhaust valve per cylinder. Wide cooling spaces between inlet and exhaust port passages. Operation by camshaft through ball-ended push-rods, and tappets housed in the crankcase, the camshaft running direct in the crankcase casting with a bronze thrust bearing at the front end from which end the camshaft is driven through spur gears. The timing gears are at the front of engine and have a small timing cover in electron.

IGNITION.—Two fully-screened B.T.H. SG4-2 magnetos (one with impulse starter) are driven from the crankshaft through spiral gears. Distributors face downwards. Integrally-screened sparking-plugs. Plessey-Breeze screening harness.

CARBURATION.—Claudel-Hobson downdraught carburettor, with independent mixture control and an Amal flame-trap, and is

The 90 h.p. Cirrus Minor Series I engine.

The 100 h.p. Cirrus Minor Series II air-cooled engine.

A rear view of the Cirrus Major Series II or III Engine.

operation. Provision for fire-fighting equipment is made on the hot and cold intake. Dual fuel-pumps can be fitted and are operated by cams on the magneto driving-shafts.

LUBRICATION.—Gear-type oil-pump, incorporating Auto-clean filter is fitted. Pressure-feed system to main and big-end bearings. Gravity drain system. An extension of the oil-pump spindle provides a power take-off point.

ACCESSORIES.—Optional. Amal fuel-pumps, electric starter, screening harness, Kigass primer.

AIRSCREW DRIVE.—Direct left-hand tractor.

DIMENSIONS.—Overall length less spinner and starter 1,013 m/m., Height 650 m/m., Width 455 m/m., Bearer feet centres as Minor Series I.

WEIGHT.—Complete with airscrew hub and spinner, two fuel pumps. and pipe-lines, bearer feet and rubbers, cooling chute and baffles, exhaust stubs and flame-trap. 248 lb. ± 2 lbs. (112.6 kg. ± 0.9 kg.).

PERFORMANCE.—Normal 90 h.p. at 2,300 r.p.m., Maximum 100 h.p. at 2,600 r.p.m., Fuel consumption, full throttle at 2,300 r.p.m. 6.6 gals. per hr., Cruising at 80% full power at 2,300 r.p.m., 5.2 gals. per hr., Oil consumption 1-2 pints (0.57-1.4 litres) per hr.

OCTANE RATING.—77 (D.T.D. 224) minimum. Fuels containing tetra-ethyl-lead can be used.

mounted on a cast induction manifold. Dual fuel pumps can be fitted at rear of crankcase, one on either side, operated through plungers by cams on magneto driving-shafts.

LUBRICATION.—Pressure feed system by oscillating piston-type of oil-pump driven from rear end of camshaft. Gravity drain system. Pressure oil filter contained in separate unit on side of crankcase at rear end.

ACCESSORIES.—Optional. Amal fuel pumps, electric starter, screening harness. Kigass primer.

AIRSCREW DRIVE.—Left Hand tractor.

DIMENSIONS.—Length 960 m/m. (37.8 in.), Height 636 m/m. (25 in.), Width 440 m/m. (17.32 in.). Bearer feet bolt centres, front to rear 402 m/m. (15.8 in.). Alternative widths between centres 386 m/m. (15.2 in.), 423 m/m. (16.65 in.), 469 m/m. (18 in.).

WEIGHT.—Complete with boss, spinner, two fuel pumps and pipe-lines, bearer feet and rubbers, screening harness, cooling chute and baffles, exhaust stubs and flame trap. 238 lb. ± 2 lb. (108 kg. ± 0.9 kg.).

PERFORMANCE.—Normal 80 h.p. at 2,300 r.p.m. Maximum 90 h.p. at 2,600 r.p.m., Fuel consumptions full throttle at 2,300 r.p.m., 6.0 gals. per hr., Cruising at 80% full power at 2,300 r.p.m., 4.59 gals. per hr., Oil consumption 1-2 pints (0.57-1.4 litres) per hr., Octane rating 70.

THE 150 h.p. CIRRUS MAJOR SERIES II.

TYPE.—Four-cylinder in-line air-cooled inverted.

CYLINDERS.—Bore 120 m/m. (4.72 in.), Stroke 140 m/m. (5.5 in.), Capacity 6.3 litres. Compression ratio 5.8 : 1. Barrels are machined from high-grade steel ingots and are located in crankcase by large spigot and four short studs securing cylinder base flange. Cylinder-heads are of aluminium-alloy with one inlet and one exhaust valve. Heads attached to barrels by twelve securing studs.

PISTONS.—Slipper type of Y-alloy, with two tapered compression and one scraper rings.

CONNECTING RODS.—Hiduminium forgings fitted with steel-backed white-metal bearings.

CRANKSHAFT.—Robust steel forging machined all over, carried in five plain bearings. Ball thrust-bearing at front end.

CRANKCASE.—Aluminium-alloy casting with Electron top-cover. The timing-gear cover at rear carries the auxiliaries and does not disturb any gears when removed as they are housed in the crankcase.

VALVE GEAR.—Operation, etc., as in Minor (Series I).

CARBURATION.—One Claudel-Hobson downdraught carburettor, fitted with flame-trap and direct cold air intake, and having an independent mixture control, is mounted on a one-piece cast induction

THE 100 h.p. CIRRUS MINOR SERIES II.

TYPE.—Four-cylinder in-line air-cooled inverted.

CYLINDERS.—Bore 100 m/m. (3.9. in), Stroke 127 m/m. (5 in.), Capacity 3,990 c.c., Compression ratio 6.25 : 1. The high grade carbon steel cylinders with machined fins have detachable heads. The cylinders are located by short anchoring studs in the crankcase.

PISTONS.—Slipper type of Y-alloy. Fully-floating gudgeon-pins. One scraper and two compression rings.

CONNECTING RODS.—As Minor Series 1.

CRANKSHAFT.—As Minor Series 1.

CRANKCASE.—As Minor Series 1.

CYLINDER HEADS.—Pent-roof type in Y-alloy (with one inlet and one exhaust valve) attached to cylinder top flange by eight studs and nuts. A gas-tight joint is secured by a spigot on the cylinder and a copper washer. The cylinder-head forms one half of the valve-gear chamber and has a cover-box acting as an oil bath for the valve rocker gear.

VALVE GEAR.—Operated from camshaft through cup-ended tappets and ball-ended push-rods. Clearance adjusted by screwed cup in one end of rocker and a hardened striking pad on the other. Valves stellited. The camshaft runs direct in the crankcase casting with a bronze thrust-bearing at the front end from which end the camshaft is driven through spur gears. The timing gears are at the front of engine and have a small timing cover in electron.

IGNITION.—As Minor Series I. Screening harness available if desired.

CARBURATION.—A Zenith downdraught carburettor with independent mixture control, also hot and cold air intake, is fitted to a one-piece cast induction manifold. Warm air from the cowling is admitted through the flame-trap up to approximately 90% of the throttle opening, after which a direct cold air intake comes into

The 150 h.p. Cirrus Major Series II Engine.

manifold which is secured by bolts passing through bosses cast on the manifold and screwed into inserts in the cylinder-head. The cold air intake operates automatically at approximately 90% to full-throttle opening.

IGNITION.—Two B.T.H. magnetos one with impulse starter. K.L.G. sparking plugs. Screening can be provided if desired.

LUBRICATION.—Pressure feed system with scavenge pump. All oilways internal in crankcase casting. Pressure and scavenge filters embodied in the oil-pump which is of oscillating piston type.

AIRSCREW DRIVE.—Direct, left-hand tractor.

ACCESSORIES.—Optional. Amal Duplex fuel pump. Electric-starter, vacuum pump, generator, and screening if required.

DIMENSIONS.—Overall length less spinner 1,096 m/m. (42.9 in.) overall height 797 m/m. Overall width 450 m/m. Bearer feet centres front to rear 540 m/m. Bearer feet bolt centres alternative widths 544 m/m. (21.4 in.), 458 m/m. (18 in.), 386 m/m. (15.2 in.).

WEIGHT.—With airscrew hub 338 ± 5 lb. (153.4 kg. ± 2.3 kg.).

PERFORMANCE.—Normal 138 h.p. at 2,200 r.p.m. ; maximum 150 h.p. at 2,450 r.p.m., Fuel consumption, full throttle at normal r.p.m., 10 gals. per hr., Cruising at 80% full power at 2,200 r.p.m., 7.3 gals. per hr., Oil consumption 0.75 to 2 pints per hr. (0.42-1.14 litres).

OCTANE RATING.—70 minimum. Fuels containing tetra-ethyl-lead can be used.

THE 145/155 h.p. CIRRUS MAJOR SERIES III.

The Cirrus Major Series III engine is similar in general arrangement to the Major Series II, but is a higher compression engine and has a correspondingly increased output. The Major Series II and Series III engines are alike in external appearances, and the illustrations may therefore be taken to represent both types. The description of the Major Series II engine will also apply to the Major Series III, except in the following details.

COMPRESSION RATIO.—6.5 : 1.

PERFORMANCE.—Normal 145 h.p. at 2,200 r.p.m. Maximum 155 h.p. at 2,450 r.p.m. Cruising 2,100 to 2,200 r.p.m. Fuel consumption, full throttle at normal r.p.m., 10.5 gals. per hr., cruising at 80% full power at 2,200 r.p.m., 8.2 gals. per hr. Oil consumption 0.75 to 2 pints per hr. (0.42 to 1.14 litre).

OCTANE RATING.—87 minimum. Fuels containing tetra-ethyl-lead can be used.

DE HAVILLAND.

THE DE HAVILLAND ENGINE CO., LTD.

HEAD OFFICE : HATFIELD, HERTS.

ENGINE WORKS : STONEGROVE, EDGWARE, MIDDLESEX.

Directors : Major F. B. Halford (Chairman), Sir Geoffrey de Havilland, F. E. N. St. Barbe, A. S. Butler, J. L. Brodie, Hugh Buckingham and A.F. Burke (General Manager).

The de Havilland organization, entered the aero-engine industry in 1927, when they produced the first of the Gipsy light aeroplane engine series.

The Gipsy range of engines has been designed by Major Frank B. Halford, F.R.Ae.S., M.S.A.E., working in close collaboration with the Aircraft Design Department of the de Havilland Company.

The first experimental Gipsy engines, produced in July, 1927, were designed to develop 135 h.p. One was installed in the D.H. 71 Tiger Moth single-seat racing monoplane which established the then World's Speed Record for Light Aeroplanes at 186 m.p.h. (300 km.h.).

The most widely used engines in the Gipsy series, which were manufactured throughout the war, included the 130 h.p. Gipsy-Major I, the 200 h.p. Gipsy-Six I and 205 h.p. Gipsy-Six II.

For post-war use the company has developed a new series of four and six-cylinder engines brief details of which are published below.

The de Havilland Engine Co., Ltd. entered the gas turbine field early in 1941. Design of the H-1 Goblin was started in April, 1941 and bench tests began a year later. Two H-1 units installed in a Gloster Meteor first flew on March 5, 1943. The Goblin is used to power the D.H. 100 Vampire single-seat jet-propelled fighter. A D.H. H-1 jet unit was also fitted to the prototype Lockheed XP-80 Shooting Star jet fighter. For details of the Goblin see pages 4-5d.

In 1934, the de Havilland Aircraft Co., Ltd., acquired the licence for the Hamilton-Standard controllable-pitch airscrew. The Company operates airscrew factories in Great Britain and Australia and manufactures airscrews in large quantities for the British and Dominion Governments.

THE NEW SERIES DE HAVILLAND GIPSY-MAJOR AND GIPSYQUEEN.

The de Havilland Engine Co., Ltd. has developed for post-war use a new series of four and six-cylinder Gipsy engines to

The 160 h.p. D.H. Gipsy-Major 51 supercharged Engine.

THE NEW SERIES D.H. GIPSY-MAJOR AND GIPSYQUEEN ENGINES.

Particulars common to all engines : Bore × Stroke 120 m/m. × 150 m/m. (4.73 in. × 5.9 in.) Compression Ratio 6.5 : 1.

Name	Take-off Power	International Power Rating	Maximum Power Rating	Weight (dry)	Supercharger gear ratio	Airscrew gear ratio	Length (from C/L of airscrew over rear cover)	Width overall	Height overall
GIPSY MAJOR 31	160 h.p. at 2,500 r.p.m. at sea level	156 h.p. at 2,400 r.p.m. at sea level	160 h.p. at 2,500 r.p.m. at sea level	340 lbs. (154.3 kg.) + 2½% (includes cooling scoops, baffles and fuel pump unit	—	—	1,123 m/m. (44.9 in.)	436 m/m. (17.4 in.)	819 m/m. (32.7 in.)
GIPSY MAJOR 51	197 h.p. at 2,500 r.p.m. at sea level	175 h.p. at 2,300 r.p.m. at 6,000 ft. (1,830 m.)	180 h.p. at 2,400 r.p.m. at 7,000 ft. (2,135 m.)	410 lbs. (186.1 kg.) + 2½% (as above)	11.16 : 1	—	1,260 m/m. (50.4 in.)	416 m/m. (16.6 in.)	838 m/m. (33.5 in.)
GIPSYQUEEN 31	250 h.p. at 2,500 r.p.m. at sea level	245 h.p. at 2,400 r.p.m. at sea level	250 h.p. at 2,500 r.p.m. at sea level	510 lbs. (231.5 kg.) + 2½% (as above)	—	—	1,587 m/m. (63.5 in.)	513.5 m/m. (20.5 in.)	838 m/m. (33.5 in.)
GIPSYQUEEN 51	295 h.p. at 2,500 r.p.m. at sea level	260 h.p. at 2,400 r.p.m. at 6,000 ft. (1,830 m.)	270 h.p. at 2,400 r.p.m. at 7,000 ft. (2,135 m.)	560 lbs. (254.2 kg.) + 2½% (as above)	11.16 : 1	—	1,638.5 m/m. (65.5 in.)	480.5 m/m. (19.2 in.)	1,056 m/m. (42.2 in.)
GIPSYQUEEN 71	330 h.p. at 2,800 r.p.m. at sea level	285 h.p. at 2,600 r.p.m. at 7,000 ft. (2,135 m.)	305 h.p. at 2,700 r.p.m. at 6,000 ft. (1,830 m.)	660 lbs. (300 kg.) + 2½% (as above)	11.22 : 1	.711 : 1	1,787.75 m/m. (71.5 in.)	433 m/m. (17.3 in.)	847.75 m/m. (33.9 in.)

The 197 h.p. D.H. Gipsy Major 31 engine.

succeed the Series I and II Gipsy-Major and Gipsy-Six engines of 1939.

For the four-cylinder engines the name Gipsy-Major is retained, but for the six-cylinder units the name Gipsy-Six has been dropped in favour of the R.A.F. name Gipsyqueen, owing to the wide use of these engines under this name in the service during the war.

In the Gipsy-Major Series there are two basic engines—the 160 h.p. Gipsy-Major 31 and the 197 h.p. supercharged Gipsy-Major 51. In the Gipsyqueen Series there are three engines—the 250 h.p. Gipsyqueen 31, the 295 h.p. supercharged Gipsyqueen 51, and the 330 h.p. geared and supercharged Gipsyqueen 71. All five engines will take controllable-pitch airscrews and the six-cylinder units will take a new constant-speed feathering and braking airscrew. The geared and supercharged Gipsyqueen 71 is the power-plant of the D.H. 104 Dove light transport monoplane.

Each of the engines indicated above has been allocated 19 numbers, i.e. 31–49, 51–69, 71–89, and the numbers in each series will be used to indicate installation changes, various combinations of accessories and design alterations affecting interchangeability.

The new engines have a new cylinder of slightly greater bore and stroke, a 30% increase in fin area, and a new aluminium-alloy head with inserted valve seats. A standard piston is fitted giving a 6.5 : 1 compression ratio, which is suitable for fuels down to an 80 octane value in the supercharged engines. Provision is made on the supercharged engines to limit the boost where it is required to use lower octane fuels.

Most of the ignition equipment, apart from the distributors, is suitable for both four and six cylinder engines, as are the magnetos which incorporate an impulse starter. Many of the reciprocating and valve operating parts, joints, connections and small attachments are common throughout the series.

Strip-lined main bearings are fitted for improved performance, to enhance wear quality and to simplify replacement, while in the six-cylinder designs opportunity has been taken to stiffen the crankcase with cross bolts on either side of the middle journal and to apply pendulum-type dynamic dampers to a lightened crankshaft.

In the Gipsyqueen 71 a steel connecting-rod has been adopted and a Bibby-type coupling is used in conjunction with a self-centering epicyclic gear to give a smooth flexible reduction gear and a short compact gear casing.

In all engines provision has been made in the timing case and of the crankcase top cover to mount a variety of accessories. In the supercharged types the supercharger drive is taken from the front of the engine, in the case of the Gipsyqueen 71 Series through a long torsion shaft.

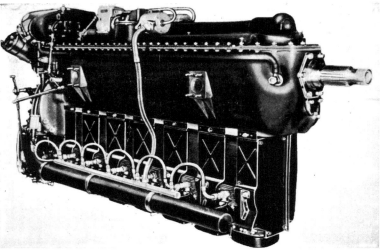

The 295 h.p. D.H. Gipsyqueen 51 supercharged engine.

If required, the normally-aspirated engines can be converted to supercharged types by fitting the supercharger unit in place of the existing rear cover. Injection-type carburettors will be a feature of the supercharged engines.

The principal particulars of the new engines will be found in the table on the previous page. Full constructional details were not available for publication at the time of closing for press.

The descriptions that follow refer to the 1939 Gipsy Major and Gipsy-Six (Gipsyqueen) engines which were maintained in production throughout the war and are still in service in very large numbers.

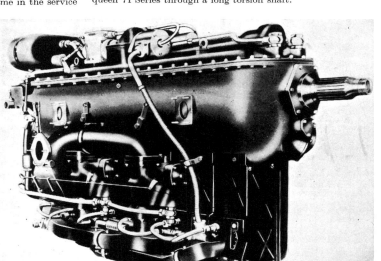

The 250 h.p. D.H. Gipsyqueen 31 six-cylinder engine.

THE DE HAVILLAND GIPSY-MAJOR SERIES I.

TYPE.—Four-cylinder in-line inverted air-cooled.

CYLINDERS.—Bore 118 m/m. (4.646 in.), Stroke 140 m/m. (5.512 in.). Capacity 6.124 litres (373.6 cub. in.). Compression ratio 5.25/1. Barrels machined all over from forgings of carbon steel. Thickness of wall and depth of finning adjusted to ensure even cooling and prevent distortion. Exposed surfaces specially treated against corrosion. Ends project far into crankcase, with oil-tight joint of "Dermatine" between barrels and latter. Detachable heads of aluminium-bronze held by long H.T. steel studs to crankcase. Copper-asbestos washers beneath heads.

PISTONS.—Slipper-type, cast in D.T.D.131. Fully-floating gudgeon pin located by external circlips and washers. One scraper and two compression rings below gudgeon pin.

CONNECTING RODS.—Machined all over from forgings of D.T.D.130 alloy and etched. Bearing caps have four H.T. bolts. Big-end has split-steel shells with white-metal.

CRANKSHAFT.—Machined all over from nickel-chromium-alloy steel forging. Statically and dynamically balanced. Five white-metal main bearings. Ball-bearing to take thrust at front end. Journals and pins bored for lightness and lubrication.

CRANKCASE.—Aluminium-alloy casting. Lower half carries the five main crankshaft bearings, which are held in position by separate caps. Top cover is of "Elektron" stoutly ribbed to resist deflection.

Valve Gear.—Fully enclosed. One inlet and one exhaust valve per cylinder seat directly against aluminium-bronze of the cylinder-head. Operation by steel rockers, tubular steel push-rods, and steel tappets off camshaft running in five bearings on port side of engine. All striking parts are hardened and replaceable. The camshaft is driven by spur-gears from the crankshaft, with a vernier arrangement of keyways between the camshaft gear and camshaft, to permit accurate valve timing.

Induction. — Claudel-Hobson AI.48 down-draught carburetter supplies the engine, and up to highest cruising speed draws through a flame-trap warmed air from the side of the engine. When the throttle is fully opened, an interconnected change-over flap is moved and air is taken from outside engine cowling. Thus freezing is prevented at cruising r.p.m. with no loss of performance at full throttle. Altitude control is provided by an air valve in the carburetter, operated from the cockpit.

Lubrication.—Oil is drawn from external tank by engine-driven gear-type pump on the rear of the engine, through a coarse gauze suction filter. This pump delivers at a pressure of 40 to 45 lbs. per sq. in., governed by an adjustable relief valve, to an "Auto-Klean" filter. Crankshaft, connecting rods, camshaft and timing gear are pressure-fed from the main oilway, which is integral with the top cover. Cylinders are lubricated by special splash arrangements from connecting rod big-ends, whereby proper lubrication of pistons is established immediately on starting. A level of oil is maintained in the valve gear covers by slight leakage past the tappets in their guides, a vent pipe within the cover maintaining constant level. Oil is drained through large openings in the crankcase and returned by gravity to the oil tank in the aircraft. Oil scavenge pumps to suit particular installations can be fitted as extras.

Cooling.—Scoops are fitted to the port side of the engine, for which suitable openings are arranged in the aircraft cowling. The air collected by these scoops is passed between the cylinders and heads and suitably deflected by special baffles on the starboard side of the engine.

Controls.—Pickup levers may be on either port or starboard side and may either pull or push to open. Throttle and magneto controls are interconnected so that correct advance is obtained for economical operation.

Ignition.—Two B.T.H. magnetos are carried on platforms on the timing-gear casing and are driven through Simms flexible "Vernier" couplings. Impulse starter.

Accessories.—Mounted on timing-gear cover. Provision made for single or dual tachometer drive.

Starting.—Rotax electric or B.T.H. electric or Rotax hand-turning gear.

Airscrew Drive.—Direct. Left-hand tractor. Airscrew boss driven off tapered extension of crankshaft by key. Airscrew is positioned by hub of boss and is driven by eight through-bolts between positively-driven front and back flanges.

Dimensions.—Length 1,227 m/m. (48.3 in.), Width 508 m/m. (20 in.), Height 752 m/m. (29.6 in.).

Weight (complete with airscrew boss and cylinder baffles).—305 lb. ± 5 lbs. (138 kg. ± 2.25 kg.). Dual D.H. A.C. fuel pump 5 lbs. (2.25 kg.), Electric starter 20 lbs. (9 kg.), Hand turning gear 10.5 lbs. (4.76 kg.).

Performance (70 octane fuel, determined by C.F.R. engine modified motor method using mixture temperature of 260°F, not containing T.E.L.).—Normal output 120 h.p. at 2,100 r.p.m., Maximum output 130 h.p. at 2,350 r.p.m., Fuel consumption at 2,100 r.p.m. sea level (approx. 95 h.p.) with mixture control adjusted to give weakest mixture for maximum power $6\frac{1}{4}$-$6\frac{3}{4}$ gallons (28.4-30.7 litre) per hour, At full throttle 2,350 r.p.m. $9\frac{1}{2}$-10 gallons (43.2-45.4 litres) per hour, Oil consumption $1\frac{3}{4}$ pints (.99 litre) per hour.

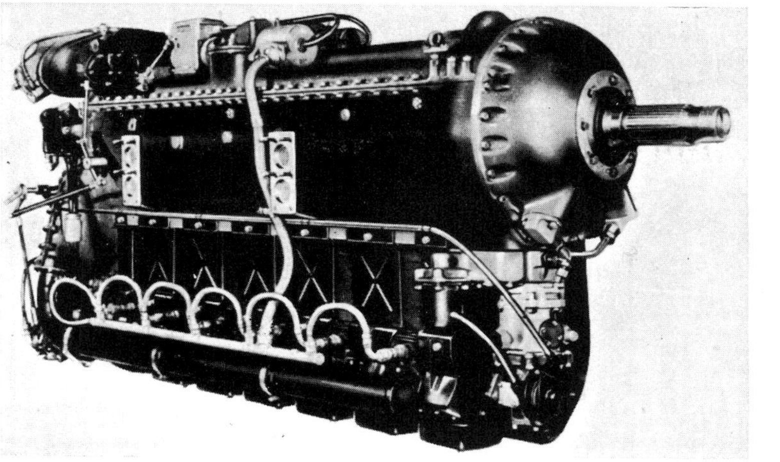

The 330 h.p. D.H. Gipsyqueen 71 geared and supercharged engine.

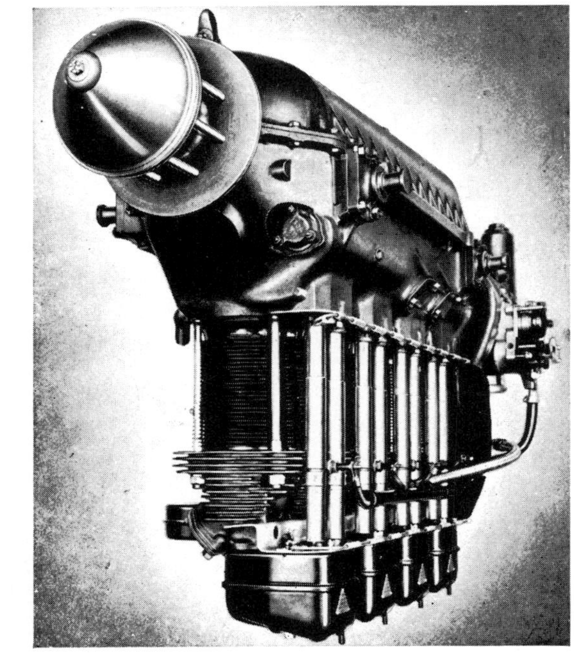

The 130 h.p. D.H. Gipsy-Major Series I engine.

THE DE HAVILLAND GIPSY-SIX SERIES I.

Type.—Six-cylinder in-line inverted air-cooled.

Cylinders.—Bore 118 m/m. (4.646 in.), Stroke 140 m/m. (5.512 in.). Capacity 9.186 litres (560.6 cub. in.), Compression ratio 5.25/1. (See Gipsy-Major.)

Pistons.
Connecting Rods. } See Gipsy-Major.

Crankshaft.—Machined all over from E.S.C. forging of nickel-chromium-alloy steel drilled for lightness and lubrication. Balanced statically and dynamically. Runs in eight steel-backed white-metal main bearings. Ball thrust-bearing at front end.

Crankcase.—Electron. Small sump at back end. Each intermediate bearing supported by stiff cross-member with separate cap. Facings for bearer-feet, breather, fuel and oil pumps, tachometer drive and starter. Top cover of Elektron carries magnetos, distributors and driving gear.

Valve Gear.—Fully enclosed. One inlet and one exhaust valve per cylinder seat directly against aluminium-bronze of head. Driven by steel rockers, tubular steel push-rods, and hardened steel tappets off camshaft running in seven bearings on port side. All striking parts hardened and replaceable. Camshaft driven off front end of crankshaft by spur-gears. Camshaft gear attached to camshaft through vernier system of keyways to give accurate valve timing.

Auxiliary Drives. — Camshaft and all auxiliaries driven off gear-wheel on front end of crankshaft between ball thrust-bearing and first crank-throw. Train of hardened gears with profile-ground teeth drive camshaft, and shaft in top cover running at 1.5 crank-shaft speed to drive magnetos. Fuel and oil pumps driven off vertical shaft at back end of camshaft. Tachometer drive and starter at back of crankcase.

Carburation. — Two Claudel - Hobson AI.48F down-draught carburetters each supply three cylinders and up to highest cruising-speed draw through a flame-trap warmed air from around cylinders. When throttle is fully opened a change-over flap is moved and air is taken from outside engine cowling. Thus freezing is prevented at cruising r.p.m., with no loss of performance at full throttle.

Lubrication.—Oil pump and filters form detachable unit at back of crankcase. Gear pump draws oil through coarse gauze filter from separate tank and delivers at 40 to 45 lbs. per sq. in. pressure by adjustable relief-valve to "Auto-Klean" filter. Main stream goes by way of cast passage in top cover to main bearings and thence to crankshaft. Oil thrown from holes drilled in big-end bearings and caps on to cylinder-walls and pistons. Cams and tappets lubricated by spray. Other stream adjusted by balanced piston arrangement to 15 lbs. per sq. in. lubricates camshaft and other accessory drives. Two scavenge pumps, each with detachable fine-mesh gauze filter, draws oil from each end of crankcase. Except for connections to tank, there are no external oil pipes.

Ignition.—Two B.T.H. magnetos, each with improved impulse-starter and Simms flexible vernier coupling and each with separate distributor, each supply one plug per cylinder. Automatic retarding for slow speeds and starting.

Cooling.—See Gipsy-Major.

Controls.—See Gipsy-Major.

Starter.—Rotax or B.T.H.

Airscrew Drive.—Direct. Left-hand tractor. Boss driven off tapered extension to crankshaft by two keys. Front flange positively driven. Eight through-bolts. Spinner quickly detachable.

Dimensions.—Length (from tip of spinner to rear of fuel pump) 1,578 m/m. (62.126 in.), Height 823 m/m. (32.4 in.), Width 485 m/m. (19.09 in.).

Weight Dry (Complete with electric starter, fuel pumps and flame-trap-type air-intake, but less airscrew boss).—468 lbs. ± $7\frac{1}{2}$ lbs. (212.7 kg. ± $3\frac{1}{2}$ kg.).

Performance (70 octane fuel, determined by C.F.R. engine modified motor method, using mixture temperature of 260°F., not containing T.E.L.).—Normal output 185 h.p. at 2,100 r.p.m., Maximum output 200 h.p. at 2,350 r.p.m., Fuel consumption at maximum cruising speed (2,100 r.p.m.) $10\frac{1}{4}$ gallons (46.5 litres) per hour, or full throttle (2,350 r.p.m.) 15 gallons (68.2 litres) per hour, Oil consumption 1-4 pints (.57-2.4 litres) per hour at 2,100 r.p.m.

THE DE HAVILLAND GIPSY-SIX SERIES II.

R.A.F. names : Gipsyqueen I (fixed-pitch) and Gipsyqueen II (constant-speed).

This version of the Gipsy-Six has been approved for use with fixed-pitch, two-pitch variable and constant-speed airscrews. It differs from the Series I engine in that it has been developed to use the higher octane leaded fuels.

Though its maximum output under fixed-pitch conditions is not greatly in excess of the Series I engine, the main purpose embodied in the design is to obtain higher consistent power outputs over the cruising range, and also a considerable increase in power for take-off purposes, made permissible by the use of controllable-pitch airscrews.

Except where stated, the specification of the Gipsy-Six Series I applies.

Cylinders.—Compression ratio 6/1. Detachable heads of aluminium-alloy held by long H.T. steel studs to crankcase. Copper-asbestos washers beneath heads.

Pistons.—Slipper-type, made from forged D.T.D.132. Fully-floating gudgeon pin located by external circlips and washers. One scraper and two compression rings below gudgeon pin.

Connecting Rods.—Big-end has split steel shells with white-metal.

Valve Gear.—Fully enclosed. One inlet and one stellited exhaust valve per cylinder seat directly against high-expansion steel valve-seats designed to permit use of leaded fuels.

Auxiliary Drives.—An extension of shaft in top cover, which runs at 1.5 times crankshaft speed to drive magnetos, rotates the constant-speed airscrew governor and vacuum pump for flying instruments. Latter may be replaced by oil servo-pump suitable for certain types of automatic pilot. Oil pressure increasing valve and hand-control for use with two-position controllable airscrews.

Carburation.—When a constant-speed airscrew is used and operational conditions may require full open throttle settings on carburetter under cruising conditions, a separately-operated flame-trap control to be used in conjunction with air-intake thermometer is fitted, so that induction temperatures may be regulated from cockpit. Altitude control is by air-valve in carburetter, operated from cockpit.

Lubrication.—Except for connections to tank, there are no external oil pipes. A small facing is provided at rear of engine to which oil tank vents may be connected, thus helping to keep the aeroplane clean.

Airscrew Drive.—Direct. Left-hand tractor. Crankshaft has been designed with specially serrated extension at front end to accept an airscrew boss suitable for wooden or metal fixed-pitch airscrews. Front flange of the propeller boss is positively driven, and eight through-bolts are provided with a spinner, which is quickly detachable. Controllable-pitch airscrews may be fitted directly to crankshaft.

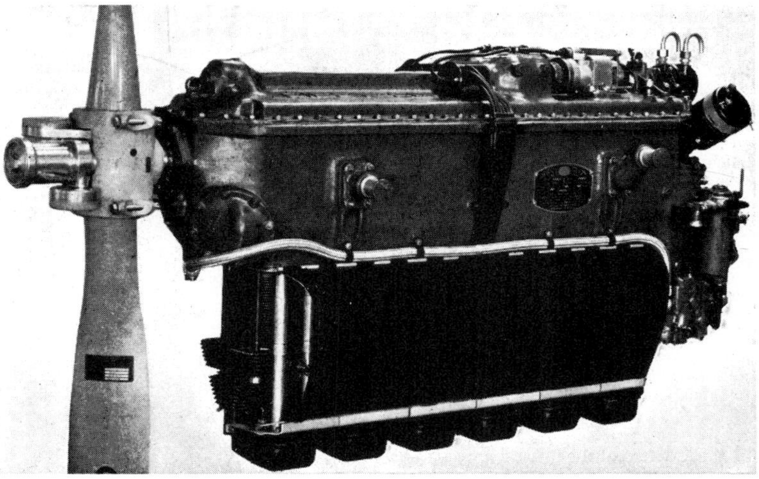

The 200 h.p. de Havilland Gipsy-Six Series II engine.

Dimensions.—Length (from spinner of fixed-pitch screw to back of fuel pump) 1,613 m/m. (63.5 in.), Height 805 m/m. (31.7 in.), Width 484 m/m. (19.06 in.).

Weight Dry.—For use with fixed-pitch airscrew, cooling baffles included, but without starter or airscrew boss 469 lbs. ± $7\frac{1}{2}$ lbs. (213 kg. ± $3\frac{1}{2}$ kg.). Weights equipped for various controllable-pitch airscrew combinations supplied on request.

Performance (77 octane fuel, determined by C.F.R. engine modified motor method, using a mixture temperature of 260°F., containing not more than 4 c.c. of tetra-ethyl lead per gallons of fuel).—Fixed-pitch airscrew normal output 185 b.h.p. at 2,100 r.p.m., Maximum output 205 b.h.p. at 2,400 r.p.m.. Rated output with controllable-pitch airscrew 205 b.h.p. at 2,400 r.p.m. Fuel consumptions: Maximum cruising $11\frac{1}{2}$ gallons (52 litres) per hour at 2,100 r.p.m.; normal cruising 10-$10\frac{3}{4}$ gallons (45-49 litres) per hour at 2,100 r.p.m.; at full throttle at 2,400 r.p.m. 16 gallons (73 litres). Oil consumption 3-5 pints (1.7-2.8 litres) per hour at 2,100 r.p.m.

NAPIER.

D. NAPIER & SON, LTD.

Head Office and Works: Acton, London, W.3.

Established : 1808. Incorporated in 1913.

Chairman : Sir George H. Nelson.

Managing Director: H. G. Nelson.

Following an unbroken period of more than one hundred years of experience of the first class in many of the varied branches of engineering the Napier Company concentrated its activities during the War 1914-1918, on the design and manufacture of aero-engines.

The Napier Lion, first produced in 1918, quickly established an enviable reputation for reliability and trustworthiness in the

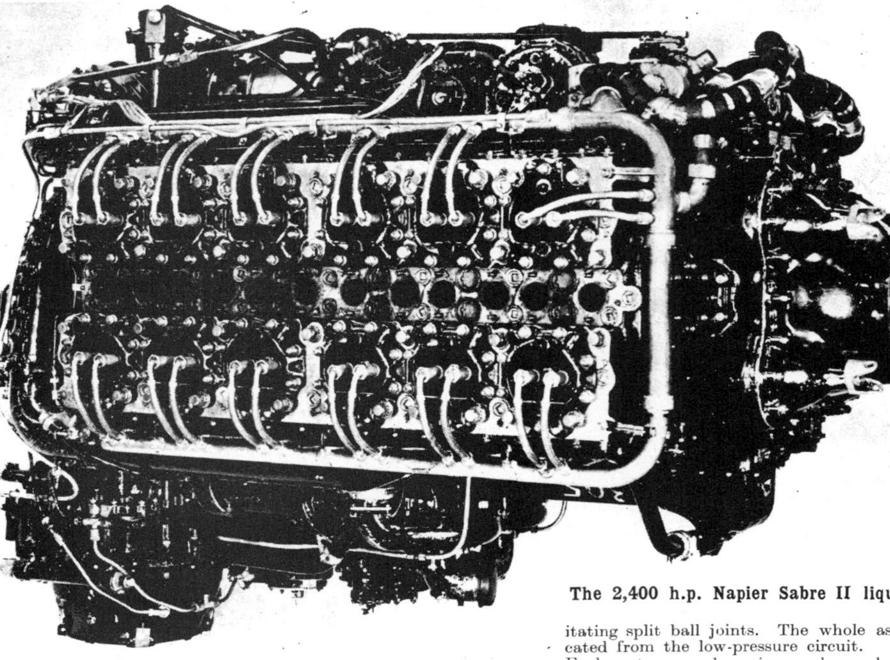

The 2,400 h.p. Napier Sabre II liquid-cooled engine.

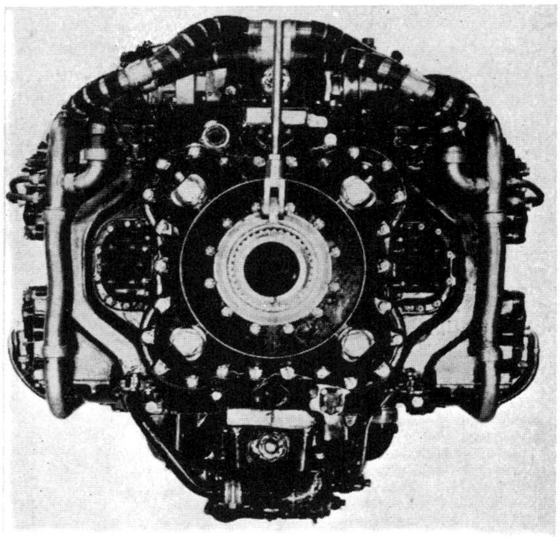

A front view of the 2,400 h.p. Napier Sabre II engine.

flying world. Even to-day, 27 years later, a marine version of the Lion re-named the Sea-Lion, is maintaining its reputation by excellent service in high-speed and other marine craft of the Fighting Services.

In 1927 a new line of development in aero-engine design was begun, that of the air-cooled in-line double-crank engine, and the Rapier and Dagger series of engines followed.

Both the Rapier and the Dagger were air-cooled vertical H-type engines, the former with sixteen cylinders and giving a maximum output of 395 h.p., and the latter with twenty-four cylinders and developing a maximum output of 1,000 h.p.

Towards the end of 1935 the Napier Company took a further step in the development of the twin crankshaft aero-engine by undertaking to build a 2,000 h.p. model incorporating a number of radical changes in design. Unlike the earlier Napier "H" engines, the new engine, now named the Sabre, is a horizontal twenty-four-cylinder "I"-type, is liquid-cooled and has reciprocating sleeve-valves in place of the former poppet valve system.

The Sabre engine passed the Air Ministry 100-hour type test in June, 1940, with a maximum power output of 2,200 h.p. at 3,700 r.p.m. It forms the power-unit of the Hawker Typhoon and the Hawker Tempest. The rocket-firing Typhoon proved to be a deadly weapon against all types of ground targets. The Tempest, introduced into service in 1944, played a notable part in the defeat of the flying-bomb attacks on Southern England in the Summer of 1944 before taking part in the concluding stages of the war in Europe.

THE NAPIER SABRE.

Type.—Twenty-four cylinder "I" type four-stroke sleeve-valve liquid-cooled, with two-speed supercharger.

Cylinders.—Bore 5 in. (127 m/m.), Stroke 4.75 in. (120 m/m.), Capacity 2,240 cub. in. (36.65 litres), Compression ratio 7 : 1. Two cast light alloy cylinder blocks each with twelve cylinders in upper and lower banks of six. Each bank has separate induction faces above and below and an exhaust face between the upper and lower banks of cylinders. Twelve jacketed passages lead from the exhaust ports to six ejector type exhaust stubs attached to the cylinder block between the cylinder heads. Each cylinder has three inlet and two exhaust ports and a compound sleeve scraper ring. Coolant jackets round cylinders with drilled passages between jackets. Coolant galleries are provided on each side of induction face above and below each block, with U-shaped coolant channels connecting outer galleries cast on front of both blocks. Inner side of each block grooved along centre-line to accommodate sleeve-drive worm shaft.

Cylinder Heads.—Each head a light alloy casting with coolant jacketing. Head is provided with compression ring and two phosphor-bronze sparking-plug adaptors and is attached to cylinder block by seven studs. There are also holes in the head flange for two of the long crankcase studs which pass through the cylinder block to the head. Four coolant jacket transfer holes and the head itself are sealed by rubber composition rings.

Sleeves.—Steel sleeves, each with four ports—two inlet, one exhaust and one combined inlet/exhaust. Sleeves are strengthened locally at inner ends for driving pins.

Sleeve Drive.—Case-hardened hollow steel drive-shaft runs in fourteen bearings in groove in inner side of each cylinder block. Each shaft in two halves, united by flanged coupling in form of an external sleeve. Three worm gears machined on each half of shaft. A drive gear bolted to the front end of the shaft meshes with an idler gear, which in turn is driven by a reduction gear pinion. Between each pair of upper and lower cylinders is a light alloy pedestal housing a worm wheel and two horizontal crank-arms with ball and socket joints into which the driving-pins of the upper and lower sleeves fit. The bronze worm wheels which drive the sleeve cranks are held in position by twin roller races mounted in each pedestal housing. The cranks are solid, necessitating split ball joints. The whole assembly is positively lubricated from the low-pressure circuit.

Each outer row has six crankcase bolts passing through both halves, and each inner row has six long tie-bolts which pass through both crankcase and cylinder blocks. The central cross web also takes eight centre-bearing bolts disposed in four rows. Finally, there are four internal steel studs in the front web to clamp airscrew shaft rear bearing.

Reduction Gear.—Gear ratio 0.2742 : 1. Airscrew-shaft helical gear on centre-line of engine with four compound reduction gears disposed symmetrically around it. Spur pinions on front ends of crankshafts mesh with the rear gears of the upper and lower pairs of reduction gears.

Induction.—A special Hobson injector type carburetter is mounted on the side of the intake bend of the supercharger. The injector incorporates the fuel entering valve, boost control, accelerator pump and the pressure-regulating valve. The fuel is supplied from the injector to the nozzle, which is situated inside the spinner. This latter, being fitted on the end of the impeller shaft, feeds the fuel into the eye of the impeller in a fine spray.

Fuel Pump.—Fuel is supplied to the injector by a Pesco pump of the vane type which is bolted to the underside of the sump. A relief valve, embodied in the pump, is differentially-controlled to allow for variations in atmospheric pressure.

Supercharger. — Hydraulically-operated two-speed single-entry centrifugal type. Gear ratios 4.68 : 1 low, 5.83 : 1 high. Inside the supercharger casing and between the impeller and the crankcase is the change-speed clutch. From the impeller the mixture passes through a ring of fixed diffuser blades and hence to four volutes cast in the supercharger casing. Each volute supplies one bank of cylinders through one of four manifolds, two above and two below the top and bottom banks of cylinders.

Lubrication.—The system comprises one main pressure pump ; a large main pressure oil-filter, a main scavenge pump with supercharger scavenge pump above it, and the front scavenge pump. The main pressure filter is housed on the left-hand side of the engine while the pumps, the high pressure relief valve and two gauze scavenge filters are housed in the bottom cover unit. Pressure oil lubricates main and big-end bearings, airscrew shaft rear bearing and reduction gear balance arms. It is also directed through numerous jets to airscrew shaft reduction gears. Two pressure-reducing valves in main pressure circuit feed a low-pressure circuit directing oil to the sleeve drives, the upper auxiliary unit and the bottom cover unit. The sleeves, pistons, cylinder bores and connecting-rods small ends are lubricated by splash oil from the crankshaft main and connecting-rod big-end bearings. Oil after completing its main and low-pressure circuits collects in the front portion of the bottom cover unit, is transferred by the front scavenge pump to the sump, from whence it is drawn by the main scavenge pump and returned to the supply tank through the carburetter throttle spindles and the supercharger inlet volute jacket.

Ignition.—Two B.T.H. type C1 SE-ES duplex magnetos mounted opposite one another on the upper auxiliary drive casing and driven by the upper auxiliary drive shaft, and two B.T.H. distributors similarly mounted and driven. Each distributor is wholly energised by one magneto and fires twenty-four plugs. Two sparking plugs per cylinder and fully-screened harness.

Auxiliary Drives.—In upper and lower auxiliary unit covers. Upper main drive shaft driven by pinion on front end of upper crankshaft through idler gear in top front portion of crankcase. Accessories on upper cover include the duplex magnetos and distributors, ignition servo control unit, airscrew governor control unit, air compressors, hydraulic and vacuum pumps, and electric generator. Lower shaft, driven off lower crankshaft through idler gear, drives two coolant pumps, main and supercharger scavenge pump, front scavenge pump, oil pressure pump, and fuel pump.

Coolant System.—Pressure liquid-cooling. Two centrifugal pumps circulate coolant from ring-type header tank in nose of cowling through engine and radiator. Thermostatic valves prevent coolant circulating to radiator until predetermined temperature is reached.

Starter.—Coffman type L.4S cartridge starter, which drives onto upper crankshaft rear pinion through idler gear, are mounted on upper crankcase.

Airscrew Drive.—L.H. tractor. Airscrew shaft embodies oil pressure ducts for operating airscrew in conjunction with airscrew governor unit. Control of governor is interconnected with ignition servo control unit.

Mounting.—Four platform faces provided on underside of crankcase act as engine mounting feet.

THE SABRE VA.

Dimensions.—Overall length 6 ft. 10¼ in. (2,089 m/m.), Overall width 3 ft. 4 in. (1,016 m/m.), Overall height 3 ft. 10 in. (1,168 m/m.).

Net Dry Weight.—2,500 lbs. (1,135 kg.).

Performance at Take-off and Altitude.—Rated power—moderate supercharge 2,165 h.p. at 3,650 r.p.m. at 6,500 ft. (1,980 m.) full supercharge 1,930 h.p. at 3,600 r.p.m. at 15,750 ft. (4,800 m.), Maximum power (combat) rating (5 mins. limit)—moderate supercharge 2,600 h.p. at 3,850 r.p.m. at 2,500 ft. (760 m.), full supercharge 2,300 h.p. at 3,850 r.p.m. at 12,750 ft. (3,890 m.), Maximum take-off power—moderate supercharge 2,300 h.p. at 3,850 r.p.m. at sea level.

SABRE VI.

The Sabre VI is basically a Series VA engine with modifications to suit its installation behind an annular nose radiator with engine-driven cooling fan.

THE SABRE VII.

The Sabre VII is, in general, similar to the Series VA except that water/methanol injection is used to obtain high powers for take-off and combat conditions. Certain components have been strengthened to enable them to stand up to increased loads. The controls have been modified to suit the altered boost pressures and speeds, and to ensure that the water/methanol cannot be used except under the appropriate conditions.

Dimensions.—Overall length 6 ft. 11 in. (2,105 m/m.), Overall width 3 ft. 4 in. (1,016 m/m.), Overall height 3 ft. 11¼ in. (1,189 m/m.).

Net Dry Weight.—2,540 lbs. (1,152 kg.).

Performance at Take-off and Altitude.—Rated power—moderate supercharge 2,235 h.p. at 3,700 r.p.m. at 8,500 ft. (2,590 m.), at full supercharge 1,960 h.p. at 3,700 r.p.m. at 18,250 ft. (5,570 m.), Maximum power (combat) rating (5 mins. limit)—moderate supercharge 3,055 h.p. at 3,850 r.p.m. at 2,250 ft. (690 m.) full supercharge 2,760 h.p. at 3,850 r.p.m. at 12,450 ft. (3,800 m.), Maximum take-off power—moderate supercharge 3,000 h.p. at 3,850 r.p.m. at sea level.

Pistons.—Machined from light alloy. One compression and one compression-cum-scraper ring above gudgeon pin and one wedge-action scraper ring below. Hollow fully-floating gudgeon-pins retained by hardened steel washers and circlips.

Connecting Rods.—Steel "H"-section forked and plain rods assembled in horizontally-opposed pairs, each pair having a common split steel-backed lead-bronze bearing. Fixed bronze small-end bearings lubricated by splash only.

Crankshaft.—Two interchangeable six-throw shafts one above the other with a lead-coated lead-bronze lined bearing between each throw. Crank webs are drilled and the seven journals and six crankpins are bored to provide oil passages. A spur pinion is shrunk on the forward end of each shaft, these pinions driving the four compound gears of the airscrew reduction gear. Rear ends of shafts are flanged. Bolted to upper shaft flange is a spur gear driven by the starter through an idler gear in the crankcase.

Crankcase.—Two light alloy castings joined on the vertical centre-line. Each half stiffened by five cross webs, the front and rear walls and the five webs providing housings for the airscrew shaft rear bearing and the crankshaft bearings. Facings for upper auxiliary unit cover and starter hand turning gear casing above and for bottom cover unit and oil sump below. Front cover unit houses the airscrew shaft, reduction gear and sleeve drive gears and comprises the gear carrier and the truncated cone-shaped airscrew shaft cover, which are attached to the front face of the crankcase by equally-spaced bolts and studs. Supercharger attached to the rear end of crankcase by a series of bolts and studs. Halves of crankcase assembled by bolts and studs in four rows.

POBJOY.

POBJOY AIRMOTORS AND AIRCRAFT, LTD.

Head Office : 20, Berkeley Square, London, W.1.

The original company was founded in 1930, but became a public company in June, 1935, with an authorised capital of £250,000 (£200,000 fully paid).

The original Pobjoy engine passed the Air Ministry 50-hour Type Test for civil purposes in 1928. In 1929, the "R" type engine was developed, giving 75/80 h.p., which model was superseded in 1934 by the 84/90 h.p. Niagara.

The last Pobjoy engine was the 130 h.p. Niagara V, which was remarkable for its increased output, as compared with its immediate predecessor, the Niagara III. It was fully illustrated and described in the 1940 edition of this Annual.

During the war the company was engaged exclusively on work on behalf of the Ministry of Aircraft Production and development of engines of its own design ceased for the duration.

ROLLS-ROYCE.

ROLLS-ROYCE, LTD.

HEAD OFFICE: DERBY

WORKS: DERBY, CREWE AND GLASGOW.

LONDON OFFICE: 14-15, CONDUIT STREET, W.1.

Established: March 15, 1906.

Managing Director: Sir Arthur F. Sidgreaves, O.B.E.

Works Director: E. W. Hives, C.H.

Chief Engineer, Aero-engine Division: A. G. Elliott, C.B.E.

Rolls-Royce, Ltd. specialises in the production of high-performance liquid-cooled aero-engines, the most recent types concerning which full descriptive details may be published being the Merlin 61 and the Griffon 65.

At the beginning of the War and during the Battle of Britain every R.A.F. first-line fighter aircraft was fitted with a Rolls-Royce Merlin engine. At the outset German aircraft had resorted to low flying tactics and to counter this Rolls-Royce, Ltd. increased the sea level power of the Merlin by 40 per cent. by an increase in supercharger pressure and this so improved the performance of the R.A.F. fighters that German aircraft were forced to fly higher. At this stage Rolls-Royce Ltd. had ready for production a new supercharger and were able to introduce the Merlin XX and the Merlin 45 into the Hurricane and Spitfire respectively and so enable the R.A.F. to maintain fighter superiority without interruption of production of either aircraft or the basic power plant.

A later stage in the development of the Merlin was the introduction of the two-speed two-stage supercharger, a system of supercharging which opened up a new era in aero-engine performance. The Merlin 61 at 40,000 ft. (12,200 m.) developed double the power given at a much lower altitude by the Merlin III, with which engine the original Spitfire was fitted in 1939-40.

A table published on a later page gives a fairly comprehensive picture of Merlin development during the war, an interesting feature of this table being the column detailing the widespread

The 2,000 h.p. Rolls-Royce Griffon 65 engine with two-speed two-stage supercharger.

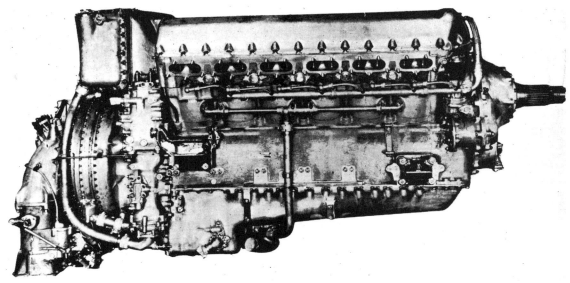

The 2,000 h.p. Rolls-Royce Griffon 65 twelve-cylinder liquid-cooled engine with two-speed two-stage supercharger.

installation of Merlin engines in British and American combat aircraft.

Altogether during the war over 150,000 Merlin engines were built in Great Britain and the U.S.A. In 1943 the combined Derby, Crewe and Glasgow factories reached an output of 18,000, or nine times the 1939 figure. The Griffon engine has also been produced in large quantities.

The Rolls-Royce Company is also engaged in the development of gas-turbine units of the Whittle type. The Gloster Meteor, the first and only Allied jet-propelled fighter to go into operational service in the European war, and also the holder of the World's Speed Record, is fitted with two Rolls-Royce units. Details of Rolls-Royce gas-turbine engines will be found on pages 7-9d.

THE ROLLS-ROYCE GRIFFON.

At the outbreak of hostilities in September, 1939, a decision was made to go ahead intensively with the production of a similar type of engine to the Merlin but of larger capacity. The Griffon as this new type came to be called, furthers the original Rolls-Royce policy of fostering the twelve-cylinder 60 degree upright-Vee type liquid-cooled power-plant. As a matter of interest it may be stated that the cylinder arrangement and dimensions of the engine are the same as those of the Rolls-Royce "R" engine which was developed for and won the 1929 and 1931 Schneider Trophy contests.

An essential requirement in the design and production of the Griffon was its availability for installation in existing Merlin-powered fighters to ensure an unbroken curve in the improvement of fighter performances. All the experience gained in the Royal Air Force and Fleet Air Arm with the Merlin has been used to the full in the design and development of the Griffon.

The Griffon incorporates a number of interesting design features including the provision of a remote gearbox, shaft-driven from the engine, on which are mounted the mechanically-driven accessories required to operate such airframe features as the retractable landing-gear, wheel-brakes, wing flaps, blind-flying instrument panel and the generator for the radio installation.

The lower marks of Griffon engine are fitted with two-speed single-stage superchargers. The Griffon II, III and IV all have

a maximum rating of 1,730 h.p. at 750 ft. (230 m.) and 1,490 h.p. at 14,000 ft. (5,270 m.) and a take-off power of 1,720 h.p. The Griffon II and III have a reduction gear ratio of .451 : 1 and the Griffon IV a ratio of .510 : 1. The Griffon II was fitted in the earlier Firefly I and II until replaced by the Griffon XII. The Griffon III and IV were both fitted in the Spitfire XII.

The Griffon VI is similar to the IV but has increased take-off and maximum boost pressure (15 lb.). This engine has a maximum rating of 1,850 h.p. at 2,000 ft. (610 m.) and 1,635 h.p. at 10,500 ft. (3,200 m.), with 1,815 h.p. available for take-off. This engine is installed in the Seafire XV and XVII.

The Griffon XII is similar to the VI but with lower supercharger gear ratios and a reduction gear ratio of .451 : 1. It has a maximum rating of 1,765 h.p. at sea level and 1,665 h.p. at 11,000 ft. (3,355 m.). It is installed in the Firefly I and II.

The Griffon 61 is fitted with a two-speed two-stage supercharger and intercooler similar to that installed in the Merlin 61 Series, and compared with the earlier Griffon models it has a considerably improved altitude performance. Its maximum rating is 2,035 h.p. at 7,000 ft. (2,135 m.) and 1,820 h.p. at 21,000 ft. (6,400 m.), with 1,540 h.p. available for take-off. The dry weight of the Griffon 65 is 1,980 lbs. (898 kg.), as compared with 1,800 lbs. (816 kg.) for the single-stage supercharged models previously mentioned. It is installed in the Spitfire 21.

The Griffon 65 is similar to the 61 but is fitted with a reduction gear ratio of .510 : 1 instead of .451 : 1. The Griffon 65 forms the power plant of the Spitfire XIV. The Griffon 66 is the same as the 65 but is fitted with cabin supercharger drive.

The Griffon 72 and 74 are modifications of the 65 to meet the requirements of the Royal Navy. Utilising the advantages offered by 150 grade fuel, a maximum boost of 25 lbs./sq. in. in F.S. gear was stipulated At this pressure the h.p. recorded at 9,250 ft. (2,820 m.) is 2,245. At sea level with 18½ lbs. boost a take-off power of 2,045 h.p. is available. The main difference between the 72 and 74 is the fitting of a Rolls-Royce Bendix-Stromberg carburettor to the former and a Rolls-Royce injection pump to the latter. The Griffon 72 was fitted in the prototype of the Firefly IV and the 74 is being installed in the production version of that aeroplane.

The Griffon 83 is of the same basic design as the 65 except

that it is fitted to drive contra-rotating airscrews. At a maximum boost of 25 lbs. the Griffon 83 has a power rating of 2,340 h.p. at 750 ft. (230 m.) and 2,120 h.p. at 12,250 ft. (3,740 m.).

The description below refers specifically to the Griffon 65 but is representative of all marks in the Griffon range fitted with the Rolls-Royce two-speed two-stage supercharger.

TYPE.—Twelve-cylinder 60° Vee liquid-cooled.

CYLINDERS.—Bore 6.0 in. (152.4 m/m.), Stroke 6.6 in. (167.64 m/m.), Swept volume 36.7 litres. Two blocks of six cylinders are mounted at 60 degrees to each other on inclined upper faces of a two-piece crankcase. Each block comprises a light alloy skirt with a separate light alloy cylinder-head. Separate cylinder liners in high carbon steel, having flanges at their upper ends, are fitted in the light alloy skirts, the flanges of the liners being sandwiched between the head and skirt making the liner practically unstressed in the static condition, thereby reducing distortion. A further advantage of this arrangement is the elimination of internal coolant leaks. Gas tightness is ensured by the use of soft aluminium-alloy jointing rings. A coolant seal on each liner at the base of the skirt is made by rubber collars located between external ribs on the liner. The cylinder assemblies are each retained to the crankcase by fourteen long studs in chrome-vanadium steel which pass through tubes in the cylinder skirt and head, these tubes being sealed against coolant leaks by rubber rings. A further series of small studs form a secondary tie between head and skirt. The heads carry renewable valve seatings in Silchrome. Inlet and exhaust valve guides are made in cast iron and phosphor bronze respectively.

PISTONS.—Machined from close forgings of R.R.59 alloy. The piston carries two compression rings and a drilled scraper ring above the gudgeon-pin and another drilled scraper ring below it. Both scraper rings and scraper ring grooves are drilled to return oil to the crankcase. A fully-floating gudgeon-pin in hardened nickel steel is located by spring wire circlips.

CONNECTING RODS.—Nickel steel forgings machined all over and having H-section shanks. Each assembly consists of a plain rod and a forked rod, the latter carrying a nickel steel bearing block, the halves of which are secured together and to the forked rod by four bolts. This bearing block retains a split flanged thin steel

A front view of the Rolls-Royce Griffon 65 engine.

shell lined with lead-bronze which runs directly on the crankpin. Similar split bearing shells are fitted to the plain rod and work on the outer surface of the forked rod block. The small end of each connecting-rod houses a fully-floating bronze bush.

CRANKSHAFT.—Clockwise rotation viewed from rear. One-piece balanced, six-throw machined forging of nitrogen-hardened chrome-molybdenum steel. Crankpins and journals are bored and fitted with oil retaining caps and the webs are drilled to allow oil to be fed axially from each end of the crankshaft to the main journal and connecting-rod bearings. Drive to the reduction gear pinion is from a serrated flange bolted to the front end of the crankshaft. The rear end of the crankshaft is connected by a flexible torsion shaft to the supercharger driving gear and also provides drives to the auxiliary gearbox, oil pumps, coolant pumps, fuel pump, tachometer and constant-speed unit. Angular movement of this flexible torsion shaft is limited by stops attached to the crankshaft.

CRANKCASE.—In two halves. Both castings of aluminium-alloy. Upper portion carries cylinders and crankshaft main bearings. The front of the crankcase forms integrally the rear housing the airscrew reduction gear and also contains the camshaft and starter motor drives. The lower portion forms the engine sump and contains the oil pump assembly consisting of the main pressure pump, supercharger change-speed operating pump and two scavenge pumps; and also the main coolant pump which is driven through the same train of gears as the oil pumps. The main bearings, of which there are seven, consist of split steel shells lined with lead-bronze alloy, which fit into semi-circular recesses machined in the top half crankcase, and are held in position by forged light alloy bearing caps and nickel-steel studs. In addition to these studs sixteen bolts pass transversely through the caps and the whole width of the crankcase, to give great rigidity but at the same time allowing withdrawal of the lower half crankcase without disturbing the crankshaft.

WHEELCASE.—Aluminium-alloy casting secured by studs at rear end of crankcase. Supercharger unit is in turn bolted onto the back of the wheelcase. The wheelcase houses the two-speed supercharger drive, drives to auxiliary gearbox coupling, engine speed indicator, airscrew constant-speed unit, intercooler pump, fuel pump, and also provides a drive to the oil and coolant pumps situated in the lower half crankcase.

VALVE GEAR.—There are two inlet and two exhaust valves per cylinder. Inlet and exhaust valves are prepared from forgings of K.E.965 steel, a protective layer of "Brightray" covering the whole of the combustion face and seat of the exhaust valve and the seat only of the inlet valve. Sodium-cooled exhaust valves. Two concentric coil springs control each valve via a steel top washer having a central taper bore containing split bronze collets which locate in a recess in the valve stem. A single central camshaft mounted in seven pedestal brackets fixed to the top of each cylinder head operates both inlet and exhaust valves through rocker arms fitted with spherical-headed adjustable tappet screws. The camshafts which are similar for both cylinder blocks are driven via spur gears, bevel gears and inclined shafts from the reduction gear wheel.

INDUCTION.—The carburetter is of Rolls-Royce-Bendix design and is of the triple-choke updraught type consisting of the following units:—throttle unit; automatic mixture-control unit; regulator unit; fuel-control unit; injector nozzle and accelerator pump. Fuel is supplied to the carburetter under pressure by a vane-type fuel-pump mounted in and driven from the port side of the wheelcase. Excess fuel is fed back to the inlet side of the pump via a relief valve. The fuel passes to the control units via filters and vapour separators. The throttle unit is similar to that used with conventional float-type carburetters and has three plate-type throttles mounted on a common shaft which is connected to the automatic-boost control unit. Each choke is fitted with a large venturi carrying eight impact tubes and two small venturi. The suction at the throat of the small venturi is a measure of the volume of air entering the engine. The pressure differential between this suction and impact tube pressure when corrected by the automatic mixture-control unit for changes in air density becomes a measure of mass air-flow. This differential is applied to the air diaphragm of the regulator unit to regulate the fuel metering pressure (or head) across the fixed jets in the fuel-control unit. The Automatic mixture-control unit consists of a sealed metallic bellows operating a contoured needle. The bellows are filled with nitrogen and a measured amount of inert oil, the nitrogen to make it sensitive to temperature as well as pressure changes, the oil to dampen vibration. The contoured valve therefore has a predetermined position for each air density encountered in flight. The regulator unit automatically adjusts the fuel pressure differential across the metering jets and therefore the fuel flow in proportion to the mass air flow through the throttle body. The unit consists of an air diaphragm, a fuel diaphragm and a balanced fuel-valve, all mounted on one stem and supported by suitable guides. Fuel enters through a strainer, passes through the balanced valve to one side of the fuel diaphragm chamber and then to the jets in the fuel control unit. Twin vapour separators are incorporated. The fuel control unit attached directly to the regulator unit contains the metering jets, fuel-head enrichment valve, an idle valve and a mixture-control valve. The enrichment valve is operated by a fuel diaphragm and provides enrichment in proportion to mass airflow through the carburetter. The idle valve is mechanically connected to the throttle and controls the mixture throughout the idle range of speeds, (*i.e.* the first 10° throttle movement). The mixture control valve provides run and idle cut-off positions. The injector nozzle is supplied with metered fuel direct from the fuel-control unit and the fuel is sprayed under pressure directly into the first stage supercharger eye. The accelerator pump of the vacuum-operated type is also supplied with metered fuel from the fuel-control unit and sprays fuel from a separate nozzle directly into the supercharger eye and at the same time causes an accelerating discharge from the main injector nozzle. The fuel/air mixture is taken through both stages of the supercharger via the intercooler to the induction manifolds in the Vee, the manifolds being provided with flame traps as a precaution against fire.

SUPERCHARGER.—Two-speed two-stage supercharger of the centrifugal type, the change-speed mechanism of which is operated by an automatic change-over mechanism incorporating an electric-pneumatic-hydraulic system operated by an atmospherically-controlled aneroid. The hydraulic oil pressure for operating the centrifugally-loaded clutches of the two-speed mechanism is supplied by the special high-pressure pump previously mentioned. Design of the clutches is such that slip is permitted under acceleration conditions to avoid overloading of gearing and also to damp out, in conjunction with the spring-drive, torsional oscillation from the crankshaft. The delivery pressure of the supercharger is controlled by an automatic servo mechanism coupled through a differential linkage to the throttle so that a constant boost-pressure is maintained at altitude up to full throttle conditions for a fixed position of the pilot's lever.

IGNITION.—Ignition is by two twelve-cylinder magnetos combined together in one unit and mounted in the Vee directly behind the reduction-gear housing. Driven by bevel gears and an inclined shaft from the port camshaft drive. Incorporates two separate circuits which are electrically independent of each other. The timing of the two magneto circuits relative to each other is fixed, but an advance and retard range is obtained by differential action in the inclined drive-shaft to the magneto. This differential action is controlled by an automatic servo mechanism coupled to the throttle lever by suitable linkage. Four metal conduits coupled with metal braiding to the magneto housing carry the ignition leads to the sparking plugs via short metal braid connections, this making the system fully screened.

LUBRICATION.—Dry-sump system. One pressure and two scavenge pumps of the gear-type driven from the wheelcase. The pressure pump delivers oil from the aircraft tank to two relief valves in one unit which controls oil pressure to a high and low pressure system. Any excess oil is spilled back directly into the crankcase. The high pressure system feeds the crankshaft journal bearings, connecting-rod bearings and constant-speed unit. The oil to the constant-speed unit is further increased in pressure by the unit for operation of the variable-pitch airscrew. High pressure oil is also taken from the delivery side of the main pressure pump through a precision gear-type pump of low capacity, where its pressure is further increased for the purpose of operating the change-speed mechanism of the two-speed supercharger drive. The low pressure system is used for feeding oil to the camshaft and rocker mechanism, oil jets feeding the airscrew reduction gears, supercharger drive gears, and various other bearings throughout the engine. Used oil drains back to the lower half crankcase, where it passes through filters to two scavenge pumps, one servicing each end of the lower half, and thence back to the aircraft tank via the oil radiator. The flow of cooling air is controlled automatically by flaps through the medium of a temperature-sensitive device.

COOLANT SYSTEM.—The coolant employed is a mixture of 70% water and 30% ethylene glycol. The coolant is circulated by a centrifugal-type pump to the cylinder blocks and from the cylinder blocks to a small-capacity header tank and from the header tank via a radiator to the coolant-pump inlet. The flow of coolant air through the radiator is controlled, whether manually or automatically, through the medium of a temperature-sensitive device. The header tank, which incorporates features to ensure the efficient separation of steam and coolant, is provided with a loaded relief valve which seals the whole coolant system up to a predetermined pressure. This pressurising of the system raises the boiling point of the coolant, and permits the use of smaller radiators. The header tank relief valve maintains the pressure in the system and also incorporates a suction-operated valve which admits air, if for any reason the pressure falls below atmospheric.

INTERCOOLER SYSTEM.—The coolant employed is a mixture of 70% water and 30% ethylene glycol which is circulated by means of a centrifugal pump from a header tank through a radiator to the jacket situated between the two stages of the supercharger and to the intercooler matrix, placed between the supercharger and induction pipe, and thence back to the header tank. This system which is entirely independent of the main engine system is pressurised and incorporates a similar design of header tank, relief valve and radiator-cooling air control as on the main system, but no thermostat. Heat exchange from the coolant is carried out by an independent radiator in the aircraft system in the normal manner.

STARTING.—The starting system is of the combustion type. Five cartridges are contained in a breech, which is indexed mechanically from the cockpit of the aircraft and fired electrically. This is piped to the starter-unit bolted to the rear face of a housing integral with the reduction-gear casing on the starboard side of the engine. The starter-unit drives through dogs and a train of gears on to the gearwheel of the airscrew-shaft. Fuel priming-nozzles are provided in the induction system to ensure easy starting.

AUXILIARIES.—All the aircraft service accessories are mounted on a separate gearbox on the bulkhead and driven by a shaft through universal joints from the top of the wheelcase. This gearbox has its own independent lubrication system and supply.

AIRSCREW DRIVE.—Left Hand Tractor. The airscrew shaft is driven through a single spur reduction gear housed partly in a casing formed integrally with the crankcase and for the remainder, in a casing bolted to the front end of the crankcase. The hollow driving pinion mounted in two roller bearings is concentric with, and is driven by, a hollow coupling shaft serrated at both ends. One end engages with a serrated driving ring on the crankshaft and the forward end with the internal serrations on the driving pinion. This coupling shaft insulates the reduction gear unit from crankshaft loadings and torsional vibrations. The hollow airscrew shaft has an integral flange which is bolted to the ring gear driven by the pinion, and is mounted in roller-bearings, axial thrust being taken in either direction by a ball thrust-bearing. A hydraulically-operated variable-pitch airscrew is centralised upon cones at each end when fitted to the airscrew shaft. High pressure oil from the constant-speed unit is supplied to the rear half of the reduction-gear casing from whence it is transferred to two concentric oil tubes, secured within, and rotating with the airscrew shaft and so to the pitch-operating mechanism of the airscrew. For the purpose of valve and ignition timing the pinion has timing marks incorporated on a bevelled face at the front end and a pointer is fitted on the pinion cover and viewed by removal of an inspection cover.

PERFORMANCE.—See Introduction.

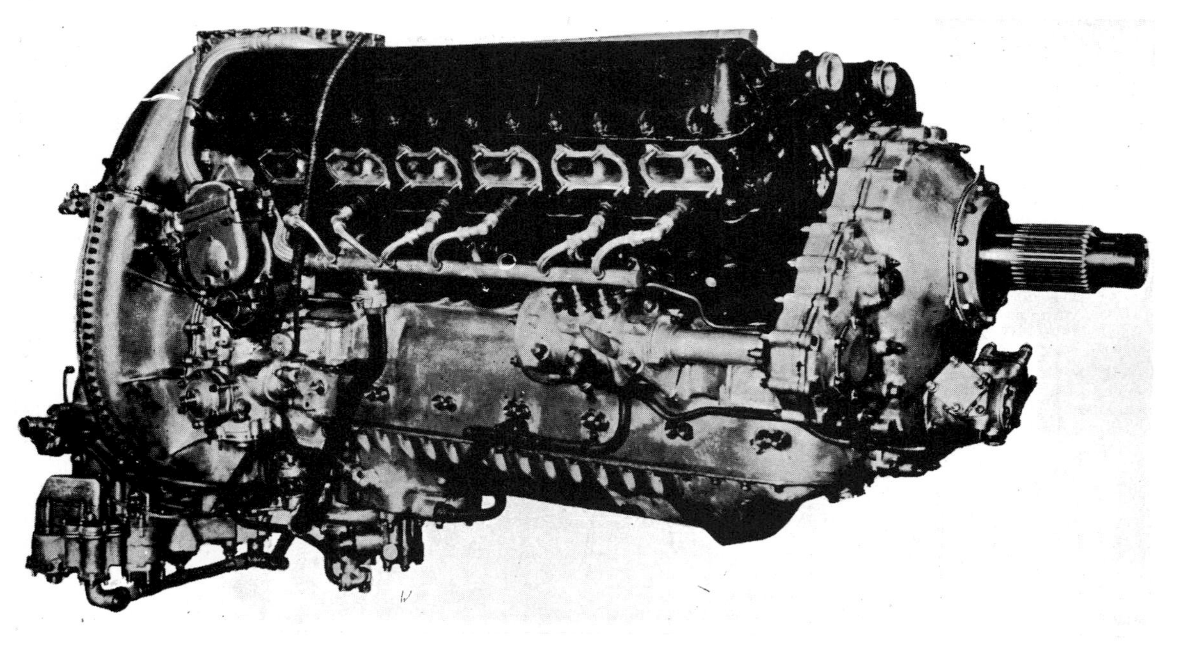

The Rolls-Royce Merlin 61 engine with two-speed two-stage supercharger.

THE ROLLS-ROYCE MERLIN 61 SERIES.

The Merlin 61 compared with its predecessors, the single-stage two-speed Merlins, has a very considerably improved performance both with regard to maximum power available and the altitude to which it is maintained. The two types of engines vary very little with respect to the features which affect installation interchangeability and it has been possible to instal the improved engine into the confined limits of a Spitfire fuselage, the only change called for being a slight lengthening (5 in.) of the nose to accommodate the extra length of the engine.

The mechanical specification is basically similar to the Merlin XX described in previous issues of this Annual, with the exception of an entirely new two-speed two-stage supercharging system.

The two-speed two-stage supercharger has two rotors driven on a common shaft and is really two separate superchargers in series. The mixture of air and petrol which is drawn through the carburettor is compressed by the first stage supercharger and is then delivered to the inlet of the second stage supercharger where it is still further compressed and is finally delivered to the main induction pipe feeding the twelve cylinders.

The process of compressing, by the superchargers, the large quantity of air required to burn the fuel results in considerable heating of the mixture and in order to reduce the mixture temperature to a normal figure, recourse is made to charge cooling, or intercooling as it is called.

The way in which this intercooling is carried out is very ingenious. A square box-like structure is mounted in the induction system between the outlet of the second-stage supercharger and the rear of the cylinder blocks. This box contains a radiator through the tubes of which water is circulated. The hot charge from the outlet of the supercharger is passed, on its way to the main induction pipe, through the matrix of this radiator and in passing its temperature is considerably reduced. In addition to this charge-cooling radiator, there is a water-jacket between the two stages of the supercharger which also contributes to the cooling of the charge.

The intercooler system is entirely separate from the main cooling system and one of the greatest advantages of this novel method is that the actual radiator from which the excess charge temperature is dissipated to the atmosphere may be placed at any convenient position on the power-plant or aeroplane.

TYPE.—Twelve-cylinder 60° Vee liquid-cooled.

CYLINDERS.—Bore 5.4 in. (137.16 m/m.), Stroke 6 in. (152.4 m/m.), Swept volume 1,647 cub. in. (27 litres). Two two-piece cylinder blocks of cast R.R.50 aluminium-alloy have separate heads and skirts. Six cylinder liners of high carbon steel in each block are directly in touch with cooling liquid. Liner is spigotted directly in skirt at top and by a loose flanged collar at the bottom, the flange of this collar being trapped between skirt and crankcase. Integral flange at top of liner beds direct into cylinder head face to make gas joint. Coolant joint at base of liner made by two rubber rings. Fourteen long studs extend in coolant tight tubes from top of cylinder block into crankcase. Twenty-four additional short studs screwed into the bottom of the cylinder-head clamp the upper liner flanges between the cylinder head and skirt. Renewable Silchrome valve seatings screwed into cylinder heads. Valve guides of cast-iron for inlets and phosphor bronze for exhausts.

PISTONS.—Machined from forgings of R.R.59 alloy. Three compression and two scraper rings. One of the latter above and other below gudgeon pin. Both grooves and rings drilled to return oil from walls. Fully-floating hollow gudgeon pins of hardened nickel-chrome steel retained in position by spring circlips.

CONNECTING RODS.—Nickel steel forgings machined to H-section all over. Each pair consists of plain rod and forked rod, latter carries nickel-steel bearing block, which accommodates the steel backed lead bronze alloy bearings. Halves of block secured together and to forked rod by four bolts. Small-end of each connecting rod houses floating phosphor bronze bush.

CRANKSHAFT.—One-piece six-throw, Machined forging of chrome-molybdenum steel. Integral balance-weights. Nitrogen-hardened. Crankpins and journals bored and fitted with oil-retaining covers.

Drive to reduction-gear pinion is through a splined coupling shaft which fits into a splined flange bolted to front end of crankshaft. To damp out irregularities in angular velocity and torque, drive from crankshaft to supercharger and timing gears and auxiliary components is through torsionally flexible shaft which provides spring drive. Twisting of this shaft is limited by hollow sleeve.

CRANKCASE.—In halves. Both castings of aluminium-alloy. Upper portion carries cylinders, bearings of crankshaft and part of housing for airscrew reduction gear. Lower portion is sump case and carries the oil pumps and filters. Main bearings, split mild-steel shells lined with lead-bronze alloy, fit into recesses machined in the crankcase. Bearings held in position by caps. Besides usual bearing cap studs, seven pairs of long bolts pass transversely through caps and across whole width of crankcase. Design gives rigidity of integrally-cast bearing cap but allows withdrawal of lower portion of crankcase without disturbing bearings.

WHEELCASE.—Aluminium casting secured by studs at rear end of crankcase. Supercharger unit goes onto back of wheelcase. Latter houses drives to the camshafts, magnetos, coolant and oil pumps, supercharger, hand and electric starters, and the electric generator.

VALVE GEAR.—Two inlet and two exhaust valves of K.E. 965 steel parellel with centre line of each cylinder block. Inlet-valves on inside of Vee have stellited ends. Exhaust valves have sodium-cooled stems and "Brightray" over crown and seating surfaces and stellited ends. Each valve has two concentric coil-springs, kept in place by collar and split wedge. Spring circlip retains valve in guide should valve-springs fail. Each valve is worked through a separate steel rocker which has a spherical-headed tappet-screw and lock-nut at the valve end for adjustment. Camshaft, along top of each cylinder-block in seven bearings, driven by inclined shaft and bevel gears from wheelcase.

INDUCTION.—Twin-choke updraught carburetter of Rolls-Royce and S.U. design supplies mixture to supercharger. Two air-passages are coupled to a single Rolls-Royce type of forward-facing air-intake. Each choke is supplied by a separate diffuser nozzle at right angles to airstream; by slow running device; by discharge orifice of accelerator-pump; and by main fuel-control jet of submerged type controlled by taper needle. Automatic mixture-control device incorporated in carburetter. One jet controlled by aneroid exposed to atmospheric pressure. In the event of failure of aneroid mixture returns automatically to full rich. Other jet controlled by aneroid subject to boost pressure and safeguarded against damage from back-fires by a disc-valve which closes the communicating vent. Positive methods against freezing; heated coolant circulates through jackets around chokes; warm scavenge oil circulates through hollow throttle-valves. Twin fuel pumps driven by independent quill shafts. If one pump fails, other has more than enough capacity to meet maximum demand. Any fuel in excess is returned through disc-valve to suction side.

SUPERCHARGER.—Two-speed two-stage supercharger, change-speed mechanism of which is operated by oil pressure from scavenge system. Delivery pressure of supercharger is controlled by automatic servo-mechanism coupled through differential linkage to throttle so that opening of latter is controlled to suit boost-pressure.

IGNITION.—Two twelve-cylinder magnetos spigot-mounted, one on each side of wheelcase. Each driven by skew-gear from upper vertical drive-shaft through serrated couplings. System fully screened. Three metal conduits coupled with metal braiding to magneto-housings. Short metal-braided connections to sparking plugs. Special heat-resisting adaptors on exhaust side. Resistors are fitted in the plug adaptors.

LUBRICATION.—Dry sump system. One pressure and two scavenge pumps of the gear type driven from wheelcase through idler gear from lower vertical drive-shaft to coolant pump. The pressure pump delivers high pressure oil from the aircraft tank, to the crankshaft and big-end bearings via a relief valve unit. High pressure oil is also delivered to the constant-speed airscrew unit where its pressure is still further increased for operation of the variable-pitch airscrew. Oil at lower pressure is delivered from the relief valve unit to the camshaft and rocker mechanism, to oil jets feeding the airscrew reduction gears, to the supercharger drive mechanism and to various other bearings and gears throughout the engine. Used oil, drains back to the lower half crankcase where it passes through filters to two scavenge pumps, one servicing each end of the lower half. The scavenge pumps deliver the used oil via the two-speed supercharger gear change operating gear and the carburettor throttles to an oil cooler and thence back to the aircraft tank. An automatic valve is fitted in the scavenge system which allows the oil to by-pass the cooler when below a predetermined temperature; the function of this valve is to maintain the oil at a constant temperature, and to safeguard the cooler against damage due to the excessive pressures which can be developed when the oil is cold.

COOLANT SYSTEM.—The coolant employed is a mixture of 70% water and 30% ethylene glycol. It is circulated by means of a centrifugal type pump from a small capacity header tank through radiators to the cylinder blocks and thence back to the header tank. The flow of cooling air through the radiator is controlled, either manually or automatically, through the medium of a temperature sensitive device. The header tank, which incorporates features to ensure the efficient separation of steam and coolant, is provided with a loaded relief valve which seals the whole coolant system up to a predetermined pressure. This pressurising of the system raises the boiling point of the coolant, and permits the use of smaller radiators. The maximum permissible coolant temperature is by this means raised to 135°C. The header tank relief valve maintains the pressure in the system, and also incorporates a suction-operated valve which admits air, if for any reason the pressure falls below atmospheric.

INTERCOOLER SYSTEM.—The coolant employed is a mixture of 70% water and 30% ethylene glycol which is circulated by means of a centrifugal pump from a header tank through the radiator to the jacket situated between the two stages of the supercharger and to the intercooler matrix, placed between the supercharger and induction pipe, and thence back to the header tank. This system which is entirely independent of the main engine system is pressurized and incorporates similar design of header tank, relief valve and radiator cooling air control as on the main system, but no thermostat. Heat exchange from the coolant is carried out by an independent radiator in the aircraft system in the normal manner.

STARTING.—The electrical equipment includes an electric starter and a dynamo capable of keeping the aircraft batteries fully charged, and to balance the current consumption required by the numerous electrically operated devices on the modern service aeroplane. Press-button electric starting is therefore available and is capable of functioning efficiently under extremely low temperature conditions. Auxiliary hand-turning gear with a reduction ratio of 13.56 : 1 operates through a portion of same gear-train as electric starter. Multi-plate clutch, common to both systems, incorporated on the starter-layshaft, is designed to slip in the event of a backfire.

ACCESSORIES.—Provision is made on the engine for driving various auxiliary units needed for aircraft services, such as air compressors for gun-turret operation, hydraulic pumps for retractable undercarriages and bomb doors, etc., engine speed indicator, vacuum pumps and the constant-speed airscrew operating pump. Necessary pipework is fitted on the engine for employment of an automatic fire-extinguishing system, and also a de-icing equipment for the airscrew.

AIRSCREW DRIVE.—Airscrew shaft driven through single spur reduction gear (.42/1) at the front end of crankcase. Hollow driving pinion in two roller-bearings co-axial with crankshaft from which it is driven by a short hollow shaft serrated at both ends. One end engages with crankshaft flange and forward end with internal serrations on driving pinion. Hollow shaft insulates pinion bearings from the crankshaft loadings. Pinion engages with toothed ring bolted to flange integral with hollow airscrew shaft. This runs on roller-bearings and has ball-bearing to take axial thrust in either direction. Airscrew shaft takes the Rotol or D.H. Hydromatic constant-speed airscrew. High-pressure oil for operation of hydraulic airscrew supplied through a tube secured within and rotating with the shaft. This tube is fed from spherically-seated oil-connection in the housing of the rear half of the reduction gear casing. Airscrew hub is centralised upon cones at each end.

PERFORMANCE.—See Table.

ROLLS-ROYCE MERLIN ENGINES.

Bore × Stroke : 5.4 in. × 6 in. (137.3 m/m. × 152.5 m/m.). Capacity : 1,647 cu. in. (27 litres.).

Engine	Take-off Power	International Rating	Maximum Power	Dry Weight (plus 2½% tolerance)	Airscrew Gear Ratio	Compression Ratio	Remarks
Merlin I	890 h.p. at 2,850 r.p.m.	990 h.p. at 2,600 r.p.m. at 12,250 ft. (3,740 m.)	1,030 h.p. at 3,000 r.p.m. at 16,250 ft. (4,940 m.)	1,385 lbs. (629 kg.)	.477 : 1	6 : 1	
Merlin II and III	880 h.p. at 3,000 r.p.m.	990 h.p. at 2,600 r.p.m. at 12,250 ft. (3,740 m.)	1,440 h.p. at 3,000 r.p.m. at 5,500 ft. (1,680 m.)	1,375 lbs. (624 kg.)	.477 : 1	6 : 1	Installed in Spitfire I, Defiant I, Hurricane I, Sea Hurricane I, Battle I.
Merlin VIII	1,080 h.p. at 3,000 r.p.m. (1,275 h.p. 100 Octane)	1,010 h.p. at 2,850 r.p.m. at 6,750 ft. (2,060 m.)	1,035 h.p. at 3,000 r.p.m. at 7,750 ft. (2,360 m.)	1,420 lbs. (645 kg.)	.477 : 1	6 : 1	Installed in Fulmar I.
Merlin X	1,075 h.p. at 3,000 r.p.m.	1,035 h.p. at 2,600 r.p.m. at 2,250 ft. (685 m.) and 960 h.p. at 2,600 r.p.m. at 13,000 ft. (3,965 m.)	1,130 h.p. at 3,000 r.p.m. at 5,250 ft. (1,525 m.) and 1,010 h.p. at 3,000 r.p.m. at 17,750 ft. (5,400 m.)	1,450 lbs. (658 kg.)	.42 : 1	6 : 1	Installed in Halifax I, Wellington II, Whitley V and VII.
Merlin XII	1,175 h.p. at 3,000 r.p.m.	1,150 h.p. at 2,850 r.p.m. at 13,000 ft. (3,965 m.)	1,150 h.p. at 3,000 r.p.m. at 14,000 ft. (4,420 m.)	1,425 lbs. (647 kg.)	.477 : 1	6 : 1	Installed in Spitfire II.
Merlin XX	1,280 h.p. at 3,000 r.p.m.	1,240 h.p. at 2,850 r.p.m. at 10,000 ft. (3,050 m.) and 1,175 h.p. at 2,850 r.p.m. at 17,500 ft. (5,340 m.)	1,480 h.p. at 3,000 r.p.m. at 6,000 ft. (1,830 m.) and 1,480 h.p. at 3,000 r.p.m. at 12,250 ft. (3,740 m.)	1,450 lbs. (658 kg.)	.42 : 1	6 : 1	Installed in Beaufighter II, Defiant II, Halifax II and V, Hurricane II and IV, Lancaster I and III.
Merlin 21	1,280 h.p. at 3,000 r.p.m.	1,240 h.p. at 2,850 r.p.m. at 10,000 ft. (3,050 m.) and 1,175 h.p. at 2,850 r.p.m. at 17,500 ft. (5,340 m.)	1,480 h.p. at 3,000 r.p.m. at 6,000 ft. (1,830 m.) and 1,480 h.p. at 3,000 r.p.m. at 12,250 ft. (3,740 m.)	1,450 lbs. (658 kg.)	.42 : 1	6 : 1	Installed in Mosquito I, II, III, IV and VI.
Merlin 22	1,280 h.p. at 3,000 r.p.m.	1,240 h.p. at 2,850 r.p.m. at 10,000 ft. (3,050 m.) and 11,75 h.p. at 2,850 r.p.m. at 17,500 ft. (5,340 m.)	1,480 h.p. at 3,000 r.p.m. at 6,000 ft. (8,130 m.) and 1,480 h.p. at 3,000 r.p.m. at 12,250 ft. (3,740 m.)	1,450 lbs. (658 kg.)	.42 : 1	6 : 1	Installed in Lancaster I and III, York I.

ROLLS-ROYCE MERLIN ENGINES—*continued*.

Bore × Stroke : 5.4 in. × 6 in. (137.3 m/m. × 152.5 m/m.).   Capacity : 1,647 cu. in. (27 litres.).

Engine	Take-off Power	International Rating	Maximum Power	Dry Weight (plus 2½% tolerance)	Airscrew Gear Ratio	Compression Ratio	Remarks
Merlin 23	1,390 h.p. at 3,000 r.p.m.	1,240 h.p. at 2,850 r.p.m. at 10,000 ft. (3,050 m.) and 1,175 h.p. at 2,850 r.p.m. at 17,500 ft. (5,340 m.)	1,480 h.p. at 3,000 r.p.m. at 6,000 ft. (1,830 m.) and 1,480 h.p. at 3,000 r.p.m. at 12,250 ft. (3,740 m.)	1,450 lbs. (658 kg.)	.42 : 1	6 : 1	Installed in Mosquito I, II, IV, VI, XII and XIII.
Merlin 24	1,620 h.p. at 3,000 r.p.m.	1,240 h.p. at 2,850 r.p.m. at 10,000 ft. (3,050 m.) and 1,175 h.p. at 2,850 r.p.m. at 17,500 ft. (5,340 m.)	1,640 h.p. at 3,000 r.p.m. at 2,000 ft. (610 m.) and 1,500 h.p. at 3,000 r.p.m. at 9,500 ft. (2,900 m.)	1,450 lbs. (658 kg.)	.42 : 1	6 : 1	Installed in Lancaster I and III, York I.
Merlin 25	1,620 h.p. at 3,000 r.p.m.	1,240 h.p. at 2,850 r.p.m. at 10,000 ft. (3,050 m.) and 1,175 h.p. at 2,850 r.p.m. at 17,500 ft. (5,340 m.)	1,640 h.p. at 3,000 r.p.m. at 2,000 ft. (610 m.) and 1,500 h.p. at 3,000 r.p.m. at 9,500 ft. (2,900 m.)	1,450 lbs. (658 kg.)	.42 : 1	6 : 1	Installed in Mosquito VI and XIX.
Merlin 28	1,300 h.p. at 3,000 r.p.m.	—	—	—	.42 : 1	6 : 1	Built by Packard (U.S.A.). Installed in Lancaster I and III, Kittyhawk II (P-40F) U.S. designation V-1650-1.
Merlin 29	1,300 h.p. at 3,000 r.p.m.	—	—	—	.477 : 1	6 : 1	Built by Packard (U.S.A.). Splined airscrew shaft. Installed in Canadian Hurricane, Kittyhawk II (P-40F). U.S. designation V-1650-1.
Merlin 30	1,300 h.p. at 3,000 r.p.m.	1,240 h.p. at 2,850 r.p.m. at 7,250 ft. (2,210 m.)	1,260 h.p. at 3,000 r.p.m. at 8,750 ft. (2,670 m.)	1,420 lbs. (645 kg.)	.477 : 1	6 : 1	Installed in Barracuda I, Fulmar II.
Merlin 31	1,300 h.p. at 3,000 r.p.m.	—	—	—	.42 : 1	6 : 1	Built by Packard (U.S.A.). Installed in Canadian Mosquito XX, Australian Mosquito 40, Kittyhawk II (P-40F and L). U.S. designation V-1650-1.
Merlin 32	1,600 h.p. at 3,000 r.p.m.	1,360 h.p. at 2,850 r.p.m. at 5,500 ft. (1,680 m.)	1,645 h.p. at 3,000 r.p.m. at 2,500 ft. (760 m.)	1,400 lbs. (636 kg.)	.477 : 1	6 : 1	Installed in Barracuda II, Seafire II.
Merlin 33	1,390 h.p. at 3,000 r.p.m.	As for Merlin 23		1,450 lbs. (658 kg.)	.42 : 1	6 : 1	Packard-built Merlin 23. Installed in Canadian Mosquito XX and Australian Mosquito 40.
Merlin 38	1,390 h.p. at 3,000 r.p.m.	As for Merlin 22		1,450 lbs. (658 kg.)	.42 : 1	6 : 1	Packard-built Merlin 22. Installed in Lancaster I and III.
Merlin 45	1,185 h.p. at 3,000 r.p.m.	1,200 h.p. at 2,850 r.p.m. at 16,000 ft. (4,880 m.)	1,470 h.p. at 3,000 r.p.m. at 9,250 ft. (2,820 m.)	1,425 lbs. (647 kg.)	.477 : 1	6 : 1	Installed in Spitfire V, P.R. IV and VII, Seafire II.
Merlin 45M	1,230 h.p. at 3,000 r.p.m.	1,165 h.p. at 2,850 r.p.m. at 10,000 ft. (3,050 m.)	1,585 h.p. at 3,000 r.p.m. at 2,750 ft. (840 m.)	1,425 lbs. (647 kg.)	.477 : 1	6 : 1	Installed in Spitfire L.F. V.
Merlin 46	1,100 h.p. at 3,000 r.p.m.	1,115 h.p. at 2,850 r.p.m. at 19,000 ft. (5,795 m.)	1,415 h.p. at 3,000 r.p.m. at 14,000 ft. (4,270 m.)	1,425 lbs. (647 kg.)	.477 : 1	6 : 1	Installed in Spitfire V, P.R. IV and VII, Seafire I.
Merlin 47	1,100 h.p. at 3,000 r.p.m.	1,115 h.p. at 2,850 r.p.m. at 19,000 ft. (5,795 m.)	1,415 h.p. at 3,000 r.p.m. at 14,000 ft. (4,270 m.)	1,450 lbs. (658 kg.)	.477 : 1	6 : 1	Installed in Spitfire VI. Fitted with cabin supercharger.
Merlin 50	As for Merlin 45			1,425 lbs. (647 kg.)	.477 : 1	6 : 1	Installed in Spitfire V.
Merlin 50M	As for Merlin 45M			1,425 lbs. (647 kg.)	.477 : 1	6 : 1	Installed in Spitfire L.F. V.
Merlin 55	As for Merlin 45			1,425 lbs. (647 kg.)	.477 : 1	6 : 1	Installed in Spitfire V, Seafire III.
Merlin 55M	As for Merlin 45M			1,425 lbs. (647 kg.)	.477 : 1	6 : 1	Installed in Spitfire L.F. V, Seafire L.F. III.
Merlin 60	1,165 h.p. at 3,000 r.p.m.	—	—	—	.42 : 1	6 : 1	Installed in Wellington VI. Obsolete.
Merlin 61	1,290 h.p. at 3,000 r.p.m.	1,400 h.p. at 2,850 r.p.m. at 12,000 ft. (3,660 m.) and 1,250 h.p. at 2,850 r.p.m. at 24,000 ft. (7,320 m.)	1,565 h.p. at 3,000 r.p.m. at 12,250 ft. (3,740 m.) and 1,390 h.p. at 3,000 r.p.m. at 23,500 ft. (7,170 m.)	1,640 lbs. (744 kg.)	.42 : 1	6 : 1	Installed in Spitfire VII, VIII, IX, P.R. XI.
Merlin 62	1,165 h.p. at 3,000 r.p.m.	—	—	—	.42 : 1	6 : 1	Installed in Wellington VI. Obsolete.
Merlin 63	1,290 h.p. at 3,000 r.p.m.	—	Over 1,650 h.p.	1,640 lbs. (744 kg.)	.477 : 1	6 : 1	Installed in Spitfire VII, VIII, IX, P.R. XI.
Merlin 64	1,290 h.p. at 3,000 r.p.m.	—	Over 1,650 h.p.	1,640 lbs. (744 kg.)	.477 : 1	6 : 1	Installed in Spitfire VII. Fitted with cabin supercharger.

ROLLS-ROYCE MERLIN ENGINES—*continued.*

Bore × Stroke : 5.4 in. × 6 in. (137.3 m/m. × 152.5 m/m.).   Capacity : 1,647 cu. in. (27 litres.).

Engine	Take-off Power	International Rating	Maximum Power	Dry Weight (plus 2½% tolerance)	Airscrew Gear Ratio	Compression Ratio	Remarks
Merlin 66	1,315 h.p. at 3,000 r.p.m.	—	Over 1,650 h.p.	1,650 lbs. (749 kg.)	.477 : 1	6 : 1	Installed in Spitfire L.F. VIII, L.F. IX.
Merlin 67	1,315 h.p. at 3,000 r.p.m.	—	Over 1,650 h.p.	1,650 lbs. (749 kg.)	.42 : 1	6 : 1	
Merlin 68	1,400 h.p. at 3,000 r.p.m.	—	Over 1,650 h.p.	—	—	6 : 1	Packard-built (U.S.A.). U.S. designation V-1650-3. Installed in Mustang III (P-51B and C).
Merlin 69	1,490 h.p. at 3,000 r.p.m.	—	Over 1,650 h.p.	—	—	6 : 1	Packard-built (U.S.A.). U.S. designation V-1650-7. Installed in Mustang III and IV (P-51C, D, F and K)
Merlin 70	1,250 h.p. at 3,000 r.p.m.	—	Over 1,650 h.p.	1,650 lbs. (749 kg.)	.477 : 1	6 : 1	Installed in Spitfire H.F. VIII, H.F. IX, P.R. XI.
Merlin 71	1,250 h.p. at 3,000 r.p.m.	—	Over 1,650 h.p.	1,650 lbs. (749 kg.)	.477 : 1	6 : 1	Installed in Spitfire H.F. VII. Fitted with cabin supercharger.
Merlin 72	1,290 h.p. at 3,000 r.p.m.	—	Over 1,650 h.p.	1,640 lbs. (744 kg.)	.42 : 1	6 : 1	Installed in Mosquito P.R. IX, B. IX, XVI, 30. Welkin I.
Merlin 73	1,290 h.p. at 3,000 r.p.m.	—	Over 1,650 h.p.	1,640 lbs. (744 kg.)	.42 : 1	6 : 1	Installed in Mosquito XVI. Welkin I.
Merlin 76	1,250 h.p. at 3,000 r.p.m.	—	Over 1,650 h.p.	1,650 lbs. (749 kg.)	.42 : 1	6 : 1	Same as Merlin 72 but fitted with cabin supercharger. Installed in Mosquito XVI, 30. Welkin I.
Merlin 77	1,250 h.p. at 3,000 r.p.m.	—	Over 1,650 h.p.	1,650 lbs. (749 kg.)	.42 : 1	6 : 1	Same as Merlin 73 but fitted with cabin supercharger. Installed in Mosquito XVI. Welkin I.
Merlin 85	1,635 h.p. at 3,000 r.p.m.	—	Over 1,650 h.p.	1,650 lbs. (749 kg.)	.42 : 1	6 : 1	Installed in Lancaster VI, Lincoln I.
Merlin 224	1,620 h.p. at 3,000 r.p.m.	As for Merlin 24		1,450 lbs. (658 kg.)	.42 : 1	6 : 1	Built by Packard (U.S.A.). Same as Merlin 24. Installed in Lancaster I and III.
Merlin 225	1,620 h.p. at 3,000 r.p.m.	As for Merlin 25		1,450 lbs. (658 kg.)	.42 : 1	6 : 1	Built by Packard (U.S.A.). Same as Merlin 25. Installed in Canadian Mosquito 25 and 26.
Merlin 266	1,315 h.p. at 3,000 r.p.m.	As for Merlin 66		1,640 lbs. (744 kg.)	.479 : 1	6 : 1	Built by Packard (U.S.A.). Same as Merlin 66. Installed in Spitfire L.F. XVI.

NOTE :—(1) Mark numbers of Merlin engines up to XX are distinguished by Roman numbers. All marks above XX are in Arabic numerals.
(2) The allotment of mark numbers in the Merlin Series of engine depends mainly on the following differences :—

(a) Supercharger gear ratio.
(b) Airscrew reduction gear ratio.
(c) Cooling system employed.
(d) Type of carburettor.
(e) Starting system.
(f) Cabin supercharger.
(g) Gearbox drive.
(h) Single or two-piece cylinder-block.
(i) In certain cases, control arrangement.

CZECHOSLOVAKIA

The former Aero-Engine Industry of Czechoslovakia consisted of the following firms :—

AVIA AKCIOVA SPOLECNOST PRO PRUMYSL LETECKY (SKODA), Praha-Cakovice.
CESKOMORAVSKA KOLBEN DANEK, Praha-Liben.
A. S. WALTER, TOVARNY NA AUTOMOBILY A LETECKE MOTORY, Praha-Jinonice.

All three of these firms were absorbed into the German Aero-Engine Industry. The Avia Company was a branch of the formerly famous Skoda armament establishment, which had been taken over by the Reichwerke Hermann Goering. The Cesko-moravska Kolben Danek was reconstituted as the Böhmisch-Mährische Maschinenfabriken A.G. The famous Walter Company became part of the German Argus Motoren G.m.b.H. The B.M.W. and Junkers combines also established aero-engine production plants in Czechoslovakia.

FRANCE

At the time of the 1940 Armistice the following were the principal firms manufacturing aero-engines for defence requirements :—

SOCIÉTÉ DES AVIONS H. M. et D. FARMAN, Billancourt.
SOCIÉTÉ DES MOTEURS GNÔME-ET-RHÔNE, Gennevilliers, Le Mans and Paris (Bd. Kellermann).
SOCIÉTÉ D'EXPLOITATION DES MATERIELS HISPANO-SUIZA, Bois Colombes and Tarbes (Hte. Pyrenées).
SOCIÉTÉ NATIONALE DE CONSTRUCTION DE MOTEURS (LORRAINE), Argenteuil.
SOCIÉTÉ ANON. DES MOTEURS RENAULT POUR L'AVIATION, Billancourt and Porte St. Cloud.
SOCIÉTÉ DES MOTEURS SALMSON, Billancourt.

As the result of an agreement between the German authorities and the Vichy Government in July, 1941, the French aero-engine factories partially resumed their activities, the factories in the Southern zone on orders from the Vichy Government (Hispano-Suiza 12Y and 12Z and Gnôme-Rhône 14N and 14R) and those in the Northern zone mainly on orders from the occupying authorities.

Of the latter, the Société des Moteurs Gnôme-et-Rhône, the Société Générale de Mechanique et d'Aviation (formerly S.N.C.M. (Lorraine) in liquidation) and the Société Voisin were engaged in the production of the Gnôme-Rhône 14M and 14N, the BMW 132T and parts for the BMW 801 ; the Société Anon. des Moteurs Renault in the production of the Renault 6Q and Argus As 411 ; and the Société Hispano-Suiza in the manufacture of parts for the DB. 610.

In addition to building German engines, however, the Gnôme-Rhône company continued the development of its own radial designs. A new series of double-row radial engines of fourteen and eighteen cylinders, the 14R and 18R, was produced and development of a twenty-eight-cylinder four-row radial derived from the 14R and 18R was undertaken. The new engine was provided with a cooling-fan in front and had two superchargers and direct fuel injection. Drive was also available for co-axial oppositely-rotating airscrews. It was to have had an output of 3,750 h.p. at 6,000 m. (19,680 ft.). The standard Gnôme-Rhône 14N radial was used in several German aircraft, notably the Messerschmitt Me 323, and the Gotha Go 244. The Gnôme-Rhône 14M was fitted in the Henschel He 129.

The Hispano-Suiza company was also engaged on engine development while fulfilling sub-contracts on behalf of the German aero-engine industry. Two new Hispano-Suiza engines were announced during the period of occupation—the 12Z, a development of the pre-war 12Y but with four valves per cylinder and a maximum output of 1,400 h.p. ; and the 24H, which used the cylinders of the 12Z and was claimed to have a maximum output of 3,000 h.p.

After the occupation of the Southern Zone, the entire aero-engine industry, which had already suffered very heavy damage (the Hispano-Suiza factory at Tarbes was pillaged by the enemy) was compelled to work for the occupying authorities. In consequence its many factories were heavily bombed by the R.A.F. and the U.S. 8th Air Force, notably Billancourt (Renault),

Argenteuil (S.G.M.A.), Gennevilliers, Le Mans, Limoges (Gnôme-Rhône), Bois Colombes (Hispano Suiza), Saint Etienne (S.C.E.M.M.) and Vénisseux (S.I.G.M.A.).

The technical bureaux for aero-engine development which were established in the free zone in the South (Hispano-Suiza at Tarbes, Gnôme-Rhône at Limoges and Béarn at Pau) ceased all activities after November 11, 1942, and all experimental work had to be abandoned.

Since the liberation of France the aero-engine industry has received orders from the Government for the following engines :—

Hispano-Suiza : 12Z twelve-cylinder liquid-cooled.

Gnôme-Rhône : Completion of orders for BMW 132 and for Gnôme-Rhône 18R, 14R and 14N radials.

Renault : In the meantime taken over by the Government. Completion of orders for Argus As 411 to French account and for Renault 4P and 6Q in-line air-cooled.

S.C.E.M.M. : Béarn 6D in-line air-cooled.

The French Government is engaged in putting into practice a programme for the reorganization of the Aircraft and Aero-engine Industries which was drawn up before the liberation of France. This programme involves ultimate complete nationalisation of both industries. A Government Technical Committee, to become eventually the permanent governing body, has been set up to deal with the general organization.

GERMANY
TURBO JET AND ROCKET UNITS

System of Nomenclature.

Early in the war the German Air Ministry introduced a system of abbreviations for use when referring to the turbo-jet or rocket units. These were :—

R   Rocket.
TL   Turbo-jet.
PTL   Airscrew turbine unit.
L   Propulsive duct ("Athodyd" or "Ram jet").
IL   Intermittent propulsive duct (Flying-bomb "tube" unit).
RL   Combined Rocket and Athodyd.

A six-figure code number was also introduced, the first three numbers (109) indicating turbo-jet or rocket units as a class. The second group of three figures indicated the particular unit. Thus, the Heinkel-Hirth He S 11 was officially the 109-011. Later the final figure of the second group was used to indicate the manufacturing firm. Thus, all Heinkel-Hirth designations ended in "1" (109-011, 109-121, etc.), Junkers units in "2" (109-012, 109-022, etc.), BMW units in "8" (109-018, 109-028, etc.). Occasionally the figure 9 was used in place of 109.

When the second group of figures was above 500, the designation applied to a rocket unit. Thus the propulsion unit for the Me 163 was designated 109-509.

ARGUS.

ARGUS MOTORENGESELLSCHAFT M.B.H.

HEAD OFFICE : BERLIN-REINICKENDORF-OST.

The Argus company developed the intermittent propulsive duct unit with which the FZG 76 Flying-bomb was powered. This unit, carrying the official designation 109-104, was also installed experimentally in the Me 328 single-seat fighter but the vibrations initiated by the pulsations of the "flying-bomb" unit caused the project to be abandoned.

THE ARGUS 014 PROPULSIVE DUCT.

The 014 intermittent propulsive duct unit used in the flying-bomb consisted of a welded steel tube "stove-pipe" about 3,350 mm. long, in the front end of which was a bank of steel spring air valves and nine backward-facing fuel nozzles. The forward speed of the unit opened the spring valves and forced air into the combustion space, into which the fuel was injected and ignited. Pressure of combustion closed the one-way valves so that the only outlet for the heated and expanded gas was out of the rear end of the tube. Inertia of the escaping gas reduced pressure in the combustion chamber below atmospheric, permitting the valves to re-open. This process was repeated 40-45 times per second in the case of the flying-bomb installation, giving the bomb a forward speed of about 390-410 m.p.h.

Fuel feed was regulated to maintain a correct mixture strength according to forward speed and altitude through compensating mechanism controlled by a pitot head and diaphragm.

A single spark-plug in the top of the combustion chamber was used for starting only. Three auxiliary fuel nozzles in the combustion chamber were fed from an external source with Butane until the walls of the chamber became hot enough for auto-ignition. Thereafter the unit was self-igniting.

The thrust of the FZG 76 propulsion unit at normal speed was estimated to be the equivalent of about 750 h.p.

B.M.W.

BAYERISCHE MOTORENWERKE A.G. ENTWICKLUNGSWERK.

HEAD OFFICE : MUNICH.

Preliminary work on jet propulsion was started by BMW in 1934 and work on the BMW 003 project was begun in 1939. This unit first ran in August, 1940.

THE BMW 003 A-1.

The BMW 003 had a seven-stage axial compressor and an annular combustion chamber with sixteen burners. The single-stage turbine had hollow air-cooled stator and rotor blades. The adjustable propelling nozzle had internal cooling.

DIMENSIONS.—Overall length 3,534 mm. Maximum diameter 690 mm,
WEIGHT.—1,252 lbs.
PERFORMANCE.—Rotational speed 9,500 r.p.m. Static thrust 1,760 lbs., Consumption 2,550 lbs./hr., Thrust (sea level, 560 m.p.h.) 1,550 lbs., Consumption 3,240 lbs./hr.
FUEL.—B 4 (87 Octane petrol).

THE BMW 018.

This unit was projected but not completed. It had a twelve-stage axial compressor, an annular combustion chamber with 24 burners, a three-stage turbine and an adjustable propelling nozzle. A static thrust of 7,500 lbs. was hoped for.

THE BMW 028.

This was projected as a BMW 018 unit modified to drive

The port side of the BMW 003 turbo-jet unit.

contra-rotating airscrews. An additional turbine stage was added and the drive to the airscrews taken through the main compressor shaft and transmitted through planet gears.

WEIGHT (without airscrews).—7,700 lbs.
PERFORMANCE.—H.P. delivered to airscrews 7,700, Equivalent h.p. developed at 500 m.p.h. 14,000, Fuel consumption 8,150 lbs./hr.

DAIMLER-BENZ.

DAIMLER-BENZ AKTIENGESELLSCHAFT.

HEAD OFFICE : STUTTGART.

Professor Leist started development of the 007 turbo-jet with the Daimler-Benz company and one unit was built and run in the Autumn of 1943. Work on the project was then stopped by the German Air Ministry because the design was more complex than those of other firms.

The 007 unit had several special features, the compressor and ducted fan being mounted on two contra-rotating drums. The inner drum carried nine stages of compressor blading, while the outer drum carried eight stages of compressor blading internally and three stages of fan blading externally. The turbine was cooled by partial admission over 30% of its circumference of air drawn from the ducted fan circuit, the remaining 70% receiving the working gases. Four tubular combustion chambers were used.

HEINKEL-HIRTH.

ERNST. HEINKEL AKTIENGESELLSCHAFT WERK HIRTH-MOTOREN.

HEAD OFFICE : STUTTGART.

The Heinkel company has a controlling interest in the Hirth Moteren G.m.b.H.

The Heinkel-Hirth turbo-jet unit programme began in 1936 and up to 1944 there were three experimental units and six projected units The He S 3 unit was installed in the Heinkel He 178 which first flew on August 27, 1939.

The He S 11 (later known as the He S 011) was begun in 1944, culminating in the series-produced 011.

THE HEINKEL HIRTH-He S 011.

The He S 011 was the outcome of the development work on the He S 11. It has an impeller at the intake, a compressor consisting of a diagonal stage and three axial stages, an annular combustion chamber with turbulance "fingers" and sixteen injection nozzles, and an axial two-stage turbine with hollow blades. An adjustable jet nozzle having two positions, fully in for idling and fully out for all other conditions, is fitted.

DIMENSIONS.—Overall length (nozzle extended) 3,510 mm. Maximum diameter 875 mm.
WEIGHT.—2,090 lbs. + 2%.
STATIC THRUST.—2,860 lbs.
FUEL.—J 2 (light diesel oil) or in emergency K 1 (diesel oil).

The port side of the Heinkel-Hirth He S 011 turbo-jet unit.

THE HEINKEL HIRTH-He S 021.

A unit designated 021 was projected and was to have been a He S 011 adapted for driving an airscrew. The output at the airscrew was intended to be 3,300 h.p. at a speed of 560 m.p.h.

JUNKERS.

JUNKERS FLUGZEUG UND MOTORENWERKE A.G.

Head Office : Dessau.

Preliminary work on the development of jet propulsion was undertaken by the Junkers company in 1937. By the end of 1939 the designing of a full-scale turbo-jet had begun. Construction of the Jumo 004 A was begun early in 1940 and the first unit was run in December, 1940. Several 004 A units were ready in the Summer of 1941.

First flight tests with the 004 installed in a Me 110 were made at the end of 1941 and soon afterwards units were installed in various experimental aircraft.

The Jumo 004 B, embodying several modifications, was designed at the end of 1941 and the first unit ran at the end of 1942. In the early Summer of 1943 a prototype Me 262 was flown with two Jumo 004 B units.

Large scale production was planned to start in the Summer of 1943 but was not fully achieved until May or June, 1944.

THE JUNKERS JUMO 004 B.

The designation 004 A identified the first development model. 004 B-1 to B-4 were operational versions with the following modifications :—(*a*) improved entry to compressor, (*b*) improved stator blade design for compressor, (*c*) modified turbine entry, and (*d*) separate compressor discs. The B-4 was the first model to have hollow turbine blades. The description below applies to the 004 B.

Type.—Eight-stage axial-flow compressor with single-stage turbine.

Compressor.—Light alloy compressor casing built in two halves and bolted together. Compressor rotor consists of eight light-alloy discs bolted together and located by spigots. A tie-rod passes through the centre of the discs. Discs increase in diameter from the low to the high-pressure end. Outer casing diameter uniform throughout its length. The blades are dove-tailed into staggered grooves on the periphery of the discs and are fixed by grub-screws through each root. Stagger of the blades increases and the chord decreases in successive stages through the compressor and the width of the disc heads becomes correspondingly smaller. All the blades are constructed of light alloy. Between each compressor stage are stator blades fixed to the outer casing and built up in two half-rings. There is a row of entry guide vanes and a row of stator vanes between each compressor stage, making seventeen rows in all. The entry guide vanes and the first row of stator blades are of fairly thick aerofoil-section light alloy, the second row being of thinner aerofoil section, and the remainder of cambered sheet steel. The rotor turns on two steel shafts which are attached to the outside faces of the first and last discs. The front compressor bearing is made up of three ball-races, each capable of taking end-thrust. The rear bearing consists of a single roller race. Cooling air is bled off between the 4th and 5th compressor stage and is led into the double skin which surrounds the whole of the combustion chamber assembly. A small amount of air is allowed to pass into the space between the combustion chambers and the inner wall. Most of the air passes down one of the exhaust cone struts to circulate inside the cone and to pass through small holes to cool the downstream face of the turbine disc. Some of this cooling air also passes into a double skin which extends to within 2 feet of the final nozzle. After the last rotor stage, air is bled off internally and is taken through tunnels in two of the ribs in the casting to cool the upstream face of the turbine disc. More air is taken through three tunnels in the central casting into the space between the two plate diaphragms in front of the turbine disc. Most of this air then passes into the hollow turbine nozzle guide vanes, emerging through slits in the trailing-edge.

Combustion Chambers.—There are six chambers disposed radially around the central casting carrying the rear compressor bearing and the turbine shaft bearing. They are numbered 1 to 6 from the rear, No. 1 being horizontal on the left. Sparking-plugs for initial combustion are in chambers 1, 3 and 5. Interconnectors are provided between the combustion chambers. A fuel injector in each chamber injects fuel upstream. Swirl vanes are fitted to the forward end of each chamber, with baffles at the rear, the hot gases passing through "slot mixers" formed in the rear side wall. The hot gases then mix with the cold air which by-passes the combustion chambers. The chambers are built up from aluminised mild steel sheet and the combustion chamber housings are free to slide at the forward end to cater for expansion.

Turbine.—There are sixty-one turbine blades, fixed into the disc by forked blade roots secured in position by rivets. Later, to economise in material and to permit higher operating temperatures to be used, hollow turbine blades were fitted. The hollow blades are placed on lugs formed in the periphery of the disc and fixed by a special soldering process, as well as by a 5 mm. peg. Cooling air is directed inside the blades. The blades are manufactured from heat resisting steel containing 30% nickel and 15% chromium.

Tail-Pipe.—Mounted in the tail-pipe is a movable "bullet" operated by a servo-motor through the throttle lever. A rack-and-pinion device moves it longitudinally. On the ground the bullet is fully forward under 50% of the max. r.p.m., and fully back (restricted orifice) between 50% and 90% of max. r.p.m. At the beginning of take-off the bullet is near the end of its backward travel, but in flight, above 20,000 ft. and at a speed of 400 m.p.h., the bullet can be moved even farther back to provide maximum thrust. The servo-motor control is interlinked with a capsule surrounded by atmospheric pressure and having ram pressure inside it, so that the position of the bullet is adjusted according to the ram pressure or the forward speed. The rear portion of the tail-pipe has a double skin, and air passing over the nacelle is directed into it for cooling purposes.

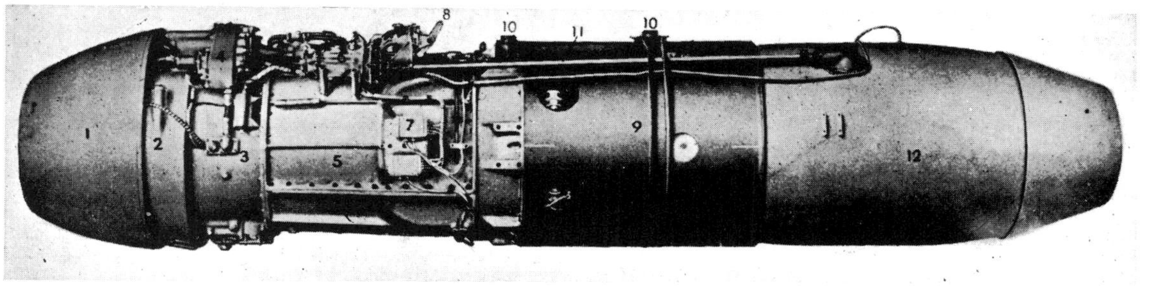

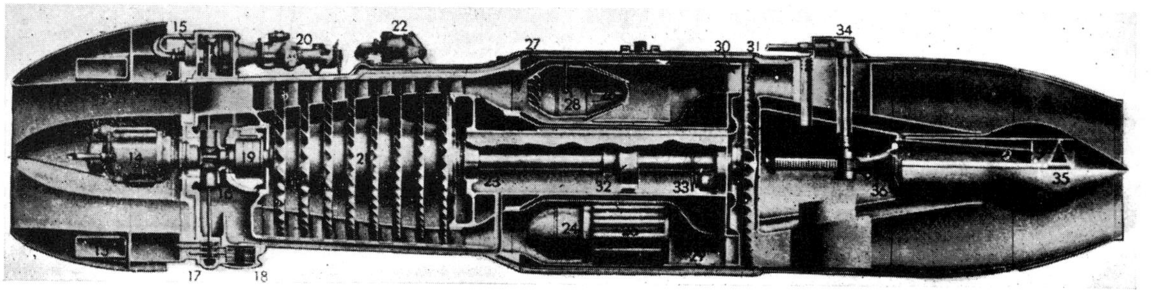

Port side and sectional views of the Junkers 004B turbo-jet unit. The numbered references are as follows :—1. Nose cowling. 2. Oil tank. 3. Entry casing. 4. Auxiliary gear box. 5. Compressor casing. 6. Servo motor. 7. Ignition Apparatus. 8. Control lever. 9. Outer casing. 10. Attachment points. 11. Movable bullet control shaft. 12. Exhaust casing. 13. Annular fuel tank. 14. Riedel starter. 15. Injection pump. 16. Auxiliary drive. 17. Oil pump. 18. Oil filter. 19. Front compressor bearing. 20. Speed regulator. 21. Compressor rotor. 22. Fuel filter. 23. Rear compressor bearing. 24. Flame tube. 25. Combustion chamber muffle. 26. Diffuser grill. 27. Combustion Chamber. 28. Injection nozzle. 29. Turbine entry ducting. 30. Turbine stator blades. 31. Turbine. 32. Forward turbine bearing. 33. Rear turbine bearing with oil scavenge pump. 34. Movable bullet operating gears. 35. Movable bullet. 36. Movable bullet support.

Lubrication.—Oil is carried in an annular nose tank. There are two pressure pumps, one supplying oil to the r.p.m. regulator, oil servo motor and compressor front bearing. The second pump supplies the rear compressor bearing and the two turbine rotor bearings. These three bearings are enclosed in an oil-tight case and a jet sprays oil into the interior of the splined shaft between the compressor and turbine shaft. Two scavenge pumps remove oil from the rear of the bearing casing and the rear turbine rotor bearing and return it to the tank. Oil from the front of the casing drains into the bottom of the auxiliary drive casing, from whence it is removed to the tank by a scavenge pump.

Auxiliaries.—An auxiliary drive casing is arranged above and driven from the front compressor shaft. From this casing are driven the fuel injection pump, the r.p.m. governor and the pump for the thrust regulator and bullet servo-motor.

Starting System.—A Riedel two-cylinder two-stroke starter engine (10 h.p. at 10,000 r.p.m.) is mounted in the air intake co-axially with the compressor shaft. It can be started electrically from the cockpit or by hand by means of a cable and pulley. Fuel for the starter motor is contained in a tank of 3 litres capacity mounted in the nose, forward of the oil tank. Starter fuel for the turbo-jet unit is contained in a semi-circular tank mounted forward of the oil tank. Starter fuel is petrol.

Installation.—The complete turbo-jet unit is fixed at three pick-up points, two above the rear compressor bearing and one above the combustion chamber housing. All pipe lines and electrical connections are brought to a small panel above the compressor casing in order to simplify installation procedure.

Instruments.—The aircraft instrument panel contains an injection pressure gauge, an r.p.m. indicator, an exhaust gas temperature gauge, and exhaust pressure gauge and an oil pressure gauge. The r.p.m. indicator has an inner and outer scale, the inner scale reading from 0 to 3,000 being used for starting, and the outer scale reading from 2,000 to 14,000 being used during flight. The exhaust pressure gauge is connected to both the tail-pipe and compressor intake.

Dimensions.—Overall length (without movable bullet) 3,864.5 mm. (Bullet projects 200 mm. maximum), Maximum diameter (intake cowling) 805.6 mm.

Weight.—1,585 lbs. + 3%.

Performance.—Maximum r.p.m. 8,700.

Height (ft.)	Speed (m.p.h.)	Thrust (lbs.)	Consumption (lbs./hr.)
0	273	1,605	2,920
0	560	1,890	3,680
8,200	273	1,300	2,290
8,200	560	1,600	2,920
36,000	536	572	1,080
36,000	560	715	1,275

Fuel.—Diesel oil (J 2 = specific weight .815-.845 kg./litre, or K 1 = specific weight .81-.85 kg./litre).

THE JUNKERS JUMO 004 C.

This was an improved Jumo 004 B with increased thrust and auxiliary fuel injection. The maximum thrust at sea level was 2,200 lbs. Weight : 1,540 lbs. + 3%.

THE JUNKERS JUMO 004 D-4.

A development of the Jumo 004 B with a new regulator, which prevented too rapid throttle movement, and two-stage fuel injection. With this unit a thrust of 2,200 lbs. was permissible at all heights and speeds.

THE JUNKERS JUMO 004 E.

The Jumo 004 E was the 004 D-4 with a shorter tail-pipe.

THE JUNKERS JUMO 012.

This projected unit was intended for a fast bomber, the Junkers Ju 287. It had an eleven-stage axial compression system and a two-stage turbine. The designed thrust was estimated to be from 6,000 to 6,400 lbs. and the weight 4,400 lbs. The specific consumption was expected to be 1.2 lbs./hr./lb. The length of this unit was about 17 ft.

Up to the time of the German collapse no unit or component had been tested.

THE JUNKERS JUMO 022.

A unit designated as Jumo 022 was projected. This was to be a Jumo 012 with gearing for contra-rotating airscrews.

LIQUID ROCKET UNITS

WALTER.

THE HWK 509 BI-FUEL ROCKET UNIT.

This unit was employed in the Me 163 B which was the first operational aircraft in the World to be powered solely by rocket motor. The weight of the unit was only 365 lb. and it developed a maximum thrust at sea level of 3,300 lb. Unlike the reciprocating engine and turbo-jet unit the liquid rocket motor gives increased rather than reduced power to altitude. Thus at 40,000 ft. the thrust of the 509 was about 10 per cent. greater than at sea level. The unit could be throttled to give a minimum thrust of 220 lb. The fuels employed, known to the Germans as T-Stoff and C-Stoff, gave a specific impulse of 180 to 190 lb. per lb./sec. In other words, a thrust of approximately 184 lb. was obtained for a consumption of 1 lb. of fuel per sec. For comparison with turbo-jet units it is more convenient to express the consumption in lb. per hour per lb. thrust and on this basis the figure for the 509 was 19 to 20 lb. as compared with 1.3 to 1.5 lb. for contempory German turbo-jet units.

T-Stoff is concentrated hydrogen peroxide and C-Stoff is a mixture of hydrazine hydrate and alcohol. In addition to its use as a fuel C-Stoff was employed to cool the double-walled combustion chamber. The two fuels were contained in separate tanks and were delivered to the combustion chamber jets under pressure from two turbine-driven pumps. At full thrust the rate of consumption was about 17.75 lb. per sec. or more than 1,000 lb. per minute.

Only a fraction of the full thrust was required to maintain a fairly high speed in level flight. Under conditions of partial thrust, however, the efficiency of the rocket motor falls off rather rapidly. For this reason the HWK 509 C unit was developed for the 8-263 aircraft. This had a main combustion chamber giving a maximum thrust of 3,740 lb. and a separate auxiliary chamber with a thrust of 660 lb. Both combustion chambers could be used together to give a total thrust of 4,400 lb. For cruising only the small chamber was employed and enabled a given thrust to be obtained for a lower fuel consumption than would have been possible by throttling the larger unit.

INTERNAL COMBUSTION ENGINES

System of Nomenclature.

German aero-engines were designated by a number made up of three figures, the first figure identifying the manufacturer and the two remaining figures the engine series. For this system the principal aero-engine manufacturers were allotted the following numbers :—

1 or 8	BMW
2	Junkers.
3	Bramo
4	Argus.
5	Hirth.
6	Daimler-Benz.
7	Bücker or Klöckner-Humbolt-Deutz.

Examples of designations conforming to this system are BMW 132 or 801, Junkers Jumo 211, Bramo 323, Argus As 411, Hirth HM 508, Daimler-Benz DB 605, and Bücker M 700 or Klöckner-Humboldt-Deutz Dz 710.

ARGUS.

ARGUS MOTOREN GESELLSCHAFT m.b.h.

HEAD OFFICE : BERLIN-REINICKEN-DORF-OST.

The Argus Company entered the German automobile industry in 1902, and produced, about 1906, the first German aero-engine—a four-cylinder vertical water-cooled type. By 1912, the Argus engine was the most widely used aero-engine in Germany.

During the War 1914-18, Argus engines of the traditional German six-cylinder vertical type of 100 to 190 h.p. were extensively used.

After the War, the firm ceased to build aero-engines, but in 1926 they re-entered the German Aero-engine Industry with two new engines of high power. These were discontinued, and a successful light aeroplane engine, known as the As 8, was produced in 1928. Then came the As 10, an inverted air-cooled eight-cylinder Vee of 240 h.p. and in 1938 the As 410 of 450 h.p.

During the war 1939-45 the As 410 and As 411 were used in advanced training and light communications aircraft.

In the jet propulsion field the Argus company was responsible for the development of the As 014 propulsive duct unit which formed the power-plant of the FZG 76 flying-bomb.

THE ARGUS As 410 A-1.

The As 410 A-1 was originally developed in 1938. In later years it was made available as a complete "power-egg," with cowling, cylinder baffles, exhaust system, etc. In this form it carried the designation As 410 MA-1.

TYPE.—Twelve-cylinder air-cooled inverted 60° Vee, supercharged and geared.

CYLINDERS.—Bore 105 m/m. (4.134 in.), Stroke 115 m/m. (4.528 in.). Capacity 12 litres (732.3 cub. in.). Compression ratio 6.4/1. Steel barrels, heat-treated aluminium-alloy heads. Exhaust-valve seating of steel, inlet seating, valve-guides and sparking-plug adaptors of bronze.

PISTONS.—Aluminium-alloy stampings. Three compression and one scraper rings.

CONNECTING RODS. — H-section forgings machined all over. Bearing surfaces nitrided. Seven main bearings of lead-bronze in steel shells.

CRANKSHAFT.—Six-throw steel forging machined all over. Bearing surfaces nitrided. Seven main bearings of lead-bronze in steel shells.

CRANKCASE.—Cast "Elektron" of deep box form.

VALVE GEAR.—One inlet and one exhaust-valve per cylinder at right angles so that exhaust outlets are inside Vee to get greatest cooling. Valve-rockers and push-rods in oil-tight casings. Tappet clearance (cold) .45 mm.

INDUCTION SYSTEM.—Single Argus-Hobson carburetter with automatic boost and altitude controls. Air warming device. Duplex self-regulating fuel pump.

SUPERCHARGER.—Centrifugal with spring-drive.

IGNITION.—Single Bosch duplex magneto with automatic advance mechanically-hydraulically coupled to throttle. Whole system screened.

LUBRICATION.—Dry sump pressure system. One pressure and two scavenge pumps, metering pump for accessory drives. Three coarse filters and one fine filter.

The 450 h.p. Argus As 410 twelve-cylinder air-cooled engine.

STARTER.—Bosch hand/electric starter.

AIRSCREW DRIVE.—Clockwise rotation. Spur-wheel reduction gear with incorporated spring-drive. Gear ratio .667 : 1. Flange-fixing for Argus vane-operated controllable-pitch airscrew.

DIMENSIONS.—Overall length 1,585 mm. Width 660 mm. Height 970 mm.

WEIGHT.—315 kg. (694.5 lbs.).

PERFORMANCE.—Take-off and emergency 465 h.p. at 3,100 r.p.m. at 1.4 ata. at sea level, 485 h.p. at 3,100 r.p.m. at 1.4 ata. at 2,630 ft. Climbing 355 h.p. at 2,820 r.p.m. at 1.2 ata. at sea level, 380 h.p. at 2,820 r.p.m. at 1.2 ata. at 5,750 ft. Maximum cruising 315 h.p. at 2,820 r.p.m. at 1.15 ata. at sea level, 340 h.p. at 2,820 r.p.m. at 1.15 ata. at 6,900 ft.

FUEL CONSUMPTION.—.45 lbs./h.p./hr. maximum cruising, sea level.

THE ARGUS As 411 A-1.

The As 411 A-1 was similar in general construction to the As 410 A-1 but had a different reduction gear ratio (.572 : 1) and increased r.p.m. The ignition system layout was also modified. It was also available as a complete power-unit under the designation As 411 MA-1.

DIMENSIONS.—Overall length 1,620 mm. Width 700 mm. Height 992 mm.

WEIGHT.—385 kg. (847 lbs.).

PERFORMANCE.—Take-off and emergency 580 h.p. at 3,300 r.p.m. at 1.8 ata. at sea level, 600 h.p. at 3,300 r.p.m. at 1.8 ata. at 2,000 ft. Climbing 440 h.p. at 3,250 r.p.m. at 1.45 ata. at sea level, 495 h.p. at 3,250 r.p.m. at 1.45 ata. at 8,000 ft. Maximum cruising 350 h.p. at 3,100 r.p.m. at 1.35 ata. at sea level, 390 h.p. at 3,100 r.p.m. at 1.35 ata. at 8,500 ft.

FUEL CONSUMPTION.—.436 lbs./h.p./hr. maximum cruising, sea level.

THE ARGUS As 403 P5 AND P9.

These designations were applied to two projected radial engines to be fitted with two-stage superchargers. The P5 had a projected take-off output of 3,250 h.p. and a rated altitude of 32,800 ft. The P9 had a projected take-off output of 2,500 h.p. and a rated altitude of 42,500 ft.

THE JUNKERS-ARGUS As 413.

The As 413 was a projected liquid-cooled "H" engine with an output of 4,000 h.p. It was intended to drive contra-rotating airscrews.

The 1,600 h.p. BMW 801 A radial engine.

A starboard side view of the Argus As 411 MA-1 power-unit.

BMW

BMW FLUGMOTORENBAU G.m.b.H.

HEAD OFFICE : MUNICH.

Founded originally in 1916, this company, under the name of Bayerische Motoren Werke A.G., achieved prominence towards the end of the War 1914-18 by producing a vertical engine, generally of the normal German six-cylinder type, with oversized cylinders and a high compression ratio for operation at heights.

Shortly after the War, the company took up the manufacture of Kuntze-Knorr compressed-air brakes for railway carriages and wagons. Subsequently the engine department, the manufacturing rights of the various engines, and the name of the company were bought up by the Bäyerische Flugzeug-werke, which changed its name to BMW Flugmoterenbau G.m.b.H.

In 1939 the BMW concern took over the Brandenburgische Moterenwerke G.m.b.H. and this company became known as the BMW Flugmotoren-werke G.m.b.H.

The BMW 801 was the first high-performance radial air-cooled engine of completely new design to be produced in Germany after the outbreak of War.

The introduction of positive air-cooling, incorporating a

cooling-fan in the cowl nose opening, operating at approximately three times the airscrew speed, and a system of internal baffles had made it possible to eliminate all external cowling excrescences. Positive air pressure built up in the cowling in front of the engine was used for cooling the cylinders, cylinder-heads, crankcase, accessories and the oil, as well as for combustion. Air could also be taken from within the cowling for cabin and wing heating.

The BMW 801 was provided with a single-stage centrifugal supercharger with two automatically changing speeds, direct fuel injection and a centralisation of controls which permitted the operation and control of boost pressure, engine speed, ignition timing and blower speed by a single lever. In addition, the engine was fitted with a VDM airscrew pitch-changing and constant-speed regulating device which in normal operation automatically maintained the selected speed by oleo-hydraulic means.

The BMW company began preliminary work on jet propulsion power-units in 1934 and its first turbo-unit, the 109-003, was first run in August, 1940. Details of BMW turbo-jet developments will be found on p. 34d.

THE BMW 801 A, B, C AND L.

The main difference between the 801 A, B, C and L was in the type of airscrew control fitted. All had right-handed rotation except the 801 B. The complete cowled power-plants incorporating these engines were designated 801 MA, MB and ML, the 801 C being supplied only as a bare engine.

Type.—Fourteen-cylinder two-row air-cooled supercharged radial with direct fuel injection.

Cylinders.—Bore 156 m/m. (6.15 in.), Stroke 156 m/m. (6.15 in.). Capacity 41.8 litres (2,560 cub. in.). Steel barrels with screwed and shrunk-on light alloy heads. One inlet and one exhaust valve per cylinder, both facing aft, with aluminium-bronze inlet and steel exhaust valve-seats. Two sparking-plugs per cylinder facing forward, one inboard of each valve. Fuel injection nozzle facing aft. Cylinders attached to crankcase by closely-spaced small diameter studs with vertical serrations so that they can be positioned relatively close to the barrel and only a narrow flange is required.

Connecting Rods.—H-section single-piece steel master-rod and six auxiliary rods in each bank of cylinders. Master-rods in No. 9 front and No. 8 rear cylinders, which are the lowest on the port side of each row. Lead-bronze big-end and bronze little-end bearings.

Crankshaft.—Two-throw four-piece crankshaft on one central single-row ball-bearing and two roller-bearings in forward and rear sections of crankcase. Shaft consists of two central webs each with crank-pin and half the centre journal, and front and rear webs with integral journals. The halves of the centre journal are hollow and screw-threaded internally. A screwed bushing splined internally for the assembly tool draws the halves together against differential threads, the actual joint being in the form of a Hirth serrated coupling. The hollow crank-pin ends are tapered internally and externally and are pressed in bronze bushes in the outer webs and secured by copper-plated steel bushes which are pressed into the ends of the pins. The bushes are threaded internally for an extracting tool. All four webs have integral balance-weights and provision made in the rear web for a torsional vibration damper.

Crankcase.—The main case is of steel and in three sections split on the centre-lines of the two rows of cylinders. Bolted to the flanged forward section is the light alloy housing enclosing the airscrew reduction gear, cooling fan increasing gear, magneto drives and airscrew pitch-changing mechanism. At the rear of the main case is the flanged blower casting in two parts. The front section contains the forward bearing of the blower shaft, the impeller and has fixed baffles and air intakes round its circumference. The rear section contains the supercharger drive, rear bearing of the blower and various accessory drives. These two sections and a channeled and bossed light alloy mounting ring seated on the rear face of the rear section are assembled to the steel crankcase by long bolts. The accessory housing containing drives for the fuel feed and injection pump, control device, starter, etc., is separately bolted to the rear half of the blower casing.

Valve Gear.—One inlet and one exhaust valve per cylinder. Exhaust valves are sodium-cooled. Totally-enclosed valve gear with overhead rockers, tubular push-rods and roller-ended tappets facing forward in the front cylinders and aft in the rear cylinders. Two cam rings, one forward and one aft, driven at one-eighth crankshaft speed and in same direction. Pressure lubrication of valve gear through push-rods.

Induction.—Two flat intakes with dust grids located inside cowling are fed with air delivered by the nose fan through shallow ducts, one on either side of the cowling, which by-pass the cylinder baffling system. After passing through the blower the air is delivered by individual pipes from the blower casing to each inlet port. Two intake throttles are geared to an oil servo-operated variable-datum boost control.

Supercharger.—Two-speed centrifugal blower. 24-bladed semi-shrouded light alloy impeller has hollow shaft through which rear extension of crankshaft carrying the supercharger and accessory drive gears passes. The drive unit comprises an output shaft on which are freely mounted two gears with multiple-plate clutches and a sliding selective clutching member which is hydraulically-operated from the control unit. For the higher ratio (7.46 : 1) the drive is taken directly from the crankshaft pinion to the forward gear on the output shaft. The low ratio (5.07 : 1) is obtained when the rear free gear is clutched.

Fuel Injection.—A Deckel cylindrical fuel-injection pump, flange-mounted on rear of engine, comprises fourteen individual pumping elements lying parallel to and arranged concentrically around the longitudinal axis. The pumps are actuated by a three-nosed cam driven through a train of spur gears from the crankshaft at one-sixth engine speed. A pump forces the fuel from the main tank through two lines to a float and pendulum de-aerator and thence to a chamber in the rear engine cover, from which tangential passages lead to the axially-mounted tube projecting into the common fuel gallery for the pumps. The metered fuel is fed through long high-pressure lines to the injector nozzles, one to each cylinder, mounted between the valves.

Ignition.—Vertically-mounted twin Bosch ZM14 CR10 magneto, mounted on nose casing with single drive unit from front end of crankshaft, serves two plugs per cylinder, one inboard of each valve.

Airscrew Drive.—Epicyclic reduction gear .542 : 1 ratio. Airscrew shaft mounted in lead-bronze bushing in nose of hollow crankshaft and on thrust ball-bearing in nose of gear casing. An external gear on the casing of the epicyclic unit drives the cooling fan through a lay-shaft at 1.72 times crankshaft speed. The airscrew pitch-change is by hydraulic pump mounted on the engine nose casing, the pump being controlled by an electric motor. An adjacent hydraulic speed governor interconnected with the throttle control constitutes an automatic control selected by the control unit. Electrically-operated fluid and slinger-ring de-icing system may be fitted. In order to pass fluid through the fan to the airscrew two slinger-rings are employed, one on the fan with passages drilled through the fan-hub to the second slinger-ring on the airscrew.

Lubrication.—Oil is fed from the tank by an auxiliary pump to the main pressure pump via the oil-coolers in the leading-edge of the cowling and thence through an Autoklean-type filter. A relief-valve limits the oil pressure through the coolers to a maximum of 12.5 atm. (184 lbs./sq. in.) and a further capsule-controlled temperature-sensitive valve maintains the main supply to the engine to a normal pressure of 8–9 atm. (118–132 lbs./sq. in.). The return of oil from the crankcase, supercharger case and accessory mounting is from the oil sump via the main return pump. Two additional return pumps drain the gear casing and a further pump drains the valve-rocker boxes. A small oil tank at the rear of the engine supplies a separate oil-pressure pump to lubricate the injection pump and boost control oil servo controls.

Accessories.—Accessory casing bolted to rear of blower section. Extended end of crankshaft passes through hollow impeller shaft and carries the auxiliary drives and starter dog for the coaxially-mounted Bosch electric or hand-energised inertia starter. The auxiliaries directly driven from the crankshaft by spur gears include a 2-kilowatt Bosch generator, an Askania vacuum pump, a Maihak fuel supply pump and the fuel-injection pump.

Cooling.—Low-drag cowling 1,320 m/m. (52 in.) in diameter and 1,473 m/m. (58 in.) long closely fits the engine and is supported by front and rear rings and an inter-cylinder baffle, all attached to several valve rocker boxes by rubber-bushed bolts. A twelve-bladed fan 813 mm. (32 in.) in diameter and driven from the airscrew reduction gear at 1.72 times crankshaft and 3.17 time airscrew speed, rotates in the cowling front opening. The cylinders and heads are closely baffled to ensure that both rows of cylinders are scavenged separately by compressed fresh air from the pressure region behind the fan. To avoid cooling losses the cylinder head baffles are extended to form a dividing wall between the two rows of cylinders and are sealed to the cowling by a rubber ring. Oil coolers are located in the leading-edge ring of the cowling and air from inside the cowling passes through them in reverse flow and out through an annular slot. In the 801A and 801B models the width of this slot and, consequently, the flow of air through the cooler, can be varied by a ring which may be moved fore and aft electrically. Exit of air which has passed over the cylinders is through an annular slot at the trailing-edge of the cowling. In 801A and 801B models this slot is controlled by an electrically-operated sliding gill ring.

Exhaust System.—All exhaust pipes extend aft from exhaust port and pass through the rear cowling slot.

Control Unit.—A master-control ("Kommandogerät") controls boost pressure, engine speed, mixture, ignition timing and supercharger speed change so that the pilot can chose the operating conditions of his power plant by means of a single operating lever. For the circulation of the required hydraulic pressure and lubricating oil, special pressure and drain pumps are fitted. These operate a circuit of thin temperature-resisting oil.

Dimensions.—Overall length 2,006 mm., Diameter (801 A) 1,307 mm., Diameter (801 C) 1,290 mm.

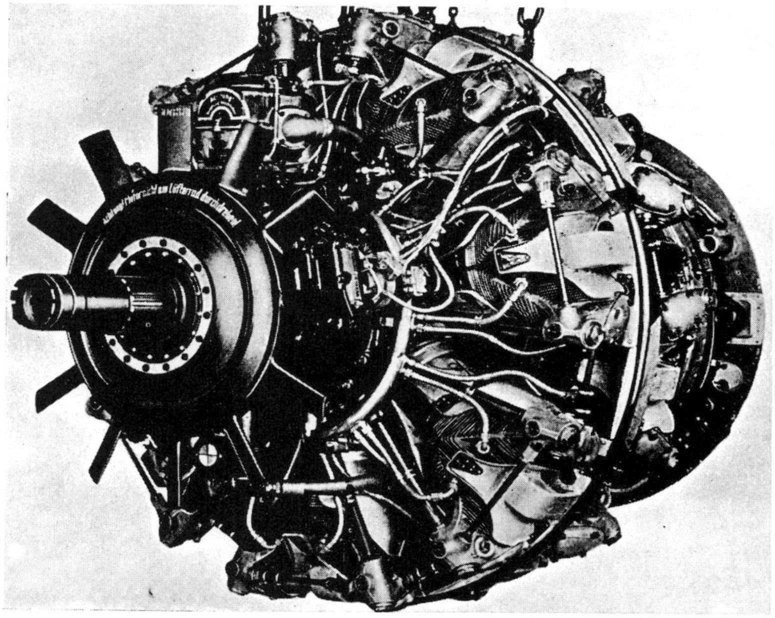

A three-quarter front view of the BMW 801 G power-plant for multi-engined installations.

Weights.—(801 A) 1,213 kg. (2,669 lb.), (801 B) 1,228 kg. (2,702 lb), (801 C) 1,055 kg. (2,321 lb.).

Performance.—Take-off and emergency 1,600 h.p. at 2,700 r.p.m. at 1.32 ata. at sea level, 1,380 h.p. at 2,700 r.p.m. at 1.3 ata. at 15,100 ft. Climbing 1,460 h.p. at 2,400 r.p.m. at 1.25 ata. at sea level, 1,310 h.p. at 2,400 r.p.m. at 1.25 ata. at 14,500 ft. Maximum cruising 1,280 h.p. at 2,300 r.p.m. at 1.15 ata. at sea level, 1,170 h.p. at 2,300 r.p.m. at 1.15 ata. at 15,000 ft. Fuel consumption .506 lb./h.p./hr. maximum cruising, sea level.

THE BMW 801 D, G AND Q.

Similar in general construction to the 801 A but operating on 96 Octane fuel. The 801 D was a bare engine, the 801 G was a power-plant for multi-engine installations, and the 801 Q was fitted with a bi-fuel system and provision for nitrous-oxide injection.

Compression Ratio.—7.22 : 1.

Supercharger Drive Ratios. 5.31 : 1 and 8.31 : 1.

Performance (801 D and G).—Take-off and emergency 1,700 h.p. at 2,700 r.p.m. at 1.42 ata. at sea level, 1,440 h.p. at 2,700 r.p.m. at 1.42 ata. at 18,700 ft. Climbing 1,500 h.p. at 2,400 r.p.m. 1.32 ata. at sea level, 1,360 h.p. at 2,400 r.p.m. at 1.32 ata. at 17,000 ft. Maximum cruising 1,300 h.p. at 2,300 r.p.m. at 1.2 ata. at sea level, 1,215 h.p. at 2,300 r.p.m. at 1.2 ata. at 18,000 ft. Fuel consumption .54 lb./h.p./hr. maximum cruising, sea level.

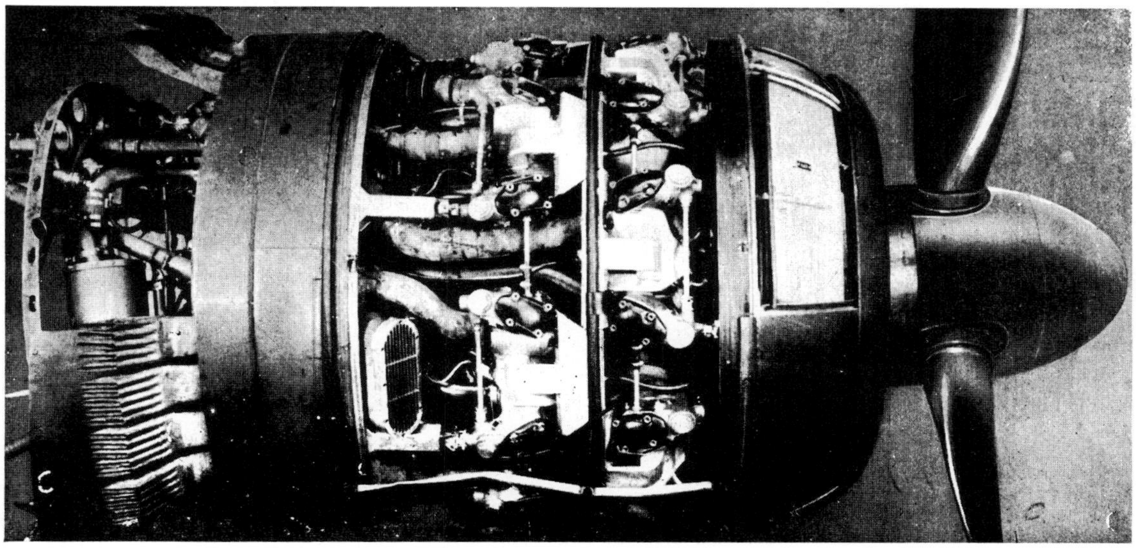

The 1,600 h.p. BMW 801 A Engine as installed in the Dornier Do 217 bomber.

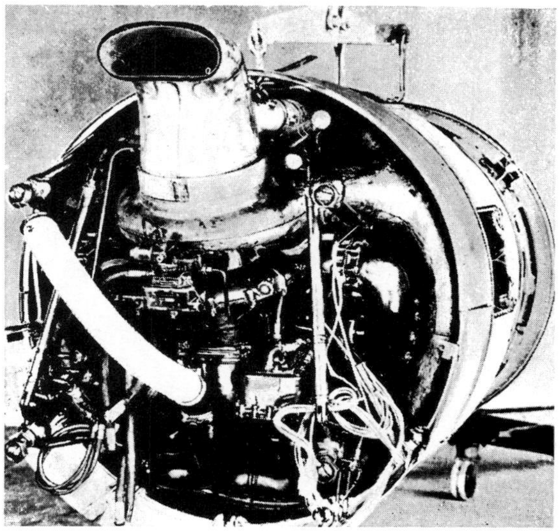

A rear view of the BMW 801 TJ engine showing the turbo-supercharger installation.

The port side of the 2,000 h.p. BMW 801 E fourteen-cylinder radial air-cooled engine.

THE BMW 801 E, F AND S.

Similar in general construction to the 801 D but fitted with different supercharger gear ratios. Modifications to the 801 S consisted of an improved and simplified master-control, chrome cylinder liners, modified rocker housing cover, modified piston rings and altered magneto timing.

SUPERCHARGER DRIVE RATIOS.—6 : 1 and 8.3 : 1.
PERFORMANCE.—Take-off and emergency 2,000 h.p. at 2,700 r.p.m. at 1.56 ata. at sea level, 1,700 h.p. at 2,700 r.p.m. at 1.65 ata. at 18,700 ft. Climbing 1,650 h.p. at 2,500 r.p.m. at 1.45 ata. at sea level, 1,500 h.p. at 2,500 r.p.m. at 1.45 ata. at 18,000 ft. Maximum cruising 1,440 h.p. at 2,400 r.p.m. at 1.3 ata. at sea level, 1,340 h.p. at 2,400 r.p.m. at 1.3 ata. at 19,000 ft. Fuel consumption .545 lb./h.p./hr. maximum cruising, sea level.

THE BMW 801 R.

Similar in general construction to the 801 E but fitted with a two-stage four-speed supercharger. 96 Octane fuel.
SUPERCHARGER DRIVE RATIOS.—4.2 : 1, 5.4 : 1, 6.5 : 1 and 7.25 : 1.
DIMENSIONS.—Overall length 2,741 mm. Diameter 1,360-1,390 mm.
WEIGHT.—1,800 kg. (3,960 lb.).

THE BMW 801 TJ.

This engine was the 801 D fitted with an exhaust-driven turbo-supercharger. 96 Octane fuel
SUPERCHARGER DRIVE RATIOS.—5.3 : 1 and 8.3 : 1.
DIMENSIONS.—Overall length 2,525 mm. Diameter 1,440 mm.
WEIGHT.—1,610 kg. (3,542 lbs.).

PERFORMANCE.—Take-off and emergency 1,810 h.p. at 2,650 r.p.m. at 1.55 ata. at sea level, 1,500 h.p. at 2,650 r.p.m. at 1.55 ata. at 40,000 ft. Climbing 1,630 h.p. at 2,425 r.p.m. at 148 ata. at sea level, 1,380 h.p. at 2,425 r.p.m. at 1.48 ata. at 38,400 ft. Maximum Cruising 1,330 h.p. at 2,300 r.p.m. at 1.28 ata. at sea level, 1,230 h.p. at 2,300 r.p.m. at 1.28 ata. at 40,000 ft. Fuel consumption .536 lb./h.p./hr. maximum cruising, sea level.

THE BMW 801 TQ.

This engine was the 801 E with an exhaust-driven turbo-supercharger. 96 Octane fuel.
SUPERCHARGER DRIVE RATIOS.—6 : 1 and 8.3 : 1.
DIMENSIONS.—Overall length 2,525 mm. Diameter 1,440 mm.
WEIGHT.—1,610 kg. (3,542 lbs.).
PERFORMANCE.—Take-off (with methanol/water injection and increased boost) 2,270 h.p. at 2,700 r.p.m. at 1.75 ata. Climbing 2,000 h.p. at 2,500 r.p.m. at 1.55 ata. at sea level, 1,715 h.p. at 2,500 r.p.m. at 1.55 ata. at 40,000 ft.

THE BMW 802.

The 802 was an eighteen-cylinder two-row radial of similar construction and arrangement to the 801. It had a take-off output of 2,400 h.p.

Although this engine was known to have been under development for some years it did not appear in any operational aircraft.

THE BMW 803.

The 803 was a twenty-eight-cylinder liquid-cooled four-bank radial engine fitted with a two-stage four-speed supercharger and driving contra-rotating airscrews.

The engine had the appearance of two fourteen-cylinder engines joined together, the cylinders of each unit being in twin in-line pairs disposed radially around the crankcase. The exhaust valves of the pairs of cylinders in each unit are on different sides when viewed from the front, the two fourteen-cylinder units being placed back-to-back.

The superchargers and all auxiliaries are driven from the rear of the engine.

CYLINDERS.—Bore 156 mm. (6.15 in.), Stroke 156 mm. (6.15 in.), Capacity 83.5 litres. One inlet and one exhaust valve per cylinder. The two cylinders in each pair have a common cylinder head casting and camshaft. The camshafts are driven by inclined drive shafts, the shafts being located at the front for the forward set of fourteen cylinders and aft for the rear set.
AIRSCREW DRIVE.—The front fourteen-cylinder unit drives the front airscrew through an extended shaft, and the rear unit drives the rear airscrew through a series of auxiliary shafts which pass between the cylinder skirts of the front set of cylinders. The gears of these auxiliary shafts mesh with a large gear wheel to which the rear airscrew is attached.
DIMENSIONS.—Length 3,786 mm. Diameter 1,600 mm.
WEIGHT DRY.—2,950 kg. (6,490 lbs.).
WEIGHT OF COMPLETE POWER PLANT.—4,130 kg. (9,086 lbs.).
PERFORMANCE.—Take-off and emergency 3,900 h.p. at 2,950 r.p.m. at 1.5 ata. at sea level, 4,000 h.p. at 2,950 r.p.m. at 1.5 ata. at 4,000 ft. Climbing 3,350 h.p. at 2,600 r.p.m. at 1.3 ata. at sea level, 2,550 h.p. at 2,600 r.p.m. at 1.3 ata. at 40,000 ft. Fuel consumption .54 lb./h.p./hr. maximum climb and combat.

THE BMW 132 F, J, K, M AND N.

The main differences between the F, J, K, M and N sub-types were in the airscrew reduction gear and the supercharger gear ratios. These differences are referred to in the following general description which applies to these models.

Of the earlier sub-types, the A, E and H were fitted with Pallas-Stromberg carburettors, all other engines, including the Do, Dc, T, W, Y, Z, L and U, being of the direct-injection type.

TYPE.—Nine-cylinder air-cooled supercharged radial with direct fuel injection.
CYLINDERS.—Bore 155.5 m/m. (6.125 in.), Stroke 162 m/m. (6.375 in.). Capacity 27.7 litres (1,690 cub. in.). Compression ratio 6.93 : 1. Closely finned chrome-molybdenum steel barrel onto which is screwed and shrunk an aluminium-alloy head with integral rocker-boxes. One inlet and one exhaust valve per cylinder. Valve ports in domed combustion chamber on opposite sides and set at 35° to cylinder axis. Valve seatings, of aluminium-nickel-iron bronze for inlet and nickel-chrome-tungsten steel for exhaust, are shrunk into head, the skirt of the latter being rolled into the port. Two spark-plugs in front of cylinder and fuel injection valve at rear.
PISTONS.—Silicon-aluminium alloy pistons are flat-topped, recessed to clear valve head rims and internally webbed. Three compression rings and one channelled and drilled oil control ring above gudgeon pin and one bevelled scraper ring below. Hollow gudgeon pins located by floating steel keeper rings held by spring circlips.
CONNECTING RODS.—One-piece master-rod and eight articulated H-section rods. Lead-bronze big-end bearing and phosphor-bronze gudgeon and wrist-pin bearings.
CRANKSHAFT.—Single-throw two-piece shaft built up on a frictional-grip maneton joint. Two roller-bearings and one ball-thrust bearing. Shaft and crankpin integral with the forward crankweb. Integral with the rear crankweb is a mounting for the rear main bearing. Each crankweb carries a two-piece riveted-on balance weight of hardened and tempered carbon steel.
CRANKCASE.—Aluminium-alloy casting. Main portion in two halves bolted together with nine bolts. Pegged in each half are steel rings to form housings for crankshaft roller-bearings. Outside of each half is faced to make spigot joints with the camwheel casing in front and supercharger casing in rear. Each half drains separately to the oil sump.
VALVE GEAR.—One inlet and one sodium-filled exhaust valve per cylinder. Exhaust valves of austenitic steel, inlet valves of solid silicon-chrome steel. Two concentric springs per valve, held by collars and split cone cotters. Steel valve rockers actuated through steel ball-ended push-rods and plain bearing roller tappets by two cam rings, one inlet and one exhaust. Each cam track has four cams and the complete cam wheel is driven through reduction gearing at one-eighth crankshaft speed.
SUPERCHARGER.—Single-speed centrifugal supercharger housed in aluminium-alloy casing partitioned by two bulkheads between which a volute air duct leads from the twin overhead intakes to the centre of a 24-bladed impeller. Air intake thus located between supercharger and crankcase and no fixed guide vanes are provided for incoming air. Twelve vanes of impeller are full-bladed, the remainder being cut away at the entry. Impeller delivers through 18-vaned diffuser integral with the front wall of the accessories gear case to an encircling induction manifold from which the air passes by tangential pipes to the cylinder ports. Double air-intake throttles, front controlled by automatic fixed datum boost pressure control, and rear connected direct to pilot's lever. Supercharger drive by spur gear off rear end of crankshaft with single intermediate compound pinion. Gear ratios : F and J = 11.4 : 1, K and M = 7 : 1, N = 10.14 : 1.
FUEL INJECTION.—Petrol from tank is fed by engine-driven pump via a Bosch de-aerator to a Bosch injection pump, whence it is supplied through nozzles to the cylinders. Injection pump consists of nine plunger elements mounted in two blocks of four and five in inverted Vee formation on engine rear cover. Plungers operated by single five-lobe camshaft. Fuel injection regulated by an automatic unit which varies in quantity in accordance with boost air pressure and temperature effects on a capsule, the response of which moves injection pump plunger control rack through an oil servo.
IGNITION.—Bosch duplex magneto supplying two Siemens two-electrode plugs per cylinder through screened harness.
LUBRICATION.—Pump unit housed in sump beneath main crankcase. Unit divided into four individual sections, the lowest containing the double gear pressure pump. Above this are the main scavenge and two auxiliary scavenge sections. Main body of sump partitioned horizontally into upper and lower scavenge chambers, lower section vented by vertical pipe to top of upper. Remaining space forward occupied by pumps and pressure filter chamber which opens through spring-loaded non-return valve into delivery distribution chamber.
AIRSCREW DRIVE.—Epicyclic reduction gear. Ratios : F, M and N = .62 : 1, J and K = .72 : 1.
ACCESSORIES.—Accessories and auxiliaries driven through several trains of spur pinions radially disposed about a central driving shaft in the auxiliary gearbox at the rear of the engine, on which the units are mounted.
DIMENSIONS.—Diameter over valve-rocker boxes 1,372 mm., Length (airscrew mounting flange to rear of starter) 1,256 mm.

The 2,400 h.p. BMW 802 eighteen-cylinder radial air-cooled engine.

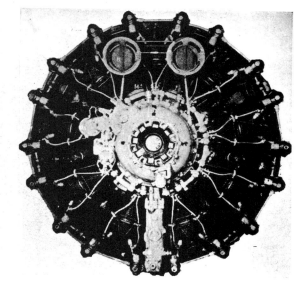

The starboard side of the BMW 803 twenty-eight cylinder liquid-cooled engine.

The 960 h.p. BMW 132K engine.

WEIGHT DRY.—525 kg. (1,155 lbs.).
PERFORMANCE (132 F and J).—Take-off and emergency 800 h.p. at 2,350 r.p.m. at 1.4 ata. at sea level, 890 h.p. at 2,350 r.p.m. at 1.4 ata. at 11,500 ft. Climbing 720 h.p. at 2,250 r.p.m. at 1.3 ata. at sea level, 810 h.p. at 2,250 r.p.m. at 1.3 ata. at 12,400 ft. Maximum cruising 650 h.p. at 2,200 r.p.m. at 1.2 ata. at sea level, 740 h.p. at 2,200 r.p.m. at 1.2 ata. at 14,000 ft.
PERFORMANCE (132 N).—Take-off and emergency 865 h.p. at 2,450 r.p.m. at 1.35 ata. at sea level, 960 h.p. at 2,450 r.p.m. at 1.35 ata. at 9,850 ft. Climbing 765 h.p. at 2,350 r.p.m. at 1.25 ata. at sea level, 865 h.p. at 2,350 r.p.m. at 1.25 ata. at 11,000 ft. Max-

imum cruising 670 h.p. at 2,250 r.p.m. at 1.15 ata. at sea level, 765 h.p. at 2,250 r.p.m. at 1.15 ata. at 12,800 ft.
PERFORMANCE (132 K and M).—Take-off and emergency 960 h.p. at 2,550 r.p.m. at 1.3 ata. at sea level, 970 h.p. at 2,550 r.p.m. at 1.3 ata. at 1,480 ft. Climbing 810 h.p. at 2,250 r.p.m. at 1.2 ata. at sea level, 830 h.p. at 2,250 r.p.m. at 1.2 ata. at 2,780 ft. Maximum cruising 715 h.p. at 2,200 r.p.m. at 1.1 ata. at sea level, 750 h.p. at 2,200 r.p.m. at 1.1 ata. at 4,900 ft. Fuel consumption (132 F, J and N) .54 lb./h.p./hr., (132 K and M) .505 lb./h.p./hr. maximum cruising, sea level.

BRAMO.

B.M.W. FLUGMOTOREN-WERKE BRANDENBURG G.m.b.H.
HEAD OFFICE : BERLIN-SPANDAU.

The Brandenburgische Motorenwerke G.m.b.H. was formed in 1936 to take over the aero-engine department of the Siemens Apparate und Maschinen G.m.b.H., which had some 25 years experience of building air-cooled radial engines. In their early days those engines were known by the name Siemens-Halske.

In 1939 the Brandenburgische Motorenwerke G.m.b.H. was acquired by the Bayerische Motorenwerke A.G., manufacturers of the well-known BMW engines, and was later known as the BMW Flugmotoren-Werke Brandenburg G.m.b.H.

The original Siemens concern, in addition to building radial engines of its own design, held a licence to build the Bristol Jupiter. Its successor continued to manufacture the Siemens Sh 14 seven-cylinder radial and also produced the Bramo Fafnir (later Bramo BMW) 323 nine-cylinder radial.

THE BRAMO BMW 323 A AND B.

TYPE. Nine-cylinder air-cooled radial with two-speed supercharger and direct fuel injection.
CYLINDERS.—Bore 154 m/m. (6 in.), Stroke 160 m/m. (6.3 in.). Capacity 26.82 litres (1,636.6 cub. in.). Compression ratio 6.4 : 1 Y-alloy head with integral rocker-boxes screwed and shrunk into chrome-steel barrel. One inlet and one exhaust valve per cylinder, both inclined at 35° at centre-line. Valve-seats, inlet bronze and exhaust stellite-faced steel, shrunk into head. Bronze valve-guide inserts.
PISTONS.—Aluminium-alloy trunk type with two compression and three scraper rings above gudgeon pin and further scraper ring below. Piston crown flat with two recesses to clear valve heads. Fully-floating gudgeon pin located by aluminium-alloy end pads.
CONNECTING RODS.—Solid H-section master-rod and eight articulated rods carried between two flanges formed on big-end by hollow chrome-molybdenum wrist-pins. Big-end runs on lead bronze bearing cast on steel bush which is shrunk onto crank-pin and located by dowel. Fixed bronze bushes at both ends of articulated rods.
CRANKSHAFT.—Two-piece chrome-molybdenum steel shaft joined at rear of crank-pin by maneton joint. Balance weights rigidly bolted to extensions of crank webs. Front end of shaft is splined to take a toothed coupling for the reduction gear drive and is fitted internally with a bronze bush to form a bearing for the tail end of the airscrew shaft. Rear end of shaft engages spring drive for auxiliary lay-shaft and supercharger.
CRANKCASE.—In five sections, comprising split main body, reduction gear housing, supercharger housing and auxiliary drives casing. Detachable sump fitted below main body between two lowest cylinders. Main body comprises two aluminium-alloy forgings joined on centre-line of cylinders by nine bolts. Extension of front half houses cam gear and eighteen tappet guides. Steel housings pressed and pinned into both halves for main crankshaft bearings. Reduction gear housing is a magnesium-alloy casting. A steel member pressed in from front houses airscrew thrust and journal bearing and at its rear end acts as anchorage for stationary bevel in reduction gear. A magnesium-alloy nose-piece diaphragm carries bearing for nose of crankshaft. Supercharger casing is an aluminium-alloy casting and auxiliary drive casing is a magnesium-alloy casting.
VALVE GEAR.—One inlet and one exhaust valve per cylinder. Silicon-chrome inlet valve with hardened tip. Nichel-chrome steel exhaust valve tipped with stellite. Both valves hollow, the exhaust valve sodium-cooled. Two springs per valve. Rockers, on needle roller-bearings in rocker-boxes integral with heads, operated by push-rods and tappets by cam-ring driven by gear train off front end of crankshaft. Entire valve gear enclosed.
AIRSCREW DRIVE.—Farman type epicyclic reduction gear. Ratio A = .622 : 1, B = .71 : 1.
SUPERCHARGER.—Induction air drawn through forward-facing intake

The 985 h.p. Bramo BMW 323 engine.

on starboard side of cowling with shutter to provide alternative entry for warm air from inside cowling. Supercharger driven from rear end of crankshaft through spring coupling. Gear ratio : 11.4 : 1. Steel impellor has sixteen radial blades curved at inlet edge to form entry guide vanes. Nine diffuser guide vanes cast integral with magnesium-alloy plate closing rear of impellor chamber.
FUEL INJECTION.—Bosch direct injection pump with nine cylinders in two banks. Bosch injection valves in front of cylinder heads, 87 Octane fuel.
LUBRICATION.—Scavenge and pressure pumps mounted as single unit on auxiliary gear box. Pressure oil passes into ducts in wall of auxiliary gear box and to edge-type filter provided with external cleaning handle and thence through non-return valve and cored passage in lower part of supercharger casing to all components. Drainage from all parts of engine to magnesium-alloy sump on underside of crankcase, scavenge oil being drawn through wire-gauze filter in bottom of sump.
IGNITION.—Bosch duplex magneto mounted on upper part of auxiliary gear box and provided with draught of cooling air through a duct. Two plugs per cylinder.
AUXILIARY DRIVES.—Auxiliary gear box is a magnesium-alloy casting mounted on rear of supercharger casing. Drive taken from gear wheel formed on supercharger spring drive to gear of same size on layshaft, after end of which is machined with claws for inertia starter. Train of gears drive magneto, tachometer, oil pumps, vacuum pump, petrol pump, injection pump and generator.
DIMENSIONS.—Overall diameter 1,388 mm., Length 1,420 mm.
WEIGHT DRY.—550 kg. (1,210 lbs.).
PERFORMANCE.—Take-off and emergency 900 h.p. at 2,500 r.p.m. at 1.45 ata. at sea level, 1,000 h.p. at 2,500 r.p.m. at 1.45 ata. at 10,200 ft. Climbing 720 h.p. at 2,350 r.p.m. at 1.5 ata. at sea level, 820 h.p. at 2,350 r.p.m. at 1.23 ata. at 14,000 ft. Maximum climbing 640 h.p. at 2,200 r.p.m. at 1.45 ata. at sea level, 710 h.p.

at 2,200 r.p.m. at 1.15 ata. at 14,000 ft. Fuel consumption .572 lb./h.p./hr. maximum cruising, sea level.

THE BRAMO BMW 323 C AND E.

These engines were similar to the 323 A and B except for a change in supercharger gear ratio (9.52 : 1). Increased boost for take-off.
AIRSCREW GEAR RATIO.—C = .71 : 1, D = .622 : 1.
PERFORMANCE.—Take-off and emergency 1,000 h.p. at 2,500 r.p.m. at 1.53 ata. at sea level. Climbing 820 h.p. at 2,350 r.p.m. at 1.27 ata. at sea level, 840 h.p. at 2,350 r.p.m. at 1.27 ata. at 6,600 ft. Maximum cruising 680 h.p. at 2,200 r.p.m. at 1.15 ata. at sea level, 710 h.p. at 2,200 r.p.m. at 1.15 ata. at 8,500 ft. Fuel consumption .511 lb./h.p./hr. maximum cruising, sea level.

THE BRAMO BMW 323 P, R AND T.

These engines were similar to the 323 D in general construction, but were fitted with a two-speed supercharger (Ratio 9.6 : 1 and 12.4 : 1).
DIMENSIONS.—Overall diameter 1,400 mm. Length 1,700 mm.
WEIGHT DRY.—600 kg. (1,320 lbs.).
PERFORMANCE.—Take-off and emergency 1,000 h.p. at 2,500 r.p.m. at 1.5 ata. at sea level, 940 h.p. at 2,500 r.p.m. at 1.5 ata. at 13,120 ft. Climbing 800 h.p. at 2,250 r.p.m. at 1.25 ata. at sea level, 770 h.p. at 2,250 r.p.m. at 1.25 ata. at 14,700 ft. Maximum cruising 630 h.p. at 2,100 r.p.m. at 1.1 ata. at sea level, 660 h.p. at 2,100 r.p.m. at 1.1 ata. at 16,500 ft. Fuel consumption .42 lb./h.p./hr. maximum cruising, sea level.

The sub-type 323 R-2 was equipped with methanol/water injection for take-off at 2,600 r.p.m. and 1.64 ata. boost, and developed 1,200 h.p. at sea level.

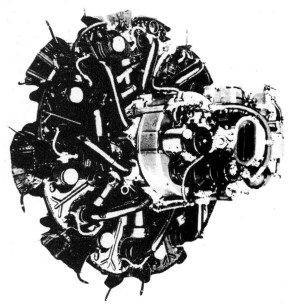

A rear view of the Bramo BMW 323 engine.

BÜCKER

BÜCKER FLUGZEUGBAU G.m.b.H.
HEAD OFFICE : RANGSDORF BEI BERLIN.
The Bücker Flugzeugbau originally specialised in the production of light training aircraft. It entered the aero-engine

manufacturing field in 1943 with a light four-cylinder inverted air-cooled engine, which the company specially developed to equip the Bücker Bü 182 Kornett single-seat advanced training monoplane, the reason for this step being the inability of the

German aero-engine manufacturers to meet the production demands of the Bücker company.
The Bücker M 700 engine has a maximum power output of 80 h.p. at 2,500 r.p.m.

DAIMLER-BENZ.

DAIMLER-BENZ AKTIENGESELLSCHAFT.

HEAD OFFICE : STUTTGART-UNTERTÜRKHEIM.

This concern, which was the descendant of the oldest automobile factory in the World, took its present form in 1926 by the amalgamation of the former firms Benz & Cie., Mannheim and Daimler Motoren Gesellschaft, Stuttgart-Berlin, originally founded by the inventors Carl Benz and Gottlieb Daimler respectively.

The Daimler firm supplied, up to 1911, all the petrol engines required by Count Zeppelin for his dirigibles. Up to 1911, the factories of Daimler and Benz developed petrol aero-engines, and were most successful in very many air displays and aero records. In 1913, both firms took part most successfully in the German Kaiserpreis-Wettbewerb for aero-engines.

During the War 1914-18, both firms were the main suppliers of all the more powerful aviation engines, with which German aircraft were fitted.

By the Treaty of Versailles, both firms were forced to stop the construction and building of aero-engines of any kind.

In 1926, the former type of 120 h.p. Mercedes D IIa six-cylinder engine was rebuilt and a small 20 h.p. air-cooled twin-cylinder aero-engine developed.

In 1928, the 800/1,000 h.p. F.2 twelve-cylinder water-cooled petrol aero-engine appeared. From this, in 1930, a similar 750 h.p. Diesel aero-engine was developed for long-distance air traffic.

From these successful experiences Daimler-Benz produced, in 1933-34, a new 900/1,200 h.p. water-cooled sixteen-cylinder airship Diesel engine for the Zeppelin L.Z.129 *Hindenburg*.

In November, 1937, the new Daimler-Benz DB 600 appeared. This was a particularly interesting technical development as the twelve cylinders were arranged in inverted Vee formation thus, with the crankcase, forming an inverted Y. The new engine established a number of important records for Germany.

A re-design of the DB 600 to incorporate direct fuel injection and improved supercharging capacity resulted in the DB 601, which established further records. The racing version of the DB 601, which set up a World's Speed Record of 469.2 m.p.h. (750.7 km.h.) in a special Messerschmitt Bf 109 R monoplane in 1939, was specially boosted to develop a maximum of 1,800 h.p. at 3,500 r.p.m., in contrast to the normal maximum output of 1,050 h.p. at 2,400 r.p.m. for the then standard engine.

The Daimler-Benz engines most widely used during the war were the DB 601, DB 603 and DB 605. The DB 606 and 610 coupled engines were installed in the Heinkel He 177.

Series production of DB engines was undertaken at Stuttgart-Untertürkheim, Genshagen - bei - Berlin, Berlin - Marienfelde, Mannheim, Brunswick-Querum (Niedersachsische Moterenwerke), Kassel - Altenbauna (Henschel), Stettin - Arnimswalde (Pommersche Motorenwerke) and Wiener-Neustadt (Henschel).

The Daimler Benz company also undertook development of the turbo-jet and one unit was built and run in the Autumn of 1943. Work on the project was then stopped by the German Air Ministry because the design was more complex than those of other firms.

THE DAIMLER-BENZ DB 603 A, B, C AND D.

TYPE.—Twelve-cylinder inverted Vee liquid-cooled. In general this engine is an enlarged version of the DB 605 with certain improvements.

CYLINDERS.—Bore 162 mm., Stroke 180 mm., Capacity 44.5 litres, Compression ratio 7.5 : 1 (left block), 7.3 : 1 (right block). Cylinders in two banks of six set at 60°. Cylinder blocks, including barrels, water-jackets, cylinder-heads and valve pockets are one piece alloy castings. Dry steel liners are screwed into barrels leaving portions of liner projecting. Attachment to crankcase by internally-threaded rings which are screwed onto projecting portions of liners, the rings pulling each cylinder sleeve down onto crankcase. A feature found on the DB 603 only is the provision of a rubber ring for a joint between cylinders and crankcase. Two inlet and two exhaust valves per cylinder. One sparking-plug on each side of cylinder, a departure from the usual DB practice.

PISTONS.—Forged light alloy concave-headed pistons of normal design with floating gudgeon pins. Three compression rings.

CONNECTING RODS.—One forked and one plain rod in each pair of cylinders. Both rods split at bearing centre-line with Vee-serrated joints. Retaining nuts are splined for special assembly tool. Either three-row roller or lead-bronze plain big-end bearings fitted with four dowels to prevent fretting of the faces. Tin flash coating absent on some engines.

CRANKSHAFT.—One-piece type with six cranks at 120° and eight balance weights. Hollow crank-pins and main journals. Shaft runs in seven plain lead-bronze bearings in the main crankcase,

FUEL SYSTEM.—Bosch direct-injection pump located between the cylinder blocks with automatic mixture regulator. Twelve-lobe camshaft within pump body driven at half crankshaft speed. Twin gear type pump at rear of engine supplies fuel under pressure to the injection pump from the main tanks via a de-aerator. Fuel injected through 3 mm. bore steel pipes from pumps to injector nozzles in cylinder heads, one between each pair of valves.

SUPERCHARGER.—Centrifugal type driven through a hydraulic coupling. The cross-section of the volute is circular instead of rectangular as in previous DB types.

IGNITION.—Bosch ZM 12 CR8 dual magnetos. Screened ignition system. Automatic advance and retard mechanism.

LUBRICATION.—Pressure lubrication provided for journal and big-end bearings, camshafts, fuel pumps, injection pump, reduction gear bearings, supercharger hydraulic coupling and auxiliaries. Oil each bearing carried in heavily-webbed section with transverse tie-rod running across the crankcase and through each bearing-cap. Front end of shaft splined to take splined mounting sleeves of reduction-gear pinion. Rear end fitted with starter dog and accessory drive gear-wheel.

CRANKCASE.—Light alloy casting with reinforcing webs in regions of crankshaft bearings. Thin light alloy top cover secured by stud and dowelled. Tubular mounting at rear end of case and below crankshaft for installation of cannon to fire through airscrew shaft.

VALVE GEAR.—Two inlet and two exhaust stellited valves per cylinder. Sodium-cooled exhaust valves. Single bevel-driven underhead

The 1,750 h.p. Daimler Benz DB 603 A twelve-cylinder inverted Vee liquid-cooled engine.

A rear view of the Daimler-Benz DB 603 L showing the two-stage supercharger.

camshaft to each block with one cam operating one inlet and one exhaust valve through short rocker arms with needle roller bearings. Ball joints interposed between rockers and valve stems. Tappet clearances (cold) inlet .3 mm. exhaust .6 mm. scavenged from camshaft covers and supercharger drive casing. Double mechanically-cleaned filters.

AIRSCREW DRIVE.—Plain spur gear type embodying pitch-change mechanism for VDM airscrew. Front bearing outrigged 10 inches ahead of gear wheel. This results in an extended reduction gear casing, the most noticeable external alteration from previous DB types. The space is probably for the fitting of reversible-pitch airscrew mechanism. Drive ratios A and D = .518 : 1, B = .465 : 1, C = .417 : 1.

DIMENSIONS.—Overall length (including electric starter and airscrew shaft) 2,610.5 mm., Width 830 mm., Height 1,156 mm.

WEIGHT.— 910 kg. (2,002 lbs.).

PERFORMANCE.—Take-off and Emergency 1,750 h.p. at 2,700 r.p.m. at 1.4 ata. at sea level, 1,620 h.p. at 2,700 r.p.m. at 1.4 ata. at 18,700 ft. Climbing 1,580 h.p. at 2,500 r.p.m. at 1.3 ata. at sea level, 1,510 h.p. at 2,500 r.p.m. at 1.3 ata. at 18,700 ft. Maximum cruising 1,375 h.p. at 2,300 r.p.m. at 1.2 ata. at sea level, 1,400 h.p. at 2,300 r.p.m. at 1.2 ata. at 17,700 ft. Fuel consumption .474 lb./h.p./hr. maximum cruising, sea level.

THE DAIMLER-BENZ DB 603 E.

The DB 603 E was similar to the A except that it had a supercharger of increased diameter and automatic airscrew-pitch control.

DIMENSIONS.—Overall length 2,706 mm., Width 830 mm., Height 1,167 mm.

WEIGHT. 925 kg. (2,035 lbs.).

PERFORMANCE.—Take-off and emergency 1,800 h.p. at 2,700 r.p.m. at 1.48 ata. at sea level, 1,550 h.p. at 2,700 r.p.m. at 1.48 ata. at 23,000 ft. Climbing 1,575 h.p. at 2,500 r.p.m. at 1.35 ata. at sea level, 1,430 h.p. at 2,500 r.p.m. at 1.35 ata. at 23,150 ft. Maximum cruising 1,395 h.p. at 2,300 r.p.m. at 1.25 ata. at sea level, 1,325 h.p. at 2,300 r.p.m. at 1.25 ata. at 22,000 ft.

The 2,660 h.p. Daimler-Benz DB 604 twenty-four cylinder X-type liquid-cooled engine.

THE DAIMLER-BENZ DB 603 AA AND AS.

These engines were similar to the DB 603 A but were fitted with superchargers of increased diameter.

DIMENSIONS.—Same as for DB 603 A.

WEIGHT.—915 kg. (2,013 lbs.).

PERFORMANCE.—Take-off and emergency 1,670 h.p. at 2,700 r.p.m. at 1.4 ata. at sea level, 1,450 h.p. at 2,700 r.p.m. at 1.4 ata. at 24,000 ft. Climbing 1,510 h.p. at 2,500 r.p.m. at 1.3 ata. at 23,600 ft. Maximum cruising 1,325 h.p. at 2,300 r.p.m. at 1.2 ata. at sea level, 1,280 h.p. at 2,300 r.p.m. at 1.2 ata. at 22,600 ft.

THE DAIMLER-BENZ DB 603 G AND K.

Similar to the DB 603 A but with increased compression ratio 8.3 : 1 left block, 8.5 : 1 right block).

DIMENSIONS.—Overall length 2,680 mm., Width 830 mm., Height 1,167 mm.

WEIGHTS.—DB 603 G 930 kg. (2,046 lbs.), DB 603 K 990 kg. (2,178 lbs.).

PERFORMANCE.—Take-off and emergency 1,900 h.p. at 2,700 r.p.m. at sea level, 1,560 h.p. at 2,700 r.p.m. at 24,300 ft. Climbing 1,580 h.p. at 2,500 r.p.m. at sea level, 1,450 h.p. at 2,500 r.p.m. at 24,200 ft. Maximum cruising 1,375 h.p. at 2,300 r.p.m. at sea level, 1,350 h.p. at 2,300 r.p.m. at 23,000 ft.

THE DAIMLER-BENZ DB 603 L AND M.

These engines were similar to the DB 603 E but were fitted with a two-stage supercharger and aftercooler.

DIMENSIONS.—Overall length 2,740 mm., Width 1,008 mm., Height 1,203 mm.

WEIGHT.—975 kg. (2,145 lbs.).

PERFORMANCE.—Take-off and emergency 1,280 h.p. at 2,700 r.p.m. at 1.4 ata. at sea level, 1,400 h.p. at 2,700 r.p.m. at 1.4 ata. at 32,800 ft. Climbing 1,675 h.p. at 2,500 r.p.m. at 1.3 ata. at sea level, 1,325 h.p. at 2,500 r.p.m. at 1.3 ata. at 30,200 ft. Maximum cruising 1,500 h.p. at 2,300 r.p.m. at 1.2 ata. at sea level, 1,230 h.p. at 2,300 r.p.m. at 1.2 ata. at 27,600 ft.

THE DAIMLER-BENZ DB 603 N.

The DB 603 N was similar to the L but had re-designed cylinders and increased r.p.m. The power figures quoted below are for the DB 603 N with a mechanically-driven low-gear supercharger and hydraulic coupling for high gear. It was intended to develop sub-types of this engine with various arrangements of supercharger gears. Compression ratio 8.3-8.5 : 1. 96 Octane fuel.

PERFORMANCE.—Take-off and emergency 2,830 h.p. at 3,000 r.p.m. at 2 ata. at sea level, 1,930 h.p. at 3,000 r.p.m. at 2 ata. at 32,800 ft. Climbing 2,225 h.p. at 2,750 r.p.m. at 1.65 ata. at sea level, 1,750 h.p. at 2,750 r.p.m. at 1.65 ata. at 32,200 ft.

THE DAIMLER-BENZ DB 603 U.

This engine was the DB 603 E with a Hirth turbo-blower in addition to the normal mechanically-driven supercharger.

REDUCTION GEAR RATIO.—.483 : 1.

PERFORMANCE.—Take-off and emergency 1,810 h.p. at 2,700 r.p.m. at 1.48 ata. at sea level, 1,600 h.p. at 2,700 r.p.m. at 1.48 ata. at 42,000 ft. Climbing 1,560 h.p. at 2,500 r.p.m. at 1.35 ata. at sea level, 1,410 h.p. at 2,500 r.p.m. at 1.35 ata at 44,000 ft. Maximum cruising 1,320 h.p. at 2,300 r.p.m. at 1.25 ata. at sea level, 1,225 h.p. at 2,300 r.p.m. at 1.25 ata. at 44,400 ft.

THE DAIMLER-BENZ DB 604 A AND B.

The DB 604 was a 24-cylinder X-type liquid-cooled engine with two-speed supercharger. Development was stopped in September, 1942.

CYLINDERS.—Bore 135 mm., Stroke 135 mm., Capacity 46.5 litres, Compression ratio 7 : 1.

AIRSCREW REDUCTION RATIO.—.334 : 1.

WEIGHT.—1,080 kg. (2,376 lbs.).

PERFORMANCE.—Take-off and emergency 2,660 h.p. at 3,200 r.p.m. at 1.42 ata. at sea level, 2,410 h.p. at 3,200 r.p.m. at 1.42 ata. at 20,600 ft. Climbing 2,270 h.p. at 3,000 r.p.m. at 1.3 ata. at sea level, 2,410 h.p. at 3,000 r.p.m. at 1.3 ata. at 21,000 ft. Maximum cruising 1,830 h.p. at 2,800 r.p.m. at 1.15 ata. at sea level, 1,860 h.p. at 2,800 r.p.m. at 1.15 ata. at 20,000 ft.

THE DAIMLER-BENZ DB 605 A, B AND C.

The DB 605 was a development of the DB 601 and was very similar in basic construction to that power-unit. The main improvements were an increase in the permissible r.p.m.; altered valve-timing, which increased the inlet period and improved the scavenging to give greater volumetric efficiency at the higher r.p.m.; complete re-design of the cylinder block to obtain the maximum possible bore with existing cylinder centres; and re-positioning of the sparking-plugs. The big-end bearings were also modified.

TYPE.—Twelve-cylinder inverted Vee liquid-cooled.

CYLINDERS.—Bore 154 mm., Stroke 160 mm., Capacity 35.7 litres. Compression ratio 7.3 : 1 (left block) 7.5 : 1 (right block). Two inlet and two exhaust valves per cylinder.

BIG-END BEARINGS.—Roller bearing big-ends discarded in favour of flanged lead/bronze-lined bearings with tin flash coating.

FUEL SYSTEM.—Bosch direct-injection pump mounted between the cylinder blocks. Injectors on inside of cylinder blocks. Special slow-running system which by-passes the main throttle. 87 Octane fuel.

SUPERCHARGER.—Centrifugal impellor with 16 blades. Hydraulic coupling drive. The coupling is automatically regulated by a control capsule subjected to atmospheric pressure which varies the supply of oil to the hydraulic coupling. This form of coupling has been retained from the DB 601, but has been considerably modified in order to reduce the operating temperature of the coupling. High temperature was a fault which occurred in the DB 601 supercharger drive. Gear ratio (no slip) 10.07 : 1.

IGNITION.—Dual Bosch magnetos mounted at the top of the rear cover.

LUBRICATION.—Pressure pump delivers oil to each of the seven main bearings, which feed pressure oil to each crankpin and big-end bearing surface. Pressure oil is also supplied by the pump to the hydraulic supercharger gear, and to the interior of the camshaft. The oil is scavenged from each camshaft cover.

STARTER.—Bosch hand/electric inertia starter.

AIRSCREW DRIVE.—Spur gear type. The detachable airscrew shaft of the DB 601 has been discarded in favour of a longitudinally splined gear shaft extension. Gear ratio A = .594 : 1, B = .534 : 1, C = .497 : 1.

DIMENSIONS.—Overall length (including starter and airscrew shaft) 2158.5 mm., Width 760 mm., Height 1,037 mm.

The 1,475 h.p. Daimler-Benz DB 605 A twelve-cylinder inverted Vee liquid-cooled engine.

The 2,000 h.p. Daimler-Benz DB 605 D engine with supercharger of increased diameter.

WEIGHT (with starter).—756 kg. (1,663 lbs.).

PERFORMANCE.—Take-off and emergency 1,475 h.p. at 2,800 r.p.m. at 1.42 ata. at sea level, 1,355 h.p. at 2,800 r.p.m. at 1.42 ata. at 18,700 ft. Climbing 1,310 h.p. at 2,600 r.p.m. at 1.3 ata. at sea level, 1,250 h.p. at 2,600 r.p.m. at 1.3 ata. at 19,000 ft., Maximum cruising 1,075 h.p. at 2,300 r.p.m. at 1.15 ata. at sea level, 1,080 h.p. at 2,300 r.p.m. at 1.15 ata. at 18,000 ft., Fuel consumption .473 lb./h.p./hr. maximum cruising, sea level.

THE DAIMLER-BENZ DB 605 AM.

Similar to the DB 605 A but with provision for methanol/water injection into the eye of the supercharger.

PERFORMANCE.—Take-off and emergency 1,800 h.p. at 2,800 r.p.m. at 1.7 ata. at sea level, 1,700 h.p. at 2,800 r.p.m. at 1.7 ata. at 13,500 ft. Other performance figures as for the DB 605 A.

THE DAIMLER-BENZ DB 605 AS.

Similar in general construction to the DB 605 A but fitted with a supercharger of increased diameter.

PERFORMANCE.—Take-off and emergency 1,435 h.p. at 2,800 r.p.m. at 1.42 ata. at sea level, 1,200 h.p. at 2,800 r.p.m. at 1.42 ata. at 26,200 ft. Climbing 1,275 h.p. at 2,600 r.p.m. at 1.3 ata. at sea level, 1,150 h.p. at 2,600 r.p.m. at 1.3 ata. at 25,600 ft. Maximum cruising 1,075 h.p. at 2,400 r.p.m. at 1.25 ata. at sea level, 1,050 h.p. at 2,400 r.p.m. at 1.15 ata. at 25,200 ft.

THE DAIMLER-BENZ DB 605 D, E, F, DB AND DC.

Similar in general construction to the DB 605 A but fitted with supercharger of increased diameter and methanol/water injection system. Increased compression ratio 8.3/8.5 : 1.87 or 96 Octane fuel.

AIRSCREW REDUCTION GEAR.—D = .594 : 1, E = .534 : 1, F = .497 : 1.

PERFORMANCE.—Take-off and emergency (DB 605 DC) 2,000 h.p. at 2,800 r.p.m. at 1.98 ata. at sea level, 1,800 h.p. at 2,800 r.p.m. at 1.98 ata. at 16,700 ft., (DB 605 DB) 1,800 h.p. at 2,800 r.p.m. at 1.8 ata. at sea level, 1,530 h.p. at 2,800 r.p.m. at 1.8 ata. at 19,600 ft. Climbing 1,275 h.p. at 2,600 r.p.m. at 1.3 ata. at sea level, 1,150 h.p. at 2,600 r.p.m. at 1.3 ata. at 25,600 ft. Maximum cruising 1,075 h.p. at 2,400 r.p.m. at 1.15 ata. at sea level, 1,050 h.p. at 2,400 r.p.m. at 1.15 ata. at 25,200 ft.

NOTE :—The additional letter after the sub-type letter is used to signify the following : "S" denotes a special engine, "B" is used when the power has been increased by a higher boost pressure and 87 Octane fuel with methanol injection, "C" is used when the power has been increased by a higher boost pressure and 96 Octane fuel with methanol injection.

THE DAIMLER-BENZ DB 605 L.

Similar to the DB 605 A but fitted with two-stage mechanical supercharger. 96 Octane fuel.

PERFORMANCE.—Take-off and emergency 1,700 h.p. at 2,800 r.p.m. at 1.75 ata. at sea level, 1,350 h.p. at 2,800 r.p.m. at 1.75 ata. at 31,400 ft. Climbing 1,400 h.p. at 2,600 r.p.m. at 1.43 ata. at sea level, 1,150 h.p. at 2,600 r.p.m. at 1.43 ata. at 31,400 ft. Maximum cruising 1,160 h.p. at 2,400 r.p.m. at 1.2 ata. at sea level, 930 h.p. at 2,400 r.p.m. at 1.2 ata. at 31,000 ft.

A rear view of the Daimler-Benz DB 605 L showing the two-stage supercharger.

THE DAIMLER-BENZ DB 606 A AND B.

The DB 606 consisted of two DB 601 engines mounted side-by-side and driving a single airscrew through a common reduction gear and extended airscrew shaft. The two engine units were inclined so that the inner banks are disposed almost vertically.

In place of the normal reduction gear housing on each engine there was a single large gear casing which connected the two crankcases. The two crankshaft pinions drove the single airscrew shaft either directly or indirectly through idler gears, according to the desired direction of the airscrew. Provision was made for declutching the individual engines from the airscrew by means of a clutch and lever in the cockpit. The superchargers, normally mounted on the port side of each engine, were located on the outer sides of the twin unit.

AIRSCREW REDUCTION GEAR.—Ratio .413 : 1. A right-handed rotation, B left-handed rotation.
DIMENSIONS.—Overall length (including starter but without airscrew shaft) 2,082 mm., Width 1,630 mm., Height 1,046.5 mm.
WEIGHT (with starter).—(DB 606 A) 1,515 kg. (3,333 lbs.), (DB 606 B) 1,565 kg. (3,443 lbs.).
PERFORMANCE.—Take-off and emergency 2,700 h.p. at 2,700 r.p.m. at 1.42 ata. at sea level, 2,650 h.p. at 2,700 r.p.m. at 1.42 ata. at 15,800 ft. Climbing 2,400 h.p. at 2,500 r.p.m. at 1.3 ata. at sea level, 2,400 h.p. at 2,700 r.p.m. at 1.3 ata. at 16,000 ft. Maximum cruising 2,000 h.p. at 2,300 r.p.m. at 1.15 ata. at sea level, 2,080 h.p. at 2,300 r.p.m. at 1.15 ata. at 16,700 ft. Fuel consumption 600 litres/hour, maximum cruising, sea level.

THE DAIMLER-BENZ DB 609 A, B AND F.

The DB 609 was a sixteen-cylinder inverted Vee liquid-cooled engine using cylinders of similar dimensions to the DB 603. It was fitted with a three-speed two-stage supercharger. Development stopped in April, 1943.

CYLINDERS.—Bore 165 mm., Stroke 180 mm., Capacity 61.8 litres. Compression ratio 8.5 : 1.
AIRSCREW DRIVE.—A and B right-handed, F left-handed rotation. Gear ratios A = .518 : 1, B = .467 : 1, F = .417 : 1.
WEIGHT.—1,400 kg. (3,800 lbs.).
PERFORMANCE.—Take-off and emergency 2,660 h.p. at 2,800 r.p.m. at 1.42 ata. at sea level, 2,450 h.p. at 2,800 r.p.m. at 1.42 ata. at 21,600 ft. Climbing 2,270 h.p. at 2,500 r.p.m. at 1.3 ata. at sea level, 1,980 h.p. at 2,500 r.p.m. at 1.3 ata. at 28,500 ft. Maximum cruising 1,950 h.p. at 2,300 r.p.m. at 1.2 ata. at sea level, 1,780 h.p. at 2,300 r.p.m. at 1.2 ata. at 26,200 ft.

THE DAIMLER-BENZ DB 610 A AND B.

The DB 610 consisted of two DB 605 engines coupled together in the same manner as in the DB 606.

AIRSCREW DRIVE.—A right-handed, B left-handed rotation. Gear ratio .413 : 1.
DIMENSIONS.—Overall length 2,129 mm., Width 1,620 mm., Height 1,036 mm.
WEIGHTS.—A = 1,540 kg. (3,388 lbs.), B = 1,580 kg. (3,476 lbs.).
PERFORMANCE.—Take-off and emergency 2,950 h.p. at 2,800 r.p.m. at 1.42 ata. at sea level, 2,700 h.p. at 2,800 r.p.m. at 1.42 ata. at 18,700 ft. Climbing 2,620 h.p. at 2,600 r.p.m. at 1.3 ata. at sea level, 2,500 h.p. at 2,600 r.p.m. at 1.3 ata. at 19,000 ft. Maximum cruising 2,160 h.p. at 2,300 r.p.m. at 1.15 ata at sea level, 2,160 h.p. at 2,300 r.p.m. at 1.15 ata. at 18,000 ft. Fuel consumption .474 lbs./h.p./hr. maximum cruising, sea level.

THE DAIMLER-BENZ DB 610 C AND D.

AIRSCREW DRIVE.—C right-handed, D left-handed rotation. Gear ratio .413 : 1.
WEIGHT.—1,570 kg. (3,454 lbs.).
PERFORMANCE.—Take-off and emergency 2,870 h.p. at 2,800 r.p.m. at sea level, 2,560 h.p. at 2,800 r.p.m. at 25,000 ft. Climbing 2,550 h.p. at 2,600 r.p.m. at sea level, 2,400 h.p. at 2,600 r.p.m. at 24,300 ft. Maximum cruising 2,100 h.p. at 2,300 r.p.m. at sea level, 2,040 h.p. at 2,300 r.p.m. at 23,000 ft.

THE DAIMLER-BENZ DB 613 A AND B.

The DB 613 consisted of two DB 603 G engines coupled together to drive a single airscrew and was similar in general layout to the DB 610.

AIRSCREW DRIVE.—A right-handed, B left-handed rotation. Gear ratio .408 : 1.
DIMENSIONS.—Overall length (without airscrew shaft) 2,224 mm., Width 1,770 mm., Height 1,135 mm.
WEIGHTS.—A = 1,960 kg. (4,312 lbs.), B = 2,000 kg. (4,400 lbs.).
PERFORMANCE.—Take-off and emergency 3,800 h.p. at 2,700 r.p.m. at sea level, 3,120 h.p. at 2,700 r.p.m. at 24,200 ft. Climbing 3,160 h.p. at 2,500 r.p.m. at sea level, 2,900 h.p. at 2,500 r.p.m. at 24,200 ft. Maximum cruising 2,750 h.p. at 2,300 r.p.m. at sea level, 2,700 h.p. at 2,300 r.p.m. at 23,000 ft.

THE DAIMLER-BENZ DB 627 A AND B.

The DB 627 was the DB 603 G fitted with a two-stage mechanical supercharger and after-cooler. Development was stopped in March, 1944.

AIRSCREW DRIVE.—Right-handed rotation. Gear ratio A = .518 : 1, B = .483 : 1.

The Daimler-Benz DB 605 T which served as the central engine in the "HZ Anlage". The two-stage compressor supplied induction air to the superchargers of the two DB 603 engines in the wings.

The 1,750 h.p. Daimler-Benz DB 607 Diesel engine of similar dimensions to the DB 603.

The Daimler-Benz DB 610, made up of two DB 605 engines coupled together to drive a single airscrew.

DIMENSIONS.—Overall length (including airscrew shaft) 2,745 mm., Width 945 mm., Height 1,230 mm.
WEIGHT.—1,020 kg. (2,244 lbs.).
PERFORMANCE.—Take-off and emergency 2,000 h.p. at 2,700 r.p.m. at 1.5 ata. at sea level, 1,325 h.p. at 2,700 r.p.m. at 1.5 ata. at 34,200 ft. Climbing 1,660 h.p. at 2,500 r.p.m. at 1.3 ata. at sea level, 1,240 h.p. at 2,500 r.p.m. at 1.3 ata. at 36,400 ft. Maximum cruising 1,400 h.p. at 2,300 r.p.m. at 1.2 ata. at sea level, 1,150 h.p. at 2,300 r.p.m. at 1.2 ata. at 32,500 ft. Fuel consumption .462 lb./h.p./hr. maximum cruising, sea level.

THE DAIMLER-BENZ DB 628 A AND B.

The DB 628 was similar in general arrangement to the DB 605 A but was fitted with a two-stage mechanical supercharger, the first stage being mounted on and driven from the reduction gear. The air intake was behind the airscrew and an induction cooler was fitted. Development was stopped in March, 1944.

AIRSCREW DRIVE.—Gear ratio A = .594 : 1, B = .534 : 1.
DIMENSIONS.—Overall length 2,754 mm., Width 903 mm., Height 1,227 mm.
WEIGHT.—860 kg. (1,892 lbs.).
PERFORMANCE.—Take-off and emergency 1,475 h.p. at 2,800 r.p.m. at 1.42 ata. at sea level, 1,200 h.p. at 2,800 r.p.m. at 1.42 ata. at 36,000 ft. Climbing 1,310 h.p. at 2,600 r.p.m. at 1.3 ata. at sea level, 1,110 h.p. at 2,600 r.p.m. at 1.3 ata. at 36,000 ft. Maximum cruising 1,075 h.p. at 2,300 r.p.m. at 1.15 ata. at sea level, 975 h.p. at 2,300 r.p.m. at 1.15 ata. at 32,800 ft. Fuel consumption .474 lb./h.p./hr. maximum cruising, sea level.

The 3,180 h.p. Daimler-Benz DB 613 engine, made up of two coupled DB 603 engines.

THE DAIMLER-BENZ DB 632.

The DB 632 was the DB 603 N with a modified supercharger and was fitted to drive contra-rotating airscrews.

WEIGHT (with airscrew drive).—1,000 kg. (2,200 lbs.).

PERFORMANCE.—Take-off and emergency 2,400 h.p. at 3,200 r.p.m. at 1.65 ata. at sea level, 1,625 h.p. at 3,200 r.p.m. at 1.65 ata. at 27,000 ft. Climbing 1,790 h.p. at 3,000 r.p.m. at 1.3 ata. at sea level, 1,500 h.p. at 3,000 r.p.m. at 1.3 ata. at 27,000 ft. Maximum cruising 1,520 h.p. at 2,700 r.p.m. at 1.2 ata. at sea level, 1,350 h.p. at 2,700 r.p.m. at 1.2 ata. at 25,200 ft.

OTHER DAIMLER-BENZ ENGINES (Development stopped).

DB 607 A. A diesel engine of similar dimensions to the DB 603. Take-off power : 1,750 h.p. Abandoned in October, 1942.

DB 612 A. The DB 601 with re-designed cylinder-heads incorporating rotary valves. Take-off power : 1,350 h.p. Abandoned.

DB 614 A, B and F. A development of the DB 603 G. Take-off power : 2,000 h.p. Abandoned in June, 1942.

DB 615 A and B. Consisting of two DB 614 engines in tandem and driving contra-rotating airscrews. Take-off power : 4,000 h.p. Abandoned in June, 1942.

DB 616 A and B. A DB 605 development. Abandoned in June, 1942.

DB 617 A, B and F. A development of the DB 603 for long-range flight.

DB 618 A. Coupled DB 617 engines.

DB 619 A and B. Consisted of two coupled DB 609 sixteen-cylinder inverted Vee engines driving a single airscrew. Capacity : 123.6 litres. Take-off power : 5,240 h.p. Abandoned in April, 1943.

DB 620 A and B. Coupled DB 628 engines. Take-off power : 2,950 h.p.

DB 621. A DB 605 D with two-stage supercharger. Take-off power : 1,620 h.p. Abandoned in September, 1942.

DB 622. A DB 603 with a two-stage mechanical supercharger and turbo supercharger. Take-off power : 1,970 h.p. Abandoned in January, 1943.

DB 623 A, B and F. The DB 603 G with twin turbo-superchargers. Take-off power : 2,265 h.p. Abandoned in January, 1943.

DB 624 A. A DB 603 G with two-stage supercharger and turbo blower. Take-off power : 1,900 h.p. Abandoned in April, 1943.

DB 625 A, B and C. The DB 605 D with turbo supercharger. Take-off power : 1,755 h.p. Abandoned.

DB 626 A, B and F. The DB 603 G with twin-turbo superchargers and induction cooler. Take-off power : 2,125 h.p. Abandoned in November, 1942.

DB 629 A, B and F. The DB 609 A/F with two-stage supercharger and turbo blower. Take-off power : 2,650 h.p. Abandoned in April, 1943.

DB 630. A 36-cylinder "double-W" engine. Bore : 142 mm. Stroke : 155 mm. Capacity : 89 litres. Take-off power : 3,900-4,100 h.p. Abandoned in April, 1943. Was to have been the basic engine for a new series.

DB 631 A. The DB 603 G with a three-stage supercharger. Take-off power : 1,900 h.p.

"HZ Anlage." This power-plant layout consisted of two DB 603 S or T and one DB 605 T engines. The first installation was incorporated in the design of the Henschel Hs 130 E. The DB 605 engine was mounted in the fuselage amidships and drove a Roots-type two-stage compressor to supply induction air to the superchargers of the two DB 603 engines mounted in the wings, each driving a single four-blade constant-speed airscrew. Total take-off power : 3,500 h.p. Rated altitude 45,300 ft. Abandoned in February, 1944.

The Daimler-Benz DB 612 A engine, a development of the DB 601 with re-designed cylinder heads.

A three-quarter rear view of the Daimler-Benz DB 625 engine showing the turbo-supercharger installation.

A rear view of the Daimler-Benz DB 623 showing the turbo supercharger installation.

HIRTH.

HIRTH-MOTOREN G.m.b.H.

HEAD OFFICE AND WORKS : STUTTGART-ZUFFENHAUSEN.

Hellmuth Hirth, famous as a pre-war pilot, founded after the end of the War 1914-18 the Versuchsbau Hellmuth Hirth and developed the HM 60 aero-engines. The great successes of this engine in several air races led, on 1931, to the foundation of the Hirth-Motoren G.m.b.H. Herr Hellmuth Hirth died after a short illness in June, 1938.

A special feature of Hirth engines was their built-up crankshafts, a patent of Dr. Albert Hirth. This design made possible the use of roller-bearings for crankshaft and connecting rods. Another feature was the very economical fresh-oil lubrication obtained by metering the amounts for each cylinder and all bearings. The very low consumption of Hirth engines was due to this lubricating system.

Ernst Heinkel A.G. owned a controlling interest in the Hirth Motoren G.m.b.H. These two companies collaborated in the development of jet propulsion, their investigations beginning as far back as 1936. The first Heinkel-Hirth unit—the He S 3—was installed in the Heinkel He 178 and flew for the first time on August 27, 1939. Details of the Heinkel-Hirth jet units will be found on pages 35-36d.

THE HIRTH HM 504 A.

TYPE.—Four-cylinder inverted in-line air-cooled.

CYLINDERS.—Bore 105 m/m. (4.128 in.), Stroke 115 m/m. (4.52 in.). Capacity 3.984 litres (243 cub. in.). Compression ratio 6 : 1. Special cast-iron barrels spigotted deeply into crankcase. Light

alloy heads, with valve-boxes incorporated, attached by long bolts from crankcase.

PISTONS.—Nelson-Bohnalite. Three compression and one scraper rings.

CONNECTING RODS.—Heat-treated chrome-nickel steel H-section rods with roller-bearings in big and little ends. Raceways case-hardened.

CRANKSHAFT.—Built-up shaft carried on five roller-bearings. Ball thrust-bearing.

CRANKCASE.—"Elektron" casting. Top cover embodies oil tank.

VALVE GEAR.—Fully-enclosed. One inlet and one exhaust valve per cylinder. Inlet valve seat of special bronze. Exhaust valve seat of special steel. Valve-rockers, on needle bearings, operated through push-rods and ball-ended tappets off camshaft running in roller-bearings.

CARBURATION.—One Pallas-Zenith 40 VAH carburettor suitable for inverted flying and fitted with automatic mixture-control.

IGNITION.—Two Bosch JFR.ARS.48 and 49 magnetos, one with impulse-starter. System fully-screened.

LUBRICATION.—Crankcase cover serves as oil tank. Metered oil feeds to airscrew thrust-bearing and cylinders. Big-end and main bearings oil-splashed.

STARTER.—Hand-turning crank with back fire safety device.

AIRSCREW DRIVE.—Right-hand tractor. Direct-drive. Hirth hub.

DIMENSIONS.—Length 960 mm., Height 780 mm., Width 520 mm.

WEIGHTS.—Dry and bare 112 kg. (245 lbs.), Fully equipped 124 kg. (274 lbs.).

PERFORMANCE.—Maximum 105 h.p. at 2,530 r.p.m., Rated 85 h.p. at 2,360 r.p.m., Cruising 75 h.p. at 2,270 r.p.m., Cruising fuel consumption 220 gr. (.485 lb.) per h.p. hour, Cruising oil consumption 3 grs. (.0066 lb.) per h.p. hour.

The 280 h.p. Hirth HM 508 D-1 engine.

THE HIRTH HM 506 A.

TYPE.—Six-cylinder inverted in-line air-cooled.

CYLINDERS.—Bore 105 m/m. (4.128 in.), Stroke 115 m/m. (4.52 in.). Capacity 5.976 litres (364.7 cub. in.). Compression ratio 6 : 1. Construction as HM 504.

CRANKSHAFT.—Hirth patented built-up type carried on seven ball-bearings and one radial thrust-bearing.

CRANKCASE. — Elektron casting of U-section with open bearing-brackets. Top of crankcase closed by cover embodying oil tank.

VALVE GEAR.—Same as for HM 504.

CARBURATION.—Two Sum down-draught carburettors with automatic mixture control and suitable for inverted flying.

IGNITION.—Two Bosch magnetos, one with impulse coupling. Screened for radio.

LUBRICATION.—Crankcase cover embodies oil tank. Oil metered to six cylinder barrels and radial thrust-bearing. Rocker gear works in oil baths. One filter and scavenge pump.

STARTER.—Hand-turning gear or Bosch starter.

AIRSCREW DRIVE.—Right-hand tractor. Direct-drive. Hirth nose-piece and airscrew hub.

DIMENSIONS.—Length 1,276 m/m. Height 735 m/m. Width 490 m/m.

WEIGHTS.—Dry and bare 149.0 kg. (328 lbs.), Fully equipped 174 kg. (383 lbs.).

PERFORMANCE.—Maximum 160 h.p. at 2,500 r.p.m., Normal 145 h.p. at 2,420 r.p.m., Cruising 135 h.p. at 2,360 r.p.m., Cruising consumptions per h.p. hour : Fuel 225 gr. (.475 lb.), Oil 3 gr. (.0066 lb.).

THE HIRTH HM 508 D.

TYPE.—Eight-cylinder 60° Vee inverted air-cooled, geared, supercharged.

CYLINDERS.—Bore 105 m/m. (4.128 in.), Stroke 115 m/m. (4.52 in.). Capacity 7.97 litres (486.4 cub. in.). Compression ratio 6 : 1. Construction as HM 504.

PISTONS. — Y-alloy. Three compression and two scraper rings.

CONNECTING RODS.—H-section rods of heat-treated chrome-nickel steel. Roller-bearings in big and little ends. Raceways case-hardened.

CRANKSHAFT.—Hirth type built-up four-throw shaft running in five roller-bearings and one radial thrust-bearing.

INDUCTION SYSTEM.—Centrifugal supercharger with light alloy rotor driven at 4.46 times crankshaft speed fed by Pallas-Zenith carburettor with automatic mixture control and suitable for inverted flying. Fuel-air mixture is distributed at low-supercharge by external manifolds to two banks of cylinders.

IGNITION.—One double Bosch magneto with automatic advance. System fully screened.

AIRSCREW DRIVE.—1.5 : 1 reduction through patent Stoeckicht sun and planet gear in which three satellite gears are carried in casing affixed to airscrew shaft. Satellite gears roll off internal gear on crankshaft and on gear suspended on gimbals and elastically supported in gear housing.

LUBRICATION.—Fresh-oil lubrication. Supply to eight cylinder-barrels and five crankshaft-bearings metered. Splash lubrication for supercharger gear and camshaft. Reduction gear lubricated by oil at high pressure. Scavenge pump draws excess oil from crankcase and forces it through filter to tank.

STARTER.—Bosch hand-turning gear or Bosch electric starter.

DIMENSIONS.—Length 1,289 m/m., Width 683 m/m., Height 815 m/m.

WEIGHTS.—Dry and bare 208 kg. (458 lbs.), Fully equipped 221 kg. (486 lbs.).

PERFORMANCE.—Maximum 280 h.p. at 3,000 r.p.m., Climb 258 h.p. at 2,920 r.p.m., Rated 225 h.p. at 2,790 r.p.m., Cruising 200 h.p. at 2,690 r.p.m.

THE HIRTH HM 512 A.

TYPE.—Twelve-cylinder 60° Vee inverted air-cooled, geared, supercharged.

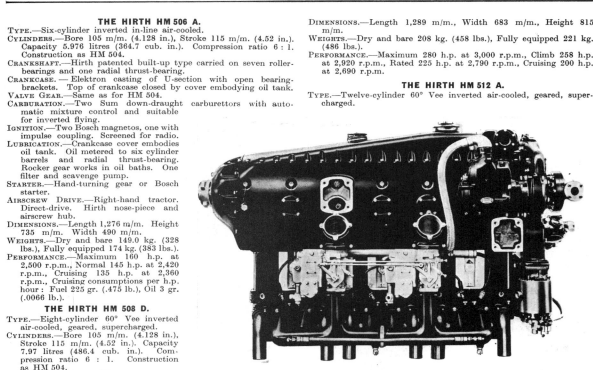

The 160 h.p. Hirth HM 506 A six-cylinder air-cooled engine.

The 400 h.p. Hirth HM 512 A engine.

The 105 h.p. Hirth HM 504 A-2 engine.

CYLINDERS.—Bore 105 m/m. (4.128 in.), Stroke 115 m/m. (4.52 in.). Capacity 11.94 litres (728.6 cub. in.). Compression ratio 6 : 1. Construction as HM 504A.

PISTONS.—Y-alloy. Two compression and two scraper rings.

CONNECTING RODS.—H-section rods of chrome-nickel steel. Roller-bearings in big and little ends. Raceways case-hardened.

CRANKSHAFT.—Hirth patent built-up shaft running in seven roller-bearings.

INDUCTION SYSTEM.—Two Pallas-Zenith 65VAH2 carburettors with automatic mixture control feeds centrifugal supercharger with light alloy rotor driven at 4.4 times crankshaft speed.

IGNITION.—One double Bosch magneto with automatic advance. Complete system fully screened.

AIRSCREW DRIVE.—1.5 : 1 reduction through patent Stoeckicht sun and planet gear. See HM 508.

LUBRICATION.—As for HM 508.

STARTER.—Bosch hand-turning gear or Bosch electric starter.

DIMENSIONS.—Length 1.542 m/m., Width 665 m/m., Height 815 m/m.

WEIGHTS.—Dry and bare 270 kg. (593.3 lbs.), Equipped 316 kg. (696.7 lbs.).

PERFORMANCE.—Take-off power 400 h.p. at 3,100 r.p.m., Maximum 360 h.p. at 3,000 r.p.m., Rated 300 h.p. at 2,810 r.p.m.

JUNKERS.

JUNKERS FLUGZEUG-UND-MOTORENWERKE A.G.

HEAD OFFICE : DESSAU.

Not only was Professor Junkers famous as a designer and builder of all-metal aeroplanes, but his opposed-piston Diesel engine was well-known and widely used before the War. The Junkers Motorenbau G.m.b.H. was founded in 1923, and besides the production of stationary Diesel engines, carburettor aero-engines were built. The development of the compression-ignition aero-engine was also pushed ahead, and in 1929 the first of this type was successfully flown. Development was continued throughout the war with the Jumo 205 and 207.

On July 15, 1936, Junkers-Motorenbau was taken over by Junkers Flugzeugbau, and the two were amalgamated as the Junkers Flugzeug-und-Motorenwerke A.G.

During 1937, two new types of petrol engines appeared, the Jumo 210 and 211 of 19.7 and 35 litres capacity. In 1938 new versions of these engines appeared in which the carburettors were replaced by a system of direct fuel-injection.

The Jumo 211 was widely used in the first years of the war but it was superseded by the Jumo 213 in the later years. Production of Jumo engines was undertaken mainly in the Dessau, Kothen and Magdeburg plants of the Junkers company.

The Junkers company began work on jet-propulsion in 1937 and the design of the first Junkers turbo-jet unit was begun late in 1939. Several prototype Jumo 004 jet units were ready in the Summer of 1941 and the first test flights were made before the end of the year. Large scale production of the Jumo 004B was planned to start in the Summer of 1943 but was not fully achieved until the early Summer of 1944.

The Jumo 004B was the only German axial-flow turbo-jet unit to be used operationally,—in the Messerschmitt Me 262 and the Arado Ar 234. Full constructional details of the 004 will be found on pages 36-37d.

THE JUNKERS JUMO 205 A, B, C AND D.

TYPE.—Six-cylinder vertical opposed-piston compression-ignition two-stroke.

CYLINDERS.—Bore 105 m/m. (4.13 in.), Stroke 2 × 160 m/m. (2 × 6.3 in.). Capacity 16.62 litres (1,014 cub. in.). Compression ratio 17 : 1. Six steel open-ended barrels, pressed into the main crankcase casting. Two sets of ports at opposite ends of cylinders, the upper for exhaust and the lower for intake.

PISTONS.—Two opposed deep-skirted pistons, of light alloy in each cylinder. Five compression and two scraper rings. Fully-floating gudgeon pins.

CRANKSHAFT.—Two six-throw crankshafts, one above and one below cylinders, geared together by a train of gears down the front of the crankcase. Airscrew shaft on intermediate gear in the train.

CRANKCASE.—One-piece casting of light alloy, with upper, lower and front covers.

WORKING CYCLE.—Two-stroke. Two opposed pistons in each cylinder compress air between them on their inward stroke. Fuel is pump-injected at or near their common dead-centre and ignited by the heat of the compressed-air charge. Combustion and expansion occur on the outward stroke. Before the end of this stroke one piston uncovers the exhaust ports, and shortly after this the other piston uncovers the inlet port, through which a rotary blower forces fresh air, the spiral motion of which scavenges the cylinder. On the return stroke, compression begins as soon as both sets of ports are covered, and the cycle is repeated.

FUEL FEED.—One fuel delivery pump on the rear end of each camshaft housing. Each cylinder is supplied by two fuel-injection pumps operated by two camshafts, one on each side of the engine. Fuel is injected into the cylinders in the form of a spray by four injector-nozzles.

SCAVENGING.—Gear-driven blower with impeller ratio of 8.9 : 1 mounted on rear of engine and delivering air through manifolds and each side of cylinder block.

STARTING.—Electric inertia-starter or cartridge-starter of conventional type.

LUBRICATION.—Forced, with one pressure and two scavenge pumps.

AIRSCREW DRIVE.—Right-hand rotation. Ratios A and D =.614 : 1, B = .602 : 1, C = .725 : 1.

The 1,200 h.p. Junkers Jumo 211 D twelve-cylinder inverted Vee liquid-cooled engine.

DIMENSIONS.—Length 1.943 m., Height 1,325 m., Width 600 mm.
WEIGHT (without airscrew hub).—520 kg. (1,144 lbs.).
PERFORMANCE (Jumo 205 C).—Take-off output 600 h.p., Cruising power 510 h.p., Maximum r.p.m. 2,200, Fuel consumption .37 lb./h.p./hr. maximum cruising.
PERFORMANCE (Jumo 205 D).—Take-off output 700 h.p., Cruising power 590 h.p., Maximum r.p.m. 2,600, Fuel consumption same as for Jumo 205 C.

THE JUNKERS JUMO 207 A, B AND C.

The Jumo 207 was a development of the Jumo 205 but was fitted with two centrifugal superchargers in series, the first being driven by an exhaust turbine. An aftercooler was fitted between the engine-driven supercharger and induction galleries. The general constructional features of the two engines are similar except for the following details.

PISTONS.—Pistons have crowns of heat-resisting steel secured to aluminium-alloy skirts by four anchor bolts. An unsplit junk ring between the stepped crown and the skirt. Five compression and scraper rings positioned in grooves lower down the skirt.

CONNECTING RODS.—H-section with double-row splash-lubricated needle bearings in the small ends. Big-end bearings have steel shells with copper-lead alloy linings. Lubricated by high-pressure oil.

SUPERCHARGERS.—Two centrifugal superchargers in series, an engine-driven blower being mounted beneath a turbine-driven unit. The engine-driven blower has radial vanes and aluminium-alloy entry guide vanes. Gear ratio 8 : 1. The exhaust-driven blower consists of a nozzle ring, turbine rotor and outlet volute. Twin waste-gates, by-passing the rotor, are used to control the effective mass flow of exhaust gas.

LUBRICATION. — Four gear-type pumps driven by the lower crankshaft. Two (pressure and scavenge) are housed at the rear end of the lower crankcase, and two (scavenge and auxiliary) are located at the front cover. All main and big-end bearings are pressure-lubricated. Oil is scavenged from the lower crankcase cover.

AIRSCREW DRIVE.—Right-handed rotation. Ratio .569 : 1.

DIMENSIONS.—Length 2,173 mm., Width 910 mm., Height 1,480 mm.

WEIGHT (without airscrew hub).—865 kg. (1,903 lbs.).

PERFORMANCE (Jumo 207 B-3).—Take-off 1,000 h.p. at 3,000 r.p.m. at sea level, 800 h.p. at 2,600 r.p.m. at sea level. Climbing 750 h.p. at 2,500 r.p.m. at sea level, 750 h.p. at 2,700-2,800 r.p.m. at 30,000-40,000 ft. Maximum cruising 680 h.p. at 2,700-2,800 r.p.m. at 30,000-40,000 ft. Fuel consumption .374 lb./h.p./hr. maximum cruising at 40,000 ft.

THE JUNKERS JUMO 207 D.

The Jumo 207 D was similar to the previously-described engine except that the bore was increased by 5 mm. from 105 mm. to 110 mm. This engine had a take-off output of 1,200 h.p.

THE JUNKERS JUMO 208.

The Jumo 208 was a development of the Jumo 207 but no details are available.

THE JUNKERS JUMO 211 A.

TYPE.—Twelve-cylinder 60° inverted Vee liquid-cooled with direct fuel injection.

CYLINDERS.—Bore 150 m/m. (5.9 in.), Stroke 165 m/m. (6.5 in.). Capacity 35 litres (2,136 cub. in.). Compression ratio 6.56 : 1. Steel cylinder barrels, each with four external lugs at their upper ends. Four long wet studs draw each barrel against 45-degree seating on cylinder-head. Each block of six barrels and one-piece cylinder-head and coolant jackets attached to crankcase flange by fourteen studs. Tin-plated copper shims seal barrels and cylinder-heads. Rubber packing at bottom of cylinder-studs seal coolant. Rubber gaskets in grooves in head seal crankcase/cylinder joints. Top end of barrels sealed to crankcase by pairs of radial rubber seals. Coolant supplied to head by long distributor tube passing through length of head. Holes in this header direct jets against all valve-seats and to coolant passages round exhaust valve-guides and injection nozzles.

PISTONS.—Forged aluminium-alloy trunk type, with three compression and two oil scraper rings, one of the latter being above the gudgeon-pin. Fully-floating gudgeon-pins located by light alloy end-caps spigoted with a sliding fit into the pins.

CONNECTING RODS.—One forked and one plain rod clamped to outer diameter of big-end bearing for each pair of cylinders. 80/20 copper/lead steel-backed big-end bearings. Little-end bearings have floating cast-iron bushes.

CRANKSHAFT.—Six-throw one-piece shaft running on eight lead/bronze steel-backed bearings, the additional bearing being placed on the forward side of the airscrew reduction gear. The fourth bearing from the rear is flanged to take crankshaft end thrust. All webs are in form of flat plates and are extended to form balance weights, the shape of each pair of webs on each side of each main bearing through holes drilled in journals and crankpins. Short tubes are fitted internally to each hole to prevent sludge entering bearings and possibly to reduce the stresses in the shaft around the holes.

CRANKCASE.—Main case of cast aluminium, integral with the cylinder blocks and airscrew reduction gear casing, carries the main bearings in Vee diaphragms, the legs of which are tied together by ribs through which the cannon tube runs. Top cover well ribbed and attached to main body by fourteen studs. Lower cover with oil strainer screen acts as oil collector from crankcase scavenge holes.

VALVE GEAR.—Underhead camshaft with rocker-arms operating two inlet and one exhaust valve per cylinder. Camshaft bearing pedestals are cast integrally with the single-piece aluminium-alloy cylinder-head. Inlet valves of chromium martensite steel. Hollow sodium-filled exhaust valves of austenitic steel. Both valves have welded stem tips. Camshafts, on seven aluminium-iron alloy bearings, driven by level and spur gears from the lower end of the auxiliary gear box. Rockers oscillate on short spindles which are bolted to bosses on the cylinder head, thus dispensing with bearing caps. Contact between cams and rockers is on rollers.

SUPERCHARGER.—Two-speed centrifugal supercharger mounted on starboard side of engine and driven off rear end of crankshaft by main accessory drive shaft. Housing and fully-shrouded impeller are magnesium-alloy forgings. A pair of bevel gears drive layshaft connected to impeller shaft by two intermediate gears. Low-ratio intermediate gear (7.85 : 1) coupled to shaft by roller clutch. High-ratio gear (11.37 : 1) by mechanically-operated friction clutch. Barometric capsule-operated automatic two-speed gear change operated through a hydraulic servo incorporating an automatic override to prevent operation in high ratio below 3,050 m. (10,000 ft.). Barrel-type throttle with automatic boost control between supercharger and engine.

FUEL INJECTION.—Dual pump draws fuel from feed tank through de-aerator to Junkers 12-plunger Vee-type injection pump mounted in engine Vee by flexible metallic mountings. Plungers operated by single camshaft driven at half engine speed by a long splined shaft from the lower end of the gear train for the oil scavenge pumps. Pressure temperature control unit. Boost pressure controlled by fully-variable-datum oil servo units. Single-orifice centrifugal-type injection nozzles on insides of Vee and spray horizontally across cylinders.

IGNITION.—Two Bosch high-tension magnetos, one supplying exhaust side plugs and the other the intake plugs. Four sparking-plug holes per cylinder but only two used. Sparking-plugs located for accessibility, being 180 degrees apart on eight cylinders and 120 degrees apart in remainder.

AIRSCREW DRIVE.—Plain spur type. Ratio .645 : 1. Both the driving and driven gears are splined to the shafts and are centralised by split bronze cones. The driven shaft is mounted on a roller race at the rear end and on a combined roller and thrust ball race at the front housing cover. The airscrew shaft is detachable from

A three-quarter rear view of the Junkers Jumo 207 B-3 heavy-oil engine.

the gear shaft, to which it is secured by face serrations and eight bolts.

ACCESSORY DRIVES.—Cast aluminium accessory drive case on rear of crankcase. All drives taken from end of crankshaft through short drive-shaft and all gears have both their bearings in case so that alignment is not disturbed when case removed. Eighteen drives include two camshaft, one generator, two magneto, one supercharger, three scavenge pumps, one oil pump, one vacuum pump, one tachometer, one starter, one injection pump, one fuel pump, one coolant pump and two unused auxiliary drives.

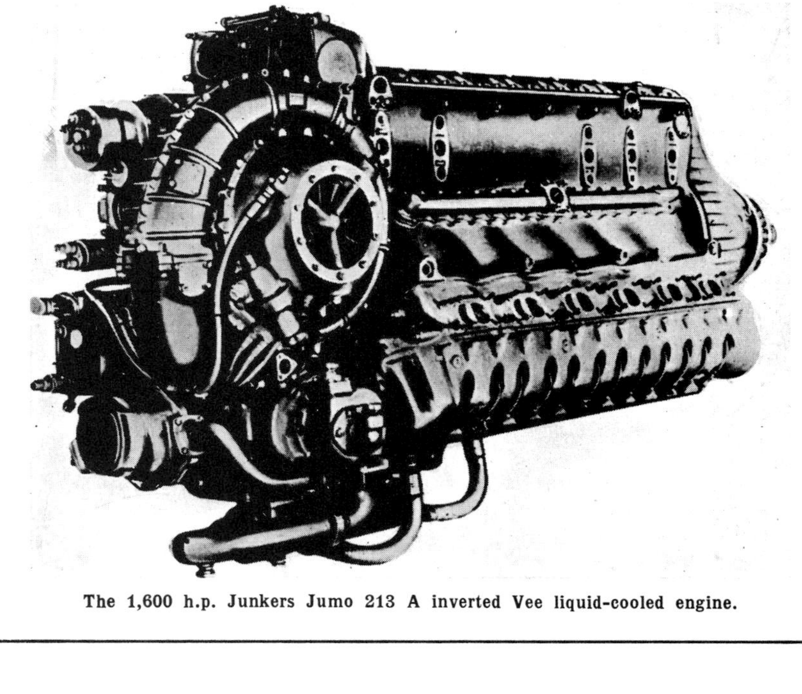

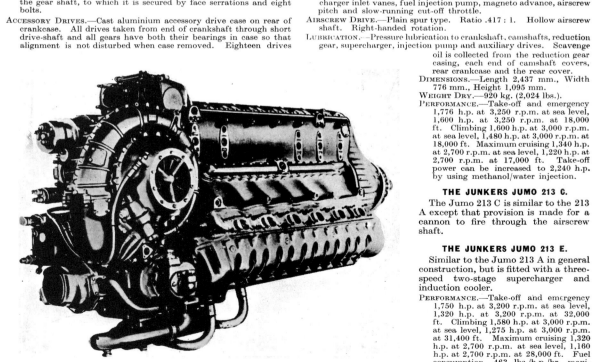

The 1,600 h.p. Junkers Jumo 213 A inverted Vee liquid-cooled engine.

LUBRICATION.—One oil pressure and six scavenge pumps, latter in three assemblies of two each. Double scavenge pump at rear end of each camshaft cover, pair of main pumps in accessory case, one at top and one at bottom. All pumps of straight spur-gear type. Oil flow from pressure pump and strainer assembly through cored passages to rear auxiliary drive-case and thence outward through external line to reduction gear case. Tee at approximate centre of line supplies oil to fuel injection pump and second tee forward diverts oil through two lines to camshaft housings. Internal piping within reduction gear case feeds main reduction gear, and through pressure line and cored passage to centre-line of crankshaft. All scavenged oil drains to bottom crankcase cover where it is picked up and delivered to oil coolers and tank. Outlet oil passes through disc strainer, rotation of which is supplied by ratchet from throttle linkage so that any changes of throttle cleans filter.

DIMENSIONS.—Length (without airscrew shaft) 1,745 mm., Width 804 mm., Height 1,659 mm.

WEIGHT DRY.—640 kg. (1,408 lbs.).

PERFORMANCE.—Take-off and emergency 950 h.p. at 2,200 r.p.m. at 1.2 ata. at sea level, 1,000 h.p. at 2,200 r.p.m. at 1.2 ata. at 17,000 ft. Climbing 850 h.p. at 2,200 r.p.m. at 1.1 ata. at sea level, 870 h.p. at 2,200 r.p.m. at 1.1 ata. at 17,000 ft.

THE JUNKERS JUMO 211 N AND P.

These engines were developments of the 211 F and J, with increased r.p.m. and boost pressure.

PERFORMANCE (Jumo 211 P).—Take-off and emergency 1,500 h.p. at 2,700 r.p.m. at 1.45 ata. at sea level, 1,410 h.p. at 2,700 r.p.m. at 1.45 ata. at 14,100 ft. Climbing 1,300 h.p. at 2,500 r.p.m. at 1.32 ata. at sea level, 1,280 h.p. at 2,500 r.p.m. at 1.32 ata. at 15,100 ft. Maximum cruising 950 h.p. at 2,250 r.p.m. at 1.15 ata. at sea level, 1,010 h.p. at 2,250 r.p.m. at 1.15 ata. at 17,000 ft.

THE JUNKERS JUMO 211 Q.

The Jumo 211 Q was the 211 F/J fitted with a turbo-supercharger. It had a take-off output of 1,500 h.p., developed 1,530 h.p. at 4,250 ft. and 1,380 h.p. at 33,000 ft.

THE JUNKERS JUMO 213 A.

TYPE.—Twelve-cylinder 60° inverted Vee pressure-cooled with direct fuel injection.

CYLINDERS.—Bore 150 mm. (5.9 in.), Stroke 165 mm. (6.5 in.), Capacity 35 litres (2.136 cu. in.). Compression ratio 6.5 : 1. Wet cylinder liners spigoted into the detachable cylinder heads and each retained by four chromium-plated studs. Two inlet and one large exhaust valves per cylinder. Fuel injector situated close to the inlet valves. Two sparking-plugs symmetrically equi-distant from the inlet valves and the single exhaust valve. Access to the plugs is through tunnels in the camshaft covers.

PISTONS.—Apparently die-cast aluminium-alloy with concave heads. Three compression and a double scraper ring above gudgeon-pin, chamfered scraper ring below.

VALVE GEAR.—Underhead camshaft driven by bevel gears. Steel flywheels are fitted at each end of the camshaft. Cam profiles provide quick valve lift.

BEARINGS.—Big-end and crankshaft bearings of lead-bronze.

SUPERCHARGER.—Twelve-bladed DVL fully-shrouded impeller of 270 mm. diameter. Fifteen diffuser ring blades. Fan-like series of eleven blades mounted in the supercharger inlet casing to form variable air inlet. These blades movable about their axes, the movement being automatically controlled.

FUEL INJECTION.—Junkers direct injection pump mounted between cylinder blocks.

IGNITION.—Dual Bosch ZM 12 CR magneto.

MASTER CONTROL.—Control box mounted at the rear of the engine. Amplifies cockpit lever motion into control of boost pressure, supercharger inlet vanes, fuel injection pump, magneto advance, airscrew pitch and slow-running cut-off throttle.

AIRSCREW DRIVE.—Plain spur type. Ratio .417 : 1. Hollow airscrew shaft. Right-handed rotation.

LUBRICATION.—Pressure lubrication to crankshaft, camshafts, reduction gear, supercharger, injection pump and auxiliary drives. Scavenge oil is collected from the reduction gear casing, each end of camshaft covers, rear crankcase and the rear cover.

DIMENSIONS.—Length 2,437 mm., Width 776 mm., Height 1,095 mm.

WEIGHT DRY.—920 kg. (2,024 lbs.).

PERFORMANCE.—Take-off and emergency 1,776 h.p. at 3,250 r.p.m. at sea level, 1,600 h.p. at 3,250 r.p.m. at 18,000 ft. Climbing 1,600 h.p. at 3,000 r.p.m. at sea level, 1,480 h.p. at 3,000 r.p.m. at 18,000 ft. Maximum cruising 1,340 h.p. at 2,700 r.p.m. at sea level, 1,220 h.p. at 2,700 r.p.m. at 17,000 ft. Take-off power can be increased to 2,240 h.p. by using methanol/water injection.

THE JUNKERS JUMO 213 C.

The Jumo 213 C is similar to the 213 A except that provision is made for a cannon to fire through the airscrew shaft.

THE JUNKERS JUMO 213 E.

Similar to the Jumo 213 A in general construction, but is fitted with a three-speed two-stage supercharger and induction cooler.

PERFORMANCE.—Take-off and emergency 1,750 h.p. at 3,200 r.p.m. at sea level, 1,320 h.p. at 3,200 r.p.m. at 32,000 ft. Climbing 1,580 h.p. at 3,000 r.p.m. at sea level, 1,275 h.p. at 3,000 r.p.m. at 31,400 ft. Maximum cruising 1,320 h.p. at 2,700 r.p.m. at sea level, 1,160 h.p. at 2,700 r.p.m. at 28,000 ft. Fuel consumption .463 lbs./h.p./hr. maximum cruising, sea level.

THE JUNKERS JUMO 211 B, D, G AND H.

Similar to the Jumo 211 A but with different gear ratios and increased r.p.m.

AIRSCREW DRIVE.—Ratios B and G = .538 : 1, D and H = .645 : 1.

PERFORMANCE.—Take-off and emergency 1,200 h.p. at 2,400 r.p.m. at 1.35 ata. at sea level, 1,210 h.p. at 2,400 r.p.m. at 1.35 ata. at 820 ft. Climbing 930 h.p. at 2,300 r.p.m. at 1.15 ata. at sea level, 930 h.p. at 2,300 r.p.m. at 1.15 ata. at 16,500 ft. Maximum cruising 790 h.p. at 2,100 r.p.m. at 1.1 ata. at sea level, 800 h.p. at 2,100 r.p.m. at 1.1 ata. at 14,700 ft. Fuel consumption .462 lbs./h.p./hr. maximum cruising, sea level.

THE JUNKERS JUMO 211 F AND J.

Similar to the Jumo 211 A in general construction. The principal differences were a strengthened crankshaft, a fully-shrouded DVL supercharger impeller, modified boost control, modified injection-pump control, simplified plungers and a pressurised coolant system The Jumo 211 J had an induction air-cooler fitted below the rear of the engine.

AIRSCREW DRIVE RATIO.—.545 : 1.
SUPERCHARGER DRIVE RATIOS.—8.8 : 1 and 12.4 : 1.
PERFORMANCE (Jumo 211 F).—Take-off and emergency 1,340 h.p. at 2,600 r.p.m. at 1.4 ata. at sea level, 1,350 h.p. at 2,600 r.p.m. at 1.4 ata. at 820 ft., Climbing 1,120 h.p. at 2,400 r.p.m. at 1.25 ata. at sea level, 1,060 h.p. at 2,400 r.p.m. at 1.25 ata. at 17,000 ft. Maximum cruising 910 h.p. at 2,250 r.p.m. at 1.15 ata. at sea level, 920 h.p. at 2,250 r.p.m. at 1.15 ata. at 19,500 ft.
PERFORMANCE (Jumo 211 J).—Take-off and emergency 1,400 h.p. at 2,600 r.p.m. at 1.4 ata. at sea level, 1,410 h.p. at 2,600 r.p.m. at 1.4 ata. at 820 ft. Climbing 1,200 h.p. at 2,400 r.p.m. at 1.25 ata. at sea level, 1,200 h.p. at 2,400 r.p.m. at 1.25 ata. at 16,500 ft. Maximum cruising 950 h.p. at 2,250 r.p.m. at 1.15 ata. at sea level, 1,000 h.p. at 2,250 r.p.m. at 1.15 ata. at 16,700 ft. Fuel consumption .462 lbs./h.p./hr. maximum cruising, sea level.

THE JUNKERS JUMO 213 F.

Similar to the Jumo 213 E but fitted with a three-stage supercharger. No intercooler. Methanol/water injected before the third stage.

PERFORMANCE.—Take-off and emergency 2,060 h.p. at 3,250 r.p.m. at sea level, 1,800 h.p. at 3,250 r.p.m. at 17,700 ft. Climbing 1,590 h.p. at 3,000 r.p.m. at sea level, 1,260 h.p. at 3,000 r.p.m. at 32,000 ft. Maximum cruising 1,320 h.p. at 2,700 r.p.m. at sea level, 1,070 h.p. at 2,700 r.p.m. at 28,000 ft.

THE JUNKERS JUMO 213 J.

Developed from the Jumo 213 A. Fitted with four valves per cylinder instead of three. Three-speed supercharger. Increased r.p.m.

PERFORMANCE.—Special emergency 2,600 h.p. at 3,700 r.p.m. at sea level, 2,000 h.p. at 3,700 r.p.m. at 26,600 ft. Take-off 2,240 h.p. at 3,700 r.p.m., Maximum take-off 2,240 h.p. at 3,700 r.p.m., 1,730 h.p. at 3,700 r.p.m. at 30,000 ft.

THE JUNKERS JUMO 213 S.

The Jumo 213 S was a development of the 213 A for low-altitude performance. It was rated at 2,400 h.p. at 8,000 ft.

THE JUNKERS JUMO 213 T.

The Jumo 213 T was fitted with a turbo-supercharger. It had a take-off output of 1,750 h.p., and developed 1,760 h.p. at 1,650 ft. and 1,600 h.p. at 38,000 ft.

THE JUNKERS JUMO 222 A AND B (SERIES I).

TYPE.—Twenty-four cylinder multi-bank liquid-cooled radial. Cylinders in six banks of four disposed radially around the crankcase.

CYLINDERS.—Bore 135 mm., Stroke 135 mm., Capacity 46.5 litres. Compression ratio 6.5 : 1. Wet liners mounted in crankcase. Cylinder heads are detachable and form part of coolant jacket. Each cylinder liner has a flange into which four waisted studs are screwed, the studs projecting through the cylinder head and serving to pull the liners against a conical seating around the combustion chamber. An aluminium sealing ring makes a gas-tight joint. Two inlet and one sodium-cooled exhaust valve per cylinder. Fuel injector mounted between the two inlet valves. Two diametrically opposed sparking-plugs per cylinder. Access to plugs through camshaft covers. Cylinder blocks numbered clockwise from the front, No. 1 being the horizontal block on the left. Cylinders numbered from the front of each block.

CRANKSHAFT.—Four-throw flat shaft supported in lead-bronze bearings. The centre bearing is of larger area and the bearing surface is continued around the side faces to provide axial location.

CONNECTING RODS.—Split master rod and five articulated rods in each of the four banks of cylinders. Lead-bronze big-end bearings. Master-rods are in cylinders 17, 22, 23 and 20. From the front they are in the lower right, lower left, lower left and lower right cylinders.

VALVE GEAR.—Single camshafts in nine split bearings for each block of four cylinders. Two inlet and one sodium valves per cylinder. Valves operated by light alloy rocker arms with hardened steel rollers.

SUPERCHARGER.—Two-speed supercharger driven by plain spur gears from rear end of crankshaft. Rectangular air intakes with "eyelid" throttles lead air through variable-pitch guide vanes into the eye of the supercharger. A master control-box is mounted above the air intakes.

INDUCTION SYSTEM.—Three separate fuel injection pumps, one between 2 and 3, 4 and 5, and 6 and 1 cylinders. Each pump feeds two blocks of cylinders. Three delivery trunks from superchargers volute casing, each of which branches into two pipes and feeds two cylinder blocks. Balance pipe between blocks 1 and 6, 2 and 3, and 4 and 5.

IGNITION.—Two duplex magnetos. One driven from camshaft driving gears of No. 2 block serves Nos. 1, 2 and 6 blocks, the second driven from No. 3 block serves the remaining blocks. Two cylinders fire together, firing order being 5 and 18, 1 and 14, 24 and 11, 7 and 20, 2 and 13, 22 and 9, 8 and 19, 4 and 15, 21 and 10, 6 and 17 3 and 16, 23 and 12.

AIRSCREW DRIVE RATIOS.—A Series (AOC, A-1, A-2, A-3) = .366 : 1, BOC = .368 : 1, B Series (B-1, B-2, B-3) = .364 : 1. A Series left-hand rotation, B Series right-hand rotation.

DIMENSIONS.—Length 2,469 mm., Width 1,159.4 mm.

WEIGHTS.—A Series 1,088 kg. (2,394 lbs.), B Series 1,120 kg. (2,464 lbs.)

PERFORMANCE (Jumo 222 A/B-1).—Take-off and emergency 2,500 h.p. at 3,200 r.p.m. at sea level, 2,200 h.p. at 3,200 r.p.m. at 16,400 ft., Climbing 2,260 h.p. at 2,900 r.p.m. at sea level, 2,090 h.p. at 2,900 r.p.m. at 16,400 ft., Maximum cruising 1,900 h.p. at 2,700 r.p.m. at sea level, 1,700 h.p. at 2,700 r.p.m. at 17,000 ft. Fuel consumption .477 lb./h.p./hr. maximum cruising, sea level.

THE JUNKERS JUMO 222 A AND B (SERIES 2 AND 3.)

These were developments of the Series 1 with increased capacity (bore 140 mm.) and modified ignition system.

PERFORMANCE (Jumo 222 A/B-2).—Take-off and emergency 2,500 h.p. at 2,900 r.p.m. at sea level, 2,490 h.p. at 2,900 r.p.m. at 1,640 ft. Climbing 2,250 h.p. at 2,700 r.p.m. at sea level, 2,020 h.p.

A starboard side view of the 1,340 h.p. Junkers Jumo 211 F and J engine.

THE JUNKERS JUMO 222 E AND F.

The Jumo 222 A/B with two-stage supercharger and aftercooler.

AIRSCREW DRIVE RATIOS.—E (left-hand rotation) = .368 : 1. F (right-hand rotation) = .364 : 1.

PERFORMANCE.—Take-off and Emergency 2,500 h.p. at 3,000 r.p.m. at sea level, 1,930 h.p. at 3,000 r.p.m. at 29,500 ft. Climbing 2,220 h.p. at 2,700 r.p.m. at sea level, 1,680 h.p. at 2,700 r.p.m. at 36,000 ft. Maximum climbing 1,840 h.p. at 2,500 r.p.m. at sea level, 1,400 h.p. at 2,500 r.p.m. at 34,600 ft. Fuel consumption .454 lb./h.p./hr. maximum cruising, sea level. at 2,700 r.p.m. at 16,400 ft. Maximum cruising 1,900 h.p. at 2,500 r.p.m. at sea level, 1,750 h.p. at 2,500 r.p.m. at 16,400 ft. Fuel consumption .449 lb./h.p./hr. maximum cruising, sea level.

PERFORMANCE (Jumo 222 A/B-3).—Take-off and emergency 2,500 h.p. at 3,000 r.p.m. at sea level, 2,410 h.p. at 3,000 r.p.m. at 9,200 ft. Climbing 2,250 h.p. at 2,700 r.p.m. at sea level, 1,980 h.p. at 2,700 r.p.m. at 21,000 ft. Maximum cruising 1,860 h.p. at 2,500 r.p.m. at sea level, 1,640 h.p. at 2,500 r.p.m. at 21,000 ft. Fuel consumption .463 lb./h.p./hr. maximum cruising, sea level.

THE JUNKERS JUMO 222 C AND D.

A further development of the Jumo 222 A/B-3 with increased capacity (Bore 145 mm., Stroke 140 mm.) and increased r.p.m.

PERFORMANCE.—Take-off output 3,000 h.p. at 3,200 r.p.m. at sea level. Climbing 2,600 h.p. at 2,900 r.p.m. at sea level.

A three-quarter rear view of the Junkers Jumo 222 twenty-four cylinder liquid-cooled engine.

THE JUNKERS JUMO 222 G AND H.

This designation covered the Jumo 222 A/B fitted with an exhaust-driven turbo-supercharger. It had a take-off output of 2,500 h.p.

THE JUNKERS JUMO 223 A.

The Jumo 223 was a power-unit made up of four Jumo two-stroke Diesel engines arranged in "box" form with four crankshafts. It was abandoned in favour of the Jumo 224 which developed a higher output.

CAPACITY.—29 litres.

DIMENSIONS.—Length 2,560 mm., Width 1,240 mm., Height 1,310 mm. Frontal area 1.25 sq. m.

WEIGHT (complete power-plant).—2,370 kg. (5,214 lbs.).

PERFORMANCE.—Take-off output 2,500 h.p. Rated altitude 20,000 ft. Fuel consumption .385 lb./h.p./hr. maximum cruising, sea level.

THE JUNKERS JUMO 224.

The Jumo 224 was a power-plant of similar type to the Jumo 223. It had a take-off rating of 4,500 h.p. and a climbing power of 3,000 h.p. No further details are available.

KLÖCKNER-HUMBOLDT-DEUTZ.

KLÖCKNER-HUMBOLDT-DEUTZ A.G.

HEAD OFFICE : COLOGNE.

This concern, which operated several shadow factories for the manufacture of standard types of aero-engines, developed a 16-cylinder opposed liquid-cooled two-stroke Diesel engine under the designation Dz 710.

THE KLÖCKNER-HUMBOLDT-DEUTZ DZ 710.

CYLINDERS.—Bore 160 mm., Stroke 160 mm., Compression ratio 15 : 1. Two horizontally-opposed banks of eight cylinders. Capacity per cylinder 3.22 litres.

DIMENSIONS.—Width 1,350 mm., Length 2,400 mm.

WEIGHT.—1,450 kg. (3,190 lbs.).

PERFORMANCE.—Maximum power 2,700 h.p. Fuel consumption

(cruising) .33 lbs./h.p./hr.

THE KLÖCKNER-HUMBOLDT-DEUTZ DZ 720.

The Dz 720 was a project for combining two Dz 710 engines in "H" form, with a maximum output of 5,400 h.p. This unit had an estimated weight of 2,900 kg. (6,380 lbs.), a width of 1,650 mm. and a length of 2,700 mm.

GERMAN POWER-BOOSTING SYSTEMS

METHANOL-WATER INJECTION.

Fluid. The mixture is designated MW 50 (Methanol-Wasser 50%) or MW 30 according to the proportion of methyl alcohol present. MW 50 fluid consists of 49.5 parts (by volume) of tap water, 0.5 parts of anti-corrosion fluid (Schutzöl 39) and 50 parts of methanol. MW 30 consists of 69.5 parts of tap water, 0.5 parts of anti-corrosion fluid and 30 parts of methanol.

Installation. The mixture was carried on the Me 109 in a cylindrical tank of 25 gallons capacity situated behind the pilot. Boost pressure from the supercharger was utilised to apply pressure to the tank, forcing the mixture along a pipe to an injection nozzle in the eye of the supercharger. The flow of mixture was controlled by solenoid valve, actuated by an automatic throttle switch and a master switch in the cockpit. A pressure gauge indicated the pressure of the mixture in the supply line. Provided that the master switch was on, the mixture was automatically injected when the throttle was opened fully.

Performance. The system was used to obtain extra power below the rated altitude of the engine. The mixture was injected into the intake side of the supercharger and acted as an anti-detonant, providing charge cooling and enabling higher boost pressures to be used. A 4% increase in power could be obtained even at constant boost pressure.

The increased power could be used for a maximum of 10 minutes at a time, and at least 5 minutes had to elapse between successive periods of operation. At this increased power the sparking-plugs had a life of only 15 to 30 hours.

On the Me 109, injection into the supercharger of the DB 605 AM engine was at the rate of approximately 35 gallons per hour. The normal fuel consumption at the take-off rating was 106 gallons per hour, but this was increased to 141 gallons per hour when using the MW 50 system with higher boost pressure.

The following table shows the performance of the Focke-Wulf Ta 152 B single-engined fighter with and without the MW 50 system.

ETHANOL-WATER INJECTION.

An ethanol-water mixture could also be used in the MW 50 installation on the DB 605 and Jumo 213 A engines.

The mixture consisted of 49.5 parts of tap water, 0.5 parts of anti-corrosion oil and 50 parts of ethyl alcohol.

PURE WATER INJECTION.

A pure water injection system had been used on the BMW 323 R and Jumo 213 A engines with air temperatures above 0°C. The engines were checked after every 50 hours running time for signs of corrosion.

The Jumo 213 A, with a basic power of 1,610 h.p. in high supercharger gear and + 8 lb. boost pressure developed 1,650 h.p. with water injection and 1,670 h.p. with MW 50 injection. These figures apply only to the increase in power obtained by fluid injection with constant boost pressure. A greater increase in power was obtained when the boost pressure was also increased.

NITROUS-OXIDE INJECTION.

Fluid. This power boosting system was first referred to by the Germans by the code-name "ha-ha", nitrous oxide or "laughing gas" being injected into the supercharger. The nitrous oxide was retained under pressure in liquid form. The system was designated as GM 1.

Installation. In a twin-engined aircraft (Ju 88 S) the liquid was carried in three cylindrical containers arranged pyramid fashion, located in the fuselage. Later aircraft had a single 75-gallon cylindrical container. Compressed air cylinders contained the air used for forcing the liquid along the pipe lines to the engines. The complete installation weighed 400 lb. (dry) and the weight of the nitrous oxide was 900 lb. assuming full tanks. The tanks were heavily lagged with glass wool and enclosed in a shell of light alloy to prevent evaporation.

In the Ju 88 S-1 (BMW 801 G-2 engines) injection was arranged at two rates,—"normal" 7.95 lb. per engine per minute and "emergency" 13.2 lb. per engine per minute. The endurance of the system at the two rates was 27 mins. and 45 mins. respectively.

Performance. This power-boosting system was used above the rated altitude of the engine. The nitrous oxide provided additional oxygen for the engine, and also acted as an anti-detonant. Part of the increased power obtained was due to its charge-cooling qualities.

The Ta 152 B aircraft with a DB 603 E engine had a maximum speed of 417 m.p.h. at 27,000 ft. When the GM 1 system was used, at an injection rate of 13.2 lb./min. the maximum speed was increased to 348 m.p.h. at 32,800 ft. The increase in h.p. of the DB 603 E engine was 350 h.p. at 32,800 ft.

With the Jumo 213 E engine installed in the Ta 152 B these rates of injection were used. The maximum speed without GM 1 was 439 m.p.h. at 35,000 ft., and this was increased to 44,300 ft. with the maximum rate of injection of 19.8 lb. per minute. This represents an increase of 418 h.p. in the engine power.

PETROL INJECTION INTO AIR INTAKE.

This system was used on the BMW 801 D engine to increase the emergency performance. It provided for over-riding of the

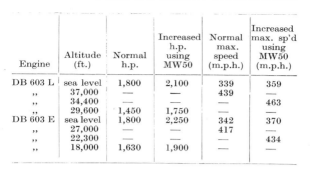

Engine	Altitude (ft.)	Normal h.p.	Increased h.p. using MW50	Normal max. speed (m.p.h.)	Increased max. sp'd using MW50 (m.p.h.)
DB 603 L	sea level	1,800	2,100	339	359
,,	37,000	—	—	439	—
,,	34,400	—	—	—	463
,,	29,600	1,450	1,750	—	—
DB 603 E	sea level	1,800	2,250	342	370
,,	27,000	—	—	417	—
,,	22,300	—	—	—	434
,,	18,000	1,630	1,900	—	—

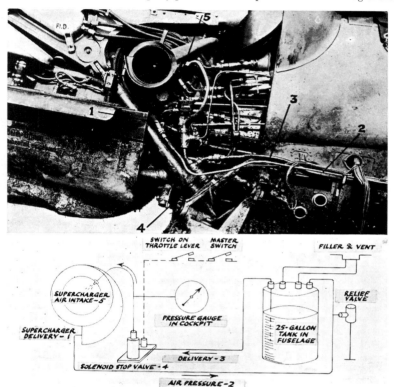

The installation of the MW 50 (methanol-water injection) system on a DB 605 AM engine in a Messerschmitt Me 109 G-14. The diagram below shows the layout of the system.

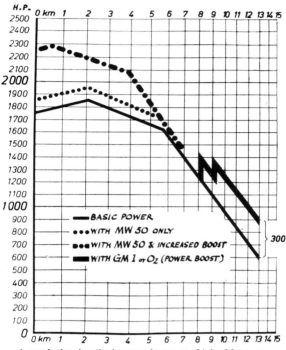

A graph showing the increase in power obtained by means of various German power-boosting systems.

boost control and a simultaneous injection of 96 octane fuel into the port air intake to prevent detonation and provide internal cylinder cooling.

The pilot had a push-pull control which operated two cocks. The first cock opened an air bleed in the boost pressure regulator chamber, causing the regulator to open the butterfly throttle to provide + 8.8 lb. boost instead of + 5.5 lb. boost at sea-level. The second cock opened a pipe line from the fuel pump to a spray nozzle fitted in the port air intake. The nozzle was calibrated to pass 14.3 ± 1.43 gallons per hour at a pressure of 18 to 25 lb./sq. in. Although no specific time limit was laid down, the system could only be operated as long as was necessary during extreme emergency.

The fuel consumption at the normal take-off boost of + 5.5 lb. and 2,700 r.p.m. was 146 gallons per hour, and this was increased to approximately 185 gallons per hour using 8.8 lb. boost and the additional fuel injection system.

Performance. The BMW 801 D engine developed 1,730 h.p. for take-off. This could be increased to 1,870 h.p. using higher boost and petrol injection system.

The Fw 190 (with BMW 801 D) had a maximum speed of 344 m.p.h. at sea-level. This speed could be increased to 360 m.p.h. when using the injection system.

ITALY

Italy capitulated to the Allies on September 8, 1943, but the German forces fighting on Italian soil did not surrender unconditionally until April 29, 1945. The four great firms constituting the Italian aero-engine industry—Alfa-Romeo, Fiat, Isotta-Fraschini and Piaggio all suffered heavily during the war, first by air bombardment and latterly by the forced transference of machinery and workpeople to Germany. Production of Italian aero-engines had virtually ceased by the end of 1943.

ALFA ROMEO.

SOCIETÀ ANONIMA ALFA ROMEO.

HEAD OFFICE AND WORKS : MILAN.

This company entered the Italian aero-engine industry in 1917, when it undertook the production of a series of engines of outside design for the Italian Government. After the War 1914-18 this work was abandoned but with the advent of the Fascist regime it was asked to co-operate in the regeneration of Italian aviation. At the outset only overhaul work was undertaken, but in 1925 the company acquired the licence to build

the Bristol Jupiter engine for the Regia Aeronautica, and the licence for the Armstrong Siddeley Lynx was also taken up.

Experience with these two engines led the firm, in 1930, to produce an engine of original design—the D.2—which the makers claimed to be the first in the World to have had a displacement supercharger equipped with an automatic device to control at low levels the power absorbed by the blower.

In 1931, the company acquired the licence for the Bristol Mercury and Pegasus engines, and it was with an Alfa

Pegasus engine that Commendatore Donati, in April, 1934, put up the then World's Height Record to 14,443 m. (47,360 ft.).

From the Pegasus engine the firm developed the Alfa 125 R.C.35 military and 125 R.C.10 civil engines. From these engines were derived, in 1936, the Alfa 126 R.C.34 and Alfa 126 R.C.10 respectively.

After Italy's entry into the War the Alfa-Romeo company undertook the manufacture of Daimler-Benz liquid-cooled engines.

FIAT.

SOCIETÀ ANONIMA F.I.A.T.

HEAD OFFICE : TURIN.

The Fiat Company was incorporated in 1898 and started on a bold policy which catered for all forms of locomotion. It began with motor vehicles and gradually extended its ramifications to include tractors, heavy-oil engines, railway trucks, tanks, aircraft and aircraft engines.

The first Fiat aero-engines were built in 1908. During the War 1914-18 more than 15,000 Fiat aero-engines were delivered.

After the War, the company pursued a very intensive research programme, devoted to the development of the twelve-cylinder Vee liquid-cooled engine. Later in its life the company turned its attention to the air-cooled radial and abandoned the

liquid-cooled engine.

The Fiat series of radials included the 840 h.p. A.74 R.C.38, the 770 h.p. A.74 R.C.42, the 900 h.p. A.74 R.C.18, the 1,000 h.p. A.76 R.C.40, the 1,000 h.p. A.80 R.C.41, the 1,100 h.p. A.80 R.C.20, the 1,250 h.p. A.82 R.C.40 and the 1,400 h.p. A.82 R.C.42.

ISOTTA-FRASCHINI.

FABBRICA AUTOMOBILI ISOTTA-FRASCHINI.

HEAD OFFICE: MILAN.

The Isotta-Fraschini Company was incorporated in 1898 in Milan for the manufacture of automobiles and internal combustion engines, and since the earliest days of flying was engaged in the design and manufacture of aero-engines.

Before the War 1914-18 a number of Isotta-Fraschini engines were used in Italian airships, aeroplanes and seaplanes. During the War, nearly 5,000 Isotta-Fraschini engines were made, and nearly all the aero-engines produced in Italy were made under Isotta-Fraschini licence.

The most recent engines of Isotta-Fraschini design included the 700 h.p. Delta R.C. 351 and 500 h.p. Gamma R.C.151, both twelve-cylinder inverted Vee air-cooled units; the 450 h.p. Astro 7.C.40 and 890 h.p. Astro 14.C.40, both air-cooled radials; the 900 h.p. Asso L.121.R.C.40 twelve-cylinder upright Vee liquid-cooled; and the 1,500 h.p. Asso L.180 R.C.I.45 eighteen-cylinder inverted W liquid-cooled engine.

PIAGGIO.

SOCIETA ANONIMÀ PIAGGIO & C.

HEAD OFFICE: GENOA.

This firm of railway-wagon manufacturers and shipbuilders, founded by the late Rinaldo Piaggio, entered the Aircraft Industry in 1916. A few years later the firm began to build aero-engines at Pontedera. It started by acquiring licences for Bristol and Gnôme-Rhône engines, and from the latter it developed its own series of engines.

This series included the 460 h.p. P.VII C.16, the 500 h.p. P.VII C.35 and P.VII C.45 seven-cylinder radials; the 700 h.p. P.X.R., 700 h.p. P.XVI R.C.35 and 625 h.p. P.X. R.C.35 nine-cylinder radials; the 1,000 h.p. P.XI *bis* R.C.40 fourteen-cylinder radial; and the 1,500 h.p. P.XII R.C.35 and 1,700 h.p. P.XXII R.C.35 eighteen-cylinder radial engines.

JAPAN

AICHI.

AICHI TOKEI DENKI KABUSHIKI KAISHA (The Aichi Watch and Electric Machinery Co. Ltd.).

HEAD OFFICE AND WORKS: 15, CHOTOSE FUNAKATACHO, NAGOYA.

TOKYO OFFICE: KOBIKICHO, KYOBASHIKU, TOKYO.

Established: 1899.

The Aichi Tokei Denki K.K., a well-known Japanese aircraft constructing firm, has since 1931 embarked on the production of aero-engines of its own design, and their first model, which has passed its official type tests, has been described and illustrated in previous issues of this Annual.

The company was originally responsible for building the 400 h.p. and 450 h.p. Lorraine engines under licence for the Japanese Navy.

It now holds the licence to build the Daimler-Benz twelve-cylinder inverted Vee liquid-cooled engine and now produces versions of the DB601 under the Japanese name "Atsuta" for the Japanese Navy.

ISHIKAWAJIMA.

TOKYO ISHIKAWAJIMA ZOSENJYO KABUSHIKI KAISHA (Aeronautical Department of the Tokyo-Ishikawajima Shipbuilding Co. Ltd.).

Established: October, 1939.

HEAD OFFICE: TOKYO.

This is a recently-established branch of the Tokyo Ishikawajima Shipbuilding Co. Ltd. It builds engines of Nakajima design under licence.

KAWASAKI.

KAWASAKI KOKUKI KOGYO KABUSHIKI KAISHA (Kawasaki Aircraft Engineering Co. Ltd.).

HEAD OFFICE: HIGASHI-KAWASAKI-CHO, HYOGO, KOBE.

This firm originally held the licence to build the German BMW engine, and large numbers of Kawasaki BMW power-units were supplied to the Japanese flying services.

The Kawasaki Company is the only Japanese concern to develop liquid-cooled engines of so-called original design. The 800 h.p. Type 95 and the 900 h.p. Type 98 were both liquid-cooled 60° Vee engines, and were the only Japanese power plants of this type to go into series production. They were both largely based on the BMW VI engine.

The Company now builds the Daimler-Benz DB 601 twelve-cylinder inverted Vee liquid-cooled engine for the Japanese Army under the Type 2 designation, and also builds the 950 h.p. Nakajima Type 99 and 1,450 h.p. Type 2 fourteen-cylinder radial air-cooled engines under licence, also for the Army.

MITSUBISHI.

MITSUBISHI JUKOGYO KABUSHIKI KAISHA (Mitsubishi Heavy-Industries, Ltd.).

AIRCRAFT AND AERO-ENGINE WORKS: NAGOYA, OHSACHICHO AND MINATOKI.

The Mitsubishi organisation has an important branch devoted to the manufacture of aero-engines. Licences were held for the Hispano-Suiza, Armstrong Siddeley and Junkers aero-engines, as well as for Farman reduction gears and compressors, Claudel-Hobson carburetters, Herzmark and Letombe engine-starters and Levasseur airscrews.

In 1935, the company acquired the licence for the Hispano-Suiza 12X and 12Y series aero-engines.

The Mitsubishi concern is now concentrating on the development and production of radial air-cooled engines, of which the fourteen-cylinder "Kasei," "Kinsei" and "Zuisei" engines are the best-known and most widely-used.

THE MITSUBISHI "KINSEI" ("GOLDEN STAR") SERIES.

TYPE.—Fourteen-cylinder two-row radial air-cooled.

CYLINDERS.—Bore 140 m/m. (5.5 in.), Stroke 150 m/m. (5.92 in.). Capacity 32.3 litres (1,970 cub. in.). Compression ratio 6.6 : 1. Nitrided steel barrels with aluminium-alloy heads cast integral with valve rocker-boxes. Closely-spaced fins machined on both barrels and heads. Two sparking-plugs per cylinder.

VALVE GEAR.—One inlet and one exhaust valve per cylinder. Tulip-type inlet valve with chromium-plated head. Exhaust valve of hollow head and stem type with welded stellite tip and base. Two springs per valve. Cadmium-plated steel valve rockers on pressure-lubricated plain tin-bronze bushings operated by steel-tube push-rods with pressed in ball ends. Valve clearance adjustment in rocker-arm push-rod ball-socket by screw and lock-nut. Valve gear operated by double-track cam ring. Cam drive through pair of spur gears from crankshaft to intermediate cam-drive.

PISTONS.—Aluminium-alloy forgings with six rings in five grooves. Flat-faced compression rings, chromium-plated on their outside diameters, fill the first two grooves. Tapered compression ring with scraping edge down in third groove. Two scalloped oil-control rings with their outer faces radiused at the upper sides and stepped to form oil drainage spaces below the scraping edges in fourth groove. Typical 45-degree oil scraper ring in fifth groove.

CONNECTING RODS.—One-piece master-rod and six articulated rods in each bank of cylinders. All rods are "I"-section and master-rod has lead-lined bearing.

CRANKSHAFT.—Two-throw three-piece steel shaft with riveted-on steel counter-weights and running in four main bearings. Shaft is split near centre-line of each crank-pin for assembly of one-piece master-rods.

CRANKCASE.—Three-piece aluminium-alloy case split on centre-line of each bank of cylinders and held together by one bolt between each cylinder.

REDUCTION GEAR.—Planetary type. Gear ratio 0.7 : 1. Large internal gear splined to crankshaft extension drives six planet pinions mounted on trunnions pressed into a machined slit cage splined to the airscrew shaft and retained in place by a large nut.

SUPERCHARGER.—Centrifugal single-speed supercharger running at 8.48 times crankshaft speed driven from main accessory drive and starter shaft, which operate through a splined coupling from the rear main bearing journal. Drive completed by a casehardened cluster gear and pinion mounted on a shaft fixed in the supercharger rear housing. Twelve-vane aluminium-alloy impeller (244 m/m.= 9.62 in. diameter) on square splines on shaft.

IGNITION.—Magneto driven by spur gear integral with crankshaft extension through an intermediate magneto drive-shaft. Two mica-insulated sparking-plugs per cylinder. Radio-shielding, including sparking-plug elbows and spring contactors in the sparking-plug wells, for all parts of ignition system other than magneto.

ACCESSORY DRIVES.—All accessories other than magneto driven by spring-loaded accessory gear drive through a centrally-located idler gear. Electric generator and electric starter are fitted.

LUBRICATION.—Three-section oil pump, comprising one pressure and two scavenge pumps, on rear cover. This source also supplies a two-position airscrew control with the requisite pressure.

MOUNTING.—Seven longitudinal bolts in bosses cast at alternate intake pipe connections on the supercharger front housing.

DIMENSIONS.—Overall diameter 1,218 m/m. (47.9 in.), Overall length 1,646 m/m. (64.8 in.).

DRY WEIGHT.—545 kg. (1,200 lbs.).

PERFORMANCE.—Take-off power 1,000 h.p. at 2,500 r.p.m., Rated output 990 h.p. at 2,400 r.p.m. at 2,800 m. (9,185 ft.), Maximum output 1,075 h.p. at 2,500 r.p.m. at 2,000 m. (6,560 ft.).

THE MITSUBISHI "ZUISEI" ("HOLY STAR") SERIES.

The "Zuisei" is a development of the "Kinsei." It is based on the same design but has a reduced stroke and overall diameter and is fitted with a two-stage supercharger.

The "Zuisei" 21, with constant-speed governor, automatic boost control and machine-gun synchroniser, has the following main characteristics.

TYPE.—Fourteen-cylinder two-row radial air-cooled.

CYLINDERS.—Bore 140 m/m. (5.5 in.), Stroke 130 m/m. (5.1 in.), Capacity 28 litres. Compression ratio 6.5/1.

AIRSCREW REDUCTION GEAR.—.727 : 1.

BLOWER RATIO.—8.5 : 1.

DIMENSIONS.—Overall Diameter 1,118 m/m. (44 in.), Overall length 1,564 m/m. (61.4 in.).

WEIGHT (Dry).—546 kg. (1,200 lbs.), with accessories 576 kg. (1,270 lbs.).

PERFORMANCE.—Maximum rated output 865 h.p. at 2,540 r.p.m. at 4,000 m. (13,120 ft.).

THE MITSUBISHI "KASEI" ("MARS") SERIES.

The "Kasei," which is also supplied to the Japanese Army under the designation Ha 32, is still a further development of the "Kinsei" engine.

Engines in this series include the "Kasei" 21, 22 and 25, all with two-speed superchargers and rated at 1,350 h.p. at 3,000 m. (9,840 ft.) and 1,260 h.p. at 6,000 m. (19,680 ft.) and with 1,825 h.p. for take-off, the "Kasei" 23 with direct fuel injection and a take-off power of 1,870 h.p., and the "Kasei" 24 with contra-rotating airscrew drive. No other details available for publication.

NAKAJIMA.

NAKAJIMA HIKOKI KABUSHIKI KAISHA (Nakajima Aircraft Co., Ltd.).

HEAD OFFICE: YURAKUKAN, MARUNOUCHI, TOKYO.

AERO-ENGINE WORKS: OGIKUBO, TOKYO-FU.

This company held the licences to build Lorraine and Bristol engines, and large numbers of 450 h.p. Lorraine and Nakajima Jupiter engines were built for the Japanese Air Services.

The Nakajima Company has since developed several radial air-cooled engines of its own design, notably the "Kotobuki" ("Congratulation"), a nine-cylinder radial based on the Jupiter, the 700 h.p. nine-cylinder "Hikari" ("Splendour") the 950 h.p. fourteen-cylinder "Sakae" ("Prosperity") and the 2,000 h.p. eighteen-cylinder "Homari" ("Honour") engine.

THE NAKAJIMA "HOMARE" ("HONOUR") SERIES.

The "Homare" (Army designation Ha 45) is an eighteen-cylinder development of the "Sakae" and incorporates all modern developments such as steel crankcase, dynamic crankshaft balancers, water injection, etc.

The "Homare" has the same cylinder dimensions as the "Sakae" but an increased capacity of 1,940 cu. in. (32 litres). The "Homare" 21 has the following characteristics.

DIMENSIONS.—Overall diameter 46.5 in. (1,182 m/m.), Overall length 70 in. (1,778 m/m.).

PERFORMANCE.—Take-off output 1,970 h.p., Maximum military output 1,700 h.p. at 19,680 ft. (6,000 m.), Normal rated continuous output 1,150 h.p. at 8,000 ft. (2,440 m.) and 1,000 h.p. at 22,000 ft. (6,710 m.).

THE NAKAJIMA "MAMORU" ("PROTECTOR").

The "Mamoru" is a fourteen-cylinder two-row radial with cylinders of larger dimensions than the "Sakae." No details of this engine are available for publication.

THE NAKAJIMA "SAKAE" (PROSPERITY") SERIES.

TYPE.—Fourteen-cylinder two-row radial air-cooled.

CYLINDERS.—Bore 5.12 in. (130 m/m.), Stroke 5.91 in. (150 m/m.), Capacity 1,700 cu. in. (27.8 litres), Compression ratio 7 : 1. Steel barrels and aluminium heads. Two valves per cylinder, one inlet and one sodium-cooled exhaust, operated by push-rods.

CRANKCASE.—Three-piece barrel type of aluminium-alloy.

CRANKSHAFT.—Three-piece two-throw counter-balanced shaft supported on three bearings, one ball and two roller.

SUPERCHARGER.—Gear-driven two-speed supercharger. Blower ratios 6.38 and 8.43 : 1.
AIRSCREW DRIVE.—Farman-type epicyclic gear. Gear ratio 12 : 7.
CARBURATION.—Nakajima twin-choke carburettor with automatic mixture and boost control.

IGNITION.—Two fourteen-cylinder magnetos, each firing one plug per cylinder. Fully-shielded ignition harness.
DIMENSIONS.—Overall diameter 45 in. (1,144 m/m.), Overall length 63 in. (1,600 m/m.).
WEIGHT (Dry).—1,175 lbs. (533.4 kg.) approx.

PERFORMANCE ("Sakae" 21).—Take-off output 950 h.p. at 2,600 r.p.m., Rated output 1,020 h.p. at 6,400 ft. (1,950 m.) and 885 h.p. at 15,700 ft. (4,790 m.).

TOKYO GASU DENKI

TOKYO GASU DENKI K.K. (Tokyo Gas & Electric Engineering Co., Ltd.).
HEAD OFFICE AND WORKS : OHMORI, TOKYO.

The Tokyo Gasu Denki K.K. or Tokyo Gas & Electric Engineering Co., Ltd. was one of the first Japanese concerns to develop a successful aero-engine of domestic design.

It eventually produced a series of radial air-cooled engines, the five-cylinder 110 h.p. "Hatakaze" the seven-cylinder 180 h.p. "Kamikaze" and the nine-cylinder 360 h.p. "Amakaze."

THE TOKYO GASU DENKI "HATAKAZE."
TYPE.—Five-cylinder radial air-cooled.
CYLINDERS.—Bore 4.5 in. (114 m/m.), Stroke 4.7 in. (119 m/m.). Compression ratio 5.3 : 1.
WEIGHT (Without airscrew hub).—309 lbs. (141 kg.).
DIMENSIONS.—Overall diameter 38.1 in. (970 m/m.), Overall length 40.9 in. (1,040 m/m.).
PERFORMANCE.—Normal output 90 h.p. at 1,650 r.p.m., Maximum output 110 h.p. at 1,840 r.p.m.

THE TOKYO GASU DENKI "AMAKAZE."
TYPE.—Nine-cylinder radial air-cooled.
CYLINDERS.—Bore 5.1 in. (130 m/m.), Stroke 5.9 in. (150 m/m.), Capacity 17.9 litres. Compression ratio 5.2 : 1.
WEIGHT (dry with accessories).—710.3 lbs. (326.35 kg.).
DIMENSIONS.—Overall diameter 50 in. (1,272 m/m.), Overall length 43.65 in. (1,109 m/m.).
PERFORMANCE.—Take-off output 360 h.p. at 2,100 r.p.m.

POLAND

The aero-engine manufacturers in production at the time of the invasion of Poland by Germany and Russia on September 1, 1939, were :—

"AVIA" WYTWORNIA MARZYN PRECYZJNYCH, Warsaw.
PANSTWOWE ZAKLADY INZYNIERJI (P.Z.I.), Warsaw.
PANSTWOWE ZAKLADY LOTNICZE WYTWORNIA SILNIKOW (P.Z.L.), Okecie-Warsaw.

The products of these three companies have been fully illustrated and described in issues of this Annual published before 1939.

RUSSIA

The Russian aero-engine industry has in the past been mainly engaged in producing engines of foreign design, notably the Wright Cyclone (M-25 and M-63), the Hispano-Suiza Y Series (M-100) and the Gnôme-Rhône K-14 Series (M-85). From this basis development has proceeded along original lines but no information concerning the latest types of aero-engines being built in Russia is available.

According to a German source, there were fourteen plants engaged on aero-engine manufacture at the outbreak of the Russo-German War, and at that time elaborate plans were put into effect for the strategic dispersal of existing plants and the erection of many new production factories in the Ural region for the evacuation of those plants likely to be endangered by invasion from the West.

SPAIN

ELIZALDE.

ELIZALDE S.A.
HEAD OFFICE : CALLE DE VALENCIA 302, BARCELONA.
WORKS : PASEO DEL GENERAL MOLA, 39, BARCELONA.
Managing Director : Don Julio de Renteria.

This important Spanish industrial concern had its origin in 1910 and made motor-cars until 1925. From that year it occupied itself with the manufacture of aviation engines exclusively. It began its career in this field by manufacturing Lorraine engines under licence and produced just prior to the outbreak of the Civil War two types of air-cooled engines, known as the Elizalde Dragon IX and Super-Dragon.

Having reorganized and re-equipped its factories and installations the company has resumed its activities with the design and development of a new series of low-powered engines known as the Tigre series. The first of the series is the four-cylinder Tigre IV, of which there are two models A and B with outputs of 125 and 150 h.p. respectively.

Under development in the series are engines of six, eight and twelve-cylinders which will be known as the Tigre VI, VIII and XII respectively. All will be derived from the Tigre IV but will be supercharged.

The Elizalde Tigre IV inverted air-cooled engine.

During 1944 the Elizalde company produced a new 450 h.p. seven-cylinder radial air-cooled engine, the Sirio S-VII-A.

THE ELIZALDE TIGRE IVA and IVB.
TYPE.—Four-cylinder in-line inverted air-cooled.
CYLINDERS.—Bore 120 m/m. (4.72 in.), Stroke 140 m/m. (5.512 in.), Capacity 6.3 litres (386.3 cub. in.), Compression ratio 6 (IVA) or 6.5 (IVB) : 1. Cast "Y" alloy cylinder heads. Forged and machined chrome-molybdenum steel barrels. Heads attached to barrels by six studs. Aluminium-bronze inlet valve seats. Austenitic steel exhaust valve seats.
PISTONS.—Aluminium-alloy. Fully-floating gudgeon-pins.
CONNECTING RODS.—Forged aluminium-alloy. Copper-lead big-end bearings, special bronze small-end bearings.
CRANKSHAFT.—Forged and machined chrome-nickel steel four-throw shaft on four copper-lead main bearings and one ball thrust bearing.
CRANKCASE.—Main case of Electron AZG-60. Forged aluminium-alloy top cover.
CARBURATION.—"IRZ" NB-60 carburettor.
IGNITION.—Bosch dual magneto, type ZJ.4.CR5.
LUBRICATION.—Pressure by triple pump driven from rear end of camshaft. Triple oil filter.
DIMENSIONS.—Length 1,114 m/m. (43.89 in.), Width 400 m/m. (15.76 in.), Height 877 m/m. (34.55 in.).
WEIGHT.—120 kg. (264 lbs.).
PERFORMANCE.—Normal output (type IVA) 125 h.p. at 2,200 r.p.m. (type IVB) 150 h.p. at 2,500 r.p.m.

THE ELIZALDE SIRIO S-VII-A.
TYPE.—Seven-cylinder radial air cooled.
CYLINDERS.—Bore 150 m/m. (5.9 in.), Stroke 145 m/m. (5.75 in.), Capacity 17.92 litres. Finned steel barrels with cast aluminium head screwed on. One inlet and one sodium-cooled exhaust valve per cylinder.
PISTONS.—Aluminium alloy. Floating gudgeon-pins. Three compression rings and two scraper rings.
CONNECTING RODS.—Master rod and six auxiliary connecting-rods carried on wrist pins. Lead alloy little-end bearings.
CRANKSHAFT.—Single-throw shaft in two halves clamped and keyed together. On two roller bearings and one ball bearing for the tail shaft.
CRANKCASE.—Of cast Elektron, comprising the main case a small front cover giving access to the distribution assembly and carrying the main thrust bearing, and a rear case and corresponding cover, which houses the compressor and all accessories. The rear crankshaft bearing rests on a flat platform of aluminium alloy which is rigidly secured to the main case.
VALVE-GEAR.—Fully-enclosed valve gear comprising push-rods, rocker-arms, etc. with pressure lubrication and scavenge return.
LUBRICATION.—Four pumps in the lower part of the rear crankcase, one pressure and three scavenge pumps. A filter at the outlet of the pressure pump is easily accessible for cleaning.
IGNITION.—Two Scintilla automatic-advance magnetos.

The 450 h.p. Elizalde Sirio S-VII-A radial engine.

CARBURATION.—One inverted "IRZ" carburettor with heater, warm air intake and automatic boost control.
SUPERCHARGER.—Centrifugal type with a gear ratio of 7.75 : 1.
OCTANE NUMBER.—80 octane fuel.
DIAMETER.—1,111 m/m. (43.7 in.) overall.
WEIGHT.—295 kg. (650 lbs.) complete, but without electric generator and starter.
PERFORMANCE.—Maximum power 450 h.p. at 2,300 r.p.m. at 2,500 m. (8,200 ft.), Power at sea level 430 h.p. at 2,300 r.p.m.

HISPANO-SUIZA.

HISPANO-SUIZA FABRICA DE AUTOMOVILES, S.A.
HEAD OFFICE : AVENIDA DE JOSÉ ANTONIO, 7, MADRID.
AERO-ENGINE WORKS : LA SAGRERA, 279, BARCELONA.

President and Chairman : D. Miguel Mateu Pla.
Managing Director : D. José Gallart Folch.

This company manufactures Hispano-Suiza engines for the Spanish Government, licences to build which it originally held from the French company. By the middle of 1939 the works at Barcelona had been re-conditioned after the Civil War and were in full production.

SWEDEN

SVENSKA.

SVENSKA FLYGMOTOR A.B.

HEAD OFFICE : TROLLHÄTTAN.

WORKS : TROLLHÄTTAN, GÖTEBORG, SKÖVDE AND ULVSUNDA.

This concern was originally formed as the Nohab Flygmotor-fabriker A.B. by the well-known Swedish engineering concern Nydqvist & Holin, to manufacture Bristol "Mercury" and "Pegasus" engines under a licence granted by the Bristol Aeroplane Co., Ltd., to the Swedish Government.

In 1941 the A.B. Volvo, of Göteborg, the leading Swedish motor company, bought a controlling interest in the Nohab concern, bought outright the A.B. Ulvsunda Verkstäder of Stockholm, and changed the name of the Nohabs Flygmotor-fabriker A.B. to Svenska Flygmotor A.B., the resulting organization becoming the largest industrial engineering organization in Sweden with four well-equipped factories at Trollhättan, Göteborg (main Volvo works), Skövde (branch Volvo works), and Ulvsunda, near Stockholm. The share capital of the company has been increased from four to eight million Kroner, all shares being held by A.B. Volvo (62.5 per cent.) and A.B. Bofors (32.5 per cent.), the additional capital to be used to expand Swedish aircraft-engine production.

The Trollhättan plant is one of the most extensive in Sweden and is situated close to the largest electric generating stations in Europe, power being obtained from the waterfalls alongside the factory.

The company is now building under licence the Pratt & Whitney Twin-Wasp radial air-cooled engine and the Daimler-Benz DB 603 twelve-cylinder inverted Vee liquid-cooled engine.

SWITZERLAND

WINTERTHUR.

THE SWISS LOCOMOTIVE AND MACHINE WORKS.

HEAD OFFICE AND WORKS : WINTERTHUR.

Telegraphic Address : Locomotive-Winterthur.

The eight and twelve-cylinder engines manufactured by this firm have been described in previous issues of this book.

The firm is manufacturing engines for the Swiss Government under licence from Hispano-Suiza.

THE UNITED STATES OF AMERICA

THE DESIGNATION OF AMERICAN SERVICE AERO-ENGINES.

The U.S. Army and Navy systems for the designation of aero-engines are similar. All service engines are designated by a letter indicating their basic type (*i.e.* R= radial, V= upright Vee, L= line, O= opposed), followed by the displacement of the engine in cubic inches to the nearest multiple of 5 and, finally, the Service model or modification number, (*i.e.* R-1830-65, V-1650-1, R-1820-56, R-2600-8, etc.). The final model or modification number of engines ordered to an Army specific-ation is always an odd number. Engines ordered by the Navy always carry even model numbers. This applies even if the basic engine model is identical, so long as the engines are ordered separately. For example, the R-1830-9 (Army) is the same engine as the R-1830-64 (Navy), both being service versions of the Pratt & Whitney R-1830-SBG engine.

There are now, however, an increasing number of cases where one of the services has adopted a type of aircraft originally built to a specification by the other, and in these cases, where the two service versions are in production together, the original power-units carrying their original model numbers are invariably used for both versions to avoid production difficulties. Certain training engines are built to an Army/Navy standard specification and these carry an AN model number, viz. R-1340-AN-1.

The following lists the principal American engine designations common to both the Army and Navy.

O-170	Continental A65		V-770	Ranger SGV-770
O-200	Franklin 4AC-199		R-830	Jacobs L-5
O-235	Lycoming O-235		R-915	Jacobs L-6
O-290	Lycoming O-290		R-975	Wright Whirlwind 9
O-300	Franklin 6AC-298		R-985	Pratt & Whitney Wasp Jr.
L-365	Menasco C-4		R-1340	Pratt & Whitney Wasp
O-435	Lycoming O-435		R-1535	Pratt & Whitney Twin-Wasp Jr.
R-440	Kinner B-54		V-1650	Packard Merlin
L-440	Ranger 6-440-C		R-1690	Pratt & Whitney Hornet
R-500	Warner Super Scarab 165		V-1710	Allison V-1710
R-540	Kinner R-55 or 56		R-1820	Wright Cyclone 9
R-550	Warner Super Scarab 185		R-1830	Pratt & Whitney Twin-Wasp
R-670	Continental W-670		R-2000	Pratt & Whitney Twin-Wasp
R-680	Lycoming R-680		R-2600	Wright Cyclone 14
R-755	Jacobs L-4		R-2800	Pratt & Whitney Double Wasp
R-760	Wright Whirlwind 7		R-3350	Wright Duplex Cyclone or Cyclone 18

ALLISON.

THE ALLISON DIVISION, GENERAL MOTORS CORPORATION.

HEAD OFFICE AND WORKS : INDIANAPOLIS 6, IND.

General Manager : E. B. Newill.

Assistant to General Manager : H. L. Wilson.

Chief Engineer : R. M. Hazen.

Assistant Chief Engineer : T. S. McCrae.

Works Manager : W. G. Guthrie.

The Allison Division of the General Motors Corporation is engaged in the production of high-performance liquid-cooled aircraft engines, reaction-propulsion power units, and aircraft engine bearings.

Other divisions of the General Motors Corpn., including Cadillac, Chevrolet, Delco-Remy, New Departure, Hyatt Bearing, Delco Products, Packard Electric, A.C. Spark Plug, Antioch Foundry, Harrison and Inland, as well as a number of individual firms and sub-contractors, contribute to Allison production by supplying raw material, semi-finished and finished parts.

The design and development of the Allison V-1710 twelve-cylinder Vee liquid-cooled engine was initiated in 1930. The first V-1710-A completed a 50 hour development test at a rating of 750 h.p. at 2,400 r.p.m. in 1932.

The V-1710-B was a re-design of the A for airship use. It was unsupercharged and possessed a reversing feature which enabled the engine to be reversed from full power in one direction to the same condition in the other in 8 seconds. With the abandon-ment of the U.S. Navy rigid airship programme after the loss of the *Akron* and *Macon* further development of the B engine ceased. The first V-1710-C was delivered to the U.S. Army in 1933 and an engine of this type completed a 50 hour develop-ment test at a rating of 1,000 h.p. at 2,650 r.p.m. in the Spring of 1935. The first practical flight installation of the C model was made in 1937 in the Curtiss XP-37. This engine was the V-1710-C10 with exhaust-driven turbo-supercharger. The first altitude-rated C engine with integral supercharger, the V-1710-C13, was installed in the Curtiss XP-40 in 1938 and this engine was put into production as the V-1710-C15 in 1939. In 1937 a left-hand rotation C engine was specially developed for use in the Lockheed XP-38.

The D and E models were both produced to meet the require-ments of the Bell Aircraft Corpn., the D to operate as a pusher and drive an airscrew through a 5 foot extension shaft for instal-lation in the XFM-1 Airacuda, and the E to drive a tractor airscrew through an 8 foot extension shaft and remote gear-box for installation in the XP-39 Airacobra.

The development of the V-1710-F paralleled that of the E with which it was almost completely interchangeable. The F was designed for considerably higher outputs than the C model, has 10% less frontal area, a higher airscrew thrust-line, shorter overall length and is furnished in both right and left-hand tractor models.

Details are given below of successive production developments of the V-1710 engine, with the equivalent U.S. Army designations and the aircraft types in which they have been installed.

*C15	V-1710-33	(P-40, P-40B, P-40C).
D2	V-1710-23	(YFM-1).
*E4	V-1710-35	(P-39C, P-39D, P-39F).
*E6	V-1710-63	(P-39D, P-39K, P-39L).
E11	V-1710-93	(P-63A).
E12	V-1710-59	(P-39J).
E18	V-1710-83	(P-39L, P-39M, P-39N, P-39Q).
E19	V-1710-85	(P-39M, P-39N, P-39Q).
*F2R	V-1710-27	
*F2L	V-1710-29	(P-38, P-38D, P-38E, F-4).
*F3R	V-1710-39	(P-40E, P-51).
*F4R	V-1710-73	(P-40K, P-40M).

F5R	V-1710-49	
F5L	V-1710-53	(P-38F, F-5).
*F10R	V-1710-51	
*F10L	V-1710-55	(P-38G, P-38H, F-5A).
F17R	V-1710-89	
F17L	V-1710-91	(P-38H, P-38J, F-5B).
F20R	V-1710-81	(P-40M, P-40N, P-51A).
F21R	V-1710-87	(A-36A).
F26R	V-1710-99	(P-40N).
F30R	V-1710-111	
F30L	V-1710-113	(P-38L).
F31R	V-1710-115	(P-40N).

*Described in previous issues.

General descriptions of the latest models in production in 1944-45 are given below. These include the F30, which weighs 1,395 lbs. (633.5 kg.) and has a take-off rating of 1,475 h.p., the E11, weighing 1,620 lbs. (735.5 kg.), and the E21, weighing 1,660 lbs. (748.2 kg.), both equipped with an Allison-built auxiliary-stage supercharger assembly and capable of developing a maximum war emergency output of 1,825 h.p.

Development continued on the V-3420 twenty-four-cylinder double Vee liquid-cooled engine, which has a current take-off rating of 2,600 h.p. at 3,000 r.p.m. and a normal rating of 2,100 h.p. at 2,600 r.p.m. at 25,000 ft. (7,525 m.).

One section of the Allison factory was devoted to the manu-facture of steel-backed lead-bronze bearings, widely used in all types of high-powered aircraft engines. Another section is engaged in the development and manufacture of aircraft reaction-propulsion units.

THE ALLISION V-1710-F31R.

TYPE.—Twelve-cylinder 60° Vee liquid-cooled geared and super-charged.

CYLINDERS.—Bore 5.5 in. (139.7 m/m.), Stroke 6 in. (152.4 m/m.),

Capacity 1,710 cub. in. (28 litres). Compression ratio 6.65 : 1. Two cylinder blocks of six cylinders each comprising a cast aluminium-alloy head, six hardened steel cylinder barrels and a cast aluminium-alloy cooling jacket. Barrels held in head by a shrink-fit and are enclosed by coolant jacket. Jacket secured to head by studs and to cylinders by nut threaded over each barrel. Each cylinder-block secured to upper half of crankcase by fourteen stud-bolts extending through the head. Combustion chamber has two intake and two exhaust valves and two diametrically-opposed sparking plugs. Steel intake valve inserts. Forged steel stellite-faced exhaust valve inserts.

PISTONS.—Machined from aluminium-alloy forgings. Three compression rings above gudgeon pin, one keystone ring in the top groove and two conventional rings, and two oil-control rings in a single groove below. Floating gudgeon pin retained by snap rings at each end.

CONNECTING RODS.—Fork and blade type made from steel forgings machined and shot-blasted. Connecting rod bearing consists of two flanged steel shells lined with nickel-silver-tin, and is clamped in the forked end by two bearing caps. Centre portion of the outside diameter of the bearing is covered with an overlay of nickel-silver-tin which acts as journal for the blade rod. Blade rod fits around the overlay and is held in place by a single steel cap. Bronze bearings pressed into small end. Big-end bearings lubricated under pressure from crankshaft. Little-end bearings lubricated by splash.

CRANKSHAFT.—Counter-balanced six-throw seven-bearing type. Each end of the shaft has a nine-bolt flange which provide mountings at the front for a flexible splined coupling for driving the reduction gear pinion and at the rear for a dynamic torsional vibration balancer. Splined to the hub of the dynamic balancer is the outer member of a hydraulic damper. An inner member is connected to the outer rigid member by a flexible quill shaft and reacts against the outer member through a hydraulic medium to minimize single-node low-frequency torsional vibration. This damper provides the driving connection between the accessories housing and the crankshaft.

CRANKCASE.—Two aluminium castings split on horizontal centreline. Large studs on the face of the upper half pass through main bearing webs on lower half to clamp the two halves over the bearing shells. All main bearings are steel flanged shells lined with nickel-silver-tin. Centre main bearing provided with faced flanges which bear on the centre crank cheeks to provide axial location for the crankshaft. Cast magnesium-alloy oil pan bolts to the bottom of crankcase lower half and provides breathing passages between crankcase compartments. Oil is scavenged from both ends of the oil pan.

VALVE GEAR.—Two inlet and two exhaust valves per cylinder.. Stellite-faced sodium-cooled nichrome-alloy valves. Single camshaft operates six rocker-arm assemblies on top of each cylinder-block. Each camshaft driven by bevel gears through separate inclined shafts from the accessory housing. Pressure lubrication through hollow camshaft.

INDUCTION.—Bendix Stromberg Model PD-12K2 two-barrel injection type carburetter with automatic mixture control on rear of accessories housing. Supplies fuel directly on the supercharger impeller which delivers the fuel-air mixture to the ramshorn-type intake manifolds.

SUPERCHARGER.—Contained in the accessory housing and is driven from the flexible inner member of the hydraulic vibration damper. The impeller unit consists of two components, one having 15 radial vanes and the other 15 matched curved guide vanes, maintaining matched relationship through a common spline on the impeller shaft. Fuel-air mixture flows through a six-vane diffuser into the scroll and thence through the branched manifold system in the Vee between the cylinder-blocks. Backfire screen in each branch manifold.

IGNITION.—Dual high-tension Scintilla Type DFLN-5 magneto and two distributors driven by camshafts.

AIRSCREW DRIVE.—2 : 1 reduction. External spur gear. Airscrew shaft supported at front end by the ball thrust bearing and at the rear by a large roller-bearing. The pinion gear is mounted between two plain bearings and is splined to and driven by the crankshaft flexible coupling. The airscrew shaft-line is 8¼ in. above the crankshaft centre-line. The front scavenging oil pump is located in the reduction gear housing and the airscrew governor is mounted on the rear of the housing in the Vee of the cylinder-blocks. The housing is also provided with oil passages to supply both governor and engine oil pressure for hydromatic airscrew operation. Reduction gear teeth are lubricated by an oil nozzle supplying three jets of oil directly on the teeth.

LUBRICATION.—Pressure system. Circulation maintained by single pressure pump and two scavenge pumps, all of the simple gear type. Constant pressure maintained by a pressure-sensitive balanced relief valve. Spring-loaded check valve prevents oil entering system when engine is stopped. Large tube in upper half of crankcase distributes oil to main bearings, through which it enters hollow portions of crankshaft. This tube also carries oil to reduction gears, reduction gear pinion bearings, and airscrew governor pad. Oil for accessory drives and valve gear is carried by tubes and drilled passages in accessory housing. Oil from valve gear drains to crankcase through passages at both ends of cylinder-block. Oil for the hydraulic vibration damper operation is also supplied from the engine pressure system.

ACCESSORIES.—Accessory housing mounted directly on the rear of the crankcase and contains the supercharger and drives for the coolant pump, camshafts, fuel pump, two vacuum pumps, main oil pump, tachometers, generator and magneto.

DIMENSIONS, WEIGHTS AND PERFORMANCE.—See Table.

THE ALLISON V-1710-F30R and F30L.

The V-1710-F30R and F30L (right and left-hand airscrew drive), which were used in the Lockheed P-38L twin-engined fighter monoplane, are similar to the V-1710-F31R except that they are fitted with exhaust-driven turbo-superchargers, details of the installation of which are not available for publication.

THE ALLISON V-1710-E11.

The V-1710-E11 is basically similar to the previously-described V-1710-F31R except that it has its external spur reduction gear driven by an 8-ft. extension shaft, and a variable hydraulic drive to a second-stage auxiliary supercharger. This engine is installed in the Bell Kingcobra in which the power-unit is mounted in the fuselage behind the pilot.

AIRSCREW DRIVE.—Outboard reduction gear box and airscrew mounting connected to the engine by an extension shaft composed of two flanged shafts, each 2.5 in. (63 m/m.) in diameter and 48 in. (1.22 m.) long and supported at the centre by a self-aligning ball-bearing mount. The reduction gear casing consists of two aluminium-alloy castings which support the airscrew shaft, thrust-bearing, reduction gear and pinion gear. The reduction gear is an external spur gear bolted to a flange on the airscrew shaft. The airscrew shaft is supported at the front end by a ballthrust-bearing and at the rear by a large roller-bearing. The pinion gear is

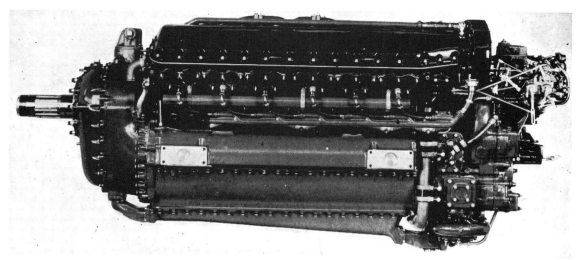

The 1,475 h.p. Allison V-1710-F30 twelve-cylinder Vee liquid-cooled engine.

The 1,325 h.p. Allison V-1710-E11 engine with second-stage auxiliary supercharger.

The 2,600 h.p. Allison V-3420 twenty-four cylinder liquid-cooled engine.

mounted between two roller-bearings and is driven by the extension shaft through an internally splined flexible coupling. Reduction gear teeth are lubricated by an oil nozzle supplying three jets of oil directed on the teeth. A combined pressure and scavenge oil pump is mounted on the front of the reduction gear housing and provides oil pressure to the oil nozzle and scavenges the case. Oil is supplied from a separate external tank. On the rear face of the casing drives are provided for two gun-synchronizers and an airscrew governor. Drive to the extension shaft is transmitted through a flexible splined coupling to a flange bolted to the front end of the crank-shaft.

WEIGHTS AND PERFORMANCE :—See Table.

THE ALLISON V-3420.

The V-3420 is a twenty-four-cylinder four-bank double-crankshaft version of the V-1710 for which an Air Corps experimental contract was originally received in 1937. It is virtually two V-1710 60° Vee twelve-cylinder units mounted on a common crankcase with a 30° angle between the centre-lines of the inner banks of cylinders, the two side-by-side crankshafts being

ALLISON LIQUID-COOLED ENGINES

Engine Type	V-1710-E11	V-1710-E19	V-1710-F30R and F30L	V-1710-F31R	V-3420
No of Cylinders ..	12	12	12	12	24
Bore and Stroke ..	5.5 in. × 6 in. (193.7 × 152.4 m/m.)	5.5 in. × 6 in. (139.7 × 152.4 m/m.)	5.5 in. × 6 in. (139.7 × 152.4 m/m.)	5.5 in. × 6 in. (139.7 × 152.4 m/m.)	5.5 in. × 6 in. (139.7 × 152.4 m/m.)
Capacity ..	1,710 cu. in. (28 litres)	1,710 cu. in. (28 litres)	1,710 cu. in. (28 litres)	1,710 cu. in. (28 litres)	3,420 cu. in. (56 litres)
Compression Ratio ..	6.65 : 1	6.65 : 1	6.65 : 1	6.65 : 1	6.65 : 1
Blower Ratio ..	—	9.6 : 1	8.1 : 1 (plus turbo-supercharger)	9.6 : 1	—
Gear Ratio ..	0.447 : 1	0.488 :1	0.5 : 1	0.5 : 1	0.4 : 1
Octane No. ..	100	100	100	100	100
Take-off Power ..	1,325 h.p. at 3,000 r.p.m.	1,200 h.p. at 3,000 r.p.m.	1,475 h.p. at 3,000 r.p.m.	1,200 h.p. at 3,000 r.p.m.	2,600 h.p. at 3,000 r.p.m.
Ratings—Normal (max. continuous)	1,000 h.p. at 2,600r.p.m. at 21,000 ft. (6,410 m.)	1,000 h.p. at 2,600 r.p.m. at 13,200 ft. (4,030 m.)	1,100 h.p. at 2,600 r.p.m. at 30,000 ft. (9,150 m.)	1,000 h.p. at 2,600 r.p.m. at 14,000 ft. (4,270 m.)	2,100 h.p. at 2,600 r.p.m. at 25,000 ft. (7,625 m.)
Military (15 min. only)	1,150 h.p. at 3,000r.p.m. at 24,200 ft. (7,386 m.)	1,125 h.p. at 3,000 r.p.m. at 15,000 ft. (4,575 m.)	1,475 h.p. at 3,000 r.p.m. at 30,000 ft. (9,150 m.)	1,125 h.p. at 3,000 r.p.m. at 15,000 ft. (4,575 m.)	2,600 h.p. at 3,000 r.p.m. at 25,000 ft. (7,625 m.)
Weight Dry ..	1,620 lb. (735,5 kg.)	1,435 lb. (651.0 kg.)	1,395 lb. (633.5 kg.)	1,385 lb. (628.8 kg.)	2,600 lb. (1180.4 kg.)
Dimensions : Length	—	194.00 in. (4.928 m.)	85.81 in. (2.180 m.)	85.81 in. (2.180 in.)	100.00 in. (2.532 m.)
Height	—	36.56 in. (9.30 m.)	37.65 in. (0.958 m.)	36.75 in. (0.932 m.)	34.00 in. (0.863 m.)
Width	—	29.28 in. (0.744 m.)	29.28 in. (0.744 m.)	29.28 in. (0.744 m.)	56.00 in. (1.421 m.)

geared together to drive a single airscrew shaft.

Nearly all parts of the power section are interchangeable with the V-1710E and F series. These include crankshafts, connecting-rods, pistons, complete cylinder assemblies including valve-gear and holding-down studs, intake manifolds, ignition assemblies and radio shielding. This leaves only the crank-case assembly and main bearings which are not interchangeable.

The reduction gear bolts on to the front of the crankcase, and several parts of this gear are interchangeable with that of the V-1710F model.

The accessory housing is designed for building up for either crankshaft rotation simply by the addition of an opposite-hand starter-dog. By special machining of the housing the crank-shafts can be rotated in opposite directions to give a practically zero-torque power-plant, with advantages for single-engine installation.

Each crankshaft has its own damping provisions but the dampers are geared in such a way as to damp between shafts as well. With this arrangement practically any type of extension shaft and reduction gearing combination can be applied to the engine.

The 1,325 h.p. Allison V-1710-E11 engine with remote airscrew drive and a second-stage auxiliary supercharger.

The engine is provided with a gear-driven single-speed super-charger, augmented by a General Electric exhaust-driven turbo-supercharger. Carburation is by a Bendix-Stromberg PT-12E1 three-barrel injection-type downdraught carburettor with automatic mixture control.

DIMENSIONS, WEIGHTS AND PERFORMANCE.—See Table.

BUICK.

THE BUICK MOTOR DIVISION, GENERAL MOTORS CORPORATION.

AERO-ENGINE WORKS : FLINT, MICH., AND MELROSE PARK, ILL.

General Manager : H. H. Curtice.

During the war the Buick Motors Division of General Motors held contracts for the manufacture of Pratt & Whitney R-1830 radial air-cooled engines. A new factory was built at Melrose Park where machining operations and the assembly of engines was undertaken. The Flint plant manufactured parts.

By April, 1942, Buick output was up to that planned for December and the original scheduled output for 1942 was completed in the first six months of the year.

The 1944 output exceeded that of 1943 and by the end of that year the company had produced over 62,000 engines.

Immediately after the capitulation of Japan all war contracts were cancelled. The Division has now reverted to automobile manufacture.

CHEVROLET.

THE CHEVROLET DIVISION, GENERAL MOTORS CORPORATION.

AERO-ENGINE WORKS : BUFFALO AND TONAWANDA, N.Y.

The Chevrolet Motor Division of the General Motors Corporation held contracts for the manufacture of Pratt & Whitney radial air-cooled engines for bombers, fighters and transports. Three models—the Pratt & Whitney R-2800-C, R-1830-43 and R-1830-92—were built. The manufacture and assembly of these engines involved seventeen of the company's plants.

Throughout the Division's widespread manufacturing system, plants were engaged on a variety of war-time aviation projects. Four plants were engaged in the production of aluminium aircraft forgings including airscrew blades, airscrew hubs and pistons, landing-gear trunnions, and aircraft engine pistons and crank-case sections. Steel forgings and numerous small steel parts were also produced for aircraft engines. A major part of Chev-rolet's large grey iron foundry in Michigan was converted to the production of magnesium castings for aircraft engines.

A newcomer to the light metals field with the conversion to war production, Chevrolet became one of the two largest producers of aluminium aircraft forgings in the World.

Immediately after the capitulation of Japan all war contracts were cancelled. The Division has now reverted to automobile manufacture.

CHRYSLER.

THE CHRYSLER CORPORATION.

HEAD OFFICE AND WORKS : DETROIT 31, MICH.

The participation of the Chrysler Corporation in the national war programme involved 5,900 war commitments. In the aviation field these included the manufacture of aircraft parts and assemblies, the large-scale production of Wright R-3350 eighteen-cylinder radial air-cooled engines, and the experimental development of the IV-2220 twelve-cylinder inverted Vee liquid-cooled engine of original design.

CONTINENTAL.

THE CONTINENTAL MOTORS CORPORATION, AIRCRAFT ENGINE DIVISION.

HEAD OFFICE : MUSKEGON, MICH.

WORKS : MUSKEGON AND DETROIT, MICH., AND GARLAND, TEXAS.

President and General Manager : C. J. Reese.
Executive Vice-President and Secretary : B. F. Tobin.
Vice-President in charge of operations : L. P. Kalb.
Vice-President and Manager, Aircraft Division : A. Wild.

Vice-President in charge of Sales and Service, Aircraft Division : D. H. Hollowell.
Vice-President and Chief Engineer, Aircraft Division : T. Jackson.
Treasurer : H. W. Vandeven.

In 1928, Continental Motors Corporation, one of the largest automobile manufacturers in the World, produced a sleeve-valve radial air-cooled aero-engine, incorporating the Argyll (Burt-McCollum) patents, purchased by the Corporation from the Argyll Company in 1925.

In 1931 the 38 h.p. A40 flat-four was put on the market. This was followed by the A50, A65, A75 and A80 engines, the popularity of which resulted in over 8,000 Continental flat-four engines being produced up to the outbreak of war. In 1940 out of all light aeroplanes built by four manufacturers in the United States, approximately 5,090 had Continental engines.

For post-war use five new engines have been developed and have passed all tests. These new models designated as the

C75, C85, C115, C125 and C140, consist of two four-cylinder engines of 75 and 85 h.p. and three six-cylinder models of 115, 125 and 140 h.p., the last-mentioned engine being fitted with an airscrew reduction-gear unit.

Production during 1944-45 centred on the W-670 radial air-cooled engine which, with minor changes was suitable for use in either training aircraft or tanks.

The Continental Motors Corpn. was designated by the War Department to build the Packard Rolls-Royce Merlin V-1650 engine. Production began in 1944 in the company's Muskegon plant. The Detroit plant was engaged in tank engine manufacture.

A subsidiary of the Continental Motors Corpn.—the Continental Aviation and Engineering Corpn.—has for many years been engaged on the development of a high-powered liquid-cooled engine. This power-plant, which carries the designation I-1430, is a twelve-cylinder inverted 60° Vee geared and supercharged engine with a cubic capacity of 1,425 cu. in. The most recent model has a war emergency power output of 2,100 h.p. at 3,400 r.p.m., which gives a power/weight ratio of .69 lbs./h.p. The I-1430 has been installed in a number of experimental types of aircraft, including fighters built by Curtiss, Bell, Lockheed and McDonnell.

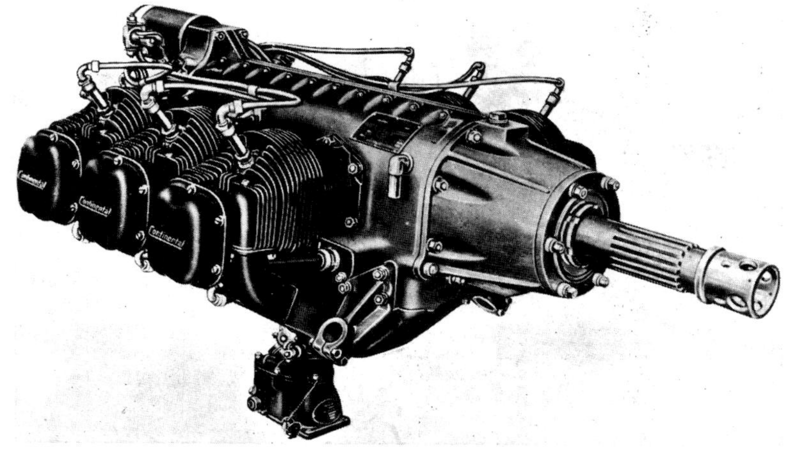

The Continental C140-1 six-cylinder geared engine.

THE CONTINENTAL A65 SERIES.

The Continental A-65 was adopted by the U.S. Army as the standard engine for use in all light liaison aircraft of the Grasshopper type under the designation O-170. Aircraft using this engine include the Taylorcraft L-2, Aeronca L-3 and Piper L-4.

Type.—Four-cylinder horizontally-opposed air-cooled.

Cylinders.—Bore $3\frac{7}{8}$ in. (98.43 m/m.), Stroke $3\frac{5}{8}$ in. (92 m/m.). Capacity 171 cub. in. (2.8 litres). Compression ratio 6.3 : 1. Heat-treated cast aluminium-alloy heads screwed and shrunk on to each forged-steel barrels. Valve-seat inserts and spark-plug bushings of aluminium-bronze. Bronze valve-guides.

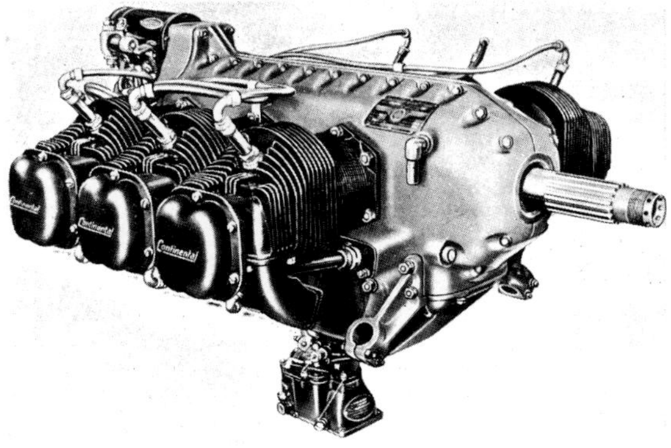

The Continental C115-1 or C-125-1 six-cylinder engine.

Pistons.—Lo-Ex duralumin-alloy. Trunk type. Full floating gudgeon pin located by end-plugs. Two compression, two scraper rings, one above and one below gudgeon pins.

Connecting Rods.—Forged steel. Split big-ends carry replaceable thin-shell steel-back cadmium bearings. Bronze bushings pressed into gudgeon pin ends.

Crankshaft.—One-piece, four-throw, chromium-nickel-molybdenum steel forging, drilled for lubrication, runs in three steel-backed cadmium bearings, one of which is at middle of shaft. Plain thrust faces on airscrew-end throw and on shoulder near airscrew so that either tractor or pusher airscrews can be used.

Crankcase.—Two-piece heat-treated aluminium casting divided at vertical lengthwise plan through crankshaft. Rigid transverse webs carry main bearings and camshaft journals. Rawhide seal prevents oil leakage at airscrew. Four engine-mounting bosses for $\frac{3}{8}$-in. bolts at rear of crankcase.

Valve Gear.—One hardened steel inlet-valve and one heat-resisting austenitic exhaust-valve per cylinder, each operated through rocker-arm, ball-ended push-rod and Wilcox-Rich hydraulic tappet,—all sealed to prevent external oil leakage. Cast "Preferall" camshaft has six hardened cams (intake cams are common to opposing cylinders). Three hardened journals and overhung eccentric at airscrew end to run fuel pump.

Induction System.—Single up-draught Stromberg NA-S3A1 carburettor supplies mixture to cast-aluminium "X" manifold with exhaust-heated hot-spot. Steel intake pipes connect manifold to intake ports. Fuel injection system available as alternative. Engine-driven injector runs at half engine speed and has four reciprocating plungers, one for each cylinder. Each supplies fuel to automatic discharge nozzle in intake pipe to each cylinder. Fuel flow to injector controlled by one needle valve in central passage from which all plungers are supplied. Constant-pressure engine-driven pump supplies fuel to injector unit. Air throttle valve at entrance to engine intake manifold. Manual control to injector unit adjusts mixture in flight.

Ignition.—Scintilla SF-4R dual magnetos.

Lubrication.—Oil at 30 lbs. per sq. in. passes through hollow crankshaft to crank-pins and also passes through tappet, push-rod and rocker-arm to rocker-arm bushing and valve-tip. Valve-stem and guide lubricated by splash. Oil returned to crankcase by way of push-rod housings. Pressure filter and relief-valve in crankcase.

Airscrew Drive.—R.H. tractor. Direct. No. 0 S.A.E. taper.

Dimensions, Weights and Performance.—See Table.

THE CONTINENTAL C75 SERIES.

This Series includes the C75-10 and 10J with dual magnetos but without provision for starter; the C-75-11 and 11J with dual magnetos and Hummer Starter; and the C75-12 and

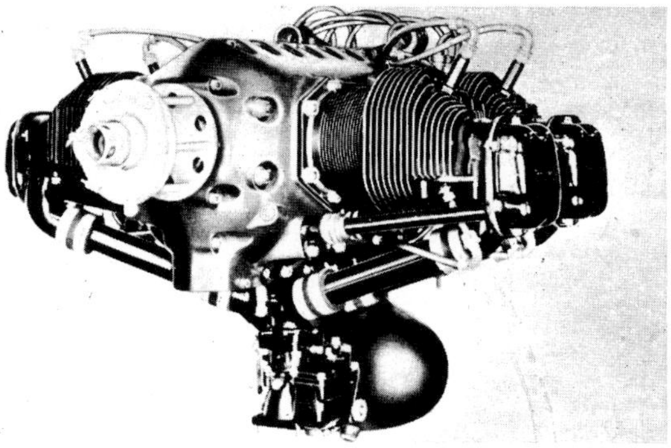

The Continental A65 four-cylinder air-cooled engine.

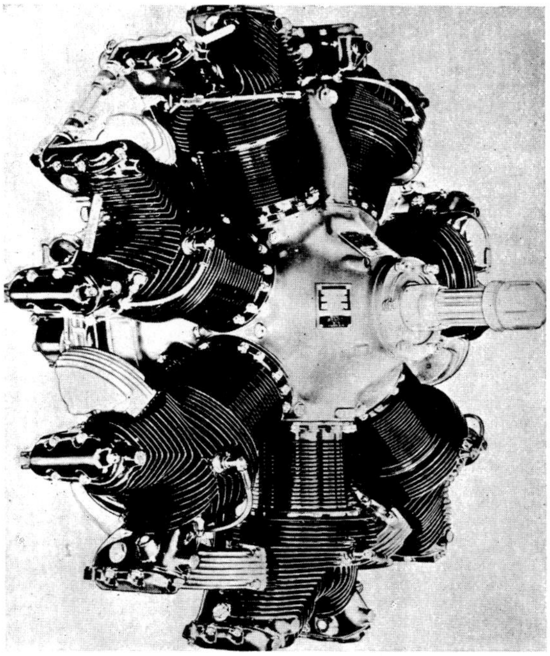

The 220 h.p. Continental W-670-6A radial engine.

THE CONTINENTAL HORIZONTALLY-OPPOSED ENGINES.

	A65-8 (0-170)	C75-12	C85-12	C115-1	C125-1	C140-1
No. of Cylinders	4	4	4	6	6	6
Bore	$3\frac{7}{8}$ in. (98.43 m/m.)	$4\frac{1}{16}$ in. (101.7 m/m.)	$4\frac{1}{16}$ in. (101.7 m/m.)	$4\frac{1}{16}$ in. (101.7 m/m.)	$4\frac{1}{16}$ in. (101.7 m/m.)	$4\frac{1}{16}$ in. (101.7 m/m.)
Stroke	$3\frac{5}{8}$ in. (92 m/m.)	$3\frac{5}{8}$ in. (92 m/m.)	$3\frac{5}{8}$ in. (92 m/m.)	$3\frac{5}{8}$ in. (92 m/m.)	$3\frac{5}{8}$ in. (92 m/m.)	$3\frac{5}{8}$ in. (92 m/m.)
Capacity	171 cub. in. (2.8 litres)	188 cub. in. (3 litres)	188 cub. in. (3 litres)	282 cub. in. (3 litres)	282 cub. in. (3 litres)	282 cub. in. (3 litres)
Rated output	65 h.p. at 2,300 r.p.m.	75 h.p. at 2,275 r.p.m.	85 h.p. at 2,600 r.p.m.	115 h.p. at 2,350 r.p.m.	125 h.p. at 2,550 r.p.m.	140 h.p. at 3,000 engine r.p.m. and 1925 airscrew r.p.m.
Cruising r.p.m. (engine) ..	2,150	2,125	2,400	2,200	2,350	2,700
Cruising r.p.m. (airscrew) ..	2,150	2,125	2,400	2,200	2,350	1,732
Weight Dry	175 lbs. (79.45 kg.)	186 lbs. (84.4 kg.)	186 lbs. (84.4 kg.)	262 lbs. (118.9 kg.)	262 lbs. (118.9 kg.)	298 lbs. (135.3 kg.)
Octane No.	73	73	73	80	80	80
Height (including carburettor)	$20\frac{5}{16}$ in. (516 m/m.)	$21\frac{1}{4}$ in. (540 m/m.)	$21\frac{1}{4}$ in. (540 m/m.)	$24\frac{3}{4}$ in. (628 m/m.)	$24\frac{3}{4}$ in. (628 m/m.)	$24\frac{3}{4}$ in. (628 m/m.)
Height (including air filter) ..	$24\frac{1}{2}$ in. (620 m/m.)	$25\frac{7}{16}$ in. (646 m/m.)	$25\frac{7}{16}$ in. (646 m/m.)	$28\frac{1}{4}$ in. (718 m/m.)	$28\frac{1}{4}$ in. (718 m/m.)	$28\frac{1}{4}$ in. (718 m/m.)
Length	$30\frac{13}{32}$ in. (722 m/m.)	$31\frac{5}{8}$ in. (804 m/m.)	$31\frac{5}{8}$ in. (804 m/m.)	$41\frac{5}{8}$ in. (1,058 m/m.)	$41\frac{5}{8}$ in. (1,058 m/m.)	$46\frac{5}{8}$ in. (1,058 m/m.)
Width	$31\frac{1}{2}$ in. (800 m/m.)	$31\frac{1}{2}$ in. (800 m/m.)	$31\frac{1}{2}$ in. (800 m/m.)	$31\frac{1}{2}$ in. (800 m/m.)	$31\frac{1}{2}$ in. (800 m/m.)	$31\frac{1}{2}$ in. (800 m/m.)
Magneto (Scintilla)	SF-4R	SF-4R	SF-4R	SF-6L-8	SF-6L-8	SF-6L-8
Carburettor (Stromberg or Marvel)	NA-S3A-1	NA-S3A-1	NA-S3A-1	MA-3-SPA	MA-3-SPA	MA-3-SPA

THE CONTINENTAL W-670 SERIES RADIAL ENGINES.

Model	Bore and Stroke	Displacement	Compression Ratio	Normal Output	Fuel Octane No.	Remarks
W-670-6A	$5\frac{1}{8}$ in. × $4\frac{5}{8}$ in. (120 m/m. × 164 m/m.)	668 cub. in. (10.94 litres)	5.4 : 1	220 h.p. at 2,075 r.p.m.	73	Army Air Forces R-670-5 model
W-670-6N	$5\frac{1}{8}$ in. × $4\frac{5}{8}$ in. (120 m/m. × 164 m/m.)	668 cub. in. (10.94 litres)	5.4 : 1	220 h.p. at 2,075 r.p.m.	73	U.S. Navy R-670-4 model
W-670-9A	$5\frac{1}{8}$ in. × $4\frac{5}{8}$ in. (120 m/m. × 164 m/m.)	668 cub. in. (10.94 litres)	6.1 : 1	250 h.p. at 2,400 r.p.m.	80	Ordnance tank engine
W-670-K	$5\frac{1}{8}$ in. × $4\frac{5}{8}$ in. (120 m/m. × 164 m/m.)	668 cub. in. (10.94 litres)	5.4 : 1	225 h.p. at 2,175 r.p.m.	73	Commercial
W-670-M	$5\frac{1}{8}$ in. × $4\frac{5}{8}$ in. (120 m/m. × 164 m/m.)	668 cub. in. (10.94 litres)	6.1 : 1	240 h.p. at 2,200 r.p.m.	80	Commercial
W-670-16	$5\frac{1}{8}$ in. × $4\frac{5}{8}$ in. (120 m/m. × 164 m/m.)	668 cub. in. (10.94 litres)	5.4 : 1	220 h.p. at 2,075 r.p.m.	73	Army Air Forces R-670-11 model Same as R-670-4 except NA-R6G carburettor
W-670-17	$5\frac{1}{8}$ in. × $4\frac{5}{8}$ in. (120 m/m. × 164 m/m.)	668 cub. in. (10.94 litres)	5.4 : 1	220 h.p. at 2,075 r.p.m.	73	U.S. Navy R-670-8 model with damper crankshaft
W-670-18	$5\frac{1}{8}$ in. × $4\frac{5}{8}$ in. (120 m/m. × 164 m/m.)	668 cub. in. (10.94 litres)	5.4 : 1	220 h.p. at 2,075 r.p.m.	73	Army Air Forces R-670-6 model Radio-shielded U.S. Navy airship engine

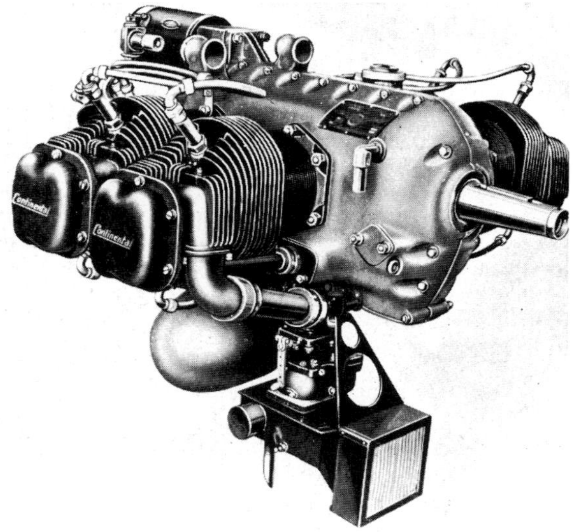

The Continental C75-12 or C85-12 four-cylinder engine.

12J with dual magnetos and Delco-Remy Starter and Generator. The J following the series number signifies that fuel injection is substituted for the Stromberg carburettor. The J engines are approximately $2\frac{1}{2}$ lbs. heavier than the carburetted models.

General constructional details are similar to those of the previously described A65 Series. For other details see Table.

THE CONTINENTAL C85 SERIES.

The C85 Series is identical to the C-75 Series except that the normal rated r.p.m. is increased from 2,275 to 2,600 and the cruising r.p.m. from 2,125 to 2,400. The rated output is consequently increased from 75 to 85 h.p. For other details see Table.

THE CONTINENTAL C115-1.

The C115 is a six-cylinder horizontally-opposed engine using the cylinders of the C75 engine. General constructional details are the same as for the previously-described models. For further details see Table.

THE CONTINENTAL C125-1.

The C-125 is similar to the C-115 except that the normal rated r.p.m. is increased from 2,350 to 2,550, with a consequent step-up in power from 115 to 125 h.p. For further details see Table.

THE CONTINENTAL C140-1.

The C140 is a geared version of the C115. It is fitted with an epicyclic airscrew reduction gear with a ratio of 1.6 : 1. For further details see Table.

THE CONTINENTAL W-670 SERIES.

Type.—Seven-cylinder air-cooled radial, direct drive.

Cylinders.—Bore $5\frac{1}{8}$ in. (120 m/m.), Stroke $4\frac{5}{8}$ in. (117.5 m/m.), Capacity 668 cub. in. (10.94 litres).

Pistons.—Plain trunk-type forgings, of heat-treated aluminium-alloy. Compression rings in grooves 1, 2 and 4. Oil scraper in No. 3. Internally finned.

Valve Gear.—Valves operating through steel-tube push-rods and forged steel rocker-arms. Two valves per cylinder. Sodium-cooled exhaust valves, of chrome-nickel silicon steel. Intake valves tulip-shaped head of stainless steel. See also "Lubrication."

Crankcase.—Two-piece aluminium-alloy casting. Breather in rear casting.

Induction System.—Fuel supplied by single barrel vertical carburettor Stromberg NA-R6D to ring manifold cast into rear crankcase. Individual pipes lead from manifold to cylinder intake ports.

Ignition.—Two Scintilla model MN7-DF magnetos.

Lubrication.—Dry sump system. One main pressure pump. One main scavenge pump. Rocker boxes, etc.

Airscrew Drive.—R.H. tractor. Direct. No. 20 S.A.E. spline shaft.

Dimensions.—Diameter 42.5 in. (1,079.5 m/m.), Length $34\frac{3}{16}$ in. (868.4 m/m.), Diameter of mounting circle (8 bolts) 20 in. (508 m/m.).

Weight (Models K and M less carburettor air scoop, manifold and airscrew hub).—465 lbs. (211 kg.).

Performance (Model K).—Department of Commerce rating 225 h.p. at 2,175 r.p.m., Fuel consumption at rated output 54 lbs. (.245 kg.) per h.p./hour., Fuel consumption at cruising r.p.m. 13/15 U.S. gallons (49/57 litres) per hour, Oil consumption at cruising r.p.m. .40 U.S. gallons (1.5 litres) per hour.

Performance (Model M).—Department of Commerce rating 240 h.p. at 2,200 r.p.m., Fuel consumption at rated output .50 lbs. (.226 kg.) per h.p./hour. Fuel consumption at cruising r.p.m. 13/15 U.S. gallons (49/57 litres) per hour, Oil consumption at cruising r.p.m. .40 U.S. gallons (1.5 litres) per hour.

FORD.

THE FORD MOTOR COMPANY.

Head Office and Works: Dearborn, Mich.
President and Founder: Henry Ford.
Executive Vice-President: Henry Ford II.
Vice-President and Treasurer: B. J. Craig.
Secretary and Assistant Treasurer: H. L. Moekle.

In addition to its large commitments in the production of Consolidated Liberator B-24 bombers for the Army Air Forces (see under "Ford," Section C), the Ford Motor Company holds contracts for the manufacture of large numbers of Pratt & Whitney R-2800 engines for the U.S. War Department.

To undertake this work the Company erected a new aero-engine plant at River Rouge. In July, 1943, a second assembly line went into operation in order to meet military production requirements.

In August, 1944, at the request of the Air Technical Service Command, U.S.A.A.F., the Ford company undertook to develop an impulse jet propulsion unit similar to that used in the German FZG-76 flying-bomb. The first Ford-built jet unit designed and built from information supplied from Great Britain was operating within three weeks of the work being put in hand.

FRANKLIN.

THE AIRCOOLED MOTORS CORPORATION.

Head Office and Works: Syracuse, N.Y.
President: Lewis E. Pierson, Jr.
Vice-President and Chief Engineer: Carl T. Doman.
Vice-President and General Sales Manager: C. F. B. Roth.
Secretary and Treasurer: Charles F. Carr.

In developing the Franklin aero-engine, the Aircooled Motors Corporation is carrying forward the experience of more than forty years. The Corporation owns the name, trade-mark and all the patents of the former Franklin Automobile Company under which all Franklin air-cooled engines are built.

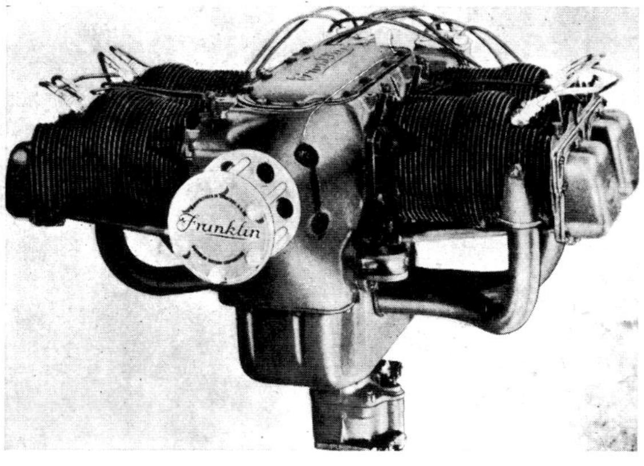

The Franklin 4AC-176-B2 four-cylinder engine.

The Corporation produced the first of its very successful series of light horizontally-opposed air-cooled engines in 1938. Since then it has placed on the market engines of four and six cylinders ranging in output from 65 to 150 h.p. It has been the object of the Aircooled Motors Corpn. to design a series of engines so that it is possible to interchange parts to get a broad power range.

The Aircooled Motors Corpn. had not finalised its post-war engine production programme by the end of 1944, but it had taken the decision to limit its products to a range of four 65 to 175 h.p., all models under 100 h.p. being four-cylinder and over 100 h.p. six-cylinder horizontally-opposed air-cooled engines. It will also discontinue the production of geared engines as being too expensive to manufacture for use in small commercial aircraft.

The Corporation has developed a number of interesting engines for the U.S. Government but no information concerning this branch of its war activities may yet be published.

FRANKLIN AIR-COOLED ENGINES.

Type.—Four or six-cylinder horizontally-opposed air-cooled.

Cylinders.—Nickel-iron barrels on to which aluminium-alloy heads are screwed and shrunk with gasket in between. Attached to crankcase by flanges on barrels and eight studs and nuts.

Pistons.—Aluminium-alloy, interchangeable between the four basic engines.

Crankshaft.—One-piece steel forging. Main bearings steel backed and copper-lead faced.

Crankcase.—Aluminium-alloy in two halves split vertically. Detachable oil-sump underneath. Cover plate above.

Valve Gear.—One overhead inlet and one overhead exhaust valve per cylinder actuated by push-rods from camshaft supported in steel-backed babbit-faced bearings. Exhaust valve-seat is an insert of stainless steel. Friction-dampers fitted on valve springs and Wilcox-Rich hydraulic valve-lifters are used on push-rods to ensure accurate functioning at all speeds. Valve gear totally enclosed.

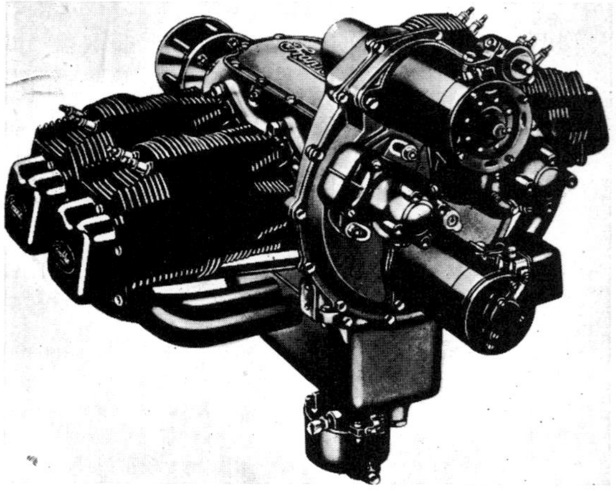

The Franklin 4AC-199-E3 four-cylinder engine.

Carburation.—Marvel-Schebler MA-3 up-draught carburettor flange-mounted on underside of oil sump with individual induction pipes to each cylinder.

THE FRANKLIN 4AC-176.

TYPE.—Four-cylinder horizontally-opposed air-cooled.
CYLINDERS.—Bore 4 in. (100 m/m.), Stroke 3½ in. (87.5 m/m.). Capacity 176 cub. in. (2.8 litres). Compression ratio 6.3 : 1 in Models B, C and D. 7 : 1 in Model F.
OCTANE No.—73 in Models B, C and D. 80 in Model F.
WEIGHTS.—Models B1 and C1 175 lbs. (79.4 kg.), Models B2, C2 and D2 182 lbs. (82.6 kg.), Models B3, C3 and D3 216 lbs. (98 kg.), Model F2 183 lbs. (83 kg.), Model F3 217 lbs. (98.5 kg.).
PERFORMANCE.—Rated output : B Models 65 h.p. at 2,300 r.p.m., C Models 75 h.p. at 2,500 r.p.m., D Models 80 h.p. at 2,650 r.p.m., F Models 80 h.p. at 2,500 r.p.m.

THE FRANKLIN 4AC-199.

TYPE.—Four-cylinder horizontally-opposed air-cooled.
CYLINDERS.—Bore 4½ in. (106.2 m/m.), Stroke 3½ in. (87.5 m/m.). Capacity 199 cub. in. (3 litres). Compression ratio 6.3 : 1 in D Models. 7 : 1 in E Models.
OCTANE No.—73 in D Models, 80 in E Models.
WEIGHTS.—Models D2 and E2 190 lbs. (86.3 kg.), Models D3 and E3 224 lbs. (101.7 kg.).
PERFORMANCE.—Rated output : D Models 85 h.p. at 2,500 r.p.m., E Models 90 h.p. at 2,500 r.p.m.

The Franklin 6AC-298-E3 six-cylinder engine.

THE FRANKLIN 6AC-298.

TYPE.—Six-cylinder horizontally-opposed air-cooled.
CYLINDERS.—Bore 4½ in. (106.2 m/m.), Stroke 3½ in. (87.5 m/m.). Capacity 298 cub. in. (4.7 litres). Compression ratio 6.3 : 1 in D Models, 7 : 1 in F Models.
OCTANE No.—73 in D Models, 80 in F Models.
WEIGHTS.—Model D2 260 lbs. (118 kg.), Model D3 294 lbs. (133.5 kg.), Model F2 261 lbs. (118.5 kg.), Model F3 295 lbs. (134 kg.).
PERFORMANCE.—Rated output : D Models 130 h.p. at 2,600 r.p.m., F Models 130 h.p. at 2,550 r.p.m.

THE FRANKLIN 6ACV-405.

The 6ACV-405 is a helicopter engine which the Air-cooled Motors Corpn. has designed, developed and produced for installation in the Sikorsky R-6 and other military helicopters.

The only information that is permitted to be published is that this unit develops a maximum power output of 245 h.p. It is completely pressure-cooled, the fan, which absorbs approximately 10 h.p., having ample capacity to cool not only the engine but also to supply the necessary air for oil cooling.

GUIBERSON.

THE GUIBERSON DIESEL ENGINE COMPANY.

HEAD OFFICE AND WORKS : 1,000, FOREST AVENUE, DALLAS, TEXAS.

This firm was organised in 1932 to manufacture aero-engines of the Diesel type after the Guiberson Corporation, who are manufacturers of oil industry equipment, had experimented for three years on the principles involved. Their first engine was granted Approved Type Certificate No. 79 by the U.S. Department of Commerce at a rating of 185 h.p.

The Model A-1020 engine, described below, received its A.T.C. No. 220 in February, 1940, and since installation in a Stinson Reliant monoplane has flown over 1,000 hours on test.

The Company has been unable to produce this engine commercially owing to the fact that its full capacity was used to manufacture engines for U.S. Army tanks. The Model T-1020, which is basically similar to the A-1020 aero-engine, was specially designed for tank use and develops 210 h.p. at 2,200 r.p.m. The Model T-1400, produced for medium tank and marine use, develops 250 h.p. at 2,200 r.p.m.

THE GUIBERSON A-1020 DIESEL.

TYPE.—Seven-cylinder four-cycle Diesel radial.
CYLINDERS.—Bore 5.125 in. (130.175 m/m.), Stroke 5.5 in. (139.7 m/m.). Capacity 1,021 cub. in. (16.73 litres). Compression ratio 15/1. B.M.E.P. for rated output 113 lbs. per sq. in.
VALVE GEAR.—One inlet and one exhaust valve per cylinder operated through push-rods and overhead rocker-gear. Combined timing and injection control. Decompression device, controlled by throttle, allows airscrew to turn freely in the air or on ground.
INDUCTION SYSTEM.—One Guiberson pump per cylinder forces fuel at 2,200 to 2,500 lbs./sq. in. pressure through one Guiberson injector into each cylinder. No supercharger.
STARTING.—Eclipse electric inertia or Coffman air starter.
DIMENSIONS.—Diameter 47.125 in. (1,198 m/m.), Length (including starter) 38.6 in. (976 m/m.).
WEIGHT.—653 lbs. (296.4 kg.).
PERFORMANCE.—Rated 310 h.p. at 2,150 r.p.m. at sea level, Fuel consumption Diesel Index No. 50 .382 lb. (.181 kg.) per h.p. hour, Oil consumption .02 lb. (.009 kg.) per h.p. hour.

The Guiberson A-1020 nine-cylinder Diesel engine.

The Franklin 6ACV-405 helicopter engine.

JACOBS.

THE JACOBS AIRCRAFT ENGINE COMPANY.

HEAD OFFICE AND WORKS : POTTSTOWN, PENNSYLVANIA.

Chairman of the Board : J. Andrew Harris 3rd.

President : C. J. Abbott.

Vice-President, Treasurer and General Manager : H. B. Knerr.

Vice-President and Engineering Manager : Henry M. McFadgen.

Vice-President and Secretary : J. Story Smith.

The Jacobs Aircraft Engine Company has been concentrating on the production of two basic engines, the R-755 and R-915, each of which has variants for different specific installations. For example, the R-755A1 is fitted in the Cessna AT-17 and UC-78 for the U.S. Army Air Forces and the Cessna Crane for the Royal Canadian Air Force. The R-915A1 was used in the Canadian Avro Anson II.

The Company has also conducted large-scale production of Pratt & Whitney engines for the U.S. Government under licence during the war.

The Jacobs R-755 Series are unsupercharged conservatively-rated engines, featuring simplicity of design. The absence of high cylinder pressures, combined with large bearing areas and rating at moderate r.p.m. permit operations at a high proportion of the rated power for extended periods without damage. This engine has been used to power a major percentage of the United Nations twin-engined trainers. In military training operation it has proved its reliability under the most severe conditions and is operating up to 1,200 hours between overhauls.

The Jacobs R-915 Series engines are also unsupercharged conservatively-rated engines of increased bore and stroke. Construction is similar to the R-755 engines except that many parts have been strengthened to absorb the increased horse-power. In spite of the unusually ample displacement and conservative rating, the power/weight ratio of the R-915A engine is only 1.68 lbs./h.p.

THE JACOBS R-755A1 (L-4MB).

TYPE.—Seven-cylinder air-cooled radial.
CYLINDERS.—Bore 5.25 in. (133 m/m.), Stroke 5 in. (127 m/m.),

Capacity 757 cub. in. (12.4 litres). Barrels machined from steel forging with closely-spaced fins. Aluminium-alloy heads screwed and shrunk on. Aluminium-bronze valve-seats shrunk into heads.
PISTONS.—Forged aluminium-alloy. Three compression rings above gudgeon pin and one scraper ring below. Fully-floating, nitrided gudgeon pins.
CONNECTING RODS.—One-piece steel master-rod and forged aluminium-alloy link-rods, the aluminium bearing directly on nitrided steel pins.

CRANKSHAFT.—Two-piece clamp type, made from chrome-nickel molybdenum steel forgings.
CRANKCASE.—Built up of five parts. First, magnesium-alloy front case, carrying the thrust ball-bearing and valve-operating gear ; second, front half of main crankcase, aluminium-alloy casting which supports the front crankshaft roller-bearing ; third, rear half of main crankcase, magnesium-alloy casting, which supports the rear crankshaft roller-bearing and incorporates a ring-type

The 225 h.p. Jacobs R-755A1 (L-4MB) radial air-cooled engine.

The 330 h.p. Jacobs R-915A1 (L-6MB) radial air-cooled engine.

intake manifold ; fourth, magnesium-alloy rear plate, which carries additional crankshaft ball-bearing and supports accessory drives ; magnesium-alloy rear case, which carries accessories.

Valve Gear.—The whole valve gear (cam, drive gears, tappets and push-rods) is in the nose section. All moving parts enclosed. Tulip-type inlet valves, and sodium-cooled exhaust valves. Two springs per valve.

Carburation.—A single Stromberg NA-R7A carburettor.

Ignition.—One Scintilla magneto and one Scintilla battery distributor, incorporating automatic spark advance.

Lubrication.—One pressure and two scavenger pumps, of gear type, built into one unit. Dry sump. Pressure to all main bearings. A take-off to operate an adjustable-pitch or constant-speed airscrew can be incorporated. Automatic valve lubrication is standard equipment.

Fuel.—73 octane.

Airscrew Drive.—R.H. tractor. Direct. No. 20 SAE spline.

Dimensions.—Diameter 44 in. (1,118 m.), Length (to rear of mounting plate $27\frac{1}{4}$ in. (692 m/m.), Overall length $40\frac{7}{32}$ in. (1,020 m/m.).

Weight.—505 lbs. (229 kg.).

Performance.—Rated output 225 h.p. at 2,000 r.p.m., Cruising 175 h.p. at 1,900 r.p.m. Take-off rating 245 h.p. at 2,200 r.p.m.

THE JACOBS R-755A3 (L-4M).

This engine is similar to the R-755A1, except that ignition is from two Scintilla magnetos. Provision is made for mounting an electrical generator and direct cranking electric starter.

THE JACOBS R-915A1 (L-6MB).

Except where stated, the construction of the R-915A1 is as for the R-755A1 but dimensions are increased and stressed parts strengthened.

Type.—Seven-cylinder air-cooled radial.

Cylinders.—Bore $5\frac{1}{2}$ in. (139.7 m/m.), Stroke $5\frac{1}{2}$ in. (139.7 m/m.). Capacity 914 cub. in. (14.97 litres). Compression ratio 6/1.

Pistons.—Forged aluminium-alloy, waffle-head design.

Connecting Rods.—Link-rods are of forged chrome-molybdenum steel. Bronze bushes for gudgeon pin and knuckle pin bearings.

Carburettor.—Stromberg NA-R7A.

Ignition.—One Scintilla magneto and one Scintilla battery distributor incorporating automatic spark advance. Eclipse 25-amp. generator.

Airscrew Drive.—R.H. tractor. Direct drive. S.A.E. No. 20 spline.

Dimensions.—Diameter $45\frac{5}{8}$ in. (1,160 m/m.), Length $40\frac{9}{16}$ in. (1,030 m/m.), Diameter of mounting bolt ($8 \times \frac{3}{8}$ in.) circle $16\frac{1}{2}$ in. (419.1 m/m.).

Weight (including magneto, battery distributor, coil, radio shielding carburettor, automatic valve lubrication and oil strainer).—555 lbs. (252 kg.).

Performance.—Take-off 330 h.p. at 2,200 r.p.m., Rated 300 h.p. at 2,100 r.p.m., Cruising 220 h.p. at 1,900 r.p.m., Fuel consumptions at cruising speed .53 lbs. (.24 kg.) per h.p. hour.

JACOBS R-915A3 (L-6M).

This engine is similar to the R-915A1, except that ignition is supplied by two Scintilla magnetos. Weight 557 lbs. (253 kg.).

JACOBS R-915A4 (L-6MBA).

This engine is similar to the R-915A1, except that a power drive is supplied for an Autogiro rotor.

KINNER.

KINNER MOTORS INC.

Head Office : 635, W. Colorado Boulevard, Glendale, California.

President and General Manager : John N. Gladden.
Vice-President : G. Brashears.
Vice-President in charge of Manufacturing : W. G. Milka.
Vice-President in charge of Sales : Gunnar Edenquist.
Secretary, Treasurer and Comptroller : Victor E. Semrau.
Assistant Secretary and Treasurer : M. E. Sears.

Kinner Motors, Inc. succeeded the former Kinner Airplane & Motor Corpn. in 1939 and in 1941 it became the largest producer of aero-engines on the West Coast. The Kinner B-4 was supplied in quantity to equip the Fleet Finch primary training biplane used in Canada under the Commonwealth Joint Air Training Plan and the B-54 used in Ryan trainers ordered by the U.S. Army and Navy. The R-56 has been installed in several types of aircraft, including the Fairchild 24 and Meyers Model OTW.

Production of the company is principally devoted to the three models, the 125 h.p. B-54, the 160 h.p. R-55 and the 160 h.p. R-56. While a large percentage has gone into military service, Kinner has been able to supply commercial users with many of their requirements.

During 1944 the company announced a new line of horizontally-opposed air-cooled engines ranging in power from 225 h.p. to 250 h.p.

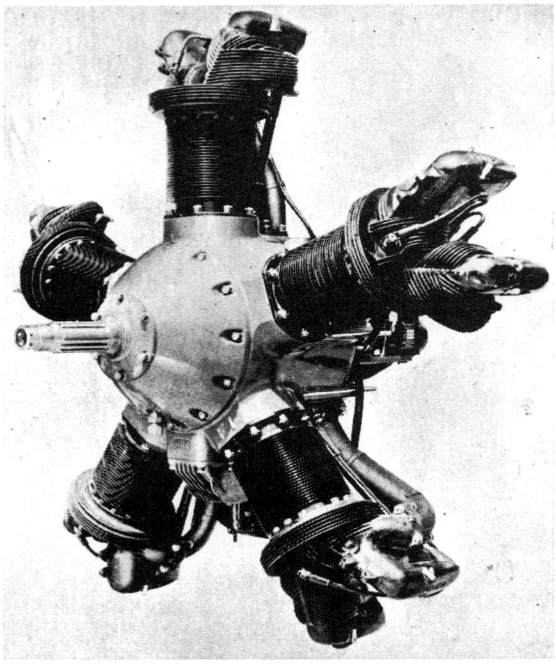

The 125 h.p. Kinner B-54 five-cylinder radial engine.

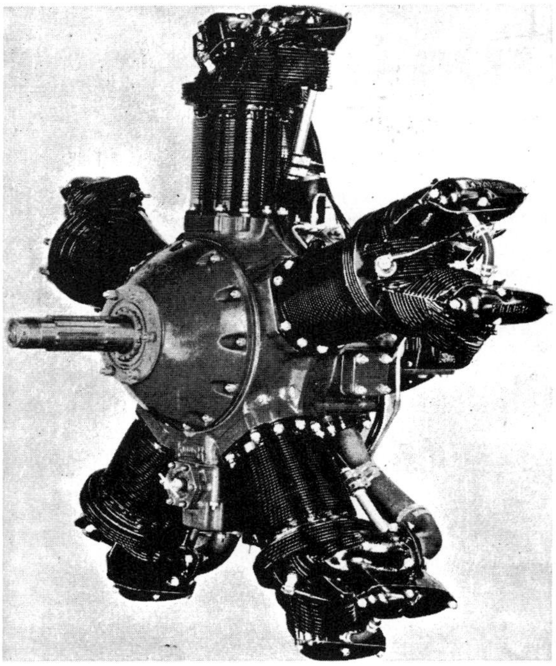

The 160 h.p. Kinner R-56 five-cylinder radial engine.

THE KINNER K-5 SERIES II.

Type.—Five-cylinder air-cooled radial.

Cylinders.—Bore $4\frac{1}{4}$ in. (108 m/m.), Stroke $5\frac{1}{4}$ in. (133.5 m/m.). Swept volume 372 cub. in. (6.1 litres). Compression ratio 5/1. Forged steel barrel bolted to crankcase, has aluminium-alloy head secured by 16 studs. Bronze valve-seats shrunk and rolled in.

Pistons.—Aluminium-alloy trunk type. Three compression rings and one scraper ring above fully-floating gudgeon pin, which is located by aluminium end plugs.

Connecting Rods.—Heat-treated alloy-steel forgings. Split master big-end, H-section auxiliary rods.

Crankshaft.—One-piece heat-treated and ground alloy-steel forging, carefully counterbalanced, runs in plain babbit bearings and thrust taken by a ball bearing.

Valve Gear.—One inlet and one exhaust valve per cylinder operated through rockers and push-rods and roller cam-followers off five separate camshafts driven at $\frac{1}{2}$ engine speed.

Carburation.—Stromberg Model NAR5A or Holley Model 419 arburettor.

Ignition.—Two Bendix Scintilla magnetos. Battery ignition also offered.

Lubrication.—High pressure. Pressure pump at 100 lbs. feeds through crankshaft to main and connecting rod bearings. Separate scavenge pump.

Airscrew Drive.—Direct. SAE No. 20 spline.

Dimensions.—Diameter $45\frac{3}{8}$ in. (1,153 m/m.), Length $31\frac{1}{2}$ in. (800 m/m.), Mounting bolt circle 14 in. (35.6 m/m.).

Weights.—Dry, without carburettor air heater, exhaust collector ring, starter or propeller hub nut, 304 lbs. (137 kg.).

Performance.—Rated output 100 h.p. at 1,810 r.p.m.

THE KINNER B-5 AND B-54.

Type.—Five-cylinder air-cooled radial.

Cylinders.—Bore $4\frac{5}{8}$ in. (117.5 m/m.), Stroke $5\frac{1}{4}$ in. (133.5 m/m.). Swept volume 441 cub. in. (7.2 litres). Compression ratio 5.25/1. Other details as for K-5.

Pistons.—Aluminium-alloy trunk type. Three compression rings and one scraper ring above fully-floating gudgeon pin, which is retained by aluminium end plugs.

Connecting Rods.—Split master big-end and H-section auxiliary rods.

Crankshaft.—Counterbalanced single-throw one-piece alloy-steel shaft runs in plain bearings, with single-row radial thrust-bearing.

Crankcase.—Barrel type aluminium-alloy, of normal design.

Valve Gear.—Five separate camshafts driven at half engine speed, with normal type cams, followers and tappets. Enclosed overhead rocker-arms actuated by push-rods.

Carburation.—One Holley or Stromberg carburettor.

Ignition.—Two Bendix Scintilla magnetos driven off the rear end of the crankshaft by spur wheels.

Lubrication.—Circulating dry sump system. Pressure feed.

Accessories.—Drives and mountings for the usual accessories.

Airscrew Drive.—Direct No. 1 spline on B5, SAE No. 10 on B-54.

Dimensions.—Diameter overall $45\frac{3}{8}$ in. (1,153 m/m.), Length overall $31\frac{1}{2}$ in. (800 m/m.).

Weight Dry (without air-heater, exhaust collector ring, starter or airscrew hub).—312 lbs. (142 kg.).

Performance.—Rated output 125 h.p. at 1,925 r.p.m., Consumptions per h.p. hour : Fuel .60 lb. (.273 kg.) ; Oil (Max.) .025 lb. (0.011 kg.).

THE KINNER R-5 SERIES II AND R-55.

The construction of the Kinner R5 Series II is practically the same as the B-5. All oil passages in the R5 Series II, however, are contained within the crankcase.

The main difference between the R-55 and the R-5 Series II is that the former has an SAE No. 20 spline shaft whereas the R-5 has a No. 1 taper shaft.

Cylinders.—Bore 5 in. (128 m/m.), Stroke $5\frac{1}{2}$ in. (140 m/m.), Swept volume 540 cub. in. (8.85 litres). Compression ratio 5.5/1.

Weight Dry (without airscrew hub, air-heater, exhaust collector ring, starter, generator or fuel pump)—R-5 Series II 335 lbs. (152 kg.), R-55 345 lbs. (156 kg.).

Dimensions.—Diameter overall $45\frac{5}{8}$ in. (1,159 m/m.), Length overall R-5 Series II $31\frac{15}{32}$ in. (800 m/m.), R-55 $33\frac{5}{8}$ in. (853 m/m.).

Performance.—Rated output 160 h.p. at 1,850 r.p.m.

THE KINNER R-53.

The R-53 is similar to the R-55 but develops a greater output by a slight increase in compression ratio and r.p.m. Its

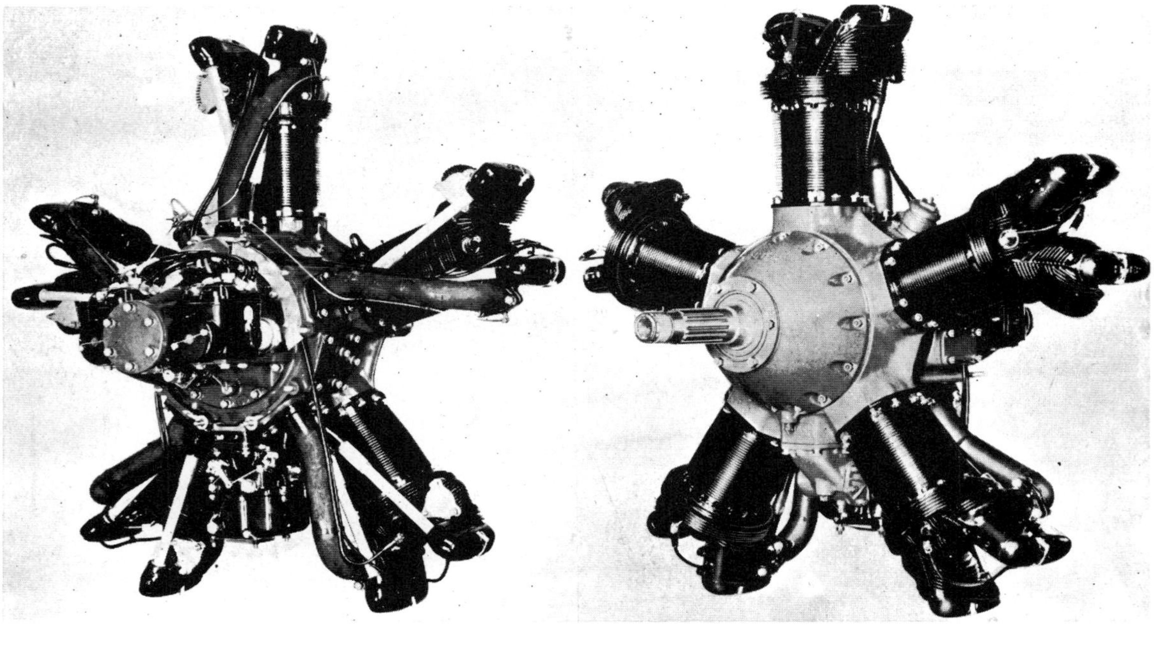

The 160 h.p. Kinner R-55 five-cylinder radial air-cooled engine.

mounting dimensions are identical to those of the B-54 and R-55, it is interchangeable with the R-55 and can be substituted for the B-54 with only slight installation alterations.

WEIGHT DRY.—351 lbs. (159.3 kg.).
DIMENSIONS.—Same as R-55.
PERFORMANCE.—Rated output 175 h.p. at 2,100 r.p.m.

THE KINNER R-56.

TYPE.—Five-cylinder air-cooled radial.
CYLINDERS.—Bore 5 in. (128 m/m.), Stroke 5.5 in. (140 m/m.), Swept volume 540 cub. in. (8.85 litres), Compression ratio 5.5/1. Forged steel barrels and cast aluminium-alloy heads bolted together. Valve-seat inserts of special bronze pressed and rolled into place. Rocker-arm supports cast integrally with head.
PISTONS.—Aluminium-alloy trunk-type. Three compression rings and one scraper ring all located above the gudgeon-pin.
CONNECTING RODS.—Articulated type H-section. Master-rod fitted with steel-backed copper-lead bearing.
CRANKSHAFT.—One-piece forged steel shaft with dynamic damper counterweights, supported on a roller front main bearing, a ball thrust bearing and a sleeve type steel-backed rear main bearing.
CRANKCASE.—Barrel type of cast aluminium-alloy. Front cover carries front crankshaft bearings, rear wall supports rear crankshaft bearing and bearings for five camshafts. Rear case includes cast aluminium manifold from which intake pipes radiate to cylinder heads and supports auxiliaries.
VALVE GEAR.—Two valves per cylinder operated by enclosed push-rods and rocker arms from individual camshafts at the rear of cylinders.
CARBURATION.—One Holley or Stromberg carburettor.

LUBRICATION.—Dry sump, with pressure lubrication to rocker boxes, etc. Gear type pressure and scavenge pumps.
ACCESSORIES.—Drives and mountings on rear crankcase cover.
DIMENSIONS.—Diameter overall 45⅝ in. (1,153 m/m.), Length overall 33¹³⁄₃₂ in. (853 m/m.).
WEIGHT DRY (without air-heater, exhaust collector ring, starter or airscrew hub).—362 lbs. (164.3 kg.).
PERFORMANCE.—Rated output 160 h.p. at 1,850 r.p.m.

THE KINNER O-552

The new O-552 six-cylinder horizontally-opposed engine is available in either direct-drive (O-552-H) or geared (O-552-HG) forms. No constructional details are available.

TYPE.—Six-cylinder horizontally-opposed air-cooled.
CYLINDERS.—Bore 5¼ in. (133.5 m/m.), Stroke 4¼ in. (108 m/m.), Swept volume 552 cub. in. (9 litres), Compression 6.5/1.
AIRSCREW DRIVE.—Direct (O-552-H) or geared (O-552-HG), Reduction gear ratio 1.47/1.
CARBURATION.—Stromberg Model NAR6 carburettor.
PERFORMANCE.—Rated output O-552-H 225 h.p. at 2,400 r.p.m., O-552-HG 250 h.p. at 2,800 engine r.p.m. and 1,905 airscrew shaft r.p.m.

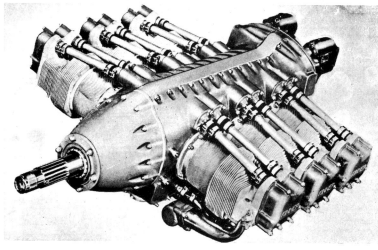

The 250 h.p. Kinner O-552-HG six-cylinder opposed engine.

LYCOMING.

THE LYCOMING DIVISION OF THE AVIATION CORPORATION.

HEAD OFFICE : 420, LEXINGTON AVENUE, NEW YORK, N.Y.
PRODUCTION AND SALES OFFICES : WILLIAMSPORT, PENNA.
President : I. B. Babcock.
Executive Vice-President : William F. Wise.
Vice-President, Secretary and General Counsel : R. S. Pruitt.
Vice-President and Treasurer : W. A. Morgensen.
Vice-President in charge of Manufacturing : Bert Conway.
Vice-Presidents : L. I. Hartmayer and I. J. Snader.
Chief Engineer : S. K. Hoffman.

The Lycoming Division is the aero-engine and airscrew manufacturing division of The Aviation Corporation which on January 1, 1936, acquired the assets and manufacturing rights of the Aviation Division of Lycoming Manufacturing Company, Williamsport, Penna.

The first aero-engine developed by Lycoming in 1928 was the nine-cylinder Model R-680, development of which was begun in 1928. The first production model (215 h.p.) was delivered early in 1931. Models now being made range from 225 to 300 h.p.

Manufacture of the horizontally-opposed air-cooled series was started in 1938 with a 50 h.p. model. This series of engines now includes nine four-cylinder and five six-cylinder models. These are put into two series : from 55-75 h.p. and from 100-220 h.p. With the exception of the O-235 100 h.p. engine all the engines ranging from the 125 h.p. O-290 to the 220 h.p. GO-435-B have the excellent feature of the major parts being interchangeable. This interchangeability also holds true for the 50-75 h.p. O-145 series engines.

The entire output of the Corporation has been devoted for several years to the military programme. The R-680 radial series was used in single and twin-engined primary and advanced trainers and the horizontally-opposed series engines were used in light trainers, liaison and light cargo aircraft and in other special military equipment.

The adaptability of the Lycoming "flat" engine is well demonstrated by the O-435 engine, which forms the power-plant of the Stinson L-5 Sentinel liaison-observation and ambulance monoplane, the Sikorsky R-6 helicopter and the "Locust" airborne tank.

THE LYCOMING O-145 AND GO-145 SERIES.

TYPE.—Four-cylinder horizontally-opposed air-cooled direct-drive (O-145) or geared (GO-145).
CYLINDERS.—Bore 3⅝ in. (92 m/m.), Stroke 3½ in. (89 m/m.). Capacity 144.5 cub. in. (2.37 litres). Two cylinders integral with each half of cast semi-steel crankcase. Cylinder cooling fins cast directly on barrels. Cast aluminium heads attached to cylinders by studs and nuts. Cylinder heads are furnished with Helicoil inserts into which the sparking-plugs are screwed.
PISTONS.—Aluminium-alloy pistons with two compression rings, one oil-regulating ring and one oil scraper ring. Full-floating gudgeon pins with aluminium-alloy retaining plugs each end.
CONNECTING RODS.—Forged steel "H"-section rods. Bronze bushing in piston end and split copper-lead steel-backed bearing at crankpin end.
CRANKSHAFT.—One-piece forged alloy-steel shaft with four throws

The 100 h.p. Lycoming O-235-C four-cylinder engine.

and three main bearings. Drilled throughout for lightness and oil passages. Spur gear to drive camshaft attached to rear of shaft with dowels and capscrews. On direct-drive models airscrew hub flange is forged integral with crankshaft. On geared models reduction gear and airscrew hub rear flange forged integral with steel airscrew shaft supported by two replaceable steel-backed lead-bronze-lined bearings. Airscrew shaft driven by gear attached to crankshaft by keyway and nut threaded on crankshaft.
CRANKCASE.—Integral crankcase and cylinder block split vertically and held together by studs, nuts and capscrews. Internal webbing support camshaft bearings and three replaceable steel-backed copper-lead main bearings.
VALVE GEAR.—Heat-treated alloy-steel camshaft with hardened lobes drilled for lightness and to provide oil passages. Mushroom type steel cam-followers with hardened faces and sockets operate directly in crankcase sections. Push-rods of steel tubing with hardened ball ends. Forged steel rocker-arms supported on full-floating pins in cylinder-head and secured by end-plugs. One inlet and one exhaust valve per cylinder may be adjusted by screw and locknut in rocker-arms. Single valve-springs secured with tapered collars and split-type valve-keys.
INDUCTION.—Marvel Model MA-2 single-barrel carburettor attached to bottom of oil sump. Centre-zone induction system, cast directly in oil sump, is submerged in heated engine oil to insure thorough and uniform vaporisation of fuel. Each cylinder has interchangeable steel intake pipe attached at both ends with rubber sleeves and clamps.
IGNITION.—Single or dual Scintilla magnetos. Single magneto driven directly from camshaft. Dual magnetos driven by spur gear from camshaft.

LUBRICATION.—Full-pressure type except for valve mechanism which is lubricated by gravity-fed engine oil. Oil is forced by pressure pump through camshaft to all cam bearings, crankshaft main bearings and connecting-rod bearings. Crankshaft is bored to provide centrifugal sludge removers at all passages leading to the main and connecting-rod bearings. Pistons, gudgeon pins and accessory drive gears are lubricated by splash. Screen oil-baffle provided between crank-case and oil sump, which has a capacity for 1 U.S. gallon (3,758 litres) of oil.
ACCESSORIES.—On all standard O-145 and GO-145 models accessory housing incorporates pressure oil pump, oil relief valve, and tachometer connection. The oil pump and tachometer shafts are driven directly from the camshaft. On O-145-A3, O-145-B3, O-145-C3 and GO-145-C3 provision is made for the installation of an aircraft type generator and starter. The starter jaw is located directly at the rear of the crankshaft, the generator is directly above the starter and is driven through a spur gear and idler gear by the crankshaft ; a fuel pump of the plunger type is driven by an eccentric located on the oil pump shaft. Models O-145-A4, O-145-B4, O-145-C4 and GO-145-C4 are furnished with automotive type generator and starter. The starter drives through a spur ring gear connected integral with the crankshaft, generator oil pump and tachometer are driven directly from the crankshaft through spur gears. Magnetos are driven through a spur gear by the crankshaft.
DIMENSIONS, WEIGHTS AND PERFORMANCE.—See Table.

THE LYCOMING O-235-B.

This engine, which is rated at 104 h.p., is identical to the O-290 except that the bore is decreased from 4⅞ in. (123.7 m/m.) to 4⅜ in. (111 m/m.), the displacement being correspondingly decreased. For structural details see description of the O-290 and for specifications see Table.

THE LYCOMING O-350.

The Model O-350 is a direct-drive six-cylinder horizontally-opposed air-cooled engine rated at 150 h.p. with an airscrew r.p.m. of 2,500, using 73 octane fuel.

In design and construction this engine is identical to the 190 h.p. O-435-C engine with the exception of the bore and stroke, these being identical to the 104 h.p. O-235-B engine.

THE LYCOMING O-290 AND O-435 SERIES.

TYPE.—Four-cylinder (O-290) six-cylinder (O-435) horizontally-opposed air-cooled incorporating the same major components.
CYLINDERS.—Bore 4⅞ in. (123.7 m/m.), Stroke 3⅞ in. (98.4 m/m.). Aluminium-alloy heads screwed and shrunk on to steel barrels. Cylinder assemblies attached to crankcase by studs and nuts. Two aluminium-bronze spark-plug bushings screwed and shrunk into heads on opposite sides.
PISTONS.—Aluminium-alloy pistons with two compression and two oil control rings. Fully floating gudgeon-pins with aluminium-alloy retaining plugs.
CRANKCASE.—Aluminium-alloy casting split on the vertical centre-line. Four copper-lead steel-backed main bearings on the four-cylinder model. Additional ball-thrust bearing at forward end

The 75 h.p. Lycoming O-145-C four-cylinder engine.

The 125 h.p. Lycoming O-290-C four-cylinder engine.

The 190 h.p. Lycoming O-435-C six-cylinder engine.

LYCOMING FLAT-FOUR ENGINES

	O-145-A	O-145-B	O-145-C	GO-145-C	O-235-B	O-235-C	O-2 90-C	GO-290-A
No. of Cylinders	4	4	4	4	4	4	4	4
Bore × Stroke	$3\frac{5}{8}$ in. × $3\frac{1}{2}$ in. (92×89 m/m.)	$3\frac{5}{8}$ in. × $3\frac{1}{2}$ in. (92×89 m/m.)	$3\frac{5}{8}$ in. × $3\frac{1}{2}$ in. (92×89 m/m.)	$3\frac{5}{8}$ in. × $3\frac{1}{2}$ in. (92×89 m/m.)	$4\frac{3}{8}$ in. × $3\frac{7}{8}$ in. 111×98.4 m/m.)	$4\frac{3}{8}$ in. × $3\frac{7}{8}$ in. (111×98.4 m/m.)	$4\frac{7}{8}$ in. × $3\frac{7}{8}$ in. (123.7×98.4 m/m.)	$4\frac{7}{8}$ in. × $3\frac{7}{8}$ in. (123.7×98.4 m/m.)
Capacity	145 cu. in. (2.37 litres)	145 cu. in. (2.37 litres)	145 cu. in. (2.37 litres)	145 cu. in. (2.37 litres)	233 cu. in. (3.85 litres)	233 cu. in. (3.85 litres)	289 cu. in. (4.75 litres)	289 cu. in. (4.75 litres)
Comp. Ratio	56.5 : 1	6.5 : 1	6.5 : 1	6.5 : 1	6.25 : 1	6.25 : 1	6.5 : 1	7.5 : 1
Normal Output	55 h.p. at 2,300 r.p.m.	65 h.p. at 2,550 r.p.m.	75 h.p. at 3,100 r.p.m.	75 h.p. at 3,200 r.p.m.	104 h.p. at 2,600 r.p.m.	104 h.p. at 2,600 r.p.m.	125 h.p. at 2,600 r.p.m. (130 h.p. Take-off) at 2,800 r.p.m.)	145 h.p. at 3,000 r.p.m.
Octane No.	73	73	73	73	73	73	73	87
Weight Dry	A2 : 163.4 lb. (74.0 kg.) A3 : 165.3 lb. (75.0 kg.) A4 : 200.36 lb. (90.9 kg.)	B2 : 163.4 lb. (74.2 kg.) B3 : 165.6 lb. (75.3 kg.) B4 : 200.5 lbs. (91 kg.)	C2 : 163.4 lb. (74.2 kg.) C3 : 165.6 lb. (75.3 kg.) C4 : 200.5 lbs. (91 kg.)	C2 : 196.4 lb. (89.2 kg.) C3 : 198.6 lb. (90.2 kg.) C4 : 233.5 lb. (106 kg.)	239 lb. (108.5 kg.)	244.3 lb. (110.9 kg.)	241.8 lb. (109.8 kg.)	330.26 lb. (149.9 kg.)
Overall Length	A2, A3 24.62 in. (0.625 m.) A4 : 26 in. (0.658 m.)	B2, B3 24.62 in. (0.625 m.) B4 : 26 in. (0.658 m.)	C2, C3 24.62 in. (0.625 m.) C4 : 26 in. (0.658 m.)	C2, C3 29.31 in. 0.744 m.) C4 : 30.69 in. (0.78 m.)	30.09 in. (0.763 m.)	31.54 in. (0.802 m.)	30.09 in. (0.763 m.)	—
Overall Width	A2, A3, A4 29.56 in. (0.75 m.)	B2, B3, B4 29.56 in. (0.75 m.)	C2, C3, C4 29.56 in. (0.75 m.)	C2, C3, C4 29.56 in. (0.75 m.)	32.32 in. (0.821 m.)	32.32 in. (0.821 m.)	32.32 in. (0.821 m.)	32.32 in. (0.821 m.)
Overall Height	A2 : 20.59 in. (0.518 m.) A3 : 22.59 in. (6.573 m.) A4 : 23 in. (0.584 m.)	B2 : 20.59 in. (0.518 m.) B3 : 22.59 in. (0.573 m.) B4 : 23 in. (0.584 m.)	C2 : 20.59 in. (0.518 m.) C3 : 22.59 in. (0.573 m.) C4 : 23 in. (0.584 m.)	C2 : 20.59 in. (0.518 m.) C3 : 22.59 in. (0.573 m.) C4 : 23 in. (0.584 m.)	25.2 in. (0.64 m.)	25.2 in. (0.64 m.)	26.64 in. (0.677 m.)	26.64 in. (0.677 m.)
Gear Ratio	Direct	Direct	Direct	17 : 27	Direct	Direct	Direct	77 : 120

LYCOMING FLAT-SIX ENGINES

	O-435-A*	O-435-C	GO-435	GO-435-B
No. of Cylinders ..	6	6	6	6
Bore × Stroke ..	$4\frac{7}{8}$ in. × $3\frac{7}{8}$ in. (123.7 × 98.4 m/m.)	$4\frac{7}{8}$ in. × $3\frac{7}{8}$ in. (123.7 × 98.4 m/m.)	$4\frac{7}{8}$ in. × $3\frac{7}{8}$ in. (123.7 × 98.4 m/m.)	$4\frac{3}{8}$ in. × $3\frac{7}{8}$ in. (123.7 × 98.4 m/m.)
Capacity	434 cu. in. (7.1 litres)	434 cu. in. (7.1 litres)	434 cu. in. (7.1 litres)	434 cu. in. (7.1 litres)
Compression Ratio ..	6.5 : 1	6.5 : 1	6.5 : 1	7.5 : 1
Normal Output ..	190 h.p. at 2,550 r.p.m.	190 h.p. at 2,550 r.p.m.	210 h.p. at 3,000 r.p.m. (airscrew speed 1,925)	220 h.p. at 3,000 r.p.m. (airscrew speed 1,935)
Octane No.	73	73	73	73
Weight Dry	379.37 lb. (172.2 kg.)	350.12 lb. (158.9 kg.)	399.2 lb. (181.2 kg.)	401.10 lb. (182.1 kg.)
Overall Length ..	46.32 in. (1.177 m.)	45.48 in. (1.156 m.)	47.70 in. (1.232 m.)	47.70 in. (1.232 m.)
Overall Width ..	32.32 in. (0.823 m.)	32.32 in. (0.821 m.)	32.32 in. (0.821 m.)	32.32 in. (0.821 m.)
Overall Height ..	28.04 in. (0.713 m.)	28.04 in. (0.713 m.)	29.61 in. (0.752 m.)	29.61 in. (0.752 m).
Gear Ratio ..	Direct Drive	Direct Drive	77 : 120	77 : 120

* Letter "A" denotes automotive type accessories are furnished with the engine. All other models are furnished without accessories but include accessory drives for use with Eclipse type equipment.

of case on the six-cylinder model. Halves of case secured by studs and nuts.

Induction.—Marvel-Schebler single barrel carburettor attached to bottom of oil sump casting. The distributing zone is submerged in oil. Separate induction pipes lead to inlet valves.

Ignition.—Dual Scintilla magnetos driven by spur gears from the timing gear.

Lubrication.—Full pressure type, including valve mechanism. Crankshaft equipped with centrifugal sludge-removers. Pistons, gudgeon pins and accessory drive gears lubricated by splash. Sump capacity (O-290) 2 U.S. gallons (7.516 litres) and (O-435) 3 U.S. gallons (11.355 litres).

Accessories.—Drive for dual magneto, starter, generator and single tachometer are standard. In addition drives for fuel pump, vacuum pump, generator and dual tachometers can be supplied.

Dimensions, Weights and Performance.—See Table.

LYCOMING HELICOPTER ENGINES.

Lycoming opposed air-cooled engines for use in helicopters are arranged to be mounted with the crankshaft in a vertical plane. The standard AN splined drive-shaft is replaced with a flange for close-coupled attachment to the free-wheeling device or clutch.

As a helicopter operates without any particular velocity relative to the surrounding air it is necessary to provide a power-driven cooling-fan. Lycoming engines are equipped with an axial-flow fan mounted on the upper end of the crankshaft with diffuser-vanes below the fan. Cowling is provided to direct the air flow around the cylinders for proper cooling and through a duct to an oil cooler.

Owing to height limitations the six-cylinder engines are operated dry sump. The accessories are mounted radially and the bottom of the accessory housing provides a small sump for the scavenge pump.

The four-cylinder engines being shorter are arranged with a wet sump below the accessory housing. The accessories are arranged parallel to the crankshaft centre-line.

The induction system is disposed on the side of the engine opposite the cooling air cowling for use with a vertical carburettor.

The following particulars relate to the O-435-D engine which forms the power-plant of the Sikorsky R-6 helicopter.

Number of Cylinders	6
Bore and Stroke ..	$4\frac{7}{8}$ in. × $3\frac{7}{8}$ in. (123.7 × 98.4 m/m.)
Capacity	434 cu. in. (7.1 litres)
Compression Ratio ..	7.50 : 1
Normal Output ..	212 h.p. at 3,000 r.p.m. at sea level
Octane No.	100
Weight dry	433 lbs. (196.58 kg.) with cooling fan and cooling system
Height	43.50 in. (1.105 m.)
Width (maximum) ..	33.50 in. (0.824 m.)
Width (minimum) ..	30.00 in. (0.762 m.)

THE LYCOMING R-680 SERIES.

The production models of the Lycoming nine-cylinder radial air-cooled engines are divided into two groups: the R-680-E Series and the R-680-B4E Series. The basic design features and the construction details are essentially similar for both series, thus providing maximum interchangeability of parts. The R-680-E series engines only may be equipped with either controllable or fixed-pitch airscrews. The R-680-B4E is available as a trainer engine with front exhaust collector for use without cylinder air baffles.

Type.—Nine-cylinder air-cooled radial.

Cylinders.—Bore $4\frac{5}{8}$ in. (117 m/m.), Stroke $4\frac{1}{2}$ in. (114 m/m.). Displacement 680.4 cub. in. (11.15 litres). Forged steel barrels with integral fins heat-treated between machining operations. Aluminium-alloy heads screwed and shrunk on. Hemispherical combustion chamber. Cylinder-head, with enclosed-type valve-rocker boxes and cooling fins integral, is machined from an aluminium-alloy casting. Intake and exhaust valve-seats of aluminium-bronze, hardened steel exhaust-valve guide, aluminium-bronze intake-valve guide, and aluminium-bronze spark-plug bushings are shrunk into head.

Pistons.—Forged aluminium-alloy, ribbed on inside for increased strength and cooling. Three compression rings and one oil regulator ring above gudgeon pin, one scraper ring below. Gudgeon pins float in both pistons and connecting rods.

Connecting Rods.—Solid "H"-section master-rod of forged chrome-nickel steel with eight interchangeable articulated rods. The solid big-end carries a steel-backed high-lead bronze bearing and is provided with flanges on each side which form the supports for the link-pins of the articulated rods. Articulated rods are of forged steel. Bronze bushings in both ends of articulated rods which in turn bear directly on "Nitralloy" link-pin and gudgeon pins. The articulated rod link-pins are locked into the master-rod by clamping plates, one for each two pins. Master rod is in No. 7 cylinder, one of the lower cylinders, to insure proper lubrication when starting and idling.

Crankshaft.—Single-throw two-piece forging of special alloy steel—hollowed for oil circulation and lightness. Counterweights are forged integral with the crank-cheeks. Shaft carried on two main

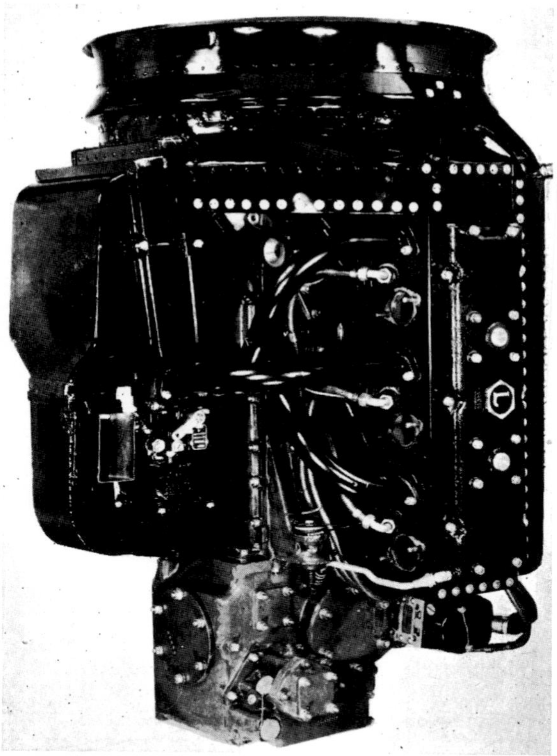

The 212 h.p. Lycoming O-435-D helicopter engine.

ball-bearings and one deep-groove ball-thrust bearing. Rear crankshaft section consists of rear crankcheek, with integral counterweight, and rear main bearing hub. End of crankcheek is split through crank-pin bore, to permit proper clamping action on crank-pin when clamping bolt and nut are tightened. Rear main bearing hub is bored for removable splined bushing which drives accessory drive-shaft.

Crankcase.—Four component sections, secured together on flanged surfaces by studs and nuts to form rigid assembly. Thrust-bearing housing (front section) and accessory-drive housing (rear section) are machined from magnesium-alloy castings. Front main bearing plate is machined from aluminium-alloy forging. Each section is heat-treated prior to final machining. Eight mounting lugs on rear circumference of main crankcase section. Front main bearing plate, attached to front of main crankcase, supports front main ball or roller-bearing and cam-idler assembly. Thrust-bearing housing supports airscrew thrust ball-bearing and contains cam followers and guides. This section is drilled for operation of hydro-controllable airscrew. Accessory-drive housing, at rear of main crankcase, supports a self-aligning ball-bearing for accessory-drive shaft.

Valve Gear.—One inlet and one exhaust valve per cylinder at 30° to centre-line, both of tungsten steel, first is solid, second sodium-cooled.

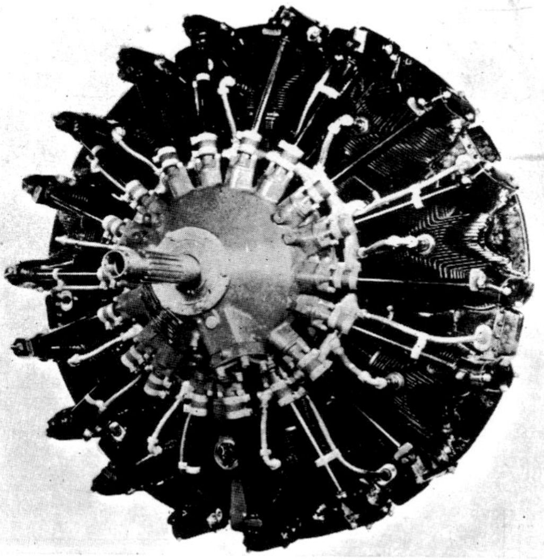

The 285 h.p. Lycoming R-680-E3A nine-cylinder radial engine.

Carburation.—Bendix-Stromberg Model NA-R7A single-barrel carburettor, with economiser, metering-type mixture control, and accelerating pump. A 12⅜ in. dia. cast magnesium impeller.

Ignition.—One dual Scintilla magneto fires two sparking-plugs per cylinder through two distributors on rear case.

Lubrication System.—Full-pressure type, except for reduced-pressure engine oil led to valve-rocker bearings. Cylinder walls and gudgeon pins are lubricated by excess oil thrown from crank-pin. One pressure pump and two scavenging pumps in one complete unit, mounted in lower left side of accessory drive housing.

Airscrew Drive.—Direct. Rotation, from airscrew end, anti-clockwise. Splines AN Std. No. 20.

Dimensions (R-680 all types).—Overall diameter 43.5 in. (1,104.9 m/m.), Overall length 37.03 in. (940.5 m/m.), Diameter of mounting bolt circle 19.25 in. (489 m/m.), Mounting bolts (8) Diameter ⅜ in. (9.53 m/m.).

Weights and Performance.—See Table below.

LYCOMING R-680 RADIAL SERIES

	R-680-B4E	R-680-E3A
No. of Cylinders ..	9	9
Bore	4⅝ in. (117 m/m.)	4⅝ in. (117 m/m.)
Stroke	4½ in. (114 m/m.)	4½ in. (114 m/m.)
Capacity	680 cu. in. (11.15 litres)	680 cu. in. (11.15 litres)
Compression Ratio ..	5.5/1	7/1
Rotation	R.H. Tractor	R.H. Tractor
Gear Ratio	Direct	Direct
Diameter	43.5 in. (1,105 m/m.)	43.5 in. (1,105 m/m.)
Length	37.5 in. (953.1 m/m.)	37.5 in.) (953.1 m/m.)
Octane No.	73	87
Weight	492 lb. (223.5 kg.)	515.46 lb. (233.9 kg.)
Take-off Power ..	—	300 h.p. at 2,300 r.p.m.
International Rating	225 h.p. at 2,100 r.p.m.	285 h.p. at 2,200 r.p.m.

PACKARD.

THE AIRCRAFT ENGINE DIVISION OF THE PACKARD MOTOR CAR COMPANY.

Head Office and Works: Detroit, Mich.

President and General Manager: G. T. Christopher.
Vice-President in charge of Engineering: J. G. Vincent.
Factory Manager: R. N. Brown.
Director of Engineering: Arthur Nutt.

The Packard Motor Car Co. was incorporated in 1900 for the purpose of manufacturing automobiles, and first entered the Aircraft Industry in 1915. The first experimental Liberty engines were developed by the company and 6,500 of these engines were built under contract during the War.

In 1928, the Packard Company developed the first Diesel air-cooled radial aero-engine. This engine had an official rating from the U.S. Department of Commerce of 225 h.p. at 1,950 r.p.m., and on May 25-28, 1931, a World's Non-refuelling Endurance Record of 84 hrs. 33 mins. was made at Jacksonville, Fla., by Messrs. Walter Lees and Frederick Brossy, in a Bellanca Pacemaker fitted with one of these engines.

In September, 1940, the Packard Company undertook to build the Rolls-Royce Merlin engine for both the American and British Governments. The first two Packard-built Merlin engines to be completed were set in motion on their test-beds at a special ceremony which was held at the Detroit works on August 2, 1941.

Packard-built Rolls-Royce Merlin engines were in full production from 1942. The original Merlin 28 was built under the designation V-1650-1 and supplied for installation in the Curtiss P-40F Warhawk and in the D.H. Mosquito and Avro Lancaster, both British and Canadian built.

In 1944-45 the Packard company was producing the V-1650-3 and V-1650-7. These engines were substantially the same as the Merlin 61 with two-speed two-stage supercharger and were installed in the North American P-51D and R.A.F. Mustang III.

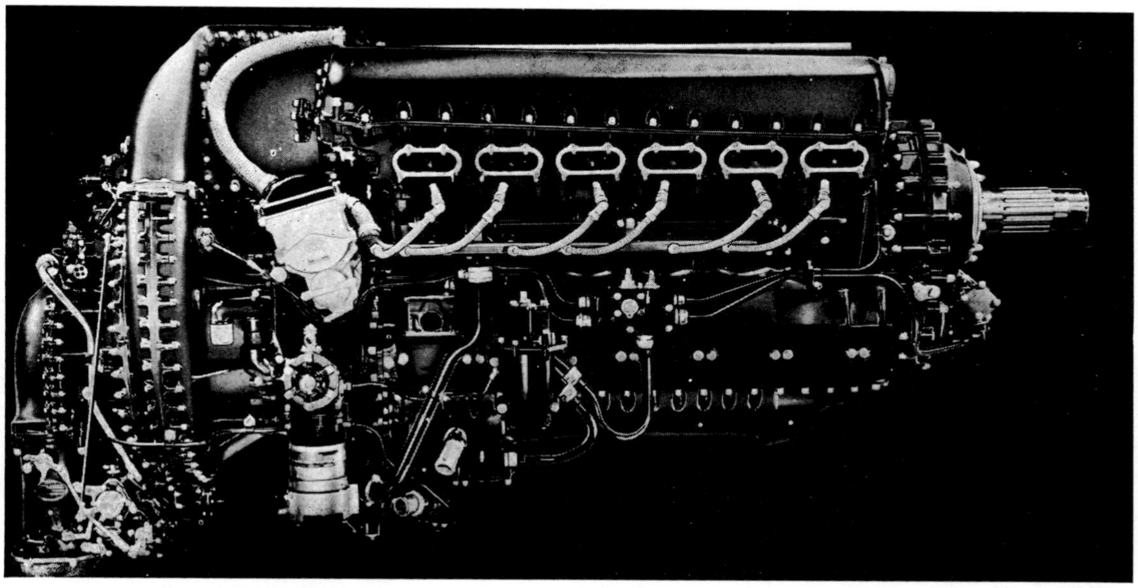

The Packard V-1650-3 (Rolls-Royce Merlin 68) twelve-cylinder Vee liquid-cooled engine with two-speed two-stage supercharger.

Packard-built Rolls-Royce Merlin 68, Merlin 69 and Merlin 266 engines of the two-speed two-stage supercharger type were used in the later versions of the D.H. Mosquito, Avro Lancaster and Supermarine Spitfire.

PRATT & WHITNEY.

THE PRATT & WHITNEY AIRCRAFT DIVISION OF THE UNITED AIRCRAFT CORPORATION.

Head Office and Works: East Hartford 8, Connecticut.
Established: 1925.
General Manager: William P. Gwinn.
Engineering Manager: Wright A. Parkins.
Chief Engineer: A. V. D. Willgoos.
Sales Manager: T. E. Tillinghast.
Factory Manager: G. H. D. Miller.

The Pratt & Whitney Aircraft Division of the United Aircraft Corpn. concentrates on the manufacture of high-powered radial air-cooled engines. It was founded in 1925 by a small group of aeronautical engine experts as the Pratt & Whitney Aircraft Company and has since become affiliated as a division of the United Aircraft Corpn.

During the war period, military requirements for Pratt & Whitney engines necessitated continual and very large expansion of production facilities. New construction at the main plant in East Hartford was supplemented by the establishment of five satellite plants within a twenty-five mile radius. The organization's licensees also expended proportionately. Four automotive companies—Ford, Buick, Chevrolet and Nash-Kelvinator—and two aviation companies—Jacobs and Continental—were building Pratt & Whitney engines at a nominal licence fee of $1 per engine.

In addition to the above expansion and production by licensees, the Pratt & Whitney Aircraft Corporation of Missouri also operated a new government-financed plant at Kansas City.

THE PRATT & WHITNEY WASP-JUNIOR R-985 SERIES.

Type.—Nine-cylinder air-cooled radial.

Cylinders.—Bore and Stroke $5\frac{3}{16}$ in. (131.76 m/m). Capacity 985 cub. in. (16.14 litres). Compression ratio 6 : 1. Built up of cast-aluminium head with integral valve mechanism housing screwed and shrunk on a forged chrome-molybdenum-steel barrel having integral fins. Individually removable baffles, providing uniform air distribution under severe flight conditions.

Pistons.—Machined from aluminium-alloy forgings. Pistons have flat heads with recesses for both intake and exhaust valves. Underside of piston head ribbed for strength and increased cooling area. Three compression rings and two dual oil-control rings and one oil-scraper ring each.

Connecting Rods.—Solid master-rod, in which big-end lead-bronze bearing bears directly on crank-pin. Eight "I"-section articulated rods attached by knuckle-pins to master-rod. Each rod bronze-bushed for both gudgeon and knuckle-pin.

Crankshaft.—Single-throw two-piece type, machined from forged alloy-steel. Shaft supported by three bearings, one roller on each side of crank, with ball thrust-bearing in nose section.

Crankcase.—Nose section is a hemispherical magnesium casting. It encloses cam and operating mechanism and carries valve-tappets. Main crankcase, in two similar sections machined together, divided

THE PRATT & WHITNEY WASP-JUNIOR R-985 SERIES.

Engine Model	Take-off Power	Normal Rating	Military Rating	Compression Ratio	Blower Ratio	Gear Ratio	Weight Dry	Diameter	Octane No.
T1B3	450 h.p. at 2,300 r.p.m.	450 h.p. at 2,300 r.p.m.	—	6 : 1	10 : 1	Direct-drive	668 lb. (303 kg.)	46.06 in. (1.170 m.)	91
SB3	450 h.p. at 2,300 r.p.m.	400 h.p. at 2,200 r.p.m. at 5,000 ft. (1,525 m.)	450 h.p. at 2,300 r.p.m. at 3,500 ft. (1,065 m.)	6 : 1	10 : 1	Direct-drive	668 lb. (303 kg.)	46.06 in. (1.170 m.)	91

THE PRATT & WHITNEY WASP R-1340 SERIES.

Engine Model	Take-off Power	Normal Rating	Military Rating	Compression Ratio	Blower Ratio	Gear Ratio	Weight Dry	Diameter	Octane No.
S1H1	600 h.p. at 2,250 r.p.m.	550 h.p. at 2,200 r.p.m. at 8,000 ft. (2,440 m.)	600 h.p. at 2,250 r.p.m. at 6,200 ft. (1,890 m.)	6 : 1	12 : 1	Direct-drive	864 lb. (392 kg.)	51.75 in. (1.314 m.)	91
S3H1	600 h.p. at 2,250 r.p.m.	550 h.p. at 2,200 r.p.m. at 5,000 ft. (1,525 m.)	600 h.p. at 2,250 r.p.m. at 3,000 ft. (915 m.)	6 : 1	12 : 1	Direct-drive	864 lb. (392 kg.)	51.75 in. (1.314 m.)	91
S1H1-G	600 h.p. at 2,250 r.p.m.	550 h.p. at 2,200 r.p.m. at 8,000 ft. (2,440 m.)	600 h.p. at 2,250 r.p.m. at 6,200 ft. (1,890 m.)	6 : 1	12 : 1	3 : 2	930 lb. (422 kg.)	51.75 in. (1.314 m.)	91

THE PRATT & WHITNEY TWIN-WASP R-1830 SERIES

Engine Model	Take-off Power	Normal Rating (low blower)	Normal Rating (high blower)	Military Rating (low blower)	Military Rating (high blower)	Compression Ratio	Gear Ratio	Weight Dry	Diameter	Fuel Grade *
S1C3-G	1,200 h.p. at 2,700 r.p.m.	1,050 h.p. at 2,550 r.p.m. at 7,500 ft. (2,285 m.)	—	1,200 h.p. at 2,700 r.p.m. at 3,700 ft. (1,130 m.)	—	6.7 : 1	.667 : 1 or .5625 : 1	1,438 lb. (652 kg.)	48.13 in. (1.222 m.)	125
S3C4-G	1,200 h.p. at 2,700 r.p.m.	1,100 h.p. at 2,550 r.p.m. at 6,200 ft. (1,890 m.)	1,000 h.p. at 2,550 r.p.m. at 12,500 ft. (3,810 m.)	1,200 h.p. at 2,700 r.p.m. at 4,900 ft. (1,495 m.)	1,050 h.p. at 2,700 r.p.m. at 13,100 ft. (3,995 m.)	6.7 : 1	.667 : 1 or .5625 : 1	1,460 lb. (662 kg.)	48.13 in. (1.222 m.)	125
S4C4-G	1,200 h.p. at 2,700 r.p.m.	1,050 h.p. at 2,550 r.p.m. at 7,500 ft. (2,285 m.)	900 h.p. at 2,550 r.p.m. at 15,400 ft. (4,695 m.)	1,200 h.p. at 2,700 r.p.m. at 3,700 ft. (1,130 m.)	900 h.p. at 2,700 r.p.m. at 17,400 ft. 5,305 m.)	6.7. : 1	.667 : 1 or .5625 : 1	1,460 lb. (662 kg.)	48.13 in. (1.222 m).	125

* Fuel Grade 125. Anti-knock value, lean mixture 99 by A.S.T.M. D. 357-41 T method.
Anti-knock value, rich mixture S × 1.0 cc. by C.F.R. 3C method.

on centre-line of cylinders and united by through-bolts and cylinder flanges, is forged from aluminium-alloy. Blower section contains centrifugal supercharger and mounting lugs for installing engine. Accessory section, in rear, carries all accessories and has integrally-cast vanes in carburettor intake elbow for balanced diffusion of mixture.

VALVE GEAR.—Completely enclosed. Cam-drum, rotating counter-clockwise at one-eighth crankshaft speed, drives overhead valves through push-rods and rocker-arms.

INDUCTION SYSTEM.—Stromberg self-priming carburettor with idle cut-off, primer tubing and distributor. Mixture is fed from carburettor through intake elbow containing the diffuser vanes mentioned above to the supercharger and diffuser in the blower section and thence to cylinders by tangential intake pipes.

SUPERCHARGER.—Built-in centrifugal type. Impeller-shaft in line with crankcase and driven from it through a spring-coupling mounted inside the rear crankshaft gear.

IGNITION.—Two Scintilla magnetos located on accessory section, each firing spark-plugs in all nine cylinders independently. Pratt & Whitney type dual ignition manifold, front and rear, provides shorter leads to spark-plugs. Radio shielding is incorporated.

LUBRICATION.—Forced lubrication by gear pump in rear section. Oil is passed through blower section, then through lower part of the power section above sump and into separate line in nose section which contains airscrew control-valve. Pressure oil from the nose is led through distributing grooves around the tappets, to metering ports, whence push-rods and valve-gear are automatically lubricated under constant pressure. Master-rod bearing, knuckle-pin bushings, cam and cam-gear are all force-lubricated from pressure oil. Accessory shafts and supercharger gearing are lubricated by drilled passages from oil-strainer chamber in rear section and an oil-jet in the main oil-feed line. All other parts are lubricated by mist or spray from pressure-oiled parts.

ACCESSORY DRIVES.—Accessories all grouped in rear, driven by three lay-shafts extending entirely through blower and rear sections ; Each shaft carries a spur-gear at its forward end, which engages drive-gear attached to rear of crankshaft. Upper shaft provides drive for starter and generator. Each of two lower shafts drives one magneto through an adjustable coupling. By a bevel-gear on each lower shaft four vertical drives are provided. The upper ends of these are drives for various types of accessory pumps or gun-synchronisers. Two tachometers projecting outwards from the rear case are driven through worm gears at right angles to the vertical shafts. The lower shafts driven from the same bevel gear drive the oil pump on the right and the fuel pump on the left. On the left side of the engine a third bevel gear suitable for driving a vacuum pump or hydraulic pump meshes with bevel gear on the magneto drive shaft. Drives or accessory pumps (or gun-synchronisers) and two tachometers. Lower shafts drive oil pump on right and fuel pump on left : also provision for angle-drive on lower left side.

DIMENSIONS, WEIGHTS AND PERFORMANCE.—See Table.

THE PRATT & WHITNEY WASP R-1340 SERIES.

The description of the "Wasp" is generally similar to that of the "Wasp Junior" except for the following.

CYLINDERS.—Bore and Stroke 5¾ in. (146 m/m.), Displacement 1,344 cub. in. (22 litres).

CRANKCASE.—On geared-drive engines, the nose section is a hemispherical aluminium forging, which houses the planetary reduction gears. There is a pad for mounting the airscrew governor. The

The 450 h.p. Pratt & Whitney "Wasp-Junior" R-985 radial air-cooled engine.

airscrew thrust bearing is mounted at the front end of the nose section. The front main crankcase also supports the cam and cam reduction gear. Valve tappets mounted in guides are located in an extension of front main crankcase directly over the cam track.

LUBRICATION.—Direct-drive engine lubricated by gear type pump located in rear section as in "Wasp-Junior," except for internal piping instead of drilled passages in the lower part of the lower section. Geared engines are similar except that there is an oil feed pipe in the reduction gear housing that carries oil to the ball thrust bearing and reduction gears.

REDUCTION GEAR.—Comprises a drive gear splined to the crankshaft and supported by a roller bearing in the anchor plate. A fixed gear is bolted to the nose section and meshes with the six pinions in the gear cage that is splined to the airscrew shaft. Gear ratio 3 : 2.

DIMENSIONS, WEIGHTS AND PERFORMANCE.—See Table.

THE PRATT & WHITNEY TWIN-WASP R-1830 SERIES.

TYPE.—Fourteen-cylinder two-row air-cooled radial.

CYLINDERS.—Bore and Stroke 5½ in. (139.50 m/m.), Capacity 1,830 cub. in. (30 litres). Compression ratio 6.7 : 1. Built up of cast aluminium head, with integral valve mechanism housing, screwed and shrunk on a forged steel cylinder barrel having integral fins. Exhaust ports have shrunk-in stainless-steel liners providing slip joint with exhaust steel pipes. Chrome-molybdenum cylinder-barrels are machined from steel forging, tapered towards hemispherical combustion chamber, thus compensating for expansion and providing longer life. Aluminium-bronze valve-seats for intake, steel for exhaust, are shrunk into head. Pressure-baffles to provide uniform cooling to entire cylinder in all flight conditions standard.

PISTONS.—Forged aluminium, ribbed on under side of head for strength, have finned inner skirts for additional cooling surface. Three compression rings, one oil scraper ring and one dual oil control ring each.

CONNECTING RODS.—Two-piece master-rod, with detachable big-end cap and lead-silver bearing and six "I"-section articulated rods for each row. Each articulated rod is bronze-bushed for both gudgeon and knuckle-pins.

CRANKSHAFT.—Two-throw one-piece type, supported by three roller-bearings in crankcase sections, and located by the front main bearing. Airscrew-shaft is supported within crankshaft by lead-copper pilot bearing and in nose section by deep-groove ball-bearing which absorbs engine thrust.

CRANKCASE.—In six sections. Power sections machined together from aluminium forgings. Nose section houses reduction gears and has provision for Hamilton-Standard Hydromatic full-feathering, or other controllable airscrews. A drilled oil passage in upper part of nose section provides means for operating airscrew pitch control. Power sections joined by through-bolts. Blower section, bolted to power section, contains supercharger and carries bronze-bushed forged steel lugs for mounting bolts. Blower intermediate section, bolted to blower section, carries down-draught carburettor and impeller gear train. Accessory section of new design is bolted to blower intermediate section.

VALVE GEAR.—One inlet and one exhaust valve per cylinder. Exhaust valves are sodium-cooled and have stellite seats. Actuated by ball-bearing rocker-arms and push-rods of heat-treated aluminium-alloy with hardened steel ball-ends. Two shelf-mounted cams, one in front power section and one in rear, are driven by spur reduction gears directly off crankshaft at one-eighth crankshaft speed. All valve gear, including push-rods, is completely enclosed and oil-tight. Internally-drilled passages provide lubrication for push-rods and rocker-arm bearings.

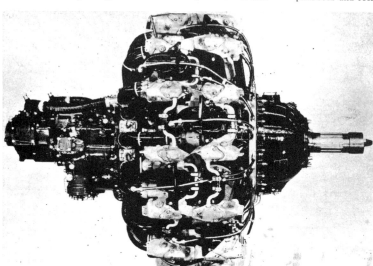

A Buick-built 1,200 h.p. Pratt & Whitney R-1830 Twin-Wasp engine.

SUPERCHARGER.—Several types available, such as single-stage single-speed, single-stage two-speed, or two-stage two-speed. Large diameter impeller of improved design, carried by high-capacity ball-bearings, is driven by dual intermediate gears containing spring-type flexible drives to absorb shocks and to equalize driving loads.

INDUCTION SYSTEM.—One Stromberg injection carburettor with automatic mixture control, idle cut-off, primer tubing and distributor, from which mixture passes through vanes in intermediate rear section of supercharger, through diffuser plate and induction passages, providing uniform distribution and contributing to improved performance at height levels.

IGNITION.—Two Scintilla flange-mounted magnetos each operate independent set of spark-plugs through single ignition manifold which is attached to the front of the power section to simplify maintenance and provide shortest possible leads. Radio shielding is standard.

LUBRICATION.—Forced-feed lubrication by gear type oil pump with separate low-pressure system to accessory drives in rear-section regulated by independent low-pressure relief-valve. Inter-rocker box and inter-cylinder drain-pipes connect to separate sump from which the return oil is scavenged by pump located in nose.

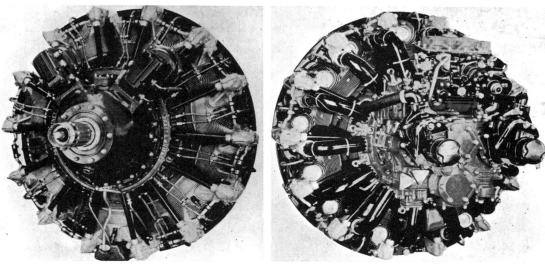

The Pratt & Whitney Twin-Wasp R-1830 fourteen-cylinder radial air-cooled engine.

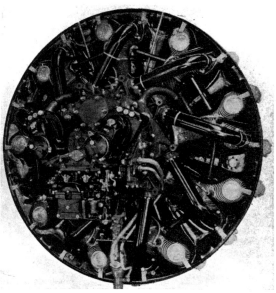

The Pratt & Whitney Wasp R-1340 nine-cylinder radial air-cooled engine.

REDUCTION GEAR.—Pratt & Whitney planetary reduction gear. Optionally, spur gear .667 : 1, or bevel gear .5625 : 1.

ACCESSORY DRIVES.—All accessories are grouped in the rear and are driven through an intermediate gear train by a single-drive shaft splined directly to the rear of the crankshaft. Provision is made to drive two gun-synchronizers or auxiliary accessory pumps, two magnetos, two tachometers, vacuum pump, oil pump, fuel pump, starter and generator drives. Generator drive may be used as a 30 h.p. take-off to drive a remote accessory gear-box. Pressure lubrication through drilled passages is provided for vacuum pump drive and gun-synchronizer or auxiliary drives.

DIMENSIONS, WEIGHTS AND PERFORMANCE.—See Table.

THE PRATT & WHITNEY TWIN-WASP R-2000 SERIES.

The R-2000 Twin-Wasp is a development of the R-1830 Series. As its designation implies it is of slightly bigger capacity and has a maximum output of 1,350 h.p.

The R-2000 has new cylinders with the bore increased to 5.75 in. (146 m/m.), but retains the crankcase, crankshaft, connecting-rods, etc., of the R-1830. It was designed for use in the Douglas DC-4 (C-54) and is not installed in any other aeroplane.

THE PRATT & WHITNEY DOUBLE-WASP R-2800 SERIES.

The general construction of the Double-Wasp is similar to that of the Twin-Wasp previously described.

TYPE.—Eighteen-cylinder two-row air-cooled radial.

CYLINDERS.—Bore 5¾ in. (146 m/m.), Stroke 6 in. (152.4 m/m.). Capacity 2,804 cub. in. (45.9 litres). Compression ratio 6.7 : 1.

INDUCTION.—Stromberg PT-13F1 injection carburettor with automatic mixture control and idle cut-off, primer tubing and distributor.

IGNITION.—One double Scintilla DF-3 shielded and compensated magneto and two distributors mounted on the reduction gear casing. Complete radio shielding.

REDUCTION GEAR.—Spur-gear planetary type. Alternate ratios of .400, .500 or .5625 : 1 are available.

ACCESSORIES.—All accessories are grouped in the rear and are driven through an intermediate gear train by a single-drive shaft splined directly to the rear of the crankshaft. Standard drives provided for generator, fuel pump, dual tachometer, vacuum pump, airscrew governor, dual side angular drives for either auxiliary or gun synchroniser drives.

DIMENSIONS, WEIGHTS AND PERFORMANCE.—No data available.

The Pratt & Whitney Double-Wasp R-2800 eighteen-cylinder radial air-cooled engine.

RANGER.

RANGER AIRCRAFT ENGINE DIVISION OF THE FAIRCHILD ENGINE AND AIRPLANE CORPORATION.

HEAD OFFICE AND WORKS : FARMINGDALE, L.I., N.Y.

Chairman of the Board : Sherman M. Fairchild.

President : J. Carlton Ward, Jr.

Vice-President and General Manager : Harold H. Budds.

Chief Engineer : A. T. Gregory.

The Ranger Aircraft Engine Division directs its entire activity to the development of inverted, in-line, air-cooled aircraft engines of six and twelve cylinders.

The Division has devoted its greatly enlarged facilities entirely to the production of engines for the American Armed Forces. Two basic models have been in production, the six-cylinder 6-440C and the twelve-cylinder geared and supercharged SGV-770C-1. Considerable development is being undertaken with the latter engine.

The 6-440 has been used in various training aircraft, notably the Fairchild PT-19 and PT-26. The SGV-770C-1 was the power-plant of the Curtiss SO3C Scout-observation monoplane.

The development of a new inverted Vee twelve-cylinder engine for installation in post-war commercial aircraft was announced in October, 1944. This engine, the SGV-770D-5 is described and illustrated on page 85d.

THE RANGER 6-440C SERIES.

TYPE.—Six-cylinder in-line inverted aircooled.

CYLINDERS.—Bore $4\frac{1}{8}$ in. (104.8 m/m.), Stroke $5\frac{1}{8}$ in. (128.8 m/m.). Capacity 441 cub. in. (7.2 litres). Compression ratio 6.5 : 1. Chrome-molybdenum steel forgings with integral fins and mounting flange. Cast aluminium-alloy heads have integral fins, spherically-machined combustion chamber and are screwed and shrunk on the barrels.

Aluminium-bronze valve-seats, one inlet and one exhaust, are shrunk on to the heads. Two sparking-plug inserts are shrunk in and screwed.

PISTONS.—Machined from aluminium-alloy. Three $\frac{3}{32}$-in. compression rings and one oil scraper ring. Gudgeon pins are of heat-treated alloy, retained by snap rings.

CONNECTING RODS.—I-section machined from chrome-molybdenum steel forgings. Steel-backed cadmium silver bearing shells used for main rod bearings and bronze bushings for the little ends.

CRANKSHAFT.—Six-throw, seven bearing shaft, statically and dynamically balanced to close limits. Main journals and crank-pins are hollow and fitted with oil plugs. These plugs act as

The Ranger 6-440-C six-cylinder inverted air-cooled engine.

The 700 h.p. Ranger SGV-770D-5 twelve-cylinder inverted Vee geared and supercharged engine.

centrifugal oil cleaners and also as oil transfers from main journals to crank-pins. Crank cheeks are drilled for two-way feeding of oil from main journals to crank-pins. Rear end of shaft carries standard starter jaw. Front end has a Standard No. 20 S.A.E. spline for the airscrew hub. Two pendulum-type vibration dampers are located on the first throw (rear) of the crankshaft.

CRANKCASE.—Barrel type of heat-treated aluminium-alloy ribbed for seven main bearings split longitudinally and clamped together by long studs anchored in the upper webs and extending through lower webs. Front section carries airscrew thrust bearing and gears for driving accessory drive shaft and vertical camshaft drive shaft. Rear section carries drive gears for the accessories.

VALVE GEAR.—Underhead camshaft is a heat-treated alloy steel forging carried in housing bolted direct to cylinder-heads. Supported on eight bearings, one at each end and one adjacent to each of six pairs of cams. Valves operated by rocker-arms, provided with crowned roller cam followers and ball-type adjusting screws. From hollow camshaft pressure oil is fed direct to camshaft bearings. Holes drilled in camshaft between each pair of cams supply a spray of oil to rocker-arms, cam followers and adjusting screws. Camshaft housing and cover of magnesium-alloy, cover serving as engine oil sump. Torsional vibration damper on rear of camshaft.

CARBURATION.—One Stromberg or Marvel Schebler updraught carburettor supported on a dividing Tee bolted to crankcase on left side between cylinders 3 and 4. Tee connects carburettor with two pipes leading to two manifolds, each of which supplies three cylinders.

IGNITION.—Two Bendix-Scintilla type SB6R magnetos mounted on upper crankcase at rear. Plain ignition wiring and sparking-plugs. Shielded wiring and sparking-plugs optional.

ACCESSORY DRIVES.—Drives for all accessories, and mounting pads and connections located at convenient points on rear of engine. They consist of starter, generator, fuel pump, vacuum pump and tachometers. Drives are protected from crankshaft torsional vibration and shock loading by a long hollow flexible shaft in top of crankcase upper section. This shaft transmits the drive from the airscrew end to the accessory drives in the rear section and isolates them from any detrimental vibrations. Accessory drive shaft carried in seven main bearings in the crankcase webs and acts as a header for the distribution of oil to main bearings and front end of engine.

LUBRICATION.—Full pressure type. Pump on crankcase rear section feeds oil through hollow engine shafts and cast-in passages, there being no external pressure oil pipes on engine. Return oil draws from crankcase from camshaft housing through camshaft vertical drive shaft and front and drain pipe at rear. Double suction scavenge pump on rear of camshaft housing returns oil through either end of housing to supply tank.

COOLING.—Pressure-type cylinder baffles are standard equipment.

DIMENSIONS.—Length overall 53.156 in. (1.351 m.), Width overall 21.594 in. (0.549 m.), Height overall 33.50 in. (0.854 m.).

WEIGHTS AND PERFORMANCE.—See Table.

THE RANGER SGV-770C-1.

CYLINDERS.—Bore 4 in. (101.6 m/m.), Stroke 5.125 in. (120 m/m.). Capacity 773 cub. in. (12.6 litres). Otherwise as for 6-440C Series.

PISTONS.—Same as for 6-440C Series.

CONNECTING RODS.—Fork-and-blade type. Lead-plated steel-backed copper-lead bearings held in the forked rods, the blade rods bearing on the outer diameter of the shells between the forks.

CRANKSHAFT.—Same as for 6-440C Series.

CRANKCASE.—Same as for 6-440C Series.

VALVE GEAR.—Two underhead camshafts, each driven from a separate vertical drive shaft from front end of crankshaft. Gear and lubrication as for 6-440C Series.

CARBURATION.—Holley non-icing carburettor feeds inlet side of the supercharger housing in the crankcase rear section.

IGNITION.—Scintilla double magneto with two twelve-cylinder distributors on upper crankcase at rear. Radio shielding.

ACCESSORY DRIVES.—Similar to 6-440C Series except that the accessory drive shaft is located in the lower section of the crankcase at the point of the Vee formed by the cylinder-blocks. Accessory drives for starter, generator, gun synchroniser, magneto, distributor, fuel pump, vacuum pump, hydraulic mechanism fuel pump, mechanical tachometer and electric tachometer.

LUBRICATION.—Same as for 6-440C Series.

REDUCTION GEAR.—Gear ratio 3 : 2. Herring-bone type. A short flexible quill shaft with gear-tooth splines at both ends provides drive from the crankshaft to the pinion gear installed concentrically over the quill shaft. This unit floats on two sets of roller-bearings

RANGER AERO-ENGINES

	6-440C-2 Six-cylinder	6-440C-3 Six-cylinder	6-440C-4 Six-cylinder	6-440C-5 Six-cylinder	SGV-770C-1 Twelve-cylinder geared and supercharged
Bore	$4\frac{1}{8}$ in. (104.8 m/m.)	$4\frac{1}{8}$ in. (104.8 m/m.)	$4\frac{1}{8}$ in. (104.8 m/m.)	$4\frac{1}{8}$ in. (104.8 m/m.)	4 in. (101.6 m/m.)
Stroke	$5\frac{1}{8}$ in. (128.8 m/m.)	$5\frac{1}{8}$ in. (128.8 m/m.)	$5\frac{1}{8}$ in. (128.8 m/m.)	$5\frac{1}{8}$ in. (128.8 m/m.)	$5\frac{1}{8}$ in. (120 m/m.)
Capacity	441 cu. in. (7.2 litres)	441 cu. in. (7.2 litres)	441 cu. in. (7.2 litres)	441 cu. in. (7.2 litres)	773 cu. in. (12.6 litres)
Compression Ratio	6.0 : 1	6.2 : 1	6.8 : 1	7.5 : 1	6.5 : 1
Gear Ratio	—	—	—	—	3 : 2
Weight (Dry) including standard equipment	376 lb. (170.7 kg.)	376 lb. (170.7 kg.)	376 lb. (170.7 kg.)	376 lb. (170.7 kg.)	730 lb. (331.4 kg.)
Take-off Power	—	—	—	—	520 h.p. (3,150 r.p.m.)
Rated Power	175 h.p. at 2,450 r.p.m.	180 h.p. at 2,450 r.p.m.	190 h.p. at 2,450 r.p.m.	200 h.p. at 2,450 r.p.m.	450 h.p. at 3,000 r.p.m. to 12,000 ft. (3,660 ft.)
Octane No.	65	73	80	87	87

and is located axially by the meshing of the herring-bone teeth with the teeth of the driven reduction gear. The latter is bolted to the airscrew shaft which, in turn, is mounted directly above the quill shaft on two roller-bearings. Thrust ball-bearing locates the airscrew shaft. Lubrication by controlled metering jet from the pressure lubricating system.

SUPERCHARGER.—Single-speed single-stage type which produces manifold pressure of 45″ of mercury at take-off. Rated manifold pressure is 38.3″ of mercury. Impeller is driven from the flexible accessory drive shaft, thus eliminating need for clutch in supercharger drive. Distribution from supercharger is through two induction pipes. A special Y-fitting on each induction pipe divides the charge equally and distributes it to two cylinders, each of which supplies one bank of cylinders. A special Y-fitting on each induction pipe divides the charge equally and distributes it to two cylinders, each of which supplies three cylinders. Blower ratio 9.5 : 1.

DIMENSIONS.—Length overall 62 in. (1.573 m.), Width overall 28 in. (0.71 m.), Height overall 32.25 in. (0.823 m.).

WEIGHT AND PERFORMANCE.—See Table.

RIGHTER.

RIGHTER MANUFACTURING COMPANY.

HEAD OFFICE AND WORKS : BURBANK, CALIFORNIA.

The Righter Manufacturing Company produces light two-stroke engines which have been used in pre-flight trainers, experimental models and pilotless target aircraft by both the U.S. Army and Navy.

The Righter 2-GS-17 (O-15) engine is a 6 h.p. two-cylinder horizontally-opposed air-cooled two-stroke which can drive either a single direct-drive or two oppositely-rotating tandem propellers.

Several model Righter engines are under development which are considered suitable for or adaptable as auxiliary power units for gliders and sailplanes.

STUDEBAKER.

THE STUDEBAKER CORPORATION.

AERO-ENGINE WORKS : SOUTH BEND, IND., FORT WAYNE, IND., AND CHICAGO, ILL.

During the war The Studebaker Corpn. held contracts for the manufacture of Wright Cyclone R-1920 radial air-cooled engines. Three plants were in operation. The main assembly plant was at South Bend and plants at Fort Wayne and Chicago acted as feeder plants, the former manufacturing gears and the latter connecting rods and precision parts.

WARNER.

THE WARNER AIRCRAFT CORPORATION.

HEAD OFFICE AND WORKS : 20263, HOOVER AVENUE, DETROIT, MICH.

President : W. O. Warner.
Vice-President and Sales Manager : L. A. Faunce.
Vice-President and Chief Engineer : L. A. Majneri.
Secretary : W. J. Jarvie.

The first Scarab was produced by Aeronautical Industries, Inc., in April, 1927. In October of the same year the company assumed its present name. The Warner Scarab-Junior was introduced in 1930, and during 1933, a larger engine, the 145 h.p. Warner Super-Scarab, was designed and built.

The earlier 90 h.p. Scarab Junior, 125 h.p. Scarab and 145 h.p. Super-Scarab engines have been illustrated and described in earlier volumes. Descriptions of the Super-Scarab Model 165 and 185 engines are given below.

THE WARNER R-500 SUPER-SCARAB 165.

TYPE.—Seven-cylinder air-cooled radial.

CYLINDERS.—Bore 4.625 in. (118 m/m.), Stroke 4.25 in. (108 m/m.). Capacity 499 cub. in. (8.2 litres). Compression ratio 6.4 : 1. Alloy steel barrels machined all over and amply provided with cooling fins. Heat-treated aluminium-alloy heads shrunk and bolted to barrels. Intake valve-seats of aluminium-bronze, exhaust valve-seats of austenitic steel.

PISTONS.—Heat-treated aluminium-alloy castings, machined all over. Two compression rings and one scraper ring. Full-floating gudgeon pins.

CONNECTING RODS.—Heat-treated alloy-steel forgings of "I"-section. Master-rod is split type with replaceable lead-bronze steel-backed bearing shell at the crank-pin end. Link-rods are assembled to the master-rod by wrist-pins locked in the link-rods and operating in bronze bearings which are drilled to provide full forced-feed lubrication. Bronze bearings pressed into the small ends.

CRANKSHAFT.—One-piece alloy-steel drop forging, machined all over and heat-treated. Airscrew end machined to an S.A.E. No. 20 spline.

CRANKCASE.—Barrel type of heat-treated aluminium-alloy, cast in two halves and bolted together on the transverse centre-line. In the rear half is inserted a heat-treated machined steel bearing cage and this and two bronze bearing sleeves, which are shrunk and pinned in the front half of the crankcase, form definite locating media for the main shaft ball-bearings, thereby preventing local bearing loads from being transmitted directly to the aluminium crankcase.

VALVE GEAR.—One inlet and one exhaust valve per cylinder. Inlet valve of cobalt chrome steel, exhaust valve of austenitic steel. Rocker-arms completely enclosed in housings cast integral with cylinder-heads. Cam ring is a machined alloy-steel drop forging and hardened on all wearing surfaces. It operates on a replaceable bronze bushing which floats on the heat-treated main bearing sleeve. All valve mechanism is lubricated automatically by a combination pressure-gravity system which originates in the rocker-arm bearings of No. 1 cylinder.

CARBURATION.—One Holley Model 419 carburettor attached to the lower part of the induction housing which is bolted directly to the rear of the crankcase. Separate intake pipes lead directly to each cylinder.

THE RANGER SGV-770D-5.

The SGV-770D-5 is a twelve-cylinder inverted Vee air-cooled engine which has been developed for post-war commercial use. Besides being approximately one-quarter lighter than engines of comparable output, the new engine is far more compact than the ordinary aircraft power-plant. Weighing 870 lbs. (395 kg.), complete with standard accessories the engine is expected to develop 700 h.p. for take-off, or nearly one horsepower per cub. inch of displacement.

Basically the new engine is composed of five major units ; the crankcase and cylinders, right and left camboxes, the nose section and the rear section. In dissembling all can be removed by a single mechanic without the use of a chain-hoist and with a minimum of time and special tools.

The power sections are made of aluminium-alloy. The six-throw crankshaft is dynamically-balanced and the connecting-rods are of the fork and blade type. Ignition is by high tension dual magnetos. The fuel induction system is designed round a new advanced type of pressure carburettor.

Pressure lubrication is of the dry sump type. The hollow accessory drive shaft is the main oil gallery, splash and spray lubricating the cylinder walls, pistons and gudgeon-pins. Valve mechanisms are pressure lubricated.

Pressure air-cooling is employed, the cooling characteristics being enhanced by aluminium cooling fins chemically bonded to the steel barrels by use of the Fairchild Al-Fin process.

The engine will be available with two airscrew reduction gear ratios : 1.65 : 1 and 2.37 : 1. Planetary reduction gears are used. At 3,600 r.p.m. for take-off, the airscrew shaft speed will be 2,180 with the first and 1,520 with the second ratio.

The new engine has an overall height of 31.11 in. (0.79 m.) is 74.92 in. (1.9 m.) long and 33.28 in. (0.846 m.) wide.

The 165 h.p. Warner R-500 Super-Scarab 165 seven-cylinder radial air-cooled engine.

IGNITION.—Dual Scintilla Model VMN7-DF magnetos flange-mounted on rear cover. Two sparking-plugs per cylinder.

ACCESSORY DRIVES.—Mounting pads provided on rear cover for starter, generator, fuel pump, tachometer drive and there are two additional drives. Two drives also provided for the magnetos.

LUBRICATION.—Combination pressure and gravity system. Rocker-arm bearings of No. 1 cylinder are lubricated by oil forced from the pressure system to the rocker-arm shafts. This oil is drained into the rocker-arm housings and, from the housings, is gravity fed to the remaining cylinders, accumulating in the covers of the exhaust rocker-arm housing of No. 5 cylinder and the intake rocker-arm housing cover of No. 4 cylinder. These two covers also act as a sump for the oil which is drained from the crankcase through the push-rod tubes. The scavenging pump picks up the oil at this point and returns it to the oil tank. Crankshaft and connecting rods drilled for forced feed. Pistons and cylinder walls lubricated by splash.

DIMENSIONS.—Overall diameter 37.25 in. (947 m/m.), Overall length (without starter) 30.5 in. (775 m/m.).

WEIGHT DRY (with unshielded ignition and without optional accessories).—341 lbs. (154.8 kg.).

PERFORMANCE.—Rated power at sea level 165 h.p. at 2,100 r.p.m., Take-off power 175 h.p. at 2,250 r.p.m., Fuel consumption at rated output .58 lb. (.263 kg.) per h.p. hour, Oil consumption at rated output .025 lb. (.0114 kg.) per h.p. hour.

THE WARNER R-550 SUPER-SCARAB 185.

The R-550 Super-Scarab is, except for a slight increase in bore, identical to the R-500 model.

DIMENSIONS.—Bore 4.875 in. (124 m/m.), Stroke 4.25 in. (108 m/m.), Capacity 555 cub. in. (9.1 litres), Overall dimensions same as for 165 h.p. Model.

WEIGHT DRY (with unshielded ignition and without optional accessories).—344 lbs. (156.2 kg.).

PERFORMANCE.—Rated power at sea level 180 h.p. at 2,100 r.p.m., Take-off power 200 h.p. at 2,475 r.p.m., Consumptions as for 165 h.p. model.

The 200 h.p. Warner R-550 Super-Scarab 185 seven-cylinder engine.

WRIGHT.

THE WRIGHT AERONAUTICAL CORPORATION.
(A DIVISION OF THE CURTISS-WRIGHT CORPORATION.)

HEAD OFFICE : 30, ROCKEFELLER PLAZA, NEW YORK CITY, N.Y.

PRODUCTION FACTORIES : PATERSON, NEW JERSEY, AND CINCINNATI, OHIO.

President : GUY W. VAUGHAN.
Executive Vice-President : G. M. WILLIAMS.
Vice-President and Acting General Manager : P. B. TAYLOR.
Vice-President and Manager of Cincinnati Plant : W. D. KENNEDY.
Secretary : E. S. CRAMER.
Treasurer : C. C. KING.

Celebrating the 25th anniversary of its corporate existence, the Wright Aeronautical Corporation, during the year 1944 reached a peak of production equal to 22 times that of its 1939 output, but owing to the advances made in manufacturing methods, and especially through the application of automatic special-purpose machine-tools, this was achieved with only 11 times the number of employees.

From the outbreak of war to the end of 1944 the company produced Cyclone and Whirlwind engines totaling 315,201,000 horsepower, and while the total number of engines built during the first 20 years was only 20,000, the total from all plants since 1939 exceeded the 200,000 mark.

Manufacture of the Whirlwind series was discontinued entirely in the Wright plants, all production being in the hands of licensees who built these engines for use in training aircraft and in tanks and tank destroyers.

Production of the Cyclone 9 in the lower horsepower models was also discontinued, and the bulk of the output of the 1,200 h.p. G-200 series was left in the hands of the Studebaker Corporation on a licence arrangement. A new model, the Series H, was introduced with a rating of 1,350 h.p., and was placed in production in the Paterson plants.

More than 50,000 Cyclone 14's of the B series were manufactured at the Cincinnati plant up to the end of 1944, when arrangements were made to switch to production of the Cyclone 18. The new 1,900 h.p. Cyclone 14 was also put into production at Paterson replacing the 1,600 h.p. series A which was discontinued.

The emphasis placed on the heavy bomber programme resulted in a concentration on the production of the Cyclone 18, rated at 2,200 h.p., of which more than 5,000 were produced in the new Wood-Ridge plant on the outskirts of Paterson, while others were manufactured under licence by the Dodge-Chicago Plant, Division of the Chrysler Corporation.

A new method of cylinder-barrel finning, know as the "W" fin, was introduced on the Cyclone 14, and later adopted on the nine and eighteen-cylinder engines. Formed from sheet aluminium and caulked into grooves cut into the barrel walls, this new fin provides greater cooling area and has been largely responsible for the increase in power of the new models. Cylinder manufacture is simplified, and fins damaged by accident or enemy action can be replaced in the field.

Engine cooling fans of both the airscrew speed and gear-driven types were introduced, and production was started on a Wright turbo-supercharger of 1,200 h.p. A development programme was undertaken on the gas turbine, and engines of this type are expected to be introduced in the near future.

THE WRIGHT WHIRLWIND SERIES.

Wright Whirlwind engines are no longer manufactured by the Wright Aeronautical Corporation, but are produced in considerable quantities by Continental Motors Corporation under a licence agreement. These engines, of 450 h.p. are in wide use in M-3 and M-4 tanks, and in M-7 and M-12 tank destroyers, as well as in several types of basic training aircraft. Production of both the seven and nine-cylinder models is also being undertaken in a new factory erected by the Brazilian Government, and which operates under licence arrangements.

TYPE.—Seven (R760) and nine-cylinder (R975) air-cooled radials.

CYLINDERS.—Bore 5 in. (127 m/m.), Stroke 5½ in. (140 m/m.), Capacities (R-760) 756 cub. in. (12.4 litres), (R-975) 973 cub. in. (15.9 litres). Steel barrels with integral fins screwed and shrunk into aluminium-alloy heads. Two inclined valves per cylinder. Exhaust ports at the side with finned aluminium elbows. Finned caps fitted as spark-plug coolers. Inter-cylinder and cylinder-head air deflectors for efficient cooling. Increased thickness of barrels permits two re-grinds.

PISTONS.—High-tensile aluminium-alloy forgings. Flat heads with recesses for intake and exhaust valves for engines with 6/1 and 6.3/1 compression ratio.

CONNECTING RODS.—Master-rod with solid big-end and steel-backed antifriction metal bearing.

CRANKSHAFT.—Single-throw type, in two sections, to permit use of solid big-end. Dynamic damper incorporates pendulum counter-weight instead of rigidly-mounted counterweight. Dynamic damper vibrates at explosion frequency, but out of phase with explosion impulses in such a way that it introduces a counter-torque in the crankshaft which balances out the torque fluctuations which cause vibration.

CRANKCASE.—Cylindrical body, heat-treated, with mounting bosses for cylinders. Front cover carries only thrust-bearing. Intermediate section carries support for front main bearing. Rear section houses accessory drives and carries mounting lugs.

VALVE GEAR.—Carried in rear of main crankcase body. Two-row cam-ring on steel sleeve, concentric with crankshaft, spur-gear driven through lay-shaft. Roller tappets, totally-enclosed push-rods, and enclosed overhead rockers operate one inlet with solid stem and one exhaust valve with hollow stem per cylinder. Exhaust valves are tulip-shaped on all models, except higher-powered units, which have salt-cooled valves whose flat heads raise compression ratio from 6.1/1 to 6.3/1.

CARBURATION.—Stromberg carburettor, below engine centre-line. All models (except R-760ET) are equipped with a General Electric Co's. supercharger, geared from crankshaft. Supercharger drives at seven to ten times crankshaft speed.

LUBRICATION.—Normal dry sump system.

IGNITION.—Two Scintilla magnetos one on each side of rear cover.

ACCESSORIES.—Mountings and drives at rear of engine for petrol pump, starter, two gun-synchronizers, two rev-counter drives and dynamo drive. Spring-coupling in main accessory drive gear bolted to crankshaft. Two-piece drive-shaft joined through spline coupling.

AIRSCREW DRIVE.—S.A.E. 20 spline. Clockwise rotation, seen from anti-airscrew end. All models have direct drive and provision for hydraulically-controllable-pitch airscrews.

DIMENSIONS.—Overall diameter 45 in. (1.143 m.).

WEIGHT AND PERFORMANCE.—See Table.

THE WRIGHT CYCLONE 7 R-1300 SERIES.

The Cyclone 7 is a new seven-cylinder radial engine of 1,300 cu. in. displacement which incorporates many components of the Cyclone 9. It has been developed specifically for commercial purposes to meet the requirements of small transport and feeder-line aircraft.

The new engine used the new type of forged cylinder head and W-type cooling fins originally introduced in the Cyclone 9H Series. It incorporates an exhaust-driven turbo supercharger and the combustion chamber has been designed to permit the use of fuels of varying Octane rate.

Valve-gear lubrication makes use of a series of external oil tubes and oil jets in the crankcase direct a continuous flow of oil into each cylinder barrel.

No further details of this engine were available at the time of writing.

THE WRIGHT CYCLONE 9 R AND GR-1820 F-50 AND F-60 SERIES

TYPE.—Nine-cylinder air-cooled radial.

CYLINDERS.—Bore 6.125 in. (155.6 m/m.), Stroke 6.875 in. (174 m/m.), Capacity 1,823 cub. in. (29.88 litres). Nitrided steel barrels screwed and shrunk into aluminium-alloy heads, with integral rocker support boxes. Two inserted valve-seats in each head. Intake and exhaust ports face rear.

PISTONS.—Forged aluminium-alloy, trunk type. Three compression and two oil-scraper rings each.

CONNECTING RODS.—Master-rod with solid big-end and steel-backed, plated silver bearing.

CRANKSHAFT.—Dynamically-balanced single-throw type (see "Whirlwind"), in two sections, to permit the use of solid big-end master-rod. Runs in three bearings.

VALVE GEAR.—One inlet and one exhaust valve per cylinder. Latter is sodium-filled, stellited and seats on stainless steel insert. Push-rods completely enclosed. Rocker-arms enclosed in support boxes cast integral with cylinder-head.

CRANKCASE.—Main crankcase of aluminium forgings, divided in plane of cylinders, the two sections held together by nine through-bolts and the cylinder flanges. Nose section is a hemispherical casting of aluminium-alloy and carries the ball-thrust bearing, and valve tappets and encloses the cam. Mounting section at rear of main crankcase carries nine mounting lugs and forms front wall of diffuser chamber. Supercharger impeller and its mating diffuser plate are mounted in the rear section. Accessories are carried on supercharger rear housing cover.

Two views of the Wright Whirlwind R-975-E nine-cylinder radial air-cooled engine.

CARBURATION.—Stromberg NAF7 down-draught carburetter on the top of supercharger section. Mixture fed through annulus to G.E.C. supercharger blower on diffuser plate and to cylinders through tangential intake pipes. Blower 11 ins. diameter and rotates on plain bearings. Provision is made for heating intake air to carburettor.

IGNITION.—Two Scintilla magnetos, two sets of spark-plugs.

LUBRICATION.—Lubrication is dry sump full pressure type. One pressure and one scavenging pump at rear of engine. All parts of valve gear are lubricated automatically.

ACCESSORIES.—Mountings and drives provided at rear of engine for petrol pump, starter, dynamo, two gun-synchronizers, and two revolution counter drives. Angle-drive for vacuum pump.

AIRSCREW DRIVE.—Geared or direct, according to model. Rotation clockwise, viewed from anti-airscrew end.

DIMENSIONS.—Overall diameter 54.12 in. (1.375 m.), Overall length (R Models—direct-drive) 43.38 in. (1.102 m.), Overall length (GR Models—geared) 47.81 in. (1.214 m.).

WEIGHT AND PERFORMANCE.—See Table.

THE WRIGHT CYCLONE 9 R AND GR-1820 G SERIES.

Except where differences are given below, see F50 and F60.

CYLINDERS.—Barrel and head have total cooling fin area of 2,800 sq. in. Exhaust and intake ports at rear of cylinder-head. Inter-cylinder and cylinder-head air deflectors for maximum cooling efficiency. Intake valve seats of bronze; exhaust valve-seats of steel.

PISTONS.—Under side ribbed to increase strength and improve cooling.

LUBRICATION.—All parts of valve gear lubricated automatically through an internal system devoid of any external tubes or lines.

ACCESSORIES.—Mountings and drives are provided at rear of engine for petrol pump, starter, dynamo, two gun synchronizers, two revolution-counter drives, and vacuum pumps. Provision is also made for mounting an "Eclipse" two-position supercharger regulator on the rear cover.

EXHAUST GAS ANALYZER.—Exhaust gas analyzer or mixture indicator has been designed for all Wright Cyclone engines, to provide means of controlling fuel consumption in flight.

AIRSCREW DRIVE.—Geared 16 to 11 or direct, according to model. Rotation clockwise, viewed from anti-airscrew end.

DIMENSIONS.—Overall diameter 54.25 in. (1.378 m.), Overall length (R Models—direct-drive) 43.25 in. (0.933 m.), Overall length (GR Models—geared) 47.75 in. (1.211 m.).

WEIGHT AND PERFORMANCE.—See Table.

THE WRIGHT CYCLONE 9 GR-1820 G100 SERIES.

TYPE.—Nine-cylinder air-cooled radial.

CYLINDERS.—Bore 6.125 in. (155.6 m/m.), Stroke 6.875 in. (174 m/m.). Capacity 1,823 cub. in. (29.88 litres). Aluminium-alloy cylinder-heads, with integral rocker support boxes, screwed and shrunk on to nitrided steel barrels. Cylinder-head and barrel have total cooling fin area of 2,800 sq. in. Exhaust and intake ports at rear of cylinder-head. Intake valve-seat bronze; exhaust valve-seat steel. Intake ports streamlined to give minimum resistance to mixture flow into combustion chamber. Improved exhaust port design for scavenging of burnt gases.

PISTONS.—Forged aluminium-alloy, trunk type. Ribbed on the underside and finned on thrust and anti-thrust sides for strength and cooling. Three compression rings and three oil control rings.

CONNECTING RODS.—Master-rod with solid big-end and steel-backed, plated silver bearing. Master-rod is of "H"-section. Articulated rods of "I"-section.

CRANKSHAFT.—Dynamically-balanced single-throw type (see Whirlwind) in two sections, to permit the use of solid big-end master-rod, incorporates Wright dynamic damper. Runs in three bearings.

VALVE GEAR.—One intake and one exhaust valve per cylinder. Latter sodium filled, stellited and seats on stainless steel insert. Valves actuated by cam on sleeve on crankshaft in front section, through push-rods and rocker-arms. Push-rods enclosed. Rocker-arms enclosed in support boxes cast integral with cylinder-head. All parts of valve gear lubricated automatically through internal system devoid of external lines or tubes.

IGNITION.—Two Scintilla magnetos, two independent sets of finned spark-plugs.

CRANKCASE.—Main crankcase of two steel forgings, divided in plane of cylinders, the two sections held together by nine through-bolts and the cylinder flanges. Nose section aluminium-alloy forging, carries ball-thrust and valve tappets and encloses cam. Supercharger impeller runs inside vaned diffuser plate in rear section. Accessories on flat plate of magnesium-alloy, which forms rear crankcase cover.

CARBURATION.—Holley 1375F down-draught non-icing altitude compensating carburettor on top of supercharger section. Mixture fed through annulus to supercharger impeller and to cylinders through tangential intake pipes. Impeller 11 ins. in diameter and rotates on plain bearings. This carburettor eliminates necessity for conventional type carburettor air preheaters to prevent icing.

LUBRICATION.—Lubrication of dry sump full pressure type. One pressure and one scavenging pump contained in same housing at rear of engine. Oil supply for main bearings and front sections of engine enters at rear of crankshaft. Master-rod bearing, knuckle-pins, cam, supercharger drive mechanism, and accessory drives also lubricated by pressure. All parts of valve gear lubricated automatically. Oil pressure available for operation of hydraulic type constant-speed full-feathering airscrew.

ACCESSORIES.—Mountings and drives at rear of engine for petrol pump, starter, dynamo, two gun synchronizers, two revolution-counter drives, and vacuum pumps. Spur-gear accessory drive provides power for various equipment or instruments. Provision for a 3 or 12-jaw starter and for mounting an "Eclipse" two-position supercharger regulator on rear cover.

EXHAUST GAS ANALYSER.—Exhaust gas analyser or mixture indicator has been designed for all Wright Cyclone engines, to provide means of determining proper mixture control adjustment in flight.

AIRSCREW DRIVE.—Geared 16 : 11 rotation clockwise, viewed from anti-airscrew end.

DIMENSIONS.—Overall diameter 55.1 in. (1.39 m.), Overall length 48.12 in. (1.22 m.).

WEIGHT AND PERFORMANCE.—See Table.

THE WRIGHT CYCLONE 9 R-1820 G200 SERIES.

The G200 Series is generally similar to the G100 Series but differs in the following respects. The cylinders are similar

The 1,100 h.p. Wright Cyclone 9 GR-1820 G100 Series radial air-cooled engine.

THE WRIGHT WHIRLWIND SERIES

Engine Model	Take-off Power	Normal Rating at Sea Level	Rating at Height	Compression Ratio	Blower Ratio	Dry Weight	Octane No.
R-760-ET	—	235 h.p. at 2,000 r.p.m.	—	6.1 : 1	—	540 lb. (245 kg.)	73
R-760-E1	300 h.p. at 2,250 r.p.m.	285 h.p. at 2,100 r.p.m.	—	6.1 : 1	7.05 : 1	570 lb. (259 kg.)	73
R-760-E2	350 h.p. at 2,400 r.p.m.	320 h.p. at 2,200 r.p.m.	—	6.3 : 1	9.17 : 1	570 lb. (259 kg.)	91
R-975-E1	—	365 h.p. at 2,100 r.p.m.	—	6.1 : 1	7.80 : 1	660 lb. (300 kg.)	73
R-975-E3	450 h.p. at 2,250 r.p.m.	412 h.p. at 2,200 r.p.m.	420 h.p. at 2,200 r.p.m. at 1,400 ft. (430 m.)	6.3 : 1	10.15 : 1	675 lb. (306 kg.)	91

THE WRIGHT CYCLONE 9 R AND GR-1820 F50 AND F60 SERIES

Engine Model	Take-off Power	Normal Rating at Sea Level	Normal Rating (low blower)	Normal Rating (high blower)	Compression Ratio	Blower Ratio	Dry Weight	Octane No.
R-1820-F52	890 h.p. at 2,200 r.p.m.	745 h.p. at 2,100 r.p.m.	775 h.p. at 2,100 r.p.m. at 5,800 ft. (1,770 m.)	—	6.40 : 1	7 : 1	1,000 lb. (454 kg.)	91
GR-1820-F52	875 h.p. at 2,200 r.p.m.	730 h.p. at 2,100 r.p.m.	760 h.p. at 2,100 r.p.m. at 5,800 ft. (1,770 m.)	—	6.40 : 1	7 : 1	1,095 lb. (497 kg.)	91
R-1820-F53	785 h.p. at 2,200 r.p.m.	685 h.p. at 2,100 r.p.m.	745 h.p. at 2,100 r.p.m. at 9,600 ft. (2,930 m.)	—	6.40 : 1	8.31 : 1	1,000 lb. (454 kg.)	91
GR-1820-F53	770 h.p. at 2,200 r.p.m.	670 h.p. at 2,100 r.p.m.	730 h.p. at 2,100 r.p.m. at 9,600 ft. (2,930 m.)	—	6.40 : 1	8.31 : 1	1,095 lb. (497 kg.)	91
R-1820-F56	785 h.p. at 2,200 r.p.m.	695 h.p. at 2,100 r.p.m.	755 h.p. at 2,100 r.p.m. at 11,300 ft. (3,450 m.)	—	6.40 : 1	8.83 : 1	1,000 lb. (454 kg.)	91
GR-1820-F56	770 h.p. at 2,200 r.p.m.	680 h.p. at 2,100 r.p.m.	740 h.p. at 2,100 r.p.m. at 11,300 ft. (3,450 m.)	—	6.40 : 1	8.83 : 1	1,095 lb. (497 kg.)	91
R-1820-F55 / GR-1820-F55	875 h.p. at 2,200 r.p.m.	730 h.p. at 2,100 r.p.m.	760 h.p. at 2,100 r.p.m. at 5,800 ft. (1,770 m.)	675 h.p. at 2,100 r.p.m. at 15,300 ft. (4,670 m.)	6.40 : 1	7.14 : 1 and 10 : 1	1,012 lb. (459 kg.) / 1,107 lb. (503 kg.)	91
R-1820-F62 / GR-1820-F62	900 h.p. at 2,350 r.p.m.	760 h.p. at 2,100 r.p.m.	760 h.p. at 2,100 r.p.m. at 5,800 ft. (1,770 m.)	—	6.40 : 1	7 : 1	1,000 lb. (454 kg.) / 1,095 lb. (497 kg.)	91
R-1820-F65 / GR-1820-F65	900 h.p. at 2,350 r.p.m.	760 h.p. at 2,100 r.p.m.	760 h.p. at 2,100 r.p.m. at 5,800 ft. (1,770 m.)	675 h.p. at 2,100 r.p.m. at 15,300 ft. (4,670 m.)	6.40 : 1	7.14 : 1 and 10 : 1	1,012 lb. (459 kg.) / 1,107 lb. (503 kg.)	91

THE WRIGHT CYCLONE 9 R AND GR-1820 G SERIES

Engine Model	Take-off Power	Normal Sea Level Rating	Normal Rating (low blower)	Normal Rating (high blower)	Compression Ratio	Blower Ratio	Dry Weight	Octane No.
R & GR-1820-G2	1,000 h.p. at 2,200 r.p.m.	820 h.p. at 2,100 r.p.m.	850 h.p. at 2,100 r.p.m. at 5,800 ft. (1,770 m.)	—	6.45 : 1	7 : 1	R : 1,103 lb. (501 kg.) GR : 1,198 lb. (544 kg.)	91
R & GR-1820-G3	875 h.p. at 2,200 r.p.m.	760 h.p. at 2,100 r.p.m.	840 h.p. at 2,100 r.p.m. at 8,700 ft. (2,650 m.)	—	6.45 : 1	8.31 : 1	R : 1,103 lb. (501 kg.) GR : 1,198 lb. (544 kg.)	91
R & GR-1820-G3B	900 h.p. at 2,350 r.p.m.	820 h.p. at 2,100 r.p.m.	820 h.p. at 2,100 r.p.m. at 8,800 ft. (2,680 m.)	—	6.20 : 1	8.31 : 1	R : 1,103 lb. (501 kg.) GR : 1,198 lb. (544 kg.)	91
R & GR-1820-G5 / R & GR-1820-G5E	1,000 h.p. at 2,200 r.p.m.	850 h.p. at 2,100 r.p.m.	850 h.p. at 2,100 r.p.m. at 6,000 ft. (1,830 m.)	750 h.p. at 2,100 r.p.m. at 15,200 ft. (4,640 m.)	6.45 : 1	7.14 : 1 and 10 : 1	R-G5 : 1,115 lb. (506 kg.) GR-G5 : 1,210 lb. (549 kg.) R-G5E : 1,139 lb. (517 kg.) GR-G5E : 1,234 lb. (560 kg.)	91

THE WRIGHT CYCLONE 9 GR-1820 G100 SERIES

Engine Model	Take-off Power	Normal Rating (low blower)	Military Rating (low blower)	Normal Rating (high blower)	Military Rating (high blower)	Compression Ratio	Blower Ratio	Gear Ratio	Dry Weight	Octane No.
GR-1820-G102A	1,100 h.p. at 2,350 r.p.m.	900 h.p. at 2,300 r.p.m. at 6,700 ft. (2,045 m.)	1,100 h.p. at 2,350 r.p.m. at 1,500 ft. (458 m.)	—	—	6.3 : 1	7 : 1	.6875 : 1	1,275 lb. (579 kg.)	91
GR-1820-G103A	1,000 h.p. at 2,350 r.p.m.	860 h.p. at 2,300 r.p.m. at 11,100 ft. (3,385 m.)	1,000 h.p. at 2,350 r.p.m. at 8,000 ft. (2,440 m.)	—	—	6.3 : 1	8.31 : 1	.6875 : 1	1,275 lb. (579 kg.)	91
GR-1820-G105A	1,100 h.p. at 2,350 r.p.m.	900 h.p. at 2,300 r.p.m. at 6,700 ft. (2,045 m.)	1,100 h.p. at 2,350 r.p.m. at 1,500 ft. (458 m.)	775 h.p. at 2,300 r.p.m. at 17,300 ft. (5,276 m.)	800 h.p. at 2,350 r.p.m. at 17,100 ft. (5,215 m.)	6.3 : 1	7.134 : 1 and 10.04 : 1	6875 : 1	1,287 lb. (584 kg.)	91
718-C9GB1 (105A)	1,100 h.p. at 2,350 r.p.m.	900 h.p. at 2,300 r.p.m. at 6,700 ft. (2,045 m.)	1,100 h.p. at 2,350 r.p.m. at 1,500 ft. (458 m.)	775 h.p. at 2,300 r.p.m. at 17,300 ft. (5,276 m.)	800 h.p. at 2,350 r.p.m. at 17,100 ft. (5,215 m.)	6.3 : 1	7.134 : 1 and 10.04 : 1	.6875 : 1	1,287 lb. (584 kg.)	91

THE WRIGHT CYCLONE 9 R-1820 G200 SERIES

Engine Model	Take-off Power	Normal Rating (low blower)	Military Rating (low blower)	Normal Rating (high blower)	Military Rating (high blower)	Compression Ratio	Blower Ratio	Gear Ratio	Dry Weight	Octane No.
702-C9GC (G202A)	1,200 h.p. at 2,500 r.p.m.	1,000 h.p. at 2,300 r.p.m. at 6,900 ft. (2,100 m.)	1,200 h.p. at 2,500 r.p.m. at 4,100 ft. (1,250 m.)	—	—	6.70 : 1	7 : 1	.666 : 1	1,310 lb. (595 kg.)	91
GR-1820-G203A	1,100 h.p. at 2,500 r.p.m.	950 h.p. at 2,300 r.p.m. at 9,100 ft. (2,780 m.)	1,100 h.p. at 2,500 r.p.m. at 7,400 ft. (2,260 m.)	—	—	6.70 : 1	8.3 : 1	.666 : 1	1,310 lb. (595 kg.)	91
704-C9GC (G205A)	1,200 h.p. at 2,500 r.p.m.	1,000 h.p. at 2,300 r.p.m. at 6,900 ft. (2,100 m.)	1,200 h.p. at 2,500 r.p.m. at 4,200 ft. (1,280 m.)	900 h.p. at 2,300 r.p.m. at 15,200 ft. (4,640 m.)	1,000 h.p. at 2,500 r.p.m. at 14,200 ft. (4,330 m.)	6.70 : 1	7.134 : 1 and 10.04 : 1	.666 : 1	1,320 lb. (599 kg.)	91 and 100
728-C9GC	1,200 h.p. at 2,500 r.p.m.	1,000 h.p. at 2,300 r.p.m. at 6,000 ft. (1,830 m.)	—	—	—	6.30 : 1	7 : 1	.666 : 1	1,310 lb. (595 kg.)	91
730-C9GD	1,200 h.p. at 2,500 r.p.m.	1,000 h.p. at 2,300 r.p.m. at 6,900 ft. (2,100 m.)	—	—	—	6.20 : 1	7 : 1	.666 : 1	1,310 lb. (595 kg.)	91

except that the cylinder barrel fins are more closely spaced and deeper to provide further cooling area. The cylinder-heads have also been redesigned for deeper fins, new valves, valve ports and valve-seats.

An innovation in the G200 crankshaft is the incorporation of the Wright Dynamic Damper in both counterweights instead of solely in the rear counterweight as formerly. The use of two dampers allows a higher take-off r.p.m. than used hitherto, with a decrease in airscrew stress.

Two reduction gear ratios are available. The 3 : 2 gear is the standard G100 type and the 16 : 9 is the type used in the GR2600 Series engines. The airscrew shafts in both cases include accommodation for a hydromatic airscrew.

The nose section of the crankcase, which encloses the reduction gear unit, has been modified to provide for the vertical mounting of the governor for constant-speed airscrews, which is driven through bevel gears from the cam intermediate gear.

The main crankcase, consisting of the two halves bolted together at the centre-line of the cylinders, is of steel as in the G100, but the nose section and the front and rear supercharger housings are machined from magnesium-alloy instead of from aluminium-alloy castings. The two halves of the main case are now bolted together internally and an integral flange is provided for the attachment of the nose section.

A greatly improved bearing surface between the master connecting rod and the crank-pin has been provided to withstand the loads imposed by increased crankshaft speed and output. Lubrication of the master-rod bearing and the cylinder walls has also been improved.

Accessory drives are similar to those of the G100. Ignition is by two Scintilla type SF9L-3 magnetos, incorporating a compensating spark timing arrangement for the equal advance on all cylinders. A stainless steel magneto and ignition wiring assembly is assembled in front of the push-rods and is in two identical halves for ease of assembly.

DIMENSIONS—Overall diameter 55.125 in. (1.399 m.), Length 50.04 in. (1.272 m.).

WEIGHT AND PERFORMANCE.—See Table.

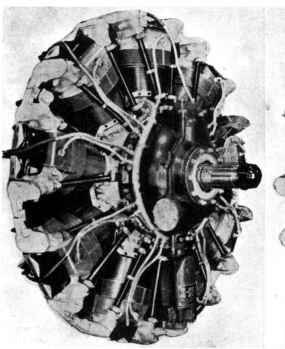

The 1,350 h.p. Wright Cyclone 9 R-1820 H Series engine with the new W-type aluminium cylinder cooling fins and forged aluminium-alloy heads.

The Wright Cyclone 9 R 1820-G200 Series engine.

THE WRIGHT CYCLONE 9 R-1820 H SERIES.

The new H series of the Cyclone 9 is similar in many respects to the earlier G200 series, and has the same overall diameter. Major differences, however, are observable in the cylinders which are constructed with forged aluminium-alloy heads, having the fins machined-out, and in the application of the new Wright "W" fin to the cylinder barrels. With a rated power of 1,350 h.p. for take-off and a weight of only 1,315 lbs. (597 kg.), this engine represents the lowest weight/horsepower ratio achieved thus far in an engine of this type. The Wright Torque-meter is built into the lower part of the nose section, of which it forms an integral part.

This new engine is available with two different blower ratios, and is designed to operate on 100/130 Octane fuel.

TYPE.—Nine-cylinder air-cooled radial.

CYLINDERS.—Bore 6.125 in. (155.6 m/m.), Stroke 6.875 in. (174 m/m.), Capacity 1,823 cub. in. (29.88 litres), Barrels, machined from nitralloy steel forgings, have inner surfaces nitrided and are screwed and shrunk into forged aluminium heads. Cylinder-head has a hemispherical combustion chamber with two inclined valves operating in bronze bushings shrunk into head. Valve rocker-arms and springs are enclosed in housing cast integrally with the head. Cylinders have W-type aluminium cooling fins rolled into grooves cut on outside of the barrel. This arrangement provides maximum cooling effect.

PISTONS.—Are full trunk type made from aluminium-alloy forgings. The Wright "uniflow" piston has six ring grooves, three compression rings and three oil control rings, the bottom ring being inverted. Piston pins, of tubular design, float in the articulated rod bushings and in the pistons and are locked in place by plug-type retainers in piston at each end of pin.

CONNECTING RODS.—Single piece H-section master-rod and eight of articulated rods machined from solid forgings. The crankpin end of the master-rod is provided with a loose pre-fit silver-plated bearing. A bearing oil-seal assembly on each master-rod improves master-rod bearing and knuckle-pin lubrication by providing a seal against excessive oil leakage from the master-rod. Knuckle pins are made from alloy-steel with nitrided bearing surfaces and are centre-drilled and tapped on one end to accommodate a locking screw. The articulated rods are alloy-steel and have split bronze bushings pressed into both ends.

CRANKSHAFT.—Two-piece single-throw clamping type permitting use of single-piece master-rod and machined from alloy-steel forgings. The assembly is adequately supported by two main roller-bearings securely assembled on the shaft and in the crankcase diaphragm. The front section includes the drive shaft, front crankcheek, front dynamic damper counter-weight and the crankpin. The rear section includes the crankshaft rear crankcheek, rear dynamic damper and crankshaft rear bearing journal. This journal carries internal splines for the accessory and starter drive-shaft coupling.

CRANKCASE.—The engine crankcase is composed of six principal sections located from front to rear as follows : crankcase front section, crankcase front main section, crankcase rear main section, supercharger front housing, supercharger rear housing, and supercharger rear housing cover. The magnesium-alloy front section houses the thrust ball-bearing ring, governor drive-shaft, torque-meter if used, and the reduction-gear assembly. The main section consists of two alloy-steel forgings which are internally bolted together. The magnesium-alloy supercharger front and rear housings provide space for the impeller, diffuser, induction passage to impeller, supercharger drive gears, all engine-driven accessories, etc.

VALVE GEAR.—Two valves per cylinder. Intake and exhaust valves have mushroom-shaped heads and hollow stems. The exhaust valve stem is partially filled with sodium mercury and the intake valve stem is empty. Push-rods are totally enclosed. The cam-ring is driven by means of intermediate gearing from the front end of the crankshaft at one-eighth engine speed.

CARBURATION.—Stromberg Model PD12K10 injection downdraft fully-automatic non-icing carburettor is located on top of the supercharger rear section. Mixture is fed through induction passage to supercharger impeller and to cylinders through radial intake pipes. The 11-inch diameter impeller rotates on plain bearings. This carburettor automatically compensates for varying density of the air and special fuel requirements for acceleration.

LUBRICATION.—Lubrication of dry sump, full-pressure type. One pressure and one scavenging pump contained in the same housing is attached to supercharger rear housing cover. An additional scavenging pump is provided in the engine sump located at the front of the engine. The drive is effected through a shaft with scavenge gear teeth milled on one end and a spline on the opposite end which engages one of the accessory drive mechanisms. Oil pressure. Cylinder walls, piston-pins, dynamic damper pins

THE WRIGHT CYCLONE 9 R-1820 H SERIES.

Engine Model	Take-off Power	Normal Rating (low blower)	Military Rating (low blower)	Normal Rating (high blower)	Military Rating (high blower)	Compression Ratio	Blower Ratio	Gear Ratio	Dry Weight	Octane No.
R-1820-C9HC	1,350 h.p. at 2,700 r.p.m.	1,200 h.p. at 5,000 r.p.m. at 5,000 ft. (1,520 m.)	1,300 h.p. at 2,600 r.p.m. at 4,000 ft. (1,220 m.)	—	—	6.55	7 : 1	.5625 : 1 and .666 : 1	1,315 lb. (596 kg.)	100/130
R-1820-C9HC	1,350 h.p. at 2,700 r.p.m.	1,200 h.p. at 2,500 r.p.m. at 5,500 ft. (1,680 m.)	1,300 h.p. at 2,600 r.p.m. at 4,000 ft. (1,220 m.)	900 h.p. at 2,500 r.p.m. at 18,500 ft. (5,640 ft.)	1,000 h.p. at 2,600 r.p.m. at 17,500 ft. (5,330 m.)	6.55 : 1	7.134 : 1 and 10.04 : 1	.5625 : 1 and .666 : 1	1,333 lbs. (605 kg.)	100/130

THE WRIGHT CYCLONE 14 GR-2600 SERIES

Engine Model	Take-off Power	Normal Rating (low blower)	Military Rating (low blower)	Normal Rating (high blower)	Military Rating (high blower)	Compression Ratio	Blower Ratio	Gear Ratio	Dry Weight	Octane No.
579-C14AC1 (-A2A)	1,600 h.p. at 2,400 r.p.m.	1,350 h.p. at 2,300 r.p.m. at 6,200 ft. (1,890 m.)	1,600 h.p. at 2,400 r.p.m. at 1,500 ft. (458 m.)	—	—	6.85 : 1	7 : 1	.5625 : 1	1,935 lb. (878 kg.)	100
GR-2600-A2B	1,600 h.p. at 2,400 r.p.m.	1,350 h.p. at 2,300 r.p.m. at 5,800 ft. (1,770 m.)	1,600 h.p. at 2,400 r.p.m. at 1,500 ft. (458 m.)	—	—	6.30 : 1	7 : 1	.5625 : 1	1,935 lb. (878 kg.)	91
GR-2600-A5A	1,600 h.p. at 2,400 r.p.m.	1,350 h.p. at 2,300 r.p.m. at 5,000 ft. (1,525 m.)	1,600 h.p. at 2,400 r.p.m. at 1.500 ft. (458 m.)	1,275 h.p. at 2,300 r.p.m. at 12,000 ft. (3,660 m.)	1,400 h.p. at 2,400 r.p.m. at 11,500 ft. (3,510 m.)	6.85 : 1	7.14 : 1 and 10 : 1	.5625 : 1	1,950 lb. (885 kg.)	100
GR-2600-A5B	1,600 h.p. at 2,400 r.p.m.	1,350 h.p. at 2,300 r.p.m. at 5,000 ft. (1,525 m.)	1,600 h.p. at 2,400 r.p.m. at 1,000 ft. (305 m.)	1,275 h.p. at 2,300 r.p.m. at 11,500 ft. (3,510 m.)	1,400 h.p. at 2,400 r.p.m. at 10,000ft. (3,050 m.)	6.30 : 1	7.14 : 1 and 10 : 1	.5625 : 1	1,950 lb. (885 kg.)	91
585-C14BA	1,700 h.p. at 2,500 r.p.m.	1,500 h.p. at 2,400 r.p.m. at 6,700 ft. (2,040 m.)	1,700 h.p. at 2,500 r.p.m. at 4,100 ft. (1,250 m.)	—	—	6.9 : 1	7.3 : 1	.4375 : 1	1,965 lb. (892 kg.)	100
586-C14BA	1,700 h.p. at 2,500 r.p.m.	1,500 h.p. at 2,400 r.p.m. at 6,700 ft. (2,040 m.)	1,700 h.p. at 2,500 r.p.m. at 4,100 ft. (1,250 m.)	1,350 h.p. at 2,400 r.p.m. at 15,000 ft. (4,575 m.)	1,450 h.p. at 2,500 r.p.m. at 14,100 ft. (4,300 m.)	6.85 : 1	7.06 : 1 and 10.02 : 1	.5625 : 1	1,980 lb. (900 kg.)	100
GR-2600-C14 BB	1,900 h.p. at 2,800 r.p.m.	1,600 h.p. at 2,400 r.p.m. at 5,000 ft. (1,525 m.)	1,750 h.p. at 2,600 r.p.m. at 3,200 ft. (975 m.)	1,350 h.p. at 2,400 r.p.m. at 14,800 ft. (4,510 m.)	1,450 h.p. at 2,600 r.p.m. at 15,000 ft. (4,575 m.)	6.9 : 1	7.06 : 1 and 10.06 : 1	.4375 : 1 and .5625 : 1	2,045 lbs. (930 kg.)	100/130

and crankshaft roller and ball-bearings are lubricated by spray. Pressure oil is available for operation of hydraulic-type constant-speed full-feathering airscrew.

ACCESSORIES.—The magnesium-alloy supercharger rear housing cover is machined in the familiar Cyclone pattern. The cover carries petrol pump, tachometer, two magnetos, starter, generator and the dual accessory drive. All main drives are effected by spur gearing and operate from pinion gears. All gears are machined from steel forgings, have hardened teeth and operate in bushings in the rear cover so that the entire system may be removed with cover.

DIMENSIONS.—Overall diameter 55.12 inches (1.40 m.), Length 47.29 in. (1.20 m.).

WEIGHTS AND PERFORMANCE.—See Table.

THE WRIGHT CYCLONE 14 GR-2600 SERIES.

The Cyclone 14 of the first, or "A" series, equipped with an aluminium-alloy crankcase, has been discontinued entirely, and there has been a steady decline in the production of the 1,700 h.p. "B" series. A new model, known as the "BB" series, was, however, placed in production during 1944, and while following the general lines of the earlier models, it is rated at 1,900 h.p. for take-off, and is equipped with cast aluminium cylinder heads and the new Wright "W" cylinder barrel fins.

CYLINDERS.—Bore 6.125 in. (155.6 m/m.), Stroke 6.312 in. (160.2 m/m.), Capacity 2,603 cub. in. (42.7 litres). Barrels of the A and BA series are machined from nitralloy steel forgings, have inner surfaces nitrided and are screwed and shrunk into aluminium-alloy heads. The cooling fins of the A and BA series are machined on the outside of the barrels the BB series have W-type aluminium fins rolled into grooves cut on the outside of the barrels. All engines in this series have a hemispherical combustion chamber with two inclined valves operating in bronze guides shrunk into head. Sparking-plug bushings on opposite sides of head between valves. Valve rocker-arms and springs enclosed in housings cast integrally with the head. Complete system of pressure baffles to provide efficient cooling for barrels and heads of front and rear rows of cylinders.

PISTONS.—Wright "uniflow" type pistons with three compression rings and three oil control rings, the bottom ring being inverted. Case hardened piston pins have bevelled ends and are retained by coiled spring retainers bedding in annular grooves at ends of piston pin holes.

CONNECTING RODS.—Single-piece "H" section master-rod and six articulated rods machined from solid forgings. Main crank-pin bearing of copper-lead alloy with steel backing in the "A" series, and of plated silver in the "B" series. A steel spider ring with a silver-plated face is fitted over one end of the bearing and provides oil passages outside the master-rod to lead excess oil from the main bearing to the knuckle pins and also secures them in place. At other end of bearing is a silver-plated slip ring.

CRANKSHAFT.—Two-throw clamping type permitting use of single-piece master-rods. Each crankcheek carries movable dynamic-damper counterweights on hardened steel rollers. Forward section of shaft splined to accommodate the driving bell-gear, rear section splined inside the rear bearing journal to receive the accessory drive shaft.

CRANKCASE.—Main case for the "A" series consists of three aluminium-alloy forged sections divided through the centre-lines of both banks of cylinders. Through-bolts tie the centre-section to the two outer sections between each pair of cylinders in each bank. For the "B" series the crankcase sections are steel forgings attached

to each other by means of small internal lugs. Front and rear sections accommodate valve-tappet mechanism. The combined sections contain the three main crankshaft roller-bearings. Magnesium-alloy reduction-gear section and supercharger housings bolted on fore and aft. Supercharger front housing serves as engine-mounting section.

VALVE GEAR.—Two valves per cylinder. Intake valves have concave heads and solid stems, exhaust valves hollow sodium-cooled stems, convex heads and stellite facings. Cam-rings driven off both ends of crankshaft through intermediate gearing at one-sixth engine speed. Totally-enclosed push-rods.

CARBURATION.—The single-speed blower engine has a Holley Model 1685F variable-venturi downdraft carburettor and the two-speed blower engine has a Stromberg Model PR 48A pressure-injection downdraft carburettor. Both are non-icing, fully automatic and compensate for varying densities of the air and special fuel requirements for acceleration. The mixture is fed through induction passage to supercharger impeller and to cylinders through radial intake pipes. The 11 in. diameter impeller rotates on plain bearings.

LUBRICATION.—Dry sump full-pressure type. One pressure and one or two scavenge pumps contained in same housing at rear of engine. Oil supply for main bearings and front sections of engine enters at rear of crankshaft. Main bearings, knuckle-pins, cams, supercharger drive mechanisms, and accessory drives also lubricated by pressure. All parts of valve gear lubricated

automatically. Oil pressure available for operation of hydraulic type constant-speed full-feathering airscrew.

ACCESSORIES.—Accessory section follows standard "Cyclone" practice. Magnesium-alloy rear cover plate carries two magnetos, oil pump and provision for fuel pump, large and small vacuum pumps, starter and generator. Gears driving all accessories are of the spur type, driven by a central spring-loaded gear on the tail-shaft. All gears are machined from steel forgings, have hardened teeth and operate in bushings in the rear cover so that the entire system may be removed with cover.

DIMENSIONS.—Overall diameter 55 in. (1.397 m.), Length 62.06 in. (1.576 m.).

WEIGHT AND PERFORMANCE.—See Table.

THE WRIGHT CYCLONE 18 GR-3350 SERIES.

Held under secrecy for some time, a new model of the Cyclone 18 was released during 1944. Known as the series "BA", this engine is rated at 2,200 h.p., and replaces the 2,000 h.p. "B" series. Two different models are available, one having blower ratios of 10.06 and 6.06, and the other 8.81 and 6.61. Used in the original Martin XPB2M-1 Mars patrol bomber, these engines are now standard for the Mars JRM-1 Transports and for the Lockheed Constellation Airliners. Their most important service, however, at the present time, is in the Boeing B-29 Superfortress,

The Wright Cyclone 14 GR-2600 Series fourteen-cylinder radial air-cooled engine.

THE WRIGHT CYCLONE 18 R-3350 SERIES.

Engine Model	Take-off Power	Normal Rating (low blower)	Military Rating (low blower)	Normal Rating (high blower)	Military Rating (high blower)	Compression Ratio	Blower Ratio	Gear Ratio	Dry Weight	Octane No.
R-3350-C18-BA	2,200 h.p. at 2,800 r.p.m.	2,000 h.p. at 2,400 r.p.m. at 3,000 ft. (915 m.)	—	—	—	6.85 : 1	6.06 : 1	.4375 and .5625	2,646 lbs. (1,200 kg).	100/130
R-3350-C18-BA	2,200 h.p. at 2,800 r.p.m.	2,000 h.p. at 2,400 r.p.m. at 3,000 ft. (915 m.)	—	1,800 h.p. at 2,400 r.p.m. at 14,000 ft. (4,260 m.)	—	68.5 : 1	6.61 : 1 and 8.81 : 1	.4375 and .5625	2,670 lb. (1,212 kg).	100/130

and to meet the tremendous demand for these installations, Wright has devoted the entire capacity of its Wood-Ridge plant to their construction. The Cincinnati plant was being changed over in 1944 from the Cyclone 14 to the Cyclone 18, and steadily

The 2,200 h.p. Wright Cyclone 18 GR-3350.

increasing production was being obtained from the Dodge-Chicago Plant, Division of the Chrysler Corporation, where Cyclone 18's are being built under a licence agreement.

TYPE.—Eighteen-cylinder double-row geared and supercharged radial.

CYLINDERS.—Bore 6.125 in. (155.6 m/m.), Stroke 6.312 in. (160.2 m/m.) Capacity 3,347 cub. in. (5,456 litres). Barrels, machined from nitralloy steel forgings, have inner surfaces nitrided and are screwed and shrunk into aluminium-alloy heads. Cylinder-head has a hemispherical combustion chamber with two inclined valves operating in bronze bushings shrunk into head. Valve rocker-arm and springs are enclosed in housings cast integrally with the head. Front and rear-cylinders are staggered and each has W-type aluminium cooling fins rolled into grooves cut on outside of the barrel. This arrangement provides maximum cooling effect.

PISTONS. Wright "uniflow" type pistons with three compression rings and three oil control rings, the bottom ring being inverted. Case-hardened piston-pins have bevelled ends and are retained by coiled spring retainers bedding in annular grooves at ends of piston-pin holes.

CONNECTING RODS.—Single-piece H-section master-rod and eight articulated rods machined from solid forgings. Main crank-pin bearing is silver-lead indium-plated with steel backing and has a .001-.0035 in. loose fit in the large bore of the master-rod. A bearing oil-seal assembly on each master-rod improves master-rod bearing and knuckle pin lubrication by providing a seal against excessive oil leakage from the master-rod. Knuckle pins are chrome-steel with nitrided bearing surfaces and are centre-drilled and tapped at one end to accommodate a locking screw. The articulated rods are chrome-nickel steel and have split bronze bushings pressed into both ends.

CRANKSHAFT.—Two-throw clamping type permitting use of single-piece master-rod. The assembly is adequately supported by three main roller bearings securely assembled on the shaft and in the crankcase diaphragm. Adjacent to and directly opposite each crankpin are dynamic damper counterweights to counteract disturbing forces. Forward section is splined to accommodate reduction driving gear and front cam driving gear splines. An extension on the rear section forms a journal for the rear main roller bearing and carries internal splines for the accessory and starter-drive shaft coupling.

CRANKCASE.—The engine crankcase is composed of five major sections located from front to rear as follows : front section, main section supercharger front housing, supercharger rear housing and supercharger rear housing cover. The magnesium-alloy front section houses the airscrew reduction-gear assembly, the driving gears for the front lubricating oil-pump, gearing for the distributors airscrew governor pump, and valve tappets and guides for front row of cylinders. The main section comprises three steel forgings which are internally bolted together. The magnesium-alloy supercharger front and rear housing provide space for the impeller diffuser, induction passage to impeller, supercharger drive gears all engine-driven accessories, etc.

VALVE GEAR.—Two valves per cylinder. Intake valves have tulip shaped heads and solid stems, exhaust valves have mushroom shaped heads and hollow sodium cooled stems. Cam rings driven off both ends of crankshaft through intermediate gearing at one-eighth engine speed. Push rods are totally enclosed.

CARBURATION.—Chandler-Evans model 58-CPB-4, downdraft fully-automatic non-icing carburettor is located on top of the supercharger rear section. Mixture is fed through induction passage to supercharger impeller and to cylinders through radial intake pipes. The 13 in. diameter impeller rotates on plain bearings. This carburettor automatically compensates for varying density of the air and special fuel requirements for acceleration.

LUBRICATION.—Lubrication of dry-sump full-pressure type. One pressure and one scavenging pump contained in same housing at front and rear of engine. Pressure oil for main bearings, rear section and part of front section is supplied from rear pump. Reduction gears, torque meter and oil booster-pump receive supply from front pressure pump. Master-rod bearings, knuckle pins, cam supercharger drive mechanism, and accessory drives also lubricated by pressure. All parts of valve-gear are lubricated automatically. Oil pressure is available for operation of hydraulic type constant-speed full-feathering airscrew.

ACCESSORIES.—The magnesium-alloy supercharger rear housing cover is machined in the familiar Cyclone pattern. The cover carries tachometer, double magneto, hydraulic pump, vacuum pump, starter, two generators, and provision for a spare accessory-drive. Gears driving all accessories are of the spur type and are powered either directly from a gear on the rear of the accessory drive-shaft or indirectly through pinion gears. All gears are machined from steel forgings, have hardened teeth and operate in bushings in the rear cover so that the entire system may be removed with cover.

DIMENSIONS.—Overall diameter 55.78 in. (1.42 m.), Length 76.26 in. (1.93 m.).

WEIGHTS AND PERFORMANCE.—See Table.